CW01025232

THE VICTORIA HISTORY OF THE COUNTIES OF ENGLAND

A HISTORY OF ESSEX

VOLUME IX

Oxford University Press, Walton Street, Oxford OX2 6DP
Oxford New York Toronto
Delhi Bombay Calcutta Madras Karachi
Kuala Lumpur Singapore Hong Kong Tokyo
Nairobi Dar es Salaam Cape Town
Melbourne Auckland Madrid

and associated companies in
Berlin Ibadan

Oxford is a trade mark of Oxford University Press

Published in the United States
by Oxford University Press Inc., New York

British Library Cataloguing in Publication Data
A catalogue record for this book is available
from the British Library

ISBN 0 19 722784 8

Distributed by Oxford University Press until 1 January 1997
thereafter by Dawsons of Pall Mall

Typeset at the University of London Computer Centre
Printed in Great Britain
on acid-free paper by
The Bath Press, Avon

THE VICTORIA HISTORY OF THE COUNTIES OF ENGLAND

EDITED BY C. R. ELRINGTON

THE UNIVERSITY OF LONDON
INSTITUTE OF
HISTORICAL RESEARCH

INSCRIBED TO THE

MEMORY OF HER LATE MAJESTY

QUEEN VICTORIA

WHO GRACIOUSLY GAVE THE TITLE TO

AND ACCEPTED THE DEDICATION

OF THIS HISTORY

A HISTORY OF THE COUNTY OF ESSEX

EDITED BY JANET COOPER

VOLUME IX

THE BOROUGH OF COLCHESTER

PUBLISHED FOR
THE INSTITUTE OF HISTORICAL RESEARCH
BY
OXFORD UNIVERSITY PRESS
1994

CONTENTS OF VOLUME NINE

LIST OF PLATES

For permission to reproduce material in their possession thanks are offered to Colchester Archaeological Trust, to Colchester Borough Council (Operational Services and Community Services), to Colchester Museums (Colch. Mus.), to Essex County Library, Local Studies Collection held at Colchester Library (E.C.L. Colch.), to the Essex Society for Archaeology and History, to the Essex Record Office (E.R.O.), and to the National Buildings Record (N.B.R.) of the Royal Commission on the Historical Monuments of England.

LIST OF PLATES

LIST OF MAPS AND OTHER TEXT FIGURES

FIGURES 3–5 were produced by Colchester Archaeological Trust. Figure 25 was drawn by Pamela Studd. All maps except figures 3–5 and 8 were drawn by Pamela Studd from drafts prepared by Janet Cooper, Beryl Board, Shirley Durgan, Pamela Studd, and C. C. Thornton. Figure 32 is based on Ordnance Survey 1/2,500 map (1882 edn.); the remaining maps are based on Ordnance Survey 6-inch maps (1881 edn.). For permission to reproduce material in their possession thanks are offered to the Bodleian Library, Oxford, to the British Library, to Colchester Museums (Colch. Mus.), to Essex County Library Local Studies Collection held at Colchester (E.C.L. Colch.), to the Essex Record Office (E.R.O.), and to the Society of Antiquaries.

EDITORIAL NOTE

THIS volume of the *Victoria History of Essex* is the ninth to be published under the co-operative system described in the editorial note to volume IV. The Essex Victoria County History Committee, under the chairmanship until 1988 of Sir William Addison (whose death in 1992 is deeply regretted) and thereafter of Mr. Frank Sainsbury, has continued to supervise the progress and funding of the work. The Hon. John Petre (from 1989 Lord Petre) succeeded Mr. Sainsbury as Vice-Chairman in 1988. Mr. William H. Liddell has continued as Hon. Secretary of the Committee; Mr. Geoffrey J. Clements was succeeded as Hon. Treasurer in 1992 by Mr. Geoffrey Hare. Mr. Kenneth H. Sleat died in 1986 and was succeeded as Hon. Assistant Secretary in 1987 by Mr. George Saddington. To all of them, and to all the members of the Committee, the University of London offers its warm thanks. It also records its deep gratitude to the Local Authorities which have provided the funds of the Committee and have thus enabled the present volume to be compiled, namely Essex County Council and the Councils of the London Boroughs of Barking and Dagenham, Havering, Newham, Redbridge, and (until 1993) Waltham Forest.

The generous help of the Local Authorities has recently been given in a period of extreme pressure on their finances, which prompted the launch in 1994 of an Essex V.C.H. Appeal Fund to supplement the resources of the Committee. Subscribers to that fund are thanked most sincerely, as are its Chairman, Mr. Robert G. E. Wood, and its Hon. Secretary, Mrs. Lynn Marston.

The present volume was planned by the former County Editor, Mr. W. R. Powell, and the work was begun under his editorship in 1983 before the staff turned their attention to the *Bibliography Supplement*. He was succeeded as County Editor in 1986 by Dr. Janet M. Cooper. In 1984 Mrs. Shirley Durgan, formerly research officer, succeeded Mrs. Norma Knight as assistant editor and Mrs. Pamela Studd was appointed editorial assistant. In 1992 Mrs. Beryl A. Board retired as senior assistant editor, and Dr. Christopher C. Thornton was appointed as assistant editor.

The *General Introduction* to the *Victoria County History*, published in 1970, and its *Supplement* published in 1990 give an outline of the structure and aims of the series as a whole, with an account of its origin and progress. As in volumes IV–VIII of the Essex History, the brief descriptions of the earlier parochial registers of each parish, commonly included in the topographical volumes of the *V.C.H.*, have not been considered necessary, because of the publication by the County Council of *Essex Parish Records, 1240–1894* (1950; revised edn. 1966).

The authors and editors of the present volume have again received help from many persons. Especial thanks are due to Mr. J. Bensusan-Butt, Dr. R. H. Britnell, Dr. A. F. J. Brown, Dr. M. Byford, Mr. A. Phillips, and Mr. J. Walter for extensive help over the whole period of the preparation of the volume. Mr. A. Borges, Miss J. V. Dansie, the late Miss H. E. P. Grieve, Dr. L. Higgs, Prof. G. H. Martin, the late Dr. J. B. Penfold, Brig. A. F. F. H. Robertson, and Mr. B. Usher have also provided information or commented on drafts, and their help is gratefully acknowledged. Particular thanks are also given to the staff of the Essex Record Office, especially those of the Branch Office at Colchester, the staff of the

Local Studies section of Essex County Libraries, and the staff of the Colchester Museum; the staff of the Archaeology Section of Essex County Council, of the Colchester Archaeological Trust, and of the Department of Environmental Services of Colchester Borough have all provided valuable information. Others who have given help with a specific part of the volume are named in the footnotes or in the list of illustrations; they too are sincerely thanked.

Nationally, a Victoria History Trust has been established: its initial endowment was in the form of a generous gift from Mr. and Mrs. Maurice Tattersfield in memory of their daughter Patricia (Pippa) Tattersfield (1937–92), who from 1966 to 1992 was the General Editor's secretary and Executive Officer of the V.C.H. and whose skilful and loyal work for the series over a long period was of outstanding value.

ESSEX
VICTORIA COUNTY HISTORY COMMITTEE

As at 1 January 1994

President

THE LORD BRAYBROOKE, J.P.
Lord Lieutenant of Essex

Vice-Presidents

COL. SIR JOHN RUGGLES-BRISE, BT., C.B., O.B.E., T.D., J.P.
G. J. CLEMENTS ESQ., F.S.A. F. G. EMMISON ESQ., M.B.E., F.S.A., D.U.
M. F. B. FITCH ESQ., C.B.E., D. LITT., F.B.A. D. L. FORBES ESQ., J.P.
W. R. POWELL ESQ., M.A., M. LITT., F.S.A.

Chairman

F. SAINSBURY, ESQ., B.E.M.

Vice-Chairman

THE LORD PETRE, D.L.

The following representatives of the contributing Local Authorities

COUNCILLOR P. BOLGER, COUNCILLOR E. W. CRUNDEN, COUNCILLOR D. F. REX, G. HARE ESQ.
(Essex County Council)
COUNCILLOR MISS K. A. GOLDEN, COUNCILLOR T. M. BIRD, A. HILL ESQ.
(London Borough of Barking and Dagenham)
COUNCILLOR C. W. PURNELL, COUNCILLOR MISS L. R. HAWTHORN, G. SADDINGTON ESQ.
(London Borough of Havering)
COUNCILLOR R. MANLEY, COUNCILLOR I. CORBETT, R. MCMASTER ESQ.
(London Borough of Newham)
COUNCILLOR H. W. MOTH, COUNCILLOR T. F. COBB, M. TIMMS ESQ.
(London Borough of Redbridge)
COUNCILLOR N. S. MATHAROO, C. RICHARDSON, ESQ.
(London Borough of Waltham Forest)

Representatives of the following Local Authorities within Essex

Basildon, Braintree, Brentwood, Castle Point, Chelmsford, Colchester, Epping Forest, Harlow, Maldon, Tendring, Thurrock, Uttlesford

Representatives of the following Bodies

Barking Historical Society
Essex Archaeological and Historical Congress
Hornchurch Historical Society
Thurrock Historical Society
Woodford Historical Society
Brentwood Historical Society
Essex Society for Archaeology and History
Romford Historical Society
Waltham Abbey Historical Society
University of Essex

Co-opted Members

C. ATTENBOROUGH ESQ. J. H. BOYES ESQ. MISS N. R. BRIGGS
D. G. BUCKLEY ESQ., County Archaeological Officer K. HALL ESQ., County Archivist
MRS. M. S. PRESTON MRS. P. V. WAWN R. G. E. WOOD ESQ.

Officers

Hon. County Secretary: W. H. LIDDELL ESQ.
Hon. County Treasurer: G. HARE ESQ.
Hon. Assistant Secretary: G. SADDINGTON ESQ.
Hon. Auditor: K. S. PLATT ESQ.
General Editor: PROFESSOR C. R. ELRINGTON
County Editor: DR. J. M. COOPER

LIST OF CLASSES OF DOCUMENTS IN THE PUBLIC RECORD OFFICE

USED IN THIS VOLUME

WITH THEIR CLASS NUMBERS

Clerks of Assize

ASSI 35	Indictments

Court of Bankruptcy

B 3	Files
B 4	Docket Books (Registers)

Chancery

C 1	Proceedings, Early
C 44	Tower series
C 47	Miscellanea
C 54	Close Rolls
C 60	Fine Rolls
C 66	Patent Rolls
	Inquisitions post mortem
C 133	Series I, Edw. I
C 134	Edw. II
C 138	Hen. V
C 139	Hen. VI
C 141	Ric. III
C 142	Series II
C 143	Inquisitions ad quod damnum
C 258	Writs of Certiorari
C 260	Recorda

Court of Common Pleas

CP 25(2)	Feet of Fines, Series II

Board of Customs and Excise

CUST 21	Miscellaneous Books

Exchequer, Treasury of the Receipt

E 32	Forest Proceedings

Exchequer, King's Remembrancer

E 101	Accounts, Various
E 122	Customs Accounts
E 126	Decrees and Orders, Series IV
E 134	Depositions taken by Commission
E 149	Inquisitions post mortem, Series I
E 159	Memoranda Rolls
E 163	Minute Books, Miscellanea
E 178	Special Commissions of Inquiry
E 179	Subsidy Rolls, etc.
E 190	Port Books

Exchequer, Augmentation Office

E 301	Certificates of Colleges and Chantries
E 310	Particulars for Leases
E 317	Parliamentary Surveys
E 318	Particulars for Grants

Department of Education

ED 15	Private Schools, Returns
ED 21	Elementary Education, School Files
ED 32	Special School Files
ED 35	Secondary Education, Institution Files
ED 49	Elementary Education, Endowment Files

Home Office

HO 45	Correspondence and Papers, Domestic and General, Registered Papers
	Census Papers
HO 107	Population Returns
HO 129	Ecclesiastical Returns

Indexes

IND 1	Institution Books

Board of Inland Revenue

IR 18	Tithe Files

Justices Itinerant, Assize and Gaol Delivery Justices, etc.

JUST 1	Eyre Rolls, Assize Rolls, etc.
JUST 3	Gaol Delivery Rolls

Court of King's Bench

KB 2	Affidavits (Supplementary)
KB 9	Ancient Indictments
	Plea Rolls
KB 27	Coram Rege Rolls
KB 28	Crown Rolls
KB 145	Recorda

Maps

MFQ 74	Map in WO 44/61
MPB 33	Map in E 178/6990

Ministry of Health

MH 13	General Board of Health and Local Government Act Office, Correspondence

Privy Council

PC 2	Registers

Prerogative Court of Canterbury

PROB 11	Registered Copy Wills

Court of Requests

REQ 2	Proceedings

Registrar General

RG 9 Census Returns, 1861
RG 10 1871
RG 11 1881
RG 31 Register of Places of Worship, 1689–1852

Special Collections

SC 6 Ministers' and Receivers' Accounts
SC 8 Ancient Petitions

State Paper Office

State Papers Domestic
SP 12 Eliz. I
SP 14 Jas. I
SP 16 Chas. I
SP 18 Interregnum
SP 23 Committee for Compounding with Delinquents
SP 29 Chas. II

Court of Star Chamber

STAC 2 Proceedings, Hen. VIII

War Office

WO 44 Ordnance Office, In-letters
WO 79 Private Collections, Various

V.C.H. ESSEX KEY TO PUBLISHED VOLUMES

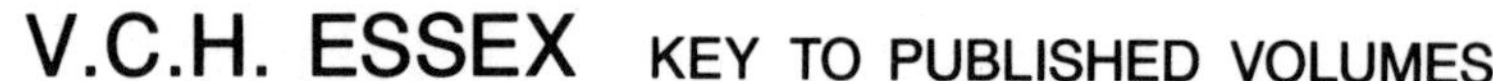

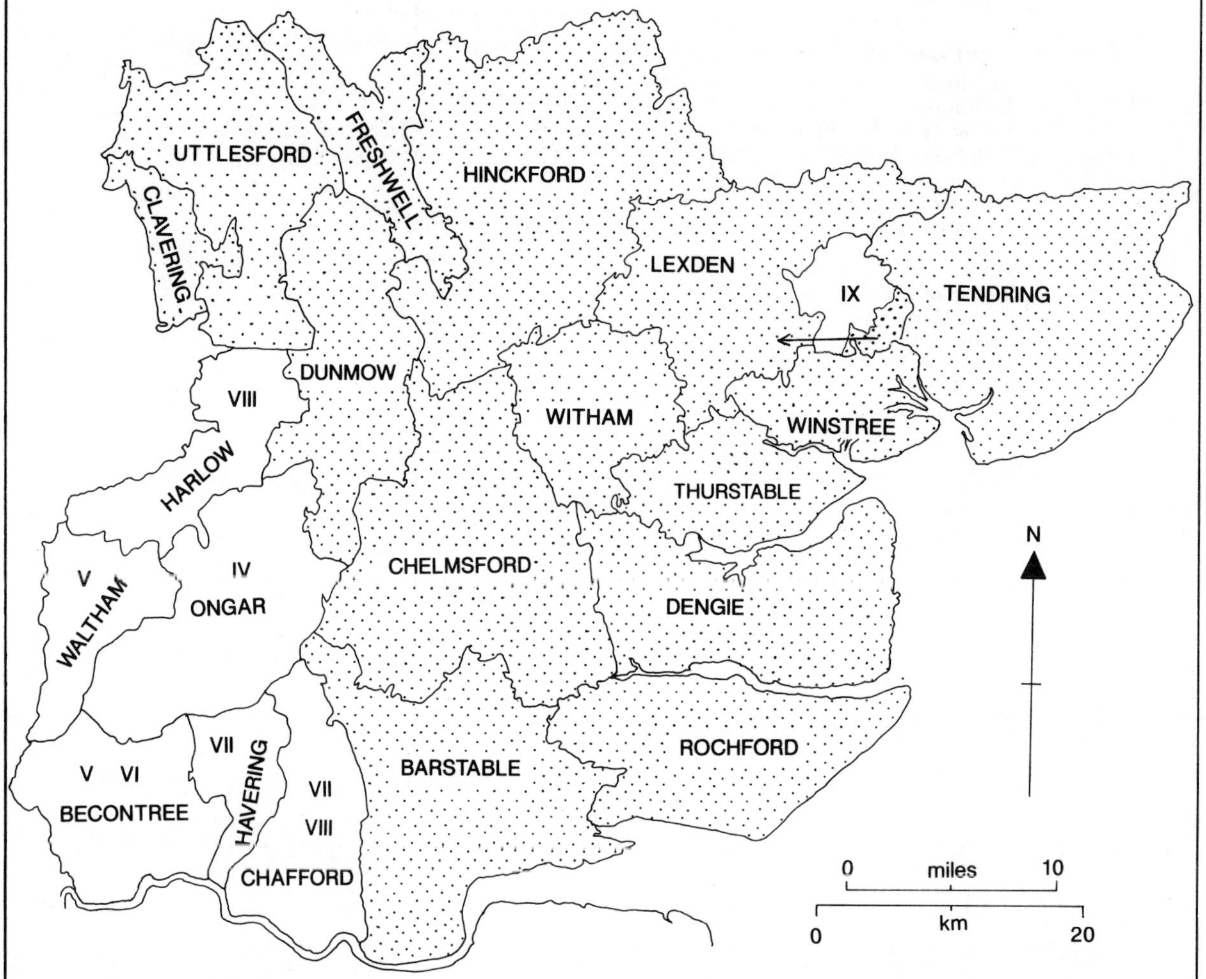

I Natural History, Prehistory, Domesday

II Ecclesiastical, Political, Social and Economic

III Roman Essex

IV Ongar Hundred

V Waltham Hundred, Becontree Hundred (pt.)

VI Becontree Hundred (cont.)

VII Havering Liberty, Chafford Hundred (pt.)

VIII Chafford Hundred (cont.), Harlow Hundred

IX Colchester Borough

Bibliography and Bibliography Supplement

Volumes yet to be published

LIST OF CLASSES OF DOCUMENTS IN THE ESSEX RECORD OFFICE

USED IN THIS VOLUME WITH THEIR CLASS NUMBERS

The records are divided between the main office at Chelmsford and the branch office at Colchester. Most of the records relating to Colchester, other than official County Records, are held at Colchester.

County Council of Essex

C/DA	Architect's Department
C/ME	Education Committee Minutes
C/MPa	Public Assistance Committee Minutes
C/T	Title Deeds of Properties
C/TE	School Deeds (some documents may no longer be available)
N/CME	Education Committee Minutes

Deposited Records

D/AB	Bishop of London, Commissary in Essex and Herts.
D/AC	Archdeacon of Colchester
D/AL	Bishop of London, Consistory Court
D/AZ	Archdeacons, Miscellaneous Extracts and Indexes
D/B	Borough Records
D/C	Diocesan Records (many sub-classes, D/CC to D/CV)
D/D	Estate and Family (many sub-classes, D/DA to D/DZ)
D/E	Ruridecanal Records
D/F	Business
D/NB	Nonconformist, Baptists
D/NC	Nonconformist, Congregationalists
D/NM	Nonconformist, Methodists
D/P	Parish Records
D/Q	Charities
D/TX	Essex Turnpikes Trust
D/Y 2	Morant Papers
D/Z	Miscellaneous Archives

Education Records

E/ML	School Log Books
E/P	Plans of New Schools
E/S	Subscription and Punishment Books, Salaries, Vouchers, etc.

Poor Law Guardians

G/Co	Colchester Union

Petty Sessions

P/Co	Colchester Division

Court of Quarter Sessions (Essex County)

Q/AB	Bridges
Q/AG	Gaols, Houses of Correction
Q/AM	Minor Functions
Q/CR	Clerk of the Peace, Parliamentary Returns
Q/RDc	Enclosure Awards
Q/RPl	Land Tax Assessments
Q/RSm	Freemasons
Q/RSr	Charities
Q/RTh	Hearth Tax Assessments
Q/RUm	Public Undertakings, Plans of Schemes
Q/RUo	Public Undertakings, Acts and Orders
Q/RUt	Turnpike Trusts
Q/SB	Sessions Bundles
Q/SMg	Sessions Books
Q/SO	Order Books
Q/SR	Sessions Rolls

Sound Archive

S/A

Transcripts

T/A	Originals in public repositories
T/B	Originals in private custody
T/M	Maps
T/P	Material for parish histories
T/R	Parish Registers
T/Z	Miscellaneous

COLCHESTER BOROUGH MUNIMENTS

The Colchester borough muniments, most of which had been divided between the muniment room in Colchester castle, the public library, and the town hall, were deposited in the Colchester branch of the Essex Record Office from 1985. Those records already listed in mid 1993 are identified by their catalogue mark; those uncatalogued are described or identified by their accession number, for example, items in Acc. C1 are part of the accession which came from the castle muniment room, those in Acc. C3 came from the library, and those in Acc. C4 from the town hall. Where an accession is a large one, box numbers have been cited to aid retrieval.

The following are the main classes used:

D/B 5 Aa	Chamberlain's accounts
D/B 5 Ab	Chamberlain's Bills and Papers
D/B 5 Cb	Court Books
D/B 5 Cr	Court Rolls
D/B 5 Gb	Assembly Books
D/B 5 R	Entry Books
D/B 5 Sb	Sessions Books
D/B 5 Sr	Sessions Rolls

D/B 5 R1 and D/B 5 R2 were calendared by W. G. Benham as *The Oath Book of Colchester* and *The Red Paper Book of Colchester*.

NOTE ON ABBREVIATIONS

Among the abbreviations and short titles used are the following:

A.-S.	Anglo-Saxon
Abbrev. Plac.	*Placitorum Abbreviatio* (Record Commission, 1811)
Abbrev. Rot. Orig.	*Rotulorum Originalium Abbreviatio, temp. Hen. III, Edw. I* (Record Commission, 1805)
acct.	account
Acts of P.C.	*Acts of the Privy Council of England* (H.M.S.O. 1890–1964)
Agric. Hist. Rev.	*Agricultural History Review*
Alum. Cantab. to 1751; 1752–1900	*Alumni Cantabrigienses, to 1751, 1752–1900*, ed. J. Venn and J. A. Venn (Cambridge, 1922–7, 1940–54)
Alum. Oxon. 1500–1714; 1715–1886	*Alumni Oxonienses, 1500–1714, 1715–1886*, ed. J. Foster (Oxford, 1888–92)
Antiq.	Antiquaries
App.	Appendix
Arch.	Archaeology, Archaeological
B.A.R.	British Archaeological Reports
B.L.	British Library
Bapt.	Baptist
bd.	board
biog.	biographical
bk.	book
Bk. of Fees	*The Book of Fees* (H.M.S.O. 1920–31)
Bodl.	Bodleian Library
Brit.	Britain, British
Britnell, *Growth and Decline*	R. H. Britnell, *Growth and Decline in Colchester, 1300–1525* (1986)
Brown, *Colch. 1815–1914*	A. F. J. Brown, *Colchester 1815–1914* (1980)
Bull. Inst. Hist. Res.	*Bulletin of the Institute of Historical Research*
C.J.	*Journals of the House of Commons*
Cal. Assize Rec. Essex, Eliz. I	*Calendar of Assize Records, Essex Indictments, Elizabeth I*, ed. J. S. Cockburn (H.M.S.O. 1978)
Cal. Chart. R.	*Calendar of the Charter Rolls preserved in the Public Record Office* (H.M.S.O. 1903–27)
Cal. Close	*Calendar of the Close Rolls preserved in the Public Record Office* (H.M.S.O. 1892–1963)
Cal. Cttee. for Compounding	*Calendar of the Proceedings of the Committee for Compounding, etc.* (H.M.S.O. 1889–92)
Cal. Cttee. for Advance of Money	*Calendar of the Committee for the Advance of Money, 1642–56* (H.M.S.O. 1888)
Cal. Doc. in France	*Calendar of Documents preserved in France* (H.M.S.O. 1899)
Cal. Exch. Jews	*Plea Rolls of the Exchequer of the Jews* (Jewish Historical Society of England, 1905–92)
Cal. Fine R.	*Calendar of the Fine Rolls preserved in the Public Record Office* (H.M.S.O. 1911–62)
Cal. Inq. Misc.	*Calendar of Inquisitions Miscellaneous (Chancery) preserved in the Public Record Office* (H.M.S.O. 1916–68)
Cal. Inq. p.m.	*Calendar of Inquisitions post mortem preserved in the Public Record Office* (H.M.S.O. 1904–87)
Cal. Inq. p.m. Hen. VII	*Calendar of Inquisitions post mortem, Henry VII* (H.M.S.O. 1898–1955)
Cal. Lib.	*Calendar of the Liberate Rolls preserved in the Public Record Office* (H.M.S.O. 1917–64)
Cal. Mem. R.	*Calendar of Memoranda Rolls, 1326–7* (H.M.S.O. 1968)
Cal. Papal Reg.	*Calendar of the Papal Registers: Papal Letters* (H.M.S.O. and Irish MSS. Com. 1891–1986)

NOTE ON ABBREVIATIONS

Cal. Papal Pets.	*Calendar of Entries in the Papal Registers relating to Great Britain and Ireland, Petitions to the Pope, 1342–1419* (H.M.S.O. 1896)
Cal. Pat.	*Calendar of the Patent Rolls preserved in the Public Record Office* (H.M.S.O. 1891–1982)
Cal. S.P. Dom.	*Calendar of State Papers, Domestic Series* (H.M.S.O. 1856–1972)
Cal. S.P. Scot.	*Calendar of State Papers relating to Scotland* (Edinburgh, 1898–1969)
Cal. S.P. Ven.	*Calendar of State Papers and Manuscripts relating to English Affairs in Venice and Northern Italy* (H.M.S.O. 1864–1947)
Cal. Treas. Bks.	*Calendar of Treasury Books 1660–1718* (H.M.S.O. 1904–69)
Camd., Camd. Soc.	Camden Series, Camden Society
Cart. Sax. ed. Birch	*Cartularium Saxonicum*, ed. W. de Gray Birch (1883–99)
Cart. St. John of Jerusalem	*The Cartulary of the Knights of St. John of Jerusalem in England: Secunda Camera, Essex*, ed. M. Gervers (Records of Social and Economic History, new series vi)
Cat. Anct. D.	*A Descriptive Catalogue of Ancient Deeds in the Public Record Office* (H.M.S.O. 1890–1915)
ch.	church
Ch. Bells Essex	C. Deedes and H. B. Walters, *The Church Bells of Essex* (1909)
Ch. Plate Essex	G. M. Benton, F. W. Galpin, and W. J. Pressey, *The Church Plate of Essex* (1926)
Char.	Charity
chart.	charter, charters
Chelm.	Chelmsford
Chelm. Dioc. Yr. Bk.	Diocese of Chelmsford, *Year Book*
Chron.	*Chronicle*
Close R.	*Close Rolls of the Reign of Henry III preserved in the Public Record Office* (H.M.S.O. 1902–75)
Colch.	Colchester
Colch. Arch. Rep.	P. Crummy, *Colchester Archaeological Reports* (Colchester Archaeological Trust, 1981–, in progress)
Colch. Cart.	*Cartularium Monasterii Sancti Johannis Baptiste de Colecestria*, ed. S. A. Moore (Roxburghe Club, 2 vols. 1897)
Colch. Charters	*Charters of the Borough of Colchester*, trans. W. G. Benham (Colchester Borough Council, 1904)
Colch. Gaz.	*Colchester Gazette* (from 1970 *Evening Gazette*)
Colch. Expr.	*Colchester Express*
Colch. Institute	Colchester Institute, Sheepen Road, Colchester
Colch. Mus.	Colchester Museums, Resource Centre, 14 Ryegate Road, Colchester
Coll.	College
colln.	collection(s)
Com.	Commission, Commissioners
Complete Peerage	G. E. C[ockayne] and others, *The Complete Peerage* (2nd edn. 1910–59)
Corp.	Corporation
ct.	court
Cur. Reg. R.	*Curia Regis Rolls preserved in the Public Record Office* (H.M.S.O. 1922–79)
cttee.	committee
D.N.B.	*Dictionary of National Biography*
Davids, *Nonconf. in Essex*	T. W. Davids, *Annals of Evangelical Nonconformity in Essex from the time of Wycliffe to the Restoration* (1863)
Dict.	Dictionary
dioc.	diocese
Dir.	*Directory*
Dugdale, *Mon.*	W. Dugdale, *Monasticon Anglicanum*, ed. J. Caley and others (6 vols. 1817–30)
E.A.T.	*Transactions of the Essex Archaeological Society* (from 3rd series iv, 1972, *Essex Archaeology and History*)
E.C.L. Colch.	Essex County Library, Local Studies Collection held at Colchester Library
E.C.S.	*Essex County Standard* (*Essex Standard* 1831–92)

E.H.R.	*English Historical Review*
E.J.	*Essex Journal*
E.R.	*Essex Review*
E.R.O.	Essex Record Office
E.S.A.H.	Essex Society for Archaeology and History (formerly Essex Archaeological Society)
eccl.	ecclesiastical
Econ. H.R.	*Economic History Review*
Educ.	Education
Educ. Enq. Abstract	*Abstract of Answers and Returns relative to the State of Education in England*, H.C. 62 (1835), xliii
Educ. of Poor Digest	*Digest of Returns to the Select Committee on the Education of the Poor*, H.C. 224 (1819), ix (2)
Eng.	England, English
enq.	enquiry
Essex C.C.	Essex County Council
Essex Map (1777)	J. Chapman and P. André, *Map of Essex from an actual survey taken in 1772, 1773, and 1774* (1777)
Essex Tel.	*Essex Telegraph* (1858–1908), *Essex County Telegraph* (1908–1951)
Feet of F. Essex	*Feet of Fines for Essex* (Essex Archaeological Society, 5 vols. 1899–1991)
Feud. Aids	*Inquisitions and Assessments relating to Feudal Aids preserved in the Public Record Office* (H.M.S.O. 1899–1920)
G.L.R.O.	Greater London Record Office
G.R.O.	General Register Office, later Office of Population Censuses and Surveys
Gant, 'Hist. Berechurch'	L. H. Gant, 'History of Berechurch', MS. in possession of the Friends of Colchester Museum
Gent. Mag.	*Gentleman's Magazine*
Geol. Surv.	Geological Survey
Guildhall	London, Guildhall Library
H.C.	House of Commons
H.L.	House of Lords
H.M.S.O.	Her (His) Majesty's Stationery Office
Hist.	History, Historical
Hist. MSS. Com.	Royal Commission on Historical Manuscripts
Jnl.	*Journal*
L.J.	*Journals of the House of Lords*
L. & P. Hen. VIII	*Letters and Papers, Foreign and Domestic, of the Reign of Henry VIII* (H.M.S.O 1864–1932)
Lamb. Pal. Libr.	Lambeth Palace Library
Lond. Gaz.	*London Gazette*
man.	manor, manorial
Min.	Ministry
mins.	minutes
Morant, *Colch.*	P. Morant, *The History and Antiquities of Colchester* (1768 edn. in *The History and Antiquities of Essex*)
Morant, *Essex*	P. Morant, *The History and Antiquities of Essex* (2 vols. 1768)
Mun.	Muniments
mus.	museum
Nat.	National
Newcourt, *Repertorium*	R. Newcourt, *Repertorium Ecclesiasticum Parochiale Londinense* (2 vols. 1710)
O.E.D.	*Oxford English Dictionary*
O.S.	Ordnance Survey
P.N. Elements	A. H. Smith, *English Place-Name Elements* (English Place-Name Society, xxv, xxvi, 1956)
P.N. Essex	P. H. Reaney, *The Place-Names of Essex* (English Place-Name Society, xii, 1935)

P.O. Dir. Essex	*The Post Office Directory of Essex*
P.R.O.	Public Record Office
P.R.S.	Pipe Roll Society
par.	parish
parl.	parliament, parliamentary
Pat. R.	*Patent Rolls of the Reign of Henry III preserved in the Public Record Office* (H.M.S.O. 1901–3)
Pevsner, *Essex*	N. Pevsner, *The Buildings of England, Essex* (2nd edn. 1965)
Phillips, *Ten Men*	A. Phillips, *Ten Men and Colchester: Public Good and Private Profit in a Victorian Town* (1985)
Pipe R.	*Pipe Rolls* (Pipe Roll Society and other publications)
Poor Law Abstract, 1804	*Abstract of Returns relative to the Expence and Maintenance of the Poor* (printed by order of the House of Commons, 1804)
Poor Law Abstract, 1818	*Abstract of Returns to Orders of the House of Commons relative to Assessments for Relief of the Poor*, H.C. 82 (1818), xix
priv. print.	privately printed
Proc.	*Proceedings*
R.C.H.M. *Essex*	Royal Commission on Historical Monuments (England), *An Inventory of the Historical Monuments in Essex* (4 vols. 1916–23)
R.O.	Record Office
Rec.	Records
Rec. Com.	Record Commission
Reg. Baldock	*Registrum Radulphi Baldock, Gilberti Segrave, Ricardi Newport et Stephani Gravesend, episcoporum Londoniensium* (Canterbury & York Society, 1911)
Reg. Regum Anglo-Norm.	*Regesta Regum Anglo-Normannorum*, ed. H. W. C. Davies and others (1913–69)
Rep.	Report
32nd Rep. Com. Char.	*32nd Report of the Commissioners for Inquiring concerning Charities*, H.C. 108 (1837), xxv
Rolls Ser.	Rolls Series
Rot. de Ob. et Fin.	*Rotuli de Oblatis et Finibus* (Record Commission, 1835)
Rot. Hund.	*Rotuli Hundredorum temp. Hen. III & Edw. I* (Record Commission, 1812–18)
Rot. Litt. Claus.	*Rotuli Litterarum Clausarum, 1204–27* (Record Commission, 1833–44)
Rot. Litt. Pat.	*Rotuli Litterarum Patentium, 1204–16* (Record Commission, 1835)
Rot. Parl.	*Rotuli Parliamentorum* (1783, 1832)
sch.	school
Sel.	Select
Smith, *Eccl. Hist. Essex*	H. Smith, *The Ecclesiastical History of Essex under the Long Parliament and Commonwealth* [*c.* 1931]
Tax. Eccl.	*Taxatio Ecclesiastica Angliae et Walliae auctoritate P. Nicholai IV circa A.D. 1291* (Record Commission, 1802)
Trans. R.H.S.	*Transactions of the Royal Historical Society*
uncat.	uncatalogued
V.C.H.	*Victoria County History*
Valor Eccl.	*Valor Ecclesiasticus temp. Hen. VIII auctoritate regia institutus* (Record Commission, 1810–34)
Westm. Abbey Mun.	Westminster Abbey Muniments

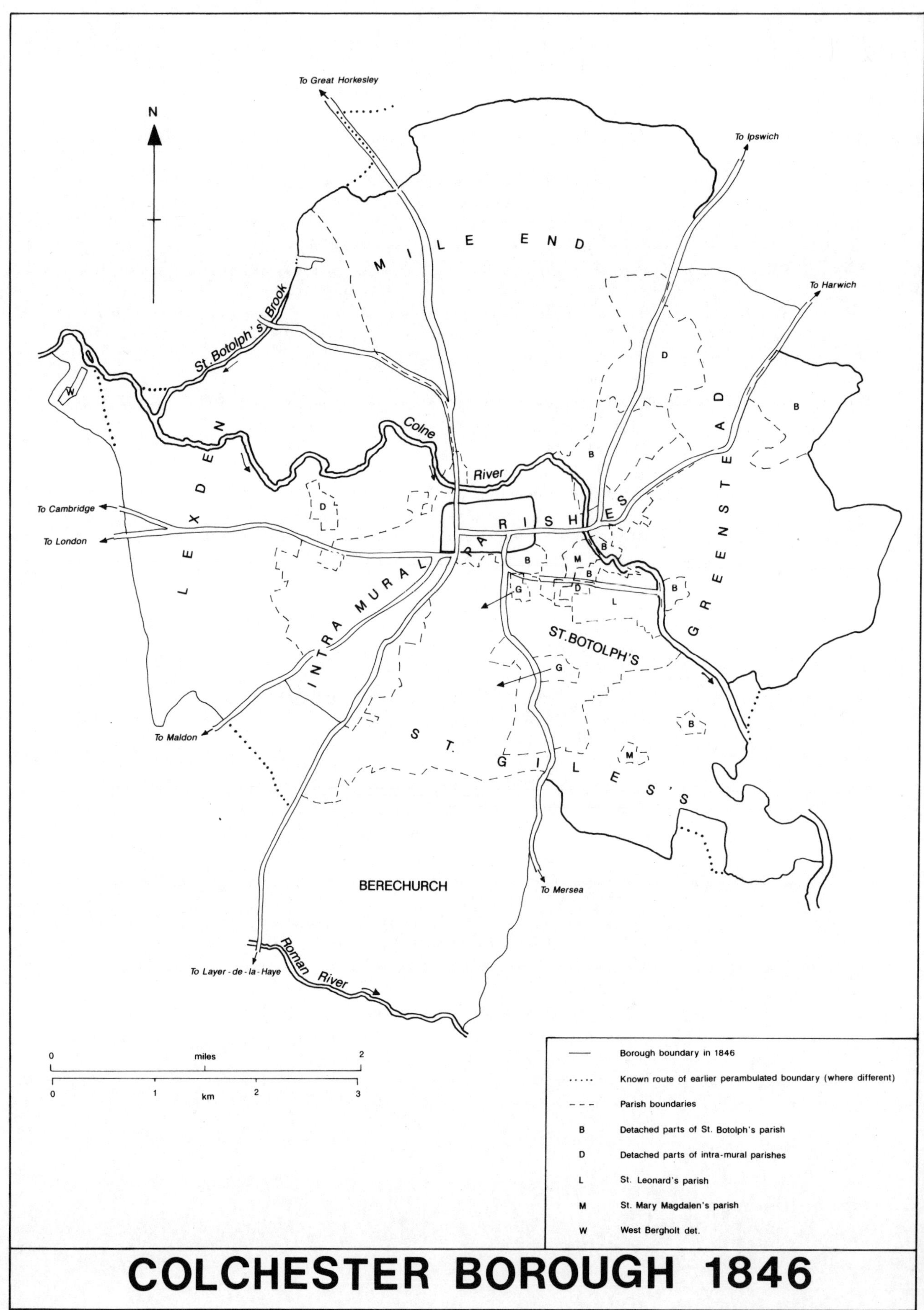

COLCHESTER BOROUGH 1846

THE BOROUGH OF COLCHESTER

COLCHESTER lies on the river Colne, at the upper limit of navigation and the lowest crossing-point of the river, a position which attracted settlement from the late Iron Age. The stronghold of Cunobelin was succeeded by the Roman *colonia* whose walls were re-used by the Anglo-Saxon *burh* and the medieval town. Through its port at the Hythe the town was able to carry on both coastal and overseas trade, and its position on the road from London to East Anglia and the main east coast ports provided good inland communications. Colchester lies at the centre of a rich agricultural area, and much of its early prosperity and importance was as a market for agricultural produce. By the late 12th century, however, the town had started to specialize in textiles, and the arrival *c.* 1570 of Dutch refugee bay- and say-makers gave new impetus to the trade, which continued until the mid 18th century. By the 17th century Colchester was also known for its oysters. The town was slow to industrialize, but became a centre of engineering in the later 19th century. In the 20th century it has become a retail and tourist centre.

Although it was the oldest town in Essex, and until the 20th century the largest, its position in the north-east corner of the county robbed Colchester of most administrative functions. Colchester castle was the seat of the sheriff in the Middle Ages, but Chelmsford became the county town, and when Essex was given its own bishop in 1914 the see was established there. Colchester, however, was chosen as the site of Essex University in 1962.

In the late 20th century Colchester prided itself on being the oldest recorded town in Britain, the name Camulodunum having been used by the early 3rd-century writer Dio Cassius in his account of the Emperor Claudius's conquests in 43 A.D.[1] The identity of Colchester with Camulodunum was finally established only in the 19th century,[2] and the association with Shakespeare's Cymbeline (Cunobelin) was not exploited. In the Middle Ages the town was known for the legend of King Coel and his daughter St. Helen, but more recently the identity of the Colchester king with the Old King Cole of the nursery rhyme has been questioned.[3] There appears to be no evidence to support the suggestion, popularized *c.* 1980, that another nursery rhyme, Humpty Dumpty, derives from the destruction of a cannon at the siege of Colchester in 1648.[4] Daniel Defoe leased an estate in Mile End from 1722, and set the first part of *Moll Flanders* in Colchester.[5]

The extent of the borough remained virtually unchanged, covering *c.* 11,333 a., from the 14th century or earlier until 1974, apart from minor adjustments made in 1931.[6] The built-up area of the town has remained within those boundaries, except for some 20th-century housing and commercial building on the eastern edge of Stanway parish.[7] The following account deals with the area of the ancient borough, including its outlying parishes of Berechurch or West Donyland, Greenstead, Lexden, and Mile End, and takes no account of the large area brought into the borough in 1974.

1 *P.N. Essex*, 367.

2 Morant, *Colch.* 12–17; Camden, *Britannia* (1806), ii. 122–3; B.L. Add. MS. 33659, ff. 65–89.

3 *Oxf. Dict. Nursery Rhymes*, 134–5; below, Med. Colch. (Intro.).

4 *Colch. Express*, 1 Dec. 1972; *E.C.S.* 7, 14 Jan. 1983.

5 D. Defoe, *Moll Flanders*; below, Outlying Parts (Mile End, Manors).

6 *Census*, 1901, 1931.

7 Below, Fig. 13.

LATE IRON-AGE AND ROMAN COLCHESTER

The Iron-Age Fortress

Camulodunum was the Romanized form of the British name Camulodunon, meaning 'fortress of Camulos', the Celtic war-god.[1] At the time of the Roman conquest of 43 A.D. it was the principal centre of the Trinovantes, a tribe thought to have occupied an area roughly corresponding to Essex and south Suffolk.[2] The tribe first appears in the written record in 54 B.C. when Mandubracius, a young Trinovantian prince, fled to Julius Caesar for help after his father was killed by Cassivellaunus, king probably of the neighbouring Catuvellauni. After Caesar's defeat of Cassivellaunus, Mandubracius was allowed to return presumably to become king.[3]

According to the accepted history of Camulodunum during the earlier 1st century A.D.,[4] Tasciovanus became king of the Catuvellauni *c.* 20 B.C.; he used the mint mark VER (with variations) for Verulamium (St. Albans) and his coins circulated in an area centred on modern Hertfordshire. Two of his neighbours, Addedomaros of the Trinovantes and Dubnovellaunus of Kent, also issued coins, Addedomaros apparently in the Colne valley if not at Colchester. About 17 B.C. Tasciovanus struck some coins with the mint mark CAM showing that he had gained control of Camulodunum. Soon afterwards Addedomaros held sway at Colchester for *c.* 10 years until he was replaced by Dubnovellaunus who himself was driven out of Camulodunum *c.* 5–10 A.D. by Cunobelin, a son but not the successor of Tasciovanus. Cunobelin quickly expanded his newly made kingdom by acquiring Verulamium and its territory, and by *c.* 25 A.D. he had annexed Kent. In 40 A.D. Cunobelin expelled one of his sons, Adminius, who appealed to the Roman emperor Caligula for help. By 42 A.D. Cunobelin was dead and in the following year the Romans invaded under Aulus Plautius. Cunobelin's sons Caratacus and Togodumnus were defeated and Togodumnus died. The climax of the campaign was the emperor Claudius's entry into Camulodunum at the head of his army.

Much of that history is now the subject of debate. Opinions differ on the significance of the distribution of coinage, and the relative chronology has also been challenged. It has been argued that Addedomaros and Dubnovellaunus both held Camulodunum before Tasciovanus, and even that there were two contemporary leaders called Dubnovellaunus, one in Essex and the other in Kent. It has also been suggested that the late coins of Tasciovanus overlapped the earliest of Cunobelin. Various dates have been proposed for Addedomaros, Dubnovellaunus, and Tasciovanus, the most radical being 40–30 B.C., 30–25 B.C., and 25–10 B.C. respectively. It has also been argued that to attempt to ascribe precise dates at all is misleading, and that the arrival of Cunobelin at Camulodunum, for example, should be dated not *c.* 5–10 A.D., but simply to the early 1st century A.D.[5]

[1] A. L. F. Rivet and Colin Smith, *Place-Names of Roman Britain* (1981), 295. Mr. Paul Sealey is thanked for his help with specific points in this chapter.

[2] R. Dunnett, *The Trinovantes.*

[3] Julius Caesar, *De Bello Gallico*, v. 2.

[4] *Archaeologia*, cv. 1–46; *Britannia*, vi. 1–19; C. F. C. Hawkes and M. R. Hull, *Camulodunum*; S. Frere, *Britannia* (3rd edn.), 29–35.

[5] B. Cunliffe, *Coinage and Society in Britain and Gaul*, 29–39; *Oppida in Barbarian Europe*, ed. B. Cunliffe and T. Rowley, 258–63; R. D. Van Arsdell, *Celtic Coinage of Britain*, 99, 349–84; C. Haselgrove, *Iron Age Coinage in South-East Eng.* (B.A.R., Brit. ser. clxxiv), 94; cf. *Brit. Numismatic Jnl.* lix. 235–7; N. E. France and B. M. Gobel, *Romano-British Temple at Harlow*, 62.

The name Camulodunum, abbreviated CAM, first occurs on rare coins of Tasciovanus of the late 1st century B.C.[6] The date corresponds approximately to the earliest available archaeological evidence for the settlement which thus may not have been the centre from which the Trinovantes struck their first coins, and indeed may not have existed when Caesar invaded the country in 54 B.C. Most of Camulodunum lay on a block of land bounded on the north by the river Colne and on the south by Roman River. It was protected by a series of earth dykes 24 km. (15 miles) long. The system is the largest of its kind and date known in Britain and is testimony to the considerable importance of Camulodunum in late Iron-Age Britain. The settlement was turned into a stronghold by a careful combination of man-made earthworks and natural features such as valleys, rivers, and dense woodland. The plan of the dyke system points to a long sequence of unstructured development. There is unlikely to have been any long-term master plan, but instead each new dyke seems to have been added to provide some specific enhancement to the existing system. The complexity and scale of the system suggests that it was not just an extravagant proclamation of status but was a defensive arrangement which was repeatedly needed and frequently upgraded. Clearly the appearance of Cunobelin at Camulodunum did not mark the start of a long period of stability in the area.

Most of the dykes consisted of a **V**-shaped ditch and a bank formed from the upcast. There was no berm between the ditch and the bank and there is little evidence for any timber structures such as palisades, revetments, or gates. The depth of the ditches varied from dyke to dyke, from *c.* 5 ft. to *c.* 13 ft., with banks in proportion up to *c.* 10 ft. high. Thus the dykes provided barriers up to 25 ft. high which would have been especially effective against chariots. Most dykes faced west to provide protection from attack from that direction. Prettygate Dyke had a ditch to either side of its bank, and Triple Dyke consisted of three small dykes side by side. Most of the dykes run transversely valley to valley (north to south) to provide sequential lines of defence but a few were placed laterally (some **U**-shaped in section) so that they provided barriers between the entrances of some of the transverse dykes. Such variations and oddities were probably designed to control the movement of the chariots, and to a lesser extent of the mounted warriors, of defenders and aggressors alike. At places where the rivers could easily be crossed the dykes seem to have been continued beyond the Colne and Roman River, to prevent an opponent from circumventing the lines of north–south dykes.

The earliest part of the system[7] is Heath Farm Dyke which protected the Gosbecks area; the latest seems to have been Gryme's Dyke which, if not post-Boudican, was certainly post-conquest.[8] The appearance of the name Cam[ulodunum] 'fortress of Camulos' on the late 1st-century B.C. coins of Tasciovanus suggests that some dykes had been constructed by that date. It has been suggested that the construction of each major phase of the earthworks was linked to changes in the size and position of the defended area,[9] but there is no evidence for the demolition of any dykes, apart from the late destruction of Sheepen Dyke. Nor is it likely that Gosbecks was ever outside the system.

Farming was concentrated at Gosbecks and in the fertile lands along the northern edge of the Roman River valley, while the industrial and commercial centre was the riverside site of Sheepen. Much agricultural and industrial produce was

[6] Van Arsdell, *Celtic Coinage*, nos. 1684 (Mack 186), 1694 (Mack 187); *E.A.T.* 3rd ser. xiii. 35–7.

[7] *Colch. Arch. Rep.* xi (forthcoming).

[8] Ibid. A Claudian coin and a sherd of *terra sigillata* were found under the bank of Gryme's Dyke in 1977.

[9] *Oppida in Barbarian Europe*, 339–59.

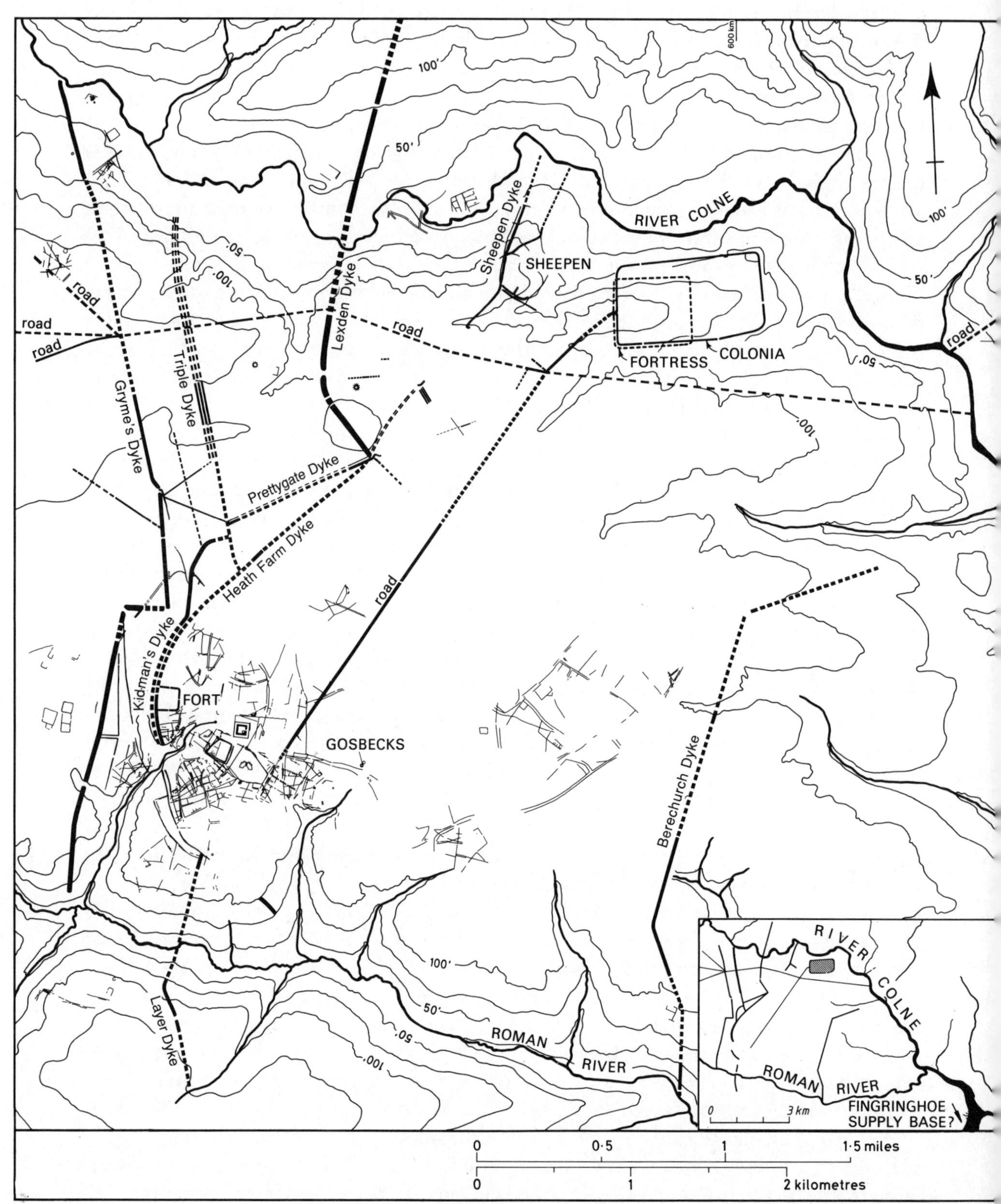

FIG. 3. CAMULODUNUM, SHOWING ROMAN ROADS AND THE LEGIONARY FORTRESS

imported and exported along the Colne, and in its heyday Camulodunum served a great hinterland north of the Thames, encompassing the Trinovantian and neighbouring Catuvellaunian territories and beyond. All that could have been achieved through large, regular markets where much of the region's produce was exchanged. The closely connected activities of providing such markets and striking money presumably underpinned Cunobelin's economic success.

Two distinct periods of occupation or activity can be detected at Gosbecks.[10] The area was at first given over mainly to native farming, but later, presumably some time after the Boudican revolt of 60–1 A.D., the site became an important tribal sanctuary with a temple[11] and a theatre.[12] The temple stood inside a square ditched enclosure which was probably laid out in the late Iron Age as an important cultural site. Against the inside of the innermost dyke was a small Roman fort of the conquest period,[13] sited to police the area while causing minimal disturbance to its layout. Gosbecks was probably the site of a pre-Roman market and the Roman authorities were probably keen to maintain such a major regional market for its economic benefits. The frequent association in antiquity of markets and religious sites explains the presence of the temple, and of the large bronze statuette of Mercury, the Roman god of merchandise, found at Gosbecks.[14]

The heart and earliest part of the Gosbecks site was an exceptionally large native farmstead, the main buildings of which stood in a large trapezoidal enclosure which on analogy with similar sites elsewhere probably contained round houses. Complicated multi-period systems of trackways, ditched fields, and defensive dykes all lead to the main enclosure and possibly represent a century or more of development. The main enclosure was remodelled several times. In its first phase, the enclosing ditch was over 10 ft. deep and clearly defensive. Without excavation it is not possible to determine the relationship between the defended farmstead and the earliest of the dykes, but it cannot be assumed that the defences around the farmstead predate the earliest dykes.

Sheepen provided a manufacturing and trading base, first for the Iron-Age settlement, then for the Roman fortress, and finally for the pre-Boudican town. Despite its industrial nature, finds from Sheepen are extraordinarily plentiful and of high quality, particularly when compared with the material recovered from the earliest levels in the town centre. Products from Sheepen[15] in the pre-conquest period included moulds generally thought to have been for the production of coin blanks.[16] After the Boudican revolt the site became a native sanctuary with the construction of at least four temples.[17] The pattern of change is reminiscent of Gosbecks and prompts the question whether Sheepen too was a market site. Such a market may have catered for manufactured goods rather than livestock and agricultural produce, which could have been the primary concern of Gosbecks.

Most of the late Iron-Age burials have been found at Lexden, between Sheepen

[10] *Aerial Arch.* iv. 77–82; *Temples, Churches and Religion: Recent Research in Roman Britain*, ed. W. Rodwell, 258–64.

[11] *V.C.H. Essex*, iii. 120–1; M. R. Hull, *Roman Colch.* 261–4; *Temples, Churches and Religion*, 259–60.

[12] *Britannia*, ii. 27–47.

[13] Ibid. viii. 185–7; *Aerial Arch.* iv. 77–82.

[14] Hull, *Roman Colch.* 264; *E.A.T.* N.S. xxiv. 43–6; J. M. C. Toynbee, *Art in Britain under the Romans*, 72–3.

[15] For the 1930s excavations, Hawkes and Hull, *Camulodunum*; cf. *Kongress-Akten der Beitrage am Limes-Kongress in Aalen 1983*, (Sonder Forschungen u. Berichten zur vor- u. frühes Baden-Wurttemberg); C. Haselgrove, *Iron Age Coinage in South-East Eng.* 163–71. For the 1970 excavation, R. Niblett, *Sheepen: an Early Roman Industrial Site at Camulodunum* (Council for Brit. Arch. Research Rep. lvii); cf. P. R. Sealey, *Amphoras from the 1970 Excavations at Colchester, Sheepen*; R. M. Luff, *A Zooarchaeological Study of the Roman North-Western Provinces*, 26–72.

[16] Use of the 'moulds' for coin production has been questioned by various writers, e.g. *Kongress-Akten der Beitrage am Limes-Kongress in Aalen 1983*.

[17] Referred to as Temples 2–5. For Temples 2 and 3: Hull, *Roman Colch.* 224–36; *Britannia*, vii. 427; for Temples 2–5 especially Temples 4 and 5 which are otherwise not published, *Temples, Churches and Religion*, 248–56; M. J. T. Lewis, *Temples in Roman Britain.*

and Gosbecks, the most important being the Lexden tumulus.[18] The remarkable collection of grave goods, dated to *c.* 15–10 B.C.,[19] included figurines of a boar and a bull, a candelabrum, at least 17 amphoras, chain mail with a leather under-garment, thread-like gold strips, and a silver medallion of the head of Augustus. They were accompanied by a small amount of cremated human bone and were mostly on or near the floor of a deep pit under the barrow mound. Some of the objects had been deliberately broken at the time of the cremation and the grave pit seems to have contained a square wooden chamber.[20] Although remarkable, the surviving grave goods provide only a very incomplete picture of a quite exceptional group which may have included various pieces of furniture such as a couch or a litter, a large wooden chest and a folding stool, vessels such as a bronze bowl and a bronze jug, and items incorporating silver- and gold-embedded textiles. The size of the group, the richness of the objects in it, and the rarity of the burial rite suggest a king's burial. The medallion of Augustus may be of great significance since heads based on that of Augustus appear on some of the more Romanized Celtic coins of the period.[21] The numismatic evidence as presently understood is of limited help in identifying the person buried, although Addedomaros is an obvious candidate.

About 200 m. north-west of the tumulus was a flat cremation cemetery which over a period of years has yielded *c.* 30 vessels from at least 9 burials. The material is typically mid 1st-century B.C. to early 1st-century A.D., but the absence of any Gallo-Belgic pottery suggests that the burials predate the Lexden tumulus by up to 30 years. The group thus provides the earliest available evidence for occupation at Camulodunum.[22]

Members of the native aristocracy were buried in wooden chambers at a special funerary site at Stanway, a short distance west of Gosbecks.[23] Each of the chambers had been placed symmetrically in large, roughly square, ditched enclosures up to 80 m. across. There were five enclosures in two rows. Each of the chambers was as large as a small room and contained the remains of a rich collection of grave goods which had been ritually smashed and scattered throughout the backfill of the chamber. Cremated human remains were also sprinkled throughout the backfill, and a least one of the chambers seems to have been broken up as part of the ritual. Near the largest of the chambers were two secondary graves, both made *c.* 10 years after the Roman invasion. Grave goods in the richer of them included over 20 vessels of pottery, metal, and glass, a set of glass gaming counters, a possible gaming board, a spear, and probably a shield.

Although the grave assemblages were not as rich and varied as that in the Lexden tumulus, the people with whom they were buried were of high status and presumably related to each other by marriage or birth. The largest chamber dated to *c.* 30 A.D., when Cunobelin was in power, was probably the grave of one of his relatives. The latest chamber dates to *c.* 60 A.D. or later and was presumably for a woman since it contained beads from a broken necklace. She may have been a daughter or a niece, or perhaps a daughter-in-law, of Cunobelin. Such a burial after the Roman conquest indicates something about the relationship between the Romans and at least one element of the local aristocratic class. Not only did the British nobles buried at Stanway see no moral dilemma in using Roman or

[18] *Archaeologia*, xxvi. 241–54; J. Foster, *Lexden Tumulus* (B.A.R., Brit. ser. clvi).

[19] Foster, *Lexden Tumulus*, 178.

[20] Ibid. 167–9.

[21] e.g. coins of Tasciovanus, Van Arsdell, *Celtic Coinage of Britain*, nos. 1794 (Mack 163), 1814 (Mack 176).

[22] *Colch. Arch. Rep.* xi (forthcoming). For a plan see Foster, *Lexden Tumulus*, 2.

[23] *Current Archaeology*, cxxxii. 492–7; *Colch. Archaeologist*, v. 1–5; vi. 1–5.

Romanized 'consumer goods' but they were allowed to live alongside the Roman colony with sufficient freedom to continue their own customs. The secondary grave with the arms appears to be the burial place of someone who enjoyed a particularly favoured status with the Roman authorities. It may be that after conquering Camulodunum Claudius installed a pro-Roman Briton such as Adminius as the native leader, and that the latest chamber was for a member of a pro-Roman faction of which Adminius was or had been the key person.

Camulodunum, or at least its immediate environs, was densely inhabited; the presence after the conquest of the fortress and the Gosbecks fort implies a large indigenous population in the vicinity and so too does the scale of the native defences and the large investment of man-hours which their construction represents. Yet the focus of the settlement was the comparatively small trapezoidal enclosure at Gosbecks to which the trackway systems led. The convergence suggests that within the enclosure were the houses of the successive native kings and that Camulodunum was in essence a large royal estate, which, by developing its role as a port and regional market place, provided its owners with far-reaching political and economic power.[24]

That interpretation is supported by the use of the site as a sanctuary in the Roman period. The locating of a theatre and temple beside the trapezoidal enclosure can be no accident and suggests that the latter was a place of great cultural significance for the Britons. The site of the trapezoidal enclosure appears to have been retained in the Roman period and its defensive ditch replaced with a more modest boundary. The architectural styles of the major buildings reflect native taste, and thus presumably some degree of native control of the site. The theatre is not an orthodox type,[25] unlike the more classical theatre in the colony,[26] and the temple in its square-ditched enclosure is not of a purely Graeco-Roman style like the great temple of Claudius in the colony but is of the Romano-Celtic type. In the light of the excavations at Stanway, it is conceivable that Gosbecks in the post-conquest period was more than a sanctuary on a site of great historical significance to the native population, and that Cunobelin was buried within the square-ditched enclosure.

The Legionary Fortress

Shortly after Claudius's entry into Camulodunum the army consolidated its gains with the construction of a legionary fortress. The new base[27] was carefully sited: inside the defences of the native settlement, but on unoccupied land so as to cause as little disruption as possible; near the river to take advantage of waterborne transport and yet sufficiently high to command a good view of the surrounding area; guarding the main river crossings into the oppidum; close to a good supply of water. The site which met all the requirements was a spur of land immediately downstream from Sheepen, and work began there *c.* 44 A.D. The longitudinal axis of the fortress was placed on an east–west ridge formed by the steep slope down to the river Colne on the north and the more gentle slope to the south. The fortress was aligned on true north and its east and principal gate (*porta praetoria*) faced seaward. On the east was a large annexe, the precise size and position of which have not been established but which is assumed to have been about a third the size of the original fortress. The fortress may have been preceded by a much smaller

[24] *Aerial Arch.* iv. 77–82.
[25] *Britannia*, ii. 43.
[26] Ibid. xiii. 299–302; *Colch. Arch. Rep.* vi. 367–8.
[27] *Fortress into City*, ed. G. Webster, 24–41; *Colch. Arch. Rep.* vi. 7–14.

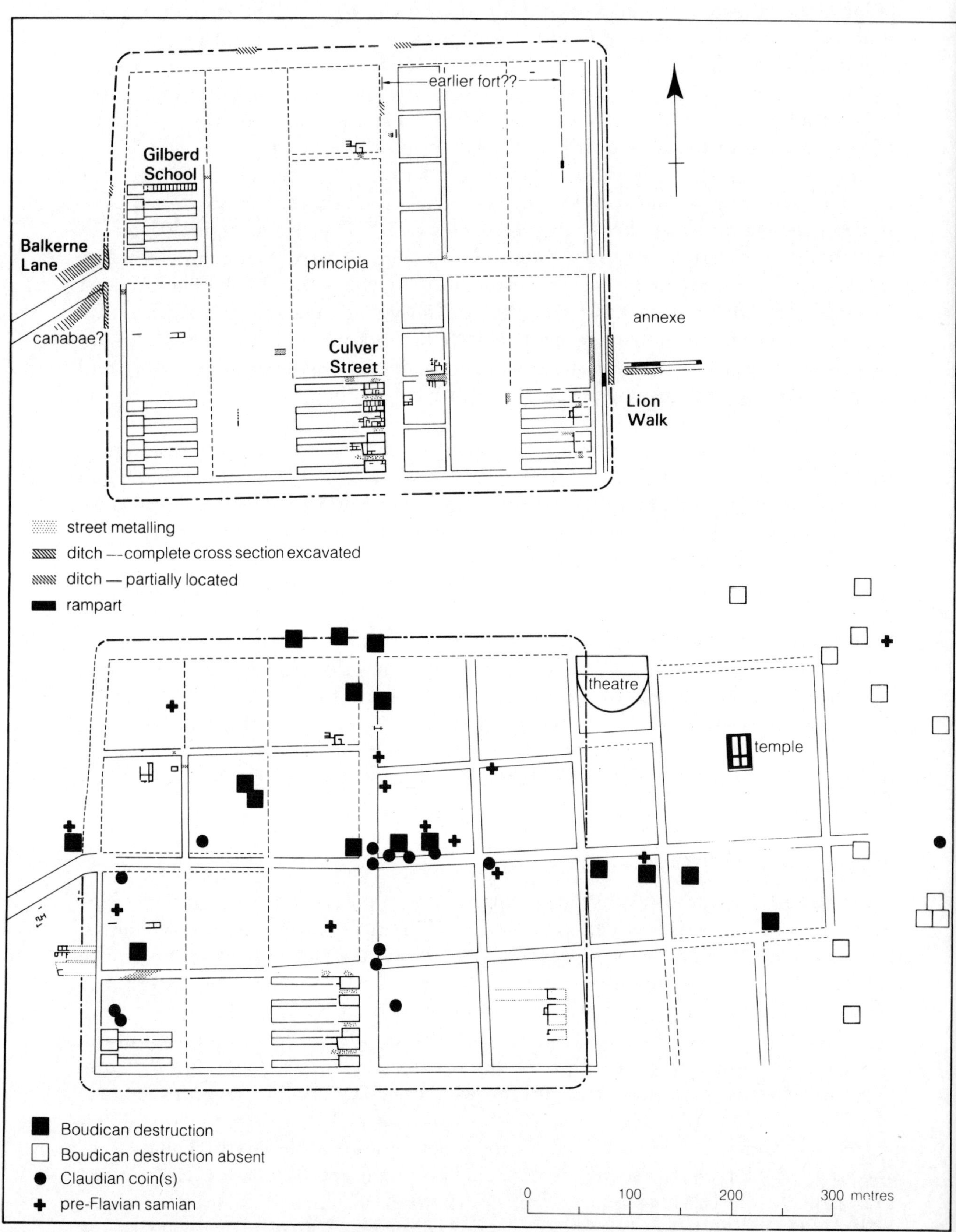

FIG. 4. THE LEGIONARY FORTRESS (TOP) AND THE PRE-BOUDICAN COLONY (BOTTOM)

unfinished Roman military base whose existence is suggested by a deep pre-Boudican north–south ditch and an early east–west rampart about 175 m. (190 yd.) east of the ditch.[28]

The layout of the fortress has been established clearly enough to show that the plan of the streets determined the plan and shape of the buildings. The plan was formulated mainly in terms of multiples of 100 Roman feet (*pedes monetales*).[29]

The defences of the fortress and its annexe were of identical construction. The ditch was **V**-shaped in profile and *c.* 2.5 m. (8 ft.) deep and *c.* 5 m. (16 ft. 6 in.) wide. The rampart was made of sand revetted with vertical faces of coursed blocks of sun-dried sandy clay. The annexe rampart seems to have been slightly wider than that of the fortress proper, 3.8 m. (12 ft. 6 in.) as opposed to 4.1 m. (13 ft. 6 in.). In each case, the topsoil was removed and the rampart built over a layer of timbers laid across its full width. There was a berm at least 1.8 m. (5 ft. 11 in.) wide between the rampart and the ditch. The street around the inside of the defences (*via sagularis*) was set back 9 m. (29 ft. 6 in.) from the inner face of the rampart. No *via sagularis* has been recognized in the annexe.[30] Nothing is known of the fortress gates except their locations.

Few of the buildings in the fortress have been examined, and of those none have been more than half uncovered. There were presumably at least 60 barracks – more if an auxiliary unit was garrisoned with the legion – and stables for the horses of the cavalry unit. Other buildings presumably included stores, workshops, latrines, a hospital, a headquarters building (*principia*) in the centre of the fortress, and the legionary commander's house (*praetorium*).

Each barrack was at least 69 m. (227 ft.) long and accommodated a 'century' of soldiers. About one third of each barrack was occupied by the centurion and took the form of a semidetached block at the end of the barrack on either the *via principalis* or the *via sagularis*. Some of the rooms were heated with hearths placed against a wall.[31] The floors, usually of sand or sandy clay, were rudimentary, except in one centurion's quarters where at least two were of planks.[32]

Apart from the barracks, the only known buildings in the fortress are two large ones which fronted on the east side of the *via principalis*.[33] They were presumably two of the eight large buildings which normally took up the entire length of one side of that street in Roman fortresses. Six of those buildings are usually thought to have been occupied by tribunes (a class of officer) so one, if not both, of the two known Colchester buildings is likely to have been so used. The southern building, however, had in its northern range of rooms a series of hearths and shallow burnt pits used for working in brass which suggest that it may have been a workshop.

The annexe was probably used for stores and, more important, may have contained the large set of baths needed for the comfort of the soldiers. Any legionary baths were almost certainly kept for civilian use in the new colony, but their site has not been found.

The buildings of the fortress were soundly made, using several different construction techniques. The load-bearing walls of the barracks had three main structural components: a mortar and stone plinth, a pair of oak ground-plates, and a superstructure of coursed sandy-clay blocks. Most of the internal walls consisted of a timber frame, the ground-plate bedded directly on top of the natural sand and

[28] *Colch. Arch. Rep.* iii. 5.

[29] Ibid. vi. 7–14; *Fortress into City*, 36–40; *Roman Towns: the Wheeler Inheritance*, ed. S. Greep (Council for Brit. Arch. Research Rep. forthcoming).

[30] *Colch. Arch. Rep.* iii. 31.

[31] Ibid. 31–5; vi. 39–49, 130, and Fig. 4.2.

[32] Ibid. vi. 25, 41.

[33] Ibid. 24–5, 50–6.

the panels between the uprights filled with wattle and daub or sandy-clay blocks.[34] In contrast, at least three of the large buildings on the east side of the *via principalis* were built in a manner normally associated with the Roman army. Trenches were dug up to 1 m. deep along the lines of the intended walls. Substantial posts of roughly square section were then dropped into the trenches as they were backfilled. The gaps between the posts were filled with daub blocks and the finished walls left unplastered.[35] The walls of buildings outside the base were formed much more simply, by applying sandy clay as a daub to a frame made by hammering a row of stakes into the ground and then weaving wattles round them.[36]

The streets of the fortress, like those of the later Roman town, were made of packed gravel. Metalling the streets was not a priority in the fortress, and some streets between barracks were left unmetalled. In one place wheel ruts and a hoof print of an ox, cow, or bull were impressed in sandy soil underlying the earliest metalling.[37]

In addition to the fortress the army built a small fort, known only from crop marks, at Gosbecks. It covers *c.* 1.6 ha. (4 a.) inside its ramparts, implying a garrison of cohort size (about 500 men).[38] There may have been another small fort at a landing area further downstream at Fingringhoe where Roman military equipment and substantial quantities of pottery and coins have been found.[39]

Two early tombstones indicate the likely garrison. One was erected in honour of Marcus Favonius Facilis,[40] a centurion with Legio XX, who is not said to have been a veteran and so was presumably a serving soldier when he died. The other was to Longinus Sdapeze,[41] an officer of the 1st squadron of the Thracian cavalry unit, who had served only 15 years and is also likely to have been in the army at the time of his death. Both stones stood by the side of the main street leading into the town. Longinus may have been stationed at the fort at Gosbecks or have been part of a unit attached to the legion and based in the fortress. The monuments are not, however, unequivocal evidence that the units were stationed at Colchester. Either man could have died while on temporary duty there during the early years of the colony[42] or while part of a small garrison based in the colony in the 50s A.D.: Tacitus recorded just such a unit at Colchester at the time of the Boudican revolt.[43]

Large numbers of copper-alloy coins were struck at unidentified mints in the north-western provinces of the Roman Empire as imitations of Claudian *aes* produced in Rome between 41 and 54 A.D. Since Colchester is the most prolific site in Britain for such coins it has been suggested that it had a mint at that time.[44]

The Roman Colony

The name of the Roman town is uncertain. A 2nd-century inscription refers to '*colonia Victricensis* which is at Camulodunum',[45] making a clear distinction between the Roman colony and the Iron-Age fortress. It has been suggested that originally the official name was *colonia Claudia* and that the colony was renamed *colonia Victricensis* when it was refounded after its destruction during the Boudican revolt.[46] Later the town seems to have become known simply as *Colonia*.[47]

The Roman colony was founded *c.* 49 A.D. after the legion had been withdrawn.

34 Ibid. iii. 20, 22, 31; vi. 21–3, 39–40; *Fortress into City*, 31–4.
35 *Colch. Arch. Rep.* vi. 50–2.
36 Ibid. iii. 107; *Fortress into City*, 32, 35.
37 *Colch. Arch. Rep.* vi. 49.
38 *Britannia*, viii. 185–7; *Aerial Arch.* iv. 77–82.
39 *V.C.H. Essex*, iii. 130–2.
40 Hull, *Roman Colch.* 15, pl. I; *Britannia*, vi. 102–5; Toynbee, *Art in Britain under the Romans*, 185.
41 Hull, *Roman Colch.* 6, pl. I; Toynbee, *Art in Britain under the Romans*, 189–90.
42 P. Salway, *Roman Britain*, 94.
43 Tacitus, *Annales*, xiv. 32.
44 *Colch. Arch. Rep.* vi. 295–307.
45 J. Wacher, *Towns of Roman Britain*, 110–11.
46 *Antiq. Jnl.* xliii. 123–8.
47 Rivet and Smith, *Place-Names of Roman Britain*, 312.

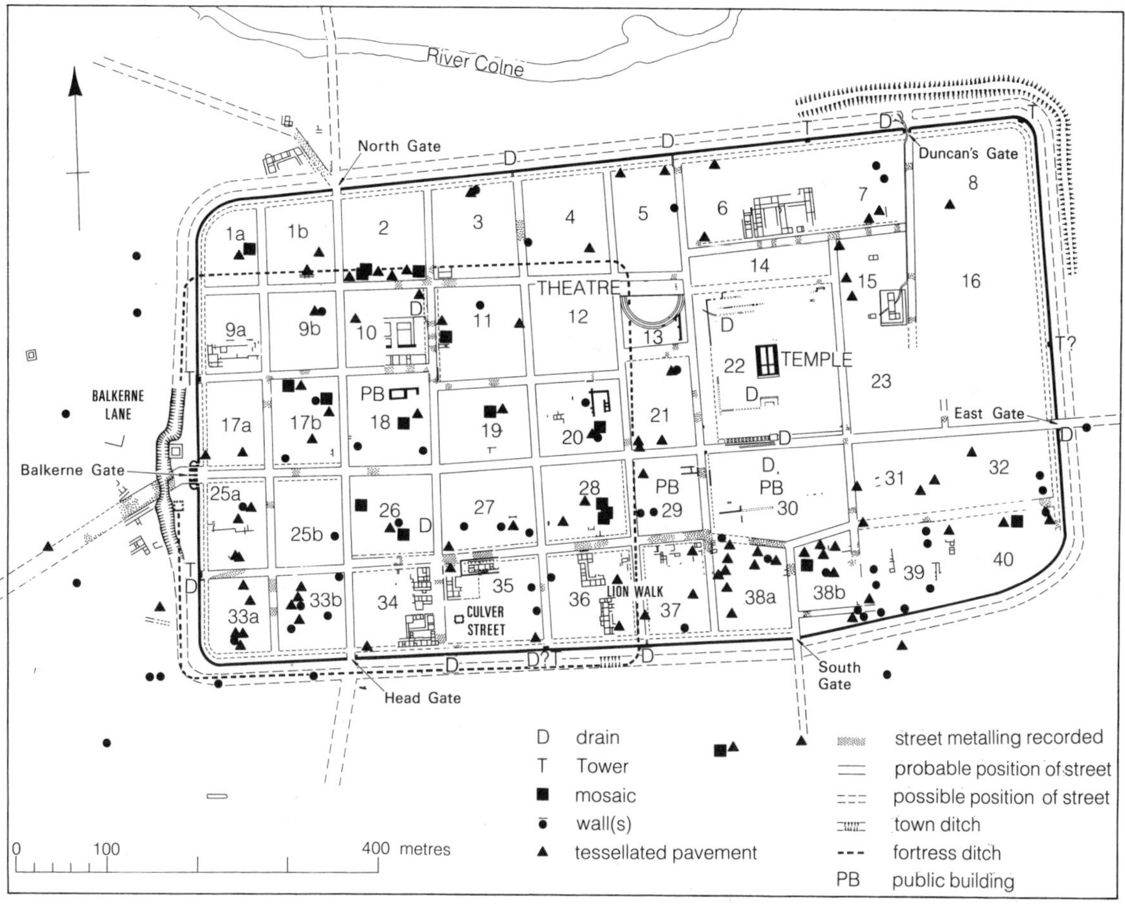

FIG. 5. ROMAN COLCHESTER, 2ND–4TH CENTURY

The buildings in the fortress had been well constructed and intended to last, so it is not surprising that the decision was made not to demolish the fortress when it was no longer needed by the army but to convert it into a town.[48] The process involved considerable building work. The legionary defences were dismantled and a new street grid laid out at a slightly different angle on the site of the annexe. The *via principalis* and the north–south street to the west were retained. The *via sagularis* was also kept, except on the east side of the colony where it was replaced by a new street built over the levelled legionary defences. About two thirds of the *c.* 18 military buildings so far excavated were burnt in the revolt of 60–1 A.D. That, combined with the number of re-used streets, suggests that a substantial proportion of the military buildings survived the transition from fortress to town. Nevertheless, the laying out of the east–west streets at the foundation of the colony necessitated the demolition of many buildings.

Parts of many barracks, apparently including all the barracks of the First Cohort,[49] were re-used as houses in the new town. In the south-east corner of the fortress, however, only the four most northerly of the six barracks were kept; the southern pair was demolished and the site left vacant, later to be cultivated.[50] On the west side of the fortress the barracks were demolished well before 60–1 and a new street lined with buildings constructed to the north.[51] The centurions' quarters were suitable for re-use as houses because they fronted at one end on a principal street

[48] *Colch. Arch. Rep.* iii. 5–11; vi. 10–14; *Fortress into City*, 32, 35.

[49] *Colch. Arch. Rep.* vi. 26–7.

[50] Ibid. iii. 31–40.

[51] Ibid. vi. 127–35.

and were divided up internally into small rooms. The men's quarters were not so readily converted being in effect a series of small independent compartments fronting on minor streets.

There was probably insufficient space in the former fortress for all the large civic buildings which the colonists required. Accordingly the military defences were levelled so that much of the annexe could be used for such buildings. Tacitus recorded that in 60–1 the settlement was easy to destroy because it had no walls: 'That was a matter which Roman commanders, thinking of amenities rather than needs, had neglected'.[52] Those 'amenities' were presumably the group of public buildings laid out after the defences had been levelled. The colony was indeed unprotected in 60 A.D.; houses burnt in the revolt had been constructed over the levelled military defences, and those defences were not replaced until after the fire.

The buildings on the site of the military annexe included the temple of Claudius,[53] the theatre,[54] and at least two others, one in Insula 29 and another in Insula 30.[55] The building or buildings in Insula 29 seem to have had columns covered with fluted stucco. The excavated theatre may be later than the one referred to by Tacitus in his description of the omens seen in Colchester before the Boudican disaster,[56] but the remains of a pre-Boudican theatre may lie underneath it.[57] The temple of Claudius which dominated the site was a lavish building decorated with marbles and porphyry imported from various parts of the Mediterranean world.[58] On the west side of the colony a monumental gate of two arches, part of which survives as the Balkerne gate, was erected on the site of the *porta decumanus*. There is some uncertainty about the date of the arch but it was probably erected *c.* 50 A.D. to commemorate the foundation of the colony.[59]

Quite how the veterans acquired redundant military buildings is obscure. The army usually gave veteran soldiers either allotments of land or a lump sum to provide an annuity for their retirement. The land was normally divided on a grid system (centuriation) and the blocks apportioned accordingly. Such a scheme has not yet been positively recognized in Colchester, probably because its traces are difficult to detect.[60] Tacitus indicated that sometimes the process of land acquisition in Colchester was not as orderly as it ought to have been. 'The settlers drove the Trinovantes from their homes and land, and called them prisoners and slaves. The troops encouraged the settlers' outrages, since their own way of behaving was the same – and they looked forward to similar licence for themselves.'[61] The apparent free-for-all could be taken to imply the absence of centuriation, but more probably Tacitus was referring to large-scale unofficial excesses after the initial allocation of centuriated land, excesses which were to be one of the contributory factors to the revolt. The relationships of the fortress and the Gosbecks fort to the occupied areas of the native settlement hint that the Roman army made some attempts to live with the local population in as unabrasive a manner as the circumstances would allow. Rather than court conflict in the way described by Tacitus, the Romans may have initially acted diplomatically by not centuriating the most sensitive land. Tolerance of native rights and traditions allowed the survival of the Gosbecks site throughout the Roman period (it was clearly never confiscated for centuriation) and the development of the native sanctuary.

52 Tacitus, *Annales*, xiv. 32.

53 Hull, *Roman Colch.* 162–8; *Temples, Churches and Religion*, ed. Rodwell, 243–8; *Britannia*, iii. 164–81.

54 *Britannia*, xiii. 299–302.

55 *E.A.T.* N.S. xxv. 301–28.

56 Tacitus, *Annales*, xiv. 32.

57 *Britannia*, ii. 27.

58 *E.A.T.* N.S. xxv. 24–61.

59 *Colch. Arch. Rep.* iii. 121–3; vi. 17–18.

60 Inf. from Tony Symes.

61 Tacitus, *Annales*, xiv. 32.

Just before the fire the town seems to have been well populated, although it was only *c.* 10 years old. The only empty space yet seen inside the former fortress area before the fire was on the site of the two barracks in the extreme south-east corner.[62] As it was a colony and thus technically a self-governing extension of Rome itself, only Roman citizens could hold land in the settlement. Retired veteran soldiers and their families were presumably the most important component of the population. Those without Roman citizenship perhaps occupied the area to the west of the town, where deep, narrow buildings huddled along the frontages of the road to London.

The story of the Boudican revolt and the burning of the town is well known.[63] The destruction was comprehensive; there are few places in the town where there is no evidence of the fire. Nevertheless, after the revolt it was possible to re-establish the earlier street system and to build new houses on pre-Boudican plots.[64]

The fire preserved evidence of life in the early *colonia*, including organic remains which, but for being carbonized, would not have survived.[65] In a pottery and glass shop in the street underlying High Street were fragments of what had been thousands of imported pottery and glass vessels, the pottery mainly red glazed *terra sigillata* and much of the glass thin-walled and delicately coloured.[66] Another shop, in the same street which was presumably a major commercial thoroughfare, stocked pottery, apparently only *terra sigillata*, besides foodstuffs including whole figs, coriander, cones of stone-pine, spelt, barley, and lentils.[67] Parts of a building in Insula 10 seem to have been used as a store rather than a shop. Separate rooms and a corridor contained large quantities of carbonized wheat, at least 30 unused and almost identical mortaria, more than 80 almost identical flagons, and 20 amphoras of various types.[68] Other organic finds from the Boudican destruction layer in the town include dates, a plum, and flax seeds. Most remarkable was a charred bed, consisting of two mattresses, in the corner of a room.[69]

It is difficult to say how quickly the town recovered after the fire. Rebuilding probably started immediately but the town never recovered its former density of buildings. Some areas, mainly those next to the town wall, were left empty and were used for cultivation when eventually a sufficiently fertile soil cover developed. Large cultivated areas are known in Insulae 17a, 34, 35, and 36.[70] Part of a ploughshare[71] was found in cultivated soil in Insula 35, while in Insula 34 there were impressions of the tips of spades.[72] A small tower granary in Insula 35 stood within an area of cultivated soil.[73] Much later, possibly in the 4th century, the site of the granary was occupied by a corn-drying kiln[74] and to the north was a large barn probably for agricultural use.[75] The clearest evidence for cultivation came from just outside the walls, near the Balkerne gate, where a large area of cultivated soil incorporated a series of raised parallel beds.[76]

The town walls were probably built soon after the revolt and presumably as a consequence of it. They have been dated to *c.* 65–80 A.D.,[77] exceptionally early for Roman town walls, and were presumably an expensive statement that such devastation was not to happen again. The extent and quality of the later building

62 *Colch. Arch. Rep.* iii. 37.

63 G. Webster, *Boudica*; Salway, *Roman Britain*, 113–21; Frere, *Britannia* (3rd edn.), 70–3.

64 *Colch. Arch. Rep.* vi. 27–30.

65 Ibid. iii. 40, 105, 108, 110; vi. 45, 330–2; *Arch. Jnl.* cxxxix. 32; Hull, *Roman Colch.* 103.

66 *Roman Colch.* 153–8; *Britannia*, xviii. 93–127.

67 *Roman Colch.* 198–202; Colch. Mus., archive rep. on excavation at 45–6 High Street by G. M. R. Davies.

68 *Arch. Jnl.* cxxxix. 32–3, 48–51.

69 *Colch. Arch. Rep.* iii. 42–7.

70 Ibid. 37; vi. 27, 33, 59–61, 137.

71 Ibid. vi. 186.

72 Ibid. 60.

73 Ibid. 108–10.

74 Ibid. 108–12.

75 Ibid. 112–16.

76 Ibid. iii. 138–41.

77 Hull, *Roman Colch.* 62–3; *E.A.T.* 3rd ser. iii. 69; *Colch. Arch. Rep.* vi. 14–15.

outside most if not all the gates underline the token nature of the early wall as a defensive structure.

The period between the mid 2nd and the early 3rd century saw in Colchester, as in other towns, the appearance of substantial, well built town houses.[78] Areas which had been used for cultivation were built over in response to the need for new building land within the walls.[79] The houses themselves were often larger and of better quality than earlier ones, the courtyard house making its first appearance. Rubble foundations became the norm, especially for internal walls, and floors were frequently tessellated. Clearest testimony to the increase in affluence is the widespread introduction of mosaic pavements. Over 30 mosaics have been recorded in the town and, as far as can be judged, the overwhelming majority are of the period 150–250.

While the size and quality of the houses implies a period of prosperity, the population did not necessarily grow. Estimating its size with any degree of confidence is almost impossible, but if Insulae 34 and 36 were typical of the *c.* 41 insulae which did not contain public buildings, then the average such insula probably contained *c.* 6–8 houses. That suggests only *c.* 300 houses in the entire town and a population of perhaps only a few thousand. There were a number of localized fires in the town in the Antonine period, but no evidence has been found for a major fire which might have affected the town's development.[80]

From its earliest days, the colony appears to have been markedly agricultural in character and to have served as the main regional market for agricultural produce of all types. Opportunities presumably abounded in a fast-developing commercial and industrial town. The expanding civilian population (containing many men newly retired from the army with substantial cash sums), the port, the large native population in the area, and the prospect of lucrative military contracts to help supply a large campaigning army presumably combined to draw the skilled craftsman and the determined entrepreneur alike, regardless of whether or not he was a veteran soldier. Immigrants, especially from Gaul, may have figured prominently among them. A workshop that made clay lamps provides proof of artisan activities within the limits of the colony proper in the pre-Boudican period.[81] Other evidence, mainly in the form of waste products or specialist structures, points to metal working in iron and copper alloys,[82] glass working,[83] bone working,[84] and pottery and tile making. The pottery industry in particular was important to the local economy. It was active from the Claudio-Neronian period to at least the late 3rd or early 4th century, and was at its most successful from *c.* 140 to *c.* 200 when large quantities of pottery were being exported to other parts of the country, especially to forts on the northern frontier.[85] Coins may have been struck in Colchester in the late 3rd century but the evidence is ambiguous. There were at least two mints in Britain at that time, one denoted by the mint

[78] *Colch. Arch. Rep.* vi. 31.

[79] Ibid. vi. 31; iii. 52.

[80] Cf. *Small Towns of Roman Britain*, ed. W. J. Rodwell and R. T. Rowley (B.A.R. xv), 85–102, esp. 93–4; Dunnett, *Trinovantes*, 53.

[81] Discovered in 1964 but unpublished: see *Fortress into City*, 44.

[82] e.g. *Colch. Arch. Rep.* iii. 26 (waste products, structures); vi. 193–7 (crucibles, waste products, smith's tongs, structures); Hawkes and Hull, *Camulodunum*, 340–6 (crucibles, waste products, smith's tongs); Niblett, *Sheepen*, 112–13. A copper-smith, Cintusmus, erected a plaque at Temple 6: Hull, *Roman Colch.* 239; *Roman Inscriptions of Britain*, i, no. 194.

[83] *Colch. Arch. Rep.* vi. 118; *V.C.H. Essex*, iii. 113; *Ateliers de Verriers de l'Antiquité à la Période Pré-industrielle*, ed. Danièle Foy and Geneviève Sennequier, 24–5. It has been suggested that the letters CCV on the bases of square glass bottles refer to *Colonia Claudia Victricensis* and are thus an indicator of a glass industry in the town (*V.C.H. Essex*, iii. 113), but it seems more likely that the letters are the abbreviations of a personal name: *Colch. Arch. Rep.* viii (forthcoming), chapter 14.

[84] *Colch. Arch. Rep.* ii. 150–60; Hull, *Roman Colch.* 208; *V.C.H. Essex*, iii. 113.

[85] M. R. Hull, *Roman Potters' Kilns of Colch.*; *E.A.T.* 3rd ser. xiv. 15–76; V. G. Swan, *Pottery Kilns of Roman Britain*, 92–5; *Colch. Arch. Rep.* x (forthcoming); *Proc. Soc. Antiq. Scot.* cx. 257–68.

signature C or occasionally CL, which some numismatists consider stood for Colonia (i.e. Colchester).[86]

The distinction between Camulodunum and the Roman colony made in the 2nd-century inscription is reflected in the locations of the two types of temple erected in the settlement. Within the walls of the Roman town was the temple of Claudius,[87] the great classical temple worthy of Rome itself, whereas scattered across Camulodunum were at least seven temples of Romano-Celtic type, including those at the native sanctuaries at Gosbecks and Sheepen.[88]

It has been suggested that with the coming of Christianity the front of the temple of Claudius was radically remodelled in the 4th century to convert it to a church and that integral to that remodelling was the addition of an apse which was to become a dominant feature of the plan of the Norman castle.[89] The evidence is inconclusive and the fact that the White Tower in London, which is like Colchester in many respects although it is not built on Roman foundations, has a very similar apse, might suggest a Norman date for the Colchester apse. Structural changes were made to other religious buildings at a similar date, although their significance is not clear. The ambulatory of the Romano-Celtic temple outside the Balkerne gate (Temple 10/Building 52) was demolished and its foundations robbed out in the later 4th or the early 5th century.[90] The temple stood across the street from a building which may also have been a temple (Building 53) and which was completely demolished and its foundations removed, probably in the 5th century.[91] When the other temples were demolished is unknown, though Temple 2 appears to have been in use at least until the late 4th century.[92]

The church and its associated cemetery at Butt Road indicate that a substantial part of the population of the 4th-century town was Christian. The cemetery contained at least 600 inhumations, possibly a great many more. The church started *c.* 330 as a rectangular building, but an apse was later added to its east end. The building had an outer wall of rubble, a tiled roof, and a simple floor of sand. Later, wooden posts were inserted into its eastern half to form aisles. There may have been as many as three graves near the east end; the earliest may have predated the church and been the grave of an important local Christian. Large quantities of animal bone indicate that funerary meals were consumed in the building and that large chicken and young pig were especially favoured. A femur and the skull (but without mandible) of a small, middle-aged woman had been placed at the base of a deep pit inside the building near the apse, probably in the 5th century when it was dilapidated. Both bones appear to have belonged to the same person and may represent an early occurrence of the practice of depositing relics in a church.[93]

The function of the building in Insula 15 once identified as a mithraeum is now uncertain.[94] The presence of a spring in the building indicates that its purpose involved water, and the most obvious explanation is that it housed some kind of lifting or pumping device for the water supply. The iron shackles[95] from the building point to the use of slaves to drive the equipment.

The cemeteries of Roman Colchester, providing one of the largest pools of information about Romano-British urban cemeteries and burial practice, have

[86] *Colch. Arch. Rep.* iv. 50.

[87] Hull, *Roman Colch.* 162–8. The positions of the solid parts of the podium provide information on the plan of the superstructure, probably a eustyle pseudoperipteral building with an octastyle front: *Temples, Churches and Religion*, 243–50.

[88] *Temples, Churches and Religion*, 275.

[89] *Britannia*, xv. 7–50.

[90] *Colch. Arch. Rep.* iii. 123–5.

[91] Ibid. 126–7.

[92] *Temples, Churches and Religion*, 272–4.

[93] *Colch. Arch. Rep.* ix (forthcoming).

[94] Hull, *Roman Colch.* 107–13; *V.C.H. Essex*, iii. 103–4; *Temples, Churches and Religion*, 271–2.

[95] Hull, *Roman Colch.* 111 and pl. XXI.

yielded more than 1,400 graves and about 2,000 objects, excluding coffin nails and human bones.[96] There was a concentration of tombstones and sculptured stone on the frontages of the main approach road to the west side of the colony, the most esteemed of the cemetery areas. Among them were the tombstones of Facilis and Longinus, a 'walled cemetery',[97] and a monument incorporating the so-called Colchester Sphinx.[98]

Most cremation burials in Colchester seem to have consisted of a cinerary urn and possibly one other vessel. The richest burials tend to come from the area on the south-west side of the town. There is no clear evidence for the date of the change from cremation to inhumation. Either the transition occurred *c.* 260 or for a long period until then the rites were used concurrently.[99]

At the cemetery at Butt Road 742 inhumations were found. There were effectively two cemeteries, the first and smaller being of the 3rd and early 4th century with burials arranged roughly north–south. In the second cemetery most inhumations were east–west and of the 4th century; they were probably Christian and contemporary with the cemetery church. More than half the graves of the first cemetery contained at least one object. In the second cemetery grave goods were rarer: only 6 per cent of adults and 12 per cent of children were accompanied by objects, mostly the personal adornments of women and girls.[1]

Over 90 per cent of the excavated inhumations at Colchester were in wooden coffins. Coffins made of split tree trunks were found at Butt Road, but at least 21 other recorded coffins from the town were either entirely of lead or were of wood lined with lead. Stone coffins seem to have been very rare in Roman Colchester, only two being attested. The bodies in at least four lead coffins and seven wooden ones, all but one from Butt Road, had been covered or at least partly covered by some kind of plaster. The objects in the graves do not seem to have been specially made funerary pieces but to have been in everyday use, and it seems likely that some were important or favoured possessions of the dead person. Some vessels were poorly made and of inferior quality, even including wasters. Often they are coated internally with lime-scale showing prior use. A large proportion of the objects are small examples of their type. Presumably such objects usually indicate the graves of children, with whom small pots and lamps could have been associated in life.[2]

The Decline of the Colony

The threat of Saxon raids along the east coast appears to have become serious in the period 268–82 when major improvements were made to the coastal defences in south-east England. Two forts in the system, Bradwell-on-Sea and Walton Castle (Suff.), are near Colchester and probably belong to the period 276–85.[3] Colchester lies less than 10 miles from the coast and, although protected to an extent by those two forts, was still vulnerable to sea-borne raiders especially via the mouth of the river Colne. Three coin hoards from the Colchester area, all dating to *c.* 275,[4] attest the feelings of insecurity widespread at the time. Steps were taken to improve the defences of the town. Initially the town ditch was substantially widened and a counterscarp bank formed with the soil dug from it,

[96] The cemeteries are discussed in Hull, *Roman Colch.* 250–8; *Colch. Arch. Rep.* ix (forthcoming).

[97] *Arch. Jnl.* ci. 69–90; above, this chapter, Legionary Fortress.

[98] Toynbee, *Art in Britain under the Romans*, 112–13.

[99] *Colch. Arch. Rep.* ix (forthcoming).

[1] Ibid.

[2] Ibid.

[3] S. Johnson, *Roman Forts of the Saxon Shore*, 109; *Saxon Shore*, ed. D. E. Johnston (Council for Brit. Arch. Research Rep. xviii), 5–6.

[4] *Colch. Arch. Rep.* iv. 69–76.

but before the end of the century sterner measures had been taken. The Balkerne gate was closed when the town ditch was extended to cross in front of it, and traffic was diverted, probably through Head gate. Duncan's gate, in the north-east part of the town, may have been similarly closed by continuing the town ditch across the front of it.[5] The Balkerne gate was probably blocked because its incorporation of the earlier monumental arch made it unsatisfactory as a defensive structure.[6] Duncan's gate may have been sacrificed because it was small, only one carriageway wide, and little used as there was not much space between it and the river for buildings.

While the changes were being made to the town defences, the built-up area of the town was shrinking. The change was most marked in the extramural areas outside the Balkerne gate and North gate where practically all the buildings were demolished during the period 275–300,[7] presumably because of their exposed positions. The decline of the extramural built-up areas is indicated by changes in the distribution of burials. Most inhumations (datable broadly to the 3rd and 4th centuries) are closer to the walls than most of the cremations (datable to the 1st and 2nd centuries): areas where burial was permitted crept inwards as the built-up part of the town shrank.[8]

The near-extinction of the suburbs was not matched by an increase in the built-up area inside the defences, and in the 4th century the open areas within the walls became larger as houses were knocked down and not replaced. At the Culver Street site, the only 4th-century building seems to have been the barn referred to above,[9] and at the Lion Walk site half of the six houses had been knocked down by the middle of the 4th century.[10] Late pottery and coins show continued activity in the court of the temple of Claudius until at least *c.* 365. The same material has been used to argue that after that date the buildings forming the court were modified for use as some kind of domestic citadel.[11]

The population of the late Roman town was not necessarily diminishing; the pattern of occupation within the walls may have been changing. It is striking that the intramural sites with the highest proportion of late Roman material (the Cups Hotel and the Angel Yard)[12] are both in High Street. The demolition of extramural and intramural houses may have been matched by the growth of a medieval-style town where the houses were smaller and focused on one street.

There have been suggestions that Roman Colchester came to a dramatic and violent end. The bones of a young woman lying obliquely on a tessellated floor of a building in Insula 40 have been interpreted as evidence of that end,[13] but it is far more likely that the body was buried in a shallow grave whose digger stopped when he reached the floor. Duncan's gate has been thought to provide convincing evidence of an assault which met with some success, but that evidence, from an excavation of 1927–9,[14] cannot be reassessed. The gate appears to have been burnt on at least two occasions in the late Roman period. The second fire was the more serious. Brushwood was piled up against the outer face of the wooden doors and set alight causing the doors to collapse inwards. The heat was so intense that many stones turned red. The two fires are not closely datable but the first was probably no earlier than 367 and the second substantially later. The fact that there were two

5 Ibid. iii. 18.
6 Ibid. 111.
7 Ibid. 16–18, 70, 113–15.
8 Ibid. vi. 18–19; ix (forthcoming).
9 Ibid. vi. 108–12.
10 Ibid. iii. 19.
11 *Britannia*, xv. 7–50.
12 *Colch. Arch. Rep.* vi. 333; *E.A.T.* 3rd ser. xxv (forthcoming).
13 Hull, *Roman Colch.* 218; G. Martin, *Story of Colch.* 9.
14 Hull, *Roman Colch.* 36–41; *Colch. Arch. Rep.* iii. 18–19.

fires shows that the town survived the first assault (if indeed that was the cause of the first fire). The debris from the second fire, however, does not appear to have been cleared away, implying that the gate was never repaired. If the interpretation of the excavation is correct, then the gate may provide proof of a violent end to the Romano-British administration.

A small hoard of clipped silver coins[15] provides evidence of the breakdown of centralized Roman government *c.* 409. By then Britain had in effect ceased to be part of the Roman empire and the local British councils, the *civitates*, had taken steps to provide for their own defence. The hoard belongs to a rash of groups of clipped coins which appeared in Britain at the period. Apparently the clipping of coins had until then been controlled by the imposition of severe penalties on offenders but with the break from Rome the practice became commonplace.[16]

Three huts within Colchester's walls and a scatter of contemporary finds show that the town was one of the many places where the Saxons settled.[17] The fate of the Romano-British population of Colchester is unclear but life in the town was certainly radically different by the mid 5th century, the date of the earliest known Saxon hut.[18] Before the change, there is likely to have been a period when the population was in rapid decline. Traditional customs may have started to break down. Two decapitated burials from the grounds of East Hill House may belong to the period, since contrary to normal practice they were inside the walls.[19] It is uncertain whether elements of the Romano-British population survived the transition. Some houses were left standing and unoccupied so that topsoil and broken roof-tile accumulated on their floors.[20] Public buildings such as the theatre and the temple of Claudius became ruins (if they had not already been so in the late Roman period) and even minor structures like the probable corn-drying oven at Culver Street seem to have been left to decay.

15 *Colch. Arch. Rep.* iv. 69–76.
16 *Britannia*, xv. 163–8.
17 *Colch. Arch. Rep.* i. 1–23; iii. 73–5; vi. 118–20.
18 Ibid. i. 22–3.
19 Ibid. vi. 323, 378.
20 Ibid. iii. 70.

MEDIEVAL COLCHESTER

Anglo-Saxon Colchester

Archaeological evidence suggests some early Anglo-Saxon settlement inside the walls of Roman Colchester, but there is no documentary record of the town until 917 when Edward the Elder expelled the Danes from it.[1] In the early 8th century London was the chief town of the East Saxons,[2] and as a port and trading centre Colchester may also have been overshadowed by neighbouring Ipswich. Nevertheless, it seems likely that the survival of the Roman wall, and perhaps of usable Roman buildings, made Colchester attractive as an administrative, perhaps royal, centre for at least the eastern part of Essex. After its recapture and refortification by Edward the Elder, the town was certainly such a centre. Two kings, Athelstan in 931 and Edmund in 940, held councils there, Athelstan's being attended by at least 13 ealdormen, 37 thegns, and 15 bishops, including the archbishop of Canterbury and the bishop of Chester le Street.[3] The bishop of London's soke, or estate with its own court, which he held in the town by the early 12th century,[4] may have originated as the bishop's residence in an East Saxon royal centre. At Old Heath, known as Old Hythe in the 12th century, *c.* 2 miles south-east of the town there was a harbour or beaching point for boats on the Colne, but it was probably always difficult to reach. Placename and topographical evidence suggests that Harwich may have been the main port for Colchester and north-east Essex before the Danish invasions, but no archaeological evidence of early settlement has been found and Harwich, which was in Dovercourt parish, was first recorded in 1229.[5] Colchester, like other Anglo-Saxon boroughs, presumably had a market, but the fact that there were no moneyers there until *c.* 991 indicates that the settlement was of little economic importance in the 10th century.

By the mid 10th century Colchester was the centre of an important and extensive group of estates held by the ealdormen of Essex.[6] Among those estates were four surrounding the walled town: Lexden, Greenstead, Donyland (including East Donyland), and Stanway. They may, with Colchester itself, have earlier formed a single, large estate, perhaps in the hands of a king or subking of the East Saxons. The ealdormanic estate was broken up in the late 10th century or the early 11th by Ealdorman Aelfgar's daughters Aethelflaed and Aelfflaed. Aethelflaed divided Donyland into four parts, at least one of which was outside the liberty of Colchester in 1086, and Aelflaed granted Stanway and Lexden to King Ethelred II. Part at least of Lexden, east of the Iron-Age dyke system, remained in Colchester, but Stanway, except for two or three detached parts, was outside the liberty in 1086.[7]

It was presumably the impressive Roman ruins, together with popular etymology, which, probably in the late Anglo-Saxon period, gave Colchester its mythical history of King Coel and his daughter St. Helen, wife of the Emperor Constantius, mother of the Emperor Constantine, and discoverer of the true cross. The story that Constantine was born in Britain to the concubine Helen was known *c.* 700.

1 *A.-S. Chron.* ed. D. Whitelock, 65.

2 *A.-S. Eng.* xiv. 27.

3 *Cart. Sax.* ed. Birch, ii, p. 357; *Glastonbury Cart.* iii (Somerset Rec. Soc. lxiv), p. 648; S. Keynes, *Diplomas of Aethelred the Unready*, 269.

4 Below, this chapter, Boro. Govt.

5 E. Ekwall, *Old English wic in Place-Names* (Nomina Germanica xiii), 16, 19; S. Reynolds, *Intro. to Eng. Med. Towns*, 25; *P.N. Essex*, 339.

6 *An Essex Tribute*, ed. K. Neale, 70–1.

7 *A.-S. Wills*, ed. D. Whitelock, pp. 36, 38; *V.C.H. Essex*, i. 432, 574; below, Outlying Parts.

Helen's connexion with Colchester was known to Henry of Huntingdon who recorded *c.* 1133 that Constantius's wife Helen had been the daughter of a British king Coel, and had built the walls of Colchester and London.[8] Geoffrey of Monmouth, writing a few years after Henry, had a more elaborate story, telling how Coel duke of 'Kaelcolim' or Colchester killed a rival and became king of England. He made peace with Constantius who was threatening to invade the kingdom, but he died eight days later, whereupon Constantius married his daughter Helen.[9] The version of the myth known in 14th-century Colchester was that Coel, who later became king of Britain, founded the town in 219 A.D. Constantius, arriving in Britain from Spain in 260, besieged Colchester for three years before the conflict was ended by his marriage to Helen. Their son Constantine was born at Colchester the following year. The account continues with the story of Constantine's succession as emperor and Helen's journey to the Holy Land.[10] The myth of Coel and Helen was only one of the stories which gathered around Colchester's prominent ruins. Gaimar, writing about the same time as Geoffrey of Monmouth, had an entirely different story about a Danish king 'Adlebrit' and his conquest of Kair Koel or Colchester.[11] Walter Map in the 1180s knew that Colchester was St. Helen's birthplace, but his main interest in the town was as the site of a mythical battle fought between 'Gado and Offa' and the Romans.[12]

King Coel of Colchester is a back formation from the placename, perhaps reinforced by stories of an historical or semihistorical Coel who occurs in the Welsh genealogies and appears to have been active in the region between the Trent and Hadrian's wall about the early 5th century.[13] The legend of St. Helen's British birth may have arisen from a confusion between her and the supposedly British wife of Magnus Maximus, whom the Welsh sources call Helen, and the saintly empress's reputation was enhanced by a further confusion between her and a Celtic water spirit originally called Alauna.[14] The merging of the legends of St. Helen and of King Coel may have occurred in northern England or Wales, where the two legends were known independently, or in Colchester itself where something in the Roman ruins, perhaps a mosaic, may have suggested a connexion with St. Helen.[15] There was certainly a St. Helen's chapel in Colchester by the early 12th century, and by the late 14th she was supposed to have built it with her own hands.[16] The invocation is unusual in south-east England,[17] and suggests an early cult of the saint in Colchester, where there was also a St. Cross chapel by the early 13th century. There was a St. Helen's well, but, unlike the well at St. Anne's chapel on Harwich Road east of the town, it was not a holy well in the Middle Ages.[18] St. John's abbey, which owned St. Helen's chapel in the 12th and 13th centuries, seems to have made no attempt to exploit the legend or to encourage St. Helen's cult, but St. Helen appeared on the earliest known, 13th-century, borough seal and on its 15th-century replacement, as well as on the illuminated initial of Henry V's charter to the borough.[19] The story of Coel and Helen, which gained a wide currency in the later Middle Ages, probably developed as an origin

[8] Hen. of Huntingdon, *Hist. Anglorum* (Rolls Ser.), 29–30.

[9] Geoffrey of Monmouth, *Hist. Regum Britanniae*, ed. A. Griscom, 338; *Jnl. Brit. Arch. Assoc.* N.S. xxv. 229–41.

[10] E.R.O., D/B 5 R1, f. 20 and v.; Bodl. MS. Gough Essex 1, ff. 19–21.

[11] *L'Estoire des Engleis* (Anglo-Norman Texts xiv–xvi), p. 3.

[12] Walter Map, *De Nugis Curialium*, ed. M. R. James, rev. C. N. L. Brooke and R. A. B. Mynors, pp. xxxix–xl.

[13] J. Morris, *Age of Arthur*, 213; C. Kightly, *Folk Heroes of Britain*, 56–93.

[14] *Landscape Hist.* viii. 67–70.

[15] Cf. St. Helen's-on-the-Walls, York: J. R. Magilton, *Church of St. Helen-on-the-Walls, Aldwark* (C.B.A. for York Arch. Trust), 18.

[16] E.R.O., D/B 5 R1, f. 20v.; below, Chapels.

[17] *Landscape Hist.* viii. 60.

[18] E.R.O., D/B 5 Cr5, rot. 5; below, Chapels.

[19] Below, Arms, Seals, etc.; H. Harrod, *Rep. on Colch. Rec.* (Colch. 1865), 2.

myth in 10th- or 11th-century Colchester as the town grew in size and self awareness.

The Early Medieval Town

In 1086 Colchester and Maldon were the only boroughs in Essex, and Colchester was much the more important. It contained at least 419 houses, suggesting a population of *c.* 2,500 or more, and placing the town in the middle rank of English boroughs. It may have approached the size of Ipswich which had at least 538 burgesses in 1066 but only 210 in 1086. Unlike many other English towns, Colchester does not seem to have declined in the years after the Conquest and no waste was reported there in 1086. Indeed the town may even have prospered as its annual farm rose from £15 5*s.* 3*d.* in 1066 to a probably extortionate £80 in 1086.[20] The proportional increase was greater than that recorded for any other borough except Rochester, whose farm increased sixfold, and it placed Colchester's farm equal fourth with Wallingford's among known borough farms, behind only those of London (£300), York and Lincoln (£100 each), and Norwich (£90).[21] By 1130, however, the farm had been reduced to £40, and on the basis of aids paid to the king Colchester has been ranked only 27th of the provincial towns in the reign of Henry I.[22] Despite its comparative decline, Colchester like many other boroughs achieved self government in the course of the 12th century, although it was slow to develop a full hierarchy of borough officers. There seem to have been no financial officers and no council until 1372, and the two bailiffs remained the chief officers throughout the Middle Ages.[23]

At times in the early Middle Ages, Colchester assumed an importance as a centre for the defence of eastern England. The massive Norman castle, built on the foundations of the Roman temple of Claudius, was probably begun in the 1070s under the threat of Danish or Flemish invasion, and perhaps in response to a Danish attack on the town in 1071.[24] It was completed *c.* 1100 when Henry I was consolidating his hold on the kingdom, and Henry visited castle and town *c.* 1132.[25] Colchester seems to have played no part in the civil wars of Stephen's reign, although it was the centre in Essex of the honor of Boulogne which belonged to his queen, Maud.[26] Following his Whitsun crown-wearing at Bury St. Edmunds Henry II was in Colchester for a week in May 1157; his court there was attended by the archbishops of Canterbury and York, the bishops of London, Lincoln, Chichester, and Exeter, the earls of Leicester and Salisbury, Warin FitzGerald, and the chancellor, Thomas Becket.[27] In 1173 a large contingent of the army to oppose Earl Hugh Bigod assembled at Colchester.[28] King John visited Colchester and its castle in 1204 and 1205, in the aftermath of his loss of Normandy, and again in 1209, 1212, and 1214.[29] The castle was besieged and captured by King John's army early in 1216, and John himself came to Colchester in March; later that year the town was ravaged by a baronial army.[30]

Henry III visited Colchester in 1242, presumably staying in the castle where his 'houses' or apartments had been repaired for him. At that visit, or another one

[20] *V.C.H. Essex*, i. 574–8; *V.C.H. Suff.* i. 429.

[21] J. Tait, *Med. Eng. Boro.* 152, 154, 184. Winchester's farm, presumably large, is unknown.

[22] *Pipe R.* 1130 (Rec. Com.), 138; *New Hist. Geog. Eng.* ed. C. Darby, 134.

[23] Below, Boro. Govt.

[24] E.R.O., D/B 5 R2, f. 20; Bodl. MS. Gough Essex 1, f. 21; *Mare Balticum*, ed. W. Paravicini, 101–10.

[25] *Reg. Regum Anglo-Norm.* ii, no. 1734; below, Castle.

[26] R. H. C. Davis, *King Stephen*, 59–60.

[27] R. W. Eyton, *Itin. Hen. II*, 26–7; A. Saltman, *Theobald, Archbishop of Canterbury*, 83, 156, 243.

[28] *Pipe R.* 1173 (P.R.S. xix), 183; Ralph de Diceto, *Ymag. Hist.* (Rolls Ser.), i. 378.

[29] *Rot. Litt. Pat.* (Rec. Com.), Intro.

[30] Matthew Paris, *Chron. Majora* (Rolls Ser.), ii. 664; Roger of Wendover, *Flores Historiarum* (Rolls Ser.), ii. 192; *V.C.H. Essex*, ii. 212.

before 1248, the townsmen promised him £10 for three palfreys.[31] In 1256 the king stayed for two days in Colchester on his way from Walsingham (Norf.) to London, again in the castle.[32] A Mile End man was later accused of having supported the baronial party against Henry III,[33] but otherwise Colchester escaped involvement in the troubles of the 1250s.

Disputes between Colchester and the lords of neighbouring manors, probably often over grazing or other territorial rights,[34] seem to have caused more violence than civil wars and national upheavals in the 13th and 14th centuries, although at times in the early 14th century national events may have supplied the occasion for disturbances whose origins were really local. In 1319 as many as 174 Colchester men, including the leading burgesses Joseph of Colchester or Joseph Eleanor, Ellis son of John, Matthew Glasswright, Ralph Ode, and Hubert Bosse, were accused of attacking a tenant and servants of Hugh de Neville, lord of several Essex manors including Langham just north of Colchester, when they came to the town to get horses, wagons, and arms for the Scottish war.[35] Hubert Bosse and Ralph Ode were among the Colchester men who were alleged to have assaulted John Dagworth, lord of the manor of Bradwell by Coggeshall, who seems also to have held land in or near Colchester, as he made preparations at Colchester to go to Scotland in 1324.[36] Disturbances at Colchester in 1327 may have been associated with the deaths of William Drury of Colchester and William Christian of Cambridge at the time of St. John's fair that year and the earlier death of Henry Savary,[37] rather than with the deposition of Edward II.

Disagreements between St. John's abbey and the town erupted into violence in 1253 when up to 40 Colchester men including the leading burgesses Oliver and John sons of Ellis were accused of destroying the abbot's gallows and tumbrels at West Donyland and Greenstead, and cutting the ropes of his ships at 'Cryclynsoye', perhaps Brightlingsea. That and other disputes over Colchester market and over the abbot's jurisdiction and free warren in West Donyland were settled in 1255.[38]

In 1312 a number of townsmen, including the merchant Henry Denny, were said to have carried off the goods in Colchester of Robert FitzWalter of Lexden, broken his park at Lexden, and hunted there.[39] A series of disputes with the FitzWalters and their tenants over pasture rights, jurisdiction, and the liability of Lexden men to contribute with Colchester to subsidies, came to a head in 1342 and 1343. In May 1342 a Lexden man was killed in Mile End; John FitzWalter, Lord FitzWalter, objected to the inquest held by the borough coroner and brought in the county coroner, infringing the liberties of the borough. Neither inquest seems to have produced the desired verdict, and FitzWalter attacked members of the juries, finally extending his attacks to all Colchester men, including one found at Southminster and one on the road from Colchester to Maldon. The attacks developed into a siege of the town which lasted from 20 May to 22 July and ended only when the burgesses paid a fine of £40. There seems to have been a second siege, perhaps precipitated by another attack on FitzWalter's park at Lexden, from 7 April to 1 June 1343; that too ended with the burgesses paying £40.[40]

[31] *Close R.* 1237–42, 444, 489; *Pipe R.* 1242 (ed. H. L. Cannon), 216; *Cal. Lib.* 1245–51, 203.

[32] *Close R.* 1254–6, 286; *Cal. Lib.* 1251–60, 278, 297.

[33] P.R.O., JUST 1/238, rot. 27.

[34] *E.A.T.* 3rd ser. xix. 164.

[35] *Cal. Pat.* 1317–21, 474–5, 479; *Cal. Inq. p.m.* vii, p. 474; *Med. Essex Community: the Lay Subsidy of 1327*, ed. J. C. Ward (Essex Hist. Docs. i), 19.

[36] *Cal. Pat.* 1324–7, 135, 137, 146; *Cal. Inq. p.m.* vii, p. 310.

[37] *Cal. Pat.* 1327–30, 158; P.R.O., JUST 3/18/5, rot. 5.

[38] *Abbrev. Plac.* (Rec. Com.), 131; *Close R.* 1251–3, 463; E.R.O., D/B 5 R2, loose folio.

[39] *Cal. Pat.* 1307–13, 530–1; *E.A.T.* 3rd ser. xix. 163–4.

[40] P.R.O., KB 27/366, Rex rot. 30; *Essex Sessions of the Peace*, ed. E. C. Furber, 88; *Cal. Pat.* 1343–5, 98–9; 1350–4, 411–14.

Lionel of Bradenham, lord of Langenhoe and a tenant of FitzWalter's, besieged Colchester from August to November 1350, damaging houses in the eastern suburb and taking grain and hay from Greenstead. The townsmen eventually bought him off for £20. The origins of the quarrel are not clear, but may have lain in a dispute over the fishery and obstruction of the river. When the burgesses brought legal proceedings against Bradenham in 1362 they accused him of having built six large weirs in 1349, although his worst offence, placing piles in arms of the Colne, was not committed until 1360. Disputes may also have arisen over access for Langenhoe men to Colchester market.[41]

Colchester remained the largest and in many respects the principal town in Essex throughout the Middle Ages. Its castle was the seat of the sheriff, and contained the county gaol until the mid 17th century, but royal justices sat at Chelmsford in 1202–3, and from 1218 the justices in eyre sat there regularly. In the course of the 14th century Chelmsford became the usual administrative centre for the county.[42] The choice of the bishop of London's new town for the role was no doubt dictated by its central position within the county, but Colchester's failure to develop as the county town may help to explain its relative stagnation or decline in the early 14th century.

Topographical evidence confirms that Colchester grew during the later 12th and the 13th century. By 1312 there were at least 518 adult males, excluding paupers, in the liberty, suggesting a population of 3,000–4,000. That probably marked the peak of Colchester's early medieval growth; like many other towns and much of rural Essex, it seems to have stagnated or declined in the earlier 14th century.[43] Although the largest in Essex, the early 14th-century town was relatively small and unimportant. Even in comparison with other towns in the county, it was not exceptionally prosperous. In 1327 Colchester's subsidy assessment of £14 0*s*. 8*d*. was less than those of Barking and Waltham Holy Cross and only 6*d*. higher than that of Writtle. The number of subsidy payers was highest at Writtle, where 127 people contributed, compared with 125 at Colchester, 120 at Waltham Holy Cross, and 119 at Barking.[44] In Suffolk, Ipswich and Bury St. Edmunds both outranked Colchester in assessment and numbers.[45] In 1334 Colchester at *c*. £261 ranked fourth in Essex in assessment, behind Writtle as well as Barking and Waltham Holy Cross. Ipswich's assessment was more than double Colchester's. On a national scale, Colchester ranked about 46th among provincial towns.[46]

The Later Middle Ages

Colchester like other towns suffered severely from the Black Death. The plague probably arrived in the winter of 1348–9 and continued throughout the summer and possibly into the autumn of 1349. The abbot and probably also the prior of St. John's abbey were dead by August 1349, perhaps from plague. Nothing is known of the fate of other religious houses or of the parish clergy. Among the townspeople 111 wills were proved in the borough court between September 1348 and September 1349, and 25 in the year 1349–50, compared with an average of 2–3 a year in the decades before and after.[47] Those figures cannot, of course, be

[41] P.R.O., C 260/74, no. 55; *E.A.T.* 3rd ser. xxvi. 67–75.

[42] H. Grieve, *Sleepers and Shadows*, 11–12.

[43] Britnell, *Growth and Decline*, 16, 20–2; L. R. Poos, *A Rural Soc. after the Black Death*, 106–7.

[44] *Med. Essex Community*, ed. Ward, 16–17, 34–5, 85–7, 105–6.

[45] *Suff. in 1327* (Suff. Green Books ix), 215–22.

[46] R. E. Glasscock, *Lay Subsidy 1334*, 80–9, 294; *New Hist. Geog. Eng.* 181–4.

[47] C. Creighton, *Hist. Epidemics in Britain*, i. 117–18; *V.C.H. Essex*, ii. 101; E.R.O., D/B 5 R1, ff. 35–44v.; Britnell, *Growth and Decline*, 22.

interpreted as indicating relative death-rates as no doubt extra care was taken to make and enrol wills in time of plague and confusion, but they do suggest an unusually high death rate. The number of those amerced for breach of the assize of ale, which probably reflected the consumption of ale in the town, dropped by *c.* 25 per cent, from 94 at Michaelmas 1345 to 70 at Michaelmas 1351, but the much smaller number of bakers amerced for breach of the assize of bread shows no such drop. Mortality in rural north central Essex has been estimated to have been as high as 45 per cent;[48] what little evidence there is suggests that Colchester's may have been slightly lower.

Whatever the town suffered in 1349, Colchester recovered rapidly in the 1350s. Recovery was due mainly to a flow of immigrants attracted by the town's growing cloth industry. In the 1340s on average *c.* 15 burgesses were admitted from outside the town each year; in the 1350s the average grew to *c.* 22, including, unusually, a few women.[49] The second plague of 1360–1 does not seem to have halted Colchester's physical or economic growth, and in 1377 a total of 2,951 people paid poll tax, making Colchester the eighth largest provincial town in England, and suggesting a total population of *c.* 4,500–5,000, higher than in 1312.[50] The evidence of the numbers involved in victualling trades suggests that Colchester continued to grow in the late 14th century and the first decade of the 15th, its medieval population reaching a peak *c.* 1410 when it may have been as much as a third higher than it had been in 1377. Numbers seem to have remained steady from then until *c.* 1450, and then to have fallen slowly until the early 16th century when the decline accelerated. By 1524 the population had probably been reduced to *c.* 4,000. Even then, Colchester ranked eleventh among English provincial towns on the basis of subsidy paid.[51] Both the growth and fall in population were governed by immigration, and the falling numbers of the later 15th century may reflect the decline in population of England as a whole as much as any economic decline in Colchester, which continued to attract immigrants from all parts of the country, and which showed few signs of serious economic or physical decay before 1500.

The increase in size and wealth in the later 14th century was not accompanied by any increase in Colchester's administrative functions. The castle was allowed to fall into decay, and seems to have been used only as a prison. Royal visits to the town were infrequent and usually for a single night. Edward III seems to have been at Colchester for a day in 1354 when his chancery was there, and Henry VI was in the town in 1445.[52] The chancery, and presumably Henry VII, was at Colchester briefly in 1487, and the king visited the town in 1491. When Humphrey duke of Gloucester visited Colchester in 1423 he was received by a party of burgesses in gowns and red hoods, presumably the bailiffs and aldermen in their liveries.[53]

There were fewer disturbances in Colchester than in some other Essex towns during the rising of 1381, even though at least one of the leaders of the revolt had probably lived there. One Kent jury described Wat Tyler as 'of Colchester' and others said he was from Essex, but other evidence suggests he was a Kentishman. John Ball described himself as 'sometime St. Mary priest of York and now of

48 Britnell, *Growth and Decline*, 22, 91; Poos, *Rural Soc.* 107.

49 E.R.O., D/B 5 R1, ff. 35–44v. There is no record of admissions of burgesses born in the town.

50 Britnell, *Growth and Decline*, 91, 94–5; Poos, *Rural Soc.* 294–9; W. G. Hoskins, *Local Hist. in Eng.* 238.

51 Britnell, *Growth and Decline*, 95–6, 193–202; Hoskins, *Local Hist. in Eng.* 239.

52 *Cal. Close*, 1354–60, 2; E.R.O., D/B 5 R1, f. 92v. A visit by Richard II in 1381, mentioned in B. Bird, *Rebel before his Time: Study of John Ball and the Eng. Peasants' Revolt*, 115–17 is not supported by any evidence.

53 *Cal. Pat.* 1485–94, 168–9, 171, 346; Britnell, *Growth and Decline*, 225.

Detail of Roman Mosaic from Middleborough

Roman Church

Balkerne Gate and Wall

The Rose and Crown Inn, 1898

The George Inn, 1929

Headgate Court (formerly the King's Head Inn), 1993

The Red Lion Inn, 1993

Colchester'.[54] He was certainly in London diocese when in 1364 he was excommunicated there, and in 1367 he was still preaching erroneous and scandalous sermons in Bocking deanery. He was in the area again in 1376 when two Colchester men were among those ordered to apprehend him.[55] Several men surnamed Ball were recorded in Colchester in the late 14th century, including at least three called John; one of them, a chaplain living in lodgings in East Street in 1377, may have been the peasants' leader.[56] At the outbreak of the revolt, however, Ball was in Kent, imprisoned at Maidstone.[57]

A group of rebels from the town and surrounding countryside seem to have gathered at Colchester about 13 June, when the bailiff of Tendring allegedly sent men to join them there before they left for Mile End in Stepney (Mdx.) on 14 June.[58] Other rebels were apparently at Colchester on 15 June, but the main disturbances there were on 16 June, when the moot hall and St. John's abbey were attacked. The attackers threatened to burn the borough muniments, but seem not to have done so although the court rolls were removed, presumably for safe-keeping, so that no courts could be held for five weeks. At St. John's the rioters, who included at least two Brightlingsea men, did carry off and burn court rolls, including those for Greenstead and West Donyland. On 17 June men from Stanway carried off muniments from St. Cross chapel in Crouch Street, which was in Stanway parish.[59] Rebels fleeing from their defeat at Billericay at the end of June failed to stir up further trouble in the borough, but some disorder, directed mainly against Flemings, apparently lasted from May to November 1381.[60] The decision to repair the town walls in 1381 was presumably a reaction to the revolt, suggesting that the town authorities saw it as a threat from outside the borough. St. John's abbey too strengthened its defences after 1381.[61]

An affray outside 'King Coel's castle' (Balkerne gate) in 1391 involving 12 armed retainers of the abbot of St. John's may have arisen from a dispute with the town, or perhaps with St. Botolph's priory, over rights of common on Balkerne field. The following year a violent dispute between the abbot and his monks spilt into St. John's green and terrorized the town.[62]

Colchester was one of the towns which in 1398 received a quarter of the traitor Henry Roper, who had been involved in an abortive uprising in Oxfordshire.[63] The election as bailiff in 1398 of the wealthy merchant Thomas Godstone, a newcomer who had held no other borough office, suggests that the borough was looking for a powerful leader in uncertain times. Godstone was a Surrey landowner who had served Richard II in Picardy and in Essex.[64] His loyalty to Richard II was shown in 1404 when he was involved, with three other prominent Colchester men, John Beche and his sons Richard and John, in a conspiracy led by the countess of Oxford and the abbots of St. John's and St. Osyth's to depose Henry IV and restore Richard II to the throne. All four Colchester men seem to have escaped punishment, although the countess and the abbots were arrested.[65] The involvement of the abbot of St. John's seems to have emboldened the town to make an

[54] A. J. Prescott, 'Judicial Records of the Rising of 1381' (Lond. Ph.D. thesis, 1984), 105; R. B. Dobson, *Peasants' Revolt of 1381*, 381.

[55] *Cal. Pat.* 1374–7, 415; *E.A.T.* N.S. xxv. 110–11.

[56] E.R.O., D/B 5 Cr16–19, *passim.*; D/B 5 R1, f. 47.

[57] Dobson, *Peasants' Revolt*, 136–7, 371; cf. Bird, *Rebel Before His Time*.

[58] Poos, *Rural Soc.* 236; *Essex and the Great Revolt of 1381*, ed. W. H. Liddell and R. G. E. Wood, 57–8; *Revue Roumaine D'Histoire*, xxvi. 337.

[59] P.R.O., KB 145/3/6/1; E.R.O., D/B 5 Cr21, rott. 1d., 2, 4; D/DH VI D11A; ibid. St. John's ledger bk. f. 267v.;

[60] Dobson, *Peasants' Revolt*, 312; *Cal. Pat.* 1381–5, 551.

[61] Below, Walls; Religious Houses.

[62] E.R.O., D/B 5 Cr27, rot. 14; D/B 5 Cr28, rot. 17.

[63] *Sel. Cases in K.B.* vii (Selden Soc. lxxxviii), pp. 94–5.

[64] *Cal. Pat.* 1396–9, 311; 1399–1401, 62, 429; *V.C.H. Surrey*, iv. 271.

[65] J. H. Wylie, *Hist. Eng. under Hen. IV*, ii. 417–27; P.R.O., E 163/6/28; *Sel. Cases in K.B.* vii (Selden Soc. lxxxviii), pp. 151–2; E.R.O., D/B 5 R2, f. 46.

unusual number of complaints against him in the borough lawhundred in 1405,[66] complaints which were repeated at intervals in the earlier 15th century even after a formal pacification and agreement had been made in 1415.[67]

Although Colchester was a centre of Lollardy, only one man, Thomas at Brook, cobbler, joined Oldcastle's rising; he may have been the same as the Thomas Pelle, cordwainer of Colchester, who was later accused of treason for his part in the uprising.[68] Roger Wyke of Colchester was involved in a planned rebellion in Kent in 1449. There were two men of that name, but the rebel was probably the Roger Wyke, fuller, who in 1453 was ordered to appear before the justices with 92 other men, all probably involved in disturbances in the aftermath of Cade's rebellion. He was related to the Roger Wyke who was bailiff of the town in 1446 and 1448.[69] In 1450 proclamations against riotous meetings were issued at Colchester and Sudbury as well as other places in south-east England.[70] Colchester does not seem to have been affected by Cade's rebellion in May that year, but in September over 100 men took up arms claiming that Cade was still alive. They broke the town gaol and threatened to kill Nicholas Peek, one of the bailiffs.[71]

At least three Colchester men joined the earl of Oxford and his brother Thomas Vere in supporting the restoration of Henry VI in 1470 and 1471,[72] but otherwise the town escaped any involvment in the Wars of the Roses. Plans were made to include Colchester in a rising against Henry VII in favour of the earl of Warwick in 1489, but there is no evidence that they received any support in the town.[73]

THE ECONOMY

The Early Middle Ages

Tenth-century Colchester, like other *burhs*, presumably functioned as a market for the surrounding countryside, but it was probably little more. It had no moneyers until *c.* 991, which suggests that despite its port, probably amounting only to a beaching place for small boats, traders did not bring foreign coin to the town to be reminted. What little foreign trade there was in 10th-century Essex seems to have been through Maldon, which had a more accessible port. From *c.* 991, however, the Colchester mint was a busy one, indicating a growth of foreign trade in the town. That perhaps reflected a decline at Ipswich, which had been sacked by the Viking army in the 991 campaign.[74] The fair held from *c.* 1104 by St. John's abbey at the feast of St. John the Baptist may have started in the 11th century, and the massive rise in the farm paid by Colchester to the Crown, from *c.* £15 in 1066 to £80 in 1086, may reflect increasing prosperity as well as Norman extortion.[75]

Growth in the 11th century seems to have been succeeded by relative decline in the earlier 12th, as the farm had been reduced to £40 by 1130.[76] Although the town retained four moneyers under William I and William II and probably under Henry I and Stephen, the number was reduced to one *c.* 1157 and minting ceased

66 E.R.O., D/B 5 Cr35, rot. 13d.

67 e.g. ibid. D/B 5 Cr39, rott. 5–6; D/B 5 Cr49, rot. 22d.; *Cal. Close* 1413–19, 201–2.

68 *E.H.R.* xxix, 101–4; *Cal. Close* 1413–19, 148; *Cal. Pat.* 1413–16, 271.

69 *Cal. Pat.* 1446–52, 338; P.R.O., KB 9/26/2, no. 175; ibid. PROB 11/4, f. 97.

70 J. H. Ramsey, *Lancaster and York*, ii. 120.

71 *Cal. Pat.* 1446–52, 415; *Cal. Close* 1446–52, 503; lists in P.R.O., KB 9/26/2 probably relate to same event.

72 *Cal. Pat.* 1467–77, 317–18.

73 *Rot. Parl.* vi. 436–7.

74 *Battle of Maldon: Fiction and Fact*, ed. J. Cooper, 208–9; *A.-S. Chron.* ed. D. Whitelock, 82.

75 Below, this chapter, Boro. Govt.; Markets and Fairs.

76 *Pipe R.* 1130 (Rec. Com.), 138.

in 1166.[77] The fair granted to St. Mary Magdalen's hospital in 1189, and St. Dennis's fair, held outside St. Botolph's priory by 1310, may, with the St. John's fair, have helped stimulate trade from the late 12th century.[78] In the 14th century the three fairs were attended by men from London, Greenwich, Cambridge, Bury St. Edmunds, Tunstead (Norf.), and Sudbury (Suff.),[79] but they were never among the major English fairs and do not seem to have attracted foreign merchants.

Trade seems to have been principally in provisions. Ten Colchester men were amerced in 1198 for exporting grain to Flanders, and oats and other corn was bought at Colchester in 1206 for shipment to other parts of England. Four Colchester men were amerced in 1195 for selling wine contrary to the assize.[80] Most goods were probably carried by ship from Colchester's port at the Hythe across the North Sea or round the south and east coasts of England. A Colchester merchant traded in the count of Holland's territory in 1197. Others were at Winchelsea and Rye (Sussex) *c.* 1216 when they were harassed and their goods seized in retaliation for the depredations of Stephen Harengood, constable of Colchester castle.[81] The Colchester merchant who sold goods to Henry II's army in Wales,[82] had probably taken them by sea. Adam of Colchester, who travelled to Gascony with Richard of Cornwall in 1225, was at Falmouth in 1226.[83] In 1204 Colchester, although ranked 19th or 20th out of 33 seaports assessed for subsidy, was apparently one of the principal east coast ports, its assessment of £16 8*s.* or £16 12*s.* 8*d.* being higher than those of Norwich, Ipswich, Dunwich, and Orford, although less than half that of Yarmouth.[84] If the assessment reflects Colchester's importance as a port, that importance was short-lived. Even though the river Colne had probably been straightened in the 11th or 12th century, improving access to the Hythe, large ships could reach the port only on spring tides. When Henry III requisitioned ships capable of carrying 16 or more horses for his expedition to Gascony in 1229, only two Colchester ships were suitable.[85]

Colchester was important enough to attract Jewish settlement between 1159 and 1182.[86] Seven Colchester Jews paid a total of £41 13*s.* 4*d.* to the Northampton *donum* in 1194, the ninth largest contribution, but one man, Isaac of Colchester, paid £25 of that sum.[87] Isaac lent money to several prominent townsmen, including Richard and Simon sons of Marcian, and resentment of his outstanding wealth may have contributed to the violence against the Jews which broke out in Colchester, as in other towns, in the early 1190s.[88] Richard son of Marcian and his son Hubert were still indebted to four Jews, three of them from Colchester, in 1238.[89] Colchester Jews, like others, had links with Jewish communities throughout England. About 1220 debts were due, presumably at Colchester, to nine Colchester Jews, three Jews from London, and one each from Norwich, Canterbury, and Oxford.[90] Josce son of Aaron of Colchester married Rose, daughter of the prominent Lincoln Jew Isaac Gabbay; he lent money to a London man before 1268, and in 1275 he lived in Dunwich. Cok of Colchester, apparently his brother, was in London in 1272 and in Lincoln in 1276.[91] Another Josce of Colchester, a

77 *Brit. Numismatic Jnl.* v. 118–20; *Pipe R.* 1156–8 (Rec. Com.), 135; 1167 (P.R.S. xi), 158.

78 Below, Markets and Fairs.

79 P.R.O., JUST 3/18/5, rott. 5, 24.

80 *Pipe R.* 1195 (P.R.S. N.S. vi), 14; 1198 (P.R.S. N.S. ix), 137; 1199 (P.R.S. N.S. x), 97; *Rot. Lit. Pat.* (Rec. Com.), 61; *Rot. Lit. Claus.* (Rec. Com.), i. 69.

81 *Pipe R.* 1197 (P.R.S. N.S. viii), 73; *Pat. R.* 1216–25, 169.

82 E. A. Webb, *Bk. of Foundation of St. Bart.'s Lond.* 46–7.

83 *Pat. R.* 1216–25, 574; 1225–32, 23.

84 *Pipe R.* 1204 (P.R.S. N.S. xviii), 218.

85 *Pat. R.* 1225–32, 264, 344, 370–3.

86 V. D. Lipman, *Jews of Med. Norwich*, 4; *Pipe R.* 1182 (P.R.S. xxxi), 69. On Colch. Jewry see *E.A.T.* 3rd ser. xvi. 48–52.

87 *Jewish Hist. Soc. Miscellany*, i, p. lxiv.

88 *Feet of F. Essex*, i. 16; *Pipe R.* 1194 (P.R.S. N.S. v), 36.

89 *Close R.* 1237–42, 51.

90 Westm. Abbey Mun. 9007.

91 *Cal. Exch. Jews*, i. 119, 162, 166, 229, 294; ii. 268; iii. 43; P.R.O., E 32/12, rot. 3d.

Jew of Lincoln, had houses in Oxford at his death in 1246.[92] Isaac of Colchester was living in Lincoln in 1268, Ellis son of Jacob of Colchester in London in 1273, and Aaron of Colchester in Dunwich in 1275.[93]

By 1220 the Colchester Jewish community had its own bailiff, Benedict, whose son Isaac was one of its principal members in 1255.[94] In 1258 a rabbi, Samuel son of the rabbi Jechiel, was given 15 years' tenure of a house in East or West Stockwell Street which may have contained the synagogue recorded in 1268.[95] Before 1285 the synagogue moved to a solar at the west end of High Street.[96] There was a Jewish 'chaplain' in Colchester in 1267 and 1276–7.[97] A 14th-century tradition held that Henry II had given the Jews a council chamber on St. John's green, but that in 1251 St. John's abbey had converted it into a chapel.[98] Although the details are questionable, such a grant by Henry II is not unlikely.

No later Colchester Jew was as wealthy as Isaac of Colchester, whose debts had passed to the king by 1209,[99] and the Colchester community ranked 16th among those which contributed to an aid in 1221.[1] It was one of the poorest Jewish communities in 1255 when two of its principal members were widows,[2] and, like other English Jewries, it declined further in the later 13th century as a result of royal exactions. Samuel and Josce sons of Aaron sold their houses in St. Runwald's parish to the wealthy burgess William Warin in 1275 to raise money to pay their tallage.[3] By 1290 there were only eight Jewish householders in Colchester, most of them comparatively poor.[4]

Although Colchester was not among the cloth towns recorded in 1202, an industry developed in the second quarter of the 13th century, and by 1247 there was a fulling mill in the liberty.[5] Surnames recorded between *c.* 1230 and *c.* 1265 include 2 chaloners, 2 drapers, 3 dyers, 5 fullers, and 3 weavers. Henry III bought 20 russet cloths in Colchester in 1249 to clothe his servants, 500 ells in 1252, and a further 30 cloths in 1254. Some of the last may have been used to make the robes of Colchester russet trimmed with rabbit fur given to Sir Richard Foliot and his wife and daughter in 1254.[6] Other cloth was acquired for Henry III from Colchester men at Boston fair in 1248 and at Ipswich fair in 1249.[7] Russet cloth was stolen in Colchester *c.* 1250, and in 1251 in the course of a dispute between a Colchester woman and Winchester merchants some was distrained by borough officers. Russet cloth was also among goods confiscated in Mile End in 1265.[8] In the later 13th century a draper, 2 fullers, and 3 weavers were recorded in charters or rentals, and surnames suggest the presence of 2 chaloners, a fuller, and 5 weavers. Worsted and blanket were recorded in 1300 and blanket was the Colchester cloth exported through Ipswich about that date.[9] Woad stolen in 1312 may have been to dye russet, or perhaps blue cloth like that stolen from a tailor in 1328.[10] Linen cloth was recorded *c.* 1316, in 1319, and, in Mile End, in 1337.[11]

Merchants who exported cloth imported wine. In 1272 six men, including the former or future bailiffs Richard of Bergholt, Henry Goodyear, and his brother

92 *Cal. Pat.* 1232–47, 488.
93 *Cal. Exch. Jews*, i. 172; ii. 38, 296.
94 *Cal. Exch. Jews*, i. 32, 60, 73, 81; *Cal. Pat.* 1247–58, 440, 444.
95 M. D. Davis, *Shetaroth or Hebrew Deeds of Eng. Jews*, p. 365; *Cal. Exch. Jews*, i. 193.
96 *Trans. Jewish Hist. Soc.* ii. 90; B.L. Lansd. MS. 416, f. 49v.
97 P.R.O., E 32/12, rot. 3d.
98 *E.A.T.* 3rd ser. xvi. 50–1.
99 *Pipe R.* 1209 (P.R.S. N.S. xxiv), 89.
1 Lipman, *Jews of Med. Norwich*, 6.
2 *Cal. Pat.* 1247–58, 439–44.
3 *Cal. Exch. Jews*, ii. 235–6; *Cal. Pat.* 1274–81, 42.
4 *Cal. Pat.* 1292–1301, 18; *Trans. Jewish Hist. Soc.* ii. 90.
5 *Pipe R.* 1202 (P.R.S. N.S. xv), p. xx; P.R.O., JUST 1/232, rot. 11d.
6 *Cal. Lib.* 1245–51, 254; 1251–60, 97, 280; *Close R.* 1247–51, 198; 1251–3, 135; 1254–6, 8, 24, 46.
7 *Cal. Lib.* 1245–51, 316.
8 P.R.O., JUST 1/233, rot. 36; JUST 1/238, rot. 27.
9 Ibid. JUST 3/18/4, rot. 4d.; *E.A.T.* 3rd ser. xx. 47.
10 P.R.O., JUST 3/19/2, rot. 33; JUST 3/19/8, rot. 31.
11 Ibid. JUST 3/18/5, rott. 22, 38d.; ibid. KB 27/312, rot. 16.

Geoffrey, sold cloth contrary to the assize; Richard and three others including the bailiff Richard Pruet, sold wine. In 1285 the Goodyears and Richard Pruet were among the six men who breached the assize of cloth, while as many as 14 men, including both the Goodyears, Richard of Bergholt, and Richard Pruet, sold a total of at least 325 tuns of wine.[12]

Leather-working, important by 1300, seems to have developed later than cloth, but a cobbler and four tanners were recorded in the mid 13th century and a cobbler and a skinner after *c.* 1265. Late 13th-century surnames indicate the presence in the town of 1 cordwainer, 2 lorimers, and 4 tanners. Other trade surnames included cutler, goldsmith, mustarder, coalman, glasswright, and vintner. At least seven pottery kilns, probably late 12th- or early 13th-century, stood behind the street frontage at Middleborough, immediately outside North gate, and there were others in Mile End. They produced a fairly coarse ware which was used only in north-east Essex. In the late 13th century or the 14th, however, Colchester kilns produced elaborate louvres which have been found as far away as Chelmsford, Great Easton, and possibly Rickmansworth (Herts.).[13]

Detailed subsidy assessments of 1272–3, 1296, and 1301, show the importance of the wool, cloth, and leather trades in Colchester. Of the 167 people recorded in the incomplete assessment of 1272–3, a total of 25 were assessed on cloth, and a further 6 were called weavers, 4 dyers, 3 fullers, and 2 carders. In addition 3 people had wool, and 2 linen. Of the cloths specified, 9 were russets valued at between 6*s.* and 15*s.* a piece; there was a piece of 'huregray' worth 15*s.*, and a piece of higher quality woollen cloth worth 30*s.* Four of those assessed on cloth were also assessed on leather or hides. Another 2 were assessed on leather alone, and 3 shoemakers and 2 tanners can be identified.[14]

The 1296 and 1301 assessments suggest that the leather trades had expanded to employ almost as many people as the cloth trades. Three of the 14 men assessed on goods worth over £4 in 1296 were tanners, including Henry Pakeman and John of Stanway, the wealthiest tradesmen, while 4 were assessed on wool or cloth, 1 on shoes, and 1 on meat. As many as 30 out of the 180 people assessed had wool or cloth; 2 of them were called dyer and 1 fuller. There were 31 leather-workers, including 16 shoemakers and 11 tanners. Four of the 22 people assessed on goods worth over £4 in 1301 (excluding the heads of the religious houses and Robert FitzWalter of Lexden) were assessed on wool or cloth, 2 were tanners, and 1 was a butcher. As many as 36 wool- or cloth-workers, including 6 fullers and 3 dyers, were assessed, compared with 30 leather-workers, including 11 tanners, 12 shoemakers, and a glover. A total of 12 men in 1296 and 18 in 1301 were assessed on 'merchandise' including silk and muslin, gloves, belts, and needles, and spices such as pepper, ginger, saffron, and fennel; 38 people were assessed on ready money for trading. Six men in 1296 and 11 in 1301 were assessed on iron (probably imported), 3 in 1296 and 1 in 1301 on sea coal; 3 men were assessed on salt in 1296. In 1301 twelve men were assessed on boats or shares in boats.[15]

Only 39 out of the 180 people assessed in 1296 (in an area excluding the outlying parishes) and only 148 out of the 388 assessed in the whole liberty in 1301 had no grain or livestock. Although some of the grain held by townsmen was for brewing or baking, and many of those who had only one cow or a few sheep may have

[12] Ibid. JUST 1/238, rot. 59; JUST 1/242, rot. 112.

[13] *Colch. Arch. Rep.* iii. 186–9, 211–14; *E.A.T.* 3rd ser. vii. 33–54.

[14] B.L. Campb. Ch. ix. 2, 4, 5.

[15] *Rot. Parl.* i. 228–65, summarized and analysed in *E.A.T.* N.S. ix. 126–55.

grazed them on the half-year common lands to supplement their income from their trade or craft, many of the most prosperous inhabitants of the town derived their income wholly or mainly from land, much of it probably in the fields south-west, south-east, and north-east of the town. Of the 14 men assessed in 1296 on goods worth over £4 four, including the two wealthiest William Warin and Adam Plaunting, and the former bailiff Henry Goodyear, were assessed only on agricultural produce; only one, Edward of Bernholt who was assessed on salt, iron, and sea coal, had no grain or livestock liable to subsidy. In 1301 all those assessed at £4 or more had some grain or livestock. Henry Pakeman, the wealthiest townsman, had retired from the tannery he ran in 1296.[16] By contrast, at Ipswich in 1283, where the ratio of those assessed on cloth, leather, iron, and 'mercery' was not dissimilar to that at Colchester, a much higher proportion of subsidy payers were assessed on boats and ships, and a smaller proportion on grain and livestock.[17] The chief crop at Colchester was oats, of which *c.* 269 qr. were recorded in 1296 and *c.* 276 qr. in 1301; there was nearly as much barley as oats in 1296, but in 1301 only *c.* 168 qr. were recorded. There was slightly less rye, *c.* 118 qr. in 1296, 144 qr. in 1301. Only 56½ qr. of wheat was recorded in 1296 and 24 qr. in 1301, and some of that may have been imported.[18] Small quantities of peas and beans were grown. Nearly 1,100 sheep and lambs were recorded in 1301, a startling increase over the 305 recorded in 1296. A total of 189 cows and calves were assessed in 1296 and 344 in 1301.[19] The evidence for the burgesses' agricultural practice fits well with that for the cultivation of the royal demesne, which included the land north-east of the castle and Sholand along Maldon Road, between 1276 and 1281. There the chief crop was oats, although rye and probably barley were also grown; the 20 qr. of wheat accounted for in 1280–1, like the 7 qr. 1 bu. in 1276–7, may have been toll corn from Middle mill. About 100 sheep were kept, and 11 cattle were sold in 1280–1.[20]

The men of Colchester were ordered to arrest Norwich merchants in their town in 1272, and toll was taken from Kings Lynn merchants in 1298. Two Yarmouth merchants were involved in the settlement of a tenement in Colchester market place *c.* 1275.[21] In 1305 Colchester was one of the towns in which French merchants from Amiens and St. Omer traded,[22] and a Dutch merchant was robbed of cash, cloth, and other goods at the Hythe *c.* 1316.[23] Few Colchester ships seem to have been involved in overseas trade in the 1280s and 1290s, but two brought wine to London in 1303 and another robbed French merchants off the Brittany coast in 1311.[24] John Lucas of Colchester, who was involved in coastal trade with his ship the *St. Mary* in 1325, was arrested with three other Colchester merchants carrying French wines in 1327, but the four Colchester ships arrested that year were outnumbered by six from Harwich and seven from Brightlingsea.[25]

Although the cases brought in the borough court and the numbers amerced for breach of the assize of ale in the 1330s and 1340s suggest that Colchester was then declining in population and perhaps in wealth,[26] the seeds of the town's rapid recovery and growth in the period after the Black Death were presumably sown then. One factor in the town's later success may have been the improvement of

16 *Rot. Parl.* i. 228–65.

17 *Proc. Suff. Institute of Arch. and Nat. Hist.* xii. 141–57.

18 Cf. P.R.O., E 122/193/33.

19 *Rot. Parl.* i. 228–65.

20 P.R.O., SC 6/1089/7, 17–18.

21 *Cal. Pat.* 1266–72, 707; *Abbrev. Plac.* (Rec. Com.), 238; *Cart. St. John of Jerusalem*, p. 154.

22 *Cal. Fine R.* 1272–1307, 520.

23 P.R.O., JUST 3/18/5, rot. 38d.

24 Ibid. E 122/50/2, 4, 8; N. S. B. Gras, *Early Eng. Customs System*, 400–1; *Cal. Pat.* 1307–13, 446.

25 *Cal. Pat.* 1324–7, 119; *Cal. Mem. R.* 1326–7, p. 130.

26 Britnell, *Growth and Decline*, 20–1.

the navigation and the extension of the quays at the Hythe. In 1339–40 and in 1341–2 the bailiffs leased to John Allen, John Peldon, Nicholas Chapman, and John Lucas, all merchants or ship owners, a total of 100 yd. of river bank below the Hythe with the meadow behind on which to build quays and warehouses.[27] In 1341 the borough reached an agreement with Sir John de Sutton, lord of Battleswick, allowing the building of quays lower down the river at Woodsend, perhaps near Hull mill, and the making of yards there for building and repairing ships.[28] A Flemish ship was arrested at Colchester in 1341, perhaps having reached one of the new quays although usually only barges and lighters could reach the Hythe.[29] Of the eight sailors or shipmen known to have been admitted to the freedom between 1327 and 1500, six were admitted between 1329–30 and 1340–1.[30] As a port, Colchester may have benefited from the decline of Ipswich in the 1330s and 1340s, a decline whose effects seem to have persisted for much of the 14th century.[31]

The Later Middle Ages

Colchester's later medieval prosperity was based on its cloth trade, which was able to develop and adapt freely, untrammelled by the restrictive practices of an independent weavers' or fullers' guild. The availability of water power for mechanical fulling may also have been important in a time of rising wages, and in the later 14th century all five mills on the Colne north and east of the town were rebuilt or adapted for fulling.[32] Colchester's wool and cloth trades were at least holding their own in the years before the Black Death. In 1340 the future bailiff William Buck and his partner contributed 5 sacks of wool to the 26,000 granted to Edward III by parliament, and in 1341 another Colchester man brought 5 sacks of wool, 200 woolfells, and 36 oxhides from Suffolk to Colchester.[33] In the same years at least 20 Colchester men were ordered to be arrested for illegally exporting wool or cloth. They included John Fordham, bailiff that year, and three future bailiffs, Adam Colne, Thomas Dedham, and John Warin the elder. Most of the wool and cloth was carried in Flemish ships, whose cargoes also included grain, cheese, and timber.[34] The export of wool and cloth through Colchester was presumably a comparatively recent development. When a merchant exported 28 sacks of wool to the staple at Bruges through the town in 1341 a customs official had to be sent from Ipswich or London to cocket the sacks.[35] Nevertheless, that year the Colne was sufficiently busy for seven Colchester men, four of whom had themselves been accused of exporting uncustomed wool, to be appointed deputies of the king's serjeant at arms to search ships in the river and estuary for uncustomed wool and other goods.[36] In 1344 a cargo of 714 ells of cloth, 20 qr. of salt, 28 weighs of cheese, and 70 qr. of crushed bark for tanning belonging to three Colchester merchants was impounded in Zeeland. Another merchant had licence to ship 30 Essex cloths from Colchester to Gascony in 1351.[37]

The growing trade led the bailiff William Reyne to tighten up the regulation of the cloth market and to reorganize two wool fairs in 1373.[38] The town continued

27 E.R.O., D/B 5 R1, ff. 35v., 37.
28 Ibid. D/B 5 R2, f. 139.
29 *Cal. Pat.* 1340–3, 286; P.R.O., KB 2/22/1; B.L. Cott. Ch. xviii. 9.
30 E.R.O., D/B 5 R1, ff. 30–113, which seldom records the occupations of new burgesses.
31 G. H. Martin, 'Borough and Merchant Community of Ipswich 1317–1422' (Oxf. Univ. D. Phil. thesis 1955), 104, 128–9, 131; *New Hist. Geog. Eng.* ed. C. Darby, 184; Hoskins, *Local Hist. in Eng.* 238.
32 Britnell, *Growth and Decline*, 76–7.
33 *Cal. Pat.* 1340–3, 296, 317; 1343–5, 539.
34 P.R.O., KB 9/22/1–2.
35 *Cal. Close*, 1341–3, 204–5, 292.
36 P.R.O., KB 9/22/1–2; *Cal. Pat.* 1340–3, 256, 286.
37 *Cal. Close*, 1343–6, 478; *Cal. Pat.* 1350–4, 130.
38 E.R.O., D/B 5 R2, ff. 4–5, 8 and v.

to specialize in medium quality russet cloths, which were sent to other parts of England and abroad. Colchester russets were known in Oxfordshire in the early 15th century. Wool was brought from a distance; a Colchester woolman was mainpernour for a Lechlade (Glos.) man in 1419.[39] Colchester merchants' debtors and creditors in the late 14th century came from as far away as Southampton, Lewes, Norwich, Westminster, and York.[40] A Flemish merchant brought woad, presumably for dying cloth, to Colchester via Great Yarmouth in 1379, and the Londoner Sir Nicholas Brembre had 'a great number' of tons of woad in the town at the time of his execution in 1388.[41]

Trade in grain and dairy products continued. In 1358 a Flemish merchant was allowed to export 24 qr. of wheat from Colchester. William Reyne, William Buck, and William Fermery, all former bailiffs, were accused of smuggling wool and corn out of Colne Water in 1362.[42] In 1364 Geoffrey Daw and William Hunt had licences to export cloth to Gascony and to buy wine and salt there for import into England. A London merchant carried on a similar trade from Colchester to Gascony and Spain in the same year, and in 1374 a Bordeaux merchant was licensed to sell 9 tuns of wine by retail in Colchester.[43] In 1366 Geoffrey Daw exported corn and ale to Flanders and Zeeland, and in 1367 Ipswich merchants were accused of shipping uncustomed wheat, meat, and other foodstuffs from Ipswich and Colchester to Flanders and France.[44] In 1463 and 1478 Colchester merchants were to take foodstuff to Calais.[45]

The leather industry seems to have declined after the early 14th century; almost the only known later medieval leather-worker of consequence was Adam Frating who was allowed to transport hides from London to Colchester by sea in 1338. He may have been the same man as the tanner Adam son of Stephen, who dealt with a London glover in 1345 and who bought 165 hides in London in 1357.[46] Timber was presumably readily available in the woods round Colchester, but the only record of its trade is the carriage from Colchester to Norwich in 1395 of timber to build a stathe.[47]

The predominance of the cloth industry in late 14th- and early 15th-century Colchester is demonstrated by the occupations of those admitted to the freedom, about a fifth of which were recorded in the period 1375–1425. Between 1375 and 1400, a total of 19 cloth-workers were admitted, including 6 dyers, 7 fullers, and 4 weavers. Only 9 men, including 2 cordwainers, 3 glovers, and 3 skinners, were engaged in the leather trade, but 15, including 9 butchers, 2 bakers, and 2 brewers, were victuallers. Five men were described as merchants. Between 1400 and 1425 there were 22 cloth-workers, including 12 weavers, 4 dyers, and 2 fullers; only 5 leather-workers, including 3 cordwainers, but 21 victuallers, including 10 butchers and 9 bakers. The 5 tailors and 1 capper recorded over the whole period may reflect Colchester's importance as a market centre rather than its cloth trade.[48]

In the later 14th century Colchester merchants extended their markets, so that their cloth reached the Mediterranean and the Baltic. The Mediterranean trade was largely carried on through Italian merchants in London, but the Colchester merchant William Ody was in Spain *c.* 1480.[49] Colchester men were more directly

39 *Romania*, xxxii. 54; *Cal. Close* 1419–22, 49.

40 *Cal. Pat.* 1374–7, 421; 1381–5, 40; 1396–9, 10, 115; E.R.O., D/B 5 Cr16, rot. 13d.

41 *Cal. Close*, 1377–81, 258; 1385–9, 362, 376.

42 Ibid. 1354–60, 438; *Cal. Pat.* 1361–4, 291.

43 *Cal. Pat.* 1361–4, 497, 511, 515, 521; 1374–7, 3.

44 Ibid. 1364–7, 211; 1367–70, 67.

45 Ibid. 1461–7, 265; 1476–85, 64.

46 *Cal. Close*, 1337–9, 596; 1343–6, 542; 1354–60, 375.

47 *Sel. Rec. City of Norwich*, ed. W. Hudson and J. C. Tingey, ii. 51.

48 E.R.O., D/B 5 R1, ff. 51v.–81.

49 Britnell, *Growth and Decline*, 65–7; P.R.O., C 1/66, no. 230.

involved in the Baltic trade; William Sedbergh took cloth to Sweden in 1361, and a Prussian merchant was in Colchester in 1375.[50] Colchester merchants were among those encountering difficulties in Prussia in the 1380s, and three or four of them were assessed to contribute to the cost of an embassy to Prussia in 1388, a small number compared with other towns.[51] Hanseatic merchants looked to the citizens of London, York, Colchester, and Kings Lynn for security for payment of debts in 1406.[52] Colchester merchants were in the Baltic again in 1441 and 1451.[53]

Colchester's rapid growth ended in the second decade of the 15th century as its traditional markets, Gascony and Prussia, faced war and depopulation. Perhaps as a result, its clothmakers abandoned their traditional russet cloths *c.* 12 yd. long and 2 yd. wide for cloths *c.* 24 yd. long and 2 yd. wide, which were nearer to standard English cloths. In the 1420s they turned to more expensive cloths which could more profitably be exported in a time of rising transport costs. Already in 1406 a London draper had five Colchester blue medleys, and blue cloth was produced throughout the 15th century. The output of fine grey musterdevillers, like the one paid towards the price of a house in 1486, increased, but from the late 1430s the most successful Colchester cloths were the new greys like the two 'beautiful' new grey cloths acquired by a Hanseatic merchant in 1453.[54]

Hanseatic merchants were in Colchester in the 1390s when two sold expensive red 'grain' dye to Vincent van der Beck, a Colchester burgess of Flemish origin.[55] In the period 1403–61 Hanseatic merchants sued or were sued *c.* 123 times in the Colchester courts.[56] The Cologne merchant Otto Bogylle was in Colchester several times between 1410 and 1428, but Hanseatic activity in Colchester was at its height in the mid 15th century, after the treaty with the Hanseatic League in 1437.[57] The three Hanseatic merchants whose houses and goods in the town were attacked by members of the duke of Buckingham's household in 1447 may have acted as resident agents for other German merchants.[58] In 1450 the bailiffs of Colchester were among those ordered to arrest Hanseatic merchants, but the merchants were back in 1452 when one was robbed in Colne Water of woad worth £72 which he had brought from London. Other Hanseatic merchants were robbed of woollen cloth from a ship anchored in Colne Water in 1454.[59] By 1470, when Richard Lowth of Colchester bought woad from the Cologne merchant Alexander Tacke, Hanseatic influence in the town was probably declining. Tacke soon returned to Germany and his attorney who later sued Lowth for debt may well have been English.[60] Hanseatic merchants were occasionally recorded in Colchester until the end of the century, but the last of them, Herman van A, was a goldsmith.[61]

In the mid 15th century Hanseatic merchants dominated the Colchester cloth trade, importing dyestuffs, notably woad, and exporting 80 to 90 per cent of the finished cloths, but control of the manufacturing processes remained largely in

[50] *Cal. Close*, 1360–4, 248; Britnell, *Growth and Decline*, 64–5; *Recesse und Akten der Hansetage 1256–1430*, iii, p. 309.

[51] *Cal. Close*, 1385–9, 67, 163, 481, 566; *Hansisches Urkundenbuch*, iv, p. 434.

[52] J. H. Wylie, *Hist. Eng. under Hen. IV*, iv. 2.

[53] *Hansisches Urkundenbuch*, vii (1), p. 351; viii, p. 75.

[54] P.R.O., C 1/81, no. 70; *Cal. Lond. Plea and Mem. Rolls*, 1413–37, 3; *Hansisches Urkundenbuch*, viii, p. 176; Britnell, *Growth and Decline*, 163–7, 181.

[55] P.R.O., C 1/68, no. 228; Vincent van der Beck was admitted a burgess in 1390–1, and one of the Hanseatic merchants, Frowyn Stepyng, was in London in 1392: E.R.O., D/B 5 R1, f. 62; *Hansisches Urkundenbuch*, iv, p. 32.

[56] S. Jenks, *Periodizität der hansischen Englandhandels*, 403. Not all the identifications are correct. John Friday who occurs 1403–4, identified as the German Johann Vridach, was more probably John Friday of Chelmsford who became a burgess of Colchester in 1406–7: E.R.O., D/B 5 R1, f. 72; Grieve, *Sleepers and Shadows*, 49–50.

[57] Jenks, *Periodizität der hansischen Englandhandels*, 398; Britnell, *Growth and Decline*, 169–72.

[58] Jenks, *Periodizitat der hansischen Englandhandels*, 409–10.

[59] B.L. Cott. Ch. xviii. 9; *Cal. Pat.* 1446–52, 431, 579; 1452–61, 223–4.

[60] Britnell, *Growth and Decline*, 175–7; P.R.O., C 1/11, no. 512; cf. Jenks, *Periodizität der hansischen Englandhandels*, 415–20.

[61] *Hansisches Urkundenbuch*, viii, p. 176; x, p. 67; xi, pp. 352–4, 365–7, 381; P.R.O., C 1/29, no. 440; C 1/46, no. 320.

English hands. The German Eberhard Cryte sued an East Bergholt fuller in 1458 for six woollen cloths in circumstances which suggest that he may have been involved in the production as well as the export of cloth, but he was apparently unusual.[62] Nor was Hanseatic control of the sale of dyestuffs complete. A London merchant sold woad, madder, and alum in Colchester in 1427, John Trew bought woad from a Melton Mowbray merchant *c.* 1430, an English woader John Werkwode was in Colchester in 1429, and the will of Thomas Ruffle, woader, was proved in the borough court in 1462.[63]

Trade with north-west Europe declined in the later 15th century, and Colchester merchants, like those of other cloth-producing areas, turned increasingly to trade through London.[64] The sheriffs of London were accused in the late 14th century of charging a Colchester draper toll, contrary to the liberties of his town, and linen cloth and woad were shipped from Colchester to London for three London mercers in 1449–50.[65] Some Colchester ships took part in the London trade: in 1480 Richard Cely shipped wool and wool fells from London to Calais in the *Nicholas* of Colchester,[66] and two other Colchester ships, the *Anne* and the *Christopher*, arrived in London that year with linen cloth, soap, and wax.[67] Thomas Bosse, a member of a leading Colchester family and a borough councillor, owed £70 in London in 1423, part of it to a Lincoln merchant, and £20 to a London mercer and a woolmonger in 1426, when he was said to be late citizen and grocer of London.[68] In 1422 Bosse and another Colchester merchant, John Brandon, seem to have owed money to an Ipswich and a Brentwood man, and in 1446 Bosse owed money to two citizens of Norwich. Brandon was described as late citizen and grocer of London in 1423 when he owed money to Norwich merchants. The dyer John Edrich, chamberlain 1442–4, owed money to two London grocers in 1456.[69] Two late 15th-century bailiffs, Thomas Smith and Richard Barker, owed money in London, Smith to a pewterer and a draper in 1482, and Barker to two mercers in 1481. In 1439 a London merchant and a Dutchman conspired to send 26 stone of wool to Colchester by road, disguised as woollen cloth.[70]

Some wool was brought from Kent. In the 1420s a London grocer, in partnership with the wealthy Colchester merchant Thomas Godstone, shipped fleeces from Faversham to Colchester.[71] Forty sacks of wool were shipped from Sandwich to Colchester in 1415, and 24 sarplers in 1421. Other Kentish wool was sent to Colchester by road and the ferry at Tilbury in 1441.[72] The town also maintained close links with the cloth-producing area of north-east Essex and south-east Suffolk. A Colchester fuller owed £15 to a Lavenham man in 1457, and Peter Barwick of Colchester Hythe owed a Hadleigh (Suff.) clothmaker £4 10*s.* in 1472; a Bury St. Edmunds coverlet-maker owed a Colchester man £8 in 1460.[73] Members of the Spring family of Lavenham were involved in the town *c.* 1470; a Nayland weaver bought a large quantity of wool there in the later 15th century, and William Christmas bought wool from a Bury St. Edmunds man *c.* 1499, paying for it partly in woad.[74]

The occupations of 68 bailiffs in the 14th and 15th centuries are recorded. Before

62 Jenks, *Periodizitat der hansischen Englandhandels*, 414.

63 P.R.O., C 1/7, no. 112; E.R.O., D/B 5 Cr47, rot. 22d.; D/B 5 R1, ff. 83v., 99; cf. Jenks, *Periodizitat der hansischen Englandhandels*, 396–426.

64 Britnell, *Growth and Decline*, 171–7.

65 E.R.O., D/B 5 R1, f. 154v.; *Cal. Pat.* 1401–5, 337; P.R.O., C 1/13, no. 147a.

66 *Cely Papers* (Camd. Soc. [1st ser.], clxix), 42.

67 *Overseas Trade of Lond. 1480–1* (Lond. Rec. Soc. xxvii), pp. 2–3.

68 *Cal. Lond. Plea and Mem. Rolls*, 1413–37, 164; *Cal. Pat.* 1422–9, 311.

69 *Cal. Pat.* 1416–22, 413; 1422–9, 147; 1441–6, 388; 1452–61, 270.

70 Ibid. 1476–85, 267, 291; *Sel. Cases before King's Council* (Selden Soc. xxxv), 103.

71 *Cal. Pat.* 1422–9, 457, 525.

72 *Cal. Close*, 1413–19, 236; 1419–22, 141; 1435–41, 418, 420.

73 *Cal. Pat.* 1452–61, 321, 618; 1466–77, 321.

74 P.R.O., C 1/48, no. 135; C 1/61, no. 420; C 1/195, no. 36.

the mid 15th century all were merchants dealing in cloth, wool, or wine, except the dyer Robert Selby, bailiff 1428, 1435, 1438, 1446, 1448; the wealthy vintner Thomas Francis, bailiff 12 times between 1381 and 1414, may have been a spicer also.[75] Most of the bailiffs in the later 15th century were merchants, but John Sayer (1454, 1457) and William Rede (1464) were shearmen, John Baker (1451), Richard Barker (1489, 1494, 1496, 1499), John Bardfield (1490, 1492, 1505), and William Colchester (1472, 1474, 1477) were fullers,[76] and Seman Youn (1455) was a pewterer, although he also exported cloth.[77] At the end of the century three bailiffs, Richard Plomer, Richard Hervey, and John Thirsk, were called clothmakers.[78] One alderman, John Pake (1398), was a draper, and seven other drapers between 1398 and 1455 were evidently substantial men.[79]

Evidence for trades other than cloth- and leather-working is sparse. Of 98 men summoned to appear before the justices in 1453, as many as 34 were cloth-workers (14 fullers, 12 weavers, 6 dyers, a shearman, and a cloth-sealer); a further 7 were victuallers (4 butchers, a brewer, a grocer, and a spicer), and 5 were leather-workers (2 glovers, a cordwainer, a skinner, and a currier). Among the others summoned were 3 shipmen, 7 tailors, 7 smiths, a tiler, a brickman, a pinner, and a painter.[80] Two forges in the east ward paid rents to the borough in the late 14th century, and a further four 'traves' or frames to hold a horse being shod had encroached on the roads before 1501.[81] At least 14 smiths were admitted to the burgage in the later 14th century and the 15th. A furber was recorded in 1492–3.[82] Two pewterers conveyed land in Lexden in 1425, and Colchester was among the towns in which the London pewterers' company seized substandard pewter in 1474.[83] Ten carpenters were admitted to the freedom between 1370 and 1407, a sawyer was admitted in 1395–6, a mason in 1426–7, a plumber in 1445–6, and a tiler in 1443–4. Enrolled deeds record a thatcher in 1328–9, carpenters in 1342–3 and 1377–8, plumbers in 1428–9 and 1451–2, and tilers in 1448–9 and 1490–1.[84] Tilers swore fealty in the borough in 1451 and 1472. A dispute over the sale of 15,000 tiles and 4,000 crest tiles reached the borough court in 1394, and cattle broke more than 500 tiles, apparently in a tileyard, in 1400.[85] There is surprisingly little evidence of ship-building after 1341, but the town was ordered to repair a small ship for the king's use in 1382 and to build one in 1401. In 1466 a boat building yard had recently been started at the Hythe.[86]

Although few fishermen appear in the records, Colchester undoubtedly benefited from the fishery which had been confirmed to the burgesses by Richard I in 1189. The oysters which were to be important in the economy of the modern town were less valuable than fish in the Middle Ages,[87] but they were sold: an oyster-stall in the market place was recorded in 1337. In the same year the bailiffs leased two fishing weirs. Men were presented in the borough court for illegal fishing in 1351 and 1356, and there were disputes over the sale of oysters at the Hythe in 1366 and over fishing with illegal nets in 1377.[88] In 1362 Lionel of Bradenham was

75 E.R.O., D/B 5 R1, f. 74v.; D/DCm 218/9.

76 Ibid. D/B 5 R1, ff. 91v., 99, 112; *Cal. Pat.* 1476–85, 267; Britnell, *Growth and Decline*, 211.

77 P.R.O., C 1/17, no. 198.

78 Britnell, *Growth and Decline*, 184.

79 P.R.O., C 1/85, no. 53; *Cal. Pat.* 1401–5, 337, 341; 1436–41, 239; 1446–52, 300; *Cal. Close*, 1422–9, 464; 1429–35, 355; *Feet of F. Essex*, iii. 229.

80 P.R.O., KB 9/26/2, nos. 175–7.

81 E.R.O., D/B 5 R2, f. 165 and v.; Bodl. MS. Rolls Essex 2.

82 E.R.O., D/B 5 R1, f. 111.

83 Ibid. Acc. C104, box of family and estate papers 1425–1893; *Med. Industries*, ed. J. Blair and N. Ramsay, 68.

84 E.R.O., D/B 5 R1, ff. 35–110v.

85 Ibid. D/B 5 R2, ff. 143v., 150v.; D/B 5 Cr28, rot. 24; Cr31, rot. 17d.

86 *Cal. Close*, 1381–5, 145, 181; 1399–1402, 239; E.R.O., D/B 5 Cr73, rot. 1d.

87 *Cal. Chart. R.* 1226–57, 411, translated in *Colch. Charters*, 2; J. E. T. Rogers, *Hist. Agric. and Prices in Eng.* i. 606–8, 617; iv. 538.

88 E.R.O., D/B 5 Cr5, rott. 6d., 8d.; Cr9, rot. 1d.; Cr11, rot. 2; Cr15, rot. 3; *Cal. Inq. Misc.* iii, p. 406.

accused of inclosing parts of the creeks running into the Colne, presumably for his own fishery, and thus preventing the burgesses and others from fishing there. Similar allegations may have played a part in Bradenham's violent confrontation with the town in 1350.[89] The burgesses' strong, and ultimately successful, opposition to the grant of the river to the earl of Oxford in 1447 was largely due to their need to protect their fishery.[90] In the 15th century presentments of burgesses for using illegal nets or traps, of foreigners for fishing, and of fishermen for taking oysters out of season became more frequent,[91] perhaps as the fishery became more valuable. The proclamation made by the bailiffs on the river Colne in 1382 included prohibitions on forestalling fish, obstructing the river, and dredging oysters out of season.[92] Colchester oysters and mussels were taken to Great Yarmouth in 1413. In 1486 a Sudbury man sued a Dunwich man for £6 8*s*. owed for fish apparently bought in Colchester.[93]

A list of the late 14th century of goods on which customs were payable at Colchester included wool, flax, and hemp for weaving; yellow and green dyes, madder, woad, and ashes for dyeing; and fullers earth, as well as woollen cloth, broadcloth, and Irish cloth. There were also leather and hides, and bark for tanning them; tallow, wax, grease and oil, cotton, and wicks for the chandlers; several kinds of wood, including wainscot and deal, for carpentry; stone, lime, and marble, timber, tiles, and shingles for building; and iron, steel, lead, and tin for metal-working. Masts and oars of various sizes, ropes and cables, were used by ship-builders or repairers. Among the livestock and provisions were corn, pigs, cows, sheep, poultry, eggs, fish, including salmon, eels, and porpoises, and fruit, as well as the more exotic garlic, onions, pepper, figs, raisins, dates, almonds, and rice. Household furniture and utensils were imported, as were furs, millstones, and mortars. Most of those goods appear in late 14th- and 15th-century customs accounts, along with large quantities of wine, salt, and linen cloth, and smaller amounts of soap, bitumen, litmus, ginger, saffron, and walnuts, and manufactured goods including hats, mirrors, cushions, and two feather beds. The craftsmen who paid custom included cardmakers, dyers, and quiltmakers; tailors and haberdashers; skinners, tanners, cordwainers, curriers, and saddlers; smiths, spurriers, furbishers, lattoners, pewterers, and bellmakers; carpenters, carvers, and joiners; painters; bookbinders and scriveners; turners and coopers; bowyers and fletchers; masons; chandlers; and butchers.[94]

There is some evidence for craft organizations, mainly under the control of the borough authorities. The earliest recorded was the butchers', whose wardens, responsible for the quality of meat sold in the market, were recorded from 1311. Overseers of the fish trade were appointed in 1365 after complaints had been made about the lack of supervision.[95] In each instance the officials' activity was confined to the market. The keepers of the tanners' art recorded in 1336 may have represented a more independent organization since they do not seem to have been elected in the borough court until 1443.[96] The bailiffs and council laid down a scale of charges for tawed hides in 1424 or 1425, and at the same time forbade the tanners and white-tawyers to pollute the river by placing their hides in it.[97] In 1425 the

[89] P.R.O., C 260/74, no. 55; *E.A.T.* 3rd ser. xxii. 67–75.

[90] Morant, *Colch.* 90–1.

[91] E.R.O., D/B 5 Cr32, rot. 15d.; Cr36, rott. 2d., 21; Cr39, rott. 1, 2, 3; Cr41, rot. 1d.; Cr55, rot. 3; Cr56, rot. 17d.; Cr57, rot. 2d.; Cr72, rot. 19d.; Cr74, rot. 23.

[92] Ibid. D/B 5 R1, f. 21.

[93] *Cal. Close*, 1413–19, 7; P.R.O., C 1/81, no. 56.

[94] E.R.O., D/B 5 R1, ff. A–C; P.R.O., E 122/193/33; E 122/52/42.

[95] E.R.O., D/B 5 Cr1, rot. 5; Cr14, rot. 10d.

[96] Ibid. D/B 5 Cr14, rot. 1; Cr59, rot. 3.

[97] Ibid. D/B 5 R2, ff. 65v.–66.

'artificers of the art of leather-working called the cordwainers' came to the borough court and asked for a number of ordinances, which had already been subscribed by all the cordwainers in the liberty, to be enrolled. All the ordinances dealt with Sunday observance, and the four masters of the cordwainers who took their oaths later that year presented only breaches of those ordinances; they did not appear before the borough court again, unless they were the wardens of the guild of St. Crispin and St. Crispian in the Greyfriars' church who sued for debt in 1525.[98] The incident of 1425 suggests that there was a pre-existing cordwainers' organization which made the new ordinances. In 1456–7 four supervisors of the curriers' craft were elected in the borough court. The masters of the wax chandlers were sworn in in the borough court in 1451.[99]

The first sign of a cloth-workers' organization was the election in the borough court in 1407 of two 'overseers and masters of the weavers' art'.[1] Two of a number of ordinances made by the bailiffs in 1411–12 were designed to regulate the cloth trade and protect the spinners and weavers. Standard weights were to be provided for weighing wool for spinning; no wool was to be sent out of the liberty for spinning, and weavers were not to be paid in food or merchandise. In 1425 a weaver and two fullers were presented in the borough court for taking part of their wages in goods rather than money.[2] In 1418 the fullers, in an effort to tighten the regulation of their trade, asked the bailiffs to form them into a guild of fullers whose two masters, elected annually on Monday after Michaelmas at St. Cross chapel, were to oversee all the master fullers within the liberty. The regulations provided that no man might exercise the crafts of both weaving and fulling, that no master weaver or fuller should take an apprentice for less than five years, and that disputes between weavers and fullers over the fulling of cloth should be settled by the masters of the guild. The guild seems to have been established, as a breach of its regulations was reported in 1419.[3] A fuller accused in 1427 of teaching his art to a man who had not been apprenticed was presented at the borough court by the lawhundred jury, not by the guild, but he was accused both of acting in derogation of his art and of breaching its ordinances.[4] Two masters of the clothiers' craft and two masters of the shearmen's craft were sworn at the Michaelmas lawhundred in 1448.[5] In 1452 it was ordained that every spinner or weaver should take an oath before the bailiffs to observe regulations as to payment for their work, which seem to have been those laid down in 1411.[6]

The tightening of craft regulations in the 15th century may have been partly the result of stagnation or decline in the town's economy. Cloth production, after falling in the 1410s and 1420s, reached its peak in the 1440s with the increasing Hanseatic trade. The later 15th century was marked by a slight decline in the number of cloths produced, and by a tendency for the sale of those cloths to be concentrated in the hands of a relatively small number of clothmakers. At the same time, Colchester increased its share of the contracting local cloth market at the expense of smaller towns in the area. Other indicators, notably the farms of the land and water tolls, also suggest declining economic activity. The farm of the borough houses and cranes at the Hythe and of the water tolls fell fairly steadily from a high point of £56 in 1438–9 to £35 in 1484–5, while the farm of the land

98 Ibid. D/B 5 Cr45, rott. 16d., 27.

99 Britnell, *Growth and Decline*, 245.

1 E.R.O., D/B 5 Cr36, rot. 23d.

2 Ibid. D/B 5 R2, f. 13; D/B 5 Cr45, rot. 25; *V.C.H. Essex*, ii. 383.

3 *V.C.H. Essex*, ii. 384; Britnell, *Growth and Decline*, 242–3.

4 E.R.O., D/B 5 Cr47, rot. 22d.

5 Britnell, *Growth and Decline*, 244–5.

6 *V.C.H. Essex*, ii. 383–4.

tolls and of the wool market in the moot hall cellar fell from a total of £22 in 1443–4 to £16 in 1484–5.[7] The decline in the number of pleas of debt in the borough courts is more difficult to interpret,[8] but it too may indicate reduced trade. Such reduced trade, however, undoubtedly reflected a reduced population, both in the borough and in its hinterland, and is not incompatible with continuing or even increasing prosperity among the surviving burgesses. Whatever Colchester's later 15th-century decline, it does not seem to have provoked complaints of poverty from the townsmen or pleas for the reduction of the borough's farm or subsidy assessment.[9]

GROWTH OF THE TOWN

The Saxon and Norman Town

The Anglo-Saxon town developed in the ruins of the Roman one, but archaeological evidence suggests there was little or no continuity between them. North Hill, Head Street, and High Street follow the lines of Roman streets, but those lines were dictated by North gate, Head gate, and East gate, all of which continued in use. The main Roman gate, the Balkerne gate, was blocked in the late Roman or Anglo-Saxon period to make a stronghold later sometimes called King Coel's castle.[10] The road from London was diverted southwards to enter the town at the south-west gate, the medieval Head or principal gate. Pottery finds and the sunken huts excavated in Lion Walk and Culver Street suggest scattered early and middle Anglo-Saxon settlement within the Roman town walls, at least in the areas between Head Street, Culver Street, and Lion Walk, and between North Hill and West Stockwell Street.[11] From the late 10th century the population seems to have increased, and settlement expanded along both sides of High Street, North Hill, and Head Street.

It has been suggested that the intramural area west of the line of Maidenburgh Street and Queen Street, apart from that between High Street and Culver Street, was laid out on a 4-pole unit, probably at the time of Edward the Elder's conquest in 917.[12] Such a replanning, which occurred in many other towns at that date, is inherently likely, but the suggestion that the area between High Street and Culver Street was laid out later than the rest of the town seems dubious, for Culver Street is the back lane for houses on the south side of High Street, and fits well into an early 10th-century plan. The streets show no other clear sign of late Anglo-Saxon town planning, and Maidenburgh Street, on the eastern edge of the 'planned' area seems to date from the early 14th century.[13] Any 10th-century town planning presumably involved laying out building plots, including the large urban estates typical of many late Anglo-Saxon towns. The Roman temple precinct, which became the site of the Norman castle, may have been one such urban estate, belonging to the ealdorman or possibly to the king. The site, like much of Colchester, seems to have been uninhabited in the 7th or 8th century when there was a cemetery in its north-west corner, but about the 10th century part of the blind arcade along the southern edge of the temple site was re-used. The first

7 Britnell, *Growth and Decline*, 181–92, 277–8.
8 Ibid. 206–8; *Econ. H.R.* civ. 184–5.
9 Cf. *Proc. Suff. Institute of Arch. and Hist.* xxxvi. 76, 97.
10 e.g. D/B 5 Cr21, rot. 30; below, Walls. The castle was also associated with King Coel: below, Castle.
11 *Colch. Arch. Rep.* i. 1–6; *E.A.T.* 3rd ser. xiv. 137.
12 *A.-S. Studies in Arch. and Hist.* i (Brit. Arch. Rep. lxxii), 149–64.; *Colch. Arch. Rep.* i. 50–1, 71.
13 Below, this chapter, this section.

post-Roman buildings on the site, immediately south of the temple podium, probably included a timber hall and seem to have been part of a high status, 10th-century dwelling.[14] Another estate belonged to the bishop of London. In the early 12th century the south-west corner of the town, bounded by Church Street on the north and Church Walk on the south, Head Street on the east, and the town wall on the west, formed the bishop's soke. It contained the church of St. Mary-at-the-Walls, an otherwise unrecorded chapel of St. Andrew, and the bishop's own house, and presumably also the 14 houses and 4 a. of land which the bishop held in 1086. The bishop also held 2 hides in the fields south-east of the town, extending from the small tributary of the Colne near the later Hull mill as far north as St. Leonard's parish.[15]

Of the ten medieval churches within or near the town walls, at least six and probably a further three were Anglo-Saxon foundations. St. Peter's at the top of North Hill, whose churchyard seems originally to have extended as far as High Street, was held by two priests in 1066, and may have been the principal church of the early town. Until the 13th century Mile End was within its parish.[16] The surviving tower of Holy Trinity, south of Culver Street, was added in the late 11th century to an existing nave,[17] and the tower of St. Martin's also contains pre-Conquest work. Both St. Nicholas's and All Saints' churches seem to follow the late Anglo-Saxon alignment of High Street and hence to have been built before the street was diverted southwards round the Norman bailey wall *c.* 1100,[18] and its dedication to an obscure Mercian saint suggests that St. Runwald's, in the market place in High Street, was founded before or soon after the Conquest. St. Mary's-at-the-Walls, in existence by the earlier 12th century,[19] was presumably built as a private church of the bishop of London; early, possibly 9th-century, graves have been found south of its churchyard, and its parish like St. Peter's extended well beyond the walls.[20] St. Botolph's, just outside the south gate of the town, was a parish church in the later 11th century, and another probably late Anglo-Saxon church, identified with the St. John the Evangelist's church said to have been on or near the site of St. John's abbey, stood a little further south, just east of the medieval St. Giles's church.[21] Both St. Botolph's and the putative St. John's lie in or near Roman cemeteries, but there is no evidence that either originated as a sepulchral chapel. At the end of the 11th century St. Botolph's was the home of a community of secular canons, who adopted the Augustinian rule *c.* 1100, but that community was probably of recent origin, not the survivor of an earlier minster church. Its parish, which presumably originally included land both inside and outside the walls, was probably enlarged after 1100 by grants of tithe to the Augustinian priory.[22] The only large estate south-east of the town which did not belong to the priory or to St. John's abbey, Battleswick manor, was in St. Giles's parish, and that suggests that the precursor of St. Giles's, not St. Botolph's, was the original parish church of Donyland in the south-east of the liberty.[23]

In 1086 a total of 354 houses paid customary dues and a further 51 which had paid in 1066 no longer did so.[24] Those, with the 14 houses on the bishop of

[14] *Arch. Jnl.* cxxxix. 384–90.

[15] *Feet of F. Essex*, i. 39; *V.C.H. Essex*, i. 440; *Cur. Reg. R.* iii, p. 181; iv, pp. 74–5; *Colch. Cart.* ii. 545–6.

[16] *V.C.H. Essex*, i. 578; *Colch. Cart.* ii. 442.

[17] Below, Churches (Holy Trinity).

[18] W. J. and K. Rodwell, *Hist. Churches*, 30–1.

[19] *Cur. Reg. R.* iii, p. 181; iv, pp. 74–5.

[20] Rodwell, *Hist. Churches*, 33.

[21] *Colch. Arch. Rep.* i. 41–6.

[22] *Cart. Holy Trinity Aldgate* (Lond. Rec. Soc. vii), 226; J. C. Dickinson, *Origins of Augustinian Canons*, 22–108; below, Boundaries.

[23] Below, Outlying Parts (West Donyland).

[24] *V.C.H. Essex*, i. 574–8; C. Darby, *Domesday Eng.* 364–8.

London's soke, make a total of 419, and there may have been other houses which had never paid dues. Although there was considerable open space within the walls throughout the Middle Ages, settlement extended outside the them by 1086. Besides their houses, individual burgesses and other landowners held a total of *c.* 1,304 a. of land, most of it in parcels of between 1 a. and 10 a. It probably lay mainly in the fields north, south-west, and south-east of the town; Bury St. Edmunds abbey's 30 a. may already have included the 'wic' which it held in Mile End in the 13th century.[25] The burgesses as a body also held 51 a. of meadow, perhaps along the Colne at the Hythe, 8 perches of land around the walls, and 80 a. in their common, probably waste land within the walls and along some of the roads leading out of the town. The borough owned land in all those places in the 14th century.[26] The rural settlements in Greenstead, Lexden, and West Donyland, and possibly Mile End were distinct from the town in 1086. Indeed, part of what was later West Donyland seems to have been in Lexden hundred, and the status of Lexden itself was disputed.[27]

The late 11th century and the 12th were marked in Colchester as in many other towns by a spate of building work. The construction of the first phase of the castle *c.* 1076 changed the physical appearance of the town, but may not have altered its layout if the site was earlier a royal residence. High Street was diverted southwards by the building of the south wall of the bailey *c.* 1100. The foundation of St. John's abbey in 1095 on a small hill south of the town, and of St. Botolph's priory in the existing parish church just outside the south gate *c.* 1100 transformed the south-east corner of the town.[28] During the 12th century both houses erected impressive churches and conventual buildings, and their presence almost certainly attracted lay settlement. St. James's church, at the east end of High Street, was built in the 12th century or earlier, and St. John's abbey built St. Giles's church in its graveyard in the early 12th century. The leper hospital of St. Mary Magdalen was founded early in the 12th century ½ mile south-east of the town.[29] Much building was done with re-used Roman stone and tile, and the quarrying of surviving Roman buildings for materials probably cleared areas within the walls, particularly perhaps Maidenburgh and Eldland north of Eld Lane, for medieval development.[30]

The Early Middle Ages

Throughout the Middle Ages the principal houses and most of the shops stood in or near the market, which was held in High Street between its junction with North Hill and the castle gate near the corner of Maidenburgh Street. There is little evidence for the concentration of the shops of different trades in specific areas, but there were cobblers' shops at the south end of East Stockwell Street in the 13th century.[31] There may have been more specialization by the 1380s when Cook Row near the moot hall, 'la Bacherie', and Cordwainers' Row, were recorded.[32] The butchers' shambles were in the middle of the market, near the moot hall, possibly round St. Runwald's church, and the fish market was nearby, west of the church. The corn market was at the west end of High Street.[33] The fullers, dyers, and tanners, who needed water, worked along the Colne between North bridge and Middle mill, and at East bridge. Fullers held land under the wall between Rye-

25 B.L. Lansd. MS. 416, f. 48v.; below, Commons.
26 E.R.O., D/B 5 R1, ff. 30–66.
27 Below, Outlying Parts.
28 Below, Religious Houses.
29 *V.C.H. Essex*, ii. 184.
30 *Colch. Arch. Rep.* i. 47–8.
31 Westm. Abbey Mun. 6702: printed by M. D. Davis in *East Anglian*, N.S. iii. 154, who translates 'sutorum' as 'tailors'.
32 E.R.O., D/B 5 Cr21, rot. 21d.; Cr22, rott. 2d., 47, 53d.
33 Below, Market.

High Street from the East, 1858

with St. Runwald's church and the 19th-century town hall in the background; the circular object at top left is the clock of St. Nicholas's church projecting over the street

High Street, *c.* 1910

with the new town hall and, in the background, the water tower called Jumbo

Hythe Hill, 1887
with the tower of St. Leonard's church

Maidenburgh Street in the 1890s

gate and North gate in the 1220s; *c.* 1242 a tanner, a tenterer, and a fuller had houses outside North gate, and in 1328 Edmund le Chaloner sold his tenement beyond North bridge to a fuller.[34] John Dyer, a clothmaker if not actually a dyer, owned at least two houses in East Street and a tenter at East mill at his death in 1330.[35]

Of the six known 12th-century stone houses, three, including the moot hall, were on the north side of High Street, one on the south side of the street at the corner of Pelham's Lane, one on the corner of Culver Street and Lion Walk, and one in East Stockwell Street. Most seem to have had solars above undercrofts, and the moot hall had a solar block at its east end by the mid 13th century. They were set well back from the street frontage which may already have been occupied by smaller houses and shops.[36] The Pelham's Lane house belonged to Joan daughter of Richard Marcian, one of the leading men in early 13th-century Colchester; in 1306 its plot extended from High Street to Culver Street.[37] Conveyances of part of a messuage in the market in the 1240s and disputes over half a messuage in 1248 and 1285[38] suggest the division of properties in the more sought-after parts of the town. St. Runwald's church was probably an early encroachment on the market place, and by the later 13th century there were shops around it.[39] The bailiffs leased a plot 9 ft. by 6 ft. on the south side of the church, presumably for building, in 1331–2.[40]

In 1258 a house in East or West Stockwell Street had upper and lower rooms, and the occupier was expected to enlarge it.[41] A lease, probably made in 1263–4, of a tenement in the market excluded the room under the solar called 'Tholuhus',[42] perhaps either a room for the collection of market tolls or 'the oil house'. By 1290 there were houses in the market with cellars below and solars above the shops or selds built in front of them.[43] Most houses were probably of timber and plaster, like the one near East gate, half of which was granted to a widow in 1321.[44]

The Friars Minor acquired a large site in the north-east quarter of the town, between High Street and the wall, before 1237. The land, like that which Henry III gave them in 1237, may have been part of the castle estate. St. Cross hospital, in a detached part of Stanway parish outside Head gate, was founded before 1272, and both St. Anne's chapel and hospital on the Harwich road and St. Catherine's hospital in Crouch Street were founded by the mid 14th century. Comparatively little work was done on the parish churches, but St. Giles's was rebuilt or remodelled, presumably by St. John's abbey, in the 13th century, and the lower stages of the tower of St. James's may have been built in the early 13th century.[45]

A house beyond East bridge, held of St. John's abbey with cultivable land and meadow in the late 12th century, may have been on the abbey's manor of Greenstead; other houses beyond the bridge in the mid 13th century seem to have been part of the town,[46] although apparently separated from it by East Hill which was sparsely populated. The settlement at East bridge may have been associated with quays, like that recorded in 1439. Permission to build a footbridge at the Hythe in 1407 was conditional on boats being able to reach East bridge, and a

34 B.L. Arundel MS. 145, ff. 12–13v.; *Colch. Cart.* ii. 331.
35 E.R.O., D/B 5 Cr3, rot. 5.
36 *Colch. Arch. Rep.* i. 53–70.
37 B.L. Campb. Ch. ii. 5; *Cal. Exch. Jews*, i. 235.
38 Westm. Abbey Mun. 9077; P.R.O., JUST 1/231, rot. 34; JUST 1/242, rot. 41d.
39 *Colch. Cart.* ii. 575.
40 E.R.O., D/B 5 R1, f. 31.
41 M. D. Davis, *Shetaroth or Hebrew Deeds of Eng. Jews*, p. 365.
42 Westm. Abbey Mun. 6723.
43 *Cart. St. John of Jerusalem*, p. 152.
44 E.R.O., St. John's abbey ledger bk. f. 101 and v.
45 Below, Religious Houses; Churches (St. Giles's, St. James's); Chapels.
46 *Colch. Cart.* ii. 316, 598.

similar provision was made when the footbridge was replaced by a cart bridge in 1473.[47] Three houses outside the walls in Head ward, presumably in Headgate or Crouch Street, were recorded about the 1220s. There were houses outside North gate *c.* 1242, and beyond North bridge by the 1270s.[48] The two 11th-century churches outside South gate, St. Botolph's and St. John the Evangelist, imply early settlement there, but there is no documentary evidence for it until the 13th century when there were houses in Lodders Lane (later Abbeygate Street) and Berisland (later Vineyard Street). In 1297 St. John's abbey owned land and buildings in Stanwell Street on St. John's green, and by that date there were houses outside Schere gate.[49] There was at least one house in Moor Street (later Priory Street) in 1296. Magdalen Street seems to have developed as an agricultural suburb by 1300.[50]

Behind the main streets there was still empty space, like the curtilage in Culver Street recorded *c.* 1270.[51] A house in Wyre Street was leased in 1271 with two selions of land 17 ft. wide, a term which suggests it was or had recently been arable,[52] and Queen Street, which runs diagonally from just south of High Street to South gate, may have originated as a path across agricultural land. The borough leased an empty plot in Wyre Street 50 ft. by 20 ft. in 1335–6; a plot of town land at the end of the street, in Eldland, seems to have been empty in 1360, but another plot there had houses on it in 1340–1.[53]

The borough repaired the town walls *c.* 1312, but no other major public building work can be securely ascribed to the earlier 14th century. Maidenburgh Street was developed in the 1330s, plots 18 ft. wide being leased by the borough. At least one lease required the tenant to build a house on the plot, and an adjoining plot had been built up by 1342–3.[54] The northern ends of East and West Stockwell Streets may have been developed about the same time; part of a 14th-century hall survives at no. 30 East Stockwell Street.[55] There was still pasture land or 'moor' in Maidenburgh in 1354–5, possibly near a watercourse which flowed from St. Helen's well near St. Helen's chapel to the castle ditch.[56]

The Later Middle Ages

As the population increased in the later 14th century, so did the development of areas behind the main streets, notably Maidenburgh, and of land outside the walls. The bailiffs leased a partly built-up plot *c.* 6 yd. by *c.* 8½ yd. near St. Helen's well in 1377–8, and in 1381–2 they leased empty plots *c.* 14 yd. long by the castle ditch and St. Helen's chapel. Further empty plots in Maidenburgh were recorded in 1387–8 and 1390–1.[57] The bailiffs leased land between the north wall and the river to extend a tannery in 1368–9, and in East Hill in the 1360s and 1370s. A newly built-up plot on the west side of North gate was recorded in 1387.[58] By 1357 there were shops in High Street as far east as the castle ditch.[59] About the 1370s William Reyne acquired or built 'new rents', the later Red Row, on High Street in front of St. Peter's churchyard. A newly built house in Eldland was recorded in 1396–7.[60]

Pressure was increasing on street frontages even away from the market; a tenement on the north side of High Street in All Saints' parish was divided into three or

[47] E.R.O., D/B 5 Cr36, rot. 32d.; Cr56, rot. 18; Cr75, rot. 7.
[48] *Colch. Cart.* ii. 319–20, 331; B.L. Arundel MS. 145, f. 13v.
[49] B.L. Arundel MS. 145, ff. 19v., 20v., 31v.–32.
[50] Ibid. f. 29 and v.; *Rot. Parl.* i. 230.
[51] E.R.O., Acc. A8173.
[52] *Cart. St. John of Jerusalem*, p. 151.
[53] E.R.O., D/B 5 R1, ff. 33v., 36; D/B 5 Cr12, rot. 18.
[54] Ibid. D/B 5 R1, ff. 34v.–35v., 37v.; D/B 5 Cr4, rot. 12d.
[55] Dept. of Env. '13th List of Buildings of Archit. or Hist. Interest', p. 46.
[56] E.R.O., D/B 5 Cr35, rot. 14; D/B 5 R1, f. 43.
[57] Ibid. D/B 5 R1, ff. 53 and v., 56 and v., 61, 62.
[58] Ibid. ff. 49, 52v.–53, 58 and v., 161; D/B 5 R2, f. 20.
[59] Ibid. D/B 5 Cr11, rot. 9.
[60] Ibid. D/B 5 R1, ff. 65v., 159; D/B 5 Cr24, rot. 46d.; Rodwell, *Hist. Churches*, 28.

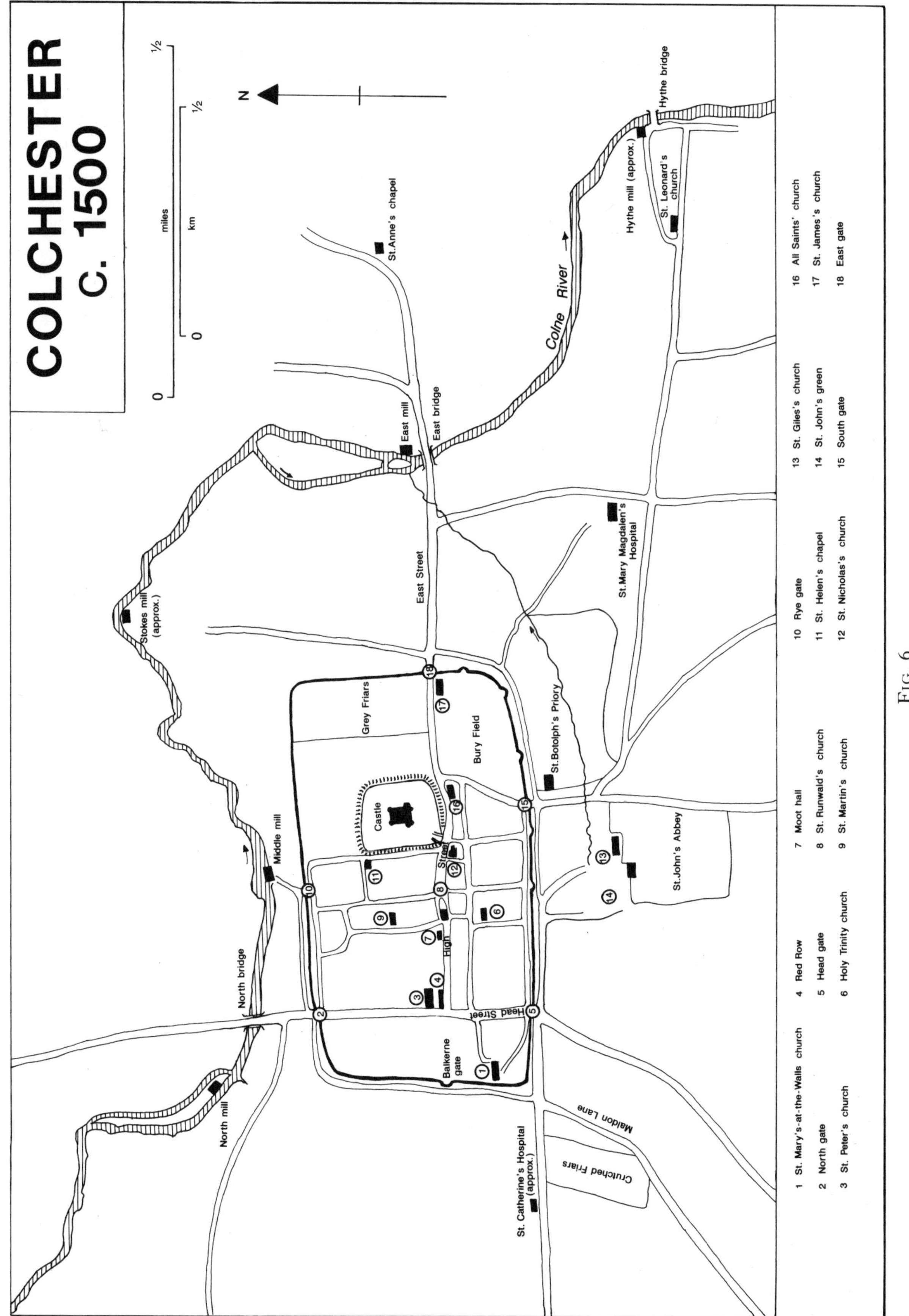
COLCHESTER
C. 1500
0 miles ½
0 km ½
N
St. Anne's chapel
East mill
East bridge
Colne River
Hythe mill (approx.)
St. Leonard's church
Hythe bridge
Stokes mill (approx.)
East Street
St. Mary Magdalen's Hospital
Grey Friars
Bury Field
Castle
St. Botolph's Priory
Middle mill
St. John's Abbey
North bridge
High Street
Head Street
Balkerne gate
North mill
St. Catherine's Hospital (approx.)
Maldon Lane
Crutched Friars
1 St. Mary's-at-the-Walls church
2 North gate
3 St. Peter's church
4 Red Row
5 Head gate
6 Holy Trinity church
7 Moot hall
8 St. Runwald's church
9 St. Martin's church
10 Rye gate
11 St. Helen's chapel
12 St. Nicholas's church
13 St. Giles's church
14 St. John's green
15 South gate
16 All Saints' church
17 St. James's church
18 East gate

Fig. 6

more parts in 1366. In 1366–7 a house between North gate and North bridge was only *c.* 18 ft. wide. A house outside North gate had been divided by *c.* 1380 when Colne priory received a rent from the part between its great gate and the town wall.[61] A house in the corner of Sholand, perhaps at the top of Maldon Road, was recorded in 1349–50, and there were houses in Childwell Lane by 1384.[62] Cloth-workers were established along the brook which ran eastwards from Stanwell across St. John's green into St. Botolph's priory precinct: a John le Dyer had a tenter at Stanwell in 1361, and a Sudbury draper acquired a tenement with a broad lead gutter there from John Pod, dyer, before 1383.[63]

By the early 15th century building along High Street was probably continuous as far as East gate. In 1428 the owner of a house adjoining the Greyfriars was forbidden to place his timbers on the friars' wall. Although in 1402 there were only eight tenements in High Street between Queen Street and St. James's church, each may have contained several houses; in 1480 three tenements in the market, in St. Nicholas's parish, contained a total of 12 separate houses.[64] In 1420 a plot with a stall on it on the north side of High Street near the castle was only 9 ft. long by 5 ft. wide. The shops in the middle of High Street round St. Runwald's remained, and by the late 14th century there were at least five under the church wall. Middle Row, east of church and shops, had been built by 1488 when a 31 ft. long gutter from one house discharged at the corner of the church.[65] In 1481 and 1482 John Howard, Lord Howard, built new houses in Colchester, one of which, on the south side of High Street, became the New inn, later the Red Lion.[66] The building was put up in several stages, the earliest being the late 15th-century western block to which a hall and east range were added early in the 16th century. The hall was set back from the street behind a small court. The frontage, which was elaborately decorated and jettied, incorporated a row of shops. Apart from the Saracen's Head, on the main London road opposite the Crutched Friars, all the nine known medieval inns or taverns were in High Street, all but one of them in the market. There is no evidence that any were purpose-built, and they were probably in large houses.[67]

Away from the main streets, a plot of land near St. Helen's chapel was built on shortly before 1411. Four newly built rents in St. Helen's Street (probably Maidenburgh Street) were recorded in 1416. In 1430 the bailiffs leased an empty plot in All Saints' parish *c.* 21 yd. square on condition that the tenant built houses on it within three years. St. John's abbey had two new shops in Wyre Street in 1478.[68]

In East Street, outside the walls, a new house was built on to an existing house in the early 15th century, a new rented building was recorded in 1416, a new cottage in 1422, and buildings on a once empty plot in 1485.[69] Part of a divided tenement there was conveyed in 1420, and there was a dispute about an eavesdrop between a cottage and two houses on the north side of the road in the same year. There were disputes about similar eavesdrops outside South gate in 1405 and beyond East bridge in 1419.[70] In 1414–15 a house outside South gate seems to have had a street frontage of only 12 ft.[71] In 1435 the town court heard a dispute

61 E.R.O., D/B 5 Cr15, rot. 5; D/B 5, R1, f. 48; D/DPr 5.
62 Ibid. D/B 5 R1, f. 41; D/B 5 Cr24, rot. 58.
63 Ibid. D/B 5 Cr13, rot. 8; Cr33, rot. 7.
64 Ibid. D/B 5 Cr33, rot. 7; Cr48, rot. 14d.; Cr78, rot. 15d.
65 Ibid. D/B 5 Cr42, rot. 24d.; D/B 5 R1, f. 168; D/B 5 R2, f. 92 and v.
66 J. Harvey, *Eng. Med. Architects* (1984), 302.
67 E.R.O., D/B 5 Cr69, rot. 1d.; Morant, *Colch.* 150.
68 E.R.O., D/B 5 Cr37, rot. 35; Cr40, rot. 45; Cr50, rot. 22d.; B.L. Arundel MS. 145, f. 4v.
69 E.R.O., D/B 5 Cr40, rot. 45; Cr43, rott. 5, 22d.; Cr81, rot. 30.
70 E.R.O., D/DRg 7/4; D/B 5 Cr41, rot. 33d.; Cr42, rott. 12, 20d.
71 Ibid. D/B 5 R1, f. 76.

over a contract for rebuilding a hall and two solars in North Street. The bailiffs demised a newly built house on a plot 93 ft. long and 16 ft. wide outside North gate, probably between the wall and Balkerne Lane, in 1430.[72] Other land between the north wall and Balkerne Lane was newly built on in 1470. There were houses between St. Mary Magdalen's hospital and the Hythe by 1408.[73]

Apart from the repair of the town wall, which included the addition of bastions on the south-east, between 1381 and *c.* 1413, there was little public building in the later 14th century. In the following century, however, there was considerable church building, at St. Martin's, St. Peter's, and St. Leonard's early in the century, All Saints' in the middle, and Holy Trinity, St. Leonard's , and St. James's later.[74]

Most of the late medieval houses whose plans are known from excavation or from surviving buildings comprised a hall and one or two cross wings, the hall usually long side on to the street. Other wings might be added at the back. All but the two major inns, the Red Lion and the George, are of two storeys, and all are timber-framed.[75] A number of shop fronts, which are characterized by one or two wide and formerly open windows, survive. Along High Street and other main streets there were probably many small shops in front of the domestic buildings, as at the George and no. 136 High Street, and at the Rose and Crown at the east end of East Street. Shops also occurred in buildings which look like cross wings but which may have been self-contained units with living quarters at the back and on the upper floor. No. 73 High Street and no. 3 West Stockwell Street may have been of that type although they could have been commercial adjuncts to adjacent houses. A shop in the front room of a service wing, which also incorporates a cross passage, is the probable explanation of the plans of no. 93 Hythe Hill and no. 7 Queen Street. All of the halls that survive or are known from excavation are aligned on the street. Those in Middleborough and Stockwell Street, as well as those presumed to have existed at the Minories in High Street, were on the street frontage. At the George in High Street, as at the moot hall, shops separated the hall from the street, and at the Rose and Crown there was a small courtyard between them. A similar arrangement may have existed at Tymperleys in Trinity Street where the central range has been rebuilt but appears to have been set back far enough for a street range and a courtyard. The number and arrangement of other rooms in the street range was largely determined by the width of the plot. In the 14th century two houses in Middleborough had only the hall and service rooms on a plot of *c.* 40 ft., a common width, and the later cross wings were developed partly at the expense of the hall.[76] At 30 East Stockwell Street the cross passage is the only part of the hall range to have survived in what appears to have been a structurally integrated hall and cross wing. By the later 15th century wings were often built down one or both sides of the plot behind the hall. Tymperleys, the west wing of the Rose and Crown, and nos. 13–15 North Hill are examples of rear wings with high-quality carpentry which were probably parlour wings.

Two or more houses under one roof, like the two houses under one roof surrendered to the bailiffs in 1341–2, may have been divided buildings, or terraced housing like the three rents under one roof in East Street conveyed in 1433 with a latrine, a small chamber called a counting house, and an outhouse called a lodge.

[72] Ibid. D/B 5 Cr50, rot. 22d.; Cr53, rot. 7.
[73] Ibid. D/B 5 Cr38, rot. 9; Cr76, rot. 30d.
[74] Below, Walls; Churches.
[75] Dept. of Env. '13th List of Buildings of Archit. and Hist. Interest, *passim*; *Colch. Arch. Group Bull.* xxxi. 27–9; xxxiii. 9–11; *Colch. Arch. Rep.* iii. 189–209.
[76] *Colch. Arch. Rep.* iii. 189–208.

Similar speculative housing is known from other towns.[77] Two shops surrounded by one large house on three sides in 1412[78] had apparently been built to face the street in front of a hall, between its two projecting wings. Other late medieval houses were also complex structures. In 1447 one called the warehouse, apparently in St. Botolph's parish, had 'houses' or rooms and a hall above it. A house in High Street in 1453 had a parlour with a chimney as much as 43 ft. behind the street frontage. In 1404 a hall and a kitchen with a solar above it were devised apart from the rest of the house, with access to them through the cart gate.[79] In the market place a house called the Hart, possibly an inn, had at least four chambers in 1462. In the late 15th century a widow sold the greater part of her house to her son but reserved for her own use the lower parlour, three 'houses', and the chamber over the great parlour.[80]

Gates called 'burgates', which may originally have led into small urban estates,[81] were a feature of some Colchester houses. They were recorded in Head Street in 1346 and 1382, on the south side of High Street in 1363, on the north side of High Street in All Saints' parish in 1366, in or near Eldland (at the bottom of Wyre Street) in 1396–7, in Queen Street in 1402, and on the south side of High Street in All Saints' parish in 1467.[82] One, at the end of Moor Street in 1425,[83] was outside the wall. The Head Street burgate led into a courtyard containing a barn for storing corn, a beer house and presumably other outbuildings. Other houses had large porches, encroaching on the street, like the great timber penthouse complained of in 1422–3. One porch, at the entrance to West Stockwell Street was *c.* 7½ ft. by *c.* 2 ft. in 1401–2.[84] 'Poys', which seem to have been lean-to constructions with solid walls at their short ends, were also added to many houses. Plots leased for the walls of a poy in 1364–5 were 9ft. by 3½ ft., and for another, outside Head gate in 1391, 8 ft. by 2 ft.[85]

Despite the increased building, there was open land within the town wall. Castle field still lay between the castle and Greyfriars in 1478, when it was being encroached on for gardens.[86] In the south-east corner of the town the Bury field survived throughout the Middle Ages, although in 1353 a man was presented for inclosing part of it.[87]

Bequests for tithes in 14th- and 15th-century wills suggest the relative wealth of different parts of the town. The richest townspeople seem to have lived in the part of High Street in St. Runwald's and St. Nicholas's parishes, and in East and West Stockwell Streets, which extended into St. Martin's parish. The west end of High Street and perhaps North Hill, in St. Peter's parish, was probably also a wealthy area: while the evidence of wills is not strong, five bailiffs are known to have lived there. Although few of the richest men lived in St. James's, the parish produced the highest number of surviving wills, suggesting a large population of middling merchants and tradesmen; the parishioners were able to rebuild the church on a grand scale in the later 15th century. The southern part of the town was a poor area: the wills of Holy Trinity parishioners were comparatively few and poor and St. Mary-at-the-Walls seems to have been poorer than any parish except

77 E.R.O., D/B 5 R1, f. 37; D/B 5 Cr51, rot. 18d.; C. Platt, *Med. Southampton*, 184.

78 E.R.O., D/B 5 Cr38, rot. 21d.

79 Ibid. D/B 5 Cr36, rot. 4d.; Cr62, rot. 4; Cr65, rot. 24d.

80 Ibid. D/B 5 Cr72, rot. 23d.; P.R.O., C 1/40, no. 2.

81 Cf. *Gesetze der Angelsachsen*, ed. F. Liebermann, i. 390, 456.

82 E.R.O., D/B 5 Cr7, rot. 8; Cr15, rot. 5; Cr22, rot. 10d.; Cr33, rot. 7; Cr76, rot. 30d.; D/B 5 R1, f. 65v.; *Cal. Close*, 1360–4, 525.

83 E.R.O., D/B 5 Cr46, rot. 4d.

84 Ibid. D/B 5 Cr44, rot. 11d.; D/B 5 R1, f. 68.

85 Ibid. D/B 5 R1, ff. 47v., 62v.

86 Ibid. D/B 5 Cr77, rot. 21d.

87 Ibid. D/B 5 Cr10, rot. 1; Cr33, rot. 7.

the small, rural, St. Mary Magdalen. St. Leonard's at the Hythe, on the other hand, was richer than many of the intramural parishes.[88] The subsidy assessment of 1487 on the whole confirms the evidence of wills; parts of Holy Trinity, however, where average payment was the highest in the borough but few parishioners were liable for subsidy, may have been becoming more prosperous, while St. Martin's where average payment was the second lowest, was becoming poorer.[89]

The Hythe

The settlement at the Hythe or New Hythe, Colchester's port, was physically distinct from the town, being separated from it by arable fields, although it was legally and constitutionally part of the town. It presumably began about the 11th century when the port moved north from the old hythe or Old Heath.[90] The move at Colchester, as at other ports, was probably associated with the construction of quays and possibly with the first improvements to the river. A cut across the marshes in Wivenhoe parish opposite Old Heath was made after the parish boundary had been fixed but probably before the surviving borough records begin in the early 14th century. St. Leonard's church at the Hythe was founded before the mid 12th century, but its compact parish contrasts with the dispersed parishes of the intramural churches and suggests that it was relatively late.[91] In the late 12th century and the early 13th the settlement was called Heia as well as Hythe, the former name presumably referring to inclosures, perhaps of meadow, made when the port was laid out. A tenement there was given to St. John's in 1160, and a rent from a house there in the later 12th century.[92] St. Leonard's church stands half way up Hythe Hill, well back from the water front and probably on the edge of the 12th-century settlement; there was still arable land near it in the mid 13th century.[93]

The Hythe was developed, both as a port and as a suburb, in the 14th century, the borough leasing land for quays and warehouses in the 1330s and 1340s.[94] By the mid 14th century the quays and the road behind them may have extended some distance southwards from the bottom of Hythe Hill. Buildings were similar to those in the rest of the town, and there are indications of pressure on street frontages. A shop with a solar above it had apparently been built on a tenement at the Hythe by 1384. A new building encroached on the road in 1392–3.[95] Most if not all houses stood along Hythe Hill or behind the quays, but by 1352 there was a back lane, North Lane or Church Lane, behind houses on the north side of Hythe Hill. South Lane, recorded in 1427, may have been the road behind the quays.[96] A footbridge built across the river in 1407 was replaced by a cart bridge in 1473–4,[97] but there was no building on the eastern bank of the river in the Middle Ages.

[88] Bequests in 65 of the 110 surviving wills in E.R.O., D/B 5 Cr3–73, *passim*; P.R.O., PROB 11/1–12, *passim*.

[89] B.L. Stowe MS. 828, ff. 14–25.

[90] Below, Port.

[91] Below, Churches (St. Leonard's).

[92] *Colch. Cart.* i. 67, 87, 95; ii. 306–7, 320; *P.N. Elements* i. 214.

[93] B.L. Arundel MS. 145, f. 18v.

[94] E.R.O., D/B 5 R1, ff. 35v., 37.

[95] Ibid. D/B 5 Cr24, rot. 26d.; D/B 5 R1, f. 63.

[96] *Cat. Anct. D.* i, C 205; vi, C 3939; E.R.O., D/B 5 Cr47, rot. 15.

[97] E.R.O., D/B 5 Cr36, rot. 32d.; Cr75, rot. 7; Morant, *Colch.* App. p. 1.

BOROUGH GOVERNMENT

The Development of Liberties

Anglo-Saxon Colchester presumably enjoyed a number of liberties, including burgage tenure, by custom without the need of formal grant.[98] Its burgesses had developed some sense of corporate identity by 1086 when they claimed 5 hides in Lexden and held 80 a. 'in their common',[99] but there is no evidence as to who qualified as a burgess at that date. By 1310 'foreigners' were admitted as burgesses in the borough court, taking an oath and finding sureties.[1] All men born within the liberty, whether or not they were the sons of freemen, were entitled to take up their freedom without any fee, and such admissions were recorded only if there was doubt as to the place or circumstances of the birth.[2] An ordinance of 1452 required anyone born in the borough who wished to enjoy its liberties and franchises to take his oath before the bailiffs according to the old custom, and lists of those sworn into tithing, which start in 1451, include freemen by birth,[3] but the list of those admitted to the freedom between 1452 and 1500 contains no men from Colchester. 'Foreigners' admitted to the freedom were required to live in the borough for at least a year, but other freemen, like the rector of Widdington who died in 1382, were non-resident.[4]

The earliest known charter to Colchester was granted by Richard I in 1189 in return for a fine of 60 marks,[5] but its close resemblance to the London charter of 1133 suggests that it was a modification of an earlier Colchester charter obtained before 1155, when London received a new charter which served as a model for many other boroughs. Colchester's charter granted the burgesses the right to elect their bailiffs and a justice to hold the pleas of the Crown in the moot hall, a significant step in the growth of the borough's liberties if it was granted in the 1130s or 1140s, and one which was certainly enjoyed from 1178.[6] Other judicial rights included exemption from the *murdrum*, from miskenning, and from the judicial duel and the right to acquit the borough by four men before the justices in eyre. The last right does not seem to have been exercised, for in all recorded 13th-century eyres Colchester was represented by 12 men, but it was allowed by the justices in the forest eyre in 1291–2.[7] No burgess was to be amerced at more than his 'wer', 100*s.*, and amercements were to be affeered by oath of other burgesses. The right to gallows was not specifically granted but was claimed in 1274.[8]

Colchester's financial privileges included quittance from scot, lot, and Danegeld, and from toll, lastage, passage, pontage, and other customs throughout England. Any toll or custom taken from Colchester burgesses in other towns or vills might be recovered from the town or vill concerned. Debtors of Colchester burgesses were to pay their debts, or else to prove at Colchester that they did not owe them; if any refused the burgesses might distrain on goods in the debtor's county. The charter also freed the burgesses from billeting members of the king's household, gave them the right to hunt fox, hare, and cat within the liberty, and to have their

[98] A. Ballard, *Brit. Boro. Chart.* pp. xliv, xlvi–xlvii.
[99] *V.C.H. Essex*, i. 574–8.
[1] E.R.O., D/B 5 Cr1, rot. 4.
[2] e.g. E.R.O., D/B 5 Cr11, rot. 4d.; Cr17, rott. 4d., 17d.; Cr18, rot. 3d.
[3] Ibid. D/B 5 R2, ff. 141v.–151v.
[4] Ibid. D/B 5 Cr10, rot. 7d.; Cr11, rot. 2d.; Cr22, rot. 29.
[5] *Cal. Chart. R.* 1226–57, 410–11; translated in *Colch. Charters*, 1–2; *Pipe R.* 1190 (P.R.S. N.S. i), 111.
[6] Below, this chapter, Officers.
[7] P.R.O., JUST 1/233, rot. 59; JUST 1/238, rot. 45d.; JUST 1/242, rot. 64d.; ibid. E 32/13, rot. 8.
[8] *Rot. Hund.* (Rec. Com.), i. 163.

fishery in the river Colne. It also granted them the customs of the river bank, whoever owned the land, towards the farm of the town, and declared that Colchester market was not to be harmed by any unauthorized markets. The last two privileges were unique to Colchester among English boroughs;[9] the others, with the exception of that relating to the judicial eyre, could all have dated from the reign of Henry I or Stephen.

The charter of 1189 was adduced by the burgesses several times in the 13th century in support of their privileges. In 1227 and 1248 they produced it before the justices in eyre in support of their claim to devise real property by will,[10] an aspect of burgage tenure not mentioned in the charter. In 1254 they claimed that it gave them the right to make their bailiffs coroners, presumably as successors to the justice granted by the charter.[11] The only privilege formally added to the borough's liberties in the 13th century was the return of writs, given by Henry III in 1252, the year in which he required such privileges to be warrantable by charter.[12] The last substantial alteration to Colchester's liberties was made by Edward II in an *inspeximus* and confirmation of the charters of 1189 and 1252 in 1319. He withdrew Colchester's exceptional privileges to distrain for debt in other counties, but granted or confirmed the profits of St. Dennis's fair. He also granted quittance from murage, picage, and pavage, confirmed that the burgesses should not be impleaded or plead outside the borough for lands or tenements inside it, and declared that assizes, juries, and inquisitions on trespasses, contracts, or felonies committed within the borough should normally be carried out by burgesses.[13]

Later charters confirmed or clarified the borough's rights,[14] usually by *inspeximus*, like the charters of 1362, 1378, 1400, and 1413. Henry VI in 1447 issued a new charter which, among other provisions, defined the geographical liberty as covering the vills of Lexden, Greenstead, Mile End, and Donyland, and granted the borough its own justices of the peace. Edward IV, while ignoring Henry VI's charter, added similar definitions to his charter of *inspeximus*, and also confirmed that the bailiffs and commonalty of the borough were a perpetual community, able to act in law and to have a common seal, the last a privilege which they had certainly enjoyed since the early 13th century.[15] In 1484, 1488, and 1511 the Crown inspected and confirmed Edward IV's charter.

The burgesses did not enjoy their rights and privileges throughout the liberty. Even within the walls there were areas outside their jurisdiction, like the castle and the bishop of London's soke in the parish of St. Mary's-at-the-Walls. The bishop's rights, confirmed by Henry I between 1120 and 1133, included jurisdiction over his men, who were not to plead outside the soke unless the bishop had failed to give them justice.[16] The soke, which had already been leased to three generations of a Colchester clerical family, was confirmed in 1206 to the burgess William son of Benet at a rent of 5*s*. a year.[17] Its holder in 1311, the wealthy clerk John of Colchester, claimed a three-weekly court, although the soke was then within the jurisdiction of the borough court.[18] The last known holder was Thomas Francis (d. 1416), who held in Head Street a demesne called Haymsokne paying 5*s*. a year

[9] Ballard, *Brit. Boro. Chart.* 201, 236.

[10] P.R.O., JUST 1/229, rot. 17; JUST 1/231, rot. 33.

[11] Ibid. JUST 1/233, rot. 58; R. F. Hunnisett, *Med. Coroner*, 138.

[12] *Colch. Charters*, 3–5; *Trans. R. Hist. S.* 5th ser. xvii. 59–82.

[13] *Colch. Charters*, 6–9.

[14] Ibid. 10–57.

[15] Below, Arms, Seals, etc.

[16] *Reg. Regum Anglo-Norm.* ii, no. 1824.

[17] *E.A.T.* N.S. xiv. 137–41; *Feet of F. Essex*, i. 39.

[18] E.R.O., D/B 5 Cr2, rot. 5d.; Morant *Colch.* Appendix, 3 n.

to the bishop of London, but there is no evidence that he claimed a court.[19] In the 12th century the part of the soke outside the walls south-east of the town passed to St. Botolph's priory and St. John's abbey.[20]

St. John's abbey, lord of Greenstead and West Donyland manors, the FitzWalters, lords of Lexden manor, and St. Botolph's priory all enjoyed extensive legal privileges in their lands within the liberty. In 1272 and 1287 the abbot of St. John's was accused of bringing the coroner of Lexden hundred into the liberty to hold an inquest on St. John's green.[21] In 1274 the burgesses complained that the abbot's gallows and tumbrel infringed their liberties, and in 1285 or 1286 they further complained that the abbot was distraining burgesses to attend his court on St. John's green, had established gallows and a cucking stool in Greenstead, in West Donyland, and at Bourne ponds (the last perhaps a relic of the jurisdiction of the bishop's soke), and held the assize of bread and of ale.[22] In 1318 the burgesses complained about Robert FitzWalter's view of frankpledge in Lexden, as well as about the abbot's in Greenstead and Donyland. About the same date they prepared a suit against FitzWalter who was apparently trying to remove Lexden from the liberty.[23] There was further friction with St. John's abbey in the early 15th century, and in 1413 the abbot was presented in the borough court for several offences, including arresting and imprisoning burgesses and usurping the borough courts and view of frankpledge by holding courts for Greenstead and West Donyland. The West Donyland court, which claimed jurisdiction over the suburb south of the town walls, was particularly galling to the burgesses. In 1414 the prior of St. Botolph's was also accused of holding a court within the liberty, presumably for Canonswick or for his manor of Shaws.[24]

The Fee Farm and Borough Finances

In the 11th and 12th centuries Colchester's relations with the Crown revolved around the payment of the annual farm. In 1066 Colchester paid a farm of £15 5*s.* 3*d.* a year; by 1086 it had risen fivefold, to £80 and 6 sestars of honey or 40*s.*, but by 1130 the farm had been halved to £40.[25] In 1269 it was said to be *c.* £41 or £42, but the sum actually paid to the Exchequer was probably only £35, when allowance had been made for the loss of revenue from the moneyers (£4) and from Kingswood (£2), and for alms to the abbot of St. John's (£1).[26] Attempts by the Crown in 1371, 1397, and 1400 to enforce payment of the full £42 failed.[27]

The borough and its farm seem to have been held in the Conqueror's reign by Waleram and then by Bishop Walchelin of Winchester, who held them in 1086.[28] Eudes the sewer held the borough from 1101, and possibly from 1089, until his death in 1120; he was succeeded by Hamon of St. Clare (d. 1150), and Hamon probably by his son Hubert (d. 1155).[29] Richard de Lucy farmed the borough as sheriff in 1156, and retained it until his retirement as justiciar in 1178 or 1179, accounting annually at the Exchequer.[30] The burgesses farmed the borough from 1178, and in 1198 they bought the fee farm for 20 marks.[31] Nevertheless, the sheriff

[19] E.R.O., D/B 5 Cr40, rot. 45.

[20] *Colch. Cart.* ii. 545–6.

[21] P.R.O., JUST 1/238, rot. 59; E.R.O., D/B 5 R2, ff. 46v., 47v.

[22] *Rot. Hund.* (Rec. Com.), i. 163; E.R.O., D/B 5 R2, f. 48 and loose folio.

[23] E.R.O., D/B 5 R2, ff. 56, 67–8; Britnell, *Growth and Decline*, 30.

[24] E.R.O., D/B 5 Cr39, rott. 5, 19.

[25] *V.C.H. Essex*, i. 578; J. Tait, *Med. Eng. Boro.* 152, 154, 184; *Pipe R.* 1130 (Rec. Com.), 138.

[26] *Cal. Pat.* 1266–72, 311, 358; *Pipe R.* 1168 (P.R.S. N.S. xii), 48; 1220 (P.R.S. N.S. xlvii), 115.

[27] E.R.O., D/B 5 R1, ff. 11v.–17; *Cal. Close*, 1399–1402, 372.

[28] *V.C.H. Essex*, i. 419, 578.

[29] *Colch. Arch. Rep.* i. 26, 29; *Reg. Regum Anglo-Norm.* ii, no. 552; *Pipe R.* 1130 (Rec. Com.), 138; below, Castle.

[30] *Pipe R.* 1156–8 (Rec. Com.); ibid. 1159–1178 (P.R.S. i–xxvii); Tait, *Med. Eng. Boro.* 188.

[31] *Pipe R.* 1179–99 (P.R.S. xxviii–N.S. x), esp. 1198 (P.R.S. N.S. ix), 134.

as keeper of the borough accounted for the farm in 1212, and later in the 13th century Stephen Harengood, William of Sainte-Mère-Église bishop of London, and Guy of Rochford, all held the farm as constables of the castle.[32] From 1269 to 1369 the farm of Colchester was assigned to the queen's dower.[33] In 1384 it was granted to Robert de Vere, earl of Oxford, who presumably held it until his attainder in 1388, and in 1399 to John Doreward, who surrendered it in 1404 for its grant to Henry IV's son Humphrey of Lancaster, later duke of Gloucester.[34] Humphrey presumably held the farm, with Colchester castle, until his death in 1447, when it was granted to Queen Margaret, wife of Henry VI.[35]

In 1086 the sources from which the farm was paid included the king's demesne in Colchester and a payment of 2 marks a year by the king's burgesses, besides, presumably, the customary dues from houses in the town. The royal demesne was separately farmed by 1280, and was probably removed from the burgesses' control when the castle, with which it was later held, was granted to Eudes the sewer in 1101.[36] The £4 a year paid by the moneyers was part of the farm before the Conquest, but by 1086 Colchester and Maldon between them owed £20 for their mints over and above their farms. In addition to the farm each house in Colchester owed 6*d.* a year to the king, a payment originally made to support the army.[37] The charter of 1189 granted or confirmed the customs of the river and its banks towards the payment of the farm.[38] In 1254 the burgesses claimed the market tolls also as part of the farm, and it was probably no coincidence that by 1310 the tolls, presumably both from the market and from the river, were leased for £35 a year, the exact amount of the farm due at the Exchequer.[39] Two sums claimed by the burgesses from the abbot of St. John's in 1285, 3*s.* a year for his fair and 16*d.* 'shrebgavel',[40] may also have been part of the farm. The element 'gavel' suggests that the shrebgavel was a pre-Conquest rent; in the late 14th century land and a house in Shreb or Shrub Street (part of Maldon Road) paid to the borough shrebgavel totalling 11*s.* 11*d.*[41] About 1322 the burgesses claimed to have difficulty paying the farm, and obtained permission to inclose and let out parcels of waste within the borough to the value of 10*s.* a year.[42] An agreement between the incoming bailiff William Reyne and the community in 1360 which appears to have been in the nature of a mortgage of half the profits of the hundred court for £10,[43] suggests that the borough then had difficulty finding cash to pay the farm. By *c.* 1400 the borough received *c.* £13 a year in rents, mostly for encroachments on the streets and other parts of the borough waste.[44] The charter of 1447 gave or confirmed to the bailiffs, towards the farm, chattels forfeited within the vill.[45]

The farm remained the single largest item of borough expenditure throughout the Middle Ages, but by 1501 fees, allowances, liveries, and stipends to borough officers, including £10 to the bailiffs and £6 3*s.* 4*d.* to the town clerk, amounted to *c.* £27.[46] By then the chamberlain also paid for the maintenance of the borough properties, and rents and legal charges due from them. The most important sources

[32] *Cal. Pat.* 1216–25, 167; *Pipe R.* 1212 (P.R.S. N.S. xxx), 54; 1218 (P.R.S. N.S. xxxix), 78; *Cal. Lib.* 1260–7, 34.

[33] *Cal. Pat.* 1266–72, 311, 358, 433–4, 460; 1272–81, 439; 1282–91, 368; 1292–1301, 451; 1307–13, 216; 1327–30, 67, 212; 1343–5, 447–8; 1358–61, 238.

[34] *Cal. Close*, 1381–5, 462; *Complete Peerage*, x. 231; *Cal. Pat.* 1399–1401, 154; 1401–5, 467–8.

[35] E.R.O., D/DRg 1/71; *Cal. Pat.* 1452–61, 340; *Cal. Close*, 1447–54, 391; below, Castle.

[36] P.R.O., SC 6/1089/7, 17–18; *Reg. Regum Anglo-Norm.* ii, no. 552.

[37] *V.C.H. Essex*, i. 419–22, 574–8.

[38] *Colch. Charters*, 2.

[39] P.R.O., JUST 1/242, rot. 110; E.R.O., D/B 5 Cr1, rot. 1d.

[40] P.R.O., JUST 1/242, rot. 110.

[41] E.R.O., D/B 5 R1, f. 169v.

[42] P.R.O., SC 8/5, no. 238; SC 8/159, no. 7906; *Rot. Parl.* i. 397.

[43] E.R.O., D/B 5 Cr12, rot. 18.

[44] Ibid. D/B 5 R1, ff. 158–70; Britnell, *Growth and Decline*, 70.

[45] *Colch. Charters*, 39.

[46] Bodl. MS. Rolls Essex 2.

of income were the tolls and the leases of equipment at the Hythe and of the moot hall cellar. They reached a peak of *c.* £80 in 1400–1,[47] but had fallen to *c.* £41 by 1501–2. In the latter year other rents and farms brought in *c.* £20, profits of court *c.* £16, and felons' goods *c.* £8. Total income was put at £127 8*s.* 7*d.* against expenditure initially set at £108 1*s.* 5½*d.*, a credit balance which seems to have been consumed by further expenses allowed after the account. At the end of the 15th century the borough resorted to paying the expenses of its members of parliament by assigning rents to them, an expedient which reduced the borough's disposable income.[48]

Officers

The first recorded borough officers were the reeves Walter Haning and Benet who witnessed a charter of Hamon of St. Clare to St. John's abbey *c.* 1150.[49] Although they were probably burgesses (Walter Haning was a member of a family prominent in 13th-century Colchester), they may have been Hamon's officers, like Hamon's servants of Colchester addressed with him by Henry I between 1120 and 1133,[50] rather than borough officers. Between 1178 and 1194 ten men, all of whom seem to have been burgesses, accounted at the Exchequer for the farm, usually in pairs; in 1187 and 1188 they were called reeves. The fact that they changed every two years suggests that they were elected by the burgesses rather than being royal appointees. From 1194 to 1198 Walter of Crepping, who may have been a county landowner, accounted for the farm, once with the burgess Simon son of Marcian.[51] Between 1239 and 1327 (when the surviving list of bailiffs in the Oath Book starts) at least 68 men are known to have served as bailiffs, 22 of them more than once. The number suggests that the bailiffs were being drawn from a slightly larger body of men than they were later in the 14th century.[52]

The bailiffs were in origin royal officers, and their chief duties were to pay the farm and to hold the borough courts. Their late 14th-century oath emphasized their judicial functions and their duty to the king; significantly it made no reference to any duty to the commonalty.[53] The close relationship to the king characterized borough bailiffs in the Middle Ages, and encouraged in most English towns the creation of the office of mayor, whose reponsibility was to the community. Colchester's failure to create its own chief officer may suggest a lack of cohesion among the commonalty (possibly related to the absence of a merchant guild or other focus for communal action); alternatively the infrequency of royal intervention in the borough may have meant that the burgesses felt no need for their own officers. In the mid 13th century the bailiffs took office at Michaelmas.[54] In the mid 14th elections seem to have been held on or soon after 8 September (the Nativity of the Virgin Mary) and to have been made by a group which included the sitting bailiffs. William Reyne's agreement in 1360 to pay £10 if the bailiffs and others elected him bailiff for the ensuing year was made on 7 September with two former bailiffs who were acting for the community.[55]

In the earlier 13th century the bailiffs were also coroners.[56] By 1287 the two offices had been separated, although the coroners were usually past or future bailiffs.[57] There is no clear evidence for a town clerk until *c.* 1372, and the first named clerk

47 Britnell, *Growth and Decline*, 277.
48 Ibid. 80–1.
49 *Colch. Cart.* i. 155.
50 *Reg. Regum Anglo-Norm.* ii, no. 1824.
51 *Pipe R.* 1179–1198 (P.R.S. xxviii–N.S. ix), *passim.*
52 Below, List of Bailiffs and Mayors.
53 E.R.O., D/B 5 R2, f. 5v.
54 P.R.O., JUST 1/242, rot. 36.
55 E.R.O., D/B 5 Cr12, rot. 18.
56 P.R.O., JUST 1/233, rot. 58.
57 E.R.O., D/B 5 R2, f. 47v.

was Michael Aunger who served from 1380.[58] The farmers of the tolls, who were *de facto* responsible for the payment of the farm, occur from 1310 and took an oath to collect the tolls fairly for the benefit of the king and the community of Colchester, but how far they were borough officers is not clear. Two or three underbailiffs appear regularly in the earlier 14th century as assistants to the bailiffs, usually in the borough court.[59] Two of the four bailiffs recorded in 1251 were probably underbailiffs, as was Henry le Parmenter, the bailiff who collected a tallage or subsidy in 1276, and as perhaps were the three leading burgesses, all past or future bailiffs, who ordered the collection of market tolls in 1253.[60] The common chest, recorded in 1372[61] does not seem to have been a new institution then. Its keys may have been held by the bailiffs, but keykeepers, who were usually aldermen, were among the officers elected by the courts from 1392. Three serjeants were recorded from 1310; their duties included collecting toll and making arrests and distraints. In 1380 their number was increased to four, making one for each of the four wards.[62] No ward officers were recorded, unless Thomas Webbe, in charge of a 'ward' in South ward in 1271, was such an officer.[63]

The bailiffs sometimes consulted and acted with other leading burgesses, notably in the course of disputes with St. John's abbey. An agreement between the town and the abbey in 1254 was made by the bailiffs and 10 other men including at least one former bailiff and three future bailiffs.[64] Neither that list nor the witness lists of charters headed by the bailiffs suggests that there was anything approaching a formal council in the 13th century or the early 14th, and indeed Colchester seems to have managed without a council until 1372. Ordinances and decisions affecting the community were made in assemblies of burgesses in the hundred court. In 1311, for instance, 28 burgesses agreed *in plena congregatione* that the bishop of London's men from Chelmsford and Braintree should be required to pay toll in Colchester, and a similar assembly of 22 burgesses decided later in the year to imprison some thieves until the next gaol delivery.[65] Such informal arrangements were unusual in 14th-century boroughs,[66] and may have been workable in Colchester only because of its small size.

The borough government was reorganized in 1372,[67] apparently as a result of financial irregularities, but also perhaps because the earlier system had been strained by the town's rapid growth in the 1350s and 1360s. The preamble to the new constitutions declared that previously the profits of rents, tolls, fines, and amercements, had been spent by the bailiffs at their pleasure, to the damage of the commonalty and contrary to earlier constitutions. The new constitutions tightened the rules for the election of the bailiffs and created two new officers, the receivers, later called chamberlains, who were to receive all the town's income. On the election day, the Monday after 8 September, one man who had not been bailiff was to be chosen from each of the four wards, 'by the advice of the whole commonalty'. Those four were then to chose a further 20 'of the more worthy and sufficient commons who have hitherto not been bailiffs' and the 24 men thus chosen were to elect the bailiffs and other officers, the receivers being chosen from among the

58 *E.A.T.* 3rd ser. xiv. 96, 99–100, which finds no evidence to support the statement by W. G. Benham in *Colch. Ct. R.* i, pp. viii–ix, that Richard of Layer and Robert Beche were town clerks.

59 e.g. E.R.O., D/B 5 Cr1, rot. 12; Cr2, rott. 1, 4d.; Cr7, rot. 6 and d.

60 P.R.O., JUST 1/233, rott. 36, 37; *Sel. Cases in Exchequer of Pleas* (Selden Soc. xlviii), p. 82.

61 E.R.O., D/B 5 R1, f. 23.

62 Ibid. D/B 5 Cr1, rot. 4d.; Cr2, rot. 1d.; D/B 5 R2, f. 12.

63 P.R.O., JUST 1/238, rot. 59.

64 *Colch. Cart.* ii. 505.

65 E.R.O., D/B 5 Cr1, rott. 11, 14.

66 Tait, *Med. Eng. Boro.* 272–89.

67 E.R.O., D/B 5 R1, ff. 22v.–23v.

men who had not served as bailiff. The 24 were also to elect eight worthy men as auditors, later called aldermen, and the bailiffs and auditors, or some of them, were to audit the receivers' accounts each year at the beginning of September. It is not clear from the constitutions whether the auditor's was a new office created in 1372, but no earlier reference to auditors has been found.

There was at first some confusion as to which officers should be elected at the same time as the bailiffs and which on the second election day, the Monday after Michaelmas, but by the end of the 14th century the bailiffs, receivers, and auditors were elected on the first day, the town clerk and the serjeants on the second.[68] The constitutions also created Colchester's first council, laying down that in the week after Michaelmas the bailiffs and auditors should choose 16 of the wisest and wealthiest men in the borough who with the auditors should form a council of 24 which should meet at least four times a year. This innovation too seems to have been designed to end an abuse, for the constitutions forbade anyone to make 'common clamour' in the court before the bailiffs on any matter touching the commonalty, but ordered them instead to present a written bill to the council. The effect of the creation of the council of 24 seems to have been to take the day to day government of the borough away from the borough court. The old assembly of all the leading burgesses was still occasionally held, as in 1489 when it agreed to the arrangements for rebuilding Hythe mill.[69]

The charter of 1447 gave the burgesses the right to elect four J.P.s to sit with the bailiffs to hear Crown pleas, but the J.P.s were not regularly elected until 1463 after their office had been confirmed by the charter of 1462. That charter also created the office of recorder, and a second council, the common council, composed of four men from each of the four wards.[70] Although recorders were regularly elected from 1462, the second council was not recorded until 1519. A borough ordinance of 1447 laid down that bailiffs, J.P.s, coroners, and keykeepers must be chosen from among the aldermen, the aldermen from among the councillors,[71] but it seems simply to have confirmed the usual practice. In the 50 years before 1447, of the 25 men who served as bailiff only two, Thomas Godstone in 1398 and John Ford in 1399, both elected in troubled years at the end of Richard II's reign, were certainly not aldermen at the time of their election, and only six others may not have been. Of the 40 men elected alderman 12 may not have been councillors. Another, undated, ordinance, probably made between 1438 and *c.* 1449, restricted attendance at elections to self-employed householders contributing to subsidies and tallages.[72] The two ordinances might seem to reflect a growing tendency towards oligarchy in borough government, but they did not in practice narrow the field of potential bailiffs. Between 1327 and the new constitutions of 1372 a total of 40 bailiffs served an average of 2.25 years each; between 1372 and 1446 only 45 served an average of 3.29 years each, and between 1447 and 1499 a total of 44 served an average of 2.36 years each. Some bailiffs held office for several years, three for more than ten: Warin son of William served 14 times betweeen 1309 and 1334, Thomas Godstone 13 times between 1398 and 1429, Thomas Francis 12 times between 1381 and 1414, and Thomas Christmas 11 times between 1474 and 1499. Others held office only once: 21 between 1327 and 1371, 17 between 1372 and 1446, and 20 between 1447 and 1499.[73] In 1372 a bailiff's fee was set at 60*s.*

[68] *E.A.T.* 3rd. ser. xiv. 96–7.
[69] E.R.O., D/B 5 R2, ff. 188–189v.
[70] *Colch. Charters*, 38, 49–50.
[71] E.R.O., D/B 5 R1, f. 145v.
[72] *E.A.T.* 3rd. ser. xxi. 104.
[73] Problems in distinguishing between men of the same name may distort the figures slightly.

a year, and a livery robe worth 20*s*; by 1501 it had risen to £5.[74] Their seal of office, recorded from 1373, may have been made in 1372.[75] Although 15th-century aldermen increasingly held office until death or retirement, it was not until 1523 that an ordinance decreed that no alderman should be removed by the 24 electors without the consent of the majority of the other aldermen.[76] The number of chamberlains was reduced from two to one between 1460 and 1463, but rose to two again in 1470. It had been reduced to one again by 1497, presumably because of difficulties in filling an office which could be expensive for its holder.[77]

Courts

The borough court, a hundred court because Colchester was a hundred in itself,[78] met fortnightly in the moot hall. At three special meetings, called lawhundreds, at Michaelmas, Hilary, and Hock day, view of frankpledge was held, a jury presenting such matters as treasure trove, the raising of hue and cry, bloodshed, encroachments, overcharging the common, breaches of the assize of ale and of weights and measures, and nuisances.[79] Until 1271 the court appears to have claimed to hear some Crown pleas, including those initiated by appeals, but in that year the justices in eyre ruled that because the court could not conclude the plea without reference to the justices no more appeals should be prosecuted there.[80] Because the burgesses enjoyed the privilege of not having to answer for their land or tenements outside the borough, the court heard pleas concerning real property in the borough, and because real property was devisable by will, wills disposing of land or houses in the borough were proved and enrolled there. The charter of 1319 confirmed the court's right to hear all pleas, assizes, or complaints arising from land or tenements in the borough.[81] Some 14th-century land disputes were heard by the central courts at Westminster, although the bailiffs several times successfully claimed their liberty and had the case removed to the borough court.[82] In the 15th century suits concerning land or houses in Colchester were regularly heard in Chancery, apparently without interference from the borough officers.[83]

By 1310 the fortnightly meetings of the hundred, almost always on Mondays, could not cope with all the legal business of the borough, and they had been augmented by extra 'pleas' which seem to have been adjourned sessions of the hundred. They could be held on any day of the week, and at times served as a court of pie powder, dispensing quick justice by meeting on successive days or several times in one day. There was no clear distinction between the two courts in the business done, but cases involving real property tended to be heard in the hundred court, where burgesses were normally admitted, wills proved, and deeds enrolled. Cases could be adjourned from hundred to pleas or vice versa. There may have been some difference in the composition of the court; some 14th-century business was done in the 'full hundred', suggesting that attendance at the fortnightly hundred court was greater than at the pleas, its adjourned sessions. In the late 13th century the coroners seem to have sat with the bailiffs in the hundred court; in 1338 they sat in the lawhundred.[84] Some enrolments made in 'pleas' were

74 E.R.O., D/B 5 R1, f. 22v.; Bodl. MS. Rolls Essex 2.

75 E.R.O., D/B 5 Cr16, rott. 11, 12d., 13d.; below, Arms, Seals, etc.

76 E.R.O., D/B 5 R2, f. 30v.

77 Ibid. D/B 5 Cr71, rot. 1; Cr72, rot. 1; Britnell, *Growth and Decline*, 229–30.

78 P.R.O., JUST 1/238, rot. 59d.

79 E.R.O., D/B 5 Cr1–81, *passim*; D/B 5 R1, ff. 175v.–176.

80 P.R.O., JUST 1/238, rot. 59d.

81 *Colch. Charters*, 9.

82 e.g. E.R.O., D/B 5 R1, ff. 171–3, 176v.; D/B 5 Cr20, rot. 7; Bracton, *Note Bk.* ed. F. W. Maitland, ii. 596–8; *Year Bk.* 8 Edw. II, 1315 (Selden Soc. xxxvii), 77; *Sel. Cases in K.B.* (Selden Soc. lxxvi), 105–7; *Feet of F. Essex*, i–iii, *passim*.

83 P.R.O., C 1/7–188, *passim*.

84 Ibid. JUST 1/238, rot. 59d.; ibid. KB 27/312.

made before only one bailiff, but it is not clear that one bailiff could hear pleas alone.

In the later 14th century the adjourned pleas, which were held only occasionally earlier in the century, came to be held more regularly, increasingly on Thursdays or Fridays. From 1411 their proceedings were enrolled as those of a separate court, called the foreign court,[85] so named presumably because its more frequent meetings made it more attractive to those from outside the liberty, although it was by no means restricted to cases involving outsiders, and outsiders could and did still plead in the hundred court. The two courts continued to deal with the same business, although pleas involving real property continued to be heard more often in the hundred court than in the foreign court. Most cases remained in the court in which they had been started, but some moved from one court to the other. From 1448 onwards courts of pie powder were occasionally held; they followed the same procedure as the hundred and foreign courts, but were adjourned from hour to hour or day to day rather than from week to week or fortnight to fortnight. The charter of 1462 defined the court days as Monday and Thursday. It called both courts the king's court, but laid down that pleas involving real property were to be held fortnightly on Mondays, a ruling which confined them to the hundred court.[86]

The commonest pleas in both the hundred and the foreign courts were debt and trespass. The court asserted in 1311 its power to hear pleas of debt over 40*s*., but in practice until the earlier 15th century most claims for sums greater than that amount were made by an action for breach of covenant. Procedure was normally by complaint, originally presumably oral, but increasingly during the 14th century written. The process allowed three essoins after the first hearing of the case; in 1389 the council agreed that if a defendant did not appear on the third day (altered before 1398 to the second) he should be distrained at once, thus reducing the essoins to two and then to one.[87] Cases were occasionally instituted by writ, either writ of right patent or, in possessory assizes and dower, the appropriate writ addressed to the bailiffs. In 1233, in the course of an assize of novel disseisin, it was stated that the custom of the borough was that the jury should be composed of six burgesses and six outsiders.[88] In the earlier 14th century several men made their law with one burgess and one outsider.[89] As in other boroughs, the assize of fresh force was commonly used in the later 14th century. Recognizances of debt were enrolled from 1353.[90]

The charter of 1447 exempted Colchester from the jurisdiction of the admiral.[91] The town had probably enjoyed some immunity earlier, and fishing offences, which would otherwise have come within the purview of the admiralty court, were dealt with in the borough court. In 1425 Thomas Rose was accused of summoning Colchester men to the admiral's court, to the injury of the borough's liberty.[92] In 1493, 1494, and 1495, however, admiralty courts were held at Colchester for an area which seems to have included the whole of the river Colne from the Hythe to the sea.[93]

Parliamentary Representation

Colchester regularly sent two burgesses to parliament from 1283, except in 1306 when only one member was returned.[94] In addition, the bailiffs and six burgesses were summoned, with representatives of other east coast towns, to a meeting at Kings Lynn in 1322 to discuss a subsidy for the Scottish war, and in 1327

[85] E.R.O., D/B 5 Cr38, *passim*.
[86] *Colch. Charters*, 49.
[87] *E.A.T.* 3rd. ser. xvii. 133, 135.
[88] Bracton, *Notebk.* ii, pp. 596–7.
[89] e.g. E.R.O., D/B 5 Cr2, rott. 4, 10.
[90] Ibid. D/B 5 Cr10, rot. 3.
[91] *Colch. Charters*, 39.
[92] E.R.O., D/B 5 Cr45, rot. 15.
[93] Ibid. D/B 5 R1, ff. 21v.–22; D/B 5 R2, ff. 213v.–216v.; D/B 5 Cr1–81, *passim*.
[94] M. McKisack, *Parl. Rep. Eng. Boroughs in Middle Ages*, 6–7, 11.

Colchester was one of 57 towns ordered to send one or two discreet wool merchants to York to discuss the wool trade with the king.[95] Although the burgesses were exempted from sending representatives to parliament between 1382 and 1425, in consideration of their expenses in repairing the town wall, burgesses were elected throughout the period.[96]

The M.P.s were chosen by the burgesses without interference from the sheriff.[97] In 1455 the electors were the 'more substantial burgesses' resident in the town,[98] a description which implies that the elections, in contrast to municipal elections, were direct, but were made by only part of the freeman body. The burgesses elected to parliament were also burgesses of the 'more substantial' sort. Of the 83 known medieval M.P.s 61 had been or were to be bailiffs, 3 were or became aldermen, and one was a councillor; a further 11 were, or were probably, free burgesses. The remaining 7 M.P.s cannot be identified, but there is nothing to suggest that they came from outside the borough.[99] Several men served in more than one parliament, notably Ellis son of John who served 12 times between 1294 and 1343, Thomas Francis who served 10 times between 1372 and 1413, and Thomas Godstone who served 9 times between 1401 and 1428; all three also served several times as bailiff. John Rattlesdon, M.P. 13 times between 1312 and 1341, was a wealthy merchant, and John Hall, M.P. 9 times between 1357 and 1369, was a councillor in 1381 and may have held other offices earlier. Most later medieval M.P.s were merchants, but two 15th-century members were lawyers, and Michael Aunger, M.P. in 1382–3, was town clerk.[1]

The cost of M.P.s' expenses worried the borough in the late 14th century and the early 15th, but how the expenses were paid is unknown until the 1490s, when the rate seems to have been 2*s*. a day. In 1490 the bailiffs assigned part of the revenue of the Hythe mills to Thomas Christmas to cover his expenses in the parliaments of 1488 and 1489, and in 1494 they assigned other rents to Thomas Jobson for the parliament of 1491.[2] M.P.s apparently reported back to the bailiffs, and one such report, for the parliament of 1485, survives. That year the M.P.s were also responsible for discharging the annual fee farm at the Exchequer.[3]

TOWNSPEOPLE

In 1086 houses in Colchester belonged to 11 Essex manors: Ardleigh, Elmstead, West Mersea, Great Wigborough, Tolleshunt, Birch, Feering, Great Tey, Rivenhall, Terling, and Shalford. In addition, the bishop's nephew William who held two houses in Colchester has been plausibly identified with William the deacon who held Peldon.[4] Such houses probably served as town houses for the manorial lords or their servants, but their use declined after the 11th century. Only one connexion can be traced after 1086, and that suggests that the house, if indeed it still existed, was of little use to its owner: in 1312 Philip de Verly, lord of Tolleshunt D'Arcy, leased to St. John's abbey a plot of land in Colchester with permission to remove the stone walls on it.[5] Few 13th-century Colchester householders seem to have been county landowners. William de la Haye, who held at least one house in

95 *Cal. Close*, 1318–23, 536; 1327–30, 237.

96 *Cal. Pat.* 1381–5, 214; 1385–9, 505; 1391–6, 379; 1401–5, 355; 1408–13, 199; 1413–16, 23; list in Morant, *Colch.* 103–4.

97 McKisack, *Parl. Rep. Eng. Boroughs in Middle Ages*, 12.

98 *Hist. Parl. 1439–1509, Register*, 642.

99 Lists in Morant, *Colch.* 103–4; *Hist. Parl. 1439–1509, Register*, 642–3; the unidentified men all served in the early or mid 14th century when evidence for both freemen and borough officers is incomplete.

1 *Hist. Parl. 1439–1509, Register*, 643; E.R.O., D/B 5 R2, f. 257.

2 E.R.O., D/B 5 R2, ff. 218–24.

3 Ibid. ff. 87–9; N. Pronay and J. Taylor, *Parl. Texts of Later Middle Ages*, 177–93.

4 *V.C.H. Essex*, i. 385, 418, 462.

5 E.R.O., St. John's abbey ledger bk. ff. 238v.–239; *Feet of F. Essex*, ii. 154.

Colchester in 1226 and at his death *c.* 1229, was perhaps the lord of Layer de la Haye,[6] and Arnulph or Arnold Mounteny, bailiff 1319–20, seems to have been heir to an estate in Mountnessing in 1321.[7] Richard Baynard, who made his will in Colchester in 1278, was probably a member of the family which held Little Maldon, Messing, Rayne, and St. Lawrence, but his connexion was with St. John's abbey, where he may have lived, rather than with the town.[8] Other medieval immigrants to Colchester, with the striking exceptions of Thomas Godstone (d. 1431–2) and Nicholas Peek (d. 1464),[9] seem to have been of humbler origin, until in the late 15th century a few London merchants invested in Colchester land. Thomas Cook, knight, who held a house and land in Colchester *c.* 1475 may have been the London alderman of that name, and Sir Henry Colet, father of Dr. John Colet, dean of St. Paul's, held land and three stalls in Colchester of St. John's abbey at his death in 1505.[10]

Few Colchester men seem to have invested in land outside the borough liberty in the earlier Middle Ages, and none established a county family, perhaps a reflection of the relative poverty of the borough in the 12th and 13th centuries. In the 14th century some burgesses did acquire land elsewhere in Essex and in Suffolk, but they usually held on lease and had at most a life interest. The early 14th-century bailiff Ellis son of John, possibly son of the prominent 13th-century burgess John son of Ellis, married before 1303 Gillian, widow of Henry de Merk (d. 1291), and acquired her life interest in the manor of Latton Merk near Harlow and an estate in Belchamp St. Paul and Marks Tey; in 1327 he was assessed for subsidy in Marks Tey and Belchamp St. Paul as well as in Colchester.[11] Joseph Eleanor, bailiff eight times between 1311 and 1342 and the founder of an important chantry in Colchester, gave land in Greenstead and Ardleigh to St. Botolph's priory in 1337 and endowed his chantry with land in Colchester in 1338; he retained over 100 a. of land in Wigborough and Salcott. In 1327 he was assessed for subsidy in Layer Breton with Salcott Virley.[12] The future bailiff Warin Atwell may have been acting for St. John's abbey when he acquired land in North Benfleet in 1332, for he gave it to the abbey in 1336. With William Brome of Greenstead he bought land in Little Yarmouth and Gorleston (Suff.) in 1330, and conveyed other land in Suffolk in 1331.[13]

The merchant and future bailiff William Buck held land in West Mersea in 1336 and acquired a house in Great Wigborough in 1354. Two thirds of the Mersea land was held in 1375 by another Colchester merchant William Hunt and his wife Philippa, Buck's daughter; the remaining third was held by the former bailiff Alexander Cogger and his wife Agnes, presumably Buck's widow, in dower. That year Hunt and Philippa conveyed their part of the estate to the wealthy Colchester merchant and bailiff Thomas Francis. Alexander Cogger also held land in Grundisburgh and Clopton (Suff.).[14] Thomas Francis gave land in Great and Little Clacton to St. Osyth's in 1393, but his principal estates were in Colchester. His daughter Christine married a Norwich merchant.[15] Another merchant and former bailiff, Geoffrey Daw, who came from Alresford, had a life tenancy of the manor

6 *Cur. Reg. R.* ix. 369; *Close R.* 1227–31, 205.

7 Britnell, *Growth and Decline*, 32.

8 E.R.O., Acc. C47, CPL 880; cf. *Cal. Inq. p.m.* iii, p. 170; *Feet of F. Essex*, ii. 82.

9 Below, this section.

10 P.R.O., C 1/66, no. 400; *Cal. Inq. p.m. Hen. VII*, iii, p. 36.

11 *V.C.H. Essex*, viii. 189; *Med. Essex Community*, ed. J. C. Ward (Essex Hist. Doc. i), 16, 18, 57.

12 P.R.O., C 143/243, no. 12; C 143/245, no. 9; *Med. Essex Community*, 26.

13 E.R.O., St. John's abbey ledger bk., ff. 199, 200v.–201; *Cal. Suff. Fines*, ed. W. Rye, pp. 166, 170.

14 *Feet of F. Essex*, iii. 39, 108, 176; *Cal. Suff. Fines*, p. 255.

15 P.R.O., C 143/416, no. 28; E.R.O., D/DCm 218/9; D/B 5 Cr40, rot. 45.

there in 1375.[16] At his death in 1367 the clothier William Mate held land in Colchester and ploughs, carts, and livestock in Horkesley.[17] John Clerk (d. 1444), son of the bailiff Thomas Clerk who was a considerable landowner in Colchester, acquired land in West Mersea and Boxted and a house in London at Holborn; in 1439, when he owed 20 marks to the dean of Lincoln cathedral, he was styled gentleman.[18]

Robert, the son of Stephen Flisp, a merchant of the Hythe who acquired land in Boxted, Wormingford, and Great and Little Horkesley in 1405, was described as a gentleman of Tendring in 1434, but he, like his father, seems to have been a merchant and he had retained land in Colchester.[19] John Sumpter, bailiff in 1422, who seems to have come from St. Osyth's, married Margery, daughter of Sir Geoffrey Brockhole and Helen de Roos through whom his son John inherited a moiety of the manors of Brockhole's in Radwinter and Giffard's in Great Sampford.[20] Thomas Jopson or Jobson, from Heslington (Yorks. E.R.), was already wealthy at his admission as a burgess in 1462–3, suing for a debt of £20 in 1463. In 1478 and 1483 he bought land in Langenhoe, and in 1488 held freehold land in West Bergholt,[21] but the family did not establish themselves in the county until his grandson Francis Jobson made his fortune at the Dissolution of the monasteries.[22]

Thomas Godstone, who was admitted as a burgess of Colchester in 1387–8, inherited the manors of Chelsham Wateville and Warlingham (Surr.) and land in adjoining parishes.[23] From his wife Christine, daughter of the bailiff John Ford,[24] he acquired the manors of Ramsey and East Newland (St. Lawrence's parish) and probably a small estate in Peldon. The Peldon land was sold in 1402 but Thomas bought the manor of Braiswick in Lexden and Mile End, within Colchester. Thomas and Christine may have planned to establish their son John, to whom Christine devised Ramsey, as a country gentleman, but John predeceased his father, and on his death in 1431 Thomas devised most of his land to his brother, another John Godstone, who was already established at Rainham.[25] Thomas seems to have devised East Newland to Nicholas Peek, a member of a Suffolk gentry family who was admitted as a burgess in Colchester in 1440–1 and served as bailiff in 1442–3, 1444–5, and 1449–50. His widow Catherine held it when she died, without issue, in 1466.[26]

Other families can be traced in the town for several generations. Peter Christmas, a fuller, was assessed for subsidy in Colchester in 1272–3, and William Christmas, presumably a descendant, was bailiff in 1372–3 and died in 1391 leaving a son John.[27] The family rose to prominence in the late 15th century when Thomas Christmas the elder served as bailiff nine times betweeen 1474 and his death in 1500, and Thomas the younger eight times between 1497 and 1519.[28] Another long-lived family descended from Warin of Colchester, who lost goods off the Kent coast in 1233.[29] His son William son of Warin bought houses and rents in

[16] *Cal. Inq. p.m.* xiv, p. 101.

[17] E.R.O., D/B 5 Cr22, rot. 15.

[18] Ibid. D/B 5 Cr31, rot. 25d.; Cr61, rot. 9; *Cal. Pat.* 1436–41, 323.

[19] *Feet of F. Essex*, iii. 244; P.R.O., PROB 11/2B, f. 52v.; ibid. C 131/63/15.

[20] Morant, *Essex*, ii. 526, 536; P.R.O., C 138/37, no. 1.

[21] E.R.O., D/B 5 Cr72, rot. 10d.; *Feet of F. Essex*, iv. 76, 82; Britnell, *Growth and Decline*, 260.

[22] Below, Tudor and Stuart Colch. (Intro.); Outlying Parts (West Donyland).

[23] *V.C.H. Surr.* iv. 271, 334; above, Intro.

[24] E.R.O., D/B 5 Cr23, rot. 26; Cr45, rot. 39.

[25] Ibid. D/B 5 Cr45, rot. 39 and d.; P.R.O., C 1/11, no. 67; C 1/75, no. 38; *Feet of F. Essex*, iii. 236; *V.C.H. Essex*, vii. 168.

[26] P.R.O., C 1/9, no. 328; C 1/16, no. 247; ibid. PROB 11/5, f. 93; *Hist. Parl. 1439–1509: Biographies*, 672; *Cal. Pat.* 1446–52, 154; *Cal. Suff. Fines*, pp. 256, 281.

[27] B.L. Campb. Ch. ix. 2; E.R.O., D/B 5 Cr27, rot. 13.

[28] Below, List of Bailiffs and Mayors.

[29] *Close R.* 1231–4, 211.

Colchester market place from impoverished Jews in 1275 and held an estate in Colchester, Mile End, and Lexden, in 1293.[30] William's son, Warin son of William, sold land to Joseph Eleanor in 1332, but had died by 1338 leaving three sons, Adam, John, and John.[31] Adam, known as Adam Warin, was bailiff 1358–9 and granted land in Michaelstow, Ramsey, and Abberton to St. Osyth's abbey in 1380. At his death in 1381 he held extensive lands in Colchester and its liberty, including Braiswick in Lexden and Mile End. One of his brothers had moved to Bury St. Edmunds; the other, John Warin the elder, a wool merchant, served as bailiff 1344–5, apparently the year of his death, although there may have been two men of the name. Adam's son, Ralph Warin the chaplain, who died *c.* 1407, was the last known member of the family.[32]

John of Fordham and his son Walter were recorded in Colchester in 1265 when John was probably a borough officer.[33] The wool merchant John Fordham, bailiff in 1341 and 1342, may have been a descendant. He died in 1345–6 leaving four sons, William, George, Simon, and John,[34] of whom William was not recorded again in Colchester. A George Fordham was apprenticed to a London fishmonger and ran away to Colchester in 1352; he or an older man of the same name was bailiff in 1362–3 and owed money to a London vintner in 1379.[35] Simon, who married Mary or Mariot daughter and heir of the bailiff William Reyne,[36] was bailiff five times between 1382 and 1395. At his death, apparently childless, in 1400 he held at least 12 houses in Colchester with arable land and meadow in the suburbs, and employed his own chaplain. John, son and heir of George Fordham, conveyed land in the borough in 1439, but he or another man of the same name died that year, and the family disappeared from Colchester.[37] Several men surnamed Ford were prominent in 14th-century Colchester, but they may not all have been related. John Ford, bailiff in 1304–5, had land in the liberty in 1311.[38] Another John was bailiff eight times between 1350 and 1374, and a Robert Ford eight times between 1352 and 1379; both seem to have been merchants. John's son John was probably the John Ford bailiff eight times between 1399 and 1418; his daughter Christine married Thomas Godstone.[39] Another John Ford was bailiff six times between 1451 and 1466, and a William Ford nine times between 1454 and 1483.

For much of the Middle Ages Colchester seems to have drawn principally on north-east Essex and south-west Suffolk for its immigrants. The 13th-century evidence is scarce, but 54 people assessed for subsidy in 1272–3, 1296, or 1301 bore surnames derived from place names, 41 of which can be reasonably certainly identified. Of those, 14 are within 10 miles of Colchester, fairly evenly distributed around the borough, 11 are in north-east Essex or southern Suffolk, and 5 in northern Suffolk or Norfolk. Three of the four remaining Essex names are of places on or near the road from London (Moulsham, Waltham, and Terling). Other names include London, Leicester, Wiston (Sussex), and Wyham (Lincs.).[40] From 1327 the places of origin of some new burgesses were recorded. No consistent pattern can be seen in the recording, and it can probably be assumed that the places recorded provide a fair sample of the places of origin, or at least of last residence,

[30] *Cal. Pat.* 1279–81, 42; *Cal. Exch. Jews*, ii. 235–6, 276; *Feet of F. Essex*, ii. 74.

[31] B.L. Add. Ch. 41691; P.R.O., C 143/245, no. 9; E.R.O., D/B 5 Cr21, rot. 51d.

[32] E.R.O., Acc. A8173; ibid. D/B 5 Cr21, rot. 51d.; D/B 5 R1, f. 38; P.R.O., KB 9/22/1; *Cal. Pat.* 1377–81, 541.

[33] P.R.O., JUST 1/238, rot. 27.

[34] Ibid. KB 9/22/1; E.R.O., D/B 5 Cr7, rot. 8.

[35] *Cal. Letters from Mayor and Corpn. Lond. c. 1350–70*, ed. R. R. Sharpe, 39; *Cal. Pat.* 1377–81, 388.

[36] E.R.O., D/B 5 Cr35, rot. 23d. For Reyne see above this chapter, Econ. Hist.

[37] E.R.O., D/B 5 Cr31, rott. 23d.–24; Cr56, rott. 5d., 6d.; Cr57, rot. 15d.

[38] Ibid. D/B 5 Cr2, rot. 1d.

[39] Ibid. D/B 5 Cr23, rot. 26; Cr45, rot. 39.

[40] B.L. Campb. Ch. ix. 2, 4–5; *Rot. Parl.* i. 228–65.

of later medieval Colchester burgesses. In the period 1327–75 just over two thirds of the 94 burgesses whose place of origin was recorded came from within 10 miles of Colchester and almost all the remainder from elsewhere in Essex or Suffolk. No places of origin were recorded between 1375 and 1380–1, but by 1380–1 the numbers of new burgesses coming from parts of Essex and Suffolk more than 10 miles from Colchester was slightly greater than the number coming from nearer the town. A few came from Norfolk or Cambridgeshire, but more came from elsewhere in England, including London, Bristol, Gloucester, Ludlow, Canterbury, Sandwich, Manchester, and York. The pattern between 1400–1 and 1449–50 was very similar, although the number of more distant migrants grew in the early 15th century and did not drop in the second quarter as numbers from Colchester's more immediate hinterland declined; they came from most parts of England, notably from coastal counties such as Yorkshire and Kent, and from Wales, Ireland, and Calais. In the later 15th century the number of new burgesses coming from Essex and Suffolk continued to decline while the number coming from outside East Anglia fell only slightly so that they formed about a quarter of all new freemen whose places of origin were recorded. They included eight men from the Low Countries and one from Calais.[41]

Although the first burgesses stated to be from the Low Countries were not admitted until 1451–2, Vincent Van der Bek admitted in 1390–1 was almost certainly from there, and 'Flemings' had lived in Colchester from the 12th century or earlier. Boidin the Fleming was reeve of the town in 1181–2 and 1182–3; John the Fleming was bailiff in the 1260s; and at least five other Flemings were recorded in 13th- century Colchester.[42] Flemings appeared increasingly often in the borough courts from the late 14th century, and two allegedly murdered a fuller from Mount Bures at Colchester in 1395.[43] Many of the *c.* 38 aliens living in Colchester in the 1440s were probably Flemings, like the 11 given permission to stay in England in 1436, but others may have been Scottish or French.[44] One of the most successful later medieval immigrants was Edmund Harmanson from Brabant, a beer brewer admitted as a burgess in 1465–6. He does not appear to have held borough office, but he was master of the important St. Mary's guild in St. Leonard's parish in 1482–3. His wife then was Maud Barwick, perhaps a relation of Peter Barwick of the Hythe, founder of a chantry in St. Leonard's.[45] He was clearly a rich man when he died, probably childless, in 1502. His cash legacies totalled *c.* £224, he increased the endowment of Barwick's or the parish chantry, and founded a chantry of his own in St. Leonard's. His widow Elizabeth died in 1505, bequeathing cash legacies totalling *c.* £177, including £40 to found a fellowship at Cambridge and another £40 to be distributed at her burial.[46]

Emigration from Colchester is less easy to trace, but Walter of Colchester who held land in Shirley (Hants) in 1227 and a house in Southampton in or before 1258 may have been from the town.[47] John Lambyn of Colchester, citizen of London, was a benefactor of Bermondsey priory in the mid 14th century, and in 1447 John

41 E.R.O., D/B 5 R1, ff. 29v.–113. A few other places of origin could be recovered from the court rolls. On migration, see J. A. Galloway, 'Colch. and its Region, 1310–1560: Wealth, Industry and Rural–Urban Mobility in a Medieval Society' (Edinburgh Univ. Ph.D. thesis, 1986), pp. 277 sqq.

42 *Pipe R.* 1182 (P.R.S. xxxi), 102; 1199 (P.R.S. N.S. x), 97; *Colch. Cart.* ii. 606; *East Anglian*, N.S. iii. 154; P.R.O., JUST 1/242, rot. 111; *Cal. Pat.* 1258–66, 235.

43 E.R.O., D/B 5 Cr25, rot. 39; Cr26, rot. 24d.; Cr31, rot. 16d.; P.R.O., C 258/31, no. 14.

44 P.R.O., E 179/108/113, 114; E 179/270/31, rot. 50; *Cal. Pat.* 1429–36, 543–85; 1446–52, 324; 1476–85, 200; E.R.O., D/B 5 Cr73, rot. 29d.

45 P.R.O., C 47/37/5, f. 37v.; E.R.O., D/B 5 R1, f. 107; Britnell, *Growth and Decline*, 197; below, Churches (St. Leonard's).

46 P.R.O., PROB 11/13, f. 79v.; PROB 11/15, f. 2 and v.

47 *Pat. R.* 1225–32, 160; *Sel. Cases of Procedure without Writ* (Selden Soc. lx), p. 35.

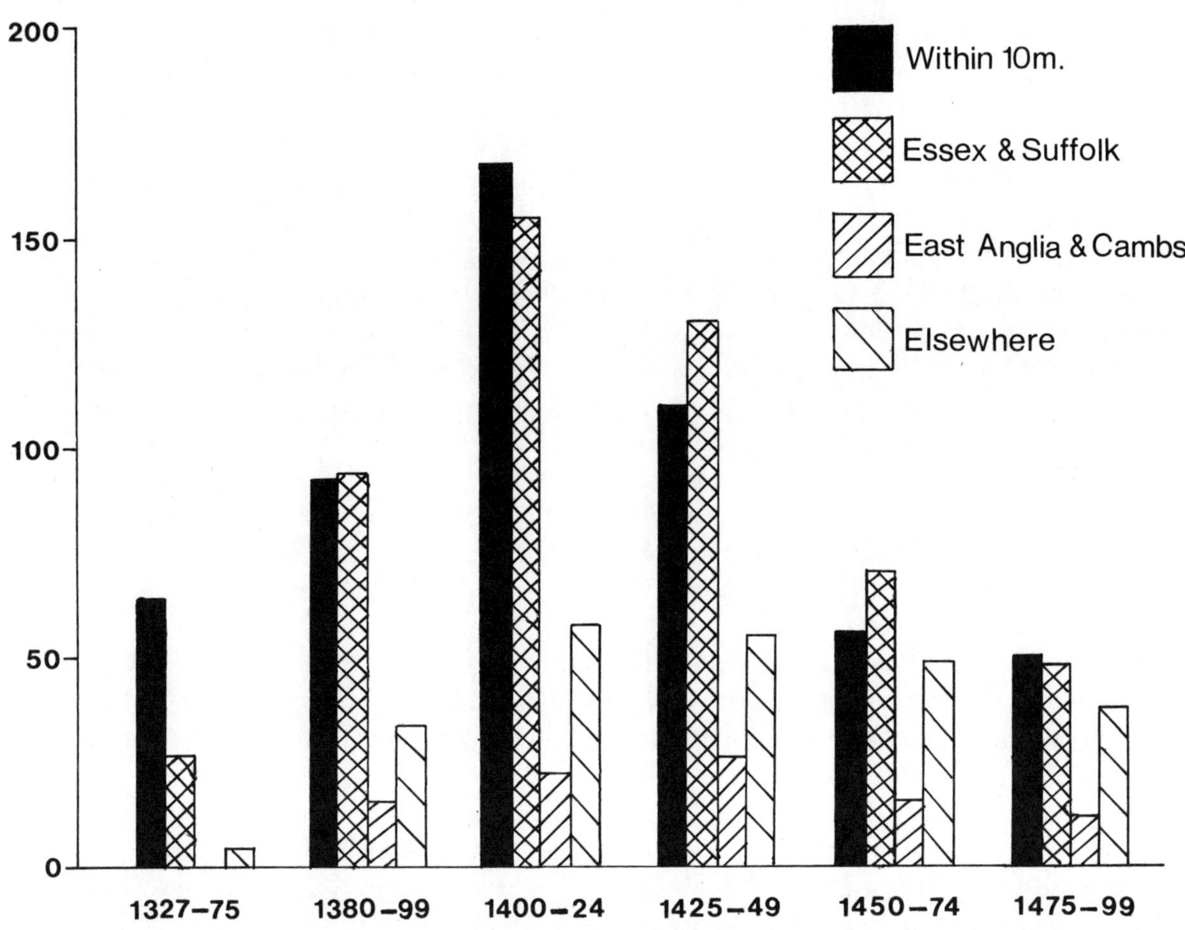

FIG. 7. ORIGINS OF FREEMEN, 1327–1499

Brigge of Colchester was a citizen or late citizen of London.[48] About 1480 a freemason, probably from a Colchester family, moved from Colchester to London to find work.[49] Colchester's most distinguished emigrant was William Colchester, abbot of Westminster 1386–1420, who came from St. Nicholas's parish.[50]

In 1272–3 the richer burgesses were assessed for subsidy on clothes and ornaments including gold rings, silver buckles, and silk belts, and on household goods including silver cups, silver spoons, mazers, and tablecloths. Similar goods were assessed in 1301, besides ewers, basins, and cooking utensils including brass pots and pans.[51] Goods stolen from humbler townsmen in the earlier 14th century ranged from the two silver cups and a small iron-bound chest of coins taken in 1346 and the 5 marks in silver taken from the parson of All Saints' church in 1317 to the brass pan and two linen sheets taken in Hythe Street in 1320 and a small bacon and cheese stolen in Mile End in 1317.[52] In the late 14th century and the 15th wealthier burgesses enjoyed a relatively high standard of living. William Christmas in 1391 bequeathed two pieces of silver plate, one with a cover, and 12 silver spoons. Robert Prior in 1443 owned at least two standing dishes and covers and two other pieces of silver gilt plate.[53] Wallhangings included the red cloth

48 *Cal. Pat.* 1340–3, 254; *Cal. Close*, 1354–60, 295; 1441–7, 479.

49 P.R.O., C 1/64, no. 780.

50 *Cal. Pat.* 1405–8, 188; E. H. Pearce, *Monks of Westminster*, 103.

51 B.L. Campb. Ch. ix. 2, 4–5; *Rot. Parl.* i. 243–62.

52 P.R.O., JUST 3/18/5, rott. 22, 33; JUST 3/129, rot. 15.

53 E.R.O., D/B 5 Cr27, rot. 13; Cr58, rot. 20.

embroidered with two figures left by John Clerk to St. Nicholas's church in 1444 and the stained cloths with pictures of St. Mary and St. Anne and two other stained cloths with figures on them left by Agnes Bounde in 1508.[54] William Wheeler had a coverlet with birds and flowers on it, and in 1452 John Primerole's bed hangings were woven with primeroles (primroses).[55] Catherine, widow of Nicholas Peek, died in 1466, leaving among other goods her chalice and mass book, and a great long coffer in her chapel. Her hall and parlour were furnished with hangings, tables and forms, and a hanging candlestick, and her silver included a standing piece and cover weighing 16¼ oz., at least two salts, one weighing 8¼ oz., and a little silver goblet.[56] By contrast, a tailor who died in 'great poverty' in 1482 had only latten basins, pots, and lavers, four candlesticks, a spit, an andiron, and trivet, a few pieces of furniture including a bed with its mattress, coverlet, pair of blankets and pair of sheets, six cushions, an old painted cloth, a russet gown, and an old broken mazer.[57]

The burgesses had the right to hunt fox, hare, and cat within the liberty,[58] but they also hunted deer when they could. In 1267 a group of Christians and Jews chased a deer into the town and killed it there, but the bailiffs confiscated the carcass.[59] In 1291 John de Galingal of Colchester was among those imprisoned in the Tower of London for taking deer in Langham park, and Ellis son of John, William son of Warin, and two other Colchester men were accused before the forest justices of similar offences. Several prominent Colchester men were accused in 1324 of taking deer in Kingswood.[60] The burgesses were jealous of their own rights, accusing four 'foreigners' in 1407 of taking partridges, pheasants, and other birds within the liberty.[61]

Archery was presumably common in medieval Colchester, but it left few records. In the 18th century the butts were said to have been in the later Butt Road, but the only medieval reference is to shooting in the court of St. John's abbey in 1319.[62] The bearstake at the junction of High Street and North Hill was used for baiting bulls before slaughter, but a bear was baited there in 1365.[63] Gambling and dicing were commonplace, and in 1373 a chess player was accused of playing all night in a tavern.[64] Tennis seems to have been popular from 1382, and in 1425 a labourer was presented as a night vagrant and tennis player.[65] Respectable burgesses entertained themselves walking with their families in the castle bailey.[66] Waits or minstrels were recorded in 1379, 1384, and 1406; the first two were maintained by the borough.[67] A miracle play involving a death's head mask and a tunic with tails, both borrowed from Dovercourt, was performed in 1377. In 1490 the parishioners of St. James's gathered for games or entertainment in the street outside the church. The event, to raise funds for the church, may have been part of a patronal festival.[68] A boy bishop ceremony was held on St. Nicholas's day at St. Nicholas's church in the early 15th century. The grammar school took part, and in 1425 the master was accused of having assaulted the boy bishop and demanded unreasonable payments from his cross-bearers in 1422.[69]

54 Ibid. D/B 5 Cr61, rot. 9; P.R.O., PROB 11/16, f. 61.
55 P.R.O., PROB 11/9, f. 183; E.R.O., D/B 5 Cr66, rot. 22.
56 P.R.O., PROB 11/5, f. 93 and v.
57 E.R.O., D/B 5 Cr81, rot. 5d.
58 *Colch. Charters*, 2.
59 P.R.O., E 32/12, rot. 3d.
60 *Cal. Pat.* 1281–92, 445; P.R.O., E 32/13, rot. 8d.; E 32/16, rot. 21.
61 E.R.O., D/B 5 Cr36, rot. 21.
62 P.R.O., JUST 3/19/8, rot. 21.
63 E.R.O., D/B 5 Cr3, rot. 3d.; Cr14, rot. 14.
64 Ibid. D/B 5 Cr15, rot. 13; Cr16, rot. 6d.; Cr46, rot. 12.
65 Ibid. D/B 5 Cr21, rot. 30; Cr39, rot. 30; Cr43, rot. 19; Cr45, rot. 15.
66 Ibid. D/B 5 Cr42, rot. 22.
67 Ibid. D/B 5 Cr19, rot. 8; Cr24, rot. 1; Cr36, rot. 2.
68 Ibid. D/B 5 Cr18, rot. 17; D/B 5 R2, f. 193v.
69 Ibid. D/B 5 Cr45, rot. 15.

The borough appears, intermittently at least, to have encouraged the cult of St. Helen as its patron. A chapel, possibly with some parochial functions, was dedicated to her by the early 12th century, and she appeared on the early 13th-century borough seal. The chantry founded in the chapel in 1328 may have had an associated guild from the first; there was certainly a St. Helen's guild by 1383 when it appointed the chantry priest, and it owned plate and vestments in 1389.[70] By 1400 it was associated with St. Cross chapel and hospital, and in 1407 it was refounded there as a guild or fraternity for men and women led by one or two wardens; it was to maintain five chaplains to pray for Henry IV and for the guild members. Those responsible for the refoundation, Thomas Godstone, Thomas Francis, John Ford, and John Sumpter, were among the wealthiest and most influential men in Colchester.[71] The guild received bequests of land and rents from Edmund Haverland in 1409 and Thomas Francis in 1416.[72] Thomas Godstone between 1424 and his death in 1431 gave land to the guild to found a chantry in St. Cross dedicated to God, the Virgin Mary, St. Helen, and St. Catherine for his soul and those of his wife Christine and son John, and of all the guild members.[73]

There were 65 members of St. Helen's guild in 1418, among them 'the countess of Hertford', probably Joan widow of Humphrey de Bohun earl of Hereford and Essex, a benefactress of Walden abbey and guardian of Richard de Vere earl of Oxford. Sir John Howard of Wivenhoe, Sir Gerard Braybroke of Danbury, and Helen, widow of Sir Geoffrey Brockhole and mother-in-law of John Sumpter, also belonged to the guild.[74] In 1442 there were 49 paid-up members, including the bailiff John Rouge, five other past or future bailiffs, and two aldermen. The abbots of St. John's and St. Osyth's were members, but perhaps surprisingly the prior of St. Botolph's was not. Some members lived in Harwich, others probably in Ipswich. Most were burgesses, but John Doreward of Bocking, who had held Olivers and Belhus in Stanway, Thomas Knevett of Stanway, and another unidentified gentleman had also paid their dues.[75] Richard Baynard of Messing (d. 1433 or 1434),[76] an associate of both Doreward and Knevett, left the guild the reversion of a house and land to support prayers for his soul. The 87 members in 1491 included the abbot of St. John's and John Bourchier, Lord Berners, but the guild may have been declining in popularity as it received only one further recorded bequest, of 20*d.* in 1486.[77] In 1518 the wardens were Sir John Rainsford of Bradfield, who had obtained Stanway by marriage, and Thomas Bonham, gentleman, the town clerk.[78] The guild held a feast on St. Helen's day each year.[79]

Most parish churches had at least one guild. Among the more important were St. Mary's guild in St. Leonard's church, which seems to have been responsible for the maintenance of the causeway to Hythe bridge and of a tumbrel, and to have paid for some work on the church; it was probably associated with St. Mary's light in the same church, which had been endowed with rents worth 11*s.* 6*d.* by *c.* 1500.[80] The endowments of the Jesus guild in St. Peter's church, first recorded in 1447, included Chiswell meadow, the source of much of the town's water. In 1537 all the parishioners of St. Peter's seem to have been members of the guild, one of

[70] Ibid. D/B 5 R2, f. 259v.; below, Chapels.

[71] E.R.O., D/B 5 Cr32, rot. 16d.; Morant, *Colch.* Appendix, p. 13.

[72] Morant, *Colch.* 157; E.R.O., D/B 5 Cr40, rot. 45.

[73] Morant, *Colch.* 157.

[74] Ibid. 150 n.; Morant, *Essex*, ii. 526; *Complete Peerage*, vi. 473–4; x. 234.

[75] E.R.O., Boro. Mun., Compotus of St. Helen's guild, 1441–2.

[76] Morant, *Essex*, ii. 176.

[77] Morant, *Colch.* 150 n.; P.R.O., PROB 11/8, f. 317v.

[78] B.L. Stowe MS. 834, f. 77; Morant, *Essex*, i. 464; ii. 191.

[79] E.R.O., Boro. Mun., Compotus of St. Helen's guild, 1441–2.

[80] P.R.O., C 47/37/5, f. 37v.; B.L. MS. Stowe 834, ff. 84–85v.

whose wardens was the alderman Robert Leche. The guild was probably connected with the Jesus mass recorded from 1456, which seems to have enjoyed particularly strong support in the early 16th century, and with the Jesus chapel recorded from 1488.[81] The St. Anne's guild to which small sums were bequeathed in 1486 and 1517 was probably associated with St. Anne's chapel and hospital, which received regular bequests of money, sheets, and other goods in the late 15th century and the early 16th.[82] There were guilds of St. Mary and of St. Crispin and St. Crispian in the Greyfriars' church.[83]

Every parish church probably had at least a light dedicated to the Virgin Mary. The next most popular saint appears to have been St. Barbara who had a guild in St. Peter's church in 1457 and 1512 and an altar there in 1501 besides a guild in All Saints' in 1512.[84] St. Peter had chapels in St. James's and St. Leonard's and a guild in St. James's, and there was a St. John's chapel in St. Nicholas's besides a guild of St. John the Baptist in St. Peter's and a chapel of St. John the Evangelist in St. Martin's.[85] St. Anthony had a statue in St. Nicholas's and a light in St. Giles's in the early 16th century.[86] Other saints honoured in Colchester included St. Paul, who had a statue in St. Leonard's church in 1492, St. Francis, who had a guild, probably in St. James's, in 1435, and St. Catherine who had an altar in Holy Trinity in 1514 and a statue and perhaps a chapel in St. Giles's church in 1526.[87] There was a Corpus Christi guild in St. Nicholas's church in 1448, and Corpus Christi was the holy day of St. Leonard's church in the 1480s.[88]

The chantries founded in St. Helen's chapel by John of Colchester in 1322 and by Richolda Cofford in the late 14th century and that founded in St. Nicholas's church by John Bayn in 1383 seem to have been lost during the 15th century.[89] Chantries were founded in the parish churches of St. Mary-at-the-Walls by Joseph Eleanor in 1348, of St. Nicholas by Thomas Francis in 1416, and of St. Leonard by Peter Barwick *c.* 1480 and by Edmund Harmanson in 1502; all four survived until 1535 or 1546, as did Thomas Godstone's chantry in St. Cross chapel.[90] In addition to the perpetual chantries, 19 people between 1384 and 1500 left money to pay for temporary chantries, most for only one year, but others for 2, 3, or 5 years, and one, founded by Thomas Francis in St. Martin's, for 10 years.[91] William Bergholt in 1400 left 10 marks to a man to go to Rome on pilgrimage for his own and his wife's souls.[92] The Friars Minor received 20 bequests from townsmen in the late 14th century and the 15th, many more than any other religious house. Perhaps surprisingly in view of the frequent conflicts between the abbey and the town, St. John's received six bequests, compared with St. Botolph's five, and St. Osyth's two.[93]

Suspected Lollard books, in English, were confiscated from several townsmen in 1405, but were returned after examination by the prior of St. Bartholomew's, London. In 1414 at least ten men, including a friar and a parish clerk, had English

[81] E.R.O., D/ACR 1–2, *passim*; D/B 5 Cr70, rot. 13; P.R.O., PROB 11/4, f. 93; PROB 11/8, f. 136v.; B.L. MS. Stowe 834, f. 80.

[82] P.R.O., PROB 11/8, f. 317v.; PROB 11/10, f. 54; PROB 11/13, ff. 23, 79v.; PROB 11/19, f. 79v.; E.R.O., D/ACR 2, f. 58; D/B 5 Cr111, rot. 6.

[83] E.R.O., D/DACR 2, f. 58; D/B 5 Cr95, rot. 14d.; Cr96, rot. 3d.

[84] P.R.O., PROB 11/4, f. 149; E.R.O., D/ACR 1, ff. 30 and v., 127, 200.

[85] P.R.O., PROB 11/4, ff. 93, 149; PROB 11/5, f. 93; PROB 11/10, f. 54; PROB 11/12, f. 104; PROB 11/13, f. 79v.; E.R.O., D/B 5 Cr47, rot. 4d.; Cr54, rot. 16d.; Cr58, rot. 20; Cr61, rot. 10; Cr62, rot. 9.

[86] E.R.O., D/ACR 1, f. 19; 2, f. 9v.

[87] Ibid. D/ACR 2, ff. 1, 197; D/B 5 Cr62, rot. 9; P.R.O., PROB 11/9, f. 103.

[88] E.R.O., D/B 5 Cr62, rot. 12; P.R.O., C 47/37/5.

[89] Below, Churches (St. Nicholas's); Chapels; *Reign of Ric. II*, ed. C. M. Barron and F. R. H. DuBoulay, 251.

[90] Morant, *Colch.* 157–8; below, Churches.

[91] P.R.O., PROB 11/4–12; E.R.O., D/B 5 Cr1–81, *passim*, esp. D/B 5 Cr40, rot. 45.

[92] E.R.O., D/B 5 Cr32, rot. 4.

[93] Ibid. D/B 5 Cr3–79, *passim*; D/ACR 1–2, *passim*; P.R.O., PROB 11/1–27, *passim*. Bequests to individual friars, monks, or canons, and those to St. Botolph's by its parishioners have been omitted.

books which they read both alone and in groups. The only man to join the Lollard rising that year was not among the book-reading group, but a Lollard cordwainer pardoned later in 1414 may have been.[94] Colchester was a centre of Lollardy in the late 1420s. A Norfolk Lollard confessed in 1430 to having attended a Lollard 'school' or meeting in the town, and others had visited the houses of two leading Lollards there, John Finch and John Abraham. Abraham and another Lollard, a tailor, were burnt in the town in 1428 or 1429.[95] Another man was falsely accused of Lollardy in 1428, and in 1428 or 1429 the abbot of St. John's, in the course of an acrimonious dispute with the town over Hythe mill, claimed that some of the townsmen were Lollards.[96] There are no other references to Lollards in the 15th century, apart from the use of 'Lollard' as an insult in 1438, but the sect flourished in the early 16th century.[97]

Two apparent instances of witchcraft came before the town court, one in 1420 when the parish clerk of St. Peter's was accused of practising magic and using devils' names, and one in 1456 when a man and his wife were accused of trying to kill boys by witchcraft.[98]

94 P.R.O., KB 9/205/1, nos. 10, 11; *E.H.R.* xxix. 101–4; *Cal. Pat.* 1413–16, 271; *Cal. Close*, 1413–19, 148.

95 A. Hudson, *Premature Reformation*, 138, 181, 186–7; *Norwich Heresy Trials 1428–31* (Camd. 4th ser. xx), 146, 152, 181–3, 185; E.R.O., D/B 5 R2, f. 71 and v.

96 E.R.O., D/B 5 Cr48, rot. 25d.; D/B 5 R2, f. 73 and v.

97 Ibid. D/B 5 Cr56, rot. 18; Hudson, *Premature Reformation*, 162, 477–9; below, Tudor and Stuart Colch. (Religious Hist.).

98 E.R.O., D/B 5 Cr42, rot. 21d.; D/B 5 Cr66, rot. 19.

TUDOR AND STUART COLCHESTER

THE earlier 16th century was a period of contraction in Colchester as the cloth trade, on which the town's economy depended, declined. The borough began to recover about the middle of the century, and its economy was greatly boosted from 1565 by the arrival of Dutch immigrants who introduced the manufacture of new draperies, the lightweight bays and says which were the mainstay of Colchester's cloth industry throughout the 17th century, and the foundation of its prosperity and growth.[1] The town was also known for its oysters and for its candied eryngo or sea holly, a sweetmeat and reputed aphrodisiac; both were presented to important visitors and sent to the borough's patrons and friends at court. Borough government was reorganized by Charles I's charter of 1635 which, among other provisions, gave the town a mayor in place of the two bailiffs who had hitherto been its chief officers.[2]

Colchester's population, declining from the mid 15th century, may have continued to contract in the early 16th.[3] Estimates based on the subsidy returns of 1524–5 suggest a figure in the range of 3,500–5,000, with one of *c.* 4,000 probably closest to the truth.[4] That figure is consistent with another estimate, based on the numbers taking the oath of allegiance to the heirs of Henry VIII and Anne Boleyn, of *c.* 3,600 (excluding clergy) in 1534, at a time when the town's population may have reached its nadir. From then on there are signs of slow recovery, the population reaching *c.* 4,600, including 431 Dutch immigrants, in the 1570s. Thereafter the trend was distinctly upward, despite short-lived interruptions in the early 1590s and between 1606 and 1610, producing a total of *c.* 11,000 by the 1620s, including 1,535 Dutch. An estimate of 10,400 for 1674 suggests only slight contraction by that date, despite the ravages of the siege of 1648 and the great plague of 1665–6. Thereafter numbers seem to have at best stagnated and by the mid 18th century Colchester, with *c.* 2,342 households,[5] was falling well behind other more rapidly developing towns.

Part of the town's growth was due to natural increase, a surplus of births over deaths, despite the appearance of small deficits in both the 1590s and the 1620s, and another larger shortfall during the quinquennium 1601–5 caused mainly by the severe plague epidemic of 1603–4.[6] Although births did outnumber deaths over the period 1561–1640 as a whole, the surplus is insufficient to account for the extent of the expansion achieved. Immigration, from elsewhere in England and from overseas, played an essential part in the growth, a feature of the town's development that was of great concern to the urban authorities in the later 16th and early 17th century.[7]

Colchester's growth was punctuated by outbreaks of epidemic disease. The years 1514, 1545, 1557–9, 1569–70, 1586–8, 1597, 1603–4, 1625–6, 1631, 1651, 1665–6,

1 *Immigrants and Minorities*, i. 263–80; L. Roker, 'Flemish and Dutch Community in Colch. in the 16th and 17th Cent.' (Lond. Univ. M.A. thesis, 1963); *Reg. of Baptisms in Dutch Ch. in Colch.* ed. W. J. C. Moens, (Huguenot Soc. xii).

2 *Diary of John Evelyn*, ed. W. Bray, i. 314–15; *O.E.D.* s.v. eryngo; E.R.O., D/B 5 Aa1/1–26; Aa1/35, ff. 1–90.

3 The following paragraphs are based on N. Goose, 'Economic and Social Aspects of Provincial Towns: a comparative study of Cambridge, Colchester, and Reading *c.* 1500–1700' (Camb. Univ. Ph.D. thesis, 1984), 248–51.

4 Cf. Britnell, *Growth and Decline*, 201–2.

5 Morant, *Colch.* 107–36; the figure excludes Mile End and Berechurch.

6 Goose, 'Econ. and Social Aspects', 263–7.

7 Below, this chapter, Soc. Structure.

and 1679 had particularly high mortality.[8] The high mortality of 1557–9 was probably caused by the national epidemic of influenza and typhus in those years,[9] while that of 1597 was possibly due to either famine or disease induced by malnutrition, the result of four successive years of high grain prices.[10] Plague appears to have been responsible for most of the other years of high death rate, and was active in the town at other times, producing peaks of mortality in particular parishes. St. Botolph's, for instance, experienced additional years of high mortality in 1578, 1583, and 1610–11, St. James's in 1580, Lexden in 1595, and St. Leonard's in 1638–9. The frequency with which the poor parish of St. Botolph experienced such crises demonstrates the close relationship between poverty and epidemic disease.[11] None of the epidemics was capable of stemming the town's growth. Although plague was a frequent visitor to the town, only in 1597, 1603–4, and 1625–6 did mortality reach double the average level for a sample of parishes representing the town as a whole, and under 10 per cent of total mortality in the early 17th century was due to the additional deaths that such crises produced.

The plague of 1665–6 was of a completely different order of magnitude. The death toll was variously given as 5,259 for the 17 months between August 1665 and December 1666, of which 4,731 were from plague, and 5,034 for the 67 weeks from 8 September 1665 to 21 December 1666, of which 4,526 were from plague.[12] Approximately half the town's population perished in the epidemic, probably making it the most destructive outbreak experienced by any large town in early modern England. The full resources of the corporation were mobilized. Two new pest houses were built, in St. Mary's-at-the-Walls and at Mile End, while searchers and bearers of the dead were appointed to dispose of the bodies.[13] Funds collected in Colchester churches quickly proved inadequate to relieve the sufferers, and were supplemented by a tax on villages within 5 miles of the town, authorized by the J.P.s and producing £217 a month. Early in 1666 an additional £250 a month for three months was ordered to be levied in the hundreds of Lexden, Dunmow, and Hinckford, and by July funds were also being raised in the hundreds of Clavering, Uttlesford, and Ongar, and in Witham half hundred. In May 1666 weekly collections were made in London churches by order of Charles II, amassing a total of £1,307 10*s*. In all *c.* £2,700 was raised in taxes and donations for the relief of the town, a sum that was administered with painstaking diligence by the corporation and its officials, despite the absence of the mayor and several aldermen, assistants, and councillors during October and November 1666.[14] A surplus of £400 of the money collected for the poor remained in the corporation's coffers some 18 years later.[15]

The immediate impact of the epidemic was profound, but both the population and the economy recovered surprisingly rapidly. Already in March 1666, when the months of peak mortality were still to come, 279 houses stood empty. By 1674, however, only 63 houses were empty, showing that Colchester had conformed to the typical pattern whereby urban population losses were quickly made good by an influx of migrants.[16] Cloth production also quickly recovered, and achieved new heights as early as 1668.[17]

Disturbances, some politically as well as economically motivated, marked mid

8 Goose, 'Econ. and Social Aspects', 300–21; *E.A.T.* 3rd ser. iv. 134–45.

9 *Econ. H.R.* xviii. 120–9; xlvi. 291–4.

10 Below, this chapter, Soc. Structure.

11 P. Slack, *Impact of Plague in Tudor and Stuart Eng.* 112, 116, 124–6.

12 B.L. Stowe MS. 840, ff. 44–5; E.R.O., D/P 200/1/6 (unfoliated), following baptisms.

13 E.R.O., D/B 5 Aa1/23; D/B 5 R1, f. 217.

14 E.R.O., D/B 5 Gb4, ff. 315v.–346v., 356; P.R.O., PC 2/59, pp. 5–6; *Cal. S.P. Dom.* 1665–6, 398; *E.A.T.* 3rd ser. iv. 141–2.

15 *Cal. S.P. Dom.* 1683–4, 258.

16 P.R.O., E 179/246/22; *E.A.T.* 3rd ser. iv. 145; *Medical Hist.* xix. 333–41; *Crisis and Order in Eng. Towns 1500–1700*, ed. P. Clark and P. Slack, 170; J. Patten, *Eng. Towns*, 132.

17 Below, this chapter, Econ.

and later 16th-century Colchester.[18] A few attracted the attention of the government in London. A Norfolk priest spread rumours of Kett's rebellion in the town in 1549, and two Colchester men were pardoned for 'treason and insurrection' that year. On 31 August another six men, presumably rebels but not, apparently, from Colchester, were condemned by the earl of Oxford and Sir Thomas Darcy and hanged at the town gates and in the market place.[19] Jerome Gilberd, a lawyer who was to be recorder of the town in the first year of Mary's reign, seems to have been suspected in 1550 of writing two seditious bills,[20] and in 1563 a shearman was accused of repeating 'slanderous reports' of the queen.[21] Between 1577 and 1579 Robert Mantell or Blosse, a seaman who had claimed at Maldon to be Edward VI, was imprisoned in Colchester castle.[22] While there Mantell built up a following in the town which included the councillor Stephen Holt, who with the gaoler and his assistant was suspected of aiding his escape in July 1579.[23] Mantell was recaptured, imprisoned in Newgate, and executed in 1581.[24] In 1584 Thomas Debell, a servant of Catherine Audley of Berechurch and like his mistress a suspected popish recusant, was imprisoned by the bailiffs for 'very dangerous' speeches pointing out that Mary Queen of Scots was the next heir to the throne and complaining that Mantell had been executed on the evidence of only one instead of two witnesses. The town clerk and the Privy Council took a less serious view of the matter, and Debell seems to have been released.[25]

In 1588 the borough supplied a ship and perhaps a pinnace for service against the Armada, and in April that year sailors from as far down the Colne as Brightlingsea were ordered to appear at the moot hall, presumably so that crews could be found.[26] Apart from the Civil War, national affairs did not impinge on Colchester again until the 1680s. In 1683, while the assembly of mayor, aldermen, and assistants duly presented a loyal address to Charles II on the discovery of the Popish plot, other burgesses were feared to be 'dangerous to the peace and government' of the country, and a drunken townsman boasted that he had fought against the old king and would fight against the present one if necessary.[27] The earl of Oxford's regiment was stationed in the town for about a month during Monmouth's rebellion in the summer of 1685.[28] In December 1688 the assembly ordered the distribution of arms to some burgesses, and troops were again quartered in the town.[29] In 1691 the recorder and the M.P., Sir Isaac Rebow, examined some 'very dangerous persons' who had been trying to escape overseas.[30]

Royal and other important visits to the town were few, but generally costly. When Catherine of Aragon came to Colchester in 1515 on her way to Walsingham (Norf.) she was given a purse and £10.[31] In 1544 the bailiffs were ordered to prepare provisions for 1,600–2,000 horse accompanying Henry VIII to Harwich.[32] Colchester declared for Mary at her accession on 19 July, and the queen travelled through the town on 26 July 1553, on her way from Framlingham to London. The streets were mended in preparation for her visit, and she was presented with a

[18] Below, this chapter, Soc. Structure.

[19] *Cal. Pat.* 1549–51, 2; B.L. Stowe MS. 829, f. 32; *Rebellion, Popular Protest, and the Social Order in Early Modern Eng.* ed. P. Slack, 52, 71.

[20] *Acts of P.C.* 1550–2, 138, 159; E.R.O., D/B 5 Cr120, rot. 1.

[21] E.R.O., D/B 5 Sb2/1, f. 22v.

[22] *Cal. Assize Rec. Essex, Eliz. I*, p. 175.

[23] E.R.O., D/Y 2/6, p. 13; D/Y 2/8, p. 207; *Acts of P.C.* 1580–1, 29.

[24] *Cal. Assize Rec. Essex, Eliz. I*, p. 215.

[25] E.R.O., D/B5 Sb2/4, ff. 36v.–37; D/Y 2/7, p. 199; D/Y 2/8, pp. 319, 323; B.L. Stowe MS. 150, f. 33.

[26] E.R.O., D/B 5 Gb1, 6, 15 April, 1588; D/Y 2/3, p. 53; *V.C.H. Essex*, ii. 221.

[27] E.R.O., D/B 5 Gb5, f. 207; D/B 5 Sb2/9, f. 319 and v.; *Cal. S.P. Dom.* 1683, 89.

[28] *William Holcroft His Book*, ed. J. A. Sharpe, pp. vi, 33, 49.

[29] E.R.O., D/B 5 Gb5, ff. 308–9.

[30] *Cal. S.P. Dom.* 1690–1, 252.

[31] E.R.O., D/B 5 R1, f. 118.

[32] S. Dale, *Hist. and Antiq. Harwich*, 249; E.R.O., D/Y 2/9, p. 355.

silver gilt cup and cover and £20.[33] Elizabeth I spent two or three days in Colchester in 1561; she was presumably met by the bailiffs, aldermen, and councillors in their livery gowns, welcomed by the recorder, and presented with a silver gilt cup and £20, as was planned for cancelled visits in 1578 and 1579. When the duke of York, later James II, visited the town in 1667 he was presented only with a box of candied eryngo, and a similar present was given to his son-in-law the future William III in 1681.[34] An expensive entertainment was planned for William on his journey to Harwich and the Netherlands in 1691, but on the return journey he was merely offered an oyster.[35] The duke of Marlborough visited Colchester in 1704, but his entertainment apparently cost only £2.[36]

Although it was overshadowed in the region by Ipswich, Colchester was by far the largest town in Essex,[37] and its castle housed the county gaol until 1666. The county town, however, was Chelmsford, where both the assizes and the county quarter sessions were usually held. Colchester acquired none of the legal and other business which those courts generated; it had fewer inns than the much smaller Chelmsford, and seems to have attracted fewer lawyers.[38] Nevertheless a number of professional men settled in Colchester, some in pursuit of their careers, others in retirement. Thomas Audley, a lawyer from Earls Colne who moved to Colchester as town clerk in 1514 and ended a career in the royal service as Lord Chancellor and Baron Audley of Walden,[39] was perhaps the town's most distinguished burgess. Although he resigned as town clerk in 1531 he had by then settled at Berechurch within the liberty, and retained his links with the town until his death in 1544.[40] Francis Jobson, son and grandson of Colchester bailiffs, also made a career in the royal service, becoming lieutenant of the Tower of London in 1564, and acquiring former monastic lands including West Donyland with its house at Monkwick, within the liberty. He married Elizabeth, daughter of Arthur Plantagenet, Viscount Lisle, thus connecting himself with her half brother John Dudley, later duke of Northumberland, father of Lady Jane Grey. He served as M.P. for Colchester in 1552, in 1553–4, and 1555.[41]

Samuel Halsnoth or Harsnett (d. 1631), son of a Colchester baker William Halsnoth, obtained his degree at Cambridge and returned to the town briefly as master of the grammar school 1587–8. He ended his career as archbishop of York; although he had not lived there since 1588 he left his library to the borough.[42] His cousin Adam Harsnett followed him to Cambridge where he took his B.D. in 1612; he was later known as a moderate Puritan theologian.[43] William Gilbert or Gilberd (d. 1603), son of Jerome Gilberd, also went from Colchester to Cambridge. He became physician to Elizabeth I and James I, but his reputation rests chiefly on his pioneering study of magnetism, *De Magnete* (1600).[44] Thomas Skinner, physician and biographer of General George Monk, duke of Albemarle, practised in Colchester where he died in 1679.[45] The madrigal

33 E.R.O., D/Y 2/2, pp. 29, 31–3.

34 *E.J.* xxiii. 66–7.

35 E.R.O., D/B 5 Gb5, ff. 337, 348.

36 Ibid. D/B 5 Ab 1/24.

37 W. J. Petchey, *Prospect of Maldon*, 10, 12.

38 Ibid. 138; H. Grieve, *Sleepers and Shadows*, vol. ii, chapter 1 (forthcoming).

39 E.R.O., D/B 5 Cr86, rott. 1, 2d.; *Complete Peerage*, i. 348–9.

40 *E.A.T.* 3rd ser. xv. 86–7; below, Outlying Parts (West Donyland, Manors).

41 *D.N.B.*; *Lisle Letters*, ed. M. St. Clair Byrne, vi, p. 280; Morant, *Colch.* 104, 137.

42 *D.N.B*; below, Soc. and Cultural (Libraries).

43 *D.N.B.*

44 Ibid.; Morant, *Colch.* App. p. 20.

45 Morant, *Colch.* 118.

composer John Wilbye lived in retirement at Colchester from *c.* 1628 until his death in 1638, as a member of the household of Mary Darcy, Countess Rivers, daughter of his earlier patron Sir Thomas Kitson of Hengrave (Suff.).[46]

The Civil War

Growing religious differences between opponents and followers of Archbishop Laud fuelled factionalism in borough government and may have led to the arrest and trial of John Bastwick, later a leading parliamentarian writer, in 1634.[47] Most borough officers in the 1630s favoured a presbyterian or independent form of church government, but Robert Buxton, mayor 1636–7 and 1645–6, supported Laud's reforms and may have had links with the court through his trade in candied eryngo.[48] In January 1642 the town petitioned parliament against bishops, chancellors, and archdeacons and their ceremonies, as well as against 'idle, double-faced, scandalous, and ignorant ministers', probably a reference to the hated Thomas Newcomen, Laudian rector of Holy Trinity church.[49] The town defended itself in the courts against the extension of the forest bounds in the 1630s.[50] It seems to have paid the £400 assessed for ship money in 1635 and 1636 although both payments, like others from the county, were late, but in 1638 it refused to pay, and in 1639 petitioned for a reduction in its assessment.[51]

The first violence, in June 1640, was directed against the recusant Anne, wife of Sir Henry Audley of Berechurch, and its underlying cause may have been as much the distress resulting from a decline in the cloth industry and resentment against the billeting of soldiers in the town as fear of papist plots. When two strange Irishmen appeared in the town at the end of May the rumour spread that Lady Audley, or her fellow recusant Bestney Barker at Monkwick, was gathering armed papists, apparently led by the archbishop of Canterbury and the bishop of Ely, and even that the queen's mother, Marie de Medici, was expected there. A group of apprentices and other young men led by a drum marched from the town to the Hythe intending to go to Berechurch and Monkwick, but most were stopped by the borough constables before they reached either house.[52] The following year a papist's house in the town was searched for weapons and for letters from Ireland.[53]

Violence in 1642 was directed against the Lucas family at St. John's Abbey. They and the burgesses had been in dispute throughout the 1630s over the inclosure of common lands and over the damage caused by the pipes of the town waterworks.[54] Sir John Lucas's entertainment of Marie de Medici on her way from Harwich to London in 1638 may also have been unpopular.[55] Early in 1640 there was a further dispute, over the activities of saltpetremen who, Sir John alleged, had done considerable damage to St. John's Abbey but had not even visited other houses in the town.[56] In 1641 Sir John infringed the borough liberties by prosecuting those involved in an inclosure riot at Rovers Tye in the House of Lords instead of in the borough court.[57] In June 1642 he seems to have been suspected of stockpiling

[46] D. Brown, *Wilbye*, 9, 53; *Complete Peerage*, xi. 26.

[47] F. M. Condick, 'Life and Works of Dr. John Bastwick' (Lond. Univ. Ph.D. thesis, 1982), 61–79; below, this chapter, Boro. Govt.; Religious Life.

[48] *Colch. Hist. Studies*, ed. D. Stephenson, 6.

[49] *C.J.* ii. 387; *Petition of Inhabitants of Colch. to Parl.* (1642): copy in E.R.O.

[50] E.R.O., D/B 5 Gb3, ff. 164v., 167, 194.

[51] Ibid. f. 200; *Cal. S.P. Dom.* 1635–6, 435; 1637, 532; 1637– 8, 419; Morant, *Colch.* 54.

[52] E.R.O., D/B 5 Sb2/7, ff. 277v.–278; P.R.O., SP 16/458/12, 13; *Rebellion, Popular Protest, and the Social Order in Early Modern Eng.* ed. Slack, 131–2.

[53] *Jnl. of Sir Simonds D'Ewes*, ed. W. H. Coates, 125.

[54] Below, Commons; Public Services.

[55] E.R.O., D/B 5 Gb3, f. 187; *Exact Catalogue of Essex Malignants* (1648): copy in E.C.L. Colch.

[56] P.R.O., SP 16/449, no. 25; SP 16/451, no. 25.

[57] Hist. MSS. Com. 3, *4th Rep. H. L.* p. 86; *L.J.* iv. 307; *Jnl. of Peasant Studies*, ii. 133–58.

arms and ammunition.[58] When, at the end of August, his plans to join Charles I became known, a drum was beaten and a crowd said to be several thousand strong assembled and broke into St. John's Abbey, where they seized arms and armour as well as household goods. They went on to attack the Lucas tombs in St. Giles's church. Sir John and his family and Thomas Newcomen, who had been going to accompany Sir John, were taken and imprisoned in the moot hall. Lucas and Newcomen were removed safely to London only by the intervention of two M.P.s, Sir Thomas Barrington and Harbottle Grimston.[59] The crowd went on to attack Sir Henry Audley's house at Berechurch and then that of Countess Rivers at St. Osyth before moving further afield.[60]

In August 1642 the county committee thanked Colchester for its zeal in raising money and plate and in offering horses for the army.[61] By October that year the trained band under John Langley was at Brentwood on its way to London, and the town was being asked for £285 10*s.* to pay its troops, as well as for horses for dragoons. The money was still unpaid in November, and the soldiers were becoming discontented.[62] That month Harbottle Grimston urged the mayor to fortify the town against an expected royalist attack, and Henry Barrington was given command of the town's ordnance.[63] Early in 1643 Colchester sent a company of troops to Cambridge, but in March it was 54 men short and its pay in arrears.[64] Requests for men and money were repeated in July and September, by which time the company was only 20 men short.[65] In October the borough tried unsuccessfully to have the trained band recalled to defend Colchester from the enemy or from its own 'unruly multitude'.[66] In December the band was still short 33 properly equipped men, and three months' assessment was unpaid.[67] Almost all the leading burgesses subscribed to the earl of Essex's army in June 1643.[68]

A Colchester committee for the sequestration of delinquents, composed of the mayor, the recorder Harbottle Grimston, and alderman Henry Barrington, was set up in March 1643, and a similar, although slightly larger, committee for the defence of the Eastern Association in September that year.[69] In July that year representatives of the county gentry and some inhabitants of Colchester petitioned parliament for the appointment of an M.P. as governor of the town.[70]

In 1642 or 1643 Grimston's relations with the town deteriorated as many leading burgesses moved away from the presbyterianism he supported towards more extreme forms of protestantism. There may also have been rumours that he had been profiteering at a time when the townsmen were suffering from the collapse of the cloth trade. Grimston alleged he was 'traduced and libelled', not only by the poor but also by many of the better sort.[71] Some opposition to parliament seems to have appeared in 1643, when the county committee complained of the slow collection of rates, and a man at the Hythe grumbled that parliament would not listen to the king.[72] In June the mayor was warned to take care to prevent disorders and riots at the coming midsummer fair.[73] In 1644 Colchester failed to

58 *C.J.* ii. 615.
59 Hist. MSS. Com. 9, *10th Rep. App. VI, Bray*, pp. 146–7; *Mercurius Rusticus or the Countries Complaint* (1723), 1–6; *C.J.* ii. 732, 736, 882.
60 *Mercurius Rusticus*, 13–15, 37; *Cal. S.P. Dom.* 1641–3, 377; E.R.O., D/B 5 Sb2/7, ff. 300v.–303; *V.C.H. Essex*, ii. 231.
61 B.L. Stowe MS. 189, f. 5.
62 E.R.O., D/Y 2/8, pp. 39, 173, 177–8; Morant, *Colch.* 55.
63 E.R.O., D/Y 2/8, pp. 44–5; D/B 5 Gb3, f. 232v.
64 Ibid. D/Y 2/7, p. 299; D/Y 2/9, pp. 81, 83, 87.
65 Ibid. D/Y 2/8, p. 59; D/Y 2/9, pp. 107, 111, 115.
66 B.L. Egerton MS. 2647, f. 361; ibid. Stowe MS. 189, f. 19.
67 E.R.O., D/Y 2/9, p. 123.
68 Ibid. D/Y 2/2, pp. 219–35; *Colch. Hist. Studies*, ed. Stephenson, 5, 13.
69 *Acts and Ordinances of the Interregnum*, ed. C. H. Firth and R. S. Rait, i. 112, 292–3.
70 *C.J.* iii. 184.
71 E.R.O., D/Y 2/8, p. 67; A. Fletcher, *Outbreak of Eng. Civil War*, 294.
72 B.L. Stowe MS. 189, f. 12; E.R.O., D/Y 2/8, p. 158.
73 *L.J.* vi. 102.

impress enough soldiers for the earl of Manchester's army, and the same year the borough petitioned parliament for relief from its heavy weekly assessment.[74] The petition seems to have had little effect, for in 1645 the total collected rose from £4,406 to £6,280. In all, between the start of the civil war in 1642 and Michaelmas 1648 the town contributed £30,177.[75] In addition, voluntary collections were made, such as those for shoes for the earl of Essex's soldiers in 1644 and for the garrison of Gloucester in 1645.[76]

A parliamentarian writer accused Robert Harmer, town lecturer 1640–8, of stirring up the people against the 'heretics and schismatics' of the army, and the townsmen of abusing the soldiers quartered on them.[77] In January 1648 some townsmen did refuse to accept soldiers billeted on them.[78] After a 'riotous and tumultuous' assembly on 30 April 1648 the trained band was called out to keep the peace on May Day. Two days later the county band had to be ordered to suppress the 'tumult' in the town, which parliament no doubt feared was related to similar risings in Suffolk, notably at Bury St. Edmunds.[79] Shortly afterwards a disgruntled townsman expressed the hope that now the troopers were gone he would have some of the best beer, and even 'a day to plunder the roundheads and the Independents'.[80]

The election of the moderate John Shaw as mayor in September 1647 suggests that opinion, at least among the free burgesses, was swinging against the army, and Shaw's removal by the army presumably added to its unpopularity. When a royalist force of *c.* 5,600 under George Goring, earl of Norwich, commonly known as Lord Goring, approached the town on 12 June 1648 the gates were shut against them, but were opened after a brief skirmish. The royalists, whose officers included Sir Charles Lucas, younger brother of Sir John, seem to have been searching for supplies and men and intended to stay in Colchester only a few days.[81] On 13 June, however, a pursuing parliamentarian force under Thomas Fairfax, Lord Fairfax, reached Colchester, and having failed to defeat the royalists in a skirmish around Head gate settled down to besiege the town.

The siege lasted until 28 August and caused serious physical damage to the town and temporary disruption to its trade.[82] The town was unprepared, and although at first the royalists managed to bring in food and ammunition from the Hythe and from the countryside north-east of the town, the completion of encircling siege works in mid July cut them off from further supplies. In the almost nightly sallies and skirmishes in June and early July both sides burnt or pulled down houses outside the wall. Grimston's house at Crutched Friars was at first occupied by the royalists but taken by the besiegers at the end of June. St. John's Abbey was held by the royalists until it was successfully stormed in mid July; having plundered the house the parliamentarian troops broke into the Lucas family vault in St. Giles's church and dismembered the bodies there.[83] The burgesses' request to Fairfax

74 B.L. Stowe MS. 189, f. 25; E.R.O., D/B 5 Gb3, f. 245v.

75 Morant, *Colch.* 56.

76 E.R.O., D/B 5 Gb3, ff. 246, 253v.

77 *True Relation of the Taking of Colch.* (1648): copy in E.C.L. Colch.

78 B.L. Stowe MS. 842, ff. 10–12.

79 Ibid. f. 14; *C.J.* v. 550; *Diary of Ralph Josselin*, ed. A. Macfarlane, 124; *V.C.H. Suff.* ii. 192.

80 E.R.O., D/B 5 Sb2/9, f. 17.

81 Matthew Carter, *True Relation of the Expedition of Kent, Essex, and Colch. 1648*, 59; *Exact Narrative of Every Day's Proceedings since the Insurrection in Essex*, 4–5: copy in E.C.L. Colch.; J. Rushworth, *Hist. Colln.* ii. 1160; *Diary of Ralph Josselin*, 128; *Colchester's Tears* (1648), 12–13; B. P. Lyndon, 'Second Civil War in Essex' (TS. in E.R.O.), 2–3; cf. Hist. MSS. Com. 27, *12th Rep. IX, Beaufort*, pp. 22–3; Hist. MSS. Com. 17, *14th Rep. App. IX*, pp. 281–2; *Colch. Hist. Studies*, 8.

82 Morant, *Colch.* 58–69; Carter, *True Relation*, 59–94; Hist. MSS. Com. 17, *14th Rep. App. IX*, 281–90; *Diary and Plan of Siege of Colch.*: copy in E.C.L. Colch.; Lyndon, 'Second Civil War in Essex', 1– 297.

83 *Last News from Colch.* (1648); *Great and Bloody Fight at Colch.* (1648); *Letter to Wm. Lenthall of Late Fight at Colch.* (1648): copies in E.C.L. Colch.; Carter, *True Relation of the Expedition*, 71; Hist. MSS. Com. 27, *12th Rep. IX, Beaufort*, p. 28.

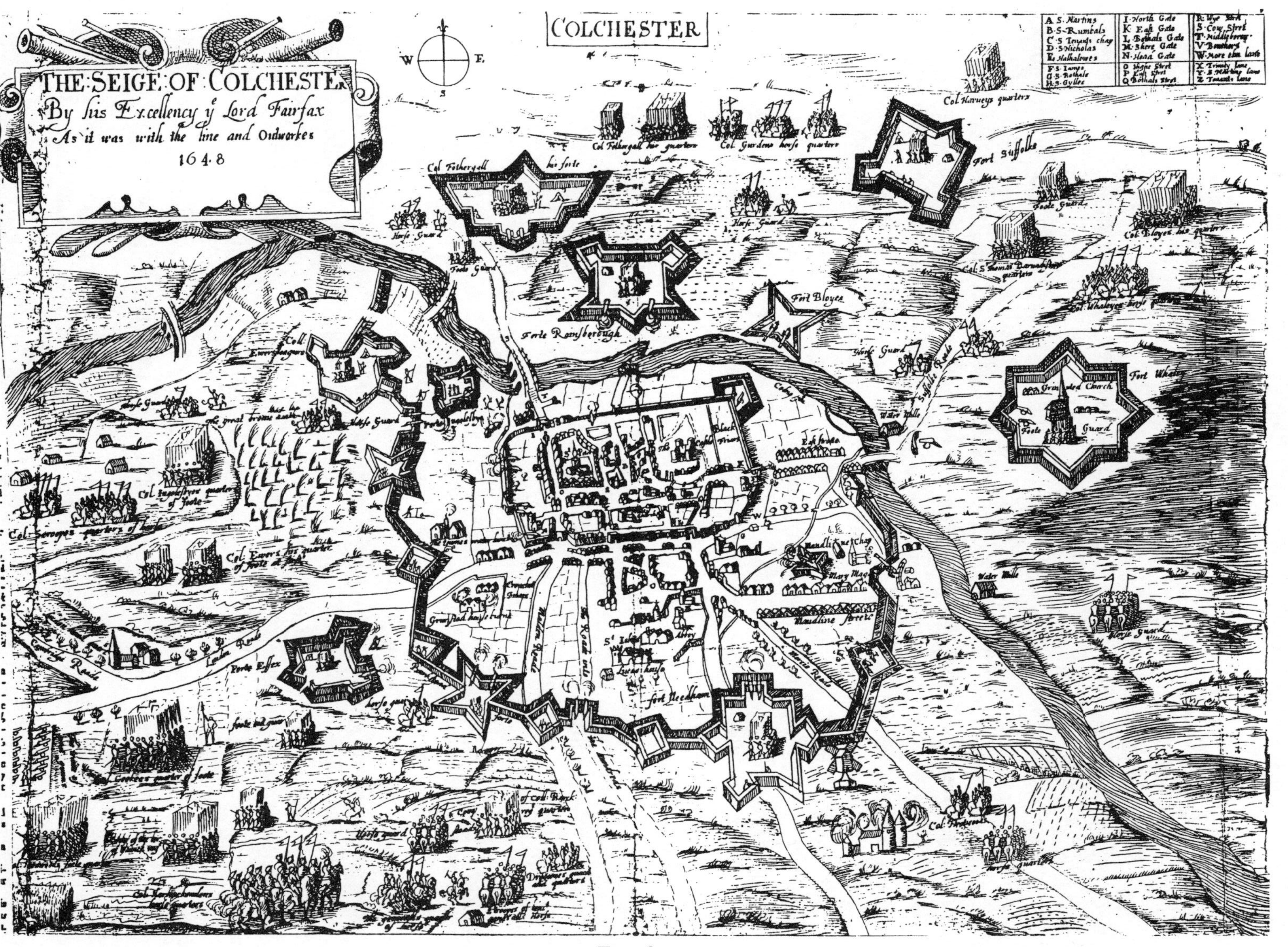
THE SEIGE OF COLCHESTER
By his Excellency ye Lord Fairfax
As it was with the line and Outworkes
1648
COLCHESTER
W
E
S
Fort Bloyes
Fort Suffolke
Fort Whaley
Forte Essex
Col Harveys quarters
Horse Guard
Foote Guard

FIG. 8

early in the siege that they might continue exporting bays was not surprisingly refused, as was their request on 7 August that non-combatants be allowed to leave the town. Both sides were accused of plundering and even killing townspeople, and the townspeople, particularly the poorer ones, suffered severely as the town was starved into submission. By the end of July the besieged were reduced to eating horsemeat, and by the end of the siege dogs and cats had also been consumed. The poor diet and the lack of water after the besiegers had cut the town's water-pipes at the end of July, caused 'fluxes' from which some townsmen died.[84]

Sir Charles Lucas, who was blamed by the parliamentarians for bringing the royalist army to Colchester,[85] had apparently expected to be able to recruit from among the impoverished weavers there.[86] He and Goring may have expected some support from the borough assembly, and after the siege several borough officers, including three aldermen, suspected of royalist sympathies were removed. One of them, Robert Buxton, with 'one Leomans', probably Henry Leming, allegedly encouraged Goring to hold out in the early days of the siege.[87] On the other hand, a royalist officer recorded that during the siege the townspeople, their 'inveterate enemies', were always ready to help foment mutiny among the soldiers and that the mayor, William Cooke, refused to co-operate with Goring in the distribution of bread.[88] On 27 August the historian John Rushworth reported from Fairfax's camp that negotiations were going on both with the royalist delegation and with 'many of our people in town'.[89] Of those sequestered or fined after the siege only Henry Leming was from Colchester.[90] Parliament, however, blamed the townspeople for the siege. Fairfax, in refusing permission for the baymakers to carry on their trade, said they should have considered their trade before they let the royalists into the town,[91] and the committee of both houses, writing on 27 July 1648 to Yarmouth which was threatened by the royalist fleet, pointed out that Colchester was suffering grievously for being 'very forward to invite and receive the enemy'.[92]

On 27 August the royalists agreed to Fairfax's stern conditions for surrender. All soldiers and officers below the rank of captain were to have fair quarter; captains and above were to surrender at mercy. On Fairfax's orders Sir Charles Lucas and Sir George Lisle were executed at once, outside the castle, an unprecedented action taken to satisfy 'military justice' and to avenge the innocent blood which they had caused to be spilt.[93] Fairfax also imposed a fine of £12,000, £2,000 of which was later returned for the poor, on the town. Half the fine was paid by the Dutch congregation. Of the rest, £3,293 was collected in Head ward and North ward, no fewer than 17 individuals contributing £100 or more, and the remainder was presumably paid by South and East wards. Such contributions were exacted from those who had already suffered considerable losses; in 1654 a total of 19 inhabitants claimed to have lost almost £7,000 between them during the siege.[94]

The town remained suspect, and in October the mayor was warned of the many 'disaffected persons' who with others lately in arms had 'dangerous designs' in

[84] *True Relation of the Taking of Colch.* (1648); Rushworth, *Hist. Colln.* ii. 1242.

[85] *True Relation of the Taking of Colch.* (1648).

[86] Carter, *True Relation of the Expedition*, 59.

[87] *To Wm. Lenthall, Speaker of the Ho. of Commons* (1648), 4: copy in E.C.L. Colch.; *Colch. Hist. Studies*, 9; below, this chapter, Boro. Govt.

[88] Carter, *True Relation of the Expedition*, 67, 78.

[89] Bodl. MS. Tanner 57/1, f. 247.

[90] *Cal. Cttee. for Advance of Money*, 944, 1140.

[91] Hist. MSS. Com. 38, *14th Rep. App. IX, Round*, p. 285.

[92] *Cal. S.P. Dom.* 1648–9, 219.

[93] *Letter from Ld. Fairfax concerning Surrender of Colch.* (1648); *True Relation of the Taking of Colch.* (1648): copies in E.C.L. Colch.

[94] *Cal. Cttee. for Compounding*, 134, 141; *Reg. Dutch Ch. in Colch.* (Huguenot Soc. xii), 136; E.R.O., D/Y 2/2, pp. 243, 319; *E.J.* xviii. 39–47; P.R.O., SP 23/155, nos. 601–3; Morant, *Colch.* 73.

hand.[95] One man was accused in 1649 of saying that he wished all the roundheads were hanged, and the following year two Colchester men thought Cromwell a rogue.[96] There were fears in 1651 that royalists would seize Colchester for Charles II, then in Scotland. A drummer who spread prophecies of the overthrow of Cromwell may have reflected the mood of some poorer townsmen. A garrison of 300 men from the county trained bands was placed in the town, and after an initial delay the defences built during the earlier civil war and siege were destroyed.[97] During the early 1650s a party opposed to Henry Barrington and the 'Cromwellians' gained the upper hand in borough government, leading to a purge of the corporation in 1655.[98] Four Colchester men were arrested in connexion with the abortive 'Salisbury insurrection' of 1655. One of them, 'Capt. Barker', may have been Robert Barker of Monkwick.[99] Troops were quartered in the town in 1656 and 1657, and there was 'great talk of Cavalier attempts again',[1] but in June 1659 the town offered to raise a troop of horse for parliament.[2]

ECONOMIC HISTORY

The Early 16th-Century Economy

In the early 16th century Colchester ranked ninth among English provincial towns in terms of taxable wealth and seventh in terms of size of taxable population.[3] It had fared well compared to many other towns in the later Middle Ages; its high position in the urban rankings testifies to the vigour of its growth after the Black Death of 1348–9, as well as to its relatively gentle later decline. The town's early 16th-century economy exhibited a diversity typical of developed early modern towns which served as manufacturing centres and markets both for their immediate areas and for a wider hinterland, and also performed administrative functions. Most large towns also possessed an economic specialism, and Colchester's economy depended heavily upon its cloth industry, allied to its role as a port.

Diversity and specialization are both revealed in the town's occupational structure (Tables I and II). The number and range of occupations, *c.* 56 in the earlier 16th century and 102 in the 17th, mark Colchester off from the smaller towns of Essex. Its important market, held three times weekly, and its three annual fairs brought outsiders to the town and encouraged the growth of service industries, and the port attracted mariners and other transport workers. Nevertheless, as many as 47 per cent of the sample for the period 1500–79 were manufacturers, and the dominant group among them were producers of woollen cloth.

The fundamental importance of cloth production and trade to the town in the early 16th century is even more apparent from the distribution of wealth in 1524 and 1525,[4] when the occupations of 252 of the 996 individuals included in either of the two subsidy assessments are known.[5] Of the seven men with taxable wealth of £100 or more, four were clothiers, one was a merchant and clothier, one a merchant, and the other, John Christmas, had made his wealth in cloth and trade. Of those assessed at between £40 and £99, 11 were clothiers or merchants, 2 were

95 *Cal. S.P. Dom.* 1648–9, 307–8.
96 E.R.O., D/B 5 Sb2/9, ff. 26v., 39.
97 Ibid. f. 57; *Cal. S.P. Dom.* 1651, 90, 108, 185, 281.
98 Below, this chapter, Boro. Govt.
99 *Cal. S.P. Dom.* 1655, 367–8; *V.C.H. Essex*, ii. 239; below, Outlying Parts (W. Donyland, Manors).
1 *Cal. S.P. Dom.* 1656–7, 171; 1658–9, 123; *Diary of Ralph Josselin*, 381.
2 *C.J.* vii. 698.
3 Goose, 'Econ. and Social Aspects', Tables 1.1 and 1.2, pp. 35, 37.
4 P.R.O., E 179/108/147, 162, 169.
5 Occupations identified mainly from wills and borough court rolls.

TABLE I: COLCHESTER OCCUPATIONAL STRUCTURE

	1500–79		*1580–1619*		*1620–59*		*1660–99*	
	no.	*per cent*	*no.*	*per cent*	*no.*	*per cent*	*no.*	*per cent*
Textiles	65	26.5	104	26.4	194	37.1	82	40.0
Clothing	21	8.6	49	12.4	37	7.1	48	6.8
Leather (raw)	3	1.2	5	1.3	6	1.1	8	1.1
Household	30	12.2	24	6.1	38	7.3	53	7.5
Tools and Arms	5	2.0	1	0.3	12	2.3	27	3.8
Housing	9	3.7	18	4.6	9	1.7	38	5.4
Food and Drink	29	11.8	52	13.2	60	11.5	81	11.5
Transport	28	11.4	45	11.4	42	8.0	45	6.4
Service	19	7.8	27	6.9	22	4.2	19	2.7
Education	–	–	2	0.5	1	0.2	5	0.7
Medicine	2	0.8	6	1.5	8	1.5	22	3.1
Miscellaneous	34	13.9	61	15.5	94	18.0	77	10.9
	245	99.9	394	100.1	523	100.0	705	99.9

Sources: Wills proved in Prerogative, Consistory, and Archdeaconry Courts in P.R.O. and E.R.O. 1500–1699.

TABLE II: LEADING OCCUPATIONS IN COLCHESTER

1500–79		*1580–1619*		*1620–59*		*1660–99*	
1	Clothier	1	Clothier	1	Baymaker	1	Weaver
2	Mariner	2	Mariner	2	Weaver	2	Baymaker
3	Weaver	3	Weaver	3	Mariner	3	Mariner
4	Smith	4	Baymaker	4	Merchant	4	Shoemaker
5	Tailor	5	Shoemaker	5	Shoemaker	5	Carpenter
6	Butcher	6	Tailor	6	Tailor	6	Woolcomber
7=	Mercer	7=	Draper	7=	Brewer	7	Grocer
	Shearman		Merchant		Draper	8=	Draper
9=	Brewer	9	Baker	9	Miller		Merchant
	Carpenter	10=	Butcher	10=	Baker	10	Tailor
11=	Merchant		Brewer		Clothier	11=	Cardmaker
	Miller	12	Carpenter	12=	Grocer		Maltster
					Innholder		Miller
							Webster

Note: Baymaker includes saymaker; smith includes blacksmith; weaver includes weavers of all types of cloth; draper includes woollendraper and linendraper; mariner includes shipsmaster and sailor.

Sources: Wills proved in Prerogative, Consistory, and Archdeaconry Courts in P.R.O. and E.R.O. 1500–1699.

simply gentlemen and the others a tallow chandler, a brewer, and a yeoman. The lists are dominated by the wealth of John Christmas, assessed initially at £1,000 in movable goods, then at £600, and finally at £400. He was the son of the merchant and bailiff Thomas Christmas, who at his death in 1520 owned lands and houses in St. Runwald's, St. Botolph's, St. Mary's-at-the-Walls, St. Leonard's, St. Martin's, and Holy Trinity parishes, and in Mile End, Greenstead, Lexden, and Old Heath. He also held manors in Bradwell-on-Sea, Beaumont cum Moze, and the unidentified 'Downwell', besides land in Birch,

Copford, Clacton, Kirby-le-Soken, Mundon, Thorpe-le-Soken, and South Hanningfield, and Newbridge mill in West Bergholt. He bequeathed 200 marks cash and 100 marks in plate to his wife Joan and a further 200 marks cash to his daughters. The recorder Thomas Bonham, the town clerk Thomas Audley, Sir John Rainsford, and the abbot of St. John's were supervisors of his will. His bequests to his shearmen, fullers, weavers, and 'ginners' indicate the origins of his wealth, which testifies to the profits that could be made from cloth production and trade in Colchester, even in a relatively stagnant economy.[6]

Readjustment and Recovery, 1500–1570

The period has been seen either as one of continuing economic decline for English provincial towns or as one of readjustment and recovery from the late medieval depression, and the evidence from Colchester tends to support the latter view.[7] There, as in many towns, the fortunes of the cloth industry were crucial. Contemporary comment,[8] government legislation,[9] and case studies of Norwich, Coventry, and York,[10] all testify to the migration of textile production from town to countryside in the early 16th century, suggesting that the expanding national cloth production of those years was based on rural areas rather than towns. Occupational data from wills indicate that the Colchester industry may have been in decline: the proportion of the occupied male testators engaged in cloth production fell from almost 30 per cent in the period 1500–39 to 18 per cent in the period 1540–79.[11] Furthermore, of the 101 burgesses admitted to the freedom between 1550 and 1570 for whom an occupation is recorded only 16 were textile workers.[12]

As early as 1528 the Colchester clothmaker John Boswell the younger reported difficulty in selling his cloths in Colchester Hall in Blackwell Hall cloth market, London, but his complaint may have been special pleading to extend his credit with his wool suppliers.[13] The difficulties of the mid-century slump in the English cloth industry[14] are evident in Colchester not only in an increasing concern with poverty and unemployment,[15] but also in the charges of sedition levelled at malcontented clothworkers in 1566. One of three weavers indicted had declared 'we can get no work nor we have no money... Then will up two or three thousand in Colchester and about Colchester', while another had complained that 'weavers' occupation is a dead science nowadays and it will never be better before we make a rising'.[16]

In 1515 there were arrears of almost £10 on the duke of Norfolk's rent roll of £25 4*s.* 5*d.* in the borough.[17] The town was included among those in need of 're-edification' by the statute of 1540, but that and lists of houses destroyed or in need of repair in Head ward and among the possessions of St. John's abbey may indicate long-term decay and may indeed be preludes to a concerted renewal.[18] A

[6] P.R.O., PROB 11/19, ff. 28 sqq.

[7] *Towns in Societies*, ed. P. Abrams and E. A. Wrigley, 159–69; *Urban Hist. Yrbk.* (1978), 60–72; *Econ. H.R.* 2nd ser. xxxix. 182–4.

[8] *Tudor Econ. Doc.* ed. R. H. Tawney and E. Power, iii. 117–18; *Discourse of Commonweal of Realm of Eng.* ed. M. Dewar, 76–7, 91.

[9] 25 Hen. VIII, c. 18; 1 Mary Stat. III, c. 7; 2 & 3 Ph. & Mary, c. 11; 4 & 5 Ph. & Mary, c. 5.

[10] *Towns in Societies*, 178–9; *Past and Present*, xl. 61; W. R. D. Jones, *Mid-Tudor Crisis 1539–1563*, 122–3; *Past and Present*, xxxiv. 49–69; C. Phythian-Adams, *Desolation of a City*, 31–67; D. Palliser, *Tudor York*, 162, 201, 208–10.

[11] Sources cited for Tables I and II.

[12] Burgess admissions extracted from E.R.O., D/B 5 Cr117–134.

[13] *L. & P. Hen. VIII*, iv (2), p. 1831.

[14] *Econ. H.R.* 1st ser. x. 153, 160; G. D. Ramsay, *Eng. Overseas Trade During the Centuries of Emergence*, 22; J. D. Gould, *Great Debasement: Currency and the Economy in mid-Tudor Eng.* 140–1.

[15] Below, this chapter, Soc. Structure (Early 16th century).

[16] *Cal. Assize Rec. Essex, Eliz. I*, p. 51; F. G. Emmison, *Elizabethan Life: Disorder*, 62–4.

[17] B.L. Add. Ch. 215.

[18] 32 Hen. VIII, c. 18; E.R.O., D/Y 2/2, p. 13; P.R.O., E 310/13/40; *Urban Hist. Yearbk.* (1978), 63; below, this chapter, Topography (Town to 1640).

much longer list of the abbey's lands in 1539 gives no suggestion of general decay.[19] The occasional record of decay in the chamberlain's account for 1548–9 is offset by more frequent references to new buildings, and many more townsmen were assessed for subsidy on land and houses in 1547 than in 1524–5.[20] In 1550 the corporation thought it worthwhile to invest £284 5*s.* in buying former chantry lands and houses in Colchester and the surrounding parishes.[21] Monastic or chantry lands changed hands time and again in later 16th-century Colchester, providing a significant stimulus to the land market, and John Lucas's acquisition of St. John's Abbey provided the townsmen with the custom of a substantial landed seat to replace that lost by the demise of the monastery.[22]

Returns of Colchester's overseas and inland trade in the earlier 16th century were included under those for the headport of Ipswich. If the Ipswich figures reflect Colchester's experience, the later 15th and early 16th centuries witnessed expansion rather than decline, and the town may have escaped the recession that affected so many provincial ports between the 1520s and 1550s as trade became increasingly concentrated upon London.[23] It is also possible that the growth of coastal traffic benefited Colchester as it did other east coast ports in the earlier 16th century; a predominantly coastal trade may explain the small average tonnage of the 23 vessels belonging to the town in 1550.[24] The annual farm of tolls and profits of the Hythe, which may have fallen from £29 in 1501–2 to £24 in 1504–5 and then rose only to £28 in 1521–2, the sum still paid in 1548–9, is not necessarily a reliable index.[25] There were difficulties with the Colne channel, which in 1536 had reportedly been 'much filled' with silt for 10 or 12 years past. A voluntary collection for its repair failed to raise a sufficient sum, and in 1549 a rate was levied on the borough which, with other contributions, yielded £290 for repairs.[26]

Ordinances enacted in the 1560s provide indirect evidence of the level of internal trade. Between 1562 and 1565 the corporation showed considerable concern with the regulation of marketing in general and that of 'foreigners' or non-freemen in particular.[27] Careful licensing of chandlers was introduced to ensure adequate provisions and fair prices. Detailed charges were imposed upon all 'foreigners' buying hides and skins in Colchester market, while every tanner was enjoined to bring as much tanned leather into the market as he took hides and skins out. The two wardens of the butchers continued to be sworn annually, one chosen by the butchers and the other by the bailiffs and aldermen. No 'foreign' butcher was to sell meat in the market after 2 p.m. between All Saints' and Shrove Tuesday, and after 3 p.m. between Easter and All Saints'. Only butchers living in the town and those who had served a seven-year apprenticeship might be admitted free, but a butcher's widow might carry on his trade. Other regulations were designed to ensure adequate quality and supply of meat. New regulations were enacted for the fishery in 1567 when there were said to be twice the customary number of oyster dredgers.[28] Only those licensed by the bailiffs were to dredge for oysters, on pain

[19] P.R.O., SC 6/Hen. VIII/976.

[20] B.L. Stowe MS. 829, ff. 12–40; below, this chapter, Soc. Structure (Early 16th century).

[21] E.R.O., Boro. Mun. Acc. C1: Misc. Deeds, item 2; *Cal. Pat.* 1549–51, 420–1.

[22] *Cal. Pat.* 1547–8, 204, 252–7; 1548–9, 86; below, Religious Houses.

[23] D. Burwash, *Eng. Merchant Shipping 1460–1540*, 145–64 and App. II, Tables of Group IV; E. M. Carus-Wilson and O. Coleman, *Eng.'s Export Trade 1275–1547*, 71–4, 114–19; R. Davis, *Eng. Overseas Trade 1500–1700*, Table 1, 52.

[24] *Econ. H.R.* 2nd ser. xiii. 338–9.

[25] Britnell, *Growth and Decline*, 278; Bodl. MS. Rolls Essex 2; B.L. Stowe MS. 829, f. 14.

[26] E.R.O., D/B 5 R2, loose fol.; B.L. Stowe MS. 829, ff. 26 and v., 55 and v.

[27] E.R.O., D/B 5 R5, ff. 91v.–92v., 93v., 102–104v.

[28] Ibid. ff. 111–12.

of 40*s*. fine, while all oysters, mackerel, and other fish were to be sold in the market at the Hythe, unless bought by householders for their own consumption.

A more general attempt to regulate economic activity was made in 1562, when the town was said to be very much decayed by immigrants intent on 'their own singular lucre', whose activities brought into contempt the authority of the corporation. The main problem was those non-freemen who kept open shops and warehouses in Colchester and thus profited from the town without contributing to it. No 'foreign' retailer or artisan was to live in the borough unless he first compounded with the bailiffs and aldermen for his freedom or for his foreign fine, on pain of 40*s*. No 'foreigner' was to buy any corn, grain, salt, coal, herring, fish, merchandise, or anything else from any other 'foreigner', on pain of forfeiture. No goods were to be 'foreign bought and sold' without payment of appropriate fines, while inhabitants were required to sue only in the borough courts unless granted special licence to sue elsewhere.[29] Taken together the ordinances represent a concerted attempt by the corporation to keep control over economic activity in the town, to protect the interests of the inhabitants, particularly of the freemen, against a perceived threat from the activities of outsiders. In 1565 regulations for taking up the freedom by birth were tightened.[30]

Had the town still been in economic decline there would have been little need to protect the burgesses from competition, and further proof of the borough's attraction to traders is provided by the limits and bounds of St. Dennis's or the Pardon Fair set out in 1562. On the south side of High Street stood fletchers, bowyers, saddlers, collarmakers, ropers, glovers, smiths, haberdashers, hollandshiremen, grocers, linendrapers, and mercers, their stalls extending from East gate to St. Runwald's church. On the north side of the road were the fishmongers and salters, then the shoemakers whose stalls extended up to the butchers' shambles. 'Foreign' linendrapers were set apart, and next to them were the pewterers, brasiers, and tinkers, town dwellers or 'foreign', followed by the tanners and soapers, who stood near St. Runwald's church. Beyond them, towards the cornmarket, stood nailmen, ironmongers, 'Ipswich men being coverlet men', foreign woollendrapers and hosiers, turners, basketmakers, 'bowlmen', and traders in butter, cheese, and corn. The goldsmiths also had an appropriate, but unspecified, location. The injunction that stalls were only to line the streets and not to be placed crossways or alongside each other implies competition for space, a bustling hive of activity for the eight days of the fair.[31] It may well be that in mid 16th-century Colchester, as in Norwich, increasing internal trade and manufacture for home consumption compensated for a depressed textile industry.[32]

The number of burgesses admitted to the town supports that interpretation. The total admitted each decade by purchase remained roughly stable during the earlier 16th century, at a level comparable to that of the later 15th.[33] That it was still proving difficult to attract migrants is perhaps suggested by the frequent concession of 3*s*. 4*d*. of the standard 23*s*. 4*d*. fine early in the century, until a sum of 20*s*. became the norm in the 1530s.[34] Evidence of the desire to attract inhabitants of the right calibre is provided by the agreement to reduce the fine payable by John Neve, clothmaker, of Stowmarket in 1516, from 20*s*. to 10*s*. provided he remained in

29 Ibid. ff. 90v.–91v.
30 Ibid. ff. 107v.–108; below, this chapter, Boro. Govt.
31 E.R.O., D/B 5 R5, ff. 89v.–90.
32 *Past and Present*, xxxiv. 49–69.
33 Burgess admissions from E.R.O., D/B 5 Cr83–163; D/B 5 Cb1/2–4; D/B 5 Cb2/2–4. Figures for 15th cent. are in Britnell, *Growth and Decline*, 279–80.
34 E.R.O., D/B 5 Cr82–109.

Colchester for at least five years. Remain he did, immediately becoming a common councillor, later an alderman, and eventually bailiff four times before his death in 1542.[35] He was among the wealthiest townsmen in the 1520s, being assessed for subsidy on £40 in goods. By 1542 his wealth had increased substantially, and he left £400 to buy lands and houses worth £20 a year to pay annuities.[36] In the 1550s there was a decisive increase in the numbers purchasing the freedom of the town, to 107 from 59 in the 1540s. If the complaints of the 1560s are to be believed, many more were assuming the freemen's privileges without paying for them. Despite the textile depression a distinct quickening of economic activity is evident in mid 16th-century Colchester, enough to sustain the urban economy through a difficult period for its staple industry and to permit some demographic growth across the second and third quarters of the century.

Growth and Development, 1570–1700

The town's economy grew decisively in the final third of the 16th century, and the key to that growth was the revival of its cloth industry. The lesson of the mid-century crisis in the English cloth export trade was that demand for the traditional heavy woollen product was inelastic, and that it was dangerous to rely so heavily upon one type of cloth,[37] whether exported in its raw state or dyed and dressed as in Colchester. Innovation was widespread, and in Colchester such innovation was inspired by the arrival of Dutch immigrants in the 1560s.[38] Late in 1561 the corporation agreed that the bailiff Benjamin Clere should treat with the Privy Council for the taking in of Dutch refugees, and the first 55 persons in 11 households arrived in 1565.[39] In 1571 there were 185 resident aliens, 431 two years later, and 1,291 by 1586. Only then did the influx slow, a census of 1622 recording 1,535 aliens.[40] The annual average number of baptisms in the Dutch church in the mid 17th century stood at 48,[41] suggesting that the size of the community had stabilized at about 1,500 in a total population of some 10,500–11,000.

The immigrants were granted considerable privileges, most notably control of the Dutch Bay Hall to which all 'new draperies' were taken for inspection and sealing before sale. Despite recurrent disputes with English weavers during the later 16th and early 17th century those privileges were repeatedly upheld.[42] The introduction of the new worsted draperies, particularly bays and says, was the key contribution of the Dutch, for those cloths were relatively light and cheap, and appealed to a wide market in southern as well as northern Europe.[43] The quality control imposed by the Dutch, although limited in 1631 to bays and says, was crucial to the reputation of the Colchester cloth, which was frequently reported to be sold simply upon inspection of its seals. Colchester bays became a byword for quality in the 17th century, and were still known in the early 18th century 'over most of the trading parts of Europe'.[44]

The revival of the Colchester textile industry is evident from the town's

35 Ibid. D/B 5 Cr87, rot. 23; Cr89, rot. 1; Cr96, rot. 1.

36 P.R.O., E 179/108/147; ibid. PROB 11/29, f. 1.

37 *Econ. H.R.* 2nd ser. xxii. 423–5.

38 *Immigrants and Minorities*, i. 261–80.

39 E.R.O., D/B 5 R5, f. 92; Roker, 'Flemish and Dutch in Colch.' 85.

40 P.R.O., SP 12/78, no. 9; SP 12/190, no. 2; SP 14/129, no. 70; E.R.O., D/B 5 R7, ff. 296v.–299.

41 Calculated from *Reg. Dutch Ch. of Colch.* (Huguenot Soc. xii).

42 *Immigrants and Minorities*, i. 266, 269–72.

43 *Econ. H.R.* 2nd ser. xxii. 424; Ramsay, *Eng. Overseas Trade*, 50–4; Davis, *Eng. Overseas Trade*, 20–5; *Univ. Birmingham Hist. Jnl.* vii. 50–1.

44 *Cal. S.P. Dom.* 1619–23, 247; 1635, 266–7; *Acts of P.C.* 1592, 76; 1630–1, 200; Hist. MSS. Com. 2, *3rd Rep.* p. 71; Hist. MSS. Com. 6, *7th Rep. I, H.L.*, p. 131; Hist. MSS. Com. 7, *8th Rep. I, H.L.*, p. 134; D. Defoe, *Tour*, ed. G. D. H. Cole (1927), i. 17.

occupational structure (Tables I and II). In the period 1580–1619 the percentage of the occupied population engaged in cloth production and distribution rose to 26, with baymaker fourth among the town's leading occupations. By the period 1620–59 baymakers had achieved first position, and 37 per cent of the occupied male population was employed in cloth production and sale. That figure rose to 40 per cent later in the century, by which time Continental producers were attempting to emulate the English product.[45] In the period 1660–99, only 2 clothiers, 3 clothworkers, and 3 dyers were found in a sample of 705 occupations, showing that the dominance of the new draperies over the old in Colchester was complete. Occupations of Colchester apprentices enrolled between 1580 and 1630 tell the same story, the proportion involved in textile production rising from little more than a quarter in the 1580s to almost a half in each of the first three decades of the 17th century.[46] In 1629 it was claimed, with typical exaggeration, that 20,000 persons were maintained by bay and say manufacture in Colchester alone, producing 400 bays and as many says each week.[47] In the early 18th century it was suggested that the town returned '£30,000 weekly in ready money for these stuffs'.[48] Celia Fiennes found that 'the whole town is employed in spinning, weaving, washing, drying, and dressing their bays',[49] while Defoe's impression was that 'The town may be said chiefly to subsist by the trade of making bays' and that the whole county was employed, and in part maintained, by spinning wool for the bay trade of Colchester and neighbouring towns.[50]

The industry's progress was not entirely trouble free, particularly in the unstable trading conditions of the 1620s and 1630s.[51] Hostility between England and Spain in the 1620s resulted in the prohibition of exports to that important market, reportedly reducing weekly production of Colchester bays from 400 pieces to 50, and leaving over £6,000 worth unsold in 1629, besides says to a similar value.[52] By 1631 Colchester's poor were petitioning against an abatement of their accustomed wages,[53] and in 1635 the bailiffs and J.P.s, in response to another complaint by the bayweavers, imposed a sliding scale of payment, 10*s.*–12*s.* a bay depending on the current market value of each ell of cloth.[54] Two years later weavers accused a baymaker of paying low wages and forcing them to accept payment in kind,[55] and attempts to cut costs may have led to the abuses in bay manufacture of which London merchants complained in 1635, a year in which exports from Colchester slumped.[56]

Notwithstanding such vicissitudes, the long-term trend in production of new draperies in Colchester was decidedly upward. The officers of the Dutch Bay Hall collected 'rawboots', fines for faulty workmanship by English manufacturers, which from 1636 provide an index of bay production (Table III). The decennial average figure rose steadily until the 1690s when a combination of poor harvests and warfare caused difficulties for English foreign trade in general.[57] The impact of the siege of Colchester of 1648 is clear, as is that of the plague of 1665–6,[58] but the speed

45 E. Kerridge, *Textile Manufactures in Early Modern Eng.* 242.

46 Apprenticeships from E.R.O., D/B 5 Cr142–186; D/B 5 Cb1/2–9; D/B 5 Cb2/3–11; D/B 5 Gb1–3; Goose, 'Econ. and Social Aspects', Table 3.1, p. 94.

47 *17th Cent. Econ. Doc.* ed. J. Thirsk and J. P. Cooper, 224.

48 T. Cox, *Magna Britannia*, i. 707.

49 *Journeys of Celia Fiennes*, ed. C. Morris, 142.

50 Defoe, *Tour*, i. 17.

51 B. Supple, *Commercial Crisis and Change in Eng. 1600–1642*, 52–8, 108–12, 122–4; *Econ. H.R.* 2nd ser. xxii. 239–40; cf. *Univ. Birmingham Hist. Jnl.* vii. 49.

52 *17th Cent. Doc.* 225.

53 *Acts of P.C.* 1630–1, 358–9; *Cal. S.P. Dom.* 1625–49, 430.

54 E.R.O., D/B 5 Cb1/10, f. 84v.

55 P.R.O., PC 2/47, pp. 389–90; *Cal. S.P. Dom.* 1637, 32, 44, 70, 87–9, 115.

56 P.R.O., PC 2/45, pp. 15, 37–8, 312, 435–6; *Cal. S.P. Dom.* 1635, 266–7, 306, 603; *Econ. H.R.* 2nd ser. xxii. 245.

57 Morant, *Colch.* 79; D. C. Coleman, *Econ. of Eng. 1450–1750*, 135.

58 Above, this chapter, Intro.

with which production recovered from each setback and then rose to new heights testifies to the resilience of the industry.

Colchester's economy flourished in other ways from the later 16th century. The thrice-weekly market continued to sell a variety of foodstuffs including 'garden stuff', the Dutch having stimulated the development of horticulture.[59] As a corn market Colchester was unrivalled in the county,[60] and the importance of its grain trade in the 17th century is shown by the appearance of maltsters among its leading

TABLE III: 'RAWBOOTS' FINES FOR ENGLISH BAYS

Year	*£*	*Year*	*£*	*Year*	*£*	*Year*	*£*
1636	33	1652	38	1668	101	1684	233
1637	34	1653	41	1669	115	1685	172
1638	39	1654	61	1670	121	1686	198
1639	39	1655	59	1671	125	1687	200
1640	48	1656	58	1672	120	1688	214
1641	41	1657	55	1673	140	1689	215
1642	25	1658	54	1674	143	1690	188
1643	34	1659	53	1675	139	1691	174
1644	46	1660	83	1676	125	1692	144
1645	53	1661	86	1677	134	1693	128
1646	42	1662	77	1678	139	1694	197
1647	38	1663	94	1679	124	1695	200
1648	36	1664	97	1680	165	1696	183
1649	67	1665	92	1681	188	1697	162
1650	73	1666	31	1682	225	1698	173
1651	49	1667	61	1683	248	1699	174

Source: E.R.O., D/B 5 Gb3–6, *passim*.

tradesmen. Pontage was levied in 1635 on corn, timber, firewood, straw, hay, clay, sand, bricks, tiles, household implements, and wool carried to and from the town by road.[61] Hides, skins, and pelts were particularly important in the town, which possessd its own leather hall.[62] In the later 16th century a new shambles and a new market cross were built, to improve and perhaps enlarge the market.[63] The twice-weekly woolmarket was reorganized in 1592 and 1595 and continued throughout the 17th century. Nevertheless, wool was still sold in inns and private houses, the lessee of the market claiming in 1685 that the aldermen and common councillors were the greatest offenders.[64] In 1624 the meat market was 'of late years much increased', while a succession of complaints against trade in meat and hides after the appointed market hours and outside the market place suggest that private marketing was growing too.[65] The 1693 charter granted a new Tuesday market and a new fair in July; both concentrated on livestock, building upon a long established trade in horses and cattle.[66] Growing numbers of inns, alehouses, and

59 E.R.O., D/B 5 Gb1, 31 July, 29 Nov. 1592; 6 Nov. 1598; D/B 5 Gb3, ff. 4, 38v.–39, 42v.; Gb4, ff. 217, 227; Gb5, f. 264; J. Norden, *Description of Essex*, 14; Cox, *Magna Britannia*, i. 707; W. Cunningham, *Alien Immigrants to Eng.* 177; E. Kerridge, *Agric. Revolution*, 269; Morant, *Colch.* 76; *Agrarian Hist. Eng. and Wales*, v. 503–7.

60 F. Hull, 'Agriculture and Rural Society in Essex 1560–1640' (Lond. Univ. Ph.D. thesis, 1950), 127–8.

61 E.R.O., D/B 5 Gb3, f. 140.

62 E.R.O., D/B 5 R5, f. 92v.; D/B 5 Gb1, 2 Nov. 1579; Gb2, f. 130v.; D/B 5 Aa1/2, 5, 14; D/Y 2/10, f. 128.

63 Ibid. D/B 5 Gb1, 2 June 1595; below, Markets.

64 Ibid. D/B 5 Gb1, 2 June 1595; Gb2, ff. 147v., 185 and v.; Gb4, ff. 54v., 228v.; Gb5, f. 177v.–178v., 238–241v.; Gb6, p. 113.

65 Ibid. D/B 5 Gb1, 2 Nov. 1579; 6 Nov. 1598; Gb3, ff. 38v.–39; Gb4, f. 150; Gb5, ff. 236, 283v.

66 P.R.O., PC 2/75, pp. 120–1; PC 2/77, pp. 376–7; *Colch. Charters*, 174; W. Walker, *Essex Markets and Fairs*, 32.

taverns catered for those attending the markets.[67] The increased overland traffic, transporting cloth to and raw wool from London, was probably chiefly responsible for the worsening roads; in 1616 the highways between Colchester (and other Essex towns) and London were being badly damaged by overloaded wagons.[68] By the later 17th century considerable quantities of raw wool were also brought from inland counties, even though the coastal supplies were becoming increasingly important.[69]

The town's overseas trade tended to follow the fortunes of its cloth industry. Port books suggest an expanding export trade in the late 16th century and the early 17th, based chiefly upon the new draperies.[70] Exports of new draperies increased approximately fourfold in the 17th century, with rapid expansions in the periods 1600–30 and 1670–1700, a slump in the 1630s, and a slow recovery to 1670. Exports of traditional woollen cloths, depressed in the 1590s, mirrored the general recovery of that trade in the early 17th century, only to fall off steadily after 1622.[71]

In 1571–2, apart from cloth, Colchester exported hides, leather and leather goods, coal, beer, wax, rough horns, and 'woadnets' (perhaps 'woadnuts' or balls of woad), all in small quantities.[72] In 1607–8 and 1621–2 cloth was supplemented by coal, beer, salt, aquavitae, sheepskins, iron, wax, mustard seed, peas, hats, deal, stockings, cordage, and old wool-cards, while in 1638–9 exports included hops, starch, ginger, cinnamon, paper, lead, copperas, oil, lime, and haberdashery wares.[73] In the later 17th century the range of commodities narrowed while the quantities of particular items increased. A little coal, some old wool-cards, hops, rapeseed, saffron, peas, some clothing, a ton of 'old iron', and the occasional horse appear, but quantities of dressed calfskins, leather, rye, wheat, and oysters dominated the non-textile export trade. Export of oysters grew remarkably, the annual average for the four years 1679–80 and 1700–1 amounting to 1,140 bu., while in the peak year of 1682 over 4,000 bu. were shipped overseas.[74]

Imports also grew and diversified. In 1571–2, apart from various types of cloth, Colchester imported some Spanish wool and unspun cotton, handles for cards and wire, new wool-cards and combs, teazles, and red and green dyestuffs. Several shipments of salt were received, besides luxuries such as sugar, prunes, raisins, pepper, cloves, and ginger. Household items included French knives and drinking glasses, bottles, brown and white paper, pins, and thread.[75] By 1660–1 a great deal of French and Rhenish wine was imported, as was iron, iron wire, iron vessels, oil, and various household items. Battery, copper wire, stone bottles, cordage, quern stones, rope, fish oil, vinegar, spirits, French salt, Spanish salt, Norway deal, 'timber to make cardboard', Holland cheese, clapboards, prunes, cloves, refined sugar, pickled herrings, wine lees, Osnabruck and broad Hamburg cloth and other manufactured items, foodstuffs, and raw materials came to the town, largely from Rotterdam but also from ports in France and Norway.[76] By 1678–80 Dutch and German cloth was becoming more prominent, until between 1699 and 1701 various types of Dutch and German linen (particularly osnaburgs, duck, holland, and burlaps) and broad and narrow German cloths predominated; there were also

[67] P.R.O., SP 12/116, no. 12; *Cal. Pat.* 1569–72, 14–15; E.R.O., D/B 5 Gb2, ff. 119v.–121v.; below, this chapter, Soc. Structure (Economic and Social Regulation).

[68] *Cal. Assize Rec. Essex, Eliz. I*, p. 167.

[69] *C.J.* xiii. 570, 720; K. H. Burley, 'Econ. Development of Essex in later 17th and early 18th cents.' (Lond. Univ. Ph.D. thesis, 1957), 300–2, 310–11; P. J. Bowden, *Wool Trade in Tudor and Stuart Eng.* 66–7; R. B. Westerfield, *Middlemen in Eng. Business*, 262, 269.

[70] *Econ. H.R.* 2nd ser. xxxix. 170–1 and Table 1.

[71] Ibid.; ibid. xxii. 245; P.R.O., E 190/610/3; E 190/610/11; E 190/612/12; E 190/620/4.

[72] P.R.O., E 190/589/7; *O.E.D.* s.v. woad.

[73] P.R.O., E 190/599/5; E 190/602/1; E 190/605/1.

[74] Ibid. E 190/610/3; E 190/610/11; E 190/612/12; E 190/620/4; Burley, 'Econ. Development', 87.

[75] P.R.O., E 190/589/7.

[76] Ibid. E 190/606/5.

pantiles and stone of various kinds, stone pots and earthenware, Norway wood, haberdasheries, paper, bullrushes, 'prepared metal', and household goods.[77] By then the range of imports was even wider, still mainly from Rotterdam, indicating the growing importance of Colchester as a centre of consumption and redistribution.

Despite its expanding trade, Colchester was not in the front rank of English provincial ports. Figures for customs payments in the 1590s place it 14th out of the 19 ports for which evidence survives,[78] while on the basis of the annual average cloth custom and subsidy paid by 15 ports between 1600 and 1640 Colchester stood in 10th place, paying less than half the total collected at Ipswich and less than an 11th of that paid by Hull.[79] Most of the growing export trade in the town's new draperies was conducted through London. In 1635, during a dispute with Colchester merchants, the Merchant Adventurers Company claimed that the town could boast only four or five merchants trading overseas, and that those bought only a fraction of the cloth made at Colchester, most bays being taken to London to be bought by the Merchant Adventurers and others.[80] Little had changed by the end of the century. In the four years 1697–1701 the annual average national export of double bays was 36,872 cloths, of which 1,137 (3.1 per cent) were exported directly from Colchester. Only 3.6 per cent of the says, serges, and perpetuanas exported nationally left from Colchester, 0.4 per cent of the single bays, and none of the treble bays.[81] Coastal shipments of bays to London in 1698–9 amounted to nearly 25,000 cloths, twenty times the town's direct exports.[82]

The geographical horizons of Colchester's trade were not extended by its expanding new drapery exports. In 1571–2 Colchester traded almost exclusively with Rouen and la Rochelle in France, with Flushing in the Netherlands, and with 'Camphere' (perhaps Quimper, France, or Kampen, Netherlands). One or two ships went to Bordeaux and Dieppe (France), to Danzig (now Gdansk, Poland), to Hamburg and Stade in Germany, and to the unidentified 'Newhaven'. Imports were additionally received from the unidentified 'Olderne' and 'Borwage' (possibly for Norway), and from Emden (Germany).[83] By the 1590s trade was heavily concentrated upon Middelburg (Netherlands), and in the earlier 17th century on 'Camphere' and Rotterdam. Occasional shipments were made to Seville (Spain), the Spanish Islands and the Azores, but the bay trade to the Mediterranean was dominated by London.[84] Colchester played little part in the Eastland trade in which Ipswich was so heavily involved.[85] Only an occasional Colchester vessel sailed to the Baltic between the 1560s and 1590s, and relatively few thereafter apart from flurries of activity in the 1600s, the 1680s, and at the very end of the 17th century, which never exceeded seven passages each way in any one year.[86] The alderman John Hunwick was a member of the Eastland Co. and of the Spanish and Portuguese Cos. in 1583. His apprentice John Eldred was a member of the Eastland

[77] Ibid. E 190/610/3; E 190/610/11; E 190/619/12; E 190/620/4.

[78] Calculated from Hist. MSS. Com. 9, *Salisbury*, v. 393; T. S. Willan, *Studies in Elizabethan Foreign Trade*, 75.

[79] Calculated from *Econ. H.R.* 2nd ser. xxii. 244–6.

[80] *Cal. S.P. Dom.* 1635, 103.

[81] P.R.O., E 190/612/12; E 190/620/4; Burley, 'Econ. Development', Table XL; calculated from E. B. Schumpeter, *Eng. Overseas Trade Statistics 1697–1808*, Table XIV, and p. 44.

[82] P.R.O., E 190/618/15; E 190/618/18.

[83] Ibid. E 190/589/7.

[84] Ibid. E 190/599/6; E 190/602/1; E 190/605/1; *Cal. S.P. Dom.* 1625–49, 121; 1629–31, 209; 1631–3, 27; Willan, *Studies in Foreign Trade*, 75; A. Friis, *Alderman Cockayne's Project and the Cloth Trade*, 65, 116, 128.

[85] R. W. K. Hinton, *Eastland Trade and the Commonweal in 17th Cent.*; J. Fedorowicz, *Eng.'s Baltic Trade in Early 17th Cent.: Study of Anglo-Polish Diplomacy*; H. Zins, *Eng. and Baltic in Elizabethan Era.*

[86] N. E. Bang, *Tabeller over Skibsfart og Varetransport gennem Oresund 1497–1660*; N. E. Bang and K. Korst, *Tabeller over Skibsfart og Varetransport gennem Oresund 1661–1783*.

Co. by 1608, and of the Muscovy Co. by 1624.[87] John Braxted was described as a merchant adventurer in 1604,[88] and although in 1619 the town claimed to have no merchants free of any company John Wiles of Colchester, who had served his apprenticeship with John Eldred, was a merchant adventurer in 1622.[89] In 1634, however, the restoration of the privileges of the Merchant Adventurers Co. of London led to a Privy Council order confining Colchester merchants to trade with Rotterdam.[90] Despite occasional shipments to Norway, Hamburg (Germany), Dunkirk and Bordeaux in France, and 'Stockholland', the Rotterdam connexion dominated the town's overseas trade throughout the later 17th century and into the 18th.[91]

Colchester's coastal trade centred upon London throughout the later 16th and 17th centuries. In 1568–9 cheese and butter were the main goods sent to the capital, followed by wheat, oats, malt, wood, and faggots. A greater variety of products was received in return, notably dyestuffs, soap, oil, groceries, ironware, coal, and canvas. A few shipments of butter and cheese went to Faversham, Gravesend, and Sittingbourne (Kent), occasional journeys were made to Southampton and Exeter, while Newcastle received considerable quantities of rye. Trade with Newcastle was second in importance only to that with London: of 77 inward cargoes in 1568–9, 44 were from London and 25 from Newcastle, the latter consisting largely of coal and salt.[92] Colchester merchants had been sending grain to Newcastle since the early 16th century, when Ambrose Lowth was accused of attempting to store a shipment of wheat and rye at Newcastle until he could set his own price.[93] In 1510 Lowth was presented in the borough court for regrating salt coming to Colchester market.[94] By the 1590s, Colchester vessels were venturing to the Scottish coast for salt.[95]

The importance of the coastal connexion with London grew as bay and say manufacture developed, until by 1649 two vessels laden with draperies sailed twice a week between Colchester and London.[96] Towards the end of the century the exchange of cloth for wool dominated the traffic, and by 1698–9 as many as 117 of 135 outward coastal cargoes were destined for London. London-bound cargoes contained coarse locks, grain, potash, household goods, ironware, beeswax, groceries and spices, leather, and foreign linens, many presumably imported from Rotterdam. Large quantities of wool for textile manufacture were received in return, followed in importance by oil, soap, tobacco, wine, iron, and various drapery, grocery, and household wares. Ten cargoes to Newcastle, four to Sunderland, and three to Whitby, consisted largely of rye and peas, supplemented by barley, beans, hay, chairs, and 'many other goods', whose diversity apparently defeated the patience of the customs officers.[97]

In 1619 Colchester possessed 26 vessels, including fishing boats and hoys, the six largest being coal ships averaging *c.* 100 tons.[98] By 1702–4 the 25 Colchester vessels involved in the coal trade with Newcastle averaged *c.* 48 tons.[99] In 1612, out of a total of 2,407 shipments of coal from Newcastle, 48 were made in Colchester ships, placing the town tenth among provincial ports involved in the trade, while a return of the tax collected under the new coal excise in 1651 places Colchester eighth of 57 provincial ports.[1] By the end of the

[87] E.R.O., D/B 5 Cr145, rot. 8d.; D/B 5 Cb2/7, f. 191; *Acts of P.C.* 1623–5, 393.

[88] E.R.O., D/B 5 Cb1/5, f. 416v.

[89] P.R.O., SP 14/105, no. 114; E.R.O., D/B 5 Cb2/7, f. 191; Friis, *Alderman Cockayne*, 116.

[90] P.R.O., PC 2/45, p. 15.

[91] Ibid. E 190/606/5; E 190/610/3; E 190/610/11; E 190/619/12; E 190/620/4; E 190/627/8; *Bull. Inst. Hist. Res.* xxix. 229–30.

[92] P.R.O., E 190/587/10; E 190/588/1; Hist. MSS. Com. 73, *Exeter*, 375.

[93] P.R.O., REQ 2/12, no. 206.

[94] E.R.O., D/B 5 Cr83, rot. 1d.

[95] Hist. MSS. Com. 9, *Salisbury*, iv. 543–4.

[96] *Cal. S.P. Dom.* 1649–50, 317.

[97] P.R.O., E 190/618/15; E 190/618/18.

[98] Ibid. SP 14/105, no. 114.

[99] Westerfield, *Middlemen*, 229 n.

[1] P.R.O., SP 18/17, no. 93; J. U. Nef, *Rise of Brit. Coal Ind.* ii. 26 n. London and Newcastle are excluded from the calculations.

17th century Sunderland had overhauled Newcastle as the main source of coal. In 1698–9 as many as 47 cargoes of coal were received from Sunderland, only 27 from Newcastle, but the latter also contained salt, glass, tanned calfskins, butter, and grindstones. Other imports, mainly of raw wool and fuller's earth, came largely from Kentish ports, particularly Rochester and Faversham.[2]

Colchester's developing trade led to a fairly steady growth in the mercantile tonnage owned by the town (Table IV). The check in that growth in the late 16th and early 17th centuries may well have been due to the increased involvement in Colchester trade of merchants from the Low Countries. Whereas in 1571–2 London merchants had competed for Colchester cloth exports, in the exceptional year 1605 'strangers' carried 1,095 double and 614 single bays out of the town.[3] In 1621–2 while trade with Rotterdam, Calais, and

TABLE IV: COLCHESTER SHIPPING

Date	*Number of Vessels*	*Total Tonnage*
1550	23	840
1582	42	1,246
1619	26	*c.* 1,080
1629	13	1,460
1676	49	*c.* 3,930
1702	34	3,675

Sources: 1550, G. V. Scammell, 'English Merchant Shipping at the end of the Middle Ages: some East Coast Evidence', *Econ. H.R.* 2nd ser. xiii. 338; 1582, P.R.O., SP 12/156/45; 1619, P.R.O., SP 14/105/114; 1629, 1676, 1702, Burley, 'Econ. Development', Table XIII.

the Azores was dominated by Colchester and Wivenhoe vessels, shipments to 'Camphere', 'Rickade' and 'Crill', *c.* 40 per cent of exports, were monopolized by 'strangers'.[4] There may have been some truth in the town's complaint in 1616 that a 'great concourse of strangers' shipped into the port and carried away the goods of both English and Dutch merchants, and in the claims made in 1616 and 1619 that Colchester's shipping was much decayed.[5] Shipping had recovered by 1629, and the middle years of the century saw considerable growth. By the end of the century Colchester vessels and Colchester merchants dominated the town's export trade, importing Dutch and German linens and a vast array of other products from Rotterdam, and also wood, iron, and pitch from Norway.[6] In 1582 there were 106 mariners in the town, 344 by 1702.[7] The annual rent payable for the lease of the tolls and profits of the Hythe increased only from £24 in 1504–5 to £42–£44 between 1597 and 1665, but whereas no fine appears to have been paid for the lease in 1504–5, and only 30*s.* in 1597, the sum charged in 1642 was £101 and in 1665 £150.[8] Through a combination of its overseas and coastal trade Colchester had done far more than hold its own in the face of the increasing activities of the capital, and it was described in 1707 as very rich and populous, inhabited by merchants of considerable estates and great traders.[9]

[2] P.R.O., E 190/618/15; E 190/618/18; T. S. Willan, *Eng. Coasting Trade 1600–1750*, 120–1, 124, 130, 137, 139, 141; C. W. Chalklin, *17th-Cent. Kent*, 177–8.

[3] P.R.O., E 190/589/7; ibid. SP 14/17, no. 66.

[4] Ibid. E 190/602/1.

[5] *Cal. S.P. Dom.* 1616–17, 59–60; P.R.O., SP 14/105, no. 114.

[6] P.R.O., E 190/606/5; E 190/610/3; E 190/610/11; E 190/619/12; E190/620/4.

[7] P.R.O., SP 12/156, no. 45; Burley, 'Econ. Development', 240.

[8] E.R.O., D/B 5 R2, f. 78v.; D/B 5 Gb1, 3 Aug. 1597; Gb3, f. 229v.; Gb4, f. 314.

[9] J. Brome, *Travels Over Eng., Scotland and Wales*, 112.

SOCIAL STRUCTURE

BETWEEN the 1520s and the 1670s Colchester's population perhaps trebled and its relative size in comparison with other provincial towns increased slightly, from seventh in terms of taxable population in 1524–5 to sixth in terms of recorded hearths in the 1670s.[10] Economic growth undoubtedly accompanied demographic

TABLE V: DISTRIBUTION OF TAXABLE WEALTH 1523–5

	No. of Taxpayers	*per cent*	*Taxable Wealth (to nearest £)*	*per cent*
Wages:				
at £1	402	40.4	402	6.1
over £1	82	8.2	160	2.4
Goods or Lands:				
£2–4	305	30.6	763	11.5
£5–9	77	7.7	502	7.6
£10–19	69	6.9	889	13.4
£20–39	27	2.7	658	9.9
£40–99	25	2.5	1,218	18.4
£100 or more	9	0.9	2,028	30.6
	996	99.9	6,620	99.9

Note: The returns for the 3 years 1523–5 have been conflated by nominative linkage because it is clear that the assessments of the wealthiest individuals were substantially scaled down in 1524 and 1525, and because the substantial differences between the lists for 1524 and 1525 can be explained partly by tax evasion, perhaps particularly among wage-earners. For fuller discussion of this methodology, see Goose, 'Econ. and Social Aspects', 57–62.

Sources: P.R.O., E 179/108/147; E 179/108/162; E 179/108/169.

growth, the town successfully overcoming periods of difficulty, short-lived reversals and slumps, and the impact of plague and the Civil War, but the price which it paid for its success was a greater polarization of society between rich and poor.

Social Structure in the Early 16th Century

Already in the mid 1520s Colchester, like other English towns, exhibited a steeply graduated hierarchy of wealth (Table V).[11] Of the 996 taxpayers recorded in Colchester between 1523 and 1525, 484 (49 per cent) were assessed on wages,[12] a figure comparable with those for other towns whether or not they were centres of cloth production.[13] Other wage earners may have been assessed on goods and yet others may have evaded taxation in both 1524 and 1525 as many apparently did in each year (Table VI). Dependent wage earners thus probably made up at least half the adult male population in the 1520s.

[10] Goose, 'Econ. and Social Aspects', p. 37.

[11] e.g. J. Pound, *Tudor and Stuart Norwich*, 31–3; D. Palliser, *Tudor York*, 134–8; W. T. MacCaffrey, *Exeter 1540–1640*, 247–50; *V.C.H. Oxon.* iv. 101–3; *V.C.H. Glos.* iv. 81.

[12] P.R.O., E 179/108/147, 162, 169. The more comprehensive 1525 list alone produces a slightly lower ratio of 43 per cent.

[13] C. Platt, *Med. Southampton*, 264 sqq.; Hoskins, *Provincial Eng.* 83–4; MacAffrey, *Exeter*, 12, 250; *V.C.H. Yorks. E.R.* i. 159; A. D. Dyer, *City of Worcester in 16th Cent.* 175; *V.C.H. Oxon.* iv. 102; *Northants. Past and Present*, vi. Table 1; Palliser, *Tudor York*, 136–7; *Early Modern Town*, ed. P. Clark, 130–1.

Only eight people were assessed on lands or houses, and all of them except for Thomas Audley's mother-in-law Elizabeth Barnardiston, assessed in 1524 on £55 worth, held estates worth less than £10. That such a high proportion of taxpayers paid on their movables presumably reflects the depths to which land values had

TABLE VI: COMPOSITION OF CONFLATED LISTS OF TAXPAYERS 1524–5

	All Taxpayers	*Wages Only*
Number in 1524 list	758	356
Number in 1525 list	783	333
Number in both lists	545	150
Number in 1524 list only	213	161
Number in 1525 list only	238	173
Total number of taxpayers	996	484

Sources: P.R.O., E 179/108/162; E 179/108/169.

sunk by the early 16th century.[14] In 1547, by contrast, 50 out of 286 people (17 per cent) paid on lands,[15] a figure which may suggest the growing attractiveness of investment in urban property. In 1628, after a century of population growth and inflation, 125 of 261 taxpayers (48 per cent) were assessed on land or houses rather than on movable goods or as aliens.[16]

Nine people were taxed on £100 or more (Table V), fewer than in Norwich or Exeter, much the same as in Kings Lynn and Bury St. Edmunds, more than in Great Yarmouth, Worcester, York, or Southampton.[17] Those nine, less than 1 per cent of the taxable population, owned as much as 30 per cent of the taxable wealth in the town. The 34 individuals, only 3.4 per cent of the taxable population, who were recognized as rich and required to pay in anticipation on goods worth £40 or more, owned virtually half the town's taxable wealth.

As in other towns, *c.* 80 per cent of the taxable population paid on £4 or less in goods or wages.[18] They were not all 'poor', as real wages were remarkably high in the early 16th century; in both Coventry and Cambridge substantial numbers assessed in the £2–£4 range kept servants.[19] The occupations of 83 men assessed on goods worth £2–£4 have been identified; they followed 34 different trades, and included 8 weavers, 5 shoemakers, 5 carpenters, 5 mariners, 4 husbandmen, 4 tailors, 4 tanners, 4 barbers, and 4 labourers. Occupations could be traced for 66 wage earners, in 33 trades, including 6 shoemakers or cordwainers, 5 mariners or watermen, 4 weavers, 4 cappers, and 4 butchers. A few people were truly indigent: in 1510 William Baker was accused of harbouring beggars and in 1514 a tailor was indicted for keeping and lodging beggars and vagabonds,[20] but both poverty and vagrancy were lesser problems than they were to become in the early 17th century.

[14] Hoskins, *Provincial Eng.* 77–8; *Northern Hist.* xiv. 72–3; *Southern Hist.* i. 42–3.

[15] P.R.O., E 179/109/308.

[16] Ibid. E 179/112/643.

[17] Pound, *Norwich*, 33; MacCaffrey, *Exeter*, 248; Dyer, *Worcester*, 175; Palliser, *Tudor York*, 136–7.

[18] Dyer, *Worcester*, 175; *Northants. Past and Present*, vi. 74; *V.C.H. Oxon.* iv. 102; MacCaffrey, *Exeter*, 250; *Early Modern Town*, ed. Clark, 131; *V.C.H. Yorks. E.R.* i. 159; Goose, 'Econ. and Social Aspects', 75.

[19] Phythian-Adams, *Desolation of a City*, 133–4; *Economica*, xxiii. 296–314; J. Hatcher, *Plague, Population and the Eng. Econ. 1348--1530*, 50; F. R. H. du Boulay, *Age of Ambition*, 13–16, 35–41. In Cambridge 28 (41 per cent) of those identified as employing servants fell into the £2–£4 assessment band: Goose, 'Econ. and Social Aspects', 73–4.

[20] E.R.O., D/B 5 Cr82, rot. 10; D/B 5 Cr86, rot. 5.

The Growth of Poverty, and Poor Relief

The price of wheat in Colchester rose from 5*s.* a quarter in August 1510 to 6*s.* 6*d.* in November that year, to 8*s.* in December 1511, and to between 12*s.* and 13*s.* 6*d.* in the winter 1512–13, before falling to 8*s.* a quarter in October 1514 and to 6*s.* in November.[21] By 1560 wheat prices had approximately doubled, to 24*s.* a quarter, but fell to 20*s.* a quarter in 1566 and 16*s.* a quarter in 1567.[22] In 1577 wheat was 22*s.* 6*d.* a quarter.[23] Long-term inflation and short-term fluctuations in the price of grain, and hence of bread, severely affected the urban poor. It is little wonder that in 1570 the bailiffs complained to the Privy Council that the common estate of the town had decayed.[24]

In 1557, a year of both dearth and sickness, the corporation introduced a compulsory poor rate of 8*d.* in the noble on all houses worth more than 3*s.* 4*d.* a year, to be assessed by specially appointed parish officers. Householders were forbidden to receive any stranger unless he could show that he would not fall to begging. Those accepting 'gatherers and collectors of wood' as tenants, or buying their wood, were to be fined.[25] In 1562 the corporation ordered that alms be collected at every sermon for the relief of the poor and impotent.[26] The alms were regularly collected between 1579 and 1595, as much as 52*s.* 6*d.* being given in 1588–9.[27]

The loss of St. Mary Magdalen's hospital and of other, poorly endowed, medieval hospitals and almshouses may have exacerbated the problem of the poor, although in 1563 the borough was using St. Catherine's hospital as a workhouse. In 1565 the corporation ordered the establishment of a common hospital for 'idle youths and poor children' born in the town, to be financed by the inclosure and letting of some of the half-year lands.[28] The hospital was being built in the early 1570s,[29] children from the poorhouse were baptized at St. Mary's-at-the-Walls in 1574, and in 1579 Richard Hall, proctor of the Colchester poorhouse, was granted protection to gather contributions in Essex and Hertfordshire.[30]

In 1572, in 12 of the town's 16 parishes,[31] 300 people paid poor rate; 102 people, almost all apparently heads of households, received relief. As the population of those parishes was *c.* 3,700,[32] it seems that *c.* 8 per cent of the total population paid a poor rate which was distributed to just under 3 per cent, excluding dependents. Assuming an average household of 4.5 people, and 2.2 in pauper households,[33] over 36 per cent of households contributed, while over 12 per cent (*c.* 224 people or 6 per cent of the total population) received relief. Of 102 named recipients, 44 were widows. Four orphans were being maintained by St. Leonard's parish, and two men in St. Mary Magdalen's were burdened 'with a charge of children'.[34]

In 1582, in the whole town, 114 people received weekly payments, a slightly lower proportion of the total population than ten years earlier. The number of

21 Ibid. D/B 5 Cr82, rot. 29; Cr83, rot. 6; Cr85, rott. 14, 15; Cr86, rot. 30.

22 E.R.O., D/B 5 R5, ff. 87v., 94, 95, 96 and v., 100 and v., 106, 109v.

23 Ibid. D/B 5 Cr140, rot. 2d.

24 E. L. Cutts, *Colch.* 154–5.

25 E.R.O., D/Y 2/2, pp. 37–8.

26 Ibid. D/B 5 R5, f. 94v.

27 Ibid. D/Y 2/2, pp. 42–59; ibid. Boro. Mun., Acc. C1, Contribution Book to the Poor, unfoliated, end of vol.

28 *Cal. Pat.* 1547–8, 356; 1557–8, 249; 1560–3, 415; 1563–6, 237; E.R.O., D/B 5 R5, ff. 106v.–107.

29 E.R.O., D/ACR 6/219; P.R.O., PROB 11/54, f. 17; PROB 11/55, f. 2.

30 E.R.O., D/P 246/1/1; Hist. MSS. Com. 9, *Salisbury*, xiii. 170.

31 E.R.O., D/B 5 R7, ff. 307–18.

32 Estimate based upon extant parish registers for 6 parishes, adjusted in proportion to numbers given in 1534 return of those swearing fealty to the king.

33 *Population Studies*, xxiii. 199–224; *Social Hist.* v. 363–4; *Crisis and Order in Eng. Towns 1500–1700*, ed. P. Clark and P. Slack, 177.

34 E.R.O., D/B 5 R7, ff. 307v., 309v., 311v.

paupers varied widely from parish to parish. None was known in St. Runwald's or St. Martin's, but 20 weekly payments were made in St. Giles's, many of them to widows and other women and several for keeping children. A total of 513 people made regular contributions to the poor rate, suggesting some expansion of the tax base since 1572, the sum collected weekly amounting to 52*s.* 9¾*d.*[35]

An array of fines was also devoted to poor relief, including those for overstocking the commons, for breaching the statute of artificers or the assize of bread and of ale, for inadequate tanning of leather, for refusing office, and for not wearing livery gowns to meetings of the borough assembly.[36] The 'rawboots' fines (Table III) were distributed to the poor from 1586 or earlier,[37] as were proceeds from the town lottery and rents from some town land, probably inclosed half-year land.[38] In 1652 part of the profits from the new coal excise was earmarked for the poor, and in 1656 meat forfeited by 'foreign' butchers was ordered to be given to the needy.[39]

The corporation administered the loan charities of Lady Judd (£100), John Hunwick (£300), and Thomas Ingram (£100),[40] which were used to set the poor on work, usually in spinning, carding, combing, and flax- or hemp-beating. Interest on the loans was applied to poor relief.[41] Poor children were apprenticed to trades- and craftsmen, often in exchange for the master's freedom of the town. In 1599 the keeper of the poorhouse was given the freedom in return for maintaining two poor girls;[42] the previous year William Ware had been admitted in return for keeping his parents from becoming a charge on the poor rate.[43]

The corporation ordered parish overseers to distrain the goods of those who refused to pay poor rates,[44] and Elizabeth, widow of Sir Thomas Lucas, appealed to the Privy Council in 1627 after the St. Giles's overseers had distrained a cow and calf for £3 rates.[45] When 23 inhabitants of All Saints' parish refused in 1629 to contribute to the relief of St. Botolph's poor, their churchwardens and overseers seem to have supported them, claiming to be unable to find any goods to distrain.[46] The corporation ordered additional assessments to be made in periods of particular need. In 1623, when high grain prices aggravated distress caused by depression in the new drapery trade, most inhabitants and occupiers of land in the town were ordered to be rated 'for 52 weeks over and above their weekly contribution'.[47]

Dearth and Depression

During the dearth of 1527 the 'substantial people' in Colchester were accused of stockpiling grain for themselves, and Cardinal Wolsey intervened to ensure that wheat in the town was actually sold to the inhabitants.[48] In 1551, another year of bad harvests, the Privy Council required the J.P.s of Kent to provide Colchester with 560 qr. of grain at reasonable prices.[49] In April 1563 the bailiffs and aldermen

35 Ibid. Boro. Mun., Acc. C1, Contribution Book to the Poor, unfoliated.

36 Ibid. D/B 5 Gb2, ff. 119v.–121v.; Gb3, ff, 62v.–63, 64, 81; Gb4, ff. 214, 229v.–230, 248; D/B 5 Cb1/10, f. 353; Cb1/11, f. 383; D/B 5 Cb2/13, f. 7; D/Y 2/2, p. 65.

37 Ibid. Boro. Mun., Acc. C1, Contribution Book to the Poor, unfoliated, end of vol.; ibid. D/B 5 Gb3, f. 162v.; for 'rawboots' above, this chapter, Econ. (Growth and Development).

38 E.R.O., D/B 5 Gb2, f. 163; ibid. Boro. Mun., Acc C.1, Contribution Book to the Poor, unfoliated, end of vol.

39 Ibid. D/B 5 Gb4, ff. 72, 150.

40 Ibid. D/B 5 Gb1, 1 Sept. 1590; 14 June 1591; 7 Aug. 1592; 18 June 1593; 10 Nov. 1595; Gb2, ff. 53v., 55; below, Charities.

41 E.R.O., D/B 5 Gb1, 14 June 1591; 7 Aug. 1592; 18 June 1593.

42 e.g. ibid. D/B 5 Cb1/6, f. 243; Cb2/6, ff. 222v., 249v.; Cb2/10, f. 51; D/B 5 Gb1, 1 Mar. 1599.

43 Ibid. D/B 5 Gb1, 19 Apr. 1598.

44 Ibid. D/B 5 Cb1/10, f. 82v.; Cb1/11, f. 107.

45 Ibid. D/B 5 Cb2/10, f. 240; *Cal. S.P. Dom.* 1627–8, 497.

46 E.R.O., D/Y 2/2, p. 41.

47 Ibid. D/B 5 Gb3, f. 31; D/B 5 Cb1/7, 221; B. Sharp, *In Contempt of All Authority: Rural Artisans and Riot in West of Eng. 1586–1660*, 25–6.

48 *L. & P. Hen. VIII*, iv (2), pp. 1629, 1781; *Agric. Hist. Rev.* xix. 152.

49 *Acts of P.C.* 1550–2, 329, 450; *Agric. Hist. Rev.* xix. 153; R. B. Outhwaite, *Dearth, Public Policy and Social Disturbance in Eng. 1550–1800*, 20.

took charge of the distribution of 500 qr. of grain brought from Danzig by alderman John Best, evidently in response to the bad harvest of the previous year.[50] In 1586, another year of dearth, the borough assembly levied a compulsory loan from the inhabitants to provide 400 qr. of Danzig rye.[51]

The years 1594–7 witnessed four successive bad harvests.[52] Between 1590 and 1593 the price of wheat averaged *c.* 23*s.* a quarter,[53] but by September 1594 it had risen to 42*s.* 10*d.*; it peaked at 48*s.* in November 1596 and remained at that level until August 1597.[54] Only in 1598 did the price fall back, to 32*s.* 6*d.* a quarter in October.[55] The response of the borough authorities was immediate. In November 1594 every alderman was ordered to lend £20, every first councillor £10, and every second councillor £5 for corn for the poor. In December a baker was appointed for each ward to bake three 'seams' of the town's grain for the poor. By May 1595 £408 had been collected and £380 spent on 289 qr. of grain; the small cash balance was distributed to the poor.[56] In December 1597 the bailiffs feared that many poor people would perish, in spite of the loan and of high poor rates which overburdened other townsmen, and in January 1598 Sir Robert Cecil allowed 400 qr. of grain to be shipped to Colchester from Norfolk despite the general restraint on the movement of corn.[57]

All that activity may not have been enough to prevent the poor from either starving or dying from disease induced by severe malnutrition. Although plague was not recorded, mortality reached double its average level in 1597 in four of the five parishes for which burial registers survive.[58] The poor parish of St. Botolph's was particularly severely affected, while St. James's, St. Leonard's, and St. Mary's-at-the-Walls also suffered. Numbers of deaths rose in July, and remained very high between September and December, a pattern at least compatible with a growing shortage of food towards the end of the harvest year 1596–7, capped by yet another bad harvest in 1597. The below-average number of baptisms in 1598 presumably reflects a shortfall in conceptions the previous year, perhaps induced by malnutrition and hence amenorrhea.[59] Furthermore, burials, particularly in St. Botolph's, fell sharply in January 1598, coinciding with the acquisition of grain from Norfolk.[60]

In other years the corporation's relief measures generally helped stave off such dire consequences.[61] The next period of severe difficulty started in 1629, when the bailiffs tried to prevent the export of 1,000 lasts of grain from Colchester because of the high local prices and the great number of poor in the town.[62] By December 1630 they were seeking to purchase rye in Norfolk for the poor with money lent or given, and in February 1631 they complained with effect to the Privy Council that local farmers, notably two Layer Breton yeomen, neglected to supply the town's market so that the poor were 'almost ready to famish and to commit outrages for want of corn'.[63] The harvest of 1630 was again very bad, the price of wheat and rye in Colchester rising to 46*s.* and 34*s.* a quarter respectively,[64] and the

[50] E.R.O., D/B 5 R5, f. 95v.; *Agric. Hist. Rev.* xix. 153; Outhwaite, *Dearth*, 20.

[51] E.R.O., D/B 5 Gb1, 12 Sept. 1586; *Cal. S.P. Dom.* 1581–90, 350; *Agric. Hist. Rev.* xix. 154; Outhwaite, *Dearth*, 20.

[52] *Agric. Hist. Rev.* xix. 154; Outhwaite, *Dearth*, 20.

[53] E.R.O., D/B 5 Cb1/3, ff. 200v., 348v.; D/B 5 Cr155, rot. 2d.

[54] Ibid. D/B 5 Cb1/4, ff. 40v., 134, 192v., 266v.

[55] Ibid. f. 340; D/B 5 Cb1/3, f.348v.; Cb1/4, f. 266v.

[56] Ibid. D/B 5 Gb1, 11 Nov., 2 Dec. 1594; 27 May 1595.

[57] Hist. MSS. Com. 9, *Salisbury*, vii. 526; *Acts of P.C.* 1597–8, 230–1.

[58] Goose, 'Econ. and Social Aspects', 306; P. Slack, *Impact of Plague in Tudor and Stuart Eng.* 73–6; A. B. Appleby, *Famine in Tudor and Stuart Eng.* 137–9; Outhwaite, *Dearth*, 29.

[59] Goose, 'Econ. and Social Aspects', 320; Appleby, *Famine*, 8–9.

[60] E.R.O., D/P 203/1/1, pp. 63–5.

[61] e.g. ibid. D/B 5 Gb2, f. 84.

[62] Ibid. D/Y 2/7, p. 247.

[63] Ibid. D/B 5 Gb3, f. 98; *Cal. S.P. Dom.* 1629–31, 500; *Acts of P.C.* 1630–1, 243.

[64] *Agric. Hist. Rev.* xix. 155; Outhwaite, *Dearth*, 20; E.R.O., D/B 5 Cb2/11, f. 143.

standard size of loaves of bread being reduced to that of the worst years of the 1590s.[65] Nevertheless plague rather than famine seems to have caused the doubling of the average mortality rates in St. Leonard's and St. Mary's-at-the-Walls in 1631.[66]

The dearth of 1630–1 was aggravated by the slump in the new drapery trade. In April 1631 it was reported that the suffering in Essex was particularly bad in the bay-making areas where the clothiers were not giving work to poor weavers.[67] In May 1631 the Privy Council, on the petition of 300 poor inhabitants of Colchester, ordered the bailiffs and aldermen to raise wages to their former level, or to provide a stock to set the poor on work, as had been done at Sudbury, or to take other measures to relieve the poor.[68] The Colchester authorities argued that raising wages would only reduce the amount of work given to the poor,[69] and the clothiers, ordered to raise wages by a sixth, replied that they could not provide employment even if they cut wages by a sixth.[70]

Further depression in the bay and say trade late in 1636 and in 1637 produced renewed controversy. Four weavers, claiming to speak for 2,000 others, petitioned the Privy Council against their low wages and troublesome work, alleging that many of them with their children were 'ready to perish'. Particular complaints were made against Thomas Reynolds, baymaker, for 'forcing them to take dead commodities such as they cannot put off'.[71] Reynolds had already, the previous January, been forced to recompense weavers to whom he had given overvalued says in lieu of wages. He denied the new charges, saying that he had given the men work and even lent them looms, and accusing three of them of being involved in burning down his house. Although he was supported by six Colchester clothworkers, the Privy Council concluded that he had oppressed and abused poor weavers. He was committed to the Fleet until he had paid each of the petitioners double the wages he had defrauded them of, and was ordered to withdraw all actions against them and pay all their expenses. Within a week he had made full satisfaction and was released.[72]

Economic and Social Regulation

In the absence of independent craft guilds the corporation played a major role in economic regulation. It controlled wages and set the assize of bread, and also appointed bakers' and butchers' wardens, searchers of leather, and overseers of the town lands. Trade disputes were often settled in the borough courts.[73] The Dutch had achieved a high degree of success in regulating the bay trade,[74] and from the later 16th century the corporation also devoted increasing attention to cloth production. In 1602 it established or re-established a weavers' company governed by two wardens, one chosen by the bailiffs and aldermen, the other by the freemen weavers. The wardens swore to ensure that all weavers performed their work skilfully and faithfully, and to enforce many of the provisions of the Statute of Artificers of 1563. The company laid down rules governing the length of apprenticeships, and the conditions of employment for journeymen, regulations repeated

65 E.R.O., D/B 5 Cb2/11, f. 143; D/B 5 Cb1/4, ff. 192v., 266v.; D/B 5 R5, ff. 96v., 100 and v., 106, 109v.; D/B 5 Cr140, rot. 2d.; Cr141, rott. 7, 15.

66 Goose, 'Econ. and Social Aspects', 306; E.R.O., D/P 245/1/1; D/P 246/1/1.

67 Sharp, *In Contempt*, 30.

68 *Acts of P.C.* 1630–1, 358–9.

69 *Cal. S.P. Dom.* 1625–49, 430.

70 W. Hunt, *Puritan Movement: Coming of Revolution in an Eng. County*, 244.

71 P.R.O., PC 2/47, ff. 389–90; *Cal. S.P. Dom.* 1637, 32, 44.

72 *Cal. S.P. Dom.* 1637, 44, 87–9, 115; P.R.O., PC 2/47, ff. 390, 422.

73 E.R.O., D/B 5 Cr82–186; D/B 5 Cb1/2–24; D/B 5 Cb2/3–34.

74 *Immigrants and Minorities*, i. 266–7; above, this chapter, Econ. (Growth and Development).

in 1608 and 1609.[75] In 1618 a company of English bay and saymakers was established, parallel to the Dutch company, for the reform of 'deceits and abuses' in the craft.[76] Among other matters the new company was required to regulate wages and impose reasonable rates, and was apparently doing so more assiduously than the Dutch company in 1622.[77]

The weavers' and other trade ordinances discriminated against 'foreigners', as did the borough authorities. Despite the welcome extended to the Dutch settlers in 1565,[78] it was ordered in 1580 that no more Dutch be allowed to settle without the consent of the bailiffs and aldermen. In 1584 householders were forbidden to receive tenants likely to prove a charge on the town, and in 1591 they were forbidden to let houses or rooms to anyone who had not lived in the town for three years or else given two sureties of £20. The constables were ordered to eject recent immigrants from employment and put longer-term residents in their places, and to remove from the town all the poor who had been there for less than three years.[79] The corporation claimed in 1613 that the increasing number of 'incomers' was the main cause of the rising numbers of poor, and in 1622 that the failure to exclude immigrants was the principal cause of the great poverty in the town.[80] Restrictions on immigrants continued in force into the 1630s.[81] In 1637 the corporation attempted to protect the interests of those who had been born free or served long apprenticeships by raising the fine for purchasing the freedom to £10, and requiring the consent of six free burgesses of the same trade to the admission.[82]

Nevertheless considerable numbers of people settled in Colchester in the late 16th and early 17th centuries, enough to sustain a population growth well above that obtainable by natural increase.[83] On average 150 migrants were apprenticed in Colchester each decade between *c.* 1580 and 1630. Of the 1,014 apprentices whose indentures record their place of origin (Table VII),[84] a quarter came from Colchester itself, a further third from elsewhere in Essex and a fifth from Suffolk. Less than a fifth came from outside East Anglia, mainly from the south midlands, particularly the cloth-working areas of Cambridgeshire. Trading contacts with south and east coast ports probably account for the *c.* 5 per cent of apprentices from the east midlands, the south, and the south-east. Very few came from the more westerly regions of the country.

Burgess admissions similarly record predominantly short-range migration and a distinct bias towards the east coast of England among those moving longer distances. Birthplaces can be identified for 1,425 of 1,500 men admitted in the 16th and early 17th centuries.[85] Of those, 435 (30.5 per cent) were born in Colchester, a further 386 (27.1 per cent) elsewhere in Essex, and 232 (16.3 per cent) in Suffolk. Significant numbers came from Yorkshire (46), Norfolk (31), London and Middlesex (26), Cambridgeshire (21), Kent (21), Lincolnshire (18), Hertfordshire (15), Lancashire (13), Buckinghamshire (12), Staffordshire (11), and Northumberland (10). Thirty-five were born overseas.

Migrants arriving to take up apprenticeships or to purchase the freedom stood

75 E.R.O., D/B 5 Gb2, ff. 23–24v., 74, 82–3.

76 P.R.O., SP 14/115, no. 28; *Cal. S.P. Dom.* 1611–18, 550; *Univ. Birmingham Hist. Jnl.* vii. 49.

77 P.R.O., SP 14/129, no. 70 (1).

78 Above, this chapter, Econ. (Growth and Development).

79 E.R.O., D/B 5 Gb1, 17 Oct. 1580; 17 Mar. 1584; 17 June 1591.

80 Ibid. D/B 5 Gb3, f. 172 and v.

81 Ibid. D/B 5 Gb2, 23–24v., 74, 82–3, 157; Gb3, ff. 13v., 83 and v., 157v.–158, 169v.–180.

82 Ibid. D/B 5 Gb2, ff. 119v.–121; Gb3, ff. 14–16v.

83 Goose, 'Econ. and Social Aspects', 266–7; above, this chapter, Intro.

84 E.R.O., D/B 5 Cr142–86; D/B 5 Cb1/2–9; D/B 5 Cb2/3–11; D/B 5 Gb1–3. All but a handful fall between the years 1580 and 1630.

85 E.R.O., D/B 5 Cr82–186; D/B 5 Cb1/2–9; D/B 5 Cb2/3–11; D/B 5 Gb1–3.

at the more respectable end of the social spectrum. Others less respectable and less welcome also found their way to Colchester. Many such vagrants had come from other towns, and a high proportion of them had travelled considerable distances. Of the 236 predominantly single men or women apprehended in and expelled from the town between 1630 and 1664 whose place of origin is known, a little over 28 per cent had moved over 100 miles, while over 70 per cent had moved more than 40 miles. Only 88 (37.3 per cent) came from East Anglia, 42 (17.8 per cent) from London and Middlesex, and as many as 20 (8.5 per cent) from Ireland. The dearth

TABLE VII: ORIGINS OF COLCHESTER APPRENTICES *c.* 1580–1630

	Number	*per cent*
Colchester	258	25.6
Essex (other)	358	35.6
Suffolk	196	19.5
Norfolk	13	1.3
Total East Anglia	825	82.0
Cambridgeshire	57	5.7
Hertfordshire	12	1.2
Huntingdonshire	14	1.4
Total South Midlands	96	9.5
Lincolnshire	18	1.8
Total East Midlands	28	2.8
Middlesex (including London)	12	1.2
Total South and South-East	26	2.6
Total North	19	1.9
Total South-West	7	0.7
Total West Midlands	3	0.3
Total Other	2	0.2
TOTAL	1,006	100.0

Note: Regional groupings as follows:
East Anglia: Essex, Suff., Norf.
South Midlands: Beds., Bucks., Cambs., Herts., Hunts., Northants., Oxon.
East Midlands: Derb., Leics., Lincs., Notts., Rut.
South and South-East: Berks., Hants, Kent, Mdx., Surr., Suss.
North: Ches., Cumb., co. Dur., Lancs., Northumb., Yorks., Westmld.
South-West: Cornw., Devon, Dors., Som., Wilts.
West Midlands: Glos., Herefs., Mon., Salop., Staffs., Warws., Worcs.
Other: Ireland, Scotland, Wales, Overseas.

Only counties from which 10 or more apprentices came to Colchester are listed separately.

Sources: E.R.O., D/B 5 Cb1/2–9; Cb2/3–11.

years 1630 and 1631 produced particularly large numbers of long distance immigrants.[86]

The whipping and expulsion of vagrants was only one part of an often punitive policy towards the poor. Alehouses were attacked in 1598 as 'harbourers of thieves, harlots, and other lewd persons' and blamed for beastliness and drunkenness which was 'the utter undoing' of many poor people.[87] Alehouse keepers, like Thomas Wilson in 1601, had to swear to prohibit cards, dice, and other unlawful games, not to permit drunkenness, and to forbid all drinking during the times of church services. They were to sell food and drink only to legitimate wayfarers or to the poorer sort of townsmen, to take no lodgers for more than a day and a night unless they could vouch for them, to control the sale of goods in their houses, and to admit the constables and other officers at all times.[88] The town was well supplied with inns and alehouses: 7 innkeepers and 69 tipplers were recorded in 1574, and 5 taverners, 5 innkeepers, and 38 alehouse keepers in 1577.[89] In 1613 the borough ordered a reduction in the number of alehouses and stricter vetting of their keepers to keep out 'incomers' and to suppress idleness,[90] but in 1686 the town was second only to Chelmsford in the county in the number of beds (198) available in its inns, and there were still at least 31 inns or alehouses in 1705.[91]

Begging by any but the 'very lame and aged not able to work' had been prohibited in 1591. Six years later an overseer and a beadle, paid for by an additional poor rate, were appointed to prevent able-bodied men from begging.[92] From 1622 four beadles were appointed to seek out unlicensed beggars, and to control the licensed ones, who were to be confined to particular parishes.[93] In 1613 a new workhouse was founded to employ the poor, lame, and impotent.[94] It was governed by four aldermen and sixteen common councillors who appointed other officers to punish and order the idle persons brought there. The new institution was clearly both workhouse and house of correction. Indeed, it was regularly called the house of correction, and its inmates included men like the Norfolk tailor committed in 1636 for drunkenness and swearing and for abusing the high constable. In 1622 detailed regulations were made for providing work for the more respectable poor in their own homes.[95]

Between 1622 and 1639 the clerk entered in the register the condition or occupation of many of those buried in St. Botolph's parish.[96] Poverty was widespread. Of the 11 people buried in June 1622, for instance, 6, including 3 widows, were 'poor' and 1 'very poor'. Many of those buried were described as weavers or 'poor weavers', a substantial number were Dutch, and a few were vagrants. The high proportion of children among them may be further evidence of poverty. By the later 17th century there appears to have been less official concern about poverty. The problem had apparently been relieved by the stabilization of population and prices and the reduction in immigration, combined with the continued growth of the town's economy.[97] The substantial increase in 'rawboots'

86 *Migration and Society in Early Modern Eng.* ed. P. Clark and D. Souden, 49–76; cf. *Crisis and Order in Eng. Towns 1500–1700*.

87 E.R.O., D/B 5 Gb1, 12 Dec. 1598.

88 Ibid. Boro. Mun., Tradesmen's Recogs. 1599–1605, ff. 13v.–14.

89 Ibid. D/B 5 Sb2/2, ff. 1–20v.; F. G. Emmison, *Elizabethan Life: Disorder*, 215.

90 E.R.O., D/B 5 Gb2, ff. 119–121v.

91 Ibid. D/B 5 Sr76, rott. 7–9; W. J. Petchey, *Prospect of Maldon*, 138.

92 E.R.O., D/B 5 Gb1, 14 June 1591; 18 Nov. 1597.

93 Ibid. D/B 5 Gb3, f. 16 and v.

94 Ibid. D/Y 2/2, p. 60; D/B 5 Gb1, 1 Mar. 1599; Gb2, ff. 119–121v.

95 Ibid. D/B 5 Sb1/4, 11 July 1636; D/B 5 Gb2, ff. 130v., 161; Gb3, ff. 14–16v.; Gb4, ff. 100, 174; Gb5, f. 313; Gb6, p. 70; below, Mun. Bldgs. (Prison).

96 E.R.O., D/P 203/1/1.

97 Ibid. D/B 5 Gb2–6; E. A. Wrigley and R. S. Schofield, *Population Hist. Eng. 1541–1871: a Reconstruction*, 210–11; *Past and Present*, lxxxiii. 81–3; R. B. Outhwaite, *Inflation in Tudor and Early Stuart Eng.* 14; above, this chapter, Intro.; Econ. (Growth and Development).

TABLE VIII: TAXED AND EXEMPT HOUSEHOLDS IN COLCHESTER 1674

Parish	*Taxed*	*Exempt*	*Total*	*per cent Exempt*
St. Botolph	116	204	320	63.8
St. Giles	100	194	294	66.0
St. James	106	155	261	59.4
St. Peter	163	88	251	35.1
St. Mary-at-the-Walls	103	92	195	47.2
St. Nicholas	78	77	155	49.7
St. Leonard	70	83	153	54.2
St. Martin	70	42	112	37.5
Lexden	33	64	97	66.0
All Saints	60	22	82	26.8
Greenstead	26	40	66	60.6
St. Mary Magdalen	17	41	58	70.7
St. Runwald	40	13	53	24.5
Mile End	21	30	51	58.8
Holy Trinity	35	16	51	31.4
West Donyland	10	–*	10	–
Total	1,048	1,161	2,209	52.6

* All those exempt in West Donyland were paupers, needing no exemption certificate, and hence not included with the exempt.

Source: P.R.O., E 179/246/22.

as bay manufacturing expanded presumably helped to alleviate poverty, but special relief payments were necessary on several occasions. By 1678 the declining Dutch community was having considerable difficulty in maintaining its poor, as it had agreed to do when it was first established.[98] At the close of the 17th century Colchester petitioned parliament for the establishment of a new workhouse to cope with the increasing numbers of poor, to prevent idleness and disorders among the 'meaner' people, and to reduce the burden of the poor rate. An Act of 1698 authorized the establishment in the town of a workhouse under the control of a corporation of the poor.[99]

Social Structure in the Later 17th Century

The hearth tax return of 1674 (Tables VIII and IX), indicates that 53 per cent of households were too poor to be taxed. To those must be added a figure, *c.* 10 per cent of the population, for the paupers who were omitted from the returns, making altogether 1,406 households, or 57 per cent of the total.[1] The base of the social pyramid, the poor or relatively poor, was a broad one, broader than that found in most other provincial towns.[2] That reflects the town's economic structure, for the poverty of many weavers and other workers in the labour-intensive cloth

[98] E.R.O., D/B 5 Gb5, ff. 133, 153, 175, 213v., 352v., 364; D/B 5 Sb3/1, pp. 3, 8, 19, 42–4, 46–7, 119; *Cal. S.P. Dom.* 1683–4, 258.

[99] E.R.O., D/Y 2/2, pp. 61–4; D/B 5 Gb6, pp. 146, 200; ibid. Q/SR 554/8; *C.J.* xii. 165–6, 207, 263, 265, 273; P. Slack, *Eng. Poor Law 1531–1782*, 46; 9 & 10 Wm. III, c. 37 (Priv. Act).

[1] Goose, 'Econ. and Social Aspects', 325–7, 339.

[2] W. G. Hoskins, *Industry, Trade and People in Exeter* (1968), 117; *Suff. in 1674*, ed. S. A. H. Hervey, 52; *V.C.H. Yorks. E.R.* i. 161; R. Howell, *Newcastle Upon Tyne and the Puritan Revolution*, 350–1; *Salop. Hearth Tax Roll 1672*, ed. W. Watkins-Pitchford; *Jnl. of Chester and North Wales Archit. Arch. and Hist. Soc.* xxxvi. 31; *V.C.H. Leics.* iv. 156–9; Goose, 'Econ. and Social Aspects', 338–42.

industry was amply attested by contemporaries, and the Essex textile areas all exhibited relatively high proportions of people exempt from hearth tax.[3] The high proportion of small or exempt households in St. Botolph's and St. Giles's parishes is explained by the number of weavers there: of 109 weavers and clothworkers identified in the town in the period 1620–99 as many as 47 (43 per cent) lived in

TABLE IX: HOUSEHOLDS OF DIFFERENT SIZES IN COLCHESTER, 1674

	1 Hearth		*2 Hearths*		*3–5 Hearths*		*6–9 Hearths*		*10+ Hearths*		*Total*
	no.	*per cent*	*no.*	*per cent*	*no.*	*per cent*	*no.*	*per cent*	*no.*	*per cent*	
St. Botolph	152	47.5	98	30.6	51	15.9	15	4.7	4	1.3	320
St. Giles	186	63.3	79	26.9	22	7.5	7	2.4	–	–	294
St. James	133	51.0	59	22.6	45	17.2	20	7.7	4	1.5	261
St. Peter	86	34.3	55	21.9	89	35.5	16	6.4	5	2.0	251
St. Mary-W.	72	36.9	69	35.4	37	19.0	14	7.2	3	1.5	195
St. Nicholas	67	43.2	39	25.2	34	21.9	12	7.7	3	1.9	155
St. Leonard	52	34.0	56	36.6	31	20.3	11	7.2	3	2.0	153
St. Martin	44	39.3	32	28.6	31	27.7	4	3.6	1	0.9	112
Lexden	56	57.7	14	14.4	21	21.6	6	6.2	–	–	97
All Saints	21	25.6	21	25.6	30	36.6	8	9.8	2	2.4	82
Greenstead	37	56.1	15	22.7	13	19.7	1	1.5	–	–	66
St. Mary M.	45	77.6	6	10.3	6	10.3	1	1.7	–	–	58
St. Runwald	5	9.4	15	28.3	22	41.5	9	17.0	2	3.8	53
Mile End	31	60.8	11	21.6	9	17.6	–	–	–	–	51
Holy Trinity	16	31.4	16	31.4	11	21.6	6	11.8	2	3.9	51
West Donyland	3	30.0	3	30.0	2	20.0	–	–	2	20.0	10
Total	1,006	45.5	588	26.6	454	20.6	130	5.9	31	1.4	2,209

Source: P.R.O., E 179/246/22.

those two parishes.[4] St. Giles's and St. Botolph's also received the largest abatements for poverty, £6 7*s.* and £5 15*s.* respectively, in Colchester in the poll tax of 1667.[5]

The funds generated by a labour-intensive industry were produced at the cost of the depression of a large section of the urban labour force. The figures reflect the impact of population growth and inflation throughout the 16th century and the early 17th, and possibly also the development of increasingly capitalistic methods of production, the decline of the independent weaver or small clothier, and a growth in the numbers of dependent textile wage workers. The corporation attempted to limit the size of units of production, in 1613, for instance, prohibiting the employment of more than five weavers, or the use of more than two broad looms and one narrow or three narrow looms and one broad. Its failure to halt the trend is demonstrated by the claims of Thomas Reynolds and others in the 1630s to employ large numbers of hands, and by the distress of many workers during the textile slumps of the 1620s and 1630s.[6]

At the other end of the social scale economic development generated considerable wealth. In 1674 *c.* 7 per cent of those assessed for hearth tax lived in households

[3] E. Kerridge, *Textile Manufactures in Early Modern Eng.* 206; Burley, 'Econ. Development of Essex', 339–44, 361; Supple, *Commercial Crisis*, 8–14; *Textile Hist. and Econ. Hist.* ed. N. B. Harte and K. G. Ponting, 3.

[4] Goose, 'Econ. and Social Aspects', 223.

[5] E.R.O., D/Y 2/2, loose material.

[6] Ibid. D/B 5 Gb2, f. 121 and v.; G. Unwin, *Studies in Econ. Hist.* 272, 281, 292; D. C. Coleman, *Ind. in Tudor and Stuart Eng.* 29; Sharp, *In Contempt of All Authority*, 7, 259–60; above, this chapter, Econ. (Growth and Development).

with 6 or more hearths, and there was a distinct contrast between the poorer suburban parishes, like St. Giles's and St. Botolph's, and the central and wealthy St. Runwald's, where over 20 per cent of households fell into that category. Of the 9 heads of household with 10 or more hearths whose occupations can be traced, 5 were merchants, 2 were bay- or saymakers, 1 was a joiner, and 1 an innholder. Twenty-six occupiers of dwellings with 6–9 hearths could be identified by occupation. Eleven were bay- or saymakers, and 3 were merchants; the only other occupation to feature twice was that of brewer. As in the 1520s, cloth production and mercantile activity were the main, though not the only, avenues to prosperity in the town.

Some members of the Dutch community amassed substantial wealth from the new draperies which they had introduced. Francis Hockee in 1638 bequeathed a total of £660 in cash to his children, while Francis Pollard left over £520 cash in 1630, and another Francis Pollard, saymaker, left well over £1,000 in 1670. In 1687 Andrew Fromanteel devised a number of houses in Colchester, besides lands at Frating, Great or Little Bentley, and Stanway (Essex), at Aldham, Hadleigh, and Stratford (Suff.), and at Bennington and Boston (Lincs.). George Tayspill, saymaker, bequeathed over £3,000 in money in 1666, and the Tayspill family became one of the wealthiest and most important in the town.[7]

The profits of saymaking were not confined to the Dutch. William Johnson bequeathed £1,400 in cash in 1634, besides the 'competent estate' he had already settled upon his son William. In 1652 Robert Smith, baymaker, left £800 to two of his children, and £30 a year to his wife from his lands and houses in St. James's parish, and in Copford and Birch. Henry Franklin, another baymaker, in 1683 made bequests of over £1,300 in cash and devised houses and land in All Saints' parish and in Wimbish, Thaxted, Lamarsh, Alphamstone, Thorpe-le-Soken, and Tendring. Drapers also prospered; Ralph Creffield the elder in 1666, having already provided for two daughters, bequeathed £700 cash, and lands and houses in St. Peter's, St. James's, and St. Botolph's, and in Great and Little Wigborough, Elmstead, Alresford, Frating, Thorrington, and Great Bentley. Two years later Edmund Thurston of St. Runwald's, draper, left cash bequests totalling over £2,600 to his wife and children, besides his land and houses in Colchester and in Dedham, Great Horkesley, Colne Engaine, Thorpe-le-Soken, Little Holland, St. Osyth, Fingringhoe, Wix, and Walton, and in Stoke-by-Nayland (Suff.).[8]

Among the other later 17th-century tradesmen and craftsmen to leave several hundred pounds, usually in addition to both town and rural land, were a vintner, a brewer, a maltster, a coalmerchant, an ironmonger, a cutler, a carpenter, a cooper, and a tanner. As early as 1624 Geoffrey Langley, grocer, bequeathed almost £1,000 in cash besides an impressive landed estate in Colchester and elsewhere. In 1686 John Furley the elder, merchant, bequeathed over £2,000 in cash, and land in Essex, and houses in Holy Trinity and at the Hythe. In 1696 Isaac Shirley left £1,000 and his lands and houses to his four children, and in 1698 William Talcott of All Saints', whose daughter Ann had married into the Furley family, left enough land, including an 117-a. wood at Stanway and an 111-a. one at East Donyland, to underwrite bequests of £80 a year besides *c.* £1,000 in cash.[9]

[7] E.R.O., D/ABW 55/49; D/ACW 11/188; P.R.O., PROB 11/320, f. 136; PROB 11/333, f. 446; PROB 11/388, f. 287; *Immigrants and Minorities*, i. 271; *Proc. Hug. Soc.* xxi. 24.

[8] E.R.O., D/ACW 17/180; D/ACR 8/58; P.R.O., PROB 11/166, f. 152v.; PROB 11/223, f. 226; PROB 11/373, f. 143.

[9] P.R.O., PROB 11/382, f. 233; PROB 11/430, f. 161v.; PROB 11/444, f. 59.

By the later 17th century several men described themselves as gentleman or esquire. Some were still clearly engaged in trade, like Henry Lamb esquire who in 1688 bequeathed his three ships, *Anne, Abigail and Thomas*, and *Resolution*, besides houses in St. Runwald's, St. Martin's, St. Giles's, and St. Nicholas's and over £1,200 in cash. Others may have retired from trade or have been country landowners attracted to the town by the lure of urban society. Such urban gentlemen often exhibited considerable wealth. In 1690 Joseph Thurston, probably a descendant of Thomas Thurston woollendraper and alderman, bequeathed over £3,400 in cash as well as a large urban and rural estate. Ralph Harrison of St. Leonard's left over £2,000 in cash in 1655, and Thomas Reynolds of St. James's over £3,500 in 1665; both were aldermen and gentlemen and both also owned lands and houses.[10]

The resilience of the town's economy was demonstrated by its rapid recovery from the siege of 1648 and from the plague of 1665–6.[11] Despite the recent expense of caring for its own sick poor, in October 1666 Colchester collected £103 8*s*. 9*d*. for the relief of London after the Great Fire.[12] Although by the late 17th century borough finances were precarious, with indebtedness preventing the construction of a new fishmarket in 1687,[13] the town was able to tap into the wealth of its leading citizens, and also to take advantage of an asset that had been a key to its economic success for over 100 years, when it mortgaged the Dutch Bay Hall and its profits besides the borough lands to wealthy burgesses.[14]

Social Disturbance

Seventeenth-century Colchester witnessed the simultaneous growth of wealth and poverty, and the development of political and religious factions, its inhabitants being called a factious multitude by the bishop of London's commissary in 1623,[15] but the urban social fabric held together remarkably well. In the early 1640s, however, religious and political differences were aggravated by economic distress as the cloth trade, which had been sluggish for 18 months, ground to a halt in 1642. There was a spate of petitions to parliament from Colchester and other towns and counties. Rumours grew of profiteering by the town's M.P., Harbottle Grimston, while the weavers spread the view that M.P.s only sat 'for their own ends to enrich themselves'.[16] Such grievances fuelled the flames of the Civil War factions.[17]

On occasion purely economic grievances did lead to riots, but such disturbances were infrequent. In 1538 some 23 Colchester men had been involved in an inclosure riot.[18] Two inclosure disturbances broke out in 1603, one said to involve 100 people, the other 400. Pales, posts, and rails on St. John's green were pulled down, possibly with the encouragement of Sir Thomas Lucas, who maintained that the pales encroached on the green.[19] More immediately related to the condition of the urban economy was the abortive rising of under-employed weavers in 1566.[20] There is little evidence of rioting in the town in the earlier 17th century, despite recurrent hardship resulting from harvest failure and depression of the cloth trade.[21]

[10] E.R.O., D/ABR 7/290; D/ABR 11/308; P.R.O., PROB 11/144, f. 115; PROB 11/247, f. 146v.; PROB 11/316, f. 382; PROB 11/320, f. 33; PROB 11/330, f. 35v.; PROB 11/332, f. 224; PROB 11/358, f. 13v.; PROB 11/391, f. 153v.; PROB 11/395, f. 84; PROB 11/400, f. 318; PROB 11/401, f. 295; PROB 11/408, f. 299v.; PROB 11/429, f. 184v.

[11] Above, this chapter, Intro.

[12] E.R.O., D/B 5 Gb4, f. 356v.

[13] Ibid. D/B 5 Gb5, f. 264.

[14] Ibid. D/B 5 Gb6, pp. 13, 237, 345, 436.

[15] Hunt, *Puritan Movement*, 94, 104, 176.

[16] A. Fletcher, *Outbreak of Eng. Civil War*, 223, 294.

[17] Above, this chapter, Intro.

[18] E.R.O., D/B 5 Cr107, rot. 3 and d.

[19] Ibid. D/B 5 Sb2/6, ff. 92v.–93.

[20] Above, this chapter, Econ. (Readjustment and Recovery).

[21] Sharpe, *Crime*, 136.

It was in the later 17th century, when conditions for the lower classes were generally improving and economic pressures decreasing, that the borough's textile workers next flexed their muscles.[22] In 1667 the people of St. Giles's attacked the commissioners for the collection of the hearth tax, pursuing them to the King's Head inn where the J.P.s were sitting.[23] In 1675 as many as 300 or 400 poor weavers, summoned by a horn, assembled at 2 a.m. in St. Mary's churchyard, marched to St. John's fields, where the mayor and officers failed to placate them, and thence through the town to John Furley's house, which they threatened to plunder and pull down. Their main demand was for better wages for bay weaving, although Furley's particular crime was 'selling corn out of the land'. With the help of some townsmen the rioters were eventually dispersed, but the trained bands were raised and kept on the alert for three weeks.[24]

Four years later, in 1679, a great company apparently marched through town 'in a rude and tumultuous manner' led by a man with colours flying,[25] and further rumblings were heard in the 1690s after a succession of bad harvests.[26] There were riots in April 1693, a year in which disturbances occurred in a number of towns upon rumour that corn was being bought up and exported to France.[27] In 1695–6 the borough paid for taking four rioters to Chelmsford.[28] In 1703 ten men rioted at the stocks at Lexden; like the rioters of 1675 they had been summoned by a horn, suggesting that the apparently minor affair might have developed into a more general protest.[29] In the early 18th century more serious disturbances arose from depression in the cloth trade and the consequent fall in wages. In 1711 two men declared that all baymakers who would not pay weavers 10*s*. a bay should be pulled from their beds by the poor, carried to St. John's fields, and there hung up.[30] Matters came to a head in 1715 when an assembly of 700–800 weavers stopped proceedings at the Dutch Bay Hall and effectively paralysed both government and industry in the town for three weeks.[31]

The town had weathered earlier trade slumps and poor harvests without such outbreaks of violence. It was some time before the decline of the high real wages of the early 16th century caused distress,[32] and the expansion of the textile industry after the arrival of the Dutch had shielded the town from the worst effects of trade slumps.[33] Even in years of dearth, coarse grain and fish such as sprats, 'the weavers' beef', were usually affordable,[34] and in difficult years the borough authorities were able to do enough to alleviate the short-term problem and to show their concern for the welfare of the poor.[35] By the early 18th century, however, the bay trade had started to contract, organized social protest was more common, and the borough authorities had lost some of their power to regulate the town's economy in the interests of social stability. Fewer foreigners were willing to purchase the freedom, preferring to risk fines for 'keeping open shop' in the borough.[36] The sale of the freedom for political or financial ends can only have tended to discredit the corporation.[37] In 1698 the bakers were accused of conspiring to defraud the poor by counting only 12 instead of 13 or 14 to the dozen, and other traders of

22 Wrigley and Schofield, *Population Hist.* 210–11; C. G. A. Clay, *Econ. Expansion and Social Change: Eng. 1500–1700*, i. 140–1.
23 E.R.O., D/B 5 Sb2/9, f. 166.
24 Ibid. D/B 5 Sb2/9, ff. 223v.–226v.; P.R.O., PC 2/65, ff. 17, 20; *Cal. S.P. Dom.* 1675–6, 513–14.
25 E.R.O., D/B 5 Sb2/9, f. 245.
26 *Agric. Hist. Rev.* xvi. 30; Outhwaite, *Dearth*, 20.
27 E.R.O., D/B 5 Sr56, rot. 13; P.R.O., PC 2/75, f. 146.
28 E.R.O., D/B 5 Aa1/35, f. 67.
29 Ibid. D/B 5 Sr71, rot. 13.
30 Ibid. D/B 5 Sr91, rot. 12.
31 *Bull. Inst. Hist. Res.* xxix. 220–30; Sharpe, *Crime*, 137–8.
32 *Immigrants and Minorities*, i. 269–72.
33 E.R.O., D/B 5 Sb2/6, f. 270.
34 Ibid. D/B 5 Cb1/4, f. 340; T. Fuller, *Worthies of Eng.* i. 498.
35 *Past and Present*, lxxi. 22–42.
36 E.R.O., D/B 5 Gb6, pp. 112, 116; D/B 5 Sr62, rot. 59.
37 Below, this chapter, Boro. Govt.

forestalling butter and eggs before they reached the market. Critics asked for the public display of the assize of bread so that the poor should know what they ought to have for their money.[38] In 1712 several bakers who had been punished for breaking the assize sued the mayor and aldermen.[39] That antagonism between rulers and ruled, rich and poor, contrasts with the paternalism of Thomas Christmas's will in 1520,[40] and illustrates the distance which separated early 18th-century Colchester society from that which had existed two centuries earlier.

TOPOGRAPHY

The Town to 1640

By *c.* 1500 houses extended well beyond the town walls in ribbon developments along the major roads, notably East Hill and East Street, Middleborough and North Street, and Magdalen Street, and in more compact suburbs outside South gate and Head gate. The settlement at the Hythe was still separated from the town by fields. Within the walls large areas of open ground remained, notably at Bury field in the south-east quarter, around the castle in the north-east, and between the wall and Head Street and North Hill in the west. Even in the main streets a decline in population in the later Middle Ages had reduced the pressure on space, and most houses had gardens or yards. Physical decay, particularly in the northern and south-eastern suburbs, seems to have become noticeable by the 1520s and 1530s, and the dissolution of the monasteries hastened the decline of the south-eastern suburb, which had been dominated by St. John's abbey and St. Botolph's priory.

By 1535 four cottages in Magdalen Street had fallen down, and an empty house site in the same street was recorded in 1538.[41] By 1539, of the houses owing rents to St. John's abbey, two in Stanwell Street and two in Lodder's Lane (Abbeygate Street) were 'decayed', and another, possibly in East Stockwell Street, had been knocked down, but the total of five houses was relatively insignificant in a rental of *c.* 163.[42] A house and three 'rents', small houses or cottages, at the Hythe were made into one house before 1542.[43] Before 1543 a total of 29 houses in Head ward, at least nine of them within the walls, had either been taken down or were 'sore decayed',[44] but not all were necessarily dwellings. As many as 13 houses formerly belonging to St. John's south and east of the walls had fallen down or been destroyed by *c.* 1550: 2 in Magdalen Street, 1 in Stanwell Street, 4 in Lodders Lane, at least 3 on St. John's green, 2 in East Street, and 1 in Holy Trinity parish, probably outside Scheregate. Another 34 were in need of repair. Not all the 'decay' was recent; three houses in Lodders Lane had been 'badly devastated' for 16 years, and that in Holy Trinity parish had been totally destroyed 'for a long time'. The decay of a house in East Street and of the Lamb or New inn on St. John's green was attributed to the attainder of the abbey in 1539.[45]

Two houses beyond North bridge had been made into one by 1534, and two in Wyre Street were similarly joined in 1540. Buildings on a plot in Stockwell Street, apparently developed late in the Middle Ages, had fallen down by 1541.[46] A house called Hell, on the south side of Culver Street, seems to have been demolished

[38] E.R.O., D/B 5 Sr62, rot. 17.

[39] Ibid. D/B 5 Gb7, ff. 9, 10.

[40] P.R.O., PROB 11/19, ff. 28 sqq.; above, this chapter, Econ. (Early 16th century).

[41] E.R.O., D/B 5 Cr104, rot. 6d.; Cr106, rot. 5.

[42] P.R.O., SC 6/Hen. VIII/976.

[43] E.R.O., D/B 5 Cr113, rot. 17.

[44] Ibid. D/Y 2/2, p. 13.

[45] P.R.O., E 310/13/40; E 318/20/1054.

[46] E.R.O., D/B 5 Cr104, rot. 9; D/B 5 Cr110, rot. 4d.; D/B 5 Cr113, rot. 18d.

between 1540 and 1543.[47] In 1548–9 the borough chamberlain was unable to collect rents from unoccupied houses outside Ryegate, in Bere Lane (Vineyard Street), and next to Holy Trinity church, while a house in East Street had fallen down.[48] There were still at least 2 empty plots, formerly house sites, in Stanwell Street, 1 in Lodders Lane, and 3 on St. John's green in 1581.[49]

Elsewhere there is evidence for increased occupancy and some new building or rebuilding. A house in St. Botolph's parish, divided in 1503, remained so in 1549, and ownership of part of a house there was disputed *c.* 1530.[50] Part of a large house in St. Peter's parish was sold in 1543, and Thomas Whitbread (d. *c.* 1520) divided a house in Headgate into two. A large house in West Stockwell Street seems to have been divided in 1532.[51] In 1542 the former St. Botolph's priory barn near the corner of St. Botolph's Street and Magdalen Street was converted into houses, and other parts of the St. Botolph's site developed.[52] In 1548–9 the chamberlain collected rents from 'newly built' shops and solars in front of the Red Lion inn and from 'new' buildings in Maidenburgh Street behind the George inn.[53]

When the economy began to recover in the 1550s or 1560s,[54] physical repair and expansion soon followed. In 1578 the borough required the tenant of a house west of the moot hall to rebuild the parts of it which had fallen down.[55] In 1580 alderman Robert Mott sold a house 'lately waste and recently built' in St. Martin's parish. At least one plot of land taken from Bury field had been 'lately' built on in 1581. A newly built house on the corner of North Street and Sheepen Lane was sold in 1594.[56] In 1610 the borough granted a building lease of a piece of waste in St. James's parish, and licensed building on the waste in East Stockwell Street.[57] Another building lease, of land at the Hythe, was granted in 1608, and in 1609 Henry Barrington agreed to build a new millhouse there with a cellar, a brick chimney, and two fireplaces. In 1623 the water bailiff was instructed to demolish and rebuild the warehouses on the waterfront.[58] Two new houses were built next to a house in All Saints' parish between 1559 and 1621. By 1634 the adjoining barn had been made into a cottage, and that too was divided in 1635.[59] The former no. 11 Sir Isaac's Walk may also have been converted to a dwelling-house from a barn at that time. It stands well back from the street frontage, and its plan, with three rooms on each floor and a large internal stack, is like that of a farmhouse. Before 1625 two 'rents' and a house were built in Dovehouse field on the west side of the road beyond North bridge, and the borough granted a building lease of a large plot outside Headgate in 1619.[60]

Division of houses continued: a house called the Crown, on the south side of High Street next to the Red Lion inn, had been divided into two before 1555, and in 1597 it was occupied by four households.[61] William Ingram in 1601 and 1603 sold two separate parcels of his house in Wyre Street, which itself seems once to have been part of the neighbouring house. By 1622 a house in All Saints' parish was divided between three or four tenants, some apparently occupying only one room.[62] Other divided houses were large; in 1609 one in St. Mary's parish, probably in Headgate, comprised three low rooms or chambers, one of them a shop on the

47 Ibid. D/B 5 Cr109, rot. 13; D/Y 2/2, p. 13.
48 B.L. Stowe MS. 829, ff. 19v., 20v.–22.
49 P.R.O., E 178/819.
50 Ibid. STAC 2/23, no. 122; STAC 2/24, no. 225.
51 E.R.O., D/B 5 Cr109, rot. 8; Cr110, rot. 13 and d.; D/B 5 R1, f. 127.
52 Ibid. Acc. C338; ibid. D/B 5 Cr112, rott. 6d., 15d.
53 B.L. Stowe MS. 829, f. 16 and v.
54 Above, this chapter, Econ. (Readjustment and Recovery).
55 E.R.O., D/B 5 Gb1, 17 Mar. 1578.
56 Ibid. D/B 5 Cr142, rott. 10, 29d.; Cr157, rot. 7.
57 Ibid. D/B 5 Gb2, f. 95.
58 Ibid. ff. 70v., 78v.; D/B 5 Gb3, f. 28v.
59 Ibid. D/B 5 Cb1/6, f. 221.
60 Ibid. Acc. C47, CPL 311–18.
61 Ibid. D/B 5 Cr120, rot. 13; Cr158, rot. 19.
62 Ibid. D/B 5 Cb1/5, ff. 118, 342; Cb1/7, ff. 122, 171.

street frontage, the kitchen, buttery, bakehouse, and storehouse on the ground floor, with seven chambers on the first floor.[63]

There were no clearly-defined industrial or craft areas in the town, but most mariners, not surprisingly, lived at the Hythe. So did many merchants, 10 out of the 13 whose addresses were recorded between 1500 and 1619. Clothmakers tended to live and work to the east, north, and south of the walls, where water was readily available; about two thirds of the known clothiers and baymakers between 1500 and 1619 lived in St. Peter's or St. James's parish.[64] The clothmaker Nicholas Maynard had water piped to his East Street house and workshops from the Colne at East mill in 1549. By 1571 a tenter yard and a tenter garden adjoined the house and workshops, which seem to have survived as a large group of buildings at the bottom of East Hill in 1748.[65] In 1535 and 1545 the clothier Henry Webb had permission to bring water, presumably from Chiswell, to his house in North Street,[66] probably the early 16th-century building later the Marquis of Granby inn. A beam in its east wing bears a shield with the initials HW.[67] A clothier's house beyond North bridge included a 'folding shop' and a tenter yard in 1604, and there were other tenters in a field in North Street in 1606. Other clothworkers lived near Losebrook, outside South or St. Botolph's gate, in 1511 and 1525.[68] Many butchers lived in East and West Stockwell Streets, near the shambles, and as late as 1580 had slaughter-houses there.[69]

The few borough buildings were in the western half of High Street. The moot hall, near the corner with West Stockwell Street, apparently remained substantially unchanged from 1373–4 until its demolition in 1843. At the west end of the street was the corn market, stalls or galleries erected against the building known as St. Peter's 'rents' in 1546, the Red Row by 1549. The 'rents' were apparently rebuilt by the prior of the Crutched friars before 1517. They were sold before the Dissolution, and passed through several hands before being acquired by the borough.[70] The borough repaired or rebuilt the corn market between 1627 and 1629, and by 1631 the rooms above the Red Row formed the Dutch Bay Hall.[71] West of St. Runwald's church, a market cross with an open ground floor and a room above replaced the medieval butter market or stall *c.* 1590. The town butchers' shambles, which stood in the middle of the street east of St. Runwald's, were rebuilt in 1583–4 as a substantial, two-storeyed structure. The fish market, in front of the Red Lion inn and its adjoining houses, was held in privately owned stalls.[72] When in 1557 the clerk of the market was appointed to oversee the maintenance and repair of buildings belonging to the town, only the bridges and mills were specifically mentioned; even the moot hall was included among 'other buildings'.[73] The borough repaired the 'ruinous' North and East bridges in 1631. Little attempt was made to maintain the town walls, or even, apparently, the gates.[74]

The castle, which had dominated the medieval town, was allowed to fall into decay in the 15th and 16th centuries. The bailey buildings fell down, and by 1622 much of the bailey wall had also gone, and houses were encroaching onto the site

63 Ibid. D/B 5 Cb1/8, ff. 72v.–73; D/B 5 Gb2, f. 180 and v.

64 Goose, 'Econ. and Social Aspects', 222–3.

65 E.R.O., D/B 5 Cr117, rot. 7; Cr136, rot. 4 and d.; Morant, *Colch.* map facing p. 4.

66 B.L. Stowe MS. 834, f. 82 and v.; E.R.O., D/B 5 Cr116, rot. 12 and d.

67 *E.R.* xxxiii. 103–5; R.C.H.M. *Essex*, iii. 61.

68 E.R.O., D/B 5 Cb1/5, f. 385; Cb1/8, ff. 72v.–73; D/B 5 Cr84, rot. 6; Cr95, rot. 10d.

69 Ibid. D/B 5 Cr142, rot. 10.

70 Ibid. D/B 5 Cr115, rot. 8; Cr135, rot. 3d.; B.L. Stowe MS. 829, f. 31; Morant, *Colch.* 111.

71 E.R.O., D/B 5 Gb3, f. 103v.; below, Markets.

72 E.R.O., D/B 5 Cr87, rot. 18; below, Markets.

73 E.R.O., D/B 5 Cr123, rot. 10.

74 Below, Communications (Bridges); Walls etc.

of its ditch. St. Giles's church was remodelled, and given a south porch and a new north chapel in the early 16th century. The tower of All Saints' church was rebuilt *c.* 1500, that of St. Mary's-at-the-Walls *c.* 1534, and north vestries were added to St. Leonard's and St. Peter's about the same time,[75] but no work seems to have been done after the Reformation. The tall, 'stately contrived' water house and works in Windmill field west of the town were built in 1620 by alderman Thomas Thurston.[76]

The Civil War and Siege

At the start of the Civil War in 1642 the town defences were improved, ramparts being built behind lost or weakened sections of the wall. By 1643 'forts', perhaps including an outwork on the north-east corner of the walls, had been added. The siege of 1648 caused extensive destruction, particularly in the suburbs, which were burnt by both sides to deprive the enemy of cover and to open up lines of fire. Sir John Lucas's house at St. John's Abbey, Sir Harbottle Grimston's at the Crutched Friars, and Henry Barrington's in the fields south-east of the town were among those destroyed.[77]

Eyewitnesses at the end of the siege described 'many fair houses' and 'fair streets ... of stately houses' burnt to ashes.[78] In March 1649 at least 193 tax-paying houses were still derelict having been burnt or pulled down during the siege: 53 in St. Botolph's, 51 in St. Mary's-at-the-Walls, 35 in St. James's (including the rectory house), 32 in Holy Trinity, 17 in St. Giles's, and 5 in St. Martin's.[79] Many poorer houses and cottages, particularly in St. Mary Magdalen's, were also destroyed. A tax assessment made in July 1649 confirms that the worst damage was in St. Botolph's, St. Giles's, and St. Mary's-at-the-Walls parishes, which were each granted a reduction of over a third in their tax. St. Peter's, St. James's, St. Leonard's, and St. Runwald's were each granted a reduction of between a quarter and a third, while the assessments of the remaining intramural parishes were reduced by between 15 and 24 per cent.[80]

Most private houses were quickly rebuilt or repaired; several were already under repair in December 1648.[81] The borough granted building leases of two plots of land 'in', presumably by, the postern, perhaps the sites of houses near St. Mary's-at-the-Walls destroyed in the siege, in 1651. Elsewhere, the sites of three burnt houses in St. Botolph's Street, by the priory entrance, were still tofts or parcels of ground in 1654.[82] The suburbs were said to be under repair in 1656, but sites in Crouch Street and Priory Street were still vacant then and in 1659.[83] The site of two burnt houses at the north end of North bridge seems to have remained empty for several years, although new houses had been built by 1683.[84] As late as 1698 Magdalen Street apparently still bore marks of the siege.[85] Henry Barrington's house had been rebuilt by 1656, but the Lucas house at St. John's and Sir Harbottle Grimston's Crutched Friars never recovered from the siege.[86] Three churches were 'ruined': St. Botolph's, St. Giles's, and St. Mary's-at-the-Walls; St. Martin's and St. Mary Magdalen's were 'decayed' in 1650, presumably

[75] Below, Castle; Churches.

[76] *East Anglian N. & Q.* N.S. iii. 31; below, Public Services.

[77] Above, Fig. 8.

[78] J. Rushworth, *Hist. Colln.* vii. 1242; *True Relation of the Taking of Colch.* (1648): copy in E.C.L. Colch.

[79] E.R.O., D/Y 2/2, p. 304; ibid. T/A 465/106 (Boro. Mun., Acc. C1, assessment of 1649); Smith, *Eccl. Hist. Essex*, 318–19.

[80] B.L. Stowe MS. 833, f. 64.

[81] E.R.O., D/B 5 Gb4, f. 24v.

[82] Ibid. f. 55; D/DMb T55.

[83] Ibid. D/DC 22/27; D/DO T955; *Diary of John Evelyn*, ed. E. S. de Beer, iii. 176–7.

[84] E.R.O., Boro. Mun., Ct. R. 200, rot. 8.

[85] *Journeys of Celia Fiennes*, ed. C. Morris, 142–3.

[86] E.R.O., D/Q 30/1/4, no. 2; below, Religious Houses.

as a result of the fighting.[87] All five churches remained unrepaired throughout the later 17th century; St. Runwald's was also out of repair for much of the century, and St. Nicholas's was extensively damaged by the fall of its tower *c.* 1700. Their ruins gave an aura of decay to the otherwise rebuilt town. Daniel Defoe in 1722 reported that the town 'still mourns in the ruins of a civil war' and referred to its 'battered walls, breaches in the turrets, and ruined churches'.[88]

The Later 17th Century

The built-up area continued to expand, particularly in Moor Elms Lane (Priory Street) where houses were being built on the waste in 1658 and before 1672, and another house had been divided into four by 1683.[89] Building leases were granted in 1681 for land at Knaves Acre in the Hythe and for a two-storeyed house with two rooms on each floor, 'well tiled, glazed, and finished', in the postern in St.

FIG. 9. PART OF A PROSPECT OF COLCHESTER FROM THE NORTH, 1697
showing the tower of St. Peter's church on the left, the roofless tower of St. Mary's on the right with the windmill beside it, and tenter grounds in the foreground to the right

Peter's parish.[90] A house built after the siege on the site of Botolph's barn outside South gate had been divided by 1683.[91] In the central area, division of large houses continued: ten rooms, including the hall, shop, and kitchen, with four chambers above them, had been separated from the rest of the former King's Arms or Sun inn in High Street by 1682. A messuage sold in 1684 was clearly composed of rooms once part of one or two houses; it comprised the passage from the street to the yard, the low room next to the street with the chamber over it, a chamber over part of an adjoining building, a staircase leading to the two chambers, a shop, and a back buttery.[92] Other divided houses were recorded regularly in the 1680s and 1690s.[93] When a house in St. James's parish was divided in 1706, one occupant

87 Smith, *Eccl. Hist. Essex*, 318–19.

88 Daniel Defoe, *Tour*, ed. G. D. H. Cole (1927), i. 16.

89 E.R.O., D/B 5 Gb4, f. 173; Gb5, f. 72; ibid. Boro. Mun., Ct. R. 200, rot. 4d.

90 Ibid. D/B 5 Gb5, ff. 180, 182.

91 Ibid. Boro. Mun., Ct. R. 200, rot. 11.

92 Ibid. Ct. R. 201, rot. 11.

93 Ibid. Ct. R. 200, rot. 1; 201, rott. 4, 12; 202, rot. 9; 207, rot. 1d.; 208, rot. 1; 216, rot. 5.

was required to build a new brick wall between the two portions.[94] By then demand for houses had eased. A 'newly built' house near North bridge was empty in 1708, and a house outside the walls in St. Mary's-at-the-Walls parish which fell down between 1673 and 1709 was not rebuilt.[95]

The market place was reorganized in 1659 and 1660, the fish market being moved from High Street to St. Nicholas's Street, and the country butchers' stalls demolished. The town butchers' shambles remained east of St. Runwald's church, but fewer butchers seem to have lived in East and West Stockwell Streets than in the 16th century and the early 17th.[96] The earlier concentrations of clothworkers near the river declined in the 17th century, but by the end of the century there was a large group of possibly industrial buildings in Ostrich Yard outside Ryegate besides that at the bottom of East Hill.[97] Fewer merchants were recorded in St. Leonard's at the Hythe, only 7 out of the 20 known to have lived in the town between 1619 and 1700, and the relative wealth of that parish declined.[98] Nevertheless in 1692 John Barrington was accused of building a warehouse on land there which should have contained no more than a fence, and by 1689 there was a 'new building' and a coalyard beside Hythe mill.[99] Improvements made to the navigation of the Colne under an Act of 1698,[1] presumably encouraged further commercial development in the early 18th century.

Despite the relative prosperity of the later 17th-century town, little public building was done. Indeed, the top storey of the castle was blown off with gunpowder in the 1690s and the reorganization of the market place seems to have involved more demolition than building.[2] The Red Row or Bay Hall was still in 1698 'a long building like stalls' on which the bays were exposed for sale. The streets, however, were then broad and well pitched.[3] The borough maintained North, East, and Hythe bridges, using stone from the partially demolished castle in 1696 and 1698, and borrowing £350 for the repair of the bridges, moot hall, and part of High Street in 1701. The town wall between Head gate and Scheregate was level with the ground *c.* 1700; part of East gate fell down in 1652, and more was pulled down in 1676.[4] The provision of piped water, from Chiswell, was again undertaken by individuals, not the borough; the first attempt in 1687 failed, and the waterworks did not operate until 1707.[5]

The Buildings

Most houses were timber-framed and plastered, with tiled roofs. Except in High Street and at the top of North Hill where there were three-storeyed houses, they were of two storeys with attics. Celia Fiennes observed in 1698 that 'the fashion of the country lies much in long roofs and great cantilevers and peaks'.[6] As the single-storeyed halls were rebuilt to provide more accommodation, especially when they were on the street frontage, so jettied construction, which had been usual on cross wings, became common along the whole length of frontages. The jettied northern part of no. 30 East Stockwell Street occupies the site of the medieval hall, while the southern half of the west side of Trinity Street appears to be a uniform range of jettied buildings of the 16th century. The fashion for jettying continued

94 Ibid. Ct. R. 224, rot. 2d.
95 Ibid. Ct. R. 225, rot. 6; 226, rot. 10.
96 Goose, 'Econ. and Social Aspects', 222; below, Markets.
97 Morant, *Colch.* map facing p. 4; E.R.O., Boro. Mun., Ct. R. 226, rot. 9.
98 Goose, 'Econ. and Social Aspects', 222.
99 E.R.O., D/B 5 Gb5, ff. 351, 354; ibid. Boro. Mun., Ct. R. 208, rot. 1.
1 Below, Port.
2 Below, Castle; Markets.
3 *Journeys of Celia Fiennes*, 142–3.
4 E.R.O., D/B 5 Gb6, p. 233; below, Communications (Bridges); Castle; Walls.
5 Below, Public Services (Water Supply).
6 *Journeys of Celia Fiennes*, 143.

into the later 17th century, the latest certain example being nos. 83–84 High Street, dated 1680. Whereas the early brackets were thin and had a simple curve, the later ones were broad and often incorporated a scroll. With the fashion for long jetties and heavy brackets went one for large gables rising off the eaves. Structurally the gables are secondary to the main ridge, which is normally parallel to the street, and they are sometimes jettied like the floor below. Nos. 29–32 West Stockwell Street has jetties and large gables on a house whose three-roomed plan with a large internal stack is of a characteristically rural type.

Houses varied in size from the large town houses of the duke of Norfolk and Thomas Audley, which became the Red Lion and the King's Head inns respectively, to merchants' houses with warehouses round a courtyard, like Winsleys at the eastern end of High Street, and to two-roomed cottages or 'rents'.[7] Headgate House, the former King's Head inn, is arranged around the east, north, and west sides of a courtyard off the west side of Head Street. The tall west range has walls of brick which incorporate at the south end a doorway with four-centred head and a large first-floor fireplace of similar form, perhaps part of Audley's house or that of his successor Richard Duke, clerk of the court of Augmentations.[8] A range was added to the back in the earlier 18th century to form an assembly room for the inn. The north range is timber-framed, and probably 17th-century; the east range, which incorporates the carriageway to the street, is also timber-framed. Tymperleys off Trinity Street, claimed as the house of William Gilberd (d. 1603), incorporates the 15th-century timber-framed parlour range of a house of which the hall was probably immediately to the east and parallel to the street. The range preserved in the house to the south was probably adjacent to the service end of the hall. The hall was demolished in the 16th or 17th century, and a linking range built between the parlour and the street range of the house. The parlour range was extended westwards on more than one occasion.

Tile was used for roofs of quite modest houses by the mid 16th century,[9] and brick was used in grand houses such as the former King's Head inn and for chimneys early in the century. A borough lease of 1617 required a new house to have a tiled roof and a brick chimney, and similar leases of 1619 and 1629 prohibited the use of thatch.[10] The borough was erecting a brick building in 1618, and an L-shaped brick house of *c.* 1620 survived in Northgate Street in the early 20th century. Brick warehouses were built at the Hythe in 1623.[11] Nevertheless brick houses were still sufficiently unusual in the 1680s for one outside Scheregate and one in St. Mary's-at-the-Walls to be so named, and brick-built houses were so described in 1702 and 1703.[12] Before 1698 wealthy Quakers, perhaps members of the Furley family in Holy Trinity parish, had built a few brick houses 'in the London mode'.[13] The houses may have been only brick fronted, and may indeed have been those at the north end of Trinity Street whose mid 17th-century façade of orange brick decorated with a plinth and pilasters survived, encased in a later building, in the 1980s.[14] Such refronting became more general later in the century.[15] Encroachment in front of houses in Holy Trinity parish in 1696 and in All Saints' in 1697 may have been infillings under overhanging first floors. So may that of the

7 Colch. Arch. Group, *Bull.* xxxi. 9–12; E.R.O., Boro. Mun., Ct. R. 215, rot. 4.

8 E.R.O., D/B 5 Cr114, rot. 8; Cr115, rot. 8.

9 e.g. P.R.O., STAC 2/23/122.

10 E.R.O., D/B 5 Gb2, ff. 160v., 180 and v.; Gb3, f. 88.

11 Ibid. D/B 5 Gb2, f. 165v.; Gb3, f. 28v.; R.C.H.M. *Essex*, 62.

12 E.R.O., Boro. Mun., Ct. R. 202, rot. 3; 209, rot. 4; 219, rot. 12; 220, rot. 8.

13 *Journeys of Celia Fiennes*, 142–3.

14 *Colch. Arch. Rep.* vi. 347–54.

15 R.C.H.M. *Essex*, iii. 54.

owner of the house next to the Red Lion, who in 1703 was encroaching on the road to enlarge his shop.[16]

Most houses in the main streets had shops on at least part of their street frontage, often with a parlour or hall on the street or immediately behind it. Other buildings, including warehouses, were grouped round courtyards entered by a great gate.[17] In the later 17th century the plaster of outer walls, particularly on gables, was often decorated with pargetting, described by a French visitor in 1698 as 'all raised into ornaments stamped upon the plaster, as we impress a seal upon wax; heads of beasts, festoons, cartridges, animals, and compartments, etc. all wretchedly designed and worse executed.' An early surviving example on the gable of no. 37 North Hill is dated 1666.[18] By the late 16th century merchants had glass in their windows and wainscot in their halls and parlours.[19] Re-used heraldic glass in the Siege House in East Street in 1922, apparently from another Colchester house, contained the date 1546 and the initials WS, perhaps for William Strachey, merchant, bailiff in 1555.[20] A clothier's house beyond East bridge in 1630 had a wainscoted hall with a parlour opening off it and another room opening off the parlour. A saymaker's house in St. Botolph's parish also had wainscoting and glass windows in 1638.[21] An elaborate, early 17th-century plaster ceiling survived in a house in Maidenburgh Street in 1922.[22]

Many inns stood near the town gates, like the Maidenhead on the corner of Crouch Street and Maldon Road, recorded from 1554 until its licence was revoked for disorders in 1698.[23] Others like the Crown, where plays were performed in 1566, were at the Hythe,[24] but the main inns, like other large houses, were concentrated in Head Street, North Hill, and High Street.

The Bell, the Crown, and the New inn or the White (later the Red) Lion, stood side by side on the south side of High Street in 1522.[25] The White Lion had been built as a town house for John Howard, Lord Howard, later duke of Norfolk, in 1481 or 1482, and seems to have become an inn between 1501 and 1515 when it was the New inn, with a sign on the street.[26] It was one of three inns appointed as wine taverns in 1604.[27] The Bell and the Crown were private houses by 1597.[28] The George, presumably the surviving inn on the north side of High Street, was recorded in 1551 and 1566.[29] In 1617 a total of 331 free burgesses ate an election dinner there in the gatehouse chamber, the rose chamber, the cock chamber, the George chamber, the lower parlour, the kitchen chamber, the street parlour, the hall, and the cellar.[30] The White Hart on the south side of High Street in St. Peter's parish, another of the licensed wine taverns of 1604, was an inn in 1539 and was still one in 1705. It accommodated 156 people for an election dinner in 1579.[31] The Angel, the third licensed wine tavern in 1604, was an **L**-shaped building on the corner of High Street and West Stockwell Street, probably with a hall parallel to High Street. First recorded by that name in 1517, it was an inn or at least an alehouse in 1585.[32]

[16] E.R.O., D/B 5 Gb6, pp. 70, 106, 280.

[17] e.g. E.R.O., D/B 5 Cb1/6, f. 221; Colch. Arch. Group, *Bull.* xxxi. 9–10, 27.

[18] *M.[Henri de Valbourg] Misson's Memoirs and Observations in his Travels over Eng.* (1719), 40; Colch. Arch. Group, *Bull.* xxix. 16–17.

[19] E.R.O., D/B 5 Cr154, rot. 5d.; Cr158, rot. 14d.; Cr162, rot. 9d.

[20] R.C.H.M. *Essex*, iii. 70; E.R.O., D/B 5 R1, f. 133.

[21] E.R.O., D/B 5 Cb1/9, f. 68v.; Cb1/10, f. 483v.

[22] R.C.H.M. *Essex*, iii. 63.

[23] E.R.O., D/B 5 Sb2/2, ff. 1–20v.; D/B 5 Cr120, rot. 14d.; D/B 5 Cb1/8, ff. 282v.–283; D/B 5 Sb4/2, 11 Aug. 1698; D/DU 289/13; Emmison, *Elizabethan Life: Disorder*, 215.

[24] Ibid. D/B 5 R5, f. 79v.; D/B 5 Cr153, rot. 20d.

[25] Ibid. D/B 5 Cr93, rot. 13.

[26] J. Harvey, *Eng. Med. Architects* (1984), 302; B.L. Add. Ch. 215; Bodl. MS. Rolls Essex 2.

[27] E.R.O., D/B 5 Gb2, f. 40.

[28] Ibid. D/B 5 Cr158, rot. 19.

[29] Ibid. D/B 5 Cr119, rot. 6; D/B 5 R5, ff. 76v.–77.

[30] Ibid. D/B 5 Ab1/8, rot. 19.

[31] Ibid. D/B 5 Ab1/2; D/B 5 Gb2, f. 40; D/B 5 Cr109, rot. 4d.; D/B 5 Sr76, rot. 7; ibid. Acc. C210, J. B. Harvey Colln. v, p. 51.

[32] E.R.O., D/B 5 Gb2, f. 40; D/B 5 R2, f. 105v.; D/ACA 14, f. 104v.; Colch. Arch. Group, *Bull.* xxxi. 27–9.

The King's Head, in Head Street near Head gate, was an inn in the 1550s, and in 1565 its innholder was licensed to keep a 'tennis play' as recreation for gentlemen and 'other fit persons'.[33] As many as 232 freemen ate an election dinner there in 1600, occupying 'Mr. bailiffs chamber', the little building, the lower great building, the other lower building, the street parlour, the roof parlour, Michelle's chamber, and the hall.[34] The inn was probably the house in St. Mary's parish assessed on 22 hearths in 1671, the greatest number of hearths in any house in the town.[35]

BOROUGH GOVERNMENT

COLCHESTER'S judicial liberties were established by its medieval charters, confirmed by *inspeximus* in 1488, 1547, 1553, 1559, 1605, and 1629. To earlier privileges was added exemption from service as sheriff or escheator and from the jurisdiction of the county coroner, given by the charter of 1535 granting Kingswood heath to the borough.[36] In the late 16th century, however, the town lost its immunity from purveyance. The bailiffs acquiesced in a demand for fish in 1587 although some townsmen resisted the purveyor, but when in 1593 the town was assessed at £12 a year composition for purveyance, the corporation determined not to pay. In the ensuing dispute the purveyor seized cattle from the town's commons.[37] The town seems to have accepted defeat by 1597 when the bailiffs unsuccessfully petitioned Sir Robert Cecil for a reduction in their assessment.[38] The dissolution of St. John's abbey and St. Botolph's priory removed two rival liberties within the borough, but the claims of St. John's to exemption from the borough's jurisdiction were inherited by the Audleys and the Lucases. In 1565 Thomas Audley of Berechurch tried to exclude borough officials from his manor.[39] His widow Catherine refused to muster with the borough in 1580, and the following year she and Francis Jobson of Monkwick had themselves assessed for subsidy in Lexden hundred instead of in Colchester. An attempt by the borough sub-collectors to distrain on cattle in Berechurch in 1581 led to a riot.[40] In 1582 and 1583 the borough was in dispute with Sir Thomas Lucas, owner of St. John's abbey, over waste ground in Greenstead and other matters.[41]

Extensive privileges were granted to the Dutch congregation established in 1570 or 1571.[42] The Dutch were allowed their own church, although they had to pay church rates in the parishes in which they lived, and were responsible for the maintenance of their own poor. Most important, they controlled the trade in bays and says, which they were allowed to carry on without becoming freemen of the town. The two governors of the Dutch Bay Hall and their 22 assistants made and changed regulations for the bay trade, and their officers inspected and sealed all bays made in Colchester whether by Dutchmen or, increasingly in the 17th century, by Englishmen.[43] Although the Dutch contributed to subsidies and other taxes laid on the town, and were subject to the borough courts, their economic privileges placed them apart from the English and led to friction, particularly in the early

33 *E.A.T.* 3rd ser. xv. 92; *Cal. Pat.* 1563–6, p. 329.

34 E.R.O., D/B 5 Ab1/4.

35 Ibid. Q/STh5; P.R.O., PROB 11/336, f. 143v.

36 *Colch. Charters*, 56–9, 76–80.

37 E.R.O., D/Y 2/6, pp. 17, 21, 23; D/B 5 Gb1, 29 Mar. 1593; 14 Mar. 1594; 2 Sept., 10 Nov. 1595; B.L. Lansdowne MS. 73, f. 118.

38 *Cal. S.P. Dom.* 1595–7, 162; Hist. MSS. Com. 9, *Salisbury*, vii, p. 332; ix, p. 396.

39 E.R.O., D/B 5 R5, f. 66v.

40 Ibid. D/B 5 Ab1/2; D/B 5 Gb1, 30 May, 8 Nov. 1581; D/B 5 Sb2/4, ff. 4v.–5v.; D/DRg 1/117; *Acts of P.C.* 1581–2, 124.

41 E.R.O., D/B 5 Gb1, 13 July 1582; 27 Aug. 1583; D/Y 2/7, p. 205.

42 *Immigrants and Minorities*, i. 266–70.

43 *V.C.H. Essex*, ii. 388; *Reg. Baptisms in Dutch Ch. at Colch.* (Huguenot Soc. xii), pp. i–xxvii, xli.

17th century, when they were supported by the Privy Council.[44] The governors of the Dutch Bay Hall retained their control of the bay trade until 1728.[45]

The composition of the freeman body, Colchester's governing class, became a matter of increasing concern to the borough officers in the 16th and 17th centuries. The medieval practice whereby all men born in the borough were entitled to enter the freedom without fee survived until *c.* 1550 when that right was apparently restricted to the sons of freemen.[46] In 1565 all those claiming the freedom by birth were ordered to be sworn in the borough court at the age of 20, paying no more than 2*d.* to the clerk and 4*d.* to the serjeants. Non-resident freemen were ordered to come to elections.[47] An order of 1523, repeated *c.* 1550 and in 1583, allowed the admission of a freeman's former apprentice for a fine of 3*s.* 4*d.*, provided that the apprenticeship of seven or more years had been registered at its start, and the order for such registration was repeated in 1660.[48] In 1637 the fine for the admission of 'foreigners' was raised to £10, and they were required to be approved by representatives of their craft; in 1654 the consent of the borough assembly was required.[49]

The number of active freemen fluctuated, but seems to have increased overall in the earlier 17th century, from perhaps *c.* 450 in 1619 to *c.* 900 in 1646. Numbers seem to have fallen in the later 17th century, but rose rapidly at its end, perhaps reaching *c.* 1,100 in 1704.[50] In the early 18th century freedoms were sold to raise money, and the system was also blatantly manipulated for political purposes: 234 men were admitted by birth or apprenticeship in 1700–1, and 39 bought their freedom from Ralph Creffield, mayor 1702–3. In 1705 the practice of admitting large numbers of men either by purchase or on dubious grounds was said to be 'an invasion of the rights and privileges of the honest free burgesses', but the sale of freedoms was complained of again in 1711 and 1713.[51]

Officers and Politics 1485–1635

Until 1635 Colchester was governed under the provisions of the charter of 1462. The principal officers were the 2 bailiffs who with the 8 other aldermen, 16 members of the first council, and 16 members of the second council, formed the common council of the borough, known by the 16th century as the assembly. The bailiffs and 2 aldermen, with the recorder, were J.P.s; 2 aldermen served as coroners, and 2 aldermen and 2 councillors as keykeepers, responsible for the common chest in which the borough seal, plate, records, and money were kept.[52] Those officers, with the chamberlain who was responsible for the borough's day to day finances, were elected annually. In the early 16th century the method and dates of election were those laid down in 1372. At a meeting of the borough court early in September the free burgesses elected 4 headmen, 1 from among the wealthier burgesses in each of the 4 wards, and each headman chose 5 other substantial burgesses from his ward, making a total of 24, who elected the officers. At the end of September another college of 24, similarly chosen, elected the town clerk and 4 serjeants at mace.[53] Despite the annual elections, by the 15th century aldermen and councillors normally held office for life, or until ill health or removal

[44] E.R.O., D/B 5 Cb1/6, ff. 93, 440; B.L. Lansdowne MS. 157, ff. 101–102v.

[45] Below, Georgian Colch. (Econ., Decline of Bay Trade).

[46] E.R.O., D/B 5 R2, f. 231v.

[47] Ibid. D/B 5 R5, ff. 107v.–108.

[48] Ibid. D/B 5 R2, ff. 31, 232; D/B 5 Gb1, 27 Aug. 1583; Gb4, f. 230.

[49] Ibid. D/B 5 Gb3, f. 172; Gb4, f. 125.

[50] Ibid. D/B 5 Aa1/1–26: number of election dinners paid for.

[51] Ibid. Boro. Mun., 'Colch. MSS.' 1620–1770, ff. 4 and v., 19v.–28; D/B 5 Sr75, rot. 5; D/B 5 Gb6, pp. 423–4; Gb7, f. 13.

[52] *Colch. Charters*, 40–54; E.R.O., D/B 5 Gb2, f. 147v.

[53] E.R.O., D/Y 2/2, pp. 17–20.

from the borough caused them to resign. When a vacancy occurred, new aldermen were chosen from among the first councillors.

The path to civic office started with the second council, although a few wealthy men went straight into the first council, from which their promotion was usually rapid. Of the *c*. 200 men known to have entered the first council in the 16th century, 79 became aldermen and 2 refused that office; a high proportion of the others served only a few years as councillors. There was only a small group of men like Winkin Greenrice, a Fleming, who were councillors for many years and served as keykeepers without becoming aldermen. Service as, or refusal to serve as, chamberlain seems to have been irrelevant to a man's later career in the 16th century: 34 of the 79 aldermen are known to have served as chamberlain and 11 refused, compared with the 39 chamberlains and 18 refusers who rose no higher than the first council. In the 17th century, however, service as chamberlain was more important. Only six of the 16th-century aldermen failed to reach the rank of bailiff, and that failure was probably due to premature death or retirement; only one of them, William Thompson (alderman 1594–7) served for as many as four years.

In 1591 it was claimed that by 'ancient order' aldermen should serve as bailiff only every four or five years, and on average they did so throughout the 16th century. Those who, like John Christmas between 1516 and 1547, Benjamin Clere between 1541 and 1575, and John Best between 1547 and 1571, served seven or eight terms as bailiff, did so because of their long tenure of office as alderman, 32, 35, and 26 years respectively. There is no evidence for a ruling clique within the ranks of the aldermen.[54] Most bailiffs were clothiers or merchants; one of the few who was not, Henry Osborne, was abused in 1610 as a man who lived by cutting leather and selling gloves, and a fool whose name had been 'in question for light behaviour'.[55]

Aldermen and councillors provided their own livery gowns, which were worn for council meetings and sermons and when the corporation officially visited the midsummer and St. Dennis's fairs. The aldermen wore scarlet gowns, the councillors purple until 1598 when they were ordered to provide themselves with black gowns faced with lambskin and with black and scarlet hoods, like the London livery gowns.[56]

Three incidents in the early 16th century led to attempts to strengthen the officers' position. In 1514 about 40 men, including a councillor, disrupted the annual elections.[57] In 1520 the retiring bailiff, William Debenham, refused to attend the swearing in of the new bailiffs or to serve as alderman, and the following year he, with others including the councillor Christopher Hammond, indicted two aldermen and the town clerk, Thomas Audley, at the county sessions at Chelmsford for attacking a house in Colchester.[58] Debenham took no further part in borough government, but Hammond became bailiff in 1525 and served as alderman until 1530.

Ordinances in 1523 confirmed the existing practice that no alderman could be removed from office at the annual election without the consent of a majority of the other aldermen. More detailed constitutions in 1524 repeated that ordinance, and abolished the second election day, providing that the bailiffs should appoint the

54 Ibid. D/Y 2/8, p. 157; Boro. Mun., Ct. R. Transcripts 1510–1600; J. R. Davis, 'Colch. 1600–62: Politics, Religion and Officeholding in an Eng. Provincial Town' (Brandeis Univ. Ph.D. thesis, 1980), 479–80.

55 E.R.O., D/B 5 Sb2/6, f. 200v.

56 *E.J.* xxiii. 65.

57 E.R.O., D/B 5 Cr86, rot. 5.

58 Ibid. D/B 5 Cr92, rot. 18d.; Cr93, rot. 3.

serjeants at mace, and the bailiffs, aldermen and common council the town clerk.[59] In 1529 the 24 electors were given a voice in the appointment of serjeants, being allowed to choose four men from eight nominated to them by the bailiffs and aldermen.[60]

When disputes between the officers, councillors, and free burgesses reached parliament in 1549 commissioners, among them Francis Jobson, confirmed and defined the 'ancient and laudable' custom of the town. Only free burgesses who were householders and were not victuallers, attorneys in the courts, or 'loose journeymen' might vote for the headmen, who were to be worth 40*s.* a year in lands or £40 in goods; the 20 electors chosen by the headmen were to be similarly qualified. There were to be two election days. On the first, the Monday after the beheading of St. John the Baptist (29 Aug.), the 24 were to choose the aldermen, bailiffs, J.P.s, recorder, and chamberlain. On the second, the Tuesday after Michaelmas, a new electoral college of 24 was to chose the coroners, keykeepers, town clerk, and serjeants at mace. The 16 first councillors were to be chosen by the bailiffs and aldermen on the Monday after Michaelmas, and they with the bailiffs and aldermen were then to chose 16 others, 4 from each ward, to serve on the second council. The bailiffs, aldermen, and chamberlain were to be sworn in in the moot hall on Michaelmas day.[61]

There was an unusually high turnover of councillors in the decade 1550–9, and John Beriff and two other aldermen were removed at the elections in 1559. That year William Beriff, a clothier and servant of Sir Francis Jobson, was deprived of his freedom for attacking an alderman and libelling a councillor.[62] Richard Thurston's initial refusal in 1574 to serve as alderman, an office to which he had been elected after apparently retiring from the first council, seems to have led to a series of ordinances tightening the rules for the swearing in of officers and prescribing fines for those who tried to evade office or failed to carry out its duties.[63]

Serious disputes broke out between different factions in the town in 1575 and 1576.[64] The immediate cause was the excessive punishment for adultery meted out to the mariner John Lone, but the underlying one was opposition to Thomas Upcher, rector of St. Leonard's, and other Calvinist clergy, and to their supporters, alderman Benjamin Clere and the recorder Sir Thomas Lucas. Townsmen presumably remembered Clere's cruelty to protestant martyrs in Mary's reign, and he was also accused of enriching his family at the town's expense, notably in making his teenage son master of St. Mary Magdalen's hospital.[65] In the summer of 1575 a series of increasingly scurrilous libels, directed first at Upcher and his associates then at Clere, circulated in the town. At first they seem to have generated sympathy for Clere, and that autumn he and his friend Robert Mott were elected bailiffs. John Hunwick, apparently an opponent of Lucas and the only alderman who had opposed Lone's punishment,[66] was removed from office. Their pursuit of the libellers, however, appears soon to have swung public opinion against Clere and Lucas. In the winter of 1575–6 the dispute reached both the Privy Council and Star Chamber, and the collection of an aid to defray the town's expenses added to Clere's unpopularity; both he and Lucas were removed from office at the elections of 1576. The electors chose their opponent John Hunwick bailiff, but the Privy

59 Ibid. D/B 5 R2, ff. 30–32v. Other ordinances seem to have remained in force for only a year.

60 Ibid. f. 33.

61 Ibid. D/Y 2/2, pp. 17–20.

62 Ibid. D/B 5 Cr125, rott. 1–2d.

63 Ibid. D/B 5 R7, ff. 256v.–257v.

64 M. S. Byford, 'The Price of Protestantism: Assessing the Impact of Religious Change on Elizabethan Essex: the Cases of Heydon and Colch. 1558–1594' (Oxf. Univ. D.Phil. thesis, 1988), 194–258.

65 E.R.O., D/B 5 Sr2.

66 *Acts of P.C.* 1571–5, 41, 61.

Council declared the election void because Hunwick was not then an alderman.[67] In the course of the year 1576–7 Hunwick was restored to his place as alderman and was elected bailiff in 1577. The following year Clere and his son John were accused of campaigning for office,[68] but if they did so, they were unsuccessful. Despite further libels in March 1579, the corporation was able that autumn to assure Sir Francis Walsingham, the recorder, that the controversies were over, and that the last borough election had been 'so peaceable as to be soon finished'.[69]

Further troubles and dissension in the 1580s[70] led to new attempts to control elections. In 1585 it was agreed that there should be only one election day, the Monday after the beheading of St. John the Baptist. The following year the rules for the election of the first council by the bailiffs and aldermen and of the second council by the bailiffs, aldermen, and first councillors were re-issued.[71] In 1587 ordinances restricted the number of freemen entitled to vote by excluding those convicted of adultery, fornication, drunkenness, or swearing, besides victuallers and those who were not householders. Only one man from each ward was to nominate the headman, the others were to agree or if necessary to choose between two candidates by show of hands. The financial qualifications for headmen and electors were raised to land worth £4 a year although the value of goods needed to qualify remained at £40, and at least two of the five electors from each ward were to be members of the common council. The practice of having two election days was restored, but the second was to be for the serjeants at mace only.[72] In 1588 provision was made for a deputy town clerk, to be nominated and appointed by the corporation.[73]

In 1593 John Hunwick was again elected bailiff, although he had retired as an alderman in 1586. His election was declared void, but within two days he was elected a member of the first council, an alderman, and bailiff.[74] In 1595 the town was split on religious lines; the electors refused to proceed to an election and the bailiffs, aldermen, and common council elected the officers for the following year.[75] In 1603 a shoemaker, claiming that the headmen had not been properly chosen, tried to prevent the electors getting into the court room for the election. When it was held, Thomas Hazlewood was elected bailiff although he had been removed as alderman in 1596 and had only just been re-elected to the first council.[76]

Those and other disorders and 'tumultuous assemblies' reflect a dispute between the free burgesses and the officers which led to two attempts in 1612 to reform the method of election. The first, which would have increased the number of freemen eligible to vote, failed because the bailiffs, aldermen, and common council would not subscribe the new orders; the second, which would have reduced the number, because the free burgesses refused to accept the proposals. In 1615 the orders of 1587 were confirmed.[77] The same year a dispute over the removal of two aldermen and seven common councillors at the annual election reached King's Bench. In a comprehensive settlement, Sir Francis Bacon ordered that the officers, with a third alderman who had been removed in 1608, be restored to their places. He repeated the ordinance of 1523 forbidding the removal of aldermen without the consent of the rest of the bench, and extended the rule to common councillors, thus confirming

67 E.R.O., D/Y 2/7, pp. 119–20.
68 Ibid. D/B 5 Sb2/3, f. 123.
69 *Acts of P.C.* 1578–80, 78; E.R.O., D/Y 2/9, pp. 257, 297; D/Y 2/7, p. 195.
70 Byford, 'Price of Protestantism', 279.
71 E.R.O., D/B 5 Gb1, 1 Nov. 1585; 20 Sept. 1586.
72 Ibid. 11 Aug. 1587.
73 Ibid. 14 Sept. 1588.
74 Ibid. 17, 19 Sept. 1593.
75 Ibid. 19 Sept. 1595; Hist. MSS. Com. 9, *Salisbury*, v, p. 394.
76 E.R.O., D/B 5 Gb2 f. 37; D/B 5 Sb2/6, f. 85v.; Davis, 'Colch. 1600–62', 130.
77 E.R.O., D/B 5 Gb2, ff. 109v.–112v., 115v.–118v.; Davis, 'Colch. 1600–62', pp. 131–3.

existing practice.[78] In 1624 one party in the corporation apparently wanted to exclude the free burgesses from borough elections, restricting the electorate to aldermen and councillors.[79]

A *quo warranto* brought against the borough charter between 1625 and 1631 was successfully resisted, and seems to have led to the confirmation of the borough's privileges by *inspeximus* in 1629, but further disputes resulted in a second challenge in 1633 and the resignation of the charter.[80] In 1635 a new charter reorganized borough government. The bailiffs were replaced by a mayor, the 16 first councillors were renamed assistants, and the 16 members of the second council common councillors. The mayor was to be chosen by the aldermen from two of their number nominated by those free burgesses entitled to vote under the 1587 ordinances. Aldermen, assistants, and common councillors were to hold office for life unless removed for bad behaviour by a majority of the officers and free burgesses; when a vacancy arose aldermen and councillors were to be chosen in the same way as the mayor, aldermen from among the assistants, common councillors from the free burgesses; assistants were to be chosen from among the councillors by a majority vote of the free burgesses. The recorder was to be elected by the officers, councillors, and free burgesses, and was to nominate the town or common clerk. The mayor was to have a casting vote in elections. He and the recorder might each appoint a deputy if they were unable to carry out their duties. The mayor, the recorder, the previous year's mayor, and two other aldermen were to be J.P.s. The officers to serve until the elections in 1636 were named in the charter, the aldermen, assistants, and common councillors being those elected in 1634.[81] Officers whose method of election was not specified in the charter (2 J.P.s, the coroners, keykeepers, and chamberlain) continued to be chosen by the electoral college. The assembly made special arrangements for the 1635 elections, which were not covered by the charter.[82] The charter gave the free burgesses a more direct say in the choice of mayor, aldermen, assistants, and councillors, but by finally abolishing annual elections except for the mayoralty it made more difficult the removal of serving officers.

The Civil War and Interregnum

By the 1640s there were divisions among the aldermen between those, headed by Robert Buxton, who had supported the king and Archbishop Laud, and those, led by Henry Barrington, who favoured parliament. The first mayoral election in 1647, of the royalist John Shaw, was annulled under pressure from a troop of parliamentarian horse, and the next man elected, John Cox, refused to serve.[83] After the siege of 1648 three aldermen (Robert Buxton, Thomas Laurence, and John Shaw), four assistants, and six common councillors who had supported, or were alleged to have supported, the royalists were removed, and the following year the moderate presbyterian recorder, Sir Harbottle Grimston, resigned.[84] Nevertheless two parties continued within the corporation, Henry Barrington's Cromwellian party being opposed by a more moderate group led by Thomas Reynolds. At the elections of 1654 Reynolds's party succeeded in removing Henry Barrington and his son Abraham, an assistant. Both sides petitioned Cromwell, who, after the 1655

78 E.R.O., D/Y 2/7, pp. 23–4, 241; D/B 5 Gb2, ff. 142v., 147v.

79 Ibid. D/B 5 Gb3, ff. 36, 38 and v.

80 *Cal. S.P. Dom.* 1633–4, 298, 313; P.R.O., PC 2/44, pp. 230–1. The first challenge was by Sir Robert Heath, attorney general 1625–31.

81 *Colch. Charters*, 81–103.

82 E.R.O., D/B 5 Gb3, ff. 141–2.

83 Ibid. D/B 5 Gb4, ff. 7v.–8; Hist. MSS. Com. 27, *12th Rep. IX, Beaufort*, 22–3; Davis, 'Colch. 1600–62', 337.

84 E.R.O., D/B 5 Gb4, ff. 22 and v., 31.

elections had returned a majority of the Reynolds party to office, sent Major-Gen. Hezekiah Haynes to Colchester to oversee new elections.[85] They were made in December 'with great difficulty': the removal of 'malignants' left only *c.* 100 free burgesses entitled to vote, only 74 of them 'honest', and the other party tried to elect John Shaw as recorder.[86] In 1656 a new charter abolished the 16 assistants and increased the number of councillors to 24, thus reducing the size of the corporation. It excluded the free burgesses from borough government, providing that all elections be made by the corporation alone.[87]

The Cromwellian charter was annulled in 1659. John Radhams, removed from the mayoralty in 1655, replaced Henry Barrington as mayor, and shortly afterwards Abraham Barrington and 3 other aldermen, 7 assistants, and the whole common council were removed or demoted.[88] In 1660 a further 4 aldermen, including John Furley the elder and Henry Barrington, 8 assistants, including the younger John Furley and Abraham Barrington, and 10 common councillors were replaced. John Shaw was restored to his place as alderman, and his son, another John Shaw, became recorder.[89] In 1661 an assistant and 3 common councillors, including the chamberlain, were removed.[90] The final purge of the corporation took place in 1662 under the Corporation Act. Four aldermen, including the mayor John Milbank and Jeremiah Daniell, 5 assistants, and 9 common councillors were removed.[91] Most of their replacements had little experience in borough government: Ralph Creffield, appointed alderman, was not even a common councillor.[92] A new charter of 1663 confirmed most of the provisions of the charter of 1635, but increased the number of aldermen from 10 to 12 (including the mayor), and the number of assistants and common councillors from 16 to 18 each. It also created the office of high steward.[93]

Borough Government and Politics 1663–1714

The controlling influence in the Restoration corporation seems to have been the younger John (later Sir John) Shaw, a supporter of the established church,[94] but opposition to his party grew during the 1670s. 'Scandalous' verses against Shaw and alderman William Moore circulated in 1673, and at the elections of 1676 the opposition, led by the aldermen Ralph Creffield, Nathaniel Laurence, and Thomas Green, all nonconformist sympathizers, succeeded in having Shaw removed as recorder. The resulting dispute lasted until the end of 1678, by which time Shaw was deputy to the new recorder, the duke of Albemarle.[95] In 1684 the 'loyal' aldermen John Rayner and William Boys accused Laurence, then mayor, Creffield, and Green of being covert dissenters, and 3 other aldermen and 15 assistants and councilmen of supporting them, enabling them to monopolize the office of mayor. The petition led to a threat of a *quo warranto* and to the surrender of the town's charter.[96]

The charter of 1684 reduced the number of assistants and common councillors to 15 each; it also excluded the free burgesses from elections which were to be

[85] Ibid. D/Y 2/7, p. 189; Bodl. MSS. Rawl. A 29, pp. 690, 692; Rawl. A 34, p. 125; Davis, 'Colch. 1600–62', 343–60.

[86] Bodl. MS. Rawl. A 34, pp. 121, 129.

[87] *Cal. S.P. Dom.* 1655–6, 253, 371; 1656–7, 71, 79; Davis, 'Colch. 1600–62', 361; E.R.O., D/B 5 Gb4, f. 147v.

[88] E.R.O., D/B 5 Gb4, ff. 192v., 194v.–195; Davis, 'Colch. 1600–62', 60, 364–5.

[89] E.R.O., D/B 5 Gb4, ff. 208 and v., 225, 226v.; Davis, 'Colch. 1600–62', 365–6.

[90] E.R.O., D/B 5 Gb4, f. 362.

[91] Ibid. f. 363v.; Davis, 'Colch. 1600–62', 370.

[92] T. C. Glines, 'Politics and Government in the Borough of Colch. 1660–93' (Wisconsin Univ. Ph.D. thesis, 1974), 77.

[93] *Colch. Charters*, 104–26.

[94] Davis, 'Colch. 1600–62', 372–3.

[95] E.R.O., D/B 5 Sb2/9, ff. 205, 209v., 214; Glines, 'Politics and Govt. in Colch.' 142–9.

[96] Bodl. MS. Rawl. Essex 1, ff. 113–22, 126–31; Glines, 'Politics and Govt. in Colch.' 198–9.

made by the aldermen, assistants, and common councillors only. All officers were to be communicants of the Church of England and to subscribe the declaration under the Corporation Act, and all could be removed by the king or Privy Council at will. Nevertheless, the officers named in the charter were those elected in 1683; Creffield, Laurence, and Green remained aldermen, and John Stilman, accused of being 'factious' in 1684, continued as mayor.[97] Further attempts by the 'loyal party' to purge the dissenting party failed.[98] There was some difficulty in filling vacancies in the assembly in July 1687, but only one man, a common councillor, refused to take the oaths.[99]

In January and February 1688 the Privy Council ordered the replacement of the mayor, Alexander Hindmarsh, 6 aldermen, 10 assistants, 12 common councillors, the chamberlain, the high steward, and the recorder.[1] Those purged came from both parties in the borough and included aldermen Ralph Creffield and Nathaniel Laurence as well as the 'loyal' alderman William Moore. In May the high steward and recorder were again replaced, the recorder by Sir John Shaw. In September a new charter reduced the number of aldermen to 10 (including the mayor) and the numbers of assistants and common councillors to 10 each. The purges and the charter between them replaced the entire corporation except for two aldermen, Thomas Green, who had left the town in 1687, and John Rayner.[2]

By the end of August 1689 all the officers appointed in 1688 except John Rayner and 2 other aldermen, 3 assistants, and 2 common councillors had resigned, making borough government virtually impossible. Elections in which the free burgesses participated as they had before 1684 filled the vacancies in the offices created by the charter of 1688. Most of those elected, including all the aldermen, had served before 1684 and most had nonconformist sympathies, but Nathaniel Laurence, Ralph Creffield, and William Moore, the leaders of their respective factions, were not re-elected.[3] As negotiations for a new charter started, the 'nonconformist' party was accused, probably falsely, of trying to ensure that it excluded the free burgesses from elections.[4] The 1693 charter confirmed by *inspeximus* that of 1663; it also nullified the surrender of 1684 and all subsequent acts of the corporation, except demises of lands and farms.[5]

The two parties, by then aligned with the national Whig and Tory parties, dominated borough government in the late 17th century and the early 18th. At first the Tories seem to have had the upper hand. In 1695 alderman Samuel Mott, a former mayor and one of the dissenting faction in the 1680s, was removed from office and from his freedom after 'several allegations of misdemeanour'.[6] In 1696 Isaac Rebow, who was to become the leader of the Whig party, and seven other men, supported by Edmund Hickeringill, rector of All Saints', and by the aldermen Nathaniel Laurence the younger and John Seabrook, protested at the refusal of the senior alderman, William Moore, to proceed to the election of a new mayor to replace John Bacon, who had died in office.[7] Rebow was later accused of manipulating borough elections by treating free burgesses,[8] and in 1703, supported by the mayor Ralph Creffield the younger, he succeeded in defeating the Tory

97 *Colch. Charters*, 128–48; Glines, 'Politics and Govt. in Colch.' 201–5; B.L. Stowe MS. 835, f. 37.

98 Glines, 'Politics and Govt. in Colch.' 200–5.

99 E.R.O., D/B 5 Gb5, ff. 270, 272–274v.

1 Ibid. ff. 288, 290, 296v.–297; Glines, 'Politics and Govt. in Colch.' 227–37.

2 *Colch. Charters*, 149–69; E.R.O., D/B 5 Gb5, ff. 293, 294 and v., 297v., 298v.; Glines, 'Politics and Govt. in Colch.' 229–36.

3 Glines, 'Politics and Govt. in Colch.' 256–9; E.R.O., D/B 5 Gb5, ff. 315–316v.

4 E.R.O., D/B 5 Gb6, p. 9; *Cal. S.P. Dom.* 1693, 296, 344.

5 *Colch. Charters*, 170–5; E.R.O., D/B 5 Gb5, ff. 360v., 361v.

6 E.R.O., D/B 5 Gb6, p. 36.

7 Ibid. Boro. Mun., 'Colch. MSS.' f. 7.

8 Bodl. MS. Rawl. C 441, f. 2.

candidate, Prince George of Denmark, for the office of high steward, although the prince's supporters alleged that he had at most 146 votes to the prince's 170.[9] There was trouble at the borough elections in 1713, and in 1714 Sir Isaac Rebow was rushed through the offices of councillor and assistant to that of alderman in two or three days.[10]

Finance

The main sources of the borough's income were rents from its estates, tolls from the Hythe, and profits of court, augmented in the 17th century by the farm and other profits of the Dutch Bay Hall. The acquisition of Kingswood (later the Severalls estate) in Mile End in 1535 and of the lands of Barwick's and Heynes's chantries in 1550 greatly increased the borough estates, but some of the chantry lands were sold almost immediately and the rest were mortgaged or let on such a long lease that the rents became insignificant.[11] Total income rose from £127 in 1501–2 to £161 (excluding the proceeds of a special rate for the repair of the harbour) in 1548–9, and to £537 in 1624–5.[12] It seems to have fallen in the later 17th century, and in 1667–8 there was a deficit of £78 as receipts totalled only *c.* £420, almost all from rents. Income remained well under £500 for the rest of the 17th century, enough to cover ordinary expenditure, but not such extraordinary costs as lawsuits or the acquisition of new charters.[13]

The main items of regular expenditure were the fee farm, which fell from £38 in 1596 to £24 by 1695 as allowance was made for 'taxes',[14] the fees, wages, and liveries of borough officers and servants, and the repair of town buildings and bridges. From 1557 the borough also assumed some responsibility for poor relief.[15] Dinners were provided for the officers and their guests at elections and major court days, and gifts of oysters, candied eryngo, or wine were sent to the borough's patrons and friends at court. In the 17th century freemen were given 8*d.* a head on election days, in lieu of dinner.[16]

Signs of financial problems appear in the mid 16th century. There was a deficit of £17 on the year 1548–9, and the assembly agreed that no leases or sales of land should be made, or any money paid by the borough, without its consent.[17] That 12 men refused to serve as chamberlain between 1553 and 1557 may be significant;[18] their fines of £3 6*s.* 8*d.* each were probably a source of extra income to the borough. Similar fines raised £23 in 1573 and £18 in 1574.[19] In 1577 chamberlains were forbidden to appoint deputies, and each was ordered to make his account at the moot hall on 2 January after the end of his year of office.[20]

In the 17th century the borough was increasingly involved in expensive lawsuits, arising either from the defence of its liberties or from quarrels within the corporation. In 1615 the money in the keykeepers' custody in the town chest was given to the chamberlain to pay for a suit in King's Bench over the town's liberties, and in 1629 a rate was levied to pay the expenses of the suit against Sir Roger Townsend of Wivenhoe over the borough's rights in the Colne.[21] The seizure of

9 Ibid. ff. 1–4; ibid. MS. Rawl. Essex 1, f. 123; E.R.O., Boro. Mun. vol. of Misc. Papers; cf. ibid. D/B 5 Gb6, p. 275.

10 E.R.O., D/B 5 Sr103, rot. 36; D/B 5 Gb7, pp. 20–4.

11 Morant, *Colch.* 158; E.R.O., D/B 5 Gb2, f. 45v.; D/B 5 Cr118, rot. 20d.; Cr138, rot. 10.

12 Bodl. MS. Rolls Essex 2; B.L. Stowe MS. 829, f. 26v.; E.R.O., D/B 5 Aa1/5.

13 E.R.O., D/B 5 Aa1/1–26; Aa1/35, ff. 1–90.

14 *Cal. S.P. Dom.* 1595–7, 162; Bodl. MS. Rawl. Essex 1, f. 137; E.R.O., D/B 5 Aa1/35, ff. 32v., 67, 78.

15 Above, this chapter, Soc. Structure (Growth of Poverty).

16 E.R.O., D/B 5 Aa1/1–26; Aa1/35, ff. 1–90.

17 B.L. Stowe MS. 829, f. 26v.; E.R.O., D/Y 2/2, pp. 19–20.

18 E.R.O., D/B 5 Cr120, rot. 1; Cr.121, rot. 1; Cr.122, rot. 1; Cr.123, rot. 1.

19 Ibid. D/B 5 Cr137, rot. 1; Cr138, rot. 1.

20 Ibid. D/B 5 Gb1, 20 Sept. 1577.

21 Ibid. D/B 5 Gb2, f. 147v.; Gb3, f. 84.

12 pipes of rape oil in 1630 led to a suit against Henry Barrington which cost £220, and in 1632 the borough resorted to mortgaging lands to raise £300 to cover that and other expenses.[22] Thereafter the borough regularly mortgaged its estates, and in 1655 mortgaged Archbishop Harsnett's library.[23] By 1643 at least part of the capital of one of the borough charities had been spent,[24] probably to cover extraordinary expenses.

After a period of relative stability in the 1660s the borough entered a prolonged period of financial difficulty when it was forced to pay Sir John Shaw £356 compensation for his removal as recorder in 1677.[25] The charters of 1684 and 1688 added to the borough's expenses. Already in 1680, in an effort to improve its regular income, the assembly had set up a committee to oversee the collection of rents, and in 1688 the chamberlains for the previous 16 years were all ordered to produce their accounts.[26] In December 1687 the profits of the Dutch Bay Hall were assigned to the chamberlain as security for his expenditure in a time of political uncertainty.[27] The £328 spent on the charter of 1693 was advanced by Sir Isaac Rebow, on the security of the Dutch Bay Hall. The hall was mortgaged for £100 in 1696, a sum increased to £150 in 1699 and to £500 in 1701.[28] In 1697 efforts were made to recover 'ancient fees, tolls, and duties'.[29] Despite further attempts between 1703 and 1709 to increase the efficiency of rent collection and to audit the chamberlain's accounts carefully, the interest on a £300 mortgage on Borough fields was unpaid in 1705.[30] In 1706 the borough's creditors were asked to present their demands in writing; money to pay them and later creditors was raised by further mortgages, and by the sale of freedoms.[31] In 1712 the assembly mortgaged the Severalls estate at Mile End for £1,000 to cover the costs of a lawsuit, and raised a further £70 from other borough lands for 'necessary expenses'.[32]

Courts

Courts were held by the bailiffs or mayor and the aldermen on Mondays and Thursdays, the Monday court known as the hundred until 1522 and the lawhundred thereafter, the Thursday as the foreign court. General lawhundreds, courts leet, were held three times a year until 1589.[33] The Monday court was apparently for freemen, the Thursday one for 'foreigners', but otherwise there was little distinction between them. The Monday court heard a few pleas concerning real property, and officers were elected there. Regulations were made in 1559 to speed the court process, and in 1574 the assembly drew up a rota of aldermen, four a week, to hold the courts.[34] In 1592 regulations tightened the court rules to provide quicker justice and to make the collection of fines and amercements more efficient.[35] By 1587 the court usually adjourned for the whole of September, presumably because of the borough elections, but might be held that month if necessary.[36] Attorneys were formally admitted to practice in the courts.[37]

The 1635 charter confirmed the borough's cognizance of all pleas, real, personal, and mixed, including the possessory assizes, and pleas of debt, covenant, detinue,

22 Ibid. D/B 5 Gb3, ff. 93, 108v., 111v.–112.

23 e.g. ibid. ff. 154, 229v.; Gb4, f. 135.

24 Ibid. D/B 5 Ab1/15.

25 Glines, 'Politics and Govt. in Colch.' 147–8, 164–5; E.R.O., D/B 5 Gb5, f. 134v.

26 E.R.O., D/B 5 Gb5, ff. 172v., 299–300.

27 Ibid. ff. 283v., 285.

28 Ibid. D/B 5 Gb6, pp. 12–13, 97, 176, 237.

29 Ibid. p. 111.

30 Ibid. pp. 280, 307–8, 318, 385, 550.

31 Ibid. pp. 341, 420; D/B 5 Gb7, ff. 8–10, 13.

32 Ibid. D/B 5 Gb6, p. 436.

33 The following section is based on E.R.O., D/B 5 Cr82–160; D/B 5 Cb1/2–23; D/B 5 Cb2/3–34; ibid. draft catalogue of Ct. R. and Ct. Bks.

34 E.R.O., D/B 5 Cr124, rot. 16; D/B 5 R7, f. 261.

35 Ibid. D/B 5 Gb1, 7 Aug. 1592.

36 Ibid. D/Y 2/7, pp. 227–8; D/Y 2/8, p. 339.

37 Ibid. D/B 5 Gb1, 17 June, 1591; 7 Aug. 1592; 25 Sept. 1598.

account, and trespass,[38] and the provisions were repeated in all other 17th-century charters. In the later 17th century, however, business in both the Monday and the Thursday courts declined, perhaps because of their cumbersome procedure. Although both courts could hear pleas of debt, in 1689 the borough attempted unsuccessfully to acquire a 'court of conscience' for the recovery of debts under 40*s*. 'according to the rules and methods used within the City of London'.[39]

From 1516 or earlier sessions of the peace were held by the borough J.P.s. From 1521 their proceedings were entered on the borough court rolls, but from 1576 there were separate sessions rolls. The borough sessions had all the powers of a quarter sessions court, and dealt with felonies and other offences committed in Colchester.[40]

The 1635 charter confirmed the mayor's right, exercised from 1493 or earlier, to hold an admiralty court weekly on Thursdays, but also confirmed the admiral's jurisdiction in the borough.[41] In 1588 the bailiffs had disputed the jurisdiction of the newly appointed admiral over the town and its liberty, and although by 1594 they seem to have accepted at least his rights to goods washed ashore, during a dispute with the Colne fishermen in 1630 they again claimed exemption from his jurisdiction.[42] The Colchester admiralty court dealt mainly with fishing offences and with forestalling the oyster market at the Hythe.[43]

Parliamentary Representation

The two M.P.s were elected by the bailiffs, aldermen, and councillors[44] from the 1550s or earlier until 1628 when, after a disputed election, the House of Commons opened the franchise to all free burgesses.[45] The small size of the Tudor electorate made control easy, but nevertheless one M.P. was usually a local man. In 1529 the earl of Oxford procured the election of his councillor Richard Rich; in 1555 the bailiffs, as instructed, elected Sir Francis Jobson.[46] In 1584 the assembly agreed to give Sir Francis Walsingham the nomination of both the borough M.P.s, and duly elected the two men he wanted.[47]

The opposition of the freemen seems to have prevented Robert Radcliffe, earl of Sussex, and Henry Hobart from getting their candidates elected in 1625. Despite the extension of the franchise in 1628, Robert Rich, earl of Warwick, was able to establish his control over the borough that year, but Henry Rich, Lord Holland, was unable to arrange the election of his friend Sir Thomas Ingram in 1640.[48] Later in 1640 the sitting M.P.s, Harbottle Grimston and Sir William Masham, with Robert Rich, Lord Rich, successfully urged the borough to elect Sir Thomas Barrington, who would otherwise have caused a contested election for the county seats.[49]

In 1654 the election was contested for the first time, John Maidstone defeating Col. Goffe by 102 burgesses' votes to 98. Attempts to reduce the electorate to the corporation led to a double election in 1656 when the mayor, aldermen, and councillors elected Henry Laurence, Lord President of the Council, and John

38 *Colch. Charters*, 98–100.

39 E.R.O., D/B 5 Gb5, ff. 313, 319.

40 J. Samaha, *Law and Order in Hist. Perspective*, 103 n.

41 *Colch. Charters*, 99–100; above, Medieval Colch. (Boro. Govt., Courts).

42 B.L. Lansdowne MS. 157, f. 305; ibid. Add. MS. 12505, f. 424; ibid. Stowe MS. 835, ff. 83–4; E.R.O., D/Y 2/2, p. 157; D/Y 2/8, pp. 341–2.

43 E.R.O., D/Y 2/2, p. 153; B.L. Stowe MS. 835, f. 91.

44 e.g. E.R.O., D/B 5 R2, f. 26v.; D/B 5 Gb1 4 Nov. 1588; B.L. Stowe MS. 841, f. 55.

45 E.R.O., D/B 5 Gb3, f. 70; D. Hirst, *Representative of the People?* 199–201.

46 E.R.O., D/B 5 Cr99, rot. 1d.; D/Y 2/7, p. 11.

47 Ibid. D/B 5 Gb1, 26 Oct., 2 Nov. 1584.

48 Ibid. D/Y 2/4, pp. 26–7, 35–9; Hirst, *Representative of the People?* 134; J. K. Gruenfelder, *Influence in Early Stuart Elections 1604–1640*, 11, 158.

49 E.R.O., D/Y 2/8, p. 73; D/Y 2/9, p. 53.

St. James's Church, 1824

St. Runwald's Church from the south-west, 1813

St. Nicholas's Church, 1874

St. Mary Magdalen's Church, *c.* 1780

St. Botolph's Church from the west, 1951

NOS. 59 AND 60 WEST STOCKWELL STREET, 1993

ST. MARTIN'S HOUSE, 1993

THE MINORIES, 1941

GREYFRIARS, 1941

Maidstone, steward of Cromwell's household, while the free burgesses elected John Shaw and Col. Biscoe.[50] In 1659, after another double election, the assembly petitioned the Committee for Privilege and Election for election by mayor, aldermen, and council only.[51]

After 1660, when Harbottle Grimston and John Shaw were returned, the free burgesses' vote was not disputed. The elections of 1679 and 1681 were contested, and polls were taken.[52] By 1706 the creation of freemen had become an issue at parliamentary as at borough elections. In 1710 the election of Sir Thomas Webster was overturned on petition, and in 1714 William Gore and Nicholas Corsellis successfully petitioned against the election of Sir Isaac Rebow and Sir Thomas Webster, claiming that 235 of their opponents' votes had been invalid.[53]

RELIGIOUS LIFE

The Reformation

Traditional forms of religious observance focusing upon the parish church were still in the ascendant among the majority of townspeople in the early 16th century. Bequests were made for the maintenance of chapels, guilds, chantries, altars, statues and for requiem masses and prayers for the dead.[54] In 1506, for example, alderman John Bardfield endowed an obit for himself, his parents, his two wives and all Christians for 100 years.[55] Three perpetual chantries were established in the late 15th century and another as late as 1523; major work was carried out on several parish churches *c.* 1500,[56] and the town granted land to the Crutched friars in 1516 to endow a mass 'for the further prosperity of the town'.[57]

Nevertheless, the town had been a centre of Lollardy in the early 15th century[58] and the heresy reappeared *c.* 1500 when it revived nationally. Six Colchester men did penance at St. Paul's Cross in 1506 and two abjured Colchester heretics were burnt at Smithfield in 1511.[59] In 1527 a heretical group in north-east Essex included 19 men and 14 women from Colchester, many of them from the upper levels of town society. They preached in each others' houses and read English books, including Wyclif's Bible and the New Testament, which they obtained from London.[60] Such groups provided a ready-made organization for the early reception and distribution of Lutheran books in Colchester,[61] although the identification of the author of the Mathews Bible with Thomas Mathews, a Lollard fishmonger from the town, seems unlikely.[62]

St. Botolph's priory was dissolved in 1536, the two friaries in 1538, and St. John's abbey in 1539. Most of their lands were acquired by Thomas Audley, later Lord Audley, Francis Jobson, and John Lucas.[63] Through Audley's intervention the town gained the lands of St. Helen's guild and Eleanor's chantry in St. Mary's

50 Ibid. D/B 5 Gb4, ff. 51v., 112v.–114v., 145v.–146.

51 B.L. Stowe MS. 636, ff. 78–82.

52 E.R.O., D/B 5 Gb5, ff. 156, 181.

53 Ibid. D/Y 2/2, pp. 341–3; Boro. Mun., 'Colch. MSS.', ff. 4 and v., 19v.–28.

54 Above, Med. Colch. (Townspeople); L. Higgs, 'Lay Piety in the Borough of Colch., 1485–1558' (Univ. of Michigan Ph.D. thesis, 1983), 141–54.

55 P.R.O., PROB 11/15, f. 139v.

56 Higgs, 'Lay Piety', 104–5; below, Churches.

57 *E.R.* xlvi. 85–6; E.R.O., D/B 5 Cr87, rot. 8.

58 Above, Med. Colch. (Townspeople).

59 J. E. Oxley, *Reformation in Essex to the Death of Mary*, 5–6.

60 *V.C.H. Essex*, ii. 21; *L. & P. Hen. VIII*, iv (2), pp. 1481, 1788–91, 1844–5, 1859, 1869, 1875, 1984; A. Hudson, *Premature Reformation*, 477–9; *E.A.T.* 3rd ser. xv. 84–5; Oxley, *Reformation in Essex*, 7–10.

61 A. G. Dickens, *Reformation Studies*, 376–7.

62 *E.R.* xliii. 1–6, 82–7, 155–62, 227–34; xliv. 40–2; lvi. 73–4; *E.A.T.* 3rd ser. xv. 85.

63 Above, this chapter, Introduction; below, Religious Houses; Outlying Parts (West Donyland).

church to refound the grammar school.[64] At St. John's in 1534 some monks temporarily refused to take the oath of fealty and the sub-prior called the King's council heretics. The abbot, Thomas Marshall or Beche, took little care to conceal his views against the royal supremacy and the abbey's possible dissolution and was executed at Colchester in 1539.[65]

Many priests were also hostile to the Henrician Reformation. John Wayne, rector of St. James's, and Dr. Thyrstell, at the Grey friars, urged their hearers in 1534 to ignore new books 'of the king's print', probably the propaganda tracts *The Glass of Truth* and the *Articles of the Council.*[66] In 1535 the curate of St. Nicholas's was presented in the borough court for praying for the pope and cardinals and reading a book in church called 'le sentence' which emphasized the authority of Rome.[67] That year at Lexden the rector was fined for stating that 'the blood of Hailes is the blood of Jesus Christ', and the curate in 1538 for teaching the 'paternoster'. Other clergy were presented between 1527 and 1545 for loose morals and not proclaiming royal statutes.[68]

In contrast, the townspeople appear to have readily accepted government policy. Church goods had been sold by 1534 at St. Mary's-at-the-Walls and by 1548 at St. Botolph's, St. James's, and St. Martin's.[69] A will of 1538 contained a protestant preamble and there was a swift decline in bequests to parish churches and the high altar, as gifts to the poor became more important. Requiem masses had apparently lost much of their popularity before 1547, the townspeople increasingly favouring funeral sermons.[70] By 1548 only two guilds or chantries remained at Colchester, Haynes's and Barwick's, the others having been already dissolved illegally by their patrons. Their lands were sold to the borough in 1550.[71] Audley's influence was probably an important factor in the town's attitude, his own support for reform being indicated by his endowment in his will dated 1544 of a Good Friday sermon in St. Peter's church.[72]

Among the more radical townspeople, old Lollard ideas appear to have merged with new protestant teaching on the sacraments.[73] In 1535 a group of Colchester people denied the sacrament of the altar, one man claiming that the doctrine of transubstantiation was akin to believing 'that the moon is made of a green cheese'; he also believed that gutter water was as good as holy water and that he might as well be buried in the highway as in the churchyard. In the same year the parish clerk of St. Peter's refused to go to confession, and in 1539 he was accused with four others of heretical beliefs about the sacraments.[74] Similar views continued to be propagated in Colchester in the 1540s.[75] In 1546 three Colchester heretics were executed 'to the example and terror of others', a fourth was burnt later, and another would not submit even when faced with the rack.[76]

Colchester was a focal point of opposition to Mary's Catholic government. In 1555 the town was described as 'a harbourer of heretics and ever was' and subjected to diligent searches for protestants.[77] During Mary's reign a total of 23 people were

64 *L. & P. Hen. VIII*, xiv (2), p. 222; *V.C.H. Essex*, ii. 502; *E.A.T.* 3rd ser. xv. 86–7; below, Education.

65 *V.C.H. Essex*, ii. 97–100; *Bull. Inst. Hist. Res.* xxxiii. 115–21.

66 *L. & P. Hen. VIII*, vii. 170; *E.A.T.* 3rd ser. xv. 85.

67 E.R.O., D/B 5 Cr104, rot. 3.

68 Ibid. rot. 2d.; Cr105, rot. 5; Cr108, rot. 8d; Cr112, rot. 5; Cr114, rott. 2–3; *E.R.* xlix. 165; *E.A.T.* 3rd ser. xv. 87.

69 *V.C.H. Essex*, ii. 26–7; below, Churches.

70 *E.A.T.* 3rd ser. xv. 88–9.

71 *V.C.H. Essex*, ii. 22–3; *Cal. Pat.* 1549–51, 420–1.

72 P.R.O., PROB 11/31, f. 4; *E.A.T.* 3rd ser. xv. 87.

73 Cf. C. Cross, *Church and People 1450–1660*, 70–5; Dickens, *Reformation Studies*, 381–2.

74 E.R.O., D/B 5 Cr104, rot. 3; *L. & P. Hen. VIII*, xiv (1), pp. 462–3.

75 e.g. E.R.O., D/B 5 Cr111, rot. 3; *L. & P. Hen. VIII*, xviii (2), p. 331; *E.A.T.* 3rd ser. xv. 90.

76 *L. & P. Hen. VIII*, xviii (2), p. 331; xxi (1), pp. 417, 550–1, 586, 648; *Acts of P.C.* 1542–7, 418, 464, 485.

77 *Narratives of the Days of the Reformation* (Camd. Soc. [1st ser.] lxxvii), 212.

burnt in Colchester, including 15 townspeople. Two other local protestants were martyred elsewhere and two more died in prison. The repression at the town was greater than anywhere except London and Canterbury.[78] The burnings consolidated protestant feeling, the ugly disturbances accompanying one set of executions being described as a 'slight insurrection' by the Venetian ambassador in 1555. A local Catholic priest reported that 'The rebels are stout in the town of Colchester. The ministers of the church are hemmed at in the open streets, and called knaves. The blessed sacrament of the alter is blasphemed and railed upon in every alehouse and tavern. Prayer and fasting is not regarded. Seditious talks and news are rife'.[79]

Mary's government was particularly concerned about the activities of protestant clergy and lay preachers in the Colchester district. As early as 1554 some people had been actively dissuading others from attendance at the newly restored mass.[80] One of those responsible was probably Thomas Putto, an Anabaptist tanner of Berechurch and a lay preacher during Edward's reign, who had recanted in 1549 and who had been ordained by Ridley in 1552. At the start of Mary's reign in 1554 he led a group of 20 or more heretics and sacramentarians who mustered on Mile End heath in opposition to the papacy.[81] More dangerous was George Eagles, nicknamed Trudgeover or Trudgeover-the-world, a tailor who became an itinerant preacher in the reign of Edward VI. The heaths around Colchester provided secure hiding places until he was finally apprehended at Colchester at St. Mary Magdalen's fair in 1557. He was hanged, drawn, and quartered at Chelmsford one week later, one of his quarters being sent for display in Colchester market place.[82] Most notable of all was John Pulleyne, who had been deprived of St. Peter-upon-Cornhill in London in 1555 and had then preached secretly in Colchester until he fled to Geneva in 1557.[83]

The bailiffs and aldermen were thanked by the Privy Council for their assistance at executions and in the apprehending of Trudgeover,[84] but that help was probably given as much out of prudence as religious conviction. Some aldermen were vigorous Catholics, such as Robert Maynard, bailiff 1552–3 and 1556–7, 'a special enemy to God's gospel'.[85] Others were protestant in sympathy, such as the bailiff Thomas Dibney, who was brought before the Privy Council for his 'evil behaviour in matters of religion', and had to do penance in two parish churches.[86] Yet other members of the local élite were more circumspect in their religious behaviour, the master and rector of St. Mary Magdalen's hospital combining both protestant and Catholic tenets in his 1557 will.[87] While outwardly complying with government instructions the magistrates were evidently afraid of pressing the persecution too hard lest there should be repercussions after Mary's death. Most of those martyred or presented by town juries came from the middling or lower orders particularly in the cloth trades. In 1557 the bailiffs were criticized for delaying the execution of heretics.[88]

The town apparently polarized into sectarian groups, rival alehouses identifying with the protestant or Catholic cause.[89] There is little sign, however, that Mary's

78 *E.A.T.* 3rd ser. xv. 92; M. Byford, 'The Price of Protestantism: Assessing the Impact of Religious Change on Elizabethan Essex: the Cases of Heydon and Colch. 1558–94' (Oxford Univ. D.Phil. thesis, 1988), 100, 115–17.

79 *Cal. S.P. Venetian*, vi (i), p. 45; Byford, 'Price of Protestantism', 115.

80 *V.C.H. Essex*, ii. 32; *Acts of P.C.* 1552–4, 395.

81 *Chron. of the Grey Friars of London* (Camd. Soc. [1st ser.] liii), 59; *Wriothesley's Chron.* (Camd. 2nd ser. xx), 12; Byford, 'Price of Protestantism', 113; *Acts of P.C.* 1550–52, 81; E.R.O., D/B 5 Cr122, rot. 4d.; *E.R.* l. 157–62.

82 Byford, 'Price of Protestantism', 113–14; *Acts of P.C.* 1556–8, 19, 129–31, 142.

83 Byford, 'Price of Protestantism', 112.

84 *Acts of P.C.* 1554–6, 153; 1556–58, 130–1.

85 *E.A.T.* 3rd ser. xv. 90.

86 *Acts of P.C.* 1554–6, 134, 137.

87 E.R.O., D/ABW 16/128.

88 *E.A.T.* 3rd ser. xv. 91; Byford, 'Price of Protestantism', 119–27; *Acts of P.C.* 1556–8, 135, 144.

89 Byford, 'Price of Protestantism', 118–19.

policies reversed the preference of the majority of Colchester's townspeople for religious reform. Most wills in the period 1554–8 had neutral preambles and they contained no requests for requiem masses and few bequests of traditional form.[90] Indeed, the proximity of the Continent provided both a haven for threatened protestants and an entry point for more radical ideas. When Christopher Vittels of the Family of Love arrived from Delft in 1555 he found a ready audience and allegedly debated the divinity of Christ with servants and husbandmen at a Colchester inn.[91]

The authorities acted with extreme caution after Mary's death. It was not until the day before Elizabeth's coronation that eight people held in the castle gaol on suspicion of supporting Trudgeover were released on bail, except for one man 'very evil in matters of religion'. Elizabeth's ban on unauthorized preaching led Peter Walker, Catholic rector of St. Leonard's church, to be pilloried 'for false seditious tales' early in 1559,[92] and to the arrest of the protestant preachers Pulleyne and Dodman shortly afterwards. Pulleyne and other preachers had swiftly returned from exile to provide protestant services in a town where there was popular demand for the adoption of Reformation principles. From Hock Day 1559 the borough court presented people for non-attendance at divine service, and after Pulleyne was appointed archdeacon of Colchester in December 1559, and rector of Copford in 1560, the borough assembly admitted him to the freedom, waiving the customary fine.[93]

The Elizabethan Settlement

A major problem for the ecclesiastical authorities *c.* 1560 was the lack of an effective protestant ministry for the town. Although a suffragan bishopric of Colchester had been created by Henry VIII, only two bishops were appointed, William More 1536–40 and John Sterne 1592–1607.[94] The loss of income from chantries, confessions, obits and soul-masses, which had improved clerical incomes before the Reformation, meant that Colchester's livings were very poor and often attracted pluralists or poorly qualified priests.[95] A scheme to unify town benefices put forward in 1549 had come to nothing, and several parishes remained vacant after the deprivations of 1554. In November 1560 there was not a single beneficed incumbent in the town, but only two curates at St. Leonard's and St. Peter's. By 1561 there were beneficed incumbents at Mile End and Lexden and 3 curates and 5 lectors.[96] Clerical provision had improved by the 1580s and prophesyings, at first suppressed, had been transformed into exercises for the instruction of Colchester's less learned clergy by 1586, as elsewhere in the diocese.[97] Most of Colchester's parishes remained poor, however, and another plan in 1581 to increase stipends by combining a number of Colchester's parishes came to nothing.[98]

The progress of reform in the first decades of Elizabeth's reign was greatly influenced by the opinions of the townspeople. Pressure from the lower and middling social groups, probably encouraged by Pulleyne, led the assembly to vote

[90] *E.A.T.* 3rd ser. xv. 90–1.

[91] Byford, 'Price of Protestantism', 114; *V.C.H. Essex*, ii. 34; Morant, *Colch.* 50; *Sixteenth Century Jnl.* x. 15–22; *D.N.B.*

[92] Byford, 'Price of Protestantism', 129; *V.C.H. Essex*, ii. 34; *Acts of P.C.* 1556–8, 215; 1558–70, 26, 44, 71.

[93] Byford, 'Price of Protestantism', 130–7; *Acts of P.C.* 1558–70, 89; *V.C.H. Essex*, ii. 34–5; E.R.O., D/B 5 Cr125, rot. 1d.

[94] *L. & P. Hen. VIII*, xiv (2), pp. 151–2; Addenda, i (2), p. 498; *V.C.H. Essex*, ii. 81; Morant, *Colch.* 81.

[95] Below, Churches.

[96] B. Usher, 'Colch. and Diocesan Administration 1539–1604': copy in E.R.O; Byford, 'Price of Protestantism', 138–40; Morant, *Colch.* 105–7; *E.R.* xlvi. 149, 154.

[97] W. Hunt, *Puritan Movement: Coming of Revolution in an Eng. County*, 94–6; P. Collinson, *Religion of Protestants*, 130; below, Churches.

[98] E.R.O., D/Y 2/7, p. 13; D/B 5 Gb1, 23 Jan. 1581; Morant, *Colch.* 105–7.

for the establishment of a borough preachership in 1562. The post was initially funded by voluntary contributions, both large and small, from a very broad range of Colchester society.[99] The post was held by a succession of influential but extreme protestants, the first of whom, William Cole, in office by 1564, was a fellow of Corpus Christi College, Oxford, and a Marian exile whose protestant credentials were impeccable.[1] After 1568 Cole was succeeded in the preachership by George Withers, former preacher at Bury St. Edmunds, and then by Nicholas Challoner from 1573. Pulleyne was succeeded in the archdeaconry by James Calfhill in 1565 and then by Withers in 1570. All were in the vanguard of reformed opinion and under their powerful influence the Colchester assembly set about creating a 'godly' civic commonwealth.[2]

In 1562 the assembly, probably prompted by Pulleyne and Cole, appointed overseers of church attendance and the borough court attempted to prohibit activities such as trading, gambling, and playing games during divine service. Those measures were probably not sabbatarian in nature but were aimed at largely traditional moral ends, and their widespread acceptance may partly be explained by the reformers' use of the traditional structure of the borough court.[3] Pulleyne did meet with opposition from some townspeople who, while regarding themselves as protestant, objected to his emphasis upon the reform of their personal lives. One woman, angered by the length of protestant sermons and the new subjects on which they touched, claimed that Pulleyne had preached away all the pavements and gravestones in St. Martin's churchyard.[4] Nevertheless, the magistrates' rapid assimilation of the reformers' message is indicated by the special tribunal against fornication, presided over by the bailiffs, aldermen, and archdeacon, held in 1566.[5]

The regulations for behaviour introduced by protestant reformers appear to have been more strictly enforced from the late 1570s, when Colchester entered a new phase of reformation under the guidance of Challoner and Withers.[6] Greater emphasis was placed upon the sanctity of the Lord's day rather than just the control of activity during divine service. In 1578 the assembly prohibited business or revelry on pardon Sunday (the fair day of St. Dennis's fair). As sabbatarianism was a subject of dispute in the Dedham classis in the late 1580s, and did not become a firm mark of the Calvinist tradition in England until 1600, it appears to have developed relatively early at Colchester.[7] In the same period the regulation of moral behaviour, especially sexual misconduct, grew more intense in the town. From 1576 new tribunals enquired into both the consumption of meat in Lent and the offences of prostitutes and fornicators. Persons convicted of adultery frequently received the traditional punishment of being paraded through the streets in a tumbrel. Persistent sexual delinquents were whipped, while drunkards and blasphemers were placed in the stocks.[8] By the 1580s alehouses had come under strict regulation, and searches were made to identify people engaged in profane activities.[9]

Many of the local clergy and townspeople adopted advanced protestant opinions that went beyond the Elizabethan settlement. Thomas Upcher, the extreme

[99] Byford, 'Price of Protestantism', 143–6, 155; E.R.O., D/B 5 R5, ff. 12v., 86; below, this chapter, this section (Common Preacher).

[1] Byford, 'Price of Protestantism', 162–4; *D.N.B.*

[2] Byford, 'Price of Protestantism', 164, 174–6, 310–11; Collinson, *Religion of Protestants*, 170–3.

[3] Byford, 'Price of Protestantism', 150–3, 176; E.R.O., Boro. Mun., Misc. Papers (formerly Sess. R. 20), rot. 11; ibid. Q/SR 171, f. 61d.

[4] Byford, 'Price of Protestantism', 165–7.

[5] E.R.O., D/B 5 R5, ff. 12v., 49; Byford, 'Price of Protestantism', 146–8.

[6] e.g. E.R.O., D/B 5 Cr141, rott. 2d., 3d.; Cr143, rott. 2, 2d.

[7] P. Collinson, *Godly People*, 429–32, 438–9.

[8] Byford, 'Price of Protestantism', 385–7, 397; E.R.O., D/B 5 Cr140, rott. 9, 10d.; Cr141, rot. 13; Cr142, rot. 5; Cr144, rot. 13d.; Cr145, rott. 23, 31d.; Cr152, rot. 14d.

[9] *E.R.* lii. 89–95; above, this chapter (Social Structure).

protestant incumbent of St. Leonard's, defended his refusal to wear a surplice by claiming that his congregation opposed its use,[10] and Robert Holmes, rector of St. James's, was presented before the borough court for stating that the surplice was 'a superstitious thing from the pope'.[11] Several Colchester incumbents became members of the clandestine Dedham classis, formed in 1582, which sometimes met in the town.[12] Zealous laymen abandoned their parish churches for others where the doctrine was more to their taste: three parishioners of St. Nicholas's went elsewhere for instruction because of the 'simplicity' of their minister, while another incumbent appealed to the Dedham classis for a ruling 'that a pastor should have his own people' after he had lost his congregation to the rival attraction of the common preacher.[13] By the turn of the century refusals to attend church, to have children baptized, or to kneel for communion were common, while many of the parish churches were in poor repair, lacking equipment, fittings, vestments, and books.[14]

The new protestant morality was probably popular in nature rather than imposed from above. Wills from the late 16th century frequently record gifts for the town preacher, for funeral and other sermons, and for the poor.[15] Yet there had been far more of a consensus in the town during the first decade of Elizabeth's reign than during the late 1570s and the 1580s. The 'godly' party received a considerable setback when Benjamin Clere and his supporters were displaced from the town government after their dispute with John Lone in 1576, which had revealed their own weaknesses in learning and conformity and highlighted Clere's role in the Marian persecution.[16] The dispute revealed a division within the protestant ranks between the extremists and the moderates who emphasized Christian charity.[17] The reformers continued to be opposed by townspeople who could probably be classified as among the profane, such as the two men caught playing cards in the King's Head at the time of divine service in 1589.[18]

Another source of opposition came from those townspeople who remained faithful to Catholicism. The Audleys' house at Berechurch became an important recusant centre; another prominent recusant was Richard Cousins, keeper of the White Hart.[19] In 1578, as the repression of Catholics in East Anglia gathered momentum, the bailiffs wrote to the Privy Council warning of obstinate recusants in Colchester.[20] Both Catholics and protestants energetically attempted to undermine each other's cause. A London sadler sheltering at Berechurch gave poor men money to persuade them not to attend lectures, presumably those given by Colchester's preacher,[21] while in 1587 a captured Catholic priest was forced to take part in a disputation in the moot hall with the town preacher in order to reveal the superiority of protestant learning.[22]

A few cases of witchcraft had been reported before the Reformation: in 1532, for example, a smith's wife was accused of practising magic 'to make folks believe they

10 Byford, 'Price of Protestantism', 142.

11 E.R.O., D/B 5 Sb2/4, f. 78; D/B 5 Cr150, rot. 32.

12 *Presbyterian movement in the reign of Eliz.* (Camd. 3rd ser. viii), 28–74; *V.C.H. Essex*, ii. 39 n.; Smith, *Eccl. Hist. Essex*, 12.

13 Collinson, *Godly People*, 9–10.

14 J. R. Davis, 'Colch. 1600–1662: Politics, Religion and Officeholding in an Eng. Provincial Town' (Brandeis Univ. Ph.D. thesis, 1980), 85–9; below, Churches.

15 F. G. Emmison, *Elizabethan Life: Wills of Essex Gentry and Merchants*, 249, 273–4, 281, 292, 298–9, 312, 319; F. G. Emmison, *Essex Wills*, iii. 215–16, 232, 266, 268, 358–9; iv. 105, 122, 142, 146, 153–4, 160, 166.

16 Byford, 'Price of Protestantism', 194–284; above, this chapter (Boro. Govt.).

17 Byford, 'Price of Protestantism', 259–68, 277–8.

18 E.R.O., D/B 5 Sb2/5, f. 109v.

19 Below, Roman Catholicism; Byford, 'Price of Protestantism', 158–62.

20 E.R.O., D/Y 2/5, p. 19; *Religious Dissent in East Anglia*, ed. E. S. Leedham-Green, 14–15.

21 *Essex Recusant*, v. 84.

22 Byford, 'Price of Protestantism', 335.

should have a silly (lucky) plough'.[23] By Elizabeth's reign the potentially malevolent aspects of such activity were more greatly feared. At least a dozen accusations were made against Colchester people, mostly women, who were thought to have harmed people or animals through magic.[24] Although one woman admitted diabolic possession, many cases apparently derived from popular reliance upon white magic and cunning folk. In 1573 one man confessed he had sent to 'Mother Humfrey' to lift a curse on his hogs, while in 1582 a woman who denied witchcraft admitted she had learnt a counter-spell from Goodwife George of Abberton. Specialist magical assistance was available in the town: in 1590 a couple from Lawford made a magic ointment to cure their children's sickness on the advice of a Colchester physician and in 1598 another Lawford man sent his wife to a cunning man, 'Goodin of Colchester', to help find a stolen horse.[25]

The 17th Century

The growth of separatist sects in Colchester presented a challenge both to the local incumbents and to the common preacher. In 1604 a group of Brownists clashed with Richard Harris, the preacher, whom they denounced as a non-resident and persecutor of God's people. The Brownists may have had some support from within the town government for Harris regarded one alderman as 'a spiteful enemy' and the assembly eventually dismissed him.[26] By the 1610s several separatist congregations existed in the town, among them the conventicle headed by John Wilkinson, who wrote a treatise denouncing infant baptism while in prison in 1613.[27] Nevertheless, the total number of separatists may still have been small, only 11 people in the town being presented for absenting themselves from divine service in 1618.[28] By the 1620s the rise of the Arminian party within the Church of England polarized religious differences in the town. The king's Directions for Preachers of 1622, limiting puritan evangelism, apparently caused a dispute over the choice of common preacher. The bishop's commissary, Dr. Robert Aylett, complained of the factious multitude, 'who will allow no minister but of their own calling and choice'.[29] Two years later a complaint was made to the bailiffs by a townsman that extreme protestants had been arrested and sent away as rebels or soldiers.[30] The archdeaconry court attempted to enforce attendance at church and conformity to Laudian doctrine: a number of people were charged for refusing to kneel at communion,[31] and a Greenstead man was presented in 1627 as an excommunicate, Brownist, and Congregationalist.[32]

Archbishop Laud's orders for the relocation of the communion table and erection of rails were moderately successful: by May 1636 as many as 9 of Colchester's 12 churches had complied and another did so later in the year.[33] Although a number of incumbents had initially refused to give communion at the altar rail, many others supported Laud, and by 1637 only John Knowles, the common preacher, refused to conform and receive communion at the archdeacon's visitation.[34] In contrast, Laud's attempt to undermine the membership of the Dutch reformed church, which had associated itself with the 'godly' or puritan opposition, appears to have

23 E.R.O., D/B 5 Cr101, rot. 9; K. Thomas, *Religion and the Decline of Magic*, 776.

24 E.R.O., D/B 5 Sr3; D/B 5 Sr6; D/B 5 Sb2/5, ff. 85v.–87, 97v., 165v.–166; C. L. Ewen, *Witch-Hunting and Witch Trials*, 284; A. Macfarlane, *Witchcraft in Tudor and Stuart Eng.: a Regional and Comparative Study*, 286–7, 299.

25 Macfarlane, *Witchcraft*, 290, 292; E.R.O., ACA/18, f. 132v.; ACA/24, f. 120v.

26 Davis, 'Colch. 1600–62', 90–1.

27 Ibid. 92.

28 E.R.O., D/B 5 Sr23, rott. 4–6.

29 Ibid. D/Y 2/7, p. 19; Hunt, *Puritan Movement*, 175–6.

30 Ibid. D/Y 2/6, pp. 129, 132–3.

31 Below, Churches.

32 E.R.O., D/ALV 1, f. 72v.

33 Ibid. D/ACA 51, ff. 27v., 51, 61, 78v., 81, 87 and v.; W. Cliftlands, 'The "Well-Affected" and the "Country"' (Essex Univ. Ph.D. thesis, 1987), 225.

34 Below, Churches; Smith, *Eccl. Hist. Essex*, 57.

failed.[35] Neither were the protestant townspeople easily intimidated. James Wheeler, churchwarden of St. Botolph's, refused to rail in the altar, but was excommunicated and imprisoned. He later escaped and fled into exile.[36] About 1635 scandalous verses circulated against Theophilus Roberts, rector of St. Nicholas's, who had erected an altar rail and prosecuted persons refusing to contribute to the cost. The verses suggested that he preached only once a month to little effect, and accused other Laudian clergy, Thomas Newcomen, rector of Holy Trinity, Gabriel Honifold, rector of St. Mary Magdalen's, and William Eyres, rector of Great Horkesley and formerly common preacher, of popery and dissolute life.[37] Clergy who did conform to Laud's injunctions were liable to lose their congregations, the disaffected protestants attending lectures elsewhere.[38] Laud's policies apparently failed to undermine the growth of extremist ideas. As a result the Calvinist Dutch church felt it necessary to reinforce its discipline.[39] In 1640 two Colchester weavers claimed to be the prophets mentioned in Zachariah 4:4 and to have the power to stop rain, turn waters to blood, and smite the earth with plagues. They both died in London of the plague in 1642.[40]

Thomas Newcomen frequently clashed with prominent Colchester puritans, including Samuel Burrows who attempted to prosecute Newcomen for undermining the Elizabethan settlement by refusing to administer the sacrament other than at the altar rail. Burrows was later excommunicated after he had distributed a scandalous libel in three Colchester churches on a Sunday morning, and when Newcomen publicized the sentence shots were fired outside his church.[41] Newcomen was also associated with the High Commission's investigation of John Bastwick in 1634, perhaps because Bastwick had described Newcomen as 'a mad parson' two years earlier.[42] The trial and his subsequent imprisonment turned Bastwick into a reckless pamphleteer, a career which eventually brought him before Star Chamber with Henry Burton and William Prynne in 1637, and a further fine, imprisonment, and the loss of his ears in the pillory.[43] The harsh sentences rebounded on the Laudian party: in Colchester in 1641 a nonconforming linendraper prosecuted before Aylett informed the court 'it were good or better for the church if there were a thousand more such as Bastwick was',[44] and Newcomen only narrowly escaped being beaten to death by Colchester rioters in 1642.[45]

The Civil War committees for scandalous and plundered ministers apparently sequestrated six Colchester incumbents: Cock at St. Giles's, Jarvis at Greenstead, Nettles at Lexden, Honifold at St. Mary Magdalen's, Newcomen at Holy Trinity, and Goffe at St. Leonard's. Thomas Eyres was stripped of Great Horkesley but allowed to keep Mile End.[46] Under presbyterian organization the town constituted one of the four sub-divisions of Thurstable classis, but only three ministers, from 1648, are known: Robert Harmer, the town preacher, Alexander Piggot at St. Leonard's, and James Wyersdale at Lexden.[47] There was by then little support for presbyterianism among the townspeople, who apparently preferred the independent congregational churches. Even incumbents not sequestered by parliament received

35 *Religious Dissent*, ed. Leedham-Green, 60.

36 Cliftlands, 'The "Well-Affected"', 227–8; *V.C.H. Essex*, ii. 53–4.

37 Below, Churches (St. Nicholas); *Cal. S.P. Dom.* 1631–3, 492.

38 Cliftlands, 'The "Well-Affected"', 233, 236.

39 *Religious Dissent*, ed. Leedham-Green, 64–7.

40 *False Prophets Discovered, . . . Lives and Deaths of Two Weavers late of Colch.* (1642, repr. 1844): copy in E.R.O.

41 *Cal. S.P. Dom.* 1636–7, 265; Bodl. MS. Tanner 70, ff. 107–11; Smith, *Eccl. Hist. Essex*, 413–16; Hunt, *Puritan Movement*, 276.

42 E.R.O., D/B 5 Sb1/4, 3 Mar. 1631/2.

43 *Cal. S.P. Dom.* 1640–1, 319–20; F. M. Condick, 'Life and works of Dr. John Bastwick (1595–1654)' (London Univ. Ph.D. thesis, 1982); *V.C.H. Essex*, ii. 53; *D.N.B.*

44 *Cal. S.P. Dom.* 1641–3, 520.

45 Above, this chapter (Intro.).

46 Smith, *Eccl. Hist. Essex*, 125–7.

47 *Division of Essex into Classes* (1648), 21: copy in E.C.L. Colch.; *V.C.H. Essex*, ii. 61.

rough treatment; in 1647 there were tumults all day in Lexden church when a group of extremists sang all 176 verses of Psalm 119 to stop the presbyterian minister, James Wyersdale, from preaching.[48] By 1652 the elders of the Dutch church believed that most of the inhabitants of Colchester were great Independents who despised presbyterian government,[49] and in 1656 Evelyn described Colchester as 'swarming with sectaries'.[50]

When Henry Barrington's 'godly' Cromwellian party took control of borough government in 1647 they ordered the constables to enforce strict sabbatarianism.[51] Henry Batchelor, by will proved *c.* 1647, gave to trustees rents of £60 charged on lands in Southminster to augment the stipends of three 'common preachers of God's word resident in Colchester'.[52] In the same year all property holders were asked to contribute a rate of 1*s.* in the pound towards the maintenance of 'godly, orthodox ministers'. Similar rates were charged in 1650, 1651, 1653, and 1654, but the system apparently lapsed after the Restoration.[53] To ensure frequent sermons the town authorities brought in ministers such as Ralph Josselin, rector of Earls Colne, who preached in 1646, 1650, and 1652. A plan of 1650 to reduce the number of parishes in the town from 12 to 4, each with a preaching minister, had apparently been abandoned by 1660.[54] Religious radicals visited the town, such as Lawrence Clarkson, the Baptist seeker, in the late 1640s, the Quaker James Parnell in 1650, 1652, and 1655, and the Baptist Thomas Tillam and the Fifth Monarchist Henry Jessey in 1655.[55] Some moderates were prosecuted: John Vickers was imprisoned for a sermon in Holy Trinity against regicide in 1654.[56]

During the disturbed years of the interregnum there appears to have been an increase in witchcraft accusations. A man who cut the tail off a neighbour's cat in 1651 was released from possession only after a lock of his hair had been burnt.[57] The same year John Locke, a 'practitioner of physic' from Ipswich, claimed to be able to recover goods 'by a figure in an almanac'. He also cured John Lawcell by 'some inward medicines', although Lawcell's wife had already paid £5 to a baymaker who made the strange claim that he had killed one man already and must kill another before he could cure Lawcell.[58]

In 1676 there were said to be 170 nonconformists and 2 papists as against 1,891 conformists, about twice the national average of dissenters.[59] Several post-Restoration aldermen and other members of influential Colchester families retained strong nonconformist sympathies.[60] In 1684 the families of the aldermen Ralph Creffield and Nathaniel Laurence were alleged to attend conventicles. At the bishop's visitation Creffield was reported to have encouraged the crowd to shout 'here comes the pope in his lawn sleeves' and to have refused to prosecute those who did not attend divine service.[61] In 1663 the Colchester Quakers, having been locked out of their meeting house by the mayor, held illegal meetings in private houses, led by the former alderman John Furley.[62] The following year a Quaker gathering was dispersed, with great difficulty, by the militia.[63] As late as 1686

48 E.R.O., D/B 5 Sb2/9, ff. 7v.–8; Cliftlands, 'The "Well-Affected"', 175, 185–6.

49 *Religious Dissent*, ed. Leedham-Green, 66.

50 *V.C.H. Essex*, ii. 61.

51 E.R.O., D/B 5 Gb3, f. 276; above, this section (Boro. Govt.).

52 E.R.O., D/B 5 Gb4, f. 103v.; ibid. Q/RSr3, 25; Char. Com. File.

53 E.R.O., D/B 5 Gb4, ff. 39v., 64v., 90, 115v.; Gb6, f. 219; *C.J.* vi. 416, 458; Morant, *Colch.* 106.

54 *V.C.H. Essex*, ii. 65; Morant, *Colch.* 106; E.R.O., D/B 5 Gb4, ff. 174, 213, 218.

55 Cliftlands, 'The "Well-Affected"', 169; below, Prot. Nonconf.

56 E.R.O., D/B 5 Sb2/9, f. 88v.

57 Ibid. D/B 5 Gb4, ff. 52v.–53.

58 Ibid. D/B 5 Sb2/9, f. 65 and v.; Ewen, *Witch Hunting and Witch Trials*, 285.

59 *Compton Census*, ed. Whiteman, 50; Collinson, *Godly People*, 27.

60 Above, this chapter (Boro. Govt.).

61 B.L. Stowe MS. 835, ff. 37–43v.; Bodl. MS. Rawl. Essex 1, ff. 113–17, 120–1, 126–8.

62 E.R.O., D/B 5 Sb2/9, f. 132 and v.

63 *Cal. S.P. Venetian* 1661–4, 286.

Furley was fined £20 for preaching at a meeting house in St. Martin's, an offence for which 10 others were also indicted, including a gentleman, 4 baymakers, 2 merchants, and a labourer.[64] A loyal address to the king in 1696 was signed by 126 Colchester Quakers.[65]

The Common Preacher

The preachership was initially maintained by voluntary contributions from a wide cross-section of Colchester society. There were at least 45 contributors in 1564 and 89 in 1568, giving amounts varying from 1*d*. a month to 40*s*. a year. By 1573 a rent of £20 a year from Kingswood heath had been assigned to the preacher's stipend, and later lecturers were maintained by the town, as at Ipswich.[66] The stipend, which soon outstripped the incomes of local incumbents, was probably necessary to attract good candidates from Cambridge. In 1575 Nicholas Challoner was allotted a rent of £40, as was his successor, George Northey.[67] The stipend was raised to £66 13*s*. 4*d*. in 1593 on the appointment of Richard Harris and that year an additional preacher at St. Peter's church was maintained by a collection of £20 in South and East wards.[68] The stipend was raised to £100 in 1619, but was often halved in the 17th century when the preacher held a local living and gave one lecture a week in Colchester instead of the normal two.[69] Preachers were sometimes able to negotiate additional annual payments, such as the £10 received by William Eyres for accommodation in 1610 and the £10 granted to Richard Pulley in 1663 to pay him, or an assistant, to read the Prayer Book before the sermon.[70] In the mid 1680s the sermons were provided by a 'combination' of three beneficed town clergy who were paid £1 a sermon.[71] A new preacher appointed in 1700 was financed that year by the £50 fine for the fishery lease.[72]

From the late 16th century or earlier regular weekly sermons were given on Sunday afternoons and Wednesday mornings.[73] In 1620 a curate also read prayers before the Wednesday sermon.[74] At least 30 sermons were given in 1684 by the 'combination' of three local clergymen.[75] In 1597 St. Botolph's was regarded as 'the most convenient and fittest place' for the sermon.[76] By 1610 the sermons were at St. James's on Sundays and St. Botolph's on Wednesdays, but the Wednesday sermon was transferred to St. Peter's when the preacher was appointed to that living in 1630.[77] Although the Wednesday sermon was at St. Nicholas's in 1658 it was more usually at St. Peter's in the later 17th century, while St. James's retained the Sunday sermon.[78]

The assembly's freedom of action in the selection of preachers was affected both by popular demand and by deference to the opinion of the retiring preacher. The extreme protestant George Northey was recommended by Nicholas Challoner on his deathbed in 1580, and in 1635 the outgoing preacher Richard Maden favoured John Knowles, who was duly appointed.[79] Most Colchester preachers were Cambridge-educated puritans, often college fellows. By 1618 a candidate had to be a graduate and was nominated and presented to the bishop of London.[80] The

64 Hist. MSS. Com. 38, *14th Rep. IX, Round*, p. 275.

65 E.R.O., D/B 5 Gb6, f. 88.

66 B.L. Stowe MS. 829, f. 84; E.R.O., D/Y 2/2, pp. 115, 119; Byford, 'Price of Protestantism', 155; Smith, *Eccl. Hist. Essex*, 21.

67 E.R.O., D/B 5 Cb1/2, f. 269; D/B 5 Gb1, Dec. 1580.

68 Ibid. D/B 5 Gb1, Mar., Aug. 1593.

69 Ibid. D/B 5 Gb4, ff. 271v., 310.

70 Ibid. D/B 5 Gb2, f. 97v.; Gb4, f. 288.

71 Ibid. D/B 5 Ab1/21–4; D/B 5 Gb5, ff. 201v., 242v.; for combination lectures, Collinson, *Godly People*, 467–98.

72 E.R.O., D/B 5 Gb6, f. 214.

73 Ibid. D/B 5 Gb1, Dec. 1579; Gb2, f. 76v.; Gb4, f. 23v.

74 Ibid. D/Y 2/2, p. 118.

75 Ibid. D/B 5 Ab1/21.

76 Ibid. D/B 5 Gb1, Dec. 1597.

77 Ibid. D/B 5 Gb2, f. 96v.; *Cal. S.P. Dom.* 1629–31, 258.

78 E.R.O., D/B 5 Ab1/20; D/B 5 Gb4, ff. 173, 200v., 204v.; Gb5, f. 201v.; Gb6, f. 214.

79 Ibid. D/Y 2/6, p. 83; D/B 5 Gb3, ff. 144, 146v.

80 Ibid. D/B 5 Gb2, ff. 169, 173v.

town did take some precautions; for Northey the bailiffs obtained a reference from Clare Hall, Cambridge, while Richard Harris, chaplain to the earl of Essex, had to preach to the assembly before his appointment in 1593.[81] Interested parties lobbied for particular candidates, as did Harbottle Grimston and John Duke, of Ipswich, in favour of Christopher Scott in 1627,[82] but the views of eminent Cambridge divines evidently carried much weight. In 1627 one of the bailiffs travelled to Cambridge to enquire after a 'learned divine' to be common preacher, and other officers were sent on similar errands in 1631, 1632, and 1635.[83]

The pressing need for an effective protestant ministry in Colchester led Bishop Grindal to allow Colchester's first preachers, Cole, Withers, and Challoner, some latitude in matters of conformity. In the 1580s, however, the new bishop, John Aylmer, took a much harder line, and George Northey was suspended and imprisoned for nonconformity in 1583 soon after his appointment. Aylmer recommended a replacement but between 1583 and 1585 the bailiffs attempted to secure Northey's freedom through the influence of William Cole, Sir Thomas Heneage, Sir Francis Walsingham, and the earls of Leicester and Warwick. A compromise seems to have been reached as Northey was apparently restored before his death in 1593.[84]

The stipend of Northey's successor, Richard Harris, was reduced after he had fallen out with some aldermen and he was dismissed in 1608.[85] In 1609–10 the bishop urged the bailiffs to appoint one of the existing underfunded incumbents, but they defiantly selected William Ames, an extreme Calvinist who was already suspended at Cambridge. Ames was forbidden to preach by the bishop and forced into exile in Holland.[86] His replacement, William Eyres, was apparently more acceptable to the bishop but less popular with the townspeople. He continued to claim the preachership after he became rector of Great Horkesley in 1618, interfering with the sermons and leading the local incumbents in opposition to his replacement Francis Liddell.[87] As late as 1627 Richard Maden wanted the matter settled before he would accept the preachership.[88]

Maden's appointment was also complicated by the unsuccessful attempt of the earl of Warwick and Harbottle Grimston, the recorder, to secure the appointment of a presbyterian candidate. In 1631 Maden was temporarily replaced by William Bridge, who was forced to flee to Holland after being excommunicated for puritanism.[89] To comply with Laud's regulation that lecturers must hold a benefice in their towns, Maden was presented to St. Peter's vicarage.[90] In 1633 the preachership was one of only three in Essex that survived Laud's inquiry into the conformity of lecturers.[91] On Maden's death that year Laud pressed, perhaps as a conciliatory gesture, the claims of two prominent London puritans associated with the earl of Warwick, but Maden's own choice, John Knowles, succeeded him. Knowles was a Cambridge puritan with considerable public influence, and he clashed with Laud in 1637 over the vacant mastership of Colchester grammar school. At a visitation that year it was reported that Knowles did not wear a surplice, say prayers for the king, or take and give communion. Soon afterwards Laud

81 Ibid. D/Y 2/6, p. 83; D/B 5 Gb1, Aug. 1593.

82 Ibid. D/Y 2/4, p. 139; D/Y 2/8, p. 19.

83 Ibid. D/B 5 Gb3, ff. 61v., 62, 99, 109v., 115, 144.

84 Ibid. D/Y 2/6, pp. 81–3, 85, 87, 89, 91–2, 95, 99, 105, 107, 121, 153; Smith, *Eccl. Hist. Essex*, 24; Byford, 'Price of Protestantism', 327–41.

85 E.R.O., D/B 5 Gb2, ff. 55v., 68; Davis, 'Colch. 1600–62', 95–7, 101.

86 E.R.O., D/Y 2/2, p. 123; D/B 5 Gb2, ff. 76v., 96v.; *D.N.B.*

87 E.R.O., D/B 5 Gb2, f. 179; D/Y 2/4, p. 139; D/Y 2/2, p. 118; Smith, *Eccl. Hist. Essex*, 23–4; Davis, 'Colch. 1600–62', 100–1.

88 E.R.O., D/Y 2/4, p. 183; D/B 5 Gb3, f. 72.

89 Davis, 'Colch. 1600–62', 186–8; *D.N.B.*

90 *Cal. S.P. Dom.* 1629–31, 258.

91 Ibid. 1631–3, 352.

revoked his licence and Knowles left for New England in 1639.[92] The preachership was apparently less influential in the later 17th century, although it was held by the presbyterian divine Owen Stockton (1657–62).[93]

Colchester's common preachers played a pivotal role in the religious and cultural life of the community and bore much responsibility for the town's continuing tradition of nonconformity. As the majority of church livings were in the gift of local families such as the Audleys and Lucases, the preachership was the only way that the townspeople could guarantee themselves godly instruction.[94] The preachers' popularity is revealed by the many small legacies they received in wills and by the frequent accompanying request that they provide a funeral sermon.[95] Some preachers apparently became well integrated into the social life of the town: Withers married into a Colchester family shortly before his appointment; Challoner married the daughter of alderman Benjamin Clere; and Northey later married Challoner's widow.[96] The preachers' views met with some opposition: in 1566 a man claimed that Cole should be deprived because he did not wear a tippet and square cap; another disagreed with Challoner about predestination.[97] Such doctrinal disputes may have grown sharper with the growth of separatist sects in Colchester during the 17th century. Preachers were also criticized when they addressed non-religious matters from the pulpit, and their involvement in reforming the town's moral life led to disputes with those townspeople who objected to the stricter regulation and harsher punishments that accompanied 'godly' rule.[98]

92 Davis, 'Colch. 1600–62', 188.

93 *D.N.B.*

94 Below, Churches.

95 e.g. Emmison, *Elizabethan Life: Wills of Essex Gentry and Merchants*, 273, 281, 292, 298, 312; E.R.O., D/ACR 96; D/ABW 21/168.

96 Byford, 'Price of Protestantism', 174, 313, 316.

97 E.R.O., D/B 5 R5, f. 76v.; Byford, 'Price of Protestantism', 273.

98 e.g. E.R.O., D/B 5 Sb2/3, ff. 123, 138v.; above, this section (Eliz. Settlement).

GEORGIAN COLCHESTER

COLCHESTER'S position on the route between London and Harwich and the Continent and its function as a centre for the surrounding rural area helped to foster commercial development and economic diversity, mitigating the difficulties caused by the loss of the bay trade. The establishment of a temporary garrison during the Napoleonic Wars was a further stimulus to the town's economy. Manufacturing growth was on a comparatively small scale and so Colchester did not share the problems in the late 18th and early 19th century of rapidly industrializing northern and midland towns. The port at the Hythe was important locally in attracting foreign trade but was not of great national significance, its development being inhibited by its location several miles inland.[1]

Burgesses were proud of Colchester's borough status, and during the period 1741–1763 when the borough charter was in abeyance, they felt keenly the loss of their privileges. The borough assembly was the seat of power locally and much political manoeuvring was centred around it. Minor local administration was carried out by the 16 town parishes, and from 1811 the improvement commissioners were very active in the town. The town had two elected members of parliament.[2]

The face of Colchester changed substantially over the period, with new elegant buildings emphasizing the bustling town's self-confidence. There was space, where houses had been demolished as the weaving trade declined, to build new houses and enlarge gardens. The town was surrounded by fields, enabling people easily to go into the countryside. Growth was gradual and, compared with other towns, Colchester appeared to contemporaries a pleasant place.[3] In 1795 Ann Taylor, who later became a well known writer, described the town as 'a nice old town . . . clean, open, and agreeable . . . situated on a healthful gravelly hill . . . commanding from many points a view of the Colne', and considered the high street 'quite a gay promenade'.[4]

Socially and culturally the town offered a wide range of activities, from book clubs and theatrical performances to charity work and meetings of friendly societies. Evangelicalism in the Anglican church was influential from the 1780s. Nonconformity remained strong but much of the religious rancour of the previous century had disappeared. The local social, political, and economic leaders were the town gentry together with members of the commercial and professional élites. A gulf remained between rich and poor: conflict surfaced in occasional disturbances, but law and order were never seriously threatened for long.[5]

Population, estimated at *c.* 10,400 in 1674, increased to 11,520 in 1801.[6] Numbers may have declined in the earlier decades of the 18th century. About 100 weavers, presumably with their families, left the town before 1715 and there was a high death rate from disease in the 1720s.[7] The historian Philip Morant estimated that there were 2,342 households in the town in 1748, not including Mile End and Berechurch; before then houses had been pulled down in St. Peter's, St. James's, St. Giles's, and Greenstead parishes, though some new ones had been built in Mile

1 Below, this chapter, Econ. Hist.
2 Below, this chapter, Town Govt.
3 Below, this chapter, Topog.
4 E.R.O., D/DU 1545/19/1, pp. 96–7.
5 Below, this chapter, Social Hist.
6 Above, Tudor and Stuart Colch. (Intro.); *Census*, 1801.
7 *C.J.* viii. 280; *Census*, 1801.

End.[8] Burials exceeded baptisms in the parish registers until the 1770s and did so again in the early 1780s; baptisms exceeded burials from 1786 until 1800, except in 1791, 1795, 1799, and 1800.[9] The strength of nonconformity complicates further any attempt to estimate population.[10] Smallpox and other diseases continued to claim lives, and towns like Colchester on trading routes were particularly vulnerable. In 1730, 1735, 1736, and 1737 smallpox was recorded in St. Peter's parish, and in 1741, 1747, and 1754 in St. Mary's-at-the-Walls, where six deaths from measles were noted in 1769. A smallpox case was mentioned in All Saints' in 1748 and more sickness than usual in 1749 and 1750. A newspaper notice in 1763 declared the town free of a recent smallpox outbreak.[11] In the late 18th century parishes occasionally provided inoculation at one or more inoculating houses.[12] In 1800 Dr. Jenner visited the town to inoculate with cowpox the 85th Regiment, invited by its commander-in-chief, the duke of York.[13] Migration from the town was usually over short distances, with other Essex parishes the most usual destinations, followed by London, then Suffolk, then other places.[14] During wartime there were fluctuating numbers of soldiers in the town. There is some evidence that soldiers who married local women settled there.[15] Population grew more rapidly in the early 19th century reaching 16,167 by 1831, although outbreaks of disease, such as cholera in 1834, were still serious.[16] It was only in the late 18th and early 19th century that the built-up area of the town was extended.[17]

During the Napoleonic Wars the town, alive with soldiers and troop movements, was described as 'gay and busy'.[18] In 1795, when Holland was held by the French, the prince of Orange with a party of nearly fifty stayed at the White Hart; the duke of York dined with him there and reviewed the Surrey Fencibles. The wars brought years of high food prices and an increasing burden of poor relief.[19] The Colchester Loyal Volunteers were formed in 1797, providing their own uniform and mounts, and patriotism was expressed in public celebration of victories and royal occasions.[20] During an invasion scare at the end of 1803 an attack was expected at any hour; soldiers were 'pouring in daily' and people were 'in the utmost distress and consternation'. Wealthier families left the town, the Rounds going to Bath, the Daniells to Halstead, and the Taylors to Lavenham (Suff.). The crisis passed, however, and by early the following year most had returned.[21]

Georgian Colchester was not at the forefront of industrial and economic change, but it remained an important centre for the surrounding area of north Essex and south Suffolk. Colchester people resented the role of Chelmsford as a county town, complaining of the cost and inconvenience of travelling to the county court and sending prisoners there.[22] They were proud of the continuing vitality of their own ancient town.

[8] Morant, *Colch.* (1748), Bk. II, pp. 3, 6, 9, 11, 13–16, 18, 21, 23, 25, 28–9.

[9] *Census*, 1801, p. 95, Abstract of Answers and Returns: copy in E.R.O., Q/CR 2/5/1.

[10] e.g. E.R.O., D/NC 52/1/1, 2.

[11] J. Smith, *Speckled Monster*, 23, 27; E.R.O., D/P 178/1/3; D/P 246/1/5; D/P 200/12/1, 3, 4.

[12] Below, Par. Govt. and Poor Relief.

[13] Smith, *Speckled Monster*, 94.

[14] E.R.O., Boro. Mun., Freemen's Admissions Bks. I, II.

[15] e.g. S. Foster, *Church of St. James the Less and St. Helen, Colch.* 8–9.

[16] *Census*, 1831; Phillips, *Ten Men*, 22–3.

[17] Below, this chapter, Topog.

[18] E.R.O., D/DU 1545/19/1, p. 93.

[19] E.R.O., Acc. C281, item 7, journal of Mr. Carr; below, Par. Govt. and Poor Relief.

[20] S. D'Cruze, 'Colch. and its Middling Sort, 1780–1800' (Essex Univ. M.A. thesis, 1985), 116.

[21] E.R.O., D/DU 1525/19/1, pp. 171–5.

[22] Below, this chapter, Town Govt. (Courts); see H. Grieve, *Sleepers and Shadows*, ii (forthcoming), chaps. 7–12, for comparison with Chelmsford.

ECONOMIC HISTORY

THE bay industry, well known for the quality of its products, was vulnerable in the 18th century to disruption by wars, competition from rival manufacturers, and the import of cotton cloth. Despite occasional revival the trade declined, and had ceased by the end of the Georgian period. Diversification, however, and enterprise by merchants, manufacturers, and shopkeepers, the growth of banking, insurance, and legal facilities, improved communications, the intermittent presence of a military garrison, and the attractions of the town's social life, enabled Colchester to consolidate its role, already established by its markets, fairs, and port, as a centre of commerce. The establishment of ironfoundries at the turn of the century enabled it to recover some of its local importance in manufacturing.[23]

The Decline of the Bay Trade

In 1707 the Dutch governors of the bay corporation introduced bylaws which stinted the production of bays and limited entry to the corporation to men who had been apprenticed to baymakers, whereas formerly it had been open to freemen who had served apprenticeship in any branch of the textile industry. Between 1707 and 1715 only 18 new men were admitted to the bay corporation, while *c.* 70 died or left the trade, 4 of them through bankruptcy, so that in 1715 there were 57 baymakers and only 11 of their 27 apprentices were likely to succeed them.[24] To reduce the cost of production, a new, lighter bay had been introduced that was more suitable to some markets and could be woven more cheaply. Some baymakers revived truck systems of payment and forced weavers to rent houses from them and to pay 'rawboots' money, the bay hall fines collected by the Dutch corporation for substandard products. By 1715, although the export of says, bays, serges, and perpetuanas direct from Colchester to Rotterdam continued, the post-war rise in exports of Colchester bays to Spain and Portugal through the London factors had declined.[25] Contemporary observers attributed the decline of trade to the export of British wool to France, the introduction of French manufactures into Spain, and the import of calicoes.[26]

In 1715 the weavers' resentment erupted into violence to enforce redress of their grievances. The Dutch bay governors capitulated after an armed mob had broken open the gaol to release weavers arrested by the mayor, and had threatened to pull down the bay hall and private houses. The Privy Council, responding belatedly to the mayor's appeal for help, mediated between weavers and baymakers. It reinforced anti-truck bylaws proposed by the Dutch bay governors and recommended other measures favourable to the weavers.[27] The weavers, threatened by the cheap labour of an excessive number of apprentices and the increasing employment of people not qualified as weavers by apprenticeship, demanded restoration of their former freedom to become baymakers. Although the baymakers and the London factors, who marketed Colchester bays, warned against the over-production that free entry would cause, parliament in 1716 nullified the restrictive bylaw of 1707, and enabled anyone who had served an apprenticeship in the woollen industry in Colchester to become a baymaker.[28]

23 Above, Tudor and Stuart Colch. (Econ., Growth and Development); Morant, *Colch.* 78 n.; *V.C.H. Essex*, ii. 396–9.

24 *C.J.* xviii. 280–1; E.R.O., T/A 146/10.

25 *C.J.* xviii. 171; P.R.O., E 190/627/8; E 190/636/6.

26 J. Smith, *Chronicon Rusticum-Commerciale or Memoirs of Wool* (1747), ii. 132, 148; *C.J.* xix. 231, 605.

27 *Bull. Inst. Hist. Res.* xxix. 220–2; A. F. J. Brown, *Essex at Work 1700–1815*, 18.

28 *C.J.* xviii. 171, 280–1; 1 Geo. I, c. 41.

During the next decade the baymakers had difficulty in maintaining their corporation. Their rent of the bay hall was abated in 1716 because of bad trade and two of their number were bankrupt by 1720. In the financial frenzy of that year a speculative bubble for the more effectual making of Colchester bays was floated, and the borough and workhouse corporations began a lawsuit to recover from the Dutch bay governors arrears of rent and the 'rawboots' money paid by the English, which should have been been passed to the mayor for distribution to the poor. Trade improved after 1720, when plague halted French competition, but such booms fuelled demands, made by rioting weavers in 1724, for higher wages and led to over- production.[29] In 1727 optimism rose again at the prospect of access to the Spanish market and the justices confirmed bylaws made by the weavers to regulate their trade.[30]

In 1728 the Dutch bay governors dissolved their corporation, abandoning the privileges granted to their refugee forebears. Two of those privileges, the right to make bylaws and protection by the privy council from harassment, may have seemed less secure after the events of 1715, and dissolution, made feasible by the assimilation of the Dutch into the native population, had economic advantages for the baymakers. Collectively they paid a 'foreign' fine, although many had acquired the freedom of the borough. They bore the expense of renting the bay hall, where they supervised the quality of bays produced by Dutch and English alike, and collected the bay hall fines known as 'rawboots' money.[31]

Soon after the outbreak of war with Spain in 1740 two more baymakers, Thomas Hills and William Sherman, were bankrupt.[32] After the war trade improved and optimism rose,[33] but death and bankruptcy had reduced the number of baymakers by 1749, when weavers complained that the few who remained took no apprentices, and had prospered by reducing wages from 15*s.* 6*d.* to 12*s.* 6*d.* for a bay, which took two weeks to weave. The weavers wanted to be paid by the bay or by the week.[34] Compared with wages of nearly 9*s.* a week paid to Exeter serge weavers in 1750, the Colchester rate was low, but it helped the baymakers to capture overseas markets from west country clothiers.[35] The fly shuttle, invented by John Kay in 1738 when he lived in Colchester and with which one weaver did the work of two, was not named among the weavers' complaints.[36]

Portuguese prosperity in the 1750s increased the trade in bays,[37] and in the 1760s there were 24 baymakers among voting, resident freemen.[38] Resistance to innovation, although occasionally menacing, was apparently short lived,[39] and Colchester weavers had probably accepted the fly shuttle by 1760, when it was in general use.[40] John Baker introduced a method, patented by him in 1769, of making striped baize. Isaac Boggis's intention to introduce a roughing mill, to replace the hand method of raising nap on the finished cloth, provoked a threat against him in 1762, but several such mills had been installed by 1770 and in 1782 manufacturers from Witney (Oxon.), seeking improved methods of roughing, adopted that of Colchester.[41] Although the industry received a few new men it seems to have suffered in

[29] P.R.O., B 4/3, pp. 5, 161; E.R.O., D/B 5 Gb7, pp. 37, 75, 92, 106, 179; *C.J.* xxiii. 660; W. Lee, *Daniel Defoe*, iii. 279–80; D. Macpherson, *Annals of Commerce*, iii. 98; D. Defoe, *Plan of Eng. Commerce* (1927), 201–2; Morant, *Colch.* 78 n.

[30] E.R.O., D/B 5 Sb5/2, p. 130; *Ipswich Jnl.* 24 June 1727.

[31] Morant, *Colch.* 78–9; *V.C.H. Essex*, ii. 399; *Immigrants and Minorities*, i. 261–80.

[32] P.R.O., B 4/10, p. 39.

[33] Morant, *Colch.* (1748), Bk. I. 75.

[34] E.R.O., Q/SBb 184/1.

[35] W. G. Hoskins, *Industry, Trade and People in Exeter 1688–1800*, 56.

[36] E.R.O., Q/SBb 184/1; P. Mantoux, *Industrial Revolution in 18th Cent.* (rev. edn.), 206–8.

[37] *Econ. H.R.*. 2nd ser. xvi. 219–33.

[38] *Poll Bk.* 1764.

[39] Brown, *Essex at Work 1700–1815*, 23–4.

[40] J. Bischoff, *Comprehensive Hist. Woollen and Worsted Manufacture*, i. 279–80; E.R.O., Q/SBb 184; *V.C.H. Essex*, ii. 399.

[41] Brown, *Essex at Work 1700–1815*, 19; J. Bensusan-Butt, *House that Boggis Built*, 10; *E.R.* xix. 112; xxxvi. 84–5.

North Hill, 1951
the east side

East Hill, *c.* 1905
the north side

Maldon Road, *c.* 1900

St. Mary's Terrace West, 1993

Providence Place, 1994

the general depression of the 1770s.[42] Three baymakers, James Robjent a former mayor, Benjamin Smith a former chamberlain, and Bezaliel Blomfield the younger, were bankrupt in 1772,[43] and John Baker, by will proved 1775, instructed his executors not to carry on his business.[44]

In 1782 Colchester baymakers, seeking to limit French competition, joined in opposition to the wool growers' petition to allow the export of British wool to France.[45] The preliminary peace treaty with America later that year encouraged hopes of renewed trade, but by 1788 many families traditionally employed in the cloth industry had been driven to find other work. The number of weavers who voted in elections fell from 224 in 1768 to 115 in 1790.[46] Among surviving baymakers were Michael Hills, who by 1787 had a manufactory where he employed weavers who paid rent to him, and his son-in-law Thomas Boggis (d. 1790). Thomas's brother Isaac (d. 1801) carried on the business, assisted by Peter Devall, who had bought a bankrupt baymaking business and also worked for Thomas Boggis.[47] The outbreak of war with France in 1793 was said to have reduced the weekly output of Colchester bays from 400 to 160 pieces. As late as 1802, however, there were signs of defiant optimism for the trade,[48] but in 1812 only the Mansfields, the Devalls, and William Argent remained as baymakers and Thomas Hocker, a former baymaker, had become a yarnmaker. The Mansfields' business ceased soon afterwards and Argent, whose warehouse was recorded in 1818, was dead by 1822.[49] Peter Devall, who concentrated the preparation of yarn in his two mills at Bourne Pond and Lexden and weaving in his warehouse in Priory Street, extended the range of his products and continued in business into the 1830s.[50]

Diversification from the Mid 18th Century

Some redundant spinners and weavers may have found employment in Michael Boyle's silk and ribbon factory established *c.* 1790.[51] A few years after Boyle's death in 1809 a firm in Wyre Street was producing silks, velvets, and bombazines, and after the Napoleonic war a co-operative of silk weavers began to produce materials for the local market.[52] Stephen Brown & Co. had apparently established silk mills in St. Peter's Street by 1824, when two men in St. Botolph's parish sought relief pending employment in the silk trade. In 1827 the overseers of that parish withheld relief from paupers who refused to send their children to work in the mills, and in the 1830s the industry employed mostly women and children.[53]

The clothing industry benefited from the growing demand for fashionable clothes and for uniforms when the town was garrisoned. In the early 19th century Charles Keymer, woollen draper, also traded as a tailor employing a foreman, 9 journeymen tailors, and 2 apprentices; in 1810 Alexander Fordyce Miller, wool merchant, draper, and the principal tailor in the town, employed *c.* 40 men mainly making uniforms for entire regiments. Journeymen moved from one master tailor to another, and in 1813 their representative successfully negotiated with the masters collectively for increased wages. The trade seems to have suffered little from the

[42] *Poll Bk.* 1784; T. S. Ashton, *Econ. Fluctuations in Eng. 1700–1800*, 158–63.

[43] E.R.O., Acc. C281; ibid. T/P 146/10; *Ipswich Jnl.* 24 Oct. 1772.

[44] P.R.O., PROB 11/1006, f. 266.

[45] E.C.L. Colch., Rebow scrapbook, p. 6.

[46] *E.R.* liv. 51; *Poll Bk.* 1768, 1784, 1788, 1790.

[47] P.R.O., PROB 11/1147, f. 293; Bensusan-Butt, *House that Boggis Built*, 14, 30–2, 34; A. F. J. Brown, *Essex People 1750–1900*, 80–9.

[48] *V.C.H. Essex*, ii. 402.

[49] *Poll Bk.* 1812; E.R.O., D/B 5 Sb6/10, 19 Oct. 1818; D/B 5 Gb9, p. 452; T. Cromwell, *Hist. Colch.* 289.

[50] *V.C.H. Essex*, ii. 403–4; *E.A.T.* x. 47–54.

[51] *Universal Brit. Dir.* (1793), ii. 522; *Ipswich Jnl.* 1 Nov. 1794.

[52] Brown, *Colch. 1815–1914*, 7; below, Modern Colch. (Econ., 19th-cent. town).

[53] E.R.O., D/P 203/8/2, 3; J. Booker, *Essex and the Industrial Revolution*, 58–9; *Returns of Factories*, H.C. 41, pp. 222–3 (1839), xlii.

closure of the barracks; in the 1820s even a small tailoring business had plenty of work, and in 1832 directories listed 20 tailors in the town.[54] The wholesale manufacture of clothing, important in Colchester later in the 19th century, originated in 1817 when Hyam Hyam, a pawnbroker with a quantity of cloth on his hands, speculated in ready-made clothing.[55]

Among non-textile artisans those engaged in the leather and building industries were probably the most numerous. Leather workers formed the predominant group throughout the period. Most of them were cordwainers,[56] who maintained their own constitution in 1723 and a friendly society in 1785, when they sought to restrict the trade to apprenticed men.[57] From 1800 boot- and shoemakers received nearly a third of the boys apprenticed under the poor law.[58] Local tanneries may have produced the dressed calf skins exported from Colchester in 1716, 1729, and 1730.[59] A tannery survived in Lexden in the 18th century.[60] One in St. Peter's parish seems to have ceased by 1754, but in 1770 Francis Abell, saddler in that parish, built a new tannery there,[61] which was acquired by William Swinborne *c.* 1776. At about the same time Swinborne acquired Cole's tannery, established by 1760 near East bridge, and he retained both until his death *c.* 1792.[62] Edward Capstack, currier, had the tannery in St. Peter's parish by 1798 and may have had an interest in the other at East bridge,[63] but from 1823 John Golding was tanner at East Street and Edward Goode at Middleborough. They were succeeded *c.* 1832 by Robert Dakin at Balkerne Lane and J. C. Eisdell at East Bridge. Eisdell and F. W. Warmington, tanners, curriers, and leather merchants of Colchester and Bethnal Green (Mdx.), played an important role in the development of the local shoemaking industry in the 19th century.[64]

The building trade thrived during the period as public and private buildings were improved or rebuilt. Carpenters, masons, and bricklayers added the fashionable windows, brick fronts, and interior woodwork which distinguished the town houses of the period. A few builders such as James Deane, Isaac Green, and William Phillips were locally notable.[65] Building materials, including bricks, pantiles, galley tiles, mortar, and wainscot boards, were recorded among imports from Rotterdam in the early Georgian period.[66] Brick-earth was available locally and there were kilns at Mile End and the Hythe.[67]

Many small industries recorded in Colchester in the period[68] were found in similar towns, but oysters and candied eryngo root were specialities for which Colchester was notable.[69] There were usually eight or more clock- and watchmakers in the town during the first half of the 18th century, and *c.* 375 surviving Colchester clocks have been recorded. The Hedge family started as clockmakers in 1739 and ran a factory from 1745 to *c.* 1778; Joseph Banister (d. 1875), partner and successor of Nathaniel Hedge (d. 1818), patented an improved escapement for clocks and

54 Brown, *Essex People*, 109–10, 113–14, 203; Pigot & Co. *London and Provincial Commercial Dir.* (1832), p. 291.

55 *V.C.H. Essex*, ii. 484; Brown, *Colch. 1815–1914*, 10.

56 *Poll Bk.* 1768, 1784, 1788, 1831; Pigot, *London and Provincial Commercial Dir.* (1832), 289; *Robson's Gazetteer* (*c.* 1838), 42.

57 E.R.O., D/B 5 Aa1/35, f. 97; Brown, *Colch. 1815–1914*, 107.

58 Below, Par. Govt. and Poor Relief.

59 P.R.O., E 190/627/8; E 190/636/6.

60 Below, Outlying Parts (Lexden, Econ.)

61 E.R.O., D/DU 115/21; *Ipswich Jnl.* 14 Apr., 24 Nov. 1770.

62 E.R.O., D/P 178/11/3; D/P 138/11/8–12; *Ipswich Jnl.* 30 Oct. 1762; T. Sparrow, *Map of Colch.* (1767); Brown, *Essex at Work*, 61.

63 E.R.O., D/P 178/11/4; D/P 138/11/11–13; *Universal Brit. Dir.* (1793), ii. 522; W. Cole, *Map of Colch.* (1805).

64 Pigot, *London and Provincial Commercial Dir.* (1822–3 and later edns.); *V.C.H. Essex*, ii. 460, 487–8; below, Modern Colch. (Econ., 19th-cent. town).

65 Below, this chapter, Topography.

66 P.R.O., E 190/627/8; E 190/630/6; E 190/636/6.

67 *Ipswich Jnl.* 21 May, 1757; Brown, *Essex at Work*, 62.

68 *Universal Brit. Dir.* (1793), ii. 521–5; Pigot, *London and Provincial Commercial Dir.* (1832), pp. 289–92.

69 Ibid. ii. 371–2, 425–35; below, Fishery.

watches in 1836.[70] A long-established kiln making clay tobacco pipes flourished throughout the period. A cork cutting business, recorded 1793–*c.* 1902 may have been the only one in the county.[71] Seedsmen and gardeners were recorded throughout the period, providing seeds, plants, and trees for the gardens that were attached to most town houses. The Cant family's nursery, founded in St. John's Street in 1765, continued to flourish on various sites in the 20th century.[72] John Aldus on East Hill was succeeded by his son John in 1767. Also in St. James's parish was Thomas Essex (d. 1799), nurseryman and seedsman from 1760 or earlier, who planted cherry trees in Childwell field in 1770 and enlarged his nursery in 1781.[73] John Agnis, who offered pineapple plants for sale at his nursery in East Street in 1771, survived in 1793, when there were six or more other seedsmen in the town.[74]

Some industries arose from Colchester's position as a port and a centre of an improving agricultural economy. A saltworks had been established at the Hythe by 1712, when Richard Freshfield acquired it for refining rock salt, imported mainly from Liverpool, which in 1737 shipped 9,200 bushels to Colchester.[75] By 1786 Colchester grocers were importing their own salt, probably already refined.[76] Between 1798 and 1801 only 34 qr. of salt was carried coastwise from Colchester compared with 303 qr. from Maldon, and although James Thorn was refining salt at Colchester *c.* 1812, the saltworks there closed soon afterwards.[77]

Most of the watermills that ringed the town were used for fulling at some time in the Georgian period and as the cloth industry declined they were converted for grinding seed or grain in competition with *c.* 12 windmills.[78] In the early 18th century malt was exported from Colchester to Rotterdam to supply the Dutch distilleries;[79] later in the period local maltsters and brewers established their own distilleries in Colchester and acquired many local inns. A malting established at the Hythe by 1706 was bought in 1727 by Richard Freshfield, who had a brewery in St. Giles's parish by 1735 and acquired a number of inns.[80] Samuel Todd had established a distillery near Headgate by 1749, when he bought Second mill, Lexden Road, with its malting house.[81] The mill and malting business survived Todd's bankruptcy and were said in 1785 to be extensive, but the malting and kiln had fallen into disuse by 1787.[82] In 1807 the Colchester brewery of Robert and Samuel Tabor acquired nine public houses within the borough.[83] Samuel Bawtree and George Savill bought Hull (or Distillery) mill in 1811 and built a distillery on the site and a rectifying house in Culver Street.[84] Thomas Andrews's brewery, recorded from 1774, passed *c.* 1815 to his kinsmen, the Cobbold family, who had maltings at the Hythe.[85] Cinder ovens recorded at the Hythe in 1773 and 1786 probably provided coke for malting kilns until a gasworks was established in 1817.[86]

70 B. Mason, *Clock and Watchmaking in Colch.* 22–3, 221, 329–69.

71 *V.C.H. Essex*, ii. 413, 418; *E.A.T.* 3rd ser. i. 49.

72 E.R.O., D/ACR 19/518; D/DU 559/125, 134–5; ibid. Acc. C47, C.P.L. 547; *E.C.S.* 23 May 1975; *Universal Brit. Dir.* (1793), ii. 523; *Colch. Gaz.* 23 Sept. 1815.

73 E.R.O., Acc. C281; ibid. D/P 138/11/8–10; *Ipswich Jnl.* 31 Jan. 1767; E.C.L. Colch., Crisp MSS. 'Colch. Monumental Inscriptions', v. 65.

74 *Ipswich Jnl.* 26 Oct. 1771; *Universal Brit. Dir.* (1793), ii. 522.

75 E.R.O., D/B 5 Sr98, rot. 6; D/B 5 Sb5/1, pp. 123, 223, 327; ibid. T/A 424/4/1,2; ibid. Q/SBb 68/1; Q/SBb 303/18; T. S. Willan, *Eng. Coasting Trade 1600–1750*, 185.

76 E.R.O., D/B 5 Sb6/7, ff. 111v.–112.

77 E.R.O., D/B 5 Sb6/9, 8 Jan. 1798; ibid. Acc. C32, f. 22; *2nd Rep. Cttee. on Laws relating to Salt Duties*, H.C. 142, App. 17 (1801), iii; *V.C.H. Essex*, ii. 445; Brown, *Colch. 1815–1914*, 15.

78 Below, Mills.

79 P.R.O., E 190/627/8; D. Ormrod, *Eng. Grain Exports and Structure of Agrarian Capitalism 1700–60*, 23, 31, 33, 67–8.

80 Below, this chapter, Topography; E.R.O., D/DHt T72/58, 97; D/B 5 Sb6/1, f. 12; P.R.O., PROB 11/815, f. 254.

81 E.R.O., D/DEl B3, p. 29; ibid. Acc. C47, C.P.L. 969.

82 Ibid. D/DEl B3, pp. 33–40; K. G. Farries, *Essex Windmills*, iii. 88–9.

83 E.R.O., D/DO T485.

84 Booker, *Essex and the Industrial Revolution*, 71; Cromwell, *Hist. Colch.* 295; *E.R.* lix. 198; E.R.O., Acc. C104 (estate and family papers, box 2).

85 E.R.O., D/P 178/11/3–7; *Universal Brit. Dir.* (1793), ii. 521; Pigot, *London and Provincial Commercial Dir.* (1823), p. 289; ibid. (1832), p. 674.

86 E.R.O., P/6 R3; ibid. D/B 5 Sb6/7, f. 109v.; below, Public Services (Gas Supply).

Shipbuilding was carried on at the Hythe throughout the period. Most of the vessels built there and registered in the port 1779–1822 were smacks, sloops, cutters, and yawls, of between 10 and 25 tons burthen, but some larger vessels were built there, including four sloops (67 to 108 tons), three sailing barges (82–93 tons), and a brigantine (104 tons).[87] In 1790 the Colchester yard built 13 ships, but in 1791, 1804, and 1805 the numbers were 4, 6, and 5 respectively.[88] William Stuttle, shipbuilder at the Hythe from 1790 or earlier, employed 5 shipwrights and 2 apprentices building merchant ships there in 1804. That yard had passed to Westerby Stuttle by 1818, and may have been acquired soon afterwards by Philip Sainty who built ships at Colchester from *c.* 1819 until 1848 or later.[89]

Considerable quantities of iron and some steel were imported from Sweden in the 1720s and 1730s by Colchester merchants, principally the aldermen John Blatch and his political adversary George Gray, plumber and glazier, who kept an iron warehouse.[90] Swedish and Russian iron was apparently being imported in 1767 when William Seaber the younger introduced American iron in competition with it.[91] Some of the metal was probably used by Colchester craftsmen. Among freemen voters in 1768 there were 7 whitesmiths, 4 cutlers, and an ironmonger.[92] There were at least as many in the 1780s and it is likely that whitesmiths and ironmongers were making castings for domestic ironware and the building industry before foundries were established. The later ironfounders Joseph Wallis, Richard Coleman, and William Dearn were formerly described as whitesmiths or ironmongers.[93]

Access to raw materials through the port and to limekilns and coke ovens at the Hythe, the demands of the building industry and agriculture, and the presence of skilled metalworkers made Colchester a suitable site for ironfoundries at the end of the century.[94] In 1792 Joseph Wallis built a foundry on Winnock's charity land at the west end of High Street as an adjunct to his ironmongery shop.[95] Richard Coleman, whitesmith, who probably had a business attached to his house in Wyre Street from 1802, had established a foundry at the Hythe by 1807, when he made railings for All Saints' church. Surviving examples of Coleman's ironwork include the gates of his own foundry[96] and those at St. Martin's church, Spring House, Lexden, and Trinity House, Wivenhoe. Wallis's foundry and shop were favourably situated to attract trade from farmers attending the market, and his products also included 8 cast iron columns for the office of the Essex & Suffolk Equitable Insurance Society, built on the site of the old corn exchange in 1819, and 26 castings of coats of arms in Essex churches.[97] Wallis (d. 1827) and Coleman (d. 1828) were succeeded by their sons Charles and Richard, who formed a short-lived partnership soon afterwards, leaving the Hythe and extending the High Street premises. By 1834 Coleman on his own had established the Abbeygate works.[98] William Dearn, nailmaker, who had settled in Colchester by 1816, was also an ironmonger and brazier by 1826. He built a house in St. Botolph's Street *c.* 1832 and later added a foundry to his business there.[99] John Oakes, engineer, had a foundry in the 1830s.[1]

87 E.R.O., Acc. 6323 (shipping registers).

88 *Ships and Vessels built in Gt. Brit. 1790–1806*, H.C. 243, p. 6 (1806), xiii.

89 E.R.O., Acc. 6323 (Shipping reg. no. 2); ibid. D/P 203/11/29; *Visitation of Dockyards*, H.C. 193, p. 7 (1805), viii; *White's Dir. Essex* (1848), 98.

90 P.R.O., E 190/628/10; E 190/631/11; E 190/636/6; E.R.O., D/B 5 Sb5/2, p. 301; below, this chapter, Town Govt. and Politics.

91 *Ipswich Jnl.* 28 Mar. 1767.

92 *Poll Bk.* 1768, 1784, 1788.

93 *Universal Brit. Dir.* (1793), ii. 522, 525; Pigot, *London and Provincial Commercial Dir.* (1823), 290; *V.C.H. Essex*, ii. 496 n.; *E.A.T.* 3rd ser. xiv. 102.

94 Account based on *V.C.H. Essex*, ii. 496–7; Booker, *Essex and the Industrial Revolution*, 8–12; *E.A.T.* 3rd ser. xiv. 102–10.

95 E.R.O., D/Q 31/1/2.

96 Colch. Mus., Hythe file.

97 *Guide to Essex Chs.* ed. C. Starr, 73.

98 Below, Modern Colch. (Econ., 19th-cent. town).

99 Foster, *Church of St. James the Less and St. Helen, Colch.*, 9; E.R.O., Boro. Mun., Improvement Com. Mins. 1811–33, p. 338; below, Modern Colch. (Econ., 19th-cent. town).

1 *E.A.T.* 3rd ser. xiv. 107.

Engine building and general engineering, for which Colchester and West Ham were the two main centres in Essex in the 19th century, developed after the establishment of the early foundries. A millwright's and engineering business was started *c.* 1810 by Mr. Sansom at Greenstead.[2]

External Trade

Colchester was well placed as a centre of internal and external trade to take advantage of the consumer revolution of the 18th century.[3] It was linked to English and Continental ports by sea and to London and Harwich by road also. In the early 19th century a Colchester grocer, James Lovett, bought goods not only from suppliers in London, the home counties, and East Anglia, but also from Cheshire, Lancashire, Leicestershire, Staffordshire, and Yorkshire.[4] Fairs were held five times a year between April and October. The popularity of the St. Dennis's or October fair, said to be waning in 1748,[5] suffered further when cattle sales were stopped because of disease between 1748 and 1755.[6] In 1769, however, the midsummer fair was the largest known for 20 years,[7] and goods were brought from London for sale at the October fair, by both London and Colchester tradesmen.[8] The April fair had ceased by 1803, but the other four survived at the end of the Georgian period and the town's markets continued to draw cereals, meat, and vegetables from the countryside and fish from the sea.[9]

The river Colne was navigable to large ships only as far as Wivenhoe, three miles below the Hythe, but hoys and lighters could reach the quays and a customs house there.[10] Merchants such as John Blatch, George Gray, Henry Walker, John Savill, Daniel Blyth, and John Baker and the families of Freshfield, Kendall, Rogers, and Tabor flourished throughout the period, usually dealing in more than one commodity.[11] The goods passing through the port in the early Georgian period were probably similar to those listed in 1669 as subject to tolls and other charges,[12] but with significant additions among imports. They included Holland linen, Silesia lawns, tea tables, close stools, bricks, and paper. The overseas exports were mainly bays, says, serges, and skins to Rotterdam and oysters to Dieppe and Dunkirk. In the 1720s the principal imports were iron, steel, and timber from Sweden and Norway and pantiles and brandy from Rotterdam.

Coastal shipping carried coal from Sunderland and Newcastle, rock salt from Liverpool, fuller's earth from Rochester; from London came raw wool, raw and tanned skins, foreign linen, spices, lemons, oranges, snuff, and tobacco. Bays were the main commodity sent coastwise to London, with some potash, seeds, and re-exported Holland linen.[13] Legitimate trade with the Continent was vulnerable during the wars with France. In the 1740s the export of bays was said to be hampered by the lack of proper convoys to protect ships from enemy attack,[14] although contraband traffic in tea, wine, brandy, and coffee continued.[15]

Trade recovered between the wars and in 1754 the wares of a Colchester merchant, John Rogers, included Liverpool, Bow, and foreign china, Staffordshire

2 *V.C.H. Essex*, ii. 498.

3 N. McKendrick, J. Brewer, and J. H. Plumb, *Birth of a Consumer Soc.* 1–6.

4 E.R.O., Acc. C32, ff. 14–65, 74–141.

5 Below, Markets; Morant, *Colch.* (1748) Bk. I, p. 77.

6 E.R.O., Q/Smg 16–18.

7 Ibid. Acc. C281.

8 Brown, *Essex at Work*, 68.

9 Below, Markets.

10 Below, Port.

11 P.R.O., E 190/627/8; E 190/636/6; E 190/630/10; E.R.O., T/A 424/1; S. D'Cruze, 'Middling Sort in Provincial Eng.: Politics and Social Relations in Colch.' (Essex Univ. Ph.D. thesis, 1990), 386; *Universal Brit. Dir.* (1793), ii. 526; Pigot, *London and Provincial Commercial Dir.* (1832), 290–1.

12 Morant, *Colch.* App. XII.

13 P.R.O., E 190/627/8; E 190/630/10; E 190/636/6.

14 E.R.O., Q/SBb 184/1.

15 P.R.O., CUST 21/45–9.

stoneware, Dutch stoneware and tiles, and India fans.[16] Coastwise trade continued during the 1780s but not without risk; in 1781 a cargo of rock salt bound for Colchester from Liverpool was captured by a French privateer off Beachy Head.[17] Exports of bread grains were disrupted during food crises.[18] Wheat, barley, and malt were shipped to London, Rochester, Southampton, and Berwick-on-Tweed. Cereals and malt exported from Colchester between 1780 and 1786 amounted to 152,681 qr. of wheat, 77,135 qr. of barley, and 70,571 qr. of malt, compared with 133,946 qr., 64,658 qr., and 218,314 qr. respectively from Harwich.[19] In 1800 there belonged to the port 156 vessels, totalling 4,663 tons and employing 434 men, compared with 137 vessels, 7,015 tons, and 814 men belonging to Harwich.[20] In terms of the tonnage of coastwise shipping Colchester rose in rank among 79 English ports, London excepted, from 31st to 22nd place between 1737 and 1751.[21] Estimated by tonnage of shipping owned, Colchester held fourth place among the five major East Anglian ports in 1709. All those ports increased their tonnage between 1709 and 1792, but by 1751 Colchester had lost rank to Ipswich.[22] The river channel was apparently impeded by shoals and silt by 1818, when ship owners and masters of Colchester and Maldon asked for a buoy on the southern extremity of the Colne bar and for the appointment of river and harbour pilots. Trinity House instituted a pilotage service in 1819,[23] but no major improvement was made to the channel in the Georgian period.[24] Between 1817 and 1820 coal imports rose from 22,439 chaldrons to 25,383 chaldrons, the increase being ascribed partly to the lack of wood for fuel.[25] By 1832 there were 8 or more coal merchants trading from the Hythe.[26]

Smuggling of wine and spirits from the Continent, and of tea, spices, china, and textiles from the Far East flourished along the Essex coast, as elsewhere, in the period.[27] Its effect on Colchester's economy and the extent to which local merchants and tradesmen dealt in contraband goods are not known. In 1717 attached to the custom house at the Hythe were a collector, a surveyor, a landwaiter, a searcher, two tidesmen, another searcher at Wivenhoe, two boatmen at Brightlingsea, and a boatman at Mersea Island, the collector's jurisdiction being co-extensive with the port of Colchester. The revenue vessel, based at Wivenhoe, was merely a smack in the 1720s and 1730s. It was replaced *c.* 1740 by a sloop, which was still in service in 1760, but had itself been replaced by a cutter by 1770. The number of seamen, under a commander and a mate, was increased from 9 and a boy in 1730 to 11 by 1742, and 24 and a boy by 1790.[28] Appointment to customs posts was in the Rebow family's patronage for many years.[29] The annual value of contraband goods seized within the port of Colchester usually ranged between £800 and £1,000, but in 1722 it amounted to £1,347 and in 1770 to £2,350.

Rowing boats and coasters were the most common smuggling craft taken, but in 1745 an armed cutter was seized.[30] Goods seized by the revenue men were sold at the custom house at the Hythe, and boats were broken up in local shipyards.[31]

[16] *Ipswich Jnl.* 1 June, 5 Oct. 1754.
[17] *The Times*, May, June, 1785; E.R.O., Q/SBb 303/18.
[18] Below, this chapter, this section.
[19] *Account of Wheat, Barley and Malt sent coastwise, Christmas 1780–Christmas 1786*, H.C. papers Geo. III, xlix, p. 219.
[20] D. Macpherson, *Annals of Commerce*, iv. 535–6.
[21] T. S. Willan, *Eng. Coasting Trade 1600–1750*, 220–2.
[22] P. J. Corfield, *Impact of Eng. Towns 1700–1800*, 36.
[23] E.R.O., D/B 5 Gb9, pp. 383–4; *E.C.S.* 8 Aug. 1969.
[24] Below, Port.
[25] *Rep. Sel. Cttee. on Agric.* H.C. 668, p. 177–8 (1821), ix.
[26] Pigot, *London and Provincial Commercial Dir.* (1832), p. 290.
[27] Cf. Neville Williams, *Contraband Cargoes*, 108 sqq.
[28] P.R.O., CUST 18/115, CUST 18/132, CUST 18/167, CUST 18/198, CUST 18/214, CUST 18/321, CUST 18/452; H. Benham, *Once Upon a Tide*, 173.
[29] D'Cruze, 'Middling Sort in Provincial Eng.', 436.
[30] P.R.O., CUST 21/22–73.
[31] Brown, *Essex People*, 92; *The Times*, 6 Oct. 1787; H. Benham, *Smuggler's Century*, 128–30; *Chelm. Chron.* 21 Dec. 1764; 8 Jan. 1765.

Among Colchester men identified as smugglers were Mason, a glazier (fl. 1715), John and Edward Harvey and John Johnson, indicted in 1726, Henry Hubbard taken in 1730, John Skinner, farmer at Old Heath who was hanged in 1746 for killing his servant, and Henry Sadler taken in 1770. A Colchester gang was active in 1729; similar gangs kidnapped a customs officer in 1744, retrieved contraband tea from the custom house at the Hythe in 1748, attacked a revenue sloop carrying a cargo of tea in 1778, and captured the sloop when it was an unmanned in 1781.[32] In 1779 tradesmen of Colchester and neighbouring parishes were among petitioners to parliament for relief from smuggling,[33] and the Twining family, tea traders in London and Colchester, constantly urged governments to reduce the punitive tax on tea to make smuggling less profitable.[34]

Retail Trade

The introduction in 1715 of a fine on shopkeepers who were not freemen, its enforcement by imprisonment in 1725, and the assessment of 88 'foreign' shopkeepers in 1735 suggest that the number of shops was growing early in the period.[35] By 1730 the intrusion of hawkers and pedlars was seen as a threat to resident traders and shopkeepers.[36] In 1764, when restrictions on Sunday trading were invoked after a lapse of several years, a walking draper from Epping was among those indicted.[37] The incursion of dealers into the main streets of the town, deplored by Philip Morant,[38] proceeded throughout the period as houses and warehouses, some formerly associated with the bay industry,[39] were acquired by merchants, tradesmen, and shopkeepers.[40]

Besides traditional craftsmen selling their own wares, there were shopkeepers who bought goods from both local and London warehouses, so that a wide range of food, wine, clothing, furniture, hardware, textiles, watches, clocks, and trinkets could be bought in the town as well as books, paper, prints, and music.[41] Advertisements stressed connexions with London fashion or advantage over London prices.[42] Fashionable china and glass were sold to the public direct from warehouses in the town; one on North Hill offered Liverpool ware in 1742; in the 1750s William Hassells, a Staffordshire potter, traded twice a week from his warehouse in Wyre Street, and in 1791 Christopher Potter advertised French china from his new Paris factory.[43] In 1788 the tax on retail shops in the town, valued above £5 and excluding those selling only bread, flour, meal or bran,[44] amounted to £23 15*s.* 9*d.* The largest sums were raised in the parishes of St. Runwald (£8 3*s.* 4*d.*), St. Peter (£6 10*s.* 1*d.*), and St. Nicholas (£5 2*s.* 8*d.*).

The victualling trade in Colchester sometimes provided a second line of business for other tradesmen and an opportunity for redundant clothworkers.[45] Many inns and public houses flourished in the town. The alehousekeepers' threat to withhold the annual fine of 10*s.*, imposed on non-freemen under a bylaw of 1715, and their subsequent action in King's Bench led to the borough justices being fined for

[32] P.R.O., E 190/636/6, f. 2v.; E.R.O., T/A 124, pp. 6, 8; ibid. D/B 5 Sb5/2 1723–34, p. 95; ibid. Acc. C281; Benham, *Smuggler's Century*, 21, 24, 132; *V.C.H. Essex*, ii. 299.

[33] *C.J.* xxxvii. 213.

[34] Williams, *Contraband Cargoes*, 153.

[35] E.R.O., D/B 5 Gb7, p. 19; D/DY 2/1 (Chamberlain's accounts 1736–7).

[36] *C.J.* xxi. 663.

[37] E.R.O., D/B 5 Sb6/3, ff. 69v., 87v.

[38] Morant, *Colch.* 80.

[39] e.g. *Ipswich Jnl.* 12 Sept. 1767; 10 Feb. 1781.

[40] Below, this chapter, Topography.

[41] *Universal Brit. Dir.* (1793), ii. 522–6; advertisements in *Ipswich Jnl.*; *E.R.* lxiv. 253–9; *Local Historian*, xvii. 158–61.

[42] *Ipswich Jnl.* 19 Jan. 1771, s.v. Steph. Candler; ibid. 23 Jan. 1773, s.v. Steph. Hooker; ibid. 8 May, 1773, s.v. Eliz. Shillito.

[43] E.R.O., Acc. C210, J. B. Harvey Colln. iv. 171; *Ipswich Jnl.* 8 Oct. 1791.

[44] 25 Geo. III, c. 30; 26 Geo. III, c. 9;*Local Historian*, xiv. 348.

[45] D'Cruze, 'Middling Sort in Provincial Eng.', 36, 151, 218.

misdemeanour in 1740.[46] With those of other towns they complained at the billeting of soldiers and their horses.[47] The building of infantry barracks in 1794 only partly relieved the problems of billeting, and stables were added to the barracks only in 1800.[48] The large numbers of soldiers in the town brought custom to many inns, whose names proclaimed their military connexions. A number of inns were staging posts, and kept horses and vehicles for hire. The principal inns were more than victualling houses; they provided rooms for political clubs, auctioneers, travelling salesmen, and entertainers.[49]

Banking and Insurance

Capital for business improvements was usually raised locally by mortgaging real property, and short-term circulating capital helped to prime the local economy.[50] In the earlier 18th century local merchants provided some banking services. Among them were Charles Whaley, wine merchant, and John Mills, tea dealer, whose activities gave rise to two rival banks. Mills, who was negotiating his customers' bills and notes by 1740,[51] opened a tea warehouse in High Street in association with his cousins Richard and John Twining of London in 1766, and in 1787 opened the Colchester and Essex bank in partnership with them. Mills, entitled to all profits and subject to all losses, indemnified the Twinings in every respect. The partnership was dissolved in 1797, but the bank survived in the hands of Mills's son, John Fletcher Mills, and John Bawtree.[52] Charles Whaley was a principal creditor of three Colchester bankrupts between 1737 and 1743.[53] The Whaley family joined with the Crickitts in a bank established in High Street by 1774.[54] George Round joined the firm in 1790. When Crickitt's Chelmsford bank stopped payment in the bank panic of 1825, the Round family acted swiftly to restore confidence and Crickitt withdrew from the firm.[55] The Colchester bank for savings was instituted in 1817 for the deposit of small sums which were invested by trustees drawn from the local gentry, clergy, and businessmen of the town.[56]

The incidence of bankruptcy throughout the period reflects the vulnerablility of the textile industry and the victualling trades, but also suggests confidence and expansion of business activity in the town. Among 43 Colchester men against whom bankruptcy proceedings were initiated in the period 1700–1800 there were 8 baymakers and 7 vintners or innholders; two thirds of the failures occurred after 1750. Failed tradesmen were usually indebted to other Colchester tradesmen or merchants, suppliers in London and Suffolk, or local gentry who had provided loans. Debts owed to creditors in remoter provinces include those of two woolcombers to a Leicestershire gentleman, probably for wool, in 1719 and 1722, and of a 'chapman' to a Huddersfield clothier in 1725.[57]

The Essex Militia Insurance Office was established in 1762 by William Seaber the elder, draper turned wine merchant, in partnership with William Keymer, bookseller, to insure men liable for service in the militia.[58] The Essex Equitable Insurance Society, founded in 1802 at the instigation of the banker John Bawtree, was among the earliest provincial fire insurance companies started in reaction to

46 E.R.O., D/B 5 Gb7, p. 19.
47 e.g. *C.J.* xxviii, pp. 125, 600.
48 Below, Barracks.
49 Brown, *Essex at Work*, 68–75.
50 D'Cruze, 'Middling Sort in Provincial Eng.', 40.
51 *E.R.* lxv. 19.
52 *Jnl. Bankers' Inst.* Oct. 1906, 320; *E.R.* lxi. 35; S. H. Twining, *House of Twining 1706–1956*, 44, 58–60.
53 P.R.O., B 4/9, pp. 50, 142; B 4/10, p. 277.
54 G. Martin, *Story of Colch.* 85; *Jnl. Bankers' Inst.* Oct. 1906, 320.
55 E.R.O., D/DR F62; *Ipswich Jnl.* 24 Dec. 1825.
56 T. Cromwell, *Hist. Colch.* 392–3; E.R.O., D/DEl F8.
57 E.R.O., T/P 146/10.
58 D'Cruze, 'Middling Sort in Provincial Eng.', 221; *Ipswich Jnl.* 2 Jan. 1762.

and independent of the cartel formed by the old established London companies. Its 24 directors, drawn equally from Colchester and the county, acquired a lease of the corn exchange in 1803, bought its first fire engine in 1812, in 1819 built an office on the site of the exchange, and in 1820 promoted the Essex Life Insurance Society.[59]

Colchester's economy responded quickly to some of the national financial crises of the 18th century. The vehemence of a petition to parliament from the corporation and inhabitants following the South Sea Bubble in 1720 suggests that many Colchester people suffered from the collapse, which probably caused the unusually high number of six bankruptcy cases initiated in 1720–1.[60] The frequent elections for parliament and borough offices required generous spending by the candidates which profited mainly the victualling trades, but occasionally contributed to the bankruptcy of candidates and their supporters. In the crisis year of 1772 the London bank in which the unsuccessful parliamentary candidate, Alexander Fordyce, was partner, failed. Bezaliel Blomfield, one of three baymakers brought to bankruptcy that year had supported Fordyce; he and others may have suffered financially from the involvement.[61] The failure of Daniel Whittle Harvey in the parliamentary election of 1815[62] contributed to the bankruptcy of Henry Thorn, silversmith turned rag merchant, who had bought Battleswick manor.[63]

The Poor

The vicissitudes of the bay industry immediately affected weavers working at home on a single loom and many were driven to seek poor relief.[64] By so doing they forfeited their right to vote as freemen, so that their declining numbers cannot be estimated from poll books, but 12 men identified as weavers in 1788 were recorded in other trades in 1812.[65] Some baymakers, cardmakers, and multi-loom weavers survived by acquiring real estate, taking up a secondary occupation, obtaining paid offices, or sending their sons into other trades or to other towns. In the 1730s John Skingsley was baymaker and distiller, Peter Cresswell was weaver and victualler, and Joseph Duffield was cardmaker and coal merchant; Ellis Clarke on his death in 1723 owned 8 tenements, including 2 inns. The Triggs family turned from weaving and woolcombing to innkeeping between 1768 and 1772; some members of the Shillito family survived as cardmakers and were appointed masters of the house of correction in 1744 and 1757.[66] Unemployed weavers and the old were usually the majority among recipients of parish poor relief, but Colchester did not bear the whole cost of recession in the trade for many spinners employed by baymakers lived beyond the borough and liberties.[67]

Three almshouses and a number of bread charities were founded to ease the plight of the old and the poor;[68] when war or bad harvests made food scarce and raised prices, private charity supplemented parish doles with immediate gifts of food. An ox was given to feed the poor in 1771 and in 1795 a subscription raised £700 to provide 4,000 food tickets.[69] The corporation, with no direct role in poor relief, reiterated statutory controls on bread and on weights and measures.[70]

59 B. Drew, *Fire Office; Hist. Essex and Suff. Equitable Insurance Soc. Ltd. 1802–1952*, 10–12, 14–15, 39, 49.

60 *C.J.* xix. 552; P.R.O., B 4/3, pp. 161–2, 168, 183, 219.

61 P.R.O., B 3/3675–6; E.R.O., Acc. C281; *Poll Bk.* 1768.

62 Below, this chapter, Town Govt. (Parl. Rep.).

63 P.R.O., B 3/4929–30; below, Outlying Parts (West Donyland).

64 D'Cruze, 'Middling Sort in Provincial Eng.', 395; E.R.O., Q/SBb 206/7.

65 *Poll Bk.* 1798, 1812.

66 D'Cruze, 'Middling Sort in Provincial Eng.', 36–7, 504–8; Brown, *Essex at Work*, 23.

67 Morant, *Colch.* 79; Brown, *Essex People*, 80.

68 Below, Charities.

69 E.R.O., Acc. C281; *Ipswich Jnl.* 10 Jan. 1795.

70 e.g. E.R.O., D/B 5 Sb6/3, f. 72; D/B 5 Sb6/4, ff. 71, 74v.; D/B 5 Sb6/9, 20 Jan. 1800; D/B 5 Sb6/10, 19 Oct. 1818.

Protests by and on behalf of the poor occasionally erupted into riot. In 1740 rioters threatening to stop wagons laden with corn from reaching the Hythe for shipment were prevented by a party of dragoons, and the justices appealed to parliament to restrict the export of grain.[71] In 1766 the mayor apparently dealt successfully with a threat of violence to enforce price-fixing and the borough's M.P.s promised to support prohibition of corn exports and local efforts to relieve the poor.[72] In 1772 rioters stopped farmers' carts and for a week enforced the sale of meat, flour, and wheat below market prices,[73] and James Ashwell, a prominent grocer, received a letter threatening farmers, millers, shopkeepers, and butchers in general and his own life in particular.[74] The corporation petitioned parliament for the free import of grain and other provisions, and the mayor promised to protect carts coming into the town.[75] The justices sentenced thieves of food or livestock to transportation.[76] When, in July 1789, as revolution grew in France, a mob seized a wagon of wheat, Francis Smythies, town clerk, rescued it and conducted it to the Hythe. The dragoons, summoned in case of further disturbance, arrived in the town soon afterwards.[77] During a shortage of flour in 1795 a meeting of the principal inhabitants recommended methods of economy in the use of flour and potatoes and raised a subscription for relief.[78] In the barracks the bread ration was reduced and soldiers were allowed to seek employment in the harvest fields.[79]

Protesters at the turn of the century claimed that the poor were starving to death and that a man had no choice but to steal or abandon his family. To the rising cost of poor relief[80] was added, in wartime, the maintenance of militia men and their families, which in 1797 and 1800 amounted to a 6*d.* rate. Further rates were raised to provide statutory recruits to the army and navy.[81] Supplying the garrison in time of war brought prosperity to farmers, market gardeners, and shopkeepers, some of whom suffered a severe reverse of fortune when the barracks were demolished at the end of the Napoleonic War.[82] Shipments of corn and wool through the port declined from 81,442 qr. and 3,959 cwt. respectively in 1817 to 54,463 qr. and 2,146 cwt. in 1820. A shortage of corn to ship to London caused one carrier, Charles Parker, to lay up two of his five ships in 1820. By 1821 Colchester banks restricted credit as the price of wheat fell; many farmers who had started business with high wartime prices on borrowed capital were ruined and Parker was bankrupt in 1822. The shortage of cash and credit among farmers affected the traders with whom they customarily dealt. In 1821 John Metcalf, woollen draper, estimated that his trade had declined by more than a third; he had plenty of wool to sell but few customers for his cloth. John Rouse, ironmonger, claimed that his trade in agricultural tools had declined and that blacksmiths and wheelwrights to whom farmers owed money were consequently in debt to him.[83]

The Professions

Many professional men were attracted to Colchester. The existence of 12 churches in Colchester, although most of their livings were poor, ensured the presence in the town of a number of clergymen. Lawyers and doctors established practices in

71 *Ipswich Jnl.* 24, 31 May, 29 Nov., 13 Dec. 1740.

72 E.R.O., Acc. C419.

73 Ibid. Q/SBb 269; ibid. Acc. C281; *V.C.H. Essex*, ii. 240.

74 D. Hay and others, *Albion's Fatal Tree: Crime and Soc. in 18th-Cent. Eng.*, App. III, p. 329.

75 *C.J.* xxxiii. 677; *Ipswich Jnl.* 11, 18 Apr. 1772.

76 E.R.O., D/B 5 Sb5/1–7, Sb6/1–10, *passim.*

77 *Ipswich Jnl.* 1, 15 Aug. 1789.

78 E.R.O., Q/SBb 360/37.

79 P.R.O., WO 79/51.

80 Below, Par. Govt. and Poor Relief.

81 E.R.O., D/P 200/8/4; D/P 200/11/3; D/P 200/11/4; D/P 200/17/3.

82 P.R.O., WO 79/51–6; Brown, *Essex People*, 112.

83 P.R.O., B 3/3971–2; *Rep. Sel. Cttee. on Agric.* H.C. 668, pp. 176–83 (1821), ix; cf. Pigot, *London and Provincial Commercial Dir.* (1832), p. 290.

Colchester. Attorneys were prominent throughout the period in politics and public affairs, especially in the disputes about the borough's charter, and served the borough's court of quarter sessions.[84] Attorneys also served as town clerks and on navigation, improvement, and bankruptcy commissions.[85] In private practice they were investment brokers, conveyancers, and landowners' stewards and agents.[86] Among them were Charles Gray, attorney in the quarter sessions court in 1719 and later M.P.,[87] Samuel Ennew (d. 1795), town clerk, recorder, and clerk of the peace for the county, William Mayhew (d. 1764), campaigner for the recovery of the borough charter, Francis Smythies (d. 1798), controversial town clerk and leader of a Tory faction, and Smythies's more dignified son of the same name, who as town clerk guided the old corporation in its last years.[88] Apothecaries, physicians, and surgeons were recorded in the town throughout the period. They were appointed to the gaol and, on a casual basis, attended and occasionally inoculated the poor in parish workhouses.[89] In 1779 seven of the 19 members of the Colchester Medical Society lived in the borough.[90] Directories listed 8 medical men in 1793 and 11 in 1832,[91] by which time the Essex and Colchester hospital had been established, with an honorary staff of two physicans, three surgeons, and a salaried apothecary or house surgeon.[92]

Colchester's maritime interest stimulated the teaching of mathematics and navigation, especially in nonconformist boys' schools, and produced a number of land surveyors and mapmakers. The schoolmasters William Cole, John, Joseph, and Willam Kendall, J. Nelson, and Hayward Rush were among the nine or so Colchester land surveyors and map makers active in the late 18th and early 19th century, whose work is known.[93] Cole's son-in-law Robert Hale, formerly a baker, became a land surveyor and mapmaker; his grandson, William Hale (1797–1870), who patented an hydrodynamic method of ship propulsion in 1827, was commemorated as a pioneer of rocket propulsion by the naming of Hale's crater on the moon in 1970.[94]

TOPOGRAPHY

THE migration of *c.* 100 weavers from the town before 1715 and a high death rate from disease in the 1720s,[95] relieved pressure on living space within the town early in the period. It was said in 1736 that many houses had been pulled down,[96] and in the next decade more were demolished, including many in the parishes of St. Peter and St. Giles, where weavers were numerous.[97] The density of building was reduced on some sites; a house on North Hill was said in 1792 to be on a site once occupied by 5 and later by 3 houses.[98] In 1748, when 2,196 houses were recorded in the 12 town parishes, the most populous were St. Botolph's, with 409 houses, St. James's with 314, and St. Peter's with 298.[99] Only in the late 18th and early 19th century was the built-up area extended westward by gentlemen's houses on

84 Below, this chapter, Town Govt.

85 E.R.O., T/P 146/10; ibid. D/B 5 Gb7–10, *passim*; ibid. Boro. Mun., Improvement Com. Mins. 1811–33, pp. 1, 6.

86 *E.A.T.* 3rd ser. xix. 223–4.

87 E.R.O., D/B 5 Sb5/1, p. 149; below, this chapter, Town Govt. (Parl. Rep.).

88 E.R.O., D/DEl F3; D'Cruze, 'Middling Sort in Provincial Eng.', 385; *E.A.T.* 3rd ser. xviii. 63–74; xix. 223–30.

89 e.g. E.R.O., D/B 5 Sb6/10, 19 Oct. 1818; below, Par. Govt. and Poor Relief.

90 J. B. Penfold, *Hist. Essex County Hosp.* 168; *E.C.S.* 25 Jan. 1974; *E.J.* xxvi. 47.

91 *Universal Brit. Dir.* (1793), ii. 521; Pigot, *London and Provincial Commercial Dir.* (1832), 290–1.

92 Below, Hospitals (Essex County Hospital).

93 A. Stuart Mason, *Essex on the Map: the 18th Cent. Land Surveyors of Essex*, 9, 44, 76, 112–13.

94 *Dict. Scientific Biog.*; *Spaceflight*, xv. 31.

95 *C.J.* xviii, p. 280; *Census*, 1801, p. 95.

96 *C.J.* xxii, p. 815.

97 Morant, *Colch.* 110, 122.

98 E.R.O., Acc. C47, CPL 1245.

99 Morant, *Colch.* 107, 110, 113, 115, 117–20, 122, 125, 127.

large plots along Lexden Road,[1] and south-eastwards by the erection of barracks in 1794 and 1800, which encouraged speculative house-building in Magdalen Street.[2] Although most of the military buildings were sold when the barracks were reduced after the Napoleonic Wars, the army retained its former parade grounds, which remained open land and included 14 a. of garden ground.[3] Between 1801 and 1831 the number of houses in the town parishes increased by *c.* 61 per cent from 1,793 to 2,893; growth was greatest in the south-eastern parishes of St. James's and St. Botolph's.

In 1722 the town was described as large and very populous, the streets fair and beautiful, with many very good, well built houses, although it was still marred by damage sustained in the Civil War.[4] In the Georgian period part of the town wall in Priory Street was patched in brick by the adjacent landowners, and 50 yd. of wall from East Hill to Queen Street were rebuilt in brick.[5] Much of the surviving wall, however, was robbed for stone, neglected, and occasionally built upon,[6] and *c.* 185 ft. near the top of Balkerne Hill collapsed in 1795. The remaining gates were demolished piecemeal,[7] and part of St. Giles's church was left in ruins until 1819. There was, however, much refurbishment and new building. The church of St. Mary's-at-the-Walls, completed in 1714,[8] and its landscaped churchyard were signs of the change of style that transformed the town's appearance. In the 1720s the top of St. Mary's ancient tower was rebuilt and four other churches, All Saints', St. Nicholas's, St. Leonard's, and St. Mary Magdalen's, were repaired or altered. In 1758 the central tower of St. Peter's church was replaced by a west tower.[9] Nonconformists built, enlarged, and rebuilt their meeting houses; the Quakers in East Stockwell Street, Baptists in Eld Lane, Methodists in Maidenburgh Street, and Independents in Lion Walk.[10] The castle was partially restored by Charles Gray, to designs of James Deane, and by his successor James Round between 1746 an 1804.[11] A theatre was built in Queen Street in 1812, and a hospital in Lexden Road in 1819.[12] Sir Isaac Rebow (d. 1726) gravelled and made handsome the walk between Head Street and Eld Lane.[13]

The streets were not always as fair and beautiful as Defoe found them in 1722.[14] Bad paving and obstructions were frequently reported to the justices under a paving Act of 1623, but the borough chamberlain, workhouse corporation, and parish officers failed to discharge their responsibilities and the small fines for neglect were ineffective.[15] Enforcement of the Act by the borough justices ceased when the charter lapsed in 1741 and by 1750 the streets were so ruinous that a new Act was obtained,[16] which perpetuated the responsibility of justices to enforce the regulations. County justices were responsible until the charter of 1763 nominated new borough justices. The new corporation in 1764 imposed weight limits on coal carts and tried to enforce the Act; parish surveyors were continually urged to survey and repair pavements, but infringements were frequent and one session in 1799 received *c.* 54 presentments of bad paving.[17] Main and side streets were congested

1 Dept. of Env., 13th List of buildings of archit. and hist. interest.

2 Below, Barracks; E.R.O., D/P 201/11/29; *Ipswich Jnl.* 16 Mar. 1799; below, pl. facing p. 137.

3 Below, Barracks; *32nd Rep. Com. Char.* pp. 547–8.

4 D. Defoe, *Tour*, ed. G. D. M. Cole (1927), i. 16–17.

5 Dept. of Env., 13th List of buildings of archit. and hist. interest; Morant, *Colch.* 7.

6 E.R.O., D/B5 Aa1/34, ff. 8, 11; T. Cromwell, *Hist. Colch.* 175.

7 Below, Walls; Dept. of Env., 13th List of buildings of archit. and hist. interest.

8 Below, Churches (St. Mary-at-the-Walls), Fig. 31.

9 Below, Churches.

10 Below, Prot. Nonconf.

11 Below, Castle; *E.C.S.* (magazine section), 28 Oct. 1966.

12 Below, Hospitals (Essex County Hospital); Soc. and Cultural (Theatres and Cinemas).

13 Morant, *Colch.* 4.

14 Defoe, *Tour*, i. 16–17.

15 e.g. E.R.O., D/B 5 Sr106, rot. 2; Sr112, rot. 8; Sr113, rot 2; Morant, *Colch.* 5.

16 Morant, *Colch.* 5 and App. II; 22 Geo. II, c. 19.

17 E.R.O., D/B 5 Sb5/3, ff. 72v., 73v., 88; Sb5/7, 14 Jan. 1799.

with carts, wagons, and carriages. A cart loaded with bays was overturned in Pelham's Lane by a wagon and five horses in 1772, and in 1774 the streets, particularly High Street, were cluttered with empty casks, chests, wheelbarrows, butchers' blocks, chains, cables, and goods for sale.[18] In 1781 residents complained of lack of street lights and the hazard of water discharged onto pavements from spouts.[19] Public lamps were installed in 1783.[20] Pigs, which may have belonged to migrants from the country, were a nuisance in the streets in 1789.[21] Roaming pigs and donkeys and obstruction of streets and paths by goods for sale persisted in the early 19th century.[22]

It was not until the establishment of an improvement commission in 1811 that a programme of new paving, cleansing, lighting, and clearance of obstructions was undertaken.[23] The commission improved lighting in the main streets in 1812, and by 1821 had laid cobbled footpaths in Magdalen and Priory Streets and flagstones in much of Head, High, and Wyre Streets and had repaired and partly rebuilt the abbey walls. It improved the approaches to the town, pulling down St. Botolph's and East gates and the houses on the foundations of North gate, diverted the access from Ipswich Road, and eased the gradient of East Hill. Within the town the commission widened High Street near the obelisk, Magdalen Street, and Head Street. Parts of the churchyards of St. Leonard's, Holy Trinity, and All Saints', and of the Pinnacle gardens (St. John's abbey grounds) were taken into the highway. Windows, jetties such as that of the George inn, steps, and porches that projected more than 18 in. into the main streets and 10 in. into other streets were removed, and shopkeepers took advantage of the compensation paid by the commission to fit fashionable flat windows into their shop fronts.[24] In 1825 the improvement commission began to lay macadamized roads of broken stone.[25]

At the east end of High Street gentlemen's houses and grounds covered about a third of the whole area within the town walls in the early 18th century.[26] New houses were built on the sites of earlier ones in the main streets throughout the period, but much of the change was to existing houses, achieved by plastering, fronting or encapsulating in brick, inserting sash windows, adding doorways with decorated cases and fanlights, and refitting internally.[27] The formation in 1718 of a borough committee to survey encroachments and the introduction of fines of 18*d.* a foot in the main streets and 12*d.* a foot in back streets, suggests a spate of refronting and underbuilding jetties at that time.[28] Some householders compounded for bow windows and pallisades.[29] Red brick was favoured. Early in the century it was often hard textured and dark in colour (e.g. no. 71 Culver Street), later it became brighter red and was suitable for rubbing and cutting for mouldings and decoration such as dentil cornices (e.g. no. 2 Queen Street). In 1766 a brickmaker at Stanway was producing white or grey 'Gault' bricks of the kind used by William Phillips when he built no. 107 Crouch Street, *c.* 1776.[30] They were used towards the end of the century for fashionable houses in the main streets and

18 Ibid. D/B 5 Sb5/4, ff. 78v.–79.

19 *C.J.* xxxviii. 156.

20 Below, Public Services (Street Paving, Cleaning and Lighting).

21 E.R.O., D/B 5 Sb5/6, f. 29v.

22 Ibid. Boro. Mun., Improvement Com. Mins., 1811–33, pp. 93–4, 172, 282; ibid. D/B 5 Sb6/10, 19 Oct. 1818.

23 51 Geo. III, c. 43; below, Public Services (Street Paving, Cleaning and Lighting).

24 E.R.O., Boro. Mun., Improvement Com. Mins., 1811–33, pp. 9, 12, 54, 59, 82, 92, 109–12, 118, 128, 137, 168–72, 180, 186, 226, 243, 259, 262, 285–7, 312, 315, 320, 335, 338, 346; ibid. 1833–47, pp. 32–3, 43, 54, 56; Cromwell, *Hist. Colch.* 176.

25 E.R.O., Boro. Mun., Improvement Com. Mins., 1811–33, pp. 142, 200, 219, 221, 226, 253, 255.

26 J. Bensusan-Butt, *All Saints', Colch. in 18th Cent.* 3.

27 R.C.H.M. *Essex*, iii. 54–71; Dept. of Env., 13th List of buildings of archit. and hist. interest.

28 E.R.O., D/B 5 Gb7, p. 65.

29 Ibid. D/B5 Aa1/34, ff. 6–7, 10–11; Aa1/35, ff. 203v., 207v.

30 Colch. Civic Soc. *Quarterly Bull.* i (6), pp. 5–6.

FIG. 10. HOLLYTREES HOUSE, 1748

for the early 19th-century hospital and new houses in Lexden Road. Despite the fashion for white brick the use of red brick continued (e.g. nos. 5–6 North Hill of 1809). Meanwhile in the less important streets houses of timber frame and plaster continued to be built throughout the 18th century (e.g. nos. 67–71 Crouch Street and no. 125 Crouch Street). Weatherboarding, a common finish for vernacular buildings in rural east Essex, was little used (but see nos. 95–6 Hythe Hill), perhaps because of the additional fire risk. By 1800 the main streets were lined with brick or plastered buildings, some with bow windows. Many of the older, jettied buildings, such as the Red Lion and the George in High Street, survived, their timbers and once pargetted fronts masked by plaster. A number of houses at the lower end of East Hill, beyond East bridge, and in some side streets were not refurbished, but they usually had sash windows inserted.[31]

Several surviving houses have 18th-century features and some distinguished Georgian houses were built in the town.[32] Hollytrees, built next to the ruined castle on the site of an earlier house in 1718, was given with the castle to Charles Gray in 1726. The house has a main front of five bays and a basement and three storeys rising to a parapet. It is set back from the street behind a small courtyard which is fronted by wrought-iron railings. The west wing, designed by James Deane, was added in 1748.[33] Gray laid out the Castle grounds as a small park with a raised walk, formed out of part of the earthwork defences, a canal, a summerhouse which

[31] Colch. Mus., Topography files: Head Street, High Street; *Ipswich Jnl.* 7 Dec. 1799, 26 June 1802, 14 May 1825; N. Lloyd, *Hist. Eng. House*, 343, fig. 548; R.C.H.M. *Essex*, iii. 60–2, 68–70; Dept. of Env., 13th List of buildings of archit. and hist. interest; J. Marriage, *Colch.: a Pictorial Hist.* illus. no. 37; Colch. Civic Soc. *Quarterly Bull.* ii. (5), p. 82.

[32] R.C.H.M. *Essex*, iii. 54–71; Dept. of Env., 13th List of buildings of archit. and hist. interest.; *E.C.S.* 13 Apr. 1962.

[33] *E.C.S.* 28 Oct. 1966; above, Fig. 10.

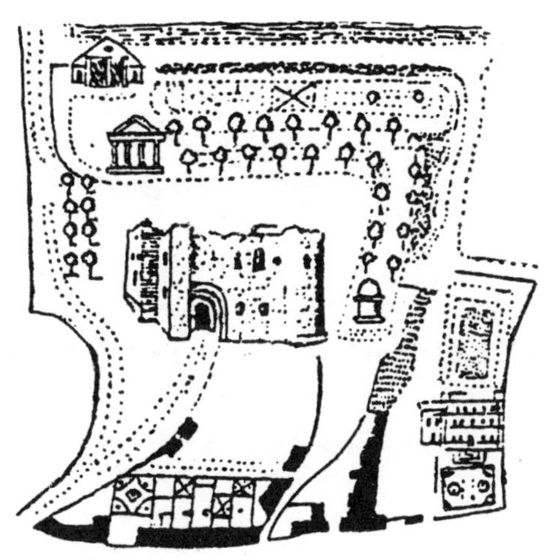

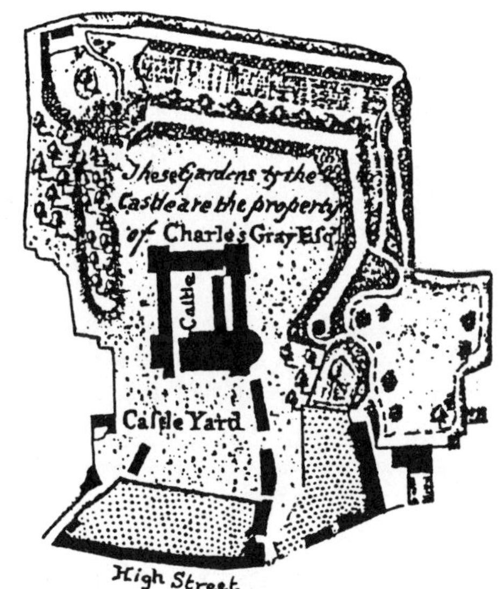

FIG. 11. THE CASTLE GROUNDS IN 1748 AND 1767

is dated 1731 and has the form of a Greek temple, and a rotunda of 1747. The many trees he planted included two cedars of Lebanon, two cedars of Bermuda, and a cork tree.[34] George Wegg built East Hill House opposite Hollytrees, pulling down nine houses to extend his grounds. The house, of three storeys, has a main front of seven bays, with a segmental pediment over a central Tuscan doorcase. Greyfriars, opposite East Hill House, was built *c.* 1755 of two storeys with attics and cellars. A garden front of five bays was added in 1780.[35] The Minories, east of East Hill House, was remodelled in 1776 in three storeys with a front of five bays, the central porch supporting a two-storeyed bay window. A Gothic summer-house from East Hill House, probably designed by James Deane, survives in the garden.[36] St. Martin's House in Angel Lane (later West Stockwell Street), with a west garden front, was built *c.* 1734 on the site of an earlier house. It was probably designed by James Deane, for Dr. Richard Daniell who laid out gardens behind it.[37] Away from High Street the better brick houses are mostly of two storeys with attics. Three-storeyed exceptions are nos. 20–22 Crouch Street, built for a merchant John Cole in mid century and having five bays, and the seven-bay nos. 44–52 Head Street of 1763–5. On the two-storeyed buildings the attic dormers are often partly hidden by a parapet. Most of the fronts are relatively plain and in a style which has evolved from that of the later 17th century. Externally there is nothing that could be described as 'Baroque' and the influence of Palladianism is limited to a few Venetian windows (e.g. on the 1748 extension to Hollytrees, the garden front of the Minories, and at Grey Friars and nos. 59–60 West Stockwell Street). The same simplicity of elevation design is continued into the early 19th century. Gothic elements occur occasionally, especially in windows (e.g. no. 31 St. John's Green of 1823) and the castellated style appears at no. 89 Lexden Road of 1818, built for Francis Smythies, which has been attributed to the Colchester-born architect Robert Lugar.[38]

[34] Colch. Boro. Council, *Hollytrees and Charles Gray*; Cromwell, *Hist. Colch.* 175; E.R.O., D/DRb F6, 7; ibid. Acc. C15, Charles Gray's notebk.

[35] Morant, *Colch.* 119; Dept. of Env., 13th List of buildings of archit and hist. interest; below, Fig. 12.

[36] J. Bensusan-Butt, *House that Boggis Built*; *E.C.S.*, 28 Oct. 1966; above, pl. facing p. 121.

[37] Morant, *Colch.* 183 and map facing p. 4; Dept. of Env., 13th List of buildings of archit. and hist. interest; *E.C.S.* 11 Apr. 1986; above, pl. facing p. 121.

[38] Pevsner, *Essex* (2nd edn.), 146; Dept. of Env., 13th List of buildings of archit. and hist. interest; above, pl. facing p. 121.

The many gardens recorded in Colchester reflect the fashionable interest in growing all kinds of plants and trees, including fruit trees, vines, and nuts.[39] By 1748 the grounds of the ruined buildings of St. Botolph's priory, St. John's abbey, and Greyfriars were laid out as orchards or gardens.[40] There were gardens where buildings had once stood, such as the site of houses near the tanyard in St. Peter's parish, which was cultivated by 1754,[41] and of St. James's rectory house on East Hill, burnt down during the siege and let as a garden in 1742.[42] Much of the ground behind houses on main streets within the walls was laid out in private gardens. Those behind houses on the east side of North Hill extended to the rear of houses in Angel Lane and on the west side there were both nursery and pleasure gardens between the streetside houses and the western town wall.[43] Sir Isaac Rebow's gardens extended eastward from Head Street towards Trinity Street, those of

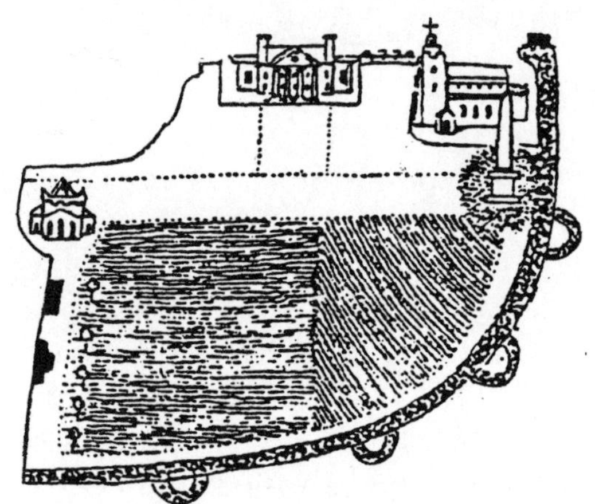

FIG. 12. THE GARDENS OF EAST HILL HOUSE IN 1748 AND 1767

Trinity House occupied almost all the centre of the square formed by Trinity and Culver Streets, Eld Lane, and Lion Walk, and a house in Queen Street had a garden of ¼ a. in 1791.[44] St. Mary's rectory had a cherry garden by 1745, and even where space was limited new gardens were planted. In 1763 the little garden of St. Peter's vicarage house was planted with nine new fruit trees.[45]

Some householders rented or bought pieces of adjoining land to enlarge their gardens. Nathaniel Laurence rented land belonging to the former hospital in St. Martin's Lane in the 1730s[46] and John Bernard acquired part of the yard of the Falcon and Queen's Head inn in High Street before 1748. Between 1748 and 1777 a small garden was laid out at the former no. 11 Sir Isaac's Walk.[47] A flower garden behind the Old Three Crowns inn in Head Street was opened to the public in 1773,[48] the garden of the Red Lion inn, bounded by Lion Walk and Eld Lane, survived until the Independent chapel was built there in 1763,[49] and that of the Three Cups until the covered market was built in 1813.[50] A botanic garden was established *c.* 1823 by the Colchester and Essex Botanical and Horticultural Society

[39] e.g. E.R.O., Acc. C47, CPL 269; ibid. D/B 5 Sb5/3, f. 50; Sb5/5, f. 69; ibid. Q/SMg 17 (Apr. 1752); *Ipswich Jnl.* 5 May, 15 Dec. 1798 (sale notices).

[40] Morant, *Colch.* map facing p. 4.

[41] E.R.O., D/DU 115/21.

[42] Below, Churches (St. James).

[43] Morant, *Colch.* map facing p. 4.

[44] E.R.O., T/M 268; *Ipswich Jnl.* 13 Aug. 1791.

[45] Morant, *Colch.* 113; E.R.O., D/P 178/1/4.

[46] E.R.O., D/B5 Aa1/34, f. 8.

[47] Morant, *Colch.* 184; Chapman and André, *Essex Map* (1777).

[48] *Ipswich Jnl.* 10 Apr. 1773; 22 Apr. 1775.

[49] *E.R.* lvii. 17.

[50] Below, Markets and Fairs.

on 8½ a. behind Greyfriars House.[51] Outside the walls there were market and nursery gardens and some houses had extensive pleasure gardens; the house on the corner of Abbeygate Street and St. John's Street had in 1754 a garden of 3 a. with a fish pond, fruit trees, and a gravel walk 100 yd. long fronting St. John's Street.[52] A house in London Road had 3 a. in 1759, another on East Hill had 5 a. in 1788, and others in St. Botolph's Street had large gardens in 1798. At a house in Magdalen Street, which was owned by the army, walnut trees survived until they were sold as timber in 1824.[53]

Some neighbourhoods, for example Head Street, part of Angel Lane, Trinity Square, and the area east and south of the castle, were occupied mainly by gentry and prosperous townspeople.[54] The reinstatement of the parochial system of poor relief after the failure of the workhouse corporation in the 1740s, however, restricted the movement of the poor between the town parishes,[55] and every parish contained some poorer housing, such as All Saints' Court behind the parish church, a yard with a well in St. Helen's Lane,[56] and the yards recorded in parishes where there were many weavers. In St. Giles's parish houses in the yard of the Star inn were demolished in the 1740s,[57] and in St. Peter's parish there was a number of yards which may have been connected with the bay trade. Soap House Yard and Downfall Yard were outside North gate. On the west side of North Hill were Green Yard and an unnamed yard, which belonged in 1707 to Robert Morfee, saymaker, and contained boxes and cisterns through which water was supplied from Chiswell meadow. Green Yard comprised 2½ a. of pasture in 1772, when it was occupied by two baymakers as tenants of James Robjent, also baymaker. Cistern Yard was built round and occupied mainly by weavers in the early 19th century, as was Pig Yard (later Manor Court) near North Bridge. Spinks Court, off North Hill, may also have been connected with the trade.[58] In 1815 tenements in North Street, Middleborough, West Stockwell Street, and Lottery Alley, Stanwell Street, were owned by James Boggis, baymaker, and occupied by his employees.[59]

In the later 18th and early 19th century large houses were divided for letting, and there was much speculative building of cottages, which were let mainly to soldiers in the 1790s, and later, on the assumption that rent could be paid as poor relief, to mechanics and labourers.[60] Even within the walls small plots of land were let on building leases, and south-east of the town, in Water Lane, there were *c.* 12 cottages which tenants were authorized to move when the lease expired in 1837.[61] They were probably those described as huts earlier in the century, when one was occupied by an old ragman.[62] Another 11 cottages were built on land belonging to the hospital of St. Mary Magdalen, 8 of them on land let at £1 15*s.* a year by the trustees and rackrented at £26 a year.[63] Some 18th-century non-parochial institutions for the poor and aged lay on the outskirts or in suburbs of the town. The

[51] T. Wright, *Hist. Essex*, i. 349; below, Modern Colch., Fig. 15.

[52] E.R.O., T/M 268; ibid. Acc. C210, J. B. Harvey Colln. iv. 172; Morant, *Colch.* 115, map facing p. 4; *Essex Map* (1777).

[53] *Ipswich Jnl.* 21 May 1759; 16 Aug. 1788; P.R.O., WO 44/61; E.R.O., D/P 203/11/29.

[54] J. Bensusan-Butt, *All Saints', Colch. in 18th Cent.*; A. Taylor, *Autobiography*, i. 93; E.R.O., T/M 268; ibid. D/P 200/12/1; D/P 246/11/2; D/P 323/11/3.

[55] E.R.O., D/P 178/13/2, 3; D/P 203/13/3.

[56] Ibid. D/DRc B18; R.C.H.M. *Essex* iii. 64.

[57] Morant, *Colch.* 79, 122; E.R.O., D/B 5 Sb2/6, f. 260v.

[58] E.R.O., Acc.47, C.P.L. 1245; Acc. C15 (part 6; brewery plans); ibid. D/ABR 16/309; Colch. Mus. Topography files: North Hill; *Ipswich Jnl.* 24 Oct. 1772; 23 Jan. 1773; Morant, *Colch.* 4; *V.C.H. Essex*, ii. 403; below, pl. facing p. 328.

[59] *Ipswich Jnl.* 25 Apr. 1821.

[60] E.R.O., D/B 5 Gb9, p. 179; D/P 303/11/29, 33, 35–7; ibid. Acc. C32; *Rep. Com. Poor Law*, H.C. 44, App. B2, pp. 41i–43i (1834), xxxvi.

[61] *32nd Rep. Com. Char.* pp. 548, 564.

[62] Colch. Mus., Capt. Crickitt's notebk. in Rebow box.

[63] *32nd Rep. Com. Char.* p. 548.

workhouse, established *c.* 1700 in the old Crutched Friars building in Crouch Street, had apparently moved to East Street by 1711. The old building was let to poor families until its demolition *c.* 1748.[64] Almshouses founded by Arthur Winsley (1727) and John Kendall (1791) were were built south-east of the town, towards Old Heath.[65] The failure of the workhouse corporation in the mid 18th century obliged the parishes to provide their own workhouses, which were consequently scattered throughout the town, and there were parochial and nonconformist almshouses and poorhouses in Bucklersbury Lane, Culver Street, East Street, Eld Lane, and St. Helen's Lane.[66]

The town's immediate surroundings were affected by the bay industry for much of the period. The use of most of the water mills for fulling contributed to the need for the many windmills that were prominent around the town.[67] Tenter frames, on which finished bays were stretched and dried, were grouped in meadows and pastures within and without the town walls. A tenterfield north of St. Mary's church in 1724 had been converted to garden ground by 1748;[68] another in St. Botolph's parish was converted to arable probably by 1734 and certainly by 1754.[69] Those north of the castle recorded in 1724 were the only ones surviving within the walls in 1777, and some extramural sites had changed,[70] but tenter frames remained on meadows outside the walls as late as 1796, when a site could be let for 10*s.* 6*d.* a year.[71] The last recorded tenterfield was near Bourne mill, in use in the early 19th century.[72]

Other industries dependent on the river for water or transport were sited mainly near the bridges over the Colne, which were all rebuilt during the period, Hythe bridge in 1737, North bridge in 1781, and East bridge in 1802.[73] On the south-eastern side of the town, and separated from it by open fields for much of the period, Hythe Street ran downhill to the Colne. The Hythe, described as the Wapping of Colchester,[74] was densely occupied by industrial buildings, yards, warehouses, and inns adjoining the quays. The town quay was on the western side of the river; in 1776 merchants were refused permission to use the eastern side, but by 1823 quays extended along both sides.[75] There were towpaths on either side of the river, leading from Wivenhoe and Fingringhoe,[76] and the prospect of the Hythe was considered pleasing.[77] The Tabor family, brewers and merchants, occupied and improved Harbour House on the quay and laid out a garden there.[78] Near East bridge and North bridge there were tanneries and breweries for most of the period.[79] At the bottom of East Hill, west of the bridge, was a large and complex group of buildings in 1748,[80] which were probably those demolished *c.* 1757 when William Lisle, ironmonger, offered their timbers and tiles for sale.[81]

In most of the town's streets and lanes there were houses with workshops and tradesmen's yards.[82] Shopkeepers and merchants usually had shops and warehouses adjoining their dwelling houses, and some developed industries on or near those sites. In 1798 Samuel Tabor, whose house was in Queen Street, had a malting and

[64] Morant, *Colch.* (1748), Bk. II, p. 43; E.R.O., D/B 5 Sr94, rot. 3d.
[65] Below, Charities.
[66] S. H. G. Fitch, *Colch. Quakers*, 114–16; below, Par. Govt. and Poor Relief; Charities.
[67] Below, Mills.
[68] V.C.H. *Essex*, ii. 404; Morant, *Colch.* illus. facing title page and map facing p. 4; Sparrow, *Map of Colch.* (1767); above, Fig. 9.
[69] E.R.O., D/DU 115/11, 21.
[70] *Essex Map* (1777).
[71] *Ipswich Jnl.* 9 Jan. 1796.
[72] *E.A.T.* N.S. x. 49.
[73] Below, Communications (Bridges).
[74] *E.R.* vi. 57.
[75] P.R.O., M.P.B. 33; D. Stephenson, *Bk. of Colch.* 93; E.R.O., D/P 203/11/29; ibid. T/A 124, p. 6; T/M 332.
[76] Below, Port.
[77] J. Pryer, *New and Exact Prospect of Colch.* (1724).
[78] E.R.O., T/B 435, pp. 7, 17, 35; *East Anglian Studies*, ed. L. Munby, frontispiece.
[79] Above, this chapter, Econ.
[80] Morant, *Colch.* map facing p. 4.
[81] *Ipswich Jnl.* 19 Mar. 1757.
[82] e.g. *Ipswich Jnl.* 28 May 1757 (sale notice); 2 July 1768; 19 Sept. 1772; 21 June 1794; E.R.O. Acc. C32, C.P.L. 269; ibid. D/P 178/11/4 s.v. Leverett; D/DDw T182; ibid. Boro. Mun., Improvement Com. Mins. 1811–33, p. 110, s.v. Brill.

warehouse in St. Botolph's Street; also in St. Botolph's Street James Ashwell, grocer, had his house, warehouse, shop, and candle-making workshop.[83] Samuel Todd, grocer at Head gate, also kept a gin distillery with mills and furnaces there in 1756;[84] Michael Boyle opened a silk factory in Head Street near his ribbon shop *c.* 1782;[85] Joseph Wallis in 1792 built an ironfoundry behind High Street, convenient to his ironmongery shop,[86] and William Jones, carver and gilder in Head Street, had a plate glass works there *c.* 1815.[87] There were other warehouses and factories in lanes off the main streets, including an iron warehouse behind the Red Lion in 1734,[88] a china warehouse there in 1787,[89] and several warehouses in Pelham's Lane in 1768.[90] A pipe kiln in George Lane flourished from the early 18th century,[91] and a bay factory in Moor Lane (later Priory Street) survived into the 19th century.[92] A linen factory was founded *c.* 1800 in St. Helen's Lane, where adjacent houses were converted as a hemp, later a worsted stocking, factory, and a silk factory was built in St. Peter's Street in 1824.[93] Brewers, profiting from increased trade while the town was garrisoned, established new breweries or enlarged existing ones on North Hill, East Hill, and in St. Botolph's Street, and a distillery in Culver Lane opened *c.* 1815.[94] Other industries, including Dearn's ironfoundry in St. Botolph's Street, and Eisdell's ropewalk off Stanwell Street, developed on the south-eastern fringe of the built-up area.[95] In 1817 William Cant's nursery in St. John's Street was put up for sale as building land.[96]

There was little change in the use and pattern of High Street in the 18th and early 19th century. The moot hall remained unchanged but a theatre was built behind it in 1764 and a debtors' prison in its yard in 1809.[97] The town's markets were held in High Street throughout the period; sites of specialist stalls were occasionally changed within it. The market cross, opposite the moot hall and in use until 1801, became a guard house and was demolished when it became a nuisance in 1808.[98] The pillory opposite the moot hall was in use in 1807, but may have been removed soon afterwards when the cage at the north-east corner of St. Runwald's church was taken down.[99] A brightly decorated pump opposite the door of the moot hall survived until *c.* 1819.[1] The Dutch bay hall, which became a market and corn exchange, was remodelled in 1800–1 and replaced in 1820 by a new corn market, with an insurance office above. The fish market and butchers' shambles were east of St. Runwald's church, and there were as many as 66 butchers' stalls on the south side of High Street by 1730. A covered market, built west of the moot hall in 1813 for all but corn and fish, was disliked by the traders, who had returned to the street by 1825.[2] Shops lined the street behind the market stalls and pens; as late as 1835 the improvement commissioners were seeking ways of keeping cattle off pavements and out of shops.[3] An obelisk, showing distances to London and other towns, was erected in 1760 east of St. Runwald's church and the butchers' shambles.[4]

83 E.R.O., D/P 203/11/29; *Ipswich Jnl.* 14 Dec. 1793.

84 E.R.O., D/DEl B3, p. 29; *Ipswich Jnl.* 4 Sept. 1756; 21 May 1757.

85 *Ipswich Jnl.* 26 Oct. 1782.

86 *E.A.T.* 3rd ser. xiv. 103–4.

87 Colch. Mus., Trade card colln. Box 5; E.C.L. Colch. Rebow scrapbk. p. 39.

88 Morant, *Colch.* 183; E.R.O., D/B 5 Sb5/2, p. 301; *E.R.* lvii. 17.

89 Colch. Mus., Trade card colln. Box 5, s.v. Minkes.

90 *Ipswich Jnl.* 28 May 1768.

91 V.C.H. *Essex*, ii. 413; *E.A.T.* 3rd ser. i. 49.

92 *Ipswich Jnl.* 21 Apr. 1821; *E.A.T.* N.S. x. 53.

93 Above, this chapter, Econ.; E.R.O., Acc. C32, C.P.L. 269; P.R.O., B3/4929–30.

94 E.R.O., T/M 268; I. Peaty, *Essex Brewers and Malting and Hop Industries of the County*, 34–47; Brown, *Colch. 1815-1914*, 9.

95 *E.A.T.* 3rd ser. xiv. 107; E.R.O., Boro. Mun., Improvement Com. Mins. 1811–33, 62; above, this chapter, Econ.

96 *Ipswich Jnl.* 26 July 1817.

97 Below, Mun. Bldgs. (Town Hall, Prison).

98 E.R.O., D/B 5 Gb9, pp. 147, 149–52; *Ipswich Jnl.* 23 Apr. 1808; *V.C.H. Essex*, ii. 241.

99 E.R.O., D/B 5 Gb9, p. 177; *E.R.* xliv, 127; lvi. 187–8.

1 E.R.O., Acc. C210, J. B. Harvey Colln. vi. 16.

2 Ibid. D/DR P12; below, Markets.

3 E.R.O., Boro. Mun., Improvement Com. Mins. 1833–47, pp. 49– 50; ibid. D/B 5 Gb9, p. 177.

4 Below, Communications (Roads); W. Cole, *Map Colch.* (1803); Colch. Mus., Topography files: Obelisk.

TOWN GOVERNMENT AND POLITICS

THE town was governed by an assembly under charters of 1693, 1763, and 1818.[5] The charter of 1693 became inoperative in 1741 after litigation removed members of the assembly from office. A new assembly was appointed by the charter of 1763; when that was similarly threatened in 1816, another charter was granted. The charter of 1693 nominated 12 aldermen, 18 assistants, and 18 common councilmen, who together formed the assembly. One of the aldermen was nominated mayor by the charter for the year 1693–4; thereafter the mayor was elected annually by the aldermen from two of their number, who had been nominated by the freemen. Aldermen, assistants, and common councilmen held office for life[6] unless they resigned or were removed for non-residence, non-attendance, or misdemeanour,[7] as in 1719 when all but two common councilmen surrendered their places or were removed for being non-resident or unsworn.[8] To fill a vacancy the assembly chose a common councilman from two men nominated by the freemen, the freemen chose an assistant from among the common councilmen, and the assembly chose an alderman from two assistants nominated by the freemen. The charter of 1693 also nominated a recorder, who acted as legal adviser and often appointed a deputy, and a high steward, whose office was largely honorary. On death or resignation their successors were to be chosen by the assembly and the freemen. There were usually two or more candidates for every vacancy. Fines for refusal to accept office were set in 1719 at £5 for an alderman, £3 for an assistant, and 30*s*. for a common councilman.[9] For declining the mayoralty Thomas Wilshire was fined £40 in 1782, and Sir Robert Smyth £105 in 1784. Wilshire's fine was later mitigated to £29 8*s*., the sum which the corporation owed him.[10] A headman chosen annually for each of the four wards by the freemen appointed five others to join with him to form a body of 24 for the borough to elect 2 coroners, 4 keykeepers, and a chamberlain from among the assembly. The mayor, his predecessor, his deputy, the recorder and his deputy, and two aldermen chosen annually by the 24 served as justices of the peace.[11] The mayor and aldermen served, with other men who were not members of the assembly, on two statutory bodies, the workhouse corporation and the navigation and improvement commission.[12] They also chose the 16 sons of freemen to be taught in the grammar school, and with the freemen elected the master.[13] The corporation was trustee of Sir Thomas White's loan charity.[14]

Men were admitted to the freedom of the borough by right of patrimony or apprenticeship, and occasionally by purchase.[15] In 1812 freedom by service was restricted to apprentices of resident freemen.[16] Members of parliament and a few other eminent men were granted honorary freedom.[17] In the mid 18th century there were, in an estimated population of 8,500,[18] more than 1,120 resident freemen[19] and about a quarter of those might have official roles, including service

5 *Colch. Charters*, 170–219.
6 Ibid. 179–82.
7 e.g. E.R.O., D/B 5 Gb7, ff. 9, 22, 73–4, 89v., 355–7; Gb8, ff. 105v., 117v., 119.
8 Ibid. D/B 5 Gb7, pp. 71–3.
9 Ibid. p. 78.
10 Ibid. D/B 5 Gb8, ff. 125v.–126, 129, 137v.
11 Ibid. *passim*.
12 Below, Port; Public Services.
13 e.g. E.R.O., D/B 5 Gb7, pp. 195, 231; Gb8, ff. 83v., 85, 95.
14 Below, Charities.
15 Morant, *Colch.* 100–1; E.R.O., Boro. Mun., 'Colch. MSS.', 1620-1770, ff. 18–38.
16 E.R.O., D/B 5 Gb9, pp. 221–2.
17 e.g. ibid. Boro. Mun., Admissions Bks. 1781–1812, pp. 15, 32; 1831–45, p. 43.
18 *Local Historian*, x. 23–6.
19 *Poll Bk.* 1741.

as jurymen, in the borough.[20] Freemen who were resident, self-employed, rate-paying heads of families, other than butchers, bakers, brewers, and alehouse-keepers, were eligible for and could be involved in election of all ranks of the assembly. Men convicted of felony, adultery, fornication, drunkenness, or blasphemy were specifically excluded from voting.[21] Resident freemen were jealous of rights which gave them not only the franchise and a role in town government, but pasture rights on half year lands, the right to send their sons to the grammar school and elect the master, and trading advantages over non-freemen, known as 'foreigners'.[22] They expected the assembly to defend those rights and were vociferous in demanding them.[23]

While the mayor and aldermen were the most powerful men in town government, all members of the assembly served on committees and filled borough offices. Promotion was not by seniority and some common councilmen never became assistants. Between 1715 and 1742, of 170 members of the assembly 38 rose to be aldermen and 15 of those became mayor. Between 1763 and 1835, of 206 members of the assembly 72 became aldermen and 39 mayor. Occasionally places were left vacant to allow promotion from freeman to alderman in one day of men, usually chosen for financial or political reasons, who were elected mayor soon afterwards and sometimes held the office for several terms. The method was used for Arthur Winsley (1719), John Blatch (1727), Samuel Ennew and Thomas Bayles (1764), William Argent, William Swinborne, Edmund Lilley, and Edward Capstack (1785), William Bunnell and William Phillips (1793–4), William Sparling and William Smith (1799), and James Boggis (1802). Argent, Lilley, Capstack, and Bunnell had been made honorary freemen shortly before their election to the assembly.[24]

Membership of the corporation and office-holding reveal the influence of family, religious, trade, and political relationships within the town. The gentry families of Creffield, Rebow, Wegg, Martin, and Round lived in or near Colchester and their involvement in borough institutions discouraged incursion by outside landed interests.[25] In the early 19th century the conduct of a faction within the corporation deterred some gentlemen from involvement in its affairs.[26] In the 18th century nonconformists were represented in the corporation roughly in proportion, about one fifth, to their presence in the population.[27] Their numbers on the corporation probably declined with the fortunes of the Whig party, and in 1834 it was said that, although nonconformists numbered a third of the population, there was none on the assembly.[28] Manufacturers and tradesmen formed the majority of the governing group, but the corporation usually included a number of professional men.[29] Among them were attorneys such as Edmund Raynham, Charles Gray, Samuel Ennew, William Mayhew, father and son, William Mason,[30] and Francis Smythies, father and son, whose influence as town clerks was strengthened by their role as legal advisers and agents of the gentry and tradesmen. The Smythies were

[20] S. D'Cruze, 'The Middling Sort in Provincial Eng.: Politics and Social Relations in Colch. 1730–1800.' (Essex Univ. Ph.D. thesis, 1990), 111–12.

[21] *Colch. Charters*, 179–86.

[22] Ibid. 194–5; E.R.O., D/B 5 Gb7, p. 19; ibid. Boro. Mun. 'Colch. MSS.', 1620-1770, f. 60; Boro. Mun., Trunk R 3/2 (lease 1745); Morant, *Colch.* 92, 102, 175; below, Common Lands.

[23] e.g. E.R.O., D/B 5 Gb7, p. 164; D/Y 2/2, pp. 351–2; M. E. Speight, 'Politics in the Boro. of Colch. 1812–47.' (Lond. Univ. Ph.D. thesis, 1969), 33–4.

[24] E.R.O., D/B 5 Gb7, pp. 71–4, 217–18; Gb8, ff. 5–6, 144–145v., 193 and v.; Gb9, pp. 13–14, 65; ibid. Boro. Mun., Admissions Bk. 1781–1812, p. 32.

[25] D'Cruze, 'Middling Sort in Provincial Eng.', 267–8.

[26] Below, this chapter, this section.

[27] D'Cruze, 'Middling Sort in Provincial Eng.', 56, 473–87.

[28] *E.C.S.* 12 Apr. 1834 (evidence to Com. on Mun. Corp.).

[29] D'Cruze, op. cit. 117.

[30] E.R.O., D/DEl B1–3, B14–18; D/B 5 Gb8, ff. 105v., 173; D/B 5 Sb5/1, p. 311; *E.A.T.* 3rd ser. xviii, 63–74.

seen as managers of the ruling group within the corporation in the late 18th and early 19th century, and their ubiquitous legal practice gave rise to popular suspicion of self-interest.[31] Frequent parliamentary elections stimulated political activity within the borough; 11 of the 33 elections held in the period 1714–1832 gave rise to allegations of partiality against the mayor or other borough official as returning officer.[32] The corporation's constitution was exploited throughout the period for political ends, and the complexity of its finances attracted allegations of extravagance and corruption.[33]

Assemblies were usually held at least four times a year, attended by 25–30 of the 48 members. *Ad hoc* committees were appointed mainly on financial matters such as debts, loans, and leases, but occasionally on such matters as encroachments and bridge maintenance.[34] A committee of aldermen audited the chamberlain's accounts.[35] In the 1780s that committee comprised eight men drawn from the assembly at large, and in 1818 all members of that body were entitled to attend meetings of a committee investigating accounts.[36]

The workhouse corporation, comprising the mayor and aldermen and 48 elected guardians, 12 from each of the four wards, operated a unified system of poor relief with a borough workhouse. The corporation also seems to have taken over the parish almshouses. Rates were levied and paid to a treasurer. He distributed money to two payers who paid outdoor relief on production of vouchers issued by twelve assistants who heard applications for poor relief every three weeks at the borough workhouse. In 1724 there were 40–50 children at the workhouse carding and spinning wool for baymaking; they were allowed 'the best of meat' three times a week, and 'the best butter and cheese' on other days. A large section of the workhouse was an infirmary for the old and infirm; they were attended by a nurse but were on fixed allowances and expected to do the same work as the children or other work of their choice.[37]

The corporation was assiduous in celebrating royal occasions and sending loyal addresses. The mayor, attended by members of the assembly in their gowns, processed to church at Easter, Whitsun, Michaelmas, and Christmas, on occasions of supplication or thanksgiving, and for charity sermons.[38] There were four sessions dinners each year and four for the grand jury. Although in 1715 the grand jury, having presented the chamberlain for not providing dinner, were warned not to repeat the complaint, the dinners were accounted for regularly.[39] Following the grant of new charters in 1763 and 1818 members of the assembly were ordered to provide themselves with gowns to be worn on public days. From 1818 failure to wear a gown incurred a fine of 5*s*., and aldermen were fined 5*s*., assistants 3*s*., and councilmen 2*s*. 6*d*. for not attending on the mayor when summoned.[40] The town mace, remade in 1730,[41] was a source of civic pride.[42] The borough's records were, in theory, kept securely in a locked chest, and a muniment room in the moot hall had been provided by 1748.[43] They were in fact sometimes dispersed among the

[31] E.R.O., Acc. C210, J. B. Harvey Colln. iv. 72; *E.A.T.* 3rd ser. xix. 23–30; *E.C.S.* 5 Apr. 1834 (evidence to Com. on Mun. Corp.); E.R.O., Boro. Mun., Council Mins. 23 Mar. 1836.

[32] H. S. Smith, *Parliaments of Eng. from 1715 to 1847* (1973), 106--7; below, this chapter, (Parl. Rep.).

[33] D'Cruze, 'Middling Sort'; Speight, 'Politics in Colch.'.

[34] e.g. E.R.O., D/B 5 Gb7, pp. 65, 75, 148, 163–4, 358; Gb8, ff. 167v.–168, 174–5; Gb9, pp. 101, 118–19, 207.

[35] Ibid. D/B 5 Aa1/35; Aa2/1, *passim*.

[36] Ibid. D/B 5 Gb8, f. 134v.; Gb9, p. 342.

[37] Morant, *Hist. Colch.* (1748), Bk. II, p. 43; *An Account of Several Workhouses, etc.* (1732): photocopies of Essex pages at E.R.O.; E.R.O., D/B 5 Sr75, rot. 3; Sr89, rot. 9; Sr94, rot. 3d.; *White's Dir. Essex* (1848), 77; *E.C.S.* 7 Aug. 1909.

[38] e.g. E.R.O., D/B 5 Gb7, pp. 25, 135; Gb8, ff. 118v., 201; Gb9, pp. 33–4, 356, 440–1, 500, 532–3.

[39] Ibid. D/B 5 Sb5/1, p. 17; D/B 5 Aa1/35.

[40] Ibid. D/B 5 Gb8, f. 7v.; Gb9, p. 356.

[41] Below, Arms, Seals, etc.

[42] *E.C.S.* 5 Apr. 1834.

[43] Below, Mun. Bldgs.; *E.C.S.* 5 Apr. 1834.

borough's officers or their executors, and the corporation occasionally had difficulty in retrieving them.[44] Thomas Glascock, dismissed as town clerk in 1715, retained books and papers in defiance of the corporation until he was threatened with imprisonment in 1724.[45] Admission books, containing the freemen lists, were found in 1755 to have been mutilated.[46] The borough's ceremonial year began at Michaelmas with a dinner given by the new mayor, followed in October by the proclamation of St. Dennis's fair.[47] In 1814 a public breakfast at the Three Cups on the opening day of the fair was attended by *c.* 100 of the local gentry. It was followed by dinner at the White Hart, a performance at the theatre, and, the next day, a ball and supper at the White Hart.[48] The borough's jurisdiction in the river Colne was proclaimed at the closing and opening of the fishery in April and September.[49] The celebrations at the opening seem to have become more elaborate after the grant of the new charter in 1818, when the corporation and neighbouring gentry dined at the Blue Posts inn, Mersea, and were entertained by a band and a sailing match.[50]

The End of the Old Charter

In the 1720s most aldermen were Whigs, led by Sir Isaac Rebow (d. 1726) M.P., high steward and recorder of the borough. He was succeeded by his grandson Isaac Lemyng Rebow (d. 1735),[51] whose relations by marriage, Matthew Martin, Robert Price, and Richard Bacon, became mayor and high steward, recorder, and town clerk respectively.[52] In the late 1720s, following a trade recession and during popular opposition to the Excise Bill,[53] five Tories quickly became aldermen. Four of them, John Blatch, James Boys, Thomas Carew, and Joseph Duffield, held the mayoralty between them from 1728 until 1741.[54] In 1728, during Blatch's first year as mayor, the freedom was sold to 56 'foreigners', most of whom later voted for Tory parliamentary candidates.[55]

In 1739, when Carew's death endangered the Tory majority on the aldermanic bench, an assembly attended by four Tory and one Whig aldermen chose Isaac Boggis, a Tory baymaker, to replace him. The conviction of George Gray, a Whig alderman, for sodomy enabled the mayor and aldermen to remove him from office in 1740, and when Gray was pardoned on the grounds that his accusers were politically motivated,[56] they defied a *mandamus* to reinstate him, electing a Tory instead.[57] Gray's supporters among the freemen countered with *quo warranto* proceedings against Blatch, Boggis, Boys, and Duffield, who they alleged had not been elected aldermen strictly according to the charter. In March 1741, during those proceedings, an assembly was called under a writ of *mandamus* to elect a mayor instead of Blatch. By that time two aldermen had died, four were subject to litigation, and one stayed away. The remaining five aldermen, all Whigs, refused to accept nominations of two Tories and chose the Whig Jeremiah Daniell as mayor. The Tory freemen filed affidavits of *quo warranto* against Daniell and the remaining aldermen and prevented the confirmation of Daniell in office by disrupting the mayoral election on charter day. The court found that none of the aldermen had

44 e.g. E.R.O., D/B 5 Gb7, pp. 229, 301; *E.C.S.* 12 Apr. 1834 (evidence to Com. on Mun. Corp.).

45 *E.R.* xlvii. 72–8.

46 *C.J.* xxvii. 205.

47 Below, Markets.

48 *Colch. Gaz.* 12 Nov. 1814.

49 *V.C.H. Essex*, ii. 434–5.

50 *Colch. Gaz.* 5 Sept. 1818.

51 E.R.O., D/P 246/1/5.

52 Ibid. D/B 5 Gb7, pp. 201–5; D'Cruze, 'The Middling Sort', 272--4.

53 D'Cruze, 'The Middling Sort', 399.

54 Below, List of Bailiffs and Mayors.

55 E.R.O., D/B 5 Gb7, p. 247; *C.J.* xxviii. 208; *Poll Bks.*

56 D'Cruze, 'The Middling Sort', 317–20.

57 P.R.O., KB 21/35, f. 161; E.R.O., D/B 5 Gb7, ff. 355 and v., 364–5.

been properly elected.[58] Consequently the charter fell into abeyance and with it the borough courts, the workhouse corporation, and the navigation commission.[59] The fishery was endangered by the lapse of the Admiralty court.[60]

The former mayor and aldermen, with the surviving assistants and common councilmen, asked parliament to reinstate the deposed men so that elections of new aldermen could be held. Parliament, by Act of 1742, restored only the workhouse corporation, appointing the former mayor and eight of the deposed aldermen to serve on it. No provision was made for the appointment or election of successors and the workhouse corporation had failed by 1745, when poor-law administration had reverted to the parish vestries.[61] The county quarter sessions took over the work of the borough court, including approval of the poor-rate.[62] An Act of 1750 vested the collection of channel dues in new navigation commissioners and the justices for the eastern division, confirmed the responsibility of parish surveyors to report paving offences to the justices, and protected the fishery, which had fallen into disorder.[63]

The Campaign for a New Charter[64]

The Tory M.P.s, Charles Gray and Samuel Savill, apparently did nothing to persuade the House of Commons to restore the borough's rights, but the cause found its champion in William Mayhew (d. 1764), an attorney who had acted against the Whig aldermen in 1741.[65] At the parliamentary election of 1747 Mayhew supported Richard Savage Nassau, the Whig candidate, in the expectation that he would help to recover the charter. Nassau was elected but took offence when the freemen petitioned him without notice in 1749, and refused to act in the matter. The desire for restitution of the borough's rights was not shared by all the inhabitants, but the freemen complained that they were deprived of the local courts and their half year lands, borough estates were being ruined and rents lost, markets were spoiled by forestallers, the fishery encroached upon, pavements in disrepair and streets obstructed.[66] In 1750 Mayhew formed a charter club at the King's Head, and in 1752 urged freemen's sons, who could not take their freedom while the charter was in abeyance, to attend there to show support for a parliamentary candidate favourable to the cause. In 1753, with an election approaching, some of the freemen demanded their pasture rights on the half year lands, although few of them kept cattle and management of the lands was probably already corrupt.[67] Their claims seem to have been silenced by the opinion of the attorney general, given that year, that the king held the common rights as donor, not the remaining freemen.[68] Philip Morant warned Lord Hardwicke that the dispute would greatly distress the candidates in the forthcoming election,[69] and neither the Tory Charles Gray nor the Whig John Olmius accepted the support of Mayhew's charter club, and the third candidate, the Whig Isaac Martin Rebow, was supported by a rival club meeting at the King's Arms. That club drafted an amended charter, which Mayhew dubbed 'charter cookery'. Olmius and, upon petition, Rebow were elected. Mayhew threatened to charge Olmius with breach of faith, on the basis of

58 P.R.O., KB 1/7(i); KB 11/35(ii); KB 21/35, pp. 369, 376, 390, 413; KB 28/159, rott. 1–8; *E.A.T.* 3rd ser. xviii. 67.

59 *C.J.* xxiv. 128; xxv. 935.

60 *V.C.H. Essex*, ii. 432–3; below, Fishery.

61 *C.J.* xxiv. 128, 166, 175–6; 15 & 16 Geo. II, c. 18; C. Gray, 'Considerations on several proposals lately made for the better maintenance of the poor', 1751: copy in E.R.O.

62 E.R.O., Q/Smg 14–19; ibid. P/CoR 1.

63 23 Geo. II, c. 19; *V.C.H. Essex*, ii. 432–3; below, Fishery.

64 Account based on *E.A.T.* 3rd ser. xviii. 63–74.

65 P.R.O., KB 1/7(i).

66 Morant, *Colch.* (1748) Bk. I, p. 71; E.R.O., Acc. C210, J. B. Harvey Colln. vi, p. 179.

67 E.R.O., D/Y 2/2, ff. 351–352v.; below, Common Lands.

68 Ibid. Boro. Mun. 'Colch. MSS.', 1620-1770, f. 60.

69 Ibid. D/Y 2/2, ff. 351–2.

a £500 wager made between them before the election, and to petition for a charter independently if the M.P.s would not act in the matter. When Olmius and Rebow eventually petitioned for a charter in 1757 they apparently sponsored the charter promoted by the King's Arms club. In 1758 a rival petition was submitted, presumably by Mayhew and the King's Head club. The Privy Council's decision was delayed by the death of George II, but before the election of 1761 Mayhew extracted from the candidates, Charles Gray and Isaac Martin Rebow, a joint commitment to the renewal of the charter. The undertaking, given at a meeting of the charter club at the King's Head, signalled the defeat of 'charter cookery'. The charter received by the borough in 1763, with public rejoicing, was in effect a confirmation of that of 1663.[70]

Revival and Discord, 1763–1818

The new corporation was at first preoccupied with reviewing its estate and reorganizing the management of its finances.[71] The charter mayor, Thomas Clamtree, was a Whig who served that office six times between 1763 and 1779.[72] The compromise between the Tory and Whig M.P.s, Gray and Rebow, tended to moderate overt political activity in borough affairs,[73] but personal and political rivalry were evident before Gray resigned in 1780, particularly in disagreements involving the town clerk, Francis Smythies, over the non-payment of salaries and the responsibility for billeting soldiers. Smythies, an able and ambitious attorney of choleric temperament who sometimes acted violently in execution of his office, was dominant in borough affairs until his death in 1798.[74] In 1779 he led the Church and Tory party in the contested election of a master of the grammar school to succeed Palmer Smythies, his father. Political and religious divisions were manifest in the ensuing pamphlet war.[75] The Tories, having persuaded the freemen that their rights were threatened by nonconformists and Whigs, won the contest and Smythies led a victory parade round the town, harassing his defeated opponents on the way.[76] A Tory faction gathered around Smythies. In 1787 the dying recorder, William Mayhew, nominated James Grimwood his deputy; Smythies stood as a rival candidate and the Tory mayor declared his election. Grimwood challenged the decision with ultimate success, but Smythies acted as recorder until ousted in 1790.[77] Thereafter Smythies served as town clerk, supported by a Tory majority in the corporation, until his death in 1798.[78]

Political activity intensified in the early 19th century,[79] and in the period 1812–35 rancorous internal disputes were prolonged by repeated lawsuits, Colchester ranking fourth among boroughs in the frequency of its appearances in King's Bench. At the mayoral election in 1812 the candidates for the freemen's nomination William Smith, William Sparling, and John Bridge, gained 133, 123, and 22 votes respectively. Francis Smythies the younger, who had succeeded his father as town clerk and alderman, reduced Sparling's majority over Bridge by rejecting votes of brewers among his supporters and, prompted by Bridge, disqualified him for not taking communion in the Church of England. The aldermen, among them two brewers, chose Bridge for mayor. He was ousted, following *quo warranto* proceedings

70 *Colch. Charters*, 198–219.

71 Below, this chapter, this section.

72 *E.A.T.* 3rd ser. xviii. 72; below, List of Bailiffs and Mayors.

73 Below, this chapter, Parl. Rep.

74 *E.A.T.* 3rd ser. xix. 223–30; D'Cruze,'The Middling Sort', 404--7.

75 E.R.O., Acc. C16, Trunk 1; ibid. D/DRc Z17.

76 Ibid. Acc. C16, Trunk 1; D'Cruze, 'The Middling Sort', 408–10.

77 E.R.O., D/B 5 Gb8, ff. 156v., 167v.; *Ipswich Jnl.* 16 Feb. 1788; 29 Aug. 1789; *E.A.T.* 3rd ser. xix. 225–6.

78 *E.A.T.* 3rd ser. xix. 223–30.

79 Account based on Speight, 'Politics in Colch.'.

in King's Bench, because he took office before Michaelmas day, and Smith was elected in his stead.[80] Bridge challenged, by *quo warranto* proceedings, the rights to office of four aldermen, one assistant, and three councilmen who were elected when the assembly lacked a quorum. Those men disclaimed, but most were reinstated by proper election. When Sparling was elected mayor in 1813, Bridge and his friends resumed their attack on him. His effigy was hanged from the gallows, and Samuel Bridge, the former mayor's brother, published anonymously *The Guild*, a high Tory satire on the self-interest of tradesmen who were members of the assembly. Prosecution of the printer inflamed the dispute, and *The Guild* became notorious. At the election of Sparling's successor as mayor in 1814, Bridge, Smythies, and a faction among the freemen objected to the nomination of John King, who had been ousted but re-elected through the ranks of the assembly. King and his successors, Edward Clay and William Argent were continually harried by Bridge's party, and in October 1816, when further litigation threatened to remove its members from office, the corporation decided to apply for a new charter.

The Last Years, 1818–35

The charter, granted in 1818 and substantially the same as that of 1763, reappointed most of the former aldermen, but not John Bridge and Francis Smythies. The appointments included 17 men whose detachment from earlier disputes might have overcome the rancour of the former corporation. Ten of them, however, declined office, among them George Round, who wrote that he despaired of ridding the new corporation of the divisions that had harmed the old one. When vacancies caused by the refusals were filled, Francis Smythies was nominated and opposed repeatedly as common councilman, assistant, and alderman. He failed to become an alderman but was reappointed town clerk in 1818 and served until the reform of 1835.[81] In the 1820s controversy within the corporation was mainly concerned with its constitution and the management of its finances, but radical opposition to the corporation was growing in the town and the freemen were formulating claims to the income of the borough estate. It had been customary since *c.* 1645 for the mayor to pay 8*d.* each to the resident freemen in lieu of dinner on charter day and the cost was usually debited to the fishery money. That practice may have given rise to the freemen's claim in 1813 to the profits of the fishery.[82] The new charter itself caused dispute by appointing seven 'foreigners'. Their right to the franchise was subsequently challenged by the freemen, who prevented the mayor from admitting them. The problem was resolved, after litigation, only by a ruling in 1824 that the king had, by appointing them, made the 'foreigners' free.[83] The freemen, whose right to the proceeds of the sale of common pasture rights was contested in the 1820s, were again at the centre of dispute in 1832 when they tried unsuccessfully to make the corporation sell the Severalls estate, and the half year lands, and distribute the proceeds among them.[84] The radical movement found a strong voice in the assembly with the conversion from Toryism of Edward Clay of the Hythe, who in 1830 canvassed the freemen to nominate him as mayor, suggesting that by proper management of the estate they might each receive 31*s.* a year.[85]

80 E.R.O., D/B 5 Gb9, pp. 219, 229–30.

81 *Colch. Charters*, 198–219; E.R.O., D/B 5 Gb9, pp. 344, 348, 362, 417; *E.C.S.* 5 Apr. 1834 (evidence to Com. on Mun. Corp.).

82 Morant, *Colch.* 99 n.; E.R.O., D/B 5 Aa1/35; Aa2/1; ibid. Acc. C210, J. B. Harvey Colln. i, p. 16.

83 Speight, 'Politics in Colch.' 33–5.

84 Below, Common Lands.

85 Speight, 'Politics in Colch.' 48–9.

In 1834 the corporation declared its willingness to co-operate with Thomas Jefferson Hogg of the Royal Commission on Municipal Corporations, but when after six days of inquiry he called the corporation 'flagitious', the mayor withdrew, bringing the inquiry to an end. Much of the criticism of the corporation voiced at the inquiry related to financial matters and some of it implicitly questioned the probity of the town clerk, Francis Smythies. Hogg complained that the mayor and town clerk initially refused to take the oath, on the advice of the recorder, and could not produce an account book of the late chamberlain. Corporation witnesses found Hogg's manner offensive and suspected him of meeting their critics privately during the inquiry.[86] Hogg, who failed to submit reports on Colchester and some other towns to the royal commission, dissented from its mainly condemnatory conclusions on municipal corporations.[87] The corporation, however, represented only *c.* 480 resident freemen out of a total population of 16,167,[88] and was dominated by Tories and churchmen. The inhabitants petitioned parliament in favour of the reform Bill; the corporation, predictably, opposed it. To the borough council formed under the Act of 1835 only one member of the old corporation, William Smith, was elected, and Francis Smythies was not reappointed as town clerk.[89]

Finance[90]

Until 1742 the corporation's finances were administered by the chamberlain, whose accounts were audited by a committee. In the period 1715–41 the annual income of *c.* £500 from rents, licences, tolls, and fines, was usually enough to meet the cost of administration, ceremony, maintenance of bridges and buildings, and payment of the fee farm rent. The corporation was frequently engaged in litigation which could not be paid for from revenue, and to meet those costs it occasionally sold the freedom[91] and repeatedly mortgaged its estate and tolls, redeeming mortgages by further borrowing.

The corporation's most valuable assets were the fishery, the waterbailiffship with a town or custom house, quay, warehouses, yards, and 20 a. of land at the Hythe, and houses and 1,000 a. of land, including Kingswood heath, at Mile End. In the town it owned a number of scattered tenements, besides the bay, leather, and wool halls. The waterbailiffship, markets, and fairs were usually let on lease, relieving the chamberlain of the task of rent collection. The fishery was leased from 1700 to 1731 to entrepreneurs, who were obliged to defend the borough's rights in the courts, and from 1807 it was administered by a company of fishermen.[92]

With the decline of the Dutch bay trade, the corporation in 1716 abated by £20 the rent of the bay hall. The corporation suffered a further loss in 1728 when the Dutch governors dissolved themselves owing arrears of rent, and the annual income from the hall had fallen to £25 by 1732.[93] In 1730, when the lease of the butchers' hall and 66 stalls was worth £75 a year, the lessee's widow payed £50 to assign it.[94] Many small rents were uncollected and the corporation often owed the chamberlain money. In 1731 the corporation leased for £10 a year 16 small tenements with a total rent of £16 11*s*.[95] The Mile End estate, called the Severalls,

[86] *E.C.S.* 5, 12 Apr. 1834; *Colch. Gaz.* 5 Apr. 1834; Brown, *Colch. 1815–1914*, 42–3; Speight, 'Politics in Colch.' 43–4; E.R.O., D/B 5 Gb10, pp. 148–4.

[87] 28 *Parl. Deb.* 3rd ser. 242–3; *Protest of Mr. Hogg* H.C. 434, pp. 32–3 (1835), xl; *D.N.B.* s.v. Hogg, T. J.

[88] *E.C.S.* 5 Apr. 1834; *Census*, 1831.

[89] E.R.O., D/B 5 Gb10, pp. 184–5, 187–9; *C.J.* xc. 369; below, Modern Colch. (Political Hist.)

[90] Section based on E.R.O., D/B 5 Aa1/30–35; Aa2/1.

[91] E.R.O., D/B 5 Gb7, pp. 114, 245.

[92] Below, Markets; Fishery.

[93] E.R.O., D/B 5 Gb7, pp. 37, 293.

[94] Ibid. pp. 10–11, 264.

[95] Ibid. p. 278.

was let in 1722 to Daniel Defoe on a 99-year lease for two fines of £500 and an annual payment of £120.[96]

In 1720 the corporation raised £1,200 by mortgaging for 1,000 years part of its estate and tolls, including the market, St. Dennis's fair, the waterbailiffship, the receivership of the woolmarket, the Hythe estate, the leather hall, and a hall with under rooms and shops at the west end of the corn market. The loan had grown to £2,700 on the security of more of the estate by 1740, when the corporation borrowed another £400.[97]

Alehouse licences raised £38 15*s.* in 1718, and fines imposed under a bylaw of 1715 on shopkeepers and alehousekeepers who were not freemen were worth *c.* £80 a year in the 1730s.[98] Following a petition by the freemen to the assembly in 1724 to enforce the bylaw on shopkeepers, two 'foreigners' were gaoled in 1725 for refusing to pay and another lost his case against the corporation *c.* 1730. The shopkeepers continued to resist: in 1735–6 only 20 of the 88 paid and arrears amounted to £103 8*s.* 6*d.* In 1739 the corporation lost its case against one of them at the county assizes. Encouraged by the outcome, the alehousekeepers decided to withhold their 10*s.* 'foreign' fines at the annual licensing. The justices forestalled the rebellion by requesting, instead of the 10*s.* fine, an equivalent contribution to maintain pavements and bridges.[99] In 1740, when the alehousekeepers alleged in King's Bench that only those who contributed were licensed, the justices were fined for misdemeanour and ordered to reimburse the alehousekeepers.[1] On their way back from London the justices, John Blatch, James Boys, and Joseph Duffield, were met by a crowd of supporters, said to be several hundred strong and presumably freemen, who welcomed their return to the town with fireworks and bell-ringing,[2] but the corporation had lost a source of revenue which it never recovered. The corporation's assets were undoubtedly jeopardized when the charter lapsed, as campaigners for its revival complained, but the fishery was protected from 1750 by the Colne Fishery Act,[3] and many of the borough's buildings, land, and tolls were let under leases granted by the former corporation or its mortgagees. Walter Bernard, alderman of the city of London, held the mortgage of land and buildings at Mile End and the Hythe. When the bankrupt lessee, Edward Morley, left the town house and quay in disrepair in 1745, Bernard granted a 14-year lease of the waterbailiffship, buildings, and quay to Jonathan Tabor. Bernard paid £50 for repairs and Tabor, paying £20 a year, was to maintain the waterbailiff's measures, collect dues and tolls (allowing freemen their customary concession), prosecute for non-payment, and defend Bernard's rights. The lease was to be void if the corporation was revived within the term. By a 21-year lease to Tabor in 1759 the rent was increased to £30, the mortgagee reserving the waterbailiffship.[4]

The new corporation, chartered in 1763, did not attempt to reinstate 'foreign' fines and its income was derived mainly from rents and fishery licences. It was unable to realize the full value of the Mile End estate, which was let under the 99-year lease of 1722 for £120 a year to Walter Bernard, who was also mortgagee of the estate. In 1767 the annual rent paid by the tenants to Bernard amounted to £510.[5] The Tabor family continued as tenants of the Hythe estate until 1789,[6] and

96 E.R.O., Acc. C47 (lease 1722).

97 Ibid. D/B 5 Gb7, pp. 93–4; ibid. Boro. Mun. Trunk R 3/1 (mortgage 1720).

98 Ibid. D/B 5 Gb7, p. 19; D/B 5 Aa1/30–35; Aa2/1.

99 Ibid. D/B 5 Gb7, p. 164; D/B 5 Sb5/2, pp. 68–9; ibid. Boro. Mun., vol. of misc. papers.

1 P.R.O., KB 21/35, p. 222; E.R.O., D/B 5 Gb7, f. 362v.

2 *Ipswich Jnl.* 6 Dec. 1740.

3 23 Geo. II, c. 19.

4 E.R.O., Acc. C47 (counterpart lease 1722); ibid. D/B 5 Gb7, pp. 25–6, 45, 302; ibid. Boro. Mun. Trunk R 3/1–3; Trunk R 4 (assignment of mortgage 1742).

5 Ibid. Acc. C47 (lease 1722); E.C.L. Colch. [Rebow] scrapbk. f. 24.

6 E.R.O., D/B 5 Gb8, f. 173.

in 1766 paid £40 10*s*. to the new corporation for 27 years' rent of a coalyard. The corporation seems to have made no systematic attempt to collect arrears,[7] but in 1764 it tried to reduce by £500 the debts inherited from its predecessor by putting up for sale all houses let for less than £5 a year. It also asked its mortgagees to repair bridges on its behalf, nevertheless in 1765 debts of £2,600 remained unpaid.[8] Litigation over the election of the recorder in 1789 left the corporation owing its solicitor, Thomas Lowten, fees of £457 and a loan of £2,000. The corporation, on the advice of the attorney general, refused to honour the bond for £2,000 because it bore only the seal of the mayor's office but in 1803 it agreed to pay interest at 5 per cent on the fees in return for a two-year delay in legal proceedings. The corporation raised £1,050 by selling land for barracks, but in 1806, with an annual income of £615, expenses of £625, and most of its estates mortgaged, its debts amounted to £7,249.[9] In 1807 the sale of common rights produced £492 but that was distributed among *c*. 515 resident freemen.[10] In the same year the corporation was obliged to borrow £1,807 to pay the cost of its defence against Lowten, his fees, and the accrued interest. In 1818, when its debts amounted to £11,844, the corporation raised £8,250 by selling land and buildings, many of them encumbered with mortgages.[11] To meet the cost of obtaining the charter of 1818 and the defence of aldermen, justices, and officers against litigation, the rest of the Mile End estate was mortgaged for £10,000.[12] In 1821, when the 99-year lease of that estate expired, the corporation took the letting of the farms and land into its own hands and by 1829 the annual income from the estate amounted to £893.[13]

The borough's complicated system of accounting, involving the chamberlain, the clerk, the mayor, and the treasurer, bred rumour and suspicion of extravagance and corruption, and the freemen believed they were being robbed of a share of the income from lucrative estates.[14] From 1763 the chamberlain was responsible for the collection of the smaller rents only, accounting for an average annual income of £132 and receiving commission of 1*s*. in the pound. William Mayhew (d. 1787) and Francis Smythies received the rent of the Mile End estate as successive agents of the mortgagee. The mayor received the income from the fishery, deducted his expenses, and paid the balance to the town clerk.[15] A treasurer appointed by quarter sessions collected the borough rate, introduced in 1812 to pay for law enforcement.[16] Edward Clay, mayor in 1815 and 1817, published his accounts in the press. A scheme for the reform of financial management proposed in 1820 by Francis Smythies, town clerk, was only partially adopted.[17] From 1821, when the lease of the Mile End estate expired, the chamberlain accounted for the rents of that estate, and from 1824 he also accounted for the fishery.[18] The corporation's failure to implement Smythies's proposal that it should distribute to the freemen not only copies of its accounts but also a share of the annual balance, probably inflamed discontent.[19] During the last decade of its life the corporation's average income from traditional sources, rents and the fishery, was £1,350. That income was supplemented by the borough rate to meet an average expenditure of *c*. £2,200, much of it spent on judicial functions. Lack of an adequate, modern gaol

7 Ibid. D/B 5 Aa1/35.
8 Ibid. D/B 5 Gb8, ff. 3v., 11, 21v.
9 Ibid. D/B 5 Aa2/1; D/B 5 Gb8, f. 175; Gb9, pp. 8, 17, 25, 44--5, 47, 51, 101, 117–19, 207; ibid. Acc. C47, CPL 1184.
10 Ibid. D/B 5 Gb9, pp. 119, 122.
11 Ibid. pp. 367–81; ibid. Boro. Mun., Trunk R 8/1, 2.
12 Ibid. D/B 5 Gb9, pp. 448, 452, 457–9.
13 Ibid. Boro. Mun. Rental 1829–35.
14 Ibid. Acc. C210, J. B. Harvey Colln. i, p. 16.
15 Ibid. D/B 5 Aa1/35; Aa2/1; ibid. Boro. Mun., Receivers' Accounts; *E.C.S.* 5 April 1834 (evidence to Com. on Mun. Corp.).
16 E.R.O., D/B 5 Sb6/9, 13 Jan. 1812.
17 Ibid. Acc. C210, J. B. Harvey Colln. iv, p. 57.
18 Ibid. D/B 5 Aa2/4.
19 Ibid. Acc. C210, J. B. Harvey Colln. iv, pp. 45, 57, 63–4; v, p. 396.

contributed to that expense by obliging the borough to send prisoners to Chelmsford. The corporation's critics claimed that the borough rate had by 1834 risen to four times the original sum, but in fact it remained at 6*d.* in the pound between 1812 and 1827, except for 1816, when there was no rate, and 1820, 1828, and 1829, when two 6*d.* rates were raised. From 1830 to 1833, when a 6*d.* rate raised £426, two annual rates were demanded, the first 6*d.* and the second 9*d.* or 1*s.*[20] The chamberlain's accounts for 1834 revealed that £600 from a sale authorized in 1819 had been almost entirely used to settle Smythies's account for five years' fees, offical entertainment, and the cost of opposing the reforming legislation. Although Smythies's claims were condemned by the corporation's successor,[21] comparison with earlier accounts shows that none of the charges was exceptional, and suggests that the new corporation could find nothing more serious with which to denigrate its predecessor.

Courts

The borough held a quarter sessions court, two petty courts, and an Admiralty court.[22] Quarter sessions sat regularly in the 18th century, except for the period during which the charter was in abeyance.[23] It dealt with appeals against the poor-rate, paving offences, petty theft and vagrancy, trading standards, domestic and neighbours' quarrels which often ended in violence, abuse of the corporation's members and officers, and more serious public disturbances. The presence of soldiers in the town tended to increase the number of bastardy cases, and deserters were occasionally brought before the court. The inhabitants tended to be litigious, especially in the implementation of laws protective of trading interests, such as those against practising a trade without having served an apprenticeship, employing unlawful helps, and on one occasion the wearing of buttons made of drugget.[24] There were occasional campaigns against false weights, swearing, and shaving on Sundays. Many offenders were fined or entered into recognizances, but until *c.* 1823 petty larceny and vagrancy were punished by whipping on market day either at the pillory, in the cart, or at the cart's tail. Women were seldom whipped publicly after 1730, and men were sometimes offered the alternative of enlisting in the king's service. From *c.* 1766 thieves, both men and women, were sentenced to transportation for seven years, but in 1777 and 1780 men were committed to hard labour on dredgers in the Thames instead.[25] In the 19th century prisoners served sentences of hard labour in Springfield prison, Chelmsford, because the borough gaol was inadequate.[26]

The borough was policed by four serjeants-at-mace, chosen by the twenty-four from among the freemen, and two constables in each parish chosen by the justices.[27] In exceptional cases the dragoons were called in, and in 1789 Francis Smythies, acting recorder, himself quelled a riot.[28] The grand jury seems to have surveyed the town occasionally to present at quarter sessions offenders against paving regulations.[29]

The availability of the courts probably encouraged litigation. Between 1759 and 1763, when Colchester had no borough sessions, a total of 35 Colchester indictments

20 *E.C.S.* 5 Apr. 1834 (evidence to Com. on Mun. Corp.); Speight, 'Politics in Colch.' 57–61.

21 E.R.O., Boro. Mun., Council Mins. 23 Mar. 1836.

22 *Colch. Charters*, 193–4; the Admiralty court is described in *V.C.H. Essex*, ii. 430–3.

23 Account based on E.R.O., D/B 5 Sb5/1–7; Sb6/1–10.

24 E.R.O., D/B 5 Sb5/1, pp. 300–1; cf. 10 Wm. III, c. 2.

25 Cf. 19 Geo. III, c. 74.

26 *3rd Rep. Cttee. on Gaols and Houses of Correction*, App. p. 310, H.L. 440 (1835), xii.

27 *E.C.S.* 5 Apr. 1834 (evid. to Com. on Mun. Corp.); E.R.O., D/B 5 Gb7–10, *passim.*

28 E.R.O., D/B 5 Ab1/32–3; *Ipswich Jnl.* 1 Aug. 1789.

29 e.g. E.R.O., D/B 5 Sb5/1, f. 209.

were heard at Chelmsford, but in a similar period following the new charter, 1764–8, there were 140 indictments at Colchester's quarter sessions.[30] The weekly petty courts dealt with personal actions, mainly for debt and trespass, against freemen on Mondays and 'foreigners' on Thursdays. The Monday court, which also dealt with admitting and swearing freemen, swearing officers, and apprenticeship, was busy in the early Georgian period. The corporation petitioned parliament in 1729 against a Bill for the easy recovery of small debts, fearing that it might prejudice the borough courts.[31] In 1735 the recorder, Robert Price, and the mayor, John Blatch, revised the rules to improve speed and efficiency in both courts and reduce the suitors' expense.[32] With the new charter of 1763 the rules were revised, but the Monday court dwindled. After 1810 it had virtually no business, except swearing the freemen, and in 1812 the mayor and inhabitants petitioned parliament for a court for speedy recovery of small debts.[33] A similar decline in the activity of the Thursday court was suddenly reversed in 1805 and the increase in the number of cases was maintained throughout the life of the old corporation.[34]

Parliamentary Representation

National politics were dominated by foreign wars and protectionist policies in the 18th century and by the issue of parliamentary reform in the early 19th, but in Colchester's parliamentary elections local matters, notably the recovery of the borough charter in the mid 18th century and political manoeuvring in the borough assembly over the whole period, were often more influential. Colchester, a parliamentary borough with a wider franchise than many others, had a better popular representation than many other parts of the country.[35] The right to vote to return two members in parliamentary elections was with the freemen, whether resident or not, unless they received poor relief. The occasional sale of freedom to 'foreigners' for financial or political purposes led to contention at parliamentary elections throughout the 18th century. Voting in national and local elections, as in the rest of England, was subject to bribery, often in the form of entertaining and sometimes by the payment of admission fees for new freemen. The number of freemen in Colchester increased substantially in election years. Nevertheless, by contemporary standards, Colchester was apparently not notably corrupt.[36] Some candidates were associated with particular parties or policies but others stood primarily to further their own careers or business interests. Personality was sometimes a more significant factor than policy.

Whigs, some having closer local connexions than others, occupied both seats until 1735. Sir Isaac Rebow, a wealthy Colchester clothier from a Dutch immigrant family and leader of the Whigs in the borough assembly, served until 1722 with Richard Ducane, a townsman who was a governor of the Bank of England.[37] Matthew Martin, M.P. 1722–7 and 1734–41, had a maritime and commercial background with the East India Co.; he bought Alresford Hall and other estates and became mayor of Colchester in 1726. Stamp Brooksbank and Samuel Tuffnell, M.P.s 1727–34, were London merchants, though Tuffnell also had a house in Great Waltham and had previously represented Maldon.[38] Isaac Lemyng Rebow, son of Sir Isaac, was returned with Matthew Martin unopposed in January 1735 but died

30 *E.J.* xxii (2), 39–42.
31 *C.J.* xxi, p. 509.
32 E.R.O., D/B 5 Cb1/27, ff. 103–4.
33 *C.J.* lxviii, p. 94.
34 E.R.O., D/B 5 Cb2/35–40, *passim.*
35 *Parl. Rep. Returns*, H.C. 112, pp. 12–95 (1831–2), xxxvi.
36 E.R.O., Boro. Mun., Admission Bks. I, II; *E.C.S.* 5 Apr. 1834; J. A. Phillips, *Electoral behaviour in unreformed Eng.*, 74–6, 80.
37 *V.C.H. Essex*, ii. 248–9; *E.R.* vi. 175, 183–4.
38 *E.J.* xxii (1), pp. 19–21; *E.R.* vi. 184–5.

in March. At the subsequent byelection the poll was the heaviest in the period. Jacob Houblon, from a prominent London merchant family, stood for the Tory opposition to Walpole's government and decisively defeated the Whig Brooksbank, apparently unpopular because of his previous bribery and corruption and his support for the Excise scheme.[39]

From 1741 until 1763 the borough charter was in abeyance and parliamentary elections were affected by disputes about it.[40] A period of party compromise followed in the 1760s and 1770s with the Tory Charles Gray and the Whig Isaac Martin Rebow, son of Isaac Lemyng, sharing election expenses and holding the two seats in three successive elections; both were respected men living in the town and taking an interest in local matters.[41]

The 1780s were an unsettled period with five parliamentary elections and a succession of candidates seeking political opportunity and spending large sums of money in pursuit of the seat. Sir Robert Smyth of Berechurch Hall, a radical Whig active in national politics, was elected in 1780 with Rebow, Gray having retired. At the byelection following Rebow's death in 1781, Christopher Potter, a large-scale baker and army contractor, beat the rival candidate Admiral Sir Edmund Affleck, a relation by marriage of the Tory Creffield family, who was supported by Francis Smythies, the town clerk. Potter was unseated on petition because of a defective qualification and Affleck was returned. In the 1784 election Affleck, though often away on foreign service, and Potter were returned. Potter's election was disallowed on petition because of his bankruptcy and the returning officer's partiality, and the seat given to Smyth, who had come third. At the byelection on Affleck's death in 1788 the Tory George Jackson, supported by Smythies, and the Radical George Tierney each recorded the same number of votes. Tierney was appointed on petition, for he would have won if Smythies and the returning officer had not manipulated the voting in Jackson's favour by opening and closing the poll at will and by creating new freemen during the voting.[42]

In the 1790 general election Smyth did not stand. The French Revolution had made his Radicalism more extreme, and Smythies' attempts to orchestrate opposition to him were helped by Smyth's ill-judged litigation to defend his fishery rights against the Colne fishermen. Jackson and Robert Thornton, an Evangelical Pittite Tory, were returned. Tierney was beaten: his vote had held up well, but polling was heavier in a general election and events in France were causing voters some anxiety about Radicalism. The tension in Evangelicalism between its social and religious radicalism and its political conservatism enabled Thornton to gain votes from both sides. By 1793 Smyth was living in Paris with other exiled English republicans; imprisoned during the Terror he was released with the help of his close friend, Thomas Paine, and died in 1802 in Paris.[43]

From 1790 until 1818 Tories, backed by the corporation and local landowning interests, held both seats, except for 1806–7 when William Tufnell, a Whig, held one. Thornton remained M.P. until he resigned in 1817 on being appointed marshal of the Court of Admiralty.[44] In 1812 the Tories, Thornton and Hart Davis, were

39 *E.A.T.* N.S. xiv. 17; *V.C.H. Essex*, ii. 249; *E.R.* vi. 185–6.

40 Above, this section; S. D'Cruze, 'Colch. and its Middling Sort, 1780–1800' (Essex Univ. M.A. dissertation, 1985), pp. 92–4.

41 *E.A.T.* N.S. xix. 224; *E.R.* lvii. 17–21; T. Thompson, 'A century of Essex politics, Boro. of Colch.': TS. in E.C.L. Colch.

42 S. D'Cruze, 'Middling Sort in Provincial Eng.' (Essex Univ. Ph.D. thesis, 1990), pp. 415–27; *E.A.T.* 3rd ser. xix. 225–8; E.R.O., T/B 251/6/4; *E.J.* iv. 124; *D.N.B.* s.v. Jackson; *C.J.* xxxviii. 597, 864; xl. 15, 289; xliv. 87, 99, 116, 125–6, 268.

43 S. D'Cruze, 'Middling Sort in Provincial Eng.', 427, 511–13; S. D'Cruze, *Our Time in God's Hands*, 26; *E.J.* iv. 124–5.

44 H. S. Smith, *Parliaments of Eng. 1715–1847* (1973), pp. 106–7; *V.C.H. Essex*, ii. 250.

strongly challenged by the popular Radical Daniel Whittle Harvey. After four days of polling Harvey was increasing his majority over Thornton, but the intervention of Col. J. H. Strutt of Terling in increasing the Tory vote apparently secured Harvey's defeat.[45]

Harvey was elected in 1818, unseated in 1820 for a defective qualification, and served again as M.P. from 1826 until 1835. A lawyer and a gifted orator, he contributed often to parliamentary debates as a moderate Radical advocating limited reform of parliament and the established church, and religious toleration, which antagonized both Tories and Whigs locally. By 1831 most electors favoured some measure of Reform. During the time that Harvey was M.P., Tories occupied the other seat, except for the period 1831–2 when local Tory support was diminished by the Tory government's legislation for Catholic emancipation. After the 1832 Reform Act questions of free trade and the importance of agricultural interests in Colchester's economy were the key local factors in elections.[46] Harvey had received strong support from the London and country out-voters who were removed under the reformed franchise. Realizing that Tory interests were likely to dominate among the town voters, Harvey did not contest the Colchester seat in the 1835 election, when two Tories were returned.[47]

SOCIAL HISTORY

COLCHESTER'S social life was influenced in the period by improved communications, by the consequences of agricultural change in the surrounding rural area and of rapid industrialization in other parts of the country, and by the indirect effects of wars, including the temporary establishment of a garrison during the Napoleonic Wars. Improved roads and methods of road transport enabled a faster interchange of commodities, and also of ideas and fashions, between the town and other parts of the country, especially London. Coaching inns were particularly important before the railway reached the town in 1843. Colchester's position on the route from London to Harwich and the Continent provided in addition an important cultural link beyond England. Newspapers, easily accessible in the town, brought news of current national and international affairs like parliamentary debates and the progress of the French Revolution. The Evangelical revival in the Anglican church, which emphasized individual faith and the spiritual worth and capacity for improvement of every person, led, particularly from the 1780s, to the establishment of Sunday schools, day schools, and hospitals, to other philanthropic work, and not least to some refinement in public behaviour. Nonconformity, strong locally, encouraged similar efforts. By the end of the period the range of social activities had widened. An increasing proportion of the town's population might be categorized as middle-ranking, but great discrepancies remained between those who could lead a reasonably comfortable and secure life and those on the borders of poverty who sometimes resorted to lawbreaking when food was in short supply or their livelihoods seemed at risk.

The remaining sections of the London–Harwich road were turnpiked under the 1725 Act, and by 1748 there was a coach to London and back, daily except Sundays, so that it was possible to make brief business and social visits to London and keep

[45] E.R.O., T/B 251/6/4.

[46] *E.R.* xxiv. 24–30, 63–70; Speight, 'Politics in Colch.' 226–42, 274–81; E.R.O., Acc. C32, Wire Colln. of political handbills and posters.

[47] *E.J.* iv. 127–36; Brown, *Colch. 1815–1914*, 82–4.

abreast of the latest developments.[48] There were 80 inns in 1762;[49] many were staging posts for travellers. Dr. Samuel Johnson and James Boswell stayed at the White Hart in 1763, as did John Wilkes in 1783. Lord Nelson visited the Three Cups in 1801, as did the Prince Regent in 1813, and the Duke of Wellington in 1823.[50] Inns were also convenient meeting places with refreshments for people such as farmers visiting the town on market days.[51] Members of political and social clubs met at certain inns: the King's Head club was started by a group promoting the return of the borough charter but continued as a Tory dining club whose members included leading Anglican clergymen and gentry; Whigs and Radicals met at the Hand in Hand club at the Red Lion.[52] Some local administration was conducted at inns: in 1783 the borough accounts committee met every Monday evening at the Waggon and Horses;[53] from the 1740s to the 1760s magistrates adjourned to the Three Cups, the White Hart, or the King's Head after quarter sessions.[54] The White Hart, which also had a coffee room, became one of the leading inns in the later 18th century, accommodating administrative and legal meetings as well as monthly assemblies and balls; it ceased trading in 1816 after its position was usurped by the Three Cups, where a new assembly room had been built in 1807.[55] New buildings and street improvements, including the provision of street lighting in the town centre from 1783 (by gas from 1819), and a wider variety of goods for sale in the shops increased the attraction of the town as a social centre.[56]

Intellectual stimulation was provided by the books and newspapers available in libraries and reading rooms, and by societies and lectures. Charles Gray set up a library in the castle in 1749, and the following year formed the Castle library book club, one of several lending libraries, which acquired a wide range of books, including works by leading contemporary philosophers and political economists.[57] In 1794, when the club's membership of 30 included 10 clergy, 4 bankers, at least 1 grocer, 1 apothecary, 1 clockmaker, and 1 captain, the writings of the Evangelical William Cowper were popular, and Byron's works were also held.[58] Thomas Paine's *The Rights of Man* was considered subversive however, and Richard Patmore, a baymaker, was indicted in 1793 for distributing part of it.[59] Colchester Medical Society, England's oldest provincial medical society, was founded in 1774 by Robert Richardson Newell. Members presented difficult or interesting cases for diagnosis and discussion, established a medical lending library, and regulated their own professional conduct.[60] In 1820 the Philosophical Society was formed, whose members, mainly professionals and traders but also one working man, each gave one of the monthly lectures at Queen Street, the subjects of which included Heat, Taste, Wit, and Electricity. The society kept a museum of antiquities which it presented to the corporation when it was dissolved in 1843.[61] Interest was developing in science as well as the arts. George Wegg of East Hill House had amassed a collection of books, manuscripts, globes, telescopes, quadrants, magnets,

48 Below, Communications; many of the notes for the following section were supplied by Mr. J. Bensusan-Butt.

49 E.R.O., Q/Sb 231.

50 *E.R.* xxiii. 10; lvi. 215; *Colch. Expr.* 12 Oct. 1972; *E.C.S.* 28 May 1965.

51 *East Anglian Studies*, ed. L. M. Munby, 160.

52 S. D'Cruze, 'Middling Sort in Provincial Eng.: Politics and Social Relations in Colch.' (Essex Univ. Ph.D. thesis, 1990), 280, 362.

53 E.R.O., D/B 5 Gb8, f. 134v.

54 Ibid. Q/Smg 14.

55 D'Cruze, 'Middling Sort in Provincial Eng.', 88; *E.R.* lvi. 215; *Guardian*, 9 Mar. 1968; *E.C.S.* 29 Dec. 1961.

56 Above, this chapter, Topog.; below, Public Services (Street Paving, Cleaning and Lighting; Gas Supply).

57 Below, Soc. and Cultural.

58 L. Davidoff and C. Hall, *Family Fortunes*, 156–7, 159.

59 E.R.O., Acc. C210, J. B. Harvey Colln. vi, p. 54.

60 *Medical Hist.* xx. 394–401; C. Joscelyne, 'Medical Practice and Medical Theory: Smallpox in Britain during the long 18th century' (Essex Univ. Ph.D. thesis, 1990), 287–9.

61 Brown, *Colch. 1815–1914*, 68; A. F. J. Brown, *Essex People*, 114.

and other mathematical and philosophical instruments by the time he died in 1777. After a successful series of lectures on astronomy at the moot hall in 1798 by a visiting lecturer, Isaac Taylor, an Independent minister in the town 1796–1810, lectured monthly in his parlour to 60–70 young people and their friends on geometry, astronomy, geography, mechanics, history, and anatomy.[62]

Local discussions were sharpened by contact with scholars and writers from further afield. Balliol College, Oxford, was patron of several town livings, and Nathaniel Forster at All Saints' was one of their presentees who was also resident; a Utilitarian writer on political economy and education, he was a friend of Jeremy Bentham. The quarrelsome Dr. Samuel Parr, an eminent classical scholar and a Whig writer, served as Forster's curate while master of the grammar school 1777–9, for which post Dr. Samuel Johnson wrote him a letter of recommendation.[63] The family of the minister Isaac Taylor was part of the small circle of intellectuals in the town. His daughters, Ann and Jane, were writers of children's stories, hymns, and poems, including 'Twinkle, twinkle little star'. The family visited friends and relations in London, Essex, and Suffolk, who included publishers, writers, medical families, clerics, and the artist, John Constable's, family at East Bergholt (Suff.). One of their Colchester friends was Benjamin Strutt, antiquary, vegetarian, amateur artist, musician, and agnostic.[64]

For much of the 18th century the established church seems to have had a limited impact on local affairs. Many of the Anglican parishes were poor livings with dilapidated church buildings, badly served by incumbents who were often pluralists and non-resident for part or all of the year. No services were held at St. Runwald's between 1723 and 1748, parishioners attending St. Peter's, and parishioners of St. Botolph's attended All Saints' until their new church was built in 1837. St. Mary's-at-the-Walls parish, however, had some wealthy inhabitants and a good rectory house to attract able clerics: Philip Morant, rector 1737–70, was author of a scholarly history of Colchester and also of Essex; Thomas Twining, son of the tea-dealer and well known as a translator of Aristotle, was resident rector 1790–1804.[65] He was acquainted with the diarist and novelist Fanny Burney.[66] All Saints' was another relatively desirable living where some of the parishioners, such as Charles Gray at Hollytrees and Thomas Boggis at the Minories, could be counted among the most influential people in the town.[67] St. Peter's church was used by the corporation for civic services.[68]

Despite various schisms old Dissent in general continued to be numerically strong, although Quakerism declined. Some dissenters were prepared to conform occasionally to qualify for civic office, and two Independents, Arthur Winsley and Jeremiah Daniell, were mayors. Others, like members of the Tabor family at Lion Walk chapel, took no interest in the corporation but were members of the navigation and improvement commission.[69] New Dissent in the form of Methodism had some early success, but declined in the 1780s, though it revived by 1800. A minister's daughter considered local dissenters *c.* 1795 to be 'men of habit more than men of piety', only a few of whom 'knew or thought why they dissented', but that condition did not continue.[70] The number of protestant dissenters was often

[62] E.R.O., Acc C47 CPL 280, George Wegg's will; ibid. D/DU 1545/19/1, pp. 123–4.

[63] *D.N.B.* s.v. Forster; Parr; *E.R.* v. 192; xxiii. 8–9; *V.C.H. Essex*, ii. 507.

[64] E.R.O., D/DU 1545/19/1, pp. 93–156; D/DU 1545/23, pp. 6, 17.

[65] Below, Churches; *D.N.B.* s.v. Morant; Twining.

[66] *E.R.* xxviii. 161–5.

[67] J. Bensusan-Butt, *All Saints' Colch. in 18th Cent.*

[68] Below, Churches (St. Peter's).

[69] D'Cruze, 'Middling Sort in Provincial Eng.', 482–3; E.R.O., D/DU 617.

[70] E.R.O., D/DU 1545/19/1, p. 98; below, Prot. Nonconf.

overestimated: in 1829 out of a population of *c*. 16,000 there were 4,330 (27 per cent) of whom 2,200 were Independents, 1,100 Baptists, 930 Wesleyan Methodists, and only 100 Quakers.[71] Roman Catholicism was insignificant in the town in the period.[72] Roman Catholics were feared: the corporation repeatedly petitioned parliament against them, for example, in 1812 about the dangers of their holding office in a protestant government, and in 1828 against granting them further concessions.[73]

The Evangelical movement revived Anglican church life from the 1780s in some parishes. By 1835 the income of many livings had also been augmented, and some of the church fabric had been improved. Robert Storry, vicar of St. Peter's 1781–1814, an early Evangelical, was succeeded by another, the enthusiastic and popular William Marsh, who stayed until 1829. Marsh instituted more Sunday services, started prayer and bible-reading meetings in the week, renovated the church, and provided more seating; he supported philanthropic activity in the parish and beyond, including missionary work and anti-slavery societies.[74] The Colchester and East Essex Church Missionary Association was established in 1816.[75] Public sermons to benefit missionary societies and on behalf of the National schools were regularly preached at St. Peter's in the early 19th century.[76] The Religious Tracts Society for Colchester and its Vicinity was formed in 1825.[77]

The influence of Evangelicalism extended beyond organized religion into the whole of private and public life, influencing personal morality and stimulating much educational and philanthropic work. The town assembly petitioned parliament against the slave trade in 1788, and Colchester Anti-Slavery Society was established in 1824.[78] Fourteen Sunday schools were opened in 1786 when Nathaniel Forster preached sermons expounding his Utilitarian view of education as a prevention rather than a cure of vice in the poor.[79] By 1833 many day-school places had been provided.[80] Some new charities were established for bread and for money for the poor.[81] The Benevolent Medical Society for Essex and Herts. was founded in 1786 for the relief of distressed medical men, their widows and children, and in 1789 Colchester Benevolent Society was established for the sick poor.[82] There were some short-lived attempts at medical provision in the late 18th and early 19th century, and in 1820 the Essex and Colchester hospital opened as a general infirmary for the poor on the initiative of Joseph Jefferson, archdeacon of Colchester, and seven other men.[83] Women of middling status, excluded from much of public life, were active in philanthropic work, such as running Colchester's Lying-In charity, set up in 1796. The Female Friendly Society, established in 1808 with a committee of 12 ladies and 114 subscribers, helped women and girls, mainly with gifts of clothing.[84]

Colchester's leaders, socially as in political and economic life, were the town gentry together with members of the commercial and professional élites.[85] Among the leading families, Charles Gray, lawyer, of Hollytrees was linked by marriage with the Creffields and the Rounds, though the Rounds were not an important

71 M. E. Speight, 'Politics in the Boro. of Colch. 1812–47' (Lond. Univ. Ph.D. thesis, 1969), 250–1.

72 Below, Roman Catholicism.

73 E.R.O., D/B 5 Gb9, pp. 227–8; Gb10, p. 14.

74 Below, Churches; C. Marsh, *Life of Revd. Wm Marsh*; J. Hurnard, *Setting Sun* (1871), 158–9.

75 *Ipswich Jnl.* 18 Apr. 1818.

76 e.g. E.R.O., D/B 5 Gb9, pp. 331, 395.

77 T. Cromwell, *Hist. Colch.* 393.

78 E.R.O., D/B 5 Gb8, ff. 158v., 159; Cromwell, *Hist. Colch.* 391.

79 *Ipswich Jnl.* 1 July 1786; N. Forster, 'A Discourse on the Utility of Sunday Schools': E.C.L. Colch.

80 Below, Educ.

81 Below, Charities.

82 Cromwell, *Hist. Colch.* 387.

83 Below, Hospitals.

84 Below, Charities; Davidoff and Hall, *Family Fortunes*, 434; Cromwell, *Hist. Colch.* 389.

85 Above, this chapter, Town Govt.; Econ.; D'Cruze, 'Middling Sort in Provincial Eng.', 135–6.

social influence in the town until the 19th century. Gray's stepdaughter, Sarah Creffield, married his friend, the lawyer George Wegg of East Hill House.[86] The Smythies, an Anglican Tory family whose members included Francis and his son Francis, both active in town politics, and also clergymen for several Colchester churches, were linked with the Twinings, the tea merchants.[87] The Smyths at Berechurch provided M.P.s for the town.[88] The increase in small workshops and the growth of retailing resulted in a significant expansion, below the gentry and above the lower levels of petty traders, artisans and labourers, of the middle-ranking groups who probably constituted about 20 per cent of the population at the end of the 18th century.[89] They usually kept female servants, and wealthier households also kept male servants. In 1780 Isaac Martin Rebow, M.P. for Colchester, had 7 male servants at Wivenhoe Park and Charles Gray 4 at Hollytrees, but only 7 Colchester houses kept as many as 2, and 50 houses had 1 each.[90] Poorer people experienced much deprivation caused by the Napoleonic Wars and the decline in the bay trade, and poor relief expenditure per head increased greatly in the late 18th century and early 19th.[91]

Different social networks, such as those of family, religion, profession, trade, or freemasonry were often intertwined. The Anglican physician, Richard Mackintosh, was part of the local Evangelical network; he was treasurer of the Castle library, vice-president of the Philosophical Society, a manager of the savings bank, active member of the Botanical and Horticultural Society and of the Colchester and East Essex Bible Society, and a founder member and voluntary physician of the Essex and Colchester hospital, all of which ensured that he was never short of patients.[92] A denominational bias was marked in social relationships, but nonconformists gradually became more integrated into social life.[93] There is some evidence to support the view that later in the period, especially in the 19th century, the spheres of middle-class women and men were becoming increasingly separated, with men's activities located predominantly in the public world and women's in the home. Maria Marsh, for example, took her role as a clergyman's wife seriously, running the home, looking after the material and moral welfare of the children and servants, undertaking some charitable work, and generally supporting her husband, whose activities were mainly outside the home; she corresponded with the Evangelical writer, Hannah More, who extolled the virtues of domesticity and the importance of women's moral influence in the home.[94]

In the 18th century men working in the cloth industry had their own supportive networks. Woolcombers held an annual procession until at least 1782 in honour of their patron saint, St. Blaize, and met at Bishop Blaize inn, Angel Lane. Other inns, like the Weavers' Arms, were frequented by other craftsmen in the industry.[95] Workers had to take care not to be seen to be breaking the Combination laws, consolidated in legislation of 1799 and 1800, and their fraternization was often disguised in the activities of friendly societies or benefit clubs. In 1793 there were 18 friendly societies in the town each with 20–40 members paying 1*s.* monthly; sick members received 8*s.* to 10*s.* a week and aged ones 6*s.*[96] By 1828 benefit and

[86] *E.R.* vi. 187; D'Cruze, 'Middling Sort in Provincial Eng.', pp. 276, 293.

[87] *E.A.T.* 3rd ser. xix. 224–5; below, Churches.

[88] Above, this chapter, Town Govt. (Parl. Rep.); below, Modern Colch., Political Hist.

[89] D'Cruze, 'Middling Sort in Provincial Eng.', 1–15, 19.

[90] J. Bensusan-Butt, *House that Boggis Built* (1972), 26.

[91] S. D'Cruze, 'Colch. and its Middling Sort', (Essex Univ. M.A. thesis, 1985), 31; below, Par. Govt. and Poor Relief.

[92] Joscelyne, 'Medical Practice', pp. 268–74; Davidoff and Hall, *Family Fortunes*, 102.

[93] S. D'Cruze, *Our Time in God's Hands*, 2–19.

[94] Davidoff and Hall, *Family Fortunes*, 123–5, 167–72.

[95] *V.C.H. Essex*, ii. 402–3; Brown, *Colch. 1815–1914*, 107.

[96] F. M. Eden, *State of the Poor*, 188.

friendly societies included those for the parishes of St. Leonard's, St. Botolph's, St. Nicholas's, and Lexden, the Samaritans Club at St. Peter's, and the Union Benefit Society.[97]

Freemasonry gave its members useful social and business contacts and by the end of the period a number of lodges existed in the town. Thomas Boggis, baymaker, was master of the Angel lodge in 1770, deputy provincial grand master of Essex in 1777, and master of the new Lodge of Unity in 1779.[98] At a masonic anniversary meeting in 1777, after the public breakfast that ladies were allowed to attend, the brethren processed to St. Peter's church where, together with the provincial grandmaster, they heard a sermon.[99] In 1799 many of the members of the Angel lodge and most of those of the North Devon lodge were soldiers. In 1834 the Angel lodge's 47 members were mainly occupied in trade and commerce, though there were a few professionals, farmers, and gentlemen.[1]

The range of social activities increased, especially for those with sufficient free time and the financial means to enjoy it. In 1790 a party of corporation gentlemen, which included two customs officers, went by sea on a two-day pleasure trip to Dunkirk; on their return they were astonished to be apprehended by another customs officer for illicit trading.[2] Colchester functioned to a certain extent like a county town in so far as people from the surrounding rural area visited the town for agricultural, judicial, and political business. Social functions were put on to coincide with particular events.[3] Monthly assemblies were held *c.* 1773 at the King's Head from November to January and at the White Hart from March to October. When fairs, like St. Dennis's, were on, special public breakfasts, dinners, suppers, balls, and theatrical performances attracted 'the most respectable families'.[4] The items included in musical concerts and at the theatre showed that Colchester was no cultural backwater. Handel's *Messiah* was performed in 1759, and there was a Handel festival at St. Peter's church in 1763 followed by a ball at the King's Head, though no musical oratorio was played again until 1790. Music by Dr. Thomas Arne accompanied a performance of *Tom Jones* at the theatre in 1769.[5] Entertainments staged at the theatre ranged from plays by Shakespeare and Sheridan to the performance in 1786 by acrobats from Sadlers Wells and the Royal Circus, which ended with a new pantomime.[6] During the Napoleonic Wars some plays were chosen by the officers of various regiments.[7] Soldiers from the garrison also brought extra custom to the town's inns, and were potential dancing and marriage partners.

Some men took part in sports. Cricket matches were sometimes played for prizes: in 1770 cricketers dined at the Cock and Pye, North Hill, before playing a match for half-guinea hats.[8] There was a race-course on Mile End heath in the 1750s, although it had gone by 1821, and a horse-race with betting was held after a cricket match on Lexden heath in 1785.[9] A new riding school was set up at the bottom of Angel Lane in 1792.[10] The town owned a subscription pack of hounds in 1754, and in 1798 the East Essex Foxhounds was established, which met quarterly for dinner at the White Hart.[11] Some early attempts at ballooning were made, and in

97 *C.J.* lxxxiii. 259.

98 Bensusan-Butt, *House that Boggis Built*, 16–17.

99 *Ipswich Jnl.* 28 June 1777.

1 E.R.O., Q/RSm 1/1, 3, 2/1.

2 *The Times*, 2 Sept. 1790.

3 *Ipswich Jnl.* 16 Jan 1773; H. Grieve, *Sleepers and Shadows*, ii (forthcoming), chapter 9, for comparison with Chelmsford, county town.

4 *Colch. Gaz.* 12 Nov. 1814.

5 *Ipswich Jnl.* 18 Aug. 1759; 9 July 1763; 9 Sept. 1769; 13 Aug. 1790.

6 Below, Soc. and Cultural (Theatres and Cinemas); *Ipswich. Jnl.* 23 Dec. 1786.

7 Theatre programmes at Colch. Mus.

8 *Ipswich Jnl.* 22 Sept. 1770.

9 E.C.L. Colch. [Rebow] Scrapbk. f. 20; Beds. R.O., L 26/1010– 11; *Ipswich Jnl.* 23 July 1785.

10 *Ipswich Jnl.* 30 June 1792.

11 Ibid. 21 Dec 1754; E.R.O., D/DHa F5, f. 1.

1829 George Green ascended from the town, reaching an altitude of nearly 3 miles.[12] Humbler folk had less leisure and little money to spend on it; some went to cockfights, forbidden by the borough court again in 1764, or indulged in poaching.[13] Both rich and poor may have enjoyed watching prizefights or visiting spectacles like the 'surprising dancing bears' on show at the market cross in 1753 or the two lions and a tiger on view at the Golden Lion in 1766.[14]

Manners, both at public events and in private visiting, at least of the social élite and of the middle-ranking groups, became more refined over the period. 'Genteel' pastimes included visiting friends and going for short walks. 'Handsome gravel walks' were laid round St. Mary's church in 1714, with lime trees planted beside them.[15] Gardens, and the growing of plants and trees, became a fashionable interest.[16] Annual spring flower shows and feasts were held in Colchester as in many English towns, and auriculas were a speciality claimed to be finer than the tulips and hyacinths of Dutch rivals.[17] Nevertheless by the early 19th century many leisure activities were considered harmful by a minority like the Evangelical William Marsh, who campaigned against the theatre.[18]

Colchester seemed a reasonably orderly town, by contemporary standards.[19] There were food riots, apparently not serious, in 1740, 1766, 1772, and 1789, when there were similar disturbances in other parts of the country.[20] Electioneering never seemed to run out of control, even though numbers of London and country voters were brought in and entertained by the rival candidates, and in 1832 part of the hustings was destroyed by the crowd.[21] Industrial action was probably most threatening early in the period when workers in the cloth industry still had some economic power: in 1715 an armed mob tried to enforce redress of weavers' grievances, and in 1724 weavers rioted for higher wages. The Luddite protests in 1811–16 against the introduction of new machinery in the stocking-making, cotton, and woollen districts in the midlands and north inspired nothing comparable in Colchester, where there was no equivalent large-scale industry.[22] The minor outbreaks of incendiarism and the breaking of threshing machines in 1815 and 1830 at Mile End were linked with a wave of agricultural unrest unconnected with the town.[23] In 1821 Queen Caroline's funeral procession, which a mob had tried to divert in London with some loss of life, stopped in the town overnight *en route* for the Continent; local people flocked to show their respect, but there was no threat to law and order.[24]

[12] *E.R.* xliv. 39, 123–4.

[13] *Ipswich Jnl.* 3 Mar. 1764; 24 Aug. 1769.

[14] *E.R.* xxiv. 187; *Ipswich Jnl.* 28 Apr. 1753; 25 Oct. 1766.

[15] Morant, *Colch.* 108; below, Churches, Fig. 31.

[16] Above, this chapter, Topog.

[17] *Ipswich Jnl.* e.g. 4 May 1754; Morant, *Colch.* 92; *Garden Hist.* x (1), 17–35; xii (1), 8–38; *E.C.S.* 15 Apr. 1966.

[18] Davidoff and Hall, *Family Fortunes*, 437.

[19] Above, this chapter, Town Govt. (Courts).

[20] Above, this chapter, Econ. Hist.; J. Stevenson, *Popular Disturbances in Eng. 1700–1870*, 91–109.

[21] Above, this chapter, Town Govt. (Parl. Rep.); E.R.O., D/B 5 Ab 1/65.

[22] Above, this chapter, Econ.; J. Rule, *Albion's People*, 215.

[23] Below, Outlying Parts (Mile End).

[24] *Ipswich Jnl.* 18 Aug. 1821.

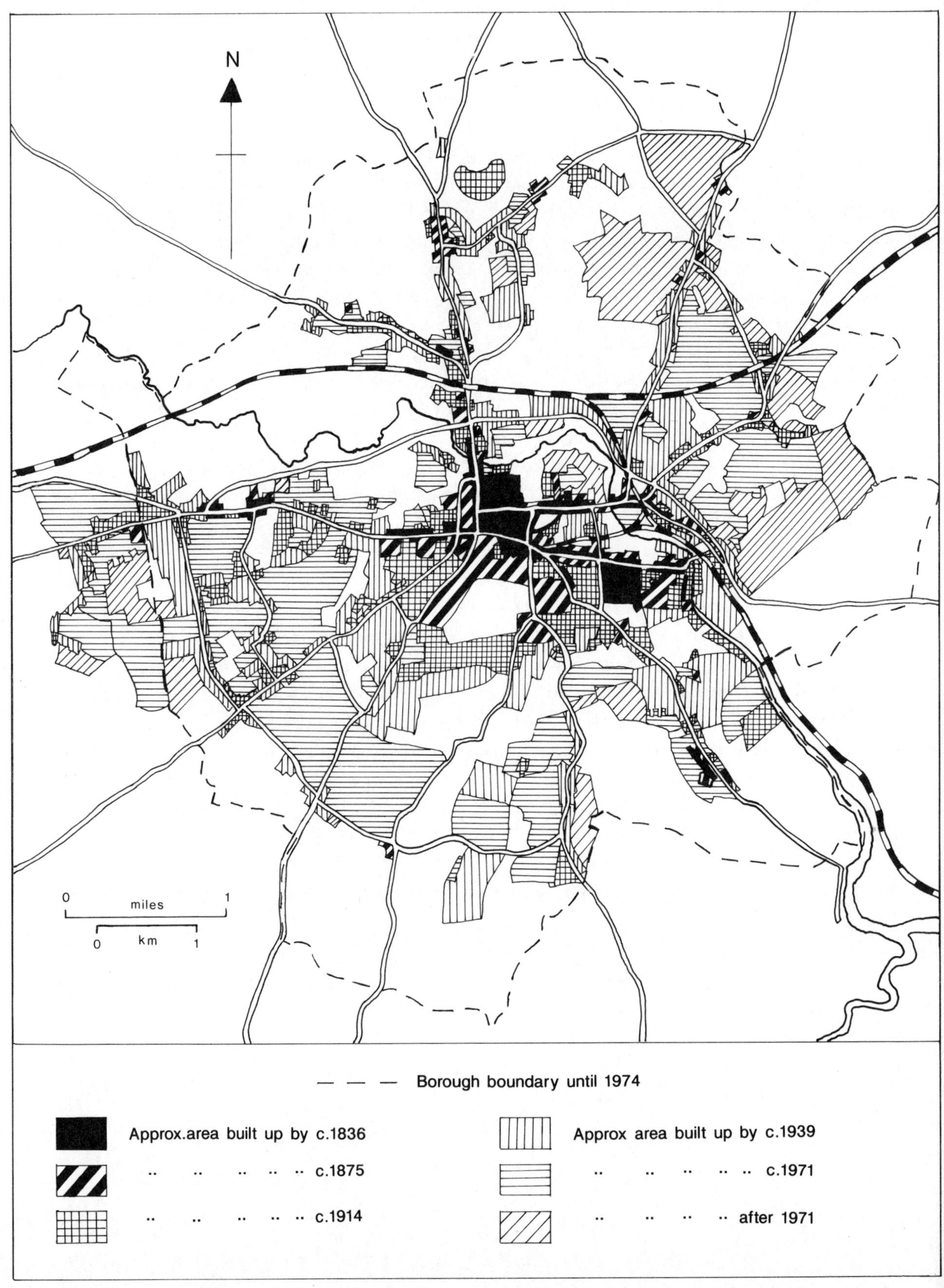

FIG. 13. THE GROWTH OF THE BUILT-UP AREA

MODERN COLCHESTER

The town's geographical position, near London and the Continent, and the re-establishment of the garrison from 1856 were both crucial factors in its modern development. In 1835, relatively unaffected by rapid industrialization in other parts of the county, Colchester remained a market town serving the neighbouring agricultural area. In the later 19th century, despite agricultural depression and helped by the garrison's demand for goods and services, its economy was able to diversify and expand, with new manufacturing enterprises developing. Both manufacturing and service industries expanded in the

TABLE X: POPULATION OF COLCHESTER ANCIENT BOROUGH, 1801–1991

Year	*Population*	*Decennial % change*	*Year*	*Population*	*Decennial % change*
1801	11,520		1901	38,373	11
1811	12,544	9	1911	43,452	13
1821	14,016	12	1921	43,393	0
1831	16,167	15	1931	49,131	13
1841	17,790	10	1941		
1851	19,443	9	1951	57,449	
1861	23,815	22	1961	65,080	13
1871	26,345	11	1971	76,408	17
1881	28,374	8	1981	82,227	8
1891	34,559	22	1991	est. 89,000	8

Sources: *Census*, 1801–1981; Colch. Boro. Council, *Colch. Counts* (Mar. 1993), 13.

20th century, but in the later 20th century manufacturing declined and the town's reputation rested on the administrative, commercial, and cultural services which it provided for the region. Borough government and poor relief had to adjust to a new reformed system after legislative changes in the 1830s. Party confrontation gave way in the late 19th century to a period of more consensual town politics which lasted until after 1945 when party rivalries increased again. Business and professional men dominated the council, though in the 20th century councillors gradually came to be drawn from a wider range of social backgrounds. Protestant nonconformity was a powerful force in the town's economic and political, as well as social and religious life. In parliamentary elections national factors became more important than local ones from the later 19th century. The town remained physically quite compact until the First World War. Afterwards suburban growth spread, but even in the later 20th century a significant amount of open space remained within the ancient borough boundaries. The pattern of development was greatly affected by the expansion of the barracks south of the town centre. The garrison gave the town a strategic importance, valuable in the context of its rivalry with other towns, and military uniforms and bands gave colour to civic events and celebrations.

The population of the ancient borough (Table X) increased steadily from 16,167 in 1831 to 38,373 in 1901 and 82,277 in 1981.[1] The estimated population in 1991 was *c.* 89,000.[2] Census figures are complicated by the garrison, whose average

[1] *Census*, 1841–1981.

[2] Colch. Boro. Council, *Colch. Counts* (Mar. 1993), 13.

strength between 1856 and 1921 was *c.* 3,000, although it rose briefly to more than 40,000 in the First World War.[3] Colchester was fortunate in having more space for its increasing population than many towns, being able to expand within its ancient boundaries, which remained virtually unchanged until 1974.[4] Advances in public health helped the death rate to fall from an average of 27.7 deaths per 1,000 of population in the period 1838–40 to 15.6 in the period 1896–1900, the rate being consistently lower than the national average from the 1850s. The infant mortality rate remained high throughout the 19th century, still averaging 130.4 per 1,000 in the period 1896–1900, but fell dramatically to average 68.8 in the period 1912–14 as infant care improved. Quinquennial recorded birth rates fluctuated between 33.7 and 31.2 per 1,000 between 1841 and 1885, but then steadily fell to a rate of 20.6 in the period 1911–14.[5] The trend continued, the death rate falling to 13.3 and the birth rate to 10.1 in 1933, both rates below the national average.[6] In the 19th century emigration was particularly to London, and immigration mostly from surrounding rural areas.[7] Twentieth-century growth was based on net immigration, much of it still from rural areas but also from London and metropolitan Essex. Commuting to London increased in the later 20th century.[8]

Colchester achieved national fame in 1884 when it was the town most affected by the earthquake which lasted for several seconds at 9.20 a.m. on April 22, when '. . . the ground and the houses with it was lifted up, shaken two or three times in a manner that made the stoutest heart quake' and then subsided 'with a kind of final shake or jerk'. People left their work to view the damage, which was minimal. There were no deaths or serious injuries. Lion Walk Congregational church spire fell, some masonry was dislodged at St. Leonard's church, and three chimneys went through the workhouse roof. Other chimneys and debris fell from buildings mostly on the east side of the town, which felt the full force of the shock. There was some damage outside the town in Wivenhoe, East Donyland, and Mersea. Well attended thanksgiving services were held at several churches the same evening and there were special services the following Sunday. Sightseers visited the town in succeeding weeks.[9] Colchester escaped the disastrous east coast floods of 1953 with comparatively minor flooding at the Hythe; the borough authorities and the garrison helped other areas more seriously affected, and the barracks provided temporary shelter for evacuees.[10]

In the First World War the town was full of troops and many local men were away serving in the forces, but daily business continued with little disruption. One German bomb caused slight damage in a garden in Butt Road in 1915.[11] A military airfield was established on a polo ground at Blackheath.[12] During both World Wars some soldiers were billeted on local families, apparently matched by rank as far as possible.[13] In the Second World War Colchester was not subjected to heavy systematic bombardment, but it did sustain smaller attacks, the heaviest loss of life occurring in 1942 when 38 patients were killed and 25 people injured at

3 A. F. F. H. Robertson, 'The army in Colch. and its influence on the social, economic and political development of the town, 1854– 1914' (Essex Univ. Ph.D. thesis, 1991), 451; Phillips, *Ten Men*, 134–8.

4 Below, Boundaries.

5 Phillips, *Ten Men*, 131, 136, 150–54; below, Public Services.

6 *Essex Tel.* 7 July 1934.

7 Phillips, *Ten Men*, 137.

8 Essex C.C. *Essex Development Plan, Rep. on First Review, Part II Towns, Colch. & District, 1964*, 2; below, this chapter, Econ.

9 *Essex Tel.* 22, 26 Apr. 1884; R. Mendola and W. White, *Rep. on the East Anglian Earthquake of 1884* (Essex Field Club Special Memoirs, i), 22–3, 44–57: copy in E.R.O.; E.R.O., D/P 245/28/13.

10 H. Grieve, *The Great Tide*, 53, 133–4, 210, 269, 280, 315, 341–2, 486.

11 G. Martin, *Story of Colch.* 111; A. Phillips, *Colch. in Old Photographs*, 77–84.

12 Gant, MS. 'Hist. Berechurch', 190.

13 e.g. E.R.O., SA 0677; Colch. Institute, Colch. Recalled oral history project, interviews 2180, 1504.

Severalls hospital.[14] In 1944 about 1,000 incendiaries and 8 phosphorus oil bombs set St. Botolph's corner on fire, badly damaging several factories and shops, but there was only one casualty and no fatality.[15] The town was an important rest centre for American troops, who regularly bussed young women out in army trucks to dances in the villages to the north and west where American servicemen were based.[16] Between 1944 and 1947 German prisoners of war were held at Berechurch in huts which were afterwards used as a military corrective centre. The prisoners of war worked on neighbouring farms in 1946 and 1947.[17]

The town's main rival in the 19th century was Ipswich, and there was keen competition over the improvement of dock facilities and the acquisition of railways.[18] From the later 19th century Chelmsford, the county town, whose importance increased when county councils were established in 1888, was Colchester's main rival, while Ipswich remained a competitor for retail trade.[19] Colchester's campaign in 1907 to become the seat of the new diocesan bishop was unsuccessful, the honour going to Chelmsford, but the score was evened in 1961 when Essex University was established at Wivenhoe Park.[20]

ECONOMIC DEVELOPMENT

The Nineteenth-century Market Town

In 1835 Colchester was primarily a market town for the surrounding agricultural area, in addition processing some of the produce and providing retailing and professional services. Nevertheless the town's proximity to the London market, its position on the road to Harwich and the Continent, and its port encouraged wider trade. The silk industry had partly replaced the earlier trade in bays and says but never assumed comparable scale or importance. Trade with the surrounding rural communities was affected by the state of agriculture, which gradually recovered from depression following the Napoleonic Wars to greater prosperity from the 1850s.[21] The re-establishment of barracks in the town from 1855[22] was a valuable stimulus to the local economy.

The port at the Hythe was an important centre of local trade with many warehouses, but because it needed improvement by *c.* 1840, Maldon was importing all the materials for Colchester's railway-building.[23] In 1838 the gasworks were built at the Hythe, and in 1848, a year after a railway goods station was built there, local traders included 26 coal merchants and 9 corn merchants, some of them owning their own ships, 3 lime-burners, 3 maltsters, 2 brickmakers, and 2 whiting manufacturers. There was one shipbuilder, P. M. Sainty, in 1848 but none in 1863, local shipbuilding being just outside the borough at Wivenhoe.[24] In the mid 19th century the coasting trade brought coal directly from northern England, and goods from the colonies and manufactures by way of London; exports were corn, malt,

[14] E.R.O., Acc. 6475, record map of aerial bombardment 1939–45; Acc. C48, file on bomb craters and other war damage; *E.C.S.* 27 Apr. 1962.

[15] *E.C.S.* 25 Feb. 1944.

[16] Colch. Recalled, interview 1502A; 'They also served', video produced by Signals: copy in Colch. Mus. Resources Centre.

[17] R. Boyes, *In Glass Houses*, 260–5; inf. from Lt. Col. R. J. Robinson; *Querschnitt* (magazine of German prisoners) 1945–7: copies in E.C.L. Colch.

[18] Phillips, *Ten Men*, 17.

[19] H. Grieve, *The Sleepers and the Shadows*, ii. chap. 12; *E.C.S.* 24 July 1992.

[20] Ibid. 20 July 1907; *Essex Tel.* 2 Nov. 1907; *Colch. Official Guide* (5th edn.), 17.

[21] *Robson's Gazetteer of the Home Counties* (1838), Essex, pp. 33, 41–7; Brown, *Colch. 1815–1914*, 15, 21.

[22] Below, Barracks.

[23] H. Benham, *Once upon a Tide*, 37.

[24] D. I. Gordon, *Regional Hist. Railways of G.B.* v (Eastern Counties), p. 58; J. B. Harvey, *Gas Lighting in Colch.* 6; *White's Dir. Essex* (1848), 68, 99–112; (1863), 122, 131.

flour, and oysters. More than 50 ships belonged to the town, but small craft from other places along the Colne also operated from the Hythe. The comparatively insignificant foreign trade consisted chiefly of wines from Spain, oil cakes from Holland, and timber from the Baltic. W. W. and C. H. Hawkins were important timber merchants. Business improved after the channel was deepened from the Hythe to Fingringhoe in 1854, allowing larger ships to berth, essential if trade was not to be lost to other ports, especially Ipswich, where a wet dock had been created in 1842. Local businessmen were able to exploit the competition between providers of transport by sea and by rail to keep down the prices charged for heavy freight.[25]

The occupational structure in 1851 reflected Colchester's position as a market town. Most people still worked in small shops, small commercial premises, or workshops, although a few were already working in larger industrial units, like the silk spinners at Brown & Moy's four-storeyed silk factory.[26] Only about one person in 20 of the employed population could be considered an industrial worker, whereas a third worked in crafts, a fifth as servants, and a tenth in trade. The leading male occupations were in agricultural and general labouring, market gardening, processing and retailing food and drink, shoemaking, tailoring, carpentry, bricklaying, upholstery, drapery, and seafaring; women and girls worked predominantly in domestic service, tailoring, millinery, laundry, and the silk industry. The employment structure was similar in the rival town of Ipswich, except that Colchester, because it covered a larger area, had proportionately three times as many agricultural labourers, equivalent to nearly a tenth of employees, most of whom worked in its outlying rural parishes. Unrecorded casual and temporary employment, and domestic and part-time work, particularly of women and children, add complexity to the apparent pattern of employment.[27]

The town's silk industry, never of great importance, had been declining from the 1820s. In 1840 the remaining 40 to 60 weavers, employed as outworkers for London firms, were earning less than farm labourers, and some at times were forced to enter the workhouse with their families. Some weavers worked at part of the former Napoleonic barracks in Military Road. Spinning was carried on mainly by low-paid young women and girls, at Brown & Moy's riverside factory in Dead Lane, but the silk industry had ceased by 1881.[28]

Many people were employed in occcupations connected with the supply of food and drink. Market gardening remained important in the borough and its hinterland, and garden seeds were produced for sale. From the 1840s trains could carry perishable produce rapidly to the expanding London markets.[29] After the repeal of the corn laws in 1846 cheaper foreign corn could be imported by river to conveniently sited mills, whilst other mills gradually went out of business. East mill had been acquired in 1840 by a branch of the Marriage family, who introduced steam power in 1844, an innovation which other mill owners adopted over the next 10 years.[30] An additional corn exchange was built in 1845 in High Street to cope with the increasing local corn trade.[31] Colchester was famous for oysters, but the fishery provided no direct employment for the town.[32]

[25] *White's Dir. Essex* (1848), 67–8, 112; *White's Dir. Suffolk* (1844), 49; Phillips, *Ten Men*, 18–22; below, Port; Communications (Railways).

[26] Brown, *Colch. 1815–1914*, 10.

[27] *Census*, 1851 (P. Tillott's occupational classification used); Brown, *Colch. 1815–1914*, 12–13, 22–3; E.R.O., D/DU 559/124.

[28] *Rep. on Handloom Weavers* [43], pp. 289–91, H.C. (1840), xxiii; E.R.O., D/DU 490; *V.C.H. Essex*, ii. 468; A. Phillips, *Colch. in Old Photographs*, 34; Brown, *Colch. 1815–1914*, 7; below, pl. facing p. 216.

[29] *Robson's Gazetteer of the Home Counties* (1838), Essex, p. 32; *White's Dir. Essex* (1848), 49, 70–1; *V.C.H. Essex*, v. 1–92.

[30] E. Marriage & Sons Ltd. *Annals of 100 years of Flour Milling*, 26–31; Booker, *Essex and Ind. Revolution*, 87–8; below, Mills.

[31] *E.C.S.* 15 Aug. 1845.

[32] Below, Fisheries.

In 1851 there were three maltings at the Hythe, convenient for the import of barley and for the export to London of malt.[33] Kimber, Gross & Nicholl's, founded in 1830 as a porter brewery behind St. Botolph's Street, had by 1851 become Charrington Nicholl's, and had moved to the bottom of East Hill. St. Botolph's beer brewery north of St. Giles's church was bought by J. P. Osborne *c.* 1835 and converted to a vinegar brewery, but ceased manufacture *c.* 1854. A brewery which C. Stopes had established at East Hill in 1828 was given to R. Hurnard in 1866 and became the Eagle brewery. Cobbold's, founded *c.* 1823, continued at North Hill. Daniell and Bishop were operating at the Castle brewery by 1863, and by 1869 had absorbed the small Northgate brewery off North Hill.[34] Of the two distilleries existing in 1835, the large Colchester Distillery at the Hythe run by George Savill, Robert Maitland Savill, and William Carrington closed in 1841, but the one in Culver Street survived until the 1870s.[35] In 1859 seven of the nine soda water and ginger beer makers in Essex were in Colchester, but by 1874 there were only four out of 17.[36]

Clothing and footwear were still supplied by small craftworkers and traders in 1851, when more than 1,100 people were employed in the clothing industry, many presumably working in their own homes, and almost 400 in boot and shoe manufacture in small workshops.[37] The introduction of bootmaking machinery, chiefly American, from the 1850s was encouraged, often with financial assistance, by F. W. Warmington & Co., tanners and leather merchants. Small and medium-sized firms could hire machines on lease, but production remained small-scale at first. The number of footwear businesses increased from 72 in 1848 to 97 in 1863 as population increased.[38]

Firms in the building industry were also small. In 1848 eight small brickmaking works, five of which were at Mile End, employed 26 men. In 1851 there were 455 tradesmen besides an unknown number of labourers employed in *c.* 38 building businesses.[39] Some of the supplies needed by the construction industry were provided by the town's early ironfoundries. The foundries, which maintained close links with the wider ironmongery trades and shops, had not been established solely to supply agricultural needs; farm implements retailed by local ironmongers were often bought from outside manufacturers.[40]

The foundries formed the basis for future expansion in the engineering industries. Wallis & Coleman's was one of the earliest ironfounding partnerships, but in 1834 Richard, son of the late Richard Coleman, set up on his own, converting former maltings in St. John's Street into engineering premises called the Abbeygate works. He remained involved with the building industry, erecting several iron bridges, including Colchester's new North bridge in 1843, and the Coggeshall gasworks, besides making agricultural implements which he exhibited at agricultural shows. He was bankrupted in 1846, but was able to resume business by 1847 having taken over premises in the Castle bailey. He ceased operating in Colchester in 1848 when he took over a Chelmsford foundry.[41] Charles Wallis continued his

33 *Census*, 1851; E.R.O., Q/RUm 2/112; Booker, *Essex and Ind. Revolution*, 73.

34 E.R.O., D/DEl B35/17; I. Peaty, *Essex Brewers and Malting and Hop Industries of the County*, 34, 36, 40; E.R.O., Acc. C210, J. B. Harvey Colln. v, pp. 275–6; *White's Dir. Essex* (1848), 101; (1863), 112; *Kelly's Dir. Essex* (1870), 71.

35 *E.R.* lix. 199; Brown, *Colch. 1815–1914*, 9.

36 Booker, *Essex and Ind. Revolution*, 71.

37 W. Hamley, 'Expansion of Victorian and Edwardian Colch.' *E. J.* xiv (2), 2.

38 *V.C.H. Essex*, ii. 487–8; *White's Dir. Essex* (1848), 100–1; (1863), 111-12.

39 *White's Dir. Essex* (1848), 101; *Census*, 1851.

40 Above, Georgian Colch. (Econ.); A. Phillips, 'Early Colch. foundries', *E.A.T.* 3rd ser. xiv. 102–10.

41 *E.A.T.* 3rd ser. xiv. 102–8; Brown, *Colch. 1815–1914*, 11–12.

father's business at the north-west end of High Street; after his death in 1849 the foundry was taken over by Thomas Catchpool, a local ironmonger and jobbing engineer who had close links with local farmers and whose foreman in the early years was James Paxman.[42] There were two other foundries, one operated in 1835 and possibly later by John Oakes and his son, and another set up in St. Botolph's Street by William Dearn, a nailmaker and ironmonger, by 1843, when he made the gates for the new town hall.[43]

The number of professionals was relatively small; in 1851 there were only 32 clergymen, 28 medical men, and 34 solicitors and lawyers.[44] Nevertheless the influence of the network of leading professionals and businessmen was very great, not only in the town's economic life but also socially and politically. Edward Williams, for example, honorary physician to the Essex and Colchester hospital 1837–49, was mayor four times.[45] F. B. Philbrick, who worked for the Liberals 1836–7 and 1880–4 and advised several public companies, was one of a succession of solicitors who exercised considerable power in the office of town clerk.[46]

Banking and insurance services became increasingly important in underpinning the local economy. In 1848 there were two small private banks, both in High Street: Mills, Bawtree, Errington, Bawtree, & Haddock, and Round, Green, & Co., the banking connexion of the Egerton Green and Round families dating from 1827.[47] The London & County Bank, which opened a High Street branch in 1852, was the first of the large amalgamated joint stock concerns to come to the town.[48] Banking services had also been extended to the working classes who could deposit small sums in Colchester Savings Bank, founded in 1817, which was also used by friendly societies.[49] The Essex & Suffolk Equitable Insurance Society, founded early in 1802 to provide fire insurance, continued as an influential institution. Charles Henry Hawkins, prominent in local politics, was one of its chairmen.[50] Specialized marine insurance was offered in 1846 by the Colchester Mutual Marine Insurance Society, which insured 70 ships, 17 of them from Colchester. The society was still operating in 1851.[51] The Colchester Permanent Benefit Building Society was founded in 1856, and the Colchester Co-operative Mutual Permanent Benefit Building Society in 1869.[52]

Industrial Growth to the Second World War

ECONOMIC CHANGE. In the late 19th and early 20th century Colchester remained an important market town for the surrounding rural area. Agriculture continued to prosper until *c.* 1875, after which it became depressed as food imports from overseas became increasingly competitive.[53] Even so, helped by the demands for goods and services of the increasing garrison in the town,[54] the local economy was able to diversify and expand, and by 1885, as agricultural depression deepened, new manufacturing enterprises were gradually helping to loosen the ties with farming. Provisions and equipment were needed for horses as well as for men at the garrison: in the 1870s, when there were *c.* 4,000 soldiers, there were also more

[42] E.R.O., D/DU 559/86; Brown, *Colch. 1815–1914*, 11, 24; for Paxman: below, this section, Industrial Growth, Engineering.

[43] *E.A.T.* 3rd ser. xiv. 107; E.R.O., D/F 23/1/41.

[44] *Census*, 1851; e.g. E.R.O., D/DU 559, papers of Dr. A. Wallace, physician.

[45] J. B. Penfold, *Hist. Essex County Hospital, Colch. 1820–1948*, 70–3.

[46] Phillips, *Ten Men*, 4.

[47] *White's Dir. Essex* (1848), 100; J. O. Parker, 'Early hist. Colch. banks', *E.R.* lxi. 39.

[48] *E.R.* lxi. 39; *White's Dir. Essex* (1863), 111.

[49] E.R.O., D/DEt F8; D/DU 551/1, 2.

[50] B. Drew, *The Fire Office, Hist. Essex and Suff. Insurance Soc. Ltd.* 29–30; Phillips, *Ten Men*, 69–70, 94; below, this chapter, Political Hist.

[51] E.R.O., D/DSu Z4.

[52] Below, this chapter, Town Development.

[53] *V.C.H. Essex*, ii. 339; *Rep. on Agricultural Distress in Essex* [C. 2778-II], pp. 366–7, H.C. (1881), xvi.

[54] *Essex Tel.* 10 Mar. 1885.

than 500 horses.[55] Demand for housing, clothing, and footwear, as for food and drink, retailing, laundering, and other services, was stimulated by population increase. Engineering developed substantially from the few small ironfoundries to become the leading industry by 1911. Firms in engineering, in the other leading manufacturing industries of footwear and clothing, and to a lesser extent in brewing, milling, and printing, gradually widened their markets at home, and some also abroad, especially in the Empire, and increasingly sought economies of scale in larger factories with modern machinery.[56] Boot and shoe manufacturers were among the leading firms in the 1890s but had disappeared by 1914, the factories mostly being taken over by clothing companies. The number of artisan workshops decreased in many different trades, but the expansion of the service sector, including the growth of both private and municipal public services, created new employment, some of it administrative and clerical. Because the town's industrial growth came later than in places in the north and midlands, it was less dependent on staple industries like cotton and iron and steel, which were threatened by competition from more recently industrialized countries in Europe and from the United States. Nevertheless, despite overall growth, there were periods of much economic uncertainty and frequent unemployment.

Railway services continued to improve, and local firms were keen to use them, capitalizing on the advantage of a fast link with markets in London and beyond. Some businessmen were already commuting daily to London before 1914.[57] The industrial centre at the Hythe expanded further, encouraged by the corporation's navigation improvement and the building of the King Edward quay between 1909 and 1912, and also because there remained a little space for new factories beside the railway.[58] In 1895 ships from London, the east coast, and South Wales brought wood, grain, stone, and coal to the Hythe; oysters, linseed oil, oil-cake, and general merchandise went to north European ports.[59] Between 1901 and 1912 Colchester was losing its share of the nationally increasing overseas trade, but gaining coastal trade. By 1912 nearly half of the small import trade was in timber, with Groom, Daniels & Co. the principal merchants. Parry's was an oil cake manufacturing and seed crushing firm.[60]

Cyclical economic fluctuations, increased mechanization, and more intense international competition caused variations in the demand for labour.[61] Deputations of unemployed men attended council meetings on many occasions demanding work not charity. Many families were reported in 1905 to be on the verge of starvation because of the breadwinners' lack of work, and some limited public works schemes were initiated by the council.[62] By 1910 the council considered local unemployment less serious than before, though the view was not shared by the unemployed.[63]

The First World War gave temporary stimulation to the production of food, the manufacture of munitions and uniforms, effective demands for higher wages, and the employment of women, but afterwards the problems of overcapacity in some parts of industry and of unemployment in the 1920s and 1930s were less severe in

55 A. F. F. H. Robertson, 'The army in Colch. and its influence on the social, economic and political development of the town, 1854–1914' (Essex Univ. Ph.D. thesis, 1991), 115–16.

56 Particular firms are treated later in this section.

57 E.R.O., SA 0677; Colch. Institute, Colch. Recalled, interview 1504.

58 Below, Port; Brown, *Colch. 1815–1914*, 34.

59 *Riparian Survey* [C. 7812], pp. 230–46, H.C. (1895), lii; J. R. McCallum, *Colch.'s Port: the Hythe and its Church*, 12.

60 *Kelly's Dir. Essex* (1902), 122, 142, 145; (1914), 161.

61 R. C. O. Matthews, C. H. Feinstein, and J. C. Odling-Smee, *British Economic Growth 1856–1973*, 321.

62 *E.C.S.* 7 Jan. 1905; *Essex Tel.* 4 Feb., 4 Mar. 1905; 9 Jan. 1909; below, this chapter, Political Hist.

63 *E.C.S.* 8 Jan., 5 Feb. 1910.

Colchester than they were in other parts of the country.[64] In 1921 the town had 2,282 registered unemployed (nearly 13 per cent of the total occupied population over 12, excluding men employed in defence), mainly because of depression in the wholesale clothing and engineering trades.[65] The local council undertook many schemes to provide work for the unemployed, claiming central government grants and loans where possible: in 1924–5 schemes included the widening of Ipswich and Mile End Roads, and the construction of a new quay and a railway siding extension at the Hythe.[66] Between 1930 and 1932 an average of *c.* 250 men a week were employed by the council in building the new bypass road, and another *c.* 20 were employed by contractors in haulage, quarrying, and other tasks; only *c.* 5 per cent of the men were brought in from depressed areas outside the borough.[67] The numbers unemployed nationally peaked in January 1933. In Colchester in the first half of 1933 on average 18 per cent of male industrial workers were out of work, but local unemployment was still increasing in early 1934 because of the discharge of men from the army. Recovery came in the later 1930s with changes in the national and international economy, and some changes in central government policies, including eventually rearmament, and some industrial reorganisation.[68] Colchester was well placed to take advantage of the growth of the new light industries in the south and east of England, and further expansion at the barracks was an additional stimulus to local trade. As conditions in more deeply depressed towns improved, the multiplier effect contributed to better economic prospects in Colchester.

Between the wars the port was further improved, King Edward quay being extended in 1925 and Haven quay built in the late 1930s, allowing larger vessels to berth, and port traffic increased during both World Wars. In 1935 grain, coal, special clay for making partition blocks, cement, linseed, timber, petrol, and road-making materials were imported by sea. Nevertheless rail and road communications were more significant for local manufacturing industries. St. Botolph's and the Hythe railway stations were used mainly for goods transport, and there were also private sidings. The Hythe district was an increasingly important industrial centre for the town, the new electricity power station being opened there in 1926 and new firms moving in during the 1920s and 1930s.[69] The coastal coal trade, carried on in ships owned mainly by northerners, continued until the mid 20th century.[70]

By the 1930s, despite the further expansion of the barracks, the town had lost ground to Chelmsford, which, as a county and cathedral town and an important centre of the new electrical and light engineering industries, was seen as the main economic rival. Although small businesses and larger family firms still dominated the private sector, the concentration in some industries into fewer and larger firms and the introduction of new technology had already begun. In Colchester as elsewhere the public sector continued to grow. Employment opportunities were starting to widen, although most unskilled workers and women still had very limited choices.[71] During the late 19th and early 20th century as a whole, despite economic depression and periods of unemployment, the standard of living at all

[64] E.R.O., Acc. C3, Colch. boro. council newspaper cuttings, *passim*.

[65] *E.C.S.* 12 Feb. 1921; *Census*, 1921.

[66] *E.C.S.* 5 Feb. 1921; *Essex Tel.* 5 July 1924.

[67] *E.C.S.* 10 Dec. 1932.

[68] Ibid. 10 Feb. 1934; B. Swann and M. Turnbull, *Recs. of Interest to Social Scientists 1919–39, Employment and Unemployment*, 19–22.

[69] e.g. *Colch. Official Guide* (1935), pp. 30–1; C. Cockerill and D. Woodward, *The Hythe, Port, Church and Fishery* [19]; McCallum, *Colch. Port*, 12; below, Port.

[70] H. Benham, *Once upon a Tide*, 62, 67.

[71] Phillips, *Colch. in Old Photographs*, 19–44.

levels improved, with a wider range of goods and services available, and working class people, when in employment, increasingly had money for pleasure as well as for necessities. The effects of periods of unemployment and sickness were mitigated by improved public services and less severe poor-relief policies.[72]

OCCUPATIONAL STRUCTURE. By 1911 (Tables XI and XII) the structure of local employment showed some significant changes from that of the mid 19th century, with engineering and machine making becoming the leading male occupational category (not counting defence, which occupied more than a quarter

TABLE XI: PRINCIPAL OCCUPATIONS, 1901

Males aged 10 or more *Occupation*	*number*	*per cent excluding defence*
Building and construction	1,396	15
Engineering and machine making	1,379	15
Conveyance of men, goods, messages	1,281	14
Food, tobacco, drink, lodging	1,058	11
Dress	877	9
Agriculture: farms, woods, gardens	704	7
Other occupations	2,723	29
Total excluding those in defence (omitted for comparative purposes)	9,418	100
Defence (29%)	3,921	
Total including those in defence	13,339	

Females aged 10 or more *Occupation*	*number*	*per cent*
Domestic service	1,578	30
Tailoring	1,289	25
Other dress	569	11
Laundry	351	7
Food, tobacco, drink, lodging	216	4
Other occupations	1,212	23
Total	5,215	100

Percentages have been calculated to the nearest whole number

Source: *Census*, 1901

of the men in the town). Conveyance of men, goods, and messages took second place, the railways alone employing 367 men, whilst numbers in the construction industry, which came third, remained about the same as in 1901 (when it had narrowly been first) but constituted a smaller proportion of the increased population. Employment was growing in food, tobacco, drink, and lodging, and also in agriculture because of increased market gardening and flower growing. Dress

[72] Colch. Institute, Colch. Recalled project, *passim*.

(clothing and footwear) employed fewer men than in 1901 because of the decline of the boot and shoe industry. In 1911 most employed women and girls were in domestic service, while tailoring and other dress trades were increasing slightly, as new clothing firms started up. More women worked in shops as retailing expanded, and clerical work was becoming a significant occupation, with 259 women employed. A few women, 231 by 1911, were able to follow careers in teaching, provided they remained unmarried, but employment opportunities for women of all classes remained much more limited than those for their male counterparts.[73]

TABLE XII: PRINCIPAL OCCUPATIONS, 1911

Males aged 10 or more *Occupation*	*number*	*per cent excluding defence*
Engineering and machine making	1,552	13
Conveyance of men, goods, messages	1,512	13
Building and construction	1,384	12
Food, tobacco, drink, lodging	1,366	12
Agriculture: farms, woods, gardens	838	7
Dress	658	6
Labouring, including in factories	517	4
Other occupations	3,751	32
Total excluding those in defence (omitted for comparative purposes)	11,578	100
Defence (26%)	4,095	
Total including those in defence	15,673	

Females aged 10 or more *Occupation*	*number*	*per cent*
Domestic service (not hotels)	1,582	27
Tailoring	1,384	24
Other dress	604	10
Food, drink, lodging	500	9
Laundry	356	6
Various clerical	259	4
Other occupations	1,255	22
Total	5,792	100

Percentages have been calculated to the nearest whole number

Source: *Census*, 1911

In 1921 (Table XIII) engineering was still the leading industry. Transport and communications were still in second place, with 688 men working in road transport, many of them on trams and buses. The construction industry had lost ground, the war having brought building almost to a standstill. New employment opportunities

[73] *Census*, 1901, 1911.

were opening up in the service sector with growth in commerce, finance, and insurance, and in public administration as central and local government expanded. More than a third of working women worked in personal service, over half of them (1,455) in domestic service although the number had already started to fall slightly. The clothing industry was still the second greatest source of female employment, but office work, usually of a routine type, was increasingly available. Already in

TABLE XIII: PRINCIPAL OCCUPATIONS, 1921

Males aged 12 or more *Occupation*	*number*	*per cent excluding defence*
Metal workers, engineering, etc.	2,003	17
Transport and communications	1,540	13
Commercial, finance, insurance (excluding clerks)	1,432	12
Builders, etc. and painters	854	7
Agricultural	829	7
Wood and furniture	568	5
Clerks, draughtsmen, typists (excluding civil service and local authority)	494	4
Textile-goods manufacture and dress	492	4
Personal service	490	4
Professional	461	4
Food, drink, and tobacco manufacture	336	3
Public administration (excluding professional and typists)	333	3
Paper, including printers	274	2
Warehousemen, storekeepers, packers	265	2
Electrical	167	1
Other	1,532	12
Total excluding those in defence (omitted for comparative purposes)	12,070	100
Defence (9%)	1,249	
Total including those in defence	13,319	

Females aged 12 or more *Occupation*	*number*	*per cent*
Personal service	2,135	35
Textile goods manufacture and dress	1,582	28
Commercial, finance, insurance (excluding clerks)	654	11
Professional	574	10
Clerks, draughtswomen, typists (excluding civil service and local authority)	405	7
Paper, including printers	102	2
Other	292	5
Total	5,744	100

Percentages have been calculated to the nearest whole number

Source: *Census, 1921*

1921 retailing employed 495 men and 498 women, and by the early 1930s as many as 50 motor buses and coaches daily were bringing people from a radius of *c.* 25 miles for shopping.[74] In Chelmsford developments were similar, except that clothing was a minor industry and work was available instead for men and women in the growing electrical industry and, for women particularly, in offices.[75]

ENGINEERING. Thomas Catchpool & Son in High Street, later Catchpool, Stannard, & Stanford, and then Stanford & Co., continued to specialize in farming equipment. The firm grew into a small manufacturing company, and by 1890 was exporting to home and foreign markets, and had also diversified into marine engine repairs. It closed in 1924.[76]

Dearn's foundry, near St. Botolph's station, was taken over in 1861 by Joseph Blomfield, an ironmonger, and his partner Thomas Mayhew Bear, who developed the Britannia works alongside Dearn's. The firm also had a London depot and showroom for *c.* 20 years. It made sewing machines, and in 1871 employed 105 people, but by the 1880s the Singer Co. dominated the sewing machine market, and the Britannia works switched to making machine tools and oil engines, supplying markets all over Britain and accepting government contracts. By 1900 the firm was in difficulties and was taken over by Victor, Hugh, and Percy Nicholson, who also made motor cars on the site, but without much success. The works were closed *c.* 1912, but reopened in 1914 for munitions work. In 1918 the Britannia Lathe & Oil Engine Co. was operating again, still owned by the Nicholsons. It closed in 1938.[77]

In 1865 James Paxman, who had been Catchpool's chief engineer from 1851, set up Davey, Paxman & Co., an engineering firm, in Culver Street, helped by capital provided by C. M. and H. M. Davey. In 1873 he opened a second factory, the Standard ironworks, off Hythe Hill, but continued to operate at Culver Street simultaneously until 1877 when, faced with a major liquidity crisis during a recession in engineering, he sold that business to A. G. Mumford. Paxman took over the entire remaining Davey Paxman business when the Daveys retired. Many new types of engines and steam boilers were made for export, being exhibited at international exhibitions and winning prizes. Paxman's engines lit the 1889 Paris exhibition, and from 1898 were used in Colchester's municipal electricity undertaking. The firm's products included engines for South African mines, refrigerating equipment for ships, and generators for factories and tramways. In 1898 Paxman's became a limited liability company, the shares being held mostly by Paxman's friends and family. Wilson Marriage joined the Paxmans in the directorship, and Percy Sanders was managing director from 1912. In 1915 the works covered more than 11 a. and employed nearly 1,000 people. During the First World War women were employed and new machinery was built to carry out secret war work for the government.[78]

The wartime interruption of international trade caused Paxman's to lose many of its overseas markets. In 1920 it joined with other firms to become Agricultural and General Engineers Ltd., which in 1926 was critical of the outdated methods used at the Standard ironworks. A.G.E. collapsed in 1932 and the Colchester part

[74] *Census, 1921*; *Colch. Official Guide* [1933–4], 24; *Kelly's Dir. Essex* (1933), 169–184.

[75] *Census*, 1921.

[76] *V.C.H. Essex*, ii. 496; *Industries of E. Counties* (*c.* 1890, Essex County Libr. reprint 1982), 192; *Kelly's Dir. Essex* (1922), 184; (1926), 194.

[77] E.R.O., D/F 23/1/35, D/F 23/1/41; Brown, *Colch. 1815–1914*, 23–4; *Inds. of E. Counties*, 177.

[78] E.R.O., D/F 23/2/11, D/F 23/2/174–81; *E.C.S.* 23 Feb. 1962; inf. from Mr. A. Phillips based on private Paxman papers; below, pl. facing p. 217.

was re-formed as Davey, Paxman (Colchester) Ltd., which in 1940 acquired the derelict Britannia Works. Improvements made under the leadership of E. P. Paxman resulted in the successful production of diesel engines, large quantities of which were produced for military purposes in the Second World War.[79]

A. G. Mumford, having bought Paxman's building in Culver Street in 1877, traded as the Culver Street Ironworks, employing *c.* 300 people by 1907 and specializing in steam pumps and small marine engines, many for British and foreign governments.[80] The firm closed in 1933, partly because the next generation of the Mumford family did not want to continue the business; the pump work continued under Truslove's in Brown's old silk factory.[81] Four engineering firms established between 1899 and 1907 at the Hythe survived the depression: Brackett's, the Colchester Lathe Co., the Pasley Engineering Co., and Wood's. Engineering firms benefitted in the 1940s from the demands of a wartime economy. Wood's, manufacturers of fans, expanded its workforce to nearly 1,000, including many women, to supply large quantities of equipment for ships, and also wireless and transmitting sets. The Lathe Co. mass-produced lathes on a larger scale. Colchester firms co-operated closely in wartime, with Paxman's providing engines and Wood's ventilation for tanks, and Mason's, a printing firm, supplying other tank components.[82]

FOOTWEAR. In the 1860s T. Harbour increased his workforce to *c.* 50 when he added a second workshop in St. Botolph's Street to his existing one in High Street. About 1860 S. G. Knopp obtained machinery from Warmington & Co., tanners and leather merchants, to make shoes in Hythe Street, and, pleased with mechanization, he built his 'Time Will Tell' factory in 1870 in Portland Road, where in 1871 he was employing 61 people, making high quality footwear for retail outlets in London and other large towns. The premises were enlarged in 1889–90, when the home demand was so great that the firm was unable to accept foreign contracts. A. C. George built a boot and shoe factory in 1881 at the corner of Kendal Road and Charles Street, and in 1890 employed more than 120 people and sold his boots and shoes all over England. W. Warren, who had a shop in High Street, another in Short Wyre Street, and a factory in Eld Lane, employed about 50 men in 1890. John Kavanagh started in the trade by repairing army boots and renovating rejected ones for resale.[83] He set up a factory in part of St. Botolph's brewery in Stanwell Street, and by 1889, when it was seriously damaged by fire, he was employing 300 people, and supplying nine London shops and a Liverpool trader. He opened a new factory lit by electricity, and had 370 employees in 1892, overtaking Knopp as the leading footwear manufacturer.[84]

The industry declined locally in the early 20th century, and by 1907 only Knopp's and George's remained of the earlier large firms.[85] G. S. Knopp, who had become sole proprietor in 1900 and made Knopp's a limited liability company in 1906, died in 1907, and the firm apparently closed soon afterwards.[86] George's factory had been sold by 1910 to E. Rose & Co., calendar-makers.[87] The 64 boot- and shoe-makers and 24 repairers remaining in 1914 were mostly very small businesses.

79 J. Booker, 'Davey, Paxman & Co.' *Business Archives*, xxxv. 12–13; E.R.O., SA 0396; ibid. D/F 23/2/179.

80 *V.C.H. Essex*, ii. 498–9; *Inds. of E. Counties*, 189.

81 Inf. from Mr. A. Phillips.

82 Brown, *Colch. 1815–1914*, 32; *E.C.S.* 29 Sept. 1919; inf. from Mr. A. Phillips.

83 *V.C.H. Essex*, ii. 487–8; Brown, *Colch. 1815–1914*, 25, 27–9; *Inds. of E. Counties*, 182, 186, 196.

84 *Essex Tel.* 29 Jan. 1889; E.R.O., Acc. C210, J. B. Harvey Colln. v, pp. 275–6; *Building News*, lviii. 644 and illus.; Brown, *Colch. 1815–1914*, 28; below, pl. facing p. 233.

85 *V.C.H. Essex*, ii. 488.

86 *Essex Tel.* 20 Apr. 1907.

87 *Kelly's Dir. Essex* (1910), 177.

Buckingham's in Head Street and Potter & Fisher's in Priory Street were relatively large, but footwear manufacture was no longer a great source of employment.[88]

CLOTHING. Some of the tailoring firms, who had been supplying outwork in the area set up factories. Moses and Simon Hyam, sons of Hyam Hyam, continued his clothing business; based in London, the firm was trading from St. Botolph's Street in 1863, but by 1870 had opened a new factory in Abbeygate Street with modern cutting and sewing machines.[89] Messrs. Hammond & Co. started in 1854 and by 1871 had *c.* 500 employees, some at their Stanwell Street factory and others working at home. H. E. & M. Moses, another London business, traded in Colchester between 1855 and *c.* 1898, opening a factory in Priory Street by 1863. In 1865 six large firms were reportedly employing 2,500 females and 200 males.[90] The clothing trade expanded as the footwear industry declined. By 1907 when Hyam's was employing 300 people at the Abbeygate Works and many others on outwork, it was considered the largest English wholesale firm dealing exclusively in ready-made clothing. Several other new local firms followed Hyam's model, including Senior, Heap & Co. established in 1890, which was taken over by Crowther's in 1900.[91] Hollington Brothers of Aldgate took over Kavanagh's boot factory in 1899 for ready-made clothing manufacture. H. Leaning & Co., wholesale clothing manufacturer specializing in men's wear, took over Knopp's 'Time Will Tell' boot factory by 1913.[92] Hart & Levy were wholesale clothiers in Magdalen Street.[93] In 1911 the Colchester firms probably employed thousands of outworkers within a radius of 20 miles.[94] Between the wars the large firms survived the depression. The Colchester Manufacturing Co., previously Hammond's, was run from the 1890s by members of the Turner family, specializing in summer clothing, often for government contracts. Peake's in East Stockwell Street, the only new firm to appear, specialized in bespoke men's wear.[95]

BREWING. The larger breweries, using new mechanized methods, grew at the expense of the smaller ones. The Stopes family, owners of Eagle brewery on East Hill, took over Cobbold's on North Hill in 1882. Those two breweries were merged in 1886 with the firm of Arthur T. Osborne, son of J. P. Osborne, which had 70 tied houses, to form the Colchester Brewing Co. which in 1894 owned 319 licensed houses, 63 of them in Colchester.[96] In 1887 the Daniell brothers at Castle brewery merged with Daniell & Son at West Bergholt, and by 1892 production was entirely at West Bergholt. The larger breweries competed with each other for control of tied houses whose numbers were limited by the licensing laws.[97] Charrington Nicholl's at East Hill remained a family firm supplying its own public houses until it was taken over *c.* 1920 by Colchester Brewing Co., which in turn in 1925 became part of Ind Coope's, which merged with Allsopp's in 1934; the takeovers were designed to accumulate more tied houses rather than more brewing plant.[98] Mallison's in William's Walk, a mineral water manufacturing business previously

88 *Kelly's Dir. Essex* (1914), 177–91; Brown, *Colch. 1815–1914*, 29.

89 *V.C.H. Essex*, ii. 484; *White's Dir. Essex* (1863), 123; *Kelly's Dir. Essex* (1870), 73.

90 *V.C.H. Essex*, ii. 483–4; Brown, *Colch. 1815–1914*, 24–5; Colch. Recalled, interview 2255.

91 *V.C.H. Essex*, ii. 484; *E.C.S.* 28 June 1968; Colch. Recalled, interview 2255; below, pl. facing p. 233.

92 Colch. Recalled, interview 2250; *V.C.H. Essex*, ii. 483–4; *Inds. of E. Counties*, 175, 183, 188–9, 195; *Colch. Official Guide* [*c.* 1920], 52; Phillips, *Colch. in Old Photographs*, 35, 37.

93 *Kelly's Dir. Essex* (1910), 173.

94 *Essex Tel.* 9 Dec. 1911.

95 *Kelly's Dir. Essex* (1937), 696; E.R.O., Acc. 6072, papers of Colch. Manufacturing Co.; *Essex Jnl.* xxviii (1), pp. 8–13; inf. from Mr. A. Phillips.

96 I. Peaty, *Essex Brewers*, 40–1; Colch. Brewing Co. recs. in possession of Ind Coope, Morland House, Romford.

97 I. Peaty, *Essex Brewers*, 43.

98 Booker, *Essex and Ind. Revolution*, 68; below, pl. facing p. 233.

owned by Charrington Nicholl's, in 1890 produced 1,500 dozen bottles a day using modern plant and had works and stores in other towns in eastern England;[99] by 1914 it was known as Colchester Table Waters Ltd., one of five mineral water manufacturers based in Colchester.[1]

MILLING. Milling became concentrated in a few larger, mechanized mills.[2] The Marriage family's business at East mill became a leading firm in the region, keeping abreast of the latest developments. In 1878 the 10 pairs of millstones were augmented with two sets of rollers, and by 1890 at least 2,500 sacks of finished flour were produced every week. The firm was controlled by the government in the First World War, and afterwards had problems of excess capacity because bread consumption fell as the standard of living improved. It managed to modernize and diversify to produce a wide range of goods: feeding stuffs, biscuit flour made from home-grown wheat, bread flour made mostly from colonial and some Russian wheat, and, until the millstone mill was dismantled in 1931, special stoneground Passover flour. Between the wars it took over Chopping's of Fingringhoe and Marriage and Hicks's at Bury St. Edmunds.[3]

PRINTING. The publication and printing of local newspapers provided a base for later expansion in the printing industry. By 1870 Benham's, a general printing firm which also produced the *Essex Standard*, employed 25 men. Newspaper proprietors included J. B. Harvey, John Taylor, and members of the Benham family, all influential figures in the town.[4] Wiles's was founded in 1869 and expanded, as did the general printing side of both the *Essex Standard* and the *Essex Telegraph* newspapers. Cullingford's printing firm was founded in 1885, and by 1913 employed 36 apprentices and printers at the works in East Stockwell Street and also had a shop in High Street. Mason's was started in 1905 as a small photographic printing business, which also produced the blueprint paper and drawing office equipment needed by local engineering firms; it pioneered photocopying. The firm grew large, diversifying into a wide range of office supplies, and opened the Arclight works in Maidenburgh Street in 1921. Rose's, calendar printers on North Hill, took over George's shoe factory in Kendal Road but remained a small-scale business. In 1908 Spottiswoode's, a large London printing firm, came to the Hythe. The printing industry survived the depression reasonably well and the number of local firms increased from 11 to 15 between 1922 and 1937. Cullingford's opened a new works in East Stockwell Street in 1927, but had some difficulties during the worst years of the depression and in 1932 temporarily reduced employees' wages. It introduced new technology from the late 1930s. Mason's expanded, in 1933 opening a branch factory in Magdalen Street for manufacturing sensitized paper, and in 1938 moving the Arclight works to a new factory in Cowdray Avenue.[5] During the Second World War Mason's developed greatly, producing equipment for cameras for aircraft reconnaissance, for war maps, and for tank landing craft, as well as supplying office furniture.[6]

GROWTH OF OTHER SECTORS. The manufacture and retailing of food and drink continued to expand, and the range of food was widened with imports from the Empire

[99] *Inds. of E. Counties*, 187.

[1] *Kelly's Dir. Essex* (1914), 1039.

[2] *V.C.H. Essex*, ii. 446–7; below, Mills.

[3] E. Marriage & Sons Ltd. *Annals of 100 Years of Flour Milling*, 26–31, 49–55; *Inds. of E. Counties*, 188; E.R.O., SA 0391, 0677–9.

[4] Brown, *Colch. 1815–1914*, 32; *V.C.H. Essex*, ii. 472–3; below, this chapter, Political Hist.; Soc. and Cultural (Newspapers).

[5] Cullingford & Co. Ltd. *Hist. Cullingfords*, [5–12]; Brown, *Colch. 1815–1914*, 32–3; *Kelly's Dir. Essex* (1922), 839–40; (1937), 1095–6; *E.C.S.* 19 May 1972.

[6] Inf. from Mr. A. Phillips.

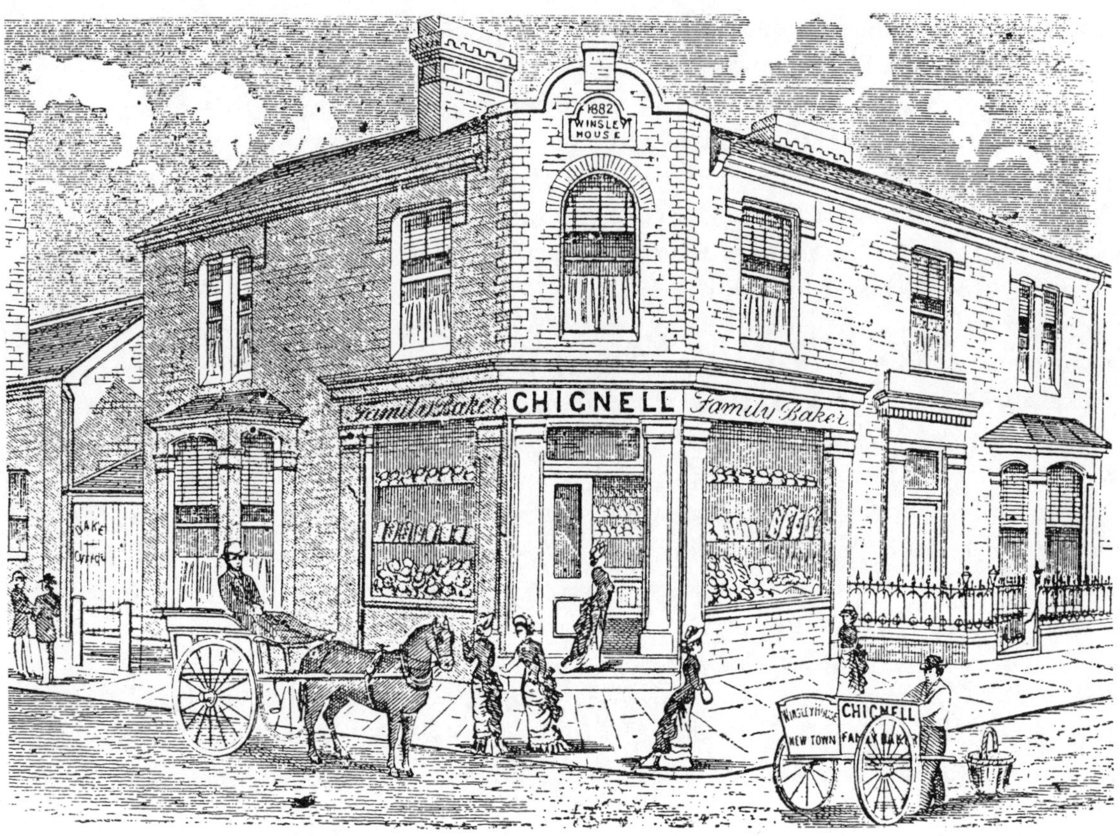

FIG. 14. A SHOP IN NEW TOWN IN THE 1880S

by retailers like Evatt Sanders & Son.[7] Many new shops and public houses were established to serve the barracks, and most food was still sold in small neighbourhood stores.[8] By 1911 the Colchester Co-operative Society was one of the largest retailers and wholesalers. It had been founded in 1861 by John Castle, a foreman in the silk industry; other skilled men including James Paxman were trustees, and the first shop opened in Culver Street. The business moved to new premises behind St. Nicholas's church in 1864–5. Much of the Co-op's growth was in New Town, which was developed from the 1880s, and by 1889 a bakery, the first grocery branch, and a butchery had opened there, besides two other butcheries in North Station Road and at the town centre site. In the 1890s the Co-op opened grocery stores at Lexden and Rowhedge, and coal depots at St. Botolph's and the Hythe. By 1911 when the first motor van was added to the 27 horse-drawn vehicles already in use for deliveries to Co-op shops, there were shops in High Street and Wyre Street, and in 1926, when a modern bakery was established in Kendall Road, transport consisted of 36 horse-drawn and 16 motor vehicles. In 1928 the Co-op opened a dairy in Wimpole Road.[9]

As the built-up area of the town grew, not only in New Town, the construction industry provided many new jobs, mostly in small family firms, though the work was often casual. In 1871 Everett's, one of the largest, employed 45 skilled men, 41 labourers, and 2 boys.[10]

The cultivation of fruit, vegetables, and flowers by small family businesses was still widespread, and produce could be transported quickly by railway to London.[11]

7 *Inds. of E. Counties*, 192, 194–5.

8 *Kelly's Dir. Essex* (1902), 125.

9 E.R.O., D/DU 490; H. W. Lewington, *Brief Hist. Acct. Colch. Co-op. Soc.*; Colch. Co-op. Soc. *100 Up, Centenary Story of Colch. Co-op.* 25: copy in E.R.O., D/DU 490A.

10 Below, this chapter, Town Development; Brown, *Colch. 1815–1914*, 126; E.R.O., Acc. C249, Working drawings of H. Everett & Son, builders.

11 *Kelly's Dir. Essex* (1929), 154; E.R.O., SA 0396.

Benjamin Cant's nursery business, which was established in 1853 and moved to Mile End in 1879, and his nephew Frank Cant's rose farm, established at Braiswick in 1875, both developed into specialist rose-growing enterprises of national and international repute. The work was still labour intensive in the early 20th century; at Mile End *c.* 50 people were employed outdoors and a few more in the office, and extra, temporary, workers were taken on seasonally for budding and other tasks.[12] The bulk of business was in field roses and seedlings, but supplying petals for rose-tipped cigarettes was an unusual sideline; as newer methods were introduced the number of employees fell from more than 50 before 1914 to 30–40 by the 1930s.[13]

The service sector, which included public services and hospitals, gradually employed more people. By 1899 the borough council had *c.* 280 employees; by 1907 about half of its wages bill was spent on its 200 teachers. In 1912 new jobs were provided when the Post Office made Colchester a regional telephone centre.[14] Banking was increasingly centralized in national banks. In 1891 Round, Green, Hoare, & Co. merged with Gurney's of Norwich, and later the same year took over the business of Mills, Bawtree, Dawnay, Curzon, & Co. which had collapsed. Barclay's of London in turn took over the business of Gurney's and Round, Green, & Co. in 1896. Parr's bank opened in 1899. By 1911 there were five banks: Parr's, two branches of Barclay's, London & County, and Capital & Counties; there were two building societies, the Equitable and the Permanent Benefit. In 1918 Parr's bank was absorbed by the London & County which amalgamated with the Westminster bank. Insurance services were provided by the Essex and Suffolk Equitable, Colchester Mutual Plate Glass, and the Association for the Protection of Property.[15]

Business and professional people, as well as the gentry, invested their capital in new ventures both at home and abroad. Leading shareholders in the Colchester Brewing Co. included London merchants and bankers, besides notable local people like Thomas Osborne, merchant of Lexden, Thomas Moy, coal merchant of Stanway Hall, and Arthur Stopes, brewer of East Hill; a few shares were held by working men like T. Moy's butler and his gardener, who probably received them as gifts from their employer.[16] The far-reaching investment interests of the physician, Alexander Wallace, were probably similar to those of other local professional and business men: he acquired brochures about photographic apparatus in Britain and Italy, timber in Australia, goldmining in Canada, and the development of the Chinese imperial railway.[17]

INDUSTRIAL RELATIONS. The growth of trade unionism locally had been hindered in the mid 19th century by the effects of low wages and by the fact that most workers still worked in small, relatively isolated units. Wages were kept low by the recruitment of factory workers from the depressed surrounding agricultural area, especially in Suffolk, by the use of women, including soldiers' wives, and young people, and by the continuing prevalence of tailoring outwork in the clothing industry.[18] Low wages were likewise widespread in Norwich where there was a

[12] *V.C.H. Essex*, ii. 481; *E.C.S.* 14 Oct. 1911; E.R.O., SA 0670.

[13] E.R.O., SA 0670, 0672.

[14] Brown, *Colch. 1815-1914*, 33.

[15] *E.R.* lxi. 39; *Colch. Almanac 1911*, [57–8].

[16] E.R.O., Acc. C235, Box 2, list in middle of large notebk. of Capt. R.

[17] E.R.O., D/DU 559/19.

[18] *1st Rep. Select Cttee. on Sweating System* [361], pp. 893–4, 896, 902, H.C. (1888), xx; *V.C.H. Essex*, ii. 337; E.R.O., T/Z 25/265–6; B. Westover, 'The Sexual Division of Labour in the Tailoring Industry, 1860–1920' (Essex Univ. Ph.D. thesis, 1984), *passim*.

similarly declining agricultural hinterland.[19] Colchester's developing engineering industry, however, like that at Chelmsford, also recruited some skilled workers from other parts of the country.[20]

In 1844 skilled men formed a branch of the Tailors' Protection Society and in 1867 were connected with the Amalgamated Society of Tailors. Shoemakers were organized long before 1840 and in 1853 they gained a wage increase from most employers. In the same year local carpenters, aware that building workers could command higher wages in London, successfully went on strike for more pay. The Colchester United Assistants' Association was formed in 1844 and its efforts together with middle class support achieved a gradual reduction in the opening hours of shops. The poorly paid girls at the silk factory in St. Peter's Street between 1843 and 1872 occasionally took industrial action but with little result in a declining industry. Skilled workers were usually better organized. A small local branch of the Amalgamated Society of Carpenters and Joiners was formed in 1863 by John Howe, but it functioned more like a friendly society than a union, with no rules about strike pay. Although there was a dispute in the engineering industry in 1872, a branch of the Amalgamated Society of Engineers was not established until 1882, probably because of the paternalism of James Paxman at the Standard ironworks and Joseph Blomfield at the Britannia works. A branch of the National Union of Boot and Shoe Riveters was set up in 1882.[21]

Factory work brought changes in working practices and the possibility of greater control by employers, but also provided better opportunities for workers to promote trade unionism. By 1891 workers at three of the largest factories were summoned to work and dismissed by a steam whistle, a sign of changing work patterns.[22] In the early 1890s trade union membership increased among unskilled as well as skilled workers, and Colchester Trades Council, founded in 1891 by John Howe, set rates of pay in 1894 ranging from 4*d.* an hour for labourers to 7*d.* for skilled building workers, which were agreed by the men and the employers' association. Union membership declined between 1896 and 1900, mainly because of economic recession but also because of political divisions in the labour movement.[23]

Most Colchester trade unionists were not militant, and disputes were few. The 1892 dispute at Kavanagh's boot factory, caused by his imposition of fines for lateness and absenteeism, resulted in union blacklisting of his firm. Knopp's was able to modernize its working practices in a less threatening fashion.[24] In 1906 a borough council employee, supported by his union, successfully took court action for alleged unfair dismissal; thereafter unions could assert that even council employees could benefit from trade union protection.[25] Paxman's factory was unexpectedly brought to a standstill for a few days in 1910 over the appointment of a 'speediator' or rate-fixer to reduce the price paid for piecework. The strike ended when the speediator resigned, as had happened in a similar dispute three months earlier at Hoffman's in Chelmsford. The Paxman's strikers were commended for their orderly behaviour, and many of them felt that the strike could have been avoided if the paternalistic James Paxman had not been ill at the time.[26]

[19] S. Cherry, *Doing Different? Politics and the Labour Movement in Norwich*, 8–11.

[20] *Census*, 1881 (ref. supplied by Mr. A. Phillips); S. Durgan, 'Laissez-faire and Interventionism in Housing: Chelmsford 1900–14, a Case Study' (Essex Univ. M.A. thesis, 1981), 15.

[21] Brown, *Colch. 1815–1914*, 124–33.

[22] *E.C.S.* 7 Feb. 1891.

[23] Brown, *Colch. 1815–1914*, 136–45; *Essex Tel.* 14 July 1894; below, this chapter, Political Hist.

[24] S. Birch, 'The Troubled Boot and Shoe Trade in Colch. during the 1890s' (Essex Univ. History B.A. project).

[25] *Essex Tel.* 12 May 1906.

[26] Ibid. 3, 7, 10, 14 May, 1910; *East Anglian Hist. Workshop Jnl.* ii (2), pp. 4–8.

Trade unions were able to negotiate wage rises and improved conditions in the days of full employment, high food prices, and inflation during the First World War, and immediately afterwards. A 48-hour week was agreed for council manual employees in 1919, but a few months later tramways employees were apparently conceded an extra 4*s.* a week only after they threatened to strike.[27] National disputes, like one in the engineering industry in 1922, sometimes affected local firms, but unions were inevitably in a weak position when unemployment was high, and militancy was not the preferred style of employees who still mostly worked in family businesses run on paternalistic lines. Even after James Paxman's death in 1922 his firm retained much of his personal style.[28] The General Strike of 1926 had far less impact than in places where labour relations were more abrasive.[29]

Employers responded to growing trade unionism by forming their own organizations. Colchester Chamber of Commerce was founded in 1904, encouraged by E. H. Barritt, a dispensing chemist, one of the many mayors who were active businessmen.[30] In 1911 it was amalgamated with the Colchester Trade Protection Society to promote members' interests and regulate local trade.[31] Freemasonry was also an important organ of mutual help for employers, and a significant local economic and political network, the number of masonic lodges increasing from 8 in 1917 to 11 in 1927.[32]

The Pre-eminence of the Service Sector

The Second World War, like the First, brought full employment and further state intervention in industry, and was a great stimulus to the town's manufacturing industries. The local engineering and clothing firms again played an important part in the war effort.[33] In the immediate post-war period interventionist reconstruction policies, particularly in housing, transport, and health and welfare, initiated and partly funded by central government, enabled full employment to continue locally. The town still provided an agricultural market for the surrounding rural area where large quantities of milk, fruit, and vegetables were produced, and was increasingly also regarded as as an administrative, commercial, and cultural centre for north-east Essex.[34] The local economy prospered in the general expansion of the 1950s and 1960s, with the engineering firms enjoying their heyday in the 1960s. The service sector grew especially fast, supported by rapid population growth. The public sector gradually employed a greater proportion of the occupied population until the late 1980s. Commuting, both in and out of the town, increased. Manufacturing was affected adversely by the fuel crises of the 1970s and subsequent periods of recession, and suffered a serious decline in the 1980s. Policies of rationalization and technological change often reduced the demand of firms for manpower. The garrison, the large number of hospitals, and, from 1961, Essex University, were stabilizing influences in a rapidly changing economic structure.[35]

27 *E.C.S.* 6 Oct. 1917; 10 May, 9 Aug. 1919.

28 Ibid. 20 Mar. 1922; E.R.O., Acc. C448, Marriage's notices to employees, 1884–1952; E.R.O., SA 0675.

29 Below, this chapter, Political Hist.

30 *Essex Tel.* 20 Feb. 1904; below, this chapter, Political Hist.

31 *Colch. Gaz.* 23 Feb. 1977; *E.C.S.* 22 Apr. 1916; Colch. Charter 800 Assn. *Colch. 800*, 76.

32 *Colch. Almanac 1911* [53]; *Kelly's Dir. Essex* (1917), 157; Ward, Lock & Co. *Colch. & District Guide* [1927], 1.

33 E.R.O., Acc. C3, dated boro. council newspaper cuttings, 1914–18, 1939–45; E.R.O., D/F 23/2/179; Colch. Recalled, interview 2246.

34 Essex C.C. *Essex Development Plan, Rep. of Survey, Colch. 1952*, 63, 65.

35 E.R.O., Acc. C3, dated boro. council newspaper cuttings 1945–53; Essex C.C. Planning papers.

TABLE XIV: PRINCIPAL OCCUPATIONS, 1951

Males aged 15 or more *Occupation*	*number*	*per cent excluding defence*
Metal manufacture, engineering, etc.	2,720	19
Commercial, finance, etc. (excluding clerical)	1,733	12
Transport	1,522	10
Builders, etc., including painters	1,370	9
Clerks, typists	1,121	8
Professional, technical (excluding clerical)	1,059	7
Unskilled	1,011	7
Personal service	686	5
Agriculture and horticulture	584	4
Other	2,819	19
Total excluding those in defence (omitted for comparative purposes)	14,625	100
Defence (20%)	3,734	
Total including those in defence	18,359	

Females aged 15 or more *Occupation*	*number*	*per cent*
Personal service	2,013	29
Clerks, typists	1,422	20
Commercial, finance, etc. (excluding clerical)	946	13
Professional, technical (excluding clerical)	941	13
Textile goods manufacture and dress	769	11
Transport	147	2
Paper, including printers	118	2
Other	707	10
Total	7,063	100

Percentages have been calculated to the nearest whole number

Source: *Census*, 1951

In 1951 (Table XIV) engineering and metal manufacture was the leading male occupational category (excluding the 20 per cent of the male working population in defence). The service sector, however, was growing fast, with commercial and financial occupations now in second place, ahead of transport and the construction industry, and with other white collar jobs well represented. The leading occupations for women and girls were in personal service, in which category about half of the jobs (1,004) were in domestic service, a declining number. Routine office jobs, and professional and technical work, particularly nursing and teaching, had overtaken work in clothing firms in the league of female occupations, and nearly as many women and girls worked as shop assistants (744) as were employed in the clothing industry (769).[36] In 1952 in Colchester and small

[36] *Census*, 1951.

areas of adjoining parishes 58 per cent of all insured workers were employed in the service industries, 30 per cent in manufacturing, and 12 per cent in extractive industries.[37]

The shift from manufacturing to service industries continued in the later 20th century. In 1977 extractive industries occupied 4 per cent of the working population in the new Colchester local government district, manufacturing accounted for 25 per cent, construction 4 per cent, and service industries 67 per cent, following the national trend; 82 per cent of female employment was in the service sector.[38] By 1987 only a fifth of the total district workforce was in industrial manufacturing.[39] Tourism, promoted from as early as 1903, and the leisure industry expanded significantly.[40]

The electrification of the railway in the early 1960s and improvements to the road network in Essex and East Anglia, besides helping local businesses, enabled more people to commute to work. In 1951, from a total working population of approaching 30,000, nearly 6,000 came into Colchester and *c.* 1,500 of the resident population travelled out to work.[41] During the following decade in-commuting increased by 43 per cent and out-commuting by 23 per cent, with a net balance of 6,700 workers coming in.[42] In 1982 only *c.* 10 per cent of the central area residents worked outside the local government district.[43]

The Hythe was the largest industrial area in 1952, but its 108 a. were only partially developed. Paxman's occupied a site of *c.* 22 a., and there were several small engineering works, a manure and skin-and-bone works, and a barge repair works. Molar clay was imported and made into fire bricks. Some sites, but not Paxman's, had railway sidings; road access was bad. Elsewhere *c.* 16 a. of industrial land south of Bergholt Road beside the railway was occupied by the Windifan works and the British Railways laundry, and *c.* 10 a., between Cowdray Avenue and the railway, by the Arclight works and a small electrical firm.[44] During the 1950s land at Gosbecks Road was allocated for light industry, but most of it was used for distribution depots.[45] Trade at the port, predominantly imports, increased until 1982, but most of the growth was below the Hythe.[46] The workers were not unionized, and so the port was used in the late 1960s during the London dockers' strikes, and in 1984 for coal imports during the national miners' strike.[47] In the later 1980s trade decreased and overheads increased, making the port's future uncertain.[48]

As new businesses moved in and existing ones expanded or amalgamated, the character of local firms increasingly changed from comparatively small family-run concerns to larger national and multinational undertakings.[49] The Colchester Lathe Co. was taken over by the (George Cohen) 600 Group after flood damage in 1953.[50] In 1964 G.E.C. bought control of Wood's, Britain's largest manufacturer of electric fans.[51] Brackett's engineering was taken over by Hawker Siddeley in 1967. Mason's, which made drawing office machinery

37 Essex C.C. *Essex Development Plan, Rep. of Survey, Colch. 1952*, 93.

38 *Census*, 1971; Colch. Boro. Council, *Colch. Borough Plan 1984*, 17.

39 M. Breheny and D. Hart, *Crossroads Colch., an Emerging Centre for Eastern England?* 55.

40 *E.C.S.* 6 June 1903; 28 Mar. 1914; 11, 18 Oct. 1991; below, Public Services (Baths and Parks); Essex C.C. Town Design Group, *Colch. an Historic Townscape*, 30.

41 Gordon, *Regional Hist. Railways*, 60; Essex C.C. *Essex Development Plan, Rep. on First Review relating to Colch. 1964*, 5.

42 Essex C.C. Town Design Group, *Colch. Land Use/Transportation Study [1965], Appendix: Employment*, 7.

43 Colch. Boro. Council, *Central Area Local Plan, 1984*, 14.

44 Essex C.C. *Essex Development Plan, Rep. of Survey, Colch. 1952*, 69–70.

45 Essex C.C. *Essex Development Plan, Rep. on First Review, Colch. 1964*, 1.

46 Below, Port.

47 *E.C.S.* 20 Jan. 1967; 8 Mar. 1985.

48 Ibid. 1 Sept. 1989.

49 *Colch. Official Guide* (1982), 17; E.C.L. Colch., Press cuttings colln.: Firms, Industries sections, *passim*.

50 *E.C.S.* 12 Aug. 1979.

51 *Colch. Expr.* 18 May 1972.

and equipment at the Arclight works, was taken over by successive companies, eventually becoming Ozalid's in 1969; the firm had declined after the retirement of Bernard Mason in 1962.[52] Marriage's milling business was taken over by Hovis McDougall in 1961 and merged with Rank's in 1962; the Colchester mill closed in 1976.[53]

Paxman's expanded in the earlier part of the period, under the direction of Sir Percy Sanders and Edward Paxman. In the 1960s, when the company was pioneering off-shore oil-drilling equipment, the workforce was *c.* 2,500. The firm faced difficulties later with problems of recession and industrial relations, but there were still 2,000 employees in 1980; however in 1992 only 650 remained. Other manufacturing firms had similar experiences, and technological change often reduced the demand for labour. The Colchester Lathe Co., which *c.* 1987 still employed *c.* 500, closed in 1992, new firms abroad having developed their own lathe-making machines to supply their own markets. Nevertheless Wood's, having become part of G.E.C., remained very successful, being one of the foremost electric fan companies in the world in 1992 when it employed 920 people.[54] The Colchester Co-operative Society, however, also stayed successful, continuing to diversify and to expand beyond the town.[55] Cheap clothing imports, particularly from the Far East, and the revival of the East London sweated clothing trade after the war affected the clothing industry adversely: Crowther's wholesale manufacturing business closed in 1968, and Hollington's closed its Colchester factory in 1983.[56]

Shops and offices were restricted in the 1950s by lack of space in the town centre. The central area was redeveloped from the 1960s to improve retailing facilities, and new sites were provided for shopping along main roads and on the outskirts of the town. Industrial zones were designated from the 1950s, and the Severalls industrial estate was developed in the 1970s.[57] The Trebor sweet factory built there *c.* 1976 was known nationally for the design of its factory buildings and for its new participative methods of work organization.[58] Efforts were made from the 1980s to encourage small businesses. The Cowdray Centre, containing small and medium sized units, was opened in 1982.[59] In 1990 a business park of 35 a. was opened off Severalls Lane and another at the Hythe to provide units for small firms.[60]

The local economy was increasingly affected by wider national and international developments, and in the early 1990s particularly by Britain's membership of the European Community and by industrial recession. By the late 1980s Colchester had developed from an agricultural market town to a potential leading regional service centre for eastern England, viewing its proximity to Europe as an asset.[61]

[52] *E.C.S.* 15 Mar. 1968; 19 May 1972.

[53] *E.C.S.* 2 May 1975; *Colch. Gaz.* 1 Apr. 1976; E.R.O., SA 0679.

[54] Essex C.C. *Essex Development Plan, Rep. on 1st Review, Colch.* 1; E.R.O., D/F 23/3/43; G. Martin, 'Paxman's Centenary', supplement, *E.C.S.* 14 May 1965; *E.C.S.* 24 Jan., 28 Feb. 1992; *Colch. Gaz.* 30 June 1986; Colch. Boro. Council, *Colch. 800*, 43; inf. from Mr. A. Phillips.

[55] Lewington, *Brief Hist. Colch. & East Essex Co-op Soc. Ltd.*, 4–7; Colch. Charter 800 Assn. *Colch. 800*, 45.

[56] *E.C.S.* 28 June 1968; 30 Nov. 1984; inf. from Mr. C. Scrivener.

[57] Essex C.C. *Essex Development Plan, Rep. on 1st Review, Colch. 1964*, 6; *Colch. Official Guide* (1982), 17; below, this chapter, Town Development.

[58] *Observer* Supplement, 2 May 1982; *Guardian*, 4 June 1986.

[59] *Colch. Gaz. Enterprise 1988, Official Programme and Guide*; Colch. Charter 800 Assn. *Colch. 800*, 43.

[60] Publicity leaflet of Colch. Business Enterprise Agency [1983]; *E.C.S.* 25 May, 6 July 1990.

[61] Breheny and Hart, *Crossroads Colch.* 53–4; *E.C.S.* 27 Nov. 1992.

TOWN DEVELOPMENT

Nineteenth-Century Growth 1835–1914

Colchester was able to avoid the extreme environmental and health problems suffered by many other towns in the 19th century because its population and industry expanded comparatively gradually, and there was space for growth. Between 1835 and 1911 the number of houses increased from 3,292 to 9,218, more than 2½ times, in a similar proportion to population growth. In 1835 buildings were concentrated in the central area within and around the town wall, with some ribbon development along the roads leading out of the town, especially on those leading eastwards towards Greenstead and the Hythe. The rest of the borough was mainly rural.[62] The topography was particularly affected by the barracks, built south of the town centre from 1855 onwards.[63] Residential and industrial development was modest. In the mid 19th century smaller houses, mainly in terraces, were built south and east of the town wall often on poorly drained low ground, and larger houses on more desirable sites to the west, beginning a spatial segregation of the social classes which had previously lived close together in the central area. A few houses were also built near Colchester North railway station and in gaps along the main roads.[64] Between 1876 and 1914 the rate of house-building increased, there was significant industrial and commercial development, and the barracks were extended;[65] by the first decade of the 20th century house completions averaged 187 a year.[66] Almost all development was south of the river Colne, which, reinforced by the railway line, formed a natural barrier between the town centre and the north part of the borough. Under public health legislation the improvement commissioners, and from 1874 the borough council, provided drainage, improved streets in the town centre, investigated industrial and other nuisances, inspected slum houses, and approved plans for new building, but town planning and wider housing powers remained permissive before the First World War.[67]

In 1845 J. P. Osborne laid out plots with frontages varying from 14 ft. to 50 ft. on his garden land, part of the Blue Posts estate, in Osborne Street south of the town centre between Stanwell and St. Botolph's Streets. In the same year new streets on Golden Acre field, on the east side of North Street near the new Colchester North railway station, were laid out for houses.[68] By 1848 terraces of working-class houses had been built in Essex, Chapel, Wellington, and South Streets, south of St. John's Street.[69] The Botanic Gardens east of the castle were to be sold in 1851, and by 1852 the National Freehold Land Society, which was affiliated with the Liberal party, had bought them and small plots had been laid out there in Castle and Roman Roads by T. Morland and C. Wilkinson; 72 lots were bought by builders, other craftsmen, merchants, and a few gentlemen, 41 of them from Colchester, the rest from the London area.[70] In the 1860s Morland and Wilkinson laid out another small estate west of North Station Road just south of

[62] *Rep. Com. on Mun. Corp. Boundaries*, H.C. 238, map s.v. Colch. (1837), xxvi; *Census*, 1831, 1841, 1911.

[63] Below, Barracks.

[64] O.S. Map 1/2,500, Essex XXVII. 4, 7, 8, 11, 12, 16; XXVIII. 1, 5, 9, 13 (1876 edn.).

[65] O.S. Maps 6", Essex XXVII, XXVIII, XXXVI (1881, 1898, 1925 edns.); *Census*, 1871, 1911.

[66] E.R.O., Acc. C246, M.O.H.'s Reps. 1901–10.

[67] O.S. Map 1/2,500, Essex XXVII. 4, 7, 8, 11, 12, 16; XXVIII. 1, 5, 9, 13 (1898 edn.); E.R.O., Boro. Mun., Improvement Com. Mins. 1835–74, *passim*; Boro. Council Sanitary Cttee. Mins. 1874–1914, *passim*.

[68] E.R.O., Boro. Mun., Improvement Com. Mins. 1833–47, pp. 248–9; *E.C.S.* 19 Sept. 1845; E.C.L. Colch., Press cuttings, notes from *E.C.S.* 1845.

[69] E.R.O., Boro. Mun., Improvement Com. Mins. 1847–53, pp. 27–8; ibid. T/M 399.

[70] E.R.O., Acc. C32, plan of part of Greyfriars estate for sale, 1847; ibid. D/DB T833; G. Martin, *Story of Colch.* 95.

the Eastern Counties' asylum consisting of Belle Vue, Colne Bank, and Essex Hall Roads, and in 1863 Meyrick and Pownall Crescents were developed by a Conservative land society.[71]

Demand for substantial houses on the west side of the town was considerable. There had been scattered development along both sides of Lexden Road in the early years of the 19th century and in 1817 the town clerk, Francis Smythies, had built a castellated villa, probably from designs by Robert Lugar, at the end of the high ground overlooking Lexden village. On the north side of the road the two parts of St. Mary's Terrace introduced a further element of architectural distinction. The west terrace of *c.* 1825 has five pairs of semidetached houses which are

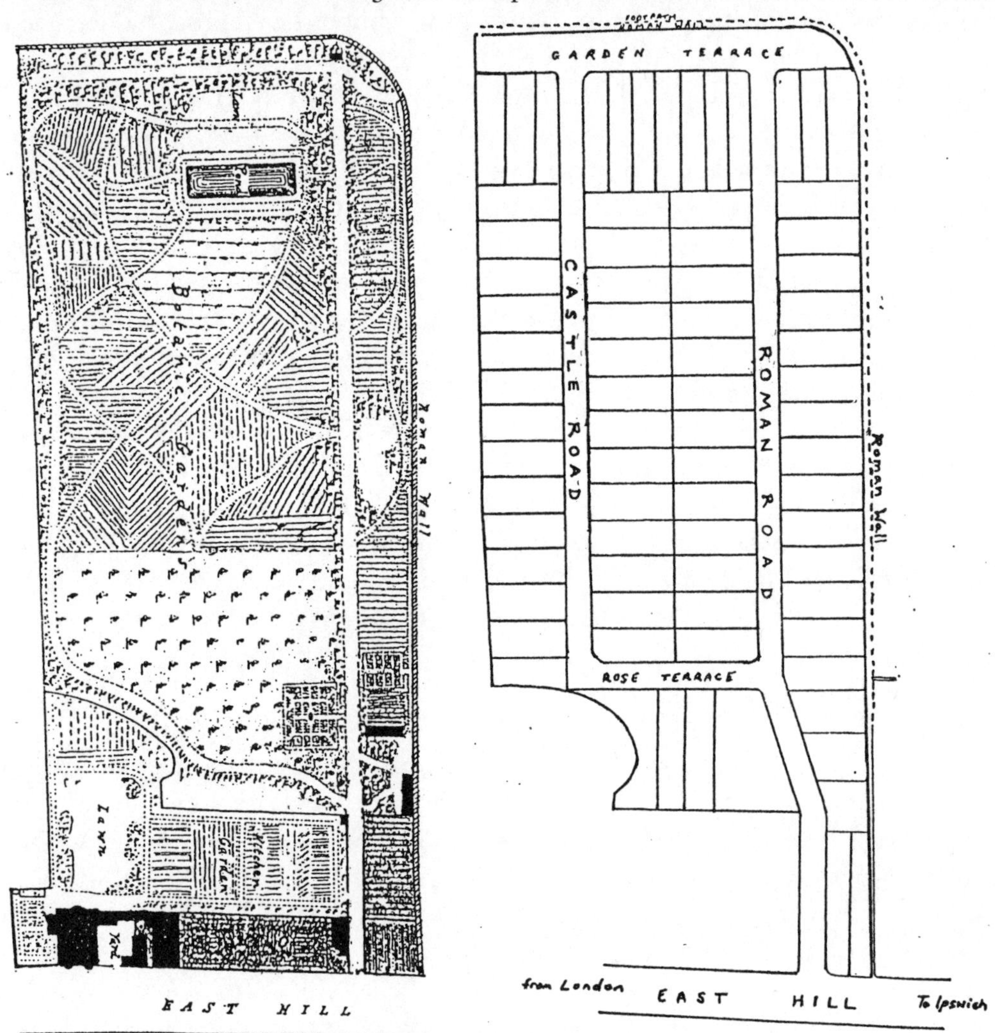

FIG. 15. THE BOTANIC GARDENS, 1847, AND THEIR DEVELOPMENT, 1852
(scale approximately 1:2687)

linked by low recessed stable blocks. The east terrace of 1837 by H. H. Hayward is a single architectural composition with accented centre and ends. Both developments were set back from the road behind gardens.[72] In the third quarter of the century there was rapid development along those new cul de sacs on the south side of the road.[73] The houses are of a variety of styles and materials but are on generous plots. Blatch (later Wellesley) Street with Blatch Square, 'a spacious

[71] E.R.O., D/DB T834.

[72] Dept. of Env., 13th List of buildings of archit. and hist. interest, 76–81; below, pl. facing pp. 232.

[73] E.R.O., T/M 399; O.S. Map 1/2,500, Essex XXVII. 12.

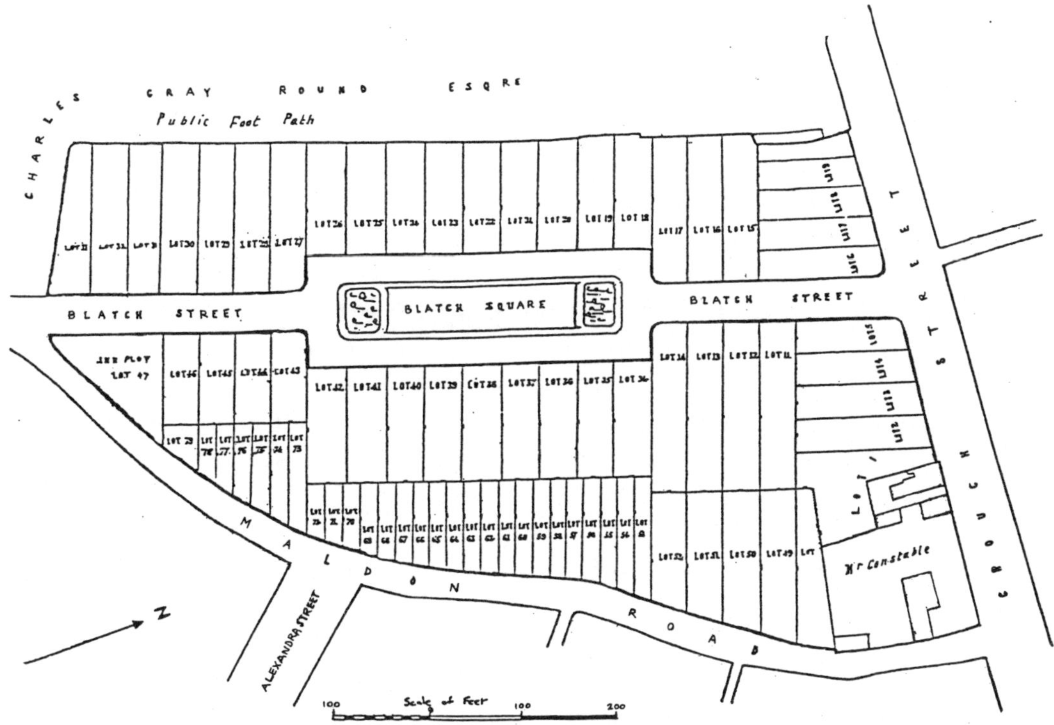

FIG. 16. BLATCH SQUARE, 1865

square planted with ornamental trees', were built south of Crouch Street, between Maldon Road and the Essex and Colchester hospital, from 1865,[74] and the West Terrace estate of large villas in the road later called The Avenue before 1868.[75] The large plots marked out often carried stipulations about development. Public houses were prohibited on the Beverley estate when plots and houses were being sold in 1874,[76] and a similar concern had been shown for the quality of development on a site near the Turrets in 1864.[77] The result was a distinctive suburb of medium size and large houses and gardens, still in the 1880s surrounded by fields.

After 1876 a further area between Lexden and Maldon Roads was developed: the executors of Charles Gray Round sold part of Hospital farm on the Creffield estate in 1876 and 1878, and spacious detached houses were built in Creffield, Oxford, Gray, and Hospital Roads;[78] Walter Chambers, a local builder, developed Cambridge, Victoria, Fitzwalter, and St. Clare Roads, and he also owned houses in the south and east quarters of the town.[79] North of Colchester North station and the new railway laundry, a small number of semidetached houses was built from 1878 on the Three Crowns estate off Bergholt Road,[80] and further houses were built along the Bergholt Road and in gaps along other main roads.[81] Between Butt and Maldon Roads Henry Jones laid out Salisbury and Beaconsfield Roads from 1879 on the Mill Field estate,[82] and before 1914 other roads were built as far south as Constantine Road.[83] The Papillon family sold land south of the workhouse, formerly part of Lord's land, in the 1880s, and Rawstorn Road and neighbouring

74 Ibid. D/DEl T293; sale cat. Blatch Street & Square, 1872: copy at E.C.L. Colch.

75 E.R.O., B4769, sale cat.; below, pl. facing p. 232.

76 Ibid. B4679, sale cat.; below, pl. facing p. 232.

77 Ibid. B4843, sale cat.

78 Ibid. Acc. C210, J. B. Harvey Colln. vii, p. 54; ibid. B119, sale cat.; below, pl. facing p. 232.

79 List of property owned by W. Chambers, in possession of Mr. J. Bensusan-Butt.

80 E.R.O., B38, B42, sale cats.

81 Colch. Boro. Planning & Devt. Dept., unpubl. map showing age of Colch. residential areas.

82 E.R.O., Acc. C8, Box 5, uncat. plans.

83 Colch. Planning Dept., unpubl. map of Colch. resid. areas.

streets were built; many employees from Mumford's engineering works in Culver Street lived there.[84]

Most growth, however, was at New Town, developed from 1878 south of the road to the Hythe, a large compact area between army land on the west and Paxman's engineering factory at the Hythe on the east: 293 houses were built there by 1885.[85] Morant, Harsnett, and King Stephen Roads were built there on the Wimpole estate between Wimpole Road and Park Lane from 1899, and Claudius, Campion, Lisle, Barrington, and part of Canterbury Roads on the Goldwell's estate (previously occupied by Bunting's nursery) on the south side of the barracks from 1901.[86] J. F. Goodey, a local builder, other members of the Co-operative movement, and local Liberals were influential in the development of New Town, hence the name Gladstone Road. The intention was to create a social mix through the provision of varied housing. Goodey himself, who specialized in precast concrete architectural detail, lived in a detached house, New Town Lodge, in New Town Road.[87] Terraced houses, with some better ones for foremen, were laid out on a gridiron road pattern and higher quality houses were built on the southern periphery in Granville and Gladstone Roads or in terraces overlooking the recreation ground.

Building societies played an important role in the expansion of the housing market. The Colchester Permanent Benefit building society, founded in 1856, and the Colchester Co-operative Mutual Permanent Benefit building society, founded in 1869, later the Colchester Equitable building society, advanced money to members to buy houses either to live in themselves or as an investment. Money was lent to women on the same terms as men, and by 1878 the number of working-class borrowers was increasing. By 1894 the Colchester Equitable had advanced £115,000 on 630 cottages, 28 businesses, 7 large houses, and 1 chapel, mostly in the town or the immediately surrounding area.[88] Colchester Co-operative Society also enabled some of its members to become owner-occupiers. In 1879, with surplus capital, it bought some plots on the New Town estate, built four cottages on them, and allotted them to members who paid for them by easy instalments; four more cottages were provided soon afterwards, and likewise four in 1884 in Rawstorn Road and four in 1886 in Pelham Road.[89]

Much new housing was of a good standard, but overcrowded and insanitary older accommodation remained, often around confined courtyards, particularly in the centre, and east and south of the town, and that facilitated the spread of infectious diseases.[90] The road from the town to the Hythe was notorious for poor housing.[91] In 1898 the medical officer of health considered that some new houses, built quickly and cheaply and sometimes on unfavourable sites, were so small that they created fresh overcrowding.[92]

In the 19th century most of the old and new trades and industries were carried on in workshops, factories, and foundries in the town centre and the Stanwell Street area, and there were breweries at East Hill and North Hill. Later in the

[84] E.R.O., D/DU 445/13; inf. from Mr. J. Bensusan-Butt.

[85] *E.C.S.* 8 Aug. 1885; below, pl. facing p. 232.

[86] E.R.O., Acc. C15, Box 8, plan of Wimpole estate 1899; Acc. C32, Sale cat. Goldwells, 1893; *Essex Tel.* 9 Feb. 1901.

[87] F. R. Rogers, 'Colch. New Town: Building of a Victorian Estate' (Cambridge Univ. Extra-mural dissertation, *c.* 1992); E.R.O., D/B 6 Pb2/369A; below, pl. facing p. 232.

[88] *Rules and Tables of the Colch. Permanent Benefit Building Soc.*; *1869–1969, Colch. Equitable Building Soc.*: copies at E.C.L. Colch.

[89] G. Phillips, *Colch. & East Essex Co-op. & Industrial Soc., Brief Hist.* 8, 10, 12.

[90] e.g. E.R.O., Boro. Mun., Improvement Com. Mins. 1847–53, pp. 27–8; Boro. Council Sanitary Cttee. Mins., 28 July 1880; Colch. Institute, Colch. Recalled, interview 2089; below, pl. facing p. 328.

[91] E.R.O., Acc. C210, J. B. Harvey Colln., iv, p. 161.

[92] Ibid. Acc. C246, M.O.H.'s Rep., 1898, pp. 10–11.

century when there was insufficient land available for industry in the central area, some new factories were built further out, like Paxman's opened at the Hythe in 1873 and George's shoe factory built in New Town in 1881. The Hythe, with its wharves and warehouses, had always been important for the port trade, but from the mid 19th century new industry was increasingly located there: the gasworks were built in 1838, the sewage works in 1884, and four new engineering factories between 1899 and 1907. Shops, inns, and commercial services were concentrated in the town centre. As trade increased and more space was required for business, some residents moved out of the central area: between 1831 and 1901 population fell in St. Nicholas's and St. Runwald's and remained almost the same in St. Martin's, all central parishes, while it increased in all other parishes. Corner shops, bakeries, and new public houses were built in the new streets beyond the town centre to serve the people living there and the soldiers from the barracks.[93]

The number of public buildings increased as the town grew. The grammar school moved in 1853 to new buildings by H. H. Hayward on the south side of Lexden Road, and many new schools were built, including the board schools by Goodey and Cressall in Barrack Street in 1896, at St. John's green in 1898, and in John Harper Street in 1900.[94] St. Botolph's church was rebuilt in 1837, St. Mary Magdalen's in 1854, and St. Michael's Mile End in 1854–5, and new churches were built: St. John the Evangelist's Ipswich Road in 1863, and St. Paul's Belle Vue Road in 1869. Most other churches were restored. New landmarks in the town included the workhouse on Balkerne Hill opened in 1837, the Essex and Colchester hospital opened in Lexden Road in 1820 with its later extensions, the Eastern Counties' asylum at Essex Hall built originally as a railway hotel, and at Mile End in the north the infectious diseases hospital and Severalls lunatic asylum opened in 1884 and 1913.[95] Jumbo, the water tower built in 1883, became a dominant feature of the town, and provided a new view at the west end of High Street.[96] There were significant changes in High Street: a new town hall replaced the old moot hall in 1845, and was itself replaced by another new building in 1902; the Albert hall was built at the west end in 1845, originally as an additional corn exchange.[97] A new corn exchange was built next door to the town hall in 1884.[98] High Street was cleared of some obstructions: the obelisk was removed in 1858, the cattle market was relocated at Middleborough in 1862, and Middle Row shops and St. Runwald's church were demolished in 1857 and 1878.[99] The tramway system also affected the appearance of the streets on the tram routes from 1904.[1]

By 1914, despite the increasing rate of building, no one lived further than about a mile from open space, and patches of market gardens still punctuated the built-up area. Countryside could still be seen from parts of the town centre because of its higher elevation. New streets had been built on the Botanic Gardens, and St. John's abbey garden was acquired by the army, but additional public open space was provided when the recreation ground was opened on the edge of New Town in 1885, and Castle park in 1892.[2] The army kept the Abbey field and Middlewick rifle ranges free of building, and the Round family preserved the Bury field south of East Hill House.[3]

93 Above, Econ.; below, Public Services (Sewerage, Gas); *E.C.S.* 8 Aug. 1885; *V.C.H. Essex*, ii. 353–4.

94 Below, Educ.; Dept. of Env., 13th List of buildings of archit. or hist. interest, 10, 74, 81, 115.

95 Below, Churches; Hospitals.

96 Anglian Water, *Jumbo 1883–1983* [11–13].

97 Below, Mun. Bldgs.

98 *Kelly's Dir. Essex* (1886), 91.

99 Booker, *Essex and Ind. Revolution*, 120; *White's Dir. Essex* (1863), 74; *E.R.* lxiv. 117–18; above, pl. facing p. 40.

1 Below, Public Services (Internal Transport); above, pl. facing p. 40.

2 Below, Public Services (Baths and Parks).

3 *E.J.* xiv (2), p. 4.

Twentieth-Century Growth 1914–92

Between the two World Wars the population increased by *c.* 10,000, the built-up area spread outwards, and the town lost its earlier compactness. The extensive Lucas estates in Mile End and Greenstead were sold in 1917 and small portions of glebe land were sold in 1918 at Mile End, St. Leonard's parish, Old Heath, and off Lexden Road, in 1920 at Mile End, and in 1922 at Monkwick; some of that land was used for building, although some of it continued as farmland until after the Second World War.[4] In 1921, when the population was 49,393, there were 9,053 occupied houses.[5] Local development was increasingly affected by central government legislation for housing and town planning. Between 1921 and 1938 much of the residential development was municipal housing in large planned estates, but there was also considerable private building in small estates, ribbon development, and in-filling, with totals of 1,029 council and 2,141 private houses.[6] The barracks expanded further, the army reserving for military use two wedges of open space in the south, between Butt and Mersea Roads and between Mersea and Old Heath Roads. Employment opportunities attracted people from neighbouring areas, some of whom moved into houses in the town. Increasing traffic congestion in the town centre was alleviated from 1933 by a new bypass north of the town, and some firms moved to sites alongside the new road. The bypass, the sections of which from west to east were known as Cymbeline Way, Colne Bank Avenue, Cowdray Avenue, and St. Andrew's Avenue, reinforced the barrier already created by the river and the railway between the town centre and the north part of the borough, and most development between the wars was in the south.

The town council, employing a mixture of direct labour and local building firms, built four housing estates between the wars to central government specifications on borough land at Mile End and on private farmland bought at Lexden on the borough boundary south of Lexden Road, at Old Heath, and between the Harwich and Ipswich roads.[7] Other council houses were built in smaller groups, like those on a site north of Castle park.[8] Nevertheless council house-building could not meet the demand for inexpensive rented houses, and the Lexden Garden Village Ltd. was formed as a public utility society to provide family homes at a reasonable rent. It raised loans from the local council and issued shares paying modest rates of interest. The scheme, initiated by Capt. R. L. Reiss, Labour parliamentary candidate for Colchester, and G. C. Bensusan-Butt, both inspired by the Garden Cities movement, was managed by men 'of all opinions and politics' who gave their professional services free. Eighty-six houses had been completed by 1926 on 40 a. bordered by Grimes Dyke on the west, Lexden Road on the north, and Lexden Straight Road on the east, but in 1927, when money for further building was not forthcoming, the remaining 9½ a. were sold to the council, which built 93 houses. The Lexden Garden Village Ltd. remained as a public company until the late 1970s when all the houses were sold, mostly to the tenants.[9]

Private detached and semidetached houses were built in new roads, mostly west, south-west, and south-east of the town centre. Gladwin Road, between Maldon

[4] E.R.O., A85, B1485, sale cats.; ibid. Acc. C32, sale cat. of glebe lands 1918; ibid. D/P 178, uncat. terrier 1943–53; Balliol Coll. Mun., Patronage Papers.

[5] *Census*, 1921.

[6] R. O'Connell, 'Council housing and the small town: Colch. 1919–50' (Essex Univ. M.A. thesis, 1984), appendix.

[7] Ibid. *passim.*

[8] H. J. Gayler, 'Colch., a Study of the Development of the Urban Landscape since 1801' (Leicester Univ. B.A. dissertation, 1963), 60.

[9] E.R.O., D/DU 906/3; ibid. Acc. C32, sale cat. 1937, stock in Lexden Garden Village Ltd.; *Essex Tel.* 7 Aug. 1926; *E.C.S.* 5 Sept. 1931; O'Connell, 'Council Housing and the Small Town', 26; inf. from Mr. J. Bensusan-Butt, son of G. C. Bensusan-Butt.

and Layer Roads, may have been typical: in 1927, Leonard Dansie, an estate agent and auctioneer, bought the first plot, employed his own builder to build a detached house, and moved into it; a few other houses were built in the same way; then Everett's, a local firm, bought the remaining plots, built semidetached houses all of the same design, and sold them separately.[10] There was also further ribbon development along main roads, including the new bypass, and spaces were filled in existing roads, farmers often being glad to sell roadside plots to speculative builders in a time of low agricultural prices.[11] Local planning regulations were drawn up before 1939, but their implementation was halted by the war.[12]

After the Second World War increased commuting, both outwards to London and inwards from towns and villages nearby, affected the expansion of the town; many commuters moved into new houses in the borough to live nearer their work. Wartime bomb damage had been slight, but some slum clearance and new building was necessary to reduce overcrowding. Because there was still plenty of space, building at high density and in high-rise blocks was not undertaken as in some other places, and Colchester was selected by Essex county council as a town for expansion.[13] Between 1945 and 1961 a total of 6,147 public and private houses were built, so that by 1961, when the population was 65,080, there were 20,229 dwellings (of which 19,825 were occupied).[14]

In the late 1940s and the 1950s the council housed 3,600 people in 1,250 new houses on 95 a. at Shrub End in the south-west corner of the borough and 3,500 people in 1,150 houses at Monkwick in the south; it also built a few houses and flats at Prettygate, north of Shrub End. Some shops, schools, and churches were provided for the new estates.[15] Private housing lagged behind public housing immediately after the war because of government restrictions. Between 1945 and 1953 only 452 private houses were built, but the number increased to 2,327 between 1953 and 1961. The first large private estate was built, mainly by W. A. Hills & Son, a local firm, in the late 1950s on 260 a. on the Home Farm and Prettygate estates in the west and south-west parts of the borough. Other developments included the war department's large Montgomery estate, built on 200 a. south of the barracks in the 1950s and 1960s. The army also built flats in 1970 in Lethe Grove near the military corrective centre, which had been built at Berechurch in the mid 1950s. There were also smaller private developments, including those off Mersea Road, west of Lexden Park, north of Colchester North railway station, between Ipswich Road and the railway, and north of East Hill, and there was much infilling.[16]

From 1955 large-scale development began north of the river with the building at Greenstead of the borough's largest council estate, most of which had been built by the mid 1960s, with infilling continuing until 1985, providing about 2,800 homes. The council also built a further 220 houses nearby at Parson's Heath.[17] The local council had in the 1950s successfully resisted the use of Greenstead for London overspill population,[18] but in 1974 in spite of local opposition the Greater

[10] Inf. from Miss J. V. Dansie, dau. of L. Dansie; *Benham's Almanac & Dir. Colch.* (1928) 113; (1932) 129.

[11] Gayler, 'Colch.' 62–4; Colch. Boro. council planning dept., unpubl. map of Colch. residential areas.

[12] E.R.O., Acc. C481, Colch. Boro. Council, *Colch. Town Planning Scheme, Preliminary Statements, 1928, 1933*; ibid. Essex C.C., NE. Essex regional planning cttee. *NE. Essex regional planning scheme (Colch. area nos. 1, 2.), 1937.*

[13] E.R.O., Acc. C481, Boro. Engineer's Dept., file of war damage 1939–45; Essex C.C. *Essex Development Plan, Rep. of Survey, Colch. 1952*, 63–76.

[14] Gayler, 'Colch.' 72; *Census*, 1961.

[15] Gayler, 'Colch.' 72–4.

[16] Ibid. 74–5; inf. from Mr. G. Broom, Colch. Boro. Planning Dept.; W. Hamley, 'Urban Structure of Colch.' (Swansea Univ. M.A. thesis, 1974), 80–1; E.C.L. Colch., Press cuttings colln., details of estates filed under their names.

[17] Inf. from Mrs. C. Edwards, Colch. Boro. Council Housing Division; *Colch. Gaz.* 18 Aug. 1977.

[18] *E.C.S.* 22 Sept. 1958.

London Council bought directly from Fairview Estates 128 private houses on the Birch Glen estate.[19] Colchester council took over those houses in 1988 after the abolition of the Greater London Council. By 1992 about a third of all council houses had been bought by their occupants, principally under the Housing Act of 1980.[20]

St. John's private housing estate was built in the 1960s in the north-east quarter of the town. Other private developments included the low-density Link homes erected on a 5.6 a. site at Welshwood Park nearby in 1972–3.[21] There was a building boom in the early 1970s,[22] but planning policies by the mid 1970s no longer designated north-east Essex as a major or medium growth area. Instead planners gave priority there to agriculture, conservation, and countryside protection, and tried to restrain Colchester's growth to allow public amenities to catch up with housebuilding.[23] From the 1960s large national firms were increasingly involved in building in the borough. In 1979 French Kier began developing the 730-a. High Woods site west of the Ipswich Road, to provide *c.* 4,000 houses and a shopping centre.[24] There was other small-scale council and private building, including small developments by housing associations like that between Forest Road and Avon Way at Greenstead in 1977 by the C.D.S. Co-operative Housing Society Ltd.,[25] bringing the total of council and private dwellings in Colchester urban area to 36,542 by the end of 1991; the population was 91,817 in 1989. In 1981 owner-occupiers formed 61 per cent of households and council tenants 25 per cent.[26]

Some of the earlier housing stock had been improved from the 1950s and there had been a little slum clearance, mainly in the 'twilight' zone around the town centre, used as car parks before being redeveloped;[27] some houses were demolished in Vineyard Street in 1962 to provide parking.[28] By 1965 there were 2,045 parking spaces,[29] and in 1966 a multistorey car park was opened in Nunn's Road.[30] Seventeenth- and early 18th-century houses in the 'Dutch Quarter', north of High Street, were renovated between 1955 and the 1980s to create a convenient residential area in the town centre; by 1984 the council had taken over 35 older buildings there and provided 147 new flats and 17 houses to blend with the older ones.[31] From 1971 there were several improvement schemes, covering St. Mary's, New Town, South Town, and Magdalen Street, to upgrade the housing stock by allowing grants to tenants for undertaking major repairs and modernization. The council improved street lighting, planted trees and shrubs, and restricted parking.[32]

Industry and commerce were after 1945 increasingly located on specific sites beyond the town centre; in 1991 the main centres were at Severalls Park, the Hythe, Cowdray Avenue, and North Station Road, and smaller ones were mainly east of the town centre and on the south-west periphery of the town.[33] Nevertheless

19 Ibid. 30 Sept. 1977.

20 Inf. from Mrs. C. Edwards, Colch. Boro. Council Housing Division.

21 *Colch. Gaz.* 11 June 1970; *E.C.S.* 17 Oct. 1975; E.R.O., B6845, sale cat.

22 *Colch. Expr.* 21 Jan. 1971.

23 Colch. Boro. Council, *Boro. Development Rep. 1975–95, 1976*.

24 *E.C.S.* 30 Oct. 1981; Essex C.C. *High Woods area, a development brief, 1976; High Woods Area, review devt. brief, 1978*; *E.C.S.* 9 Mar. 1979.

25 C.D.S. Co-operative Housing Society Ltd. *Prospectus, Aug. 1977*: copy at E.C.L. Colch.

26 Statistics from Mr. D. Collins, Colch. Boro. Planning Dept.

27 Hamley, 'Urban Structure of Colch.' 81.

28 *Colch. Gaz.* 20 Nov. 1962.

29 Essex C.C. Town Design Group, *Land Use/Transportation Study, Colch. Rep., Technical Appendix on Car Parking, 1967*, 5.

30 *Colch. Gaz.* 24 May 1966.

31 Essex C.C. *Dutch Quarter, an Approach to the Future Development of the Area, 1970*; *Colch. Gaz.* 12 July 1982; 24 Sept. 1984.

32 *E.C.S.* 16 Nov. 1973; 8 Jan. 1982; 12 Apr. 1990; E.R.O., Acc. C34, Colch. Boro. Engineering Dept., New Town improvement plans; *Colch. Gaz.* 15 Nov. 1983.

33 Above, this chapter, Econ.; Colch. Boro. Council, *Location Maps & Business Listings of Commercial Areas, 1991*.

concern grew about the problems of traffic congestion, and also about haphazard development and demolition in the central area,[34] such as the demolition of St. Nicholas's church in 1955 for a new Co-op department store, and of the Cups public house in 1972.[35] Colchester Civic Society was set up in 1964 to try to halt losses of that sort by encouraging higher standards in planning and design and by arousing public interest in the preservation and improvement of local amenities.[36] A report of 1968 on the town centre, amended by Essex county council in 1969, contained proposals for the following 14 years to redevelop the Lion Walk, Culver Street, St. Peter's Street, and St. John's Street/Vineyard areas, to make the town centre a conservation area, to build an inner relief road system and peripheral multistorey car parks, and to pay special attention to the needs of pedestrians and public transport.[37]

By 1984 parts of the plan had been amended because of financial constraints and the new preference for improvement and small-scale rather than comprehensive redevelopment. Some activities were moved out of the town centre: in 1975 the cattle market went from Middleborough to Severalls Lane, and a new swimming pool and sports centre were built in Catchpool Road on the south side of Cowdray Avenue. In the central shopping area a new public library was built, replacing the one opened in Shewell Road in 1948, some houses were converted into small shops in Trinity Street in 1975, and the Lion Walk shopping precinct was opened in 1976. Four office blocks were built in St. Peter's Street by 1976 to provide municipal offices and a telecommunications centre.[38] The southern and western sections of the new inner relief road were finished by 1981, cutting through existing road patterns and neighbourhood areas and causing the demolition of 107 houses, 50 shops, 32 other businesses, 4 factories including the Colchester Manufacturing Co. and Hollington's, the Elim church, a warehouse formerly the Empire cinema, and 4 public houses, the Carpenters Arms in Chapel Street, the old Essex Arms in Essex Street, the Plough in St. Botolph's Street, and the Woolpack at St. Botolph's Corner.[39] Multistorey car parks were built at Queen Street in 1972 (closed in 1992 because of structural faults), St. John's Street in 1977, Middleborough in 1980, and Balkerne Hill (St. Mary's) in 1981.[40] The appearance of the shops changed as chain stores with fronts in their own house-style came to dominate the streets and shopping precincts. Between 1968 and 1980 total commercial floor space increased by 45 per cent in the central area, with an increase of 35.6 per cent in the number of non-food shops and a decrease of 11.9 per cent in the number of food shops.[41] After the publication of the central area local plan of 1984 the Culver Street shopping precinct with 47 shopping units built by the Carroll Group was opened in 1987, and St. John's Walk shopping centre of 18 units and Osborne Street car park in 1990.[42] A large supermarket was included as part of the Highwoods development in the north part of the borough and another at Stanway beyond the ancient borough's western boundary.

Many more schools and churches were built in the period from 1914, but some of the previously existing ones were converted to other uses in the later 20th

[34] Essex C.C. *Colch.: an Historic Townscape 1967*; ibid. *Land Use/Transportation Study: Colch. 1967*; Colch. Boro. Council, *Town Centre Rep. 1968*.

[35] Rodwell, *Hist. Chs.* 31; *Colch. Gaz.* 19 May 1972.

[36] *Colch. Civic Soc. Qtrly. Bull.* 1964 etc.

[37] *E.C.S.* 12 July, 23 Aug. 1968; 22 Aug. 1969.

[38] Colch. Boro. Council, *Central Area Local Plan 1984*, 1; *Colch. Gaz.* 21 Feb. 1975; *E.C.S.* 3 Jan. 1976; below, Soc.and Cultural (Libraries); *Colch. Gaz.* 24 Sept. 1976; A. Duncan, *The Onflowing Stream, 1935–92* (updated hist. of Lion Walk Ch.), 155–81.

[39] Below, Communications (Roads); *E.C.S.* 22 March 1968; E.C.L. Colch., Press cuttings colln., Inner Relief Road.

[40] *Colch. Expr.* 27 Apr. 1972; *E.C.S.* 11 July 1980; 4 Dec. 1981; 31 Jan. 1992.

[41] Colch. Boro. Council, *Central Area Local Plan 1984*, 21–2.

[42] Ibid. *passim*; *E.C.S.* 30 Oct. 1987; 6 Apr., 7 Dec. 1990; below, pl. facing p. 280.

century. Community centres and neighbourhood shopping parades were built on many new estates after 1945. Other new landmarks included the war memorial designed by H. C. Fehr and completed in 1923, Hythe generating station opened at the Hythe in 1927, the Turner village part of the Royal Eastern Counties' Institution in the 1930s, the new technical college (later Colchester Institute) at Sheepen Road in 1959, Essex University at Wivenhoe Park in 1961, the new Goojerat barracks in the early 1970s replacing the old ones, the Royal London offices at Middleborough in 1982, county council accommodation at Stanwell House in 1985, the District General hospital in 1985, offices and housing beside Colchester North railway station in the late 1980s, the new police headquarters alongside Southway in 1989, and the leisure centre at Cowdray Avenue in 1991. Among earlier buildings demolished were the Hythe gasworks in 1973 and the former asylum at Essex Hall in 1985.[43]

The need to preserve some open space and to provide pleasant views became more important as the built-up area grew. Braiswick golf course north-west of the town, founded in 1909, remained free of development. The council established sports grounds and children's play areas on sites all over the borough and created artificial lakes in Castle park in 1973. The cemetery in Mersea Road was extended and landscaped, covering more than 57 a.[44] Trees were planted in 1931–2 along the western part of the bypass to create an Avenue of Remembrance, one section commemorating former citizens including 25 former mayors, the other servicemen who died in the First World War; two other avenues were planted, one in honour of the Girl Guide movement, the other called a Children's Avenue.[45] The council prohibited building on the southern slopes of the Highwoods site and on some woodland nearby, and in 1988 opened High Woods country park as public open space.[46] In 1990 the council bought from Essex county council part of Lexden park, opening it to the public in 1991 as a nature reserve.[47] In 1992 some land at the southern and northern extremities of the historic borough was still agricultural. Thus, although the built-up area of the town had increased greatly in the 20th century, a significant amount of space remained free of buildings, and, because of the varied elevations of different parts of the town, many views of open land were retained.

POLITICAL HISTORY

The Reformed Borough 1835–92

National politics, as manifested in movements like Chartism and events like the repeal of the corn laws, affected politics in Colchester, but local circumstances, such as the strength of religious nonconformity and the lack of industry in the town, were more influential. The earlier part of the period saw the adjustment locally to a new reformed system of borough government and poor relief imposed by central government legislation.[48]

Under the Municipal Corporations Act of 1835 the new corporation comprised a mayor, elected annually by the council; six aldermen, three of whom were elected

43 Below, Barracks; Hospitals; Public Services; Churches; Prot. Nonconf.; Educ.; Essex Univ.; *Colch. Official Guide* (1982), 24; *E.C.S.* 3 Jan. 1976; 12 Nov. 1982; *Colch. Gaz.* 30 June 1970; 14 Jan. 1985.

44 Below, Public Services (Cemeteries, Baths and Parks); local inf.

45 *Essex Tel.* 8 Aug. 1931; 8 Oct. 1932; E. A. Blaxill, *Opening of Colch. By-pass Road, a Hist. of the Road*, 7–8.

46 Colch. Boro. Council, *High Woods Country Park Management Plan, 1987*.

47 Inf. from Mr. M. Shepherd, Colch. Boro. Planning Dept.

48 Section based on E.R.O., Boro. Mun., G/CoM 1–16; ibid. Improvement Com. Mins. 1833–63 and Spec. Cttees. Mins.; ibid. Boro. Council Mins. 1835–45 and Spec. Cttees. Mins. 1874–92; ibid. Acc. C4, Boro. Council newspaper cuttings, 1884–92.

triennially in rotation by the council; and 18 councillors, six of whom retired annually, directly elected by ratepaying householders. The borough was divided into three electoral wards, each represented by six councillors. The corporation was allowed to retain a separate borough quarter sessions administered by eight justices with a recorder, and continued to maintain the borough gaol.[49] The borough lawhundred and foreign (Monday and Thursday) courts were in abeyance from 1878 and were abolished in 1972.[50]

In the first borough council election under the Act, in 1835, the Reformers or Liberals gained a narrow majority, of ten to eight, which they increased by electing six Liberal aldermen, and appointing Liberals as mayor, town clerk, chamberlain, treasurer, and town serjeants in place of the previous Tory or Conservative incumbents; their nominees were also appointed as J.P.s, clerk of the peace, and coroner.[51] The new council apparently met *in camera* until March 1836, but publicly in the moot hall thereafter, holding frequent special meetings in addition to quarterly ones.[52]

The new corporation, like its predecessor, had only limited powers; it administered markets, fairs, and borough charities, maintained the North, East, and Hythe bridges, managed its properties comprising the Severalls and the Chantry lands, and selected scholars for the town grammar school.[53] It still owned the fishery but had little control over it.[54] A borough police force was set up in 1836. Other important local government functions were performed by other statutory bodies: the board of guardians, composed of one or two guardians elected from each of the 16 parishes in the union together with the J.P.s *ex officio*, administered the poor law subject to central government control, and the autonomous improvement commissioners were responsible for streets, drainage, lighting, the investigation of nuisances, and the maintenance of the navigation on the Colne. The town parishes retained little more than their ecclesiastical functions. Education was left to religious and other organizations.[55]

The main problem in 1835 was the £10,000 mortgage on the Severalls taken out by the new corporation's forerunners, the unreformed corporation, to cover debts. Committees were appointed to investigate the accounts for 1834 and 1835 and the corporation's current assets. The accounts could not be passed because £600 raised from the sale of a granary and wharf at the Hythe had been spent illegally, mainly by Francis Smythies on dinners and wine, and on resisting the Municipal Corporations Bill. The borough charities of Lady Judd, Sir Thomas White, John Hunwick, Thomas Ingram, and William Turner had been lost. Nine tenths of the outstanding debt of £1,810 incurred by the previous administration in 1834–5 were unacceptable; the debts and running costs since then totalled £2,781, including £450 for providing five new cells at the borough gaol. The Severalls estate, though probably undervalued at *c.* £950 a year gross, was the largest source of income and was in a generally good condition, but total annual income from the fishery, all the other estates, and market tolls was only *c.* £1,550, clearly insufficient to pay off the debt, especially as interest of £450 a year was paid on the mortgage of the Severalls.

In January 1837 the corporation levied a rate of 9*d.* on a rateable value of £19,058, but it lacked powers to raise rates for expenses already incurred. Application was

[49] 5 & 6 Wm. IV, c. 76; *Lond. Gaz.* 7 Dec. 1835, p. 2324; E.R.O., Boro. Mun., Boro. Council Mins., 28 Dec. 1835, 1 Jan. 1836; ibid. Acc. C210, J. B. Harvey Colln. iv, p. 74.

[50] Inf. from P. Coverley, E.R.O. Colch. branch archivist.

[51] M. E. Speight, 'Politics in the Boro. of Colch. 1812–47' (Lond. Univ. Ph.D. thesis, 1969), 73–4: copy in E.R.O.

[52] Speight, 'Politics in Colch.' 74; E.R.O., Boro. Mun., Boro. Council Mins. 28 Dec. 1835; 1 Jan., 6 May 1836.

[53] *V.C.H. Essex*, ii. 502–8.

[54] Below, Fishery.

[55] Below, Par. Govt. and Poor Relief; Public Services; Educ.

made to the Treasury for permission to sell the borough estates to finance running costs and build a new town hall besides paying off debts, but only the sale of enough land to pay off debts was permitted. By October £2,648 had been raised from sales of 45 portions of the Severalls estate.

In November 1837 electors, lacking confidence in the Liberal council's ability to put the borough finances on a secure footing and perhaps fearful of the fierce opposition of some Liberal nonconformists to church rates, returned a Conservative majority, who promptly reappointed their own supporters to some of the key borough offices.[56] The corporation reduced the interest on the Severalls mortgage, and raised a rate of 6*d.* on a reassessed rateable value of almost £45,000, thus managing to balance the accounts, while accepting the necessity of continuing to carry the burden of mortgage debt. The income from the sale of more of the Severalls estate in 1840 was used to restore Sir Thomas White's charity, and that from further sales in 1842, with money raised by public subscription, financed the new town hall opened in 1845.

While the reformed system of local government was being established in the borough, the Chartist movement for radical parliamentary reforms, including universal suffrage, presented a potential threat to law and order nationally; in Colchester, however, the relatively few Chartists were essentially moderate and cautious. The Colchester Working Men's Association formed in 1838 was led by craftsmen and small traders; prominent among them was William Wire, watchmaker and antiquarian, who argued for the use of moral not physical force. Many Chartists were nonconformists and in 1838 were allied with campaigns for the abolition of church rates and for church disestablishment. The local impact of Chartism was small, but it may have encouraged those who feared its consequences to devote more of their resources to charitable giving and religious and educational work as ways of countering its influence among the poorer classes. In the 1840s former Chartists often united with the radical Liberals to oppose the corn laws, which were supported by the 'protectionist' Conservatives, and, after repeal, to promote the later parliamentary reform bills; others became involved with trade unions, and John Castle founded the Colchester Co-operative Society in 1861.[57]

The pattern of parliamentary representation in the period from 1835 to 1852 seemed affected more by local than national factors.[58] Colchester was one of only three boroughs (the others being Aylesbury and Grantham) out of 189 whose voting showed a shift to the right after parliamentary reform in 1832. The Conservatives, whose party organization through parliamentary clubs was superior to the Liberals', held both of the town's seats, except for the period 1847–50 when the Liberal J. A. Hardcastle held one seat.[59] Local newspapers, with their declared party biases, particularly the Conservative *Essex Standard*, and pamphlets and handbills exercised considerable influence.[60] Direct bribery was not widespread, voters being more affected by other pressures, and by 1852 appears to have diminished.[61] The newly enfranchised £10 householders in Colchester, unlike those in industrialized parts of the country, included many tradesmen dependent on the economy of the surrounding agricultural area. Conservative voting was encouraged by the identification of that party with

56 Speight, 'Politics in Colch.' 253–4.

57 A. F. J. Brown, *Chartism in Essex and Suff.* 36, 39–42, 60, 85–122; Brown, *Colch. 1815–1914*, 110–24; Speight, 'Politics in Colch.' 242–6; B.L. Add. MS. 27820, ff. 310–13, 346–8.

58 *Essex Tel.* 1 Dec. 1885 gives details of election results 1832–85; E.R.O., Acc. C 32, Wire Colln. of election handbills and posters 1731–1852.

59 J. Turner, 'Colch. Poll Bks. 1832–52' (Essex Univ. B.A. Project, 1979), 1; Speight, 'Politics in Colch.' 165–96; *E.R.* viii. 242.

60 Speight, 'Politics in Colch.' 197–224.

61 Turner, 'Colch. Poll Bks.' 8; E.R.O., Acc. C210, J. B. Harvey Colln. iv, pp. 136–7.

agricultural interests and by the apparent incompetence of the Liberal-controlled borough council of 1835–7. In addition the Conservative Sir G. H. Smyth of Berechurch hall, M.P. 1835–50, was popular and noted for his anti-Roman Catholicism, and the Conservative Richard Sanderson, M.P. 1832–47, was a generous local benefactor.[62] Both men successfully promoted the Stour Valley Railway Act and the Navigation Act, which were beneficial to the town.[63] Voters who consistently supported the Liberal party were usually staunch nonconformists, but Wesleyans were divided between the two political parties.[64]

Local party politics were based on national parties. Conservative majorities were returned continuously in borough elections between late 1837 and 1879, not always large but enough to keep control of the council and to invest it with a legitimacy lacking before 1835. In 1847, following Hardcastle's parliamentary victory, the Liberals gained five seats on the borough council, but their success was shortlived and the Conservatives continued to dominate municipal politics until 1867.[65]

The corporation was still in the 1860s playing only a limited part in local government, content to leave important matters like drainage and sewerage to the improvement commissioners. Water and gas were supplied by private companies and a fire brigade was provided by the Essex & Suffolk Equitable insurance society. A burial board, set up in 1854, opened a cemetery in 1856.[66] Income from rates was £879 in 1854–5, which was only 25 per cent of total receipts of £3,482, compared with Ipswich's rateable income of £3,014, 40 per cent of a total of £7,591.[67] In 1863 the corporation paid for a new cattle market by taking out a further mortgage on borough property.[68]

The achievements of the improvement commissioners in the 19th-century town were considerable. Under an Act of 1847 which granted permissive powers to intervene on public health grounds, they undertook substantial drainage and sewerage work. The board's constitution was altered by the Act: previously all ratepayers of more than £50 a year had been eligible to be commissioners; from 1847 £30 male ratepayers and owners of land adjoining the river elected annually from among their number 24 commissioners with power to appoint committees, make bylaws, levy rates, and borrow money.[69] Between 1856 and 1885 there were *c.* 250 electors, and three to six of the 24 commissioners at any one time were shipowners. J. B. Harvey, a Liberal nonconformist prominent in a wide range of local activities and member of the borough council 1847–90, was an active commissioner from 1848 and chairman from 1860. Members often had vested interests which might seem to threaten their impartiality, as in 1866 when six commissioners were connected with the gas company with which the board had a contract.[70]

Most council members of both parties were merchants and traders, or professional men; a few were gentlemen of private means; many had family or business connexions with other members or officials, and prominent men often served on other bodies. Of the 24 council members seven in 1857 and nine in 1865 were also improvement commissioners. Charles H. Hawkins, borough councillor 1844–89, mayor four times, poor-law guardian, improvement commissioner, and leader of

62 Turner, 'Colch. Poll Bks.' 30; Brown, *Colch. 1815–1914*, 83–4; Speight, 'Politics in Colch.' 265.

63 Speight, 'Politics in Colch.' 296–8; below, Public Services (Railways).

64 Turner, 'Colch. Poll Bks.' 17.

65 Brown, *Colch. 1815–1914*, 85–8.

66 Below, Public Services.

67 *Boro. Accts. 1854–5* [350], pp. 321–2, H.C. (1856), lix.

68 Brown, *Colch. 1815–1914*, 45.

69 Colch. Navigation & Improvement Act, 10 & 11 Vic. c. 281 (Local & Personal).

70 E.R.O., Acc. C210, J. B. Harvey Colln. i, p. 1; v, pp. 135, 463; Phillips, *Ten Men*, 4; below, Soc. and Cultural (Newspapers).

Colchester Conservative party, illustrates the power of a local family network: he was the son of William, a council member, son-in-law of John Bawtree, a prominent citizen, and younger brother and business partner of William Warwick Hawkins M.P., who was himself the son-in-law of Francis Smythies the elder, a former town clerk.[71] Successful local businessmen who served on the council included Thomas Moy, a coal merchant, who was mayor 1877–9, and Alfred Francis, a corn merchant, who died in 1884 during his mayoralty.[72]

Nonconformity was strong in the town, and the Independents or Congregationalists were particularly allied with the Liberal cause against the privileges of the established church, which was often aligned with Conservative interests. In 1861 after a Liberal councillor's objections to Conservative domination of the mayoralty from 1837, the new Conservative mayor promised to discharge his duties apolitically. Many local Liberals were able to overcome their frustration at being effectively excluded from council decision-making by being involved in public activities outside the borough council, as improvement commissioners, members of the gas company, educational reformers, or poor-law guardians. Party politics were not absent from other bodies. James Wicks, after his election to the board of guardians in 1869, fought successfully on behalf of the Liberals for the press to be admitted to the board's meetings.[73]

The freemen were insignificant in town government after 1835, when the municipal franchise was extended to all £10 ratepayers, their numbers on the parliamentary electoral register declining from 413 in 1835 to 323 in 1891.[74] A few of them, however, in attempting to defend their allegedly disappearing rights, occupied much of the council's time and money in repeated litigation.[75]

In parliamentary elections the freemen's influence steadily declined as the parliamentary franchise was extended. After the second Reform Act (1867) the total registered electorate was 2,970, equivalent to about an eighth of the town's population. The Liberals benefited, winning both seats in 1868. Electioneering brought some excitement to the community and participation was not for the faint-hearted: at the hustings in 1868 at one point 'a volley of stinking eggs' was thrown at Dr. W. Brewer, one of the Liberal candidates. Colchester's only longstanding Liberal M.P. during the 19th century was J. Gurdon Rebow, M.P. 1857–9 and 1865–70.[76] The 1868 election marked a turning point, Rebow being the last truly local candidate. Afterwards general election campaigns became increasingly preoccupied with national rather than local issues, with national parties rather than with local personalities. At the byelection on Rebow's death in 1870 the Liberal government's candidate was Gen. Sir Henry Storks, a strong supporter of the controversial Contagious Diseases Acts, which provided for compulsory inspection and medical treatment of prostitutes in garrison towns, including Colchester. Opponents of the legislation, including Josephine Butler, supported a rival Liberal candidate, Dr. B. Langley, and used the election in their campaign for repeal. Langley withdrew on election day, and the Conservative, Col. A. Learmonth of Edinburgh, won convincingly. The Liberal defectors, however, were those least committed to active Liberalism and nonconformity; the committed remained loyal to party rather than to a particular moral issue.[77]

[71] Phillips, *Ten Men*, 3; *E.R.* viii. 178; *Gent. Mag.* 1868 (1), p. 405.

[72] *E.C.S.* 13 Sept. 1884; 2 Jan. 1910.

[73] E.R.O., Acc. C210, J. B. Harvey Colln. *passim*; Brown, *Colch. 1815–1914*, 101; Phillips, *Ten Men*, 94–6; below, this chapter, Social Hist.

[74] Brown, *Colch. 1815–1914*, 82; *E.C.S.* 31 Oct. 1891.

[75] e.g. *E.C.S.* 22 June 1895; below, Common Lands.

[76] Brown, *Colch. 1815–1914*, 99–100; E.R.O., Acc. C210, J. B. Harvey Colln. iv, pp. 179–83; *Essex Tel.* 1 Dec. 1885; *E.C.S.* 3 June 1983.

[77] A. Phillips, 'Four Colch. Elections', *An Essex Tribute*, ed. K. Neale, 199–227.

The Conservative vote was maintained in the 1870s as Colchester continued to function as a market town for the surrounding agricultural area; the growing military presence at the garrison added to Conservative support. As local Liberalism began to strengthen,[78] however, two Liberal M.P.s, the moderate R. K. Causton, a wealthy sportsman and amateur photographer, and the radical W. Willis, a barrister whose father had been a straw hat maker, were returned in 1880 in a very close result.[79] Agricultural depression and the coming of industry from the 1880s helped the Liberal cause in the longer term, and after 1886 class divisions became increasingly significant in parliamentary campaigns. In 1885, after the third Reform Act (1884) had deprived Colchester of one of its two parliamentary seats, the Conservative, H. J. Trotter, a landowner from County Durham, won the single seat.[80] He retained it in 1886 when some leading members of the local Liberal party joined the Liberal Unionists on the Liberal split over Irish home rule. Elections still roused strong passions, and a disagreement between some rival party supporters in 1886 led to a fight in which 'some of the combatants received severe blows, the blood flowing freely' and a crowd of 200 to 300 people gathered.[81] In 1887 the revised electoral roll was composed of 4,048 householders, 355 freemen, and 17 lodgers. At the byelection in 1888, following Trotter's death in a hunting accident, the seat was won by F. R. G. Greville of Easton Lodge, Little Easton, then known as Lord Brooke, the son of the 4th earl of Warwick, whose wife Frances became well known in county and national society, but he took little interest in parliamentary matters.[82] The Conservatives held the seat in 1892, but with a new candidate, Capt. H. S. Naylor-Leyland, of the Life Guards, who had a much reduced majority.[83]

The role of the corporation started to change significantly from the 1870s as legislation forced local councils to adopt more interventionist policies. The 1848 Public Health Act had never been adopted in Colchester because public health responsibilities were shared between the borough council and the improvement commissioners, but in 1874 the commissioners surrendered to the council all their powers except those relating to the river, which was improved extensively in the 1880s.[84] The corporation in 1874 appointed an inspector of nuisances and formed a council sanitary committee to deal with water supply, sewerage and drainage, and the improvement, repair, cleaning, and lighting of streets. Colchester was one of the three healthiest towns in England in 1879, but the sanitary inspector's graphic reports of prevailing conditions in the poorer parts of the town show that even in one of the more salubrious towns like Colchester public health advances were not achieved quickly. In 1880 the inspector shrank from visiting many filthy and squalid places which lacked proper sanitation or even a water supply. Poor families with no facilities for isolation regularly suffered avoidable and often fatal illnesses.[85]

The corporation bought the water company in 1880 and in 1883 built the controversial water tower known as Jumbo in its efforts to extend the water supply. In 1884 a sewage works was built at the Hythe and a borough isolation hospital opened at Mile End. The council gradually widened its range of municipal activities: a town museum had been established by 1861; an additional volunteer fire brigade formed in 1878 was supervised by the borough chief constable; a scale

78 Para. based on D. White, *Liberal Ascendancy in Colch.* (priv. print. Brightlingsea, 1989), 159–89.

79 *E.A.T.* 3rd ser. xxiii. 84–5.

80 Brown, *Colch. 1815–1914*, 100–1; *Essex Tel.* 1 Dec. 1885.

81 *E.C.S.* 3 July 1886.

82 *E.R.* xxxiii. 45–6; *Who's Who, 1900*, 1032.

83 *E.C.S.* 3 April 1992.

84 P.R.O., MH 13/53; below, Port.

85 E.R.O., Boro. Mun., Boro. Council Sanitary Cttee. Mins. 26 Feb. 1879; 28 July 1880.

of cab fares was set in 1880. An open-air public bathing place was provided in 1883, a recreation ground in 1885, and the Castle Park in 1892. The Public Libraries Act was adopted in 1891.[86] In 1890 some of the borough farms had to be relet at reduced rents because of agricultural depression, but by then regular rates set twice a year on an increasing rateable value had placed borough finances on a more secure footing. In 1892–3 total council expenditure was *c.* £40,000 when a rate of 4*s.* 6¼*d.* was fixed on the rateable value of £116,318.[87]

The Conservative majority on the corporation was overturned only in 1879, by which time most of the improvement commissioners' duties had been transferred to the council. The Liberals then appointed a Liberal mayor and reappointed as town clerk J. B. Philbrick who had held the office 1835–37. In 1880 J. B. Harvey was the first Liberal alderman elected for 40 years, the Conservatives having opposed his nomination on four previous occasions, for fear of losing their majority. The Liberals retained power into the 20th century, except in 1884–5 when the Conservatives gained a majority mainly because of the electorate's dislike of the high rate caused by the Liberals' public works, notably in their water policy. James Wicks, the vociferous champion of the purchase of the waterworks, lost his seat on the council to the delight of his opponents, but was re-elected the following year and later relaxed his combative style enough to become mayor in 1895–6.[88]

From 1880 until 1904 was a period of consensus town politics, with the two parties agreeing not to contest elections; the mayoralty alternated on a party basis, the mayor remaining aloof from party politics during his year of office. A ratepayers' association was formed by some citizens who feared the potential results of such electoral pacts, and although the association had minimal success electorally it provided a forum for airing grievances. The Co-operative society also fielded at least one unsuccessful candidate.[89]

Council meetings had been held only quarterly as late as 1871, but by 1881, with an increasing workload, there were often two a month. The number of committees increased from only two in mid century to 12 in 1880 and 16 in 1890.[90] In 1891 there were 5,135 municipal voters (*c.* 15 per cent of the population).[91] The existing constitution of the council needed modification to enable the corporation to cope more efficiently with the demands of an increased population and a much wider range of municipal responsibilities.

Civic ceremonies, such as the annual opening of the oyster fishery, the proclamation of St. Dennis's fair, and the oyster feast, were continued after 1835. In 1838, to celebrate Queen Victoria's coronation, public subscriptions were invited to provide meat and money in the parishes and dinners in the workhouse and gaol. Food tickets were distributed in 1856 to mark the end of the Crimean war, and a public dinner was held at the corn exchange for *c.* 170 soldiers. It was the celebration of the Prince of Wales's marriage in 1863, however, which seemed to change the style of official festivities, aided no doubt by the military presence in the town. As well as the usual food provisions, there were processions, bands, sports, a military review, fireworks, and a bonfire, all setting a pattern for Queen Victoria's golden jubilee in 1887 and later occasions.[92] The oyster feast developed from a private and exclusive meal to a grand occasion promoting civic pride with

[86] E.R.O., Acc. C210, J. B. Harvey Colln. iii, p. 32; below, Public Services; Hospitals; *V.C.H. Essex Bibliog.* 325.

[87] Colch. Boro. Council, *Abstract of Accts. 1892–3*, 102–3, 106–7.

[88] D. White, *Liberal Ascendancy in Colch.* 61–5; E.R.O., Acc. C210, J. B. Harvey Colln. iii, p. 85; Phillips, *Ten Men*, 103–15; *Essex Tel.* 28 Jan. 1905.

[89] White, *Liberal Ascendancy in Colch.* 65–71.

[90] Phillips, *Ten Men*, 122.

[91] *E.C.S.* 31 Oct. 1891.

[92] E.R.O., Acc. C210, J. B. Harvey Colln. iv, p. 74; v, p. 111; vii, pp. 143–5; *E.J.* xxvi (2), 34–6.

important national figures as guests. Everything was designed to bear witness to Colchester's municipal progress in the 19th century, for which the borough council could claim increasing credit.[93]

A Century of Change 1892–1991

Local government in the period was concentrated in the borough council, whose power was at its height immediately before the First World War. Thereafter, although the council's functions continued to grow, it was increasingly subject to directives and dependent on grants and loans from the central government. Essex county council, created in 1889 to provide certain services for the county as a whole, came to play a more important role. It was responsible for Colchester's secondary and higher education from 1903, and took over the borough library in 1924 and poor-relief administration from the guardians in 1929.[94] The 16 parishes in the borough, which retained few civil functions, were amalgamated in 1897 to create one unified civil parish.[95]

In the 20th century political developments in the town were much more closely entwined than previously with those in the nation as a whole: the adoption of more interventionist policies at central and local level, the growth of the Labour party, and the participation of women through the ballot box and to a limited extent as elected representatives. By 1884 the municipal electorate included 600 women, and from the 1890s women were more directly involved in public affairs at a local level. The Colchester Women's Liberal Association, founded in 1892, was the most active in pursuing women's rights, particularly women's suffrage, but women of various political persuasions, including Conservatives, together formed the Colchester branch of the National Union of Women's Suffrage Societies.[96] In 1895 Sir Weetman Pearson, a wealthy oil contractor, won the parliamentary seat for the Liberals. He retained it at subsequent elections until he was raised to the peerage as Lord Cowdray in 1910; created a viscount in 1917, he was high steward of Colchester 1910–27 and a generous benefactor to the town. L. Worthington Evans won for the Conservatives in 1910.[97] He retained the seat in 1919 when he stood as a Coalitionist against a Labour candidate. As a member of the Cabinet he was reputed to have the loudest voice there 'if not in the House'.[98] In 1918 the borough had been merged with most of Lexden and Winstree rural district to form a new constituency of which the former Colchester constituency comprised two thirds.[99]

To take account of population growth and the borough council's wider range of functions the number of its members was increased from 24 to 32 in 1892. The municipal wards were redrawn within the borough boundaries to revert from the three existing wards created in 1835 to the four which had existed in the 18th century, north, south, east, and west, each represented by six councillors and two aldermen. At the same time the council's power was augmented by the transfer from the improvement commissioners of responsibility for the Colne navigation, for which the council set up a new harbour and navigation committee.[1] The council remained responsible for its estate, police force, sanitation, roads and drainage, water supply, street lighting, cattle market, museum and muniments, Castle park,

93 E.C.L. Colch., Press cuttings, Mayors, S. G. Cooke; D. Cannadine, 'The transformation of civic ritual . . . the Colch. oyster feast', *Past and Present*, xciv. 109–30.

94 *E.C.S.* 11 Sept. 1981; section based on E.R.O., Acc. C3, dated boro. council newspaper cuttings, 1892–1945.

95 Youngs, *Admin. Units. of Eng.* i. 135.

96 Brown, *Colch. 1815–1914*, 104–6.

97 B. Hamnett, 'Cowdray, Colch. and the British Connection', unpubl. paper, History Dept., Essex Univ.; *E.C.S.* 7 May 1927.

98 *Essex Tel.* 4 Jan. 1919; *E.R.* xl. 89.

99 *E.C.S.* 30 June 1917; Youngs, *Admin. Units of Eng.* i. 726.

1 Colch. Corp. Act, 55 & 56 Vic. c. 107 (Loc. and Priv.).

recreation ground, public bathing places, and footpaths, and for the implementation of Acts of Parliament relating to the borough. It strengthened its control of the fishery, and also continued to select scholars for the town grammar school. A school board was formed in 1892 at the council's request.[2]

In the period up to the First World War the corporation further extended its functions, opening the public library in 1893, establishing a corporation fire brigade in 1896, taking over the work of the burial board in 1896 and the school board's responsibility for elementary education in 1903, and providing allotments for the working classes from 1893, an electricity supply from 1898, and a tram service from 1904. A new town hall was opened in 1902, a symbol of municipal pride and progress, though at first the plans had been vociferously opposed by the Ratepayers' Association. Under a new scheme for the grammar school in 1909 the mayor was *ex officio* chairman of governors. The river was improved and King Edward quay built between 1910 and 1912. As road traffic increased, road improvements and road safety became of greater concern to the corporation.[3]

There were inevitably areas of conflict where the borough council's interests clashed with those of the county. In 1894 the county council accepted responsibility for only 20 of the 80 miles of main roads in the borough, a source of great dissatisfaction to Colchester corporation.[4] The county's high expenditure was resented locally by those who associated it too readily with spending on the needs of metropolitan Essex.

The poor-law guardians retained responsibility for poor relief in the early 20th century, but in times of economic depression the borough council was strongly represented in *ad hoc* schemes to give emergency outdoor relief. For example, in 1894 a central committee composed of the mayor, some councillors, and clergymen was formed to raise money for issuing 1*s.* tickets for food, fuel, and other necessities. The problem of unemployment was already on a scale beyond the guardians' resources before 1914, and the council provided temporary jobs on public work schemes on many occasions, as in 1908 when some men were employed to dig sewers for the new county asylum, preference being given to married men with families. Some underlying tension between the guardians, probably anxious about their own declining influence, and the corporation surfaced in the guardians' displeasure at receiving no invitation to the official service held by the corporation on King Edward VII's death in 1910.[5]

Gas remained in private ownership, despite the borough council's wish to take over the undertaking and its unsuccessful attempt in 1916, supported by the county council and Lexden and Winstree rural district council, to oppose the gas company's bill to increase its powers. Council members who had a pecuniary interest in the gas company were not allowed to vote on the issue; some were sympathetic to the council's view that the company had passed on excess profits to shareholders instead of reducing the price of gas, but Alderman Henry Laver, chairman of the gas company was not among them.[6]

In the period from 1892 to 1914 decisions on how far to adopt interventionist local policies, in the acquisition, for example, of public utilities or in housing, remained to a large extent in the borough council's own hands. Provided that

[2] Below, Fishery; Educ.

[3] Below, Public Services; Port; Communications (Roads).

[4] *Essex Tel.* 24 Nov. 1894.

[5] *E.C.S.* 13 Jan. 1894; 24 Feb., 4 Apr. 1908; 21 May 1910; below, Par. Govt. and Poor Relief.

[6] E.R.O., Acc. C235, Box 2, reg. of shareholders of Colch. Gas Co. 1915; below, Public Services (Gas).

Bourne mill, 1923

Greenstead Mill, 1899

Silk Mill, formerly Brown and Moy's, 1878

Jumbo Water Tower, *c.* 1950

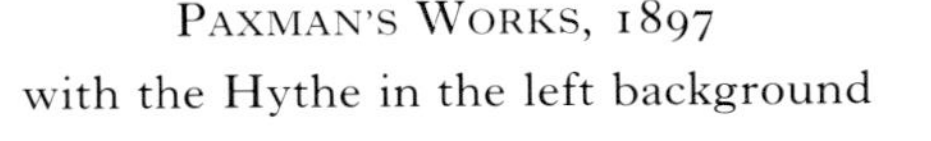

PAXMAN'S WORKS, 1897
with the Hythe in the left background

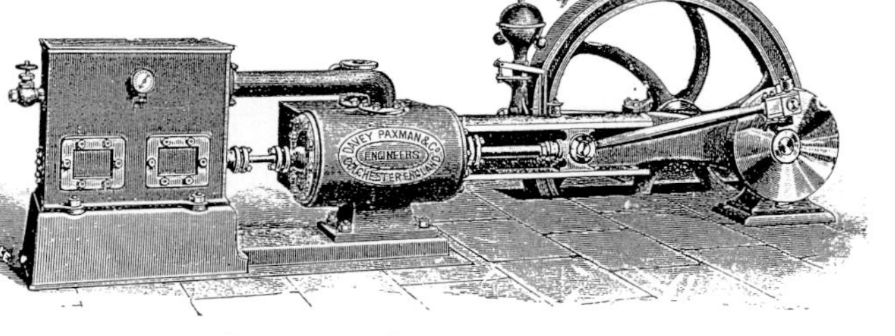

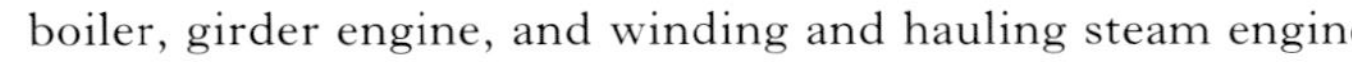

PAXMAN'S PRODUCTS
boiler, girder engine, and winding and hauling steam engine

municipal ownership of water or electricity or the fishery could show a profit, as each did in the early 20th century, any laissez-faire opposition was effectively silenced. The failure of the tramways to make a profit except in wartime led to more radical questions of whether the council should go so far as to subsidize certain public services. Early housing policies raised similar ideological issues. The council was statutorily required from 1890[7] to clear slums, but powers to provide working-class houses to replace them were permissive and no council houses were built in Colchester before the First World War.

Local government responsibilities were increased during the First World War by central government direction and control. In 1915 the borough council appointed a local tribunal composed of representatives of the army, the council, and labour to supervise military recruitment and hear appeals.[8] The council provided additional temporary buildings at the Infectious Diseases hospital, took over the voluntary maternity centre, set up a war loan scheme, introduced special 1*d.* tram fares for troops, provided communal kitchens in the New Town area, tried to regulate and conserve fuel supplies, supervised food rationing, and provided allotments for food cultivation with, in 1918, at least 25 pigs. Wartime economies included the reduction of lighting, the postponement of major road and harbour improvement schemes, and the purchase of coal in advance at summer prices. As more men enlisted, the council increasingly employed women, including 14 as tram conductresses by 1916.[9] In 1917 there were 640 council employees of whom 230 were women; only 84 of the men were of military age. A special salaries committee was set up to deal with frequent claims for higher wages and salaries to meet rising prices.[10]

Between the two world wars the borough council extended its functions even further, but its autonomy in policy-making and finance was further eroded by central legislation. The sewerage and the electricity and water supplies were improved, and further work was done on the harbour. Buses replaced the trams in 1928–9 but proved no more profitable than their predecessors. Improvements were made to roads, and a bypass was constructed between 1930 and 1933, partly funded by central government as a relief scheme for the unemployed. The cemetery was enlarged in 1937 and a new fire station opened in 1938. Facilities for sport and recreation were also extended.[11]

Colchester built no council houses until 1921, although Chelmsford had a scheme before 1914.[12] The council appointed a housing committee in 1919, which included representatives of working people. Between 1921 and 1939, with the aid of central government subsidies, 1,242 council houses, representing about a third of all new houses, were built at Mile End, Lexden, Old Heath, Shrub End, between the Harwich and Ipswich roads, and near the new bypass road. Each scheme generated a welcome, though limited and temporary, demand for builders and labourers at a time of high unemployment. The council increasingly employed direct labour and in 1936 established a housing department.[13]

To cope with its increasing functions the council was enlarged in 1937 from 32 to 36 members, and the borough rearranged into 9 new wards, each represented

7 Housing of the Working Classes Act, 55 & 56 Vic. c. 22.

8 *E.C.S.* 23 Oct. 1915.

9 Ibid. 10 June 1916; 6 Oct. 1917.

10 *Essex Tel.* 8 Dec. 1917.

11 Below, Public Services; Port; Communications.

12 S. Durgan, 'Laissez-faire and Interventionism in Housing: Chelmsford 1900–14, a Case Study' (Essex Univ. M.A. thesis, 1981).

13 R. O'Connell, 'Council Housing and the Small Town: Colch. 1919–50' (Essex Univ. M.A. thesis, 1984), 1–58, appendix.

by three elected councillors, of whom one would retire each year, and by one alderman chosen by the council; existing members were assigned to the new wards. The size of the municipal electorate had increased from 4,786 in 1892 to more than 24,000.[14] The administration of municipal services entailed a considerable increase in borough council staff. The advice of salaried chief officers as professional experts was welcomed by council members faced with the complexity of 20th-century decision-making. In 1924 the mayor publicly thanked the borough accountant for his 'kind and efficient' help which had saved the council hundreds of pounds, much more than the cost of his salary.[15] Four loyal officers retired in 1926: the town clerk had served for over 40 years, the borough librarian for 30, the superintendant of the waterworks for 46, and the museum curator for 24.[16]

A special committee set up in 1935 took precautions against air raid and fire in 1938–9. On the outbreak of war in 1939 food and fuel committees were appointed and the opening of a new town library was suspended. During the war council housebuilding and other schemes were halted. The council was subjected to even more central government regulation than in the previous war, notably in civil defence, evacuation, and rationing. In 1941 the borough fire service was transferred to central government.[17] The council provided a war-time nursery in Brook Street in 1942, to help women to contribute to the war effort in the local factories. A special committee was established in 1944, to consider post-war reconstruction and development, particularly in housing.[18]

Rates continued to be an important source of council income between 1892 and 1945, and the rateable value of the town steadily increased to £193,486 in 1913–14.[19] In 1897 of an income of £45,000 the rates contributed £28,000; the rest was derived from central government and county council grants, and the borough fishery, estates, and markets. Colchester's total borough rate was only slightly above the average of 63 towns in 1898, but the elements within it for the school board and for poor relief, which were out of the council's control, were significantly above average.[20] Expenditure gradually increased as the council provided more services. The rate rose to 7*s*. 4*d*. in 1913, doubled after the war, and was more than 18*s*. from 1921 until 1929 when the administration of poor relief passed from the board of guardians to the county council; the borough was revalued in 1929 at £271,960 and the overall rate fell from 19*s*. 4*d*. to 14*s*.[21] By 1938–9 the rateable value had increased to £344,857, and a rate of 14*s*. 8*d*. raised £237,828, but by then rateable income was less than half of the total borough income, and central government grants financed over half of total expenditure; loans outstanding at the end of the year amounted to £2,185,947.[22]

At the end of the 19th century trading and professional interests still predominated in the council chamber, though new industrialists like James Paxman, John Kavanagh, Wilson Marriage, and John Knopp were becoming influential.[23] In the first half of the 20th century the pattern was slightly modified as early Labour councillors were mainly drawn from trade union and working class backgrounds. Family connexions and freemasonry continued to provide useful introductions to civic life, and such features continued into the 20th century. A few women had been regularly appointed as guardians from 1893 and co-opted to the education

14 *E.C.S.* 7 Mar. 1936; 6 Nov. 1937.
15 Ibid. 5 Apr. 1924. 16 *Essex Tel.* 9 Oct. 1926.
17 Below, Public Services (Fire Service).
18 *Essex Tel.* 4 July 1942; 4 Mar. 1944.
19 Colch. Boro. Council, *Abstract of Accts. 1913–14*, p. xiv.
20 *E.C.S.* 5 Feb., 6 Aug. 1898.
21 Ibid. 27 Apr. 1918; 6 Apr. 1929.
22 Colch. Boro. Council, *Abstract of Accts. 1938–9*.
23 *E.R.* xxxi. 116; xli. 211; above, this chapter, Econ.

committee from 1903, but there were no female councillors until Mrs. C. B. Alderton, Liberal, and Mrs. P. R. Green, Labour, were co-opted in 1918, although women were eligible to serve from 1907.[24] Apart from them there were only a few other female members by 1945, notably Dame Catherine Hunt, Conservative, and Dr. Ruth Bensusan-Butt, Labour.[25] Nonconformist chapels, particularly Lion Walk Congregational, continued to supply a number of councillors. F. E. Macdonald Docker, champion of the unemployed, Labour councillor, and minister of Stockwell Street Congregational church, was mayor 1935–6, the first clergyman to serve that office.[26] Denominational differences became less significant in the 20th century, and party considerations dominated local politics, though to a lesser extent during the two World Wars. The Conservative P. A. Sanders served as a capable wartime mayor for an unprecedented four years, 1939–43, though the Labour councillors objected to forgoing their turn to nominate one of their own group.[27]

Between 1892 and 1904 the previous pattern of contrived political agreement by the Liberals and Conservatives continued, both party groups content to perpetuate their own existence; ward elections were contested again in 1904. The Liberals had a majority on the council until 1907, and 12 of them were accused of belonging to a secret dining club where they forged municipal schemes.[28] Thereafter the Liberal decline was mirrored by the steady rise of the labour movement. The first representative of the working classes was John Howe; associated with Chartism in his early life, he was elected as a Liberal in 1894, and pressed unsuccessfully for evening council meetings instead of the daytime ones which effectively excluded most working men from standing for election; as a poor-law guardian, he objected to the use of workhouse children as cheap labour in the gardens of the wealthy.[29] A branch of the Independent Labour Party had been formed by 1894, but that initially divided the labour movement, some members of which saw the Liberal party as their best advocate. Both the trades council, founded in 1891, and the I.L.P. had been dissolved by 1900, but both had revived by 1905, and one I.L.P. councillor, T. Smith, was elected before 1914.[30]

No elections were held during the First World War, vacancies being filled by co-option. Three Labour candidates were returned in the 1919 council election. Some local Liberals were uneasy at the rise of the Labour party: Asher Prior, a staunch Liberal, voted against the Labour candidate in parliamentary elections; E. A. Blaxill, a Liberal alderman, became a Conservative.[31] Between the wars none of the three parties had a majority in the council. The Labour party fought hard to secure their fair representation in the offices of mayor and aldermen, as the Liberals had done before them in 1879–80. T. Smith had to wait until 1928 to become the first Labour alderman on grounds of seniority. C. C. Smallwood had already been elected the first Labour mayor in 1926, after which the mayoralty passed to each party in turn until 1933.[32] Thereafter a special mayoralty committee composed of the mayor and previous mayors was set up to make a 'non-political' nomination each year. Although Labour feared that such a scheme would militate against their interests, mayors were still elected by 'gentlemen's agreement' from each of the three parties in turn. Council elections were suspended again during

24 Brown, *Colch. 1815–1914*, 105; *E.R.* lxi. 52; P. Hollis, *Ladies Elect, Women in Eng. Local Govt., 1865–1914*, 392.

25 *E.R.* lviii. 51; R. Lindsey, 'Dr. Ruth Bensusan-Butt' (Essex Univ. B.A. History project, 1987).

26 *E.C.S.* 16 Nov. 1935; 12 Feb. 1993.

27 *Essex Tel.* 15 Nov. 1941.

28 White, *Liberal Ascendancy in Colch.* 72–7.

29 Brown, *Chartism in Essex and Suff.* 120–1; *East Anglian Hist. Workshop Bull.* vi. 7–8.

30 Brown, *Colch. 1815–1914*, 142–50.

31 *E.C.S.* 9 Jan. 1926; Colch. Instititute, Colch. Recalled, interview 1516A.

32 *E.C.S.* 13 Nov. 1926; 17 Nov. 1928.

the Second World War. Party allegiances were firmly held, but personal antagonism was generally absent.

Political events between the wars in Colchester were less dramatic than in some other parts of the country. In May 1926 in the General Strike the Home Office appointed an emergency food officer, all units at the garrison were put on standby, and 30 special constables were sworn in. Some tramworkers, the railwaymen, and some union men at the local engineering works struck for just over a week, but 'for the most part the community went its way in a half-hearted manner'. An orderly demonstration on St. John's Green attended by 2,000–3,000 strikers was addressed by the Labour councillor T. Smith, chairman of the local strike committee, and by Clement Attlee, M.P. for Limehouse, London, the later prime minister.[33]

A Fascist meeting was held at the Albert Hall in 1934, and Fascist blackshirts had a small local headquarters in St. John's Street *c.* 1935.[34] The borough council, some members dissenting, allowed a Fascist meeting to be held in Castle park in 1935; several hundreds attended but there was no disturbance.[35] Sir Oswald Moseley, the Fascist leader, addressed an orderly meeting at the moot hall in 1936, but afterwards had to be escorted by police through a noisy crowd of supporters and opponents outside.[36] No support for fascism, nor for communism, was voiced in the council chamber, where moderation was the preferred style.

Between 1945 and 1950 the Labour party was in control of the borough council, but thereafter the Conservatives dominated until 1974. After 1945 councillors were drawn from a very wide range of social backgrounds, and party alignments became even more significant. The borough council's functions were further eroded. The borough police force was merged with Essex county police in 1947, and in 1948 electricity was nationalized and the borough infectious diseases hospital was transferred to the National Health Service. Borough control of the water supply was shared with neighbouring councils in 1960 when the Colchester and District Water Board was established.[37]

Housing needs were the most urgent problem in the period of post-war reconstruction, and 590 council houses were built between 1945 and 1949, many of them on the Barn Hall estate between the Old Heath and Mersea roads.[38] Between 1953 and 1958 the council finished building the Shrub End estate, developed housing at Prettygate with a private firm, and built houses at Monkwick, besides completing minor infilling schemes.[39] The town clerk successfully resisted the use of Greenstead for housing London overspill, and instead nine phases of council housing were built there for local people before 1974. Purpose-built homes for the elderly were provided from 1968.[40]

Such developments, coupled with the simultaneous private housing development in the borough, necessarily greatly increased council expenditure on sewerage, roads, and other services. More attention was gradually given to amenities and appearance. In the 1950s the council restored *c.* 50 buildings in the 'Dutch Quarter' to house elderly people.[41] A new central library was opened in Shewell Road in 1948.[42] After the war the county council had taken responsibility for all schools in

33 Ibid. 8, 15 May 1926; *Essex Tel.* 8, 11, 15 May 1926.
34 *E.C.S* 13 Oct. 1934; E.R.O., SA 0401.
35 *Essex Tel.* 10 Aug., 8 Sept. 1935.
36 *E.C.S.* 5 Dec. 1936; *Essex Tel.* 5 Dec. 1936.
37 *E.C.S.* 12 May 1950; below, Public Services; Hospitals.
38 O'Connell, 'Council Housing and the Small Town', 59–70, appendix.
39 *E.C.S.* 19 Sept. 1986.
40 Ibid. 7 June 1973; 26 Apr. 1968; *Colch. Expr.* 24 Feb. 1972.
41 *Colch. Official Guide* (1973), 25–6.
42 *V.C.H. Essex Bibliog.* 328.

the borough, but in 1964, after a struggle, the borough council was able to appoint its own education officer to administer the schools in the borough, an arrangement which lasted until 1974 when education reverted to the county council.[43]

Until the later 20th century patriotism was much in evidence in civic ceremonial, reinforced, particularly in wartime, by the participation of the garrison, with which the council's relationship was very good. The mayor and corporation in state bade farewell to departing troops and provided receptions on their return. In 1899 E. J. Sanders, the Conservative mayor, managed to revive, or institute, the observance of St. George's Day, though not everyone shared his enthusiasm. It came to be marked by a civic and military procession to a church service, the wearing of roses by council employees, and band music in the Castle park, though after the First World War only the church service remained. The mayor continued to open the fishery formally every year and proclaim St. Dennis's fair, and council members attended the friendly societies' annual parade. It was the mayor's oyster feast, however, which was the most prestigious, and expensive, event in the civic calendar. Reported extensively in the local and national press, it was considered an effective way of promoting Colchester's municipal achievements. Guests included the duke of York (later George VI) in 1924 and the Prince of Wales in 1931, among a succession of the political, religious, and military leaders of the nation. Invitations were extended even more widely in the 1930s to include prominent figures from the arts and sport, and after the Second World War the entertainment industry was well represented.[44] In the early 20th century the mayor and corporation still played a leading role in local celebrations of royal and other national events.[45] Civic and national pride were entwined, but loyalty to monarch and country may have been felt more strongly than civic pride by many citizens, and others may have felt that party and class divisions were more significant than either.

Under local government reorganization in 1974[46] Colchester borough was merged with West Mersea urban district, Wivenhoe urban district, and Lexden and Winstree rural district to form Colchester district. The new district council had 60 members. Borough status was granted and a mayor permitted as head of council; at the council's discretion the courtesy title of honorary alderman could be conferred on former councillors of eminent service who would then be entitled to participate in formal occasions only.[47] Rural interests from the area beyond the ancient borough were prominent in the new council. Power was shared between the main parties from 1974 to 1976. Thereafter there was a Conservative majority until 1987 when a minority administration was formed by the Social and Liberal Democrats.[48] That party, renamed Liberal Democrats, was still in control in 1991.[49]

The administration of river works, water supply, and sewerage was transferred to the Anglian Water Authority in 1974. The borough bus company was privatized in 1986. More leisure facilities were provided, and tourism promoted.[50] By 1973–4 the borough's rateable value had increased to £9,276,558. By then just over a third of total income was derived from rates, a small proportion from charges for council services, and most from central government grants.[51] The role of local government at borough level became less important in the later 20th century, particularly after 1974. The complexity of local government administration and constant change resulted in more decisions being made by paid chief officers than by elected representatives.[52]

43 *E.C.S* 10 Jan. 1964; below, Educ.

44 *Colch. Gaz.* 29 Oct. 1976.

45 *Essex Tel.* 24 June 1907.

46 Local Govt. Act, 21 Eliz. II, c. 70.

47 Essex C.C. *Essex County Handbk.* 74; Colch. Boro. Council, *Mins.* 3 Apr. 1974; inf. from Mr. J. Cobley, town clerk and chief executive, Colch. boro. council.

48 *E.C.S.* 29 June 1973; Colch. Charter 800 Assn., *Colch. 800*, 49.

49 *E.C.S* 19 July 1991.

50 Colch. Charter 800 Assn. *Colch. 800*, 35–6; below, Public Services (Internal Transport); above, this chapter, Econ.

51 Colch. Boro. Council, *Facts and Figures 1973–4*, 4–5, 50.

52 *E.C.S.* 19 Oct. 1973.

SOCIAL HISTORY

THROUGHOUT the period the town was a centre for social and recreational activities for the surrounding district, and the presence of the garrison helped to increase the range of facilities. An important factor was the strength of protestant nonconformity, whose relationship with the established church gradually changed from one of mutual distrust and rivalry to amicable co-operation. Philanthropy and self-help were key elements underpinning the 19th-century social structure, but in the 20th century they were replaced to a large extent by state health, welfare, and educational services. Overlapping social networks, based on economic position, religious affiliation, political interests, educational experience, kinship, and locality provided differing frameworks of social support and influence and supported a variety of leisure patterns.[53]

The garrison, established at the time of the Crimean War in 1855,[54] enriched local social life. The town and country gentry had considerable social contact with senior ranks, entertaining and attending balls during the military social season every winter. The garrison commander lived at Lexden for several years, and Scarletts, an estate south-east of the town, was rented for the district commander in the 1880s. There was keen army interest in local dramatics, sport, and freemasonry.[55] The garrison, however, also introduced or exacerbated some social problems. Many army families were destitute in the early years because commanding officers usually approved more marriages than the seven per cent allowed to the lower ranks; in 1857 only 144 out of 370 wives were 'authorized' army wives who were allowed to share their husband's rations and laundry services and enjoyed other advantages.[56] Soldiers, very visible in the uniforms of cavalry and infantry regiments, were often involved in drunken and disorderly behaviour in the town; public houses notorious for fights included the Blue Boar in Angel Lane, and the Woolpack in St. Botolph's Street. Armed military pickets were necessary in the town in the 1860s and 1870s; after Christmas 1869 it took two days to stop large numbers of men from the 18th and 33rd Foot from fighting each other and other men.[57] Prostitution was by no means a new problem, for in 1844 there had been complaints of prostitutes making the streets unsafe for respectable women after 7 p.m.,[58] but the army did bear a large responsibilty for its increase and for the spread of venereal disease. The issue became a political one in garrison towns between the passing of the Contagious Diseases Acts in the 1860s and their repeal in 1884.[59]

Relations between lower ranks and townspeople improved from the mid 1880s following army reforms.[60] Drunkenness and prostitution in the town diminished after barrack canteens were improved in 1886, encouraging men to spend more of their leisure at the camp. The temperance movement and some local churches may also have contributed to raising standards of behaviour.[61] Nevertheless soldiers continued to be involved in fights in the early 20th century, particularly with cattle

53 Below, Soc. and Cultural; Churches; Prot. Nonconf.

54 Below, Barracks.

55 A. F. F. H. Robertson, 'The Army in Colch. and its Influence on the Social, Economic and Political development of the Town, 1854–1914' (Essex Univ. Ph.D. thesis, 1991), 108–12, 195–203.

56 *Correspondence between War Dept. and Maj. Gen. Gascoigne on Destitution amongst Families of Soldiers at Colch.* [102], pp. 193–200, H.C. (1857), ix; Robertson, 'Army in Colch.' 66–9.

57 Robertson, 'Army in Colch.' 101–8.

58 *Essex Mercury*, 15 Oct. 1844.

59 Robertson, 'Army in Colch.' 76–82; above, this chapter, Political Hist.

60 Robertson, 'Army in Colch.' 144–56; e.g. *Essex Tel.* 9 June 1888.

61 Robertson, 'Army in Colch.' 178–84.

drovers, who had a tough reputation. Between the wars the borough chief constable regularly recruited to his police force army boxing champions to be used for breaking up fights; as a result the Colchester police boxing team became European champions.[62] Military parades and bands added colour to local life. In 1898 a grand tattoo, lit by *c.* 200 torches, was held on the Abbey field with 11 military bands, and many tattoos were held in the 20th century.[63] A popular Sunday morning pastime was to watch the soldiers march to the garrison church with their bands. The army's participation contributed greatly to the scale and success of special celebrations for military victories and royal jubilees, marriages, and coronations.[64] The garrison made its hospital and sports facilities available to townspeople, and played local teams in various sports, but was never needed to suppress a riot nor used to break a strike.[65] Its presence in the town was less noticeable after 1945, and from 1989, when an I.R.A. car bomb exploded beside army houses, seriously wounding a soldier, involvement in the local community had to be tempered even more carefully by security considerations.[66]

The influence of organized religion was important in the 19th century and into the 20th, but increases in church attendance may mainly reflect a rapidly rising population. In 1851 the largest congregations were recorded at Stockwell Street Congregational chapel and at St. Peter's church.[67] Many Anglican churches were extensively restored in the later 19th century and new churches and chapels of ease were built in fast growing districts, the first, All Saints' at Shrub End on the southern edge of the town in 1845, being given a new parish. To take account of problems caused by low stipends, lack of sufficient lay help in poor parishes, falling population in the town centre, and suburban growth, the parishes were reorganized several times, notably in 1911, 1953, and 1977. By 1992 only three of the twelve ancient parish churches in the town remained open.[68]

Evangelicals were strong within the Church of England in the 19th century. Prominent amongst them were Meshach Seaman, rector of St. James's 1839–49 and of Greenstead 1849–82, who was also a keen Liberal much involved in local affairs, and J. R. Cotter, rector of St. Mary Magdalen's 1877–90. St. Peter's church maintained a strong Evangelical tradition.[69] From the 1860s a High Church tradition developed at St. Leonard's and from the 1880s at St. Giles's, All Saints' and St. James's. More moderate churchmanship was dominant, however, promoted by rectors like J. T. Round, and later, J. W. Irvine, both of whom became rural dean and encouraged good relations between supporters of Anglicanism's different strands and with other denominations.[70] Colchester and District Clerical Society, founded in 1857 for monthly Bible reading and discussion, was a forum for local clergy.[71] In the early 20th century the High Church tradition followed by H. F. V. Carter and his eccentric curate G. A. Newcomen at St. Leonard's caused some parishioners to leave the church. By 1939 the succeeding rector's Anglo-Catholicism was regarded by the ecclesiastical authorities as too extreme, and the tendency was checked, later incumbents following a more moderate High Church line.[72] St. James's became the town's Anglo-Catholic church.[73]

[62] Colch. Institute, Colch. Recalled, interview 2221.
[63] *E.C.S.* 9 Apr. 1898; 12 Oct. 1990.
[64] Colch. Recalled, interview 2224; e.g. *E.J.* xxvi (2), 34–6.
[65] Below, Hospitals; *E.C.S.* 11 Apr. 1975; Robertson, 'Army in Colch.' 88–93, 184–7, 205.
[66] Colch. Recalled, interview 1505; *E.C.S.* 24 Nov. 1989; inf. from Miss J. V. Dansie.
[67] P.R.O., HO 129/8/204.
[68] Below, Churches; Modern Churches.
[69] Below, Churches; *E.C.S.* 15 Apr. 1882; E.R.O., D/P 138/28/9.
[70] Below, Churches; *E.C.S.* 31 Aug. 1860; E.R.O., D/E 4/3; Brown, *Colch. 1815–1914*, 170.
[71] E.R.O., Acc. C389, mins. of Colch. Clerical Soc.
[72] *Rep. Royal Com. on Eccl. Discipline* [Cd. 3069], pp. 326–7, H.C. (1906), xxxiii; Colch. Recalled, interviews 2002, 2003; Balliol Coll. Mun., Patronage papers.
[73] Below, Churches.

Protestant nonconformity grew in strength, although bedevilled particularly in the mid 19th century by disagreements within congregations. It was a powerful force in the town, supplying many of its leaders. Between 1840 and 1874 its places of worship, including mission rooms, increased from 8 to 20, and Sunday schools from 6 to 29. Growth continued into the 20th century.[74] Roman Catholics, recovering from their earlier exclusion from public life, built their first church in Colchester in 1837. Despite remaining anti-Catholic feeling, their numbers grew steadily thereafter.[75]

Divisions between nonconformists and Anglicans affected many aspects of town life. Clergy of various persuasions promoted education and welfare, and some supported the labour movement, but many nonconformists objected strongly to paying church rates and to government interference in education by the established church. By the end of the 19th century, although significant underlying tensions remained, disagreement between nonconformists and Anglicans was gradually disappearing. The pattern was similar at Ipswich.[76] The intense rivalry over education was apparently contained within the school board, established in 1892, which included members from both camps,[77] although in 1903 four nonconformist ministers were among 19 people summonsed for not paying the new education rate.[78] Members of different denominations increasingly joined forces to fight the commonly perceived social evils of unemployment, sickness, poverty, intemperance, and Sabbath-breaking, and many served the community on local bodies.[79] The ecumenical movement became significant from *c.* 1970.[80]

Social differences were apparent in patterns of religious observance. St. Mary's-at-the-Walls was the church preferred by the leading Conservatives.[81] In 1920 the rector of St. Paul's, a working-class parish where many men were unemployed, remarked that very few demobilized men had returned to the church after the war. In 1930 the rector of St. John's, another working-class parish, thought that declining church attendance was partly due to Sunday outings by public transport and broadcast church services on Sunday evenings. The rector of All Saints' with St. Nicholas's observed that church attendance was better among his educated parishioners.[82] In the rural outlying parts nonconformist congregations were composed mainly of labouring people,[83] but in the town the nonconformist churches attracted members from all social levels, though the social composition of different congregations varied. Many of the town's most influential people belonged to Lion Walk Congregational church. Between 1835 and 1937 it provided 59 members of the borough council, including several mayors, and 19 others associated with municipal life. Headgate Congregational's members on the other hand were more likely to be 'respectable working class'.[84] Some prominent families like the Cants and the Turners preferred their children to attend church services rather than the Sunday schools, which were apparently regarded as suitable only for lower-class children.[85] Churches and chapels provided recreational activities

74 Below, Prot. Nonconf.; Brown, *Colch. 1815–1914*, 170; E. A. Blaxill, *Hist. Lion Walk Cong. Ch.* 46–7.

75 Below, Roman Catholicism; S. Foster, *Ch. of St. James the Less & St. Helen, Colch. 1837–1987*, 13–14.

76 Phillips, *Ten Men*, 25; Brown, *Colch. 1815–1914*, 154–5; E.R.O., D/P 245/5/2; ibid. Acc. C210, J. B. Harvey Colln. iv, pp. 74, 107; *Essex Tel.* 9 July 1898; P. A. Hills, 'Division and Cohesion in the 19th-cent. Middle Class: the case of Ipswich 1830–70' (Essex Univ. Ph.D. thesis, 1989), pp. i, 315–16.

77 Below, Educ.

78 E.R.O., Acc. C203, Headgate Ch. Min. Bk. 1891–1912, 1 Sept. 1903.

79 e.g. *E.C.S.* 6 Aug., 10 Dec. 1904; above, this chapter, Political Hist.

80 Colch. Recalled, interview 1543.

81 Inf. from Mr. J. Bensusan-Butt.

82 E.R.O., D/CV 3/2, 4/3.

83 Ibid. SA 0672.

84 Blaxill, *Hist. Lion Walk Cong. Ch.* 49; Colch. Recalled, *passim*, esp. interviews 1534, 2158; E.R.O., SA 0399.

85 E.R.O., SA 0670; Colch. Recalled, interview 1543.

ranging from circulating book societies, like the three at Lion Walk Congregational in the late 19th century, to football clubs, mothers' meetings, temperance societies, and choirs.[86] E. H. Turner, organist at All Saints', borough organist, and conductor of a local choral society, was a leading figure in the town's musical life and attracted many good singers to his highly regarded church choir.[87]

Religion, especially the Evangelical type, frequently prompted charity and social concern. Churches continued to administer various charitable donations and bequests, like the small ones to provide bread and coals for the needy in St. Leonard's parish at the Hythe, a poor district.[88] George Round of East Hill House supported many public institutions, and his wife Margaret was much involved in charity work in St. James's parish and beyond. She maintained an orphanage built *c.* 1866 for ten destitute children, frequently held sewing classes for the Girls' Friendly Society and Young Women's Help Society, and provided treats for local schoolchildren. By her will, proved in 1887, she made bequests to Colchester hospital and other local charities and left £1,500 to the rector and churchwardens of St. James's, the income to be used for the infant school, the Sunday school, and clothing for the poor.[89] Wilson Marriage, teetotaller, businessman, and a leading Quaker, campaigned for public health and education, the building of a new town hall, and the closure of public houses.[90]

Philanthropy and pressure for social reform were not always directly associated with institutionalized religion. James Paxman, the industrialist, was a generous benefactor to the town, helping to establish the Albert School of Science and Art, giving a large piece of land for recreation, and financing the new town hall's clock tower.[91] H. H. Elwes, in his mayoral year 1902–3, inaugurated a distress scheme which developed into a local branch of the Charity Organization Society.[92] In the early 20th century Dr. Ruth Bensusan-Butt, women's suffragist and Fabian, campaigned to raise standards of health and welfare, especially of women and children, and for the provision of a maternity home.[93] Elfreda Sanders, mayor 1953–4, and five times mayoress to her brother, Sir Percy Sanders, did much work for the Red Cross and other charities.[94]

Self-help was encouraged through institutions like the Colchester Provident Asylum Society, established in 1833 under the chairmanship of Sir G. H. Smyth, M.P., of Berechurch Hall, which invited contributions from artisans or small shopkeepers entitling them in old age to apply for one of the society's cottages built between North Hill and Balkerne Lane.[95] Colchester Provident Labourers' Society, established in 1842 on the initiative of Revd. J. T. Round to encourage thrift and self sufficiency, enabled the poor to make payments to clothing and coal funds. Those contributions were augmented by wealthier persons who were to befriend families and set an example. Allotments were also acquired.[96]

Friendly societies offered probably the most important channel of self-help for workers. They became more popular as real wages increased and enabled more men to insure themselves in a limited way against the ever-present threat of poverty. In the early 19th century there were already several societies. The Colchester Provident Benefit Society, founded in 1809, had 270 members by 1834,

86 Blaxill, *Hist. Lion Walk Cong. Ch.* 47–8; Brown, *Colch. 1815–1914*, 178.
87 Colch. Recalled, interviews 1533, 1543.
88 Below, Charities.
89 E.R.O., D/P 138/28/9; Brown, *Colch. 1815–1914*, 93–4.
90 Phillips, *Ten Men*, 5.
91 *E.C.S.* 13 Nov. 1897.
92 Ibid. 26 Nov. 1910.
93 R. Lindsey, 'Dr. Ruth Bensusan-Butt 1877–1957' (Essex Univ. History B.A. project, 1987), *passim*; below, Hospitals.
94 *E.C.S.* 8 Oct. 1965; *Colch. Expr.* 30 Jan. 1966.
95 E.C.L. Colch., Mrs. D. Woodward's notes on Colch. Provident Asylum Soc.; Brown, *Colch. 1815–1914*, 94; below, pl. facing p. 137.
96 E.R.O., D/Z 11/1–2.

and the town's first Oddfellows' Lodge was founded in 1844. By the 1890s most working men belonged to one or more societies, the most prominent of which were local branches of the Foresters, the Oddfellows, the Hearts of Oak, the Royal Liver, and the Sons of Temperance. The smaller societies were gradually superseded by the large national organizations; by 1913 the Oddfellows and Foresters between them had *c.* 6,000 members in the town. The societies functioned as social clubs, most meetings being held in public houses, and the annual church parade with regalia and bands became a colourful public spectacle.[97] Their role diminished as state welfare provision increased in the 20th century, but branches of the Oddfellows and the Foresters survived in 1992.

The proliferation of voluntary adult educational outlets like the Mechanics' Institution founded in 1833, the university extension centre established in 1889, and church organizations enabled those who were not too tired from drudgery at work and in the home to improve themselves and become more self-sufficient.[98] There was considerable interest in the town's history, particularly its Roman period. William Wire (d. 1857), a watchmaker, was a self-educated radical and nonconformist who acquired an extensive knowledge of antiquities.[99] The Colchester Co-operative Society, founded in 1861, whose members included many temperance advocates, had its own lending library and reading room, and arranged lectures and concerts as well as co-operative trading for members.[1] John Castle, one of its founders, said the aim was to set a good example to fellow working people and improve their physical, social, and moral condition.[2] Nevertheless, despite such institutions and the increased provision of schools, educational advance before the 20th century should not be overestimated, for in 1877, when the rector of St. John the Evangelist's was widowed, 43 of the 107 parishioners sending a joint letter of condolence signed with a cross.[3]

The leaders of Colchester social life in the 19th century included the Smyths of Berechurch Hall, the Papillons of Lexden Manor, the Rebows at Wivenhoe Park, and, most of all, the Rounds who lived at East Hill House and Hollytrees in Colchester and at Birch Hall, Birch, and also owned Colchester castle. Such families, who were also socially active at county and national level, had much contact through committees, social events, and charity work with higher ranking army officers, doctors and surgeons, and clerics, and with the middle-class business and professional men who ran the town. In the 20th century, after the manorial estates were broken up, the landed interest declined, leaving a more important social role for the middle-class business and professional families whose members came to be regarded as the town's social as well as its political and economic leaders.[4]

Members of the leading families, which in the early 20th century included the Cants, Turners, Benhams, Pawseys, Marriages, Blaxills, Impeys, Bensusan-Butts, and Daniells, were often connected by marriage. Family networks established the economic and social status of their members and provided access to various formal organizations like the Rotary, golf, and political clubs, churches, and freemasons' lodges, which facilitated social and business contacts. St. Runwald's club, which

[97] Brown, *Colch. 1815–1914*, 134–5, 158, 176; e.g. *Essex Tel.* 7 June 1913.

[98] Below, Educ.

[99] E.R.O., T/A 515; A. F. J. Brown, *Essex People*, 162–3.

[1] *100 up, Centenary Story of Colch. & East Essex Co-operative Society Ltd.*, 6–7; E.R.O., Acc. C265, Colch. Co-op. Soc. Mins. 1864–72, *passim*; Brown, *Colch. 1815–1914*, 133.

[2] E.R.O., Acc. C265, Colch. Co-op. Soc. Mins. 1864–72, 9 Oct. 1867.

[3] E.R.O., D/P 525/28/4.

[4] Brown, *Colch. 1815–1914*, 152, 163; E.R.O., D/P 138/28/9; ibid. D/DRh F23; *E.R.* xii. 223; *E.A.T.* 3rd ser. xxiii. 79–90; J. Penfold, *Hist. Essex County Hosp. 1820–1948*, 65–75, 157–61; below, Outlying Parts.

met over Griffin's store in Crouch Street, was for professional men, and Colchester club for well-to-do businessmen, though the distinction was relaxed by the mid 20th century when St. Runwald's club was starting to decline. The Officers' Club at the garrison was open to local men of high enough social status.[5] In the 20th century, while the mayor's political power diminished, his leading role in the social life of the town and in charity work was emphasized.[6]

The higher the social level the more formal were social relationships. The Cants, for example, the leading family at Mile End in the early 20th century, invited friends to dinner and shooting parties, went beagling with members of the garrison, and played tennis, golf, and cricket. The family employed a cook, housekeeper, full-time gardener, a boy who later became chauffeur of the car acquired in 1912, as well as nannies and governesses when necessary. Mrs. Cant was much involved with Mile End parish church and Sunday school and charitable work in the village. Younger family members made social contacts through tennis clubs like the one at Lexden and at dances. Railway excursions, mainly to London and the east coast, had been possible from 1843, but from the early 20th century families like the Cants who could buy a motor car often preferred outings by road.[7] A very few wealthy families like the Benhams might visit the Continent, but most people who had seaside holidays usually spent them in England until the later 20th century; the Turners had holidays at Clacton, Frinton, or Felixstowe.[8] The lower middle class emulated, as far as their income permitted, the social patterns of those above them. Servants' wages were low and it was possible for people with moderate income to employ domestic help until the supply diminished after 1939. A High Street jeweller in the early 20th century lived over his shop in five-bedroomed accommodation, employed a maid, was a churchwarden and freemason, and had much social contact, mostly outside the home, with other small businessmen.[9]

As the town spread outwards in the late 19th and early 20th century there was considerable residential class segregation, but it diminished from the Second World War, which was seen as having a levelling effect. Social mobility was always considered possible, usually by the acquisition of money through success in business, and, especially in the 20th century, also through education.[10] Thomas Moy (b. 1831), son of a silk throwster, built up a very prosperous coal and building supplies business, was mayor 1877–9, and in 1880 bought Stanway manor and moved to Stanway Hall.[11] James Paxman, employed at Catchpool's as a young man, later amassed a fortune through his own engineering business, served as mayor 1887–8 and 1897–8, and bought Stisted Hall and its estate.[12] In the early 20th century a joiner's son was able to progress from his first job as an office junior to become deputy town clerk. However some other families could not afford to let their children take up the school scholarships which they won.[13]

Working-class networks were usually more informal ones based on family and kinship, neighbours, the public house, and in the 20th century a common educational background in state schools. The family provided support in childbirth, sickness, and bereavement, particularly before 1945. At the Hythe when someone died a particular local woman would come in to lay out the body, a black-painted

[5] E.R.O., SA 0670, 0672–3; Colch. Recalled, interviews 1543, 1501, 1502A.

[6] e.g. L. Dansie's scrapbook of his mayoralty in the possession of Miss J. V. Dansie.

[7] E.R.O., SA 0670–2; Brown, *Colch. 1815–1914*, 159.

[8] Colch. Recalled, interview 1543.

[9] Brown, *Colch. 1815–1914*, 156; Colch. Recalled, interview 1510.

[10] Above, this chapter, Town Development; Colch. Recalled, interviews 1502A, 1505.

[11] *E.C.S.* 8 Jan. 1910.

[12] Ibid. 13 Nov. 1897; above, this chapter, Econ.

[13] Colch. Recalled, interviews 1533, 2221.

board would be put up in the window, and neighbours would visit to pay their last respects. Other networks were based on friendly societies, trades unions, the Co-operative movement strong in the New Town district, political clubs, and churches.[14]

Working-class leisure activities tended to be different from those of the middle class. A maintenance worker at the barracks, formerly an army farrier, living at Canterbury Road in the 1920s was interested in football and gardening, was a regular customer at his local public house, and a member of the British Legion and the Old Comrades' Association; his wife was occupied mainly with the home and family and read a little; on Sundays his children went to Sunday school and church where they sang in the garrison choir, and the whole family went for a walk, usually at Middlewick.[15] Young people might join organizations like the Scouts, usually associated with churches, or the King George V mixed club in East Stockwell Street. Billiards and snooker could be played at the Co-op club in High Street and the TocH club.[16] To meet members of the opposite sex some participated in the 'monkey parade', walking down High Street from St. Nicholas's church to the west end. Dances were held at the Oak hall at the Red Lion and at the Labour club behind the Co-op in High Street. Courting was done by walking miles, large parts of the town remaining undeveloped by building. Before 1939 it was the custom on Whit Sunday for both children and adults to queue in Lower Castle park to skip through long skipping ropes.[17] Men who worked at Cant's nursery in the early 20th century were allowed to go rabbiting on Saturday afternoons.[18] Some men at New Town kept pigeons.[19] Firms like Paxman's and Wood's ran their own sports and social clubs.[20] Day rail trips to Clacton and Walton provided treats.[21] Many working-class women, however, found any spare time was taken up with outwork for tailoring firms to supplement the family income.[22]

Rowdyism and drunkenness on the streets were common in the 19th century, particularly at elections. Guy Fawkes night in 1875 was marked by vandalism and violence.[23] The distinction between 'respectable' and 'rough' people within the working class was widely made; the former were seen as honest and hardworking; the latter category included itinerants, the 'workshy', and those who had an uneasy relationship with the legal system. Before 1939 'rough' families were likely to live north of the town centre or east of it at the Hythe. In that period there was gang warfare between the north and east gangs, and in some places a soldier was said to be unsafe on his own, but the violence was apparently largely confined to those who wanted to fight. Vineyard Street in the central area, notorious for drunkenness and prostitution, was known as Harlots' Row.[24] Itinerants, among other occupations, used to bring in wild roses from the briars to Cant's nursery at Mile End.[25] Marmalade Grimes and Emma were a well-known tramping couple at the beginning of the 20th century.[26]

Class differences in leisure patterns lessened throughout the 20th century. Cricket and tennis, at first gentlemen's games, became more widely played, and football, athletics, swimming, as well as the local cinemas, theatre, and roller-skating, were popular. A successful pageant, held in 1909, illustrated Colchester's importance in

[14] Brown, *Colch. 1815–1914*, 158; Colch. Recalled, interviews 2002, 2090.
[15] Colch. Recalled, interview 1539.
[16] Ibid. interviews 2221, 2224.
[17] Ibid. interviews 2100, 1533, 2276.
[18] E.R.O., SA 0671.
[19] Colch. Recalled, interview 2224.
[20] E.R.O., D/F 23/3/47; ibid. SA 0675.
[21] Colch. Recalled, interview 2223.
[22] Ibid. e.g. 2147, 2190.
[23] A. F. J. Brown, *Essex People*, 179; idem, *Colch. 1815–1914*, 165.
[24] Brown, *Colch. 1815–1914*, 166; E.R.O., SA 0401; Colch. Recalled, interviews 2220, 2200, 2197.
[25] E.R.O., SA 0672.
[26] *Essex Tel.* 19 July 1924.

local and national history.[27] Fairs and the town carnivals provided further entertainment.[28] Colchester zoo at Stanway was another attraction in the later 20th century.[29] Improved communications increased national and international social influences; London and the Continent offered new opportunities for entertainment and holidays. The twinning of Colchester with Wetzlar, Germany, in 1969 and with Avignon, France, in 1972 led to many social and cultural exchanges.[30]

27 Ibid. 24 June 1907.

28 Brown, *Colch. 1815–1914*, 177–9; *E.C.S.* 6 Jan. 1984.

29 Reserved for treatment in a future volume.

30 E.C.L. Colch., Press cuttings filed under 'Twin Towns'.

BOUNDARIES

BOROUGH AND LIBERTY. The liberty, first defined in Henry VI's charter of 1447, covered the town of Colchester and its four hamlets (the parishes of Lexden, Berechurch or West Donyland, Greenstead, and Mile End), in addition to part of the river Colne which had been granted or confirmed to the burgesses by Richard I. In the late 13th century the burgesses claimed that a charter of Richard I had declared the four hamlets to be within the borough, but Richard's only known charter, while granting hunting rights within the 'banlieu', did not define the liberty territorially.[1] Greenstead, although it may earlier have been an independent estate, was within Colchester in 1086, and so presumably were Berechurch, West Donyland and Mile End, which were not separately recorded in Domesday Book unless the 2 hides belonging to St. Peter's church were in Mile End. The status of Lexden was disputed, and part of West Donyland in St. Giles's and St. Botolph's parishes seems to have been outside the liberty.[2] In 1277 the Colchester bailiffs claimed, apparently with success, that the St. John's abbey manors of Greenstead and West Donyland were within the liberty, but the status of the two hamlets was disputed again in 1285 and the following years.[3] The inhabitants of all four hamlets were assessed for subsidy with Colchester from 1296 if not earlier, but soon after 1313 Robert FitzWalter, lord of Lexden manor, tried unsuccessfully to establish that Lexden was outside the borough's jurisdiction.[4] There seem to have been no further serious disputes about the status of the hamlets until the 1580s when Catherine Audley revived the claim that Berechurch was outside Colchester, and some inhabitants of Lexden refused to contribute to a subsidy as part of the borough.[5] The burgesses claimed Stanway as part of the borough at the forest eyre in 1291–2,[6] but the claim, if it did relate to the whole parish and not to detached parts within Colchester, was not made again.

The borough bounds accepted in 1835 followed the outer parish boundaries of Lexden, Mile End, Greenstead, St. Giles's, and Berechurch.[7] Under the Essex Review Order of 1934 the area of the borough was increased from 11,333 a. to 12,011 a. by the addition of small areas from Ardleigh, East Donyland, Langenhoe, Stanway, West Bergholt, and Wivenhoe.[8] In 1974 the administrative borough was extended to cover the former Lexden and Winstree rural district and West Mersea and Wivenhoe urban districts.[9]

THE PERAMBULATED BOUNDARY. Perambulations of a boundary which differed at several points from the parish and later borough boundaries took place at long and irregular intervals from the 13th century to 1801.[10] Part of a later medieval description of the southern boundary survives but cannot be related to 17th- and 19th-century perambulations, and a 13th-century list of boundary marks and a similar one of 1563 are too brief to work out the exact route followed.[11] The earliest clear accounts are of 1637 and 1671; with the detailed account of the 1801 perambulation, which incorporates earlier material, they enable most of the route to be reconstructed.[12]

The 17th-century perambulations began at the Colne in the south-east corner of the liberty and followed Birch or Battles brook westwards to the lane from Old Heath to Rowhedge, then the lane to its junction with a track leading back to the brook, thus taking in a small part of East Donyland. They followed the track back to the brook, the brook to its source by Mersea Road, and then turned south along the road. The route from there to Roman River is not altogether clear, but it seems to have gone nearly due south and may have followed the parish boundary, as it did along the river to Kingsford bridge. The 17th-century route turned north along Layer Road, but the later medieval perambulation may have continued along the river to take in Olivers fee, presumably the later Olivers in Stanway.[13] From Layer Road the perambulation turned north-west along Gosbecks Road to Maldon Road, taking in part of Stanway parish. It ran straight across Maldon Road, following the parish boundary and the line of the Iron-Age ramparts across Lexden heath, then along the lane to Newbridge, leaving out a small area of Lexden north-west of Chitts hill. The line of the perambulation beyond Newbridge is not clear. In 1801 it, like the parish boundary, ran along the Colne to St. Botolph's brook and then followed the brook north-eastwards. In the 17th century it seems to have crossed the river below Newbridge, possibly by a footbridge called Motts bridge near where St. Botolph's brook falls into the Colne. It then seems to have followed field boundaries to the point at which a track from Colchester to Bergholt heath crossed the brook, apparently taking in a small area of West Bergholt. From the track it followed St. Botolph's brook and another small brook to the Horkesley road, ignoring small areas of West Bergholt and Great Horkesley east of the brooks, then turned north along the road, across Horkesley heath to the foot of Horkesley causeway where Black brook crosses the road. From that

1 *Colch. Charters*, 1–2, 37; P.R.O., SC 8/257/12813.

2 *V.C.H. Essex*, i. 432, 574, 578; below, Outlying Parts (West Donyland, Manors).

3 *Sel. Cases in K.B.* (Selden Soc. lv), 35; P.R.O., JUST 1/242, rott. 110, 112d.; E.R.O., D/B 5 R2, ff. 48, 49 and v., loose folio.

4 *Rot. Parl.* i. 228–38; E.R.O., D/B 5 R2, ff. 55, 67–8.

5 E.R.O., D/B 5 Gb1, 30 May, 8 Nov. 1581; D/DRg 1/117; Morant, *Colch.* 139 n.

6 P.R.O., E 32/13, rot. 8.

7 *Rep. on Parl. Bdys. of Cos. and Boros.* H.C. 141, p. 177 (1831–2), xxxviii; *Rep. Com. on Mun. Corp. Bounds.* H.C. 238 s.v. Colch. (1837), xxvi: the map accompanying both reports incorrectly shows the southern boundary cutting across St. Giles's par., possibly omitting the lands of the manor of Battleswick in West Donyland.

8 *Census*, 1931.

9 F. A. Youngs, *Guide to Local Administrative Units of Eng.* i. 604.

10 E.R.O., D/B 5 R1, ff. 3, 46, 217v.; D/B 5 R2, f. 7 and v.; D/B 5 Aa2/1, p. 148; *E.C.S.* 5 April 1834.

11 E.R.O., D/B 5 R1, ff. 3, 217v.; D/B 5 R2, f. 42.

12 Ibid. D/B 5 Gb3, ff. 173v.–174; Gb5, ff. 61–62v.: printed in Morant, *Colch.* 95–7; ibid. Boro. Mun., 1801 perambulation; above, Fig. 2.

13 Ibid. D/B 5 R2, f. 42.

brook the perambulation followed a rampart or causeway across Horkesley and Boxted heaths to the corner of Langham park, probably where the boundaries of Langham, Boxted, and Mile End meet. From there the perambulation followed a brook to Ipswich Road and the road to Bullock wood, taking in the small extra-parochial area on Cock Common. From Ipswich Road it followed the parish boundary through Bullock wood and along the edge of Sowen wood to Harwich Road but then went straight across the road and followed ditches or streams to Crockleford or Salary brook, taking in part of Ardleigh parish. It then followed parish boundaries along Salary brook, round Churn wood, and across Whitmore heath to the stream which flows through Wivenhoe park. At the south-west edge of the park the perambulation probably turned south-east to the old channel of the Colne and thence into the main river, taking in a small area of Wivenhoe parish.

The minor divergences between the perambulation route and the parish boundaries may have resulted from the moving of parish boundaries, either as tithes were given to a neighbouring church or as the course of streams or drainage ditches changed. That certainly seems to have happened on the West Bergholt boundary where the perambulation of 1671 states that the track leading to Bergholt was agreed by both incumbents to be the boundary between West field (in Lexden) and West Bergholt, and where the 1801 perambulation followed St. Botolph's brook, then the parish boundary. There may have been a similar boundary change at Gosbecks, whose tithes were in dispute between St. John's abbey and the rector of Stanway in 1364.[14] The parishes of Stanway and St. Mary-at-the-Walls were intermixed in the Middle Ages, and as late as 1578 part of Stanway seems still to have been within the liberties of Colchester.[15] A rationalization of the boundaries may have given Stanway the land north-east of Gosbecks.

The perambulated boundary on the north may reflect hunting rights in Kingswood forest. The forest boundary as recorded in 1298 cannot be identified on the ground, but it does not seem to follow St. Botolph's brook, and at the corner of Langham park it coincides with one of the points on the borough perambulation.[16] The rampart or causeway which was followed across Horkesley and Boxted heaths in the 17th century may have been a woodland boundary bank and ditch. Five Horkesley men accused of forest offences in 1276–7 were classed with the Colchester men, and there was a disturbance at Great Horkesley 'within the liberty of Colchester' in 1285. Part of Great Horkesley 'within Chester well' was within the liberties in the 1360s.[17]

THE RIVER. The river Colne from North bridge to 'Westness' was granted or confirmed to the burgesses by Richard I. The burgesses' rights there were acknowledged in 1285, and confirmed by later charters,[18] but the location of Westness was later disputed. In 1362 the burgesses claimed that their fishery included the Geedons between Fingringhoe and Langenhoe, and the Parrock or north part of the Pyefleet channel around Mersea Island,[19] suggesting that Westness may have been the later Westmarsh point on the north shore of the entrance to Brightlingsea creek. The limits of the liberty were not defined in 1448 when it was recovered from the earl of Oxford, to whom Henry VI had granted it, or when the borough's rights were challenged in 1579.[20] In 1629 and 1630 Sir Roger Townsend of Wivenhoe, who had built wharves on his land, and fishermen anxious to escape the borough's jurisdiction claimed unsuccessfully that Westness was opposite Wivenhoe wood, between Rowhedge and Colchester.[21] When the fishery was challenged again in 1700 the borough defined Westness as 'beyond Colne water' and 'beyond or near Chich St. Osyth', and in another dispute in 1896 the borough claimed that Westness was St. Osyth or Colne point in the open sea at the mouth of the Colne estuary.[22]

The boundaries of the borough's liberty in the Colne were marked by the bailiffs or mayor 'going down the river'. The ceremony was first recorded *c.* 1540. It was held regularly from 1580, perhaps in response to the challenge to the borough's rights in 1579. The bailiffs, and later the mayor, attended by councillors, were rowed down the river to the blockhouse near the Mersea stone where they feasted on meat, oysters, and wine.[23] In a similar ceremony *c.* 1587, while the borough's rights over the river were still in dispute, the Admiralty court judge Julius Caesar was taken by water from the Hythe to Mersea blockhouse where the borough's charter was read to him.[24] When the borough recovered control of the channel from the improvement commissioners in 1892[25] the Harbour and Navigation committee of the council resolved that they should hold a committee meeting once a year at the Mersea stone 'in continuation of the ancient custom observed by the Corporation'.[26] The custom continued in 1987.

WARDS. Head ward, the south-west quarter of the borough, was recorded in the early 13th century, and the north or North Street quarter or ward in 1254. The later four wards, North, South, East, and West or Head ward were recorded in 1272.[27] Fourteenth-century evidence suggests that the borough had been divided into four quarters, the east–west boundary running down the middle of the High Street, the north–south one running from Ryegate to Scheregate. The north-west ward, centred on North Hill and North Street, was the North

14 Ibid. St. John's abbey ledger bk. ff. 213v.–214v.
15 Ibid. D/B 5 Sb2/3, f. 26v.
16 P.R.O., E 32/15.
17 Ibid. E 32/12, rot. 1; JUST 1/242, rot. 110; E.R.O., D/B 5 R2, loose folio; cf. *Colch. Charters*, 58.
18 P.R.O., JUST 1/242, rot. 112d.; *Colch. Charters*, 1–2, 37.
19 E.R.O., D/DCr L5/2; P.R.O., SC 8/40/1971; *Cal. Pat.* 1361–4, 283; below, Fig. 23.
20 *V.C.H. Essex*, ii. 430; Morant, *Colch.* 90–1; E.R.O., D/B 5 Gb1, 25 May 1579.
21 E.R.O., D/B 5 Gb3, ff. 84, 90v.; P.R.O., E 134/5–6 Chas. I Hil./3; E 134/6 Chas. I Mic./17.
22 E.R.O., D/B 5 Gb6, pp. 213, 215; D/DCr L5/2, ff. 60–75.
23 B.L. Stowe MS. 836, f. 73; *E.J.* xxiii. 66.
24 E.R.O., D/B 5 Ab1/2; D/B 5 Cr140, rot. 28; P.R.O., E 134/5 Chas. I Mic./8.
25 Below, Port.
26 E.R.O., Boro. Mun., Harbour and Navigation Cttee. Min. Bk. 1892–6, p. 20.
27 P.R.O., JUST 1/235, rott. 18, 19d.; JUST 1/238, rot. 58d.; *Colch. Cart.* ii. 319.

ward; the north-east ward was East ward; the south-east ward (which included the South gate), South ward; and the south-west ward, centred on Head Street and Headgate, Head ward.[28] Those ward boundaries did not coincide with parish boundaries, and left all the parishes except St. Mary's-at-the-Walls divided between two or more wards. The suburbs and outlying parishes were included in the appropriate wards; Kingsmead was in East ward in 1385, the Hythe in South ward in 1386, and Bourne mill in South ward in 1407, but Dilbridge north-east of Kingsmead was in North ward in 1428.[29]

By 1748 the wards had been reorganized so that their boundaries corresponded more closely with those of the parishes. Head ward comprised St. Mary's, Holy Trinity, Lexden, and parts of St. Runwald's and St. Giles's; South ward St. Botolph's, St. Mary Magdalen's, Berechurch, and part of St. Giles's; North ward St. Peter's, St. Martin's, St. Nicholas's, Mile End, and part of St. Runwald's; and East ward All Saints', St. James's, St. Leonard's, and Greenstead.[30] Different boundaries were set out for the wards ordained for maintaining a workhouse in 1613, the whole of St. Giles's being assigned to Head ward, the whole of St. Runwald's to East ward, and St. Leonard's to South ward instead of East ward. A different arrangement again was recorded in 1764.[31] In 1837 the wards were found to be composed of complete parishes in an arrangment similar to that of 1613, except that St. Runwald's parish was in Head ward, St. Giles's in South ward, and St. Leonard's at the Hythe in East ward. One of the serjeants at mace, however, claimed that the ward boundaries did not follow parish boundaries.[32]

Under the Municipal Corporations Act of 1835 the borough was reorganized into three wards. The first comprised Berechurch, St. Botolph's, St. Giles's, Holy Trinity, and St. Mary's-at-the-Walls; the second, Lexden, St. Martin's, St. Peter's, St. Runwald's, and Mile End; and the third Greenstead, All Saints', St. James's, and St. Leonard's.[33] In 1892 a system of four wards, their boundaries approximating to those of the 18th-century wards, was restored.[34] In 1937 the borough was rearranged into nine wards: St. Mary's, Castle, New Town, Abbey, Berechurch, Lexden and Shrub End, Mile End, St. John's, and Harbour.[35]

PARISH BOUNDARIES. There were 16 parishes within the liberty, including the outlying parishes of Lexden, Berechurch, Greenstead, and Mile End. Their bounds were first recorded in the earlier 19th century.[36] Six parishes, whose churches lay within the walls, were small, any extramural lands lying intermixed in the borough fields south-west and south-east of the walled area. Their boundaries within the walls followed tenement boundaries. The area of those two fields may originally have been in two parishes: St. Mary's-at-the-Walls, whose parish covered much of Borough field south-west of the walls, and St. James's which extended round the walls on the north-east and south-east and along both sides of Harwich Road beyond the Colne. South-east of St. James's parish lay the scattered parish of St. Mary Magdalen, formed from the lands of St. Mary Magdalen's hospital, and the compact parish of St. Leonard's at the Hythe which contained a small detached part of St. Peter's parish.

The boundaries of all the parishes, with the possible exception of St. Leonard's, had been rationalized by the 19th century; in the 1590s there were more detached parts, notably those belonging to St. Nicholas's parish which had lost all its extramural land by 1748, although in the 15th century the church had tithe from part of Magdalen field south-west of the walls and as late as 1747 land north-west of Harwich Road was said to be in St. James's or St. Nicholas's.[37] An area of 242 a. in the north-east, probably once part of Greenstead, had been attached to All Saints' parish by 1542; its boundaries were altered slightly between 1794 and 1876. The poverty of the living of All Saints' in 1254 suggests that the arrangement was made after that date.[38] About 1699 St. Mary's parish exchanged meadow along the Colne for arable which had formerly been in Lexden.[39] In 1817 the bounds of Lexden, St. Mary-at-the-Walls, St. James's, and Holy Trinity in the borough fields south-west of the walled town were altered to give each parish a compact, although detached, area instead of scattered acres in each of five fields.[40]

St. Botolph's parish (905 a., half of it in detached portions) to the south and east of the walled area was composed largely of the lands of St. Botolph's priory, although the church was parochial as well as conventual. The original parish church of the area south of the town was probably the precursor of St. Giles's whose parish included Battleswick manor, the only large estate in the southern half of the liberty which did not belong to St. John's abbey or St. Botolph's priory in the Middle Ages. The Colne seems to have been Greenstead's original western boundary, but in the mid 11th century the estate there was divided into four parts, one of which passed to St. Botolph's priory and thereby became part of St. Botolph's parish. Mile End in the north was in St. Peter's parish until the 13th century. Lexden in the west was a berewick of Stanway in 1086.[41] In 1364 lands in Crouch Street belonging to St. Cross hospital, later in St. Mary's parish, were in Stanway, as was land

28 E.R.O., D/B 5 R1, ff. 158–70; ibid. D/Y 2/2, p. 13.

29 Ibid. D/B 5 Cr25, rott. 7, 44; Cr36, rot. 26; Cr49, rot. 19d.

30 Morant, *Colch.* 98 n.

31 Ibid. App. p. 17; E.R.O., Acc. C210, J. B. Harvey Colln. vi, p. 36.

32 *Rep. Com. on Mun. Corp. Bounds.* s.v. Colch.

33 5 & 6 Wm. IV c. 76; *Rep. Com. on Mun. Corp. Bounds.* s.v. Colch.; *White's Dir. Essex* (1848), 51.

34 *Colch. Corp. Act* 1892, 55 & 56 Vic. c. 107 (Local and Personal).

35 E.R.O. Boro. Mun., Council Mins. 1936–7, pp. 54–5.

36 Ibid. D/CT 89–98, 100, 152, 220, 242; Gilbert, *Colch. Map* (*c.* 1846); below, Fig. 22.

37 B.L. MS. Stowe 832, ff. 7–44; Morant, *Colch.* 114, 117, 119; Balliol Coll. Oxford Mun. C 23.11; E.R.O., D/DEt T7.

38 P.R.O., E 318/2/57; E.R.O., D/DHt P60; O.S. Map 6", Essex XXVIII (1880 edn.); *E.A.T.* N.S.xviii. 123.

39 E.R.O., D/P 273/3/4A; below, Outlying Parts (Lexden, Intro.).

40 E.R.O., D/P 273/8/1, 6.

41 *V.C.H. Essex*, i. 432.

St. Mary's Terrace East, 1993

The Turrets, Lexden Road, 1987

New Town Lodge, *c.* 1990

The Avenue, 1993

Beverley Lodge, *c.* 1885

New Town: semidetached houses, *c.* 1990

Kavanagh's Boot and Shoe Factory, *c.* 1893

East Hill Brewery, 1865

Textile Factory, Crowther Bros., *c.* 1930

belonging to the rector of St. Mary's.[42] In 1403 the rector of Stanway agreed that the warden of St. Cross hospital might serve the inhabitants of Crouch Street and Maldon Road in return for their tithes. The area was thus absorbed into the surrounding St. Mary's parish, which was called St. Mary's and St. Cross in 1487–8.[43] A field near the south-west postern, perhaps the later detached part of Lexden in St. Mary's parish, was still in Stanway in the 15th century.[44]

Most of the parish boundaries followed field or tenement boundaries, although the western boundary of St. Giles's followed Layer Road for much of its length and the eastern part of the southern boundary Birch or Battles brook. St. Botolph's and Salary brooks formed much of the northern and eastern boundaries of Lexden, Mile End, a detached part of St. Botolph's parish, and Greenstead. The southern boundary of St. Nicholas's parish followed the town wall for a short way, as did the south-western boundary of the intra-mural part of St. James's parish. The 19th-century boundaries of All Saints' parish followed the wall on the east and on much of the north, but the castle and presumably the Greyfriars site were extraparochial in the Middle Ages. In the 1590s the friary site was in St. James's parish; part was in All Saints' by 1686, but part was still claimed by St. James's in 1742.[45]

Attempts in the 16th and 17th centuries to unite some of the smaller parishes failed,[46] and all 16 parishes survived until 1897 when they were united to form the single civil parish of Colchester, although some of the detached parts had been absorbed into their surrounding parishes under the Divided Parishes Act of 1882.[47]

COMMUNICATIONS

ROADS. The most important road has been the one which from prehistoric times linked Colchester with London.[48] At Marks Tey, 5 miles west of Colchester, the Roman Stane street from St. Albans, based on an earlier track, joined the London road. In Roman times a road led north from Colchester to Stratford St. Mary (Suff.) later to become the Ipswich road, and one led north-east through Ardleigh towards Mistley, later continuing to Harwich and the sea link with the Low Countries.[49] Another road led north-west through Mile End to Nayland and by the Middle Ages continued to Sudbury (Suff.) and Bury St. Edmunds.[50] Other roads, probably also of Roman origin, ran north-west to Cambridge and south-east to Fingringhoe. The road leading south-west to Maldon existed by the Middle Ages. Minor roads linked Colchester with other settlements in north Essex.

In the Middle Ages liability for road maintenance lay with landowners, who often tried to pass it to their tenants. The borough was presumably responsible for roads in the town centre; obstructions to roads were regularly presented at the lawhundred courts.[51] Bequests helped to finance road maintenance: John Geldeforde by will proved in 1423 left money for repairing bad roads, and William Smith by will proved 1460 left 5 marks for the repair of the Nayland road in Mile End.[52] The 1555 Act made parishes, supervised by the justices, responsible for their own repairs,[53] and in the early 17th century the corporation raised rates from parishes for road maintenance.[54] From 1555 until the early 19th century the parishes and sometimes the borough were presented at quarter sessions for failure to repair main roads.[55]

A new causeway at Rovers Tye on Ipswich Road was mentioned in 1429; in 1693 the part of Ipswich Road nearer the town in Greenstead, All Saints', and Mile End parishes was referred to as the new causeway, and another section in Mile End, presumably further out, was called the old causeway.[56] Turnpiking began with an Act of 1696 when the Severalls road in Mile End and parts of the London–Harwich road were turnpiked by the justices of the peace.[57] An Act of 1707 gave the justices powers to take over further sections of the road between Brentwood and Colchester, including the stretch between Lexden Cross and Head gate.[58] Under an Act of 1725 the Ipswich road between Colchester and Langham and the remaining stretches of the London road between Shenfield and Harwich were turnpiked by trustees,[59] among them Charles Gray of Colchester, who were appointed to take over from the justices. The trustees erected in 1760 in High Street a painted obelisk, showing the distances to London and other towns; it remained there until 1858.[60] Under an Act of 1765 further roads were turnpiked including that from Lexden to Halstead.[61] In 1766 trustees set tolls ranging from 1*s.* 6*d.* for a wagon with wheels less than 9 in. (23 cm.) wide down to 1*d.* for a laden or unladen horse, mule, or ass not drawing a load.[62]

42 E.R.O., St. John's abbey ledger bk. ff. 213v.–214.
43 Ibid. D/DH VI D 11A; B.L. MS. Stowe 828, f. 14.
44 E.R.O., St. John's abbey ledger bk. f. 210v.
45 Below, Castle; B.L. MS. Stowe 832, f. 13; E.R.O., D/P 200/8/1; *E.A.T.* N.S. xii. 331.
46 Above, Tudor and Stuart Colch. (Religious Life).
47 *Census*, 1891; 1901.
48 Para. based on *V.C.H. Essex*, iii. 1, 4–5, 24–31; O.S. Map of Roman Britain (4th edn.).
49 *V.C.H. Essex*, ii. 262.
50 Below, Outlying Parts (Mile End).
51 E.R.O., D/B 5 R2, f. 56; D/B 5 Cr1–81, *passim*.
52 Ibid. D/B 5 Cr43, rot. 14d.; Cr71, rot. 13.
53 Highways Act, 2 & 3 Phil. & Mary, c. 8.
54 E.R.O., D/B 5 Gb2, ff. 85–91v., 99v.–106.
55 Ibid. Q/SR 217, 225, 273.
56 Ibid. D/B 5 Cr49, rot. 14; P.R.O., ASSI 35/134/1; ASSI 35/135/1.
57 Turnpike Act, 7 & 8 Wm. III, c. 9; for accounts of Essex turnpiking, see J. Booker, *Essex and the Industrial Revolution*, 99–133; *E.J.* xvi (2), 20–5; xvi (3), 13–20.
58 6 Anne, c. 7 (Priv. Act).
59 12 Geo. I, c. 23.
60 E.R.O., D/DR B1A, f. 8v.; Booker, *Essex and Ind. Rev.* 119–20.
61 Essex Turnpike Act, 5 Geo. III, c. 60.
62 E.R.O., D/DU 459, p. 137.

An Act of 1793 divided the Essex trust, which had apparently been set up under the 1725 Act, into two districts with Colchester one of six divisions in the first district.[63] Trustees were to meet at least four times a year.[64] The turnpike trustees sometimes co-operated with the Colchester improvement commissioners, as they did in 1811 to cut a small new section of the Ipswich road, a short distance beyond East bridge, in place of the old route past the Rose and Crown, and in 1817 to improve East Hill.[65] Under an Act of 1815 detailed new scales of tolls were set, ranging from 3*s.* for a wagon with 9-in. wheels drawn by 8 horses (with even higher charges for narrower wheels) down to 1½*d.* for a laden or unladen horse.[66] By 1820 the Colchester trustees had no outstanding debts and were able to reduce tolls by a third.[67] The arrival of the railways caused a fall in the turnpike revenues and legislation attempted to apportion responsibility for highways more carefully to various local authorities, so that the Essex turnpike trust was dissolved by 1870. From 1888 major roads were financed by the county rate.[68]

In the early 20th century road traffic through Colchester increased so much that a bypass road was constructed 1930–3, taking traffic round the north side of the town; the central government bore three quarters of the cost to provide work for the unemployed.[69] A new northern bypass, opened in 1974, superseded the earlier one, taking traffic from the London road at Stanway in a wide arc to join the Ipswich road at Ardleigh.[70] An eastern bypass, taking Harwich traffic from the northern bypass through Ardleigh, Elmstead, the Bentleys, Great Bromley, and Langham to avoid Colchester town, was opened in 1982.[71] The southern section of an inner relief road, Southway, was opened in 1973, and the western section over Balkerne hill to the old northern bypass was built 1976–81.[72] Planning permission was given in 1990 for construction of an eastern section from the Greenstead roundabout to St. Botolph's roundabout, and work on the first phase started in 1993.[73]

BRIDGES. The borough maintained North bridge and East bridge in the town, and the Falling bridge, of uncertain location, which led towards Mile End.[74] Minor bridges were maintained by inhabitants of the parishes in which they lay.[75] Bequests were sometimes made for bridge maintenance, for example, William Hefkere, by will proved 1381, left 10*s.* towards the repair of East bridge.[76] North bridge, recorded in 1189,[77] stood on the site of a Roman bridge or ford, as presumably did East bridge, recorded from 1238.[78] Masons were to build a new bridge, perhaps North or East bridge, in 1394, but the medieval North and East bridges were later said to have been made of timber.[79] North bridge was extensively repaired in timber by the borough in 1580.[80]

In 1407 the corporation allowed the inhabitants of the Hythe to build a footbridge with handrails over the Colne, provided that it was not wide enough for horses and carts and did not interfere with the navigation to East bridge.[81] Following some conflict with the corporation, the inhabitants were permitted in 1474 to build a cart bridge of stone or timber.[82] When the corporation rebuilt Hythe mill *c.* 1552 it undertook to maintain the bridge; extensive work was carried out in 1619, including lengthening the chain with 31 lb. of iron, presumably to block access to the bridge.[83]

Under the charter of 1629, when the bridges were 'ruinous', pontage was granted on all three of them for 14 years at 4*d.* for a laden cart or wagon, 2*d.* for a horse carrying a pack of wool, 1*d.* for a horse carrying half a pack of wool, and ½*d.* for each laden packhorse.[84] With the proceeds North and East bridges were repaired in 1631.[85] The tolls were leased, for example those of North bridge in 1635 for two years for £20, and those of East and Hythe bridges for £20.[86] The corporation tried to make St. Leonard's parishioners responsible for Hythe bridge again but in 1667 the Court of Chancery declared the borough liable.[87]

In 1723 the borough assembly was apparently looking for ways of passing its responsibilities to others, but the following year was resigned to raising a rate itself for bridge repairs. North bridge was repaired in 1737, as were East and Hythe bridges in 1738, and there was further work on East and North bridges in 1765.[88] In 1775 a salary of 10*s.* a year was paid to a keeper for East bridge; possibly similar arrangements were made for North and Hythe bridges.[89]

North bridge, part of which collapsed in 1775, was rebuilt in brick by William Staines by 1781.[90] In 1820 one of the western arches and the east wing and side were repaired, and the east side was widened.[91] The bridge was taken down in 1843 and replaced with a cast iron bridge of three arches built by the town council,

63 Essex Turnpike Act, 33 Geo. III, c. 145: copy in E.R.O., D/TX 1/1, 1/4.

64 E.R.O., D/TX 2/1.

65 Ibid. Boro. Mun., Improvement Com. Mins. 1811–33, pp. 12, 74–6, 83.

66 Essex Turnpike Act, 55 Geo. III, c. 90: copy in E.R.O., D/TX 1/1.

67 E.R.O., Q/RUt 1/3.

68 Colch. Boro. Council, *Centenary of Mun. Corp. Act: Souvenir* (1936), 15–16; Booker, *Essex and Ind. Rev.* 118.

69 *E.C.S.* 7 Apr. 1989; E. A. Blaxill, *Opening of Colch. By-pass Road 1933, a Hist. of the road*: copy at Colch. Mus. (pictures colln.); above, Modern Colch. (Town Devt.).

70 *Colch. Gaz.* 19 Dec. 1974; *E.C.S.* 7 Feb. 1975.

71 *Colch. Gaz.* 5 Apr., 18 Aug. 1978; *East Essex Gaz.* 18 June 1982.

72 *E.C.S.* 6 Apr. 1973; 22 Apr. 1977; 31 Oct. 1980; 30 Jan. 1981.

73 Ibid. 22 June 1990; inf. from Ms. E. Curry, Public Relations Officer, Colch. Boro. Council.

74 E.R.O., D/B 5 Cr19, rot. 1d.; Cr72, rot. 19d.; Cr82, rot. 10d.; Cr103, rot. 2d.

75 Below, Outlying Parts, *passim.*

76 E.R.O., D/B 5 Cr21, rot. 8.

77 *Colch. Charters,* 2.

78 Hull, *Roman Colch.* 11, 241–2; *Colch. Cart.* ii. 598.

79 *Cal. Pat.* 1391–6, 385; Morant, *Colch.* 3.

80 E.R.O., D/B 5 Ab1/2.

81 Ibid. D/B 5 Cr36, rot. 32d.; Morant, *Colch.* 129.

82 Morant, *Colch.* App. p. 1.

83 Ibid.; E.R.O., D/B 5 Ab1/9.

84 *Colch. Charters,* 100.

85 E.R.O., D/B 5 Aa1/9.

86 Ibid. D/B 5 Gb3, ff. 145, 149.

87 Ibid. Wire Colln. II. 24.

88 Ibid. D/B 5 Gb7, pp. 164, 181; Gb8, f. 11; D/B 5 Ab1/34.

89 Ibid. D/B 5 Aa2/1, p. 24.

90 *Ipswich Jnl.* 13 May 1775; E.R.O., D/B 5 Gb8, ff. 74v., 79v., 105v.; cf. T. Wright, *Hist. Essex,* i. 307, followed by later directories, which says that North bridge was rebuilt in 1801 by Sir William Staines.

91 E.R.O., Boro. Mun., Chamberlain's accts. 1818–30, p. 12.

increased traffic being anticipated because the bridge was on the link road between High Street and the new railway station.[92] In 1903–4 it was widened by 17 ft. 6 in. (5.3 m.) on the east side for trams.[93]

The old East bridge was replaced in 1802 by a bridge of five brick arches with stone pilasters and an iron balustrade, financed by the erection of a turnpike in Lexden Street.[94] In 1928 the bridge was widened from 29 ft. (8.8 m.) to 46 ft. (14 m.) and the steepness of the approaches reduced, half the cost being borne by the central government to provide work for the unemployed.[95]

A new Hythe bridge was built in brick with three arches in 1737, the navigation commissioners contributing £50 to the cost.[96] It was removed in 1837. A new bridge under construction fell down in 1839.[97] Another timber bridge built soon afterwards was washed away in 1876 and replaced in 1898 by an iron bridge, designed by James S. Cooke.[98] In 1968 a wider bridge of a concrete deck on steel girders, designed by the borough architect's department, was built diagonally across the river just east of the old one, which was retained for pedestrians. The central government bore three quarters of the cost because the new bridge served a principal road.[99]

As part of the new bypass road opened in 1933 a new bridge over the Colne 50 ft. in width was built of reinforced concrete. It was believed to be the first two-hinged arch bridge in the country. West of the Ipswich road another bridge on the bypass crossed the railway diagonally.[1]

ROAD TRANSPORT.[2] In 1637 carriers went to London on Thursdays, lodging at the Cross Keys in Gracechurch Street, and returning on Fridays.[3] By 1748 a coach went to London and back every day except Sundays.[4] In 1767 the stage coach took six inside passengers to and from London on six days a week, leaving the White Hart at 5 a.m. and arriving in London at 2 p.m. in time to dine, another coach making the return journey; the Colchester fly took four inside passengers to and from London twice a week from the same inn. Two common stage wagons each went to London and back once a week taking two days each way. Other coaches and carriers passing through Colchester provided services several times a week to Norwich, Ipswich, Stowmarket (Suff.), and Harwich.[5]

In the early 19th century Colchester remained an important staging post for coaches travelling to and from London, many of which carried mail. In 1822 from the Three Cups inn six coaches went daily to London, others left for Yarmouth, Harwich, and Ipswich, and every night two mail coaches left for Norwich and Yarmouth. Every day a coach from Yoxford (Suff.), Saxmundham (Suff.), and Ipswich called at the Red Lion on its way to London, as did another doing the return journey. Coaches to Braintree and Cambridge ran from the Angel. Colchester was an important centre for carriers serving the surrounding areas.[6]

In 1848 there were five horse-drawn omnibuses operating between Colchester and Braintree, Sudbury, Halstead, Walton, and Brightlingsea, but road transport faced increasing competition from the railways. Horse-drawn services were replaced from 1904 by motor buses, the first one running between Colchester and West Mersea. Services were gradually extended, particularly in the 1920s, by many local private companies. The heyday of motor bus and coach transport was from 1945 to the 1960s; thereafter the increasing use of private cars led to reductions in public transport services. Colchester borough transport department made an agreement in 1984 with the remaining private operators whereby municipal transport services extended outside the borough to Wivenhoe, West Mersea, and West Bergholt. In the 1980s some private companies provided daily coach services to London for commuters, but traffic congestion was a problem and by 1990 only one service remained.[7] In 1990 local companies provided daily services to towns and villages in Essex and neighbouring counties, including an Eastern National service to Stansted airport. National Express coaches ran a daily service to towns in the north of England.[8]

RAILWAYS. In 1843 the Eastern Counties Railway extended its line from London as far as Colchester North station.[9] At first there were four trains in each direction on weekdays and three on Sundays, but within two months there were six weekday trains each way, the journey to London *c.* 2½ hours.[10] By 1846 one of the daily trains made the journey from London to Colchester in only 90 minutes. The rival Eastern Union Railway built a line from Ipswich southwards to Colchester in 1846 and northwards to Norwich in 1849, and built a branch west to Hadleigh (Suff.) in 1847 and east from Manningtree to Harwich in 1854.[11] The Eastern Counties'

92 A. F. J. Brown, *Essex People 1750–1900*, 169, 172; *White's Dir. Essex* (1848), 69; plaque on bridge.

93 E.R.O., Boro. Mun., Special Cttee. Mins. 1902–12, p. 23; plaque on bridge.

94 E.R.O., D/B 5 Gb9, pp. 39, 50; Wright, *Hist. Essex*, i. 318.

95 Plaque on bridge; E.R.O., Boro. Mun., Roads & Drainage Cttee. 29 Dec. 1926; 7 Mar. 1927; 14 Mar. 1928.

96 E.R.O., D/B 5 Gb7, p. 329; D/Y 2/1, p. 145; Wright, *Hist. Essex*. i. 328; below, pl. facing p. 296.

97 *2nd Rep. Tidal Harbours Com.* H.C. 692, App. B, p. 625 (1846), xviii; *E.C.S.* 5 Apr. 1839.

98 E.R.O., Acc. C47, CPL 1189; *E.C.S.* 5 Apr. 1878; *Kelly's Dir. Essex* (1902), 122.

99 *Colch. Gaz.* 27 Feb., 7 Mar. 1968.

1 E. A. Blaxill, *Opening of Colch. By-pass Road*, 6; *E.C.S.* 8 Jan. 1993.

2 The following section deals with external transport; for internal transport, see below, Public Services.

3 *E.R.* xxii. 162.

4 Morant, *Colch.* (1748 edn.), Bk. I, p. 1; E. G. Axten, 'Hist. Public Transport in Colch.' (TS. in E.R.O.), *passim.*

5 E.R.O., D/DU 459, pp. 132–6.

6 *E.R.* xxv. 83–4; B. Drew, *The Fire Office, Hist. Essex & Suff. Equitable Insurance Soc. Ltd.* 157.

7 Axten, 'Public Transport in Colch.' pp. 25, 34, 36–100; *E.C.S.* 23 Sept. 1983.

8 Eastern National, National Express, Eastern Counties companies: publicity leaflets.

9 *V.C.H. Essex*, ii. 336; D. I. Gordon, *Regional Hist. Railways of G.B.* v (Eastern Counties), pp. 37–79; Phillips, *Ten Men*, 14–20, 32–5, 42–50; Axten, 'Public Transport in Colch.' pp. 17–24.

10 *Eastern Counties Railway Timetable*, 24 Apr., 1 June 1843: extracts at E.R.O., J. B. Harvey Colln. vii, pp. 208, 213.

11 Gordon, *Regional Hist. Rlwys.* v. 42; 7 & 8 Vic. c. 85 (Local); 9 & 10 Vic. c. 97 (Local).

FIG. 17. THE RAILWAY HOTEL, 1843

London–Colchester service was notoriously slow and unreliable, the company being unwilling to convey passengers efficiently to Colchester in case they continued to Norwich on the Eastern Union route instead of travelling on its own London–Norwich route via Cambridge. The bitter rivalry between the companies was contained by an agreement of 1854, whereby the Eastern Union Railway, although owning a fifth of the lines, received only a seventh of profits.[12]

In 1847 a new company, the Colchester, Stour Valley and Halstead Railway, opened a branch line from Colchester North station to the Hythe where a small station was built to serve the port, and in 1849 another line from Marks Tey to Sudbury.[13] The Tendring Hundred Railway Co. opened the Hythe–Wivenhoe railway in 1863, and extended it in 1866 by a single track line from East gate and Hythe junctions to a small central Colchester station at St. Botolph's.[14] In 1866 the line was extended from Wivenhoe to Weeley with a branch to Brightlingsea, and in 1867 it reached Walton.[15]

In 1862 the Eastern Counties, Eastern Union, East Anglian, Newmarket, and Norfolk Railway companies merged to form the Great Eastern Railway;[16] in 1883 the Tendring Hundred and the Clacton-on-Sea companies,[17] and in 1898 the Colchester, Stour Valley, Sudbury and Halstead Co., also merged with the G.E.R.[18] In 1923 the G.E.R., with the Colne Valley Co., became part of the London and North Eastern Railway, which on nationalization in 1948 became part of the British Rail Eastern Region.[19] By 1963 the London–Clacton line was completely electrified, the section from London to Colchester having been completed in 1962. The Wivenhoe–Brightlingsea branch line was closed in 1964.[20] In 1990 there were 44 trains each weekday from Colchester to London and fast trains took 50 minutes for the journey.[21]

Colchester North, the town's main railway station, was opened in 1843 and refreshment facilities, a new telegraph office, and extra sidings were added in 1854.[22] The Railway Hotel, of white brick in Italianate style, was built immediately south of the station in 1843. It had closed by 1850 when it became a hospital.[23] The station was rebuilt in 1865, and extensively remodelled and rebuilt in 1894. It was extended in 1961 when new offices were built on the north side of the railway line.[24] St. Botolph's station was restored and renamed Colchester Town in 1991.[25]

12 Gordon, *Regional Hist. Rlwys.* 42, 69–70; Phillips, *Ten Men*, 14–20, 34–5.

13 9 & 10 Vic. c. 76 (Local); Gordon, *Regional Hist. Rlwys.* 58; *E.C.S.* 6 July 1849.

14 C. Phillips, *Tendring Hundred Railway: Hist. of the Colch. to Clacton and Walton Lines*, 5–7.

15 Brown, *Colch. 1815–1914*, 20; 26 & 27 Vic. c. 143 (Local).

16 25 & 26 Vic. c. 223.

17 46 & 47 Vic. c. 56.

18 61 & 62 Vic. c. 214.

19 Booker, *Essex and Ind. Rev.* 159.

20 Gordon, *Regional Hist. Rlwys.* 60, 68; W. Hamley, 'Urban Structure of Colch.' (Swansea Univ. M.A. thesis, 1975), 6.

21 Great Eastern timetable, 1990–1.

22 Gordon, *Regional Hist. Rlwys.* 60.

23 *Builder*, i. 350; below, Hospitals.

24 Gordon, *Regional Hist. Rlwys.* 60; *E.C.S.* 11 Feb. 1893; 21 Apr. 1894; *Colch. Official Guide* (4th edn.), 23.

25 *E.C.S.* 19 July 1991.

POSTAL SERVICES AND TELECOMMUNICATIONS. Eight post horses were financed by the town assembly in 1591.[26] The government ordered a postal stage to be set up in Colchester in 1625, and by 1628 the town had a postmaster.[27] Early posting houses were usually inns, but in 1664–5 a post house was built in St. Mary's parish.[28] The service did not always run smoothly: the postmaster in 1677 was reputed to supply the worst horses on the road; coaches risked robbery and in 1687 a large quantity of uncut diamonds was stolen from the Holland mail between Colchester and Harwich.[29] By 1767 there were regular collections and deliveries at Mr. Manning's post office at the King's Head. Post coaches served London, major towns in Norfolk and Suffolk, and Dedham, Boxted, and Harwich. A direct mail service to Holland was provided twice a week by the post coach from London which passed through Colchester.[30]

A Colchester penny post was established in 1815, with three mail carts serving Thorpe-le-Soken, Boxted, and Stratford St. Mary (Suff.), and the intermediate villages.[31] Within a year of the railway's arrival in Colchester in 1843 some mail went by train.[32] In 1848 a postmaster, two clerical assistants, and two town deliverers were based at an office in Head Street, and there were receiving houses at East Hill, Hythe Street, and Lexden.[33] By 1882 there were 18 pillar and wall post boxes.[34] Motor vans replaced the remaining horse drawn mail coaches in 1909.[35] The main post office moved from the east to the west side of Head Street in 1874; the building was extended in 1936.[36] There were 15 sub post offices in the borough by 1937 and 21 in 1985.[37]

In 1803, during the Napoleonic Wars, St. Mary's-at-the-Wall's church steeple was designated as one of a series of signalling stations between the east coast and London; messages were apparently to be transmitted by hoisting a red flag.[38] A Colchester station of the Electric and International Telegraph Co. was opened in 1856.[39] The South of England Telephone Co. established an exchange in High Street in 1886. The first customer was the Essex Standard newspaper.[40] In 1891 the Eastern Counties' idiot asylum, one of the small number of customers, was linked by telephone with the police station.[41] The National Telephone Co. established a telephone exchange in 1894 in 14 St. John's Street serving 27 subscribers.[42] It was taken over by the Post Office in 1912, when Colchester was made a regional centre employing 30 to 40 people.[43] By 1924 there were 573 telephone lines and St. Martin's House in West Stockwell Street had been acquired. A new automatic exchange was opened in 1929 in a new two-storeyed building in West Stockwell Street serving 1,100 customers. An extra floor was added in 1954 when the equipment was extended to cater for 4,700 lines.[44] The first floor of the building was extended in 1963 when subscriber trunk dialling was introduced.[45] A new building was completed alongside the old one in 1969 to cope with further expansion of the service. In 1985 electronic equipment was installed. There was a staff of 168 in 1990 when the exchange was closed, a new digital exchange at Norwich taking over the work.[46]

The administrative headquarters of the General Post Office Eastern Region, employing 500 people, was moved from London to a new building in St. Peter's Street in 1969–70. The regional head postmaster, before privatization in 1984, was responsible for 22 head post offices and the regional telephone manager for 6 telephone areas.[47]

PORT

THE Anglo-Saxon port appears to have been at Old Heath, called from the 12th century Old Hythe, where a 7th-century pot of Belgian origin has been found.[48] There was still a landing place there in 1341, and a tradition that ships had once sailed up a channel or creek to unload there was apparently known to old men in 1630, but by the mid 12th century the main port was established at the Hythe or New Hythe.[49] The new harbour had presumably been made, or improved, by deepening and straightening the river above Rowhedge. Until the 20th century the borough boundary preserved the line of a former channel, once presumably the main stream of the river, which led towards Old Heath.[50] The removal of the river into a new and straighter channel leading towards Colchester would have greatly improved the navigation to the Hythe. Nevertheless, the Hythe was probably never accessible to large ships except perhaps at spring

26 E.R.O., D/B 5 Gb1, 31 May 1591.

27 *Acts of P. C.* 1625–6, 162; E.R.O., D/Y 2/9, p. 310.

28 L. J. Johnson, *The Posts of Essex*, 36–7; E.R.O., D/B 5 Aa1/23.

29 *Cal. S. P. Dom.* 1677–8, 527; 1687–9, 494.

30 E.R.O., D/DU 459, pp. 131–2.

31 Johnson, *Posts of Essex*, 19, 37.

32 Brown, *Colch. 1815–1914*, 162.

33 *White's Dir. Essex* (1848), 95.

34 *Kelly's Dir. Essex* (1882).

35 *Colch. Expr.* 21 Dec. 1972.

36 *Colch. Official Guide* (4th edn.), 38.

37 *Kelly's Dir. Essex* (1937); *Citizen's Dir. and Guide* (Colch. district edn. 1985), 13–14.

38 *Times*, 23 July 1803; R. G. E. Wood, *Essex and the French Wars* (Seax portfolio 9), no. 36.

39 E.R.O., Acc. C36: receipt for first telegraph message.

40 *E.C.S.* 6 Mar., 18 Sept. 1886.

41 E.R.O., Boro. Mun., Watch Cttee. Mins. 1881–91, p. 333.

42 Colch. Mus., G.P.O. and Brit. Telecom file; *Essex Tel.* 8 Sept. 1894.

43 Brown, *Colch. 1815–1914*, 33.

44 *Essex Tel.* 28 Jan. 1928; *E.C.S.* 13 July 1990; Colch. Mus., G.P.O. and Brit. Telecom file.

45 *E.C.S.* 24 May 1963.

46 Colch. Mus., G.P.O. and Brit. Telecom file; *E.C.S.* 13 July, 14 Dec. 1990.

47 *E.C.S.* 18 Aug. 1967; 30 Oct. 1970; *Colch. Gaz.* 15 July 1969; inf. from British Telecom.

48 Morant, *Colch.* 122–3; *P.N. Essex*, 376–7; *Colch. Cart.* ii. 307–8; *Colch. Arch. Rep.* i. 21–2. This section was completed in 1987.

49 E.R.O., D/B 5 R2, f. 139; P.R.O., E 134/5 Chas. I Mic./8; E 134/5–6 Chas. I Hil./3; *Colch. Cart.* i. 87, 95.

50 See below, Fig. 23.

tides. As early as 1327 wheat for Newcastle on Tyne had to be carried in small boats from the Hythe to Brightlingsea because the water was too low for sea-going vessels to get any higher up the river.[51]

By the 13th century weirs and piles, some of them presumably associated with the oyster fishery, were being erected in the river; in 1285 there were as many as 23 weirs between Colchester and the sea, all said to have been there from time immemorial. Navigation was also impeded by the dumping of ballast into the channel.[52] In 1353 there were further complaints that the channel was obstructed by weirs, mills, staves, palings, and kiddles, and in 1362 Lionel of Bradenham, the prior of Mersea, and six other men were ordered to remove at least 3 'enclosures' and 28 weirs which had so reduced the water in the channel that even small boats could hardly reach the Hythe.[53] Edward IV's charter of 1462 provided that no one should make weirs, kiddles, or other 'engines' without the bailiffs' licence,[54] but the provision may have been designed as much to protect the fishery as to maintain the navigation. In the late 15th century the abbot of St. John's, and in 1582 a miller, were accused of placing piles in the river.[55]

Thomas Christmas (d. 1520) left £20 for the repair of the 'creek' at the Hythe, but the money was not paid until 1548–9; in that and succeeding years the borough raised a further £290 to repair and scour the channel.[56] The early 16th-century work may have included making a new channel for the river for at least part of the distance between Colchester and Wivenhoe. A 'new channel' recorded in 1629 had been dug so long before that the details of its construction had been forgotten.[57] Henry VIII inspected Colne Water in 1543 and thought it a better harbour than the Stour at Harwich, but, apart from building a blockhouse to defend its mouth, the government seems to have done nothing to improve the river.[58] In the 1570s it was usual for sea-going ships to moor at Wivenhoe or Rowhedge and transfer their cargo to small boats for carriage to the Hythe.[59] A bill for the repair of the harbour and channel, prepared by the borough *c.* 1585, came to nothing, but in 1592 the borough assembly agreed to allow £10 a year for the repair of the channel and appointed four overseers of the channel to supervise expenditure. The borough carried out some work on the channel in 1603, and in 1614 made another unsuccessful attempt to get an Act for its improvement.[60]

An Act for the improvement of the channel was obtained in 1623, when the river was said to be impassable between Rowhedge and Hythe mill. The bailiffs or their deputies were empowered to raise money for the maintenance of the channel and the harbour by taking toll for 15 years from ships using the port,[61] but no provision was made for any major improvements. In 1629 the river at the Hythe was still only *c.* 3 ft. deep at an ordinary tide, although it might be 5–6 ft. deep at a spring tide. Thus although ships of 40–60 tons loaded could reach the Hythe at a spring tide with a favourable wind, at other times the river was navigable only by small boats.[62] In 1641 and 1685 the borough assembly promoted other bills for 'cutting the channel', alleging in 1685 that the existing channel was 'filled up and almost useless',[63] but no Act was obtained until 1698. The new Act provided for the widening, deepening, and straightening of the river, the work to be paid for by tolls to be collected by the mayor and commonalty for 21 years.[64] It also appointed commissioners for the channel, who included the mayor and aldermen of Colchester and the justices of the peace for the eastern division of Essex. Work began in 1699, and by 1701 some points of land between Wivenhoe and the Hythe had been cut through to make a 'canal', and floodgates had been erected at the Hythe, but the work does not seem to have been completed, perhaps for lack of funds.[65] An Act of 1719 extended to 1740 the period during which the borough might collect customs, but halved the duties to be collected. It also provided for the making of towpaths on either side of the river between Wivenhoe and Fingringhoe and the Hythe. The commissioners apparently used their powers and revenues under the Act to build a lock just below the Hythe.[66]

Later Acts for improving the navigation and paving the borough streets, obtained in 1740, 1749–50, 1781, and 1811, further extended the term of the Acts of 1698 and 1740, and vested in the Commissioners, then called the improvement commissioners, most of the powers held until 1742 by the corporation.[67] Most of the money raised was spent on the town's streets; what was spent on the channel was used mainly to pay for routine dredging and the repair of the river banks. The channel does seem to have been deepened, however: by the mid 18th century it was 9 or 10 ft. deep at spring tides, and 5–7 ft. deep at neap tides, and vessels of *c.* 90 tons loaded could reach the port.[68]

Despite such work, the river in 1829 was still so winding that shoals formed quickly, and a report recommended straightening it, making a new cut between Wivenhoe and the Hythe, and

51 P.R.O., E 101/556/14.

52 B.L. Add. MS. 12505, f. 265; P.R.O., JUST 1/242, rot. 112d.; E.R.O., D/B 5 R5, f. 110v.

53 *Cal. Pat.* 1350–4, 509; P.R.O., C 260/74, no. 55.

54 *Colch. Charters*, 47–8.

55 E.R.O., D/B 5 Cr143, rot. 4d.; D/B 5 R2, f. 213v.

56 P.R.O., PROB 11/19, f. 218v.; B.L. Stowe MS. 829, ff. 25v., 26 and v., 33v., 55 and v.; E.R.O., D/B 5 R2, loose folio.

57 P.R.O., E 134/5 Chas. I Mic./8.

58 *L. & P. Hen. VIII*, xviii (1), p. 418; xxi (2), pp. 432, 446.

59 E.R.O., D/B 5 Sb2/2, ff. 62v., 68; P.R.O., E 134/5 Chas. I, Mic. 8.

60 E.R.O., D/B 5 Gb1, undated meeting, meeting of 7 Aug. 1592; Gb2, ff. 34v., 134v.

61 21 Jas. I, c. 34, printed in Morant, *Colch.* App. p. 9.

62 P.R.O., E 134/5 Chas. I Mic./8; E 134/5–6 Chas. I Hil./3; E 134/6 Chas. I Mic./17.

63 E.R.O., D/B 5 Gb3, f. 211v.; Gb5, f. 230.

64 9 & 10 Wm. III, c. 19.

65 E.R.O., D/B 5 Gb6, pp. 163, 171–2, 200, 226, 234.

66 5 Geo. I, c. 31.

67 13 Geo. II, c. 30; 23 Geo. II, c. 19; 21 Geo. III, c. 30; 51 Geo. III, c. 43 (Local and Personal).

68 e.g. E.R.O., Boro. Mun., Improvement Com. Mins. 1811–33, pp. 14–15, 18, 73, 232–3, 237; Morant, *Colch.* 127.

removing the lock at the Hythe. Some work, apparently including the making of an new cut below New quay, had been done by *c.* 1846, although in 1840 the navigation committee of the improvement commissioners had declared themselves unable to make any major improvements because of insurmountable difficulties, presumably financial.[69] In 1842 the committee rejected a plan by Peter Bruff for a new cut and a new dock at the Hythe, but in 1846 they agreed to spend £6,000 as economically as possible.[70] An Act was obtained in 1847 empowering the commissioners to construct a floating basin with the necessary wharves and quays and to make a new cut or channel between Wivenhoe and the Hythe. Admiralty commissioners reported that year that only about a third of the money raised in duties between 1827 and 1846 had been spent on the river, which was in a 'most defective and neglected state', but they opposed Bruff's plan for the construction of a weir controlling a new cut to the Hythe, as it would interfere with the tidal scouring of the river.[71] Funds did not permit the construction of the canal and floating basin, but some work was carried out between 1847 and 1857, including the removal of the lock and the widening, deepening, and straightening of the river between New quay and the Hythe.[72]

In 1880 Colchester traders complained that some ships took as many as 5 or 7 days to get from Wivenhoe to the Hythe, but by 1883 the commissioners had bought a steam dredger and claimed to have deepened the channel by up to 2 ft. over the previous 25 years. In 1887 for the first time a vessel of 325 tons, drawing 10 ft. of water, reached the Hythe.[73] In 1888, however, the commissioners concluded that they had insufficient powers to develop the port and river, and in 1892 management of the navigation was transferred to the corporation.[74]

In 1892 the *c.* 3,000 vessels using the port each year were mainly Thames barges; larger ships, including small coasting vessels and small cargo steamers, drawing 9½ ft. could reach the Hythe at spring tides and those drawing 5½ ft. at neap tides. A recommendation of 1894 to deepen the water by at least 4 ft. at the Hythe and 3 ft. lower down the river was not carried out.[75] In 1907 further proposals were made for erecting a barrage at Rowhedge, making a basin at New quay, and deepening the channel from Rowhedge to Hythe bridge. The council rejected the barrage and the basin, but agreed to widen and deepen the upper part of the river. Work, mainly dredging but apparently including the making of a swinging dock, was carried out between 1909 and 1912.[76] Further improvements, including the enlargement of the swinging dock and the removal of some bends in the river, were made between 1920 and 1924, and in 1925 a ship of 750 tons was able to reach the Hythe.[77] Major improvements, including those proposed in 1894, were again considered in 1935 and 1937, and the swinging dock was further enlarged in 1938, but work seems to have been abandoned on the outbreak of the Second World War.[78]

In the later 20th century the amount of traffic using Colchester port, including wharves at Rowhedge and Wivenhoe, increased steadily; in 1984 a total of 2,501 ships carrying over 1 million tons of cargo docked there. The proportion of ships reaching the Hythe declined, however, from 46 per cent of the total in 1980–1 to 18 per cent in 1985–6, as shipping companies made increasing use of larger ships which could not reach the upper quays. Despite extra dredging in the later 1970s, the maximum draught for ships using the Hythe in 1986 was 3.7 m. at a spring tide and 2.7 m. at a neap tide.[79] Trinity House pilots, first appointed in 1819, were available to all vessels and compulsory for foreign ships using the river.[80]

Both coastal and continental trade from the Hythe was important in the Middle Ages and later. By 1637 there was a regular weekly service by hoy from the Hythe to London, perhaps by two ships as in the 1650s, and by 1714 two packets made the journey weekly.[81] Steam replaced sail in the 1830s and 1840s, reducing the journey time to 7 hours, and a twice weekly service was maintained throughout the 19th century. Steam packets apparently sailed thrice weekly in 1910 and 1912, but the service had been reduced to twice weekly by 1917 and seems to have ceased soon afterwards.[82] In the earlier 19th century there was also a regular service to Hull and Gainsborough.[83]

There was a granary at the Hythe in 1327. Between 1339 and 1342 the bailiffs leased 5 plots of land for new quays and buildings behind

69 E.R.O., Boro. Mun., Improvement Com. Mins. 1811–33, pp. 298–301, 356–7; 1833–47, pp. 165–6; G. Gilbert, *Colch. Map c.* 1846.

70 E.R.O., Boro. Mun., Improvement Com. Mins. 1833–47, pp. 203, 206–7, 276.

71 10 & 11 Vic. c. 281 (Local and Personal); E.R.O., Boro. Mun., Improvement Com. Mins. 1847–53, p. 74; Memorial of 1847, and Appendix: copy in E.C.L. Colch.; *2nd. Rep. Tidal Harbours Com.* [692], App. B, pp. 623–6, H.C. (1846), xviii; W. Wheeler, *Rep. on R. Colne* (1894), 5.

72 E.R.O., Boro. Mun., Improvement Com. Mins. 1847–53, pp. 380–2; ibid. Proc. Navigation Cttee. 1847–80, 25–8, 34, 43, 55, 66; ibid. Acc. C47, CPL 1192, 1209; Gilbert, *Colch. Map*; O.S. Map, 6" Essex XXVIII. SW. (1885 edn.).

73 Wheeler, *Rep. on R. Colne*, 6; *Return of Harbour Works in past 20 Yrs.* H.C. 313, p. 22 (1883), lxii; E.R.O., Boro. Mun., Navigation and Improvement Com. Bk. of Proc. 1882–92, p. 108.

74 E.R.O., Boro. Mun., Navigation and Improvement Com. Bk. of Proc. 1882–92, p. 126; Colch. Corpn. Act, 55 & 56 Vic. c. 107 (Local and Personal).

75 Wheeler, *Rep. on R. Colne*, 6, 8–9; E.R.O., Boro. Mun., Harbour and Navigation Cttee. Min. Bk. 1892–6, pp. 86, 152.

76 R. M. Parkinson, *Rep. on Suggested Barrage Scheme for R. Colne (1907)*: copy in E.C.L. Colch.; E.R.O., Boro. Mun., Harbour and Navigation Cttee. Min. Bk. 1906–15, pp. 3–4, 30, 40–5, 56, 58, 74–5, 79, 85, 100–3, 107, 152–4, 160.

77 E.R.O., Boro. Mun., Harbour and Navigation Cttee. Mins. 1915–22, pp. 84a, 118–19, 135, 139; 1922–33, pp. 10, 13, 25, 27, 39.

78 Ibid. 1933–47, 17–18, 61, 69, 75; copies of reps. in E.C.L. Colch.

79 Colch. Boro. Council, 'Facts & Figs.' 1954–84; idem, 'Future Viability of Colch. Port: Draft Final Rep.' (1986): copies in E.C.L. Colch.

80 E.R.O., D/B 5 Gb9, pp. 383–4; *E.C.S.* 8 Aug. 1969; Colch. Boro. Council, 'Review of Council Operations at Port of Colch.' (TS. in E.C.L. Colch., 1975), p. 2.

81 J. Taylor, *Carriers' Cosmographie* (1637); *V.C.H. Essex*, ii. 284; v. 4 n.

82 H. Benham, *Once upon a Tide*, 222–6; *P.O. Dir. Essex* (1866 and later edns.); *Kelly's Dir. Essex* (1882 and later edns.); *Descriptive Account of Colch.* [1893], 35: copy in E.R.O.

83 Benham, *Once upon a Tide*, 222–3; *Robson's Gazeteer of Home Counties* (1838), 41.

them, the building to be done by the tenants, and in 1352 a merchant owned a quay with a house, presumably a warehouse, on it. The 1462 charter gave the bailiffs control over the making of wharves and cranes, and the town built a new quay in 1548–9.[84] There was a crane, apparently newly built, by 1387, and a second one had been built by 1396. The borough collected an aid for making a new crane in 1495.[85] By 1610 or earlier the quay, warehouses, and crane were normally maintained by the water bailiff, the borough officer in charge of the port, although the borough itself seems to have carried out major repairs, as in 1738 when the chamberlain spent *c.* £30 on repairs to the crane. In 1623 the water bailiff was required to rebuild the warehousing as a brick building of 2½ storeys with a tiled roof.[86] Private quays were the responsibility of their owners who were presented in the borough courts for allowing them to fall into disrepair.[87]

In 1680 there was one legal quay, which extended *c.* 177 yd. along the west bank of the river from the end of Middle Row, a short way below Hythe bridge. It was leased in sections by the town, the tenants being responsible for maintenance and repair. A lease of the northern part in 1685 provided for the building of a new crane.[88] In 1690 Giles Sayer, a glazier, built a new quay and warehouse *c.* ½ mile below the Hythe and refused to pay rates or duties to the town for goods loaded and unloaded there. The town was unable to dislodge him, and his quay was recognized by the Act of 1698. The operations between 1699 and 1701 to straighten the channel seem to have left Sayer's wharf high and dry, and in 1701 the borough leased to him the land between his wharf and the new navigation channel, presumably for a new wharf. In 1724 the wharf was called Giles Sayer's wharf; by 1846 it was the New quay.[89]

By 1823 the quays at the Hythe extended along both sides of the river. The former town quay on the west bank, called the common quay, was 195 yd. long; north of it, immediately south of Hythe bridge, was the Ordnance Arms quay, 37 yd. long. On the east bank of the river was Grocer's quay, 235 yd. long.[90] Under the Act of 1847 a new quay *c.* 230 ft. long was built in 1857 at Lower Granary Hythe, between Hythe bridge and New quay.[91] By 1907 the quays were inadequate, and between 1910 and 1912 a new quay, King Edward quay, was built below Hythe quay on the west bank of the river; it was extended in 1925. A third public quay, Haven quay, was built below King Edward quay in the late 1930s.[92] By 1975 all but one of the private quays on the east bank of the river were disused. There were then 1,350 m. of working quay, but Hythe quay, above the turning bay, was not much used. Haven quay was extended by 40 m. in 1983.[93]

Colchester port was, for the purposes of the royal customs, a member of Ipswich from the 14th century or earlier, and by the later 17th century Mersea, Brightlingsea, Wivenhoe, Maldon, and Burnham were part of Colchester port.[94] In the 14th century Colchester port included South Geedon and Parrock fleet (part of Pyfleet channel) creeks, Hamford Water, East Mersea and Brightlingsea; similar limits were claimed, apparently successfully, in 1587.[95] In 1680 the port boundary ran southwards from the Naze point along the coast to a point of land at or near Tollesbury, then westwards, inland, covering all the creeks and streams flowing into the Colne as far as Colchester itself. In 1823 the bounds extended slightly further south towards the Thames estuary, to meet those of the port of London, but otherwise they were the same as those of 1680. In 1884 the limits of the port were extended still further southwards to Havengore Creek.[96]

From the 14th century or earlier there were both royal and borough officials of the port. Deputies to the king's butler and to the serjeant at arms for the east coast ports, including Colchester, were recorded from 1334, and one for Colchester and Maldon in 1353. A collecter of customs for Ipswich and Colchester was appointed in 1350, and a controller of customs for Colchester and Maldon in 1399.[97] Most of the medieval officers recorded later served both Ipswich and Colchester, presumably from Ipswich with deputies in Colchester, but a searcher of ships at Colchester and Maldon was recorded in 1445. Some officials, like the weigher ordered in 1341 to take the weighing beam from Ipswich to Colchester to weigh cloth there, moved from one port to the other.[98] In 1455 the bailiffs were accused of trying to prevent the packers of wool and cloth from exercising their office, perhaps an early instance of the friction between the two sets of officials recorded again in the later 17th century.[99] From the later 16th century or earlier a customer and controller, a searcher, and a surveyor for Colchester were appointed regularly, as were a collector of customs, landwaiters,

84 P.R.O., E 101/556/14; ibid. C 131/9, no. 4; E.R.O., D/B 5 R1, ff. 35v., 36v., 37; *Colch. Charters*, 47–8; B.L. Stowe MS. 829, f. 33v.

85 Britnell, *Growth and Decline*, 69; B.L. Stowe MS. 828, f. 67.

86 E.R.O., D/B 5 Gb2, f. 96; Gb3, f. 28v.; D/B 5 Ab1/34.

87 e.g. ibid. D/B 5 Cr39, rot. 18d.; Cr145, rot. 31; D/B 5 Sr10, rot. 4.

88 P.R.O., E 178/6469; E.R.O., D/B 5 Gb4, f. 263; Gb5, ff. 168v., 234; D/B 5 Sr52, rot. 9.

89 E.R.O., D/B 5 Gb5, f. 333; D/DC 22/14–21; Act 9 & 10 Wm. III, c. 19; Gilbert, *Colch. Map* (1846).

90 P.R.O., E 178/6690; ibid. MBP 33.

91 10 & 11 Vic. c. 281; E.R.O., Acc. C47, CPL 1209; ibid. Boro. Mun., Improvement Com. Mins. 1854–63, pp. 149, 155, 251.

92 Parkinson, *Barrage Scheme for R. Colne*, 2; E.R.O., Boro. Mun., Harbour and Navigation Cttee. Min. Bk. 1906–15, pp. 106–7, 152–4; 1915–22, p. 18; 1922–33, p. 143; Colch. Boro. *Centenary of Mun. Corp. Act: Souvenir* (1935), 17; O.S. Map 1/2,500, Essex, XXXVIII. 8 (1936 edn.).

93 Colch. Boro. 'Review of Council Operations at Port of Colch.' (1975); idem, 'Future Viability of Colch. Port: Draft Final Rep.' (1986), 9.

94 e.g. P.R.O., C 260/55, no. 92; ibid. E 122/193/33; E 178/6469; *Cal. Treas. Bks.* 1679–80, 201; 1681–5, 446–7, 554, 1122; 1685–9, 1555; 1689–92, 12, 927–8.

95 P.R.O., C 260/74, no. 55; B.L. Add. MS. 12505, ff. 265–7.

96 E.R.O., D/B 5 Gb5, f. 168v.; P.R.O., E 178/6990; *Lond. Gaz.* 18 March 1884, p. 1306.

97 *Cal. Pat.* 1334–8, 24, 256; 1396–9, 568, 590; *Cal. Fine R.* 1347–56, 217.

98 *Cal. Fine R.* 1437–45, 315; *Cal. Close*, 1341–3, 204.

99 P.R.O., C 1/17, no. 198; *Cal. Treas. Bks.* 1669–72, 1043, 1182.

tidewaiters, searchers, and boatmen from 1670.[1] In the mid 18th century the customs employed a comptroller, a surveyor, 2 landwaiters (at the Hythe and at Wivenhoe), a supervisor of customs, 3 riding officers, 4 coal meters, and 1 corn meter. There were still 10 customs officers in Colchester in 1985.[2]

The chief borough officer for the port was the water bailiff, recorded by that name from 1504, although the profits of the office were leased by the bailiffs from 1399 or earlier. He had charge of the crane or cranes (which all ships loading or unloading had to use) and warehouses, and was responsible for weighing and measuring merchandise and for collecting borough customs and toll, and quayage and wharfage fees. A measurer at the Hythe, presumably the water bailiff's assistant, was among the borough officers elected in 1373.[3] By 1705 the water bailiff was also responsible for overseeing the oyster fishery and the fish market at the Hythe.[4] In 1592 the borough assembly agreed to appoint 4 overseers of the channel, and in 1622 the serjeant of Colne Water was appointed beaconager to set up beacons.[5] The Act of 1623 and the following Acts empowered the bailiffs to appoint collectors of tolls or channel dues. In 1657 the assembly laid down rules for the appointment and behaviour of 4 meters or measurers at the Hythe, and 16 porters or carriers to assist them, all of whom were to swear to deal justly between buyer and seller.[6] The Act of 1847 empowered the commissioners to appoint a harbourmaster (in addition to the borough harbourmaster); they also appointed meters or measurers of coal and corn.[7] When sole control of the port passed to the council in 1892 the former commissioners' harbourmaster became deputy harbourmaster. Under the Act of 1892 the chairman of the borough Navigation Committee assumed the title of portreeve.[8] The borough still employed a harbourmaster and deputy harbourmaster in 1987.

CASTLE

COLCHESTER castle was built for William I, probably by Eudes the sewer *c.* 1076, using for the foundation of the keep the podium of the Roman temple of Claudius.[9] The surviving building, 46.3 m. × 33.5 m., is the largest Norman keep in England, larger than the White Tower of London which was built on a similar plan. The ground plan of Colchester keep, including the apse in the south-east corner, may be based on that of the late Roman building,[10] but the evidence is conflicting. The keep was built of rubble, including much septaria, stone, and tile taken from Roman buildings, with dressings of ashlar and tile.

The Crown kept possession of the castle until 1101 when Henry I granted it, with the town, to Eudes the sewer.[11] It escheated to the Crown on Eudes's death in 1120, and remained in the king's hands, although held intermittently by hereditary constables between *c.* 1120 and 1214, until it was granted in tail male to Humphrey of Lancaster, later duke of Gloucester, in 1404.[12] In 1436 it was regranted to Humphrey and his wife Eleanor in tail, but on Humphrey's death without issue in 1447 Eleanor was refused dower, and the castle reverted to the Crown.[13] In 1616 it was fraudulently included in a grant of concealed lands made to Samuel Jones and John Jones, and in the same year their interest was acquired by the life constable John Stanhope, Lord Stanhope. Although Jones and Jones were found guilty of fraud and imprisoned in 1620, Lord Stanhope's son Charles continued to claim the reversion of the castle under the grant of 1616.[14]

In 1629 Charles I granted the reversion of the castle, which was still in the possession of Charles, Lord Stanhope (d. 1675), to James Hay, earl of Carlisle.[15] The earl mortgaged his interest to Archibald Hay in 1633 and conveyed it to him outright in 1636. Archibald Hay, having failed to obtain possession from Lord Stanhope,[16] sold the reversion of the castle in 1649 to the parliamentarian Sir John Lenthall. Lenthall sold it in 1656 to Sir James Norfolk, who bought out Lord Stanhope's interest in 1662. Norfolk retained possession of the castle until his death in 1680, and his son Robert in 1683 sold the keep, but not the bailey, to a Colchester ironmonger, John Wheeley, for its stone. Wheeley, whose speculations had already driven him into debt, demolished part of the keep in the later 1690s, but the operation proved unprofitable and in 1705 he sold the keep to Sir Isaac Rebow.[17]

In 1726 Sir Isaac devised it to his grandson Charles Chamberlain Rebow who sold it the following year to Mary Webster who gave it to her daughter Sarah Creffield (d. 1751) and Sarah's second husband Charles Gray. In 1727 Mary Webster bought the bailey, presumably also for the Grays. She confirmed the grant to Gray by her will, proved in 1754.[18] On Gray's

1 P.R.O., E 190 (port bks.), *passim*; *Cal. Treas. Bks.* 1660–7, 263; 1669–72, 1166; 1681–5, 553; 1685–9, 200, 535.

2 Morant, *Colch.* 129; *E.C.S.* 4 Oct. 1985.

3 E.R.O., D/B 5 Cr31, rot. 2d.; D/B 5 R2, ff. 6v., 78v.; W. Rastell, *Colln. of Entries etc.* (1596), f. 3v.

4 E.R.O., Acc. C47, CPL 1226.

5 Ibid. D/B 5 Gb1, 7 Aug. 1592; Gb3, f. 11v.

6 Ibid. D/B 5 Gb4, f. 160v.; Gb7, p. 37; 21 Jas. I, c. 34; 9 & 10 Wm. III, c. 19; 5 Geo. I, c. 31; 13 Geo. II, c. 30.

7 10 & 11 Vic. c. 281 (Local and Personal); E.R.O., Navigation Cttee. Mins. 1847–80, pp. 1–2.

8 E.R.O., Boro. Mun., Harbour and Navigation Cttee. Min. Bk. 1892–6, p. 1.

9 *Arch. Jnl.* cxxxix. 391, 399.

10 R.C.H.M., *Essex*, iii. 51–4; *Britannia*, xv. 9–10, 31.

11 *Reg. Regum Anglo-Norm.* ii, no. 552.

12 *V.C.H. Essex*, i. 347; *Cal. Pat.* 1401–5, 468; *Rot. Parl.* iii. 670.

13 *Cal. Pat.* 1429–36, 503–6; *Feet of F. Essex*, iv. 23; *Complete Peerage*, v. 736.

14 E.R.O., D/DRe L3.

15 [J. H. Round], *Hist. and Antiq. Colch. Castle*, 126–7; E.R.O., D/DRe E1: abstract of title.

16 *Cal. S.P. Dom.* 1639–40, 57–8.

17 E.R.O., D/DRe L3; D/DRe T4; Morant, *Colch.* 9–10.

18 E.R.O., D/DRe L3; D/DRe T4, 6; Round, *Colch. Castle*, 128–9; *E.A.T.* N.S. iii. 149–51.

death in 1782 the castle passed to Sarah's granddaughter Thamar Creffield and her husband James Round of Birch.[19] It remained in the Round family until 1920 when Captain E. J. Round sold it to the borough as a war memorial; money for the purchase was given by W. D. Pearson, viscount Cowdray, high steward of the borough.[20]

Eudes the sewer was probably constable of the castle throughout the reigns of William I and William II, overseeing the completion of the keep and the construction of the bailey and putting the partly built castle into a state of defence to withstand the threatened invasion of Cnut of Denmark in 1085.[21] After his death his former under tenant Hamon of St. Clare became constable; in 1130 he accounted for the farm and aids of the borough and of Eudes's lands in Essex.[22] He seems to have held the castle throughout the civil war of Stephen's reign despite the Empress Maud's grant of it to Aubrey de Vere in 1141.[23] Hamon died *c.* 1150 and was succeeded by his son Hubert of St. Clare who was constable at his death in 1155.[24] From 1155 to 1190 the castle was probably in the sheriff's hands, except for the period 1173–4, during the rebellion of the young king, when Ralph Brito seems to have been constable. The castle was strengthened, garrisoned, and victualled in those years but was not attacked.[25]

The castle was provisioned again in 1190, the equipment including 26 military tunics presumably for a garrison.[26] The following year John son of Godfrey became constable and was granted an allowance of £12 a year from the farm of Tendring hundred to maintain his position.[27] He was succeeded in 1196 by William de Lanvalai, Hubert of St. Clare's grandson, who in 1200 bought from King John the right to continue to enjoy the custody of the castle.[28] He died in 1204 and was succeeded first by his widow Hawise and then by his son, another William de Lanvalai.[29]

Early in November 1214 King John stayed in Colchester, presumably at the castle, for two days;[30] he seems to have replaced de Lanvalai, a baronial partisan, by the sheriff, Matthew Mantell, who was almost at once ordered to hand the castle over to Stephen Harengood, probably a German or Flemish adherent of the king.[31] Mantell and Harengood carried out extensive works on the castle, and equipped and garrisoned it.[32] In July 1215, after the signing of Magna Carta, Harengood was ordered to restore the castle to de Lanvalai.[33] Colchester was thus one of the few castles not in the keeping of a royal supporter. By October 1215 de Lanvalai was in rebellion, or possibly dead, and later that year or early in 1216 the garrison was reinforced by a French contingent.[34] The castle held out against a siege by Savory de Meuleon in January 1216, but surrendered to King John in March. Harengood was reappointed constable and also made sheriff.[35] Early in 1217, however, the castle was surrendered to the French and their English associates in return for a truce.[36] It was restored to the Crown by the Treaty of Lambeth in 1218, provisioned again at a cost of £20, and committed to William of Sainte-Mère-Église, bishop of London.[37]

William handed the castle over to Eustace de Fauconberg, his successor as bishop of London, in 1223.[38] Eustace was succeeded as castellan by William Blund in 1227 and William by Randal Brito in 1229.[39] In 1230 the castle was granted to John de Burgh, who had married Hawise daughter and heir of the younger William de Lanvalai, to hold as William had held it,[40] but in 1232 John and his father Hubert de Burgh were ordered to deliver the castle to Stephen of Seagrave.[41] Stephen did not hold it long, as Ralph Gernon was constable in 1234 and delivered the castle to Hubert de Ruilli in 1236.[42] Richard de Muntfitchet was constable 1242–6 and sheriff 1244–6;[43] he may have been succeeded by the sheriff Richard of Whitsand, but in 1251 Henry of Haughton handed the castle over to John de Grey.[44] In 1255–6 the castle was committed to the sheriff Ralph of Ardern, but Guy of Rochford was keeper from 1256 until his banishment in 1258.[45]

In 1258 the castle was committed to the baronial leader Roger Bigod, earl of Norfolk, who held it until June 1262 or later although he had been ordered to surrender it to the sheriff the previous July.[46] It then seems to have remained in the sheriff's custody until October 1266 when it was transferred to Thomas de Clare who held it until 1268 when it was returned to the sheriff.[47] In 1271 the castle was granted for 5 years to the

19 *E.R.* lii. 168; lvii. 19; Round, *Colch. Castle*, 131.

20 E.R.O., D/DR F58; D/DRh Z13; ibid. Boro. Mun., Council Mins. 1919–20, pp. 148, 294, 376–7.

21 See entries in 'Colch. Chron.' discussed in *Colch. Arch. Rep.* i. 28–30.

22 *Pipe R.* 1130 (H.M.S.O. facsimile), 138–9.

23 *Reg. Regum Anglo-Norm.* ii, no. 1822; iii, nos. 634–5.

24 *E.A.T.* 3rd ser. xx. 30–4.

25 *Pipe R.* 1170 (P.R.S. xv), 110; 1173 (P.R.S. xix), 30–1; 1174 (P.R.S. xxi), 67, 74–5; 1180 (P.R.S. xxix), 2; 1190 (P.R.S. N.S. i), 104.

26 Ibid. 1190 (P.R.S. N.S. i), 3.

27 Ibid. 1191 & 1192 (P.R.S. N.S. ii), 24.

28 Ibid. 1196 (P.R.S. N.S. vii), 111; I. J. Sanders, *Eng. Baronies*, 92; *Rot. de Ob. et Fin.* (Rec. Com.), 89.

29 *Pipe R.* 1205 (P.R.S. N.S. xix), 183; 1210 (P.R.S. N.S. xxvi), 58.

30 *Rot. Litt. Claus.* (Rec. Com.), i. 177.

31 *Rot. Litt. Pat.* (Rec. Com.), 123; *Pipe R.* 1214 (P.R.S. N.S. xxxv), 1; Round, *Colch. Castle*, 40.

32 *Rot. Litt. Claus.* (Rec. Com.), i. 179, 182, 184, 187, 193–5; *Pipe R.* 1215 (P.R.S. N.S. xxvii), 62.

33 *Rot. Litt. Pat.* (Rec. Com.), 151. Cf. *Memoriale Walteri de Coventria* (Rolls Ser.), ii. 221.

34 *Rot. Litt. Pat.* (Rec. Com.), 171–2; Ralph of Coggeshall, *Chron. Anglicanum* (Rolls Ser.), 179; W. Farrer, *Honors and Knights' Fees*, iii. 289, 291; S. Painter, *Reign of King John*, 367.

35 Ralph of Coggeshall, *Chron. Anglicanum* (Rolls Ser.), 178–9; *Mem. Wal. de Coventria* (Rolls Ser.), ii. 229; *Rot. Litt. Pat.* (Rec. Com.), 171–2.

36 *Mem. Wal. de Coventria* (Rolls Ser.), ii. 235.

37 *Pipe R.* 1218 (P.R.S. N.S. xxxix), 65; *Rot. Litt. Claus.* (Rec. Com.), i. 345, 365.

38 *Pat. R.* 1216–25, 417.

39 Ibid. 1225–32, 144, 241.

40 *Close R.* 1227–31, 314; Round, *Colch. Castle*, 45; Farrer, *Honors and Knights' Fees*, iii. 289.

41 *Pat. R.* 1225–32, 496–7.

42 *Close R.* 1231–4, 499; *Cal. Pat.* 1232–47, 145.

43 *Cal. Pat.* 1232–47, 294, 477.

44 Ibid. 1247–58, 95, 98.

45 *Abbrev. Rot. Orig.* (Rec. Com.), i. 15; Matthew Paris, *Chron. Majora* (Rolls Ser.), v. 725; *Cal. Pat.* 1247–58, 482.

46 *Cal. Pat.* 1247–58, 655; 1258–66, 164, 214.

47 Ibid. 1258–66, 645, 649; 1266–72, 218, 509.

absent Prince Edward whose attorneys committed it to the sheriff in 1271 and to John of Cokefield in 1272.[48] In 1273 it was granted for life to John de Burgh who had held it from 1230 to 1232.[49] After his death in 1274 the sheriff received the castle again, and he and his successor held it until 1276 when its custody was transferred to Richard of Holebrook.[50] Holebrook may have held it until his death between November 1290 and March 1291, or the castle may have been part of the manor of Colchester assigned to Eleanor of Provence (d. 1291) in June 1290.[51] From 1291 to 1350 it appears to have been in the sheriff's custody except 1325–7, when a separate keeper was appointed. The castle was among those fortified and garrisoned in 1307–8 and again in 1321–2.[52]

From 1350 onwards, except for the period 1368–71, the keepership of the castle was held separately from the shrievalty. By then the castle was of little or no military importance, and those keepers who had more than a financial interest in it were primarily concerned with the gaol and its prisoners. Robert of Benhale was keeper from 1350 to his death in 1364; Lionel of Bradenham was constable, presumably under Benhale, in 1359.[53] From 1371, when the sheriff withdrew, the castle was kept in hand by the Crown until 1376 when it was committed to George of Felbridge at a rent of £10.[54] Felbridge held until 1384 when the castle was granted to Robert de Vere, earl of Oxford,[55] on whose attainder in 1388 it was granted successively, for their lives, to Sir Walter de la Lee, to Sir John Littlebury in 1395, and to Robert Tey in 1396.[56]

After the death of Humphrey, duke of Gloucester, in 1447 the castle, with many of the duke's other estates, was granted first to John Hampton, and then two months later to Henry VI's queen, Margaret of Anjou.[57] Hampton seems to have served as constable under Margaret, for in that capacity he was held responsible for escapes in 1455 and 1460.[58] Margaret presumably held it until her attainder in 1461, when custody of the castle was granted for life to Sir John Howard, later duke of Norfolk, who was killed at Bosworth in 1485 and was succeeded by Thomas Kendall.[59] In 1496 the castle was granted for life to John de Vere, earl of Oxford, whose possession was declared in 1509 to be hereditary, allegedly deriving from the grant by the Empress Maud to Aubrey de Vere.[60] John de Vere (d. 1513) was succeeded by his nephew John de Vere (d. 1526), who was succeeded by his cousin another John de Vere (d. 1540).[61] Custody of the castle did not pass to the third John's son and heir, another John de Vere, but was granted in 1541 to his son-in-law Sir Thomas Darcy, later baron Darcy of Chich, who was replaced on Queen Mary's accession by Anthony Kempe.[62] Kempe himself was replaced in 1559 by Henry Macwilliams of Stambourne Hall (d. 1586) who was succeeded by his son another Henry Macwilliams (d. 1599).[63] The custody for the life of Mary Cheek, widow of the elder Henry Macwilliams, was then granted to her son-in-law Sir John Stanhope, later Lord Stanhope; the grant was extended in 1603 to include Sir John's son Charles, and finally confirmed in 1607 to John and Charles Stanhope for their lives.[64] The Stanhopes were still in possession when the Crown alienated the castle in 1629.

The original arrangements for defending the castle are uncertain, and evidence for a system of castle-guard is slight, but lands in Darleigh in Little Bromley in 1248, in Wix in 1281, in Elmstead in 1317, in Great Oakley in 1327, and in Great Holland in 1331, owed castle-guard rents to Colchester castle.[65] In 1173 and 1174 and again in 1216 wages were paid to knights and serjeants in the castle,[66] and later garrisons were presumably also professional soldiers. It was claimed *c.* 1600 that the town had paid rents and owed services at the castle until the beginning of Elizabeth I's reign,[67] but there is no evidence what they were or whether they were related to castle-guard.

As long as it was in the king's hands, Colchester castle, like other royal castles, was extraparochial and outside the borough. In the later 13th century it served as an office for the sheriff.[68] In the 17th century, and probably earlier, borough officers might not arrest within the castle yard, and those who were not freemen could trade within the castle precinct without municipal disturbance.[69] In the 17th and 18th centuries the castle was usually held to be extraparochial, although John Wheeley paid rates to All Saints' parish *c.* 1690.[70] Its status was challenged in 1809 and overturned in 1810 when it was ordered that occupants of houses in the bailey be rated in All Saints' parish.[71]

The Norman castle was built in at least two main stages.[72] In the first, marked by the temporary battlements whose outline survived at first floor level in 1988, the keep was raised to

48 Ibid. 1266–72, 509, 642.
49 Ibid. 1272–81, 41.
50 *Cal. Fine R.* 1272–1307, 36, 57; *Cal. Pat.* 1272–81, 141.
51 *Cal. Pat.* 1281–92, 424; *Cal. Close*, 1288–96, 84–5, 154.
52 *Cal. Close*, 1307–13, 30, 50; 1318–23, 437; 1323–7, 423, 479.
53 *Cal. Pat.* 1348–50, 577; 1364–7, 55; *Cal. Fine R.* 1347–56, 235; 1356–68, 377; *Cal. Inq. p.m.* xi, p. 476.
54 *Cal. Fine R.* 1369–76, 141, 365; *Cal. Pat.* 1374–7, 368; P.R.O., C 260/87, no. 47.
55 *Cal. Pat.* 1381–5, 442.
56 Ibid. 1385–9, 424; 1391–6, 609; 1396–9, 1.
57 *Cal. Pat.* 1446–52, 33; Rymer, *Foedera* (1737–45 edn.), v. 170.
58 *Cal. Pat.* 1452–61, 242, 645.
59 *Rot. Parl.* v. 476, 479; vi. 382; *Cal. Pat.* 1461–7, 124.
60 *Cal. Pat.* 1494–1509, 73; *L. & P. Hen. VIII*, i (1), p. 28.
61 *Complete Peerage*, x. 239–47; *L. & P. Hen. VIII*, i (2), p. 1285; ibid. xvi. p. 457.
62 *L. & P. Hen. VIII*, xvi, p. 457; *Cal. Pat.* 1553–4, 283–4.
63 *Cal. Pat.* 1558–60, 62; Round, *Colch. Castle*, 55.
64 P.R.O., C 66/1544, m. 40; *Cal. S.P. Dom.* 1598–1601, 357; 1603–10, 15; 1580–1625, 426; Round, *Colch. Castle*, 55.
65 *Bk. of Fees*, ii. 1409; *Cal. Inq. p.m.* ii, p. 227; vi, p. 69; vii, p. 25; P.R.O., C 143/208, no. 32.
66 *Pipe R.* 1173 (P.R.S. xix), 31; 1174 (P.R.S. xxi), 67; *Rot. Litt. Pat.* (Rec. Com.), 192.
67 E.R.O., D/DRe Z3.
68 H. M. Cam, *Hund. and Hund. Rolls*, 89, 146.
69 E.R.O., D/DRe Z3; P.R.O., E 317/Essex/10.
70 P.R.O., E 134/4 Wm. and Mary Mich./5.
71 Morant, *Colch.* 10; E.R.O., D/DRe E1; D/B 5 Sb6/9, orders of 6 July, 1 Oct. 1810; ibid. Acc. C15.
72 *Arch. Jnl.* cxxxix. 391–401.

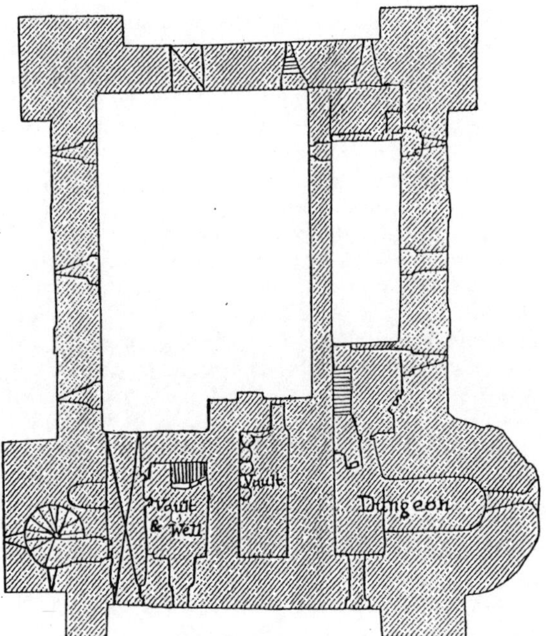

FIG. 18. PLAN OF THE CASTLE, 1876
(scale 1:667)

one storey. Shortly afterwards the corner towers were heightened. The first stage, which was almost certainly intended to be temporary, has been associated with the threatened invasion of Cnut of Denmark in 1085. Surviving Roman walls may have served as outer defences in the castle's earliest years, but by *c.* 1100 a bailey formed by an earth bank probably topped by a palisade had been built. Building work was resumed after the threat of invasion had passed. The single storey keep was levelled up to the height of the corner towers and then raised to three storeys with corner towers.

Internally the keep was originally divided into two main sections by a north–south wall, but after the completion of the upper storeys a second north–south wall was inserted into the eastern section. The ground-floor rooms had minimal lighting and were presumably designed for storage. The great hall probably occupied the western section of the first and second floors, and the central section may have been divided from it only by arcades. The eastern division presumably contained chambers on two floors. The apsidal south-east corner contained undercrofts on the ground and first floors and the chapel on the second floor. The chapel had aisles and an ambulatory and was probably lit by a clerestorey. There were two staircases, one between all floors at the south-west corner and one rising from the first floor at the north-west corner. Comparison with the White Tower and other early keeps suggests that the intended entrance would have been on the first floor, probably at the west end of the south side, but the only structurally original outer doorway to survive is a minor one, once approached by a timber stair, close to the north-west corner. The surviving main entrance on the ground floor, at the western end of the south wall just east of the south-west tower, is formed by a moulded arch of three orders which is of *c.* 1100, but was probably not intended for its present position. In the 12th century a stone forebuilding, which replaced an earlier timber stair, was constructed to give it protection.

Late Saxon buildings, including a chapel, seem to have survived immediately south of the keep and, protected by Roman walls, probably formed part of the living quarters of the first phase of the castle. Before or during the early stages of the construction of the keep in the 1070s or 1080s, a stone hall with adjoining chambers in a 'double pile' building was built south-east of the chapel and aligned with it. In the early 12th century the chapel was rebuilt and a fireplace similar to those in the surviving upper storey of the keep was inserted into the west wall of the hall.[73]

About £24 was spent on the repair of the castle in 1161, and further work was done on the castle and the king's houses in it in 1167 and 1170.[74] In 1172–3, just before the revolt of the young king, the castle was strengthened by the construction of a bailey, at a cost of £50. The work was probably the replacement of the wooden pallisade on top of the Norman bailey rampart by a stone wall, also on top of the rampart. The bailey had certainly been surrounded by a stone wall by 1182–3 when £30, including the cost of a lime kiln, was spent on its repair. Possibly, however, the bailey made in 1172–3 was the lower bailey to the north of the Norman bailey. Further work, costing over £18, was carried out in 1173–4.[75]

The castle was repaired regularly in the late 12th and early 13th century. Work on the gutters and roof of the keep was carried out in 1180 and 1181–2, and as much as £30 was spent on unspecified works in 1190.[76] In 1192 and 1195 a total of 60 marks was spent on repairs to the castle and the houses in it.[77] A further 50 marks was spent between 1199 and 1202, and smaller sums in 1204 and 1210, perhaps on preparations for King John's visits in 1203, 1205, 1209, and 1212.[78] The work may have included the remodelling of the bailey buildings: in the earlier 13th century the east end of the chapel was squared off, and the rooms east of the hall were demolished and replaced by new buildings to the west and north-east, set into the tail of the rampart.[79]

The castle was strengthened during the civil war of John's reign. A carpenter was paid 22 marks for work there in 1214; in 1215 Stephen Harengood was allowed 45 marks for its repair

73 Ibid. 396–9.

74 *Pipe R.* 1161 (P.R.S. iv), 67–8; 1167 (P.R.S. xi), 158; 1170 (P.R.S. xv), 110.

75 Ibid. 1173 (P.R.S. xix), 13; 1174 (P.R.S. xxi), 75; 1183 (P.R.S. xxxii), 19: the use of the word *castrum* implies that the stone wall was not that of the keep which is consistently referred to as the tower, *turrim*.

76 *Pipe R.* 1180 (P.R.S. xxix), 2; 1182 (P.R.S. xxxi), 102; 1190 (P.R.S. N.S. i), 104.

77 Ibid. 1191 & 1192 (P.R.S. N.S. ii), 171; 1195 (P.R.S. N.S. vi), 219.

78 *Pipe R.* 1199 (P.R.S. N.S. x), 87; 1200 (P.R.S. N.S. xii), 37; 1202 (P.R.S. N.S. xv), 259; 1204 (P.R.S. N.S. xviii), 46; 1210 (P.R.S. N.S. xxvi), 58; *Rot. Litt. Pat.* (Rec. Com.), Itin. of King John (unpaginated).

79 *Arch. Jnl.* cxxxix. 331–2, 337, 401.

and the men of Colchester were given timber to enclose it.[80] The work may have included the replacement of the early 12th-century forebuilding by a barbican, and, if it had not been done earlier, the creation of the north bailey, probably surrounded by a timber palisade, between the earlier bailey and the town wall. Repairs in 1218 and 1219 presumably made good damage sustained in the two sieges of 1216.[81]

The palisade blown down in 1218 and replaced at a cost of *c.* £6[82] probably surrounded the north bailey. It blew down again in 1237 and was re-erected at a cost of *c.* £39 in 1239. It was repaired again in 1275–6.[83] Repairs to the main structure of the castle in the 1220s included reroofing the corner towers of the keep and further work on the houses in the bailey, possibly extensions to the buildings north-west and north-east of the hall.[84] In 1237 the constable was instructed to complete works on the castle, and in 1242 the king's houses in the castle were repaired.[85] The constable spent 100 marks on the keep in 1253, possibly on the building of the barbican, if that had not already been done in 1214. Several oaks were supplied for that and other work. Major repairs were carried out in 1256.[86]

The main gate, in the south-west corner of the bailey wall opposite St. Nicholas's church, was not recorded until the 1240s[87] although it had presumably been built at the same time as the bailey wall. It was repaired in 1256 and again in 1300.[88] As late as 1669 there was a bridge over the castle ditch, presumably part of the gate.[89] There may have been a second gate, for what appears to have been the main gate, at the south end of Maidenburgh Street, was called the west gate in 1439–40 and 1459.[90]

Further work was carried out in 1258–9. Materials supplied for a hall in 1258 included four carved posts, presumably for the roof. In 1259 Roger Bigod, the constable, was allowed twelve oaks to make a chamber in the castle, timber allowed earlier having been stolen.[91] Another twelve oaks were used in 1271, presumably in the great stone chamber made about that date or in the repair of the hall. The chamber, with the wardrobe, pantry, buttery, and cellar associated with it, was near a turret, probably in the keep.[92] In 1333–4 the constable removed the house in the bailey where the justices used to sit and also the portcullis and possibly other parts of the entrance to the keep, but repairs were carried out in 1350 and again in 1422.[93] The gaol was apparently still in the bailey in 1455, but it was then so old and weak that prisoners were able to escape through a broken roof.[94] All the bailey buildings, except possibly part of one in the south-east corner, had disappeared by 1622.[95]

By *c.* 1600 the castle was no longer defensible, and the cost of repairs, including reroofing the hall and dungeon and partly blocking 25 loopholes, was estimated at £84.[96] By 1622 houses on the east side of Maidenburgh Street had encroached on the bailey ditch if not the wall.[97] By 1637 the hall roof had fallen in, and several encroachments, totalling 2 a., had been made on the bailey. The lower bailey to the north was an arable field.[98] The castle played little or no part in the seige in 1648, although the royalists considered using it as a stronghold and carried out some work including recutting the south bailey ditch. In 1650 it was reported not to be worth the cost of repair.[99]

Charles, Lord Stanhope, seems to have begun the demolition of the castle, digging up stones and levelling earthworks. In 1649 he removed 200 loads of stone from the bailey wall, and in 1656 he demolished another section of wall, presumably also in the bailey. The last sections of the bailey wall, on the south and west, were removed by Sir James Norfolk, probably in 1669 when he leased building plots on the south-west of the castle to a London bricklayer.[1] Part of the main bailey gate, however, seems to have survived in 1683 when Norfolk leased a plot of land beside it.[2] John Wheeley had licence to pull the keep down in 1683, but did not do so. In 1685 he granted building leases for lean-to houses or sheds against the west wall of the keep, and converted part of the bailey, which Norfolk had leased to him, into a bowling green. The building leases were challenged in 1694–5, and Wheeley turned to demolition, knocking down the upper storey and the corner towers of the keep with the help of screws and gunpowder. Stone from the castle was sold for the repair of town bridges in 1696 and 1698. Wheeley, or possibly Stanhope who removed 100 loads of sand from the castle site, broke into the sand-filled Roman vaults beneath the Norman structure.[3]

In 1728 and 1729 Charles Gray landscaped part of the bailey, reconstructing the north side of the bailey bank as a straight terrace walk ending in a temple-like summer house at the west end. Below it on the north he formed a regular canal in the former ditch.[4] He may also have altered the eastern bank and ditch which

80 *Rot. Litt. Claus.* (Rec. Com.), i. 179, 184, 193–5.

81 *Pipe R.* 1218 (P.R.S. N.S. xxxix), 78; 1220 (P.R.S. N.S. xlvii), 116.

82 *Rot. Litt. Claus.* (Rec. Com.), i. 389; *Pipe R.* 1218 (P.R.S. N.S. xxxix), 78.

83 *Cal. Lib.* 1226–40, 301, 316, 366; P.R.O., E 159/17, rot. 19d.; E 101/460/26.

84 *Cal. Lib.* 1226–40, 18, 55, 121; *Rot. Litt. Claus.* (Rec. Com.), i. 529; ii. 34, 202; *Arch. Jnl.* cxxxix. 403.

85 *Cal. Lib.* 1226–40, 282; *Pipe R.* 1242 (ed. H. L. Cannon), 216.

86 *Cal. Lib.* 1251–60, 96, 297; *Close R.* 1251–3, 306, 331, 453.

87 *Colch. Cart.* ii. 327–8; B.L. Arundel MS. 145, f. 4v.

88 *Cal. Lib.* 1251–60, 297; *Close R.* 1296–1302, 350.

89 E.R.O., Acc. C15.

90 Ibid. D/B 5 R1, f. 89; D/B 5 Cr69, rot. 16d.

91 *Close R.* 1256–9, 199, 341, 414.

92 P.R.O., E 101/460/26; *Cal. Lib.* 1267–72, p. 167.

93 *Cal. Inq. Misc.* ii. 346; *Cal. Pat.* 1350–4, 10; 1416–22, 443.

94 *Cal. Pat.* 1452–61, 242.

95 E.R.O., Acc. C49: map of castle estate.

96 Ibid. D/DRe Z3.

97 Ibid. Acc. C49.

98 *E.A.T.* N.S. iii. 144–5.

99 Round, *Colch. Castle*, 59; *Arch. Jnl.* cxxxix. 407; P.R.O., E 317/Essex/10.

1 E.R.O., D/DRe L3; D/DRe Z10; ibid. Acc. C15; *E.A.T.* N.S. iii. 146–7; Morant, *Colch.* 8.

2 E.R.O., D/DRe T5.

3 Ibid. D/DRe L3, 5; ibid. D/B 5 Ab1/22; Morant, *Colch.* 7–8; *E.A.T.* N.S. iii. 149.

4 E.R.O., D/DRb F6, 7.

FIG. 19. THE CASTLE FROM THE SOUTH-EAST, 1718

are aligned on his house and on which he built a rustic stone archway. Before 1732 he broke through a ground floor window in the south end of the east wall to make a doorway into the new garden. He does not appear at first to have made much use of the keep itself, leasing the western part, including the Roman vaults, the former dungeon vault west of the chapel vaults, and a large chamber or granary, to a Colchester merchant in 1733, and the eastern part, including the chapel undercroft and vaults, to the county as a prison in 1734.[5]

In 1746 Gray started work on the keep, rebuilding the south-east turret; in 1749 he restored the 'chapel' (in fact the undercroft), and in 1750 he repaired a room on the west side of the castle for use as a granary. He also strengthened foundations of the keep and the damaged vaults by covering them or filling them in with *c.* 400 loads of earth. The flat roof of re-used Roman bricks over the vault of the chapel undercroft, which survived in 1988, may have been built at that time. In 1754 and 1755 he remodelled much of the south side of the keep, creating on the first floor a library with large windows on its south side and an arcaded passage or piazza on the north. He built a similar arcade on the ground floor, to the east of the main entrance. In 1760 he raised the main staircase to the top of the surviving walls, roofing it over with a dome, and by 1767 he had built a room against the north-east tower.[6] Gray's work of restoration was apparently continued by James Round who presumably built the pitched roof which had replaced the flat roof over the chapel undercroft by 1791 and made the surviving east doorway between 1786 and 1804.[7] No further major alterations were made until 1931 when the Roman vaults were reinforced. In 1934–5 the keep was roofed in steel over a concrete frame, and a bridge was made to the main entrance where the ground had been dug away by recent excavations.[8]

The castle was used as a prison in 1226, and was delivered regularly from 1236.[9] It continued as the county prison until 1667,[10] even when the sheriff was not constable; in 1256, for example, the sheriff was ordered to keep a prisoner in the king's prison there by grant of Guy of Rochford the keeper.[11] The castle was transferred to the sheriff in 1275 expressly so that he might keep prisoners there, and when the keepership was granted to Richard of Holebrook the following year the sheriff's right of access for prisoners was reserved.[12] A grant of the keepership of the gaol made in 1343 was revoked in 1344 when it was found that the custody of prisoners belonged to the sheriff.[13] When the constableship was separated from the shrievalty in 1350 the constable or keeper was made responsible for the prisoners, and later constables were held accountable for escapes like any sheriff.[14] The sheriff resumed responsibility for the gaol under the Gaols Act of 1504.[15]

Presumably all keepers, whether sheriffs or not, appointed deputies who were effectively gaolers, like the constable's deputy who was pardoned for an escape in 1487.[16] John Flinchard and William de Roigne, constables accused of extortion in the 1270s, were probably deputies,

5 Ibid. D/DRe E7; Round, *Colch. Castle*, 130.

6 E.R.O., Acc. C15; ibid. drawings in Mint portfolio; *E.A.T.* N.S. iii. 151–3; Round, *Colch. Castle*, 101–2, 130–1.

7 E.R.O., drawings in Mint portfolio; B.L. Add. MS. 29927, f. 8.

8 *E.R.* xliv. 243–5; *Mus. Jnl.* xxxv. 453–5.

9 *Pat. R.* 1225–32, 37; R. B. Pugh, *Imprisonment in Med. Eng.* 67–9.

10 E.R.O., Q/SR 412/55; Q/SR 416/97.

11 *Close R.* 1254–6, 348.

12 *Cal. Pat.* 1272–81, 127, 141.

13 Ibid. 1343–5, 113, 157.

14 *Cal. Fine R.* 1347–56, 235; *Cal. Pat.* 1377–81, 267; 1401–5, 477; 1408–13, 114; 1452–61, 242; *Cal. Inq. Misc.* vi, p. 326.

15 19 Hen. VII, c. 10.

16 *Cal. Pat.* 1485–94, 156.

as was Edmund, constable of the castle, killed in 1283.[17] Roger Chamberlain or Gaoler (d. 1360) and his wife Helen, who may have succeeded him, were commemorated by an inscription inside the main entrance to the castle.[18] Other gaolers were recorded in 1406 (William Dych keeper of Colchester castle or gaol), 1417 (Richard Baynard gaoler of the gaol of Colchester), and 1428 (Jacolet Germain).[19]

Among medieval prisoners were the vicar of Coggeshall, imprisoned in 1296 for fishing in Coggeshall abbey fishponds, and the master of St. Leonard's hospital, Newport, and the parson of Theydon Bois, imprisoned in 1331 and 1334 for forest offences.[20] There were Jews in the gaol in 1253, pirates in 1326, 'the king's enemies', perhaps opponents of the Despensers, in 1326, and heretics in 1428.[21] Later prisoners included Robert Mantell or Blosse, who claimed to be Edward VI, in 1580, prisoners of war in 1547, 1603, and 1653, protestants in 1557, popish recusants in 1596 and 1625, royalists in 1642, and Quakers in the 1650s and 1660s.[22] In the mid 17th century the castle gaol was used only for felons and rogues; prisoners taken in civil actions such as debt or trespass were not sent there.[23]

In 1619 the gaoler was accused of keeping an unruly alehouse in the prison and his successor in 1629 killed a prisoner who attacked his house. In 1631 the building was so dilapidated that prisoners were exposed to wind and weather, the gaoler was cruel, and the food inadequate.[24] In 1633 the roof of the dungeon leaked seriously, and on one occasion in 1646 the prisoners had to stand up to their knees in water all night. The county agreed to pay £40 for repairs to make the gaol secure, but paid only £20 although the gaoler spent £30.[25] There were still prisoners in the gaol in 1667, but by 1668 the county prison had moved to the Cross Keys, Moulsham.[26]

For most of the period 1691–1835, except for the years 1703–6 and 1712–16, part of the castle was used as a county prison for prisoners from the Colchester area. At first the prison was in the vault or dungeon west of the chapel vaults; in 1727 it was moved to the vaults of the chapel undercroft.[27] A house in the north-east corner of the keep, built before 1732, was occupied by the goaler.[28] In 1780 the prison comprised a day-room for women and three cells for men, the latter divided from each other by gratings to allow the circulation of light and air from the two windows. All four rooms were in vaults below the chapel undercroft.[29] In 1787 and 1788 the gaol was enlarged by enclosing the south end of the eastern courtyard (formed by the east wall of the castle and the surviving partition wall) to make a prison of two storeys and an attic, the upper storey and attic containing two rooms for women, and the lower storey a day room and three cells for men.[30] Although the goal was in good repair in 1818 when the lease was renewed, new rules on prison accommodation introduced in 1824 made it almost useless, and it was closed in 1835.[31] The keeper's house was demolished in 1881.[32] A new county house of correction in Ipswich Road was opened in 1835 and closed in 1850.[33]

The undercroft was used as a militia armoury from 1819 to 1854; in 1855 it was dedicated by Charles Gray Round as a museum for the town. In 1865 Round gave a small room in the south-west tower as a town muniment room.[34]

Lands in Colchester were held with the castle in the early 12th century when Eudes the sewer gave the issues of the castle chapel to St. John's abbey.[35] A steward of the castle and lordship, distinct from the constable, was appointed in 1447,[36] but the office was not recorded again. Kingswood was said to belong to the keepership of the castle in 1217,[37] but it was not later included among the castle lands. In 1271 the lands were said to comprise 110 a. of arable and 28 a. of meadow.[38] The arable was reckoned at 180 a. between 1376 and 1559 but at only 124 a. in 1599, possibly a belated recognition of medieval alienations to the Greyfriars and others. The meadow was consistently reckoned at 27 a. Quit rents of 30*s.* a year were recorded from 1364.[39] In the earlier 17th century the lands lay in two main blocks. The first comprised Great and Little Sholand and Broomfield (*c.* 31 a.) between Lexden and Maldon Roads with the Long Strake (2 a.) on the other side of Maldon Road, all annexed to the bailiwick of Tendring hundred which was held with the castle. The second comprised the lands around the castle itself, the upper bailey (8 a.), Great Barley, Middle, and Home fields, (40–50 a.), Little Barley or Sheepshead field

17 *Rot. Hund.* (Rec. Com.), i. 139; P.R.O., JUST 3/35B, rott. 24, 26.

18 *E.A.T.* N.S. xvi. 42–7.

19 E.R.O., D/B 5 Cr36, rott. 2d., 3; *Cal. Pat.* 1416–22, 67; *Acts and Monuments of John Foxe*, ed. S. R. Catley, iii. 586.

20 *Cal. Close*, 1288–96, 474; 1330–3, 110; 1333–7, 245.

21 *Close R.* 1251–3, 393; *Cal. Close*, 1323–7, 479; *Cal. Pat.* 1324–7, 294; *Acts and Monuments of John Foxe*, iii. 586.

22 *Cal. S.P. Scot.* 1547–63, no. 217; *Acts of P.C.* 1630–1, p. 96; Round, *Colch. Castle*, 53–9, 62–3; *V.C.H. Essex*, ii. 67, 221; for Mantell see above, Tudor and Stuart Colch. (Intro.).

23 E.R.O., D/DRe L2, Z3.

24 P.R.O., ASSI 35/61/2, no. 20; ASSI 35/71/2, no. 4; ASSI 35/73/1, no. 10.

25 E.R.O., Q/SBc 2/13; Q/SBa 2/61–2, 64.

26 Ibid. Q/QO 1, ff. 182v., 203; Q/SR 412/55; Q/SR 416/97; *Essex Q.S. Order Bk. 1652–61*, ed. D. H. Allen, pp. xxi–xxii.

27 E.R.O., Q/SBb 1/8; Q/SBb 365/26; Q/SO 3, p. 156; Q/SO 4, pp. 117, 128, 345; Q/SO 16, p. 410; Round, *Colch. Castle*, 130.

28 B.L. Add. MS. 29927, f. 8; E.R.O., D/DRe E7.

29 J. Howard, *State of Prisons* (1780), 221; plans of 1819 and 1830 in E.R.O., Q/AGb 3.

30 B.L. Add. MS. 29927, f. 8; *Gent. Mag.* lxxiv (2), 705, 1096–8; J. Neild, *State of the Prisons* (1812), 139.

31 E.R.O., Q/SBb 452/56; 475/10/1; 476/16/1; Q/SO 34, f. 240.

32 Round, *Colch. Castle*, 107 n.

33 *2nd Rep. Inspector of Prisons, Home Dist.* [89], p. 341, H.C. (1837), xxxii; *3rd Rep.* [141], p. 216, H.C. (1837–8), xxx; E.R.O., Q/SO 40, p. 77.

34 E.R.O., Q/AMm 1/1, 1/2, 1/4; Q/SBb 452/39, 56; ibid. D/DRe Z13; *E.R.* lvi. 7–8; Round, *Colch. Castle*, 102.

35 *Colch. Cart.* i. 3.

36 *Cal. Pat.* 1446–52, 42.

37 *Rot. Litt. Claus.* (Rec. Com.), i. 345.

38 *Cal. Inq. Misc.* i, p. 131.

39 *Cal. Pat.* 1374–7, 368; 1461–7, 124; 1553–4, 283; 1558–60, 62; P.R.O., C 142/518, no. 20; Round, *Colch. Castle*, 137, 139. *Cal. Inq. p. m.* xi, p. 476 reads 80 a. of arable in 1364, but the MS. (P.R.O., E 149/23, no. 13) is torn at that point and probably originally read 180 a.

(5 a.), Great and Little Rowan meads (22 a.), and four parcels (10 a.) in King's meadow. In addition there were two arable closes (8 a.) north of King's meadow, which were annexed to the bailiwick of Tendring hundred, and Castle Grove (10 a.) a little way to the north-east in Mile End parish. Two thirds of Middle mill also belonged to the castle.[40]

The lands descended with the castle until 1683 when Robert Norfolk sold the keep to John Wheeley. He retained the lands, including the bailey, until his death in 1688 when they passed to his infant daughter Dorothy, who died the same year, and then to his sister Martha wife of Hope Gifford. Martha died without issue in 1722 and was succeeded by her heir at law Elizabeth, wife of John Embrey, who in 1725 sold half the castle lands to Francis Powell. In 1727 Powell sold to Mary Webster Castle Grove or Banks hedge, Sheepshead field, and the castle bailey, which were thus reunited with the castle.[41] Charles Gray bought the bailiwick of Tendring hundred, presumably with some of the lands annexed to it, *c.* 1750, and a further *c.* 57 a., including Sholand and Broomfield, in 1757.[42]

The tithes of the castle lands were held by St. John's abbey until the Dissolution and were then retained by the Crown until 1560 when they were granted to Sir Francis Jobson. They descended to his granddaughter Mary Jobson and to her son Edward Brooke who sold them to Sir James Norfolk in 1652. The tithes were thus merged in the castle estate, which became tithe free.[43]

WALLS, GATES, AND POSTERNS

TOWN walls *c.* 3,000 yd. long were built *c.* 65–80 A.D. when the Roman town was rebuilt after its destruction by Boudicca. The walls were originally 8–10 ft. thick, built with a core of layered septaria and mortar faced with coursed septaria and tile. A number of internal towers, *c.* 6 ft. wide and *c.* 18 ft. long, probably placed at the end of streets, served as look-out posts and as platforms for weapons. There was a ditch outside the wall, and in the later 2nd century the wall was strengthened by the construction of a rampart behind it. There were probably six gates. The exceptionally large Balkerne gate in the west wall seems to have been built as a free-standing structure about the time of the foundation of the Roman town, possibly as a triumphal monument; it had two large central arches for vehicular traffic, flanked by two smaller pedestrian arches with guardrooms on either side. The gate was closed in the 4th century when the town ditch was extended across it; it was later blocked with a rough masonry wall. The south-west gate, the later Head gate, seems to have had two large arches, and the east gate may have had a central arch flanked by two pedestrian arches. The surviving north-east gate comprises a single arch, 11 ft. wide, and the north-west gate, the medieval North gate, may have been similar. There is no evidence for the south-east gate, which may have been on the site of the medieval South or St. Botolph's gate.[44]

The Roman walls formed the basis of the medieval circuit. They were defended unsuccessfully by the Danes in 920, and were repaired by Edward the Elder in the same year; his work may have included the blocking of the Balkerne gate.[45] Excavation has revealed a mid 11th-century ditch on the south and east sides of the town, perhaps made in connexion with a strengthening of the defences at the time of the threatened invasion of Cnut of Denmark.[46] Major repairs, possibly amounting to rebuilding in places, were carried out in 1173–4, at the time of the rebellion of the young king, the burgesses being allowed at least part of the cost out of the farm of the town.[47] No further work seems to have been done in the 13th century, and by the early 14th century the walls were decayed, that at the East gate being undermined by gravel digging. Wallgavel was payable from a house outside Scheregate in the south wall in 1310, and from a moor in Moor (Priory) Street south-east of the town in 1312, as well as, presumably, from other land and houses in the borough. It was apparently insufficient for the maintenance of the wall, for in 1312 the borough levied a 'tallage' on the whole community for the repair of the walls and gates.[48] That money probably paid for extensive repairs, but by 1329 houses were being built against the wall and on the town waste adjoining it, and in the mid 14th century several people were accused of taking stones, one as many as six cartloads, from the wall. One man in 1346 removed part of the crenellation of the wall.[49]

The borough carried out extensive repairs between 1381 and *c.* 1413, removing at least one house which had been built against the wall.[50] By then part of the eastern end of the south wall had collapsed outwards, and a new wall was built

40 E.R.O., Acc. C49: map of 1622; P.R.O., E 178/5293, printed in *E.A.T.* N.S. iii. 143–5; E 317/Essex/10. For Middle mill see below, Mills.

41 E.R.O., D/DRe E7, 8; D/DRe L5; D/DRe T6; ibid. Acc. C15.

42 Round, *Colch. Castle*, 134, 139, 145; E.R.O., D/DRe T9.

43 E.R.O., Acc. C15; P.R.O., C 142/176, no. 44; C 142/684, no. 20; cf. Round, *Colch. Castle*, 143.

44 *Colch. Arch. Rep.* vi. 16–18, 64–5; M. R. Hull, *Roman Colch.* 14–63, summarized in *V.C.H. Essex*, iii. 92–6; *Colch. Archaeologist*, no. 1, 16–17; no. 2, 6–10.

45 *A.-S. Chron.* ed. D. Whitelock, 65–6; *V.C.H. Essex*, iii. 94.

46 *Colch. Arch. Rep.* i. 52–3.

47 *Pipe R.* 1174 (P.R.S. xxi), 75.

48 E.R.O., D/B 5 Cr1, rot. 6; Cr2, rott. 11d., 12d.; *Colch. Cart.* ii. 639; *Cal. Letters from Mayor and Corp. Lond. c. 1350–70*, ed. R. R. Sharpe, pp. 74–5.

49 E.R.O., D/B 5 R1, ff. 29v., 32, 33, 34; D/B 5 Cr3, rot. 1d.; Cr7, rot. 10d.; Cr9, rot. 6; Cr10, rot. 10d.; Cr12, rot. 11d.

50 E.R.O., D/B 5 Cr21, rot. 37; *Cal. Pat.* 1381–5, 214; 1385–9, 505; 1391–6, 379; 1401–5, 355; 1408–13, 199; 1413–16, 23.

on top of its remains; five regularly spaced bastions were added at the same time round the south-east corner of the wall, between East gate and Scheregate.[51] Some attempt seems to have been made to ensure the future maintenance of the wall: in 1392 three burgesses gave 2 houses, 4 a. of land, and the advowson of St. Cross hospital for the repair of the walls, and in 1394 a lease of land along the north wall from Ryegate to North bridge stipulated that the tenant should repair the wall. In 1398 another lease of land adjoining the wall reserved to the borough the right of access to the wall for its inspection and repair.[52] By 1423, however, the wall was again being undermined by sand-digging, and in 1470 stones were being removed by the cartload. Outhouses had been built against the south wall near Scheregate by 1436, and alderman Robert Leche removed the blocking from a Roman drain arch at the Balkerne gate to make a new postern in 1535.[53] In 1551 the chamberlain was accused of failing to repair the walls, the wall at Head gate being in danger of falling. The southern end of the east wall seems to have collapsed in the 16th century.[54] Sand-digging under the wall and the removal of stones from it continued, but in 1579 and 1586 the offenders were ordered to repair the wall. In 1619 a licence was granted to build on the wall provided that the holder maintained the wall on which he built.[55]

The walls were refurbished during the Civil War. In 1642, on a petition from the inhabitants, parliament voted £1,500 for improving the defences of the town and the blockhouse, presumably the one at the entrance to the harbour; Sir Harbottle Grimston urged the mayor to take advantage of the grant and to raise more money in the town if necessary.[56] By 1643 there were several forts within the town, one of them near the postern by St. Mary's-at-the-Walls, another in High Street. They do not appear to have been substantial works, and some may have been little more than pits revetted with wood, like that excavated in the south-east corner of the town.[57] Nevertheless in 1648 the walls were weak, and there was a long gap in the north part of the circuit. When the royalist army took over the town that summer they filled such gaps with earth ramparts and strengthened other parts of the wall with 'works', perhaps including the major outwork at the north-east corner of the town.[58] The walls thus strengthened withstood the onslaught of the parliamentary cannon, although the tops of two old, ruined towers, presumably bastions, were demolished. After the surrender Fairfax ordered the demolition of the walls, an order repeated by the council of state in 1649 and apparently carried out in 1651. The south-west corner of the circuit, by the royalist battery in St. Mary's churchyard, seems to have been destroyed at that time, but most of the works destroyed were probably the ramparts and siege works built in 1648.[59]

Complaints of stone-digging in the wall and building against it continued in the later 17th century,[60] and no serious effort seems to have been made to maintain it. By 1694 the wall near Scheregate was level with the ground on the town side, and in 1711 the chamberlain was accused of endangering the lives of the inhabitants by failing to make a fence on the wall from Headgate to Scheregate. Further complaints about the state of the wall were made in 1717 and 1722, and by 1724 most of the north wall west of Ryegate had gone.[61] By 1748 the walls were being maintained only by those whose gardens adjoined them.[62] About 185 ft. of the wall near the top of Balkerne Hill collapsed into the road in 1795, and 125 ft. a little further north collapsed *c.* 1850.[63] By the 1890s two bastions had been incorporated into houses or workshops, and a third had been made into a Gothic summer house.[64]

In 1866 the corporation paid the improvement commissioners to carry out minor repairs to the wall, apparently on Balkerne Hill.[65] The corporation surveyed the walls in 1879, and considered repairing dangerous sections, but were deterred by doubts as to the ownership of the wall and consequent liability for its repair.[66] In 1887 the museum committee of the borough council assumed responsibility for the wall,[67] and thereafter it was regularly inspected and repaired at the borough's expense. The committee also took steps to prevent the demolition of parts of the wall, but gave permission for a breach on Balkerne Hill in 1901 and was unable to prevent a contractor removing a section of the wall at Headgate in 1909. After excavations in 1913 the foundations of the Balkerne gate were consolidated and the remaining portions of the gate and guardroom roofed over.[68] Between 1967 and 1976 the question of the ownership of the wall again caused difficulties,

51 Hull, *Roman Colch.* 51–3.
52 *Cal. Pat.* 1391–6, 154; E.R.O., D/B 5 R1, ff. 64, 66.
53 E.R.O., D/B 5 Cr43, rot. 19d.; Cr74, rot. 2; Cr104, rot. 3; *Colch. Arch. Rep.* vi. 326–7.
54 E.R.O., D/B 5 Cr118, rot. 8; Hull, *Roman Colch.* 46.
55 E.R.O., D/B 5 Cr141, rot. 3; Cr147, rott. 34d., 36; D/B 5 Gb2, f. 184.
56 Ibid. D/Y 2/8, pp. 44–5.
57 Ibid. D/B 5 Sb2/7, f. 306; D/B 5 Gb2, f. 237; *Great and Bloody Fight at Colch.* (1648), 3: copy in E.C.L. Colch.; Hull, *Roman Colch.* 46.
58 Hist. MSS. Com. 27, *12th Rep. IX, Beaufort*, p. 25; Bodl. MS. Tanner 57/1, f. 249; M. Carter, *True Relation of the Expedition to Kent, Essex and Colch. 1648*, 60: copy in E.R.O.; above, fig. 8.
59 Morant, *Colch.* 60–1, 65–6, 68; E.R.O., D/Y 2/2, p. 241; *Cal. S.P. Dom.* 1649–50, 181; 1651, 90, 108, 281; *V.C.H. Essex*, iii. 95.
60 e.g. E.R.O., D/B 5 Gb5, ff. 224–5.
61 Ibid. D/B 5 Sr59, rot. 8; Sr95, rot. 19; Sr115, rot. 6; Sr132, rot. 40; J. Pryer, *New and Exact Prospect of Colch.* (1724).
62 Morant, *Colch.* 7.
63 Hull, *Roman Colch.* 22.
64 E.R.O., Boro. Mun., Mus. Mun. and Libr. Cttee. Min. Bk. 1882–94, p. 196.
65 Ibid. Boro. Mun., Council Min. Bk. 1863–71, p. 84; ibid. Acc. C210, J. B. Harvey Colln. vi, p. 3.
66 Ibid. Boro. Mun., Council Min. Bk. 1871–7, p. 392; 1877–80, pp. 76, 208, 234–5, 237, 276, 288.
67 Ibid. Acc. C210, J. B. Harvey Colln. vi, extra pp. 101–2; ibid. Boro. Mun., Mus. Mun. and Libr. Cttee. Min. Bk. 1882–94, p. 39.
68 Ibid. Boro. Mun., Mus. and Mun. Cttee. Min. Bks. 1882–1952, *passim.*

the town council maintaining that the wall was the responsibility of the owners of adjoining land, and the Department of the Environment being unable to prevent the demolition of parts of the wall because notice of scheduling had not been served on all owners.[69] Some repairs were carried out in 1980; in 1985 a 30-ft. section of the south wall was excavated and then demolished for the service road to the Culver shopping precinct; a major programme of restoration began in 1986.[70]

The town was surrounded by a ditch in Roman and presumably also in early medieval times, but by the 14th century much of the ditch on the north and south sides seems to have been filled in and built over. There was a curtilage under the north wall outside Ryegate before 1242, and houses outside Scheregate, presumably in the ditch, by 1337. The area between the south wall and St. John's Street was occupied by houses and gardens in 1443.[71] The western ditch survived as Balkerne Lane until the construction of the inner relief road in 1976–7.[72]

In the Middle Ages there were four main gates, Head gate and South or St. Botolph's gate in the south wall, North gate, and East gate. All, except perhaps South gate, were Roman in origin, although Head gate, the principal medieval gate, may have been just north of the site of the Roman gate: in 1635 there was a house in the corner formed by the wall on the south and the gate on the east, and no trace of medieval work has been seen in the small portion of the Roman gate which has been examined.[73] South gate, if not Roman, was in existence by 1197.[74] In addition to the main gates there were two pedestrian gates, Scheregate in the south wall, and King's Scherde or Ryegate in the north wall. The north postern was recorded in 1240 and was called King's Scherde before 1242; it or Scheregate, which was in existence in the 13th century, had given rise to the surname de la Scherde before 1254.[75] A postern in the west wall near St. Mary's-at-the-Walls, an enlarged Roman drain arch, was recorded from 1473, and another in St. Peter's parish, presumably that made by Robert Leche in 1535, in 1681.[76]

North gate, Head gate, and South gate each comprised a single large arched or square-headed gateway,[77] suggesting that they had been rebuilt in the Middle Ages; there is no evidence for the appearance of the East gate. A house or rooms had been built over the south gate by *c.* 1338 and was still there in 1604.[78] In 1358 the bailiffs and community of the town leased the north gate to a shoemaker, giving him permission to build over the gate and on an adjoining plot of land on condition that he repair the wooden gates.[79] The borough was leasing the rooms over the north gate in 1531 and in 1736, and the gate seems to have had two storeys of building above it in 1724.[80] Head gate too seems to have had a house or rooms above it, possibly the house whose foundations had been built into the wall at the gate by 1473, and a house extended over Scheregate by the late 15th century.[81] John Ellis, by will dated 1485, provided for statues of St. Helen, St. Margaret, and St. John the Baptist to be placed on the East gate.[82]

The chamberlain was accused in 1447 of failing to repair East gate and Head gate; in 1470 South gate was in ruins, and in 1474 chains at East gate and Head gate needed repair. South gate still needed repair in 1534, and in 1540 one of the aldermen was accused of selling 'the town gate at St. Botolph's',[83] perhaps part of the wooden gate at South gate. St. Botolph's gate was repaired in 1609.[84] All the gates were still standing and defensible in 1648, and withstood the siege that year. Part of East gate fell down in 1652, and more of it was pulled down as dangerous in 1676, but part of the Roman guard house on the south side of the gate survived in 1813, and that or another part of the gate was demolished by the improvement commissioners in 1819.[85] Head gate was demolished in 1753.[86] The top was taken off North gate in 1774, but the sides of the gate, incorporated into the adjoining houses, were not demolished until 1823.[87] St. Botolph's gate was demolished by the improvement commissioners in 1814.[88] Ryegate was sold, presumably for its materials, in 1659, but a staircase and the west part of the gate survived in 1671, incorporated into the adjoining house.[89] Scheregate presumably disappeared with its adjoining wall in the later 17th century, although its position was marked by Scheregate steps in 1990.

69 *Colch. Gaz.* 21 Nov. 1967; *E.C.S.* 11 June 1973; 4 June 1976.
70 *E.C.S.* 22 Feb. 1980; 4 Oct. 1985; 21 Nov. 1986.
71 *Colch. Cart.* ii. 323–4; E.R.O., D/B 5 Cr5, rot. 6d.; Cr61, rot. 22; and see, D/B 5 R1, ff. 32, 33, 38v., 84 and v., 88.
72 *Colch. Gaz.* 4 Apr. 1973; Colch. Charter 800 Assn. *Colch. 800*, 37.
73 E.R.O., D/B 5 Cb1/10, f. 169; *Colch. Archaeologist*, no. 2, 8.
74 *Pipe R.* 1197 (P.R.S. N.S. viii), 73.
75 P.R.O., JUST 1/233, rot. 35d.; *Colch. Cart.* ii. 323–6, 437–8.
76 E.R.O., D/B 5 Cr75, rot. 2; D/B 5 Gb5, f. 180.
77 Speed, *Map* (1610); Pryer, *Prospect of Colch.* (1724).
78 E.R.O., D/B 5 R1, f. 70; D/B 5 Cb1/5, f. 390.
79 E.R.O., D/B 5 R2, f. 253.
80 Ibid. Acc. C47, CPL 1184, no. 18; ibid. D/Y 2/1, p. 123; Pryer, *Prospect of Colch.* (1724).
81 E.R.O., D/B 5 Cr75, rot. 23; Bodl. MS. Rolls Essex 2.
82 E.R.O., D/B 5 R2, f. 187.
83 Ibid. D/B 5 Cr61, rot. 18; Cr74, rot. 2; Cr75, rot. 23; Cr104, rot. 3d.; Cr110, rot. 2.
84 Ibid. D/B 5 Ab1/7, f. 13.
85 Ibid. D/B 5 Gb4, f. 68v.; Gb5, f. 115; ibid. Acc. C424; Hull, *Roman Colch.* 44 and pl. ix.
86 Contemporary plaque on site.
87 *Chelm. Chron.* 11 Nov. 1774; T. Cromwell, *Colch.* 176.
88 E.R.O., Boro. Mun., Improvement Com. Mins. 1811–33, pp. 51–2.
89 Ibid. D/B 5 Gb5, f. 64.

BARRACKS

TROOPS, often en route to the Continent, were billetted in Colchester from the late 17th century.[90] In 1794 local innkeepers, concerned by the growing expense of the practice, petitioned the corporation for barracks to be built in the town and in the same year the first infantry barracks were built on 4 a. to the south-east.[91] By 1800 additional infantry barracks, artillery, and cavalry barracks had been built on an adjoining 21 a., the whole bordered by Magdalen street (later Barrack Street) on the north, Wimpole Lane on the west, and Port Lane on the east.[92] In 1805 the barracks could accommodate over 7,000 officers and men and 400 horses. Much of the building was done by Thomas Neill.[93]

After the Napoleonic Wars the barracks were reduced.[94] When the disposal of barrack buildings began in 1816 the only people in the artillery barracks were 1 barrack serjeant and 12 patients in the hospital.[95] Buildings, fixtures, and fittings of the cavalry barracks were sold in 1818.[96] The sale of the older barracks and the freehold site on which they stood started in March 1817 but was not, for technical reasons, completed until 1840.[97] In 1818 the government paid £5,000 for the continued use of 14 a. on which stood infantry barracks with accommodation for 51 officers, 800 men, and 16 horses. Those were the only barracks left in Colchester by 1821 when they were occupied by up to 16 officers and 602 men.[98] The government also retained Barrack field, 23 a. south of the barracks bought for an exercise field in 1805, and the Ordnance field, 32 a. west of the barracks between Military and Mersea Roads in St. Botolph's parish bought in 1806.[99] The 14 a. of land used in 1818 was given up before 1836, but leased again in 1856 for a temporary exercise ground.[1] In July 1856, when 10,000 men of the German Legion occupied the barracks, 2,000 of them were housed under canvas on Barrack field. Between 1865 and 1878

FIG. 20. THE BARRACKS, 1856

[90] e.g. *Cal. S.P. Dom.* 1672–3, 393; 1678, 140; E.R.O., D/B 5 Gb8, ff. 35, 108. This section was written in 1990.

[91] E.R.O., D/B 5 Gb8, f. 198; *Acct. of Money Issued by the Barrack Master Gen.* H.C. 824 (1), p. 1 (1795–6), xli; a plan of Colch. barracks in the back of a manuscript army list of 1762, B.L. Stowe MS. 484, f. 38, seems to be of the Napoleonic barracks.

[92] E.R.O., D/B 5 Gb8, ff. 204, 208v., 211; ibid. Gb9, pp. 31–2; *Garrison - Ten British Military Towns*, ed. P. Dietz, 12.

[93] *Acct. of Monies Expended on Buildings at Colchester*, H.C. 306, p. 1 (1808), vii.

[94] *Colch. Gaz.* 21 Sept. 1816.

[95] *Return of Artillery Barracks*, H.C. 499, p. 1 (1816), xii.

[96] *Colch. Gaz.* 22 Aug. 1818.

[97] P.R.O., WO 44/557.

[98] *V.C.H. Essex*, ii. 185; P.R.O., MFQ 74/2382; *Return of Barracks*, H.C. 188, p. 1 (1822), xix.

[99] *Return of all Lands and Tens.* (unpublished W.O. report, 1900), pp. 4–5: copy in Nat. Army Mus.

[1] *32nd Rep. Com. Char.* p. 546; *Return of Military Stations*, H.C. 305, pp. 32–3 (1862), xxxii; P.R.O., WO 44/719.

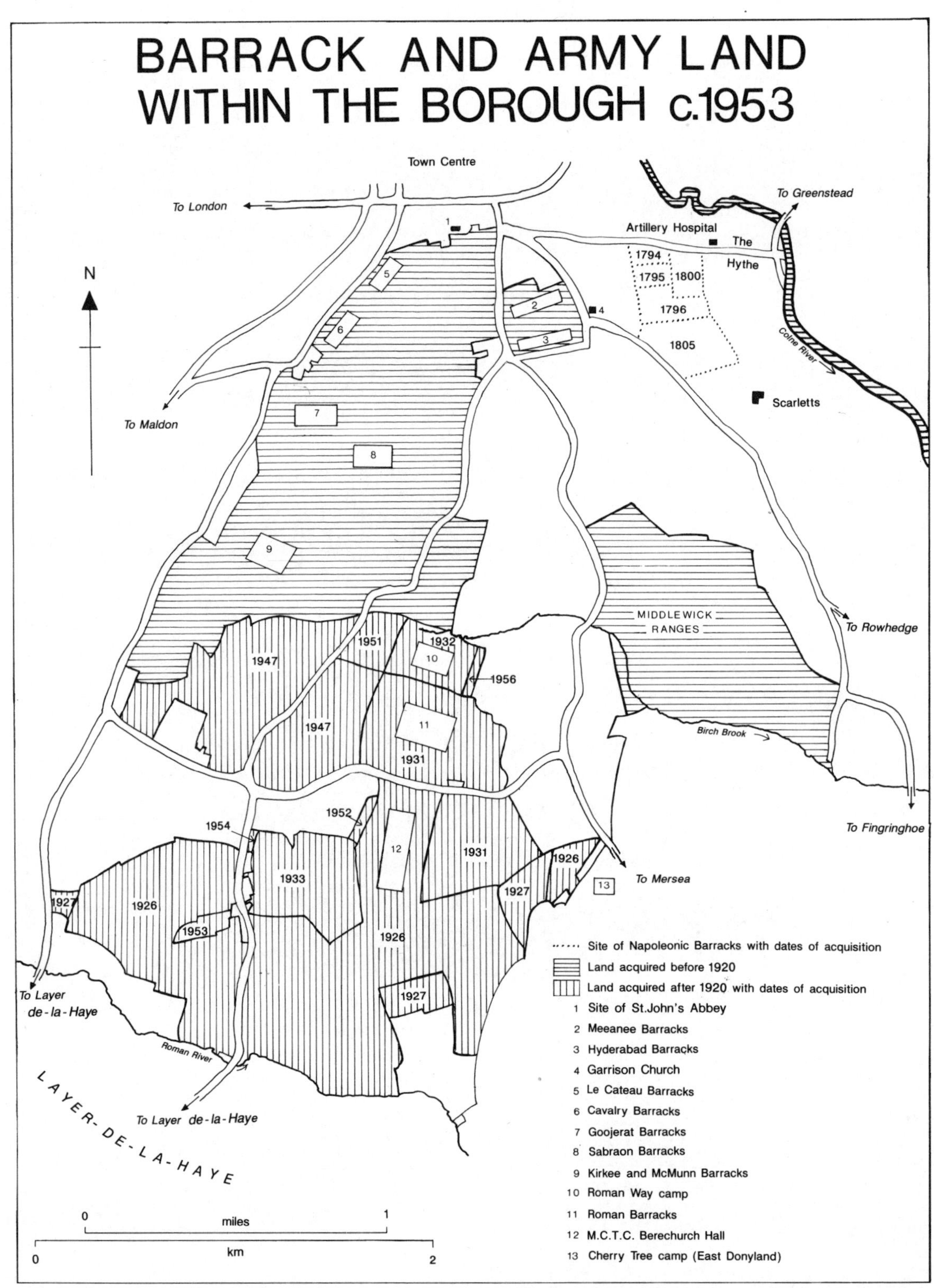
BARRACK AND ARMY LAND
WITHIN THE BOROUGH c.1953
Town Centre
To London
To Greenstead
Artillery Hospital
The Hythe
1794
1795
1800
1796
1805
Colne River
Scarletts
To Maldon
To Rowhedge
MIDDLEWICK RANGES
Birch Brook
To Fingringhoe
To Mersea
To Layer de-la-Haye
Roman River
To Layer de-la-Haye
LAYER-DE-LA-HAYE
1947
1951
1932
1956
1947
1931
1952
1954
1933
1931
1926
1927
1927
1926
1953
1926
1927
Site of Napoleonic Barracks with dates of acquisition
Land acquired before 1920
Land acquired after 1920 with dates of acquisition
1 Site of St.John's Abbey
2 Meeanee Barracks
3 Hyderabad Barracks
4 Garrison Church
5 Le Cateau Barracks
6 Cavalry Barracks
7 Goojerat Barracks
8 Sabraon Barracks
9 Kirkee and McMunn Barracks
10 Roman Way camp
11 Roman Barracks
12 M.C.T.C. Berechurch Hall
13 Cherry Tree camp (East Donyland)
0 miles 1
0 km 2

FIG. 21

the army allowed the Colchester and East Essex Cricket club to use part of the field; in 1885 the field was leased to the town as a recreation ground.[2]

In 1855 and 1856 wooden huts, intended as temporary infantry barracks for 5,000 men, were erected on the Ordnance field by Lucas Bros.[3] Laundry rooms and schoolrooms were included in the original provision. By 1857 there was a large reading room and 48 small rooms for married soldiers.[4] In the same year, because of the inconvenience of holding military exercises at Wivenhoe Park, the government bought Middlewick farm, 167 a. in St. Giles's parish south of the barracks, as a rifle range and drill ground; 20 a. in the parishes of East Donyland and St. Giles were added to the Middlewick range in 1874; and between 1889 and 1899 the range expanded with the aquisition of over 500 a. in the parishes of St. Giles, St. Botolph, East Donyland, and Fingringhoe. All the land lay south of the town.[5] The purchase of St. John's farm and the Abbey gardens in 1860 added 156 a. to the barrack land.[6] Between 1862 and 1864 brick-built cavalry barracks for *c.* 2,500 men were erected in Butt Road. In 1858 and 1859 accommodation for army families was provided in rented cottages at the Hythe; from 1859 houses in Black Boy Lane were rented until permanent married quarters were built in 1862 on another 18 a. acquired south of the Abbey gardens. A gymnasium was built on the same site.[7] During the early 1870s the garrison was further enlarged by the building of artillery barracks, later named Le Cateau, north of the cavalry barracks; the parade ground lay between the infantry barracks on the east and those of the cavalry and artillery on the west.[8] Between 1900 and 1902 Goojerat and Sabraon barracks were built on the southern edge of the camp on part of the land of Barn Hall farm, 19 a. of which was acquired in 1899.[9] Between 1896 and 1904 the old wooden huts on the Ordnance field were replaced by the brick buildings of Hyderabad and Meeanee barracks.[10] In 1866 Colchester became the headquarters of the newly created Eastern District; to accommodate the General Officer Commanding Eastern District the government rented Scarletts, an estate abutting the southern edge of the recreation ground, from 1885.[11] In 1904 the government bought Reed Hall and Bee Hive farms, comprising together 785 a. south-west of the garrison.[12] In 1914, when between 30,000 and 40,000 men were in training in Colchester, wooden huts were put up at Reed Hall. A military airfield was established on several acres of land at Blackheath; after the war it was transferred to Friday Wood.[13] Between 1926 and 1933 large areas of Berechurch parish, including Berechurch Hall, were bought for the army.[14] During the 1930s Kirkee and McMunn barracks were built at Reed Hall; Roman Way and Cherry Tree camps were established south-east of the main camp. In 1939 emergency barracks were built on various sites in the garrison area including the Abbey field, at Blackheath, and at Berechurch.[15]

In the 1950s, because of the increasing difficulties caused by the movements of large numbers of troops and military vehicles, including helicopters, so close to the town, plans were made for a more acceptable and efficient use of the 5,000 a. which the War Department owned south of the town.[16] A plan to concentrate the barracks further from the town, south of the Abbey field area, and to dispose of surplus land including the Abbey field, was accepted in 1962.[17] Hyderabad and Meeanee barracks, modernized between 1958 and 1961, remained unchanged;[18] Roman barracks were built in 1962 adjoining Roman Way camp on the south;[19] Goojerat barracks, rebuilt between 1970 and 1975, became the headquarters of the 19 Airportable Brigade formerly based in wooden huts at Cherry Tree camp, a site then offered to other government departments.[20] Sabraon Barracks, last used in 1960, were demolished in 1971.[21] Le Cateau and Cavalry barracks, whose demolition was planned in 1962, were still partially occupied in 1990.[22] In the 1980s army houses in Lethe Grove and Homefield Road were vacated and the sites sold for private development.[23]

In 1804 land in Military Road was bought as a military burial ground; in 1856 the garrison church, a timber-built, slate-roofed building for 1,500 men, opened on the site. The church was restored in 1891, the work perhaps including the replacement of the original slate roof by one of tarred felt, and again in 1989 when the roof was reslated.[24]

A hospital was built for the barracks in 1797, possibly the one, south-east of the Napoleonic barracks, which was sold in 1818.[25] An artillery hospital, in a house on the north side of Barrack

2 *E.R.* xx. 47; A. F. J. Brown, *Essex People 1750–1900*, 185; Brown, *Colch. 1815–1914*, 164; *Return of all Lands and Tens.* 1900, pp. 4, 5; E.R.O., D/Q 30/1/11.

3 *Illus. Lond. News*, 3 May 1856; *Kelly's Dir. Essex* (1859); *Acct. of Purchase of Land at Colch.* H.C. 456, p. 2 (1861), xxxvi.

4 *Return of Huts 1854–5 and 1855–6*, H.C. 267, p. 2 (1857 Sess. 2), xxvii; *Return of Barracks and Encampments 1857*, H.C. 165, p. 2 (1857 Sess. 2), xxvii.

5 P.R.O., WO 44/719; *Return of all Lands and Tens.* 1900, pp. 4–5; Nat. Army Mus. Archives Rep. 24 Apr. 1990.

6 *Return of Military Stations*, H. C. 305, pp. 32–3 (1862), xxxii.

7 Ibid.; *E.C.S.* 3 May 1862; *Return of Lands and Tens. Purchased or Rented by War Dept.* H.C. 402, pp. 28–9 (1878), xlvii.

8 *Kelly's Dir. Essex* (1874, 1878); E.R.O., Acc. C249: Everett's building plans.

9 E.R.O., D/Q 30/1/9; E.R.O., Acc. C249: Everett's building plans.

10 Inf. from Senior Public Information Officer, H.Q. Eastern District.

11 *Return of all Lands and Tens.* 1900, pp. 6–7.

12 Nat. Army Mus. Archive Rep. Nov. 1990.

13 C. Cockerill and D. Woodward, *Colch. as a Military Centre*, 31; Gant, 'Hist. Berechurch', 190.

14 Inf. from M.O.D.

15 *Garrison*, ed. Dietz, 18; Gant, 'Hist. Berechurch', 193.

16 *E.C.S.* 8 Oct. 1971.

17 *Garrison*, ed. Dietz, 18.

18 *Colch. Garrison Herald*, Spring 1985, p. 25: copy in E.C.L. Colch.

19 *Colch. Gaz.* 8 May 1962.

20 Ibid. 21 Apr. 1970; 24 Oct. 1974; *Colch. Expr.* 6 Feb. 1975.

21 *Colch. Gaz.* 10 Sept. 1971.

22 *E.C.S.* 8 Oct. 1971; inf. from H.Q. Eastern District.

23 *Colch. Gaz.* 1 Dec. 1983; 10 Sept. 1984; *E.C.S.* 18 Mar. 1988.

24 *Return of all Lands and Tens.* 1900, pp. 4–5; *Jnl. Soc. for Army Hist. Research*, xxxv. 185 n.; E.R.O., Acc. C249: Everett's building plans; *E.C.S.* 6 Oct. 1989.

25 P.R.O., WO 79/51; below, Hospitals.

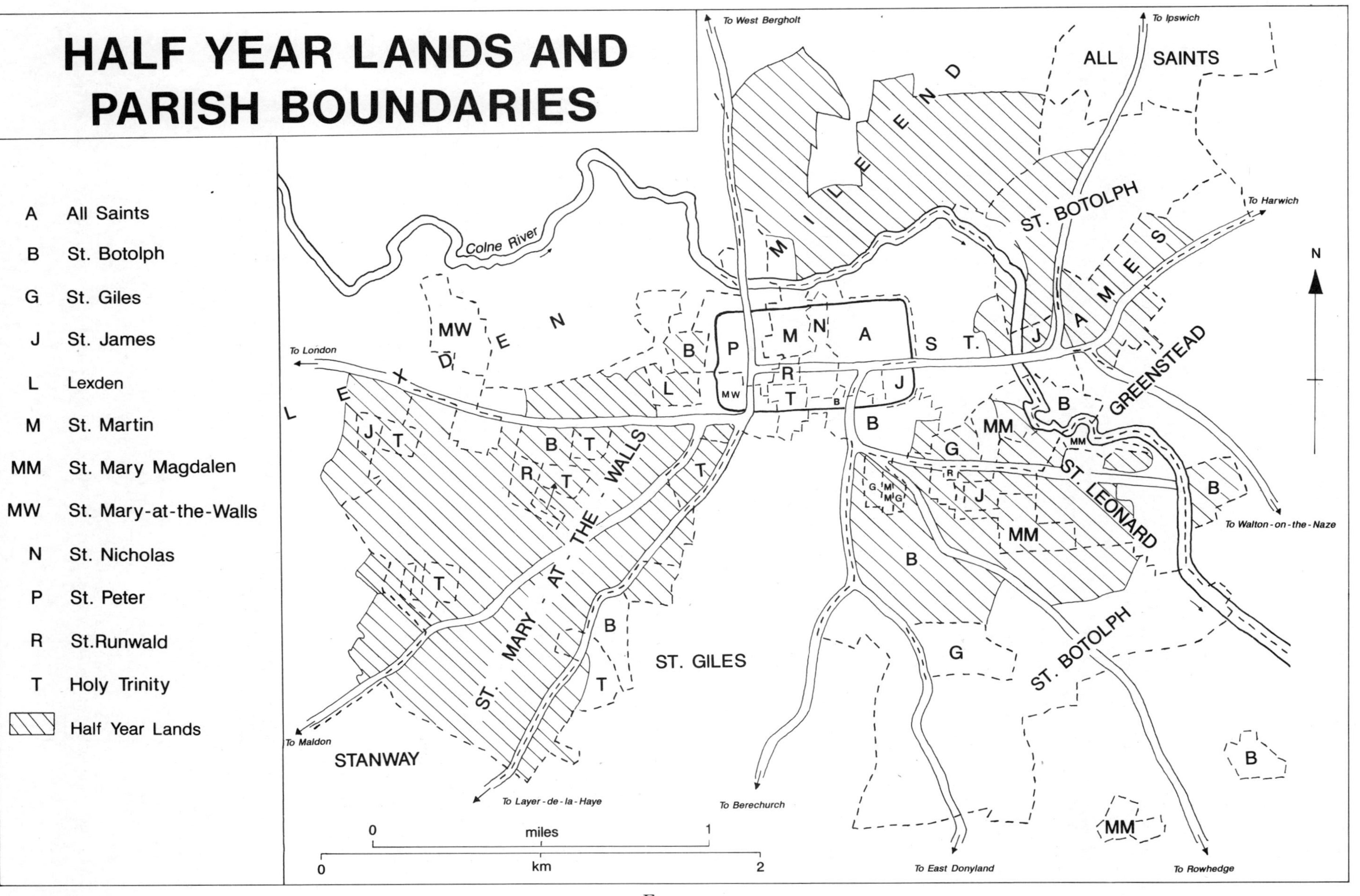
HALF YEAR LANDS AND PARISH BOUNDARIES
A All Saints
B St. Botolph
G St. Giles
J St. James
L Lexden
M St. Martin
MM St. Mary Magdalen
MW St. Mary-at-the-Walls
N St. Nicholas
P St. Peter
R St.Runwald
T Holy Trinity
Half Year Lands
ALL SAINTS
MILE END
ST. BOTOLPH
ST. JAMES
GREENSTEAD
ST. LEONARD
ST. GILES
ST. MARY AT THE WALLS
STANWAY
LEXDEN
Colne River
To West Bergholt
To Ipswich
To Harwich
To Walton-on-the-Naze
To Rowhedge
To East Donyland
To Berechurch
To Layer-de-la-Haye
To Maldon
To London
N
0
miles
1
0
km
2

Fig. 22

Street which was bought by the army in 1804, had two new wings added during the Napoleonic wars and was sold in 1824.[26] In 1856 the infantry barracks on the Ordnance field included 24 hospital huts for 216 patients.[27] An officer's hut was adapted for use as a lying-in hospital in 1870.[28] In 1873 the individual regimental hospitals were centralized into one camp hospital in huts in the north-east corner of the infantry barracks;[29] a brick ward for serious cases was added in 1888.[30] The hutted hospital closed in 1896 when a new brick-built hospital of five blocks for 221 patients was opened south of the Abbey field.[31] In 1974 Victoria House, a residential block for 100 staff, was added.[32] The building ceased to function as a hospital in 1978, but a medical reception station was later housed in the main block. By 1990 the most easterly wing of the building had been demolished.[33]

Although a temporary building for military offenders was set up in the south-west corner of the hutted camp in 1857,[34] handcuffed soldiers were marched through the town, apparently to Colchester prison, after an incident in the town in 1858.[35] In 1871 a permanent prison was built to house 47 prisoners in individual cells. Designated a military prison in 1897,[36] it was modernized in 1901 to include a laundry and gymnasium, and extended to take another 16 prisoners and by 1908 the buildings had a fully qualified staff and an armoury. In 1913 the prisoners were engaged in a variety of activities including bridge building and signalling. The prison closed in 1924, and by 1937 each barracks had its own certified detention rooms. During the Second World War hutments at Reed Hall were used as detention barracks. A camp of nissen huts was established at Berechurch Hall in 1943 for Italian prisoners of war. It was used for German and Austrian prisoners in 1944 and included a Roman Catholic seminary where 120 priests were trained; in 1947 it became the 19 Military Corrective Establishment, later the Military Corrective Training Camp. The nissen huts were replaced in 1988 by a new prison which in 1990 was the only remaining military prison in Britain.[37]

From 1854 barracks of the East Essex Regiment of militia, later the East Essex Rifles, were in the building and on grounds of the former county goal on Ipswich Road, *c.* 1 mile east of the town; the barracks were offered for sale in 1881.[38]

Headquarters for the Volunteers, subsequently the Territorial Army, were opened in Stanwell street in 1887. The building was replaced in 1964 by a new one at the corner of Butt Road and Goojerat Road.[39]

THE COMMON LANDS

THE burgesses exercised common rights over much of the liberty. The common land was divided into two types, whole year land, on which the burgesses and other landholders had common all the year round, and half year land on which the burgesses only had common from Lammas to Candlemas. The main whole year commons comprised detached areas of pasture in wood, heath, and waste in the outlying parishes, especially Mile End. The half year commons consisted of grazing rights on the borough fields, the ancient open fields of the town which lay chiefly, although not exclusively, within the parishes of the intramural churches.[40]

THE WHOLE YEAR COMMONS. The whole year commons may have originated in common rights in a large area of woodland covering the north and north-west quarters of the liberty, divided between the royal forest of Kingswood and the borough's wood or Cestrewald.[41] Kingswood had been in the hands of the burgesses before 1168 but was then reclaimed by Henry II, although the townsmen retained their common rights.[42] In the 17th century the burgesses still claimed an ancient right to feed cattle and take wood from 2,000 a. in Kingswood heath, but the area of common was by then probably much smaller because of extensive medieval inclosure and clearance in the south part and centre of Mile End parish.[43] In the 14th century the burgesses also claimed common rights in St. John's abbey's Soane wood, north-east of the town in Greenstead. By the early 16th century the burgesses' main year-round pasture was Mile End heath; they also had common rights in Parsons heath and Cross heath in Greenstead and Rovers Tye heath along the Ipswich road.[44] The rump of Kingswood, in the north part of Mile End, was acquired once more by the borough in 1535 and became known as the Severalls estate when it was leased and inclosed after 1576.[45] About 1590 the inclosures there caused *c.* 150 poor townsmen to claim that they

26 P.R.O., WO 44/61.
27 *Return of Huts 1854–6*, p. 2.
28 B.L. Add. MS. 45816, ff. 23b–24.
29 *Return of Lands and Tens.* (1878), pp. 28–9.
30 *Army Medical Rep. for 1888* [C. 6056], p. 43, H.C. (1890), xliii.
31 *E.C.S.* 17 Oct. 1896.
32 *Colch. Gaz.* 22 Jan. 1974.
33 *E.C.S.* 31 Oct. 1980, 10 June 1983; inf. from H.Q. Eastern District.
34 *Colch. as a Military Centre*, 21.
35 E.R.O., Boro. Mun., Watch Cttee. 1857–8, 2, 13 July 1858.
36 *Rep. on Military Prisons, 1897* [C. 8988], p. 20, H.C. (1898), xlvii.
37 R. Boyes, *In Glass Houses, passim*; *Times Ed. Suppl.* 15 July 1988; *E.C.S.* 11 Mar. 1988.
38 E.R.O., Q/SO 423, Jan. 1854; ibid. *Sale Cat.* B 281.
39 *Kelly's Dir. Essex* (1898); *Colch. Gaz.* 18 Feb. 1964.
40 E.C.L. Colch., E Col 1 912: Copy of Gilbert, *Map of Colch.* (*c.* 1846), belonging to J. S. Barnes, one of the conservators of the commons, with half year lands marked.
41 Above, Med. Colch. (Growth of the Town).
42 Below, Outlying Parts (Mile End); *E.A.T.* 3rd ser. xix. 162.
43 E.R.O., Boro. Mun., 'Colch. MSS.', 1620–1770, f. 2; below, Outlying Parts (Mile End).
44 E.R.O., D/B 5 R2, ff. 206–7 and loose leaf *c.* 1536; Chapman and André, *Essex Map*; E.R.O., St. John's abbey ledger bk. f. 157v.
45 *Colch. Charters*, 58; below, Outlying Parts (Mile End).

had been much injured by the loss of their common land.[46]

Certain highways were apparently whole year commons, including in the early 14th century a road leading through St. John's abbey land in Greenstead to Wivenhoe. The road along the bank of the Colne between North bridge and North mill was common in 1366, and in the same year common rights were claimed in the road through the St. Botolph's priory land south of the town towards Old Heath. In 1447 the prior was said to hold in severalty another way through his land which ought to have belonged to the commonalty of Colchester.[47] Land inclosed in 1411 for a rabbit warren apparently obstructed the burgesses's common hunting rights at Clingo Hill in Greenstead.[48] The 80 a., and the 8 p. about the town wall, in the burgesses' common in 1086 may represent whole year common land within and around the walls, where much open space survived into the medieval period, rather than the borough fields.[49]

HALF YEAR COMMONS: LOCATION AND ORIGIN. The disposition of the half year lands suggests that they probably originated as fallow and spring-field grazing rights on the open fields belonging to the borough, rather than as rights enjoyed as part of the farm of the royal demesne or a late extension of pasturage rights from Colchester's meadow land.[50] The furlongs of Borough field in St. Mary's-at-the-Walls parish do not appear to show in their layout the influence of the underlying Roman features such as roads, cemeteries, and suburban buildings, so Colchester's open fields were probably laid out in the late Anglo-Saxon period. The 1,304 a. held, mostly in parcels of 1–10 a., by 276 burgesses in 1086 were perhaps open field holdings made up of scattered strips with commensurate common rights lying within the area later covered by the borough fields.[51] Later inclosure may have severely reduced the area of commoning, for by 1599 there were only *c.* 626 a. of half year commons and *c.* 1634 there were said to be only 400–500 a.[52] In the mid 18th century the half year lands were estimated to contain 500 a., including most of the land in St. Mary's-at-the-Walls parish, although it was claimed that the commons had recently been extended.[53] Nonetheless, in the early 19th century half year lands were stated to comprise 1,020 a.: 564 a. in Head ward; 189 a. in North ward; 118 a. in East ward, and 147 a. in South ward, an area not far short of that held by the burgesses in 1086.[54]

There were three main concentrations of half year land: one south-west of the town known as Borough field, which may have originally lain entirely within St. Mary's-at-the-Walls parish; one to the south-east, which may have originally formed one great field within St. James's parish; and one to the north-east, which may once have formed a third field within Mile End and Greenstead parishes. The tithes of many lands were later transferred to other parishes, particularly with the foundation of St. Botolph's priory *c.* 1100 and St. Mary Magdalen's hospital in the early 12th century.[55] The continuation of furlongs across the boundary from St. Mary's-at-the-Walls into Lexden parish and the use of the names Borough field, Bury field, and Dole field in an area of Lexden adjoining St. Mary's-at-the-Walls suggest that the original open fields extended into Lexden.[56] The parishes of Stanway, Lexden, and St. Mary's-at-the-Walls certainly remained intermixed throughout the Middle Ages.[57] The division of tithes between the intramural parishes had the effect of fossilizing evidence of earlier agrarian arrangements including individual open field strips. In Borough field, for example, the strips, and later irregular inclosures and sub-divisions, were accommodated within a series of large curving furlongs of clearly open field type, and 'common baulks' were also identifiable as late as the 19th century.[58]

HALF YEAR COMMONS: INCLOSURE TO *c.* 1600. There is no evidence when inclosure of the borough fields began, but by the later Middle Ages consolidation had become a serious obstacle to the exercise of common rights. In 1311 the borough court recorded that all of Nicholas le Gros's newly inclosed arable lands north of the river had been half year lands from time immemorial, and in the same year John Person was charged with making several a croft near Colebaynes land.[59] The land which the bailiffs licensed Roger Moriss to inclose in 1348–9 presumably lay in the borough fields, and other inclosures which threatened to extinguish common rights were made in 1353 in Bury field within the walls, Partridge fen in Borough field, and Someres field at Dilbridge in Mile End. A croft, perhaps an assart, called la Brache or Bruche, was also made several in 1365–6.[60]

Between 1401 and 1447 common land was made several in Holmere near Butt Lane, at Bourne mill, in Bury field, at Shrub wood, in Synchedown next to North Street, and at the Hythe.[61] In 1466 a ship builder held common soil, probably meadow, beyond the crane at the Hythe as several.[62] Another phase of inclosure occurred in the later 16th century when unlawful inclosures proved a 'great impediment' to the burgesses' cattle.[63] The problem recurred a century

46 E.R.O., T/A 407/89.

47 Ibid. D/B 5 R2, ff. 40, 56; D/B 5 Cr15, rott. 1d., 12; Cr61, rot. 11; *Colch. Cart.* ii. 508–9.

48 E.R.O., D/B 5 Cr38, rot. 2.

49 *V.C.H. Essex*, i. 577; above, Med. Colch. (Growth of the Town); cf. *Antiquary*, vi. 97.

50 Cf. *V.C.H. Yorks. E.R.* vi. 211–13; Morant, *Colch.* 92–3; [J. H. Round], *Colch. Castle*, 140–3; *Antiquary*, vi. 95–8.

51 *V.C.H. Essex*, i. 574–6.

52 B.L. Stowe MS. 832, ff. 27–44; E.R.O., Boro. Mun., 'Colch. MSS.', 1620–1770, f. 1.

53 Morant, *Colch.* 92–4.

54 T. Cromwell, *Hist. Colch.* 261.

55 Above, Boundaries.

56 E.R.O., D/CT 95, 220.

57 Above, Boundaries.

58 O.S. Map 6", Essex XXVII and XXVIII (1875–6 edn.); E.R.O., D/CT 95, 100; E.C.L. Colch., E Col 1 912: 'Map of The Borough Fields'.

59 E.R.O., D/B 5 Cr2, rot. 2; *E.A.T.* 3rd ser. xix. 162–3.

60 E.R.O., D/B 5 R1, f. 40; D/B 5 Cr5, rot. 1; Cr14, rot. 4; Cr15, rot. 1d.

61 Ibid. D/B 5 Cr32, rot. 15d.; Cr35, rott. 2 and d., 14; Cr41, rot. 14; Cr47, rot. 23; Cr57, rot. 2.

62 Ibid. D/B 5 Cr73, rot. 1d.

63 Ibid. D/B 5 Cr121, rot. 2d.; Cr123, rot. 3; Cr143, rot. 4; Cr144, rot. 21d.; Cr150, rot. 33.

later, between 1654 and 1655, when the free burgesses were said to be suffering great prejudice from encroachments, tillage, and inclosure.[64] Common rights were also obstructed by agricultural improvements from the 17th century onwards, including new buildings, farmyards, and root crops.[65]

Disputes between the burgesses and St. John's abbey over grazing rights suggest that the abbey had extinguished common rights on its land south and east of the town. In the early 14th century the abbot encouraged new tenants to inclose their land in Monkdown,[66] and in 1340 the abbot inclosed his land there so that the burgesses could not common, an action which they were still disputing in 1427. In that year the abbot was also accused of keeping his boundaries open at Stowersland, in Greenstead towards East bridge, in order to impound the burgesses' cattle when they strayed from neighbouring commons.[67] The abbot had also inclosed Oldgate field or Maryland outside East gate in 1364, but the burgesses continued to demand that the land be thrown open, and in 1489 broke the abbey's closes there. The abbot retaliated by impounding their cattle.[68] The burgesses also claimed that the abbot had bought land from them in order to make it several and so had obstructed common grazing rights on a total of 400 a. of arable, meadow, and pasture which used to be common 'at the usual times', presumably a reference to half year lands.[69]

If the abbot of St. John's had encroached on some of the borough's half year lands, the borough itself had consented to the inclosure of others. In 1516 the bailiffs and commonalty gave the wardens of St. Anne's guild permission to inclose all the chapel lands, which presumably lay near the chapel along the Harwich road. At the same time they extinguished rights of common on land adjoining the Crutched friars' orchard, south of the later Crouch Street.[70] A proposal *c.* 1536 to inclose all the land in the liberty except the whole year commons and to charge the owners a rent of 3*d.* an acre for meadow and 2*d.* an acre for arable and pasture came to nothing, perhaps because of the inclosure riot that same year.[71] That or a similar plan may have led to the order, made by the commissioners appointed to settle differences in the town in 1549,[72] that inclosures or sales of commons should be made only with the unanimous consent of the bailiffs, aldermen, and common councillors.[73]

In 1564 the borough assembly agreed to inclose and lease the half year land and to use the rents to support a hospital for the poor.[74] The 5*s.* rent agreed that year by the holder of Golden field, near the later Military Road, for his intercommoning,[75] may have been one such rent for a new inclosure, and the 2*s.* 6*d.* rent agreed for a parcel of half year ground in St. Leonard's at the Hythe in 1602 was to be paid to the town's poor.[76] The provision for a workhouse partly financed by rents of half year lands was repeated in 1613 and the lease in 1618 of land on the north side of Magdalen Street, between Magdalen green and Spittleman's wash, which allowed the tenant to inclose the land may have helped to finance the scheme.[77]

HALF YEAR COMMONS: MANAGEMENT TO *c.* 1790. Where landowners and tenants farmed their half year land as arable they could not sow winter crops and had to grow oats and barley, crops which were well suited to the light sandy soils of the liberty.[78] Nearly three quarters of the crops possessed by Colchester taxpayers in 1296 and 1301 comprised oats, barley, and peas, and the court rolls also contain references to lands occupied by spring-sown crops.[79] The *c.* 500 a. of several 'rye ground' in St. Giles's parish in the late 16th century may reveal greater use of winter-sown crops outside the area of half year commonage.[80] Although the half year lands were commonable between Lammas and Candlemas the dates were probably more flexible in practice, for at Dilbridge farm in 1699 commoning was delayed until 'the corn is off'. Similarly, in the early 14th century rights were claimed 'from the carrying of hay to Candlemas' on half year land in Salt meadow and Eastmead, near the Hythe.[81] Nonetheless, when the burgesses' rights were challenged in the mid 18th century they retaliated by driving their cattle over the commons whether or not the harvest had been completed.[82]

There is no direct evidence for a stint until 1573 when it was set at three great cattle or 30 sheep for each burgess.[83] Nonetheless, from the early 14th century the commons were often overloaded with flocks of up to 400 sheep, besides cattle, horses, and pigs. Burgesses were occasionally amerced, but foreigners, having no right of common, were more frequently presented for burdening the commons to the prejudice of the commonalty. Those at fault included the prior of St. Botolph's, the almoner of St. John's, the rector of Mile End, and the tenants of the manors of Lexden and West Donyland.[84] In the late 15th century the commoners' cattle were tended by a common cowherd, who impounded

64 Ibid. D/B 5 Gb4, f. 127v.
65 e.g. ibid. D/B 5 Sr67, rot. 9d.; ibid. Boro. Mun., 'Colch. MSS.', 1620–1770, ff. 1v., 2v.
66 *E.A.T.* 3rd ser. xix. 160–1.
67 E.R.O., D/B 5 Cr6, rot. 1d.; Cr47, rot. 22d.; *Colch. Cart.* ii. 508–9.
68 E.R.O., D/B 5 R2, f. 46; D/B 5 Cr14, rot. 1d.; Cr33, rot. 20d.; ibid. St. John's abbey ledger bk. f. 277.
69 Ibid. D/B 5 R2, ff. 191, 209–12.
70 Ibid. D/B 5 Cr87, rot. 8.
71 Ibid. D/B 5 R2, loose leaf *c.* 1536; ibid. D/B 5 Cr107, rot. 3.
72 Above, Tudor and Stuart Colch. (Boro. Govt.).
73 Morant, *Colch.* 94; E.R.O., D/Y 2/2, pp. 17–20.
74 Above, Tudor and Stuart Colch. (Soc. Structure).
75 E.R.O., D/B 5 R5, f. 101v.
76 Ibid. D/B 5 Gb2, f. 21.
77 Above, Tudor and Stuart Colch. (Boro. Govt.); below, Par. Govt. and Poor Relief; E.R.O., D/B 5 Gb2, f. 168 and v.
78 Britnell, *Growth and Decline*, 42–4.
79 Above, Med. Colch. (Econ.); *E.A.T.* N.S. ix. 126–55; E.R.O., D/B 5 Cr9, rot. 2; Cr15, rot. 4; Cr16, rot. 14; Cr19, rot. 3d.
80 B.L. Stowe MS. 832, f. 30.
81 Beds. R.O., L17/185; E.R.O., D/B 5 R2, f. 40.
82 E.R.O., D/Y 2/2, p. 351; below, this section.
83 E.R.O., D/B 5 R7, f. 235.
84 e.g. ibid. D/B 5 Cr2–19, *passim.*

unauthorized beasts and reported defects and trespasses to the bailiffs; in 1538 burgesses were forbidden to put cattle on the commons except in the cowherd's charge.[85]

The management of the half year lands was one of the matters in dispute between the corporation and the burgesses in the years before 1635.[86] The disposal of money received from the land seems to have been of as much importance to the burgesses as the rights themselves. In 1627 the assembly repeated the stint of 1573 and agreed that the bailiffs should appoint 2–4 burgesses from each ward to drive the commons as often as necessary, fining owners 3*s*. 4*d*. for each beast illegally grazed. Pigs were similarly to be driven and impounded. In 1629 new ordinances confirmed the stint laid down in 1573 and provided for the election of four treasurers, one from each ward, who were to appoint the drivers of the commons and to receive the fines collected. Land already inclosed was to remain so, and no more leases were to be granted without the consent of a majority of the commonalty at a public meeting. All fines and rents were to be distributed to poor burgesses and their families.[87]

The burgesses seem to have achieved a modification of the rules for the appointment of drivers in 1633,[88] but in 1634 they claimed a stint of 3 great cattle or 90 sheep and again objected to the ordinance for the driving of the half year lands. They also complained that some aldermen had tried to prevent them from commoning by laying their several lands open to the half year lands so that cattle could be impounded for trespass, and by sowing the land with roots or by building on it. The burgesses were equally concerned that the lease of Kingswood heath made in 1572 was about to be renewed, thus again depriving them of wood and timber besides their rights of common.[89] They almost succeeded in getting a clause into the new borough charter in 1635 forbidding the inclosure or other interruption of their commons,[90] and they did succeed in having the drivers' powers confined to foreigners' cattle while freemen's cattle were to be placed under the care of one herdsman from each ward.[91]

The disputed election of 1742 led to the lapse of Colchester's charter, and in 1749 the burgesses claimed that they were deprived of their half year commons, their cattle were impounded, and they had no redress.[92] Landowners seized the opportunity to press for the abolition of the commons, which they considered hindered improvement and encouraged poor stock-keeping. In 1753 Philip Yorke, Lord Hardwicke, lord of Mile End, Greenstead, and Dilbridge manors, briefed by the historian Philip Morant, claimed that he and his fellow landowners had been powerless against 'a thousand furious fellows backed by a bullying mayor' who were determined to extend their half year lands and prepared to put their cattle on them at the beginning of August whether or not the corn was cut. Among the landowners only the wealthy widow and brewer Elizabeth Selly had refused to be intimidated. The burgesses hired an attorney to sue for their pasture rights, but in 1753 the attorney-general advised them that all their privileges, franchises, and lands had reverted to the Crown on the lapse of the charter. The dispute led to agitation in the town during the parliamentary election of 1753, in which Lord Hardwicke supported the Tory candidates.[93] The half year commons were restored to the mayor and commonalty under the 1763 charter.[94]

HALF YEAR COMMONS: MANAGEMENT AND SALE *c.* 1790 TO *c.* 1900. The dissolution of the half year lands began in the last decade of the 18th century. In 1794 the burgesses offered to surrender rights of common on land south of Magdalen Street for the barracks, and further rights were surrendered to the government in 1796. In 1806 rights of common were sold to the government on 34 a. acquired for the rapidly expanding military site. Those sales may have suggested a way of raising money at a time of serious financial problems for the borough. In 1797 a committee was appointed to examine whether compensation had been received for inclosures and to determine how far expansion at the Hythe had encroached upon common land. In 1801 the treasurers were requested to survey the half year lands, including lands which claimed to be exempt but were once common. A proposal that year to sell the half year commons to cover the corporation's debts was rejected by the burgesses, but two years later an amended proposal that a sufficient quantity be sold to redeem the corporation's land tax was approved. In 1806 another committee recommended the sale of the common rights to discharge the corporation's debts, including a £2,493 mortgage on the corporation estates.[95]

In 1807 Benjamin Strutt, the chamberlain, claimed that the treasurers and drivers were prevented from enforcing the burgesses' common rights by fear of prosecution or physical assault and 'by bribes and other treacherous dealings'. Of the money which they did collect, twice as much was spent on treats and feasts as on widows, orphans, and sick, weak, and poor burgesses, a form of embezzlement noted by Morant in 1748.[96] Strutt's condemnation resulted in a new constitution creating the 'conservators' of the commons, four men elected annually on 27 July, who were to survey and record the half year lands and might at the request of the four

85 Ibid. D/B 5 R2, ff. 182, 189–90, 225.
86 e.g. ibid. D/B 5 Gb3, f. 73.
87 Ibid. ff. 62v., 63, 64, 81.
88 Ibid. f. 124v.
89 Ibid. Boro. Mun., 'Colch. MSS.', 1620–1700, ff. 1–2v.
90 P.R.O., PC 2/44, pp. 230–1.
91 E.R.O., D/B 5 Gb3, f. 139v.
92 *E.A.T.* 3rd ser. xviii. 63–74.
93 Morant, *Colch.* 94; E.R.O., D/Y 2/2, pp. 351–3; ibid. Boro. Mun., 'Colch. MSS.', 1620–1770, ff. 60, 61v.; for Mrs. Selly see S. D'Cruze, 'The Middling Sort in Provincial Eng.: Politics and Social Relations in Colch. 1730–1800' (Univ. of Essex Ph.D. thesis, 1990), 204–7.
94 *Colch. Charters*, 196.
95 E.R.O., D/B 5 Gb9, pp. 52, 73–4, 77, 85, 101–4, 107, 122–33; above, Barracks.
96 B. Strutt, *A Plan for Regulating, Improving, and Rendering more Beneficial the Common or Half-Year Land*, 3–4, 8–10; Morant, *Colch.* 94.

treasurers or any 12 burgesses enter inclosed or cultivated fields to preserve common rights. An annual assembly, held in late July in the moot hall, was to consider proposals for the purchase of common rights at £30 an acre for meadow and £20 for arable. Where cultivation obstructed regular commoning the conservators were empowered to negotiate a licence at a rate not less than one quarter of the annual rent charge. Those moneys, together with the fines taken for illegal grazing, were to be placed in government security or used to purchase estates. The annual interest or rent was to be paid by seven trustees to the chamberlain for distribution in equal shares to resident burgesses.[97]

Initially, purchases of common rights were negligible and in 1808 the standard charge was reduced to £20 an acre for meadow and £15 an acre for arable. Sales were allowed at lower prices in 1809 and 1811, and charges were further reduced to £7 an acre for arable and pasture in 1815. From 1809 onwards the balance in the conservators' accounts arising from sales of half year rights amounted to between £100 and £200 each year, with occasional larger sales such as the 27 a. which brought in £472 in 1812. Total sales between 1805 and 1820 were 554 a., followed by a further 200 a. by 1825, leaving only 266 a. of half year land.[98]

In 1825 seven common councillors claimed that money arising from the sales had not been distributed to the free burgesses as the constitution of 1807 required and they demanded their equal share of moneys paid to Strutt between 1818 and 1824. Strutt was ordered to resist the claims and the borough assembly committed itself to defending him against any legal actions.[99] In 1829, perhaps as a result of that dispute, it was proposed that the remaining common rights be sold and the proceeds placed in 3 per cent annuities, so as to improve the income distributed annually among the burgesses. A further proposal to sell off the Severalls and land bought with money from the sale of half year lands, was successfully opposed.[1] After 1825 sales were much reduced, although 39 a. were sold in St. Mary's-at-the-Walls parish as late as 1862, and common rights in Drury farm in that parish were still subject to legal disputes and transfers of ownership in the later 19th century.[2]

A group of litigious burgesses, led by Jeremiah Prestney and James Coveney, claimed that all income derived from ancient rights of fishing, hunting, and grazing properly belonged to the freemen rather than the corporation. In one legal action brought against the corporation, as conservators of the commons, they claimed the profits of the common land but the suit was dismissed with costs awarded against the plaintiffs in 1898. The costs were still in dispute in 1904, when they were ordered to be paid out of the money invested by the trustees of the half year lands. The great expense to the town of contesting the case led to the suggestion that the freemen should be abolished, but the final verdict, and the death of Prestney in 1899 and Coveney in 1909, brought the episode to a close. The freemen continued to receive small pensions from the fund in 1993.[3]

MILLS

WATER MILLS. Three mills were recorded in Colchester, one in Greenstead, and two in Lexden in 1086. Middle mill, recorded *c.* 1101, was probably omitted from the survey with the castle to which it belonged.[4] Of the six Domesday mills, only the two Lexden mills, the later Lexden mill and North mill, can be certainly identified, but the Greenstead mill was probably the mill on the Colne which was moved, apparently to the site of Hull mill, in the mid 12th century. The mill on the bishop of London's soke, which seems to have been built between 1066 and 1086, may have been on the Colne between North mill and Lexden mill, on land which was in St. Mary's parish until 1699;[5] if so it was not recorded again. The mill belonging to St. Peter's church may have been the later Stokes mill on the boundary of Mile End parish, and another Domesday mill has been identified with East mill.[6]

For most of the 13th and 14th centuries there were eight mills, five (Lexden mill, North mill, Middle mill, Stokes mill, and East mill) on the Colne, and three (Bourne mill, Cannock mill, and Hull mill) on a small tributary south of the town. Other early mills, probaby short-lived, included a fulling mill called Haddel mill, recorded in 1247; Sebares mill at the Hythe, whose site was recorded in 1332;[7] and Crudde mill, a fulling mill apparently near East mill, recorded in 1391 and 1406.[8] The borough built a ninth mill, Hythe mill, on the Colne in the late 14th century.[9]

The presence of five, and later six, mills on the Colne within a short distance of each other, and of three mills even closer together on its small tributary, led to water shortages which were overcome by the raising of ever higher millponds. In 1407 and 1410 Middle mill pond, in 1411 East mill pond, in 1414 Bourne mill pond, and in 1429 Hythe mill pond overflowed and flooded adjoining meadows or roads.[10] The need to safeguard the water supply to Lexden mill

97 E.R.O., D/B 5 Gb9, pp. 129–33.
98 Ibid. pp. 155, 167, 198, 217, 276–7; Cromwell, *Hist. Colch.* 261.
99 E.R.O., D/B 5 Gb9, pp. 509–10.
1 Ibid. D/B 5 Gb10, pp. 41–2, 117–18.
2 Ibid. D/DEl T401–2; D/DEl 255.
3 *Essex Jnl.* xx (2), 31–3; E.R.O., Acc. C3, Press Cuttings; ibid. Boro. Mun., Special Cttee. Min. 1902–12, 150–1.
4 *V.C.H. Essex*, i. 432, 440, 574–5, 578; *Reg. Regum Anglo-Norm.* ii, p. 18.
5 Below, Outlying Parts (Lexden, Econ.).
6 *V.C.H. Essex*, ii. 446.
7 P.R.O., JUST 1/232, rot. 11d.; E.R.O., St. John's abbey ledger bk. f. 199v.
8 E.R.O., D/B 5 Cr27, rot. 11; Cr35, rot. 21; Cr61, rot. 18.
9 Ibid. D/B 5 Cr26, rot. 16d.
10 Ibid. D/B 5 Cr36, rot. 11; Cr37, rot. 14; Cr38, rot. 2; Cr39, rot. 18d.; D/B 5 R2, f. 73.

was presumably what caused John FitzWalter to force a Colchester man to sell him an unidentified mill near Lexden manor, possibly Newbridge mill in West Bergholt, in 1342.[11]

The burgesses do not seem to have owed suit to any mill, and the borough assembly's attempt in the early 1570s to force bakers to grind at Hythe mill was quickly abandoned.[12] Some tenants of St. John's abbey may have owed suit to the abbey's Stokes mill, but the only manorial mill was Lexden mill.[13] The building of windmills, mostly short-lived, by individual burgesses from the 1370s does not seem to have led to any disputes with the water mill owners.

Not all the Colchester mills operated throughout the Middle Ages.[14] Middle mill had fallen down by 1381 and was not rebuilt until *c.* 1402,[15] but its place as a corn mill may have been taken by the short-lived windmills. Stokes mill and North mill were not recorded as corn mills in the mid 14th century, and seem to have operated only as fulling mills in the 15th century. Other medieval water mills, like their early modern successors, probably contained both corn and fulling mills: St. John's abbey complained in 1429 that the burgesses were setting up roadblocks to stop men from grinding or fulling at the abbey's mills.[16]

The corn and fulling mills, particularly those on the stream south of the town, were the most valuable mills. Hull mill was valued at £7 6*s.* 8*d.* *c.* 1540, although it had been leased for only £3 13*s.* 4*d.* in 1536.[17] Bourne mill was farmed for £6 a year in 1538–9 and Cannock mill for 73*s.* 4*d.* about the same date. Middle mill was valued at £6 a year in 1541–2 and Stokes mill was farmed for 68*s.* 4*d.* a year in 1538–9.[18] Hythe mill had been farmed for 53*s.* 4*d.* *c.* 1500, and North mill for only 10*s.* in 1493, but both may have increased in value by the 1530s; Hythe mill was leased for £30 a year in 1578.[19]

Stokes mill and North mill disappeared in the late 16th century, but their place as fulling mills may have been taken by Crockleford mill on Salary brook, first recorded in 1588.[20] In 1632 there were said to be between 7 and 20 corn mills within the liberty, the higher estimates presumably counting double mills as two and including mills such as Layer mill on or near the borough boundary. The seven mills were probably Lexden mill, Middle mill, East mill, and Hythe mill on the Colne, and Bourne mill, Cannock mill, and Hull mill on its tributary. They were unable to grind enough corn for the town without the help of neighbouring mills and of three or four newly erected windmills.[21] Obtaining enough water was still difficult. The refusal of the millers of Cannock and Bourne mills to co-operate in the early 1630s led the miller at Cannock mill to dam his pond so high that it overflowed. In 1663 the raising of the floodgates and banks of Hythe mill flooded meadows there, and in 1681 the damming of water for Hythe mill interfered with East mill.[22]

Hythe mill was demolished before 1736 and Hull mill converted into an oil mill by 1733,[23] their place as corn mills perhaps being taken by some of the *c.* 10 windmills which had been built in the liberty by the later 18th century. In the 19th century and the earlier 20th the number of mills was further reduced and the surviving mills grew in size, notably East mill which was able to take advantage of the improved navigation on the Colne to grind corn from and supply flour and meal to an area much greater than Colchester borough.

Bourne mill, which belonged to St. John's abbey by 1311, may have been the mill granted to the abbey at its foundation. It takes its name, first recorded *c.* 1240, from the small stream or bourne south of the town on which it stands.[24] Like the other mills on that stream, it seems to have worked as a corn mill throughout the Middle Ages.[25] It may have been rebuilt *c.* 1326, when the abbey agreed to find large timber, ironwork, mill spindle, wheel, and stones for it.[26] Its pond was the abbey's fishpond.[27] St. John's held the mill until the Dissolution. It and its fishpond then passed through a number of hands before being sold in 1590 to John Lucas, whose descendants held it until 1917.[28] The mill was a corn mill in 1632 and seems to have remained one, perhaps with a fulling mill, throughout the 18th century. In the earlier 19th century it was a cloth mill for weaving, fulling, and finishing bays. That business closed *c.* 1840, and the mill seems to have been disused for some years. By 1860 it was a corn mill, and by 1894 it was partly steam-driven. It worked until 1935.[29] It was given to the National Trust in 1936 and converted into a house. The machinery was restored in 1966.[30]

Bourne mill lies close to the northern end of a large artificial embankment which was built to create the pond to the west. The surviving house was built as a fishing lodge in 1591 by Thomas Lucas, whose arms appear over the doorway.[31] The walls are of re-used materials, presumably taken from the site of St. John's abbey. The ornate gables are in the style which was fashionable in

[11] P.R.O., KB 27/366, Rex rot. 30 (4).
[12] E.R.O., D/B 5 R7, ff. 236v.–237, 261v., 270.
[13] Ibid. D/B 5 Cr28, rot. 36; below, Outlying Parts, (Lexden, Econ.).
[14] Britnell, *Growth and Decline*, 20–1, 86–8, 197–8.
[15] *Cal. Inq. Misc.* iv, p. 80; *Cal. Pat.* 1401–5, 189.
[16] E.R.O., D/B 5 R2, f. 73v.
[17] P.R.O., SC 6/Hen. VIII/898, m. 5d.; *Cal. Pat.* 1554–5, 332–3.
[18] P.R.O., E 318/2/57; SC 6/Hen. VIII/976, mm. 3d., 11d.–12; E 310/13/41, f. 39.
[19] Bodl. MS. Rolls Essex 2; *Cal. Inq. p.m. Hen. VII*, i, p. 396; E.R.O., D/B 5 Gb1, 17 Mar. 1578.
[20] E.R.O., D/B 5 Sb2/4, f. 184v.
[21] P.R.O., E 134/8 Chas. I Mic./18.
[22] Ibid. E 134/8 & 9 Chas. I Hil./21; E.R.O., D/B 5 Gb4, f. 289; Gb5, f. 189v.
[23] E.R.O., D/Y 2/1, p. 107; D/DHt F1.
[24] Ibid. D/B 5 Cr2, rot. 2; *Colch. Cart.* i. 37; ii. 604; *P.N. Elements*, i. 63.
[25] E.R.O., D/B 5 Cr1–81 *passim.*
[26] Ibid. St. John's abbey ledger bk. ff. 63v.–64.
[27] *Colch. Cart.* ii. 511.
[28] *L. & P. Hen. VIII*, xix (1), p. 495; xix (2), p. 195; *Cal. Pat.* 1580–2, p. 117; E.R.O., D/B 5 Cr142, rot. 12d.; Cr152, rot. 2d.; Beds. R.O., L 23/462.
[29] P.R.O., E 134/8 Chas. I Mic./18; E.R.O., T/A 163/1; *E.A.T.* N.S. x. 49–51; *Kelly's Dir. Essex* (1898, 1902); H. Benham, *Some Essex Water Mills*, 96.
[30] *Bourne Mill* (Nat. Trust); cutting from *Essex Gaz.* (n.d.) in E.C.L. Colch.
[31] R.C.H.M. *Essex*, iii. 71, 73; Pevsner, *Essex*, 145.

the Low Countries in the later 16th century. Each gable-end incorporates a chimney and originally the principal floor may have contained a single room with a fireplace at each end. By the early 19th century a fulling mill had been attached to the south end of the lodge, and in the mid 19th century the main building was converted into a corn mill, necessitating the insertion of an upper floor and a sack hoist and the cutting of additional doorways in the walls.

Cannock mill, which belonged to St. Botolph's priory, was called the mill near Wick or the old mill in the wood in 1311 and the old priory mill in the later 14th century; it was called Canwick or Cannock mill in 1404.[32] It was presumably older than the priory's new or Hull mill which seems to have been built lower down the stream in the later 12th century. The two mills were sometimes leased together in the later 15th century.[33] In 1536 the Crown granted Cannock mill to Sir Thomas Audley, who gave it to St. John's abbey.[34] The Crown kept the mill after the dissolution of St. John's, leasing it in 1565 to John Mildmay and in 1575 to Edward Lucas, who in 1576 assigned the lease to Sir Thomas Lucas. Sir Thomas bought the mill soon after taking out a new lease in 1594, and rebuilt it *c.* 1600 as an overshot mill with two ponds. It was a corn mill in 1632, and included a fulling mill in 1651.[35] It seems to have been a corn mill, perhaps with a fulling mill, in the 18th century; in 1803 and in the 1820s it was a flour and fulling mill.[36] The mill remained in the Lucas family until 1917. It was rebuilt in 1845, as an overshot mill fed by iron pipes from a high pond; new buildings were erected in 1875. It worked as a corn mill until the later 1940s when it became a store for Cramphorn's.[37] The building was restored in 1973; in 1989 it was converted into a centre for the sale of tropical fish.[38]

Crockleford mill, on Salary brook, was first recorded in 1588. It seems to have been part of Shaws farm, being held by Edmund Church before 1647 and by John Roberts in 1810 and 1811,[39] and it may have been built by William Beriff, the Colchester clothmaker who acquired the farm in 1545, although it was not listed with the farm at his death in 1595.[40] In 1657 it was rebuilt as a small bay-thickening or fulling mill.[41] It was a fulling mill in 1777, and a bay mill in 1797, but it was leased as a flour mill in 1819 and converted into an oil mill in 1823. It was sold in 1837 as a chemical plant and water mill. The London Chemical Works later produced 'Mother Liquor' there. It was a corn mill again by 1877, and worked until *c.* 1955.[42]

East mill, on the Colne at East bridge, was held by St. Botolph's in 1311, and remained in the priory's possession until the Dissolution when it was granted to Sir Thomas Audley.[43] It worked as a corn mill until the mid 15th century or later, but was a fulling mill in 1552.[44] Audley conveyed it in 1536 to John Christmas, whose son George sold it in 1554 to John Maynard.[45] The mill was a fulling mill in 1569 and in 1582 when it was run by Maynard's widow Alice. In 1624 it comprised both corn and fulling mills.[46] The corn mills were expanded by Henry and John Dunnage, millers in the late 18th century,[47] and when Edward Marriage bought the mill in 1840 it was a breast or overshot mill with six pairs of stones. An auxiliary steam engine was installed in 1844. In 1865 Marriage improved the river above the Hythe to enable London barges to reach the mills. In the 1870s further improvements were made to the mills and their machinery, including the installation of a second steam engine and the introduction of roller mills. Between 1885 and 1893 the mills were almost completely rebuilt and extended to accommodate a 6-sack roller plant, besides the old mill stones. Warehousing was extended. The mills were renovated in 1930–1, the mill stones and water wheel being dismantled.[48] The mill, then owned by Rank Hovis McDougall which had taken over the Marriage firm, was closed in 1976 and converted into an hotel in 1979.[49]

Hull mill, below Cannock mill on the stream south of the town, was recorded by that name in 1438, but it was probably St. Botolph's priory's new mill recorded in 1227, which seems to have replaced an earlier mill on the Colne at the Hythe, demolished in the mid 12th century.[50] Hull mill was known as the new or new priory mill between 1311 and 1386 and as the mill in the wood between 1387 and 1435. Like Cannock mill, with which it was leased in 1452 and 1498, Hull mill worked as a corn mill throughout the Middle Ages, and was still one in 1519. In 1405 it also contained a fulling mill.[51] At the Dissolution the mill passed to Sir Thomas Audley, reverting to the Crown on his death.[52] It was still in the Crown's possession in 1555, when it was a corn mill with two pairs of stones, but was sold to speculators in 1562.[53] In 1690 it comprised one water mill, one fulling mill, and

32 E.R.O., D/B 5 Cr1–34, *passim*.
33 Ibid. D/B 5 Cr64, rot. 20d.; P.R.O., C 1/509, no. 8.
34 *L. & P. Hen. VIII*, xi, p. 208.
35 P.R.O., E 134/8 Chas. I Mic./18; E 134/8 & 9 Chas. I Hil./21; E 310/13/41, f. 39; E 310/14/44, ff. 8, 44; E.R.O., D/B 5 Sb2/9, f. 62.
36 E.R.O., T/A 163/1; *E.A.T.* N.S. x. 50.
37 Benham, *Essex Water Mills*, 97; E.R.O., T/A 163/1; ibid. Acc. C47, CPL 661; Beds. R.O., L 23/462.
38 *E.C.S.* 15 Feb. 1973; 26 May 1989.
39 E.R.O., D/B 5 Sb2/4, f. 184v.; D/DMb T7; B.L. Stowe MS. 842, f. 29v.; P.R.O., E 134/11 Anne Mic./21; *Cal. Cttee. for Compounding*, 418, 2403–4.
40 P.R.O., C 142/244, no. 96.
41 E.R.O., Q/SR 379, rot. 26.
42 Chapman and André, *Map of Essex* (1777); E.R.O., D/DLy M84A, p. 139; O.S. Maps, 6" Essex. XXVIII. SW (1876 edn.); Benham, *Essex Water Mills*, 100.
43 E.R.O., D/B 5 Cr2, rot. 2; *L. & P. Hen. VIII*, xi, p. 208.
44 E.R.O., D/B 5 Cr1–119, *passim*; P.R.O., CP 25/2/70/578, no. 10.
45 *L. & P. Hen. VIII*, xi, p. 208; *Cal. Pat.* 1550–3, 271; 1553–4, 369; E.R.O., D/B 5 Cr120, rot. 8.
46 P.R.O., C 142/151, no. 55; E.R.O., D/B 5 Sb2/4, f. 20v.; D/B 5 Cb1/8, ff. 51v.–54v.
47 E.R.O., D/DLy M84A, pp. 102, 132.
48 [E. Marriage & Son Ltd.] *1840–1940: Annals of 100 Years of Flour Milling*, *passim*: copy in E.C.L. Colch.
49 *Colch. Gaz.* 16 July 1976; *The Leader* 15 July, 1979.
50 E.R.O., D/B 5 Cr55, rot. 18; *Colch. Cart.* ii. 539, 545.
51 E.R.O., D/B 5 Cr1–81, *passim*, esp. Cr35, rott. 6d., 16; Cr64, rot. 20d; Cr90, rot. 16; P.R.O., C 1/509, no. 8.
52 P.R.O., SC 6/Hen. VIII/898, m. 5d.; *Cal. Pat.* 1554–5, 332–3.
53 E.R.O., Boro. Mun., tin trunk, S55; P.R.O., C 66/979, m. 4.

one oil mill.[54] By 1733, when John Rootsey devised it to his son Samuel, it was an oil mill,[55] and it remained so until 1811 when it was sold to Samuel Bawtree and George Savill who demolished it and built a distillery and water corn mill on the site. The distillery went out of business *c.* 1841, and in 1843 the buildings, including the water mill with four pairs of stones, one pair of rollers, and an auxiliary steam engine, were sold.[56] The mill worked as a corn mill from 1845 until its demolition in 1896.[57]

Hythe mill, on the west bank of the Colne just above Hythe bridge, was built by the borough before 1385.[58] It was not recorded as a corn mill until 1429, when it had been rebuilt as a corn and fulling mill with two wheels, and its early lessees were clothmakers or fullers, but its high rent of 20 marks in 1387, unchanged in 1439, suggests that it had always been a corn and fulling mill. The abbot of St. John's complained that the rebuilt mill encroached on his land.[59] The mill was derelict by 1489 and was rebuilt, still as a corn and fulling mill, at the expense of Thomas Christmas the elder and Robert Barker.[60]

The mill had fallen down again by 1548, but was rebuilt soon afterwards.[61] In 1573 and 1574 the borough tried to recover the rebuilding costs by forcing bakers to grind at the mill, but had to give up the attempt in 1575. Efforts that year to 'persuade' the bakers and the Dutch community to grind there were no more successful.[62] In 1579 the tenant was allowed 4 tons of rough timber for building work, and in 1598 was ordered to pay £100 for repairs. The next tenant, Henry Barrington, agreed to build a mill house and to repair the mill.[63] By 1619 the mill comprised two corn mills and one fulling stock. The rent of £30 in the later 16th century rose to £40 a year in 1619, but fell to £20 in the 1650s and 1660s.[64] The mill seems to have been extensively repaired in 1705–6, although the mill house had been removed in 1703, but before 1736 it was demolished because it obstructed navigation.[65]

Middle mill on the Colne outside Ryegate, the king's mill belonging to Colchester castle, was recorded *c.* 1101 when Henry I granted one third of it to St. Botolph's priory. The priory retained that third until the Dissolution, when it was granted to Sir Thomas Audley.[66] It presumably escheated to the Crown on his death, and was thus reunited with the remaining two thirds of the mill. The mill descended with the other castle lands to Hope and Martha Gifford, and was conveyed to Francis Powell in 1725. It was bought by Charles Gray in 1757, and passed with the castle lands to the Round family.[67]

The mill, a corn mill, was repaired by the keeper of the castle in 1300 and *c.* 1335; further repairs were carried out in 1367, but by 1381 the mill was unoccupied and in ruins.[68] Between 1402 and 1405 Thomas Godstone built a new mill, a fulling mill perhaps with a corn mill, on the old site which he leased from the Crown.[69] In 1575 the bailiffs alleged that the mill had been used as a fulling mill for some time, but it contained a corn mill in 1593 and 1632.[70] It was a double corn and fulling mill in 1681, 1689, 1707, and *c.* 1750. John Wheeley, owner of the castle, repaired it *c.* 1690.[71] In the 19th century it was a corn mill worked by members of the Chopping family; it had an auxiliary steam engine by 1886.[72] In 1933 the millers sold out to Marriage's of East mill, who stripped out the machinery. The building was sold to the borough council the following year, and was demolished in the 1950s.[73]

North mill, on the Colne north-west of North bridge, was one of the two mills in Lexden in 1066 and 1086.[74] Hubert of St. Clare gave it to St. John's abbey between 1148 and 1154, but in 1235 the abbot quitclaimed his interest in the mill, then said to be in the suburbs of Colchester, to Hubert's successors John de Burgh and his wife Hawise de Lanvalei.[75] The mill was held of John de Burgh in 1247,[76] and later of his successors the FitzWalters. Their undertenant, Walter Galingale, gave it to his daughter Sibyl and her husband William Knapton, who in 1338 conveyed it to Sir Geoffrey le Scrope, whose descendants, barons Scrope of Masham, held it until 1493 or later.[77] The mill, a fulling mill in 1380 and 1493, was probably derelict in 1526 when it was described as an old mill; it had disappeared by 1748.[78]

Stokes mill, on the Colne at the end of Land Lane, may have been the mill belonging to St. Peter's church in 1066 and 1086. By *c.* 1225 it belonged to St. John's abbey which leased it to Nicholas son of Geoffrey Spenser for 10*s.* a year. In 1248–9 Gillian widow of Walter Baker confirmed

54 P.R.O., CP 25/2/827/2 Wm. & Mary, East.
55 E.R.O., D/DHt F1.
56 K. G. Farries, *Essex Windmills*, iii. 93; *E.R.* lix. 198–9; E.R.O., D/DHt F1; ibid. Acc. C47, CPL 148; *V.C.H. Essex*, ii. 446.
57 Benham, *Essex Water Mills*, 98.
58 E.R.O., D/DIc T43; D/B 5 Cr25, rot. 14.
59 E.R.O., D/B 5 Cr26, rot. 16d.; Cr28, rot. 29; Cr57, rot. 3d.; D/B 5 R2, f. 73; Britnell, *Growth and Decline*, 198.
60 E.R.O., D/B 5 R2, ff. 188 and v., 218v.
61 B.L. Stowe MS. 829, f. 12; Morant, *Colch.* App. p. 1.
62 E.R.O., D/B 5 R7, ff. 236v.–237, 261v., 270 and v., 274; D/B 5 Gb1, 17 Mar. 1578.
63 Ibid. D/B 5 Gb1, 25 May 1579, 18 July 1598; D/B 5 Gb2, f. 78v.
64 Ibid. D/B 5 Gb1, 17 Mar. 1578, 5 Dec. 1595; Gb2, ff. 45, 175v.; Gb5, f. 98; D/B 5 Aa1/19; Aa1/25.
65 Ibid. D/B 5 Ab1/25; D/B 5 Gb6, p. 283; D/Y 2/1, p. 107; Morant, *Colch.* 129.
66 *Reg. Regum Anglo-Norm.* ii, p. 18; P.R.O., E 318/2/57; ibid. SC 6/Hen. VIII/898, m. 5d.
67 E.R.O., D/DRe T8, 9, 12.
68 *Cal. Close*, 1296–1302, 250; 1333–7, 521; 1364–8, 333; *Cal. Inq. Misc.* ii, p. 346; iv, p. 80.
69 *Cal. Pat.* 1401–5, 189; E.R.O., D/B 5, Cr35, rot. 6d.
70 E.R.O., D/B 5 R7, f. 270v.; D/B 5 Sb2/5, f. 163; P.R.O., E 134/8 Chas. I Mic./18.
71 E.R.O., D/DRe E5; D/DRe L5; D/DRe T7, 8.
72 Benham, *Essex Water Mills*, 93; *Kelly's Dir. Essex* (1886 and later edns.).
73 Benham, *Essex Water Mills*, 93–4; E.R.O., Boro. Mun., Parks and Bathing Places Cttee. Mins. 1929–36, p. 125; *E.C.S.* 8 Apr. 1949; J. Marriage, *Colch. A Pictorial Hist.* no. 63.
74 E.R.O., D/B 5 R1, ff. 60v.–61; *V.C.H. Essex*, i. 432; *Reg. Regum Anglo-Norm.* iii, no. 236.
75 *Feet of F. Essex*, i. 107; *Colch. Cart.* ii. 599.
76 P.R.O., JUST 1/231, rot. 33.
77 Ibid. KB 27/366, Rex rot. 30, m. [4]d.; *Feet of F. Essex*, iii. 45; *Cal. Inq. p.m. Hen. VII*, i, p. 396.
78 E.R.O., D/B 5 Cr20, rott. 21, 25d.; Cr26, rot. 51; Cr96, rot. 19; *Cal. Inq. p.m. Hen. VII*, i, p. 396; Morant, *Colch.* 111.

it to the abbey.[79] In 1422–3 it was a fulling mill, although the stocks were so badly repaired that they tore cloth.[80] At the Dissolution the mill, still a fulling mill, passed to the Crown.[81] It was leased as a fulling mill in 1560, and in 1569 was owned by John Maynard, who also held East mill.[82] It had been demolished by 1610.[83]

WINDMILLS. A mill mound in Monksdown was recorded in 1325, and an old one at Old Heath in 1341 and possibly in 1349.[84] Three windmills belonging to the burgesses William Reyne, John Ford, and Henry Bosse, presumably recently built, were recorded in 1372, but one was apparently demolished after 1373 and another after 1414.[85] A windmill in Head ward, perhaps near Lexden Road, was recorded in 1451, and Windmill field by Harwich Road in St. James's parish, site of the later St. Anne's or East windmill, may already have been called Mill field in 1542.[86] Henry Barrington's, later Scarlett's, mill was built *c.* 1585, and there was a mill mound between Maldon Road and Butt Road in the 1590s.[87] There was a windmill in St. Mary Magdalen's parish in 1599, and a field south of Magdalen Street was still called Windmill field in 1631. In 1632 John Lucas complained that three recently built windmills took trade from Cannock mill.[88] All the windmills were burnt by parliamentary troops during the siege of 1648,[89] but were quickly rebuilt. In 1702 there were seven windmills on the borough's half year land south-west and south-east of the walls, and 11 or 12 windmills have been identified in Colchester in the 18th and 19th centuries.[90]

There were two windmills on the north side of Lexden Road. The *First mill*, near the waterworks, existed by 1678, but was described as lately built when it was conveyed to John Boggis in 1724.[91] In 1754 it had two pairs of stones and three boulting mills. The mill was rebuilt shortly before 1807 as a post mill with a large roundhouse. It seems to have been demolished *c.* 1819. The *Second mill*, to the west, was conveyed to Thomas Talcott in 1681. From 1749 to 1756 it was owned by a distiller, who may have used it and its malting house for distilling.[92] In 1785 the mill was described as modern built. Four millers went bankrupt in the later 18th century and the early 19th, and the mill seems to have been demolished *c.* 1824.

Butt mill, on the west side of Butt Road, was built between 1660 and 1662 when it was conveyed to John Gibson, miller of Middle mill. The mill was rebuilt soon after 1779, and again, after a fire, in 1787. In 1824 it was a post mill with three pairs of stones over a brick roundhouse. It was repaired after storm damage in 1852 but was demolished in 1881.

A mill in *Mersea Road*, was first recorded in 1726. In 1813 the post mill was replaced by a brick tower mill which in 1818 had two pairs of stones. In 1848 the mill was a self-turning one. It was closed and the machinery sold in 1859.

Two windmills, recorded from 1632, stood close together on the site of *Military Road*, one at Golden Acre, the other in Golden at the Hill, Golden Knapp hill, or Golden Noble hill.[93] The western or middle mill in St. Giles's parish was recorded again in 1666 and passed through a number of hands in the later 17th century and the 18th.[94] In 1795 it was a new post mill; by 1815 it had two pairs of stones and could be adapted to run a third pair, but in 1830 it still used only two pairs. In 1682 the eastern mill, in St. Botolph's parish, had been held by George Harrington, who was a Colchester miller in 1652. Like the middle mill it passed through a number of hands in the 18th century.[95] In 1812 it was a post mill with a roundhouse, and in 1820 it had two pairs of stones. From 1835 or earlier the two mills were held by the same millers who *c.* 1839 moved the eastern mill to a site in St. Giles's parish just north of the middle mill, adding a roundhouse of three storeys in the rebuilding. Both mills were demolished in 1862.

Distillery mill which existed by 1777 and probably by 1748, seems to have been built by the Rootseys, owners of Hull mill. It was held by successive owners of the water mill until its closure *c.* 1895. It was a brick tower mill by 1786. In 1843 it was six storeys high and had four pairs of stones, presumably three for barley and maize and one for wheat as in the later 19th century.

St. Anne's mill or East windmill in St. James's parish was one of the windmills of which John Lucas complained in 1632. It was recorded again in 1653.[96] In 1759 it was bought by Bezaliel Angier in whose family it remained for the rest of its working life. It was rebuilt as a brick tower mill after a fire in 1767. In 1832 it worked two pairs of stones, although there was room and power for a third. It ceased working *c.* 1864.

The mill later called *Scarlett's mill* was built *c.* 1585.[97] In 1656 it was a wind oil mill belonging to Henry Barrington, and it was presumably the windmill north of his house in 1648.[98] It was probably still an oil mill *c.* 1673, but by 1686, when Abraham Barrington sold it to John Scarlett, it was a wind corn mill.[99] It was recorded throughout the 18th century, but seems to have

79 B.L. Arundel MS. 145, ff. 11, 19; *Colch. Cart.* ii. 468, 599–600.
80 E.R.O., D/B 5 Cr43, rot. 25d.
81 P.R.O., SC 6/Hen. VIII/976, mm. 11d.–12.
82 Ibid. C 66/951, m. 30; C 142/151, no. 55.
83 Speed, *Colch. Map.*
84 E.R.O., St. John's abbey ledger bk. ff. 60v.–62, 106 and v.; ibid. D/B 5 R2, ff. 45v., 139.
85 Britnell, *Growth and Decline*, 87–8, 197–8.
86 E.R.O., D/B 5 Cr64, rot. 6; P.R.O., E 318/2/57; B.L. Add. Roll 25791.
87 P.R.O., E 134/8 Chas. I Mic./18; B.L. Stowe MS. 832, ff. 24, 43.
88 B.L. Stowe MS. 832, f. 39; E.R.O., D/DU 487; P.R.O., E 134/8 Chas. I Mic./18.
89 Morant, *Colch.* 65.
90 E.R.O., D/B 5 Sr67, rot. 7; Farries, *Essex Windmills*, iii. 88–99.
91 Rest of section based on Farries, *Essex Windmills*, iii. 88–99, and the documents there cited.
92 E.R.O., Acc. C47, CPL 969.
93 P.R.O., E 134/8 Chas. I Mic./18.
94 E.R.O., D/DCm T87, 88; D/DHt T72/87, 89–91, 94–5; D/DHt T337/16.
95 Ibid. D/Q 30/1/10; Q/SR 352/131; D/DHt T72/108, 111.
96 P.R.O., E 134/8 Chas. I Mic./18; E.R.O., D/DCm T65.
97 P.R.O., E 134/8 Chas. I Mic./18.
98 E.R.O., D/Q 30/1/4, no. 2; above, fig. 8.
99 E.R.O., D/B 5 Sb2/9, f. 217; D/Q 30/1/4, no. 12.

been dismantled in 1800; it may have been moved to a site on or near Magdalen green, where a windmill was recorded between 1801 and 1813, before being moved again, to Shrub End, where it worked until 1871. Its roundhouse survived until 1973.

There was a windmill in *Mile End* in 1730,[1] and two were recorded on Mile End heath in 1777. The eastern one, on the south side of the later Mill Road, seems to have been built *c.* 1764 and to have worked until the early 1880s. The western one had gone by 1806 and probably by 1791. A windmill of unknown type was recorded north of the Colne *c.* 1724.

A post mill at Old Heath operated from 1774 to 1780, when it may have been moved to a site in Greenstead opposite the Hythe, where a postmill had been built by 1784. The Greenstead mill was demolished in 1903 or 1904.[2] Another windmill was associated with East mill in 1795; it was probably built over the water mill. There was a short-lived post mill near Cannock mill in the early 1840s, owned by the miller of Cannock mill. Clubb's mill, a rag mill in North Station Road,[3] was recorded in 1832. It ceased work in 1852 after storm damage.

FISHERY

THE Colne oyster fishery, 'the most valuable asset of the borough',[4] has been the source as much of bad neighbourliness and litigation as of profit to Colchester. The charter of 1189 confirmed the fishery to the borough, but did not define the location of 'Westness', its seaward boundary. Conflicting rights were held by neighbouring lords: in 1119 Henry I had granted to St. John's abbey the fisheries and mills in Brightlingsea manor, and between 1174 and 1187 Henry II confirmed to St. Osyth's priory the manor of Chich St. Osyth with extensive rights, including those over the foreshore.[5]

In 1362, when Lionel of Bradenham claimed the creeks of the Colne in his manor of Langenhoe, Colchester was able, with some plausibility in law, to join Alresford, Brightlingsea, St. Osyth, Fingringhoe, East and West Mersea, Peldon, Pete, Wigborough, Salcott, Tollesbury, and Goldhanger, in asserting that they had had a common fishery in the river and its creeks from time immemorial.[6] With similar plausibility Colchester at the same time obtained a confirmation of its charter, a grant which may well have helped to send Brightlingsea into the arms of the privilege-conscious Cinque Ports about that time.[7]

The charter of 1447 did not mention the fishery, although it defined the liberty as including the area from North bridge to 'Westness'; indeed, the fishery had a few days earlier been granted to John de Vere, earl of Oxford, lord of Wivenhoe. The rival claims were settled in Colchester's favour before a jury of 24 'indifferent persons', the witnesses on both sides accusing each other of lying under oath, but Westness remained indeterminate,[8] and the tradition of a free fishery which Colchester had usurped persisted in the Colneside communities.

The Act of 1562 for the maintenance of the navy which had allowed the free sale and export of fish,[9] had the unintentional result of greatly increasing the number of oyster dredgers, some of whom sold their oysters away from Colchester. The borough market and its poor suffered, and the stock of oysters was over-fished to the point of destruction. In 1566 when the borough assembly found it necessary to make constitutions for it, the oyster fishery's chief role was to provide a cheap and abundant food supply for the borough poor, 'which by that provision were chiefly relieved'. To that end no oysters were to be sold anywhere except at the quayside market at the Hythe; dredgermen from the Colneside communities who sold either to 'foreigners' or in their own villages became liable to imprisonment and the forfeiture of their boats.[10]

A routine was formulated which was to continue for 400 years. A close season was declared for the breeding period, from Easter to Holy Rood day (14 Sept.). In August each year those wishing to dredge were to apply to the bailiffs for a licence, and a register of those so licensed was to be kept. In addition, however, the lords of some manors on the lower Colne and the lord warden of the Cinque Ports retained the right to nominate a small number of summer dredgers from among the poorest licensed oystermen of their parishes. The Hythe remained the sole legal oyster market and any forestaller buying oysters to ship out of the Colne was liable to lose both his cargo and his vessel, except that if the bailiffs were satisfied that Colchester was fully supplied, the surplus might be sent elsewhere.[11]

There was an immediate protest from the fishermen of the parishes along the lower Colne, who claimed that the bailiffs had interfered with their dredging and fishing.[12] When the matter came before the county assizes at Brentwood in 1567 the court concentrated on conservation. The fishermen were to supply the Colchester markets as largely and plentifully as they had in the previous 20 years. Though licences for summer dredging were to be granted as formerly, the close season was emphasized. No boat was to carry more than two persons or tow more than

1 E.R.O., D/DC 18/32.
2 E.R.O., Boro. Mun., Spec. Cttee. Mins. 1902–12, 16 Feb. 1904; above, pl. facing p. 216.
3 *E.A.T.* N.S. x. 53.
4 E.R.O., Acc. C133, Laver's draft memo. to town council.
5 *Colch. Cart.* i. 21; *Cal. Chart. R.* ii. 332–3; *Colch. Charters*, 2.
6 *Cal. Pat.* 1361–4, 283; above, Medieval Colch. (Econ.).
7 *Colch. Charters*, 10–14, where the charter is misdated 1364; *V.C.H. Essex*, ii. 267.
8 *Cal. Pat.* 1446–52, 33; *Colch. Charters*, 36–9.
9 5 Eliz. I, c. 5.
10 E.R.O., D/B 5 R5, f. 111.
11 Ibid.; ibid. D/Y 2/3, pp. 30–41.
12 *V.C.H. Essex*, ii. 431; *Cal. Assize Rec. Essex, Eliz. I*, p. 54.

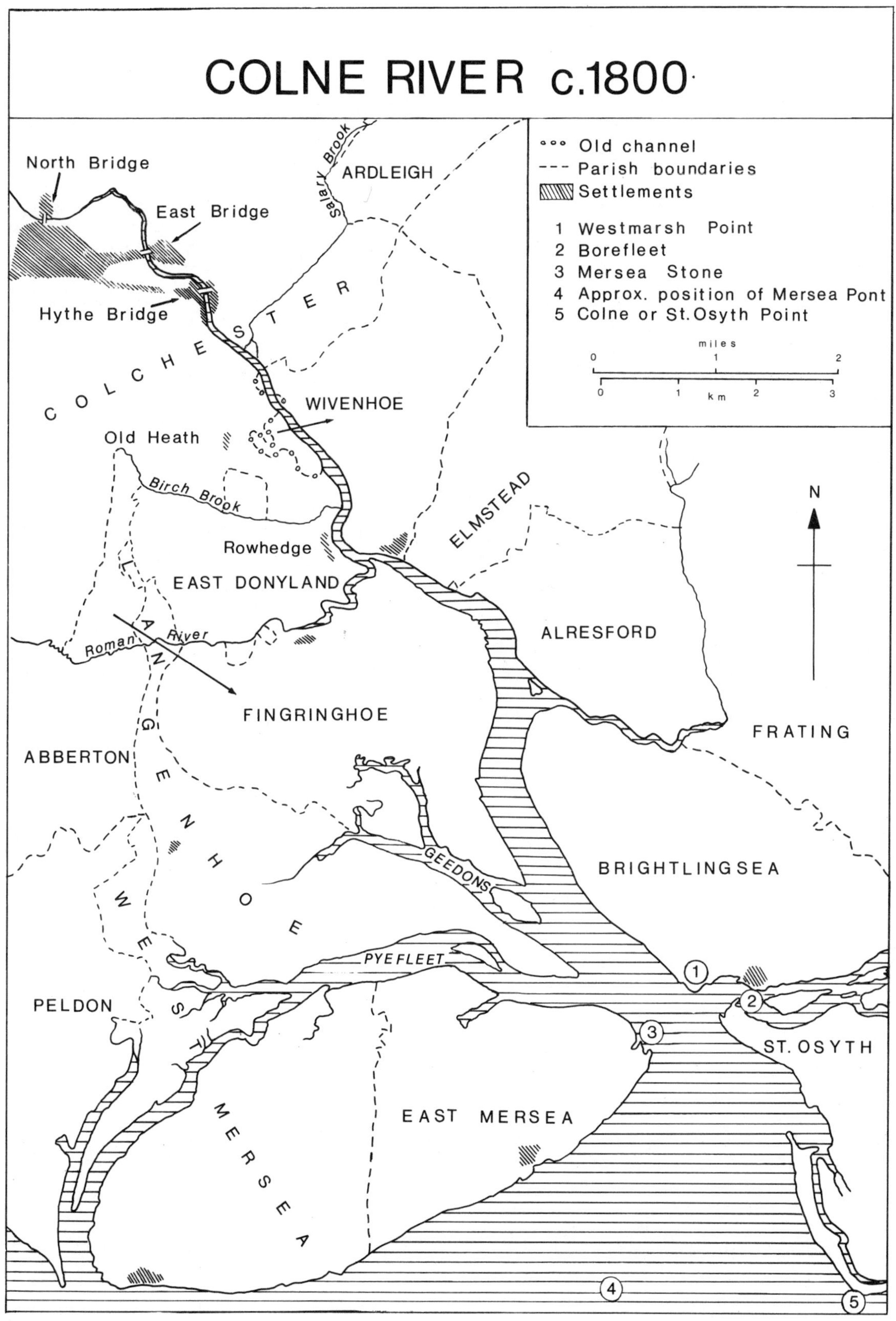
COLNE RIVER c.1800
Old channel
Parish boundaries
Settlements
1 Westmarsh Point
2 Borefleet
3 Mersea Stone
4 Approx. position of Mersea Pont
5 Colne or St.Osyth Point
miles
0 1 2
0 1 km 2 3
N
North Bridge
East Bridge
Hythe Bridge
Salary Brook
ARDLEIGH
COLCHESTER
WIVENHOE
Old Heath
Birch Brook
Rowhedge
EAST DONYLAND
ELMSTEAD
ALRESFORD
Roman River
LANGENHOE
FINGRINGHOE
ABBERTON
FRATING
GEEDONS
BRIGHTLINGSEA
PYEFLEET
PELDON
WEST MERSEA
ST. OSYTH
EAST MERSEA

Fig. 23

one dredge of the existing standard size. Summer dredgers could only go one in a boat, with a mast and sail not more than 7 ft. high. Fishermen were to sort the contents of their dredges at once and put back all brood and immature oysters. The boats which the borough had impounded were to be immediately returned; a man must not be deprived of his means of livelihood.[13] The regulations, however, were of little avail when the Act of 1564 left the door open for exporters, and by not affirming Colchester's rights and powers the justices had only publicized the uncertainty of those privileges.

In 1629, shortly before the 'oyster famine' of the 1630s, which was felt most acutely in London,[14] Colchester revived its policy of the 1560s, provoking the 'poor fishermen of Essex' to petition the Admiralty.[15] The fishermen claimed, as did Roger Townsend of Wivenhoe in his contemporaneous and related suit against the borough,[16] that Westness was at the point where the borough boundary crossed the Colne; if that were proved, Colchester would lose all the productive part of the fishery.

The 1635 charter confirmed Colchester's right to admiralty jurisdiction, but did not specify the location of Westness.[17] Nevertheless, the first action of the newly constituted assembly in July 1635 was to arrest every man and boat found summer dredging in the Colne without the mayor's licence.[18]

In 1638 a government inquiry, under Sir Henry Marten, into the extraordinary dearth of oysters in Essex and Kent found that, as a result of the insatiable demands of the export trade, Colchester and Maldon were both plundering the prime spatting ground at Mersea 'Pont' off East Mersea. Fishermen were removing cultch to private layings and 'grounds' where the spat and brood in it often died. Marten accordingly proposed to reduce exports to not more than 1,000 half-barrels a week.[19] Colchester had already taken some action with a flurry of bans and embargoes in 1633 and 1634, but in 1636 the Privy Council decreed that those applied only to foreigners, and that it was lawful to export oysters in English ships.[20] In 1638 or 1639 the Privy Council, then taking action, reprimanded the new mayor for granting too many summer licences, and transferred enforcement to the High Admiral and his vice-admirals.[21] Only the interruption of the Civil War saved the fishery from extinction.

A new complication was introduced by developments at Brightlingsea, whose sea-borne trade had collapsed totally by 1610. Its later, modest, wealth was based almost entirely on shrewd exploitation of the oyster industry, in a relationship with Colchester's fishery which might be termed symbiotic but which the borough increasingly regarded as parasitic.[22]

In the political turmoil of the Interregnum the borough found it even more difficult to control the fishery. Fishermen were regularly, but ineffectively, prosecuted at the court at the East Mersea blockhouse for dredging out of season, using a 'smack-sail' instead of a rowing boat, staking off exclusive beds in the creeks, selling brood from the river to outsiders, selling fattened oysters from the layings by the ship-load to Flemings, threatening the water bailiff and even the mayor. The fishermen simply replied that their alleged offences had been committed outside the jurisdiction of the borough's court. Not only was the borough unable to resist technical development, it was soon to find itself threatened by men of wealth and national influence.[23] In the 1650s private layings began to prosper and proliferate in the creeks of the Colne, largely in the hands of 'yeomen' dredgers, supported by manorial lords who rejected Colchester's claims to exclusive rights over their foreshores. At Brightlingsea the new lord, George Thompson, began in the 1650s by prohibiting pits on the saltings, went on to charge rent for them, and then in the 1670s to grant layings in Borefleet (Brightlingsea Creek) as copyholds.[24] By 1693 his heir had granted ten 1,000-year leases.[25] Dredgermen bought their licences, which Colchester apparently could not refuse, dredged young oysters from the river, fattened them on their own layings, and sold them at a profit in which Colchester had no share. Dredgermen actually resident in Colchester were at a disadvantage compared with Brightlingsea and Mersea men, so that from the mid 17th century onwards Colchester struggled to find a mechanism to control and profit from a fishery of which it had no working experience.[26]

In 1671 James duke of York, lord High Admiral and lord warden of the Cinque Ports, claimed the whole fishery. The borough responded by leasing the valuable Pyefleet for 14 years to its recorder, Sir John Shaw, on condition that he defend the fishery.[27] James's claim apparently lapsed with his removal from office in 1673, but in 1674 Charles II confirmed a lease he had granted to two speculators of the lower Colne and its oyster fishery.[28]

The lease apparently did not take effect, but it had shown that the borough's title to the fishery was uncertain,[29] and neighbouring landowners were to exploit the uncertainty. In 1683 the borough leased the whole fishery, apparently for the first time, to two Mersea oyster dredgers for £50 a year, the borough to bear any legal costs of defending it.[30] In 1700 the fishery was leased, for a £50 fine and a 1*s.* a year rent, to two

[13] E.R.O., Boro. Mun., Acc. C1, Ct. Entry Bk. 1571–92, ff. 145v., 146 and v.

[14] *Cal. S.P. Dom.* 1634–5, 359.

[15] E.R.O., Boro. Mun., Acc. C1, Town Clerk's Dept., Precedents/Ref. Bk. 1895–1901, 122–4. (From S.P. Dom. 20 June, 1629.)

[16] Above, Boundaries.

[17] *Colch. Charters*, 99–101.

[18] E.R.O., D/B 5 Gb3, f. 155v.

[19] *Cal. S.P. Dom.* 1637–8, 557.

[20] Ibid. 1634–5, 462; 1636–7, 206; 1637, 14.

[21] Ibid. 1638–9, 32–3, 38.

[22] E. P. Dickin, *Hist. Brightlingsea* (1939), 165–9; *Cal. Pat.* 1569–72, 15.

[23] E.R.O., Boro. Mun., Acc. C1, Fishery Papers, temp. Hen. VII–1718, papers for 1650s.

[24] Ibid. D/DDi M2; D/DU 210/1, 2.

[25] Ibid. D/DU 210/20–8.

[26] E.R.O., Boro. Mun., Acc. C1, Fishery Papers, temp. Hen. VII–1718.

[27] Ibid. D/B 5 Gb5, ff. 51–2.

[28] Dickin, *Hist. Brightlingsea*, 125.

[29] E.R.O., D/B 5 Gb5, ff. 152v., 201, 203.

[30] Ibid. Boro. Mun., Acc. C4, Pulleyne *v.* Colne Fishery Co., 1902, defendant's bk. of docs.; *V.C.H. Essex*, ii. 431.

entrepreneurs, the aldermen John Potter and Ralph Creffield, who were to defend it in the courts if necessary. The lease, which defined Westness as 'in, beyond, or near Chich St. Osyth', was extended to 1736, although the town had to bear some of the legal expenses.[31]

Despite the full co-operation of the borough and the astute impanelling of up-river juries to deal with offenders from Brightlingsea and St. Osyth and *vice versa*, Potter and Creffield had difficulty forcing some of the more prosperous Brightlingsea dredgers to comply with the regulations.[32] In 1703 they successfully prosecuted a group of interlopers, from the rivers Crouch and Roach as well as Brightlingsea parish,[33] but they were suspected of supporting attempts by West Mersea, Tollesbury, and Salcott dredgermen to fish freely in Borefleet, to which Colchester had already advanced unsuccessful claims in 1557 and 1659.[34] Isaac Brand of Brightlingsea vindicated his manorial rights so fully that Borefleet's position outside the fishery was never questioned again.[35] After an action lasting from 1724 to 1728,[36] Marmaduke Rawdon of Fingringhoe obtained an injunction against Potter and Creffield and their licensees, and the Geedons were judged to be outside the fishery. The claim advanced in 1724 by James Waldegrave, Lord Waldegrave, of Langenhoe to Pyefleet, an essential element of the fishery, was a more serious threat, but it seems to have been abandoned.[37] In 1731 the borough bought out both Creffield and Potter's successor John Colt and so resumed the fishery.[38]

After the lapse of the charter in 1741 the fishery degenerated into such a free-for-all that all parties agreed to seek an Act of Parliament.[39] The Act of 1758 vested the powers to issue licences, to appoint a water bailiff or serjeant, and to hold the court at the blockhouse in three J.P.s from the Colchester division of the county; it also identified Westness with St. Osyth point.[40] Under the Act a court of conservancy composed of nine J.P.s and a jury of 12 dredgermen at once agreed regulations which formed the basis of all later rules for the fishery. When the new charter was granted in 1763 the borough formally adopted the system and rules. The number of licensed dredgers, residents in the eight riverside parishes who had served a seven-year apprenticeship, increased from 34 in 1758 to 69 in 1764, although totals varied widely from year to year. Colchester itself was omitted from the list of parishes, and, although 8 of the 30 dredgers licensed in 1736 were from the borough, after 1758 there was none.[41]

In 1787 George Waldegrave, Earl Waldegrave, and Sir Robert Smyth of Berechurch Hall again claimed Pyefleet, but without the support of the dredgermen their claim failed.[42]

During the Napoleonic Wars many Colne fishermen joined the Fencibles, and that experience of working together may have contributed to their decision in 1807 to form themselves into a single company to control and work the fishery. Although it involved the borough's virtual abdication of its rights, the company was formed under the chairmanship of two Colchester aldermen, the elder and younger Thomas Hedge.[43] The elder Hedge had acquired a farm in Brightlingsea adjacent to the wintering beds, and his tenant at another farm there, which straddled the road from the village to the waterside, was John Noble, the foreman of the fishery jury.[44] The number of dredgermen, or 'freemen of the river', rose from 73 in 1807 to 413 in 1866. The company, with its annual share-out of the profits, inspired a blind loyalty, became the foundation for a whole further fishery (stowboating) and yachting economy, and evolved its own traditions and even mythology, but it had no basis in law.[45] In 1821 the borough, receiving *c.* £2 2*s.* for each licence, found the new system 'sufficient for every liberal purpose',[46] but after the Municipal Reform Act of 1835 the new corporation with its new-found financial competence was not so sure. It regretted what it saw as the loss of its fishery, and with the formation of a watchdog fishery committee in 1836 it took the first step on the way to recovery.[47]

In 1836 and 1841 and between 1861 and 1864 the corporation, aware that its loss of control was due partly to its ignorance of oyster-dredging, undertook investigations into the fishery.[48] Although the communal loyalty and virtual self-policing of the dredgermen had merit, the fishery company was being run as a large benefit club. The powers of the jury, particularly of the two foremen who were working dredgermen, would have been dictatorial but for the annual elections. The foremen prescribed times and conditions of work; their officers handled all buying and selling, and they could borrow up to £5,000 on the security of the fishery. They allowed licensed dredgers to take a turn at 'working their stint' in the river, and when the annual accounts had been agreed they ordered a share-out to all working members, retired members, and their widows. Apprenticeship rules

31 E.R.O., D/B 5 Gb6, pp. 213, 215–16, 280; *V.C.H. Essex*, ii. 431.

32 E.R.O., Boro. Mun., Acc. C10, box 22: Colne Fishery Co. *v.* Chapman et al. 1895, plaintiff's bk. of docs. 163.

33 Ibid. Acc. C4, Pulleyne *v.* Colne Fishery Co. 1902, defendant's bk. of docs. 121–3.

34 Ibid. D/B 5 Cr124, rot. 10; ibid. Boro. Mun., Acc. C1, Fishery Papers, temp. Hen. VII–1718.

35 Ibid. D/DU 210/20–8.

36 Ibid. Boro. Mun. Acc. C10, box 21, bdle. C, 35.

37 Ibid. D/B 5 Gb7, pp. 193, 196, 287; ibid. Acc. C1, Lord Waldegrave *v.* Mayor and Corp. (Fishery), bound fols. (a) bill (b) depositions; *V.C.H. Essex*, ii. 430.

38 Ibid. D/B 5 Gb7, p. 280; ibid. Acc. C47, CPL 1227.

39 *V.C.H. Essex*, ii. 432–3.

40 31 Geo. II, c. 71.

41 E.R.O., D/Y 2/1, p. 141; ibid. Boro. Mun., Acc. C1, Colne Fishery Co. Min. Bk. 1758–63; Colne Fishery Co. Oath & Min. Bk. 1764–87.

42 Ibid. D/B 5 Gb8, pp. 153, 156, 160, 175, 180.

43 Ibid. Boro. Mun., Acc. C1, Colne Oyster Fishery Bk. 1788–1809, pp. 113, 118, 128, 146, 150, 155.

44 Ibid. pp. 104–5, 113, 119, 125; ibid. D/DY, p. 2.

45 Ibid. Boro. Mun., Acc. C1, Colne Oyster Fishery Bk. 1788–1809; Acc. C4, Colne Oyster Fishery Bk. 1810–40, 1841–70, *passim*; *V.C.H. Essex*, ii. 433.

46 E.R.O., Acc. C210, J. B. Harvey Colln. iv, p. 45.

47 Ibid. Acc. C4, Fishery Cttee. Min. Bk. 1836.

48 Ibid. Fishery Cttee. Min. Bk. 1836, 16 May, 10 June 1836; 1861–9, 14 Nov. 1861; ibid. abortive bill of 1864; ibid. Boro. Mun., Council Min. Bk. 1839–45, pp. 98–105; 1858–63, rep. of special cttee. 27 Oct. 1862.

made membership of the company all but hereditary; it was a fishery run for fishermen.[49] To the borough the fishery was an ill-run business but a potential goldmine which could almost replace the rates. To the dredgermen the Colne estuary was common water from which the wealthier among them could replenish their private layings, and which guaranteed labouring part-time dredgers a living in the worst of years.[50]

When, in 1841, a dispute began over the destruction of an oyster bed by a ship running aground, the fishery company was happy for the corporation to take on the expense of prosecution. The case, which dragged on until 1848, established that the Colne was a fishery as well as a navigable waterway, and that the corporation was within its rights to prosecute.[51] The company found that it had connived in proving the fishery to be the property of the borough.

An attempt in 1862 by alderman C. H. Hawkins to reform the fishery by Act of Parliament, replacing the system of work sharing by day-wage labour, introducing capital investment, and levying a royalty to the corporation, met with opposition from the dredgermen.[52] That opposition was weakened, however, by their poor financial position after a series of bad spat-falls in the 1850s and early 1860s,[53] and by a division within their ranks between the 'merchants' who had their own private oyster businesses and the 'crews'. The corporation's astute insistence that in future 12 dredgermen elected by the general body must be associated with the jury led in 1867 to an unintended closing of ranks.[54]

The decision of 1848 had given the corporation the confidence to provoke a showdown with the dredgermen by refusing to grant some regular fishermen their annual licences. In 1864 one brought an action against the corporation to test whether it could refuse to grant a licence to a fully qualified dredgerman from one of the eight Colneside parishes. Judgement in 1867, and on appeal in 1868, was for the corporation.[55]

The company was advised throughout that crucial period by its clerk, the Colchester solicitor H. S. Goody, who, realising that the company had no existence in law, persuaded the dredgermen to accept in the Colne Fishery Act of 1870 the best terms he could secure.[56] Under that Act[57] Colchester recovered the fishery; the company became a legal entity, but it re-entered the fishery only on the corporation's terms, paying a rent of £500 a year and a quarter of any profits over £1,500 as well as bearing all the industry's expenses. Control was in the hands of a Joint Fishery Board composed of six men from the corporation and six from the company, but the election of the latter was so organized that the corporation could manipulate the dredgermen's choice. The fishery did, however, remain the preserve of the eight Colneside parishes, and the annual share-out or dividend continued. In those circumstances it became the undeclared policy of the company to render the fishery as labour-intensive as possible while keeping profits below £1,500. Balance sheets contained little detail, and meetings of the Joint Fishery Board were few.[58]

The fishery was revolutionized by Henry Laver, who joined the board in 1886 and quickly made himself an expert in oyster fishing.[59] Reports in 1888 and 1889 were scathing on the state and running of the fishery and on the accounting policy of the company, and between then and 1892 Laver put into effect his 'Forward Policy'.[60] Despite opposition from the company, the foremen were brought under the control of monthly meetings of the board, a steam dredger was acquired, a detachment of water police formed, and a professional manager, E. Newman, appointed.[61] For some years Newman was subjected to obstruction and contumely,[62] but he gradually won the liking and respect of the dredgermen, as Laver never did. During their joint reign, from 1892 to Newman's death in 1911,[63] a succession of hard-fought lawsuits put the extent of the fishery on a clear legal basis for the first time,[64] likely grounds of dispute were obviated by shrewd and timely purchases, and a start was made on identifying the special potential of different parts of the river.[65]

As a result of Newman's supervision the total sale of oysters rose from 675,000 in the 1893–4 season to 2.7 million in 1894–5, and even exceeded 3 million in 1897–8, but the success could not be maintained.[66] Already in 1880 the pouring of untreated or inadequately treated sewage into rivers had started a typhoid scare, and in 1895 a national inquiry showed an extraordinary coincidence of sewer outfalls and oyster beds.[67] The typhoid outbreak that year was linked to oysters

49 Ibid. D/DEl B31.
50 Ibid. Acc. C210, J. B. Harvey Colln. iv, p. 57.
51 Ibid. Boro. Mun., Acc. C4, boxes 3, 6, 11, 12, 15.
52 Ibid. Fishery Cttee. Min. Bk. 1861–9, 10 Feb. 1862; 23 Jan. 1863.
53 James Murie, *Rep. on the Sea Fisheries of the Thames Estuary* (1903), 185: copy in E.R.O. Colch.
54 E.R.O., Boro. Mun., Acc. C4, Fishery Cttee. Min. Bk. 1861–9, 10 Oct. 1867; 9 Jan. 1868.
55 Ibid. Boro. Mun. Acc. C24, boxes 4–6, 13; *V.C.H. Essex*, ii. 434.
56 E.R.O., Boro. Mun., Acc. C4, Fishery Cttee. Min. Bk. 1861–9, *passim*; *Essex Tel.* 19 Jan. 1890.
57 33 & 34 Vic. c. 85.
58 E.R.O., Boro. Mun., Acc. C10, box 7; Acc. C4, Colne Fishery Board Memoranda/White Bk. 1886–1915, 62.
59 Ibid. Acc. C4, Colne Fishery Board White Bk. *passim*; ibid. Black Bk. *passim*.
60 Ibid. Boro. Mun., Acc. C10, box 1, C. A. Russell's evidence in Colne Fishery Co. *v.* Pulleyne (1904), proc. day 8, p. 16; Acc. C133, Newman's Rep. to Fishery Bd. 1888; ibid. Short's Rep. to Bd. 1889 on Fishery Co.'s accts. 1881–9.
61 Ibid. Acc. C4, Colne Fishery Co. Min. Bk. 1871–91, 225, 318, 355, 375, 409; Colne Fishery Bd. Min. Bk. 1891–6, 8–11, 57.
62 Ibid. Colne Fishery Bd. Min. Bk. 1891–6, 63; 1896–1900, 54.
63 *E.C.S.* 1 July 1911.
64 E.R.O., Acc. C10, boxes 1–24, *passim*; ibid. Acc. C4, Colch. Fishery Co. *v.* Pulleyne (1904); ibid. Boro. Mun. Acc. C4, Colne Fishery Cttee. Min. Bk. 1896–1918, 18 Feb., 17 June 1913.
65 Ibid. Acc. C4, Colne Fishery Co. Min. Bk. 1871–91, 373–5, 416–19; 1896–1900, 82, 122–4.
66 Ibid. Colne Fishery Bd. Min. Bk. 1894–1900; 1900–21; 1928; 1930–64: manager's end of season returns.
67 *24th Rep. Local Govt. Bd.: Rep. of Medical Officer, 1894–5, on Oyster Culture in Relation to Disease* [C. 8214], pp. xi–xii, 2, 38–41, H.C. (1896), xxxvii.

from Brightlingsea Creek, outside the fishery, but demand was affected.[68]

A more persistent threat came from the slipper limpet, accidentally imported with the bluepoint oyster from the U.S.A.[69] Restrictions on cultivation imposed by the navy during the First World War allowed the pest to proliferate while conditions for the oysters deteriorated. Sales in 1920 were less than half those of 1898, and in 1930 only a seventh. In 1920, while the Ministry of Agriculture and Fisheries removed 2,000 tons of slipper limpets from the mouth of the fishery, a new mystery killer spread from the sea into the river, destroying between 20 per cent and 50 per cent of the oysters on the beds.[70] As a government inquiry decided that the new disease was unrelated to the dumping of over 1,000 tons of TNT off the coast, no compensation was paid.[71] Sales were also hampered by an increase in freight charges after the railway strike of 1919 and by a spell of unseasonably hot weather which reduced demand. The once lucrative Continental market was undermined by an unfavourable exchange rate and the reduction in the ferry service from Tilbury to Ostend.[72]

The industry enjoyed a semblance of prosperity in the 1920s and 1930s, but the great tide of 1953 smothered the layings with mud.[73] The company went to the work of rescue and rehabilitation with some success, but by 1959 a large deficit was predicted.[74] The hard winter of 1963 killed 85 per cent of the prime stock in Pyefleet and 90 per cent in the Colne, and returns were so unpromising that the corporation would not provide a loan to tide the company over. The Geedons, for which the borough had fought so hard and often, were leased to the Essex Naturalist Trust, and when it was decided that the expense of an annual meeting in 1964 was not justified, the Colne fishery was virtually at an end.[75] Most of the oysters sold in Colchester in the 1980s were imported.

MARKETS AND FAIRS

MARKETS. Colchester presumably had a market from the late Anglo-Saxon period or earlier. The charter of 1189 directed that the markets should remain as they had been when they were confirmed by the justices in eyre under Henry II.[76] No market days were specified in later charters, but in 1285 the market days were Wednesdays and Saturdays;[77] in 1380 there was a complaint about an unlicensed Thursday market. Nevertheless, the claim made in 1452 and 1464 that the common market was held every day is supported by references to the sale of goods on Monday, Tuesday, Wednesday, Thursday, Saturday, and Sunday during the 14th and 15th centuries.[78] Not all goods were sold every day; a jury for the assize of bread summoned on a Friday in 1341 quoted the price of corn in the market the previous Wednesday, implying that it had not been sold on the Thursday.[79] Orders issued in 1575 indicate that Wednesday and Saturday were market days but that Saturday was the principal day for 'foreign' butchers.[80] In 1594 the market days were Wednesday, Friday and Saturday, but Saturday was the only market day reported in 1634.[81] An attempt in 1653 to move the market to Friday seems to have failed, for Saturday was still the market day in 1670.[82] The charter of 1693 granted a weekly general market on Tuesdays in addition to the ancient markets, but by 1697 that was a separate livestock market, and in 1724 the general market days were Thursday and Saturday.[83] In 1768 Wednesday was the market day for fruit, fowls, and country goods, Friday had been the principal day for fish, and Saturday was the day for meat and all kinds of provisions.[84] In 1825 there were some stalls open on most days, but Saturday was the main market day for corn and cattle, and Wednesday for poultry and fruit. By 1837 the Wednesday market was 'of trifling importance'.[85] In 1888 the borough claimed markets on Tuesday, Friday, and Saturday, although by then the market was actually held only on Saturdays.[86] The street market was held daily in 1929,[87] but had reverted to Saturdays by 1989.

The borough courts and assemblies made orders for the market, mainly to assign standings or stalls to particular trades. Not all trades were assigned stalls, however, and the claim made in 1452 and 1464 that the market was held everywhere[88] suggests that there was less formal organization than in some towns. Market standings or stalls were for country people; freemen sold from their shops or from stalls outside their houses.[89] The sale of butcher's meat, however,

68 *Brightlingsea Par. Mag.* Jan. 1895, 6–7; Feb. 1895, 7; Mar. 1895, 6–7: copy in E.S.A.H. Libr., Hollytrees, Colch.; E.R.O., Acc. C4, Colne Fishery Board, Black Bk. 8 Apr., 27 Aug., 4 Sept. 1896; 13 Jan., 10 Feb., 28 Apr., 3 June 1897.

69 E.R.O., Acc. C4, Colne Fishery Bd. Manager's reps. Apr. 1915–July 1921, reps. of 28 Apr., 14 July, 1920.

70 Ibid. reps. of 25 Aug., 8 Sept., 13 Oct. 1920.

71 Ibid. rep. of 14 Mar. 1921.

72 Ibid. reps. of 12 Apr., 10 Sept., 8 Oct., 12 Nov. 1919; 14 Jan. 1920; ibid. Colne Fishery Bd. Min. Bk. 1922–7, 1929: manager's reps. (noted but not recorded).

73 Ibid. Colne Fishery Bd. Min. Bk. 1949–64, 11 Mar., 27 May, 8 July 1953.

74 Ibid. 22 July, 9 Sept. 1959.

75 Ibid. 25 Feb., 27 Mar., 8 May, 18 Dec. 1963; 24 Feb. 1964.

76 *Colch. Charters*, 2. This section was written in 1989.

77 P.R.O., JUST 1/242, rot. 36.

78 *Cal. Pat.* 1377–81, 475; E.R.O., D/B 5 Cr1, rot. 3; Cr2, rot. 9; Cr28, rot. 19; Cr48, rott. 4d., 28d.; Cr64, rott. 3d., 21; Cr72, rot. 31d.

79 Ibid. D/B 5 Cr6, rot. 10.

80 Ibid. D/B 5 R7, f. 266.

81 J. Norden, *Description of Essex* (Camd. Soc. [1st ser.] ix), 14; B.L. Harl. MS. 6684, f. 104.

82 E.R.O., D/B 5 Gb4, f. 98; Gb5, f. 40v.

83 *Colch. Charters*, 174; E.R.O., D/B 5 Gb6, p. 121; ibid. Boro. Mun., Q/S papers (formerly Sess. R. 136), rot. 24A.

84 Morant, *Colch.* 80.

85 T. Cromwell, *Hist. Colch.* 200; *Rep. Com. on Mun. Corp. Bounds.* H.C. 238, p. A3 (1837), xxvi.

86 *Rep. Com. on Market Rights and Tolls* [C. 5550–II], p. 79, H.C. (1888), liv.

87 *Markets and Fairs in Eng. and Wales*, pt. iv (Min. of Agric. and Fish. Econ. Ser. no. 23), 108.

88 E.R.O., D/B 5 Cr64, rot. 21; Cr73, rot. 31d.

89 e.g. ibid. D/B 5 Gb3, f. 4; Gb4, f. 227.

was limited to the market, except for one butcher at the Hythe and one in Lexden permitted by an order of 1598.[90] In 1607 the assembly set up a market bushel, which was repaired in 1645.[91] In 1726 butchers were ordered to weigh at the public scales provided by the town.[92]

The borough was leasing the market tolls by 1310, and seems to have continued to do so until *c.* 1800. In the early 19th century the tolls and other profits of the market were given to senior members of the corporation to support them in their old age.[93] The corporation appointed a collector of dues in 1835, but by 1888 the tolls were again leased to a contractor, Mr. Percy who leased the tolls of *c.* 50 other markets in England.[94] The stalls too were leased, those in the wool and butter markets by 1400.[95] In the late 14th century the town received rents from only 21 stalls and the butchers' shambles and in 1549 from only 9 stalls; other stalls, apparently in private possession, were being bought and sold in the 15th century.[96] From the 17th century the butchers' stalls were normally leased to contractors. The borough assembly agreed to lease the fish market, whole or in parcels, in 1715, and the meat and green markets in 1810.[97]

Henry VI in 1447 granted the clerkship of the market to the bailiffs, and the grant was confirmed, with the assizes of bread and of ale, of wine, and of weights and measures, by Edward IV in 1462.[98] Two clerks of the market were appointed in 1515, and a salaried deputy clerk in 1557 'for the more speedy punishment of offenders'; a head clerk of the market was recorded in 1693.[99] In 1565 the clerk of the market employed men to arrest forestallers on the outskirts of the borough; in 1656 the clerk himself was among those ordered to confiscate meat from butchers who stayed in the market after closing time.[1] Masters or overseers of butchers, leather workers, and the fish market, whose duties included presenting sellers of faulty goods or unwholesome food, were appointed in the borough courts intermittently from 1443,[2] and forestallers and other market offenders were regularly presented in the borough court in the middle ages and the 16th century and in the borough quarter sessions in the 17th century.[3] A court of piepowder was held occasionally between 1448 and 1482.[4]

The general market was held in High Street, from its junction with North Hill and Headgate down to St. Nicholas's church. The medieval shambles were in the middle of the market near the moot hall. In 1428 two butchers were presented in the borough court for throwing entrails in front of their neighbours' doors at the end of West Stockwell Street.[5] In the 16th century the free butchers' shambles adjoined the east end of St. Runwald's church.[6] The medieval fish market seems to have been on the south side of High Street, west of St. Runwald's church; in 1515 it was in front of the Red Lion inn.[7] An oyster stall recorded in 1336 may have been in a separate oyster market: in 1671 the oyster sellers were ordered to move from their old marketplace to St. Peter's parish, at the west end of High Street.[8] There was a separate fish market at the Hythe by 1443 for the sale of fish caught in the borough's water in the Colne; it continued until 1594 or later.[9] The corn market was held at the west end of High Street, called corn hill by 1336.[10] From 1463, and probably from 1400 or earlier, the butter market or butter stall was outside the moot hall.[11] The cook row, probably also near the moot hall, was recorded in 1381.[12] A permanent leather stall, possibly with an upper storey, built onto a house in the middle of the market, was leased by the bailiffs and commonalty in 1428.[13] Four leather-dressers' stalls recorded in 1548 may have been in St. Peter's parish, like the tanners' stalls recorded in the same year.[14]

In 1583–4 the free butchers' shambles at the east end of St. Runwald's church were rebuilt as a two-storeyed, timber-framed building with a tiled roof extending down the middle of High Street.[15] The country butchers had separate stalls, probably in St. Peter's parish where there was a shambles in 1604.[16] About 1590 a new fruit and poultry market, with an open ground floor and a covered upper storey, was built in the middle of High Street opposite the moot hall, on the site of the earlier butter stall.[17] It was known as the market cross by 1605, and the butter market by 1639.[18] In 1592 the assembly ordered the vegetable market to be held on the south side of High Street from the Red Lion inn down towards St. Nicholas's church, an order repeated in 1621.[19] Between 1627 and 1629 a cornmarket, probably part of the Red Row (later the Exchange) at the corner of High Street and

90 Ibid. D/B 5 Gb1, 6 Nov. 1598.
91 Ibid. D/B 5 Ab1/6, 1/16.
92 Ibid. D/B 5 Gb7, p. 210.
93 *E.C.S.* 5 Apr. 1834.
94 E.R.O., D/B 5 Cr1, rot. 1d.; D/B 5 Gb10, pp. 35, 183; *Rep. Com. on Market Rights and Tolls*, p. 78.
95 E.R.O., D/B 5 Cr1, rot. 1d.; Cr32, rot. 1.
96 Ibid. D/B 5 R1, ff. 91v., 160v., 169 and v.; D/B 5 Cr124, rot. 12; Cr138, rot. 19; D/DCm T11; B.L. Stowe MS. 829, ff. 14, 17v.; P.R.O., C 1/66, no. 400.
97 E.R.O., D/B 5 Gb2, f. 50; Gb5, f. 162v.; Gb7, p. 19; Gb9, p. 195.
98 *Colch. Charters*, 39, 49–50.
99 E.R.O., D/B 5 Cr87, rot. 1; Cr123, rot. 10; D/B 5 Sr56, rot. 14.
1 Ibid. D/B 5 R5, f. 66v.; D/B 5 Gb4, f. 150.
2 Ibid. D/B 5 Cr59, rot. 3; Cr64, rot. 3d.; Cr65, rot. 3d.; Cr74, rot. 2d.
3 e.g. ibid. D/B 5 Cr48, rot. 10; Cr57, rot. 3d.; Cr148, rot. 38d.; D/B 5 Sr55, rott. 1–18; ibid. Boro. Mun., Misc. Papers (formerly Sess. R. 20), rot. 13.
4 *E.A.T.* 3rd ser. xvii. 136–7.
5 E.R.O., D/B 5 Cr48, rot. 23.
6 Ibid. D/B 5 Cr138, rot. 19; B.L. Stowe MS. 829, f. 14.
7 E.R.O., D/B 5 Cr9, rot. 4; Cr11, rot. 11d.; Cr48, rot. 28d.; Cr87, rot. 18; D/DRg 1/90.
8 Ibid. D/B 5 Cr5, rot. 8d.; D/B 5 Sb2/9, f. 191v.
9 Ibid. Acc. C47, CPL 1230–1; Britnell, *Growth and Decline*, 245.
10 E.R.O., D/B 5 Cr5, rot. 8d.
11 Ibid. D/B 5 Cr32, rot. 1; Cr72, rot. 1.
12 Ibid. D/B 5 Cr21, rot. 21d.
13 Ibid. D/B 5 Cr48, rot. 15d.
14 B.L. Stowe MS. 829, ff. 17v., 18v.
15 E.R.O., D/B 5 Ab1/3; D/B 5 Cb1/5, ff. 457 and v.; D/B 5 Gb2, f. 50.
16 Ibid. D/B 5 Sb2/9, 61v.; D/B 5 Cb1/5, ff. 42 and v.; D/B 5 Aa1/19; D/B 5 Ab1/10.
17 Ibid. D/B 5 Gb1, 29 Nov. 1592; Speed, *Colch. Map*; Morant, *Colch.* 114, and map facing p. 4.
18 E.R.O., D/B 5 Gb2, f. 50; D/B 5 Sb2/7, f. 271v.
19 Ibid. D/B 5 Gb1, 31 July 1592; Gb3, f. 4.

North Hill, was repaired or rebuilt. Although that was a separate room or building, as it had a key, corn was also sold from stalls or galleries 'against the red row' in the mid 17th century.[20]

In 1659 and 1660 the assembly decided to let ground in the market place to the highest bidder, and perhaps in order to clear the road outside the moot hall, ordered the demolition of the country butchers' stalls, and the removal of the fishmarket to Wyre Street (presumably the later St. Nicholas's Street).[21] The country butchers' stalls were replaced by moveable stalls erected on Saturdays on the south side of High Street in the 'High Town' in St. Peter's parish. By 1698 they had spilled over onto the north side of the street.[22] A lease of land for stalls on the south side of the street in 1698 allowed the lessee to charge 12*d.* for a butcher's stall and 6*d.* each for stalls for other traders, including shoemakers, glovers, knackers, basketmakers, dishturners, pedlars, and chapmen.[23] In 1715 butchers who had no stalls stood on the south side of High Street in St. Peter's parish; more butchers' stalls were available by 1730 when there were as many as 66 of them.[24] The fishmarket in Wyre Street was replaced in 1697 by a specially built market beside the free butchers' shambles in High Street, east of St. Runwald's church. It was repaired by St. Runwald's parish in 1751, and was still there in 1803, but by 1880 it had moved to St. Nicholas's Street.[25] The shambles were extensively repaired in 1800, and the fishmarket was paved in 1804.[26] In 1765, after complaints that the market was concentrated in the Exchange, the sellers of butter, eggs, poultry and other goods, except corn, were ordered to move back to the old market cross.[27] By 1803 that market place was disused and was turned into a guard house; it was demolished in 1808.[28] The butter market had meanwhile moved back to the Exchange, the vegetable market to the south side of High Street between Pelham's Lane and the Red Lion inn.[29] In 1810 the vegetable market was moved eastwards, to a site near the obelisk, in the middle of High Street near the shambles.[30]

In 1813 a new covered market for meat, butter, fruit, and vegetables was built by public subscription just west of the moot hall on the former garden of the Three Cups hotel. The disused shambles were leased by the corporation to the improvement commissioners for demolition in 1816, but were apparently still standing when they were offered for sale in 1819. In 1821 butchers were forbidden to set up stalls in High Street.[31] The new covered market was unpopular with the traders, most of whom had returned to High Street by 1825, and in 1837 the general market was regularly held there.[32] In 1888 the market consisted of *c.* 25 stalls in High Street and St. Nicholas's Street selling sweets, fish, and birds; hawkers sold vegetables and some poultry.[33] By 1929 poultry and eggs were being sold in the cattle market in Middleborough; the remainder of the general market of 53 stalls, 40 of them for agricultural produce, was held daily in High Street.[34] The general market was moved from High Street to the east end of Culver Street in 1961 and to a site near the west end of that street in 1968. It moved back to High Street in 1981.[35]

The corn exchange, formerly the Red Row, was extensively repaired and remodelled in 1800 and 1801; its projecting central bay had a broken pediment supported by Corinthian columns, and was surmounted by a clock turret and cupola; four Doric columns supported a cornice and frieze below a flat roof which projected into the street in front of the central bay.[36] The exchange, described as the former butter market, was offered for sale in 1819 and was demolished the following year. A new exchange, designed by David Laing, was built at the expense partly of local farmers and corn merchants and partly of the Essex and Suffolk Equitable Insurance company which had occupied the upper floor of the old building. The open ground floor has a colonnade of cast-iron fluted pillars extending onto the pavement; the façade of the upper storey is balustraded with a central pediment.[37] By 1844 the new building was inconvenient, dark, and too small for the market, and in 1845 a second exchange, later the Albert Hall, with a further 50–60 stands for merchants, was built on an adjacent site.[38] In 1884 the corn exchange moved into a new building on part of the Cups hotel site (the former vegetable market) near the town hall. In 1929 there were 110 stands there and *c.* 300,000 cwt. of grain was sold.[39] The number of farmers and dealers attending the market declined in the mid 20th century, to *c.* 30 in 1962 when the corn exchange was taken over by the Metropolitan Railway Surplus Lands Company. It closed in 1967, and the building was demolished in 1972.[40]

20 Ibid. D/B 5 Ab1/12, 13; D/B 5 Sb2/7, ff. 271–272v.; D/B 5 Sr44.
21 Ibid. D/B 5 Gb4, ff. 205v., 216, 217, 221, 222v.
22 Ibid. D/B 5 Gb5, f. 40v.; Gb6, p. 142; D/B 5 Sr54, rot. 16B; B.L. Stowe MS. 842, f. 66.
23 E.R.O., Acc. C1, [box P], misc. papers.
24 Ibid. D/B 5 Gb7, pp. 11, 263.
25 Ibid. D/B 5 Gb6, p. 128; ibid. Boro. Mun., Boro. Sanit. Cttee. Mins. 1878–81, p. 105; ibid. Acc. C213, box 1, envelope of misc. notes; Morant, *Colch.* 80; T. Cromwell, *Hist. Colch.* 299; [B. or J. Strutt], *Hist. and Description of Colch.* (1803), ii. 78; J. Pryer, *New and Exact Prospect of Colch.* (1724).
26 E.R.O., D/B 5 Ab1/37; Ab1/42.
27 Ibid. D/B 5 Gb8, ff. 15–16.
28 *V.C.H. Essex*, ii. 241; *Ipswich Jnl.* 23 Apr. 1808.
29 *Colch. Gaz.* 6 Mar. 1819; [Strutt], *Hist. Colch.* ii. 78.
30 *Suff. Chron.* 1 July 1810–from TS. note among newspaper cuttings in E.C.L. Colch.
31 Cromwell, *Hist. Colch.* 199; E.R.O., Boro. Mun. Proc. Improvement Com. i, pp. 74, 158; ibid. Acc. C47, CPL 755; *Colch. Gaz.* 6 Mar. 1819.
32 Cromwell, *Hist. Colch.* 199; *Rep. Com. on Mun. Corp. Bounds.* p. 193.
33 *Rep. Com. on Market Rights and Tolls*, p. 81.
34 *Markets and Fairs in Eng. and Wales*, pt. iv, 106–8.
35 *E.C.S.* 4 May, 1979; *Colch. Exp.* 19 Sept. 1980.
36 E.R.O., D/B 5 Gb9, pp. 45, 49; D/B 5 Ab1/44; drawing, wrongly identified as the Dutch Bay Hall, in P. Giffard, *Yesterday's Town*, 39.
37 *Colch. Gaz.* 6 Mar. 1819; Cromwell, *Hist. Colch.* 191–2; White, *Dir. Essex* (1848), 71.
38 E.R.O., Acc. C210, J. B. Harvey Colln. iv, p. 99; White, *Dir. Essex* (1848), 71; *E.C.S.* 15 Aug. 1845; below, Mun. Bldgs.
39 E.R.O., Boro. Mun. Special Cttee. Min. Bk. 1878–84, Aug. 1884; *Markets and Fairs in Eng. and Wales*, pt. iv, 106–8.
40 *E.C.S.* 28 Dec. 1962; 12 Feb. 1965; 2 June 1967; *Colch. Exp.* 8 June, 10 Aug. 1972.

By 1427, when two cows were sold in the north ward,[41] the main livestock market was being held at the top of High Street, in St. Peter's parish. Another livestock market, granted by the charter of 1693, was held on Tuesdays on St. Anne's field in Harwich Road from 1694. It was held only fortnightly by 1748.[42] The market, field, and fair held there were leased in 1733, and 1738, and the fair field and tolls in 1769, by which time the market was probably no longer held.[43]

By the early 19th century the Saturday livestock market in High Street had become an obstruction and a nuisance; in 1819 it was moved briefly to a site on the east of Balkerne Hill but returned to High Street at the petition of the traders.[44] Loose cattle apparently stood east of St. Runwald's church, pigs between George Lane and the Swan inn, extending into St. Nicholas's Street if necessary, and bulls were kept near St. Runwald's church.[45] In 1855 the market's removal from High Street was an election issue, and in 1857 the town council set up a cattle market removal committee which experimented with holding the market in the castle bailey and examined other possible sites.[46] In 1861 a public inquiry recommended a site at the bottom of North Hill, and the market moved there in 1862.[47] The new market, at Middleborough, had permanent pens for animals and an octagonal settling house or office to which a small clock turret was added in 1898.[48] The cattle market moved to a new site in Severalls Lane, on the northern edge of the town, in 1975. In 1985 it was held on Tuesdays, Thursdays, and Saturdays.[49] An attempt to hold a general market on the site on Tuesdays failed after only seven months in 1976–7.[50]

A wool market was apparently held privately in a hall in St. Runwald's parish until 1373 when the bailiff William Reyne moved it into the cellar below the moot hall.[51] The market seems to have been held on Tuesdays in 1393, but sales of wool were recorded on a Thursday in 1381 and on a Friday in 1425.[52] It was moved into the room above the fruit and poultry market in 1592.[53] In 1595 the Assembly complained that wool was being sold in inns and private houses, often by false weights, and repeated the order that the market should be held on Tuesdays and Thursdays in the fruit and poultry market, from 8 a.m. to 11 a.m. and from 1 p.m. to 4 p.m. The morning market was for free burgesses, the afternoon one for both burgesses and outsiders. The town maintained two sets of scales for weighing the wool, kept by the keeper of the wool market who was entitled to charge for weighing the wool and for storing it in the room above the market.[54] In 1602 there were separate stalls for 'foreign' and 'new' wool merchants, and the foreign merchants' stalls were recorded again in 1642.[55] In 1605 the inside of the market cross was planked to make a hall for weighing wool in the market.[56] The order of 1595 was repeated in 1651, 1660, 1681, 1686, and 1720.[57] In 1729 the keepership of the wool market was granted to the keepers of the bay hall, and although the borough made a lease of both the market and the hall in 1732, the market was not recorded thereafter. It had been discontinued by 1748.[58]

FAIRS. A fair for four days at the feast of St. John the Baptist (24 June) was granted to St. John's abbey at its foundation, and confirmed by Henry I *c.* 1104.[59] The fair may have been older, for in 1285 and 1290 the burgesses claimed that the abbot should pay 3*s.* towards the farm of the town for his fair, presumably to compensate the town for some loss of revenue when the fair was granted to the abbey. Although the abbot, relying on Henry I's charter, denied that the payment was due, a jury in 1290 found that it did belong to the farm of the town.[60] The abbot was still paying 3*s.* a year *c.* 1387 when he was said to hold the fair of the commonalty of the town.[61] After a dispute between the abbot's men and townsmen at the fair in 1272, both sides claimed to have been robbed and wounded. The town accused the abbot of bringing in the county coroner to view a body found on St. John's green during the fair,[62] but the town does not seem to have made any claim to the fair itself. After the Dissolution the fair appears to have descended with the manor of West Donyland in which St. John's green lay, being held in 1836 by Admiral Nicholas Tomlinson and his wife Elizabeth and Maria Ward as lord and ladies of that manor.[63] Nevertheless, from the mid 16th century or earlier the bailiffs, aldermen, and councillors, in their gowns, perambulated the fair, presumably asserting some jurisdiction over it. The custom continued until 1695.[64]

Goods on sale at the fair in 1587 included silk ribbons and leather belts, and linendrapers from Sudbury and Hadleigh in Suffolk attended with their wares in 1590.[65] A man from Earl's Colne

41 E.R.O., D/B 5 Cr48, rot. 4d.

42 Ibid. D/B 5 Gb6, p. 23; Morant, *Colch.* 80.

43 E.R.O., D/B 5 Gb7, pp. 311, 340; Gb8, f. 44v.

44 Ibid. D/B 5 Gb9, p. 387; ibid. Acc. C210, J. B. Harvey Colln. iv, p. 49.

45 Ibid. Boro. Mun., Special Cttee. Min. Bk. 1856–78, cattle mkt. removal cttee., Mar. 1860.

46 E.R.O., Acc. C210, J. B. Harvey Colln. v, p. 82; ibid. Boro. Mun., Special Cttee. Min. Bk. 1856–78, cattle mkt. removal cttee. meetings *passim*; Phillips, *Ten Men*, 134–5.

47 E.R.O., Acc. C210, J. B. Harvey Colln. i, pp. 301–7; *Rep. Com. on Market Rights and Tolls*, p. 78.

48 E.R.O., Boro. Mun., Estate and Cattle Market Exec. Cttee. Mins. 1896–1904, pp. 17–38; O.S. Map 1/500, Essex XXVII. 8. 23 (1876 edn.); photographs in E.R.O. Mint Binder; below, pl. facing p. 329.

49 *Colch. Gaz.* 21 Feb. 1975; *E.C.S.* 18 Oct. 1985.

50 *Colch. Gaz.* 27 May, 1977.

51 E.R.O., D/B 5 R2, ff. 4–5.

52 Ibid. D/B 5 Cr21, rot. 21d.; Cr28, rot. 19; Cr48, rot. 9d.

53 Ibid. D/B 5 Gb1, 29 Nov. 1592.

54 Ibid. 2 June 1595.

55 Ibid. D/B 5 Aa1/2; Aa1/12.

56 Ibid. D/B 5 Gb2, f. 50.

57 Ibid. D/B 5 Gb4, ff. 54v., 228v.; Gb5, ff. 177v., 261 and v.; Gb7, p. 106.

58 Ibid. D/B 5 Gb7, pp. 249, 283; Morant, *Colch.* 114.

59 *Colch. Cart.* i. 2, 5.

60 P.R.O., JUST 1/242, rot. 110; E.R.O., D/B 5 R2, ff. 49, 50v.–51v.

61 E.R.O., D/B 5 R1, f. 168v.

62 Ibid. D/B 5 R2, ff. 46v.–47; *Cal. Pat.* 1266–72, 707; P.R.O., JUST 1/238, rot. 59.

63 E.R.O., D/DEl T358/45.

64 Ibid. D/B 5 Sb2/2, f. 117; D/B 5 Gb6, p. 52; cf. D/B 5 R5, f. 108v.

65 Ibid. D/B 5 Sr7, rot. 18; D/B 5 Sb2/5, f. 114.

brought a horse to sell at the fair in 1613, and the fair was described as a horse fair in 1767.[66] The fair was for sheep, cattle, and 'other merchandize' in 1836, but was said to be a cattle fair in 1837.[67] By 1861 it was a pleasure fair, and was blamed by many in the town for exercising a 'most demoralizing influence', particularly over working class girls.[68] It was abolished in 1872.[69]

Richard I in 1189 granted St. Mary Magdalen's hospital an annual fair on the eve and feast of St. Mary Magdalen (21 and 22 July).[70] In 1318 it was attended by traders from Greenwich (Kent), London, Sudbury (Suff.), Bury St. Edmunds (Suff.), and Tunstead (Norf.), among them a garlicmonger. Badly tanned leather was sold there in 1439 and salt in 1498.[71] The fair, held on Magdalen green, continued until 1872, but does not seem to have been of much importance.[72] Its profits, which belonged to the master of the hospital, were uncertain in 1582.[73] The fair, held on 2 August after the change in the calendar, was a toy fair in 1767; in 1825 it was known as 'Scalt Codlin fair', apparently a reference to the baked apples sold or consumed at it.[74] In 1863 it was only a small fair for 'pleasure and pedlary'.[75]

A third fair was granted to the burgesses by Edward II in 1319, to be held on the eve and feast of St. Dennis (9 Oct.) and on the six following days.[76] The grant may simply have regularized a fair already being held, for in 1310 there was a dispute over a leather-seller's stall, set up under the wall of St. Botolph's priory outside the town, on the Saturday and Sunday after St. Dennis's day.[77] That stall appears to have been for a fair rather than for the general market, and Bury field, in which part of St. Dennis's fair was held by the mid 16th century,[78] extended as far as the priory walls. London merchants attended the fair in 1364.[79]

In 1562, when new orders were made for it, the fair began under East gate and extended along both sides of High Street as far as the town well, presumably the later King Coel's pump near the junction with North Hill. It was then attended by, among others, fletchers, bowyers, sadlers, soapers, tanners, glovers, shoemakers, blacksmiths, goldsmiths, rope-makers, haberdashers, linendrapers, woollendrapers, hosiers, upholsters, coverlet-makers, mercers, grocers, pewterers, brasiers, ironmongers, turners, basket-makers, fishmongers, salters, and sellers of butter and cheese, from Colchester itself and from as far away as Ipswich, Bungay (Suff.), and London. Outsiders had standings assigned to them, according to their crafts; freemen stood in front of their market stalls.[80]

In 1578 the borough forbade the holding of the fair on a Sunday, and the charter of Charles I in 1635 reduced it from eight to four days.[81] Late 16th- and early 17th-century references to the sale of necklaces and bracelets, the purchase of silk, and to haberdashers' and cloth stalls[82] indicate that it was still a general fair, but it was also referred to as a horse fair in 1599 and 1613.[83] In 1662 the fair was attended by 'an incredibly large crowd of people, country folk, gentry and all', musicians played everywhere, and all sorts of goods were on sale.[84] It seems to have declined by the early 18th century; its profits, usually leased with the butchers' stalls in the market, were only *c.* £5 in 1736 and 1737. In 1698 the lessee was allowed to take only 2*d.* a square yard from freemen and 4*d.* a square yard from foreigners for stalls.[85]

In the 1760s the fair was for cattle, horses, cheese, butter, and toys.[86] The cattle and horses were sold in Bury field for four days;[87] the other goods on the north side of High Street from the exchange to the market cross.[88] Among the attractions in 1785 was a 'learned pig' which had previously performed in London.[89] In 1809 the cattle were moved to St. Anne's field because there was not room in Bury field for the large numbers brought to the fair.[90] In 1822 as many as 1,500–2,000 bullocks, 800 sheep, and 40 horses were sold.[91] The general fair in High Street was declining in 1825.[92] Despite attempts to move them to St. Anne's, traders were still setting up stalls in High Street in 1848, although by then the fair had dwindled to 'a toy and gingerbread fair of the lowest description'. It continued on the north side of the street into the later 19th century, reduced to one day by 1888, but by 1910 it was only a cattle and horse fair, and its tolls had declined from £13 in 1905 to £8 14*s.* in 1909.[93]

The bailiffs, later the mayor, and the aldermen permabulated the fair from 1563 or earlier; from 1715 the ceremony was described as one to proclaim the fair.[94] In 1814 the mayor and corporation were led by a band as they walked

66 Ibid. D/B 5 Sb2/6, f. 82; D/DU 459, p. [139].
67 E.R.O., D/DEl T348/45; *Rep. Com. on Mun. Corp. Bounds*. p. A3.
68 Press cuttings in E.C.L. Colch.
69 P.R.O., HO 45/9307, 12356.
70 *Cal. Chart. R.* 1257–1300, 99.
71 P.R.O., JUST 3/18/5, rot. 24; E.R.O., D/B 5 Cr57, rot. 2d.; D/B 5 Cb1/1, f. 82.
72 P.R.O., HO 45/9306, 12132; [Strutt], *Hist. Colch.* ii. 79.
73 Morant, *Colch.* 81, App. p. 8.
74 E.R.O., D/DU 459, p. [139]; Cromwell, *Hist. Colch.* 297.
75 White, *Dir. Essex* (1863), 73.
76 *Colch. Charters*, 9.
77 E.R.O., D/B 5 Cr1, rot. 3d.
78 B.L. Stowe MS. 829, f. 18v.
79 *Cal. Letters from Mayor and Corp. Lond. c.* 1350–70, ed. R. R. Sharpe, p. 105.
80 E.R.O., D/B 5 R5, ff. 89v.–90: printed in Morant, *Colch.* App. p. 14.
81 E.R.O., D/B 5 Gb1, 17 Mar. 1578; *Colch. Charters*, 100–1.
82 E.R.O., D/B 5 Sb2/3, f. 141; Sb2/4, f. 72; Sb2/5, f. 144; Sb2/6, f. 63v.
83 Ibid. D/B 5 Gb1, 13 Sept. 1599; D/B 5 Sb2/6, f. 239v.
84 *Jnl. of Wm. Schellinks' Travels in Eng.* (Camd. 5th ser. i), 164.
85 E.R.O., D/Y 2/1, pp. 145, 167; ibid. Acc. C1, [box P], misc. papers.
86 Ibid. D/DU 459, p. [139].
87 Ibid. D/B 5 Gb8, f. 9.
88 Morant, *Colch.* 81.
89 *E.R.* xlv. 15.
90 E.R.O., D/B 5 Gb9, pp. 163–4; D/DHt T337/10A.
91 E.R.O., Acc. C210, J. B. Harvey Colln. iv, p. [24]: newspaper cutting.
92 Cromwell, *Hist. Colch.* 297.
93 E.R.O., Acc. C210 J. B. Harvey Colln. iv, p. 107; *Rep. Com. on Market Rights and Tolls*, p. 79; newspaper report of 15 June 1912; *E.C.S.* 22 Oct. 1910: cuttings in E.C.L. Colch.
94 E.R.O., D/B 5 R5, ff. 108v.–109; D/B 5 Gb7, 10 Oct. 1715.

from the moot hall to Bury field. In 1910 the procession was led by the town serjeant carrying the borough mace and the four constables carrying the ward maces.[95] The fair was formally proclaimed for the last time in 1932.[96]

The charter of 1693 granted the town a fair for live cattle, goods, and merchandize, on 12 and 13 July each year.[97] In 1694 the assembly directed that the new fair be held near St. Anne's, in the fair field.[98] In the 18th century the mayor and corporation attended it, as they did the older fairs.[99] By 1861 the fair was a pleasure fair, and like that on St. John's green was blamed for corrupting the populace.[1] It was abolished in 1873.[2]

William III, in a charter of 1699 reincorporating the tailors of Colchester, granted to the mayor and his successors a cattle fair in St. Anne's field every year on the second Tuesday in April and the three days following.[3] It was called the Tailors' fair in the 18th century, and was said in 1767, possibly in error, to be for wholesale tailors.[4] It had ceased by 1803.[5]

Henry I in 1157 granted St. John's abbey a fair for two days at the feast of the Invention of the Cross (3 May), to be held on the castle waste between St. Helen's chapel and High Street.[6] The grant by Henry III in 1256 to the keeper of the castle of a fair for eight days at Whitsun[7] may have been an attempt to revive or replace the abbey's fair, but if so it failed, for there is no further record of either fair. In 1373 the bailiff William Reyne claimed to have reorganized a wool fair, held annually on the nativity of St. John the Baptist and the feast of St. Mary Magdalen.[8] There is no later reference to such a fair, and it seems likely that it was simply an expanded wool market held to coincide with the St. John's and St. Mary Magdalen's fairs.

A pleasure fair, whose attractions included custard throwing, was held at Easter and Whitsun in Middleborough in the late 18th century. It was known as the Wilderness fair from a wilderness or maze belonging to Lexden park which lay just north-west of North bridge. It was still held, without the custard throwing, in 1843,[9] and was probably the small Easter Tuesday pleasure fair wrongly identified with the Tailors' fair in 1863.[10]

MUNICIPAL BUILDINGS

TOWN HALL. The town had presumably had a hall in which to hold its courts since the earlier 12th century when it was given the right to have its own justices,[11] and a common hall, later called the moot hall, was recorded in 1277.[12] The building on the north side of High Street, demolished in 1843, was of the 12th century and originally comprised a stone house, *c.* 40 ft. long, lengthwise to the street, with a first floor hall.[13] It had doorways in the north and south walls, the south one at least being original, which perhaps marked a screens passage separating the hall from its chambers to the north. Both doors were approached by steps, and the south one had an 'entry' encroaching on the market place by 1367.[14] The north door opened into a large court or garden where market stalls were erected.[15] The south doorway was flanked by two elaborately carved windows, one of which survived largely intact, but blocked, in 1843. It was of two orders, both with decorated capitals, the outer with colonettes, the inner with standing figures; the inner archivolt was carved with pine cones or bunches of grapes, the outer with a leaf design and a human head at the apex. The carving has been shown to be from the same workshop as the west doorway of Rochester cathedral, built *c.* 1160.[16]

By the later 14th century the hall was out of repair and old fashioned, and it was remodelled in 1373–4 at the instigation of the bailiff William Reyne. Reyne rebuilt the steps to the doors, the north ones in tiled stone, the south ones in marble. The south steps and the outer door were covered by a two-storey porch with an overhanging upper storey jutting out into the market place; shops or stalls with solars above them were built in the space between the south wall of the hall and the street frontage, on either side of the new porch. Reyne also restored the undercroft below the hall, enlarging the windows to make it suitable for the wool market. He refurnished the main hall with benches and triple sedilia.[17]

No major alterations seem to have been made to the hall before its demolition in 1843, although repairs were carried out at intervals in the 16th, 17th, and 18th centuries, notably *c.* 1701 when the corporation borrowed £350 for the repair of the moot hall, the bridges, and part of High Street.[18] A turret, presumably the bell turret above the entrance, was recorded in 1583, and the room under the bell in 1618.[19] The hall was taxed on three hearths in 1680 and 1681, but the number was reduced to two in 1684.[20] Descriptions of the hall in 1579, 1748, and 1803

95 *E.C.S.* 22 Oct. 1910; MS. note from a newspaper of 1814 in E.C.L. Colch. newspaper cuttings.

96 E.R.O., Boro. Mun., Council Mins. 1932, Council-in-Cttee. 21 Oct. 1932.

97 *Colch. Charters*, 174.

98 E.R.O., D/B 5 Gb6, p. 23.

99 e.g. ibid. p. 260.

1 Press cutting, 1861, in E.C.L. Colch.

2 P.R.O., HO 45/9335, 20369; E.R.O., Boro. Mun., Council Min. Bk. 1871–7, p. 72.

3 *Cal. S.P. Dom.* 1699–1700, 265.

4 Morant, *Colch.* 81; E.R.O., D/DU 459, p. [139].

5 [Strutt], *Hist. Colch.* ii. 80.

6 *Colch. Cart.* i. 24.

7 *Cal. Pat.* 1247–58, 534.

8 E.R.O., D/B 5 R2, f. 8 and v.

9 A. F. J. Brown, *Essex People 1750–1900*, 167, 170.

10 White, *Dir. Essex* (1863), 73.

11 Above, Medieval Colch. (Boro. Govt.)

12 E.R.O., D/B 5 R2, f. 1v.

13 Drawings reproduced in *Colch. Arch. Rep.* i. 62–7; dimensions from E.R.O., D/DR P21.

14 E.R.O., D/B 5 Cr15, rot. 18d.

15 Ibid. rot. 6d.; Cr35, rot. 1d.

16 *Colch. Arch. Rep.* i. 63–7.

17 E.R.O., D/B 5 R2, ff. 6–9.

18 Ibid. D/B 5 Gb6, p. 233.

19 Ibid. D/B 5 Ab1/3, 1/9.

20 Ibid. D/B 5 Ab1/21.

FIG. 24. THE TOWN HALL OF 1843

suggest that the internal arrangements changed little. On the first floor was the main hall or moot hall with, to the north, the exchequer which had been partitioned by 1748 to provide a muniment room. Above the exchequer and muniment room was the council or freemen's chamber.[21] By 1683 other public buildings, including the gaol, adjoined the hall, probably on the west on land owned by the corporation in the early 19th century.[22]

In 1764 the corporation leased to the Norwich Company of Comedians, who had been performing in the moot hall since 1725, part of the moot hall yard on which to build a theatre.[23] In 1828 the corporation leased the disused building back for a term of 50 years as a sessions house and additional gaol accommodation.[24]

The new town hall designed by John Blore and R. Brandon was opened on the same site in 1845.[25] Built at a cost of £6,000 raised mainly by public subscription, it was a three-storeyed stone building, its front divided into five bays by six Roman Doric pilasters surmounted by a cornice and a balustrade; the borough arms were carved on the raised central compartment. It contained a large assembly hall called the moot hall, a court room, a magistrate's room, committee rooms, a police station and cells, and offices for the gaoler; by 1882 there were two court rooms.[26] By 1878 the hall was inadequate and its foundations unstable; neighbouring properties were bought to extend and buttress the building, but the work was not carried out, and in 1897 the hall was demolished.[27]

In 1902 the third town hall on the site was opened by the former Liberal prime minister, Archibald Philip Primrose, earl of Rosebery. The red brick and Portland stone building was designed by Sir John Belcher in Renaissance style.[28] The tower, windows, pictures, statues, and furnishings of the hall were provided by gifts and benefactions amounting to *c.* £12,000. The capitals of the façade are decorated with wheat, roses, and oyster shells; in niches around the building at second floor level are set six life-size marble statues of Eudes *dapifer*, Thomas Audley Lord Audley, Dr. William Gilberd, Archbishop Samuel Harsnett, King Edward the Elder, and Boudicca. The 162-ft. high Victoria tower was given by James Paxman and named after the queen with her special permission; on the top is a bronze statue of St. Helen. In the upper angles of the tower are four bronze ravens symbolizing the port of Colchester and in the lower angles figures representing engineering, fishery, agriculture, and military defence. In the tower is a chiming clock with five bells and a bell of *c.* 1400 believed to have come from the medieval moot hall. Two law courts are on the ground floor, from which rises an elaborate staircase of coloured marble. On the first floor are the mayor's parlour, the grand jury room, and the council members' room, which can all be opened into one large room; also on the first floor is the council chamber, its ceiling painted to John Belcher's design with figures representing the months; the three stained glass windows were made by Messrs. Powell and Sons of the Whitefriars glass works.[29] Carved figures of a boy and girl of the Bluecoat school are on the side walls of the upper staircase leading to the second floor. Most of that floor is taken up by the moot hall, the principal assembly room, which has coupled Corinthian columns surmounted by a frieze, an elaborate cornice, and a barrel-vaulted coved ceiling.[30]

In 1965 the corporation bought the Cups hotel, west of the town hall, to provide additional office accommodation; in 1975 part of the Treasurer's department moved to Rebow chambers in Sir Isaac's Walk. By 1985 council departments were housed in buildings throughout the town, including the old public library in Shewell Road, East Lodge and the Gatehouse in East Hill, Northgate House in North Hill, and Lexden Grange in Lexden.[31] New council offices, Angel Court, were built in 1988 east of the town hall connected to it by a tunnel beneath West Stockwell Street.[32]

PRISON. The bailiffs used private houses to imprison suspected offenders *c.* 1250,[33] but by 1285 they had custody of a gaol, which was delivered from 1300.[34] In 1367 it was probably below the moot hall, presumably with a door and

21 Ibid. D/B 5 Sb2/3, f. 110v.; Morant, *Colch.* (1748), Bk. II. 9–10; [B. or J. Strutt], *Hist. and Description Colch.* ii. 20.

22 E.R.O., D/B 5 Gb5, f. 202; D/DR P21.

23 Ibid. D/B 5 Aa1/35, f. 106; D/B 5 Gb5, f. 3v.; below, Soc. and Cultural.

24 E.R.O., D/B 5 Gb10, p. 33.

25 A. F. J. Brown, *Essex People 1750–1900*, 171; *E.C.S.* 4 May 1845.

26 *White's Dir. Essex* (1848); *Kelly's Dir. Essex* (1882).

27 *P.O. Dir. Essex* (1878); G. H. Martin, *Colch.* 107; *Kelly's Dir. Essex* (1890); *Essex Tel.* 23 Jan. 1897; *E.C.S.* 6 Feb., 27 Mar., 14 Aug. 1897.

28 Design published in *The Builder* in 1899 and reproduced in C. Cunningham, *Victorian and Edwardian Town Halls* (1981), 158.

29 *E.R.* xi. 33–48.

30 D. T.-D. Clarke, *Town Hall Colch.* 15–16; *E.A.T.* 3rd ser. v. 232.

31 Colch. Civic Soc. 'Quarterly Bull.' ii. 13; *E.C.S.* 4 Jan. 1963; 23 Jan. 1968; 25 Jan. 1985; *Colch. Expr.* 30 Jan. 1975.

32 *E.C.S.* 2 May 1986; 8 Oct. 1987.

33 P.R.O., JUST 1/238, rot. 27.

34 Ibid. JUST 1/242, rot. 110; JUST 3/18/4, rot. 4d.

a window on the north side of the building as prisoners were alleged to escape over an unrepaired wall into St. Runwald's churchyard. William Reyne's improvements in 1373 included placing outside the moot hall door posts to which the prisoners could be chained to beg; hitherto they had had to stand in the 'shaft' which gave access to the prison.[35] In 1618–19 the prisoners were supplied with a leaded basket to gather food, presumably by begging from passers by, which suggests a window or other opening giving on the street.[36] By 1579 there was a separate women's gaol in an upper room in the moot hall,[37] perhaps in the room over the porch.

In 1608 a house of correction was made out of some chambers in the moot hall,[38] apparently in the building west of the original hall. In 1624 or 1625 it appears to have been moved to other, possibly new, buildings on the same or an adjoining site.[39] Its equipment included a treadmill, housed in a separate building in 1628–9.[40] The house of correction may have been the bridewell recorded in 1681 which, in 1703, was equipped with a handmill for grinding malt.[41] The bridewell was turned into a gaol in 1730 when an earlier gaol, presumably in adjoining buildings, was converted into houses.[42] In 1748 the gaol was below the moot hall and adjoining buildings.[43] In 1801 it was filthy and offensive and without an outside exercise yard. There was one room for debtors and three other rooms each 7 ft. high; two on the ground floor were 16 ft. by 11 ft. and 15 ft. square respectively, one on the first floor was 15 ft. by 9 ft. All were lighted and ventilated by small grated windows. Two strongrooms, each 16 ft. by 11 ft., were probably below the moot hall cellar.[44] A separate debtors' prison was built in the north-west corner of the moot hall yard in 1809; the timber and brick building had a single day room on the ground floor with three cells above, and appears to have had windows in the west wall.[45] In 1822 all categories of prisoners were held in the gaol; those found guilty of capital offences were sent, after sentence, to the county gaol.[46]

In 1834 the cells in the old town gaol still held seven prisoners, and there were three cells in the debtors' prison. There was no room for a treadwheel and sentences of hard labour were served in the county gaol in Chelmsford.[47] By 1839 the hall of the disused theatre in the north-east corner of the moot hall yard, which had been used as extra prison accommodation since *c.* 1828, was being used as the men's exercise yard, and the gallery had been converted into six women's cells which in 1840 were made into a separate women's prison. Men were still held in the old gaol, but some of the oldest cells were not normally used. Poor drains made the whole prison 'disgustingly offensive', the cells were small and airless, and there was no open air exercise yard.[48] In 1843 the demolition of four of the seven cells in the men's prison to make way for the new town hall and the temporary use of the debtors' building to house the prison governor during the rebuilding caused serious overcrowding.[49] Cells built in the basement of the new town hall seem not to have been used for several years, and in 1849 the gaol was still 'a wretched place of confinement' totally unsuitable as a prison. Improvements had been made by 1862 when there were 2 day rooms, 2 exercise yards, and 16 cells, some presumably in the basement of the town hall.[50] The borough council could not afford to meet all the requirements of the 1865 Prison Act, and by 1868 the gaol was used only for remand prisoners and juveniles, all other prisoners being sent to the county gaol.[51] The gaol apparently closed in 1878 and was demolished, with the town hall, in 1896 and 1897.[52]

ALBERT HALL. The hall, at the west end of High Street, was built as a corn exchange in 1845 to designs by Raphael Brandon. It has a front of five narrow bays, the three recessed middle ones being divided by two Ionic columns supporting a shallow portico. Each of the central bays contains an arched doorway; the two outer bays originally contained niches holding life-size figures symbolizing ancient and modern agriculture, but the niches were replaced by windows, perhaps when the building was converted into a school in 1885. In 1991 the statues stood at the entrance to St. Mary's multi-storey car park on Balkerne Hill. A statue of Britannia above the centre of the portico was made of such soft stone that it quickly eroded and was removed. The building closed as a corn exchange in 1884 and reopened in 1885 as the Albert School of Art and Science, which became the responsibility of the borough council in 1894. The hall was used for educational purposes until 1912[53] and as a Food Control office during the First World War. After years of disuse, major alterations were made in 1926; a stage, foyer, and gallery were built and the building was used as an assembly hall, art gallery, and theatre until 1972. By 1974 it was being used as a stationery store by Cullingford and Co.[54] In 1980 the council sold it to property developers[55] and in 1991 the restored

35 E.R.O., D/B 5 Cr15, rot. 16d.; D/B 5 R2, f. 9.
36 Ibid. D/B 5 Ab1/9.
37 Ibid. D/B 5 Sb2/3, f. 110v.
38 Ibid. D/B 5 Cb1/6, f. 129v.
39 Ibid. D/B 5 Ab1/11; D/B 5 Aa1/5.
40 Ibid. D/B 5 Ab1/9, 12, 13.
41 Ibid. D/B 5 Ab1/20, 23.
42 Ibid. D/B 5 Gb7, pp. 276, 287.
43 Morant, *Colch.* (1748.), 114.
44 *Gent. Mag.* lxxiv (2), 705.
45 E.R.O., D/B 5 Gb9, pp. 149–51, 164–5; ibid. D/DR P21.
46 *Rep. to Sec. of State, pursuant to 4 Geo. IV, c. 64 and 2 & 3 Vic. c. 56*, H.C. 104, pp. 12–13 (1824), xix.
47 *3rd Rep. Sel. Cttee. H.L. on Gaols*, H.C. 440, App. p. 310 (1835), xii.
48 *5th Rep. Inspector of Prisons* [283], p. 159, H.C. (1840), xxv; *6th Rep.* [347], p. 125, H.C. (1841–II), iv.
49 *10th Rep.* [674], p. 179, H.C. (1845), xxiii.
50 *14th Rep.* [1173], p. 98, H.C. (1850), xxviii; *28th Rep.* [3215], p. 32, H.C. (1863), xxiii.
51 E.R.O., Boro. Mun., Boro. Council Mins. 1863–71, p. 295.
52 Ibid. 1877–80, pp. 97–8; ibid. Watch Cttee. Mins. 1892–96, p. 67.
53 *E.C.S.* 15 Aug. 1845; A. M. Brown, *Colch. High School: the first fifty years*, 6–8; below, Educ.
54 N. Butler, *Theatre in Colch.* 49; *Colch. Expr.* 27 Jan. 1972; 10 Apr. 1974.
55 *E.C.S.* 2 May 1980.

building housed the Co-operative Bank and the General Accident Assurances Corporation.

The PUBLIC HALL, later ST. GEORGE'S HALL, behind no. 156 High Street was not, despite its name, a municipal building. The red brick hall with apsidal ends was built in 1851 primarily for the use of the Mechanics Institution.[56] After the Institution's closure in 1860 it was used as a library and reading room, lecture room, and theatre until the owners, the Colchester New Public Hall Co. Ltd., went into liquidation in 1897. The hall then changed hands several times and had a number of uses: as a magistrates' court and cells, a clothing factory, and a club for the troops in the First World War. In 1920 it was bought by Henry Elwes, renamed St. George's Hall, and became a young men's club and then a centre for the unemployed. The neighbouring Repertory Theatre used the hall as a workshop from 1937 to 1967. Cullingford and Co. bought the premises in 1948 and rented the basement out separately. From *c.* 1960 they used half the hall as a stockroom and took over the whole of the ground floor in 1967.[57]

ARMS, SEALS, INSIGNIA AND PLATE

ARMS. The earliest known representation of the borough arms, a red shield with a green jagged cross, its arms and foot pierced with three nails, and three golden crowns, the bottom one encircling the foot of the cross, appears in the initial letter of the charter of 1413. The cross and nails probably refer to St. Helen's legendary discovery of the true cross and passion nails; the crowns may refer to her alleged discovery of the bodies of the three magi. The same arms appear on the early 15th-century common seal of the borough.[58] There appear to have been several variants in the 16th and 17th centuries, but in the version recorded at the heralds' visitation of 1558 and used until the corporation decided to revert to the medieval form *c.* 1915, the cross is silver and there are no nails.[59] In 1976 a full armorial achievement was granted to the new Colchester district. The medieval borough arms were retained, supported by a Roman soldier and a fisherman, and surmounted by a crest showing St. Helen holding the cross, with the motto 'no cross, no crown'. In 1989 the full achievement had never been used.[60]

BOROUGH OF COLCHESTER. *Gules, a jagged cross vert, its arms and foot pierced with three nails, and three golden crowns, the bottom one encircling the foot of the cross* [Recorded 1413, regranted 1976]

FIG. 25

SEALS.[61] The first, probably 13th-century, common seal of the borough, in use by 1317, was round, 3¾ in. in diameter. On the obverse was a triple-towered castle, masoned and embattled, its round-headed doorway having half-opened doors, below it, a stream spanned by three arches with a fish naiant under each arch, and round the circumference the legend, lombardic: [SIGILLUM C]OLCESTRENSIS S . . . BU[R]GI C[OMMUNE]. On the reverse was St. Helen, crowned and seated on a canopied throne, holding a long cross and the three holy nails, with the legend, lombardic: QUAM CRUX INSIGNIT HELENAM C[OLCESTRIA GIG]NIT. The seal continued in use until 1379 or later.[62] The brass matrix of the second common seal, in use by 1462, was with the borough plate in 1989. The seal is round, 3½ in. in diameter. On the obverse is St. Helen, enthroned under a canopied niche, with Christ half length in a niche above; on each side is a smaller, canopied, turreted niche with an angel holding a shield, that on the left bearing a cross and that on the right the 15th-century royal arms; below, under an arch, are the borough arms supported by lions or ravens. The legend, black letter, is SIGILLU*M* COMMUNE BALLIVORU*M* ET COMMUNITATIS VILLE DOMINI REGIS COLCESTRIE. On the reverse is a castellated town, in front of it a river crossed by a bridge or steps, on each side a lion statant surmounted by a flowering branch, with the legend, black letter: INTRAVIT IHC IN QUODDAM CASTELLUM ET MULIER QUEDAM EXCEPIT ILLUM, an adaptation of Luke 10. 38 apparently referring to St. Helen.[63] The seal remained in use until 1891 when it was replaced by an embossing seal of the same design as its obverse but bearing the modern royal arms and with the legend THE COMMON SEAL OF THE

56 Ibid. 10 Oct. 1851.

57 E.R.O., Acc. C210 J. B. Harvey Colln. iv, pp. 163–5; deeds in possession of Mr. J. C. Cross, Cullingford and Co. Ltd.; J. C. Cross, *'A Heap of Victorian Rubble' 1842–1892* (priv. print. 1992), *passim*: copy in E.C.L. Colch.

58 *Arch. Jnl.* lviii. 378; *E.R.* ix. 202–20; xxiii. 1–8.

59 *E.R.* ix. 219; xxiii. 112–13; press cuttings of 28 Oct. 1842, 25 Apr. 1915 E.C.L. Colch.; *Visit. Essex* (Harl. Soc.), i. 6.

60 Colch. Boro. Council, *Policy Cttee. Mins.* 27 July 1976; inf. from the town serjeant.

61 The following section is based on a draft by the late R. B. Pugh, revised by Janet Cooper.

62 B.M. *Cat. of Seals*, ii, no. 4825; *Colch. Arch. Rep.* i. 82; E.R.O., D/DRg 6/2; *Proc. Soc. Antiq.* 2nd ser. x. 343. The missing letters after S on the obverse are given as UI in *Oath Bk. of Colch.* ed. W. G. Benham, 226–7, which assumes an error for UM.

63 B.M. *Cat. of Seals*, ii, no. 4827; *Colch. Arch. Rep.* i. 82–3; E.R.O., D/DRg 6/5; the letters IHC represent the Greek letters beginning the name Jesus.

MAYOR ALDERMEN AND BURGESSES OF THE BOROUGH OF COLCHESTER MDCCCXCI.[64] That seal was replaced in 1976 by a new one bearing the borough arms and the legend THE COMMON SEAL OF COLCHESTER BOROUGH COUNCIL.[65] The bailiffs' seal, the silver matrix of which survives, is round, 2¼ in. in diameter; it depicts a castle or walled town with St. Helen standing in the doorway of a central tower. Outside the legend, which is black letter SIGILLUM OFFICII BALLIVORUM VILLE COLCESTRIE, is a broad border of roses and fleur-de-lis. The seal appears to be 14th-century although no impressions survive before 1546.[66]

Another seal described as a common seal of the vill survives on a chantry foundation deed of 1348. It is circular, 2 in. in diameter, with a raven facing to the right, and the legend SIGILLU*M* CUSTOD*IS* PORT*US* CO[L]ECEST'.[67] 'Custos portus' is presumably a translation of port reeve, and the seal may be an early 13th-century reeves' or bailiffs' seal. It was still one of the borough seals *c.* 1450.[68]

INSIGNIA. In 1515 two maces, presumably one for each bailiff, were carried before Catherine of Aragon when she arrived in the town.[69] By the mid 17th century, probably from 1635 when Charles I's charter substituted a mayor for the bailiffs, the town possessed a great mace which was replaced in 1698 by one weighing *c.* 100 oz. and surmounted by a globe and cross.[70] That mace and most of the borough plate were sold in 1730 to pay for a new silver gilt great mace still in use in 1989.[71] The mace is 58 in. long, ending in an open arched crown surmounted by an orb and cross; it has the royal arms and the letters GR on the flat plate at the top. Four caryatides separate the bowl into compartments which bear the borough arms, a crowned fleur-de-lis, a crowned thistle, and a crowned harp. The shaft is richly ornamented, and the hallmarks are for London 1729–30.[72] Three maces mended before Queen Mary's visit in 1553 may have been serjeants' maces.[73] Serjeants at mace were recorded in 1463–4, by which time the office was already well established, and in 1635 each carried a mace bearing the royal arms.[74] In 1989 the borough insignia included four silver gilt serjeants' maces, each *c.* 12 in. long and bearing the Stuart royal arms, which were carried in civic processions by special constables. Three of the maces probably date from *c.* 1633, but the fourth, which has a maker's mark on the stem, may have been made to replace the mace missing in 1687.[75]

The mayor's gold chain, of 506 links in 6 separate chains each of diminishing length, was presented in 1765 by Leonard Ellington, a London merchant. The mayor's badge, worn separately from the chain, is a silver gilt replica of the 15th-century borough seal in a carved ivory mount. When it was presented to W. Gurney Benham in 1935 the then mayor's badge, a golden jubilee medal of 1887 in a gold border of oak leaves and figures from the 15th-century seal, was assigned to the deputy mayor. In 1909 the Colchester pageant committee presented the mayoress's gold chain and badge showing Boudicca in her war chariot, and in 1922 a St. George's Day medal was given for the mayoress.[76] In 1825 and probably earlier the treasurer's badge of office was a silver key, but the 19th-century one had been lost by 1905 when a silver gilt key bearing the borough arms in coloured enamel was presented by C. R. Gurney Hoare.[77] The water bailiff's oar was recorded in 1689;[78] in 1989 there were two silver oars, one, 8½ in. long and hallmarked 1804–5, may have been in use in 1825; the other, 10 in. long, was hallmarked 1827–8.[79] By 1689 the water bailiff was using a gauge to check the size of oysters taken from the town's fishery.[80] In 1748 the gauge was brass,[81] but in 1825 a silver gauge was being used. That gauge, lost by 1895, may be the one hallmarked 1804–5 which was given back to the borough in 1905. In 1950 there were three gauges, two brass and one silver but by 1966 only one silver and one brass gauge remained.[82]

The bailiffs' livery gowns were first recorded in 1372. Aldermen were probably given robes *c.* 1404 and councillors received hoods from 1411–12.[83] By 1578 bailiffs and aldermen had to provide their own scarlet robes with black velvet tippets and caps,[84] and common councillors their own mulberry coloured gowns and caps. In 1598 councillors' gowns were changed to black cloth faced with lambskin, with black and scarlet hoods.[85] By 1548 salaried officials were provided with a livery which in 1665 was blue. By 1843 the councillors' gowns were purple, the town clerk's and the treasurer's black silk.[86] In 1895 the mayor's robe was scarlet with sable trimmings and black facings[87] but by 1901 it was black with gold trimmings. The change was probably made on Queen Victoria's death. Since local government re-organization in 1974 chairmen of committees have worn red robes with fur facings, honorary aldermen purple with black velvet facings, and councillors blue with fur facings.[88]

PLATE. In the 17th century several items of plate were given to the borough mostly by men who held office in the town.[89] In 1680 the 20 pieces

64 E. A. Blaxill, *Boro. Regalia*, 30.
65 *E.C.S.* 30 July 1976; inf. from the mayor's secretary.
66 *E.R.* ix. 204; Blaxill, *Regalia*, 15; *Bull. of John Rylands Libr.* xxx. 268.
67 B.M. *Cat. of Seals*, ii, no. 4831; *Colch. Arch. Rep.* i. 82; the seal is illustrated in *Colch. Guide* (1982), 63.
68 E.R.O., D/B 5 R1, f. 179v.
69 Ibid., f. 118.
70 Ibid. D/B 5 Gb7, f. 217; D/B 5 Aa1/35.
71 Ibid. D/B 5 Gb7, f. 264; *E.R.* xviii. 170.
72 Ll. Jewitt & W. H. St. John Hope, *Corp. Plate and Insignia*, i. 193–8.
73 E.R.O., D/Y 2/2, p. 31.
74 Ibid. Acc. C104, box of papers 1425–1893; ibid. D/B 5 R1, f. 99v.; *Colch. Charters*, 91.
75 Inf. from town serjeant; Jewitt & Hope, *Corp. Plate*, i. 124, 193–8; Blaxill, *Regalia*, 12; E.R.O., D/B 5 Gb5, f. 281.
76 Blaxill, *Regalia, passim.*
77 T. Cromwell, *Hist. Colch.* ii. 400–1; Blaxill, *Regalia*, 25.
78 E.R.O., D/B 5 Gb5, f. 320.
79 Cromwell, *Hist. Colch.* ii. 400–1; Blaxill, *Regalia*, 15.
80 E.R.O., D/B 5 Gb5, f. 320.
81 Morant, *Colch.* (1748), Bk. I. 92.
82 Cromwell, *Hist. Colch.* ii. 400–1; Blaxill, *Regalia*, 15–17; L. E. Dansie, *Colch. Boro. Regalia*, 2.
83 Britnell, *Growth and Decline*, 224–5.
84 E.R.O., D/B 5 Gb1, 7 July 1578.
85 Britnell, *Growth and Decline*, 224; E.R.O., D/B 5 Gb1, 30 Oct. 1598.
86 E.R.O., Acc. C210, J. B. Harvey Colln. iv, p. 97.
87 Jewitt and Hope, *Corp. Plate*, i. 198.
88 Inf. from the town serjeant.
89 E.R.O., D/B 5 Gb2, f. 132; Gb3, f. 214; Gb5, f. 157.

of town plate included silver beer and wine cups, salt dishes, and a caudle cup and cover.[90] In 1730 nineteen pieces were sold to pay for a new mace. The one remaining piece, a large, two-handled, silver gilt loving cup given in 1679 by Abraham Johnson,[91] was still in the borough's possession in 1989. Plate acquired since 1730 includes the 18th-century mayor's theatre ticket, a circular silver plaque 2 in. in diameter; four Elizabethan silver spoons and a Charles II apostle spoon presented by the Essex Archaeological Society in 1926, 1927, 1928, and 1948; a tankard, a chocolate pot, and a punch ladle by R. Hutchinson, a 17th-century Colchester silversmith, acquired in 1955 and 1961; and a silver replica of the Colchester obelisk, presented in 1962. Three of the most remarkable pieces were in the mayor's parlour in 1989: a 25½ in. long silver decanter in the shape of a 16th-century three-masted warship, given in 1913; an 18th-century punch bowl given by the United States army air force in 1945; and a silver casket with a statuette of St. Helen on the lid and enamelled side panels depicting the town hall and St. Botolph's Priory with the borough arms between, which was given to Dame Catherine Hunt in 1935 and bequeathed by her to the corporation in 1948.

PARISH GOVERNMENT AND POOR RELIEF

PARISH GOVERNMENT.[92] Except for some 17th-century vestry minutes of All Saints' and St. Leonard's parishes, surviving parish records consist of 18th- and 19th-century vestry and select vestry minutes, overseers' rates and accounts, churchwardens' rates and accounts, surveyors' accounts, and some bills and settlement papers.

Vestry meetings to appoint parish officers were held usually at Easter, and in some parishes also at Michaelmas or Christmas. There were additional meetings: up to 10 a year were recorded in the later 17th century in St. Leonard's and All Saints' parishes, but meetings in the 18th century in all parishes where the records survive were fewer.[93] Usually from 2 to 20 male parishioners of high status attended, with a larger attendance at the Easter meeting; women were seldom present.[94] Between 1798 and 1809 in All Saints' parish a monthly meeting, composed mainly of parish officers, acted as a small executive committee.[95] Following the second Sturges Bourne Act of 1819 select vestries of *c.* 20 members, incumbent, parish officers, and local gentlemen and traders, met at least once a month in All Saints', St. Botolph's, St. James's, St. Giles's, and St. Runwald's parishes, to consider applications for poor relief.[96] The rector or vicar, if present at ordinary or select vestry meetings, took the chair; otherwise a churchwarden or another parishioner of standing presided. Meetings were usually held in the vestry, and sometimes adjourned to a private house or an inn; members of the All Saints' monthly meeting met alternately at the Castle inn and the Seahorse, St. Botolph's vestry meetings were held at several different inns and at the parish workhouse, and in the 1820s St. Runwald's monthly meetings were held at three different inns.[97]

Two churchwardens and usually two overseers, but sometimes three or four, were appointed. A Quaker served as overseer in Holy Trinity in 1761 and again in 1770, and another one as overseer in St. Mary Magdalen's in 1782.[98] A woman was appointed overseer in St. Botolph's in 1754, in St. Nicholas's in 1780, and in Holy Trinity in 1786, but each time the work was done by a male deputy or deputies. From the 1820s parishes normally employed an assistant salaried overseer; St. Giles's had two in 1830 and 1831.[99] Two, or occasionally three or four, surveyors were appointed annually; Holy Trinity had a salaried one from 1836.[1] Usually two parish constables were appointed, but in June 1757, during the national unrest that preceded the elder Pitt's recall to the government, there were four additional constables in St. Botolph's and in All Saints' parishes 'for suppressing all riots and disorders'.[2] From *c.* 1800 officers were appointed to assess and collect taxes for the central government.

Vestries, besides looking after their parish churches and answering for watch and ward, undertook other public services, such as maintaining fire engines and parish pumps.[3] St. Nicholas's had a parish cage from 1760 to 1810, and St. Leonard's erected one in 1783.[4]

PARISH POOR RELIEF TO 1834. Except between 1698 and 1745,[5] the parish's main responsibility from the Tudor period was poor relief, supervised by the borough justices. In 1678 the justices ordered parish officials to badge the poor, and the poor were being badged in St. Mary's parish in 1690.[6] In 1783 the ratepayers of St. Peter's parish agreed to badge the poor, except the blind or lame or those over 70 years of age.[7] Overseers gave relief in regular or casual cash doles, or sometimes loans, supplemented by grants of clothing, shoes, bedlinen, cloth, fuel, soap, and, occasionally, tools for work. Rents, rates, or fees for burial or nursing care might be paid. Widows, children, the sick, and

90 *E.R.* ii. 16.
91 E.R.O., D/B 5 Gb5, f. 157.
92 Account based on the parish records, listed fully at E.R.O.; specific references are given where appropriate. The four outlying parishes are treated separately below (Outlying Parts).
93 E.R.O., D/P 245/8/2, 3; D/P 200/8/1–3.
94 e.g. ibid. D/P 323/8/1.
95 Ibid. D/P 200/8/4.
96 Ibid. D/P 200/8/2, 3; D/P 203/8/2, 3; D/P 138/8/7; D/P 324/8/1.
97 Ibid. D/P 200/8/4; D/P 203/8/1–3; D/P 177/8/4.
98 Ibid. P/COR 10; ibid. D/P 323/8/1.
99 Ibid. D/P 203/5/1; D/P 176/12/1; D/P 323/8/1; D/P 324/8/1.
1 Ibid. D/P 323/4/1.
2 Ibid. D/P 200/8/2; D/P 203/5/1.
3 Below, Public Services.
4 E.R.O., D/B 5 Gb9, p. 177; D/P 245/8/3.
5 Above, Tudor and Stuart Colch. (Soc. Structure), Georgian Colch. (Town Govt.).
6 E.R.O., D/B 5 Sb3/1, p. 10; ibid. Acc. C210 J. B. Harvey Colln. vi, pp. 80–1.
7 Ibid. D/P 178/12/2.

the aged were always amongst recipients of poor relief, but, especially in times of high unemployment, able-bodied men were also relieved. An incomplete survey of St. Botolph's parish poor in 1794 included many weavers; only a few of the families receiving relief had more than four children.[8]

Medical care was provided on a casual basis in the 18th century, but by the early 19th century many parishes had a salaried medical officer. Smallpox inoculation at parish expense was provided occasionally in the late 18th century in one or more inoculating houses: in 1776 a man was nursed at an inoculating house at the expense of St. Leonard's parish;[9] in 1779 St. Nicholas's parish paid for the treatment of a parishioner in the inoculating house.[10] There were no local facilities for the treatment of mental handicap and illness until the 1850s.[11] Occasionally parishes sent lunatics to the Bethlehem hospital (Lond.) and paid for their maintenance there.[12] St. Botolph's had a standing arrangement in the early 19th century to send insane paupers to Holly House lunatic asylum, Hoxton (Mdx.).[13] The pantry in St. James's workhouse was altered in 1826 to provide a lock-up for a deranged and very dangerous woman.[14] In 1830–2 St. Runwald's boarded out two harmless idiots at a house in Maidenburgh Street,[15] but presumably such paupers often remained with their own families.

Besides the overseers' difficulties in distinguishing between the workshy and those eager to support themselves, there were the perennial problems of unemployment and low wages.[16] The parishes' intention was to provide work within workhouses, but lack of workhouse accommodation often forced them to find work outside. All Saints' bought a bay loom in 1690 and bay work was given to the poor.[17] In the 1740s St. Runwald's provided spinning wheels for some female paupers; in 1779 St. Nicholas's lent a man some weaving equipment from the workhouse; and in 1801–2 St. Leonard's lent parish spinning wheels to poor people.[18] Unemployed men were sometimes given paid labouring work: in 1826–7, in a decade when jobs were particularly scarce, St. Botolph's parish employed men on the roads and at the parish gravel pit.[19] Overseers of several parishes successfully offered the improvement commissioners tenders for sweeping streets, to occupy occasionally unemployed men.[20]

Children were expected to work as soon as they were old enough. In 1771 children of applicants in St. Leonard's were to spin all day, with just a half hour break for breakfast and an hour for dinner, otherwise relief would be witheld.[21] Similarly in 1827 St. Botolph's denied relief to parents refusing to send their children to work in the town's silk mills, the millowners having requested children, presumably as cheap labour.[22] In St. Mary's-at-the-Walls, however, many parents were encouraged by the town gentry not to allow their children to work at the local silk factory for fear of corrupting their morals.[23] Younger children were sometimes boarded out by a parish, and older ones apprenticed. Before 1800 boys were apprenticed mainly to fishermen, oyster dredgers, and mariners, near Colchester or further away at Southwark, Deptford, South Shields, or Sunderland, and to weavers, mainly in Colchester. After 1800 no children were placed with weavers, but a few boys still followed nautical trades and nearly a third were apprenticed to cordwainers.[24]

Sometimes lodgings were found for paupers,[25] or houses rented for their use.[26] The large number of unendowed almshouses in the various parishes were presumably used to house paupers.[27] Ten of the 12 town parishes had their own small workhouses in the 18th century and the early 19th. Some parishes converted existing almshouses into workhouses, but many of those may have been used as pauper housing rather than as places where paupers were set to work. The former St. Catherine's hospital in Crouch Street, which had been used as a borough workhouse in the later 16th century, was used as a parish workhouse for St. Mary's-at-the-Walls in the later 18th century.[28] Almshouses on the north side of Bucklersbury Lane became St. Nicholas's workhouse by 1748.[29] In 1834 St. Mary's workhouse held 8 inmates on average.[30] A workhouse in St. Martin's from 1770 to 1788 was probably in Hospital Yard, Angel Lane, where a pest house was said to have stood.[31]

Some or all of the other parish workhouses were also converted buildings. Three houses near East bridge in East Street became St. James's workhouse in 1755; there were 14 inmates in 1834.[32] All Saints' equipped a six-roomed house as a workhouse *c.* 1753; the outbuildings were being let by 1774 and the house was being used for pauper housing by 1799; in 1801 the vestry planned to create another workhouse and by 1822 one was in use.[33] St. Botolph's had a workhouse in 1782 which may have been the one in Moor Lane (Priory Street) mentioned in 1825.[34] Between 1829 and

8 Ibid. D/P 203/18/3.
9 Ibid. D/P 245/8/3.
10 Ibid. D/P 176/12/2.
11 Below, Hospitals.
12 e.g. E.R.O., D/P 323/12/1.
13 Ibid. D/P 203/8/3; D/P 203/18/1.
14 Ibid. D/P 138/8/7.
15 Ibid. D/P 177/12/8.
16 *Rep. R. Com. Poor Law*, H.C. 44, App. pp. 43G, 43H (1834), xxxv.
17 E.R.O., D/P 200/8/1.
18 Ibid. D/P 177/12/1; D/P 176/12/1; D/P 245/12/9.
19 Ibid. D/P 203/8/2–3.
20 Below, Public Services; E.R.O., D/P 203/18/1.
21 E.R.O., D/P 245/8/3.
22 Ibid. D/P 203/8/3.
23 *Rep. R. Com. Poor Law*, App. p. 43H.
24 e.g. E.R.O., D/P 203/14/1–3; D/P 138/14/1.
25 e.g. ibid. D/P 177/8/2.
26 Ibid. D/P 138/8/8.
27 Morant, *Colch.* 170–1; below, Religious Houses.
28 E.R.O., D/B 5 Sb2/1, f. 20.
29 Morant, *Colch.* (1748), Bk. III, pp. 8–9.
30 *Rep. R. Com. Poor Law*, App. p. 43G.
31 Guildhall MS. 9557, f. 71; Morant, *Colch.* 171; E.R.O., Acc. C210 J. B. Harvey Colln. vi, p. 89.
32 E.R.O., D/P 138/18/1, 4; *Rep. R. Com. Poor Law*, App. p. 42G.
33 E.R.O., D/P 200/12/4; D/P 200/8/2–4.
34 Ibid. P/COR 10; ibid. D/P 203/8/1; D/DEl T358/48.

Head Street from the south, *c.* 1865

The Culver Centre, *c.* 1990

Aerial view of central Colchester from the south-west, *c.* 1960

The town hall and the castle, in the background, mark the line of High Street; below them the public library stands on the corner of Shewell Road and Culver Street, and the gothic Lion Walk Congregational church between Culver Street and Eld Lane

1831 there were 17–27 inmates.[35] St. Giles's had a workhouse in 1775 which admitted paupers from St. Leonard's also, and which may have been the large workhouse in Stanwell Street recorded in 1833.[36] St. Leonard's had its own workhouse by 1768, which may have been the one recorded in 1834 on the south side of Hythe Street opposite Knaves Acre.[37] Holy Trinity had a workhouse by 1749 and a poorhouse, perhaps the same house, on the north side of Eld Lane in 1818.[38] St. Peter's had a workhouse in 1779, probably the one in North Street mentioned in the 1830s; in 1820 there were 31 inmates.[39] St. Mary Magdalen's parish had four houses on the north side and two on the south side of Magdalen Street, all sold in 1837, described as a workhouse but which probably functioned rather as pauper housing.[40] St. Runwald's had no workhouse of its own, but apparently used those in neighbouring parishes.[41]

The workhouse masters usually received an annual salary and a weekly allowance per inmate, which in St. Botolph's was reduced from 3*s.* 9*d.* in 1829 to 3*s.* in 1832.[42] St. James's reduced the workhouse master's allowance from 3*s.* 6*d.* in 1821 to 3*s.* 3*d.* in 1832. Sometimes masters were also allowed proceeds from work done by inmates, or free coal or other extras; by the early 19th century their terms of service were sometimes set out in writing.[43] Spinning, weaving, and carding were the main forms of work until the beginning of the 19th century.[44] Thereafter, apart from the training of girls for household service, inmates seemed to do little more than make, repair, and launder their own clothes and help with the running of their own workhouse and garden. In 1821 the inmates of St. James's poorhouse were allowed a diet of wholesome food with 'a comfortable and hot dinner' of meat and vegetables three times a week.[45] The parishes were well aware of the expense and inefficiency of running so many small workhouses separately, and in 1818 discussed combining their resources to convert part of the garrison hospital to a shared house of industry, but it was not until after the Poor Law Amendment Act of 1834 that a union of parishes was again effected.[46]

In spite of significant differences between parishes in size of population and proportion of poor inhabitants, trends in poor relief expenditure were similar. In general, the cost of parish poor relief rose gradually in the 17th century, possibly in line with the gradual rise in population. In 1602 the total amount raised by poor rates ranged from *c.* £40 in St. Giles's to less than £3 in St. Mary Magdalen's, a very small and poor parish.[47] In 1665–6 Colchester suffered so badly from plague that parish poor rates had to be supplemented. In St. Leonard's, where the cost of poor relief had ranged from £50 to £100 a year between 1653 and 1664, almost £158, *c.* £100 of it given by the borough, was spent during the first quarter alone of 1666.[48] In 1629 All Saints' parish subsidized the poor of St. Botolph's, and in the 17th century St. Mary Magdalen's received poor relief contributions from Berechurch.[49]

In 1776 net expenditure ranged from £41 in St. Mary Magdalen's to £423 in St. Peter's, and over the period 1783–5 averaged from £76 in St. Mary Magdalen's to £552 in St. Peter's.[50] The rate of increase in expenditure accelerated in the last decade and high costs continued in the opening years of the 19th century, as the Napoleonic Wars destroyed the remnants of the local cloth industry. Between 1800 and 1805 the All Saints' overseers complained of the great distress caused by the high price of food; relief to dependants of militia men was a further wartime expense.[51] Average expenditure per head in the town and outlying parishes rose from 12*s.* 5*d.* in 1803 to 16*s.* 10*d.* in 1813, and in 1814–15 annual expenditure amounted to £8,560, ranging from £75 in St. Mary Magdalen's to £1,019 in St. Botolph's.[52]

After the end of the wars in 1815 average expenditure per head declined slightly to 16*s.* 3*d.* in 1821, and it fell further to 13*s.* 9*d.* a head in 1831. In the decade before the 1834 Act some parishes were making efforts to reduce spending, believed by many ratepayers excessive, partly because of the inefficiency and inequity involved in providing relief separately in the 12 parishes of the town.[53]

Some parishes, as St. Botolph's in 1826–8, paid higher allowances than others to the mentally handicapped and aged.[54] At the same period St. James's officers were apparently hardening their attitude towards paupers: from 1824 relief was withheld from paupers who kept dogs, in 1829 there was a plan to provide bread and flour instead of money, and from 1831 rents were no longer paid. By 1829 applications for relief in St. James's had dwindled to none.[55] In St. Runwald's on the other hand between 1829 and 1834 twenty persons on average received regular payments.[56] The use of indoor as opposed to outdoor relief before 1834 probably depended on relative costs and on the availability of workhouse accommodation within a parish. All 12 town parishes and

35 Ibid. D/P 203/18/16–17.
36 Ibid. D/P 245/18/13; D/P 324/8/1.
37 Ibid. D/P 245/12/4; *27th Rep. Com. Char.* p. 555; E.R.O., D/CT 93A.
38 E.R.O., D/P 323/12/1; ibid. T/M 268.
39 Ibid. D/P 178/12/1; D/P 178/19/1; D/P 178/8/1.
40 Notes press cuttings file in E.C.L. Colch.; E.R.O., G/CoM 2, p. 336.
41 E.R.O., D/P 177/8/4.
42 Ibid. D/P 203/18/16, 17.
43 e.g. ibid. D/P 138/8/7, 8.
44 Ibid. D/P 200/12/4; D/P 323/12/1; D/P 176/12/1; D/P 178/18/8.
45 Ibid. D/P 138/8/7; *Rep. R. Com. Poor Law*, App. pp. 42G, 43G.
46 E.R.O., D/P 178/18/5; below, this section, Poor Relief after 1834.
47 Morant, *Colch.* 181 n.
48 E.R.O., D/P 245/8/2.
49 Ibid. D/Y 2/2, p. 41; ibid. D/B 5 Sr57, rot. 28.
50 Ibid. Q/CR 1/1.
51 Ibid. D/P 200/8/4; D/P 200/17/3.
52 *Rep. R. Com. Poor Law*, App. pp. 2F, 41F; E.R.O., Q/CR 1/10.
53 *Rep. R. Com. Poor Law*, pp. 2F, 41F.
54 E.R.O., D/P 203/8/3.
55 Ibid. D/P 138/8/7, 8.
56 Ibid. D/P 177/12/8.

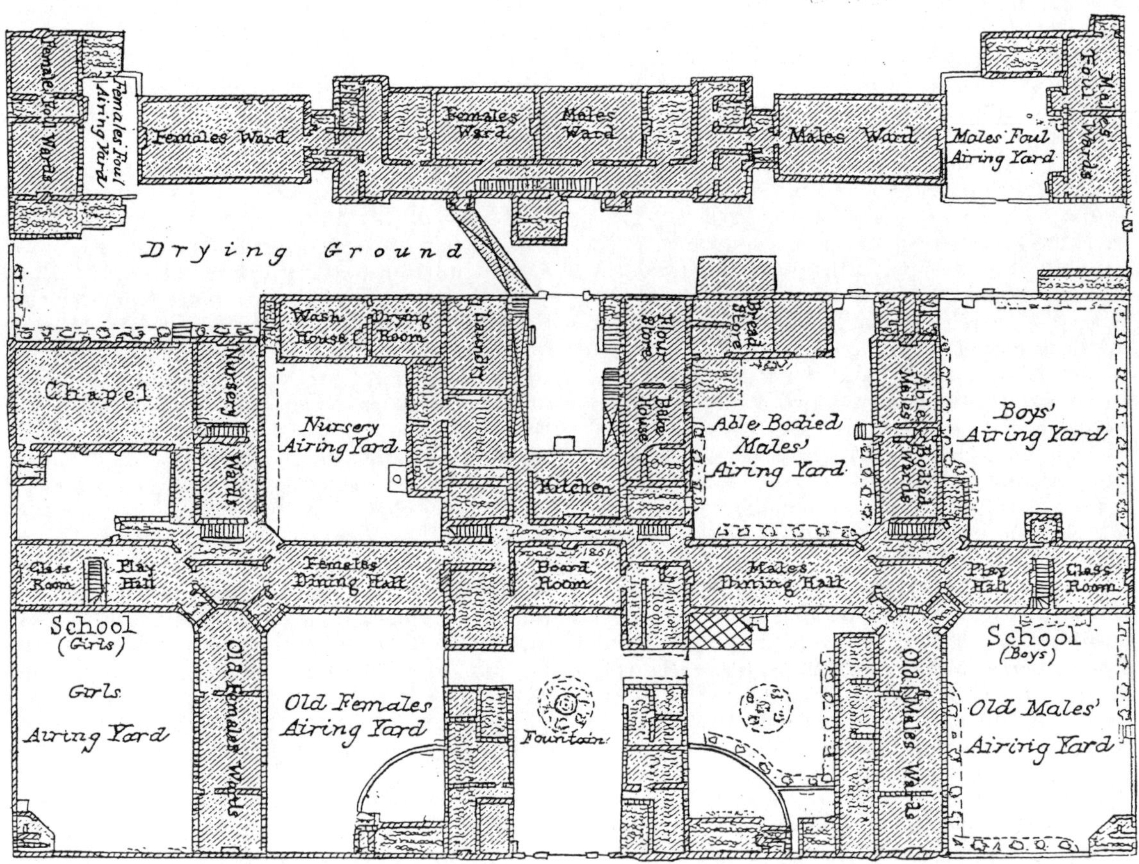

FIG. 26. PLAN OF THE UNION WORKHOUSE, 1876 (scale 1:580)

the 4 outlying parishes became part of Colchester poor law union in 1835.[57]

POOR RELIEF AFTER 1834.[58] Colchester poor law union was administered by a board of guardians composed of two elected representatives from each of St. Botolph's, St. Giles's, St. James's, St. Mary's-at-the-Walls, and St. Peter's parishes, and one from each of the 11 remaining parishes, together with the J.P.s *ex officio*. The guardians, who appointed a clerk, treasurer, relieving officer, and an auditor of accounts, met weekly. From 1836 rate collectors replaced the salaried assistant overseers of the parishes. In 1836 the borough was divided into four medical districts, each served by one or two medical officers; another two medical officers were responsible for midwifery and workhouse cases.

In 1835 and 1836 relief in the separate parishes was gradually brought under the control of the guardians. The existing parish workhouses, containing 79 inmates in 1835, were rented by the guardians and re-equipped. St. Mary's took the able-bodied, St. Giles's the infirm women, St. James's the children, and St. Peter's the infirm men. St. Botolph's received any overspill from the other houses. St. Nicholas's was too small to be useful, and St. Martin's too old and exceedingly dirty. The guardians tightened their supervision of the accounts after some confused bookkeeping by the clerk in the 1840s and by two rate collectors in the 1850s. After 1894 some women were appointed guardians.

In 1836 the guardians bought 9 a. at the top of Balkerne Hill for a union workhouse, and in 1837 paupers were moved into the new grey brick building, designed by John Brown. The parish workhouses were sold.[59] In 1848 an infirmary, later extended, was built north of the workhouse, a detached laundry was added in 1896–7, and separate casual wards in 1898.[60] The workhouse staff were a master and mistress, schoolmaster and mistress, porter, and later, nurses, all resident, a chaplain, and, from 1842, a workhouse medical officer of health. Numbers of workhouse inmates increased in 1837 to 133 and 156 in 1857. In the early 20th century there were 200–300 inmates, but about half were patients in the infirmary. There were 755 outdoor paupers in August 1837, none of them able-bodied, and another 103 wives of the sick and aged; in 1857 there were 1,245, only 97 of them able-bodied. In 1909 the number receiving outdoor relief was 569. By then the provision of other hospitals, homes, and schools, besides old

57 Ibid. G/CoM 1, pp. 1–2.
58 Account based on E.R.O., G/CoM 1–16, 30, 39–49, 52–4.
59 *4th Rep. Poor Law Com.* p. 202, H.C. (1837–8), xxviii.
60 Below, Hospitals; Essex C. C., *Public Assistance Subcttee. Rep. 26 Mar. 1930*, 48–9: copy at E.R.O.

age pensions and the expansion of workers' insurance schemes, had relieved the poor law of some of its burden.

Annual expenditure on poor relief for all 16 parishes, which averaged £10,155, equivalent to 12*s.* 5*d.* per head of population, in the years immediately before the union, decreased by about a quarter in the first few years of the new poor law with its new deterrent measures. In 1840–1 expenditure on the poor was £7,517, equivalent to 8*s.* 5*d.* per head. Thereafter costs gradually increased, and by 1858–9 expenditure on poor relief was £8,567; nevertheless, with a rapidly increasing population, that represented only 7*s.* 5*d.* per head.[61]

The Colchester guardians apparently resented their subordination to the poor law commissioners and their successors, particularly in the early decades. Their opposition focused on the imposed rule that denied relief to able-bodied men unless they and their families entered the workhouse, a policy which ignored problems of involuntary unemployment. In 1838 the chairman of the board of guardians resigned over the issue, although he remained a guardian, and the board wrote to the poor law commissioners expressing the fear that great suffering would be caused at a time of high prices.[62] In 1840 the guardians considered making loans to able-bodied men, and in 1870 preferred to employ men in stone-breaking rather than send them to the workhouse. Loans were frequently made by the 1850s.

Workhouse regulations ensured a regimented life-style, with uniform diets and clothing; visitors were allowed only on Wednesdays. In the early years unmarried pregnant women were distinguished by close mob caps over shorn heads and by blue and yellow clothing. Specific diets were intended for different classes of paupers. In 1836 the amount of meat for able-bodied inmates was reduced. In 1856 one meat dinner a week and half a pint of beer a day was added to the diet of the aged and infirm. Plum pudding was allowed for Christmas dinner, and Christmas day rations were allowed on the prince of Wales's marriage in 1863, Queen Victoria's jubilees in 1887 and 1897,[63] and the coronations in 1902 and 1911. An inspector in 1923 criticized the monotonous infirmary diet of meat, presumably boiled, and vegetables six days a week, and the guardians then allowed roast dinners at least twice a week. The workhouse diet was also improved, and in 1927 inmates were allowed 2 ounces of beef sausages, breakfast sausage, or brawn twice a week for breakfast or supper.

Workhouse inmates were set to work as far as was practicable. In 1838 children learned straw-plaiting. Boys learned shoemaking and tailoring, but from 1842 did gardening instead, probably because the house clothing store was already well stocked. Children were sent out to work in the silk factory in Dead Lane.[64] Work for adults was not meant to be pleasant, and included working hemp, picking oakum, and breaking granite, besides tasks connected with the daily running of the institution. Pigs were reared. The guardians provided oakum and granite until the First World War.

Discipline in the workhouse was meant to be strict. There were frequent cases in the early years of inmates absconding, a punishable offence if workhouse clothing was taken. The workhouse master resigned in 1846 because he no longer felt able to keep order. Men and women were not supposed to mix, and in 1849 screens were fixed to the upper parts of the facing windows of the men's and women's bedrooms so they could not make signs to each other. As late as 1900 all visits to able-bodied male and female inmates were stopped to ensure that the workhouse remained unattractive.

Some aged couples were allowed to share a room, especially if one of them was nursing the other. Old people could walk or sit outside the workhouse at certain times, and in 1844 three benches were provided. From 1892 old men were allowed an ounce of tobacco a week, and from 1893 the aged and infirm were allowed extra tea and sugar and butter or cheese for supper.

Until 1853 mentally ill paupers who could not be cared for at home were taken to lunatic asylums in neighbouring counties, many to Warburton's asylum, Bethnal Green (Mdx.). Between 1853 and 1913 the new Essex asylum at Brentwood was used, and thereafter Severalls mental hospital within the borough. In the 20th century some young mentally handicapped poor were given places at the Royal Eastern Counties' institution.[65]

Children were kept separate from other workhouse inmates as far as possible, and in 1841 came under the complete control of the schoolmaster and mistress. In 1842 the children were healthy and clean but the boys were flea-ridden and the girls short of clothing. In 1847, though, they were filthy and beyond the schoolmaster and mistress's control outside lessons; the guardians consented to the mistress's request for an assistant in 1848 when there were 54 children in the workhouse schools. In the 1860s because the children frequently suffered from ophthalmia the medical officer recommended more exercise and fresh air and more meat, bread, butter and milk, and an allowance of beer or porter.

Older boys were occasionally apprenticed, usually to mariners, and older girls and boys sometimes went into service. From 1869 orphaned and deserted children were boarded out if possible, supervised by weekly home visits. From 1873 the boys were drilled by a sergeant four times a week, from 1892 they went swimming regularly, and from 1895 went out to play football. By 1892 there were 70 children in the workhouse school, but from 1894 they attended the new board school in North Street, and were allowed to wear ordinary clothes there.[66]

In the early 20th century efforts were increasingly made to remove children from the workhouse to

61 *4th Rep. Poor Law Com.* p. 38; *11th Rep. Poor Law Com.* p. 191, H.C. (1845), xxvii; *12th Rep. Poor Law Board*, pp. 7–8, 78–9, H.C. (1859–60), xxxvii. The figures quoted relate to expenditure on poor relief as distinct from total expenditure which was always higher.

62 *E.C.S.* 7, 14 Dec. 1838.

63 *E.J.* xxvi (2), 34, 36.

64 *E.C.S.* 12 Feb. 1881.

65 Below, Hospitals.

66 Colch. Institute, Colch. Recalled, interview 2081.

other institutions and to foster homes, but the guardians' attempts to provide children's homes were unsuccessful. Some boys went to Dr. Barnardo's and Dr. Stephenson's homes, whence before the First World War some joined emigration schemes to Canada, and boys were regularly placed on the naval training ship 'Exmouth'. Other children went to Greenwood industrial home, Halstead, St. James's orphanage, Colchester, and Lexden and Winstree union's cottage homes. In 1934 only 5 children remained out of 114 inmates in the workhouse side of the institution.[67] Under the Children Act 1908[68] the guardians and their successors occasionally assumed parental rights on behalf of a child, and some children were placed for adoption.

The guardians tried to keep vagrants apart from other indoor poor. In 1841, when there was an influx of filthy and diseased wayfarers, some lodgings were found to supplement the inadequate workhouse accommodation. The police superintendant was appointed an assistant relieving officer in 1849 to keep a record of vagrants and issue tickets for the workhouse. Increased accommodation for vagrants was provided in 1885 and 1898. In spring 1935 there were 63 casuals on average, most of them men, comprising about a quarter of all inmates. The casual wards were closed in 1939.[69]

Outdoor relief continued after 1834 in both cash and kind: 570 loaves were allowed in one week in 1837. In the winter of 1840–1 able-bodied men were relieved on at least 29 occasions because of their own or their families' sickness, that being a way the guardians could circumvent the workhouse test. Loans were given for midwifery, nursing, food, medicinal brandy, and coffins. In 1868 a committee of guardians reported that the relieving officers had been too lax and were encouraging pauperism. Applications were henceforth to be investigated more carefully, relief being paid to applicants on certain days in a shed at the workhouse, except for the aged and infirm who were to be visited weekly by the relieving officers. In 1869 the three medical officers attended 1,930 cases of sickness.

By 1900 extra cash was always allowed to the outdoor poor at Christmas. From 1921 the board of guardians met fortnightly for general business and once or twice weekly to deal with the large numbers of unemployed applicants. In 1924 the guardians paid the Colne drainage board a quarter of the wages of men whom they referred to it for labouring work. By the 1920s the workhouse test was no longer applied to men unable to find work during economic depression.

In 1929 the boards of guardians were abolished and the poor law was administered by Essex county council until 1948. The union workhouse was renamed Colchester public assistance institution in 1920, and St. Mary's hospital in 1938.[70]

HOSPITALS

BEFORE the 19th century no voluntary hospital was established which survived more than a few years.[71] Alexander Fordyce, a speculative banker, built a hospital in Colchester *c.* 1768 but apparently it had closed by 1772. Other short-lived attempts at medical provision included the establishment by Dr. Loftus Woods in 1797 of a dispensary for the poor which may have closed when he died in 1804, and the setting up by four local doctors in 1816 of an eye infirmary which closed in 1818.[72]

When the Essex and Colchester hospital (later the Essex County hospital, Colchester) was opened in 1820, sick paupers remained the responsibility of the poor law authorities. Following the Contagious Diseases Acts of 1864, 1866, and 1867, which attempted to limit the spread of venereal diseases in certain military towns, including Colchester, by the compulsory treatment of infected prostitutes, a government lock hospital was built in 1867–8 in Port Lane at the east end of the town; it was closed in 1886.[73] Early attempts to contain infectious diseases included the provision of two pest houses, one at Mile End probably between Mill Road and Clay Lane, and another in St. Mary's parish, built during the severe outbreak of plague in 1665–6.[74] The borough maintained a hospital ship, apparently for infectious diseases, between 1877 and 1921.[75] In 1884 a borough isolation hospital was built (below, Infectious Diseases, later Myland, hospital).

Facilities were provided for local mentally handicapped patients, mainly children, from 1859 when the Eastern Counties' asylum for idiots and imbeciles, later the Royal Eastern Counties' Institution, was established at Essex Hall. Mentally ill patients were sent to various asylums in London and neighbouring counties until 1853; thereafter they went to the new Essex lunatic asylum at Brentwood until Severalls hospital was opened in 1913.[76] A maternity hospital was opened in 1932.[77]

In 1948 the voluntary hospitals in Colchester became part of the North East Metropolitan regional hospital board of the National Health Service. The isolation hospital was renamed Myland hospital and no longer used exclusively

67 Essex C. C., *Public Health Rep. on Institutions* (1934), p. 26: copy at E.R.O.

68 8 Edw. VII, c. 67.

69 E.R.O., C/MPa/10, p. 232; C/MPa/17, p. 508; Colch. Recalled, interview 2100.

70 E.R.O., C/MPa/16, p. 627.

71 This section was originally written in 1989. Much help was given by the late Dr. J. B. Penfold in its preparation.

72 J. B. Penfold, *Hist. Essex County Hosp. Colch. 1820–1948*, 1; *Gent. Mag.* (1772), 310–11; A. F. J. Brown, *Eng. Hist. from Essex Sources 1750–1900*, 147.

73 27 & 28 Vic. c. 85; 29 Vic. c. 35; 31 & 32 Vic. c. 80; Brown, *Colch. 1815–1914*, 167–8; E.R.O., G/CoM 52, House cttee. 14 Oct. 1886, 7 May 1889.

74 E.R.O., D/B 5 R7, f. 273v.; D/B5 Aa1/23; R.C.H.M. *Essex*, iii. 71.

75 E.R.O., Boro. Mun., Sanitary Cttee. Mins. 1874–8, 18 Apr. 1877, 17 July 1878; 1878–81, pp. 149, 259.

76 Ibid. G/CoM 1–16, 39, 52–4; *V.C.H. Essex*, viii. 91.

77 Below, this section, Colch. Maternity Hosp.

for infectious cases; together with the Essex County, Colchester Maternity, and St. Mary's hospitals, it was managed by the Colchester group hospital management committee. The Royal Eastern Counties' and Severalls each had its own separate management committee. Severalls and the Colchester group were combined in 1964 to form the St. Helena group with its own management committee. In the 1974 health service reorganization the hospitals in the St. Helena group joined with the Royal Eastern Counties' and the Tendring district hospitals, to form the new Colchester district with its own management team responsible to the Essex area health authority (an intermediate tier) and the North East Thames regional health authority. When the area authorities were abolished in 1982 the Colchester district became responsible to the North East Essex district health authority.[78] In 1992, under large-scale reorganization of the health service, three hospital trusts were established in Colchester, the Essex Rivers Health Care Trust (general), the North East Essex Mental Health Trust, and the New Possibilities Trust (learning disabilities). In 1993 the North East Essex, Mid Essex, and West Essex district health authorities merged to form the new North Essex Health Authority, with power to buy health services from hospital and other trusts. The three district health authorities had been working as one organization, the North Essex Health Consortium, since 1991.[79]

The first stage of the new District General hospital, planned to replace eventually all the existing public hospitals, was opened in 1985.

The military hospital established at the barracks in the 19th century relieved some of the pressure on the health service hospitals from 1959 until its closure in 1976. St. Helena hospice, financed by voluntary contributions, was opened at Myland (Mile End) Hall in 1985 to serve north-east Essex; the Joan Tomkins day centre opened there in 1988.[80] A private nursing home, set up by a consultant *c.* 1950 in his home in Lexden Road, became a charity, Colchester Nursing Home Ltd., in 1959. It moved in 1969 to new premises in Oaks Drive, which were extended in 1977 and 1984. Community Hospitals Ltd. took over the accommodation in 1989 to replace it with a new larger hospital.[81]

ESSEX COUNTY HOSPITAL, COLCHESTER.[82] In 1818 the Essex and Colchester hospital (renamed in 1907) was launched as a general infirmary for the poor on the initiative of Joseph Jefferson, archdeacon of Colchester. He persuaded seven other men to join with him in subscribing to buy the materials of the south wing of the military hospital. The following year, when 3 a. of land on the south side of Lexden Road were bought, the south wing was removed from the barracks and re-erected there to plans by M. G. Thompson.[83]

The hospital was financed by subscriptions, gifts, and interest on investments; receipts exceeded expenditure until the mid 1860s. By the late 19th century income was also derived from collections on Hospital Sunday from 1871, Hospital Saturday from 1883, and bazaars. The Ladies' Linen League raised money to supply linen from 1910, and the Colchester Ladies' Collection Association raised money from 1911. The hospital continued as a voluntary hospital until 1948, but there were financial problems. From 1920 in-patients were charged £1 a week for maintenance, reduced to 10*s.* for contributors to an insurance scheme started in 1910.

The management committee was under the presidency of the lord lieutenant of Essex; it was composed of a number of 'life governors', including the bishop of London, the Chancellor of the Exchequer, M.P.s representing the Essex constituencies, the mayor of Colchester, subscribers of 30 gn. or more, and executors of legacies of over £100; the ordinary governors were annual subscribers of 2 gn. or more and the overseers of subscribing parishes. The committee appointed two honorary physicians, three honorary surgeons, and a salaried staff of a house apothecary and secretary, a matron, nurses, and a porter. The building, of white brick in the classical style, was opened in 1820 with an operating room and beds for more than 80 patients in eight wards.

In 1825 a portico with double pilasters, designed by William Lay, was built on the front entrance. Two wings, designed by J. Hopper, county surveyor, were added in 1839. An isolation block of two wards with a nurses' room was built at the back of the hospital on the west side in 1847. There were major alterations to the building in 1879–80 to designs by J. H. Wyatt of London: an additional storey, to provide bedrooms, was built over the existing two floors in the centre of the building and square projections were added at each corner to contain washrooms with baths, and water closets; the existing windows were enlarged. Further extensive alterations were undertaken in 1897 to commemorate Queen Victoria's diamond jubilee, providing a new laundry and a nurses' home, converting nurses' accommodation in the central block to a children's ward and the nurses' dining room into an isolation ward, modernizing the operating theatre, and converting the porter's rooms into a casualty room.

For most of the 19th century usually only non-infectious non-pauper poor patients with a good chance of recovery were admitted, although accident cases were accepted. Patients, nominated by subscribers at weekly board meetings, were accepted on the advice of medical staff. From 1824 free vaccination was available. The hospital chiefly served the labouring population of Colchester and the surrounding countryside. In 1863 there were 90 beds but the

78 Essex area health authority, *Information Handbk.* (1979); inf. from Mr. D. J. Hooton and Mr. C. Willsher.

79 Inf. from North Essex Health Authority.

80 Deeds of 1983 in possession of Hospice; publicity leaflets [1988]; *E.C.S.* 3 Apr. 1987; 5 Feb. 1988.

81 *E.C.S.* 7 Oct. 1966; 15 Aug. 1969; 16 Nov. 1984; 1 & 29 Sept. 1989; *Colch. Gaz.* 6 May 1977.

82 Account based on Penfold, *Hist. Essex County Hosp. Colch.* and additional inf. from the author; below, pl. facing p. 344.

83 E.R.O., D/DR B10; H. M. Colvin, *Biog. Dict. Brit. Architects*, 823.

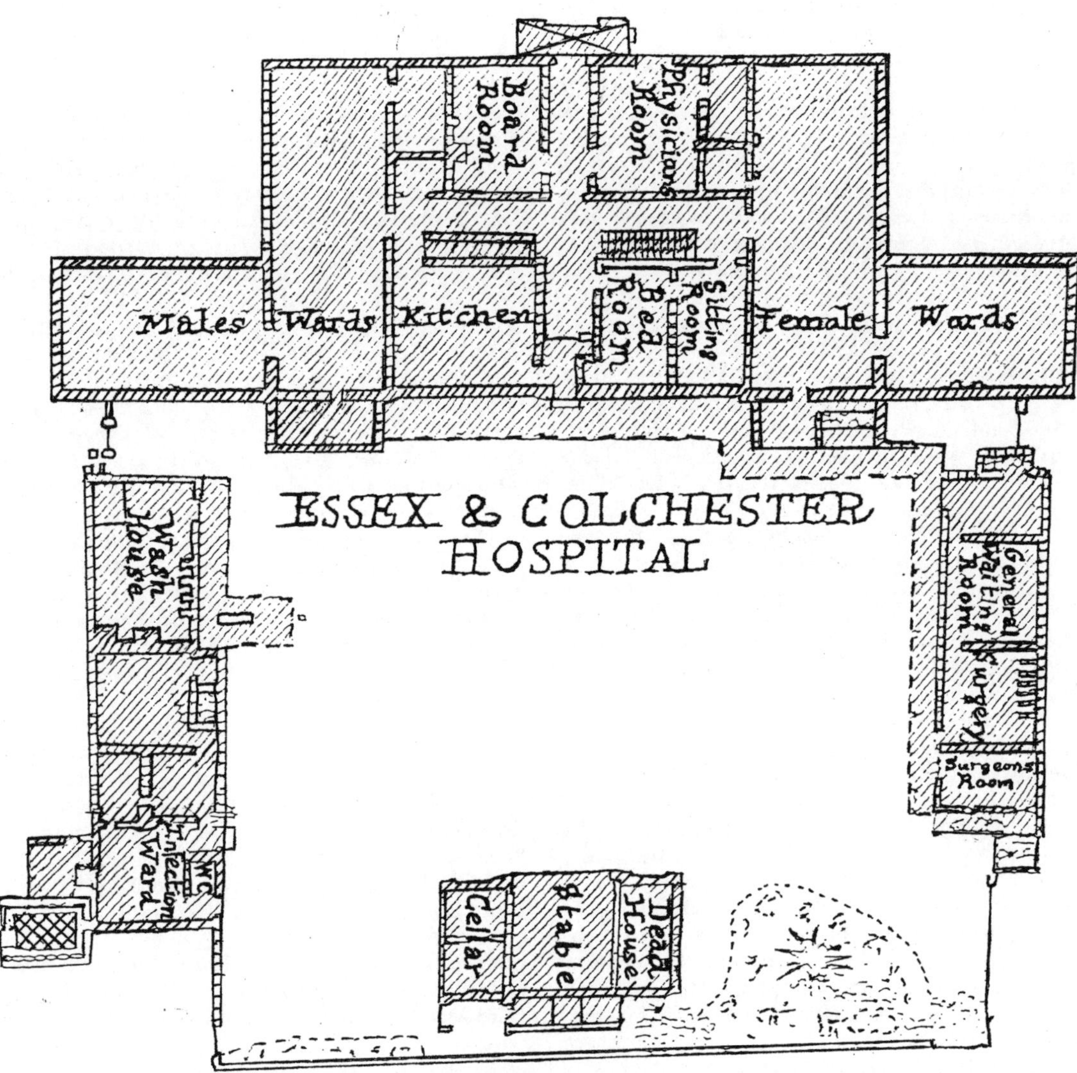

FIG. 27. PLAN OF THE ESSEX AND COLCHESTER HOSPITAL, 1876 (scale 1:333)

average daily number of patients was 50 and the average stay was 63 days. In the early days treatment was mainly by drugs, although a few operations were performed without anaesthetic. By 1870 up to 70 out-patients were attending weekly. Patients who broke the hospital rules were reprimanded, or discharged and put on a blacklist. Conditions for patients gradually improved. In 1869 part of the grounds were laid out as recreation areas. In 1877 the lower wards were painted grey and the upper ones buff, colour being used for the first time; pictures and upholstered chairs were provided; non-betting games, such as draughts and dominoes, were allowed; and fish and additional tea and sugar were added to the unimaginative diet. From 1881 the senior consulting physician and surgeon, and the chairman of the medical board sat on the committee. Admission meetings doubled to two a week from 1882. Paying patients were accepted from 1889, and in 1891 the hospital committee agreed to admit paupers in exceptional cases.

Official hospital policy was against private admission, but a private ward (not previously mentioned in reports) was abolished in order to provide a new children's ward which was opened in 1908. In 1911 a chapel and adjoining mortuary, and in 1912 a disinfecting chamber, a new isolation ward, and a new pathology laboratory were built. During the First World War the military authorities commandeered 50 of the 100 beds in the hospital, and female patients were transferred to the girls' high school in Wellesley Road. Two wooden huts were erected as temporary wards for 150 soldiers, and additional nurses and many voluntary helpers were used. In 1918 marquees in the grounds provided another 52 emergency beds. Following an inspector's criticism of the monotonous infirmary diet in 1924 at least two roast meat dinners a week and cake for Sunday tea were introduced for patients. Miss L. Jones raised funds to provide a wireless for the infirmary in 1927.

In the 1920s and 30s there were further additions and improvements. In 1924–6 a new block was built for outpatients, including dental surgeries, casualty and X-ray departments, and, on the upper floor, private patients' rooms, and doctors' quarters. In 1927 one of the wartime huts was refurbished and divided into two wards, increasing the number of beds by 20 to 160. In 1937 the hutted wards were closed and two new wards containing 40 beds were opened. During the Second World War the Essex County was graded as a first class non-teaching hospital for all types of cases and became part of the emergency medical service with its capacity temporarily increased to 269 beds.

In 1948 the hospital became part of the National Health Service. During succeeding decades facilities were further improved and the number of patients increased, though capacity was unable to keep pace with the demands of a rapidly rising local population. In 1950 the wooden huts were taken over for blood donor sessions, and were finally removed when new operating theatres were built on the site in 1955. A new radiotherapy block was opened in 1964. By 1968 there were 201 acute beds.[84] In 1969 a postgraduate medical study centre was built in Gray Road behind the hospital and the out-patients' department, pharmacy, and X-ray department were enlarged. A new children's wing was opened in 1972.[85] The number of beds at the hospital fell to 89 by 1988 as a result of the opening of the District General hospital.[86] In 1992 the postgraduate medical centre moved to a site adjacent to the District General hospital.[87]

ST. MARY'S HOSPITAL.[88] The hospital was built in 1837 as the Colchester union workhouse for sick besides destitute and aged paupers. Accommodation for the sick was already inadequate by 1844, partly because the workhouse was the only refuge for infectious cases, and a new workhouse infirmary was built in 1848. Cases of smallpox were noted particularly in 1845, 1863, 1868, and 1872, and of typhoid in 1861 and cholera in 1866. Usually lunatics were not allowed to remain in the house, but a straitjacket was provided in 1855 to be applied only by the workhouse master. In 1860 the guardians agreed to treat non-pauper women suffering from venereal disease in a building behind the workhouse, but in 1861 the poor law authorities vetoed the arrangement and in 1865 refused to agree to the workhouse's registration as a lock hospital. A 'foul ward', apparently for contagious diseases, existed by 1865 and was crowded in 1868, but the government lock hospital brought some relief from 1869. The workhouse infirmary was extended in 1869 and a dispensary established.

A detached fever ward was built north-east of the hospital in 1870.[89] In 1882 the corporation allowed the board of guardians to treat infectious cases at Hales' House on the Severalls estate. After the closure of the lock hospital in 1886 additional buildings were provided at the workhouse for cases of venereal diseases. A lying-in ward was mentioned in 1898.

From 1901 infectious paupers were accepted at the borough isolation hospital, releasing some beds at the workhouse. In 1911–12 a two-storeyed extension was added to the east end of the male infirmary, providing 40 additional beds, and the 16 beds in the former schoolhouse used for the sick since *c.* 1895 were allocated to contagious and tuberculous cases. The average number of patients in the workhouse infirmary increased from 105 *c.* 1870 to 135 in the summer quarter of 1899. By 1916 there were 10 nurses.

On the abolition of the board of guardians in 1929 the workhouse passed to Essex county council; it was taken over by the National Health Service in 1948.[90] By 1950 there were 208 beds, mainly for the chronic sick, but about a third were occupied by aged residents who were allowed to stay and for whom homes had been found by 1955. In 1958 more than half the cases were chronic sick, about a quarter acute medical, and the rest non-acute medical; the hospital secretary asserted that the idea of St. Mary's as a public assistance institution was 'a thing of the past'.[91]

By 1968 the hospital had been considerably modernized and a chest clinic built in the grounds. Medical and surgical facilities were wide-ranging, but of its 170 beds 102 were for geriatric in-patients, and there was a day centre for geriatric out-patients.[92] The day centre was extended in 1974, rehabilitation services improved in 1984, and a stroke unit was provided in 1985.[93] After the opening of the District General hospital St. Mary's became a geriatric hospital and had 125 beds in 1988.[94] The hospital was closed in 1993.[95]

INFECTIOUS DISEASES, later MYLAND, HOSPITAL. In 1884 a farmhouse on the Severalls estate at Mill Road, Mile End, was converted into a borough isolation hospital for non paupers. From 1888 infected paupers were also accepted.[96] Three small brick wards, each containing four beds, and two temporary pavilions were built, one of wood, and the other of corrugated iron. Another corrugated iron building was erected *c.* 400 m. from the main hospital with permanent accommodation for 20 patients and for a further 50 in an emergency, to serve

84 St. Helena group hosp. management cttee. *Handbk.* 1 Jan. 1968, p. 16.
85 *E.C.S.* 23 May 1969; 16 June 1972; *Colch. Expr.* 25 Sept. 1969.
86 N. E. Essex community health council, *12th Rep.* p. 28.
87 *E.C.S.* 10 July 1992; inf. from Essex Rivers Health Care.
88 Account based on E.R.O., G/CoM 1–16, 39–49, 52–4.
89 Phillips, *Ten Men*, 76–9.
90 E.R.O., C/MPa 1–17.
91 Colch. group hosp. management cttee. *Rep.* (1950–9).
92 St. Helena group hosp. management cttee. *Handbk.* 1 Jan. 1968.
93 *Colch. Gaz.* 13 Dec. 1974; *E.C.S.* 17 Feb. 1984; 4 Dec. 1987.
94 N. E. Essex community health council, *12th Rep.* p. 28.
95 *E.C.S.* 18 June 1993.
96 E.R.O., Boro. Mun., Sanitary Cttee. Mins. 1874–84, *passim*; ibid. Urban Sanitary Authority Hosp. Cttee. Mins. 1887–90.

as a smallpox hospital for north-east Essex. Three more blocks were added in 1910, 1913, and 1915. Four temporary buildings were built during the First World War for troops. The smallpox building was demolished by the fire brigade in 1936 and a new smallpox block was opened in Mill Road, Mile End, to serve the whole of Essex. In 1938–40 two new permanent blocks were built to replace a small pavilion and two temporary military wards.[97]

The hospital was taken over by the National Health Service in 1948 and renamed Myland Hospital. A hospital entirely for infectious diseases was no longer considered necessary and only 65 beds in two wards were retained for that purpose. The smallpox ward was adapted for ophthalmic patients and the remaining wards were used for general medical and surgical cases. One of the temporary blocks soon afterwards provided additional accommodation for tuberculous patients, another was used for supplies by the ambulance services. The remaining temporary block was reserved for use in any possible smallpox outbreak. Additional beds were provided for tuberculous patients in 1952, but from 1955 the demand for such beds decreased and a greater proportion of chronic sick patients were taken instead.[98] Kershaw House, a unit for 19 physically handicapped people, was opened in 1975. By 1977 the hospital contained 181 beds, almost a third of them geriatric.[99] By 1988 the number of beds had fallen to 77, for ophthalmic, geriatric, younger disabled, and infectious diseases cases,[1] and in 1989 the hospital was closed and demolished.[2]

ROYAL EASTERN COUNTIES' INSTITUTION, including TURNER VILLAGE. In 1850 the former hotel south of the main railway station was, with the help of its owner S. M. Peto, converted into a branch asylum of Park House hospital for idiots, Highgate (Mdx.), and 28 children were sent there from London. The number of mentally handicapped patients at the branch asylum, called Essex Hall, had increased to 150 by 1855 with an additional 50 accommodated elsewhere in Colchester, but between 1855 and 1858 all the patients were transferred to the newly built Royal Earlswood hospital, Surrey. In 1859 a separate Eastern Counties' asylum for idiots and imbeciles was established, based at Essex Hall, only the second such institution in England.[3] It received voluntary subscriptions and contributions from some patients, and served Essex, Norfolk, Suffolk, and Cambridgeshire. Patients, mainly but not exclusively children, were admitted by votes of subscribers and no paupers were allowed. The average number of resident patients gradually increased from 66 in 1862 to 189 in 1891 and to 245 in 1897. Patients were accepted for five years, and after 1865 up to 20 per cent of cases could be re-selected to give them a permanent home.[4] Before the institution was handed over to the National Health Service in 1948, Essex, Norfolk, Suffolk, and Cambridgeshire county councils contributed towards the costs of their own patients.[5]

From the beginning the regime was claimed not to be merely custodial but to emphasise training and teaching. In 1862 a cottage was built on the lawn near the main building to provide special care for *c.* 20 children. Some of the higher-grade patients were instructed in reading, writing, and arithmetic; others worked at tailoring, housework, gardening, and, from 1863, in the specially equipped laundry. Recreations included cricket, football, croquet, keeping animals, and watching magic lantern shows. In 1867 a detached wooden building was built for infectious patients. A new laundry was built *c.* 1882, and in 1883 a new recreation hall. In the 1890s patients made all staff uniforms, repaired shoes, clothing, and bedding, did carpentry, and made mats and mattresses. Poplar's Hall, a small farm opposite Essex Hall, was leased in 1892 and bought in 1895; cows and other livestock were provided, so that men and boys could do farm work. A seaside home, Crossley House at Clacton, was acquired in 1894 with financial help from Sir Savile Crossley, of Somerleyton (Suff.).[6]

In 1901 the Peckover schools, given by A. Peckover, lord lieutenant of Cambridgeshire, were opened on an adjoining site; they contained classrooms and workshops. Essex Hall was extended in 1903 to provide an additional 20 beds. A new block, Bristol House, named after Frederick William John, marquis of Bristol (d. 1907), a previous chairman, was opened in 1915 for another 100 patients. By that date the asylum was called the Royal Eastern Counties' institution for the mentally defective. In 1916 Hillsleigh House, East Hill, was bought to house 34 patients, and in 1918 Lexden House was leased as a school for high grade females, increasing the institution's beds to 630. Greenwood school, Halstead, was opened for 86 girls in 1922, enabling Lexden House to become a hostel; about the same time East Hill House was obtained as an upper boys' school, and Hillsleigh was then used as a school for the younger boys. In 1923 Bridge Home, Witham, was bought to provide 233 beds for patients from the institution.[7]

In 1935 eight villas for male patients were opened at Turner village in Turner Road, Mile End, with workshops, assembly hall, kitchen, laundry, administrative buildings, and playing fields; they were named after the Turner family whose members, notably J. J. C. Turner (d.

97 Colch. group hosp. management cttee. *Rep.* (1950); J. Smith, *Speckled Monster*, 170, 172; *E.C.S.* 14 Mar. 1936.

98 Colch. group hosp. management cttee. *Rep.* (1950–8).

99 *E.C.S.* 4 July 1975; 2 Dec. 1977.

1 N. E. Essex community health council, *12th Rep.* p. 28.

2 Inf. from N. E. Essex health authority.

3 W. Millard, *The idiot and his helpers* (1864): copy in E.R.O., Acc. C201; *Jnl. R. Soc. Medicine*, lxxxi. 107–8; E. Sidney, *Visit to an asylum for idiots* (1851): copy in E.R.O.

4 E. Counties' asylum, *Ann. Rep.* (1863–6, 1891–8): copies in E.R.O., Acc. C201.

5 *E.C.S.* 21 June 1974.

6 E. Counties' asylum, *Ann. Rep.* (1863–6, 1891–8); R. J. Kemp, 'Royal E. Counties' hosp. 1848–1948', unpubl. paper in possession of J. B. Penfold based mainly on (Royal) E. Counties' asylum inst. *Ann. Rep.* (1860–1948).

7 Kemp, 'Royal E. Counties' hosp.'

1913) had been closely involved with Essex Hall. From that date Essex Hall with the Peckover schools was used for female patients. The institution then had 1,850 beds in its different centres, a boys' school at Littleton House (Cambs.) and a home for young women at Great West Hatch, Chigwell, having been added.[8] In 1946 a large modern hospital was completed at Turner village to serve the whole institution, and the hospital's administrative centre moved from Essex Hall to Abbeygate House, St. John's Green, where it remained until it moved *c.* 1972 to new headquarters opposite Turner village. In 1947 Handford House, Ipswich, was acquired for 22 female patients, and Kingsmead at Lexden for a girls' hostel. Handford House was replaced *c.* 1970 by no. 1 Queen's Road, Colchester, which was used for the elderly mentally handicapped in 1989.[9]

Two additional villas were opened at Turner village in 1964 providing another 100 beds. In 1975 a 28-bed unit was built in the grounds of Lexden House off Cooks Lane.[10] An educational adventure playground of 4 a. for the mentally handicapped was created at Turner village in 1977.[11] Between *c.* 1950 and the early 1980s Barker House, Clacton-on-Sea, was used as a holiday home, and Brunswick House, Mistley, was used from *c.* 1950 to *c.* 1986 as a male hostel.[12] Essex Hall was closed and demolished in 1985, and its 12 a. site sold in 1988. Many patients had by then been moved out into the community, some to group homes, and only 640 patients remained at Turner village.[13] The home at Lexden House was closed in 1990.[14]

SEVERALLS HOSPITAL. In 1904 the corporation sold 300 a. of the Severalls estate at Mile End to Essex county council for a site for Severalls county mental hospital which opened in 1913 for 1,800 patients. The red-brick building, designed by F. Whitmore and W. H. Town, had a large central hall, wards and adminstrative offices, connected by a network of corridors, and there were villa-style wards around the high-fenced perimeter. The hospital was transferred from Essex county council in 1948 to the National Health Service under the Ministry of Health.[15] The medical superintendant had sole responsibility for all staff and patients until 1971 when departmental committees took over his tasks.[16]

Until 1930 only certified patients were admitted and the regime was severe, with force feeding and clothing restraints. By the 1960s the staff at Severalls were at the forefront of new developments in psychiatric treatment: large wards were divided, and new drugs and rehabilitation projects enabled patients to have more contact with the outside world. A psychogeriatric unit was established in 1961 for 145 men and 229 women.[17] In 1962 a laundry serving nine hospitals in the area was opened to provide employment for Severalls patients, and by 1966 there was a day hospital for 100 elderly people who attended 2 or 3 times a week. The first group home for former patients was established in 1967 by the charity Phoenix Group Homes.[18]

Increasing co-operation between Severalls and other local hospitals led in 1964 to one ward and a new operating theatre at Severalls being allocated to 30 male surgical patients from Essex County hospital's waiting list, and in 1971 an adjoining ward was designated a medical ward to take 28 patients. Larch House alcoholism unit was set up at Severalls in 1977.[19] From 1988 Severalls garden centre, with its shop staffed by the League of Friends, raised money for the hospital. With the increasing emphasis on rehabilitation in the community from 1959, the number of beds at the hospital decreased to 1,024 by 1977 and to 726 by 1988, by which time there was also more provision for the mentally ill in other Essex towns.[20]

COLCHESTER MATERNITY HOSPITAL. In 1932 an eight-bed maternity home was opened in a converted house in Lexden Road; its cause had been championed for many years by Dr. Ruth Bensusan-Butt, a general practitioner specializing in midwifery. By 1935 it had been extended to take 20 patients; the adjoining house was acquired and used as a nurses' home. Further alterations and additions enlarged the hospital to 52 beds by 1950, 22 of them in an obstetric unit opened in 1949.[21] An extra storey was built in 1967 to house a special care baby unit with 11 cots; by then the hospital had 79 beds, including 40 in an obstetric unit. A two-storeyed extension on the south side was opened in 1981; the ground floor became the special care baby unit with 18 cots, and the first floor contained delivery rooms and an operating theatre. The hospital had 86 beds in 1988.[22]

MILITARY HOSPITAL. There was a hospital in Colchester barracks during the Napoloeonic Wars. The new barracks established in 1856 included 20 hospital huts.[23] By 1870 an officer's hut

8 Royal E. Counties' inst. *Ann. Rep.* (1932–7); *E.R.* xxiii. 110.

9 Kemp, 'Royal E. Counties' hosp.'; inf. from Mr. C. Willsher.

10 *E.C.S.* 29 May 1964; 23 May 1975.

11 *Colch. Gaz.* 1 Dec. 1977; 24 Oct. 1979.

12 Inf. from Mr. C. Willsher.

13 *Colch. Gaz.* 23 Feb. 1988; *E.C.S.* 20 Sept. 1985; N. E. Essex community health council, *12th Rep.* p. 28.

14 *E.C.S.* 12 Apr. 1990.

15 E.R.O., Boro. Mun., Special Cttee. Mins. 1902–12, 18 July 1904, p. 161; *Kelly's Dir. Essex* (1908); A. Whitehead, *In the Service of Old Age: the welfare of psycho-geriatric patients*, 40, 42–3, 49; foundation stone on building.

16 *Colch. Gaz.* 18 Oct. 1971.

17 Whitehead, *In the Service of Old Age*, 41, 48–9, 53; J. K. Wing and G. W. Brown, *Institutionalisation and schizophrenia: a comparative study of three mental hosps. 1960–8*; *E.C.S.* 9 Dec. 1966.

18 *Colch. Gaz.* 19 June 1962; *E.C.S.* 9 Dec. 1966; 10 Mar. 1967.

19 *Colch. Gaz.* 7 Jan. 1964; 10 Oct. 1979; *E.C.S.* 10 Dec. 1971.

20 *E.C.S.* 9 Dec. 1977; 30 June 1989; *Colch. Gaz.* 9 July 1986; N. E. Essex community health council, *12th Rep.* p. 28.

21 R. Lindsey, 'Dr. Ruth Bensusan-Butt 1877–1957' (Essex Univ. History B.A. project, 1987), 32–3; *Colch. Gaz.* 8 May 1935; Colch. group hosp. management cttee. *Rep.* (1950).

22 St. Helena group hosp. management cttee. *Handbk.* 1 Jan. 1968, p. 16; *E.C.S.* 9 Jan. 1981; 15 Apr. 1988; N. E. Essex community health council, *12th Rep.* p. 28.

23 C. Cockerill and D. L. Woodward, *Colch. as a military centre*, 13, 17, 19; *Illus. London News*, 3 May 1856.

had been converted into a lying-in institution.[24] In 1896 new hospital buildings in red brick replaced the huts, providing for 221 patients in eight large wards and some smaller rooms.[25] A pathology laboratory was added in 1934, a reception annexe in 1951, and twin operating theatres in 1963. In 1959, after the garrison had been reduced, some patients were accepted at the military hospital from Essex County hospital's waiting list. There were 90 beds in seven wards in 1972, by which time about a third of all beds were used for civilian patients.[26] By 1975 there were 114 beds in eight wards, cared for by 150 military and 100 civilian staff. Despite local attempts to save it the hospital was closed in 1978,[27] although it temporarily reopened in 1991 during the Gulf War.[28]

COLCHESTER DISTRICT GENERAL HOSPITAL. The first stage of the Colchester District General hospital, Turner Road, containing 283 beds, was officially opened by Queen Elizabeth II in 1985. The nine wards and various departments were built in groups around landscaped courtyards.[29]

PUBLIC SERVICES

WATER SUPPLY. In the Middle Ages wells and springs in use included Stockwell, Stanwell, St. Helen's well, Childwell near Magdalen Street, and one in Chiswell meadow. Water was frequently polluted by the washing of clothes, vessels, or wool, and other noxious things; in 1406 a leprous woman allegedly contaminated Stanwell by washing there.[30] In 1279 the Friars Minor built a conduit to bring water from Coningswell to their house.[31]

Most townspeople shared access to pumps or wells,[32] but by the 16th century some wealthy burgesses piped water directly to their properties. In the mid 16th century water was conveyed in lead or wooden pipes from East mill stream to one or more clothiers' premises in East Street to be used for dyeing or washing wool.[33] By 1537 spring water from Chiswell meadow on the west side of North Hill ran, probably through pipes, to a house in North Hill near North gate.[34] There was a conduit at the Hythe by 1539.[35] Ralph Finch, by will dated 1552, left money to pipe water from a cistern, presumably near North Street, to a washing place near the foot of Balkerne hill, to ensure a purer supply. A reservoir probably existed in Chiswell meadow by the late 16th century when there may have been more than one cistern near North Street.[36]

In 1620 Thomas Thurston raised water from Chiswell meadow to a town reservoir in the highest part of the adjoining Windmill field west of the town, to provide piped water for some houses.[37] In 1626 the tenant of the Three Crowns nearby was to maintain the waterworks.[38] Thomas Lucas allowed the waterworks' pipes to cross his land in St. Mary's parish, but his son John, later Lord Lucas, frequently disputed the arrangement, and in 1633 cut off the supply.[39]

By 1687, after the disruption of the Civil War and especially of the siege when the parliamentary troops cut the water pipes, John Wheeley the younger obtained from the town assembly the lease of Windmill field and a licence to lay pipes in the streets. In partnership with John Potter and Timothy Cook he aimed to restore the supply of spring water from Chiswell meadow. The first scheme failed because of Wheeley's financial difficulties and because the reservoir, probably on the same site as Thurston's, was too far west of the town and not high enough.[40] Eventually Potter decided on a higher storage point nearer the town. In 1707, in return for connecting the rectory house to the supply,[41] he was allowed to build two cisterns in the north-west corner of St. Mary's parsonage field. He was then able to take the spring water by underground pipes from Chiswell meadow through one of the Balkerne gate arches into the garden of the Three Crowns inn and thence to the two cisterns to supply the central part of the town. The waterworks functioned well initially, but were so badly neglected in 1738 that the rector of St. Mary's, for a small payment, used bricks from the cisterns to repair his house.[42] The direct piped supply from the Chiswell meadow spring continued to serve houses at the bottom of North Hill. In the higher part of the town residents reverted to the use of public and private wells and pumps; King Coel's pump, near the Exchange in the High Street, was a brightly decorated landmark in the 18th century.[43] The conduit in St. Leonard's parish on the east side of the town was maintained.[44]

In 1808 Ralph Dodd, a civil engineer, obtained an Act granting powers to a new private Colchester Waterworks Co. to supply the town

24 B.L. Add. MS. 45816, ff. 23v.–24.

25 *E.C.S.* 17 Oct. 1896.

26 *Colch. Expr.* 27 Sept. 1973; Colch. group hosp. management cttee. *Rep.* (1959), 22.

27 *E.C.S.* 27 Mar. 1975; 31 Dec. 1976; 6 May 1977.

28 Ibid. 1 Feb. 1991.

29 Ibid. 12 Oct. 1984; 31 Oct. 1986; N.E. Essex health authority, *Opening of District Gen. Hosp., Colch.*

30 E.R.O., D/B 5 Cr9, rot. 3d.; Cr15, rot. 12; Cr36, rott. 6d.–7; Cr38, rot. 2; Morant, *Colch.* 1; *Colch. Arch. Rep.* iii. 26. This section was written in 1988.

31 E.R.O., D/B 5 Cr25, rot. 50; below, Religious Houses.

32 e.g. E.R.O., D/B 5 Cr137, rot. 15d.; Cr140, rot. 17; Cr141, rot. 16d.

33 Ibid. Cr117, rot. 7 and d.; D/DU 457/4; D/DHt T72/4.

34 Ibid. D/B 5 Cr116, rot. 12 and d.

35 P.R.O., SC 6/Hen. VIII/976.

36 Morant, *Colch.* 2; *Colch. Arch. Rep.* iii. 27.

37 E.R.O., D/B 5 Gb3, f. 1v.; Morant, *Colch.* 2.

38 E.R.O., D/B 5 Gb3, f. 59.

39 *Cal. S.P. Dom.* 1629–31, 93; 1633–4, 231, 249–50; 1639, 57.

40 E.R.O., D/B 5 Gb5, ff. 227v.–228; D/B 5 Sr57, rot. 55; Phillips, *Ten Men*, 8–9.

41 Guildhall MS. 9532/2.

42 T. Cromwell, *Hist. Colch.* 303; Morant, *Colch.* 2–3.

43 Morant, *Colch.* 1–2, 4, 111; E.R.O., D/DQ 37/49; D/ABW 81; D/B 5 Ab1/23.

44 E.R.O., D/P 245/8/3.

including East Street and the Hythe. After some initial difficulties he was able to collect water from Chiswell meadow and the Balkerne springs in two large reservoirs at the foot of Balkerne hill, where he built a pumping house to raise water by steam engine to a large reservoir built on the site of Potter's cisterns.[45]

The needs of a growing population, the greater risk of fire, and the practice of watering the dusty streets increased the demand for water, but by the mid 19th century the waterworks company provided piped water to less than a fifth of the households in the borough, and those not all the time, the remainder relying on traditional communal sources.[46] In 1849 only 12 of the 22 existing town wells, springs, and pumps were open, of which five were in private hands. Some were available only to certain businesses or tenants, others were contaminated by practices such as washing fish baskets. Elsewhere water was wasted, notably at Nicholls' brewery well where 50,000 gallons were lost every day.[47] In 1850 in the poorer north and east parts of the town almost half the people had no water on their premises and many were forced to carry water of dubious quality long distances.[48]

In 1851 William Hawkins and Peter Bruff bought the waterworks company as an investment, given the growing concern about public health and water supply. The following year Bruff, believing that Colchester's existing springs had run low, sank an artesian well on the premises of the old waterworks to the west of the town, which within a few years doubled the waterworks' output.[49] Nevertheless in 1858 the most densely populated areas of the town, including much of the east side, still had no water supply.[50] About 1860 Bruff discovered a strong spring just south of Sheepen farm and brought water from there to the Balkerne hill works, thus further increasing the supply,[51] but the private waterworks company was still unable to provide an adequate water supply for all inhabitants.[52] Some of the commissioners advocated a water tower at the top of Balkerne hill to increase the water pressure and thus improve the supply to the east of the town.[53]

In 1880 the corporation, assuming the commissioners' responsibility for public health and ensuring a satisfactory water supply, bought the waterworks.[54] Bruff's Sheepen well was abandoned in 1880, but a new one was sunk close by.[55] Loans from the Local Government Board enabled the corporation to build a 130-ft. water tower on Balkerne hill, despite vociferous local opposition on economic and aesthetic grounds. The tower, nicknamed Jumbo, which was built by Messrs. Everett with the tank and other ironwork supplied by Mumford's, was opened in 1883.[56] Water from Clark's meadow near the waterworks yard and from Sheepen springs was, for health reasons, not supplied for domestic consumption after 1890.[57] New waterworks were completed in 1894 at the foot of Balkerne hill, with a new pumping plant. By 1899 the borough council supplied water to 34,500 inhabitants, but 3,750 still relied on private sources.[58]

Lexden springs were acquired in 1906 and a further pumping plant installed there.[59] By 1949 Colchester's water supply was obtained from boreholes at Balkerne, Cooks Mill, and Aldham, and from springs at Lexden, and at Sheepen and Clark's meadows; *c.* 1 per cent came from the River Colne.[60] Colchester borough, Lexden and Winstree rural district, and West Mersea urban district councils united in 1960 to form the Colchester and District Water Board; Braintree urban district and Halstead rural district councils were included in 1969. The Colchester and District Water Board became part of the Anglian Water authority in 1974 and in 1978 the Colchester and Ipswich divisions were merged to form a new Stour Water division. Colchester's water supply in the 1980s came from boreholes in the Colne and Stour valleys from which water was pumped into Lexden and Horkesley reservoirs respectively; water from the river Colne was treated and stored at Ardleigh reservoir. The Jumbo water tower was used to balance the water distribution system of the town until 1988 when it was bought by Net Work Trust, an Evangelical Christian organization, to use as a place of worship.[61]

SEWERAGE. In the early 19th century the improvement commissioners were not obliged to provide drainage and sewerage from private houses and at first had no power to raise money to repair or alter communal drains, such responsibilities resting with individual property owners and parishes.[62] The commissioners did, however, investigate problems and suggest remedies, sometimes subsidizing the cost.[63] They frequently ordered the extension of drains, as in

45 48 Geo. III, c. 137: copy in E.R.O., D/DEl Z3 with MS. plan; *East Anglia Postal History Study Circle Bulletin*, xl. 40–1; Cromwell, *Hist. Colch.* 303; Phillips, *Ten Men*, 11–12; E.R.O., D/DU 115/23.

46 e.g. E.R.O., Boro. Mun., Improvement Com. Mins. 1833–47, pp. 44–5; Phillips, *Ten Men*, 24.

47 E.R.O., Boro. Mun., Improvement Com. Mins. 1847–53, pp. 174–81.

48 Ibid. pp. 213–15.

49 Phillips, *Ten Men*, 35–6; *Essex Naturalist*, xvii. 22; J. Brown, 'Note on the artesian well at Colch.' reprinted from *Annals and Mag. of Natural Hist.* Oct. 1853: copy in E.C.L. Colch.

50 E.R.O., Acc. C210, J. B. Harvey Colln. v, pp. 89–99.

51 *Essex Naturalist*, xvii. 23.

52 E.R.O., Boro. Mun., Improvement Com. Mins. 1854–62, pp. 341–2.

53 Phillips, *Ten Men*, 57.

54 Ibid. 58, 96–8; Colch. Water Act, 42 & 43 Vic. c. 121 (Local and Private).

55 *Essex Naturalist*, xvii. 24.

56 Anglian Water, *Jumbo 1883–1983*, [11–13]; Colch. Civic Soc., *Quarterly Bull.* i (1), p. 5; below, pl. facing p. 216.

57 *Essex Naturalist*, xvii. 23–5.

58 J. C. Thresh, *Rep. on water supply of Essex, 1901*, 137; *E.C.S.* 10 Nov. 1894; Colch. Boro. Council, *Centenary of Mun. Corp. Act*, 19.

59 Colch. Boro. Council, *Centenary of Mun. Corp. Act*, 19.

60 Colch. Corp. *Water Supply Cttee. Accts. 1949–50*; E.R.O., Acc. C254, J. E. Lee, MS. Hist. of Colch. Water Supply Dept. 1933–61.

61 Anglian Water, *Jumbo*, [13, 22]; *Colch. Gaz.* 21 Apr. 1978; 15 Aug. 1988; *E.C.S.* 9 June 1989; below, Prot. Nonconf. (Other Churches).

62 E.R.O., D/P 200/8/4; ibid. Boro. Mun., Improvement Com. Mins. 1811–33, p. 39.

63 Ibid. Boro. Mun., Improvement Com. Mins. 1811–33, pp. 44, 113–14, 116–17, 146.

1822, following complaints from householders, when they ordered the construction of a 255-ft. barrel drain to carry sewage and excess water into the sewer at the entrance of Castle inn yard.[64] A cholera epidemic in 1834 prompted an investigation by the commissioners which found a positive correlation between neglected drains and the incidence of disease, though the nature of the relationship between them was still imperfectly understood. Areas particularly badly affected included Stanwell Street, Duck Lane, Pelham's Lane, part of Eld Lane, and St. John Street. Dung heaps were an added nuisance, but provided a living for some inhabitants.[65] The investigation led to further improvements in drainage, concentrated where the need seemed greatest, but progress was dependent on the availability of funds raised from the commissioners' limited rating powers and from private subscriptions. In 1834, for example, the owners of property in Pelham's Lane contributed towards the cost of a barrel drain there, and in 1837 the owners or occupiers in West Stockwell Street had to pay to have their property connected to the new sewer there.[66] In 1847 a committee to inquire into the sanitary condition of the town reported that the south side remained very filthy and noxious from defective drainage.[67] A new Improvement Act of 1847 conferred on the commissioners greater powers, albeit still permissive ones, to intervene.[68] Between 1847 and 1854 they constructed a network of sewers and drains in the central area and reaching as far as Harwich Road, Greenstead Road, Military Road, and Maldon Road.[69] However, deficiencies in the water supply and the continuing inadequacy of the commissioners' finances limited sanitary advance.[70] The rapid growth of the barracks exacerbated the problems.[71]

The river Colne received all the town's sewage, and a report by the Registrar General in 1866 showed that, although no deaths were recorded in Colchester during the cholera epidemic that year, fever was usually found beside the river.[72] In 1871 only one house in ten in Colchester had water closets, and many of those drained into cesspits, not sewers. There was increasing concern about the pollution of the river, but the improvement commissioners were short of funds, having spent large sums on improving the navigation.[73]

In 1874 the commissioners surrendered their powers to Colchester corporation, anticipating the Public Health Act of 1875 which made borough councils into the local sanitary authorities with clearly defined statutory duties. Repeated promptings from the Local Government Board, to which the council was now responsible, together with pressure from two influential millers, Wilson Marriage and Ezekiel Chopping, led the council to investigate possible sewerage schemes.[74] Eventually in 1880 members of the council agreed to buy land at the Hythe from the coal merchant T. Moy to build a sewage works, which was opened in 1884, despite the fears of F. J. Manning, rector of St. Leonard's, about its harmful effects on his parishioners.[75]

The system was greatly extended and many of the old sewers were reconstructed over succeeding decades. Work begun in the 1930s on an important scheme to improve sewerage in the south of the borough had to be abandoned during the Second World War.[76] Major extensions to the sewage treatment works at the Hythe were opened in 1971.[77] Additional sewers were built in the 1970s.[78] Sewerage was taken over by the Anglian Water Authority in 1974.[79]

STREET PAVING, CLEANING, AND LIGHTING. Early attempts to keep the streets in good condition were uncoordinated and often ineffective. Colchester had some paving by 1417 or 1418 when the town council chose two wardens to investigate defective paving and ensure its repair.[80] In the 15th century bequests were sometimes made for street cleaning and repair.[81] An Act of 1623 compelling owners to pave and repair the streets in front of their own property proved unenforceable.[82] Wandering pigs were a perennial problem, and in 1627 two to four free burgesses from each ward were appointed to keep the town free of them, but such a measure was only a limited attempt at improvement.[83] The town assembly did not make sufficient use of its enabling power to raise occasional rates for the maintenance of streets.[84] An order of 1647, obliging householders to sweep their own street frontage and clear their own refuse on pain of fines, had to be repeated in 1682 and 1689.[85] Free burgesses enrolled from 1670 had to pay 4*s.* towards paving the street in front of the moot hall and adjoining houses.[86] In the early 18th century paving was the responsibility of parish officials round churches and other parish buildings, of the workhouse corporation round their poorhouses, and of the chamberlain in the market and beside the town wall.[87]

Colchester's main streets, Head Street, North

64 Ibid. pp. 179–80, 250, 312, 328, 347.
65 Ibid. 1833–47, pp. 29–31; Phillips, *Ten Men*, 22–3.
66 E.R.O., Boro. Mun., Improvement Com. Mins. 1833–47, pp. 35, 53–4, 63–4, 77, 82.
67 Ibid. 1847–53, p. 25.
68 10 & 11 Vic. c. 281 (Priv. Act).
69 E.R.O., Boro. Mun., Improvement Com. Mins. 1847–53, *passim*; 1854–62, pp. 1, 7, 17, 38.
70 Above, this section, Water Supply; Brown, *Colch. 1815–1914*, 46–8.
71 E.R.O., D/P 245/28/4; Phillips, *Ten Men*, 50.
72 Phillips, *Ten Men*, 52.
73 Ibid. 80–4.
74 E.R.O., Boro. Mun., Boro. Sanitary Cttee. Mins. 1874–8, 1878–81; Phillips, *Ten Men*, 84–6, 92.
75 E.R.O., Boro. Mun., Special Cttee. Mins. 1879–84, pp. 55–6; ibid. D/P 245/28/14; *E.C.S.* 2 Aug. 1884.
76 Colch. Boro. Council, *Centenary of Mun. Corp. Act: Souvenir* (1936), 18; *E.C.S.* 21 June 1968.
77 *E.C.S.* 3 Oct. 1969; *Colch. Gaz.* 1 Oct. 1971.
78 *Colch. Gaz.* 17 July 1973.
79 Colch. Charter 800 Assn. *Colch. 800*, 35–6.
80 E.R.O., D/B 5 R2, f. 59.
81 e.g. D/B 5 Cr58, rot. 19; Cr70, rot. 13.
82 Channel Act, 21 Jas. I, c. 34 (Priv. Act); Morant, *Colch.* 5.
83 E.R.O., D/B 5 Gb3, f. 64 and v.
84 Ibid. D/B 5 Gb2, ff. 85–90, 99v.–106, 145v.–146v.; D/B 5 Sr50.
85 Ibid. D/B 5 Gb2, f. 276; Gb5, ff. 197v., 319.
86 Ibid. D/B 5 Gb5, f. 40.
87 Ibid. D/B 5 Sr106; Sr113; Sr145; Sr155.

Hill, and High Street, described as wide and spacious in the mid 18th century, were compared favourably with those of other towns,[88] but the streets in general were considered ruinous and dangerous. An Act of 1750 consolidated previous legislation and obliged householders to repair and pave the street in front of their houses if it had been paved already. Parish surveyors, reimbursed by the justices for cleaning and paving public places, employed scavengers to help sweep the streets and remove refuse.[89]

It was not until the 19th century that street improvement was approached more systematically through the efforts of the improvement commissioners and from 1874 of the borough council. Despite some opposition the borough procured a further Act in 1811 for the better paving, lighting, and watching of Colchester, after which the commissioners raised rates regularly for such purposes.[90] The town was divided into nine districts for street cleaning and repair, which were contracted out, sometimes to the overseers of the appropriate parishes.[91] A sweeping machine was used in 1849 but soon returned to its owner for fear of depriving scavengers of their employment; hand road scrapers were in use by 1875.[92] Gradually more streets were paved and kerbed, beginning with the central district, and attempts were made to keep them clear of obstruction.[93] Some houses were purchased for road widening, as in Magdalen Street in 1811 and at North bridge in 1818, and compensation was paid to owners, who were often active commissioners.[94] House fronts were occasionally set back to widen the pavement, and St. Botolph's gate was demolished in 1813 in the cause of street improvement.[95] The steep descent of East Hill was made safer *c.* 1817 by widening the road, the turnpike trustees agreeing to contribute towards the costs.[96] Between 1825 and 1840 most of the main streets were macadamized, replacing cobblestones in the central streets, and other roads were treated in the following two decades.[97] Street watering, begun in 1827, was gradually extended, funded partly from the rates and partly by private subscription.[98] From 1880, because of complaints about the horrid stench of fish in St. Nicholas Street, the fish market was washed down after trading on Saturdays.[99]

In the 20th century the borough council replaced horse-drawn with mechanical transport for cleaning the streets and removing the house refuse. The use of concrete and tar for roads and pavements obviated the need for watering,[1] but between the wars the streets were still soiled by the passage of horses and cattle.[2]

The borough first provided public lamps in 1783, following an Act which empowered the corporation to use duties collected on the channel towards the costs of lighting the town.[3] In the winter of 1812–13, from September to March, 360 oil lamps were in use, provided by private contractors.[4] From 1819 gas lamps gradually replaced them.[5] Until the later 19th century lighting was financed both publicly and privately,[6] and was only slowly extended beyond the town centre; for example, it was not until 1877–8 that Greenstead Road from Hythe bridge to Harwich Road was lit.[7] Electricity was first used for street lighting in 1901.[8]

FIRE SERVICE. In 1605 the borough assembly provided for firefighting a long ladder, 2 iron hooks, and 20 leather buckets, kept in the moot hall. The 12 town parishes each kept 2–10 buckets in their churches, and from 1614 also ladders, stakes, and iron hooks.[9] By the early 18th century there were borough water engines,[10] for whose maintenance and deployment the 12 town and 4 outlying parishes combined to raise £10 10*s.* a year from 1733; the fire service was provided by a keeper or repairer of the engines and 12 firemen from different parishes, who were to be available when needed.[11] All Saints', St. Peter's, St. James's, and Holy Trinity parishes each had their own manual fire engines, the responsibility of the churchwardens. All Saints' engine was financed partly by contributions from the Essex Equitable insurance company and kept in a special house. In 1804 the company, by then called the Essex and Suffolk Equitable insurance society, undertook the maintenance of the four parish engines. It bought a carriage engine with 40 leather buckets in 1812,[12] and in 1819 paid for boards to show the position of hydrants in the town.[13] St. James's vestry agreed in 1829 to sell its fire engine, no longer considered of use.[14]

A series of fires in the 19th century drew attention to the problem of water supply for firefighting. In 1842, although the insurance

88 Morant, *Colch.* 3 n.

89 Channel Act, 23 Geo. II, c. 19; E.R.O., Boro. Mun., Improvement Com. Mins. 1811–33, p. 5.

90 E.R.O., D/P 200/8/2; 51 Geo. III, c. 43.

91 E.R.O., Boro. Mun., Improvement Com. Mins. 1811–33, pp. 5, 156, 182–3.

92 Ibid. 1847–54, p. 139; ibid. Boro. Sanitary Cttee. Mins. 1874–8, 15 Dec. 1875; A. F. J. Brown, *Essex People 1750–1900*, 180.

93 E.R.O., Boro. Mun., Improvement Cttee. Mins. 1811–33, pp. 30–2, 158, 160, 172.

94 Ibid. pp. 12–13, 71, 111.

95 Ibid. pp. 51–2, 262.

96 Ibid. pp. 74–6, 83.

97 Ibid. 1811–62, *passim*; ibid. Acc. C3, Borough press cuttings, undated item on Albert Hall and Art Gallery, Mar. 1926.

98 Ibid. Boro. Mun. Improvement Cttee. Mins. 1811–33, p. 246; 1833–47, p. 19; ibid. Acc. C210, J. B. Harvey Colln. ii, p. 111.

99 Ibid. Boro. Mun., Boro. Sanitary Cttee. Mins. 1878–81, pp. 105–6.

1 Colch. Boro. Council, *Centenary of Mun. Corp. Act: Souvenir* (1936), 16; A. Phillips, *Colch. in Old Photos.*, 102.

2 Colch. Institute, Colch. Recalled, interview 2224.

3 E.R.O., Acc. C210 J. B. Harvey Colln. vi, p. 72; ibid. D/DFg F4.

4 Ibid. Boro. Mun., Improvement Com. Mins. 1811–33, p. 35.

5 Below, this section, Gas Supply; E.R.O., Boro. Mun., Improvement Com. Mins. 1833–47, pp. 181–2.

6 E.R.O., Boro. Mun., Improvement Com. Mins. 1847–54, pp. 102–3.

7 Ibid. 1833–47, pp. 181–2; ibid. Boro. Sanitary Cttee. Mins. 1874–8, 19 Dec. 1877.

8 Below, this section, Electricity Supply.

9 E.R.O., D/B 5 Gb2, ff. 54v.–55, 132v.

10 Ibid. Gb7, p. 149.

11 E.R.O., D/P 246/28: uncat.

12 Colch. Boro. Council, *Centenary of Mun. Corp. Act: Souvenir* (1936), 44; E.R.O., D/P 200/8/1–3; D/P 245/5/2.

13 E.R.O., Boro. Mun., Improvement Com. Mins. 1811–33, p. 129.

14 Ibid. D/P 138/8/7.

society had 3 engines and 20 part-time firemen in Colchester, a fire at Wallis's, the ironmongers in High Street, spread to and destroyed St. Peter's vicarage house because the society's fire keys were lost and water could not be obtained quickly.[15] The interests of the improvement commissioners, who were statutorily responsible for supplying sufficient water in case of fire but were also concerned with providing water for general domestic and public use, conflicted with those of the insurance directors, concerned only with protection from fire.[16]

In 1878 the Colchester fire brigade was formed, a uniformed volunteer force of 14 men under the control of the local chief constable; a steam fire engine was bought by voluntary subscription and the council provided an additional 20 hydrants. The voluntary brigade was disbanded in 1886, and the insurance society's brigade in 1902. Colchester corporation fire brigade was formed in 1896, taking over the steam engine,[17] and was based in Stockwell Street until it moved to Stanwell Street in 1898.[18] A horse-drawn steam engine was used until 1921, when it was replaced with a petrol-driven motor engine which was used until 1934 when superior equipment was supplied. In 1936 there were 4 officers, 2 drivers, and 14 men, and in 1938 a new fire station in Cowdray Avenue replaced the old one.[19] Between 1938 and 1941 part-time volunteers were used in an auxiliary fire brigade as directed by the central government, and appliances were kept at times at St. Peter's Street, Maldon Road, East Street, and at the old Stanwell Street station. The fire services were transferred to the Home Office in 1941 under wartime legislation.

As it was not a county borough, Colchester did not regain control of its fire brigade in 1948. The Cowdray Avenue building became the Colchester station of the Essex county fire service, and also housed the divisional headquarters and divisional control; divisional headquarters moved to no. 2 Park Road in 1978, and control was centralized at county fire headquarters, Hutton.[20]

POLICE. Before 1836 watch was kept by unpaid part-time parish constables and by borough sergeants at mace and ward constables. In 1836 the watch committee, set up under the Municipal Corporations Act, formed a full-time police force consisting of a superintendant and 19 men based at an office next to the moot hall. Three day-sergeants served the three borough wards. The remaining 16 men were divided into two consecutive night shifts covering 8 beats. Each night-constable, his number on both sleeves, carried a truncheon and rattle, and patrolled alone.[21] In 1837 steps were taken to reduce the numbers of constables, parishes being encouraged to revert to their former practice of electing their own part-time constables. By the end of the year the night watch was reduced to one shift of five men patrolling five reconstituted beats supervised by a watch sergeant, and 100 townsmen had been made special constables. Supernumeraries were appointed to be summoned as required. Complaints in 1838 about police inefficiency led to attempts to man the police office at all times and to make more use of supernumeraries; the beats were altered and a sixth one added. Representations by inhabitants of Lexden, Mile End, and Greenstead parishes in 1839 about the inadequacy of their policing resulted in two supernumerary constables being provided for weekend duties at Lexden, and one each for the other two parishes.[22] Two full-time officers were added to the force in 1841 and thereafter the outlying parishes were served by the full-time borough police.[23]

In 1844 the force was accused of failing to suppress prostitution and disorderly public houses, but specific evidence was not produced.[24] Constables were required to keep a watchful eye on public houses, but unfortunately the task frequently resulted in dismissals for drunkenness. The presence of the garrison and the growing numbers of troops from the 1850s, as well as rapid population growth, stretched police resources. In 1857 the Colchester force was increased to 22 men and remodelled. Incidents involving soldiers often caused friction between the police and the military authorities, but through co-operation between the parties in 1860 two rooms at the green market, by the entrance from Angel Lane (West Stockwell Street), were provided for a base for a military patrol to help keep the peace. Elections were other times of potential crisis when additional policing was necessary. In 1867 a plain clothes officer was employed for the first time to investigate robberies of corn from the granaries at the Hythe.[25]

In 1883, despite continuing problems caused by the presence of large numbers of soldiers, the acting head constable reported that relations with the military authorities were 'of the most cordial character'. Attendance at fires was an important police duty, and from 1884, with the agreement of the volunteer fire brigade and the Essex and Suffolk Equitable fire insurance society, the head constable officiated at outbreaks of fire. By 1886 the borough force consisted of 32 men, including two plain clothes officers. In 1890 a sergeant and three borough constables were appointed as river police to protect the

15 *E.C.S.* 6 May 1842.

16 E.R.O., Boro. Mun., Improvement Com. Mins. 1847–53, pp. 338–48.

17 Ibid. Boro. Sanitary Cttee. 1874–8, 22 Mar., 11 Apr. 1878; Colch. Boro. Council, *Centenary of Mun. Corp. Act*, 44.

18 E.R.O., Boro. Mun., Special Cttee. Mins. 1896–1902, pp. 3, 38; *Kelly's Dir. Essex* (1902).

19 E.R.O., Boro. Mun., Watch (Fire Brigade) Sub-Cttee. Mins. 1920–34, 18 Jan. 1921; Colch. Boro. Council, *Centenary of Mun. Corp. Act*, 44; Colch. Boro. Council, *Inauguration of New Fire and Ambulance Station* (1938).

20 E.R.O., Boro. Mun., Watch (Fire Brigade) Sub-Cttee. Mins. 1938–47; *Escape* (Summer 1988), 22–3: copy in E.C.L. Colch.; *Colch. Gaz.* 15 Sept. 1978.

21 E.R.O., Boro. Mun., Boro. Watch Cttee. Mins. 1836–7, 3 and 25 Feb. 1836.

22 Ibid. 5 and 19 Jan. 1837; ibid. 1837–40, *passim*.

23 Ibid. 1840–57, 7 Oct. 1841.

24 Ibid. 2 Oct. 1844.

25 Ibid. 1857–68, 7 July 1857, 11 and 25 Sept., 2 Oct., 26 Nov. 1860, 6 Aug. 1867.

Colne fishery; in 1892 four additional constables were provided and there were three boats.[26] The hospital ship was used as a river police station when it was not needed for isolating patients.[27] A tricyle, obtained in 1884 for police use, was apparently replaced by a bicycle in 1896.[28]

In the 20th century many new borough bylaws and the increasing volume of traffic multiplied police duties. In 1904 a 10 m.p.h. speed limit was introduced in the town centre, and policemen measured the speed of cars with two special stopwatches. By 1907 the strength of the borough force was 49 men.[29] A police matron was appointed in 1912 for searching female prisoners, and two women police officers were temporarily appointed in 1918, but from 1921 women were appointed on a permanent basis. In 1923 there were 58 police officers, including one sergeant and two constables on river duty; three additional constables were employed by the Fishery Board for the protection of the oyster fishery.[30] By 1926 there were police outstations at Mile End and Lexden. From 1929 a motorcycle was used for traffic control and in 1934 a car was bought.[31]

In 1845 the borough police moved to offices in the new town hall, then in 1896 to West Stockwell Street. From 1902 the force was accommodated in the succeeding new town hall, and additional offices in Culver Street were provided in 1920 and 1934.[32] In 1940 the borough police moved to a former soldiers' home in Queen Street.

When the Essex county police force was formed in 1839, the borough force had declined to amalgamate, but offered instead 'every assistance at the outskirts of the borough'. Colchester county division, one of 14 created in 1840, was responsible only for the area surrounding the borough and had its headquarters at Stanway.[33] Colchester borough continued to resist the union of its force with the county's until 1947 when its 77 officers amalgamated with the county force under the 1946 Police Act to become the Colchester division of the Essex Constabulary with headquarters at the Queen Street station. A new police headquarters, repeatedly postponed since 1967, was opened on Southway in 1989.[34]

GAS SUPPLY. Gas lighting was introduced to Colchester by Harris & Firmin, High Street chemists, who from 1817 manufactured coal gas to light their own and adjoining shops.[35] In 1819 the improvement commissioners accepted Harris & Firmin's tender to light High Street from the top of North Hill to St. Nicholas's church, and in the 1820s gas lighting gradually replaced oil lamps in Crouch Street, Moor Lane, East Hill, and North Hill.[36] Before 1825 the gasworks were moved from High Street to Duck Lane (later Northgate Street) near the river Colne.[37]

Following Harris's retirement the Colchester Gas, Light and Coke Co. was formed in 1826 with 31 shareholders. In 1838 new gasworks at the Hythe replaced the old ones which were sold in 1839.[38] Auxiliary gasworks were built in 1843 in Dead Lane (later St. Peter's Street), west of the silk factory, to improve the supply to the north and east sides of the town, but were moved to the Hythe in 1849.[39] In 1865 a small group of consumers formed the Gas Consumers' Co. and tried to obtain an Act of Parliament to supply gas in Colchester. Members of the existing company, under the chairmanship of J. B. Harvey, felt compelled to fight their potential rivals by securing in 1866 an Act of incorporation[40] so that they could raise additional capital and increase gas supplies, and the Gas Consumers abandoned their action. Prices were reduced under pressure from the improvement commissioners, but increased coal and labour costs prevented the payment of a dividend to shareholders in 1874 and reduced payment in 1875. The gas company, despite concerted opposition from Colchester corporation, its chief customer, eventually obtained an Act in 1875 which fixed a higher maximum price and increased its powers, enabling it to raise additional capital for improvements.[41] The favourable terms secured by the town corporation for street lighting meant that the gas company could not prevent street lighting from being subsidized by private consumers. In the following two or three years the gas plant was improved and enlarged, and a telescopic gas holder was built for storing 300,000 cu. ft. of gas. New income was derived from manufacturing sulphate of ammonia.[42]

In 1916 the gas company obtained a further Act to construct new gasworks, acquire lands, raise additional capital, and extend the limits of their supply to operate beyond Colchester. The corporation, still eager to take over the gas undertaking, had petitioned against the Bill, claiming that the company had exceeded its powers, and benefited its shareholders excessively instead of reducing the price of gas.[43] The gas company, by constructing a retort house and extending its plant at the Hythe in 1920, was

26 Ibid. 1881–91, 28 Mar., 17 Apr. 1883, 21 Jan. 1884, 16 Nov. 1886, 19 Nov., 10 Dec. 1890; 1892–6, 13 Apr., 14 Sept. 1892; E.R.O., T/Z 429.

27 *Essex Tel.* 9 Jan. 1904; above, Hospitals.

28 E.R.O., Boro. Mun., Boro. Watch Cttee. Mins. 1881–91, 16 Sept. 1884; 1892–6, 9 Sept. 1896.

29 Ibid. 1903–8, 10 Aug. 1904, 17 Apr. 1907.

30 Ibid. 1912–18, 20 Nov., 18 Dec. 1912, 21 Nov. 1917; 1918–25, 18 Dec. 1918, 21 Feb. 1923; *Essex Tel.* 6 July 1918; inf. from Ms. Maureen Scollan.

31 E.R.O., Boro. Mun., Watch Cttee. Mins. 1925–35, 17 Mar., 19 May 1926, 17 July, 18 Sept. 1929, 14 Feb. 1934.

32 Above, Mun. Bldgs. (Town Hall); E.R.O., Boro. Mun., Boro. Watch Cttee. Mins. 1918–25, 21 July, 17 Nov. 1920; 1925–35, 19 Sept. 1933, 14 Feb. 1934; inf. from Ms. Scollan.

33 J. Woodgate, *Essex Police*, 8, 23; E.R.O., Boro. Mun., Boro. Watch Cttee. Mins. 7–8 Dec. 1843; *Chelmsford Chron.*, 5 *June 1840*.

34 *E.C.S.* 13 Nov. 1981; 16 June 1989.

35 Cromwell, *Hist. Colch.* 306; Booker, *Essex and Ind. Revolution*, 188–90, 192–3.

36 E.R.O., Boro. Mun., Improvement Com. Mins. 1811–33, pp. 130–1, 187, 249.

37 Cromwell, *Hist. Colch.* 307; J. B. Harvey, *Gas Lighting in Colch.* 6.

38 Harvey, *Gas Lighting*, 6.

39 Ibid. 8; A. F. J. Brown, *Essex People 1750–1900*, 172.

40 29 & 30 Vic. c. 89 (Priv. Act).

41 Harvey, *Gas Lighting*, 9–11; Phillips, *Ten Men*, 58–68; 38 Vic. c. 1 (Priv. Act).

42 Harvey, *Gas Lighting*, 13–14.

43 6 & 7 Geo. V, c. 42 (Priv. Act); E.R.O., D/F 27/2/12.

able to withstand competition from electricity and remain profitable until the nationalization of gas in 1949.[44]

In 1964 additional plant at Hythe Quay enabled gas to be manufactured from oil as well as from coal.[45] The gasworks at the Hythe were closed in 1971, and gas was supplied from Chelmsford and Hitchin through the grid until 1973 when Colchester was converted to natural gas from the North Sea. The Hythe gasworks were demolished in 1973.[46]

Gas showrooms were opened in High Street by 1922, and moved to Head Street by 1933.[47] New Eastern Gas Board headquarters were opened in 1972 on a 10 a. site in Whitehall Road.[48]

ELECTRICITY SUPPLY. Electricity was produced privately at Berechurch Hall for lighting the premises in 1882 by Crompton dynamoes driven by a Davey Paxman engine.[49] In 1882–3 Colchester corporation considered supplying electric lighting to the town's streets,[50] but it was the South Eastern (Brush) Electric Light and Power Co. Ltd. which obtained powers from the Board of Trade and began supplying electricity in 1884 to some firms and a few households in the town centre. The venture was unsuccessful and *c.* 1886 the company sold the plant in Culver Street.[51]

In 1893 the corporation secured an Act to provide electricity,[52] but made little progress because of lack of public support. Nevertheless in 1896 the corporation decided to construct electricity works, and installed a temporary plant to supply power to the military hospital.[53] The general supply began in 1898 from an electricity station in Osborne Street. By the end of 1899 the 141 consumers included businesses, chapels, and institutions. Local Government Board loans obtained for extending the supply were repaid from profits from supplying electricity. In 1901 electricity was first used for street lighting.[54] Between 1899 and 1935 Colchester corporation raised its output of electricity from 61,381 to 15,477,880 units a year and the number of its consumers increased from 137 to 22,745. In 1927 the Hythe generating station was opened to provide increased capacity, and showrooms were opened in High Street. An area of 260 square miles around Colchester was added in 1928 by Special Order, and 11,000-volt power lines were built radiating out from Colchester to Tollesbury, Wakes Colne, Brantham (Suff.), Ramsey, Walton-on-Naze, and Jaywick. In 1931 the corporation obtained a further Special Order to cover Walton-on-Naze urban district, and bought undertakings at Wivenhoe and Walton. Profits were used to reduce prices or introduce low tariffs to attract new demand. The rapid advance of domestic electrification more than compensated for the loss of the custom of the tramways, important consumers between 1904 and 1930, and of several engineering works in the depression of 1931–2. In 1935 a new turbine and alternator of 3,500 kw. capacity was installed at the Hythe station which was then linked to the national grid and became a temporary generating point under the Central Electricity Board's control.[55]

When the electricity industry was nationalized in 1948 Colchester was included in the Suffolk sub-area of the Eastern Electricity Board.[56] The Colchester showrooms moved to nos. 36–8 Head Street in the early 1960s, and from there to a new building in Culver Street West in 1986.[57] Electricity offices built on the power station site in Osborne Street were converted into offices for the corporation bus service in 1974.[58]

INTERNAL TRANSPORT. From 1855 all cabs had to be licensed by the improvement commissioners who in 1859 approved two stands for cabs, one opposite the corn exchange and the other on the east side of St. Runwald's church. In 1880 the borough council provided a scale of cab fares.[59] In 1989 the borough, through its transportation committee, was still the licensing authority for hackney carriages.[60]

By 1848 a private horse-drawn omnibus ran between the Cups and Red Lion hotels and North railway station.[61] In the late 19th century another private horse bus operated between Lexden church and St. Nicholas's church on weekdays. In 1893 the borough council made bylaws controlling omnibuses.[62]

Horse buses were superseded by trams in the early 20th century. Preparations for steam trams were made by the Colchester Tramways Co. Ltd. in 1882,[63] but the scheme was abandoned for lack of funds. The corporation bought the remaining materials and removed the track already laid from North station to Middleborough, and in 1901, with its own electricity supply available, obtained an Act to provide its own trams.[64] A municipal electric tramway system was opened in 1904 with a fleet of 16 trams from the depot in Magdalen Street operating on double tracks from Colchester North railway station to High Street, and from

44 E.R.O., D/F 27/2/15; *E.C.S.* 6 May 1949.

45 *E.C.S.* 15 Nov. 1963; 16 Oct. 1964.

46 *Colch. Gaz.* 2 Jan., 30 Mar. 1973.

47 *Kelly's Dir. Essex* (1922, 1937).

48 *Colch. Expr.* 27 Apr. 1972.

49 *Electrician,* 2 Dec. 1882, p. 67: copy in E.R.O.; Booker, *Essex and Ind. Revolution,* 214.

50 Colch. Boro. Council, *Centenary of Mun. Corp. Act: Souvenir* (1936), 40.

51 E.R.O., Q/RUm 2/302; Q/RUo 88; Brown, *Colch. 1815–1914,* 52; C. Melling, *Light in the East,* 14–15.

52 56 & 57 Vic. c. 35 (Priv. Act).

53 E.R.O., D/F 23/4/18, 19.

54 Ibid. Boro. Mun., Electricity, Light & Power Cttee. Mins. 1896–1902, *passim*; ibid. Lighting Cttee. Mins. 1896–1908, pp. 73–4.

55 Colch. Boro. Council, *Centenary of Mun. Corp. Act,* 40–2.

56 Melling, *Light in the East,* 6, 16.

57 Inf. from Mr. V. S. Gibbons and Mr. G. Stewart.

58 Inf. from Mr. E. G. Axten.

59 E.R.O., Boro. Mun., Improvement Com. Mins. 1854–62, pp. 66–9, 244, 256; ibid. Boro. Sanitary Cttee. Mins. 1878–81, p. 55.

60 E.R.O., Boro. Mun., Transportation Cttee. Mins. 1989.

61 *White's Dir. Essex* (1848), 112.

62 E. G. Axten, 'Hist. of Public Transport in Colch.' 26 (TS. in E.R.O.); *Kelly's Dir. Essex* (1902); E.R.O., Boro. Mun., Watch Cttee. Mins. 1892–6, p. 69.

63 E.R.O., Q/RUm 2/314, 324; *Colch. Gaz.* 29 Nov., 6 Dec. 1882.

64 *Essex Tel.* 25 Mar. 1899; P. Gifford, *Yesterday's Town: Colch.* 85; 1 Edw. VII, c. 182 (Priv. Act).

Hythe Bridge, *c.* 1825

The Hythe, *c.* 1930

East Bridge, *c.* 1775

Site of North Gate, 1775

there to Lexden, the Hythe, and East Street.[65] A new tram route to the recreation ground was added in 1906 and two more trams bought.[66] The trams ran at a loss, except during the First World War, but were maintained as a public service.[67]

In 1928–9 the corporation gradually replaced trams with 20-seater buses, and routes were extended from the tramway terminus at Lexden to the borough boundary and to Clairmont Road on Lexden Straight Road, and from North station to Mile End and to Bergholt Road. Additional bus routes were provided between Old Heath and St. Botolph's station and between Mersea Road and High Street in 1929, and between St. John's church Ipswich Road and Irvine Street off Shrub End Road in 1931. Bus services were reorganized in 1933 into seven routes with increased frequency. In 1939 diesel 52-seater buses were introduced and another garage was built next to the original tram depot.[68]

After the Second World War new services were gradually introduced to new residential areas.[69] The borough council had provided a central bus station in St. John's Street in 1925 for all operators, which was used until 1961 when a new bus station in Queen Street was opened, which was in turn replaced by one on East Hill in 1972.[70] In 1974 the council allowed the municipal buses to continue to run as a public service despite a large deficit in the accounts.[71] Twenty-eight fully automated Atlantean buses replaced the existing fleet in 1975–6, and an additional fleet of five smaller buses was bought in 1988.[72] The administration headquarters moved in 1974 from Magdalen Street to larger premises in Osborne Street.[73] In 1989 they moved to no. 26 St. Botolph's Street. In 1986 the borough bus services were privatized but the borough council held all the shares. Various private companies provide bus services within the borough as part of long-distance routes.[74]

CEMETERIES. In 1854 the closure of all the town churchyards was ordered, except St. Mary Magdalen's where burials continued until 1892. Representatives of all eleven parishes formed a single burial board and bought from G. Tettrell 18 a. on the west side of Mersea Road, which in 1856 was consecrated as a burial ground.[75] Two chapels and a house for the superintendant were built.[76] In 1896 Colchester corporation assumed the duties of the burial board.[77] The cemetery, extended in 1895 by *c.* 12 a., had been enlarged to more than 57 a. by 1937.[78] The borough crematorium, south of the cemetery, was opened in 1957.[79]

BATHS AND PARKS. As early as 1774 John Sauvage, a physician, built a floating bath on the Colne at Colchester, to offer bathing for medicinal purposes. There was a charge of 2*s.* each for nobility and gentry and 1*s.* for others, with a warm bath also available for 3*s.*[80] From 1808 inhabitants of sufficient means could take a warm bath at the new waterworks for 2*s.* in water heated by the steam used for the engine, or a cold bath for 1*s.*[81] Two large tepid swimming baths and individual baths, privately owned, were opened in 1847 in Osborne Street.[82] In 1883 P. O. Papillon leased to the borough a piece of the river Colne and its north bank, *c.* 450 sq. m., south of Belle Vue Road, for a public open bathing place. It was extended in 1887 and 1896.[83] When the new bypass road bridged the river at the site in 1933, an open air swimming pool further north on the river was provided instead and was used until 1978 when it was turned into a water sports centre.[84] Private slipper baths in High Street, transferred to the council in 1922, were closed in 1934 when new ones were built in Culver Street.[85]

In the mid 19th century the botanical gardens, which had been established in 1823 behind Greyfriars, and 'Mr. Jenkin's Pleasure Grounds' in St. John's Street were open to the public, on payment of an admission charge.[86] The botanical gardens were sold for building in 1851.[87] The first public open space was the recreation ground south of the town centre, formerly the old drill field of the Napoleonic barracks, leased from the War Department from 1885 until it was bought by the borough council in 1958.[88] In 1890 part of Lexden park was opened as a public garden.[89] In 1892 Castle park was opened to the public, 10 a. having been bought from the trustees of Charles Gray Round with a legacy from Mr. R. Catchpool and an additional 7 a. being leased by the borough council. The castle itself was acquired in 1920, and in 1929 Viscount Cowdray added Hollytrees house and its gardens to the park.[90] Riverside walks along the Colne and two

65 E.R.O., Boro. Mun., Special Cttee. Mins. (Tramways), 1896–1902, 1902–12; *Essex Tel.* 23, 30 July 1904.

66 Colch. Boro. Council, *Colch. Corp. Transport 1904–64* (1964).

67 E.R.O., Boro. Mun., Special Cttee. Mins. (Tramways), 1902–12; above, Modern Colch. (Political Hist.).

68 Colch. Boro. Council, *Centenary of Mun. Corp. Act: Souvenir* (1936), 39–40; Colch. Boro. Council, *Colch. Corp. Transport 1904–64.*

69 Colch. Boro. Transport Ltd. *Bus map and guide*, Oct. 1988; Axten, 'Public Transport in Colch.' *passim.*

70 Axten, 'Public Transport in Colch.' 38; Colch. Charter 800 Assn. *Colch. 800*, 39.

71 *Colch. Gaz.* 17 May, 16 Aug. 1974.

72 *E.C.S.* 21 Mar. 1975; *Colch. Gaz.* 16 Nov. 1988.

73 *E.C.S.* 31 May 1974.

74 Axten, 'Public Transport in Colch.' *passim.*

75 *Lond. Gaz.* 15 Sept. 1854, p. 2828; E.R.O., D/CC 7/4; D/P 324/8/1; D/P 381/1/13.

76 *Kelly's Dir. Essex* (1882).

77 Ibid. (1922).

78 E.R.O., D/CC 46/2; *Kelly's Dir. Essex* (1937).

79 E.R.O., Boro. Mun., Parks and Cemetery Cttee. Mins. 1953–69, 20 Dec. 1957.

80 *Ipswich Jnl.* 28 May 1774.

81 Cromwell, *Hist. Colch.* 303.

82 Brown, *Colch. 1815–1914*, 46.

83 E.R.O., D/DPa 78; ibid. Boro. Mun., Bathing Places Cttee. Mins. 1879–84; 1888–96, pp. 59, 67–8, 89.

84 Ibid. Boro. Mun., Parks and Bathing Places Cttee. Mins. 1929–36, 4 Dec. 1929, 27 Apr. 1933; *E.C.S.* 24 Aug. 1984.

85 E.R.O., Boro. Mun., Parks and Bathing Places Cttee. Mins. 1929–36, 11 Sept. 1933.

86 Cromwell, *Hist. Colch.* 351–9; Brown, *Colch.* 1815–1914, 46.

87 *E.C.S.* 19 Sept. 1851; above, Modern Colch. (Town Devt.).

88 *Colch. Official Guide* (4th edn.), 31; E.R.O., Boro. Mun., Recreation Ground Cttee. Mins. 1884, 1886–96.

89 *Essex Tel.* 26 Apr., 5 July 1890.

90 *E.C.S.* 22 Oct. 1892; E.R.O., Boro. Mun., Public Park Cttee. Mins. 1892–6; *Kelly's Dir. Essex* (1937).

artificial lakes in Castle park were created in 1972–3.[91]

The directors of Marriage's mill presented East Bay meadow to the town as a recreation ground in 1934.[92] Various other open spaces and playing fields were acquired by the borough in the 20th century, including Old Heath recreation ground, West End sports ground, Mile End recreation ground, Mill Road playing field, and King George VI playing field at Lexden.[93]

A long-awaited indoor swimming pool, the first stage of Colchester sports centre, off Cowdray Avenue, was opened in 1975; other indoor and outdoor sports facilities were provided there soon afterwards. The centre was called Leisure World from 1991. Many schools and local organizations had previously hired the garrison's indoor pool.[94] An 8-lane athletics track, financed jointly by the army, the borough council, the education authority, and the National Sports Council, was opened at the garrison in 1983.[95] In 1989 Monkwick indoor sports centre was used by pupils during the school day and open to the public at other times, as was Highwoods sports and leisure centre at Gilberd school; privately owned sports facilities were also available to the public at Essex University and at Woods leisure centre, Braiswick.[96]

SOCIAL AND CULTURAL INSTITUTIONS

NEWSPAPERS.[97] For much of the 18th century Colchester relied on the *Ipswich Journal*, printed in Ipswich by John Bagnall from 1720. At first the paper contained only London and international news, but by 1727 it advertised Colchester events, and by 1740 had a small column of local news in which Colchester occasionally figured.[98] The paper continued until 1777. A rival edition was launched in 1774 and continued throughout the 19th century.[99]

The Essex Mercury or Colchester Weekly Journal, the first Colchester newspaper, seems to have started in 1733 and was published by John Pilborough, bookseller and printer of High Street, probably the 'foreign' shopkeeper of that name who owed fines in 1736. Popularly known as 'Pilborough's Journal' to distinguish it from the *Ipswich Journal*, it continued until 1747 or later.[1]

The *Chelmsford Chronicle or Essex Weekly Advertiser*, an uncontroversial Liberal paper, was published in Chelmsford from 1764, but had an agent in Colchester.[2] In 1766, when *c.* 100 copies were distributed there, *Colchester* was added to the title, but was dropped when a new management took over in 1771 after the bankruptcy of the original owners.[3] The paper continued as the *Chelmsford Chronicle*, renamed the *Essex County Chronicle* from 1884 and the *Essex Chronicle* from 1920. A Colchester edition was published from 1867 to 1874 as the *Essex County Chronicle*.[4]

The *Colchester Gazette*, the first newspaper to be produced in the town after the *Essex Mercury*, was launched in 1814 as the *Colchester Gazette and General Advertiser for Suffolk, Norfolk, Cambridgeshire and Herts.*, a four-page Tory paper published weekly on Saturdays at 6½*d.* by Swinborne and Co. of High Street. In its first nine years ownership of the paper changed three times.[5] In 1829 the *Colchester Courier*, a Liberal paper, founded the previous year as the *Sickle* by Samuel Haddon of Manningtree, was incorporated into the *Gazette*, which was then issued jointly by Haddon and C. J. Ward. It followed an independent policy but failed to attract subscribers. It incorporated the *Essex Independent* in 1833 and was the *Colchester and Chelmsford Gazette, Essex and Suffolk Independent* in 1836 when the two outer pages were printed in Colchester and the two inner ones in Chelmsford.[6] By 1837 John Copland was the sole proprietor, *Essex and Suffolk Independent* had been dropped from the title, and the paper was printed in Chelmsford.[7] It was sold in the same year to John Bawtree Harvey who attempted to revive it as an organ of reform under the title of the *Essex and Suffolk Times or Colchester, Chelmsford and Ipswich Gazette*,[8] but his full and forthright reporting of Chartist riots led to the collapse of his newspaper business, and the paper ceased publication in January 1841.[9] The *Colchester Gazette* was revived in July 1877 by Edward Benham, owner of the *Essex Standard*, and issued weekly on Wednesdays.[10] In 1930 it was modernized and published in folio size. When it ceased publication in 1970 Essex County Newspapers Ltd. immediately launched a new daily, the *Evening Gazette*[11] which continued in 1992.

The *Essex County Standard* was founded in January 1831 as the *Essex Standard*, a weekly Tory paper which filled the gap left by the

91 *E.C.S.* 11 Aug. 1972; *Colch. Gaz.* 27 Nov. 1972; *Colch. Expr.* 25 Jan. 1973.

92 E.R.O., Boro. Mun., Parks and Bathing Places Cttee. Mins. 1929–36, 29 Oct. 1934.

93 Ibid. 1896–1953, *passim*; *Colch. Citizens' Dir. and Guide* (1988), 7.

94 *E.C.S.* 21 Feb. 1975; 11 Oct. 1991; *Colch. Gaz.* 11 Feb. 1964.

95 *E.C.S.* 3 June 1983.

96 *Citizens' Dir. and Guide* (1988), 34; E.R.O., Boro. Mun., Recreation, Tourism & Arts Cttee. Mins. 1988; inf. from Colch. Boro. recreation dept.

97 For a full list of Colchester newspapers, many of them short lived, see *V.C.H. Essex, Bibl. Suppl.* p. 31.

98 *Ipswich Jnl.* 3 Dec. 1720; 17 June 1727; 7 Jan. 1740.

99 E.R.O., Acc. C210, J. B. Harvey Colln. v, pp. 465–7.

1 *Essex Mercury*, 31 Jan. 1736, no. 151; E.R.O., D/Y 2/1, p. 135; *Ipswich Jnl.* 23 Sept. 1826.

2 M. E. Speight, 'Politics in Boro. of Colch. 1812–1847' (Lond. Univ. Ph.D. thesis, 1969), 199: copy in E.R.O.; *Chelm. Chron.* 17 Aug. 1764.

3 *Chelm. Chron.* 7 Feb. 1766; 27 Jan., 29 Mar., 5 Apr. 1771.

4 *V.C.H. Essex Bibl. Suppl.* 30.

5 *Colch. Gaz.* 22 Jan. 1814; 11 May 1816; 4 Oct. 1821; 19 Apr. 1823.

6 *E.R.* vi. 158; Speight, 'Politics in Colch.' 216; *V.C.H. Essex Bibl. Suppl.* 33; *Colch. Gaz.* 10 Sept., 29 Oct. 1836.

7 *Colch. and Chelm. Gaz.* 31 Dec. 1836.

8 Speight, 'Politics in Colch.' 210–11; *Essex and Suffolk Times*, 11 Nov. 1837.

9 *Essex Tel.* 16 Aug. 1890.

10 *Colch. Gaz.* 4 July 1877.

11 Ibid. 6 Oct. 1970.

change in policy of the *Colchester Gazette*, and was to be 'a Standard around which the loyal, the religious, and the well-affected of our County may rally'.[12] It was at first printed in Chelmsford, but was aquired by John Taylor in September 1831 and thereafter printed in Colchester. A Wednesday edition was launched in 1855 with the words *and General Advertiser for the Eastern Counties* added to the title. The paper was sold to Edward Benham, T. Ralling, and Henry B. Harrison in 1866.[13] The *Essex and West Suffolk Gazette*, founded in 1852 by rival Tories to counter Taylor's strong anti-Catholic views, was incorporated into the *Essex Standard* in 1873, and the paper was enlarged to eight pages.[14] Circulation greatly increased in 1891 when the price was reduced to 1*d.* In 1892 the title *Essex County Standard* was adopted.[15] Ralling had relinquished his interest in the paper before Benham's death in 1869, and Harrison continued as joint proprietor with Benham's widow, Mary, until he retired in 1879. Benham's son William Gurney Benham (d. 1944) became editor in 1884; his brother Charles (d. 1929) was joint editor from 1892.[16] W. G. Benham retired in 1943 and was succeeded by his son Hervey (d. 1987), who adopted an independent policy.[17] The paper was enlarged to 10 pages in 1951 when it incorporated the *Essex Telegraph*.[18] The interests of Benham and Co. were divided in 1958; the newspaper publishing side continued as Benham Newspapers Ltd.[19] In 1964 the paper was printed by web-offset lithography, a process pioneered by Benham and fellow newspaper proprietor Arnold Quick at their printing business in Sheepen Road, and the *Standard* was described by the trade paper *Printing World* as Britain's best produced weekly newspaper.[20] Hervey Benham retired from the editorship of the papers in 1965.[21] In 1970 Benham Newspapers Ltd. merged with Arnold Quick's Clacton-based publishing company as Essex County Newspapers Ltd., which in turn was acquired by the Reed International Group in 1982.[22] The *Essex County Standard* continued in 1992.

The Liberal *Essex Telegraph and Colchester, Chelmsford, Maldon, Harwich, and Eastern Counties General Advertiser* was founded in 1858 by Wright and Sons of Head Street and owned by the family until 1901.[23] In 1902 the *Colchester Mercury and North Essex Express*, a Liberal paper published by Frederick Wright and owned by his family since 1867, was incorporated into the *Telegraph*, which was then owned and published by Essex Telegraph Ltd.[24] In 1908 the title was the *Essex County Telegraph*.[25] The paper was bought by a group of Colchester businessmen in 1948 and issued as a tabloid Conservative paper; it was incorporated with the *Essex County Standard* in 1951.[26]

THEATRES AND CINEMAS. In 1720 plays were performed in the moot hall probably by the Norwich company of comedians who, by 1726, were paying an annual rent of *c.* £10 to play there regularly for five weeks from the end of October.[27] In 1764 the corporation granted the company a 99-year lease at £12 a year of part of the moot hall yard on which to build a theatre for their exclusive use.[28] The building, financed by subscription, measured *c.* 64 ft. by 38 ft. and held 300 people; the main access was through the moot hall, but the stage door was reached through a passage from Angel Lane (later West Stockwell Street).[29] The theatre opened in October 1764; the plays of Goldsmith and Sheridan and Garrick's versions of Shakespeare were among the productions in its early years.[30] The theatre's popularity waned; by 1810 the building was dilapidated and, with the agreement of the Norwich Theatre Co., was repossessed by the corporation, which paid Benjamin Strutt £200 to buy out the subscribers' interests. In 1812 Strutt opened a new theatre, later the Theatre Royal, seating *c.* 1,200, on the east side of Queen Street. The Norwich Co. was given a 53-year lease of the building, but the company's visits to Colchester were infrequent after *c.* 1839 and seem to have ceased in 1852.[31] In 1843 Colchester was said to be 'not a theatre-going town'.[32]

For over 20 years from 1852 the theatre was used only occasionally, for professional and amateur productions and for political meetings. In 1878 the run-down building was bought and refurbished by the brothers Edwin, Henry, and John Nunn and their partner Daniel Vale. Well known professional companies brought plays to Colchester, the D'Oyly Carte opera company paid regular visits, and 'grand military evenings' were arranged by the garrison. Nevertheless the owners found it impossible to make the theatre pay, and it was sold in 1889 to a company formed by E. Thompson Smith. Again the building was refurbished, electric lighting and central heating were installed in 1901, and other improvements were made in 1902 and 1907. From 1914 to 1918 the theatre had capacity audiences, but when it burnt down in 1918 it was not rebuilt.[33]

The Playhouse theatre, St. John's Street, built in pseudo-classical style by E. H. Bostock and Sons Ltd. to replace the old theatre in Queen

12 *E.C.S.* 7 Jan. 1831.
13 *V.C.H. Essex*, ii. 472; *E.C.S.* 5 Jan. 1855; 26 July 1873.
14 Speight, 'Politics in Colch.' 206.
15 *E.R.* vi. 160.
16 *E.C.S.* 5 July 1879; 16 Aug. 1884, 6 Apr. 1929; *The Times*, 15 May 1944.
17 *E.C.S.* 19 May 1944; 4 Dec. 1981.
18 Ibid. 5 May 1951.
19 *The Times*, 20 Dec. 1957.
20 *E.C.S.* 17 Apr., 20 Nov. 1964.
21 Inf. from Essex County Newspapers Ltd.
22 *E.C.S.* 31 July 1987.
23 *Essex Tel.* 1 May 1858; *V.C.H. Essex*, ii. 473.
24 *Colch. Mercury*, 11 Jan. 1868; *Essex Tel.* 4 Jan. 1902.
25 *V.C.H. Essex Bibl. Suppl.* 33.
26 *E.C.S.* 27 Apr. 1951.
27 E.R.O., D/B 5 Ab1/26; D/B 5 Aa1/35, f. 106; W. A. Mepham, 'Hist. Drama in Essex from the 15th Cent. to the Present Time' (Lond. Univ. Ph.D. thesis, 1937), 302 in E.R.O.
28 Mepham, 'Hist. Drama', 305.
29 E.R.O., D/B 5 Gb8, f. 3v.; Norf. and Norwich R.O., MS. 4697/8 10 S8, articles of agreement 1764.
30 *Ipswich Jnl.* 27 Oct. 1764; 26 Feb. 1774; 22 Sept. 1775; 1 Sept. 1779.
31 E.R.O., D/B 5 Gb9, pp. 194–5; T. Cromwell, *Hist. Colch.* i. 438; N. Butler, *Theatre in Colch.* 16.
32 A. F. J. Brown, *Essex People 1750–1900*, 172.
33 P. Sherry, *Theatre in the Family, passim*; Butler, *Theatre in Colch.* 20–33.

Street, was opened in 1929 but became a cinema in 1930.[34] It was taken over by Associated British Cinemas in 1932. The building was remodelled in 1962 and renamed the A.B.C. It was owned by E.M.I. in 1981 when it became a bingo hall.[35]

The Grand theatre, seating 1,700, opened in High Street in 1905; its name was changed later in the year to the Grand Palace of Varieties, and in 1906 to the Hippodrome. It became a cinema in 1920,[36] was later acquired by the Gaumont British Picture Corporation, and survived until 1961 when it became the Top Rank Club, a bingo hall.[37] In 1985 the club closed and the building stood empty until 1988 when it was reopened as a nightclub by Big R Leisure; after the collapse of Big R in 1990 the club was bought by Rollers U.K. Ltd.; it remained a nightclub in 1991.[38]

The moot hall, the Public Hall, and the Corn Exchange, all in High Street, the Co-operative assembly hall in Long Wyre Street, and the drill hall in Stanwell Street were used for live entertainment in the late 19th and early 20th century.[39] From *c.* 1860 music halls were held in the Colin Campbell, later the Gaiety, public house in Mersea Road; they continued into the 20th century.[40]

From 1926 the Albert Hall in High Street was used as a theatre by the amateur Colchester Stage Society and from 1937 to 1971 by the professional Colchester Repertory Company.[41] In 1969 the Colchester New Theatre Trust was formed and in one year raised £62,000 towards the cost of a new theatre to be built in the garden of the old rectory house of St. Mary's-at-the-Walls. With help from the borough council and a grant from the Arts Council the Mercury Theatre, designed by Norman Downie, was built at a cost of £260,000. The plain, irregularly shaped building contains a hexagonal stage jutting into an auditorium with inner movable walls; offices, workshops, and a restaurant were built around the periphery. The theatre, with seating for 500, opened in 1972.[42]

Films were shown in the Corn Exchange in 1898.[43] In 1910 Grand Electric Empires Ltd. opened the Electric theatre in the former Liberal club lecture hall in Headgate. The programme, which ran from 2.30 p.m. until 11 p.m., included a selection of piano pieces and several different films; afternoon tea was served in the interval. The cinema, known as the Headgate, was acquired by Ager's Cinema Circuit Ltd. in 1922 and screened Colchester's first talking picture.[44] In 1924 Arthur Askey, the comedian (d. 1982), made his professional stage debut in one of a series of concert parties in the cinema.[45] A leading cinema circuit, County, were the owners in 1937.[46] The cinema was known as the Cameo Arts cinema by 1967, when a branch of the National Film Theatre met there monthly.[47] In 1972 it became part of the Star Group of enterprises; the cinema closed in 1976.[48]

The Vaudeville Electric theatre in Mersea Road, opened by David Ager in 1911, was the town's first purpose-built cinema. The Gaumont British Picture Corporation acquired it in 1927 and renamed it the Empire. In 1959 it closed and the building was used as a warehouse; it was demolished in 1971.[49]

The Regal, opened in Crouch Street in 1931, was designed in Spanish style by the cinema architect Cecil Massey, and was the headquarters of Ager's Cinema Circuit Ltd.[50] In 1937 it was owned by the County circuit, in which Oscar Deutsch, who had opened the chain of Odeon theatres, had a controlling interest, and in 1938 it was acquired and renamed the Odeon. The building was extensively remodelled in 1964; 10 years later the interior was completely reconstructed to provide three screens, and it became the Odeon film centre;[51] a fourth screen was added in 1987 and two more in 1991 when alterations to the building gave a 30 per cent increase in seating capacity.[52] In 1992 the Odeon was the only cinema in Colchester.

MUSEUMS AND ART GALLERIES. Many antiquities found in the town in the 18th and 19th centuries were bought by private collectors, notably Charles Gray, whose collection was displayed in the castle crypt by 1756, and William Wire, who set up his own museum in 1840. In 1846 the corporation assigned a room in the town hall to store 'articles of antiquity or curiosity', but there were no arrangements for public access. In 1852 a former mayor, Henry Vint, bequeathed to the borough a fine collection of mainly Roman bronzes on condition that a suitable fire-proof building be provided for them. Charles Gray Round, treasurer of the newly formed Essex Archaeological Society, offered a room in the castle as a museum for both the society's and the corporation's collections.[53] The museum was established in 1855 and opened to the public in 1860; it was extended in 1920 when the castle was acquired by the corporation.[54] The separate collections of the Archaeological Society and the corporation were permanently amalgamated in 1926 and the museum was named the Colchester and Essex Museum.[55] In 1992 the collections covered all periods from the palaeolithic to the early modern, with a particularly fine collection of Roman objects, including

34 *E.C.S.* 16, 23 Mar. 1929; S. Peart, *Picture House in E. Anglia*, 134.
35 Peart, *Picture House*, 134, 154; *E.C.S.* 11 Sept. 1981.
36 *Kelly's Dir. Essex* (1908, 1912); Peart, *Picture House*, 66.
37 *E.C.S.* 30 Nov. 1961.
38 Ibid. 1 Feb. 1985, 24 Aug. 1990; inf. from manager, Rollers U.K. Ltd.
39 Butler, *Theatre in Colch.* 48; *Essex Tel.* 8 Oct. 1898; 6 May 1905; 9 Jan. 1909; *E.C.S.* 6 Mar. 1909.
40 Butler, *Theatre in Colch.* 18, 40.
41 Ibid. 51; *Colch. Expr.* 27 Jan. 1972.
42 *E.C.S.* 16 May 1969; Butler, *Theatre in Colch.* 91–2.
43 *E.C.S.* 26 Feb. 1898.
44 Peart, *Picture House*, 33, 153.
45 Plaque on building.
46 Peart, *Picture House*, 107.
47 *E.C.S.* 20 Jan. 1967.
48 *Colch. Gaz.* 20 Mar. 1972; *E.C.S.* 3 Dec. 1976.
49 Peart, *Picture House*, 154; *Colch. Gaz.* 11 Nov. 1971.
50 *E.C.S.* 27 Feb. 1931; 11 Jan. 1977; Peart, *Picture House*, 154.
51 Peart, *Picture House*, 107, 154; *E.C.S.* 18 Jan. 1974.
52 *E.C.S.* 11 Dec. 1987; *Colch. Gaz.* 7 June 1991.
53 Colch. Boro. Council, *Souvenir of the Centenary of the Essex and Colch. Museum*, 3–8; Brown, *Essex People*, 163.
54 E.R.O., D/DRe Z13; *E.C.S.* 5 Oct. 1860; *E.R.* lvi. 146.
55 *E.A.T.* N.S. xviii. 137.

the Colchester Mercury. A major modernization programme, begun in 1990, introduced video and audio-visual equipment to illustrate different events in the town's history.[56]

The corporation in 1929 opened Charles Gray's house, Hollytrees, acquired with the castle, as a museum of later antiquities.[57] In 1991 its collection included 18th- and 19th-century costumes, needlework, tools, and toys, and the 17th-century plaster ceiling of a former High Street house. In 1958 All Saints' church became a museum of natural history, and by 1992 an experimental wildlife garden had been established in the churchyard. Holy Trinity church became a museum of social life in 1974.[58] A clock museum was opened in 1987 in Tymperleys in Trinity Street, to display the Colchester-made clocks collected by Bernard Mason (d. 1981), which he had presented to the borough in 1973.[59]

The Albert Hall was used as an art gallery from 1926 until 1972.[60] In 1956 the Minories, a Georgian house in High Street, was bought and furnished by the Victor Batte-Lay Trust and opened as an art gallery in 1958. It was extended into the neighbouring house in 1976. With the help of funds provided by the Eastern Arts Association, concerts, lectures, and art exhibitions were held throughout the year until the gallery closed in 1992.[61]

LIBRARIES, BOOK CLUBS, AND READING ROOMS. Samuel Harsnett, archbishop of York and a native of Colchester, by will proved 1631, left his library to the corporation for the use of the clergy of the town.[62] It was placed in a room at the east end of the Dutch Bay hall and librarians were appointed from 1635; Edmund Warren, rector of St. Peter's, was the librarian in 1653.[63] The books were moved to the grammar school, in the schoolmaster's charge, before 1668 but when Philip Morant undertook their care and repair *c.* 80 years later he found them neglected and decayed; they were transferred to a room in the castle in 1749 and into the newly built library there in 1755.[64] The extensive range of theological works included those of Thomas Aquinas, Erasmus, Ulrich Zwingli, Johann Bullinger, and Roberto Bellarmino. From 1894 the collection, with its examples of early letterpress printing, was kept in successive public library buildings.[65]

Charles Gray established a library, mostly of antiquarian books, in the castle in 1749; it included Boethius's *Consolation of Philosophy* printed by William Caxton. In 1750 Gray formed the Castle Library book club; membership was initially by invitation, but seems to have been by ballot after Gray's death in 1782, when it was limited to *c.* 30 gentlemen. The library was extended by gifts including James Deane's collection of books on architecture. In 1763 Gray and Philip Morant bought travel books and the works of contemporary authors such as Addison, Newton, Swift, Voltaire, and Montesquieu with a £100 legacy. In 1788 new purchases by the book club committee included the works of David Hume and Adam Smith.[66] The club continued in 1873 but was not recorded thereafter; its collection of 959 volumes passed into the care of the public library in 1920.[67]

In 1786 William Keymer advertised a subscription library with *c.* 1,300 books at his premises opposite the Three Cups in High Street; borrowing charges in 1791 were 16*s.* a year, 5*s.* a quarter, and 1*d.* an evening. A catalogue of 3,316 books published *c.* 1797 listed many novels.[68] Among several other 19th-century subscription libraries and reading rooms were the Colchester Library established in High Street in 1803, the Conservative reading room in Head Street in 1825, a reading room in the Three Cups by 1840, the Co-operative Society reading room in Culver Street *c.* 1861, a library in the Public Hall, High Street, by 1855, and the Liberal reading room in 1863.[69] A library in the garrison in 1856, which included French and German books, was apparently well used by the military.[70] Headgate chapel ran a book society in 1878,[71] and three book societies were connected with Lion Walk church in 1883.[72]

In 1890 R. D. Catchpool, formerly of Colchester, left £1,000 to the corporation towards the cost of a free public lending library to be built within five years of his death.[73] In 1892 the corporation opened short-lived reading rooms in Lexden, Mile End, Old Heath, and Parsons Heath,[74] but the main library was not opened until 1894. It adjoined the law courts in West Stockwell Street, and was designed in neo-Jacobean style by Brightwen Binyon of Ipswich.[75] In 1902 an extra room was added in the new town hall, communicating with the original building.[76] In 1911 the library had *c.* 10,000 lending and 5,000 reference books.[77] By the 1930s a larger building was required, and the site of A. G. Mumford's iron foundry in Culver Street was acquired. A neo-Georgian building was designed by Marshall Sisson; it was built by Henry

56 *E.C.S.* 27 July 1990; 20 Mar. 1992.
57 Ibid. 28 Sept. 1929.
58 *Colch. Official Guide* (1982), 63.
59 Inf. from the curator; *Colch. Gaz.* 26 July 1973.
60 Above, Mun. Bldgs.
61 J. Bensusan-Butt, *House that Boggis Built*, 43–4; *Colch. Official Guide* (1982), 63; inf. from Eastern Arts Assoc.
62 Morant, *Colch.* 168.
63 E.R.O., D/B 5 Gb3, ff. 103v., 137v.; Gb4, f. 95.
64 Ibid. D/B 5 Gb4, f. 19; Morant, *Essex* (facsimile edn. 1978), i, Intro. p. (x).
65 W. G. Benham, *Archbishop Sam. Harsnett (1561–1631), Native of Colch.* 20; G. Goodwin, *Cat. of the Harsnett Libr. at Colch.* (1888): copy in E.C.L. Colch.; *E.C.S.* 10 Nov. 1894.
66 E.R.O., Acc. C15 Gray's notebk.; ibid. T/A 315; 'Castle Libr. Cat.' (TS. in E.S.A.H. Libr., Hollytrees).
67 *V.C.H. Essex Bibl.* 328.
68 *Ipswich Jnl.* 28 Jan. 1786; 1 Oct. 1791; S. D'Cruze, 'The Middling Sort in Provincial England' (Essex Univ. Ph.D. thesis, 1990), 87 n.
69 T. Wright, *Hist. Essex* i. 349; Brown, *Colch. 1815–1914*, 71, 155; *Pigot's Dir. Essex* (1840); *Kelly's Dir. Essex* (1855); E.R.O., Acc. C210, J. B. Harvey Colln. v, p. 209.
70 E.R.O., Acc. C60, Wm. Wire's Diary, 31 Aug. 1856.
71 Ibid. Acc. C281, Wm. Wire, Colch. Memoranda.
72 E. A. Blaxill, *Hist. Lion Walk Congregational Ch., Colch. 1842–1937*, 47–8; E.R.O., Acc. C210, J. B. Harvey Colln. vii, p. 331.
73 *V.C.H. Essex Bibl.* 328.
74 Bd. of Educ. *Questionnaire to Public Libraries Cttee.* (1925): completed copy in E.C.L. Colch.
75 *E.C.S.* 20 Oct. 1894.
76 E.R.O., Colch. Boro. Mun., Special Cttee. Mins. 1896–1902, pp. 60, 88.
77 *Colch. Almanac* (1911): copy in E.R.O.

Everett and Sons with bricks made in their Land Lane yard and was almost complete in 1939, when it was requisitioned for use as a food office. It did not open as a library until 1948.[78] The site was scheduled for redevelopment in the 1970s, and a new library in Trinity Square was opened in 1980.[79] Most of the old building was demolished in 1987 but part remained standing as a bookshop in the Culver Precinct in 1992.[80] The library, hitherto run by the borough, became part of the Essex county library service in 1974.[81] Branch libraries were opened in Prettygate and Greenstead in 1975.[82]

SPORT. Organized games were played at the garrison, the grammar school, and at some private schools in the early and mid 19th century, but sports facilities were not generally available to the public until 1885, when the corporation aquired the old barrack ground as a recreation ground.[83] By the 1880s and 1890s local firms such as Paxman's and Mumford's had started football and cricket teams; some clubs had their own pitches.[84] Rugby was apparently played in the 1870s and cycling clubs had started by 1882. The Colchester and Essex Lawn Tennis Club was formed *c.* 1878 and played on courts at Cambridge Road; it continued in the 1930s but was not recorded later.[85]

The Colchester and Essex Cricket Club, formed *c.* 1861, leased part of the old barrack ground in 1865, moving to Cambridge Road in 1878 and to Castle park in 1908.[86] Colchester Town Football Club was founded in 1873,[87] its managers founded a professional club, Colchester United, in 1937 and Town club players formed a reserve team.[88] United, popularly known as the U's, joined the Football League division 3 (south) in 1950; the club was relegated to the non-league G.M. Vauxhall Conference in 1990, but was promoted to division 3 of the Football League in 1992.[89] Colchester Town played at Cambridge Road and then on several other pitches until 1909, when it rented land in Layer Road.[90] Colchester United bought the ground *c.* 1970, but sold it in 1991 to the borough council, which leased it back to the club for three years.[91]

Colchester Swimming Club was established in 1884; members swam in the river Colne until 1932, after which they used the borough's swimming pools; sessions were also held in the garrison pool from the 1960s.[92] Colchester Rovers Cycling Club was formed in 1891; cycle races were held on the recreation ground.[93]

Colchester Bowling Club started in 1902 at Lewis Gardens off Queen Street; it moved to Castle park in 1961. The West End Bowling Club was formed in 1926 and played at Harper's sports ground, later West End sports ground, at Shrub End. The Brotherhood Bowling Club, started as a specifically Christian club at Harper's ground, was the Castle Bowling Club by 1933. Colchester Ladies' Bowling Club opened at Harper's sports ground *c.* 1931. Colchester Men's Hockey Club was founded *c.* 1908 probably at Harper's sports ground. In 1992 the club played at Castle park and on the new 'Astroturf' at Leisure World. Colchester Women's Hockey Club was founded before 1936; it played at Shrub End and Leisure World in 1992. Colchester Golf Club was formed in 1909 at Braiswick; the nine-hole course was enlarged to 18 holes *c.* 1937. Colchester Croquet Club was formed *c.* 1929 and initially played in a private garden. In 1931 the club rented land in Elinore Road; members subscribed to buy the whole ground in 1961.[94]

Among other sports clubs formed during the 20th century were those for boxing, indoor bowls, judo, orienteering, volleyball, and water ski-ing.[95] In 1980 the Triangle rollerskating rink opened off East Hill; it was replaced in 1990 by Rollerworld, which incorporated a rink of international standard, the largest in the United Kingdom.[96] Sports centres which opened in 1975 on the Thomas Lord Audley school site in Monkwick Avenue, and in 1981 at Gilberd's school, were available to the public.[97] A sports centre was built on land off Cowdray Avenue in 1975; in 1991 it was incorporated into a new leisure centre, Leisure World.[98] A private leisure centre, Arena, in Circular Road East, was opened in 1983.[99]

SOCIETIES. Of the many societies founded in Colchester in the 19th and 20th centuries, several survived for 20 years or more. The Philosophical Society, started in 1820 'for the promotion of scientific and literary pursuits', had its own library, lecture room, and museum in Queen Street; it was dissolved in 1843.[1] The Colchester and Essex Botanical and Horticultural Society was formed in 1823, and established a nursery and botanic garden on 8½ a., part of the Greyfriars site, behind High Street in 1824. The society continued to meet until *c.* 1843; the gardens had been closed by 1851.[2] Colchester Music Society was formed in 1825 and continued until 1934,

78 *E.C.S.* 29 Oct. 1948; 10 Sept. 1982.
79 Ibid. 16 May 1980.
80 *Colch. Gaz.* 29 Jan. 1987.
81 *E.C.S.* 16 May 1980.
82 *Souvenir Programme of Opening of Prettygate Branch Libr. 5 July 1975*; *Souvenir Programme of Opening of Greenstead Branch Libr. 6 Oct. 1975*: copies in E.C.L. Colch.
83 Above, Public Services.
84 Brown, *Colch. 1815–1914*, 177; C. H. Clarke, *Colch. Town Football Club*, 16.
85 Brown, *Colch. 1815–1914*, 164; E.R.O., Acc. C210, J. B. Harvey Colln. v, p. 222; Tennis club mins. in possession of Mr. P. Benham.
86 Brown, *Colch. 1815–1914*, 163–4; *E.C.S.* 21 Sept. 1907.
87 Clarke, *Town Football Club*, 7.
88 R. A. F. Handley, *Up the City! Story of Colch. United F.C.* 40.
89 Inf. from Mr. H. Mason, club press officer.
90 Clarke, *Town Football Club*, 7, 25–7.
91 *E.C.S.* 30 Jan. 1981; 22 Feb. 1991.
92 Ibid. 30 Aug. 1884; 24 Aug. 1984; *Colch. Gaz.* 11 Feb. 1964.
93 A. Heales, *Colch. Rovers Cycling Club, the First 100 Years* (priv. print. 1991), 9: copy in E.C.L. Colch.; *E.C.S.* 7 Apr. 1894.
94 Local inf.
95 *Colch. Citizens Guide and Dir.* (1992).
96 Inf. from Mr. A. Starr, Rollerworld.
97 *Colch. Gaz.* 13 June 1975; inf. from sec. of Gilberd's school.
98 *Colch. Expr.* 17 Sept. 1975; *E.C.S.* 29 Nov. 1991.
99 *E.C.S.* 3 Dec. 1984.
1 T. Wright, *Hist. Essex* i. 349; Brown, *Colch. 1815–1914*, 68.
2 *White's Dir. Essex* (1863); *E.C.S.* 19 Sept. 1851; above Fig. 15.

when it failed for lack of support.[3] Members of the Colchester Antiquarian Society, founded *c.* 1850, joined other antiquaries in the county to form the Essex Archaeological Society in 1852.[4] Meetings were held in the lecture room of the Literary Society in St. John's Street;[5] in 1985 the society became the Essex Society for Archaeology and History.[6] The Morant Club, formed in 1909 to investigate local barrows, was dissolved in 1925, and part of its funds passed to the Archaeological Society.[7] The Colchester Chess Club started in 1888 at Banks's restaurant in High Street; in 1911 it met at the Shaftesbury hotel.[8] A debating society flourished from 1926 until 1980,[9] and the Gardeners' and Allotment Holders' Association from *c.* 1945 until 1985.[10] Among the many societies in the town in the 1990s were the Art Society started in 1946, the Civic Society, started in 1964, and St. Botolph's Music Society, started in 1967.[11]

SITES AND REMAINS OF RELIGOUS HOUSES

ST. JOHN'S ABBEY.[12] The buildings of the abbey were laid out in 1095, and the first of them were completed in 1115. The cloister and domestic buildings lay north of the church, as a small hill occupied the land to the south. The abbey was burnt down in 1133. The church was rebuilt on a cruciform plan, with a massive central tower and an elaborate west front flanked by south-west and north-west towers, possibly round. Late 12th-century capitals, perhaps from the internal jambs of a window or from blind arcading, found near the abbey site, may have been from its church or chapter house.[13] Building was still in progress in 1235 when Henry III gave the abbey 15 oaks; the work may have included the transepts and chancel of the church, which appear to have had lancet windows. The chancel may have been further modified in the early 14th century, for the presbytery was apparently new when the body of Eudes the sewer was moved there in 1320. The domestic buildings were later said to have been moved from the north to the south side of the church in the rebuilding after 1133, but the cloister and some buildings, including the chapter house, seem to have remained on the north, as Eudes's body allegedly lay undisturbed in the chapter house from 1120 to 1320. Moreover, a 15th-century drawing of the church shows on the south side of the nave a 14th- or 15th-century chapel which could not have been built had the cloister, which from the evidence of a surviving fragment appears to have been of the earlier 13th century, been on that side.[14] The buildings needed repair in 1363. In the 14th or 15th century chapels were built on the south of both nave and chancel and a lantern and spire were added to the central tower. St. Mary's altar was recorded in the mid 13th century, and a chantry was founded in St. Mary's chapel in 1364. The lady chapel, perhaps the south chancel chapel, where abbots and local gentry were buried, was recorded again in 1489 and 1521.[15] The church seems to have stood in the north-east quarter of the abbey site, east of the surviving gateway; a number of skeletons and an east–west wall have been found in that area.[16]

In the late 14th century and the early 15th, perhaps as a result of the revolt of 1381, the abbey strengthened its defences, repairing the precinct wall and adding at least two towers on the north side, facing the town. The surviving two-storeyed gatehouse was built shortly afterwards. In 1453 the abbey's precinct for purposes of sanctuary, which included the whole of St. John's green, outside the precinct wall, also seems to have been defended, if only by a palisade.[17]

The abbey was dissolved in 1538. Its site was leased to Roger Williams in 1544, and on his surrender in 1545 to Sir Thomas Darcy.[18] In 1547 it was granted to John Dudley, earl of Warwick, later duke of Northumberland, who sold it to Francis Jobson in 1547.[19] Jobson sold St. John's in 1548 to John Lucas, who had already acquired Sir Thomas Darcy's lease and with it possession of the site.[20] Lucas died in 1556 and was succeeded by his son and grandson, both called Thomas Lucas. The younger Thomas (d. 1625) was succeeded by his son John (d. 1671), created Baron Lucas of Shenfield in 1645.[21] The site was confiscated during the Civil War, and in 1643 was among the lands used to secure the payment of £5,000 a year from parliament to Robert Devereux, earl of Essex.[22] In the 1660s St. John's was said to belong to John

3 Brown, *Colch. 1815–1914*, 155; *Essex Tel.* 13 Oct. 1934.

4 *E.A.T.* [1st ser.], i. 1.

5 Brown, *Essex People*, 182.

6 *Essex Arch. and Hist. News*, no. 91.

7 E.R.O., Acc. C236, correspondence of Morant Club.

8 *E.C.S.* 7 Nov. 1969; *Colch. Almanac* (1911): copy in E.R.O.

9 *E.C.S.* 17 Aug. 1973; 24 Oct. 1980.

10 Ibid. 10 May 1985.

11 *Colch. Expr.* 11 May 1972; Colch. Civic Soc. 'Quarterly Bull.' i. 1; inf. from Mrs. G. Nicholson, sec. of St. Botolph's Music Soc.

12 The institutional history of the religious houses is given in *V.C.H. Essex*, ii.

13 *Colch. Arch. Rep.* vi. 373–4.

14 Ibid. i. 28–31, 40–6; B.L. MS. Cott. Nero D. viii, f. 345, published in *E.A.T.* N.S. viii, facing p. 120; *Colch. Archaeologist*, ii. 17; *Antiq. Jnl.* vi. 450; *Close R.* 1234–7, 57.

15 *Cal. Papal Pets.* i. 444; *Colch. Cart.* ii. 330–1; P.R.O., C 143/353/6; ibid. PROB 11/8, f. 207; PROB 11/20, f. 159v.

16 Inf. from P. Crummy, Colch. Arch. Trust; Colch. Mus., file on St. John's abbey.

17 E.R.O., D/B 5 Cr30, rott. 1, 16; Cr41, rot. 2d.; *Cal. Pat.* 1452–61, 50.

18 *L. & P. Hen. VIII*, xiii (2), p. 296; xix (1), p. 372; xx (1), p. 307.

19 P.R.O., E 318/38/2042; *Cal. Pat.* 1547–8, 204; Morant, *Colch.* 144.

20 E.R.O., D/DRe Z10, no. 33; *Cal. Pat.* 1548–9, 86.

21 P.R.O., C 142/107, no. 40; Morant, *Colch.* 124.

22 B.L. Add. MS. 5497, f. 141.

FIG. 28.
ST. JOHN'S ABBEY GATEHOUSE, 1718

Cockshott,[23] but he may have been Lord Lucas's tenant. The site was apparently sold soon after 1671 to John Walkesdon, a Jacobite who fled to France with James II in 1688. It then passed through a number of hands until it was bought in 1720 by Edward Arrowsmith who, by will proved in 1760, devised it to his daughter Sarah and her husband Philip Roberts.[24] Sarah Roberts held the site in 1783, and probably in 1797. In 1834 it was occupied by Mr. Austen, presumably the nurseryman Edward Austen. It was bought by the War Office in 1860 from Thomas and Frederick Baring.[25]

John Dudley owed *c.* £658 for the lead from the church and other abbey buildings, which had presumably been unroofed, in 1552,[26] but part of the church seems to have survived in 1621. On the south the Lucas family converted part of the abbey, perhaps the abbot's lodging, into their house.[27] It was presumably there that John Lucas (d. 1556) provided for his widow to have three chambers and the use of various offices, a mill, and the granary.[28] In 1640 there were a great gate and three other gates, presumably in the precinct wall; one of them may have been the plain round-headed gateway flanked by round towers which apparently survived on the south of the site in 1648. Much of the house was destroyed in the siege that year, when it was used as a royalist outpost, and the remaining buildings were damaged by Dutch prisoners housed there in the 1660s.[29] All trace of the Lucases' house seems to have disappeared by 1748; the mansion house let with the site and some of the former abbey demesne in 1744 and 1783 was presumably outside the precinct wall.[30]

The surviving rectangular gatehouse is on the north side of the abbey precinct, facing the town, and was presumably the main entrance to the abbey. It is built of flint with flushwork decoration, of two storeys with corner turrets. The main gateway has a four-centred arch with niches above and on both sides. The upper storey, including the battlements, the window tracery and the details of the niche above the door, was blown up when the gatehouse was stormed by parliamentary troops in 1648, and was almost entirely rebuilt, probably in the 1840s. It appears to be a faithful copy of the 15th-century work. To the east of the gatehouse are the north and east walls of a 15th-century porter's lodge.[31]

ST. BOTOLPH'S PRIORY. The church, a house of secular canons in the late 11th century, was refounded *c.* 1100 as a house of Augustinian canons. The church was rebuilt in the 12th century and was dedicated in 1177.[32] It was both parochial and conventual throughout the Middle Ages, the canons presumably occupying the chancel and transepts, the parishioners the nave.[33] St. Thomas's altar was recorded in 1281 and St. Catherine's chapel in the priory church in 1406. St. Mary's chapel next to the choir, recorded in 1435, was repaired or remodelled in 1488, and there was a Trinity chapel in 1503.[34] In 1512 there was a west porch, perhaps over the 'pardon door' recorded in 1514.[35] The dormitory was being rebuilt in 1383.[36] In 1421 an indulgence was granted to those who helped with the repair of the buildings.[37] There is little evidence for the plan of the monastery, but part of the northern range of the cloister has been excavated on the south side of the nave.[38] A courtyard west of the church was entered by a gateway which survived on St. Botolph's Street until the siege of 1648. A dovecot was recorded in 1536, and the great barn, south of the church and cloister, had been converted into houses by 1542.[39] Part of the monastic buildings or outbuildings apparently survived in 1621 south-east of the church; it was probably destroyed in 1648.[40] Two foundations with adjacent floors,

23 *Cal. Treas. Bks.* 1660–7, 676; 1667–8, 421; 1669–72, 220.
24 Morant, *Colch.* 145; P.R.O., PROB 11/852, f. 359 and v.
25 E.R.O., Acc. C47, CPL 847–8, 893, 906; *E.C.S.* 4 May 1860; *Return of Military Stations*, H.C. 305, pp. 32–3 (1862), xxxii.
26 *Cal. Pat.* 1550–3, 349.
27 Speed, *Colch. Map.*
28 P.R.O., C 142/107, no. 40.
29 P.R.O., SP 16/451, no. 25; M. Carter, *True Relation of Expedition of Kent, Essex, and Colch.* (1648), 70–1; *Cal. Treas. Bks.* 1660–7, 676; above, fig. 8.
30 Morant, *Colch.* map facing p. 4; E.R.O., Acc. C47, CPL 893.
31 R.C.H.M. *Essex*, iii. 47–8; *Letter of Wm. Lenthall of Late Fight at Colch.* (1648): copy in E.C.L. Colch.; MS. note from a newspaper of 23 April 1841 in E.C.L. Colch. newspaper cuttings.
32 *E.A.T.* (3rd ser.), xi. 114.
33 E.R.O., D/ACR 2, ff. 10v., 59v.
34 *Colch. Cart.* ii. 570; *Cal. Pat.* 1405–8, 188; E.R.O., D/B 5 Cr62, rot. 4; D/ACR 1, f. 61v.; P.R.O., PROB 11/8, f. 164v.
35 E.R.O., D/ACR 1, ff. 178v., 194.
36 Ibid. D/B 5 Cr22, rot. 55d.
37 *Cal. Papal Reg.* vii. 172.
38 C. Peers, *St. Botolph's Priory* (H.M.S.O.), 17.
39 E.R.O., D/DMb T55; D/DFg T1; ibid. Acc. C338.
40 Speed, *Colch. Map.*

FIG. 29. ST. BOTOLPH'S PRIORY, 1718

which may have been from such a south-eastern building, were excavated in 1987.[41] Short lengths of three parallel walls, possibly of outbuildings, were recorded in the south-west corner of the site in 1944, and part of the precinct wall survived in the back walls of houses in St. Botolph's Street into the 20th century.[42]

The priory was dissolved in 1536 and granted to Sir Thomas Audley,[43] but the nave and aisles of the church remained in use as a parish church until they were badly damaged in the siege of 1648.[44] Audley held the priory site until 1540 when he granted it to John and Anastasia Golder who sold part, including the great barn. Anastasia granted the remainder of the site to Arthur Clark in 1548.[45] Clark died in 1553 and was succeeded by his son Alban who sold the priory site in 1589–90 to Thomas Sackville, Lord Buckhurst, created earl of Dorset in 1604.[46] Thomas's son Richard, earl of Dorset, sold it to Edward Legg in 1615.[47] In 1637 Legg sold the site to William Mott and others, who conveyed it in 1639 to John Brettle and others. The others released their interest in the site to John Brettle in 1642; Brettle by will dated 1649 devised it to his sisters Anne wife of Thomas Penneth, Margaret, and Mary. The sisters conveyed it in 1651 to Jacob, Peter, Elizabeth, Mary, Ann, Judith, Sarah, and Jane Hendrick, children of the alien Oliver Hendrick. Hendrick, by will dated 1683, devised the site to his surviving children Jacob Hendrick and Elizabeth Burkin. In 1720 Elizabeth Burkin and John Hendrick, presumably Jacob's son, conveyed their respective moieties of the estate to Matthew Martin. Martin divided the estate, conveying the southern half to his son-in-law John Price in 1733. Price, by will dated 1743, devised it to his wife for life with remainder to his son Martin and daughter Mary.[48] They seem to have sold it to Elizabeth Selly, who was occupying the site in 1745. She devised it to her son-in-law John Halls, owner of the Greyfriars site. Halls, by will proved in 1795, devised it to his nephew James Halls who held until 1797 or later. The land immediately south of the ruined church, a brewery occupied by Joseph Shepherd from *c.* 1802, was sold to St. Botolph's parish for a new church by T. Mayhew in 1835.[49]

The northern part of the estate passed, with Matthew Martin's other Colchester lands, to his son Thomas who devised it in 1772 to his wife Dorothy for life with reversion to his nephew and son-in-law Isaac Martin Rebow, later Isaac Martin Rebow Martin, husband of his daughter Mary. In 1786, after Isaac Martin's death without issue, Thomas Martin's widow Dorothy and her husband John Adams, with Mary's consent,

41 *E.A.T.* (3rd ser.), xix. 264.
42 Colch. Mus., folder on St. Botolph's.
43 *L. & P. Hen. VIII*, x, p. 419.
44 Below, Churches (St. Botolph's).
45 E.R.O., Acc. C338; *L. & P. Hen. VIII*, xvi, p. 52; *Cal. Pat.* 1547–8, 338.
46 P.R.O., C 142/98, no. 18; C 66/1350, m. 3; *Complete Peerage*, iv. 422.
47 E.R.O., D/DMb T55; *E.A.T.* N.S. xi. 38.
48 E.R.O., D/DMb T55: abstract of title.
49 Morant, *Colch.* 149; E.R.O., D/P 203/8/4; D/P 203/11/1–38; ibid. Acc. C47, CPL 44; P.R.O., PROB 11/1267, ff. 236–42.

conveyed the reversion of the estate to Thomas Martin's other daughter Sarah (d. 1807) and her husband William Fraser (d. 1813).[50] In 1813 Fraser's daughter and heir Elizabeth conveyed the ruins of the priory church to the parish. The site was placed in the care of the Board of Works in 1912.[51]

The surviving ruins of the priory church, of flint rubble with dressings of Roman brick and some Barnack and limestone, date mainly from the early to mid 12th century, and seem to be of the church consecrated in 1177. They comprise the remains of seven bays of the aisled nave, and of the elaborate west front flanked by north-west and south-west towers. Excavation has revealed a small north transept, a south transept with a crypt or undercroft beneath it, and a short, square-ended, chancel. The crypt extended under the crossing, and presumably also under at least part of the chancel.[52] The nave had a high triforium above the squat, circular piers of its arcade. The central west doorway with a round arch of five orders, four of them with chevron ornament, survives, as do two side doorways, probably of four orders, into the aisles. Above them were two tiers of intersecting wall arcade, and above that a rose window flanked by two round-headed windows. Above them was a string course terminating in two pinnacles; above that again was another intersecting wall arcade, and above that were three round-headed windows, and at the apex of the gable a small round recess. In the 14th century new windows were inserted into all but the easternmost bay of the north aisle.[53] The ruins were damaged in the earthquake of 1884 and were extensively repaired in 1887–8; further work was undertaken by the Board of Works after 1912.[54] In 1990 and 1991 the west front was cleaned and repaired, and in 1992 the position of the transepts and chancel was marked out on land recently acquired and landscaped by the borough.[55]

GREYFRIARS. The Friars Minor or Greyfriars had established a house in Colchester by 1237 when Henry III granted them a plot of land to enlarge their site which lay on the north side of High Street between the castle and East gate.[56] In 1247 he gave them 10 marks from the forest eyre, perhaps to finance building work, and in 1269 he gave 7 oaks to build their church.[57] The priory buildings were presumably nearly complete by 1279 when the friars acquired permission to bring water by an underground conduit across the king's demesne land and under the town wall to their house, although Edward I gave 6 oaks, presumably for further building, in 1306.[58] The friars received several further grants of land in the course of the late 13th century and the 14th, including 4½ a. north of their site from Edward II, so that by the Dissolution they owned a block of land between High Street, the town wall, and the castle bailey.[59] The house and gardens were bounded by a precinct wall on the south and west and by the town wall on the north and east.[60]

The friary was surrendered in 1538, most of its valuables, including the lead from roofs and water pipes, being sold, stolen, or pledged before the king's agent arrived.[61] The site, with the hall called the old hall, the infirmary house, the chambers called Sir Thomas Tyrell's lodging, the kitchen, bakery, and brewery, two small gardens and 4 a. of land within the precinct wall, was leased to Francis Jobson in 1539 and granted to him in 1544. The king reserved the right to have buildings taken down and removed, but in the event 'superfluous' buildings were sold to Jobson; the lead was melted down for the king's use.[62] Jobson conveyed the Greyfriars to William Watson in 1565.[63] Watson bequeathed the site to his nephew Brian Watson, but one third passed to his son and heir John.[64] Brian in 1586 and John's heir William Watson in 1596 conveyed their shares to Martin Basil from whom the site passed to his son and grandson, both called Martin Basil. The youngest Martin conveyed it in 1636 to Henry Leming and his son Henry who sold it in 1654 to William Peeke. Peeke's daughter Mary married Thomas Turgis who conveyed the site in 1700 to Thomas Carpenter, who settled it, after his and his wife's death, on his grandson Thomas Bayes. Bayes sold it in 1740 to Robert Potter (d. 1752). Potter or his trustees sold it to the Revd. John Halls (d. 1795), who built a new house on the street frontage and laid out a garden behind it. Halls devised Greyfriars to his nephew James Halls, from whom it passed *c.* 1814 to Thomas Baskerfield. Baskerfield, by will proved in 1817, left Greyfriars to his wife Sophia, apparently with reversion to his executor Horatio Cock and his heirs. Priory field, behind the house and its garden, was leased to the trustees of the botanic gardens from 1824. The whole estate was offered for sale in three lots in 1847, presumably on Sophia Baskerfield's death.[65] Two new streets of houses were laid out on the site of the botanic gardens,[66] but Halls's house and its southern neighbour, with their gardens, survived in 1990.

50 E.R.O., D/P 203/3/6.

51 E.R.O., Acc. C47, CPL 758; newspaper cutting of 13 Apr. 1912 in E.C.L. Colch.

52 *E.A.T.* (3rd ser.), xviii. 106; *Colch. Archaeologist*, v. 9–10.

53 R.C.H.M. *Essex*, iii. 48–9; E.R.O., T/A 633; 18th-cent. copy of 17th-cent. drawing among E.C.L. Colch. newspaper cuttings; above, Fig. 29.

54 Printed rep.: copy in E.R.O. pamphlet box C6A; *E.C.S.* 12 April 1912; 5 June 1915, in E.C.L. Colch. press cuttings.

55 *Colch. Archaeologist*, iv. 2–5; v. 10; *E.C.S.* 24 Aug. 1990.

56 *Close R.* 1234–7, 433.

57 *Cal. Lib.* 1245–51, 113; *Close R.* 1268–74, 49.

58 P.R.O., C 143/4, no. 19; *Cal. Pat.* 1272–81, 299; *Cal. Close*, 1302–7, 392.

59 P.R.O., C 143/12, no. 22; C 143/19, no. 9; C 143/77, no. 5; *Cal. Fine R.* 1272–1307, 322; *Cal. Pat.* 1292–1301, 14; 1307–13, 157, 202; 1338–40, 108; 1348–50, 85; 1422–9, 107.

60 E.R.O., D/B 5 Cr111, rot. 9.

61 *L. & P. Hen. VIII*, xiii (2), p. 437.

62 P.R.O., SC 6/Hen. VIII/963; ibid. E 318/14/649, rot. 24; *L. & P. Hen. VIII*, xix (1), p. 625.

63 Morant, *Colch.* 152; E.R.O., D/DRg 1/226.

64 P.R.O., C 60/389, no. 12; C 142/163, no. 55.

65 E.R.O., D/DRg 1/226; D/DP 200/11/1–7; D/DCT 89B; D/ABR 24/108; ibid. Q/RPl 1142; ibid. Acc. C47, CPL 792, 1040; Acc. C32, sale cat.; Morant, *Colch.* 152; above, fig. 15.

66 *E.C.S.* 19 Sept. 1851; above, fig. 15.

The site was entered through a gatehouse in Friar Street which survived in 1622. The conventual buildings were apparently set back from the street, the cloister and domestic buildings being on the north side of the church. In 1620 two parallel ranges of buildings apparently survived, but in 1718 only the walls, one containing 13th-century lancet windows, and the remains of the cloister walk remained. Fragments of wall remained in 1748, but were presumably destroyed by John Halls when he laid out his garden.[67] No trace of the medieval buildings remained in 1847, nor had any foundations been found in the course of digging in the botanic

FIG. 30. THE GREY FRIARS, 1718

gardens, but skeletons had been found in the kitchen garden north-west of the 18th-century house. In 1794 there were two ponds at the north end of Priory field, near the town wall, presumably former fishponds; before 1847, probably in 1824 when the field was converted into botanic gardens, they were made into a single pond.[68]

CRUTCHED FRIARS. The house, on the south side of Crouch Street just west of its junction with Maldon Road, originated in the 12th century or the early 13th as a hospital and chapel founded by the lords of Stanway in a detached part of that parish. It was first recorded in 1251, and Robert FitzWalter, lord of Lexden manor, quitclaimed the advowson to Thomas de Belhus of Stanway in 1285.[69] In 1383 John Stansted, a former chaplain, sold the advowson to two Colchester men who in turn conveyed it in 1392 to three leading burgesses. They conveyed it the same year to the bailiffs and commonalty for the repair of the town walls,[70] but the Crown presented in 1395, and in 1400 granted the advowson, which was said to have been forfeited to the king, to John Doreward, lord of Stanway manor. Nevertheless, in 1403 eight burgesses of Colchester were patrons.[71]

The hospital was endowed by an early master with at least 6 a. in the suburbs of Colchester, recovered by another master in 1285, but by 1401 it had fallen on hard times and the chapel, which then comprised nave, chancel, and bell-tower, and other buildings were in great need of repair. In 1403 the bishop of London, at the request of the patrons, and with the consent of John Doreward as patron of Stanway church, gave the master or warden of the hospital permission to conduct services for the inhabitants of the detached portion of Stanway parish in Crouch Street and Maldon Lane, and granted the chapel baptismal and burial rights. He endowed it with the great and small tithes and offerings of its area of the parish, but burdened the warden with an annual pension of 13*s.* 4*d.* to the rector of Stanway. The warden was responsible for the maintenance of the chapel and was to look after its goods, notably the relic of the holy cross.[72] In 1407 the guild of St. Helen, earlier associated with St. Helen's chapel, whose members included the leading burgesses and many of the neighbouring landowners, was refounded in St. Cross chapel, and undertook to support 5 chantry priests and 13 poor people in the hospital.[73] Nevertheless the old foundation survived; masters or wardens of St. Cross hospital being appointed in 1468 and 1485.[74] In the early 15th century Thomas Godstone, one of the patrons, built a chapel of St. Mary adjoining St. Cross chapel, and founded a chantry there.[75] Thus by the later 15th century there were two chapels and at least one hospital on the site.

About 1496 the Crutched friars successfully claimed St. Cross chapel and hospital, which with their endowments were quitclaimed to them by the wardens of St. Helen's guild and Edward Knevett lord of the manor of Stanway.[76] The friars presumably enlarged the buildings, taking Godstone's chapel into their church as a lady chapel; by 1510 when the endowments of Godstone's chantry were granted to them the lands were said to be for the lady altar in the conventual church.[77] Another altar, of special indulgence, was recorded in 1516.[78] Burials discovered in the 19th century in the garden of no. 38 Crouch Street presumably mark the site of the friars' graveyard.[79] Foundations were found

67 Speed, *Colch. Map*; E.R.O., Acc. C49, map of castle estate; Morant, *Colch.* map facing p. 4; below, Fig. 30.
68 E.R.O., Acc. C32, sale cat. annotated by William Wire; ibid. D/DHt P60.
69 *V.C.H. Essex*, ii. 181; *Cal. Pat.* 1247–58, 105; *Feet of F. Essex*, ii. 49.
70 Morant, *Colch.* 149; *Cal. Pat.* 1381–5, 56; 1391–6, 154; *E.R.* xlv. 33–5; P.R.O., C 143/417, no. 5.
71 *Cal. Pat.* 1391–6, 557; 1399–1401, 372; E.R.O., D/DH VI D 11A.
72 P.R.O., JUST 1/242, rot. 49; Morant, *Colch.* App. p. 13; E.R.O., D/DH VI D 11A.
73 *Cal. Pat.* 1405–8, 392; above, Med. Colch. (Townspeople).
74 *Cal. Pat.* 1467–77, 89; 1485–94, 61.
75 Morant, *Colch.* 157.
76 Ibid. 150.
77 Copies of grant in B.L. Stowe MS. 834, ff. 35–6; E.R.O., D/Y 2/2, p. 305.
78 E.R.O., D/B 5 Cr87, rot. 8.
79 *E.R.* xxxiii. 200 n.

under a house and garden in the same area in the 1930s, with further skeletons between them and the road, and the foundations of a stone building with a slate roof, possibly St. Cross chapel, were excavated near the street frontage in 1989.[80]

In 1538 the prior and community granted the church, churchyard, and priory buildings including stables, barns, and dovecotes, with all their land in Colchester and its liberty and in Stanway and West Bergholt, to Thomas Audley, later Lord Audley.[81] Audley acquired a grant of the premises from the Crown in 1541, although John Barnaby, who had married Catherine widow of Edward Knevett of Stanway, appears to have made an unsuccessful claim to it.[82] The site passed from Lord Audley to his brother Thomas Audley of Berechurch and to Thomas's son Thomas who sold it in 1563 to William Watson (d. 1571). Watson devised the Crutched Friars to his sister Elizabeth Walleys for life with succesive reversions to his nephew William Watson and to William's two sisters, both called Joan, but one third of the estate passed to his son and heir John Watson.[83] In 1573 Elizabeth Walleys quitclaimed her life interest to John Watson, reserving to herself and her husband a house and garden at the west end of the precinct wall, against the Spital house, presumably in the north-west corner of the site.[84] Joan wife of Arthur Hall, presumably niece of the elder William Watson, conveyed her interest in the estate to John Watson in 1580, and in 1583 John granted the Crutched Friars to William and Robert Woodward, who sold it the following year to Edward Barker. Barker's son James held it in 1613 but later sold it to John Stephens (d. 1620) from whom it passed to his son John (d. 1625) and presumably to the younger John's eldest son James.[85] Part of the friary buildings, a north and a south range joined by a wall, may have survived during the Stephens' tenure of the site, but they were probably demolished when Sir Harbottle Grimston Bt. (d. 1648), who bought the Crutched Friars in 1637, built a house on the site for his son Sir Harbottle, M.P. and recorder of the town. The house was fired by the retreating royalists during the seige of Colchester in 1648, and was not occupied by the Grimstons thereafter.[86]

About 1700 the surviving building was converted into a town workhouse; it appeared then to be a recent building, apart from some windows in its east wall.[87] That workhouse had apparently closed by 1711, and the Crutched Friars, owned in 1748 by Jeremiah Daniell, was used for pauper housing. Daniell by will proved 1766 bequeathed it, then occupied as two dwellings, to his daughter Sarah Daniell. Sarah devised it to her brother Peter whose estates were sold on his bankruptcy in 1784. The Crutched Friars, otherwise called the Priory or the Old Workhouse, then comprised a tenement and 10 a. of land and garden ground.[88] It was acquired by James Blatch, who by will proved 1812 devised it to his wife Elizabeth for life with reversion to his son James. James was succeeded in 1837 by John Blatch, who owned the site in 1846.[89] In 1865 James Blatch Philip Hoblyn sold the land for development, laying out Blatch, later Wellesley, Street between Crouch Street and Maldon Road.[90]

The house on the north side of Crouch Street called Crouched Friars in 1989 derives from a copyhold of Lexden manor, called the Holy Cross by 1694, which had probably been held by the Crutched friars in the early 16th century.[91] There is no evidence that it formed part of the site of their house.

HOSPITALS. St. Mary Magdalen's hospital, founded by Eudes the sewer in the early 12th century, was apparently still functioning in 1557 when the master, Thomas Gale, made one of its brothers his executor and residuary legatee.[92] In 1565, however, the hospital's lands were sold, to pass within a few months to alderman Benjamin Clere whose son Benjamin was master from 1562 to *c.* 1580. The hospital had presumably ceased to house its five poor or infirm people by 1565, and by 1580 its buildings were falling down.[93] The lands were restored in 1582, but later 16th-century masters appear to have used their office mainly as a source of income. The hospital was refounded in 1610.[94]

St. Catherine's hospital, on the north side of Crouch Street, had been founded by 1352 for a master and infirm brethren, presumably by the lords of Lexden manor, to whom the site belonged.[95] In 1378 the proctor or master was accused of assaulting three inmates, two men and a woman. The hospital was recorded again in 1382, 1406, and 1510; part of it had become a house and garden by 1545, but in 1583 that was converted into a barn because it was so close to the hospital that no one could live in it.[96] The hospital survived as almshouses in 1622 and 1671. In 1748 the six brick houses, of two rooms each one upstairs and one downstairs, were used as the St. Mary's parish workhouse.[97] St. Anne's chapel and hospital is treated elsewhere.[98]

John Savey, by will proved 1451, bequeathed 7 houses under St. John's abbey wall to house

80 Colch. Mus., file on Greyfriars; inf. from P. Crummy, Colch. Arch. Trust.
81 E.R.O., D/DH VI D 11B.
82 P.R.O., E 318/2/57; E.R.O., D/B 5 Cr114, rot. 6d.; D/ABW 3/44; D/DH VI D 11B.
83 P.R.O., C 142/163, no. 55; C 60/389, no. 12.
84 E.R.O., D/B 5 Cr138, rot. 3.
85 P.R.O., PROB 11/146, f. 58 and v.
86 Morant, *Colch.* 63, 151; Speed, *Colch. Map*; *Hist. Parl.: Commons, 1660–90*, 448.
87 Morant, *Colch.* 151.
88 E.R.O., D/DU 445/3; above, Georgian Colch. (Topog.).
89 E.R.O., D/DEl T325; D/P 246/11/1, 41; D/CT95B.
90 Ibid. D/DEl T293; above, Fig. 16.
91 Ibid. D/DEl M163–5; D/DPa 57; ibid. Acc. C126.
92 E.R.O., D/ABW 16/128; *V.C.H. Essex*, ii. 184–6.
93 P.R.O., E 178/817; *Cal. Pat.* 1557–8, 249; 1560–3, 415; 1563–6, 237.
94 Morant, *Colch.* App. IX; below, Churches; Charities.
95 *Cal. Pat.* 1350–4, 366.
96 E.R.O., D/B 5 Cr21, rott. 27, 37d.; Cr35, rot. 26d.; Cr82, rot. 10d.; D/DPa 57, extracts from Lexden Ct. R.
97 Ibid. D/DPa 57, rentals; Morant, *Colch.* 170–1; above, Par. Govt. and Poor Relief.
98 Below, Ancient Chapels.

13 poor people who were to pray for him and his benefactors; there seems to have been no endowment, and the almshouses were not certainly recorded again although there was an almshouse in the same area in 1589 and 1627.[99] Other almshouses, presumably also unendowed, were recorded in Magdalen Street in 1458 and 1559.[1] An almshouse in St. Martin's parish, recorded in 1607, was disused by 1748 although its site was still called Hospital yard.[2]

CHURCHES

Ancient Churches

ALL SAINTS'. The church's position, at an angle to the modern High Street and on the same alignment as a nearby Roman building, suggests that it existed before High Street was diverted southwards by the building of the castle bailey in the late 11th century.[3] St. Botolph's priory was patron in 1254, and retained the advowson until the Dissolution, when Henry VIII gave it to Sir Thomas Audley, later Lord Audley. The bishop presented by lapse in 1557, Robert Talcott by purchase of a turn in 1609, and the Crown by lapse in 1662, but the advowson descended in the Audley family[4] until Henry Audley sold it in 1698 to John Dane, clerk, who sold it the following year to Henry Compton, bishop of London. John English presented John Dane in 1709, presumably as a result of a grant from the same John Dane.[5] On Compton's death in 1713 his son, Hatton Compton, gave the advowson to Balliol College, Oxford, who retained it, presenting regularly,[6] until 1928 when the benefice was united with that of St. Nicholas with St. Runwald. Thereafter Balliol had two turns in four, until the new benefice of St. James with All Saints, St. Nicholas and St. Runwald was formed in 1953 with the bishop as patron and All Saints' church was closed.[7]

The rectory was valued at 1 mark in 1254.[8] No value was recorded in 1291 or 1535. Although Lord Audley, by will dated 1544, gave the rector of All Saints' all the Colchester tithes formerly held by St. Botolph's priory, the living was vacant because of poverty in 1563.[9] In 1650 the tithes were worth £30 and the parsonage house £3.[10] In 1772 Charles Gray settled a yearly rent of £10 10*s*., from a house and land in All Saints' parish, on the rector as long as he was resident. By 1810 the payment was £12 a year because funds had accumulated during a vacancy, and the rent charge was redeemed in 1921.[11] The net income of the living was £291 in 1835.[12] In 1837 tithes on *c*. 161 a., mainly arable land, were commuted for a yearly rent charge of £35. The total value of the living in 1898 was *c*. £300.[13]

There was no glebe in 1610, but by 1810 there were 5 a. of land in Mile End parish bought by the Governors of Queen Anne's Bounty with a benefaction from R. Hoblyn, rector 1798–1827, and *c*. 1 a. of meadow in St. Leonard's parish; by 1887 the meadow had apparently increased to *c*. 3 a.[14] Most of the glebe was sold in 1918.[15]

The rectory house, recorded in 1610, stood west of the church in the churchyard.[16] In 1720 Francis Powell, rector, repaired it, but it was still too small for his family to live in.[17] After improvements by a later rector, John Abbot, in 1759, the house was occupied by successive incumbents.[18] A new brick house, designed by H. Hayward, was built on or near the site of the old house in 1858.[19] It was used as a rectory house until the ecclesiastical reorganization of 1953.[20]

Medieval rectors, recorded from 1318, included John, amerced in 1337 for felling hazel trees growing on the town wall, William Robyn amerced in 1375 for assault,[21] and William Brown, amerced in 1484 for obstructing the highway with a 'whirlegigge', perhaps a turnstile.[22] A yearly rent of 12*d*. for a lamp in the church survived until 1548.[23] A rent of 6*d*., recorded in 1334, was presumably for general church purposes.[24]

Rectors often held other livings, frequently in Colchester, where most incumbents lived for at least part of the year serving All Saints' personally. John Lakyn, a future Master of Jesus, Cambridge, held the living from 1557 until the Elizabethan settlement.[25] Oliver Pigg, presumably a relative of the younger puritan of the same name, was instituted in 1569, but from 1571

99 E.R.O., D/B 5 Cr64, rot. 13d.; Cr66, rot. 27d.; Cr150, rot. 18d.; D/B 5 Cb1/8, f. 264.
1 Ibid. D/B 5 Cr68, rot. 30; Cr124, rot. 8.
2 Ibid. D/ACA 31, f. 49; Morant, *Colch.* 171.
3 *Arch. Jnl.* cxxxix. 390–419. This account was written in 1987.
4 *E.A.T.* N.S. xviii. 123; Newcourt, *Repertorium*, ii. 163–4.
5 Balliol Coll. Mun., C. 23.15, 16; E.R.O., T/A 547/1.
6 Balliol Coll. Mun., C. 23.17; E.R.O., T/A 547/1.
7 E.R.O., D/CPc 215; *Lond. Gaz.* 1 May 1953, p. 2424.
8 *E.A.T.* N.S. xviii. 123.
9 E.R.O., D/DRe Z9 (xxii); B.L. Harl. MS. 595, no. 24, f. 69.
10 Smith, *Eccl. Hist. Essex*, 318.
11 E.R.O., D/DRc Q4; Guildhall MS. 9628/2; Balliol Coll. Mun., Patronage Papers.
12 *Rep. Com. Eccl. Revenues*, H.C. 54, pp. 642–3 (1835), xxii.
13 E.R.O., D/CT 89A; ibid. T/A 645.
14 Guildhall MS. 9628/2; E.R.O., T/A 645.
15 Balliol Coll. Mun., Patronage Papers.
16 Guildhall MS. 9628/2; [B. or J. Strutt], *Hist. and Descrip. Colch.* ii. 35.
17 E.R.O., D/P 200/8/1; Guildhall MSS. 25750/1, 25754/1.
18 *E.R.* i. 145; Lambeth Palace Libr., Fulham Papers Terrick 14, ff. 313–16; ibid. Howley 48, no. 3; E.R.O., D/ACM 12.
19 E.R.O., Acc. C111 (uncat.): Par. Bk. 1851–79.
20 Ibid. D/CPc 215.
21 Ibid. T/A 237; T/A 547/1; Newcourt, *Repertorium*, ii. 163–4; E.R.O., D/B 5 Cr5, rot. 7d.; Cr17, rot. 7.
22 *E.R.* xlv. 122; T. Wright, *Dict. of Obsolete and Provincial Eng.*
23 P.R.O., E 301/30/220.
24 E.R.O., D/B 5 Cr4, rot. 7.
25 Guildhall MS. 9531/12, f. 471v.

until 1609 the parish was in the hands of John Walford, an 'unpreaching minister', who also held St. Mary Magdalen's by sequestration from 1574 until 1596. He was accused of puritan practices in 1583 but thereafter seems to have conformed. In 1586 he was 'tied to the exercises' of the less learned clergy. He resigned in 1610 and was succeeded by Thomas Talcott, rector of St. Mary's-at-the-Walls since 1604.[26] Thomas Warner, who resigned the living in 1638, was also rector of Abberton of which he was deprived in 1644.[27] Successive visitations in the late 16th century and the early 17th revealed neglect by the churchwardens. In 1584, for instance, the communion book was torn and there was no large Bible; in 1633 the church had no communion plate, and the churchwardens were ordered to remove from the churchyard two posts for drying yarn. In 1636 the churchwardens had not sworn to the articles.[28]

From 1662 to 1837 rectors held the living in plurality with the neighbouring St. Botolph's whose church had been destroyed in the siege of 1648.[29] Edmund Hickeringill, rector 1662–1708, resorted to law in 1674 and 1691 in an attempt to collect tithes from the occupiers of the former St. Botolph's priory lands and from the castle bailey. In the early 1680s he quarrelled vituperatively with Henry Compton, bishop of London, about the St. Botolph's tithes which the bishop wanted to divert to another church.[30] In 1683 the churchwardens were excommunicated for refusing three times to take the customary oath.[31] Francis Powell, rector from 1713 until his death in 1749, also complained of encroachments on the rights and revenues of the church. He held a daily service when he was at home, at least one service with a sermon on Sundays, and communion monthly and at the great festivals; he was imprisoned in the Fleet in 1747.[32]

From 1749 to 1928, except for 1890–2, the church was held by a succession of members of Balliol College.[33] Nathaniel Forster, rector 1764–90, a utilitarian writer on political economy, lived at the rectory house and seems to have served All Saints' personally, although he was also rector of Tolleshunt Knights and vicar of Ardleigh. He employed as curate Samuel Parr, who was also curate of St. James's and master of Colchester grammar school.[34] Despite Forster's residence and his interest in Sunday schools, between 1766 and 1790 the average number of communicants fell from *c.* 60 to *c.* 20–30. Services were reduced to only one on Sunday, and in 1790 communion was celebrated only *c.* 8 times a year.[35] In 1841 of the 100 families in the parish 78 were said to belong to the church. On Census Sunday 1851, out of a population of 477, attendances of 120 in the morning and 200 in the afternoon were reported, with an additional 100 Bluecoat schoolchildren from St. Nicholas's parish on each occasion.[36]

J. T. Round, rector from 1851 until his death in 1860, restored the church. It was largely as a result of his work that the new parish of St. John the Evangelist was formed, partly out of a detached part of All Saints' parish, in 1863.[37] His successor, F. Curtis, asked parishioners in 1866 not to 'thirst after change', but by 1874 had introduced a daily service and increased the number of communion services to two a month.[38] T. G. Gardiner, rector 1890–2, was concerned about the education and welfare of working people and active in the labour movement; he encouraged lay participation in parochial work.[39]

By 1907 communion was celebrated every Sunday, and the church was probably already in the 'broad church tradition' which the congregation was anxious to retain in 1933. A. W. Deakin, rector 1924–7, raised congregations from 40 to 100 on Sunday mornings, and from under 100 to a full church (330) in the evenings, but the poverty of the living forced his early resignation.[40] The church was closed in the ecclesiatical reorganization of 1953.[41]

The church of All Saints' comprises a chancel, nave, north chapel and aisle, and a fine west tower of knapped flints.[42] The walls are of stone and flint mixed with brick; the dressings are of limestone. The south wall of the nave, which was refaced in 1855, was said in the 18th century to contain herringbone work, suggesting an 11th-century date, but the width of the nave indicates that it was largely rebuilt later.[43] The chancel was rebuilt in the early 14th century, and the north chapel and aisle were added in the 15th century, probably soon after 1448. The tower was rebuilt in the early 16th century, possibly *c.* 1500, but the 14th-century tower arch was retained.[44] A small house adjoining the church with a little room over it, recorded in 1610, was probably a porch and porch chamber, for in 1720 Francis Powell pulled down a small chamber over the church porch, and a south porch existed in 1748.[45] The north arcade was demolished in 1738 and replaced by wooden piers which were themselves replaced in 1824 by four 'iron Gothic' columns. In 1771–2 a gallery

26 B. Usher, 'Colch. and Diocesan Admin.' (TS. in E.R.O.), 2, 28; above, Tudor and Stuart Colch. (Religious Life, Eliz. Settlement).

27 *E.A.T.* N.S. xi. 41.

28 E.R.O., D/AZ 1/1, f. 74; D/AZ 1/4, f. 137v.; D/AZ 1/7, f. 134; D/AZ 1/8, f. 60v.; D/AZ 1/11, f. 5; *E.A.T.* N.S. xi. 43.

29 Below, St. Botolph's.

30 *D.N.B.* s.vv. Hickeringill, Compton; E. Hickeringill, *Naked Truth* (1680); P.R.O., E 134/25–6 Chas. II Hil./5; E 134/3 Wm. & Mary Mich./5.

31 *E.A.T.* N.S. xxiii. 162.

32 Guildhall MSS. 25750/1; 25755/1.

33 Balliol Coll. Mun., C 23.17; E.R.O., T/A 547/1; *Alum. Oxon. 1715–1886.*

34 *D.N.B.*; below, St. James's.

35 N. Forster, *Discourse on the utility of Sunday Schools* (1786): copy in E.C.L. Colch.; Lambeth Palace Libr., Fulham Papers Terrick 14, ff. 313–16; ibid. Porteus 25, no. 56.

36 E.R.O., D/ACM 12; P.R.O., HO 129/8/204; *V.C.H. Essex*, ii. 353.

37 C. E. Benham, *Colch. Worthies*, 45–6; E.R.O., D/CE 77; *White's Dir. Essex* (1863).

38 E.R.O., Acc. C111 (uncat.): Par. Bk. 1851–79.

39 Brown, *Colch. 1815–1914*, 139; E.R.O., D/P 138/28/9.

40 E.R.O., D/CV 1/2; Balliol Coll. Mun., Patronage Papers.

41 E.R.O., D/P 200/28/4; *Lond. Gaz.* 1 May 1953, p. 2424.

42 R.C.H.M. *Essex*, iii. 32–3; Pevsner, *Essex*, 132; *E.A.T.* N.S. xii. 323–36.

43 Morant, *Colch.* 119; the nave is *c.* 24 ft. wide, not 18 ft. as in R.C.H.M. *Essex*, iii. 33 followed by W. and K. Rodwell, *Hist. Churches,* 30.

44 E.R.O., D/B 5 Cr62, rot. 12; D/B 5 R1, f. 113.

45 Guildhall MS. 9628/2; E.R.O., D/P 200/8/1; Morant, *Colch.* (1748), Bk. I, map facing p. 4.

was erected and a window inserted at its west end, and in 1811 another gallery was added.[46] Between 1855 and 1857 the north arcade was rebuilt in 13th-century style as part of a major restoration to the designs of H. Hayward; other work included refacing the south wall of the nave and inserting new windows in it.[47] The tower was repaired in 1878. The chancel was restored *c.* 1890 by Rolfe and Coggin.[48] The church was sold to the borough council and converted in 1957 into a natural history museum.[49]

There were five bells: (i & ii) Miles Gray, 1610, (iii) Richard Boler, 1587, (iv) Miles Gray, 1620, and (v) Miles Gray, 1682. All were rehung in Little Horkesley church between 1953 and 1973.[50] The plate included two silver cups, one of 1658, and another with silver paten cover of 1714 by Richard Hutchinson of Colchester, a silver paten of 1714 and a silver flagon of 1777, all in Colchester museum in 1987.[51]

Monuments include grave slabs in the chancel to two rectors, Edmund Hickeringill (d. 1708) and John Abbot (d. 1760). In the north aisle are marble monuments to Charles Gray (d. 1782), and to his wife, her two daughters, and her mother, Mary Webster.[52] In 1987 most of the monuments were hidden by the museum display units.

HOLY TRINITY. Architectural evidence shows that the church, which stands on the east side of Trinity Street overlying a minor Roman street junction, existed by the 11th century.[53] Until 1536 its parish included Berechurch.[54] In the 1170s the advowson was in dispute between Bury St. Edmunds abbey (Suff.) and Thomas dean of Colchester. Thomas surrendered it to the abbey, but *c.* 1205 abbot Samson returned it to him.[55] By 1254 it had passed to Richard Champneys, who gave it to St. John's abbey before 1259.[56] The king presented in 1393, believing the rectory to be vacant and the patronage lapsed, but John Mayn, presented by the abbey in 1382, recovered the living in 1397.[57] At the Dissolution the advowson passed to the Crown, which presented until 1628 except for the years 1605 and 1606, when two turns were apparently sold. The rectory was sequestered to the rector of St. Mary's-at-the-Walls from *c.* 1644 until 1735.[58] In 1702 George Compton, earl of Northampton, acting for his uncle Henry Compton, bishop of London (d. 1713), acquired the advowson from the Crown by exchange. Compton intended to give it to Balliol College, Oxford, but an error in the grant of 1702 delayed the gift until 1714. The Crown presented by lapse in 1735 when the last sequestrator died, but Balliol College presented in 1736, and regularly thereafter.[59] In 1932 the benefice was united with St. Martin's, and the college and the patron of St. Martin's presented alternately until 1953 when Holy Trinity was closed and its parish incorporated into the new parish of St. Botolph with Holy Trinity and St. Giles.[60]

The rectory was valued at 3 marks between 1182 and 1211 and in 1254, and at £6 13*s.* 4*d.* in 1535.[61] No value was recorded in 1291. An annual pension of 4*s.*, paid to the abbot of Bury St. Edmunds from 1182 or earlier until *c.* 1205, was apparently claimed later by St. John's abbey.[62] In 1510 the bishop of London annexed to Holy Trinity rectory a chantry in West Bergholt church, endowed with 2 messuages, *c.* 49 a. of land, and 33*s.* 4*d.* rent; rectors served the chantry until its suppression in 1543.[63] In 1536 Sir Thomas Audley gave a farm at Ardleigh to the rectory to compensate for the loss of Berechurch chapelry, which was then worth 43*s.* a year.[64] The farm, leased at 30*s.* in 1559, was worth £16 in 1650 but only £12 in 1683, and £11 in 1707. In 1765 the rector paid a quitrent of 5*d.* to the lord of Ardleigh manor.[65] The living was augmented in 1738 by £200 from Queen Anne's Bounty and a like sum from Edward Brookes's legacy, which with a supplement from the rector were used to buy a farm at Walton-le-Soken.[66] By 1835 the net income had risen to £158, but part of the farm belonging to Holy Trinity had been destroyed by the sea by 1843. In 1845 tithes on *c.* 60 a. of mainly arable land, 17 a. of garden ground, and 10 a. of houses were commuted for a rent charge of £23 12*s.* 2*d.* Another 12 a., which had belonged to St. John's abbey, were tithe-free. The farm at Walton was exchanged in 1853 for stock producing £90 a year.[67] The income of the living was £300 in 1890. The farm at Ardleigh was sold after 1911.[68]

A house opposite Holy Trinity churchyard was occupied by the rector *c.* 1250 and an adjacent house belonged to successive patrons in the 13th century, but there is no evidence that either was a rectory house,[69] and later medieval rectors

46 E.R.O., D/P 200/8/1, 3; ibid. T/Z 175.

47 Ibid. D/P 200/8/3; D/P 200/6/2; ibid. Acc. C111 (uncat.): Par. Bk. 1851–79.

48 Ibid. D/AZ 7/1, p. 116; D/P 200/6/3–4.

49 G. Martin, *Story of Colch.* 119.

50 *Ch. Bells Essex*, 215; *Colch. Official Guide* (1973), 43.

51 *Ch. Plate Essex*, 189–90; for Hutchinson family, *E.R.* lx. 163.

52 Morant, *Colch.* App. 21–2.

53 R.C.H.M. *Essex*, iii. 33; W. and K. Rodwell, *Hist. Chs.* 32. This section was written in 1987.

54 Below, Outlying Parts (West Donyland, Church); *L. & P. Hen. VIII*, xi, p. 154.

55 B.L. Lansdowne MS. 416, ff. 46–8; *Kal. Abbot Samson* (Camd. 3rd ser. lxxiv), pp. 161–2.

56 *E.A.T.* N.S. xviii. 123; *Feet of F. Essex*, i. 229.

57 *Cal. Pat.* 1391–6, 328; 1396–9, 264; P.R.O., C 44/12, no. 12.

58 Newcourt, *Repertorium*, ii. 181; Smith, *Eccl. Hist. Essex*, 66.

59 *Cal. S.P. Dom.* 1700–2, 512; Morant, *Colch.* 116; E.R.O., D/DR T60; Balliol Coll. Mun., C 23, 18–20, 22; Guildhall MSS. 9550, 9557; *Rep. Com. Eccl. Revenues*, H.C. 54, pp. 642–3 (1835), xxii.

60 *Chelm. Dioc. Yr. Bk.* (1933 and later edns.); E.R.O., D/CPc 228; *Chelm. Dioc. Chron.* June 1932, 95–6; *Lond. Gaz.* 1 May 1953, p. 2424.

61 *Chron. Jocelin of Brakelond*, ed. H. E. Butler, 64; *E.A.T.* N.S. xviii. 123; *Valor Eccl.* (Rec. Com.), i. 443.

62 *Chron. Jocelin of Brakelond*, 64; E.R.O., T/A 370.

63 *Cal. Pat.* 1330–34, 281; 1405–8, 330; E.R.O., D/B 5 R2, ff. 126–8; Newcourt, *Repertorium*, ii. 181; Guildhall MS. 9531/9, f. 24v.

64 *L. & P. Hen. VIII*, xi, pp. 154, 208; P.R.O., C 54/406, no. 10.

65 Guildhall MSS. 9532/2, ff. 98v.–99, 102v.–103; 9531/13, f. 13 and v.; Smith, *Eccl. Hist. Essex*, 319; E.R.O., D/ACV 9B, ff. 39–40; B.L. Add. Roll 25791.

66 C. Hodgson, *Queen Anne's Bounty*, pp. clii, cccxii–cccxiii; Morant, *Colch.* 116.

67 *Rep. Com. Eccl. Revenues*, pp. 642–3; Balliol Coll. Mun., C. 19, 23, 26, 36; E.R.O., D/CT 100.

68 *Kelly's Dir. Essex* (1890); E.R.O., D/CPc 132; ibid. T/A 645.

69 *Colch. Cart.* ii. 438–9.

lived in a house 'opposite' or 'by' the churchyard leased from the borough.[70] Trinity House, adjoining the churchyard, was given to the parish as a rectory house by A. M. Ager by will proved 1927, but it was in very bad repair and in 1932 it was sold and the money invested for the living.[71]

Thomas dean of Colchester seems to have been rector in the 1170s, assisted by his brother William.[72] Most later mediaeval rectors, recorded from *c.* 1250, held the church only briefly;[73] one, Edward Squire, was deprived in 1510 for an unknown offence.[74] William Jay, instituted in 1530, subscribed the oath of supremacy in 1534; he may have survived throughout the Reformation period, living in the parish and dying *c.* 1559.[75] William Lyon, instituted in 1561, retained Holy Trinity and Mile End, which he held in plurality, until his death in 1585.[76] His successor Robert Good, a former saddle-mender, was described as double-beneficed in 1586 and was 'tied to the exercises' for the instruction of the less able clergy in 1586 and 1589. He apparently abandoned the living in 1591 when a relative procured him the vicarage of Tolleshunt D'Arcy.[77] Good's successor, Henry Corinbeck, refused in 1592 to subscribe to the Articles, and neglected divine service. A series of short incumbencies from that year compounded neglect; in 1604 the churchwardens failed to procure even the Easter communion. In 1607 the rector, John Booty, was ordered by the archdeacon to study the Old Testament and the works of the Swiss reformer Bullinger.[78] A parishioner protested in 1616 at the curate's use of the surplice, and another in 1636 refused to receive communion from the Laudian rector Thomas Newcomen.[79]

From 1648 until 1714, while St. Mary's church lay in ruins, rectors of St. Mary's, the sequestrators of Holy Trinity, ministered to both congregations in Holy Trinity church, and in the period 1649–51 most of the recorded marriages of Colchester couples took place there.[80] In 1683 the cure was said to be served diligently by William Shillito, assistant curate 1679–99.[81] In 1723 the last sequestrator, Robert Middleton, was employing an assistant who lived in Holy Trinity parish and provided daily and Sunday services there; communion was celebrated monthly and at festivals in the two churches by turn.[82]

Charles Lidgould, rector 1736–65, lived in the parish and served it himself for most of the year, performing one Sunday service and communion every two months and at festivals.[83] His successors from 1766 until 1830 were fellows of Balliol College who did not live in Colchester and employed assistant curates to serve the parish and provide one Sunday service and communion four times a year. Peter Wright, rector 1830–9, although already 70 years old and resident on his living of Marks Tey, performed daily services at Holy Trinity.[84] He was succeeded in both parishes by Lewis Welsh Owen, rector 1839–68, who started parish day and Sunday schools,[85] restored the church, and increased the services to two on Sundays with a monthly communion. On Census Sunday 1851, out of a population of 798, congregations of 300 in the morning and 250 in the afternoon were reported, with 50 children at the afternoon Sunday school.[86] John Bush Early, rector for 33 years from 1877, started monthly afternoon services for children *c.* 1894.[87] His successor E. R. Monck-Mason, rector 1910–39, refurbished the church, built and enlarged a church hall, started a parish magazine, and encouraged meetings and social clubs for men, women and children.[88] After the union with St. Martin's in 1932 Monck-Mason was assisted by a Church Army captain in providing three services every Sunday in each church. His successor found the living too poor to pay for regular help throughout the year and from 1940 services were usually held in the two churches alternately.[89]

The church is built of flint rubble, septaria, and Roman brick, with dressings of Roman brick and Reigate stone.[90] It comprises a chancel with north and south chapels and south-east vestry, an aisled nave of three bays with south porch, and a west tower of three stages with a pyramidal cap. The Anglo-Saxon church may have been single-celled, the nave and chancel undifferentiated from each other structurally. Parts of the west wall of that church survive, and part of its east wall has been found at the south-east corner of the surviving nave. The surviving tower was added in the later 11th century. In the mid 14th century the nave was rebuilt and the chancel built or rebuilt. The south arcade and aisle and the south porch were built in the late 15th century; the south chapel was added later in the same century.

70 Morant, *Colch.*, 116–7; E.R.O., D/B 5 R1, ff. 41, 64, 74, 100v., 103 and v., 115; D/B 5 Cr108, rot. 12d.

71 Balliol Coll. Mun., Patronage Papers; *Par. Mag.* Oct. 1927, Sept. 1929, Mar. 1932.

72 B.L. Lansdowne MS. 416, f. 46.

73 *Colch. Cart.* ii. 439; Newcourt, *Repertorium*, ii. 181–2; E.R.O., T/A 237; T/A 547/1; P.H. Reaney, *Early Essex Clergy*, 68.

74 Newcourt, *Repertorium*, ii. 182.

75 ibid.; E.R.O., D/B 5 R2, f. 162; D/B 5 R1, f. 131.

76 Corpus Christi Coll. Camb., MS. 122, f. 51; *Cal. Pat.* 1560–3, 375.

77 *Seconde Part of a Register*, ed. A. Peel, ii. 159, 162; B. Usher, 'Colch. and Diocesan Admin.' (TS. in E.R.O.), 19, 37–8.

78 Newcourt, *Repertorium*, ii. 182; E.R.O., D/AZ 1/1, f. 42; D/AZ 1/2, f. 6v.; D/AZ 1/10, f. 69v.

79 *E.R.* xlv. 41; E.R.O., D/AZ 1/8, f. 51v.

80 Morant, *Colch.* 109, 116; E.R.O., T/R 124/1; below, St. Mary's.

81 *E.A.T.* N.S. xxiii. 164; plaque in ch.

82 Guildhall MS. 25750/1.

83 Ibid. MS. 9550; E.R.O., D/P 323/1/2–3.

84 Guildhall MSS. 9556–8, 9560; *Alum. Oxon. 1715–1886*; *E.R.* xxi. 14–15; E.R.O., D/ACM 7; D/P 323/1/2–3; ibid. Libr. Folder, Colch., TS. poem, 'Recollections of an Old Colch. Inhabitant'.

85 *Alum. Oxon. 1715–1886*; below, Educ.

86 P.R.O., HO 129/8/204; *V.C.H. Essex*, ii. 353; E.R.O., D/P 323/8/1A, 2.

87 E.R.O., D/CV 1/2; *Kelly's Dir. Essex* (1894); *Jarrold's Guide to Colch.* (1903), 171.

88 E.R.O., D/CV 2/2; D/CV 3/2; *Par. Mag.* 1911–39; *E.C.S.* 8 Dec. 1950; plaque in ch.

89 *Par. Mag.* June and July 1932, Jan. 1933, Apr. 1940.

90 R.C.H.M. *Essex*, iii. 33–5, with plate facing p. 34; Rodwell, *Hist. Chs.* 31–2; H. M. and J. Taylor, *Anglo-Saxon Archit.* i. 162–4; *Jnl. Brit. Arch. Assoc.* iii. 19–22.

By 1585 the walls and windows were decayed and there was neither pulpit nor reading desk.[91] The rector repaired the chancel in 1597, but it was not until 1609 that repairs to the tower and south wall of the nave were carried out.[92] The pulpit and reading desk, mentioned in 1708, may have been provided at that time.[93] By 1633, however, the chancel was dilapidated, the tower ruinous, and the churchyard used as a milking yard.[94] Some repairs were done at once, for the tower was fit to receive a new bell later that year.[95] In 1705 the chancel needed new paving.[96] In the 17th or 18th century a window was inserted in the west wall of the south aisle. A vestry was added to the east end of the chancel and south aisle in 1840. In the 1850s the church was reseated and plaster removed from the outside walls revealing two niches containing defaced statues. The statues, and a carved stone coffin in a 14th-century niche in the south wall, were destroyed.[97] The north aisle and chapel were added in 1866.[98] For nearly 20 years after the closure of the church in 1953 the building was left unoccupied and was vandalized. In 1972 the borough council, with a gift from the Soroptimists of Colchester, bought the building and in 1974 opened it as a museum of rural crafts.[99] The design of the museum retained the surviving monuments and 15th-century font.

The church's one bell, of 1633, was stolen in the 1960s.[1] The church plate included a paten of 1710 and a mazer mounted with silver-gilt, which has been ascribed to the 15th century and may have been given to the church in the 19th century.[2] An iron-bound chest, in the church in 1987, is probably of the early 17th century.[3] The 14th-century door with contemporary knocker plate and hinges was in 1987 displayed in the porch. The memorials include a marble and alabaster tablet to William Gilberd (d. 1603)[4] and a tablet to the madrigalist John Wilbye (d. 1638), erected in 1938 by the English Madrigal societies.[5] Five funeral hatchments display the arms of Sir John Shaw (d. 1690) and his wife Thamar (d. 1681), John Brasier (d. 1725), Sir Richard Bacon (d. 1773), and Thomas Talcott (d. 1685).[6] In the churchyard, which became a public garden in 1972,[7] are many 18th- and 19th- century tombs, but a pyramidal monument to Mary Darcy, countess Rivers (d. 1644), had been removed by 1748.[8]

ST. BOTOLPH'S. A church existed before the foundation of the Augustinian priory between 1093 and 1100.[9] Its functions were taken over by the priory church, which was apparently both conventual and parochial until the Dissolution. As an Augustinian foundation, the church was exempt from all ordinary jurisdiction until 1550 when it was made subject to the bishop of London.[10] After St. Botolph's church was destroyed in the siege of 1648 the benefice was regularly held in plurality with All Saints' until 1851.[11]

The ecclesiastical parish comprised many small scattered pieces.[12] In 1852 *c.* 12 a. near St. Mary Magdalen's church was transferred to that parish. In 1863 an outlying part of St. Botolph's parish east of the Harwich Road was transferred to the new parish of St. John the Evangelist. Under the comprehensive boundary reorganization of 1911 St. Botolph's parish boundaries were consolidated by the transfer of small areas to St. Mary's, St. Giles's, St. Mary Magdalen's, St. Paul's, and St. James's, and the addition of small areas of St. Giles's and St. Mary Magdalen's. In 1950 a part of St. Botolph's was transferred to the new parish of St. Barnabas, Old Heath. In 1953 under the Colchester ecclesiastical reorganization St. Botolph's became part of the new parish of St. Botolph with Holy Trinity and St. Giles.[13]

The cure was not presentative, but was supplied by the priory or its appointees until the Dissolution, when Henry VIII gave Sir Thomas Audley, later Lord Audley, the site of the priory and the rectory with all its appurtenances, including presumably the advowson or right to appoint a curate.[14] The advowson of the living, later styled a perpetual curacy, remained in the Audley family until 1698 when Henry Audley sold it, together with that of All Saints', to John Dane who sold it the following year to Henry Compton, bishop of London. On Compton's death his son, Hatton Compton, gave it to Balliol College, Oxford.[15] Balliol retained the advowson until 1870 when it was exchanged with the diocesan bishop for that of Little Tey.[16] The bishop was the patron of the united benefices of St. Botolph, St. Giles, and Holy Trinity in 1987.[17]

The church was worth *c.* 40*s.* in 1254;[18] it was not separately valued in 1291 or 1535. Most of the church's potential income was lost when Lord Audley, by will proved 1544, gave all the priory's tithes in Colchester to the rector of All Saints'.[19] Before 1548 St. Botolph's churchwardens

91 E.R.O., D/AZ 1/7, f. 143.
92 Ibid. D/AZ 1/1, f. 42; D/AZ 1/4, f. 153v.; D/AZ 1/10, ff. 36, 43v.
93 Guildhall MS. 9532/2, ff. 59v.–60.
94 *E.A.T.* N.S. xi. 40–1.
95 *Ch. Bells. Essex*, 216.
96 E.R.O., D/ACV 9A, f. 66v.
97 Ibid. D/P 323/8/1A, 2; *E.A.T.* N.S. xix. 324–6. *White's Dir. Essex* (1848), 79; ibid. (1863), 84; F. Chancellor, *Sepulchral Mon. Essex*, 206 and plate lxvii.
98 E.R.O., D/AZ 7/1, pp. 140–1.
99 *Lond. Gaz.* 1 May 1953, p. 2424; Rodwell, *Hist. Chs.* 32; *E.C.S.*. 23 Oct. 1970; 4 June, 2 July 1971; 20 Oct. 1972; notice in mus.
1 *Ch. Bells Essex*, 216, 357; inf. from curator; Bell displayed in mus. is that of Peldon (1613).
2 *Ch. Plate Essex*, 191 and plate II; *E.A.T.* N.S. iii. 76–7; xix. 50; R.C.H.M. *Essex*, iii. pl. facing p. 35; Rep. Colch. & Essex Mus. 1950–4, p. 42; paten and mazer in Colch. Mus. in 1984.
3 H. W. Lewer and J. C. Wall, *Ch. Chests Essex*, 106.
4 Chancellor, *Sepulchral Mon. Essex*, 202; *Par. Mag.* Oct. 1917; above, Tudor and Stuart Colch. (Intro.).
5 *E.A.T.* N.S. xi. 230–5; *E.R.* xlviii. 45; *D.N.B.*; above, Tudor and Stuart Colch. (Intro.).
6 *Guide to Essex Chs.* ed. C. Starr, 64; notice in mus.
7 E.R.O., D/P 323/8/1A.
8 E.C.L. Colch., Crisp MS. 'Colch. Mon. Inscriptions', ii; Morant, *Colch.* App. p. 21.
9 *V.C.H. Essex*, ii. 148. This account was written in 1987.
10 *E.A.T.* N.S. xviii. 123; *Cal. Pat.* 1549–51, 172.
11 E.R.O., D/P 203/1/5.
12 Above, fig. 22.
13 E.R.O., D/CC 5/1; D/CE 77; D/CPc 132; D/CPc 302; *Lond. Gaz.* 1 May 1953, p. 2424.
14 Newcourt, *Repertorium*, ii. 166.
15 Guildhall MS. 9628/2; Balliol Coll. Mun., C 23.15–17.
16 E.R.O., D/CPc 30.
17 *Chelm. Dioc. Yr. Bk.* (1986–7), 165.
18 *E.A.T.* N.S. xviii. 123.
19 E.R.O., D/DRe Z9.

sued the rector of All Saints' for the tithes, but evidently did not retrieve more than the small tithes, worth £10, which the curate held in 1650.[20] In 1766 St. Botolph's had no income, but in 1810 when the living was being served by the rector of All Saints', there were said to be tithes on 500–600 a. and surplice fees of £10–15. The tithes were presumably those granted to the rector of All Saints' in 1544.[21] No value was recorded in 1835, but when the new church was built in 1836 an endowment of *c.* £100 a year was proposed for the living.[22] In 1851 the income comprised a permanent endowment of £85 17*s.* 8*d.*, fees of £10, and the Easter offering of £7 10*s.*[23] Mary Montagu Thorley (d. 1861) left a house and 5 cottages in Colchester for the augmentation of St. Botolph's.[24] The Ecclesiastical Commissioners augmented the living by £82 in 1871, and by 1887 the income was *c.* £283.[25] A parsonage house in Priory Street, mentioned in 1866, became in 1953 the parsonage house for the new benefice of St. Botolph with Holy Trinity and St. Giles.[26]

A guild in the parish chapel of St. Botolph's was recorded in 1488. The church goods included some small candlesticks, a little bell, and some banners, sold by 1548.[27]

The living cannot be shown to have had a regular curate until the early 1570s, probably because the ancient priory church became, after 1559, the pulpit for the common preacher. From the early 1570s, however, the cure was served by William Kirby, rector of East Donyland 1572–91, who in 1583 failed to read the weekday services and was described as 'a sower of discord between neighbour and neighbour'.[28] Thomas Holland, curate 1586–7, was 'tied to the exercises' for the instruction of the less able clergy and was eventually suspended for failing to attend them. From about 1588 until at least 1607 the living was in the hands of Thomas Farrar, rector of St. James's from 1592.[29] In 1584 the communion table was 'naught' and certain stalls were 'broken up and thrown about', possibly in an earlier manifestation of the puritanism displayed in 1616 by two parishioners and in 1636 by another who refused to receive communion kneeling,[30] and in 1635 by the churchwarden, James Wheeler, who refused to rail in the communion table.[31]

From the siege of 1648, when St. Botolph's church was ruined, until the consecration of the new church in 1837, St. Botolph's parishioners attended All Saints' church. The new church was not licensed for marriages until 1848, but burials took place in St. Botolph's churchyard throughout.[32] Church life until 1837 suffered from the lack of a parish church, and in 1815 many parishioners attended the Baptist or Presbyterian chapels.[33] The new church with accommodation for over 1,000 enabled large congregations to attend. On Census Sunday 1851 below average attendances of 342 in the morning, including 161 Sunday school children, and 669 in the afternoon, including 168 children, were reported from a population of 3,000.[34] From 1851, when T. B. G. Moore became perpetual curate, St. Botolph's was no longer held in plurality. In 1859 there was monthly communion.[35]

J. R. Corbett, vicar 1875–1907, rural dean of Colchester 1897–1907, employed assistant curates.[36] St. Stephen's mission hall, Canterbury Road, a temporary building of 1894, was licensed as a chapel in 1899. A new permanent chapel was built alongside it in 1905 and became a separate parish church in 1953.[37] In 1920 average morning attendances were 300 at St. Botolph's and 60 at St. Stephen's, and average evening attendances were 350 and 150 respectively. In the early 20th century three priests served the parish, but after 1922 the parish could no longer support more than two, and S. T. Smith, vicar 1927–31, resigned for financial reasons.[38] Church attendance decreased as the town centre population fell, until the 1970s when P. Evans, the vicar, increased congregations by actively encouraging new members from outside the parish. Music and drama played an important part in the church's life in 1987, and the church was often used by other organizations, such as local schools and the Colchester Institute.[39]

At the Dissolution the priory church of St. Botolph became the parish church. It was also used by the corporation on civic occasions until the Civil War.[40] In 1584 the windows of the church and chancel were so broken that the church was more like a dovehouse than a place of prayer.[41] The belfry was in a poor condition in 1633 and the church windows needed glazing.[42] In 1650 the church was described as burnt and ruined from the siege, and it was left in ruins thereafter.[43]

The new church of St. Botolph, immediately south of the priory ruins, consecrated in 1837, was designed by William Mason of Ipswich in the Norman style.[44] The large white brick building

20 *E.A.T.* N.S. xiii. 167; Smith, *Eccl. Hist. Essex*, 318.

21 Guildhall MSS. 9558, f. 90; 9628/2.

22 J. S. M. Anderson, *Sermon* (1836): copy in E.C.L. Colch.; *E.C.S.* 27 Oct. 1837.

23 P.R.O., HO 129/8/204.

24 Balliol Coll. Mun., C 23.40.

25 E.R.O., D/CE 6; ibid. T/A 645.

26 *P.O. Dir. Essex* (1866), 58, 66; E.R.O., T/A 645; *Lond. Gaz.* 1 May 1953, p. 2424.

27 P.R.O., PROB 11/8, f. 164v.; *E.A.T.* N.S. xiii. 167.

28 B. Usher, 'Colch. and Diocesan Admin.' (TS. in E.R.O.), 3, 28–30.

29 Ibid. 3–4; E.R.O., D/AZ 1/7, f. 117; *E.R.* xxxii. 135; above, Tudor and Stuart Colch. (Religious Life, Eliz. Settlement).

30 E.R.O., D/AZ 1/4, f. 169v.; D/AZ 1/7, f. 126 and v.; D/AZ 1/8, f. 53.

31 *Cal. S.P. Dom.* 1635–6, 263; *V.C.H. Essex*, ii. 53–4.

32 Morant, *Colch.* 148; Lambeth Palace Libr., Fulham Papers, Terrick 14, ff. 321–4; ibid. Randolph 9, pp. 862–71; E.R.O., D/P 203/1/35.

33 Lambeth Palace Libr., Fulham Papers, Howley 48, no. 39.

34 P.R.O., HO 129/8/204; *V.C.H. Essex*, ii. 353.

35 E.R.O., T/A 547/1; ibid. D/AZ 7/1, p. 118.

36 *Chelm. Dioc. Chron.* Jan. 1921, p. 6; E.R.O., D/CV 1/2.

37 Below, Modern Churches (St. Stephen's).

38 E.R.O., D/CV 3/2; 4/3.

39 [P. Constable], pamphlet in church.

40 Above, Religious Houses (St. Botolph's); Morant, *Colch.* 148; *Colch. Archaeologist*, no. 5, pp. 6–10.

41 E.R.O., D/AZ 1/7, f. 126 and v.

42 *E.A.T.* N.S. xi. 37.

43 Smith, *Eccl. Hist. Essex*, 318.

44 E.R.O., D/DRh F25/19; ibid. Acc. C47, CPL 44, Pps. and accts. of bldg. of St. Botolph's ch.; H. E. von Stürmer, *Hist. Guide to Colch.* 25; above, pl. facing p. 120.

comprises a chancel, nave with galleried north and south aisles, south chapel, south vestry, west gallery, and west tower. Extensive alterations to the interior in 1882 included the creation of a chancel in the eastern bay of the nave.[45] A south chapel was dedicated to St. Agnes in 1933.[46] In the later 1970s the screen, choir stalls, and pulpit were removed, and the nave pews were replaced with chairs.[47]

There is one bell of 1837 by Thomas Mears. The plate is 19th-century.[48] A white marble wall monument with a female figure in classical dress, commemorating William Hawkins (d. 1843) and Mary Ann his wife (d. 1834), on the east wall south of the altar, was obscured by an internal partition in 1987.

ST. GILES'S. The church, immediately north of St. John's abbey precinct, was probably built soon after the foundation of the abbey in 1097 and may have replaced an Anglo-Saxon church dedicated to St. John the Evangelist, which stood *c.* 100 yd. away on the site of a Roman cemetery.[49] St. Giles's was recorded between 1165 and 1171 when the bishop of London confirmed it to St. John's abbey. The abbey appropriated the church *c.* 1220; no vicarage was ordained, but the abbey was to provide a suitable chaplain.[50] After the Dissolution the living was called a perpetual curacy, but it appears that from 1650 or earlier the rectory, composed of tithe only, passed to successive curates. From 1812 the living was treated as a rectory.[51]

At the Dissolution the advowson of the perpetual curacy, together with the tithes, seems to have descended with the site of St. John's abbey to the Lucas family, although Thomas Audley, nephew of Lord Audley, was said to have held it at his death in 1572.[52] John Lucas, Lord Lucas, presented in 1662. There is no later record of any presentation by him or his heirs, and in 1702 the Crown presented, presumably by lapse.[53] Francis Powell, curate of St. Giles's (d. 1749), acquired the advowson, which was sold by his executors to his successor, Charles Lind.[54] Lind mortgaged it to Jeremy Bentham who obtained possession after Lind's death in 1771 and in 1774 sold it to Nicholas Tindal. By will dated 1774 Tindal left the patronage in trust for John Morgan and Anna Maria his wife. Thomas Woodrooffe, one of the trustees, presented in 1788 and 1812, and the bishop of London by lapse in 1810. John Morgan (d. 1817) devised the advowson in trust for his son, John Woodrooffe Morgan. In 1818 the trustees presented the same J. W. Morgan, who died in 1857, leaving the advowson to his nephew, T. M. Gepp (d. 1883), who devised it to his son, N. P. Gepp. In 1913 the Gepp family transferred the patronage to G. T. Brunwin-Hales, rector of St. Mary's, Colchester, who later the same year transferred it to the archdeacon of Colchester.[55] St. Giles's benefice ceased to exist in 1953 when the new benefice of St. Botolph with Holy Trinity and St. Giles was created in the reorganisation of Colchester parishes, and the church was closed.[56]

The living was valued at 40*s.* in 1254 and £3 6*s.* 8*d.* in 1291.[57] No value was recorded in 1535, and the living was vacant because of poverty in 1563.[58] By 1650 the rectorial tithes worth *c.* £25 were attached to the living, but in 1719 its value was only £30 a year because much of the parish, the site of St. John's abbey and its demesne, was exempt from tithes.[59] The living was augmented with the reversion of a quarter share of Huntsman's Farm, Foxearth, left by Moses Cook (d. 1732), matched in 1770 with £200 from Queen Anne's Bounty. In 1824 J. W. Morgan's grant of a house and *c.* 1 a. of land worth £400 was met by two parliamentary grants of £300 each.[60] Thus the value of the living increased to £50 by the mid 18th century and to £190 by 1835.[61] Tithes on 385 a. of arable, 118 a. of meadow, 32 a. of market gardens, and 1 a. of glebe (presumably that recently given by J. W. Morgan), were commuted for a rent charge of £193 14*s.* in 1837.[62] By 1887 the value of the living had risen to *c.* £250.[63]

There was no glebe, and no parsonage house until 1824[64] when J. W. Morgan gave the parish a rectory house in Mersea Road. The house was sold in 1903 and a new one bought in Gladstone Road, no house or land being available within the parish.[65]

In 1414 John Wells, parish clerk, and four others were accused of reading books in English but were apparently treated leniently.[66] William Tey, by will proved 1514, endowed an obit in the church, presumably the one worth 8*s.* a year which survived until 1548.[67] In 1542 as many as half the 320 adult parishioners failed to attend church, some working and others frequenting the alehouse or staying in bed.[68]

About 1586 the curate William Cock was ordered to be deprived for refusing to wear the surplice; he presumably conformed for he kept St. Giles's for 34 years, although in 1605 he was accused of allowing excommunicated people to attend church.[69] Cock's son and successor,

45 E.R.O., D/P 203/3/8; D/CF 20/1.
46 *Chelm. Dioc. Chron.* Nov. 1933, p. 176.
47 [P. Constable], pamphlet in church.
48 *Ch. Bells Essex*, 216; *Ch. Plate Essex*, 193.
49 *Colch. Arch. Rep.* i. 40–6; *Jnl. Brit. Arch. Assoc.* N.S. xxv. 214. This account was written in 1987.
50 *Colch. Cart.* i. 75–6, 86–9.
51 Morant, *Colch.* 125; E.R.O., D/CP 3/34.
52 Morant, *Colch.* 125; P.R.O., C 142/163, no. 57; above, Religious Houses (St. John's); there is no record of any presentation by the Audley family.
53 P.R.O., IND 1/17005, f. 114; E.R.O., T/A 547/1.
54 Morant, *Colch.* 125.
55 E.R.O., D/CP 3/33, 34; D/DGe 542; D/CPc 139.
56 *Lond. Gaz.* 1 May 1953, p. 2424.
57 *E.A.T.* N.S. xviii. 123; *Tax. Eccl.* (Rec. Com.), 23.
58 B.L. Harl. MS. 595, no. 24, f. 69.
59 Smith, *Eccl. Hist. Essex*, 318; Morant, *Colch.* 125.
60 Morant, *Colch.* 107; C. Hodgson, *Queen Anne's Bounty*, pp. clxix, cci, cccxii–cccxiii; E.R.O., D/CP 3/33.
61 Guildhall MS. 9556, p. 122; *Rep. Com. Eccl. Revenues*, H.C. 54, pp. 642–3 (1835), xxii.
62 E.R.O., D/DGe B5.
63 Ibid. T/A 645.
64 Smith, *Eccl. Hist. Essex*, 318; Lambeth Palace Libr., Fulham Papers, Terrick 14, ff. 325–8; ibid. Howley 48, no. 127.
65 E.R.O., D/CP 3/33; G. Rickword, *Notes on Ch. of St. Giles*, 7.
66 [G. Rickword] *St. Giles, Colch.* 5.
67 P.R.O., PROB 11/17, f. 172; ibid. E 301/19/205.
68 E.R.O., D/ACA 1, f. 90v.; W. H. Hale, *Precedents*, 125.
69 T. W. Davids, *Annals of Nonconf. in Essex*, 114; Morant, *Colch.* App. 23; E.R.O., D/AZ 1/10, f. 80.

Samuel, was presented in 1627 for not reading prayers in church on Wednesday and Sunday,[70] but the reason may have been laziness rather than opposition to the established church, for in 1644 he was apparently ejected after being charged with non-residence, with forgetting to administer the wine at communion, with excommunicating those who did not come to the altar rail for communion, and with failing to prepare people to take the Covenant.[71] In 1636 one of many parishioners who did not attend communion vowed that he would be brained before he would receive communion kneeling at an altar rail.[72]

The living was vacant in 1650 and probably remained so for much of the later 17th century, being served by other Colchester clergy and by masters of the grammar school;[73] most 18th-century incumbents were pluralists. Francis Powell, rector of All Saints' and curate of St. Botolph's 1713–49, acted as curate for the absentee Edmund Heywood who was incumbent of St. Giles's from 1702 and also vicar of Great Bentley from 1708 until his death in 1728. Powell acquired the patronage of St. Giles's and appointed himself as perpetual curate.[74] He performed one Sunday service when he was at home, paying a curate to do so at other times.[75] His successor, Charles Lind, who held two other Essex livings, continued to conduct only one Sunday service and in 1766 administered communion four times a year to 20 to 30 parishioners. In 1778 the non-resident incumbent claimed to be very careful that the church was served properly.[76]

In 1810 the living was vacant, being served, as it had been for the previous 31 years, by Charles Hewitt, rector of Greenstead; there were *c.* 30 communicants.[77] Church life improved slightly under the resident J. W. Morgan, rector 1818–57, who held two Sunday services, but only *c.* 50–60 parishioners out of a population of 1,987 attended church in 1841, and on Census Sunday 1851 attendances of 123 at both the morning and afternoon services were reported out of a population of 2,443.[78] Morgan's successor, W. Goode, a firm Evangelical, resigned in 1872 and was followed by W. H. Wardell, rector until 1903, a moderate High Churchman, who inaugurated daily services and a full choral Sunday evening service. St. Barnabas's church was opened in 1875 as a chapel of ease in the growing suburb of Old Heath, and an assistant curate was appointed from 1887 to serve it. In 1903 a new parish room was built, and the church was restored in 1907 after many years of fund-raising.[79] In 1914 there were four Sunday and two daily services, in line with the moderate High Church tradition which continued in 1941.[80]

The average attendance in 1920 was 130 at the morning and 280 at the evening service, and 30 at St. Barnabas's in the evening. In 1928 a house in Claudius Road was bought for the curate, but sold in 1930 when a new house was built next to the church. By 1930 E. W. H. Harley Parker, rector 1927–31, was finding it difficult to manage with only one curate in a growing parish where there were no people of leisure to help in church organizations.[81] In 1939 a new parish hall was opened beside St. Barnabas's church, and in 1950 St. Barnabas's became the church for a new parish taken from St. Giles's, East Donyland, and St. Botolph's.[82] Already in 1942 St. Giles's was regarded by many as redundant, too close to more attractive churches, and it was closed on the reorganization of Colchester parishes in 1953.[83]

The church of St. Giles (occasionally called St. Sepulchre's in the 17th century or the early 18th)[84] comprises a chancel with north and south chapels, nave with south porch, and west tower.[85] The walls are of mixed rubble with some septaria and brick, the porch is mainly of brick, and the tower of wood. The roofs are of tiles, slates, and lead. In the west end of the surviving south wall of the nave is a small lancet window, apparently of the 12th century. The chancel was rebuilt or at least remodelled in the 13th century when the surviving, blocked lancet window was made in the south wall. The north aisle of the nave and tower were probably built in the 14th century, and further work may have been done in 1423 when £3 15*s.* or more was spent on ironwork for the windows.[86] The church was remodelled in the early 16th century, when the south porch was added, a new east window inserted, and the north chapel built or completely rebuilt; the demolished north porch may have been of the same date. The tower was repaired soon after 1514.[87]

In 1748 only the chancel and a small part of the nave were used, the rest of the church lying in ruins, probably from the 1648 siege; there was a boarded west tower,[88] perhaps that which existed in 1987, but that tower, which is constructed of re-used materials, is central to the nave and aisle as they were amalgamated in 1819. Other work in 1819 included the bricking in of empty windows, and the insertion of wooden columns to support galleries and a low-pitched

70 E.R.O., D/ALV 1, f. 72v.

71 *Walker Revised*, ed. A. G. Matthews, 148; below, St. Mary Magdalen's.

72 E.R.O., D/AZ 1/8, f. 52 and v.

73 Smith, *Eccl. Hist. Essex*, 318; idem, 'Essex Parochial Clergy', 117–24: copy in E.S.A.H. Libr., Hollytrees, Colch.; *E.A.T.* N.S. xxiii. 164; *V.C.H. Essex*, ii. 506 n.

74 *Alum. Cantab. to 1751*; Morant, *Colch.* 125.

75 Guildhall MSS. 25753/1; 25754/1.

76 [Rickword], *St. Giles, Colch.* 10; Lambeth Palace Libr., Fulham Papers, Terrick 14, ff. 325–8; ibid. Lowth 4, ff. 301–4.

77 Lambeth Palace Libr., Fulham Papers, Randolph 9, pp. 972–9.

78 Guildhall MS. 9560; E.R.O., D/ACM 12; *V.C.H. Essex*, ii. 353; P.R.O., HO 129/8/204.

79 [Rickword], *St. Giles's, Colch.* 10–11; E.R.O., D/P 324/8/2.

80 *Kelly's Dir. Essex* (1914), 171; *Par. Mag.* July 1941: copy in E.R.O.

81 E.R.O., D/CV 3/2, 4/3; D/P 324/29.

82 *Chelm. Dioc. Chron.* Mar. 1939, p. 47; E.R.O., D/CPc 302.

83 *Par. Mag.* May 1942: copy in E.R.O.; E.R.O., D/CP 3/32.

84 Morant, *Colch.* 122 n.

85 R.C.H.M. *Essex*, iii. 42–5; W. and K. Rodwell, *Hist. Chs.* 35–6; Crummy, *Colch. Arch. Rep.* i. 41.

86 E.R.O., D/B 5 Cr45, rot. 12.

87 P.R.O., PROB 11/17, f. 172.

88 Morant, *Colch.* (1748), Bk. II, p. 21.

roof.[89] Extensive alterations were made to the interior and furnishings in 1859. From 1886 funds were raised to restore the church or build a new one,[90] but it was not until 1907 that the chancel and the north chapel were restored, and a vestry added south of the chancel, designed by Sir A. Blomfield.[91]

The church was closed in 1953, and was for some years used as a store by St. John's Ambulance Brigade. In 1972 it was sold and converted into a masonic hall, opened in 1976. The interior was rearranged, an upper room, reached by a staircase in the tower, being formed at gallery level in the west end of the nave. Single storey additions were made on the south and west sides of the nave.[92]

The surviving plate, of 1826, was on display in Colchester museum in 1987.[93] The only bell, of 1627 by Miles Gray, was cracked by 1881 and unusable by 1954.[94] The north chapel contains several memorials to members of the Lucas family. A black marble memorial, originally a floor slab, to Sir Charles Lucas and Sir George Lisle, royalists shot by order of General Fairfax after the siege in 1648, has been mounted on the north wall. An arch with carved rosettes and strap ornament on its soffit also survived on the north wall, probably from the tomb of Thomas Lucas (d. 1611) and Mary his wife (d. 1613). A wall tablet to John, Lord Lucas (d. 1671), and another to Anne, Lady Lucas (d. 1660), also remain.

ST. JAMES'S. Architectural evidence shows that the church was founded by the 12th century or earlier.[95] Before 1242 the advowson was held by Ralph Somer; it was granted to Coggeshall abbey in 1253, and recovered presumably by Ralph's heirs in 1266.[96] From 1328 or earlier until the Dissolution St. Botolph's priory was patron, presenting regularly except on two occasions in 1469 when Coggeshall abbey presented. In 1536 Henry VIII granted the advowson to Sir Thomas Audley, who gave it to his brother, Thomas Audley of Berechurch. Although the Crown presented by lapse in 1585, 1622, and 1670, the advowson remained with the Audley family until 1700 when Henry Audley sold it to Henry Compton, bishop of London (d. 1713), whose executor sold it to his successor, John Robinson. On Robinson's death in 1723 the advowson passed to his widow who sold it to Samuel Hill; Hill exchanged it with the Crown in 1724 for that of Shenstone (Staffs.). The Crown presented until 1857,[97] but seems to have sold the advowson *c.* 1865 to Charles Cornwallis, Baron Braybrooke, who in 1868 exchanged it with the bishop of Rochester, then the diocesan bishop, for that of Littlebury. Since then successive diocesan bishops have presented.[98] The new benefice of St. James with All Saints, St. Nicholas and St. Runwald was formed in 1953 with the bishop as patron and St. James's as the parish church.[99]

The rectory was valued at 40*s.* in 1254 and £11 8*s.* 4*d.* in 1535.[1] No value was recorded in 1291. In 1495 a pension of 10*s.* a year was paid to St. Botolph's priory, and payments continued until the Dissolution.[2] In 1650 tithes and rates on houses levied by the town council were worth £20 and glebe 20*s.* a year.[3] Thomas Audley, Lord Audley left 10*s.* a year to the rector, but payment had ceased by the mid 18th century.[4] Moses Cook (d. 1732) left the reversion of a quarter share of the rent of Huntsman's Farm, Foxearth; the living was augmented in 1749 by £50 under the will of Susanna Hoyt, and in 1770 by £200 from Queen Anne's Bounty, to match Cook's legacy, which was used to buy a house in Bear Lane (later East Stockwell Street). A parliamentary grant of £200 in 1812, and another of £300 in 1823 to meet the £200 received from the rector and parishioners following the exchange of the parsonage house, helped to raise the gross income to £122 by 1835.[5] Tithes on 49 a. of arable, 20 a. of grass, 62 a. of gardens, and 30 a. of buildings were commuted for a rent charge of £75 14*s.* 4*d.* in 1845, and the value of the living had increased to £140 by 1863.[6] In 1865 part of the purchase money of the advowson was used to endow the living; the sum was augmented by the will of Margaret Round, proved 1887, so that by 1890 the living was worth £205.[7]

There was a rectory house near the church in the time of John Ball, rector 1372–93.[8] The house which needed repair in 1596, and was 'ready to fall down' in 1609, was probably the one on the south side of East Hill just outside East gate which was burnt down during the siege of 1648.[9] The site was owned by the rector and let as garden ground in 1742.[10] There was no rectory house until the late 18th century when a house in East Stockwell Street was acquired, presumably the one bought with the augmentation of Queen Anne's Bounty. Under pressure from the archdeacon the house was exchanged *c.* 1820 with William Walford for a house on East Hill in St. James's parish.[11] A new rectory house, designed by S. S. Teulon, was built in 1859 on

89 E.C.L. Colch., Crisp MS. 'Colchester Monumental Inscriptions', v. 3.

90 E.R.O., D/P 324/8/1, 2; C.P.L., drawing of St. Giles's church, 1890; E.R.O., Churches Collection, picture of interior of St. Giles's church before restoration, 1907.

91 Rickword, *Notes on St. Giles's Ch.* 7; *Kelly's Dir. Essex* (1910), 153.

92 E.R.O., D/CP 3/32; inf. from Masonic Hall Co. Ltd. and Mr. P. Jackson, solicitor.

93 *Ch. Plate Essex*, 193.

94 *Ch. Bells Essex*, 216; E.R.O., D/AZ 7/1, p. 120; *V.C.H. Essex*, vi. 120.

95 R.C.H.M. *Essex*, iii. 35. This account was written in 1987.

96 *Cur. Reg. R.* xvi, p. 408; *Feet of F. Essex*, i. 193, 263.

97 Newcourt, *Repertorium*, ii. 169–70; Morant, *Colch.* 120; E.R.O., T/A 547/1.

98 E.R.O., D/P 138/3/2; D/CPc 20, 26.

99 *Lond. Gaz.* 1 May 1953, p. 2424.

1 *E.A.T.* N.S. xviii. 123; *Valor Eccl.* (Rec. Com.), i. 443.

2 E.R.O., D/DM Q1; Balliol Coll. Mun. C. 23.

3 Smith, *Eccl. Hist. Essex*. 318; Morant, *Colch.* 106.

4 Newcourt, *Repertorium*, ii. 169; Morant, *Colch.* 120.

5 Morant, *Colch.* 107; C. Hodgson, *Queen Anne's Bounty*, pp. clxix, cccxii–cccxiii; E.R.O., D/CP 3/34; Guildhall MS. 9628/2; *Rep. Com. Eccl. Revenues*, H.C. 54, pp. 642–3 (1835), xxii.

6 E.R.O., D/CT 92A; *White's Dir. Essex* (1863), 84.

7 E.R.O., D/P 138/3/2; D/CPc 20; D/CP 3/36; Char. Com. files; below, Charities; *Kelly's Dir. Essex* (1890).

8 *E.A.T.* 3rd ser. viii. 287–8.

9 E.R.O., D/AZ 1/4, f. 151v.; D/AZ 10, f. 19v.; Morant, *Colch.* 120.

10 Guildhall MS. 25754/1.

11 Ibid. MSS. 25750/1; 25755/1; Lambeth Palace Libr., Fulham Papers, Randolph 9, pp. 980–7; ibid. Howley 48, no. 163; E.R.O., D/P 138/8/7.

land north of the old house.[12] It was still the rectory house in 1987.

The living was poor, but not the poorest Colchester living, and vacancies were usually filled.[13] The rector in 1406 was accused of keeping a concubine.[14] Edmund Coningsburgh, non-resident rector for under a year in 1470, was employed by Edward IV as an envoy to the pope in 1471 and became archbishop of Armagh in 1477.[15]

Anchorites were associated with the parish church in the 12th and 13th centuries.[16] A statue of St. James, in the chancel, was recorded in 1409 and 1485, and one of St. Ignatius, possibly with an associated altar, in 1500.[17] There was a guild of St. Peter in 1426, perhaps in the chapel of the saint recorded in 1500. The lady chapel was recorded in 1491.[18] Alice Strange, by will of 1409, endowed an obit in the church, but it had been lost by 1548.[19] A guild of St. Anne and St. James, in existence in 1525, had disappeared by *c.* 1546.[20]

In 1534 John Wayne, rector 1510–36, openly preached against certain new books 'of the king's print', but later rectors and their parishioners, notably the alderman and clothier John Clere (d. 1538), seem generally to have endorsed the protestant changes of the 16th century.[21] John Pekins, rector 1537–9, and John Blank, instituted 1541, were deprived of subsequent livings in Mary's reign.[22] By 1548 the churchwardens had used the 31*s.* 9*d.* raised from the sale of copper plate, wax, and latten to glaze, whitewash, and paint the church.[23] The living seems to have been vacant from 1554 or earlier until 1586.[24] In 1575 as many as 11 people were fined for repeated absence from church. The puritan curate in 1582 did not use the catechism but expounded parts of the scripture instead. Robert Holmes, rector 1586–92, also rector of Greenstead 1586–9, was accused in 1585 of 'slack administration' of the communion; in 1588 he described the wearing of the surplice as superstitious.[25] In 1595 Thomas Farrar, rector 1591–1610, was accused of serving two cures in the same day; in 1616 his successor Samuel Crick was non-resident and his curate apparently unlicensed.[26]

In 1632 the rector always wore a surplice to read prayers before the sermon he preached on the Friday before the monthly communion service, but in 1636 he was reminded to administer communion only to parishioners kneeling at the rail.[27] Robert Tuller signed the Essex Testimony, a presbyterian manifesto, in 1648, apparently as minister of St. James's, and the Independent Owen Stockton preached there on Sunday mornings from 1657 to 1662.[28]

William Shelton, rector 1670–99, who also held Stisted 1691–9, was a staunch defender of the Church of England, and opposed papists, Quakers, and other dissenters,[29] as did the non-resident Thomas Bennet, rector 1701–16, lecturer at St. Olave's, Southwark, and preacher at St. Lawrence Jewry (Lond.).[30] His successor Barnabas Simpson, rector from 1716, lived in Colchester, employing a curate to serve his country living. In 1723 there were two Sunday services and monthly communion. By 1738, when Simpson was also sequestrator of St. Nicholas's, services at St. James's had been reduced to one on most Sundays. John Milton, rector 1743–67, held only one Sunday service in 1747 when he also served Lexden.[31] By 1766 Milton, then also vicar of Fingringhoe, was in poor health and employed one curate to perform the Sunday service and another to say prayers on Wednesdays and Fridays; monthly communion was administered to 60–70 communicants. John Heath, rector 1777–81, lived in Chelmsford where he was master at the grammar school; his curates included Samuel Parr, master of Colchester grammar school.[32]

In 1810 the resident rector John Dakins provided an evening lecture as well as one full service on Sundays, and communion eight times a year for 50–60 communicants, a number little changed since 1778. By 1815, although he also served Peldon, he seems to have increased the Sunday services at St. James's to two.[33] Meshach Seaman, rector 1839–49, was an Evangelical writer of devotional and literary works.[34] In 1841 three quarters of the population of 1,439 were said to belong to the church, but on Census Sunday 1851, out of a population of 1,845, only 270 in the morning and 370 in the afternoon, including 70 Sunday school children on each occasion, attended church.[35]

St. Anne's mission hall was built before 1907 to serve the increasing population in the Ipswich road area.[36] By 1902 there were four Sunday services and two each weekday at St. James's, reflecting the high churchmanship of C. C. Naters, rector 1895–1918, who, despite the

12 M. Martin, *Ch. of St. Jas.* 22.

13 Newcourt, *Repertorium*, ii. 169–70.

14 E.R.O., D/B 5 Cr36, rot. 2.

15 *D.N.B.*

16 e.g. *Pipe R.* 1156–8 (Rec. Com.), 21; 1185 (P.R.S. xxxiv), 20; 1219 (P.R.S. N.S. xlii), 114; E.R.O., D/B 5 R1, f. 11v.; *V.C.H. Essex*, ii. 158.

17 Morant, *Colch.* 160; P.R.O., PROB 11/8, f. 122v.; *E.A.T.* N.S. xxi. 245–6.

18 E.R.O., D/B 5 Cr47, rot. 4d.; *E.A.T.* N.S. xxi. 241–2; P.R.O., PROB 11/10, f. 54 and v.

19 Morant, *Colch.* 160.

20 *E.A.T.* 3rd ser. xv. 88, 94 n.

21 *L. & P. Hen. VIII*, vii, p. 170; above, Tudor and Stuart Colch. (Religious Life).

22 Newcourt, *Repertorium*, ii. 85, 169, 586.

23 *E.A.T.* N.S. xiii. 165.

24 Corpus Christi Coll. Camb., MS. 122, f. 52; Newcourt, *Repertorium*, ii. 169.

25 E.R.O., D/AZ 1/7, f. 148v.; *E.R.* lii. 94–5.

26 E.R.O., D/AZ 1/1, f. 68v.; D/AZ 1/4, f. 104; ibid. St. Jas.'s baptismal reg. 1561–1664.

27 Smith, *Eccl. Hist. Essex*, 40; E.R.O., D/AZ 1/8, f. 46v.

28 *Calamy Revised*, ed. A. G. Matthews, 555; T. W. Davids, *Annals of Nonconf. in Essex*, 366–7.

29 T. Bayles, *Some account from Colch. of the Unfairness ... of Two Rectors 1699*, 7; *Alum. Cantab. to 1751*; W. Shelton, *Sermon before Ld. Mayor etc. at Guildhall Chapel 1680*: copy in E.C.L. Colch.

30 *D.N.B.*; *Alum. Cantab. to 1751*; T. Bennet, *Confutation of popery* (1701); copy in E.C.L. Colch.

31 Guildhall MSS. 25750/1, 25753/1, 25755/1.

32 Lambeth Palace Libr., Fulham Papers, Terrick 14, ff. 329–32; ibid. Lowth 4, ff. 305–8.

33 Ibid. Lowth 4, ff. 305–8; ibid. Randolph 9, pp. 980–7; ibid. Howley 48, no. 163; E.R.O., T/A 547/1.

34 E.R.O., D/P 138/1/1; M. Seaman, *Valedictory Address, passim*: copy in E.R.O., box C6.

35 E.R.O., D/ACM 12; P.R.O., HO 129/8/204; *V.C.H. Essex*, ii. 353.

36 E.R.O., D/CV 1/2.

opposition of many parishioners, introduced incense, vestments, processions, lights, and holy pictures, into the church. When in 1914, without a faculty, he erected a rood loft and screen, and an altar in the south chapel which obscured the monument to the philanthropist Arthur Winsley, parishioners brought a case against him in the consistory court. Naters was ordered to remove the rood loft and some of the candlesticks and pictures. When a further judgement compelled him to replace the altar with a small Jacobean table to reveal Winsley's monument, he complied, but with solemn ceremonial and a defiant sermon against state interference in religion.[37] The high church tradition was maintained by Naters's successors. The average church attendance in 1920 was 130 in the morning and 150 in the evening. C. W. James, rector from 1927, needing help especially for the growing district round St. Anne's mission hall, from 1934 had an assistant curate.[38] In 1987 the church was a focus for catholic faith and worship in Colchester and three quarters of the members lived outside the parish.[39]

The church of St. James, the largest in Colchester, stands in a commanding position just inside the former east gate at the top of East Hill. It is built of rubble with ashlar dressings, and comprises an aisled chancel with north-east vestry, aisled and clerestoried nave with north porch, and west tower.[40] The Roman brick north western quoins of an unaisled nave survive and the later medieval development suggests that in the 12th century the church may have been cruciform. The lower stages of the tower are late 12th- or early 13th-century, and the upper stage is 14th-century. The presumed transepts were extended as aisles *c.* 1300 when the two eastern bays of the arcades were built. Money for a new aisle was being collected in 1403.[41] The church underwent a major reconstruction in the late 15th century; new work was done on the chancel in 1464 and in 1490 money for the enlargement and enrichment of the church was raised by an entertainment in the street outside the church. The two western bays of the arcades were built and the arches of the eastern bays were reshaped to match them. The aisles were extended and the older parts refenestrated. The chancel and its chapels and vestry were built or rebuilt, as was the chancel arch and the matching arches between the chapels and the nave aisles. The tower was remodelled and given diagonal buttresses.[42]

The tower was said to be decayed in 1633.[43] A parish clerk's house adjoining the north side of the chancel was demolished in 1818 for highway improvements to East Hill.[44] The church was in reasonably good order in 1835 except for the north wall, but by 1870 was so dilapidated that services were no longer being held there.[45] Restoration work was carried out in 1871–2 under S. S. Teulon. The north porch and tower arch were rebuilt, and all the roofs were renewed except for those of the chancel aisles. A new organ was installed in the north chapel in 1890, and screens to designs by T. G. Jackson were erected in the south chapel in 1899–1900.[46] In 1951 the 19th-century choir stalls were removed from the chancel and the floor was lowered. In 1954 the north chapel was restored, and the existing organ removed and replaced by the organ from St. Nicholas's church. The organ console was moved to the west end of the church in the 1970s.[47]

Two brasses of the late 16th century to Alice and John Maynard survive. A large marble statue of Arthur Winsley was erected in 1738 at the east end of the south chapel. It was moved to the west end of the north aisle in 1923 when the south chapel was restored. A painting, the Adoration of the Shepherds, presented by the painter George Carter in 1778 as an altarpiece, was hanging above the north door of the nave in 1987 and a painting of the Last Supper by Sir William Archer of 1855 was above the sacristy door in the north chapel.[48]

Two bells by Miles Gray of 1622 survive; the smaller one is used as a clock bell. The church plate includes a silver gilt paten of 1705 and a pair of silver gilt flagons of 1750. An oak chest of the 16th century and one of the 17th remained in the church in 1987, and there was a medieval altar slab with consecration crosses, which belonged to St. Martin's Church.[49]

ST. LEONARD'S. The church, on the north side of Hythe Hill, was recorded *c.* 1150 when Maurice de Haie gave the church of 'Hethe' to St. John's abbey who still held the advowson in 1227.[50] The king presented in 1388, the temporalities of the abbey being in his hands,[51] and Sir Thomas Audley in 1539 by purchase of a turn. At the Dissolution in 1544 the advowson passed to the Crown which presented regularly until 1676 when the living was left vacant and sequestered.[52] In 1702 the advowson was acquired by exchange for Henry Compton, bishop of London (d. 1713), and it passed in 1714, like that of Holy Trinity, to Balliol College, Oxford.[53] The Crown presented in 1742 but the college did so regularly from 1753[54] until 1977 when the

37 *Kelly's Dir. Essex* (1902); *E.C.S.* 25, 31 July 1914; 30 Jan. 1915; *Essex Tel.* 21 Nov. 1914.

38 E.R.O., D/P 138/28/5; D/CV 3/2; D/CV 4/3; *Chelm. Dioc. Chron.* Mar. 1934, p. 40.

39 Local inf.

40 Above, pl. facing p. 120; R.C.H.M. *Essex*, iii. 35–7; Martin, *Ch. of St. Jas.* 23–48; W. and K. Rodwell, *Hist. Chs.* 34; E.R.O., T/A 641/5.

41 E.R.O., D/B 5 Cr28, rott. 12, 17d.; Cr33, rot. 28d.

42 P.R.O., PROB 11/5, f. 63; E.R.O., D/B 5 R2, f. 193v.

43 *E.A.T.* N.S. xi. 39.

44 Martin, *Ch. of St. Jas.* 22–3.

45 E.R.O., D/P 138/7/1; D/AZ 7/1, p. 122.

46 E.R.O., D/CF 9/3; D/P 138/6/5, 6; *Kelly's Dir. Essex* (1890).

47 Martin, *Ch. of St. Jas.* 36, 38; P. Rusiecki, *St. James the Great, Colch., a guide to the church*, 18.

48 Martin, *Ch. of St. Jas.* 33, 36; *E.R.* xlii. 11.

49 *Ch. Bells Essex*, 94, 216; Rusiecki, *St. James*, 18; *Ch. Plate Essex*, 193; H. W. Lewer and J. C. Wall, *Ch. Chests Essex*, 106-7; inf. from Miss K. Kelly.

50 *Colch. Cart.* i. 189; ii. 545. This account was written in 1987.

51 *Cal. Pat.* 1385–9, 453.

52 Newcourt, *Repertorium*, ii. 173–4; Smith, *Eccl. Hist. Essex*, 318.

53 *Cal. S.P. Dom.* 1700–2, 512.

54 Morant, *Colch.* 130; Guildhall MSS. 9556–7; *St. Albans Dioc. Cal.* (1878 and later edns.); *Chelm. Dioc. Yr. Bk.* (1915 and later edns.).

benefice was united with that of St. Mary Magdalen with St. Stephen. Thereafter the patronage board presented for two turns in three and the Lord Chancellor for the third.[55] The church was closed in 1983 and in 1987 was acquired by the Redundant Churches Fund.[56]

The rectory was valued at 5 marks in 1254 and £10 in 1535.[57] A pension of 5*s.* due to St. John's abbey was recorded in the late 12th century and still paid in the 13th century.[58] In 1227 there was a vicarage endowed with some small tithes, but it was not certainly recorded thereafter. St. Botolph's priory successfully claimed tithes of the Sokeham or Haymsokne in 1227, and a pension of 2*s.* due to the priory from St. Leonard's in the 1490s[59] may have been in lieu of tithes. In 1650 the income of £7 15*s.* from the 3 a. of glebe and £2 from tithes was augmented by £38 from rates on houses levied by the town council. In 1707 the total income of the living was only £16.[60] Moses Cook (d. 1732) left the reversion of a quarter share of Hunter's farm, Foxearth, and the living was augmented by grants of £200 from Queen Anne's Bounty in 1770 (to match Cook's benefaction) and 1814 and by a parliamentary grant of a further £200 in 1809.[61] The Bounty added 2 a. of meadow to the glebe in 1805 and a further 2 a. in 1810.[62] By 1835 the net income had risen to £100.[63] In 1845 tithes on 79 a. were commuted for £30.[64] The income was augmented with £24 a year in 1843, with a capital grant of £200 in 1864, and with a total of £41 13*s.* 4*d.* a year in 1868, 1875, and 1879; the sale of 4 cottages and 5 a. of glebe in 1879 raised £1,376.[65] The sum of £200 collected by Trinity church school, Springfield, in 1874 when the headmaster F. J. Manning became rector was matched by the patron, the diocese, and the Ecclesiastical Commissioners to produce an annual income of £30. By 1894 the tithe rent charge had fallen to £18, augmentation by the Bounty and the Ecclesiastical Commission amounted to £116 18*s.* 6*d.* a year, and the share in the farm at Foxearth produced £10 a year making a total income of £144 18*s.* 6d.[66] In 1916 James N. Paxman endowed the living with a rent charge of £32 out of Stisted rectory house and glebe.[67]

The medieval rectory house, recorded in 1531,[68] was probably opposite the church at the junction of Hythe Hill and Parsonage Lane, where the house stood in the 18th century.[69] The rectory house, which had seven hearths in 1662, was let to a tenant and was in disrepair in 1683.[70] Although it was described in 1748 as a large house with a good garden, it was not occupied again as a rectory house and was pulled down *c.* 1841.[71] A new rectory house was built in 1863 on open land on the north side of Hythe Hill about 325 yd. west of the church. The house, designed by H. W. Hayward, may have reused some older materials and was enlarged in 1871.[72] It was requisitioned during the Second World War.[73] After the war it was used again as a rectory house until it was sold *c.* 1970.[74]

In 1290–1 an anchoress was associated with St. Leonard's.[75] The names of rectors are known from 1311.[76] Before the Reformation incumbencies were usually short,[77] and in 1466 the rector was licensed to hold one, and in 1480 two, other benefices in plurality because of the poverty of the living.[78] An altar of St. Peter existed by 1437 and a chapel of the saint by 1502.[79] St. Mary's guild played an important part in church and parish life in the 1480s, and by *c.* 1500 St. Mary's light had been endowed with rents worth 11*s.* 6*d.*[80] Peter Barwick founded a parochial chantry *c.* 1480, giving in trust rents and a house and garden for a priest to sing mass and help serve the cure. The house was probably that on the east side of the churchyard, recorded in 1586.[81] John Honyngton, by will proved 1485, gave a field to the chantry but its future was apparently uncertain in 1486.[82] Edmund Harmanson, by will proved 1502, left a house and rent charge to the parish chantry, and a house to support another chantry priest.[83] Both chantries survived in 1546 when the parish or Barwick's chantry was worth £8 14*s.* 4*d.* and Harmanson's 10*s.*[84] A guild of St. Leonard, in existence in 1486, had disappeared by *c.* 1546. John Bardfield, by will proved 1506, and John Day the chantry priest, by will proved 1520, endowed obits which in 1548 were together worth 18*s.* 8*d.* of which 8*s.* 8*d.* was paid to the poor.[85]

In 1546 the Privy Council dismissed trivial complaints, perhaps from protestant parishioners, against William Wright, rector 1539–50.[86] Nicholas Davy, former parish chantry priest, became rector in 1550 and was probably deprived

55 *Chelm. Dioc. Yr. Bk.* (1977–8), 140.

56 *Essex Countryside*, Oct. 1983, 51; *Essex Chron.* 3 Mar. 1987.

57 *E.A.T.* N.S.. xviii. 123; xxiv. 80; *Valor Eccl.* (Rec. Com.), i. 443.

58 *Colch. Cart.* i. 67, 87, 95.

59 *Colch. Cart.* ii. 545; E.R.O., D/DM Q1; for Sokeham above, Med. Colch. (Boro. Govt.).

60 Smith, *Eccl. Hist. Essex*, 318; Guildhall MS. 11248.

61 Morant, *Colch.* 107; C. Hodgson, *Queen Anne's Bounty*, ii, pp. clxix, cccxii.

62 Guildhall MS. 9628/2.

63 *Rep. Com. Eccl. Revenues*, H.C. 54, pp. 642–3 (1835), xxii.

64 E.R.O., D/CT 93.

65 *Lond. Gaz.* 3 Oct. 1843, p. 3216; 12 July 1864, p. 3492; 8 May 1868, p. 2632; 7 May 1875, p. 2461; 11 Apr. 1879, p. 2771; E.R.O., D/P 245/3/9.

66 E.R.O., D/P 245/3/1, 9, 10; ibid. T/A 645.

67 Ibid. D/P 245/3/4; D/CP 3/39; plaque in ch.

68 E.R.O., D/B 5 Cr100, rot. 9d.

69 P.R.O., PROB 11/15, f. 139v.; Morant, *Colch.* 130.

70 E.R.O., Q/RTh1, f. 21; *E.A.T.* N.S. xxiii. 163; E. Hickeringill, *Black Nonconformist* (1682), 66–7.

71 Morant, *Colch.* 130; Guildhall MSS. 9557, 9628/2, 25754/1, 25755/1; E.R.O., D/P 245/5/1; D/ACM 12.

72 Bodl. MS. Top. Gen. C97, no. 2; E.R.O., D/CT 93; D/P 245/3/8; D/P 245/8/5; cf. Colch. Civic Soc., Schedule of Bldgs. of Archit. Interest.

73 Balliol Coll. Mun., Patronage Papers.

74 *Chelm. Dioc. Yr. Bk.* (1955 and later edns.).

75 P.R.O., C47/37/5, ff. 37–41; B.L. Harl. Ch. 44, E17.

76 E.R.O., D/B 5 Cr3, rot. 7d.

77 *Colch. Cart.* ii. 545; Newcourt, *Repertorium*, ii. 173–4; P. H. Reaney, *Early Essex Clergy*, 68; E.R.O., T/A 237; T/A 547/1; *E.A.T.* N.S. vi. 240.

78 *Cal. Papal. Reg.* xii. 491; xiii. 711.

79 E.R.O., D/B 5 Cr54, rot. 16d.; P.R.O., PROB 11/13, f. 79v.

80 B.L. Stowe MS. 834, ff. 84–85v.

81 Morant, *Colch.* 158–9; E.R.O., D/B 5 Cr148, rot. 17.

82 P.R.O., PROB 11/7, f. 138v.; PROB 11/8, ff. 317v.–318.

83 P.R.O., PROB 11/13, f. 79v.

84 Ibid. E 301/20/56, 60.

85 Ibid. PROB 11/8, 317v.; PROB 11/15, f. 139v.; ibid. E 301/19/203; E.R.O., D/ACR 2/102.

86 *Acts of P.C.* 1542–7, 475.

for marriage in 1554.[87] In 1559 the Privy Council ordered the bailiffs to pillory Peter Walker, rector since 1557, for 'false seditious tales'.[88] Walker had left the parish by 1561 and the cure was then served by the prominent radical and former Marian exile Thomas Upcher, rector of Fordham 1561–96. Upcher became rector in 1571 and held the living until his resignation in 1582.[89] His successor, Thomas Lowe, had been a founder member of the Dedham classis but withdrew from the meetings in 1584. He was shunned by the godly as double-beneficed: he held St. Mary Magdalen's, apparently by sequestration, in conjunction with St. Leonard's until his death in 1615.[90] By 1585 the church and churchyard were filthy, and in 1594 a man was presented for making sails in the church.[91] In 1632 John Wall wore the surplice but in 1635 he administered communion to parishioners in their seats; the churchwardens were said to be 'absolute Brownists'.[92] Wall was succeeded by the presbyterians William Jenkyn, 1640–44, and Alexander Piggott, *c.* 1648–60.[93] Edmund Hickeringill, rector of All Saints', unsuccessfully sought presentation to St. Leonard's in 1668 and vehemently opposed the appointment of a new sequestrator *c.* 1680. His tactics, of encouraging parishioners to withhold tithes and the tenant to refuse to vacate the rectory house, were successful, for by 1683 he was rector.[94] As late as 1705 the archdeacon had to order the placing of the communion table against the east wall.[95]

In the early 18th century the living was held by sequestrators who provided only one Sunday service and communion once a month.[96] From 1753 it was often held by rectors of All Saints', another Balliol living,[97] who employed assistant curates, among them the political economist Nathaniel Forster and the eccentric John Trussler, to provide one Sunday service and monthly communion.[98] In 1841 more than three fifths of the population were said to belong to the church,[99] but in 1850 the rector Francis Curtis chided parishioners for their apathy.[1] On Census Sunday 1851, out of a population of 1,295, congregations of 120 in the morning and 200 in the afternoon were reported, with 140 children at the Sunday school.[2] Curtis and his successors John G. Bingley, 1864–74, and F. J. Manning, 1874–86, lived in the parish, employed assistant curates, sought to remedy the effects of poverty and ignorance there, and restored the church.[3] In 1870 the slogan 'Change here for Rome—Bingley, station master' was chalked on the church wall.[4] H. T. Osborne, rector 1886–96, introduced daily services[5] and his successor, H. F. Carter, refitted the church in Tractarian style and frequently invited the ritualist A. H. Stanton to preach.[6] The Anglo-Catholic G. M. Withers, rector 1934–7, alienated many church members and by 1939 the congregation was depressed and depleted, but by 1950 attendance at church and Sunday school had increased greatly, although a moderately High Church tradition was maintained.[7] The political activities of J. R. Hale, 1964–71, briefly a member of the National Front, aroused controversy.[8] From 1972 until its closure in 1983 the church was served by a priest-in-charge who was industrial chaplain for Colchester.[9]

The church of St. Leonard comprises a chancel with north and south chapels and north-east vestry, aisled and clerestoried nave of four bays, two-storeyed south porch, and west tower.[10] The walls are of mixed rubble, septaria, flint, pebbles, brick, and freestone, with limestone dressings. The roofs of the nave and chancel are tiled; those of the aisles and tower are of lead. An earlier church comprising nave and chancel was enlarged *c.* 1335 by the building of the north aisle and the rebuilding of the chancel; the considerable difference in alignment between the nave and chancel suggests that the new chancel replaced an earlier one on faulty foundations. The west tower of three stages was built in the late 14th century and in the early 15th the embattled south aisle and porch were added. The 15th-century south door with contemporary hinges and knocker plate survived in 1983. The north and south chapels were added in the late 15th century. The parish undertook considerable building work in 1481–2 which included the reconstruction of the vestry.[11] The clerestory, mooted by 1464,[12] was built *c.* 1500; the hammerbeam roof was originally decorated with twelve carved angels, five of which were stored in the church in 1983. The north vestry was added in the 16th century and the rood stair rebuilt *c.* 1530.

The building, a royalist stronghold, was stormed by parliamentary soldiers in the siege of 1648.[13] It was repaired in 1662 and a brick font installed.[14]

87 *Cal. Pat.* 1549–51, 203; P.R.O., E 301/19/29; E.R.O., D/ACR 100/5.
88 *Acts of P.C.* 1556–70, 71.
89 Corpus Christi Coll. Camb., MS. 122, f. 50; J. W. Martin, *Religious Radicals in Tudor Eng.* 70; P. Collinson, *Archbishop Grindal*, 172; B. Usher, 'Colch. and Diocesan Admin.' (TS. in E.R.O.), 8–9, 33.
90 *Presbyterian movement in the reign of Queen Eliz.* (Camd. 3rd ser. viii), 37; *Seconde Part of a Register*, ed. A. Peel, ii. 162; Usher, 'Colch. and Diocesan Admin.' 9, 33.
91 E.R.O., D/AZ 1/7, f. 149; D/AZ 1/1, ff. 50, 52v.
92 T. W. Davids, *Annals of Nonconf. in Essex*, 171; E.R.O., D/AZ 1/8, f. 46v.; *E.A.T.* N.S. ii. 255; xi. 171.
93 *D.N.B.*; Smith, *Eccl. Hist. Essex*, 109.
94 E.R.O., D/B 5 Gb5, f. 16; D/ACV 9B, ff. 37–8; Hickeringill, *Black Nonconformist*, 66–7, 194; Anon. *Scandalum Magnatum* (1682); *E.A.T.* N.S. xxiii. 163.
95 E.R.O., D/ACV 9A, f. 69v.
96 Guildhall MSS. 9532/2, 25751, 25753/1.
97 E.R.O., T/A 547/1.
98 *D.N.B.*; Guildhall MSS. 9551, 9557, 9560; E.R.O., D/P 245/1/1, 6.
99 E.R.O., D/ACM 12.
1 Press cuttings in E.C.L. Colch.
2 P.R.O., HO 129/8/204; *V.C.H. Essex*, ii. 353.
3 Nat. Soc. file; *E.C.S.* 22 Mar. 1845; E.R.O., D/P 245/6/10; Phillips, *Ten Men*, 120–1.
4 E.R.O., D/NM 2/9/3.
5 *Kelly's Dir. Essex* (1886).
6 *Rep. Com. Eccl. Discipline* [Cd. 3069], pp. 326–7, H.C. (1906), xxxiii; *D.N.B.* s.v. Stanton; *E.C.S.* 6 Oct. 1934; *E.R.* xxiii. 155; plaques in ch.
7 E.R.O., D/P 245/28/3, 4; Balliol Coll. Mun., Patronage Papers.
8 *Eve. Gaz.* 29 Apr. 1971; *E.C.S.* 12, 19 May 1972.
9 *Chelm. Dioc. Yr. Bk.* (1972–3); *Colch. Expr.* 14 Sept. 1972.
10 R.C.H.M. *Essex*, iii. 44–6 and pl. facing p. 35; W. and K. Rodwell, *Hist. Chs.* 36–7; *E.A.T.* N.S. ii. 350–6; E.R.O., T/A 645, pp. 57–8; inf. from Council for Care of Chs.
11 P.R.O., C47/37/5, ff. 37–41.
12 P.R.O., PROB 11/5, f. 49.
13 Morant, *Colch.* 65.
14 E.R.O., D/P 245/8/2.

The church was repaired again in 1724 when a painted altar piece was set up, and by 1748 painted wooden panels depicting the patriarchs had been fixed to the chancel roof, and the tower had a battlemented parapet and cupola.[15] The top of the tower fell *c.* 1780 and was rebuilt in brick in 1788. In 1802 the south wall of the church was buttressed.[16] The painted panels, then decayed, were removed from the chancel roof in 1815,[17] and in the 1830s the church was repaired and repewed. The brick font of 1662 was broken up in 1840, buried in the north chapel, and replaced by the 15th-century font from East Donyland church.[18] In the 1860s the tower arch was opened and the chancel restored. Wall paintings in the chancel were discovered in 1866 and painted over. Restoration of the south porch may date from that time. The tower was damaged by the earthquake of 1884 and *c.* 1889 the brickwork of 1788 was replaced by flint flushwork and a double-stepped, pinnacled parapet.[19] In the period 1904–35 the interior was refurbished and screens and a rood inserted;[20] the 15th-century work incorporated in the screens may be from the pre-Reformation screen, part of which survived behind the choir stalls in 1883.[21] A flying buttress was built to reinforce the south wall in 1912. In 1987 the Redundant Churches Fund became responsible for the church.[22]

The church had six bells in 1683.[23] Of those, two survived in 1983 and another, attributed to one of the Grays, was sold in 1829 when it was damaged and useless.[24] A sanctus bell, attributed to Mot, was recorded unhung in 1904.[25] In 1983 there were six bells: (i) Bowell, 1927 (ii) Gardiner, 1755 (iii) Chamberlain, formerly attributed to Jordan, late 15th-century (iv) Kebyll, 15th-century (v) Thornton, 1719 (vi) Gardiner, 1755, recast by Bowell, 1926.[26] The plate includes an Elizabethan chalice, another of 1638, and a paten of 1713. A medieval mazer bowl was given to the church in the 18th century.[27] An oak chest and three chairs, all of the 17th century, survived in 1983. The monuments include an indent of a priest's memorial brass which has been moved from the chancel to the north chapel[28] and a wall tablet by George Lufkin to William Hawkins (d. 1812).[29]

ST. MARTIN'S. Topographical and archaeological evidence suggests that the church was founded in or before the late Anglo-Saxon period.[30] It was recorded in 1254 when the advowson of the rectory was held by St. Botolph's priory. The priory retained the advowson until the Dissolution, when it was granted to Sir Thomas Audley. The Audley family did not present after 1537, and the Crown presented, presumably by lapse, in 1616.[31] In the early 18th century Henry Audley sold the patronage to Henry Compton, bishop of London (d. 1713). Compton's executor sold it to his successor, John Robinson, and on Robinson's death in 1723 it passed to his widow, but its later descent is not clear. The Crown presented in 1760 by lapse. In 1748 and 1768 the advowson was held by Bowater Vernon of Hanbury (Worcs.),[32] but later the Vernon family's patronage was disputed. William Smythies presented in 1770, presumably having purchased a turn, and the bishop presented by lapse on the next vacancy in 1825 and thereafter.[33] The advowson remained with the bishop until 1929 when the benefices of St. Martin's and Holy Trinity were united. Succeeding presentations were made alternately by the bishop of Chelmsford and the patrons of Holy Trinity, until the reorganization of the Colchester parishes in 1953, when St. Martin's church was closed and the benefice of Holy Trinity with St. Martin's was incorporated into the new benefice of St. Botolph with Holy Trinity and St. Giles.[34]

The rectory was valued at 13*s.* 4*d.* in 1254 and £6 13*s.* 4*d.* in 1535. No value was recorded in 1291. From 1254 until 1537 an annual pension of 3*s.* was paid to the prior of St. Botolph's and in 1254 2*s.* was also paid to the rector of St. Mary's.[35] In 1650 there was no house, glebe, or tithes.[36] The living was augmented in 1714, 1749, and 1752, with sums of £200 from Queen Anne's Bounty, which were used in 1764 to buy a farm at Ardleigh. A further grant of £200 in 1802, a parliamentary grant of £800 in 1814, and two benefactions of £100 each from J. Round and the Curates' Aid Society, raised the value of the living to £45 a year in 1810 and £72 in 1835.[37] Tithes on 3 a. of garden ground were commuted for a rent charge of £2 in 1849.[38] That and a gift of £1,500 stock had increased the value of the living to £115 in 1851.[39] In 1887 the income was £188 but there was no rectory house. The farm at Ardleigh was sold in 1920.[40]

In the Middle Ages, because of its small income, St. Martin's was frequently held by

15 Morant, *Colch.* 129–30 and map facing p. 4.

16 E.R.O., D/AZ 7/1, pp. 126–9; D/P 245/6/10; D/P 245/8/3.

17 T. Cromwell, *Hist. Colch.* i. 235.

18 *E.A.T.* N.S. ii. 352; xix. 100.

19 E.R.O., D/P 245/6/10; D/P 245/28/13; *E.C.S.* 20 Apr. 1866.

20 E.R.O., D/P 245/6/13; D/P 245/28/3; *E.C.S.* 6 Oct. 1934; J. R. McCallum, *Colch. Port, the Hythe and the Ch.* 22; *E.R.* xxix. 110; *Chelm. Dioc. Chron.* July 1923, 99.

21 *E.A.T.* N.S. ii. 351.

22 E.R.O., D/P 245/6/14; D/P 245/6/20; *Essex Chron.* 3 Mar. 1987.

23 *E.A.T.* N.S. xxiii. 163.

24 E.R.O., D/P 245/8/1.

25 *Ch. Bells Essex*, 218.

26 Inf. from Council for Care of Chs.

27 *Ch. Plate Essex*, 194–5 and pl. ii, viii, xvi.

28 E.R.O., D/P 245/6/10.

29 E.C.L. Colch., Crisp MS. 'Colch. Mon. Inscriptions', viii; R. Gunnis, *Dict. Brit. Sculptors 1660–1851*, 245.

30 W. and K. Rodwell, *Hist. Chs.* 29. This account was written in 1987.

31 *E.A.T.* N.S. xviii. 123; Newcourt, *Repertorium*, ii. 176; *L. & P. Hen. VIII*, x, p. 419.

32 MS. annotation in E.R.O. copy of Morant, *Colch.* (1748), Bk. II, p. 9; Morant, *Colch.* (1768), ii. 112, 115.

33 *Rep. Com. Eccl. Revenues*, H.C. 54, pp. 642–3 (1835), xxii; E.R.O., T/A 547/1.

34 E.R.O., D/CPc 228; *Lond. Gaz.* 1 May 1953, p. 2424.

35 *E.A.T.* N.S. xviii. 123; *Valor Eccl.* (Rec. Com.), i. 443; E.R.O., D/DM Q1; Balliol Coll. Mun. C. 23.

36 Smith, *Eccl. Hist. Essex*, 319.

37 C. Hodgson, *Queen Anne's Bounty*, pp. xxxvii, ccxxxiv, cccxiii; Morant, *Colch.* 115; Guildhall MS. 9628/2; *Rep. Com. Eccl. Revenues*, H.C. 54, pp. 642–3 (1835), xxii.

38 E.R.O., D/CT 94A.

39 Hodgson, *Q. Anne's Bounty*, p. xxxvii; P.R.O., HO 129/8/204.

40 E.R.O., T/A 645.

pluralists such as Thomas Clark, rector 1438–57 who nevertheless lived in Colchester in 1444 when he was accused of several assaults including an attempted rape in the church vestry.[41] By will of 1523, Robert Everard left the proceeds from his house and lands at Mile End for an obit in the church. Another obit, endowed with land at Kings mead, was recorded in 1548.[42] About 1545 the churchwardens sold a gilt pyx and crucifix, and a silver chalice, partly to pay for work on the fabric and furnishings.[43]

For much of the period *c.* 1550–1760 the living was vacant and served, often unsatisfactorily, by curates or the incumbents of other Colchester parishes.[44] In 1582 the minister was accused of preaching false doctrine, and in 1584 the curate did not catechize. The parish had no surplice in 1585 and 1605, and no Book of Common Prayer in 1604. The curate in 1609 abused the church and parishioners by his 'naughty speeches' from the pulpit,[45] and his successor in 1634 excused his failure to read prayers on holy days by saying that no one attended them.[46] The puritan practice of sitting for communion was followed in 1635 when seats for communicants were put round the communion table inside the rail.[47]

The church fabric was allowed to decay in the earlier 17th century, and damage sustained in the siege of 1648 does not seem to have been repaired. By 1693 the church was unusable, and services for St. Martin's parishioners, taken by Robert Dickman rector of Aldham and Strethall, were presumably held in a neighbouring church.[48] Robert Turner, vicar of St. Peter's, read prayers and preached at St. Martin's on Sunday mornings from 1723 or earlier until *c.* 1727, when his voice became too weak. In 1742 Sunday services for St. Martin's, St. Runwald's, and St. Peter's parishes were held at St. Peter's church.[49]

From 1760 incumbents were appointed regularly. Yorick Smythies, presented by his father, held the living for 54 years 1770–1824; he lived most of the time in Colchester but occasionally resided on his other living of Little Bentley, performing one Sunday service with sermon at each church. Communion was administered monthly to *c.* 30 communicants in 1766, but by 1810 only quarterly to *c.* 20.[50] Most baptisms between 1735 and 1812 took place at St. Peter's.[51] Three quarters of the families in the parish were said to belong to the church in 1841, but on Census Sunday 1851, when the population was 942, only 167 in the morning and 250 in the evening (including 37 and 30 Sunday school children respectively) attended church.[52] By 1891 services had increased to three on Sundays, daily evensong, and communion on saints' days. There were Sunday classes for young girls and young men, a mothers' meeting, and a working men's club.[53]

O. D. Watkins, rector 1902–7, had worked in India for 26 years.[54] He lived in an adjoining parish and served the cure personally, but felt the need for help in a parish where three quarters of the population did not attend church and collections covered less than three quarters of church expenses. H. F. de Courcy-Benwell, rector 1913–*c.* 1930, a member of the local Labour and Independent Labour parties, read morning prayers daily, held communion weekly, and tried to visit his parishioners monthly. His efforts to make use of lay helpers foundered in the largely working-class parish.[55]

The church of St. Martin, West Stockwell Street, comprises a chancel with modern north vestry, aisled nave of three bays, with south porch, and west tower.[56] The walls are of flint rubble with Roman and later brick, and the roofs are tiled. By the 11th century the church was probably a cruciform building with chancel, nave with north aisle, and transepts. The surviving west tower, which includes much Roman brick and may have replaced a central tower, was added in the 12th century. The chancel was rebuilt in the earlier 14th century, from which date a piscina and a probable Easter sepulchre survive; its roof is supported by an open crown post truss on arch braces with wall posts running down to the floor. In the 14th or 15th century the nave, north aisle, and transepts were rebuilt and a south aisle was added; a hagioscope in the north aisle and the rood-loft staircase at the south-east corner of the nave survived in 1987. On the site of the 19th-century vestry there was a 14th-century north chapel whose south door survived in 1987.[57] A south porch was probably built in the late 14th century, but was rebuilt in the late 17th century. The tower or steeple was being built or rebuilt in 1517.[58]

The building was in bad repair in the late 16th century and the 17th. In 1607 two broken bells were removed, the tower being too weak and damaged to hold the three bells, and the windows and chancel needed repair.[59] By 1633 part of the tower had fallen down, and more was demolished during the siege of 1648.[60] Some repairs were apparently made between 1748 and 1768 and the ruined tower was covered in, but the church remained in poor condition.[61] The

41 Newcourt, *Repertorium*, ii. 176; E.R.O., D/B 5 Cr59, rot. 16; Cr60, rot. 2d.

42 P.R.O., E 301/19/200; Morant, *Colch.* 160–1.

43 *E.A.T.* N.S. xiii. 167.

44 Newcourt, *Repertorium*, ii. 174–7, 182; E.R.O., T/A 547/1.

45 E.R.O., D/AZ 1/4, f. 134v.; D/AZ 1/7, ff. 135, 142v., 146; D/AZ 1/8, f. 141v.–142; D/AZ 1/10, f. 69v.; D/AZ 1/11, f. 6v.

46 Ibid., D/ACV 2, f. 45v.

47 Ibid. D/AZ 1/8, f. 46.

48 Guildhall MS. 9628/2; Newcourt, *Repertorium*, ii. 7, 565.

49 Guildhall MSS. 25750/1; 25751; 25754/1.

50 *Alum. Cantab. 1752–1900*, ii. 582; Lambeth Palace Libr., Fulham Papers, Terrick 14, ff. 333–6; ibid. Lowth 4, ff. 309–12; ibid. Randolph 9, pp. 996–1001; ibid. Howley 49, no. 7; *Ipswich Jnl.* 20 May 1815.

51 E.R.O., D/P 325/1/3.

52 Ibid. D/ACM 12; P.R.O., HO 129/8/204; *V.C.H. Essex*, ii. 353.

53 *Par. Mags.* 1891: copies in E.C.L. Colch.

54 *E.C.S.* 14 June 1902.

55 E.R.O., D/CV 1/2; 3/2; 4/3.

56 G. Buckler, *Twenty Two Essex Chs.* 121–5; R.C.H.M. *Essex*, iii. 37–9; Rodwell, *Hist. Chs.* 26–7, 29–30; Pevsner, *Essex*, 134; E.R.O., T/A 641/5.

57 *E.R.* i. 14.

58 P.R.O., PROB 11/17, 21v.

59 E.R.O., D/AZ 1/1, ff. 41v., 60v., 65v.; D/AZ 1/2, f. 4; D/AZ 1/7, f. 156; D/AZ 1/8, ff. 141v.–142; D/AZ 1/10, f. 75; D/AZ 1/11, ff. 9v.–10.

60 *E.A.T.* N.S. xi. 41; Morant, *Colch.* 115.

61 Morant, *Colch.* (1748), Bk. II, p. 11; ibid. (1768), 115; T. W. Wright, *Hist. Essex*, 309; E.R.O., T/A 641/5.

interior was renovated and reseated shortly before 1848.[62] The nave and chancel were partially restored in 1882, the chancel roof by Sir George Gilbert Scott at his own expense.[63] Further extensive controversial restoration was undertaken in 1891 but was apparently never completed: the floor was repaved, the arcade pillars were repaired, the tower arch was reopened, and a north vestry was built.[64] Between 1903 and 1907 the tower was restored.[65]

The two bells removed in 1607 were sold and were apparently replaced in 1642 by one by Miles Gray, which was old and cracked in 1899. The church plate included a silver salver of 1741, at the Colchester museum in 1987. Two oak chests, one with an early 16th-century lock-plate, and one Jacobean with moulded panels, were still in the church in 1985.[66] A medieval altar slab with consecration crosses was being used in 1922.[67]

St. Martin's church was made redundant at the 1953 reorganisation.[68] In 1957 it was transferred in trust to the Colchester theatre group as a cultural centre.[69] The interior was painted black and a stage erected at the west end, but in 1987 the building was declared unsafe for public performances. In 1991 Essex county council bought the church for conversion to offices.[70] The graveyard, maintained by Colchester district council, contains a large sarchophagus tomb of 1816 of William Sparling.

ST. MARY'S-AT-THE-WALLS. The discovery of Anglo-Saxon graves, perhaps of the Middle-Saxon period, south of the surviving churchyard suggests that a pre-Conquest church stood on or near the site of the surviving building.[71] The church, near the western postern in the town wall, lay within the soke acquired by the bishop of London between 998 and 1066 and was recorded in 1206.[72] It was an episcopal peculiar;[73] although it was included in the archdeacon's visitation in 1683 it was exempt from his jurisdiction in 1768 and parishioners' wills were proved in the bishop of London's, not the archdeacon's, courts until *c.* 1857.[74] The advowson, retained by the bishop of London when he leased the soke in 1206, passed to successive diocesan bishops, and the bishop of Chelmsford was patron when the church closed in 1978.[75] The Crown presented in 1361 and 1596, the bishopric being vacant.[76]

The rectory was valued at 3 marks in 1254, £2 13*s.* 4*d.* in 1291, and £10 in 1535. A payment of 2*s.* from St. Martin's rectory, recorded in 1254, was apparently lost by 1291.[77] In 1429 the abbot of St. John's successfully claimed tithes on land in Monksdown in the parish.[78] In 1650 the living was worth £40 a year.[79] In 1766 Charles Gray gave the rector of St. Mary's tithes on 24½ a., formerly tithe-free lands of St. Botolph's priory.[80] A parliamentary grant of £200 in 1833 and an annual grant of £50 from that year by the patron, the bishop of London, raised the value of the living to £212 a year in 1835.[81] In 1898, when the annual net income was £275, boundary changes resulted in tithe rent charges of £48 being transferred from Lexden to St. Mary's.[82]

In 1610 the glebe comprised *c.* 10 a. of arable, 3 a. of half year land, and two small houses in St. Mary's Lane.[83] The houses apparently replaced two taken down in the 1540s and were later divided into three dwellings which were pulled down *c.* 1677.[84] By 1810 Philip Bayles, rector 1804–55, had increased the half year land to 11 a. by lease and purchase; from 1823 or earlier until *c.* 1890 he and his successors leased from the free burgesses rights of common on the glebe.[85] By 1900 all the glebe had been sold.[86]

The rector had an orchard and garden, and presumably also a house, in the early 14th century.[87] A rectory house mentioned in 1610 was probably the one opposite the church in St. Mary's Lane that had 10 hearths in 1671, and was extended eastwards *c.* 1677 by the rector, Joseph Powell. In 1739 its older west end was rebuilt by the rector, Philip Morant.[88] A new house was built in 1871, to the designs of Frederic Chancellor, north-east of the old house, which was demolished.[89] The 1871 house was pulled down and replaced in 1964–5 by a smaller one, which was sold in 1983 to the Mercury theatre and renamed Mercury House.[90]

In 1338 Joseph Eleanor or Colchester, clerk, obtained licence to alienate 2 messuages, 102 a., a toft, and 10*s.* rent to two priests to say divine

62 *White's Dir. Essex* (1848), 80.

63 E.R.O., D/AZ 7/1, p. 129; *E.R.* i. 14.

64 E.R.O., D/CF 30/2; *Par. Mags.* 1891: copies in E.C.L. Colch.; E.R.O., Boro. Mun., Mus., Mun., and Libr. Cttee. Min. Bk. 1882–94, pp. 135, 140, 142.

65 E.R.O., D/CV 1/2.

66 *Ch. Bells Essex*, 101, 219; E.R.O., T/A 645; *Ch. Plate Essex*, 195; H. W. Lewer and J. C. Wall, *Ch. Chests Essex*, 107–8.

67 *Brentwood Dioc. Mag.* ii. 46 (July 1922).

68 Rodwell, *Hist. Chs.* 29.

69 *E.C.S.* 17 Nov. 1961; inf. from Mrs. J. Jones, Colch. theatre group.

70 *E.C.S.* 30 Aug. 1991; *Colch. Archaeologist*, no. 5, p. 21.

71 W. and K. Rodwell, *Hist. Chs.* 33. This account was written in 1988.

72 C. Hart, *Early Chart. of Essex*, ii. 38; *Feet of F. Essex*, i. 39.

73 Morant, *Colch.* 107.

74 E.R.O., D/ACV 9A; Morant, *Colch.* 107; F. G. Emmison, *Wills at Chelm.* i–iii, *passim.*

75 *Feet of F. Essex*, i. 39; Newcourt, *Repertorium*, ii. 174–5; Guildhall MSS. 9550, 9556–8; *St. Albans Dioc. Cal.* (1878 and later edns.); *Chelm. Dioc. Yr. Bk.* (1915 and later edns.).

76 *Cal. Pat.* 1361–4, 74; Newcourt, *Repertorium*, ii. 175.

77 *E.A.T.* N.S. xviii. 123; *Tax. Eccl.* (Rec. Com.), 24; *Valor Eccl.* (Rec. Com.), i. 443.

78 E.R.O., D/DRe Z10; *E.A.T.* N.S. xxiv. 92.

79 Smith, *Eccl. Hist. Essex*, 318.

80 E.R.O., D/P 246/1/5.

81 C. Hodgson, *Queen Anne's Bounty*, ii, p. cccxiii; E.R.O., D/P 246: uncat. deed of grant; *Rep. Com. Eccl. Revenues*, H.C. 54, pp. 642–3 (1835), xxii.

82 E.R.O., D/CPc 95.

83 Newcourt, *Repertorium*, ii. 174.

84 E.R.O., D/Y 2/2, p. 13; D/P 246/1/2; G.L.R.O., DL/C/345, f. 149.

85 E.R.O., D/P 246: uncat. description of land and feoffment (2 items); ibid. T/A 645.

86 Ibid. D/CT 95.

87 E.R.O., D/B 5 Cr100, rot. 9d.

88 Newcourt, *Repertorium*, ii. 174; Morant, *Colch.* 109; Smith, *Eccl. Hist. Essex*, 318; G.L.R.O., DL/C/345, f. 149; E.R.O., Q/RTh 5, f. 8; ibid. D/CT 95; D/P 246/1/2; ibid. T/A 366.

89 E.R.O., D/P 246: uncat. plans; *E.R.* iii. 30; O.S. Map 1/500, Essex XXVII. 12.8 (1891 edn.).

90 N. Butler, *Theatre in Colch.* 91–2; inf. from theatre.

service in St. Mary's church.[91] In 1348 he gave the same endowment, with 100 sheep, for a chantry of St. Mary and All Saints served by two chaplains who were to pray for him, his parents and benefactors, and all faithful Christians.[92] From 1362 or earlier the chantry was served by one priest in the chapel of St. Thomas the Martyr. When Eleanor died its advowson passed to the bailiffs and commonalty, who presented until the Suppression.[93] The endowment, worth £8 6*s.* in 1535, was given by the king to the bailiffs and commonalty in 1539 for the foundation of a grammar school and other uses.[94] A chantry house in the churchyard near the north-east end of the church was demolished when the church was rebuilt in 1714.[95]

Rectors were recorded from *c.* 1220; the living was poor and in the Middle Ages incumbencies were usually short.[96] Papal authority was given in 1398 for the rector to have a portable altar, and in 1440 to allow the new rector, Robert Lardener, to hold another living, because of the poverty of St. Mary's.[97] Lardener (d. 1464) endowed two lights before the great crucifix and one at the entrance to the chancel.[98] The sale by the churchwardens of a silver and gilt pyx and other plate *c.* 1534 and the removal of painted window glass by 1548 suggest that parishioners held protestant views, as presumably did Thomas Kirkham, rector 1540–51, who was fined in 1544 for failing to read the king's statutes in the church and for living with a woman.[99] His successor, Marmaduke Smith, escaped deprivation for marriage in the spring of 1554, but took the precaution of fleeing before the arrival of bishop Bonner's episcopal visitors in October.[1]

From 1562 until 1804 rectors of St. Mary's served at least one other cure, usually in or near Colchester, and from *c.* 1644 to 1735 were sequestrators of Holy Trinity.[2] Hugh Allen, rector from 1562, also held St. Mary Magdalen and, from 1567, Tolleshunt D'Arcy. He subsequently went to Ireland with the Ardes Expedition of 1572, becoming bishop of Down and Connor (1572–82) and of Fearns (1582–9). John Walford, rector of All Saints, 1571–1609, and an unpreaching minister, held St Mary's by sequestration until 1596.[3] George Archer, formerly 'a scrivenor and an attorney in the County Court', was instituted in 1596 and also held St Nicholas's by sequestration from 1598 until his death in 1604.[4] Archer was succeeded by the conformist Thomas Talcott, 1604–41, rector of All Saints, 1609–26 and of Mile End 1626–41.[5]

In 1644 parliament replaced the non-resident Robert Mercer, who was also vicar of St. Peter's, with William Boissard, who may have had royalist sympathies as he was presented to All Saints' rectory in 1640 by Sir Henry Audley.[6] Nevertheless he remained at St. Mary's until 1660, when he became perpetual curate of St. Giles's.[7] Despite serious damage in the siege of 1648[8] St. Mary's church was used for baptisms 1654–*c.* 1663 and for marriages 1656–*c.* 1660.[9] The congregation used Holy Trinity church for services until 1714,[10] when St. Mary's church was rebuilt. John Smith, rector 1661–*c.* 1676 was also minister of the Dutch church 1668–75; he was later known as 'Narrative Smith' for his narrative of 1679 on the Popish plot.[11] The pluralist Joseph Powell, rector 1676–97, seems to have lived in Colchester at least occasionally, for he enlarged the rectory house, but an assistant curate, William Shillito, served St. Mary's and Holy Trinity 1679–99.[12]

Robert Middleton, rector 1706–34, rebuilt St. Mary's church in 1714 and from that time provided one Sunday service in St. Mary's, another in Holy Trinity, and communion once a month and at festivals in the two churches by turns. From 1723 or earlier he employed assistant curates.[13] In the later 18th century the parish, with several wealthy residents, a new church, and a good rectory house,[14] attracted two eminent scholars who preached to 'polite congregations'.[15] Philip Morant, historian of Essex, rector 1737–70, provided one full Sunday service, communion once a month and at festivals, and read prayers on Sundays between Michaelmas and Easter. He lived in the rectory house until he moved in 1767 to his other benefice at Aldham, leaving an assistant curate to serve St. Mary's.[16] Thomas Twining, translator of Aristotle, vicar of White Notley 1772–96, and curate of Fordham 1763–89, thought the living so attractive, although not valuable, that he 'used a bit of pushery' to get it in 1788. He lived at Fordham and Colchester and died in 1804.[17]

His successor Philip Bayles, rector 1804–55, served the cure himself, assisted in his later years

91 *Cal. Pat.* 1338–40, 27; E.R.O., D/DRg 6/3.

92 B.L. Campb. xxiii. 14; Morant, *Colch.* 155–6.

93 *Reg. Sudbury*, i. 231; Guildhall MSS. 9531/3, f. 89; 9531/9, ff. xiv verso, xxii verso; 9531/10, f. 18; Morant, *Colch.* 156; E.R.O., D/DRg 6/5.

94 *Valor Eccl.* (Rec. Com.), i. 443; *L. & P. Hen. VIII*, xiv (2), 222.

95 E.R.O., D/P 246/1/2.

96 Newcourt, *Repertorium*, ii. 174–5; E.R.O., T/A 237; T/A 547/1; ibid. D/P 246/1/1; P.R.O., JUST 1/231, rot. 34.

97 *Cal. Papal Reg.* v. 147; ix. 121.

98 Morant, *Colch.* 161.

99 *E.A.T.* N.S. xiii. 165; E.R.O., D/B 5 Cr114, rot. 2 and d.

1 Newcourt, *Repertorium*, ii. 175; B. Usher, 'Colch. and Diocesan Admin.' (TS. in E.R.O.), 10.

2 Above, Holy Trinity.

3 Usher, 'Colch. and Diocesan Admin.' 10; T. W. Davids, *Annals of Nonconf. in Essex*, 98, 104.

4 Usher, 'Colch. and Diocesan Admin.' 11; *A Viewe of the State of the Clargie in Essex* (1604), 15.

5 Newcourt, *Repertorium*, ii. 175, 231; Davids, *Annals of Nonconf. in Essex*, 159; H. Smith, 'Parochial Clergy in Essex' (TS. in E.R.O.), 124; E.R.O., D/P 146/1/1.

6 Lambeth Palace Libr., Comm. MSS. XIIa/9/417–18; Smith, 'Parochial Clergy in Essex', 119; Newcourt, *Repertorium*, ii. 164.

7 Newcourt, *Repertorium*, ii. 164; E.R.O., T/A 547/1.

8 Smith, *Eccl. Hist. Essex*, 318; Morant, *Colch.* 108; illus. in Lorenzo Magalotti, *Travels of Cosmo the Third through England (1669)* (1821).

9 E.R.O., D/P 245/1/1; D/P 246/1/2; ibid. T/R 124/1.

10 Morant, *Colch.* 116.

11 *D.N.B.* s.v. Oates, T.; *E.R.* xlviii. 169.

12 *Alum. Cantab. to 1751*; Morant, *Colch.* 109; tablet in Holy Trinity ch.

13 Guildhall MSS. 25750/1, 25751.

14 Ibid. 9557, f. 69; Morant, *Colch.* 109.

15 *E.R.* xxviii. 165.

16 Morant, *Essex*, i, p. viii; *D.N.B.*; Guildhall MSS. 9551, f. 58; 25754/1.

17 *D.N.B.*; *E.R.* xxviii. 164; T. Twining, *Recreations and Studies of a Country Clergyman of the 18th Cent.* ed. R. Twining (1882).

by a curate, and on Census Sunday in 1851 morning and afternoon services were attended by *c.* 400.[18] In the 1860s the rector Charles L'Oste's great age inhibited innovation, but parish life revived under his successor John W. Irvine, rector 1870–97 and rural dean from 1880, who increased the number of services and rebuilt the church and rectory house.[19] His association with G. H. Wilkinson suggests an interest in the reconciliation of ritualists and evangelicals; he also urged better relations with nonconformists.[20] The parish boundaries were altered in 1898 by an exchange of detached parts with Lexden and in 1911 by the transfer to St. Mary's of detached parts of St. Runwald's, St. Botolph's, and Holy Trinity, consolidating the parish south and west of the church.[21] Greville T. Brunwin-Hales, rector of St. Mary's 1897–1932 and vicar of Berechurch 1913–32, rural dean from 1907, was active in borough affairs and did notable work in the formation of the new diocese of Chelmsford.[22] He introduced daily matins and evensong and weekly communion, attracting many people from other parishes to St. Mary's.[23] G. A. Campbell, rector and rural dean 1933–46, replaced daily matins, which was rarely attended, with daily communion in St. Mary's or Christ Church chapel of ease.[24] In the 1970s St. Mary's was isolated from much of its parish by the new ring road, and in 1978 the church was closed.[25]

Christ Church opened in 1904 as a chapel of ease in an iron building on land in Ireton Road given by James Round. It was served by curates of St. Mary's.[26] In 1978 the iron building was replaced by a brick and slated church on the same site in Ireton Road, built to the designs of Bryan Thomas as the parish church of Christ Church with St. Mary and shared with the former Headgate Congregational church.[27]

The church of St. Mary's-at-the-Walls comprises a chancel with northern organ chamber, north-east vestries, and a south chapel, an aisled and clerestoried nave, north and south porches, and a north-west tower.[28] All but the tower are of 1872. The medieval church apparently comprised a chancel, perhaps with a chapel, a nave, south porch, and north-west tower.[29] The tower needed repair in 1385, and was replaced *c.* 1534 by the surviving tower, built of rubble containing Roman bricks and tiles, with limestone dressings.[30] The church was ruined in the siege of 1648.[31]

The repair of the church may have been mooted in 1679 when a new bell was cast, but it was not until 1709 that steps were taken to rebuild the church by brief.[32] In 1713 the remains of the chancel, nave, and porch were demolished, and a new brick church, designed by John Price, was built immediately east of the stump of the medieval tower. It comprised an aisled nave with a west gallery, a small chancel, and the tower whose the upper stage was rebuilt

FIG. 31. ST. MARY-AT-THE-WALLS, 1864

in brick in 1729.[33] Plans to crown the tower with four stone pineapples and a cupola may not have been carried out.[34] In 1853 the western gallery was removed, revealing the tower arch.[35] A south-east vestry, in imitation of Price's style, was added *c.* 1859.[36]

In 1872 the church, except the tower, was rebuilt in red and black brick to the designs of Arthur Blomfield. The chancel with south chapel and north organ chamber was built first as an extension to the existing church, but as funds increased the nave and aisles were rebuilt on the 18th-century foundations, the columns of the arcades being of cast iron. A clerestory and north and south porches were added.[37] In 1911 the tower battlements, damaged in the earthquake of 1884, were repaired and a chancel screen and choir stalls were built; the iron columns of the nave arcades were clad with light ochre terracotta and their capitals decorated.[38] In 1922 an apse was added to the south chapel which was refitted as a war memorial.[39] A rood and beam were erected in 1931. In 1936 vestries were added to

18 Lambeth Palace Libr., Fulham Papers, Randolph 9, ff. 1002–9; E.R.O., D/ACV 26; P.R.O., HO 129/8/204.
19 E.R.O., D/P 246: uncat. service register; ibid. J. B. Harvey Colln. vi, p. 129.
20 *E.C.S.* 12 July 1872; *D.N.B.* s.v. Wilkinson; E.R.O., D/E 4/3, p. 16.
21 E.R.O., D/CPc 95, 132.
22 *Crockford* (1932); *E.R.* xli. 214; G. Hewitt, *Hist. Dioc. Chelm.* 133.
23 *Par. Mag.* Feb. 1899, p. 3; July 1899, pp. 3–4; E.R.O., D/P 246: uncat. P.C.C. Mins. 1920.
24 *Par. Mag.* Feb. 1933, p. 2; *Chelm. Dioc. Yr. Bk.* (1947).
25 *E.C.S.* 25 Nov. 1977.
26 E.R.O., D/P 246: uncat. corresp.; *Par. Mag.* Sept. 1904, p. 2; *Chelm. Dioc. Chron.* Feb. 1931, p. 31; May 1934, p. 79; Mar. 1952, p. 18; Apr. 1952, p. 26.
27 *E.C.S.* 3 Sept. 1978; D. Stephenson, *Bk. of Colch.* 135.
28 R.C.H.M. *Essex*, iii. 39; Rodwell, *Hist. Chs.* 32–3; inf. from Council for the Care of Churches.
29 E.R.O., D/B 5 Sb2/7, f. 59; D/ABV 1, f. 4; Morant, *Colch.* 108, 161; Guildhall MS. 9531/9, f. xiv verso.
30 E.R.O., D/B 5 Cr24, rot. 52d.; *E.A.T.* N.S. xiii. 165.
31 Morant, *Colch.* 65, 69; Magalotti, *Travels of Cosmo the Third*, facing p. 472.
32 *Ch. Bells Essex*, 219; E.R.O., D/B 5 Sr88, rot. 3; *E.R.* xxvi. 198.
33 E.R.O., D/P 246/6: uncat. plan; *E.A.T.* N.S. xxiii. 311–20; Morant, *Colch.* 108.
34 E.R.O., D/P 246/6: uncat. estimate; Morant, *Colch.* map facing p. 4.
35 P. Sherry, *Portrait of Colch.* 28.
36 E.R.O., D/AZ 7/1, p. 130.
37 Ibid. D/P 246/6: uncat. mins. Ch. Improvement Cttee.; D/CF 10/2; *E.C.S.* 12 July 1872.
38 E.R.O., T/Z 13/10; *E.R.* xx. 153; *Par. Mag.* Feb. 1911, p. 2; July 1911, pp. 1–2.
39 E.R.O., D/P 246/6: uncat. mins. P.C.C.; *Par. Mag.* cover illus. June 1937 and later edns.; *Chelm. Dioc. Chron.* May 1922, p. 76.

the north-east end of the church,[40] and in 1937 the interior walls of the church were plastered and whitened, covering Blomfield's patterned brickwork.[41] In 1980 the building was converted to an arts centre.[42]

The church had one bell of 1679, which was moved to St. Leonard's when St. Mary's closed.[43] The plate deposited in Colchester museum includes a chalice of 1633, apparently made for the friary of Ross (Ireland); it is not known how or when St. Mary's acquired it.[44] A table font by Albert Hartshorne *c.* 1872,[45] survived in the tower in 1988. Several monuments from the 18th-century church were re-erected in 1872 and retained in 1980. Among them is a memorial to the Rebow family, with a figure of John (d. 1699),[46] and a tablet in memory of Thomas Twining, rector 1788–1804. A tablet commemorating Philip Morant was erected in 1966.[47] Mrs. Church, by will proved 1928, gave £301 stock to maintain, repair and decorate the fabric; the income of £9 a year was transferred to Christ Church in 1978.[48] Dame Catherine R. Hunt, by will proved 1950, gave £1,468 for the benefit of the church and parish.[49]

In 1714 the churchyard was levelled, tree-lined paths were laid round the church, and the place became a fashionable resort of the gentry.[50] The paths and lime trees survived in 1988 with some 18th- and 19th-century monuments.

ST. MARY MAGDALEN'S. The church may have been founded by Eudes the sewer in the 12th century as the chapel of St. Mary Magdalen's hospital,[51] but it had acquired parochial status by 1237 when the church, *ecclesia*, of St. Mary Magdalen was confirmed to St. John's abbey, and in 1254 the master of the hospital was rector of the church.[52] In 1558 the advowson was granted to the bishop of London.[53] When the hospital was refounded in 1610, the Lord Chancellor was given power to nominate the master, who was also to be rector of the parish, and the rectory was not separated from the mastership until 1953.[54] In 1977 a team ministry was set up for the parishes of St. Mary Magdalen, St. Leonard, and St. Stephen; it was dismantled in 1986 and the benefices of the three parishes were united, the patronage board presenting for two turns in every three and the Lord Chancellor for the third.[55]

The church had no separate endowment until 1953 when, after a Charity Commission inquiry, the capital sum of £11,000 and the master's house, no. 24 New Town Road, were transferred from the charity to the Ecclesiastical Commissioners.[56]

From an unknown date until 1548 a rent of 13*d.* a year from 1 a. of arable was paid for providing holy bread. Walter Ramyssen, by will dated 1457, gave a tenement in Magdalen Street for an obit in the church; it had been lost by 1548.[57] Thomas Gale, master and presumably rector 1548–57, combined protestant and Catholic tenets in his will.[58]

Benjamin Clere the younger, although described as a clerk on his appointment in 1562, was said in 1580 to be neither minister nor priest. In 1584 there was another minister, presumably a curate, but two men doubted whether he preached sound doctrine. By 1586 the mastership had been granted to Thomas Lowe, rector of St Leonard's, who was warned not to meddle with the profits of the parsonage and hospital. He continued to hold it, presumably by sequestration, until his death in 1615. On several Sundays in 1599 no services were held, and in 1604 there was no surplice.[59]

Gabriel Honifold, rector for 28 years, and rector of Ardleigh 1614–42 was ejected *c.* 1644 accused of preaching seldom, neither residing nor providing for the cure, swearing by his faith, and playing cards on Sunday.[60] He seems to have been succeeded by the royalist minister of St. Giles's, Samuel Cock, who in 1646 was ordered to give the hospital to the rector of St. Leonard's.[61] In 1650 when Henry Barrington, a former mayor and a protestant extremist, was appointed master of the hospital, the living was left vacant and the church was used as a poorhouse.[62]

The church seems to have remained in ruins and unused until 1721, when the Lord Chancellor appointed the first of a regular succession of rectors.[63] From then until 1852 the living was held by three members of the Smythies family: Palmer Smythies (1721–73), who was also rector of St. Michael's Mile End and master of the grammar school, his son John (1773–1816) also rector of Alpheton (Suff.) 1806–16, and John's son, John Robert (1816–52) one of the founders of the Royal Agricultural Society.[64] In 1768

40 Inf. from Council for Places of Worship; *Chelm. Dioc. Chron.* Dec. 1930, p. 183; Apr. 1931, p. 61; May 1936, p. 74; Dec. 1936, p. 192; E.R.O., D/P 246/6: uncat. faculty.

41 *Par. Mag.* Oct. 1937, p. 1.

42 *E.C.S.* 2 May 1980.

43 *Ch. Bells Essex*, 219; inf. from Colch. Mus.

44 *Ch. Plate Essex*, 195–6, plate facing p. 22; R.C.H.M. *Essex*, iii, plate facing p. xxxv; *E.A.T.* N.S. xviii. 140–1; E.R.O., D/P 246: uncat. corresp.

45 *E.C.S.* 12 July 1872.

46 E.R.O., D/P 246/1/2: list by P. Morant; Morant, *Colch.* App. p. 19; M. Benham, *Among the Tombs of Colch.* 30; E.C.L. Colch., Crisp MS. 'Colch. Mon. Inscriptions', xi.

47 *E.J.* i. 171.

48 E.R.O., D/P 246: uncat. corresp.; inf. from Mr. R. Burmby, ch. treasurer.

49 *Chelm. Dioc. Chron.* Dec. 1948, p. 94; E.R.O., D/P 246: uncat. corresp.

50 Morant, *Colch.* 108; E.R.O., Wire 5/14.

51 The hist. of the hosp. is treated in *V.C.H. Essex*, ii. 184–6; above, Religious Houses; below, Charities. This account was written in 1987.

52 *Colch. Cart.* i. 96; P.R.O., JUST 1/233, rot. 36.

53 *Cal. Pat.* 1557–8, 400.

54 E.R.O., D/DRc Z11; below, Charities.

55 *Chelm. Dioc. Yr. Bk.* (1976–7), 140–1; (1977–8), 140; (1986–7), 166; inf. from the Revd. J. Shillaker.

56 Smith, *Eccl. Hist. Essex*, 319; below, Charities.

57 P.R.O., E 301/19/204; Morant, *Colch.*, 161.

58 *E.A.T.* 3rd ser. xv. 86, 91; E.R.O., D/ABW 16/128.

59 *Cal. Pat.* 1560–3, 415; *E.R.* xlvi. 154; B. Usher, 'Colch. and Diocesan Admin.' (TS. in E.R.O.), 12; P.R.O., E 178/817; E.R.O., D/AZ 1/7, f. 73v., 131v.; D/AZ 1/10, 49v., 74v.

60 *Walker Revised*, ed. A. G. Matthews, 155.

61 Above, St. Giles's.

62 B.L. Add. MS. 36792, f. 5v.; *E.H.R.* xv. 641–64; Smith, *Eccl. Hist. Essex*, 319.

63 E. Hickeringill, *Works*, ii. 92–3; E.R.O., D/ACV 9A, p. 64; ibid. D/P 381/1/1.

64 *Alum. Cantab. to 1751*; *1752–1900*.

there was a sermon every Sunday.[65] On Census Sunday 1851 attendances were 150 in the morning and 180 in the afternoon (including 30 Sunday school children on each occasion) from a population of 433.[66] By 1859 there was monthly communion, and the average number of communicants increased from 7 in 1841 to 50 in 1896.[67] Assistant curates were appointed from the early 19th century until 1944 or later.[68]

Robert Bashford, rector 1900–16, also chaplain of Colchester Union workhouse, held two Sunday services, litany twice weekly, communion three times a month, and one service on saints' days. In 1906 a parish hall was built in Wimpole Road.[69] About 1920 the parish bought a smaller hall, formerly a Methodist mission hall, in Magdalen Street; it was sold in 1956. From 1965 there was close contact with Wimpole Road Methodist church.[70] St. Mary Magdalen's church was closed in 1986 on the creation of the united benefice of St. Leonard, St. Stephen and St. Mary Magdalen.[71]

The medieval church of St. Mary Magdalen stood on the north side of Magdalen green, north of the modern Magdalen Street. It seems to have comprised an aisleless nave and chancel with an adjoining chapel for the lepers. The nave contained a 13th-century south doorway and windows of the 14th and 15th centuries. A porch of unknown date survived in 1601.[72] The hospital chapel had been destroyed before 1610, and the church needed repair in 1633.[73] After the siege in 1648 it was abandoned until 1721 when Thomas Parker, the Lord Chancellor, repaired it at his own expense. The 18th-century church comprised a small brick chancel, presumably built in 1721, and the repaired medieval nave. The wooden bellcot was damaged by lightning in 1739 but afterwards repaired.[74] The church was demolished in 1852, and a new one, designed by F. Barnes in the decorated style, was built just to the south and consecrated in 1854. It comprises a chancel, aisleless nave, north and south transepts, and south porch.[75] A small polygonal south-west tower was added after 1861, damaged by the earthquake in 1884, and rebuilt in 1885.[76] Vestries on the north side of the chancel were added in 1920.[77] The tower was extensively repaired in 1931.[78]

There was one bell of 1847. The church plate included a silver chalice and cover of 1723 which passed to the united benefice.[79]

ST. NICHOLAS'S. Archaeological and topographical evidence suggest that the church, which stood on the south side of High Street, was founded in the 10th century, but it was not recorded until the early 13th century when Simon son of Marcian, the patron, confirmed a payment of 1*s*. a year to St. Botolph's priory.[80] Before 1238 he gave the advowson of the rectory to St. John's abbey, which retained it until the Dissolution when it passed to the Crown.[81] In 1702 George Compton, earl of Northampton, obtained the advowson from Queen Anne in an exchange. He conveyed it to his uncle, Henry Compton, bishop of London (d. 1713), who left it to Balliol College, Oxford. The college presented in 1742 and thereafter, except in 1771 when the Crown presented by lapse.[82] The benefice was united with St. Runwald's in 1873 and the patronage alternated between the successors of Emma Sarah Round, patron of St. Runwald's, and Balliol College. In 1928 the united benefice of St. Nicholas's and St. Runwald's was united with that of All Saints', and Balliol College presented for two turns in four until the creation of the new parish of St. James with All Saints and St. Nicholas and St. Runwald in 1953.[83]

The rectory was valued at £1 6*s*. 8*d*. in 1254, and £10 in 1535. No value was recorded in 1291. From the income a pension of 1*s*. was paid to the prior of St. Botolph's in 1254 and 2*s*. in 1495, but it appears to have been lost by 1535.[84] In 1650 the tithes and the rates on houses levied by the town council for the incumbent amounted to only £9;[85] in 1766 the income was under £25 a year.[86] The living was augmented in 1773, 1786, 1789, and 1796 with a total of £800 from Queen Anne's Bounty, and in 1813 with a parliamentary grant of £600. A benefaction of £200 from Balliol College was matched with a parliamentary grant in 1833, followed by two further parliamentary grants of £200 each, raising the value of the living to £92 in 1835 and to £135 in 1863.[87] Tithes on about 13 a. of meadow and garden ground were commuted for a rent charge of £1 10*s*. in 1849. The living was worth *c*. £298 in 1898, excluding the income from St. Runwald's Farm, Old Heath.[88] The St. Runwald's glebe land, in Queen's Road and in Old Heath, was sold in 1918, and a small piece of glebe at Monkwick in 1922.[89]

A rectory house, recorded in 1637, was worth £4 10*s*. in 1650; attached to the west end of the church over a passage into the churchyard, it was repaired by the parish in 1695.[90] By 1738 it was being let; described as small and inconvenient in

65 Morant, *Colch.* 127.
66 P.R.O., HO 129/8/204; *V.C.H. Essex*, ii. 353.
67 E.R.O., D/ACM 12; D/AZ 7/1, p. 132.
68 Ibid. D/P 381/1/4, 5, 14, 15; *Chelm. Dioc. Chron.* July 1944, p. 52.
69 *Kelly's Dir. Essex* (1908, 1912).
70 Inf. from Miss L. Boyles; E.R.O., D/P 381/29/6, 7.
71 Inf. from the Revd. J. Shillaker.
72 E.R.O., D/B 5 Sb2/6, f. 18.
73 Ibid. D/DRc Z11; *E.A.T.* N.S. xi. 43.
74 Description based on drawings in Bodl. MS. Top. Gen. e 61, f. 43, and in E.R.O., Mint binder; E.R.O., D/P 381/1/1; Morant, *Colch.* 126–7; above pl. facing p. 120.
75 E.R.O., D/CC 5/1; Pevsner, *Essex*, 135.
76 E.R.O., D/AZ 7/1, pp. 132–3.
77 Inf. from the Revd. B. Snaith.
78 E.R.O., D/CFa 1, pp. 550–1.
79 *Ch. Bells. Essex*, 219–20; *Ch. Plate Essex*, 196.
80 W. and K. Rodwell, *Hist. Chs.* 31; *Arch. Jnl.* cxxxix. 390–419; *Colch. Cart.* ii. 542. This account was written in 1987.
81 *Colch. Cart.* i. 94–7; ii. 315; Newcourt, *Repertorium*, ii. 177.
82 Morant, *Colch.* 116; *Cal. S. P. Dom.* 1700–2, 512; E.R.O., T/A 547/1.
83 E.R.O., D/CPc 34; D/CPc 215; D/CP 3/37.
84 *E.A.T.* N.S. xviii. 123; *Valor Eccl.* (Rec. Com.), i. 443; E.R.O., D/DM Q1.
85 Smith, *Eccl. Hist. Essex*, 319; Morant, *Colch.* 106.
86 Lambeth Palace Libr., Fulham Papers, Terrick 14, ff. 341–4.
87 C. Hodgson, *Queen Anne's Bounty*, ii, pp. ccxvii, cccxii–cccxiii; *Rep. Com. Eccl. Revenues*, H.C. 54, pp. 642–3 (1835), xxii; *White's Dir. Essex* (1863).
88 E.R.O., D/CT 97A; ibid. T/A 645.
89 Ibid. sale cat. A85; Balliol Coll. Mun., Patronage Papers.
90 Guildhall MS. 9628/2; Smith, *Eccl. Hist. Essex*, 319; Morant, *Colch.* 118.

Berechurch Hall, demolished 1882

Old Cottages in Magdalen Street, 1897

Cistern Yard, 1932

Opening of the Oyster Fishery, 1913

Sorting Oysters, *c.* 1910

Livestock Market at Middleborough, *c.* 1900

High Street, 1858

from the east, with the corn exchange (later the Albert Hall) and pens for the livestock market

1766, it was still being let as a shop in 1815.[91] No new house was acquired.[92]

Thomas Francis, by will made 1416, gave land and tenements in trust for 100 years to St. Helen's guild in St. Helen's chapel to pay a chaplain £6 13*s.* 4*d.* a year to pray in St. Nicholas's church for his soul and those of his family. Before 1533 Henry VIII granted the chantry to Sir Thomas Audley.[93] In 1383 John Bayn bequeathed £86 13*s.* 4*d.* to endow a chantry for himself and his family.[94] Arrangements were made in 1406 for the keeping in the church of an obit for William of Colchester, abbot of Westminster.[95]

A boy bishop ceremony, apparently for the boys of the grammar school in the parish, was held in the church in the earlier 15th century.[96] A chapel of St. John and a Jesus mass were recorded in 1456.[97] Between 1236 and 1560 almost half of recorded incumbents were known pluralists, including Richard Langridge, rector 1531–7, chaplain to two consecutive archbishops of York and archdeacon of Cleveland from 1534, who was presumably non-resident.[98] In 1535 the curate of St. Nicholas's was presented for praying for the pope and cardinals and speaking against the king's statutes.[99]

Gerard Shilbury, curate from 1578 to 1586, and rector of Greenstead 1580–7, was an unpreaching minister. His parishioners attended other churches because of his 'simplicity' and at the episcopal visitation of 1586 he was 'tied to the exercises' for the instruction of the less learned clergy. Thomas Farrar held the living by sequestration from 1586 until he was presented to St. James's in 1592. Under his successor, William Banbrick, there was neither morning nor evening prayer in 1594. George Archer, rector of St. Mary's, held the living by sequestration from 1598 until his death in 1604.[1]

The Laudian Theophilus Roberts, rector from 1609 and rector of Berechurch from 1633, was lampooned in 1632 or 1633 for railing in the communion table and proceeding against parishioners who refused to contribute to the cost.[2] In 1648 the sequestrated living was apparently served with that of St. Giles's by Nathaniel Seaman, rector of Greenstead and master of Colchester grammar school.[3] In 1683 William Shelton, rector of St. James's and sequestrator, preached on one Sunday a month and on weekdays, the church being used by the Dutch congregation at other times.[4]

In 1718 the church was in ruins and most baptisms took place at St. James's.[5] It was repaired in 1721, and in 1738 Barnabas Simpson, rector of St. James's and sequestrator, held one Sunday service at St. Nicholas's except once a month and on great festivals when he took two services at St. James's. Communion was administered *c.* 5 times a year.[6] In 1766 there were daily prayers and one sermon on Sundays.[7]

There was still only one Sunday service in 1810, usually taken by John Smythies the former rector who was acting as curate, and communion was administered four times a year to *c.* 30 communicants.[8] In 1841 only about half of the families in the parish belonged to the church; the relatively low attendances of 150 in the morning and 210 in the afternoon (including 40 Sunday school children on each occasion) reported on Census Sunday 1851, out of a population of 959, reflect the high incidence of nonconformity in the parish.[9] The early years after the union with St. Runwald's in 1873 were difficult. There was friction between the rector, J. G. Bullock former rector of St. Runwald's, who was non-resident from 1882 because of ill health, and a non-communicant churchwarden.[10]

By 1893 there was communion twice a month as well as at major festivals, and by 1906 there were three services on Sundays.[11] The congregation fell to only *c.* 30 under H. E. Legh, rector 1895–1902, but rose to 300 by 1907.[12] Attendances were still increasing in 1911, but by 1927 diminishing as many older residents moved away. Between Bullock's resignation in 1891 and 1913 there were seven rectors. In 1908 there was much activity in Sunday school and mission work and church services were described as bright but without extravagant ritual. J. M. Harris, rector 1913–28, an Evangelical, supported the labour movement and showed concern about social problems.[13] The church was closed in the reorganization of Colchester parishes in 1953.

The Anglo-Saxon church, comprising nave and chancel, seems to have been adapted from a Roman building.[14] It was rebuilt in the 14th century in flint and brick with a chancel with a north vestry, north and south transepts, and aisled nave.[15] One aisle was apparently added soon after 1384, and there was a north chapel by 1395. A bell tower was mentioned in 1409.[16] The tower was probably over the crossing where substantial piers survived in 1874. The south aisle was remodelled or rebuilt in the 15th century and extended eastwards to form a south

91 Guildhall MS. 25753/1; Lambeth Palace Libr., Fulham Papers, Terrick 14, ff. 341–4; ibid. Howley 49, no. 25.
92 E.R.O., T/A 645.
93 Morant, *Colch.* 150, 156–7, 160; E.R.O., D/DCm 218/9; B.L. Stowe MS. 834, f. 67v.
94 E.R.O., D/B 5 Cr38, rot. 15d.
95 *Cal. Pat.* 1405–8, 188.
96 E.R.O., D/B 5 Cr45, rot. 15.
97 P.R.O., PROB 11/4, f. 93 and v.
98 E.R.O., T/A 237, 547/1; Newcourt, *Repertorium*, ii. 177.
99 *E.A.T.* 3rd ser. xv. 86.
1 B. Usher, 'Colch. and Diocesan Admin.' (TS. in E.R.O.), 15; Davids, *Nonconf. in Essex*, 98; E.R.O., D/AZ 1/1, f. 75v.; D/AZ 1/7, f. 135.
2 *E.A.T.* N.S. xi. 37 n.; *Cal. S.P. Dom.* 1631–3, 492.
3 *V.C.H. Essex*, ii. 506.
4 *E.A.T.* N.S. xxiii. 162.
5 E.R.O., T/R 108/4; Morant, *Colch.* 118.
6 Guildhall MS. 25753/1.
7 Lambeth Palace Libr., Fulham Papers, Terrick 14, ff. 341–4.
8 Ibid. Randolph 9, pp. 1018–25.
9 E.R.O., D/ACM 12; P.R.O., HO 129/8/204; *V.C.H. Essex*, ii. 354.
10 E.R.O., D/P 177/8/3; D/P 176/28/2.
11 Ibid. D/P 176/7; *Kelly's Dir. Essex* (1906), 151.
12 Balliol Coll. Mun., Patronage Papers.
13 E.R.O., D/P 177/8/3; D/P 176/28/4; *E.C.S.* 14 June 1902; *E.R.* lx. 49; *Essex Tel.* 5 Dec. 1908.
14 Rodwell, *Hist. Chs.* 31.
15 R.C.H.M. *Essex*, iii. 39–41; Morant, *Colch.*, 117–18; E.R.O., T/A 641/5; T. Wright, *Hist. Essex*, i. facing p. 311, picture of church; E.S.A.H. Libr., Hollytrees Colchester, Probert colln. 1, p. 48, photo.; ibid. Stokes colln., drawing.
16 E.R.O., D/B 5 Cr23, rot. 63; Cr29, rot. 4d.; Cr38, rot. 15d.

chancel chapel, incorporating the south transept. About 1700 the tower collapsed on the nave and chancel destroying both roofs. The west ends of the nave and south aisle were repaired in 1721 and new pews installed, but the rest of the church was left in ruins. In 1729 a wooden tower surmounted by a small conical bellcot was built north of the nave, apparently above the north transept. St. Nicholas's was popularly called the Dial Church in the mid 18th century because of the clock which projected into the street from the tower.[17]

The church was restored and greatly enlarged in 1875–6 in the gothic revival style to the plans of Sir George Gilbert Scott. The north aisle, nave, chancel, north transept, and part of the tower were retained, the nave and chancel becoming the north aisle of the Victorian church and the north aisle being converted to a parish room. The tower was rebuilt and a leaden spire added, the gift of G. H. Errington of Lexden Park. A new nave, chancel, vestry, organ chamber, and south aisle were built, financed by voluntary subscriptions, against the old church on the south and east.[18] In 1920 a reredos and mural tablet were erected as a war memorial. A chapel of St. Runwald, in the north aisle, was dedicated in 1935.[19] The church was demolished in 1955.[20]

There were six bells, two 15th-century by Richard Hill and by Joan his widow, one of 1701, and three of 1803. They were bought by St. Martin's church, Basildon.[21] The church plate included an inscribed silver cup and cover of 1569, displayed in 1987 in the Colchester museum and used on special occasions in St. James's church.[22] The pews and the pulpit were moved to St. Barnabas's church.[23] Part of the churchyard, converted into a small public garden, and some tombstones survived in 1987.

ST. PETER'S. The church, on the east side of North Hill near its junction with High Street, was established before the Conquest when it was held of the king's alms by two priests. In 1086 Eudes the sewer held a quarter of the advowson and Robert son of Ralf of Hastings three quarters.[24] Eudes's quarter passed to his foundation St. John's abbey; Robert's three quarters were given by his son William to St. Botolph's priory. In the early 13th century the abbey granted its share of the advowson to the priory in exchange for confirmation of a pension of 5*s.* 4*d.* a year.[25] By 1254 the priory had created the parish of Mile End out of the north part of St. Peter's parish, and in 1319 the priory appropriated St. Peter's rectory and ordained a vicarage.[26] A presentation by the Crown in 1335 was revoked in 1336 when the priory was pardoned for appropriation without royal consent.[27]

At the Dissolution the rectory and the advowson of the vicarage were granted to Sir Thomas Audley, later Lord Audley,[28] in whose family they remained until *c.* 1700, but the Audleys presented only 8 of the 15 incumbents between 1565 and 1690. The archbishop of Canterbury presented in 1579, the Crown in 1589, and turns were sold in 1600, 1629, and 1632. During the lunacy of Thomas Audley (d. 1697) the Crown presented in 1672 and Audley's guardian in 1682. The Crown presented by lapse in 1698.[29] Henry Audley (d. 1714) sold the advowson of the vicarage *c.* 1700 to Henry Compton, bishop of London. Compton's executor sold it to the next bishop, John Robinson (d. 1723), whose widow presented in 1738 and 1739.[30] The advowson belonged to Bowater Vernon by 1748; Humphrey Carleton presented in 1760 and Charles Smith in 1781. John Thornton (d. 1790) bought the advowson, presumably from Smith,[31] to ensure the presentation of Evangelicals.[32] His trustees, dominant among them the leading Evangelical Charles Simeon, presented in 1814 and 1830.[33] Before his death in 1836 Simeon acquired the advowson and since 1854 his trustees have presented.[34]

In 1066 St. Peter's was the richest church recorded in the county, with an endowment of 2 hides, a mill, and two houses in the town, worth 30*s.* in all. By 1086 the estate's value had increased to 48*s.*, but Eudes the sewer held a quarter of it and Robert son of Ralf of Hastings claimed the rest.[35] The rectory was valued at 5 marks in 1254 and £2 13*s.* 4*d.* in 1291. In 1254 annual pensions of 5*s.* 4*d.* and 16*s.* were due to St. John's abbey and St. Botolph's priory respectively.[36] The vicarage ordained in 1319 comprised the small tithes, except those of North mill, and a house; the vicar owed an annual pension of 60*s.* to the priory.[37] The priory acknowledged the abbey's right to an annual pension of 5*s.* from St. Peter's in 1364, and by 1492 had reduced to £1 6*s.* 8*d.* its own pension from the vicarage.[38] In 1535 the vicarage was valued at £10.[39] Lord Audley, by will proved 1545 gave £1 6*s.* 8*d.* to the vicar of St. Peter's for an annual sermon on Good Friday.[40] John Bryan (d. before 1519) by will dated 1516 augmented the vicarage with a sum which seems to have been used *c.* 1545 to buy 13 a. at Mile

17 Morant, *Colch.* 117–18; above, pl. facing p. 120

18 E.R.O., D/CF 13/4, which includes plans; ibid. T/Z 13/10, which includes photos.; R.C.H.M. *Essex*, iii. 39–41.

19 E.R.O., D/P 176/28/3; D/P 200/28/2.

20 Rodwell, *Hist. Chs.* 31.

21 *Ch. Bells Essex*, 220; inf. from Mr. G. W. Crook, churchwarden of St. Martin's, Basildon.

22 *Ch. Plate Essex*, 197; inf. from Miss K. Kelly.

23 *Colch. Expr.* 30 Jan. 1975; inf. from the Revd. E. Turner.

24 *V.C.H. Essex* i. 423–4, 576, 578. This account was written in 1988.

25 *E.A.T.* N.S. xv. 94–5; *Colch. Cart.* ii. 543–6.

26 *Reg. Baldock*, 200–3, 210; Newcourt, *Repertorium*, ii. 178.

27 *Cal. Pat.* 1334–8, 185, 221.

28 *L. & P. Hen. VIII*, x, p. 419.

29 Newcourt, *Repertorium*, ii. 179.

30 Morant, *Colch.* 113; E.R.O., D/ACM 7.

31 *D.N.B.* s.v. Thornton; E.R.O., D/P 178 addl.

32 H. E. Hopkins, *Charles Simeon of Cambridge*, 155, 217.

33 E.R.O., D/P 178/6/8; *White's Dir. Essex* (1848), 87.

34 E.R.O., T/A 547/111; ibid. D/CP 3/42; *Chelm. Dioc. Yr. Bk.* (1915 and later edns.).

35 *V.C.H. Essex*, i. 578.

36 *E.A.T.* N.S. xviii. 123; *Tax. Eccl.* (Rec. Com.), 24.

37 Newcourt, *Repertorium*, ii. 178, where the pension is wrongly given as 40*s.*; *Reg. Baldock*, 210; Guildhall MS. 9531/1.

38 *Colch. Cart.* ii. 499, 502; E.R.O., D/DM Q1.

39 *Valor Eccl.* (Rec. Com.), i. 443.

40 P.R.O., PROB 11/31, f. 4.

End. In 1574 Nicholas Clere and William Hall gave in trust for the vicar *c.* 40 a. in Great Horkesley.[41]

The last two augmentations seem to have been omitted from valuations *c.* 1610 and in 1650. About 1610 the vicarage was said to comprise only the vicarage house, 1 a. of glebe, and a house on North Hill. In 1650 the glebe worth only £6 was augmented by £8 18*s.* 10*d.* rates on houses levied by the town council.[42] By 1683 the land at Mile End and Great Horkesley yielded £22 a year and in 1707 supplied most of the total income of £35.[43] Augmentations of £200 each from the patron, the bishop of London, and Queen Anne's Bounty in 1719, and from the patron in 1795 and 1805 helped to raise the gross income to £300 by 1835.[44] Tithes on 26 a. were commuted in 1845 for £20 16*s.* 3*d.*[45] In 1884 *c.* 6 a. in St. Mary's parish were sold; in 1894 St. Peter's retained 40 a. in Great Horkesley, 12 a. at Mile End, and 9 a. in St. Botolph's and St. Leonard's parishes. The farm at Great Horkesley and part of the land at Mile End were sold by 1920 and by 1953 all the land had been sold.[46]

The vicarage house stood on the east side of the churchyard in 1385, and a house on the same site was mentioned *c.* 1610.[47] In 1748 the house was low, mean, and dark.[48] It was rebuilt *c.* 1760 as a two-storeyed house fronting High Street. The parapeted front range, extending beyond the churchyard boundary, had a central, semi-hexagonal bay with a pillared portico.[49] The house was burnt down in 1842 and replaced by no. 59 North Hill, an early 17th-century house largely rebuilt in the 18th century. That house was still occupied as the rectory in 1959 but by 1963 it had been replaced by a new house built in the garden, and the old house was sold.[50]

A guild or fraternity of St. John the Baptist had been established by 1404 and survived until 1457 or later.[51] Another guild was associated with the Jesus mass, recorded from 1447 and very popular in the early 16th century, which was presumably celebrated in the Jesus chapel on the north side of the church.[52] One or both of those guilds was apparently endowed with houses and land in St. Mary's and Lexden parishes and with houses on North Hill.[53] A guild of St. Barbara was recorded in 1457 and 1525.[54] The 15th-century church also contained a chapel and statue of St. Mary.[55]

John Odolishoo, by will proved 1452, endowed an obit in the church.[56] Richard Haynes (d. by 1506)[57] gave in trust houses and land in Colchester, Lexden, Layer de la Haye, Salcott Virley, Tolleshunt, and Easthorpe to pay a priest to sing the Jesus mass and give 8*s.* a year to clothe two poor men. In 1535 the chantry was valued at £8 19*s.* 8*d.* Nicholas Bush, chantry priest in 1535,[58] may be identifiable with the canon of that name at St. Osyth's abbey in 1539 and with the clerk imprisoned in 1561 for saying mass.[59] The bailiffs and commonalty bought most of the chantry land from the king in 1550.[60]

Rectors were recorded from *c.* 1194, and the names of most medieval vicars are known. Incumbencies were usually short.[61] In 1312 the rector was dispensed to take an additional living, but in 1324 and 1331 an oath of residence was exacted.[62] John Gurdon, found guilty of assault in 1433, acquired the living in 1434, committed robbery with violence in 1438 and resigned soon afterwards.[63] Richard Cawmond, vicar 1494–1535, a Cambridge graduate and a pluralist, attended the examination of heretics at Colchester in 1528 and took the oath to Henry VIII and his heirs by Anne Boleyn there in 1534.[64] At his death in 1535 he had goods both in Colchester and at Clare Hall, Cambridge.[65] In 1539 the parish clerk was presented for opposing the particular confession of sins, and in 1543 the vicar Henry Beck was presented for neither preaching the gospel nor reading the king's statute in church.[66] The vacant living was served by a good curate in 1560.[67]

The benefice was vacant for most of the early part of Elizabeth's reign.[68] Robert Lewis, vicar 1579–89, was imprisoned for nonconformity in 1581 and was a founder member of the Dedham classis in 1582. The following year he admitted to not wearing the surplice and refused to subscribe to Whitgift's articles, and in 1586 he was threatened with deprivation for nonconformity. In 1589 he departed to take up the lectureship at Bury St. Edmunds.[69] William Cole, vicar 1593–1600, appears to have continued to serve the church in 1593 and 1594 in spite of being excommunicate and having no

41 E.R.O., D/P 178/3/3; Morant, *Colch.* 112–13.

42 Newcourt, *Repertorium*, ii. 179; Smith, *Eccl. Hist. Essex*, 319; Morant, *Colch.* 106.

43 *E.A.T.* N.S. xxiii, 161; Morant, *Colch.* 113.

44 C. Hodgson, *Queen Anne's Bounty*, pp. cxxxiii, clxxviii; *Rep. Com. Eccl. Revenues*, H.C. 54, pp. 642–3 (1835), xxii.

45 E.R.O., D/CT 98.

46 Ibid. D/P 178/3/2; D/P 178: uncat. terrier 1943–53; ibid. T/A 645.

47 *Reg. Baldock*, 210; Newcourt, *Repertorium*, ii. 179.

48 E.R.O., D/B 5 Cr24, rot. 47; Guildhall MS. 9628/3; Morant, *Colch.* 113.

49 Morant, *Colch.* 113; Guildhall MS. 9550; Colch. Mus. Topog. files: High Street.

50 E.C.L. Colch. Acc. C210: J. B. Harvey Colln. iv, pp. 95, 163-5; *White's Dir. Essex* (1863), 82; *Chelm. Dioc. Yr. Bk.* (1959–60, 1963–4).

51 E.R.O., D/B 5 Cr34, rot. 18d.; P.R.O., PROB 11/4, f. 149.

52 E.R.O., D/B 5 Cr70, rot. 13; P.R.O., PROB 11/8, f. 136v.; above, Med. Colch. (Townspeople).

53 Morant, *Colch.* 159.

54 P.R.O., PROB 11/4, f. 149; ibid. E 179/108/169, m. 5.

55 P.R.O., PROB 11/4, f. 149; *E.A.T.* N.S. xxi. 145–6.

56 E.R.O., D/B 5 Cr64, rot. 16v.

57 Ibid. D/ACR 1/133.

58 *E.A.T.* 3rd ser. xv. 88; *Valor Eccl.* (Rec. Com.), i. 443; P.R.O., E 301/19/29; E 301/30/37.

59 *V.C.H. Essex*, ii. 161; P.R.O., SP 12/17/18; SP 12/18/1; SP 12/18/7.

60 *Cal. Pat.* 1549–51, 420–1, 505; Morant, *Colch.* 158.

61 Newcourt, *Repertorium* ii. 179; E.R.O., T/A 547/1; T/A 237; P. H. Reaney, *Early Essex Clergy*, 69–70; Guildhall MSS. 9550, 9557–8, 9560.

62 *Cal. Papal Reg.* ii. 100; *Reg. Baldock*, 274, 295.

63 Newcourt, *Repertorium*, ii. 179; *E.A.T.* N.S. xxi. 139–42; xxii. 342.

64 *Alum. Cantab. to 1751*; *E.A.T.* N.S. xv. 84; E.R.O., D/B 5 R2, f. 164v.

65 P.R.O., PROB 11/25, f. 198.

66 *L. & P. Hen. VIII*, xiv, pp. 402–3; *E.A.T.* 3rd ser. xv. 86–7.

67 Corpus Christi Coll. Camb., MS. 122, ff. 50, 52.

68 B. Usher, 'Colch. and Diocesan Admin.' (TS. in E.R.O.), 16.

69 *Alum. Cantab. to 1751*; Davids, *Nonconf. in Essex*, 113–14; E.R.O., D/AZ 1/7, ff. 144–5, 169.

licence to preach. Parishioners accused him of neglecting the services, stealing the bells, and allowing the pupils of his school to break the church windows.[70] The presbyterian Edmund Warren, appointed *c.* 1653, was ejected in 1662, and replaced by Edmund Hickeringill who left St. Peter's for All Saints' in 1663.[71]

After the Restoration St. Peter's replaced St. Botolph's as the foremost town church. The bishops' and archdeacons' visitations were held there and the mayor and commonalty attended Sunday and special services.[72] By 1684 the church had a large organ, the only one in the town, and the borough paid an organist to play for festivals and town lectures, but by 1705 such payment had ceased.[73] From 1698 to *c.* 1750 when vicars of St. Peter's were usually sequestrators of St. Martin's and St. Runwald's, people from those parishes attended St. Peter's for two Sunday services with sermons, daily prayers, and monthly communion.[74] In 1748 prayers were said regularly on two weekdays and on some holy days. Although the income was insufficient for the duty, four vicars served for 20 years or more in the period 1714–1814, and from the mid 18th century assistant curates were frequently employed.[75]

William Smythies, vicar 1760–80, was a quarrelsome man who often appeared in the borough court and in 1765 was bound over to keep the peace with his wife.[76] The Evangelical Robert Storry, vicar 1781–1814, described himself as a 'gospel clergyman' and sought to attract Methodists to St. Peter's.[77] His successors maintained the Evangelical tradition and served the cure personally. William Marsh (1814–29), an impressive preacher of Calvinistic principles, established good relations with the garrison, and encouraged attendance at both Sunday services by providing dinners at the vicarage.[78] The scholar and pluralist Samuel Carr (1830–54) in 1843 erected a memorial in the church to the Marian martyrs of Colchester.[79] In 1841 he estimated that three quarters of the population of the parish were members of the church.[80] The practice of holding civic services in St. Peter's was revived in 1844 and maintained until the late 1920s.[81] By 1851 St. Peter's average attendance of 880 in the morning and 1,100 in the evening was the largest Anglican congregation in Colchester, and was rivalled only by that of Stockwell Street Congregational chapel.[82] C. T. Ward, 1895–1922, restored the church, founded boys' and girls' clubs, and held services for soldiers.[83] By boundary changes of 1911 St. Peter's parish lost an unpopulated area of Culver Street and *c.* 2 a. in the north-west corner of the parish, and gained a detached part of St. Nicholas's parish, north of High Street. In 1953 parts of the parishes of All Saints, St. Nicholas, and Holy Trinity with St. Martin were transferred to St. Peter's,[84] giving the church a compact parish. The church has maintained a vigorous life in the Evangelical tradition. In 1988 there were between two and four services on Sundays and one in the week.

The church of St. Peter comprises a chancel of one bay with north vestry over a charnel house, an aisled and clerestoried nave of seven bays with two western porches, and a west tower of three stages. The walls are of mixed rubble, septaria, brick, and ragstone, with limestone dressings.[85] The vestry is faced with knapped flint; the tower is of red brick with ashlar and white brick dressings. Ironwork on the south door, attributed to Thomas of Leighton (Buzzard) (fl. 1300), survives from a church comprising chancel, nave and central tower, perhaps with transepts,[86] which was enlarged by the addition of a south aisle in the early 15th century and a north aisle and chapel later in the century: the chapel existed by 1457.[87] A south porch, mentioned in 1632,[88] was probably of the 15th century. The north vestry was added in the early 16th century. The surviving pulpit, communion table, and chair are from a late 17th-century refitting of the church. Altar rails of the same date have been re-used in the west gallery staircase. Seats for the mayor and aldermen were made in 1701.[89]

In 1758 the church was remodelled. The central tower was taken down and replaced by the surviving west tower, surmounted by a cupola; the nave was extended eastwards, reducing the chancel to one bay, and all the windows, except the east window of the north aisle, were replaced. The 18th-century organ gallery at the west end may have been added in 1791 when a gallery was inserted in the north aisle. A gallery was built in the south aisle in 1815.[90]

The south aisle was extended eastwards in 1817. In 1832 the south doorway was bricked up on the inside and its porch probably demolished; new doorways with embattled porches were made into the west end of each aisle.[91] In 1859 the nave and aisles were reseated. A clerestory was added in 1896 but the Georgian galleries were retained. Restoration of the chancel, begun in 1896 with the replacement of the wooden chancel arch by a stone one, was completed in

70 E.R.O., D/AZ 1/1, ff. 49v., 52v., 79v.; D/AZ 1/10, 29v.; D/B 5 Sb2/5, f. 98v.

71 Davids, *Nonconf. in Essex*, 373–4; *E.A.T.* N.S. xx. 203; Smith, *Eccl. Hist. Essex*, 398; above (All Saints').

72 Morant, *Colch.* 112, 148; *E.A.T.* N.S. xix. 17–18; *E.A.T.* 3rd. ser. iv. 137.

73 E.R.O., D/B 5 Gb5, f. 223; D/ACV 9A, f. 65v.

74 Guildhall MS. 9550.

75 Morant, *Colch.* (1748), Bk. II, p. 8; Guildhall MSS. 9557–8, 9560; E.R.O., D/ACM 12; D/P 178/1/4.

76 Bensusan-Butt colln.

77 M. Benham, *Among the Tombs of Colch.* 54.

78 *D.N.B.*; C. Marsh, *Life of Revd. Wm. Marsh.*

79 *Alum. Cantab. 1752–1900*; M. Benham, *Among the Tombs of Colch.* 52–3.

80 E.R.O., D/ACM 12.

81 Ibid. Acc. C210: J.B. Harvey Colln. iv, p. 97; E.C.L. Colch., E Col. 1, 264.

82 P.R.O., HO 129/8/204.

83 E.R.O., D/P 178/8/3; D/P 178/28/4; *E.C.S.* 22 Feb. 1896; *Essex Tel.* 7 Nov. 1908.

84 E.R.O., D/CPc 132; F. A. Youngs, *Admin. Units of Eng.* i. 135.

85 R.C.H.M. *Essex*, iii. 41–2; Pevsner, *Essex*, 135.

86 W. and K. Rodwell, *Hist. Chs.* 28–9.

87 P.R.O., PROB 11/4, f. 149.

88 E.R.O., D/P 178/3/3.

89 Ibid. D/B 5 Gb6, p. 234.

90 Ibid. Q/SBb 206/7; ibid. T/Z 13/10; *E.R.* vi. 72–3, and pl. facing p. 65.

91 E.R.O., D/P 178/6/8; Wright, *Hist. Essex*, i. 306.

1902.[92] The chancel platform was later extended westwards beyond the arch. The cupola and clock bell were removed when the tower was repaired in 1903.[93] The former communion table, a large, originally secular, table of the earlier 17th century, stands at the east end of the north aisle, surmounted by the 19th-century painted reredos from St. Nicholas's church.[94]

Six bells were recorded in 1683.[95] Eight new bells were hung in 1763 and recast in 1913.[96] The plate destroyed in the fire at the vicarage in 1842 included a silver chalice and cover of 1660 and a silver salver of 1691. They were replaced by Victorian vessels and a silver paten of 1698 by Benjamin Pyne.[97] A clock, prominently mounted on a bracket on the west side of the tower in 1866, was rebuilt in 1912.[98]

Among the surviving monuments are four 16th-century memorial brasses, one of the early 17th-century, and two wall monuments, with kneeling figures, to Martin Basill (d. 1623) and his wife and to George Sayer (d. 1577) and his wives. There is a memorial to the dead of the Crimean War above the south arcade of the nave; from 1858 until 1928 the colours of the 44th (East Essex) regiment hung above it.[99] A memorial in the south aisle commemorates men of the Essex Yeomanry and the Royal Horse Artillery who died in two World Wars.

ST. RUNWALD'S. The invocation to an obscure 7th-century Mercian child saint suggests an Anglo-Saxon or possibly early Norman origin. The position of the church, on an island site in the middle of High Street within an existing market place, and its detached graveyard suggest that it was one of the later ancient Colchester churches, founded after much of the central area had been built up. It may have started as a chapel and later acquired parochial status and burial rights.[1]

In 1254 the patron was Margaret Baudechoun.[2] The advowson of the rectory seems to have passed to the Tey family by the marriage of Agnes Baude, presumably Margaret's descendant, and Sir Robert Tey, who presented jointly in 1364. It descended in the Tey family, with the manor of Marks Tey, until 1527 when Sir Thomas Tey conveyed it to Thomas Neville, perhaps on the marriage of his daughter Elizabeth to Marmaduke Neville. Marmaduke held the advowson at his death in 1545, but did not exercise it, the bishop of London presenting by lapse in 1544.[3] No presentations were made thereafter until the Crown presented by lapse in 1760, but the advowson passed with Marmaduke Neville's estate of Botingham Hall in Copford[4] to Charles Gray, who presented in 1772. Gray devised the advowson to James Round of Birch Hall whose family retained it until the union of the benefice with St. Nicholas's and the closure of St. Runwald's church in 1873.[5]

The rectory was valued at 13*s.* 4*d.* in 1254, and in 1535 was said to be worth as much as £7 13*s.* 4*d.* No value was recorded in 1291. An annual pension of 6*s.* 8*d.* was paid to St. Botolph's priory in 1495.[6] A rectory house in North Street (North Hill) was recorded in 1387, but not thereafter.[7] In 1560 the living was described as utterly destitute.[8] In 1650 its income was only £3 8*s.* 8*d.* a year from the rates on houses levied by the town council for the incumbent, and 8*s.* from tithes, and in 1707 the value was still only *c.* £3.[9] In 1768 the only certain income was tithes of *c.* 7 a. of land in Borough field (presumably the 8 a. mentioned again in 1810) and the interest on £600 of Queen Anne's Bounty.[10] Moses Cook (d. 1732) left the reversion of a quarter share of the rent of Huntsman's Farm, Foxearth. The living was augmented in 1749, in 1752, in 1770 to match Cook's legacy, and in 1797 with sums of £200 from the Bounty. Charles Round gave £200 in 1809, and the rector J. T. Round £600 in 1828; the last two sums were matched by further augmentations from the Bounty.[11] The income in 1835 was £160.[12] There was no glebe in 1650, but by 1828 more than 45 a. of land in the parishes of St. Runwald, St. Mary, and St. Giles had been bought.[13]

Between 1275 and 1544 incumbencies were often short in the poorly endowed parish. About half of the recorded rectors resigned: among them were John Best, rector 1382–92, who probably belonged to the leading Colchester family of that name, Christopher Swallow, rector 1513–16, who later founded Earls Colne grammar school, and John Farforth, found guilty of stealing £40 in 1520.[14] The parish owned some tenements in North Street in 1476.[15] Mathew Read, by will proved 1517, left a rent charge of 6*s.* 8*d.* a year to support an obit in the church. It survived in 1548.[16] A guild of St. John the Baptist was recorded in 1525. The rector presented in 1544 appears to have left after a very short time; before 1548 the churchwardens sold £12 worth of church plate, partly to pay the

92 E.R.O., D/P 178/6/6; D/P 178/6/8; D/P 178/6/13; D/P 178/8/3; D/CF 34/2; *E.C.S.* 22 Feb. 1896.

93 E.R.O., D/P 178/6/8; D/P 178/6/13–16; D/P 178/8/3; ibid. Pictorial colln.

94 Inf. from Canon E. G. H. Turner.

95 *E.A.T.* N.S. xxiii. 161.

96 E.R.O., D/P 178/5/6 (note inside cover); D/P 178/6/14; D/P 178, uncat. terrier 1943–53; *E.R.* xxii. 94; *Ch. Bells Essex*, 221–2.

97 *E.A.T.* N.S. xv. 297; xxiii. 161; *Ch. Plate Essex*, 198.

98 *Essex Tel.* 7 Nov. 1908; E.R.O., D/P 178/8/3; D/P 178/6/14.

99 E.R.O., D/P 178/28/4.

1 W. and K. Rodwell, *Hist. Chs.* 33–4; G. Buckler, *Twenty Two Chs. of Essex*, 220–2. This section was written in 1985.

2 *E.A.T.* N.S. xviii. 123.

3 Newcourt, *Repertorium*, ii. 180; Morant, *Essex*, ii. 202–3; *Feet of F. Essex*, iv. 163.

4 Morant, *Colch.* 114; Morant, *Essex*, ii. 196.

5 Guildhall MS. 9557, f. 71; E.R.O., D/DRe T12; D/CPc 34.

6 *E.A.T.* N.S. xviii. 123; *Valor Eccl.* (Rec. Com.), i. 443; E.R.O., D/DM Q1.

7 E.R.O., D/B 5 R1, f. 160v.; D/B 5 Cr141, rot. 16d.

8 Corpus Christi Coll. Camb., MS. 122, f. 51.

9 Smith, *Eccl. Hist. Essex*, 319; Morant, *Colch.* 106; Guildhall MS. 11248.

10 Morant, *Colch.* 114; Guildhall MS. 9628/2.

11 Morant, *Colch.* 107; C. Hodgson, *Queen Anne's Bounty*, pp. clxix, clxxxiii, ccix, cccxiii.

12 *Rep. Com. Eccl. Revenues*, H.C. 54, pp. 642–3 (1835), xxii.

13 Smith, *Eccl. Hist. Essex*, 319; Guildhall MS. 9628/2; E.R.O., D/DR O7; ibid. sale cat. A85.

14 Newcourt, *Repertorium*, ii. 180; E.R.O., D/B 5 Cr92, rot. 12; *V.C.H. Essex*, ii. 526 n.

15 Morant, *Colch.* 114.

16 P.R.O., E 301/19/201; E 301/30/220; E.R.O., D/B 5 R2, ff. 105 and v.

debt of £5 6*s*. 8*d*. which he owed the king, presumably for first fruits and tenths. The rest of the money was used to buy a pair of organs.[17]

The living, left vacant from the mid 16th century until 1760, was served by a succession of curates, many of whom were incumbents of nearby churches. In 1589 the church was being let out by the churchwardens as a covered market, and in 1597 the sequestrator, William Cole, sometimes said the service only once a month.[18] The royalist and Laudian views of Thomas Newcomen, rector of Holy Trinity, who served the church from *c*. 1627, led to conflict with the parishioners among whom was John Furley, a leader of the puritan party in Colchester and churchwarden in 1633.[19] Newcomen's dispute with a parishioner in 1637 over the erection of altar rails in St. Runwald's and his refusal to administer communion to those who would not kneel at them, created an uproar in the town, and involved the archbishop. Laud's behaviour in the dispute was cited against him later at his own trial.[20]

John Nettles, vicar of St. Peter's, served St. Runwald's in 1664.[21] The parish registers were signed in 1669 by Lewis Griffin, rector of Greenstead, in 1671 by William Shelton, vicar of St. James's, and in 1686 by the vicar of St. Peter's.[22] Between 1723 and 1748 there were no services at St. Runwald's, probably because of the poor condition of the building, and the parishioners attended St. Peter's.

Rectors were presented regularly from 1760. John Cantley, rector 1772–97, lived 4 miles away at Copford in 1778 and paid a curate to perform a Sunday service and preach once a fortnight; communion was administered four times a year to at least 20 people. There were 20–30 communicants in 1810 when the cure was served by a resident rector William Walford.[23] The Rounds presented two members of their family, James Round, rector 1797–1809, and James T. Round, son of Charles, rector 1824–51, rector of St. Nicholas's 1830–46 and rural dean from 1840.[24] By 1841 three quarters of the inhabitants of the parish were said to belong to the church. On Census Sunday 1851 attendances of 112 in the morning and 132 in the afternoon were reported, including 12 Sunday school children on each occasion, from a population of 324.[25] By 1859 there was monthly communion. St. Runwald's and St. Nicholas's benefices were united in 1873, because the combined population of less than 1,500 could not support two churches.[26]

The church of St. Runwald was probably built in the late 11th or early 12th century when it is thought to have comprised a small rectangular nave of coursed flint rubble and a square chancel.[27] Both nave and chancel retained a 12th-century or earlier plan. By the early 14th century the shops of Middle Row had been built against the east wall of the church. A lady chapel of three bays, on the north of the chancel, was added in the 15th century. There was a tower, presumably at the west end, by 1388.[28]

In 1595 the church was in ruins, and it needed repair in 1633.[29] The tower was taken down *c*. 1692, and replaced by a roughcast wooden turret at the east end of the nave roof, supported internally by timber framing. The chancel was repaired in 1695.[30] In 1760 the parish restored the church in brick, a pedimented surround was added to the south doorway and round-headed windows were inserted in the east and west walls; the chancel arch was probably rebuilt at the same time.[31]

The church was in a poor condition again by the mid 19th century: the removal of the Middle Row shops in 1857 left the east end of the church exposed and damaged, the foundations at the west end were defective, and the building was an obstruction in the busy High Street. It was demolished in 1878.[32] The 15th-century north arcade was re-erected in St. Albright's church, Stanway, in 1879. Some of the rubble was used in two houses, Cloisters and St. Runwald's, on the corner of Maldon Road and Salisbury Avenue.[33] The church site was sold to the town council in 1878.[34]

The churchwardens in 1765–6 paid 10*s*. 6*d*. for a font, which may be the one described in 1856 as a new and well finished octagonal font; architectural evidence does not support the claim that the 15th-century font in Little Totham church in 1985 came from St. Runwald's. A small Jacobean altar table from St. Runwald's was in St. James's church in 1985.[35]

In 1362 a plot of land 45 ft. by 43 ft. at the corner of West Stockwell Street and St. Runwald Street, 100 yards from the site of the church, was granted to John Newman, the rector, by William de Holton, chaplain, who succeeded him in 1364, to make a churchyard. It survived, slightly reduced in size, in 1985.[36]

The broken bell recorded in 1620 was probably

17 *E.A.T.* N.S. xiii. 166; 3rd ser. xv. 94, n. 41.

18 B. Usher, 'Colch. and Diocesan Admin.' (TS. in E.R.O.), 36–7; E.R.O., D/AZ 1/10, f. 41.

19 *D.N.B.* s.v. Newcomen; *E.R.* ii. 36; *E.A.T.* N.S. xi. 45, n. 3; above, Holy Trinity.

20 Bodl. MS. Tanner 70, ff. 107–11; Smith, *Eccl. Hist. Essex*, 66, 413–16; *Cal. S.P. Dom.* 1637–8, 69.

21 H. Smith, 'Parochial Clergy in Essex' (TS. in E.R.O.), ii. 121.

22 J. S. Appleby and P. Watkinson, *Par. Ch. of St. Runwald, Colch.* 23–4.

23 Lambeth Palace Libr., Fulham Papers, Lowth 4, ff. 325–8; ibid. Randolph 9, pp. 1034–41.

24 C. E. Benham, *Colch. Worthies*, 45–6; J. T. Round, *Farewell Sermon* (1851): copy in E.C.L. Colch.

25 E.R.O., D/ACM 12; P.R.O., HO 129/8/204; *V.C.H. Essex*, ii. 354.

26 E.R.O., D/AZ 7/1, pp. 138–9; D/P 177/3/2; D/P 176/8/3.

27 Description based on drawings, plans, and photographs of St. Runwald's church in Colch. Mus.; Buckler, *Twenty Two Essex Chs.* 216–20; Appleby and Watkinson, *St. Runwald*, 27–8; Rodwell, *Hist. Chs.* 33; E.R.O., D/B 5 R1, ff. 32v., 35v.; above, pl. facing p. 120.

28 Morant, *Colch.* 114 n.; E.R.O., D/B 5 Cr26, rot. 61.

29 E.R.O., D/AZ 1/1, f. 70v.; *E.A.T.* N.S. xi. 45.

30 *E.R.* xlviii. 150–4; Buckler, *Twenty Two Essex Chs.* 218.

31 Morant, *Colch.* 114; Cromwell, *Colch.* 200.

32 E.R.O., D/ACV 26; D/P 177/8/3; D/AZ 7/1, pp. 138–9; D/CF 16/3.

33 R.C.H.M. *Essex*, iii. 207–8; G. Martin, *Story of Colch.* 104–5.

34 E.R.O., D/P 177/8/3.

35 E.R.O., D/P 177/5/3; Buckler, *Twenty Two Essex Chs.* 219; Appleby and Watkinson, *St. Runwald*, 28; *E.C.S.* 4 Jan. 1985; inf. from Miss M. Benham, Revd. R. G. Bromby, and Miss K. Kelly.

36 *Cal. Pat.* 1361–4, 178; *Abbrev. Rot. Orig.* (Rec. Com.), ii. 274; Newcourt, *Repertorium*, ii. 180; O.S. Maps 1/500, Essex XXVII. 12. 3 (1876 edn.); 1/1,250, TL 9925 SE. (1982 edn.).

recast or replaced by Miles Gray in 1621; his bell was transferred to St. Nicholas's in 1878 and to the Colchester museum in 1953. A second, smaller bell seems to have been sold when the tower was demolished *c.* 1692.[37] The church plate, comprising an Elizabethan communion cup, a cup and cover of 1765, and a paten of 1708, passed to St. Nicholas's in 1878 and was in 1985 displayed at the Colchester museum, as was the 14th-century plated iron parish chest.[38]

Modern Churches

ALL SAINTS', SHRUB END. In 1845 a new parish of All Saints' Stanway was formed from parts of the east of Stanway and the west of Lexden parishes.[39] Its name was changed to All Saints', Shrub End, in 1960, after boundary changes had brought the parish into Colchester borough.[40] The patronage of the living was vested in the diocesan bishop.[41] The church was endowed with rent charges of £60 a year given by Elizabeth Papillon, £40 a year from Stanway rectory, £88 a year from the Ecclesiastical Commissioners, and a vicarage house built in 1847 in Shrub End Road. The house was sold *c.* 1975, and a new one was built in its garden.[42]

All Saints' church, built in the Decorated style in red brick with stone dressings, was designed by G. R. French.[43] It comprises a chancel, nave, and north-west tower with slated spire. A north choir vestry was added in 1958 and the nave was extended westwards in 1982.[44] The mission church of St. Cedd, Iceni Way, a simple dual-purpose brick building, was opened in 1955.[45]

ST. ANNE'S. The church, formerly a chapel of ease to St. James's, became parochial in 1953 when a new parish was formed from part of the north-west of the parish of St. James with All Saints and St. Nicholas and St. Runwald, and part of the west of Greenstead parish.[46] The patronage was vested in the bishop.[47] A vicarage house was built in Compton Road in 1953.[48]

The church, in Compton Road, was built in 1937 of red brick, comprising a large rectangular nave with a small, shallow chancel. In 1982, following the sale of the parish hall built in 1962, the western half of the nave was converted into a hall and used by the local community throughout the week.[49]

ST. BARNABAS'S. The church, formerly a chapel of ease to St. Giles's,[50] became parochial in 1950 when a new parish was taken from the parishes of St. Giles, St. Botolph, and East Donyland.[51] The archdeacon was succeeded as patron of the living by the bishop in 1956.[52] The vicarage house, no. 13 Abbots Road, was built *c.* 1930 for the curate of St. Giles's.[53]

The brick church, which in 1955 replaced the small one built in 1875, was designed as a dual-purpose building, comprising a shallow chancel and rectangular nave with a Lady chapel in a small room at the south-east corner. The parish hall, built in 1928–9, adjoins the west end. The pulpit, designed by Sir George Gilbert Scott, and the pews are from St. Nicholas's, the brass lectern given in memory of W. H. Wardell, rector of St. Giles's 1873–1903, is from St. Giles's, and the organ is from St. Martin's.[54]

ST. JOHN THE EVANGELIST'S. In 1863 an ecclesiastical district north-east of the town was formed on the initiative of J. T. Round, rector of All Saints' and St. Runwald's, to serve the increasing population from the parishes of All Saints, St. Botolph, Greenstead, Ardleigh, Langham, and Mile End.[55] A very small part of the south of the new parish was restored to Greenstead in 1961.[56] The patronage of the living was vested in the archdeacon of Colchester.[57] Tithe rent charges of £30 from Mile End, £10 from Ardleigh, and £5 from Langham, were granted to the new church.[58] The value of the living in 1887 was £250, together with the rent from two cottages with 1 a. of garden. In 1920 the land and one cottage were sold.[59] A glebe house was built in Ipswich Road, north of the church, in 1863 and replaced by a new building in Evergreen Drive in 1979.[60]

The church, in Ipswich Road, built in 1863 to designs by A. Blomfield in the Decorated style, is of red brick with yellow and blue bands and stone window tracery. It consists of a chancel and nave surmounted by a small bellcot at the west end.[61] The chancel and its fittings and part of the nave were built with money collected in memory of J. T. Round.[62]

ST. PAUL'S. The church, formerly a chapel of ease to Lexden, became parochial in 1879 when a new parish was created from part of the north-east of Lexden parish.[63] The bishop became the patron at the request of J. Papillon, rector of Lexden.[64] The income of the living was £50 a year from the Ecclesiastical Commissioners

37 E.R.O., D/AZ 1/4, f. 187; *E.R.* xlviii. 150–4; *Ch. Bells Essex*, 98, 222; inf. from Mr. M. Davies.

38 *Ch. Plate Essex*, 197; E.R.O., T/A 645; H. W. Lewer and J. C. Wall, *Ch. Chests Essex*, 109; inf. from Mr. M. Davies.

39 *Lond. Gaz.* 15 Aug. 1845, pp. 2460–2.

40 'Historic Shrub End' (TS. in E.C.L. Colch.), 2.

41 *Chelm. Dioc. Year Bk.* (1946), 85; ibid. (1986–7), 168.

42 *White's Dir. Essex* (1848), 128; E.R.O., Acc. C111: Chronicle of All Saints, Stanway, Shrub End; ibid. C117: sale cat.; inf. from the Revd. D. E. Cowie.

43 E.R.O., T/Z 13/10.

44 Inf. from the Revd. D. E. Cowie; E.R.O., Acc. C111: faculty.

45 *Colch. Official Guide* (4th edn.), 45.

46 E.R.O., D/CPc 314.

47 *Chelm. Dioc. Year Bk.* (1954), 76.

48 Inf. from the Revd. T. V. Hodder.

49 *Colch. Expr.* 5 Apr. 1962; inf. from the Revd. T. V. Hodder.

50 Above, St. Giles's.

51 E.R.O., D/CPc 302.

52 *Chelm. Dioc. Year Bk.* (1951), p. 76; ibid. (1956–7), p. 75.

53 E.R.O., D/P 324/29.

54 *Colch. Expr.* 30 Jan. 1975; inf. from the Revd. E. Turner.

55 E.R.O., D/CPc 18; *White's Dir. Essex* (1863), 90.

56 E.R.O., D/CPc 392.

57 Ibid. D/CPc 18.

58 Ibid. D/CP 3/38.

59 Ibid. D/P 525/3/4, 7.

60 Ibid. D/CC 14/1; D/P 525/3/6.

61 Ibid. T/Z 13/10.

62 Brass tablet in church: copy in E.C.L. Colch. Crisp MS. 'Colch. Monumental Inscriptions', vii. 3. A large extension was added in 1988 on the south side.

63 Above, Outlying Parts (Lexden, church); E.R.O., D/CPc 54.

64 E.R.O., D/CP 11/30.

and a tithe rent charge of £60 a year from Lexden rectory.[65] By 1937 there was a vicarage house at Braiswick; the diocese sold it in 1956 to the retiring incumbent and bought a house in North Station Road.[66] The construction in 1933 of the Colchester bypass south of the church and in 1980 of Westway to the north isolated the church from many of its parishioners.[67]

The first stage of the church in Belle Vue Road, consisting of a chancel and nave, was built in 1869. The building was completed in 1879 by the addition of a south aisle, choir vestry, and south porch designed by J. Clarke.[68]

ST. STEPHEN'S. The church, formerly a chapel of ease to St. Botolph's, became parochial in 1953 when a new parish was created from the eastern part of the parish of St. Botolph with Holy Trinity and St. Giles.[69] The parish was reduced in size in 1955 when an area in the south was transferred to Berechurch parish.[70] In 1977 St. Stephen's was combined with St. Leonard's and St. Mary Magdalen's under a New Town ministry, and in 1986 became part of the united benefice of St. Leonard, St. Mary Magdalen, and St. Stephen. The patronage of the living was held by Balliol College, Oxford, from 1953 until 1977; thereafter it was exercised by the patronage board twice and by the Lord Chancellor once in every three turns.[71]

The small red-brick church in Canterbury Road, designed by C. E. Butcher in 1904, comprises a chancel and nave, structurally undivided from each other, south vestry, and west porch, with a slated belfry over the nave. It was consecrated as a parish church in 1954.[72]

ANCIENT CHAPELS

ST. ANNE'S. The chapel, by a holy well on the south side of Harwich Road *c.* ½ mile beyond East bridge, probably existed by 1344 when Richard Shaw, chaplain, surrendered land at the well.[73] By 1379 there was a hospital there, under a proctor or warden who seems to have been a layman.[74] It was rebuilt in 1380, possibly by the St. Anne's guild who collected money that year and who held land near the hospital in the earlier 15th century.[75] The relationship of the hospital and its warden to the chaplains recorded in 1384 and 1386 and to John Newton, chaplain or hermit at St. Anne's from *c.* 1387 to 1414 or later,[76] is not clear. In 1402 the endowments were inadequate for the support of the master and brethren of the hospital, but John Vertue the elder (d. 1485) apparently increased them. He and others also left bedding to the hospital.[77] Elizabeth Harmanson founded a temporary chantry in the chapel in 1505 and another woman left stained cloths, presumably banners, of St. Anne and the Virgin Mary to the chapel in 1508.[78]

Chapel and guild apparently survived in 1536 but had been dissolved by 1549.[79] An attempt in 1559 to revive the hospital seems to have failed.[80] The chapel, presumably disused, was recorded in 1590; in 1748 the plain rectangular building was used as a barn.[81]

ST. HELEN'S. The north and east walls of the surviving building, on the corner of Maidenburgh Street and St. Helen's Lane, incorporate parts of the lower courses of the north and east walls of the Roman theatre which occupied the site,[82] but there is no evidence to support the later tradition that the chapel itself dated from the time of St. Helen. It seems likely that there were two chapels of that dedication in the 13th century and perhaps earlier. Only one was recorded in the 14th century, but after the re-establishment of St. Helen's guild in the chapel or hospital of St. Cross (later the Crutched friars) in 1407 that chapel was occasionally called St. Helen's.[83]

One chapel of St. Helen, next to the castle, was held by the king or by St. John's abbey. Eudes the sewer granted the recently restored church with 14 a. of land belonging to it to the abbey at its foundation; at the same time he gave the abbey the tithes of the castle chapel which were later associated with St. Helen's.[84] St. Helen's was not among the possessions confirmed to the abbey by Henry I, and although it was included in later papal and episcopal confirmations,[85] it is not clear whether the abbey actually obtained, or retained, possession of the chapel.

In 1157 Henry II granted to St. John's land called the castle waste, extending from St. Helen's chapel next to the castle southwards to High Street, and the land around the chapel to make a graveyard and a house for the clerks serving it.[86] Later evidence suggests that he intended to found a small chapel or college of

65 *Lond. Gaz.* 19 Mar. 1880, p. 2142; E.R.O., D/CP 3/40.
66 *Kelly's Dir. Essex* (1937), 159, 168; E.R.O., D/CP 3/41; inf. from the Revd. H. D. Winter.
67 *Colch. Official Guide* (4th edn.), 10; inf. from Colch. boro. engineer's dept.
68 E.R.O., T/P 147, p. 43.
69 Above, St. Botolph's; E.R.O., D/CPc 315.
70 E.R.O., D/CPc 331.
71 *Chelm. Dioc. Year Bk.* (1954), 75; ibid. (1978–9), 140.
72 E.R.O., Acc. C128: copy of seal of consecration, 1954.
73 Morant, *Colch.* map facing p. 4; E.R.O., D/B 5 R1, f. 38.
74 E.R.O., D/B 5 Cr19, rott. 16, 18d., 23d., 26.
75 Ibid. D/B 5 Cr20, rot. 11; Cr87, rot. 8; D/B 5 R1, f. 167.
76 E.R.O., D/B 5 Cr23, rot. 29; Cr25, rot. 44d.; Cr39, rot. 19d.; *Cal. Pat.* 1385–9, 405.
77 *Cal. Papal Reg.* v. 588; E.R.O., D/Y 2/2, p. 65; D/B 5 Cr62, rot. 22d.; D/B 5 Cr111, rot. 6; P.R.O., PROB 11/10, f. 34.
78 P.R.O., PROB 11/15, f. 2; PROB 11/16, f. 61.
79 *L. & P. Hen. VIII*, x, p. 419; B.L. Stowe MS. 829, f. 28v.
80 E.R.O., D/Y 2/2, p. 65.
81 Ibid. D/DCm T17; Morant, *Colch.* 153; Colch. Mus., engraving of 1724.
82 P. Crummy, *In Search of Colch. Past*, 59.
83 e.g. *Feud. Aids*, ii. 210; for St. Cross see *V.C.H. Essex*, ii. 181.
84 *Colch. Cart.* i. 3; *Colch. Arch. Rep.* i. 26.
85 *Colch. Cart.* i. 6, 13, 62, 67, 87, 95.
86 Ibid. 24.

clerks to pray for his soul. If so, the foundation failed, and the unendowed chapel seems to have become a liability to the abbey. A later tradition that the chapel was dedicated, or rededicated, in 1239 in honour of St. Catherine and St. Helen by Roger Niger, bishop of London, in the presence of William de Wande, abbot of Colchester,[87] may reflect a rebuilding by the abbey, but in 1265 the chapel was repaired at the king's expense, under the supervision of one of his servants.[88] In 1290, in the course of a wide-ranging dispute, the town accused the abbot of failing to maintain the chapel or to provide services there for the king and his ancestors, as he was bound to do by his possession of the tithes.[89] The arguments of both parties make it clear that there was some confusion between St. Helen's chapel and the king's chapel in the castle. The abbot was eventually ordered to provide a chaplain to celebrate three times a week in either St. Helen's chapel or the castle chapel as the constable or other keeper of the castle should direct. There are no further references to a St. Helen's chapel in which the king or St. John's abbey had an interest, and it seems likely that that chapel fell into disuse after 1290 and its functions were taken over by the castle chapel. It is tempting to identify the 12th- and 13th-century St. Helen's chapel with the chapel in the castle bailey, which appears to have been built or rebuilt in the later 11th century and remodelled in the earlier 13th century,[90] but that chapel would have been within the castle, and the area south of it would have been occupied by the bailey buildings and separated from High Street by at least an earthen bailey rampart in 1157 and so would hardly have been described as the castle waste between St. Helen's chapel and the road.[91]

In 1293–4 Master John of Colchester, apparently intending to found a small hospital, obtained licence to provide an endowment of 60 a. of land and 50*s*. rent for Nicholas, chaplain of the 'new' chapel of St. Helen, to maintain 6 poor people at the chapel to pray for his soul.[92] Nothing came of the plan, and in 1307 John obtained a new licence to grant to a chaplain celebrating there, the plot of land, held of St. Botolph's priory, on which stood 'a certain chapel of St. Helen of Maidenborough', with an endowment of 40 a. of land and 40*s*. rent.[93] No grant was made, however, until 1322 when John gave to John Bracy, the chaplain, the site of the chapel in Maidenburgh Street, 28 a. of arable, and 40*s*. rent in Colchester to found a chantry in the chapel, which had been built a long time before in honour of Jesus Christ and St. Helen.[94] The intended foundation of 1307 and that carried out in 1322 clearly relate to the surviving St. Helen's chapel; the fact that the site was held of St. Botolph's priory suggests that it was not the same as the earlier chapel granted to St. John's abbey.

In 1328 John of Colchester conveyed the advowson of his chantry to the bailiffs and commonalty, who presented fairly regularly until 1534. In 1336, however, they merely leased the buildings of the 'old' St. Helen's chapel to a chaplain for just under a year,[95] and in 1383 the fraternity of St. Helen appointed a chaplain for a year.[96] In 1416 Thomas Francis left 8 a. of land to augment the chaplain's stipend.[97] Richolda widow of Richard Cofford (d. 1395) founded another chantry in the chapel *c.* 1396, and chaplains were apparently appointed to it in the 15th century.[98] The St. Helen's hospital to which the king gave vestments and other furnishings *c.* 1414 was almost certainly St. Cross hospital, but St. Helen's guild seems to have retained some responsibility for St. Helen's chapel, providing tapers in 1441–2.[99]

St. Helen's chapel was granted in 1539 to the bailiffs and commonalty for the foundation of the grammar school, but was not so used.[1] The borough sold the chapel in 1541 to William Reve who sold it in 1557 to Jerome Gilberd.[2] In 1610 the borough confirmed the building to George Gilbert, perhaps a descendant of Jerome.[3] In 1683 the chapel was bought from Robert Torkington by Stephen Crisp and given to the Quakers as a meeting house.[4] It was repaired or rebuilt in 1701,[5] re-using old materials. The Quakers sold the chapel in 1801;[6] from 1830 the building was used by the central National school.[7] It was later used as a circulating library and as an upholsterer's warehouse. In 1883 it was bought by Douglass Round and extensively restored by William Butterfield, and in 1886 it was rededicated as a chapter house for Colchester rural deanery.[8] It was still used as a chapter house in 1923, but from 1946 was leased by the borough council for the museum service.[9]

The surviving chapel is a small, single celled, rectangular building. Much of it, including all the window tracery and the facing of the walls with their prominent brick string courses, appears to be the work of Butterfield.[10] Two 13th-century lancets in the north wall confirm the existence of a 13th-century building on the site.

87 *Colch. Arch. Rep.* i. 26.
88 *Cal. Pat.* 1264–8, 19.
89 J. H. Round, *St. Helen's Chapel* (priv. print.), 11–13, 22–3: copy in E.C.L. Colch.; E.R.O., D/B 5 R2, ff. 49, 50v.–52v.
90 *Arch. Jnl.* cxxxix. 323–8.
91 Above, Castle.
92 P.R.O., C 143/22, no. 24.
93 Ibid. C 143/65, no. 16.
94 Ibid. C 143/148, no. 4; E.R.O., D/DRg 6/1, printed in Round, *St. Helen's Chap.* 24–7; *Cal. Pat.* 1321–4, 2.
95 Round, *St. Helen's Chap.* 27; E.R.O., D/DRe Z10, no. 11.
96 E.R.O., D/B 5 Cr5, rot. 2; Cr22, rot. 30; ibid. T/A 237.
97 E.R.O., D/B 5 Cr40, rot. 1, printed in Morant, *Colch.* 154 n.
98 *Cal. Inq. Misc.* vi, p. 43; *Cal. Close*, 1396–8, 371; E.R.O., D/B 5 Cr32, rot. 16d.; Morant, *Colch.* 154.
99 *Cal. Pat.* 1413–16, 228; E.R.O., Boro. Mun., St. Helen's guild compotus roll.
1 *L. & P. Hen. VIII*, xiv (2), p. 222; P.R.O., E 178/829.
2 Round, *St. Helen's Chap.* 19; E.R.O., D/B 5 Cr124, rot. 6.
3 E.R.O., D/B 5 Gb2, f. 95.
4 S. H. G. Fitch, *Colch. Quakers*, 97.
5 E.R.O., T/A 424/7/1.
6 Fitch, *Colch. Quakers*, 95.
7 Below, Educ. (Other C. of E. Schools).
8 Round, *St. Helen's Chap.* 19–20.
9 *E.A.T.* N.S. xvi. 109; E.R.O., Boro. Mun., Council Mins. 1945–6, pp. 175, 391.
10 R.C.H.M. *Essex*, iii. 50; photographs in Round, *St. Helen's Chap.*

The east and another north window date from a later medieval, possibly 15th-century, reconstruction.

ST. MARY'S. The chapel, on St. John's green, was first recorded in 1363 when it had been damaged by flood and fire.[11] In 1392 the chapel's warden was involved, with two clerks of St. Giles's church, in a dispute with St. Mary Magdalen's hospital, perhaps over jurisdiction.[12] The chapel presumably survived until the Dissolution but had been demolished by 1581.[13]

ST. THOMAS'S. A chapel of St. Thomas outside the walls was recorded before 1238, probably *c.* 1220,[14] contradicting the 14th-century tradition that it had been the Jewish council chamber and was consecrated by Abbot William of St. John's in 1251.[15] A perpetual chantry had been founded there by 1379, and chaplains were presented by St. John's abbey in 1384 and 1386.[16] The chapel, on St. John's green, was recorded in 1476, and presumably survived until the Dissolution; its site was waste ground in 1581.[17]

ROMAN CATHOLICISM

IN the later 16th century and the early 17th Roman Catholic worship in the Colchester area centred mainly around the Audleys of Berechurch who were active recusants for over 140 years. Catherine Audley (d. 1611), her grandson Sir Henry (d. *c.* 1672), and Henry's widow Anne (d. *c.* 1704) were all supporters of the Catholic cause. In 1562 mass was said regularly in the Audleys' house.[18] In 1577 congregations of up to 30 people attended mass at Berechurch, and Catherine, described as a very wealthy and dangerous woman, was indicted for her involvement with 'riotous assemblies' of papists.[19] The daughter of Sir Richard Southwell, she was an ardent Catholic who encouraged her household and tenants to defy the authorities. Her servant, Thomas Debell, 'a notable papist and a lewd busy fellow', was imprisoned in 1584 for sedition.[20]

The 1560s and 1570s were a period of intensive Catholic activity when many papists were presented for recusancy; the bailiffs, who were very intolerant of Catholicism, did their utmost to persuade the dissidents to conform.[21] One very prominent Catholic was Richard Cousins who, in the 1550s, owned the White Hart inn in which Bishop Bonner's agents stayed. In 1562 Cousins was imprisoned in the moot hall for his papist activities.[22] Named repeatedly in the indictments was Roche Green (d. 1602), whose son Richard (d. 1590) was ordained in Rome in 1582,[23] and who, resisting earnest attempts to convert him, spent *c.* 20 years in prison, some of them in Colchester.[24] Other Essex recusants were imprisoned in Colchester castle, some for long periods.[25]

The use of Essex ports by papists crossing to and from the Continent was seen as a threat by the authorities; a priest and Mrs. Audley's son were carried to Douai, probably from Colchester, before 1577 by John Lone, a Wivenhoe mariner.[26] Other recusants on their way abroad, either from the Hythe or from Harwich, passed through Colchester; in 1578 a party of travellers which included nuns from the Low Countries was arrested at the White Hart inn on the way from Harwich to London. In 1584, in an attempt to control such traffic, commissioners were appointed to watch the port and issue passports; bonds were to be taken from all shipowners.[27]

During the 17th century and the greater part of the 18th the number of Roman Catholics in the town, *c.* 17 in 1625, declined steadily; in 1688 the mayor reported that no fines for non-attendance at church had been levied during the previous 11 years. In 1766 there were perhaps only 4 or 5 papists. The nearest priest was at Great Bromley Hall between *c.* 1720 and 1760 and at Giffords Hall in Stoke-by-Nayland (Suff.) in 1767.[28] By 1795 a small group of Irish Catholic exiles from the Continent were living in the town, ministered to by an exiled French priest.[29]

In the early 19th century large numbers of Irish Catholic soldiers arrived in the town. A priest in St. Botolph's parish who taught French to officers from the garrison in 1810 may have been Armand Benard, a French priest serving Colchester by 1812. In 1814 he recorded 11 civilian Catholics resident in the town and 12 baptisms, some presumably of soldiers' children, but no chapel seems to have been registered.[30] Many Irish Catholic soldiers settled in Colchester after the Napoleonic wars and Irish names

11 *Cal. Papal Reg.* iv. 33.

12 E.R.O., D/B 5 Cr27, rot. 14 and d.

13 P.R.O., E 178/819.

14 *Colch. Cart.* ii. 597.

15 Bodl. MS. Gough Essex 1, f. 7; *E.A.T.* (3rd ser.), xvi. 50.

16 *Cal. Pat.* 1377–81, 399; Guildhall MS. 9531/3, ff. 89v., 105.

17 E.R.O., D/DHt M146; P.R.O., E 178/819.

18 E.R.O. D/B 5 R5 f. 20; ibid. Q/SR 318/32; Q/RTh 7, 8; *Essex Recusant*, xii. 39. This account was written in 1988.

19 P.R.O., SP 12/120, f. 44.

20 E.R.O., D/B 5 Sb2/4, f. 36v.; ibid. D/Y 2/7, p. 199; D/Y 2/8, pp. 319, 323.

21 Ibid. D/Y 2/6, p. 69.

22 M. Byford, 'Price of Protestantism' (Oxf. Univ. D.Phil. thesis, 1988), 21; E.R.O., D/B 5 R5 ff. 31v.–32v.

23 G. Anstruther, *Seminary Priests*, i. 137.

24 M. O'Dwyer, 'Catholic Recusants in Essex' (Lond. Univ. M.A. thesis, 1969), p. 156.

25 *V.C.H. Essex*, ii. 43–5.

26 P.R.O., SP 12/120, f. 44.

27 E.R.O., D/B 5 Sb2/3, f. 104; Sb2/4, ff. 85v.–87; D/Y 2/5, p. 19; D/Y 2/6, p. 65.

28 *Essex Recusant*, xxv. 10–11; Bodl. MS. Rawl. D 372, f. 352 and v.; E.R.O., T/A 420; S. Foster, *Church of St. James and St. Helen*, (priv. print.), 5 : copy in E.C.L. Colch.

29 Westminster Dioc. Arch., Bp. Douglass Papers, VIII D, 1 June 1795.

30 Lambeth Palace Libr., Fulham Papers, Randolph 9, pp. 862–71, 980–7; Westminster Dioc. Arch., Poynter Papers, London Clergy, Misc. (1812–16), 111 C 9.

figure prominently in the baptismal registers up to 1817. In 1816 the military were withdrawn, Benard moved to Witham Place, and for 19 years Colchester had no resident priest; Gifford's Hall and Witham Place were the nearest Catholic centres.[31]

In 1831 William Dearne, an ex-soldier who had settled in the town as an ironmonger and nail-maker, provided a small building at the foot of North Hill where mass was said regularly by a priest from Witham.[32] There may have been a small chapel in Moor Lane (later Priory Street) before the permanent church dedicated to St. James was built there in 1837.[33] C. P. King, who had already been serving Colchester from Witham for several months, became the first resident priest of the Colchester mission which covered *c.* 120 square miles of north-east Essex. William Joseph Stourton, Lord Stourton, (d. 1846) transferred from Witham to Colchester an annuity of £100 paid by his family. The annuity was reduced to £50 in 1880 and the family continued to support the mission until 1882 or later.[34]

In 1856 the civilian congregation of fewer than 100 was greatly outnumbered by the *c.* 800 Catholic soldiers and their families who came to the garrison at the onset of the Crimean war. Civilians and soldiers continued to worship together until 1865 when an army chaplain was appointed. By 1905 the civilian Catholic population had increased to *c.* 300 and the Sisters of Mercy, who came from Brentwood in 1891, were supporting the priest in his ministry. The Bourne Institute, named after and opened by F. A. Bourne, archbishop of Westminster, was built next to the presbytery in 1910. In 1918 Colchester became a parish in the newly created Brentwood diocese.[35]

To serve the growing population on the outskirts of the town several missions opened from St. James's. By 1944 mass was said in a room in the Dog and Pheasant public house at Mile End; in 1947 parishioners helped to build and furnish the little church of St. Joseph in Mill Road.[36] Services were held in the village hall in Berechurch from 1959 until 1964 when the church of St. Theodore of Canterbury was opened in Prince Philip Road.[37] Mass was said in a rented iron building in Straight Road, Lexden, from 1933 until 1937 when the church of St. Theresa of Lisieux was built in Clairmont Road. In 1954 a priest-in-charge was appointed and Lexden became a separate parish in 1960; the building was replaced by a larger church built nearby in 1971. The church of St. John in Iceni Way, a simple brick building which opened in 1961, is served from Lexden parish.[38] Mass was said in a church hall in Greenstead in 1974; by 1979 the church of St. John Payne in Blackthorn Avenue was serving the Catholic population of Ardleigh and Greenstead. The mission was given parochial status in 1983 when it also served Mistley.[39]

The church of St. James the Greater was known as St. James the Less by 1900. St. Helen was added to the dedication *c.* 1902.[40] The church stands in Priory Street near its junction with East Hill. Built of white brick in the Norman style to the design of J. J. Scoles, it originally comprised an apsidal chancel and an aisleless nave with a west gallery.[41] In 1861 the organ was removed from the gallery which was fitted with seating for 100 soldiers.[42] In 1904 and 1910 the chancel was extended and aisles were added to the nave.[43] In 1987 the church was reordered; glass by Pugin from a redundant church was inserted in the windows of the newly formed Blessed Sacrament chapel.[44]

A permanent army chaplain, appointed in 1865, conducted services in St. James's church until 1867 when he was permitted to use the camp chapel in Military Road, but in 1904 the parish priest again had the pastoral care of Catholic soldiers from the garrison.[45] In 1949 Catholic army families were worshipping in a barrack block. The Garrison church of Christ the King was completed at Le Cateau barracks *c.* 1954. After several years of falling attendances the resident chaplain was withdrawn in 1983, and the church was closed.[46] In 1988 a weekly mass for army families was held in St. John's, Iceni Way.[47]

PROTESTANT NONCONFORMITY[48]

BAPTISTS. There was a small Baptist group in Colchester in the late 1630s; one of its members, Thomas Lamb, later a prominent General Baptist preacher in London, was imprisoned by the Court of High Commission in 1639 for keeping conventicles. In 1640 a meeting of *c.* 20 people led by Richard Lee, a tailor, was broken up by the borough authorities.[49] The congregation was apparently still meeting in 1642 when Anabaptists were reported in Colchester,[50] but there is no further record of Baptist activity in the 1640s.

The Fifth Monarchist Henry Jessey seems to have preached in Colchester in 1653, and he was followed in 1655 by the Baptist Thomas Tillam who had made *c.* 100 converts by May 1656.[51]

31 *Essex Recusant*, x. 79–80; Foster, *Ch. of St. James*, 7.
32 *Essex Recusant*, x. 81.
33 *White's Dir. Essex* (1848), 84.
34 Letters of Lord Stourton in St. James's presbytery.
35 Foster, *Ch. of St. James*, *passim.*
36 *Cath. Dir.* (1944, 1951); Foster, *Ch. of St. James*, 34.
37 *Cath. Dir.* (1959, 1965).
38 Ibid. (1934 and later edns.); inf. from par. priest.
39 *Cath. Dir.* (1974 and later edns.).
40 Ibid. (1900, 1902).
41 Pevsner, *Essex*, 133.
42 Foster, *Ch. of St. James*, 19.
43 *Kelly's Dir. Essex* (1908, 1910).
44 Inf. from the par. priest.
45 Foster, *Ch. of St. James*, 20–1.
46 Inf. from archives at P.R.C.C.(A)'s office, M.O.D. Chaplains, Bagshot Park.
47 Inf. from the par. priest.
48 This section was completed in 1988; an earlier draft was written in 1960 by John Mann.
49 E.R.O., D/B 5 Sb2/7, ff. 280–281v.; *Cal. S.P. Dom.* 1639–40, 286; 1640, 391; for Lamb see *Bapt. Quarterly*, N.S. xxvii. 4–8.
50 E.R.O., D/P 246/1/1; *Bapt. Quarterly*, N.S. xxvii. 5.
51 Much information on Tillam and on the Seventh Day Baptist congregation in Colchester has been supplied by Oscar Burdick, Graduate Theological Union, Berkeley, California.

Tillam's teachings were at first approved by the borough authorities, who gave him a church to preach in, but by 1657 he was preaching the seventh day (Saturday) sabbath, and opposition to his teaching grew.[52] In 1659 the Independent minister of St. Peter's, Edmund Warren, warned of the 'spreading of this Jewish leaven' among his flock.[53] Tillam was imprisoned in London in 1660,[54] and does not seem to have returned to Colchester.

Abraham Chaplin was pastor of the Colchester Seventh Day Baptists in 1690.[55] In 1706 he and two of his congregation registered their newly repaired meeting house in St. Leonard's parish. Joseph Davis the younger of Highgate (Mdx.), a member of the Seventh Day Baptist church in London, by will dated 1731 and proved in 1733, devised to Daniel Wright of Colchester, apparently a Seventh Day Baptist minister, the meeting house and burial ground at the Hythe for his life.[56] Four Colchester Particular Baptists joined a Sabbatarian congregation under John Ridley in 1739, but that may have been the one at Woodbridge (Suff.).[57] The Colchester congregation, which received a bequest in 1760, seems to have survived until *c.* 1770. The meeting house at the Hythe was still known as the Sabbatarian meeting in 1773, and a surviving member of the extinct congregation was admitted to Eld Lane church in 1774.[58]

Stephen Crisp was apparently minister of a Baptist, perhaps a General Baptist, congregation in Colchester for a short time before his conversion to the Society of Friends in 1655.[59] In 1697 Thomas Agnes represented the Colchester congregation at the General Assembly of General Baptists; he attended again in 1704 and was apparently still elder or pastor in 1715.[60] In 1729 the Particular Baptists made provision for General Baptists who wished to join their congregation, perhaps suggesting a crisis among the Generals, but the church continued in the 1730s when it was represented at the General Assembly by John Coolidge, and Charles Bulkeley seems to have been minister for a short time in the early 1740s.[61] It had been dissolved by 1755.[62]

Richard Tidmarsh, sent to Essex by the first General Assembly of Particular Baptist churches late in 1689, found some Baptists in Colchester worshipping with other dissenting congregations. His preaching persuaded them to set up a Particular Baptist church, and in 1690 their minister, John Hammond, registered a meeting house in St. Martin's Lane.[63] In 1703 Abednego Lord registered a room in East Street for Baptist services,[64] presumably for a separate congregation. In 1707 a total of 40 men and 53 women united to form one Baptist church under Cornelius Rayner, who had succeeded Hammond in 1695; the union was probably between Rayner's and Lord's congregations as Abednego Lord the elder died a member of the united church in 1718.[65] By 1712 the congregation was meeting in a house in Eld Lane in St. Botolph's parish, which was conveyed to trustees that year; it may earlier have met in a house on North Hill, perhaps the Baptist meeting house rated for church repairs in St. Peter's parish in 1702.[66]

Rayner died in 1708. He was succeeded by John Vicars, 1709–11, and Vicars by John Rootsey, 1711–38, both founder members of the Colchester church.[67] Rootsey, a wealthy man who described himself as a gentleman and who owned land in several parishes in Essex and Suffolk, had *c.* 200 hearers in 1715, but in 1721 a total of 29 members refused to associate with him and left the Eld Lane church.[68] Others followed in 1724, 1729, and 1730, and *c.* 1724 they acquired their own pastor, John Dunthorne from Hertfordshire. They had a meeting house in St. James's parish, probably in East Bay.[69] The schism, which seems to have been caused by Rootsey's personality or religious views (he may have had leanings towards Quakerism, asking to be buried very simply in the Quaker fashion), continued until after his death in 1738. In 1739 the two congregations reunited at Eld Lane under Dunthorne who remained pastor until his death in 1756.[70] In 1758 there was another schism when David Chapman, Dunthorne's assistant from 1753, led 5 men and 8 women away from Eld Lane to found a new church, meeting in Moor Lane (later Priory Street); another 4 men joined them in 1759.[71] Chapman seems to have left Colchester soon afterwards,[72] but his church continued, perhaps because its members refused to accept Dunthorne's successor, Thomas Eisdell, whose ministry was considered too 'doctrinal' by some of his own congregation. Most returned to Eld Lane early in the pastorate of Eisdell's successor Thomas Stephens, 1774–1802.[73]

Although he complained in 1777 of the railing

52 *Life and Death of Hen. Jessey* (1671), 83, 87; *Trans. Bapt. Hist. Soc.* [1st ser.], ii. 240; *First Publishers of Truth*, ed. N. Penney (Friends Hist. Soc.), 91, 96; *Diary of Ralph Josselin*, ed. A. McFarlane, 368; *Cal. S.P. Dom.* 1655–6, 340, 342.

53 E. Warren, *Jew's Sabbath Antiquated* (1659), preface (unpaginated).

54 P.R.O., SP 29/4, no. 18.

55 *Bapt. Quarterly*, N.S. xiv. 165.

56 E.R.O., D/B 5 Sr78, rot. 14; ibid. photocopy of Mill Yard Ch. Bk. pp. 235, 255; *Last Legacy of Joseph Davis senior of London*, ed. W. H. Black (1869), p. 73.

57 E.R.O., D/NB 4/26; *Bapt. Quarterly* N.S. xiv. 165.

58 E.R.O., D/ABR 25, f. 71; D/P 245/8/3; D/NB 4/3.

59 S. Tuke, *Memoirs of the Life of Stephen Crisp*, p. ix.

60 *Mins. of Gen. Assembly of Gen. Baptists*, ed. W. T. Whitley (Bapt. Hist. Soc.), i. 49–50, 91; *Trans. Bapt. Hist. Soc.* [1st ser.], ii. 98.

61 E.R.O., D/NB 4/1, p. 71; *Mins. of Gen. Assembly of Gen. Baptists*, ii. 12, 23, 37, 41; E. Spurrier, *Memorials of Eld Lane Baptist Ch.* 30–1.

62 *Mins. of Gen. Assembly of Gen. Baptists*, ii. 100.

63 *Memorials of Eld Lane*, 11–12; E.R.O., D/B 5 Sr53, rot. 40. For the history of Eld Lane church see also H. Spyvee, *Colch. Baptist Church–The First 300 Years 1689–1989* (1989).

64 E.R.O., D/B 5 Sb4/3, f. 10.

65 Ibid. D/NB 4/1, pp. 1, 9; *Memorials of Eld Lane*, 12, 15–16.

66 E.R.O., D/NB 4/1, pp. 34–5; ibid. T/B 286; *Memorials of Eld Lane*, 18.

67 E.R.O., D/NB 4/1, pp. 1, 12, 17; D/NB 4/24.

68 Dr. Williams Libr., MS. 38.4, p. 40; E.R.O., D/NB 4/1, p. 57; D/DHt F1.

69 E.R.O., D/NB 4/1, p. 65; D/NB 4/2 (unpaginated); D/NB 4/24; D/B 5 Sr174, rot. 14; *Memorials of Eld Lane*, 21.

70 E.R.O., D/DHt F1; D/NB 4/2; D/NB 4/35; *Memorials of Eld Lane*, 24.

71 E.R.O., D/NB 4/1, pp. 81–3; D/NB 4/3, s.a. 1744; D/NB 4/26.

72 Ibid. D/NB 4/35.

73 Ibid. D/NB 4/3; *Memorials of Eld Lane*, 25–6.

spirit which had prevailed since the beginning of the church's troubles,[74] Stephens, who founded the Essex Baptist Association and was an early supporter of overseas missions, was a successful pastor at Eld Lane, starting a mission at Mile End in 1796.[75] In 1795 the meeting house was enlarged, and a baptistry was added. Earlier baptisms had taken place publicly at Rootsey's mill (Distillery Pond); they had provided opportunities for evangelization but had often provoked jeering from the large crowds which gathered to watch.[76]

Argument over Stephens's successor, perhaps exacerbated by doctrinal differences within the congregation which in 1796 was described as 'Arminians, Methodists, or Baptists', led to another schism in 1803 when 16 people followed an unsuccessful candidate to a meeting room in St. Runwald's parish. Most of the seceders returned in 1804 at the start of the pastorate of George Pritchard, 1804–12.[77] By 1811 there was considerable dissatisfaction with Pritchard's ministry, and a dispute that year over his refusal to allow the 'antinomian' John Church to preach at Eld Lane caused several members to secede in 1812 and join a new church in Stanwell Street on St. John's green.[78] Numbers of both members and hearers increased under Pritchard's successor George Francies, 1815–36, although his claim to have a membership of 800–900 in 1829 was much exaggerated; there were 165 members in 1838. The mission at Mile End was reregistered in 1816 and one at Lexden in 1821.[79] In 1834 a new chapel, to seat 1,000, was built on a site adjoining the old one, largely at the expense of Benjamin Nice, one of the deacons.[80]

For 30 years after Francies's resignation in 1836, Eld Lane suffered from an ineffective ministry due partly to the ill health of successive pastors and partly perhaps to continuing doctrinal differences. The presumably extreme views of Thomas Rust, pastor 1838–41, caused the Congregational minister to withdraw from the joint missionary prayer meetings which had previously been held.[81] Rust was supported by most of his congregation, but in 1848 dissatisfaction with his successor led 28 members, apparently believers in closed communion, to resign to form a new church in Military Road.[82] In spite of those and other resignations, Eld Lane reported congregations on Census Sunday 1851 of 350 in the morning, 600 in the afternoon, and 200 in the evening, in addition to 60 Sunday school children.[83] Moves towards strict communion in 1856 and 1857 led to further resignations, and in 1858 there were only 144 church members.[84]

The church was revived by E. Spurrier who served, first as assistant and then as pastor, from 1866 to 1908. He reorganized the church, introducing the office of elder in 1876 to help with pastoral work, and he was almost certainly responsible for the adoption of open communion in 1867. By 1883 meetings were being held at Parsons Heath and at a chapel in Ipswich Road, and missions were opened at Parsons Heath in 1885[85] and at Blackheath in 1889. A mission room in Magdalen Street was in use in 1892. At Eld Lane itself a Sunday school building erected in 1868 was extended in 1889. Spurrier was twice president of the Essex Federation of Free Churches and twice of the Essex Baptist Union.[86] Church membership rose from 212 in 1888 to 281 in 1893 and reached a peak of 430 in 1959. The church's success was at least partly due to the work of P. H. Warwick Bailey, pastor 1944–72 and mayor of Colchester in 1949.[87] It was still flourishing in 1988. The missions at Parsons Heath and Blackheath were then independent churches.

The church built in 1834 was restored in 1883 to plans by the Colchester architect F. E. Morris; a vestry, a library, and a Sunday school room, designed by J. F. Goodey, were added on the west side of the church in 1889.[88] The plain building, of white brick with a pedimented front,[89] was thoroughly renovated in 1978.

A church in Stanwell Street, St. John's green, was built in 1812 by a group of Independents and Baptists, some of them seceders from Eld Lane. The congregation, which had followed John Church, had worshipped in a barn in St. Mary Magdalen's parish earlier in 1812. It adopted a Calvinist declaration of faith in 1813.[90] The church suffered from financial problems as well as from tensions between Baptists and Independents, but it was held together by its pastor, Henry Dowling, who preached three times on Sundays and held weekly services in the town and surrounding villages. He claimed a congregation of *c.* 400 in 1829, although in 1833 there seem to have been only *c.* 50 members. Dowling resigned in 1834 to become a missionary in Tasmania, and in 1835 the church was dissolved.[91]

The chapel was bought by William Day, a Baptist member of the original congregation, and reopened as a Particular Baptist church. In 1851 congregations of 50 in the morning, 90 in the afternoon, and 57 in the evening were reported.[92] Numbers fell after the resignation in 1864 of the pastor who had served since 1835, but by 1872 the church had revived sufficiently to erect a new building.[93] About 1900 some members seem to have seceded to form Providence church, Burling-

74 E.R.O., D/NB 4/3.

75 Ibid.; P.R.O., RG 31/3; *Bapt. Quarterly*, N.S. xi. 55–6.

76 E.R.O., D/NB 4/3, s.a. 1778, 1780, 1785, 1790, 1795; *Memorials of Eld Lane*, 37.

77 E.R.O., D/NB 4/4; *Memorials of Eld Lane*, 50; P.R.O., RG 31/3.

78 E.R.O., D/NB 4/5; P.R.O., RG 31/3; *Memorials of Eld Lane*, 51; *Bapt. Mag.* (1853), 4.

79 P.R.O., RG 31/3.

80 E.R.O., D/NB 4/6; ibid. Q/CR 3/2/31; ibid. Acc. C281, item 1, p. 35; *Memorials of Eld Lane*, 52–3; E. A. Blaxill, *Nonconf. Ch. of Colch.* 15.

81 E.R.O., D/NB 4/6; D/NB 4/29.

82 Ibid. D/NB 4/6; *Memorials of Eld Lane*, 55.

83 P.R.O., HO 129/8/204.

84 E.R.O., D/NB 4/6.

85 G.R.O. Worship Reg. no. 29134.

86 E.R.O., D/NB 4/15; D/NB 4/16; D/NB 4/35; *Memorials of Eld Lane*, 56; Blaxill, *Nonconf. Ch. of Colch.* 15; *E.R.* xxvii. 146–7; *Essex Tel.* 18 July, 1884.

87 *Essex Bapt. Union Rep.* (1887/8 and later edns.); *E.C.S.* 13 Apr. 1973; *Essex Chron.* 18 July, 1984.

88 E.R.O., D/NB 4/42.

89 Pevsner, *Essex*, 137; *E.C.S.* 14 Apr. 1978. A block of offices and meeting rooms was added on the east side of the church in 1991: *Evening Gaz.* 30 Sept. 1991; below, pl. facing p. 345.

90 P.R.O., RG 31/3; E.R.O., D/NB 6.

91 E.R.O., D/NB 6; ibid. Q/CR 3/2/32; *Life of Hen. Dowling* (Melbourne, priv. print. 1871), 28: copy in E.C.L. Colch.

92 P.R.O., HO 129/8/204; E.R.O., D/NB 6.

93 E.R.O., T/Z 8, no. 36; *Kelly's Dir. Essex* (1890).

ton Road,[94] but they returned to St. John's green in 1910. The church was without a pastor from 1926 to 1936 and again from 1946. It closed in 1955. The building was sold in 1957 to the Elim Pentecostal church.[95]

In 1961 Strict Baptists started meeting at the former Town Mission hall in King Harold Road. A school-hall and classrooms designed by H. P. Stevens, a church member, were built in Prettygate Road in 1964, partly with money from the sale of the St. John's green church. A permanent church was built in 1976.[96]

The believers in closed communion who seceded from Eld Lane in 1848 built the Ebenezer chapel in Military Road, and in 1851 reported congregations of 100 in the morning and 150 in the afternoon. Another Baptist congregation of 30 in the morning, 50 in the afternoon, and 35 in the evening, led by a shoemaker, James Waterman, and meeting in a warehouse in the same road, had been licensed in 1850. It dissolved later in 1851, and its members seem to have joined the Stanwell Street church.[97] In 1857 and 1859 the congregation from the Ebenezer chapel met in the Bible Room in Lion Walk. It seems to have dissolved by 1866, when a new Calvinistic or Particular Baptist church was formed in the Bible Room with Waterman as minister. It continued until 1874 when financial difficulties and declining numbers forced the trustees to sell the room.[98]

SOCIETY OF FRIENDS. The Quaker missionary James Parnell visited Colchester early in 1655 and made several converts, including John Furley, a member of a prominent Colchester family, and Stephen Crisp, a Baptist who became a leading Quaker in the town and a missionary in England, Holland, and Germany.[99] Parnell was arrested at Coggeshall later in 1655 and imprisoned in Colchester Castle where he died the following year.[1] Late in 1655 another missionary, Martha Simmonds from London, walked through Colchester barefoot in sackcloth and ashes.[2] By *c.* 1660 the Quakers in Colchester seem to have been organized into a two weeks meeting and, with Quakers from neighbouring villages, into a monthly meeting. They acquired their first property in 1659 when Thomas Bayles gave them a burial ground in Moor Lane (later Priory Street).[3]

Persecution of the Colchester Quakers, mainly for their refusal to pay church rates or tithes, was particularly fierce during the mayoralty of William Moore who in 1663–4 had the meeting house boarded up and then ordered troops to break up Quaker meetings in the street, beating and imprisoning many of those attending; he again prevented Quakers from using their meeting house during his second mayoralty in 1670–1. They suffered further violent persecution in 1685, apparently at the instigation of the town clerk, Samuel Shaw; meetings were broken up and John Furley was fined for preaching.[4]

The Quakers met in a rented house or room until 1663 when the lease expired; in spite of the persecution they were then suffering, in 1663–4 they built a large meeting house[5] on a site adjoining St. Martin's church and extending from West to East Stockwell Street, including the later Quaker Alley. It was acquired by the Quaker Thomas Bayles in 1663 and was sold to trustees for the Colchester two weeks meeting in 1672. It was enlarged in 1672–3.[6] In 1683 the Friends bought St. Helen's chapel in Maidenburgh Street which became known as the little meeting house, but evening meetings in private houses continued until 1695.[7] William Penn attended an evening meeting in Jonathan Furley's house in 1677.[8] In 1701 the meeting house in St. Martin's Lane was enlarged and St. Helen's chapel repaired and licensed as a meeting house.[9]

In 1702 Colchester was still seen by opponents as a centre of Quakerism, although membership of the meetings was probably already declining from its peak in the 1680s.[10] Joseph Besse, schoolmaster and author of *The Sufferings of the People called Quakers*, was among the five Colchester Quakers who affirmed instead of taking the oaths of allegiance and abjuration in 1716, and as many as 47 Quakers affirmed instead of taking the oaths in 1723.[11] Distraints, sometimes punitive, for unpaid church rates were taken fairly regularly throughout the 18th century, mainly from the leading and wealthier members of the community like Richard Freshfield, Matthew Hawkins, and John Kendall (1726–1815), a benefactor to the Colchester poor and a missionary in England, Scotland, and Holland.[12] Quakers also suffered, presumably from mobs, for refusing to illuminate their houses on coronation days.[13]

The two weeks and the monthly meetings maintained their separate existence until 1760, although there was a considerable overlap in membership and both used the same meeting

94 *Kelly's Dir. Essex* (1902).

95 Inf. from Pastor P. A. Grist (1984) and Revd. G. Stormont (1959).

96 G.R.O. Worship Reg. nos. 69075, 69508; *Colch. Expr.* 20 Feb. 1964; *Colch. Gaz.* 24 Sept. 1976.

97 E.R.O., D/NB 4/6; ibid. T/Z 8, no. 36; P.R.O., HO 129/8/204. The location of the Ebenezer chapel is confirmed by E.R.O., D/NB 4/6.

98 E.R.O., D/NB 4/6; D/DU 559/1, 27; cf. ibid. T/Z 8, no. 68.

99 *First Publishers of Truth*, ed. N. Penney (Friends Hist. Soc.), 91–2, 96; S. Tuke, *Memoirs of Life of Stephen Crisp* (1824).

1 J. Besse, *Sufferings of Quakers* (1733), i. 87–91; B.L. Stowe MS. 834, ff. 22–3.

2 *Jnl. Friends' Hist. Soc.* liii. 31–5, 315–16.

3 *Stephen Crisp and his Correspondents*, ed. C. Fell Smith, 48; S. H. G. Fitch, *Colch. Quakers*, 107.

4 E.R.O., D/DRg 1/186; D/B 5 Sb2/9, f. 132; *Cal. S.P. Venetian*, 1661–4, 286; *First Publishers of Truth*, 94–8; Fitch, *Colch. Quakers*, 50–4.

5 *First Publishers of Truth*, 94–8, 100.

6 E.R.O., T/A 424/7/1; T/A 424/3/1; ibid. D/DSb T16; *First Publishers of Truth*, 95.

7 *First Publishers of Truth*, 49; E.R.O., T/A 424/7/1, printed in Fitch, *Colch. Quakers*, 42.

8 *E.R.* xliv. 174.

9 E.R.O., T/A 424/7/1.

10 F. Bugg, *Quakerism Deeply Wounded* (1702); idem, *Quakerism Drooping* (1703): copies in E.C.L. Colch.; Fitch, *Colch. Quakers*, 59–62.

11 E.R.O., D/B 5 Sr108, rot. 9; D/B 5 Sb5/1, pp. 29, 320–42; *D.N.B.* s.v. Besse.

12 E.R.O., T/A 424/4/1–2; Fitch, *Colch. Quakers*, 80–1; below, Charities.

13 E.R.O., T/A 424/4/1, p. 42.

house. Friction between them on matters of jurisdiction was first recorded in 1711, and grew so bad that in 1723 the two weeks meeting ceased to send representatives to the monthly meeting. In 1727 the two weeks meeting similarly ceased to send representatives to the Essex quarterly meeting, recognizing only the yearly meeting in London. The effect of the withdrawal of the two weeks meeting was to reduce the monthly meeting, which was left with only the small rural preparative meetings, to insignificance. Relations were presumably made worse in the period 1730–2 by the behaviour of Benjamin Lay who was accepted by the monthly meeting after he had been expelled from the two weeks meeting for disorderly conduct. The rift was healed in 1760 when the two weeks meeting was reconstituted as a monthly meeting for the town only, the two remaining rural meetings becoming the Manningtree monthly meeting. The two monthly meetings merged in 1772.[14]

The number of Quakers in Colchester and its neighbourhood continued to decline throughout the 18th century and the figures of 80 members and 20 other attenders reported in 1829 may have been fairly accurate.[15] Nevertheless, between 1800 and 1802 the meeting house in Quaker Alley was remodelled and extended at a cost of *c.* £900, part of which was raised by selling St. Helen's chapel with its associated five almshouses and a further four almshouses adjoining it on the south, and the disused burial grounds in Moor Lane and Almshouse Lane. From 1826 to 1835 the Colchester monthly meeting had to be subsidized by the other Essex meetings.[16] In 1851 the meeting house could hold 767, but the congregations on Census Sunday were only 58 in the morning and 48 in the afternoon.[17]

Curiously the revival of Quakerism in Colchester seems to have coincided with the burning down of the meeting house in 1871. A new meeting house on a more convenient site in Sir Isaac's Walk opened in 1872 and was remodelled in 1892. In 1881 the Sudbury monthly meeting was united to the Colchester meeting for religious matters. A mission was started at Lexden before 1889 and another, apparently short-lived, at Mile End in 1893. Membership of the Colchester monthly meeting increased to a peak of 193 in 1924.[18] The meeting house in Sir Isaac's Walk, which had proved expensive to maintain, was sold in 1938 and a new one built in Shewell Road.[19] That site was compulsorily purchased for redevelopment in 1974 and the Friends moved to St. Mary's House, Church Street, which they remodelled and extended.[20] In 1984 there were 150 members.[21]

Colchester Quakers benefited from several charities. Five houses, part of the St. Helen's chapel estate bought in 1683, were used as almshouses in the 18th century. Four small almshouses adjoining them on the south were built by Stephen Crisp or his wife Gertrude Losevelt for poor widows. All nine houses were sold in 1802.[22] Thomas Braybrook by will dated 1669 left to Quaker trustees three houses in East Street, but possession was not obtained until after his widow's death in 1708. By 1784 the houses were not worth repair; the site was sold and the proceeds added to the monthly meeting's funds for the poor.[23] In 1700 Robert Nicholas was allowed land in St. Helen's chapel yard to build four houses for poor Friends to live in, and the houses were built, partly by subscription, in 1701.[24] By 1837 the houses seem to have been let and the rent applied to the relief of the poor. They were demolished and the site sold after the earthquake of 1884, and the proceeds were invested for poor Quakers.[25] Giles Sayer, by will proved 1708, left to his executor Richard Ashby 3 a. of pasture near Magdalen field for the benefit of poor Quakers, and a £50 mortgage interest in land in Peldon and West Mersea for poor Quaker widows. In 1709 Ashby conveyed the land in Peldon and West Mersea as well as that in Colchester to Quaker trustees.[26] Mary Cockerill, by will dated 1717, left the rents and profits of a house, later two houses, in East Stockwell Street to the women's meeting. The building was sold to the town council in 1956 and the proceeds invested for women Friends.[27] Benjamin Lay, by will dated 1731, left £100 to the Coggeshall monthly meeting to assist emigrants to America, or in default of suitable emigrants to help poor members of the Colchester monthly meeting. The interest was received by the Colchester monthly meeting in 1962.[28] Mary Liversidge and Joan Bloys, by wills dated 1814, and Elizabeth Davison, by will dated 1823, gave £50, £19 19*s.*, and £100 respectively to the monthly meeting for poor Friends. All three legacies were invested in 1835.[29] James Hurnard in 1878 gave £1,000 in railway stock, the income to meet the general expenses of the monthly meeting.[30] Wilson Marriage, by will proved 1932, left £500 to build and endow a caretaker's and meeting house by the burial ground in Roman Road. In 1964 the charities produced a total income of £79 0*s.* 10*d.*[31]

INDEPENDENTS and PRESBYTERIANS, later CONGREGATIONALISTS and UNITED REFORMED CHURCH. Owen Stockton, the ejected town lecturer, preached in his house until he was forced to leave Colchester in 1665. In 1672 he was licensed as an Independent teacher in a meeting house in St. Martin's Lane in Colchester, and as a Presbyterian preacher in Ipswich and Hadleigh (Suff.).[32] Edmund Warren, the

14 Fitch, *Colch. Quakers*, 10–20, 82–3.
15 E.R.O., Q/CR 3/2/29.
16 Fitch, *Colch. Quakers*, 30, 94–5, 107–8, 114–15.
17 P.R.O., HO 129/8/204.
18 Fitch, *Colch. Quakers*, 31–2, 35, 65.
19 Ibid. 101.
20 *E.C.S.* 9 Nov. 1984.
21 *Colch. Gaz.* 24 Oct. 1984.
22 Fitch, *Colch. Quakers*, 114–15.
23 Ibid. 115.
24 E.R.O., T/A/424 7/1.
25 Fitch, *Colch. Quakers*, 116.
26 E.R.O., T/A 424/3/8.
27 Char. Com. file; Fitch, *Colch. Quakers*, 117–18.
28 Fitch, *Colch. Quakers*, 84.
29 Char. Com. file.
30 Fitch, *Colch. Quakers*, 118.
31 Char. Com. file.
32 Dr. Williams's Libr., MS. 24.7; *Cal. S.P. Dom.* 1671–2, 332–3; 1672, 41, 378; T. W. Davids, *Annals of Nonconf. in Essex*, 370.

ejected minister of St. Peter's, was licensed in the same year to preach to a Presbyterian congregation in John Rayner's house.[33] Independents and Presbyterians seem to have worshipped together in the 1670s and 1680s, Stockton and his successor William Folkes alternating as preachers with Warren. The joint congregation was later said to have met for a time in a room in the castle.[34] In 1691 Folkes's successor as Independent minister, William Rawlinson, built a meeting house in Moor Lane (later Priory Street), and in 1693 Warren's successor, Daniel Gilson, registered a newly built Presbyterian meeting house in St. Helen's Lane.[35]

Rawlinson's successor John Gledhill apparently found the Independent congregation very divided when he arrived in 1693,[36] possibly partly because of the recent split with the Presbyterians and partly because of internal disputes: another Independent congregation in Colchester, presumably a breakaway group, registered two meeting houses in St. Nicholas's parish in 1711.[37] Gledhill revived the Moor Lane congregation, claiming to have 600 hearers in 1715.[38] Among the members of the 18th-century congregation were Arthur Winsley and Jeremiah Daniell, both of whom, as occasional conformists, became mayors of Colchester.[39] Winsley apparently paid for a rebuilding of the meeting house in 1735.[40] In 1764, at the start of the ministry of John Crisp, members and occasional communicants totalled 105.[41] Land in Lion Walk was bought in 1763, and in 1765–6 a new meeting house was built there.[42]

By 1773 a substantial portion of the congregation, including four deacons, was dissatisfied with Crisp's preaching, which they found insufficiently evangelical, experimental, and spiritual. The minister resigned, but further disagreements arose over the choice of his successor.[43] By 1809, possibly because of the minister's illness, numbers had fallen to 66 members and 12 occasional communicants.[44] The church revived under John Saville, 1809–28, who registered a mission room in St. Leonard's parish in 1822.[45] There were 110 members at Lion Walk by the end of his ministry and his successor claimed a congregation of 1,000 in 1829.[46] By 1828 there were again dissensions in the church. Part of the fault may have lain with Saville, whose next ministry, at Braintree, ended unhappily after only two years, but the differences seem to have been exacerbated by the behaviour of Joseph Herrick, the minister of the St. Helen's Lane church.[47] The resignation of Saville's successor, Henry March, in 1839 was precipitated by an abusive letter from Herrick, but there had for some time been 'painful hindrances' to his ministry, including disputes which led to the departure of some of the congregation to St. Helen's Lane *c.* 1836.[48] In spite of the difficulties, membership of Lion Walk increased to 168 during March's ministry.[49]

After a two-year vacancy Thomas W. Davids, probably Lion Walk's most outstanding minister, was appointed, and served until 1874. The early years of his ministry were not easy, and in 1843 and 1844 a total of 27 members resigned to form a new church, later Headgate Congregational church. Nevertheless by 1845 membership at Lion Walk had risen to 215 and preaching stations had been opened at Shrub End (1842), Harwich Road, Greenstead (1844), and Old Heath (*c.* 1845). There was a church Benevolent Society; a teachers' Bible class had been started in 1841 and a lay preachers' association in 1844. Another mission was opened at the Hythe *c.* 1846.[50] On Census Sunday 1851 below-average congregations of 588 in the morning, 681 at a children's service in the afternoon, and 325 in the evening were recorded at Lion Walk, and congregations of 91 at Shrub End, 100 at the Hythe, and 115 at Greenstead. Membership of Lion Walk rose to 253 in 1855.[51] By 1858 the chapel was in need of improvement, and in 1863 it was completely rebuilt to designs by Frederick Barnes of Ipswich. The 'popery' of the Early English architecture, notably its spire, aroused opposition and provoked at least one resignation,[52] but to those who had planned it the new building symbolized Lion Walk's growing importance in the life of the town.[53] Davids himself was active in nonconformist affairs both in the town and in the county, being secretary of the Essex Congregational Union 1858–73, but he became known best as author of *Annals of Evangelical Nonconformity in Essex* published in 1863.[54]

The remainder of the 19th century and the early 20th were marked by shorter ministries and long vacancies during which the deacons led the church. In 1880 a group of church members, led by the deacons E. F. Blaxill and J. Barber, bought a site extending from Culver Street to the church for new Sunday school buildings which were erected in 1887–8.[55] The congregation was enlarged by a secession from Headgate

33 *Cal. S.P. Dom.* 1672–3, 176.
34 Davids, *Nonconf. in Essex*, 374.
35 E.R.O., D/B 5 Sr57, rot. 21; Fitch, *Colch. Quakers*, 97.
36 E. A. Blaxill, *Hist. Lion Walk Cong. Ch.* 13.
37 Guildhall MS. 9579/1.
38 Dr. Williams's Libr., MS. 38.4, p. 37.
39 Blaxill, *Hist. Lion Walk*, 9–10.
40 E.R.O., D/B 5 Sb5/3, f. 12.
41 E.R.O., Acc. C250, Lion Walk reg. 1702–1840, ff. 1–2v.
42 Ibid. Lion Walk misc. papers *c.* 1765–1935.
43 Ibid.
44 Ibid. Lion Walk reg. 1702–1840, f. 12.
45 P.R.O., RG 31/3.
46 E.R.O., Acc. C250, Lion Walk reg. 1702–1840, f. 12; ibid. Q/CR 3/2/35.
47 Ibid. Acc. C250, Lion Walk ch. mtgs. 1809–39; Blaxill, *Hist. Lion Walk*, 28.
48 E.R.O., Acc. C210, J. B. Harvey Colln. vii, p. 114: cutting from *Essex Standard*, 8 Mar. 1839; ibid. Acc. C250, *Essex Standard*, obit. of Herrick.
49 Ibid. Acc. C250: Lion Walk ch. mtgs. 1809–39; Blaxill, *Hist. Lion Walk*, 32.
50 T. W. Davids, *Substance of a Statement to Members of the Church of Christ in Lion Walk* (priv. print. [1845]): copy in E.C.L. Colch.; Blaxill, *Hist. Lion Walk*, 32–4; idem, *Nonconf. Chs. of Colch.* 23.
51 P.R.O., HO 129/8/204; Blaxill, *Hist. Lion Walk*, 41.
52 *Essex Tel.* 25 Oct. 1862; J. A. Tabor, *Nonconf. Protest against the Popery of Modern Dissent* (Colch. priv. print. 1863): copy in E.R.O., D/NC 56/6/2.
53 Blaxill, *Nonconf. Ch. of Colch.* 23; idem, *Hist. Lion Walk*, 32–4.
54 *D.N.B.*; Blaxill, *Hist. Lion Walk*, 47; *Essex Tel.* 22 Apr. 1884, cutting in E.R.O., Acc. C250, Lion Walk misc. papers *c.* 1765–1935.
55 Blaxill, *Hist. Lion Walk*, 54–5.

Essex and Colchester Hospital, *c.* 1880

Kendall's Almshouses in the early 20th century

Eld Lane, 1951
with the Darcy almshouses demolished in 1962

Lion Walk Congregational Church, *c.* 1864

Eld Lane Baptist Church, 1994

Lion Walk Congregational Chapel, *c.* 1860

Culver Street Methodist Church, *c.* 1900

church in 1881,[56] and Lion Walk continued to flourish, particularly under Frank Leggatt, 1902–7.[57]

The 20th century has been marked by co-operation between Lion Walk and other Congregational churches in Colchester, although union with Headgate church was rejected in 1947.[58] The Hythe mission chapel closed in 1938,[59] but the other missions, including one at Lexden founded in 1931, flourished and became independent churches. By 1975 congregations were as large as 300, and total membership was over 400. The church building aroused controversy again in 1975 when plans, carried out in 1985, were revealed to redevelop the site with shops on the ground floor and a church above.[60]

The meeting house in St. Helen's Lane, later known as the old meeting, was described as Presbyterian in 1715 when Daniel Gilson was said to have 600 hearers.[61] Gilson, who served from 1692 until his death in 1728, encountered some opposition from a party within the congregation, perhaps the unlicensed group to whom John Richardson, apparently a Presbyterian, was preaching in 1700.[62] His successor John Tren (d. 1738) was much respected, and James Throgmorton, minister 1742–54, was known for his moderation and goodness.[63] Throgmorton and his predecessors were Presbyterians, but his successors tended towards Unitarianism.[64] Nevertheless in 1796 the congregation called Isaac Taylor, an Independent, to the ministry, and he made a Calvinistic confession of faith at his ordination.[65] Although he had some success with well attended evening lectures and with village preaching, Taylor encountered opposition from the Unitarian element in his congregation; numbers declined, and he resigned in 1810.[66] The support of some of the congregation for the antinomian John Church, who preached at St. Helen's Lane in 1810–11, led to further dissension and the secession of some members to the new Stanwell Street church in 1812.[67] Matters came to a head early in the ministry of Joseph Herrick who came to the church in 1814. In 1816 the Unitarian trustees removed the roof of the meeting house, forcing Herrick and his supporters to meet in the Lion Walk chapel or in Herrick's own house. Herrick, supported by 28 or more members of the congregation, opened his own chapel on the other side of St. Helen's Lane at the end of 1816. The trustees reopened the old chapel, probably in 1817, as a Unitarian chapel, but the congregation was small and the chapel closed in 1823.[68]

The first 20 years of Herrick's ministry at the new chapel although successful were stormy, perhaps reflecting a crisis in Congregationalism in Colchester as a whole as well as the personality of the minister.[69] Besides disputes with 'impertinent' and 'obstructive' members of his own congregation there was friction with the Lion Walk church, for the first time facing direct competition from another flourishing Congregational body. Nevertheless missions were opened in Lexden in 1821 and in Barrack Street in 1824.[70] The St. Helen's Lane chapel was enlarged in 1824, but in 1828 and 1829 there was further trouble with 'antinomians', which seems to have culminated in the removal of some members of the congregation to the Stanwell Street church. A secession to St. Helen's Lane from Lion Walk church led to the further enlargement of the chapel in 1836; the work included the building of a new front on Stockwell Street, and the chapel was thereafter known as Stockwell Street chapel. The enlargement of the chapel resulted in a debt which was used by some of the trustees and deacons, who were opposed to Herrick's ministry, to gain control of the chapel.[71] After protracted wrangling the mortgagees, who supported Herrick's opponents, seized the chapel for debt in 1843, and Herrick and his supporters were forced to agree to buy the chapel back by paying off the mortgage, which they did in 1844. During the dispute some members of the congregation seem to have moved to Lion Walk chapel. A vestry was added to the chapel in 1845, without incurring further debt. In 1851 Herrick claimed a connexion of *c.* 1,500.[72]

Herrick remained at Stockwell Street, where he was long remembered as a gifted preacher,[73] until his death in 1865. The remainder of his pastorate was peaceful. His successor T. Batty, 1866–1906, built new schoolrooms in 1868, remodelled the chapel in 1875, and established a mission in Mile End, where a chapel was built in 1880.[74] For most of the earlier 20th century the church suffered from short pastorates and frequent vacancies. From 1946 to 1950 the church was served jointly with Shrub End Congregational church, but plans for uniting the two churches were not carried out. After 1950 Stockwell Street had no minister, and by 1960 its membership had fallen to 20.[75] It closed in 1966. Despite public protests the building remained empty until it was sold in 1979 for conversion to offices.[76]

In the late 1830s there was considerable dissatisfaction with both the existing Congregational churches in Colchester.[77] Between 1837 and 1841

56 J. W. Newby, *Story of Headgate*, 31.
57 Blaxill, *Hist. Lion Walk*, 56–65.
58 *Lion Walk Ch. Mag.* Dec. 1947; for the history of the church in the 20th century see A. Duncan, *Onflowing Stream 1935–1992* (1992).
59 Inf. (1959) from the Revd. A. E. Simmonds.
60 *E.C.S.* 26 Sept. 1975; 11 Mar. 1977; 1 Apr. 1977.
61 Dr. Williams's Libr., MS. 38.4, p. 37.
62 E.R.O., D/B 5 Sr64, rot. 20d.; for Richardson see Davids, *Annals of Nonconf. in Essex*, 512.
63 *Trans. Cong. Hist. Soc.* vii. 254; E.R.O., D/P 246/1/5, 25 Jan. 1754.
64 *Trans. Cong. Hist. Soc.* vii. 257.
65 D. M. Armitage, *Taylors of Ongar*, 34; E.R.O., D/NB 4/3, Eld Lane Baptist Ch. Bk.
66 *Taylors of Ongar*, 35; *Trans. Cong. Hist. Soc.* vii. 258.
67 *Trans. Cong. Hist. Soc.* vii. 258; above, this section, Baptists.
68 *Trans. Cong. Hist. Soc.* vii. 259–60; P.R.O., RG 31/3; J. Herrick, *Immanuel* (priv. print. 1819), pp. xv–xix: copy in E.C.L. Colch.; *Trans. Unit. Hist. Soc.* v. 332; xviii. 236; cf. T. Cromwell, *Hist. Colch.* 405.
69 *Colch. Hist. Studies*, ed. D. Stephenson, 22–32.
70 P.R.O., RG 31/3.
71 E.R.O., Acc. C210, J. B. Harvey Colln. vii, p. 120.
72 P.R.O., HO 129/8/204.
73 Press cutting of May 1914, in E.C.L. Colch.
74 E.R.O., Stockwell St. Cong. Ch. Gen. Cttee. Min. Bk. 1873–1906, *passim*; Blaxill, *Nonconf. Ch. of Colch.* 14.
75 Blaxill, *Nonconf. Ch. of Colch.* 14; *Trans. Cong. Soc.* vii. 254; inf. (1960) from the church secretary.
76 *E.C.S.* 13 Oct. 1978; 2 July 1982.
77 *Colch. Hist. Studies*, 22–32.

five meeting places were registered by groups mainly composed of members or former members of Lion Walk, Stockwell Street, and the dissolved Baptist and Independent congregation at Stanwell Street. Samuel Hubbard, a deacon at Stockwell Street in 1839–40, was minister of congregations in St. Peter's parish in 1839 and St. Martin's parish in 1841.[78] Some of the registrations may have been of the meetings in private houses to which Joseph Herrick of Stockwell Street objected in 1840, but in 1843 several of those involved in the earlier meetings joined in the foundation of a new Congregational church. The leading members of the group were the surgeon David Morris who had resigned from Lion Walk in 1842, the newspaper proprietor and local politician J. B. Harvey, the solicitor H. S. Goody who had also been a member of Lion Walk, and the solicitor and Liberal activist F. B. Philbrick. They met for a short time in a room in the Mechanics' Institution before building their new chapel at Headgate, designed by W. F. Poulton, early in 1844.[79] Alexander Fraser, the first minister, was called in 1844 by 30 members of the new church. Membership increased rapidly in the first few years, 13 people being admitted in 1844 (only 5 of them from Lion Walk church), 22 in 1845, and 17 in 1846.[80] Relations with Lion Walk were cordial throughout the 19th century, but those with Stockwell Street were less close.[81]

By 1865 open-air services were being held in neighbouring villages, and in 1868 it was necessary to increase the accommodation at Headgate itself by building side galleries.[82] In 1881, however, a dispute between the hitherto popular minister Edmund Miller and his deacons led to the departure of over 40 members, including J. B. Harvey and H. S. Goody.[83] The church recovered in the remainder of Miller's ministry and those of his successors, membership reaching a peak of 225 in 1902 after a successful mission by 'Gypsy' Smith in 1901. New schoolrooms were built in 1903.[84]

In the earlier 20th century the church was strongly pacifist, 12 members being conscientious objectors during the First World War. In 1933 as many as 50 members were pacifists and in 1939 the church published *A Christian Protest against Conscription* written by the minister Wallis Hayward.[85] Membership of Headgate, as of other churches, declined in the earlier 20th century, but a proposed union with Lion Walk was rejected in 1947. The church was gutted by fire in 1968 but was restored and reopened in 1970.[86] In 1974 it was closed and the congregation joined with that of the parish church of St. Mary's-at-the-Walls to build Christ Church, Ireton Road, which in 1988 was shared by the two congregations.[87] The old church was sold to the Labour party.

The church in King Harold Road, Shrub End, remained a mission of Lion Walk until 1946 when it was joined with Stockwell Street in a joint pastorate. By 1948 Shrub End was almost self-supporting and became an independent church. In 1955 a new church, built by the Essex Congregational Union, was opened in Plume Avenue.[88]

The chapel in Harwich Road, Greenstead, was enlarged in 1877. In 1936 the assistant minister at Lion Walk was given sole charge of the chapel, which was rebuilt in 1938. The church became self-supporting in 1946 and fully independent in 1948.[89] By 1985 the congregation had united with that of Headgate at Christ Church, Ireton Road.

The mission at Old Heath seems to have been closed before 1851, but it was later reopened and was enlarged in 1888 and again in 1899; in 1960 it was still a mission of Lion Walk,[90] but by 1985 it was independent and unlike Lion Walk had remained Congregational. The mission hall at Lexden, founded in 1931, was replaced by a permanent church in 1936.[91] In 1985 it was an independent Congregational church.

WESLEYAN METHODISTS. The Wesleyan preacher Laurence Coughton came to Colchester in the summer of 1758, and by the time John Wesley visited the town in October that year the society had a membership of 120, despite fierce opposition from other ministers and clergy. Early Wesleyan meetings were often disrupted by the mob who let birds into the meeting room to put out the candles, and on one occasion drove a donkey into the room. Wesley visited Colchester several times in 1759, often preaching on St. John's green because the hired meeting room at the bottom of North Hill was too small. On his advice the Colchester Methodists built their own meeting house in Maidenburgh Street, which was licensed in 1761. Wesley, preaching in the shell of the twelve-sided building in 1759, described it as 'the best building of the size for the voice that I know in England'.[92] The church suffered from internal disputes between 1763 and 1766 but had recovered by 1769 and was still growing in 1772 despite the 'uncommon stumbling blocks' being placed in its way; it became the head of a circuit in 1765.[93] Among the early ministers was Francis Asbury (1768) who became the first bishop of the Methodist Episcopal Church in the U.S.A.[94] Because of the

78 P.R.O., RG 31/8; E.R.O., D/NB 6; ibid. Stockwell Street Min. Bk. 1816–63; ibid. Lion Walk reg. 1702–1840.
79 E.R.O., D/NC 45/2/1; *Story of Headgate*, 1–11, 24.
80 E.R.O., D/NC 45/1/1.
81 e.g. *Story of Headgate*, 24, 26–7, 37; E.R.O., D/NC 24/2/2, s.a. 1862.
82 E.R.O., D/NC 45/2/2; *Story of Headgate*, 29.
83 E.R.O., D/NC 45/2/2; ibid. Acc. C210, J. B. Harvey Colln. vii, p. 230; *Story of Headgate*, 31.
84 E.R.O., Headgate Ch. Min. Bk. s.a. 1901; *Story of Headgate*, 42.
85 *Story of Headgate*, 56, 60, 64.
86 *Colch. Gaz.* 12 Nov. 1968; *E.C.S.* 26 Sept. 1969; 14 June 1974.
87 *E.C.S.* 20 Dec. 1974; 3 Mar. 1978.
88 G.R.O. Worship Reg. no. 65183; inf. (1959) from the Revd. A. Mead.
89 G.R.O. Worship Reg. no. 58635; *Lion Walk Ch. Mag.* Jan. 1946; Apr. 1948.
90 Inf. (1959) from Pastor R. Biggs and Miss B. Russell; *Lion Walk Ch. Mag.* Feb. and Sept. 1946; G.R.O. Worship Reg. no. 75094. The mission made no return in 1851.
91 Blaxill, *Nonconf. Ch. of Colch.* 25; G.R.O. Worship Reg. nos. 54127, 56635.
92 *Letters of John Wesley*, ed. J. Telford, iv. 56, 58–9; *Works of J. Wesley* (1872), ii. 462, 466, 468–9, 514, 521–2; E.R.O., D/NM 2/9/3, notes at the end of the vol.; ibid. Q/SMg 19.
93 *Works of J. Wesley*, iii. 153, 241, 272, 301, 420, 482; *Hall's Circuits and Ministers*, ed. T. G. Hartley, 132–3.
94 K. B. Garlick, *Mr. Wesley's Preachers*, 6; *Proc. Wesley Hist. Soc.* xxxii. 76.

'ill conduct' of the preachers the Colchester society declined in the early 1780s, and Wesley made several visits to strengthen it. Numbers had risen to 60 by the time Wesley visited the church for the last time in 1790, but he still found the congregation 'lessened and cold enough' and the spirit of Methodism lost. The society's problems were compounded by the Evangelical vicar of St. Peter's, who opposed the creation of a separate Methodist church; he apparently ceased trying to attract Methodists to St. Peter's after Wesley had publicly accused him of sheep stealing.[95] Methodist numbers revived, and in 1800 the meeting house was rebuilt to accommodate 700–800.[96]

Missions from Maidenburgh Street were opened at Lexden and at the Hythe in 1822.[97] The Lexden house, or another in the same parish, was licensed again in 1823, as was a house in St. Botolph's, both by John Wood, a Wesleyan.[98] In the same year two Chelmsford Wesleyans, Thomas Page a schoolmaster and Ambrose Freeman the circuit minister, licensed houses in St. Runwald's and in St. Giles's, and Page licensed a chapel in St. Giles's in 1824.[99] All the meetings were probably short lived, and their relationship to Maidenburgh Street is not clear. In 1827 a former Sunday school room in St. Nicholas's parish was licensed, presumably as a mission from Maidenburgh Street, by R. C. Coleman, probably Richard Coleman a lay preacher in the Colchester circuit, and William Dennis who was a member of Maidenburgh Street by 1832.[1] In 1829 the minister claimed a congregation of 700 at Maidenburgh Street and of 100 at a meeting in a former Primitive Methodist chapel in Magdalen Street, although membership was only 229 at Maidenburgh Street and 11 at Magdalen Street. The Magdalen Street meeting seems to have closed later that year.[2]

In 1835 the church bought a site in Culver Street, and a new chapel was opened in 1836. It stood behind the street frontage, approached through an archway; the two cottages on the street were used by the church.[3] The later 1830s and 1840s were a time of expansion, the meeting house or preaching station in Magdalen Street being reopened 1836–43 and 1848–9, one at the Hythe 1840–8, and one at Old Heath 1848–59.[4] The Wesleyan Reform schism reduced membership in the late 1840s, but average congregations of 700 in the morning and 650 in the afternoon were reported in 1851 although actual congregations on Census Sunday that year were 500 in the morning and 330 in the afternoon.[5]

The preaching station at Old Heath was reopened 1861–2, and that at the Hythe was revived in 1864 and replaced by a chapel in 1869.[6] Mission work was begun at Mile End in 1884.[7] At Culver Street the schoolroom was enlarged for both school and church purposes in 1869, and in 1878 the chapel was repaired and reseated, increasing the accommodation.[8] In 1900 the church was remodelled to plans by W. Cressall and J. F. Goodey, providing a suite of rooms and a caretakers' house in place of the old cottages, and an imposing new façade with twin flanking towers. The interior was remodelled with a new choir gallery and rostrum. The church was gutted by fire in 1926, but was rebuilt on its former plan and reopened in 1928.[9]

In 1970 the Culver Street church was closed and sold for redevelopment as part of the shopping precinct. A new church was built at the entrance to Castle park on a site between Ryegate Road and Maidenburgh Street, near that of the 18th-century meeting house. The buildings, designed by Kenneth C. Cheeseman to fit the irregular plan of the site, are low with a flat, copper roof. The interior arrangements are flexible, with a movable partition between the church and a hall. In the vestibule is the pulpit from the original meeting house.[10]

The preaching station at the Hythe was replaced in 1869 by a chapel in the back lane, later Spurgeon Street; it closed in 1956.[11]

In 1899 the New Town Wesleyan Chapel Trust was formed and land for a church bought; the church, in the later Wimpole Road, opened in 1904.[12] In its early years the church was well filled, with membership reaching 148 by 1914. Progress was revived after the First World War, and the ministry of G. H. Simpson, 1929–33, was outstanding. When the Hythe and Artillery Street churches closed in the 1950s some of their members transferred to Wimpole Road, which in 1963 reached a membership peak of 262.[13] By 1972 the minister also served Elmstead Market, Rowhedge, and Fingringhoe.[14]

PRIMITIVE METHODISTS. The Primitive Methodist Samuel Chapman registered a chapel in a converted house in Magdalen Street in 1824, and Colchester, with 19 members and a resident preacher, was part of the Norwich circuit in 1825.[15] The chapel was being used by the Wesleyans in 1829, and there is no further record of Primitive Methodism in Colchester until 1839 when the society, which then had 55 members, built a chapel near the Barracks, in the later Artillery Street.[16] C. H. Spurgeon (1834–92), the

95 *Works of J. Wesley*, iv. 220, 240, 265, 295, 497; E.R.O., D/NM 2/9/3, at end of vol.; J. A. A. Baker, *Hist. Methodism in Colch.* 7.

96 Cromwell, *Hist. Colch.* 404.

97 P.R.O., RG 31/3; E.R.O., D/NM 2/1/14.

98 P.R.O., RG 31/3; inf. (1960) from Meth. Bk. Steward's office.

99 P.R.O., RG 31/3; *Hall's Circuits and Ministers*, 119.

1 P.R.O., RG 31/3; E.R.O., D/NM 2/1/2; D/NM 2/1/14.

2 E.R.O., Q/CR 3/2/31; D/NM 2/1/14; D/NM 2/9/3 p. [28].

3 E.R.O., D/NM 2/3/5; D/NM 2/8/14; Baker, *Hist. Methodism in Colch.* 9.

4 E.R.O., D/NM 2/1/25.

5 Ibid. D/NM 2/1/2; P.R.O., HO 129/8/204; below, this section, United Methodist Free Church.

6 E.R.O., D/NM 2/1/25; D/NM 2/5/24.

7 Baker, *Hist. Methodism in Colch.* 19.

8 E.R.O., D/NM 2/3/1, 5; D/NM 21/9/3, loose papers; Baker, *Hist. Methodism in Colch.* 10.

9 E.R.O., D/NM 2/3/2, 3; below, pl. facing p. 345.

10 *Castle Meth. Ch.* (1970): copy in E.C.L. Colch.; *Colch. Gaz.* 20 Oct. 1970.

11 E.R.O., D/NM 2/5/24; inf. (1959) from the late Mr. L. E. Dansie.

12 G.R.O. Worship Reg. no. 40401; *Wimpole Road Meth. Ch. Golden Jubilee*: pamph. in E.C.L. Colch.

13 M. Broom, *Wimpole Road Methodist Church, 1904–79*; *Colch. Meth. Circuit Plans* (1954–5, 1972); E.R.O., D/NM 2/5/39.

14 *Colch. Expr.* 14 Dec. 1972.

15 P.R.O., RG 31/3; E.R.O., D/NM 2/9/3, p. [28]; H. B. Kendall, *Origin and Hist. Prim. Meth. Ch.* ii. 215; J. Petty, *Hist. Prim. Meth. Connexion*, (1864 edn.), 463.

16 E.R.O., D/NM 2/2/1; D/NM 2/9/3, p. [28].

Baptist preacher, was converted in the Artillery Street church in 1850 by a sermon from a lay preacher, probably Samuel Nightingale; he preached there himself in 1864.[17] On Census Sunday 1851 congregations of 183 (including 60 children) in the morning, 239 (including 80 children) in the afternoon, and 117 in the evening were reported. A preaching room at Greenstead, closed by 1860, reported congregations of 22 in the afternoon and 50 in the evening.[18] The Artillery Street church became the head of a circuit in 1859.[19] In 1873 it reported a membership of 70 and congregations of 300.[20] Numbers declined in the later 1870s, but by 1887 they had recovered to 66 members and a congregation of 250. The church was remodelled in 1892. It closed in 1957.[21]

In 1869 a group of Primitive Methodists started worshipping in the former Old Meeting or St. Helen's chapel.[22] They moved to the new Ebenezer chapel in Nunns Cut (later Nunns Road) in 1873.[23] The membership was 33 and the average congregations 100 in 1873.[24] By 1887 both membership and congregation had fallen to 10 and strenuous efforts were being made to revive the church. Numbers rose steadily in the 1890s until in 1905 there were 30 members and congregations of 130.[25] The church closed in 1946.[26]

UNITED METHODIST FREE CHURCH. A number of members seceded from the Culver Street Wesleyan church in the late 1840s. Some of them were worshipping at the New Jerusalem church, formerly the Presbyterian Old Meeting, in St. Helen's Lane in 1851 when they reported congregations of 200 in the afternoon and 300 in the evening.[27] In 1853, the New Church congregation having apparently died out, they formed a new trust for the chapel. The following year J. C. Houchin, formerly a Primitive Methodist lay preacher, became minister and the church adopted Congregational principles of order and church government while remaining associated with the United Methodist Free Church. In 1860 Houchin registered the chapel as Methodist Free Church,[28] but the following year the congregation declined to join the London district meeting of the United Methodist Free Church and in 1863 it formally declared itself a Congregational church. Houchin resigned for financial reasons in 1864 and in 1865 the congregation called Mr. Reynolds, a Baptist, to be their minister. The church founded in 1853 seems to have dissolved soon afterwards, but the chapel continued in use under T. Delight, one of the original trustees. He gave the Primitive Methodists permission to use it in 1869 and they retained possession until their move to Nunns Cut in 1873 despite an attempt *c.* 1870 by the United Methodist Free Church to recover the building.[29]

A United Methodist Free Church in Magdalen Street, apparently in the former Primitive Methodist and Wesleyan chapel, was recorded in 1863.[30] By 1876 it was an undenominational mission hall under the direction of John Bawtree.[31] In 1881 it was again recorded, possibly in error, as a Methodist Free Church, but it had closed by 1897.[32]

THE NEW JERUSALEM CHURCH. A public meeting was arranged in Colchester in 1816 by members of the New Church already established at Brightlingsea. Opposition from local clergy and ministers caused the borough council to withdraw permission for the use of the town hall, but 400–500 people attended a meeting in the Angel inn.[33] In 1823 the bookseller U. W. Mattacks, registered a meeting house, almost certainly the Old Meeting, for the New Church; Mattacks was still leader in 1851 when the congregation of 20 shared the building with a breakaway Methodist group.[34] The church had died out by 1853 when a new, Methodist, trust was formed for the meeting house.[35]

The church was revived in 1881 by Joseph Deans, then minister at Brightlingsea, and a society was formed in 1882. It met in the Shaftesbury hotel in Culver Street, and by 1887 had 51 members.[36] By 1890 most of the 37 members of the Colchester society, unlike other British members of the church, had adopted the Academy view that Emanuel Swedenborg's writings were a direct revelation of divine truth. The following year they withdrew from all connexion with the British General Conference of the church and affiliated themselves to the American General Church of the Advent of Our Lord.[37] A few members, who continued to subscribe to the views of the British Conference, formed a separate society which continued to meet in the Shaftesbury hotel; it moved *c.* 1910 to the Masonic hall, Abbeygate Street, and *c.* 1912 to the Oddfellows hall, George Street, where it remained until it was dissolved *c.* 1927.[38] The main Colchester society also met in the Shaftesbury hotel, although it also used a room, formerly the St. Botolph's Infant school, in Osborne Street from 1898 to 1901. In 1902 it moved to a room in Priory Street and reorganized itself as the Colchester Society of the

17 *E.R.* lix. 87; Kendall, *Hist. Prim. Meth. Ch.* ii. 239.
18 P.R.O., HO 129/8/204.
19 E.R.O., D/NM 2/2/1; *Prim. Meth. Conf. Mins.* (1858, 1860).
20 E.R.O., D/NM 2/2/22.
21 *Kelly's Dir. Essex* (1894); E.R.O., D/NM 2/5/31.
22 Ibid. D/NM 2/2/18.
23 Ibid. D/NM 2/5/45; G.R.O. Worship Reg. no. 21757.
24 E.R.O., D/NM 2/2/22.
25 Ibid. D/NM 2/2/23–5.
26 Ibid. D/NM 2/5/45.
27 Ibid. D/NM 2/1/2; P.R.O., HO 129/8/204.
28 G.R.O. Worship Reg. no. 10293.
29 E.R.O., D/NM 2/2/18; ibid. Acc. C69.
30 Ibid. D/NM 2/9/3, p. [28]; *White's Dir. Essex* (1863), 91.
31 *Goody's Colch. Almanac* (1876).
32 *Benham's Colch. Dir.* (1881 and later edns.); O.S. Map 1/2,500, Essex XXVIII. 12 (1876 and 1897 edns.)
33 A. L. Wakeling, *Brightlingsea Soc. of the New Ch.* (1968, reproduced from TS.), pp. 11–12: copy in E.C.L. Colch.
34 P.R.O., RG 31/8; ibid. HO 129/8/204.
35 Blaxill, *Nonconf. Ch. of Colch.* 20; above, this section, United Meth. Free Ch.
36 Blaxill, *Nonconf. in Colch.* 21; Wakeling, *Brightlingsea Soc.* 34–5; *Colch. New Ch. Monthly*, no. 2: copy in B.L.
37 *New Ch. Monthly*, i, *passim*.
38 *Kelly's Dir. Essex* (1902 and later edns.); Blaxill, *Nonconf. Ch. of Colch.* 21.

General Church of the New Jerusalem. A new church was built in Maldon Road in 1924 and extended in 1967.[39]

SALVATION ARMY. Early in 1882 William Booth, the founder of the Salvation Army, bought through an agent the former skating rink in St. John's Street.[40] The Army licensed rooms in the theatre in Queen Street shortly afterwards and in June, after an outdoor meeting in the cattle market, opened their barracks in the converted skating rink.[41] Early meetings there provoked violent and unruly behaviour from some bystanders, but the Army's right to hold services there and out of doors was upheld by the mayor and other justices.[42] A building on Hythe Hill licensed in 1888 had closed by 1895.[43] William Booth visited Colchester several times, preaching to large congregations.[44] The barracks in St. John's Street were demolished in 1973 to make way for the inner relief road, and a new citadel was opened in Butt Road. It was extended in 1975.[45]

UNDENOMINATIONAL MISSIONS. Thomas Flory, a builder, registered the Gospel Band Hall in Queen Street in 1886. In 1902 a new Gospel Band Mission Hall, seating 300, was erected in Abbeygate Street; it became well known for the hearty singing of Moody and Sankey hymns, accompanied by organ and 12-piece band, and in its early days was well filled. In 1966 the mission became affiliated to the Fellowship of Independent Churches and was renamed Colchester Evangelical church.[46]

The Colchester Town Mission was founded in 1839 by the businessman J. B. Harvey, who served as its secretary for over 40 years, to visit the 'multitude who never attend public worship'.[47] A missionary was employed, but the mission had no permanent headquarters until 1956 when it bought the former Congregational church at Shrub End.[48] The building was taken over by the Baptists in 1961, and the mission moved to Maldon Road. It had closed by 1988.[49]

Cottage meetings for railwaymen were held in 1892 by Harry Thorogood, a signalman from St. Botolph's station, and Mrs. Nottidge. An old carpenter's shop at Mrs. Nottidge's house, no. 1 Colne Bank Road, was converted into a mission hall. Meetings were held there and in rented rooms until 1896 when a Railway Mission hall, seating 250, was built in North Station Road. The first salaried superintendent was appointed in 1924.[50] The mission became the Emmanuel Evangelical church *c.* 1979.[51]

The British Christian Mission rooms in Lion Walk were registered in 1891 by John Adams, a wholesale and retail clothier; they were disused by 1895.[52] The Friends Evangelistic Band registered the Vineyard Street Mission hall in 1930, and the Christian Alliance of Women and Girls registered two rooms at no. 4A Bank Passage in 1937; both seem to have been short-lived. In 1967 a meeting room in Wimpole Road was registered for 'Christians not otherwise designated'.[53]

OTHER CHURCHES. The Brethren were active in Colchester by 1844 when C. T. Rust of Eld Lane Baptist church accused them of taking members from other churches.[54] No congregation was recorded in 1851, but members of Eld Lane resigned to join the Brethren in 1867 and 1868, and in 1871 there were two Brethren meetings in the town with a total of 350 sittings.[55] Brethren registered rooms at no. 70A High Street in 1884 where they remained until 1917. They met at the Burlington hall, Burlington Road, from 1917 to 1921 and then successively at the Literary hall, St. John's Street and the Gospel Hall, North Station Road. In 1933 they built the Assembly hall in Maldon Road, whose name was changed to the Maldon Road chapel in 1979.[56] Another group which was meeting in Cedars Road in 1906 seems to have continued until 1960 or later. Other meetings, mainly short-lived, were recorded in Culver Street from *c.* 1874 to 1894 and in 1947, Sir Isaac's Walk from *c.* 1878 to 1882, in 1894, and from *c.* 1902 to 1926 or later, Lion Walk from *c.* 1898 to 1926 or later, Gilberd Road from *c.* 1898 to 1902, and Osborne Street in 1906.[57]

Missionaries from London established a branch of the Church of Jesus Christ of the Latter Day Saints at Colchester in 1850.[58] In 1851 they claimed congregations of 30 in the morning and 120 in the evening in a converted shop in St. Peter's parish, probably on North Hill where the presiding elder lived,[59] but actual membership was probably never much more than 30 and had fallen to 5 by 1854 when the church was disbanded. It was revived in 1857 but was disbanded again *c.* 1860.[60] There was no further Mormon activity in Colchester until 1949 when a new church was founded. Meetings were held in a hired hall until a church was built in Straight Road between 1963 and 1966.[61]

39 Blaxill, *Nonconf. Ch. of Colch.* 21; G.R.O. Worship Reg. nos. 47944, 49960; *E.C.S.* 21 Apr. 1967.

40 E.R.O., Acc. C210, J. B. Harvey Colln. vii, p. 56, newspaper cutting.

41 G.R.O. Worship Reg. nos. 26306, 26349; Blaxill, *Nonconf. Ch. of Colch.* 23–4.

42 E.R.O., Acc. C210, J. B. Harvey Colln. vii, pp. 327–8.

43 G.R.O. Worship Reg. no. 30806.

44 Blaxill, *Nonconf. Ch. of Colch.* 24.

45 G.R.O. Worship Reg. no. 73717; *Colch. Gaz.* 4 Sept. 1972; 24 Apr. 1975; *E.C.S.* 2 Nov. 1973.

46 G.R.O. Worship Reg. nos. 29583, 45152; foundation stone on bldg.; *Kelly's Dir. Essex* (1890, 1894); inf. (1959) from the superintendent Mr. E. C. Betts; *E.C.S.* 7 Jan. 1966.

47 *Colch. Christian Mag.* (1845), 13: copy in E.C.L. Colch.; E.R.O., Acc. C210, J. B. Harvey Colln. v, p. 214.

48 Inf. (1959) from Mr. Ira Miller.

49 *Benham's Colch. Dir.* (1961 and later edns.); above, this section, Baptists.

50 *The Railway Mission, 1896–1956*; *Kelly's Dir. Essex* (1894).

51 *E.C.S.* 4 June 1976; G.R.O. Worship Reg. no. 42229.

52 G.R.O. Worship Reg. no. 32852; *Kelly's Dir. Essex* (1890).

53 G.R.O. Worship Reg. nos. 52461, 57663, 71152.

54 C. T. Rust, *The Brethren* (1844).

55 E.R.O., D/NB 4/29; *The Nonconformist*, 8 Jan. 1873.

56 G.R.O. Worship Reg. nos. 28315, 46973, 55402; *Kelly's Dir. Essex* (1906 and later edns.).

57 *Kelly's Dir. Essex* (1878 and later edns.); G.R.O. Worship Reg. no. 61713; inf. (1959) from D. Parkes.

58 *E.J.* xviii. 57–8.

59 P.R.O., HO 129/8/204.

60 *E.J.* xviii. 58.

61 G.R.O. Worship Reg. no. 70566; *Colch. Gaz.* 21 May 1963; *E.C.S.* 19 Feb. 1965; 3 June 1966.

A Christadelphian fellowship was formed in 1907 by C. J. Cole, a tailor. Meetings of about 20 were held in a hut in Winnock Road, later successively in the Co-operative reading room, New Town Road, St. George's hall, High Street, the Foresters hall, Winnock Road, and the Friends meeting house, Shewell Road. During the First World War dissension arose on the question of non-combatant service, and some members seceded to form a separate fellowship. In 1959 one fellowship met in Shewell Road and the other in the Oddfellows hall, George Street.[62] Only one fellowship, meeting in the Oddfellows hall, Williams Walk, survived in 1984, and it had closed by 1988.

Christian Science meetings, begun in a cottage in Bergholt Road in 1909, quickly moved to a room in the Masonic hall, Abbeygate Street. From 1912 services were held at no. 150A High Street, and in 1919 a Christian Science Society was formed. In 1923 premises in Lion Walk were bought and remodelled to provide a hall seating 100, a reading room, and a schoolroom, on two storeys. The society became the First Church of Christ Scientist, Colchester, in 1931, and in 1938 the church was dedicated. The church was demolished as part of the redevelopment of Lion Walk, and a new church was built in 1975 in Trinity Street and dedicated in 1977. The building, designed by Bryan Thomas to fit its constricted site, has reading rooms on two storeys on the street frontage with behind them an octagonal room for worship, surmounted by a glass spire.[63]

Jehovah's Witnesses began meeting in Colchester in 1936. They registered rooms at no. 41C Head Street as a Kingdom hall in 1939 and moved to no. 41A Head Street in 1948. Between 1954 and 1957 services were held in the Colchester and County Liberal club, and in 1953 the swimming pool at Bath Place was used for baptisms.[64] A Kingdom hall in George Street, formerly the Oddfellows hall, was dedicated in 1962. A new hall in Elmstead Road was built in a single day in 1984 by *c.* 1,200 members of the church from all over the country.[65] In 1988 there were also meetings at the Hythe and Lexden.

Following a mission in 1930, a resident Elim Pentecostal minister was appointed for Colchester, and meetings were held in a hall, possibly the Oddfellows hall, in Osborne Street. In 1931 a tabernacle, intended to be temporary, was erected in Fairfax Road; it was occupied until 1957 when the church moved to the former Strict Baptist chapel in Stanwell Street. The chapel was demolished to make way for the new inner relief road and a new Elim Pentecostal church was built in Walsingham Road and opened in 1971.[66]

After preliminary meetings in a private house and in the Shrub End social hut, members of the pentecostal Assemblies of God in 1936 set up a Full Gospel mission which moved in 1939 to rooms in a house in Straight Road. A permanent church was opened in a hall there in 1946.[67]

A Seventh Day Adventist church was founded in 1939 by Pastor J. M. Howard, and the former Gospel hall in North Station Road was acquired in 1940. The hall was rebuilt and registered for worship in 1966.[68]

The Gospel Acres Evangelistic team reopened the former Artillery Street Primitive Methodist church as the Spurgeon Memorial church *c.* 1960. In 1966 it was taken over by the Datchet Evangelical fellowship and its name altered to Spurgeon Evangelical church.[69]

House meetings were started on the Greenstead estate in 1964, and the Greenstead Evangelical fellowship was founded in 1966. It acquired a site in Magnolia Drive in 1970 and built the Greenstead Free church.[70] The Jesus Centre, the coffee-bar church, was established in the former town mission hall in King Harold Road, Shrub End, in 1969.[71] Mount Zion Free church at no. 328 Ipswich Road was registered for Evangelical Christians in 1972.[72] The Colne Valley community church, a member of the Evangelical Alliance, was founded in 1977; in 1987 its members were instrumental in forming Net Work which in 1988 bought the disused water tower, Jumbo, for use as a prayer centre. In 1988 the church opened a school in its premises at Braiswick.[73]

Christian Spiritualists began meeting in a private house in Wellesley Road in 1930, and in 1934 they built All Kin hall in Maldon Road. The hall was demolished in 1967, and the congregation met in a succession of temporary premises.[74] Christian Spiritualists registered a room at no. 117 Shrub Road as the Temple of Light in 1973.[75] They were still meeting there in 1988; another group met in Port Lane South. A Spiritualist society was apparently founded in Colchester in 1928 and a branch of the National Spiritualist association in 1934; in 1962 its members built a church in Priory Street which in 1988 was affiliated to the Spiritualist National Union.[76]

62 Inf. (1959) from Mr. F. W. Bennell (Shewell Road) and Mr. L. H. W. Wells (George Street).

63 G.R.O. Worship Reg. nos. 51896, 73973, 74170; Blaxill, *Nonconf. Ch. of Colch.* 25; *First Church of Christ Scientist, Dedication Service* (1977): copy in E.C.L. Colch.; *Colch. Gaz.* 4 Sept. 1972; 24 Apr. 1975; *E.C.S.* 2 Nov. 1973.

64 G.R.O. Worship Reg. nos. 59002, 62079; inf. (1959) from R. J. Pistell, overseer of cong., and from Liberal club; E.R.O., Boro. Mun., Parks and Bathing Places Cttee. Mins. 1942–53, meeting of 20 Mar. 1953.

65 G.R.O. Worship Reg. nos. 68609, 76693; *Colch. Expr.* 15 Oct. 1962; *Colch. Gaz.* 22 Oct. 1984.

66 G.R.O. Worship Reg. nos. 53627, 68004, 72753; *Colch. Expr.* 5 Aug. 1971; 23 Apr. 1975; *Colch. Gaz.* 8 Nov. 1971; inf. (1959) from Revd. G. Stormont, sec. to the Brit. Pentecostal Fellowship.

67 G.R.O. Worship Reg. nos. 58901, 61513; inf. (1959) from Pastor R. C. Bolt; *E.C.S.* 1 Feb. 1991.

68 G.R.O. Worship Reg. no. 70387; inf. (1959) from Mr. I. R. Kennersley; *E.C.S.* 13 Aug. 1965; *Colch. Gaz.* 29 March 1966.

69 G.R.O. Worship Reg. no. 68090; *E.C.S.* 25 Feb., 25 March 1966.

70 G.R.O. Worship Reg. no. 73501; *E.C.S.* 30 June 1967; *Colch. Gaz.* 2 June 1970.

71 *Colch. Expr.* 2 Apr. 1975.

72 G.R.O. Worship Reg. no. 73100.

73 *E.C.S.* 16 Feb., 23 Nov. 1990; 30 Aug. 1991; inf. from the pastor, P. Prothero.

74 *Kelly's Dir. Essex* (1937); inf. (1959) from Mr. F. H. Allcock; *Colch. Gaz.* 22 Aug. 1975.

75 G.R.O. Worship Reg. no. 73571.

76 G.R.O. Worship Reg. no. 69018; *Colch. Expr.* 15 Mar. 1962; 29 Mar. 1973; inf. (1959) from Mrs. M. Weaver.

FOREIGN CHURCHES. A Dutch church was established by 1562.[77] Its first known minister, Jan or John Migrode a refugee from Zeeland, was living in Colchester in 1563. His successor Theodorus van den Berghe, a distinguished scholar, served the church from 1572 until his death in 1598, refusing two calls to return to Holland.[78] Two later ministers, Jonas Proost, 1600–44 and Jan Ruytinck, whose name was anglicised John Ruting, 1645–63, served as masters of the Colchester grammar school.[79] The Dutch congregation were later said to have worshipped at first in St. Giles's church; by the 1680s they were using St. Nicholas's, and in the early 18th century All Saints', contributing to its repair in 1704, 1705, and 1712. In 1716 they acquired their own church in a house in St. Mary's parish near the corner of Head Street and St. Mary's Lane.[80]

In 1612 James I confirmed the privileges of the Dutch congregation, including the use of their own order in their church.[81] In the 1630s Archbishop Laud attempted to assimilate the Dutch to the Church of England, ruling that only aliens and the first English-born generation might use the Dutch service; others were to attend their parish churches. Laud's vicar general reported that the Dutch ministers and elders at Colchester were very ready to obey, and were indeed as conformable as any clergy in the diocese, having agreed to translate the Book of Common Prayer into Dutch,[82] but privately they opposed the measures and were the last of the foreign churches to accept Laud's injunction.[83] Although by the later 17th century the Dutch community was being assimilated, ministers continued to be appointed, among them Jan Smit or John Smith, who was also rector of the parish church of St. Mary-at-the-Walls. The Dutch church closed in 1728 or 1729.[84]

Forty-three members of the French church in Colchester were reported in 1573. The church was still in existence in 1593, but presumably came to an end when the Huguenots returned to France after the Edict of Nantes in 1598.[85] The year after the revocation of the Edict in 1685 a group of refugees, including seven ministers and their families, moved from Maldon to Colchester, and the son of a French minister was buried in St. Nicholas's in 1688.[86] The French poor in Colchester were relieved regularly from 1698 to 1718 or later, and French ministers were recorded in 1691, 1696, 1698, 1716, and 1717.[87] The church was last recorded in 1722.[88]

NON-CHRISTIAN RELIGIOUS BODIES

JUDAISM.[89] In 1763 Hyman Waag, a Jewish lapidary, was living in Colchester, and Levi Alexander traded in the town as a silversmith and watchmaker in 1775.[90] In 1791 a Jewish marriage took place in Synagogue Yard which adjoined Quakers Alley in West Stockwell Street,[91] but there is no record of a synagogue there after 1794.[92] In 1796, when two Colchester men were among the trustees for a Jewish graveyard in Ipswich, Colchester Jews seem to have been worshipping there.[93] Tradesmen with Jewish names lived in Colchester in the 19th century, notably in 1848 when Michael Samuel, pawnbroker and silversmith, and Moses and Simon Hyam, tailors, were recorded,[94] but there is no evidence for a synagogue or any worshipping Jewish community in the town.[95] At least one member of the Hyam family became a Christian.[96]

The Colchester and District Jewish Association was formed in 1952. Between 1961 and 1969 the Jewish community met in a hall in Northgate House. In 1969 a new synagogue was built in Fennings Close to serve north Essex.[97]

BAHA'I. Members of the Baha'i faith first met in Colchester *c.* 1970; a Spiritual Assembly was formed in 1976 and members met regularly in private houses in 1988.[98]

77 F. G. Emmison, *Essex Wills*, ii, p. 138.

78 *Reg. of Baptisms in the Dutch Ch. of Colch.* (Huguenot Soc. xii), pp. ii, 89; L. Roker, 'Flemish and Dutch Community in Colch. in the 16th and 17th Cent.' (Lond. M.A. thesis, 1963), pp. 149–51; *Proc. Huguenot Soc.* xxi. 20–1; E.R.O., D/B 5 R5, f. 94v.

79 Morant, *Colch.* 177; Roker, 'Flemish and Dutch Community', 154, 157–8; *Religious Dissent in E. Anglia*, ed. E. S. Leedham-Green, 56.

80 E.R.O., D/P 176/1/2; D/P 200/8/1; D/B 5 Sb5/1, p. 52; *E.A.T.* N.S. xxiii. 162; Morant, *Colch.*, 79 n.; Blaxill, *Nonconf. Ch. of Colch.* 26.

81 Morant, *Colch.* 77.

82 *Cal. S.P. Dom.* 1637, 233; Smith, *Eccl. Hist. Essex*, 52.

83 *Religious Dissent in E. Anglia*, ed. Leedham- Green, 60; Roker, 'Flemish and Dutch Community', 164.

84 *Reg. Baptisms of Dutch Ch.* 90–1.

85 Ibid. 105; *Acts of P.C.* 1592–3, 138.

86 Bodl. MS. Rawl. C. 984, ff. 73, 74v., printed in *Proc. Huguenot Soc.* ii. 476; E.R.O., D/P 176/1/2.

87 E.R.O., D/B 5 Sb5/1, p. 48; *Proc. Huguenot Soc.* i. 327; vii. 153; xi. 276, 281, 285; xii. 274–87.

88 Defoe, *Tour*, ed. Cole (1927), i. 44.

89 This section was written in 1988. For Jews in medieval Colchester, above, pp. 27–8.

90 *Trans. Jewish Hist. Soc.* xxv. 155; B. Mason, *Clock and Watchmaking in Colch.* 390.

91 *Anglo-Jewish Assoc. Quarterly*, iii (2), 22.

92 E.R.O., D/P 325/11.

93 *Trans. Jewish Hist. Soc.* ii. 134.

94 *White's Dir. Essex*, (1848), 109, 111.

95 *Trans. Jewish Hist. Soc.* xvii. 182.

96 E.R.O., Stockwell St. Cong. Ch. Bk. 1816–64.

97 *E.C.S.*, 24 Jan. 1969; G.R.O. Worship Reg. no. 68180; *Colch. Expr.* 23 Oct. 1969.

98 Inf. from Mrs. B. Begent.

EDUCATION

A SCHOOL[99] was founded in Colchester in the early 12th century.[1] Schoolmasters were mentioned in 1357, 1383, and 1425; in 1460, 1464, and 1512 they were apparently associated with a school adjoining St. Mary's churchyard, east of the postern gate.[2] By the early 16th century there was provision for even a charity child to be taught until the age of ten.[3] A grammar school in All Saints' parish, founded and endowed in 1520, was refounded in 1539 and survives as the Royal grammar school. In the 16th and early 17th century the names of several schoolmasters were recorded. Most of them seem to have kept writing schools,[4] but William Cole, vicar of St. Peter's 1583–1600 and a licensed teacher, kept a grammar school for 30–50 children.[5] The borough assembly tried to protect the free grammar school from competition,[6] but from the late 17th century dissatisfaction with that school's curriculum, its religious bias, and its low teaching standards[7] prompted the opening of several boys schools, including one kept by Quakers. The Dutch were running a school in 1714. In the 18th century a group of undenominational and nonconformist charity Sunday schools was started, two charity day schools were founded, one by Churchmen and one by nonconformists, and there were usually two or three Quaker schools where some charity children were taught. The aspirations, however, of the urban middle class and of local farmers stimulated a demand for schools which was not met by the grammar and charity schools, and many private schools were opened. In 1812 two central day schools were created by the union of the nonconformist day and Sunday schools and of the Church day school with the undenominational Sunday schools. By 1818 the central National and British schools were attended by *c.* 300 and *c.* 210 children respectively. They and a few dame schools provided education for the poor and there were several middle-class private schools.[8] By 1833 Churchmen had opened a day school for girls and three for infants. The central schools provided for older children, and the parish and nonconformist churches maintained Sunday, preparatory, and infant schools, so that a total of 1,360 children attended day schools for the poor. Some of those were among the 950 who attended Sunday schools, and the number of dame and private schools had grown.[9]

Between 1833 and 1853 Churchmen opened five parish day schools, a branch of their central school, and an evening school, while nonconformists opened a Wesleyan school and six Congregational schools, and Roman Catholics opened a day school. In 1844, the managers of the British school, which was mainly supported by Congregationalists, declared their opposition to government 'interference' in education, and in 1847 and 1855 Colchester nonconformists protested against the extension of state aid and inspection.[10] Sectarian rivalry and a growing demand for well-trained domestic servants stimulated the provision of schools, but clergymen also advocated education to remedy the moral degradation caused by poverty and industrial conditions and to maintain social order.[11] In the period 1835–76 six evening schools were opened. A Ragged school, started in 1854, was supported by Churchmen and nonconformists and in 1867 an industrial school for girls and a Quaker Sunday school for adults were opened. By 1850 teaching methods were improving; the monitorial system adopted in the early 19th century was losing favour and, as pupil teachers replaced monitors, certificated teachers were increasingly appointed, and teachers' associations began to hold meetings in Colchester.[12]

By 1870 there were 14 voluntary day schools, and although some nonconformists favoured the establishment of a school board, Churchmen, who had provided eight of the schools, opposed it, insisting that a deficiency of *c.* 600 places could be met by further voluntary effort.[13] The Wesleyan school, which had closed in 1863, was reopened with a new branch, and Roman Catholics strove to improve their school. Churchmen, led by J. W. Irvine, rector of St. Mary's-at-the-Walls, began a vigorous effort which provided six more schools by 1875; they enlarged existing schools and, in 1890, built another so that by that date Anglicans provided three quarters of the places available.[14] The Quaker adult schools flourished and in 1875 the Co-operative society started evening courses on scientific subjects. Factory owners and businessmen led a similar voluntary effort which in 1885

99 This article, of which an early draft was written by A. F. J. Brown in 1958, was completed in 1987. Unless otherwise stated the numbers of schools and children given do not include those of Greenstead, Lexden, Mile End, or W. Donyland, which are covered below, Outlying Parts.

1 *Introduction to Cur. Reg. R.* (Selden Soc. lxii), p. 280; *Feet of F. Essex*, i. 39; *E.A.T.* N.S. xiv. 137–41.

2 E.R.O., D/B 5 Cr11, rot. 8; Cr22, rot. 44d.; Cr45, rot. 15d.; Bodl. MS. Rolls Essex 2; Morant, *Colch.* 171; Guildhall MS. 25630, no. 2 1560-75, f. 140, 9 Oct. 1565. E.R.O., D/B 5 Cr10, rot. 3: *magnum Scoland* was misread by I. H. Jeayes in *Colch. Ct. Rolls*, ii. 9 as 'the great school'.

3 P.R.O., PROB 11/16, f. 61.

4 e.g. E.R.O., D/B 5 Cr110, rot. 20; D/B 5 Sb2/3, f. 25v.; D/ACA 14, f. 88; D/ACA 17, f. 71; D/ACA 21, ff. 285, 314; D/ACA 29, f. 52.

5 E.R.O., D/ACA 21, f. 460; D/ACA 24, f. 113.

6 Ibid. D/B 5 Gb1, 10 Jan. 1583; Gb4, f. 294v.

7 *V.C.H. Essex*, ii. 507; E.R.O., D/B 5 Gb5, f. 52.

8 E.R.O., Boro. Mun., Legal Precedent Bk. 1629–1770, f. 21v.; *Returns Educ. Poor*, H.C. 224, pp. 245–68 (1819), ix (1).

9 *Educ. Enq. Abstract*, H.C. 62, pp. 271–2 (1835), xli.

10 Brit. and Foreign Sch. Soc. *39th Rep.* (1844), 76; E.R.O., Acc. C210 J. B. Harvey Colln. iv, p. 107; *E.C.S.* 16 Mar. 1855.

11 N. Forster, *Discourse on the Utility of Sunday Schs.* (1786), 31–3; E.R.O., Acc. C210 J. B. Harvey Colln. iv, p. 107; Nat. Soc. files; *Ipswich Jnl.* 7 Mar. 1812; *E.C.S.* 28 Mar. 1845; 11 Mar. 1855; 27 May 1859; Brown, *Colch. 1815–1914*, 55–6.

12 *E.C.S.* 11 Dec. 1846; *Goody's Colch. Almanac* (1876), 13; Brown, *Colch. 1815–1914*, 61–2.

13 *E.C.S.* 23 Dec. 1870; 20 Dec. 1872.

14 Ibid. 14 Dec. 1889; Brown, *Colch. 1815–1914*, 170.

established an adult school of art and science. By 1891 there were 15 voluntary elementary schools, but some used hired and ill-adapted buildings, playground space had been reduced by new classrooms, and cramped urban sites precluded further enlargement.[15] The Board of Education estimated that 528 places were needed at once in the borough and liberties and another 1,512 in the near future to allow for population growth and the closure of condemned schools. Nonconformist support for a school board had grown, the proportion of the population capable of subscribing to the schools decreased as factories attracted more poor families to the town, and voluntary bodies could no longer find resources to replace condemned schools and educate all the children of the poor. Teachers hoped that a school board would reduce classes to 60 children and restrict the role of pupil teachers.[16] In 1892, when Churchmen announced the impending closure of three of their schools,[17] a board of 11 members was formed at the request of the borough council. The first board consisted of 6 Churchmen, 2 nonconformists, and 3 representatives of the Co-operative society and the trades council.[18] The board quickly took over five Church schools, the British school, and one Wesleyan school, using the old buildings until it could replace them; it built six new schools between 1894 and 1903. In 1895 *c.* 3,910 children attended schools and of those, 1,977 (*c.* 50 per cent) were at 10 voluntary schools. The transition from the denominational system was eased by a non-sectarian syllabus of religious instruction, devised by J. W. Irvine in co-operation with nonconformists.[19] By 1899 there were 4,406 at school of whom 1,834 (42 per cent) attended the 10 voluntary schools. Evening classes were established at the new board schools,[20] and from 1896 there were classes for pupil teachers at the Albert school of science and art. By 1903 there were in the borough 6 board and 7 voluntary schools (5 Church, 1 Wesleyan, and 1 Roman Catholic), and 5 more Church schools in Greenstead, Lexden, and Mile End.

The school board was replaced in 1903, under the 1902 Education Act, by the borough education committee, a Part III authority with responsibility for elementary education.[21] In 1905 elementary schools in Colchester provided no separate, graded classes for children over 11 years of age. There were then 95 boys at the grammar school, 37 boys and 135 girls at the pupil teacher centre, and 87 boys and 190 girls of secondary school age at the principal private schools. No state secondary education for girls was available, and provision for further education was inadequate.[22] In 1907 the pupil teacher centre became a secondary school for boys and girls, but it was superseded in 1909 by a county high school for girls, a junior technical school for boys, and a technical institute opened in a new building. From 1909, when the garrison schools closed, the council became responsible for educating soldiers' children.[23] In 1907 the borough education committee took over and rebuilt one Church school, but 10 voluntary schools survived in the 1920s. In the 1930s three Church schools closed and another was taken over by the council, and a new council school was built. By 1939 all but the Roman Catholic school had been reorganized in line with the Hadow report, one central and two elementary schools had become senior schools, and a new senior school had been built. Three classes for handicapped children were opened between 1906 and 1924, and in 1938–9 three nursery departments were added to existing infant schools.

Under the 1944 Education Act Colchester was merged in the north-east division of the county, but was a separate division from 1962 to 1974.[24] Under the 1944 Act all secondary schools, except the Royal grammar, the girls secondary, and the technical schools, became secondary modern, mixed schools. Under the 1976 Education Act all secondary schools, except the Royal grammar and the girls high schools, became comprehensive.[25] After the Second World War many schools were overcrowded, the school population was further increased by an influx of children from new army housing estates, and temporary buildings were used.[26] Between 1953 and 1987 the education authorities built 1 special, 12 primary, and 3 secondary schools, and Roman Catholics built a secondary school; new buildings were provided for 2 county primary, 2 county secondary, 1 Roman Catholic, 4 Church schools, and the technical institute. In 1985 three secondary schools were damaged by fire, probably caused by arson.[27] Secondary schools were reorganized under the 1976 Act in 1986 and 1987: a sixth-form college was opened in the former premises of the Gilberd school, North Hill, and only the Royal grammar and girls high schools retained their own sixth forms.[28]

THE ROYAL GRAMMAR SCHOOL. The history of the school to 1905 given in a previous volume[29] needs some correction. Thomas Christmas, by will proved in 1520, founded and endowed a grammar school at his house called Westons in All Saints' parish. He instructed his heirs, or failing them the town bailiffs, to pay a priest £10 a year to teach grammar to 24 Colchester

15 *E.C.S.* 19 Dec. 1891.

16 Ibid. 5 Mar., 9 Apr. 1892; *Essex Tel.* 28 May 1892.

17 *Colch. Boro. Council Mins.* (1891–2), pp. 107, 121, 138, 173; *E.C.S.* 5 Mar. 1892.

18 *E.C.S.* 4 June 1892; *Colch. Boro. Council Mins.* 1891–2, pp. 121, 138, 173.

19 Brown, *Colch. 1815–1914*, 170.

20 *E.C.S.* 22 Feb. 1896; *Returns Elem. Educ. 1899* [Cd. 315], p. 340, H.C. (1900), lxv (2); E.R.O., Colch. Sch. Bd. Mins. 1899–1903, pp. 1, 67.

21 *Colch. Boro. Council Mins.* 1902–3, pp. 777–8. Numbers of schools include those in Greenstead, Lexden, and Mile End.

22 M. E. Sadler, *Rep. on Secondary and Higher Educ. in Essex*, 229–39, 246, 265–6.

23 *Colch. Boro. Council Mins.* 1908–9, p. 885.

24 Inf. from Essex Educ. Dept.; *Educ. in Essex 1960–64*, p. 11.

25 E.R.O., N/CME 5, p. C6–9; Essex Educ. Dept., Lists of Schs.

26 E.R.O., C/ME (Educ. Cttee. Mins.) *passim*; *Colch. Boro. Council Mins.* 1967–8, p. 507.

27 *E.C.S.* 24 May, 7 June 1985.

28 Inf. from Essex Educ. Dept.

29 *V.C.H. Essex*, ii. 502–8.

children.[30] When the bailiffs and commonalty implemented the scheme to provide a free grammar school under Henry VIII's grant of 1539, they seem to have adopted the existing grammar school at Westons, for in 1574 John Christmas was patron of the free school. The masters to whom in 1553 and 1558 the borough paid the salary stipulated by the royal grant were probably masters of the school at Westons, as they were in 1574 and 1583. In 1585 the borough bought the house[31] and the free grammar school continued there until it moved in 1853 to new buildings in Lexden Road, designed by H. W. Hayward.[32] In 1900 there were only 29 boys at the school. By 1905 attendance had risen to 107, but although the buildings had been enlarged, the school needed laboratories, playing fields, more classrooms, an art room, a better library, and a larger and stronger teaching staff.[33] New buildings, including a laboratory, were added in 1910, a swimming pool was opened as a war memorial in 1923, six classrooms were built in 1928, and in 1937 the laboratory was enlarged. Gilberd House was acquired as a hostel in 1903, and three more neighbouring houses were added in 1920 and 1934. In 1933 foundation scholarships were abolished and admission by open examination was introduced.[34] By 1942 attendance had risen to 645 and under the 1944 Education Act the school acquired Voluntary Controlled status. The school was enlarged in 1959 and 1963-4.[35] In 1987 it survived as a selective grammar school.

CHARITY SCHOOLS. *The Bluecoat school.*[36] The school opened in 1710 as a Church charity school for the whole town[37] to prepare *c.* 100 boys and girls for apprenticeship or service. By 1711 the school and teachers' dwellings occupied three houses in Culver Street.[38] It was supported by subscriptions, benefactions, and, at first, voluntary payments from some children. Subscribers and benefactors had the right to nominate children and might partly clothe them. The blue coats and stockings for the boys and blue gowns for the girls supplied from 1715 gave the school its name, and in 1719 figures of a boy and a girl in the distinctive dress were set over the school door. The children were instructed in religious knowledge and practice, including daily prayers and attendance at church on Sunday, and in proper behaviour; boys were also taught reading, writing, and arithmetic and girls to read, sew, and knit. From 1720 the trustees apprenticed two boys each year to local tradesmen and increased the number as more money was subscribed. In 1764 the school taught and clothed 50 boys and 19 girls. The master's salary increased from £30 in 1755 to £50 in 1769, and the mistress's from 14 to 16 guineas in 1772. By 1780 however, income had fallen to £92, barely enough to maintain the school, without the clothing charity. The trustees revived charity sermons, encouraged new subscribers, and limited the number of boys to 40. The master's salary was maintained in view of his diligence, but the girls school, which had declined under a neglectful mistress, was temporarily closed. The school had revived by 1788 when 50 boys and 20 girls attended. By 1811 the school had 128 subscribers and there were plans to enlarge it, but in 1812 it was united with 12 undenominational Sunday schools to form a central National school for all 16 Colchester parishes.

The Bluecoat charity trustees contributed to the cost of the National school and clothed the charity children who were taught there. In 1816 they revived the practice, which had apparently lapsed, of apprenticing two boys a year and extended it to put not more than five girls into domestic service. By 1837 the Bluecoat charity was given to children who had distinguished themselves at the National school and were taught more arithmetic than other children.[39] Nevertheless in the 1870s several charity girls were below the standard formerly required and in 1875 an inspector observed that many of the charity children were dunces. From that time Bluecoat candidates were selected more carefully. From 1886 the Magdalen Street branch National school was open to the charity children. In 1890 the trustees clothed 74 boys and 44 girls, but the distinctive dress was unpopular among girls, and in 1902 *c.* 50 boys and only 25 girls were clothed.[40]

The charity, endowed by a series of benefactors from 1711 onwards, had an annual income of £298 in 1906. In 1913 a farm at Wickham St. Paul's, given by William Naggs in 1747, was sold and the proceeds invested in £676 stock. The endowments of the Bluecoat and National schools were regulated by a Scheme of 1927. The income of those of William Naggs, Sarah Edwards, and Edward Snell to the Bluecoat school and of Margaret and Mary Round to the National school, which then amounted to £363, was to be used to maintain Church of England schools in Colchester, and to provide bibles, clothes, and assistance with further education. Any residue was to be applied to the secondary and further education of Church of England residents in the borough. In 1986 payments to Church of England and county schools amounted to £600 out of an income of *c.* £675.[41]

The Greencoat school[42] originated as a charity day school, apparently connected with the Independent meeting in Moor Lane. It had been

30 P.R.O., PROB 11/19, f. 219.

31 *L. & P. Hen. VIII*, xiv (2), p. 222; E.R.O., D/B 5 R7 f. 249; D/B 5 Gb1, Jan. 1573, Aug. 1585; Morant, *Colch.* 171.

32 *E.C.S.* 12 Aug. 1853.

33 Sadler, *Rep. Sec. and Higher Educ. in Essex*, 229–39, 264.

34 G. H. Martin, *Hist. Colch. Royal Gram. Sch.* 33, 36; E.R.O., C/ME 16, p. 395; C/ME 30, p. 181; C/ME 32, p. 398; *E.R.* xix. 200; P. S. Jeffrey, *Some Chapters in Hist. Royal Gram. Sch.*

35 E.R.O., C/ME 38, p. 348; *Educ. in Essex 1956–60*, 26; *1960–64*, 23.

36 Based on E.R.O., T/A 613; ibid. D/Q 48 (Mins. Trustees, 1810–1914; Mins. Subscribers, 1811–1927); Morant, *Colch.* 179; *Short Acc. of the Church of Eng. Char. Schs. in Colch.* (1868); *E.R.* xlix. 125–33; *E.C.S.* 16 Dec. 1966.

37 S.P.C.K., ALB 2/2041, 2058; *V.C.H. Essex*, ii. 562, where the foundation date is incorrect.

38 S.P.C.K. *Acc. of Char. Schs.* 22.

39 *32nd Rep. Com. Char.*, p. 551.

40 *Kelly's Dir. Essex* (1890, 1902); P. Gifford, *Yesterday's Town*, 46.

41 *32nd Rep. Com. Char.* 548–51; P.R.O., ED 49/2041, 2043, 2046; E.R.O., D/DEl T358/48; ibid. Q/RSr 3, pp. 26–7, 29: *V.C.H. Essex*, ii. 562.

42 Based on E. A. Blaxill, *Hist. Lion Walk Cong. Ch. 1642–1937*, 36; J. A. Tabor, *Brief Hist. Lion Walk Independent Chapel*, 68–9; Morant, *Colch.* 179.

established by 1726 when Arthur Winsley, by will proved 1727, gave £3 a year to teach a boy and a girl. That school survived in 1748.[43] The meeting, which had moved in 1766 to Lion Walk, in 1767 converted the old meeting house to a school. In 1787 the school was named Greencoat from the children's charity clothes.[44] It flourished under William Cole, master 1765–1807, and by the end of the 18th century had 80 children. It was combined in 1812 with Lion Walk Independent Sunday schools to form a British school.[45]

The Charity Sunday Schools. In 1786 a group of Sunday schools was formed, probably at the instigation of Jonathan Tabor whose daughter married William Fox, founder of the Sunday School society. The group comprised five schools for boys and seven for girls, open to all denominations, and a school for nonconformist boys and girls. In 1812 the schools were merged in the central National and British schools.[46]

PAROCHIAL SCHOOLS. ALL SAINTS' parish contained the Royal grammar school until 1853 and the Bluecoat school until 1812, when the central National school opened in the neighbouring parish of St. Nicholas. In 1818 there were many schools, which were probably private,[47] and no parochial school seems to have been established in the early 19th century. Infants probably attended schools in St. James's parish, but by 1851 there was a Church Sunday school in All Saints' parish attended by 100 children from the central National school.[48]

HOLY TRINITY. By 1841 a Church Sunday school for *c.* 20 children had been opened in a room in Lady Darcy's almshouses in Eld Lane. It was a National Sunday school with 26 children by 1846, and 50 by 1851.[49] In 1859 *Holy Trinity National day school* for 40 was built in Eld Lane. It survived in 1882, but had closed by 1886. The schoolroom in the almshouse continued to be used, presumably by the Sunday school.[50]

ST. BOTOLPH'S parish contained the central British school;[51] no parochial day school was established, but by 1841 there was a Church Sunday school for 300 children, supported by subscriptions. By 1851 it was attended by *c.* 160 children and 106 children from the parish attended the central National school,[52] which in that year opened its Magdalen Street branch to accommodate them.[53]

ST. GILES'S. In 1832 an infant school maintained by subscription and pence opened at Old Heath with *c.* 150 children. It survived in 1841 and was not then restricted to Church children, but by 1846 it had become a National school with 114 infants, and a Church Sunday school had been opened with 70 older children, who attended the central National day school. The infant school, which survived in 1866, had closed by 1870.[54] In 1872 a new infant school for 65 was opened, but the rented building soon proved unsuitable, and in 1875 the school moved to a new building in Old Heath Road, which was also used as the district church of St. Barnabas. It was built by subscription and diocesan and National Society grants, but by 1887 the rector was supporting the school with little help.[55] In 1893 the school had accommodation for 63 children and an average attendance of 53. It was replaced by a board school in 1894.[56]

ST. JAMES'S. A Sunday school, started in 1823, survived in 1829 but had failed by 1833.[57] A new Sunday school had been started under the patronage of George Round by 1839, when 70 children were being taught in the church. By 1846 the school had 130 children who also attended the central National day school, and a few were taught in the evening.[58] Soon afterwards the boys were transferred to St. Nicholas's Sunday school, but in 1859 a Sunday school for boys and girls was built in St. James's parish in a lane, later Guildford Road, off East Hill.[59] A Church day school for infants was opened *c.* 1836 in East Street. Attendance there rose from 52 in 1839 to 95 in 1846, but the school was short of money and, although it survived in 1852, it seems to have closed soon after.[60] A new infant school, under the patronage of Margaret Round, was opened *c.* 1864 in a hired building in East Street. In the 1870s it was usually attended by *c.* 140 children, and from 1878 it received annual government grants. The building was condemned in 1891, and in 1894, when the National branch school vacated its East Hill building,[61] St. James's infants moved there.[62] In 1899, to prevent the establishment of a board school in the parish, the rector, C. C. Naters, started a girls school and soon afterwards a boys school

43 E.R.O., D/Q 30/6/1; Morant, *Colch.* (1748) Bk. III, p. 17.

44 Anon. *Hist. and Antiquities Colch.* (1789), 128.

45 Below, this section, Nonconf. Schs.

46 N. Forster, *Discourse on the Utility of Sunday Schs.* (1786), pp. 31–3; *32nd Rep. Com. Char.* p. 560; *E.C.S.* 25 Mar. 1864; *D.N.B.*; below, this section, Other Church of England Schs.; Nonconf. Schs.

47 *Returns Educ. Poor*, H.C. 224, p. 245 (1819), ix (1).

48 P.R.O., HO 129/8/204.

49 E.R.O., D/ACM 12; Nat. Soc. *Inquiry 1846–7*, Essex, 6–7; MS. by W. J. D. Raven in possession of D'Arcy charity trustees; P.R.O., HO 129/8/204.

50 *Kelly's Dir. Essex* (1878, 1882, 1886); *Official Enq. into Colch. Chars. 1886*; *E.C.S.* 24 Apr. 1897.

51 Below, this section, Nonconf. Schs.

52 *Returns Educ. Poor,* p. 267; E.R.O., D/ACM 12.

53 P.R.O., HO 129/8/204; E.R.O., D/DRb F11.

54 *Educ. Enq. Abstract,* p. 271; E.R.O., D/ACM 12; D/DRb F11; Nat. Soc. *Inquiry 1846–7*, Essex, 6–7; *Kelly's Dir. Essex* (1866 and later edns.).

55 *E.C.S.* 20 Dec. 1872; Nat. Soc. file; E.R.O., D/P 324/8/2; ibid. T/A 645.

56 *E.C.S.* 4 Feb. 1893; below, this section, Board Schs. (Old Heath).

57 E.R.O., D/P 138/3/2; D/P 138/8/7; *Educ. Enq. Abstract*, p. 271.

58 E.R.O., D/P 30/28/18; Nat. Soc. *Inquiry 1846–7*, Essex, 6-7.

59 M. Seaman, *Valedictory address to the parishioners of St. James's, Colch.* (1850), 8: copy in E.R.O., Box C6; *E.C.S.* 13 May 1859.

60 E.R.O., D/P 30/28/18; ibid. T/M 399 (map 1848); Nat. Soc. *Inquiry 1846–7*, Essex, 6–7; *E.C.S.* 23 July 1852.

61 Below, this section, Other Church of England Schs.

62 E.R.O., D/P 138/28/9 (1884, 1886); E.R.O., Colch. Sch. Bd. Mins. (1892), p. 5; Nat. Soc. file; *Rep. Educ. Cttee. of Council, 1878–9* [C. 2342–I], p. 886, H.C. (1878–9), xxiii; *Kelly's Dir. Essex* (1890); *E.C.S.* 19 Dec. 1891.

in the East Hill building, and moved the infants to St. Anne's mission, Harwich Road. In 1906 he closed St. James's boys department, which was threatened by the building of East Ward council school, and moved the infants back to East Hill.[63] In 1930 *St. James's Church of England school* was reorganized for juniors and infants. In 1949 it was granted Aided status and moved in 1961 to a new building for 120 children, opposite the old one. Seven new classrooms were added between 1962 and 1971 to accommodate *c.* 345 children.[64] Margaret Round, by will proved 1887, gave £1,500 in trust to pay £15 a year to the infant school and £10 to the Sunday school.[65]

ST. LEONARD'S. A Church Sunday school was founded in 1780[66] and in 1836 an infant day school was added. Both schools were supported by subscription and pence. In 1839 the Sunday school was attended by 90 children, of whom 20 also attended the central National day school; there were 50 children in the infant school, and there were also four small dame schools, mostly kept by Church people.[67] Attendance at the infant school had declined to 60 by 1841 and in 1845 Francis Curtis, rector 1839–61, who was concerned about immorality among girls in his parish, reorganized the school for girls of any age above 5 and boys from 5 until their admission to the central National school.[68] By 1846 St. Leonard's day school was attended by 28 girls and 18 boys, but by 1848 the school was attended by infants only and by 1850 the schoolroom had been given up, although children were still being taught.[69] By 1851 *c.* 48 older children from the parish attended the National school, which in that year opened a branch in Magdalen Street, and only the Sunday school survived at St. Leonard's, attended by 110 children.[70] By 1868 *c.* 50 children from the parish attended Magdalen Street National school and an evening school for factory workers had been started by John G. Bingley, rector 1864–74,[71] but many Church children were attending a 'wretched little school' which Bingley wanted to replace by a Church school. He overcame government opposition to a school solely for infants, and in 1869 built *St. Leonard's National school* on Hythe Hill by subscription and grants for 150 infants.[72] The school received annual government grants from its opening.[73] In 1873 it became a mixed school with an infant department,[74] but by 1875 the infant room was too small. Teaching was disrupted by many unruly and unwilling children, driven to school by enforcement of the 1876 Education Act. By 1885 children were being turned away from the day school, Sunday attendance had risen to 270, and some older boys were being taught at the Rectory. In that year the school was enlarged by subscription and government grant for 300 mixed and infant children.[75] In 1891 the older boys were sent to other schools, but St. Leonard's school was still overcrowded.[76] It was taken over by the school board in 1894 and replaced by Barrack Street board school in 1896.[77]

ST. MARTIN'S. A Church Sunday school, supported by subscription, had been founded by 1833, when it had 100 children, who probably worked in a local silk factory. By 1841 attendance had fallen to 32,[78] and by 1843 the school had failed; in that year 25 infants from St. Martin's attended St. Peter's day school. In 1845, William Murray, rector 1836–50, started a day school for infant girls. In 1847, aided by subscription and a National Society grant, he built a day and Sunday school in the churchyard in East Stockwell Street for 95 infant girls.[79] Attendance rose from 39 in 1846 to *c.* 70 in 1851.[80] The school seems to have become a mixed infant school by 1871 and from that year received annual government grants. By 1891 the school was overcrowded, but its cramped site made enlargement impossible and in 1892 it was taken over by the school board.[81] An evening school teaching reading, writing, arithmetic, and needlework to young women and girls was being held in the infant school by 1876. It survived in 1878 but was not recorded thereafter.[82]

ST. MARY'S-AT-THE-WALLS. In the early 19th century there was no parish Sunday school to complement the central National day school, which St. Mary's children attended. In 1843 *c.* 15 children from the parish attended St. Peter's infant school but by 1859 a Church Sunday school and a dame school had been established, probably by C. A. L'Oste, rector 1855–70. In 1859 those schools were teaching *c.* 100 children. In 1864 the Sunday school moved from the church to a room built by subscription on land at St. Mary's Steps, Balkerne Lane, given by L'Oste. In 1873 St. Mary's Church infant day school was started there by J. W. Irvine, rector 1870–97.[83] From 1875, when it was attended by 35 infants, the school received annual government

63 Nat. Soc. file; *Colch. Boro. Council Mins.* 1905–6, p. 911.

64 *Colch. Boro. Council Mins.* 1929–30, p. 573; E.R.O., D/P 138/28/5; inf. from sch.

65 Char. Com. file.

66 Centenary celebrations, 1880: D. Weston, 'Indexes and extracts from log bks. of St. Leonard's sch.' (TS. in E.R.O.); E.R.O., D/P 245/5/2.

67 E.R.O., D/P 30/28/18.

68 Ibid. D/ACM 12; *E.C.S.* 28 Mar. 1845.

69 Nat. Soc. *Inquiry 1846–7*, Essex, 6–7; E.R.O., T/M 399; *Essex Tel.* 12 Feb. 1850.

70 E.R.O., D/DRb F11; P.R.O., HO 129/8/204.

71 Nat. Soc. file; E.R.O., T/A 547/1.

72 E.R.O., D/P 245/28/16; ibid. E/P 35; O.S. Map 6", Essex, XXVIII (1881 edn.).

73 *Rep. Educ. Cttee. of Council*, 1870–1 [C. 406], p. 455, H.C. (1871), xxii.

74 E.R.O., D/P 245/28/17.

75 Nat. Soc. file; Weston, 'Indexes and extracts'; *Kelly's Dir. Essex* (1890).

76 P. Quinlivan, *Hist. Wilson Marriage Secondary Sch.* 7.

77 Nat. Soc. file; E.R.O., E/ML 129/1.

78 *Educ. Enq. Abstract*, p. 271; E.R.O., D/ACM 12; ibid. T/M 399.

79 Nat. Soc. file; *E.C.S.* 6 Jan. 1843; 11 Dec. 1846.

80 Nat. Soc. *Inquiry 1846–7*, Essex, 6–7; *E.C.S.* 11 July 1851.

81 *Rep. Educ. Cttee. of Council, 1871–2* [601], p. 257, H.C. (1872), xxii; *E.C.S.* 19 Dec. 1891.

82 *Goody's Colch. Almanac* (1876), 17; (1878), 17.

83 *E.C.S.* 6 Jan. 1843; 8 July 1859; 13 Apr. 1864; 12 July, 20 Dec. 1872.

grants, and by 1882 attendance had risen to 99.[84] In 1885 attempts to replace the building failed, and although it was enlarged for 131 in 1887,[85] by 1891 it was overcrowded. Another building appeal failed in 1892, when a school board was impending.[86] The school continued to be supported by subscription and government grants,[87] and in 1903 was officially commended for its instruction and discipline. It suffered from school board competition and attendance declined;[88] in 1930 Board of Education recognition was withdrawn, and the school closed.[89]

ST. MARY MAGDALEN'S. By 1833 subscribers were supporting a Church Sunday school of 40 children who contributed pence, and three day schools attended by 182, but the parish was very poor and by 1846 only a Church Sunday school of 8 children survived.[90] Although by 1851 attendance had risen to 30, it was far lower than in other parts of the town, and only 7 children from the parish attended the central National day school.[91]

ST. NICHOLAS'S. The central National school opened in the parish in 1812 and *c.* 1832 a Church Sunday school, maintained by subscription, was opened in the central day school building. Attendance rose from 27 boys and 23 girls in 1839 to 111 boys and 45 girls by 1846, but in 1851 only 40 children attended and some of those were apparently boys from St. James's parish. No parish school for infants was established and by 1843 a few attended St. Peter's day school.[92]

ST. PAUL'S. A Sunday school was opened in the early 1870s at St. Paul's chapel of ease, North Street. In 1875 a day school for 150 infants was built by subscription and grant in Belle Vue Road, to serve the growing population near North Street railway station.[93] The school received annual government grants from 1880, when it was attended by 31 children.[94] Numbers rose to 70 in 1890 and in the autumn of 1891 more than doubled to reach 193 by December. In 1894, when North Street Board school opened, numbers fell to 146 and St. Paul's school began to decline. It closed in 1901.[95]

ST. PETER'S. In 1818 there were two girls schools in the parish, supported by voluntary contributions. They had apparently failed by 1823, when a dame school for 30 girls was opened. John Mills, by will dated 1822, gave 25*s.* a year to support a Church Sunday school which may also have opened in 1823.[96] By 1826 William Marsh, vicar 1814–29, had built a schoolroom next to the vicarage house and opened the first Church infant school in Colchester. His successor, Samuel Carr, took over the dame school and its 30 girls in 1833. There were then 192 children at the infant school, and 340 in the Sunday school.[97] He apparently started a central evening school, where *c.* 70 boys aged 6–16 were being taught in the period 1835–7,[98] and in 1836, aided by a government grant, bought a room in Crispin Court and converted it to a school for *c.* 150 girls. In 1839 St. Peter's Church day schools were attended by 150 infants and 70 girls, and the Sunday school, supported by Mills's charity, by 250 children. The day schools were supported by subscription and pence.[99] In 1843 many children from neighbouring parishes attended the infant school, but after a successful master's departure in 1851 the day schools declined and by 1859 they had only 74 infants and 40 girls, taught by untrained teachers.[1] Nevertheless the infant school was enlarged in 1886 and by 1891 had *c.* 147 children, still taught by untrained teachers. It escaped official condemnation, but the girls school was too bad for government recognition.[2] Both schools were closed by 1893.[3] An evening school for young women existed in 1861.[4]

ST. RUNWALD'S. A Sunday school was attended by 20 boys and 6 girls in 1841, and 9 infants from the parish were attending St. Peter's school in 1843. By 1846 a day school, supported by subscriptions, had been opened in the parish, but it and the Sunday school had only nine children each.[5] By 1851 Sunday school attendance had risen to 12; in that year a branch of the National day school opened in Magdalen Street, and St. Runwald's day school seems to have closed.[6]

OTHER CHURCH OF ENGLAND SCHOOLS.[7] *The Central National school* was formed in 1812 by the union of the Bluecoat charity school with a group of Sunday schools. The school, held in a converted warehouse in Maidenburgh Street, adopted the Madras monitorial system,

84 *Rep. Educ. Cttee. of Council 1875–6* [C. 1513–I], p. 532, H.C. (1876), xxiii; *1882–3* [C. 3706–I], p. 652, H.C. (1883), xxv.

85 Nat. Soc. file; *E.C.S.* 28 Jan. 1888; *Returns Elem. Educ. 1893* [C. 7529], p. 164, H.C. (1894), lxv.

86 *E.C.S.* 19 Dec. 1891; 23 Apr. 1892; Nat. Soc. file; E.R.O., D/DVv 76.

87 *Returns Elem. Educ. 1893* [C. 7529], p. 164, H.C. (1894), lxv; *1899* [Cd. 315], p. 324, H.C. (1900), lxv (2).

88 E.R.O., E/S 3/16–17.

89 *Colch. Boro. Council Mins.* 1929–30, pp. 349, 574.

90 *Educ. Enq. Abstract*, p. 272; Nat. Soc. *Inquiry 1846–7*, Essex, 6–7; *E.C.S.* 19 Jan. 1844.

91 P.R.O., HO 129/8/204; E.R.O., D/DRb F11; *E.C.S.* 25 July 1851.

92 E.R.O., D/P 30/28/12, 18; Nat. Soc. *Inquiry 1846–7*, Essex 6–7; P.R.O., HO 129/8/204; *E.C.S.* 6 Jan. 1843.

93 Nat. Soc. file; *Kelly's Dir. Essex* (1882).

94 *Rep. Educ. Cttee. of Council, 1880–1* [C. 2948–I], p. 576, H.C. (1881), xxxii.

95 *Kelly's Dir. Essex* (1890, 1894); *E.C.S.* 19 Dec. 1891; Nat. Soc. file.

96 *Returns Educ. Poor*, H.C. 224, p. 269 (1819), ix (1); *Educ. Enq. Abstract*, p. 272; *32nd Rep. Com. Char.* p. 562; E.R.O., D/P 178/5/2.

97 E.R.O., D/P 178/6/1; D/P 30/28/18; ibid. T/A 645; *Returns Parl. Grants for Educ. 1834–7*, H.C. 395, p. 10 (1837–8), xxxviii; *Educ. Enq. Abstract*, H.C. 62, p. 272 (1835), xli; Nat. Soc. file.

98 E.R.O., D/P 178/28/10.

99 Nat. Soc. file; E.R.O., D/P 30/28/18; *32nd Rep. Com. Char.* p. 562.

1 *E.C.S.* 6 Jan. 1843; 25 Apr. 1851; *Rep. Educ. Cttee. of Council, 1859–60* [2681], p. 6, H.C. (1860), liv.

2 *E.C.S.* 19 Dec. 1891; E.R.O., T/A 645.

3 *Returns Elem. Educ. 1893* [C. 7529], p. 164, H.C. (1894), lxv.

4 *E.C.S.* 16 Aug. 1861.

5 E.R.O., D/ACM 12; *E.C.S.* 6 Jan. 1843; Nat. Soc. *Inquiry 1846–7*, Essex, 6–7.

6 P.R.O., HO 129/8/204.

7 From 1907 'National' was omitted from titles of schs.: *Colch. Boro. Council Mins.* 1906–7, p. 486.

which enabled large numbers to be taught by a few teachers. By 1817 it was attended by 206 boys and 112 girls; from 1830 St. Helen's chapel was used for extra classrooms[8] and by 1839 numbers had risen to 330 boys and 115 girls. In the 1850s the National school committee clothed 80–90 children.[9] The school was supported by subscription, fees, sermons, and collections at the annual school festival, and from 1856, by government grants.[10] It was highly praised by government inspectors,[11] but the building was unsuitable, and in 1861 a new school was built by subscription and grants in St. Helen's Lane.[12] Although in the 1870s the standard achieved by most of the girls was low, the school continued to flourish under successive headmasters, among them a former Bluecoat boy who had also been a pupil teacher there, and in 1878 the school was enlarged.[13] Competition from board schools after 1892 reduced the National school's subscriptions and enrolment, and in 1896 the master left to become headmaster of Barrack Street Board school.[14] The number of boys attending the National school fell from 430 in 1890 to 350 in 1902, but the number of girls remained constant at 180.[15] In 1904 the school was reorganized as a mixed school and enlarged. In 1920, when a central council school was opened, the National central school was renamed *Bluecoats*.[16] By 1937 only 153 children attended. The transfer of senior children to St. Helena council school in 1938 left only 50 juniors at the school and it closed in 1939.[17]

Magdalen Street National branch school was opened in 1851 for 200 children from the parishes of St. Mary Magdalen, St. Leonard, St. Botolph, St. Giles, and St. James. It flourished under Thomas Shave, who had 20 years experience at St. Peter's infant school.[18] From 1856 Magdalen Street school received annual government grants, and by 1866 it was one of the best mixed schools in the Essex and Suffolk inspectorate.[19] In 1879, to relieve overcrowding, the school was reorganized for boys only. It was reorganized for juniors and infants in 1935 and closed in 1936.[20]

Osborne Street National infant school probably started in 1857 as the Ragged infants' school in Osborne Street, later taken over by St. Botolph's parish. A new infants school was built in 1870 in Osborne Street.[21] By 1891 it was attended by *c.* 200, but there was no room on the site for enlargement. It was taken over by the school board in 1892 and replaced in 1898.[22]

Stanway All Saints' National school was opened at Bottle End, Lexden, in 1861 for more than 70 children in the parish of All Saints' Stanway taken from the parishes of Stanway and Lexden. The school was enlarged in 1882 and 1910. In 1930 the school became a council school called Shrub End junior mixed and infants school. It closed between 1965 and 1974.[23]

East Hill branch National school opened in 1873 in St. James's Sunday school building. Attendance increased from 91 in 1879 to 118 in 1891.[24] It closed in 1892.[25]

Stanwell Street National school opened in 1873 in the Ragged school building in Stanwell Street.[26] It received annual government grants from its beginning and, although the building was inadequate and had no playground, attendance rose from 43 in 1874 to 101 in 1878 and 153 in 1886.[27] The school was taken over by the school board in 1892 and replaced in 1898 by St. John's Green school.[28]

Kendall Road National, later *Church of England, school* for girls and infants was built for 356 children by subscription and National Society grant in 1890.[29] Attendance rose from 269 in 1893 to 326 in 1899.[30] In 1935 it was reorganized for junior girls and infants, although boys were admitted to the first year of the junior school. In 1937 the school was reorganized for mixed juniors and infants. It was granted Controlled status in 1953 and moved in 1975 to new buildings for 280 in Recreation Road,[31] where it continued in 1987.

ROMAN CATHOLIC SCHOOLS. In 1838 a day school was opened in the basement of the new church in Priory Street and by 1841 it had *c.* 24 children.[32] Although in 1845 it was alleged that *c.* 40 children needed free education, only 17 attended in 1851, and in 1859, when the

8 *Returns Educ. Poor*, H.C. 224, p. 268 (1819), ix (1); *32nd Rep. Com. Char.* pp. 548–51; *Rep. of National Sch. at Colch.* (1852); ibid. (1855) (Pamphs. in E.C.L. Colch.).

9 *Short Acct. of the Church of Eng. Schs. in Colch.* (1868), 6; *Nat. Soc. Rep.* (1817); *E.R.* xlix. 127–8.

10 E.R.O., D/P 30/28/18.

11 *Mins. Educ. Cttee. of Council, 1856–7* [2237], p. 94, H.C. (1857 sess. 2), xxxiii; *Rep. Educ. Cttee. of Council, 1859–60* [2681], p. 59, H.C. (1860), liv; E.R.O., D/Q 48 (Mins. Bluecoat trustees, 1857).

12 *E.C.S.* 26 Mar. 1858; 25 Oct. 1861; 10 May 1865; Nat. Soc. file; E.R.O., E/P 33; *Short Acct. Ch. of Eng. Schs. in Colch.* (1868), 13.

13 E.R.O., D/Q 48 (Mins. Bluecoat trustees); *Kelly's Dir. Essex* (1866–90); *E.C.S.* 9 June, 1871; 29 Mar. 1872; *Colch. National Schs.* (1879) (Pamph. in E.C.L. Colch.)

14 E.R.O. D/Q 48 (Mins. Bluecoat trustees).

15 *Kelly's Dir. Essex* (1890, 1902).

16 *Colch. Boro. Council Mins.* 1903–4, p. 868; ibid. 1904–5, p. 508; E.R.O., Boro. Mun., Educ. Cttee. Mins. 1917–22, p. 265.

17 *Colch. Boro. Council Mins.* 1937–8, p. 785; *E.R.* xlix, p. 133.

18 *E.C.S.* 25 Apr.; 25 July 1851; E.R.O., D/DRb F11.

19 *Mins. Educ. Cttee. of Council, 1856–7* [2237], p. 94, H.C. (1857), xxxiii; *Rep. Educ. Cttee. of Council, 1866–7* [3882], p. 86, H.C. (1867), xxii.

20 *Colch. National Schs.* (1879) (Pamph. in E.C.L. Colch.); *Colch. Boro. Council Mins.* 1934–5, p. 760; ibid. 1935–6, pp. 74, 758.

21 F. Lord, 'The Colch. Ragged Schools, 1854–80' (Essex Univ. B.A. project), 36.

22 *E.C.S.* 19 Dec. 1891; 1 July 1893; 22 Feb. 1896; E.R.O., Colch. Sch. Bd. Mins. 1892, pp. 5, 9, 31.

23 E.R.O., T/P 173; Essex Educ. Dept., List of Schs. (1974).

24 Nat. Soc. file (St. James's par.); *E.C.S.* 20 Dec. 1872; 15 Oct. 1873; 19 Dec. 1891; *Colch. National Schs.* (Pamph. in E.C.L. Colch.).

25 *E.C.S.* 5 Mar. 1892.

26 *E.C.S.* 20 Dec. 1872; *Kelly's Dir. Essex* (1894).

27 *Rep. Educ. Cttee. of Council, 1874–5* [C.1265–I], p. 317, H.C. (1875), xxiv; *1878–9* [C. 2342–I], p. 887, H.C. (1878–9), xxiii; *1886–7* [C. 5123–I], p. 518, H.C. (1887), xxviii.

28 *E.C.S.* 1 July 1893.

29 Nat. Soc. file; *Building News*, lvii. 482.

30 *Returns Elem. Educ. 1893* [C. 7529], p. 164, H.C. (1894), lxv; *1899* [Cd. 315], p. 322, H.C. (1900), lxv (2).

31 Log bks. in possession of headmaster; *Colch. Boro. Council Mins.* 1934–5, p. 760; ibid. 1936–7, p. 730; Essex Co. Architect's Dept. *Kendall Sch.* (Plans in E.R.O.).

32 S. Foster, *Ch. of St. James the Less and St. Helen, Colch. 1837–1987* (priv. print.), 13; E.R.O., D/ACM 12.

children of Irish soldiers attended the garrison schools, there were only 12 children on the school roll.[33] The school survived in 1864, but in 1866 it had no master. Although the Catholic Poor Schools Committee gave a small building grant that year, it was not until 1870 that two schoolrooms for a total of 80 children were added on the north side of the church.[34] The school failed in 1880 but reopened in 1883.[35] From 1891 it was taught by Sisters of Mercy, who had recently moved from Brentwood, and by 1893 it had 100 children. A new school for 240 was built south of the church in 1896, and in 1902 it was enlarged for 292.[36] Many of the children were of the poorest classes of all quarters of the town and some were unacceptable to other schools.[37] Priory Street school was enlarged again in 1951. In 1953 it was renamed *St. Thomas More school*, and in 1952 was granted Voluntary Aided status. It was reorganized in 1963 for juniors and infants, and in 1967 a new infant building was added. In 1974 the building of 1896 was demolished and replaced by a new block, linking the 1902 building with that of 1967.[38]

St. Benedict's Voluntary Aided Roman Catholic secondary school, Norman Way, opened in 1963 when *c.* 180 seniors from St. Thomas More school moved to new buildings for 300. St. Benedict's was enlarged in 1974 for 600, and in 1976 it became comprehensive.[39]

St. Teresa's Roman Catholic Voluntary Aided primary school, Clairmont Road, Lexden, opened for 280 in 1967.[40]

NONCONFORMIST SCHOOLS. *The central British School* was formed in 1812 by the union of the Greencoat and Lion Walk Independent Sunday schools. It was conducted on Joseph Lancaster's monitorial system and maintained by subscription and pence. Some children were clothed, as they had been in the Greencoat school, and in 1819 all were outfitted. The trustees continued to clothe a few children until 1848 or later.[41] By 1815 early indiscipline had been overcome and enrolment grew from 135 boys and 95 girls in 1815 to 176 boys and 141 girls in 1817. Boys always outnumbered girls but in the 1830s the proportion of girls attending the school fell from 44 per cent to 33 per cent. The school prospered and an infant school was added *c.* 1834.[42] An evening school, opened in 1849, had 70 pupils by 1855 but many soon lost interest and the school seems to have failed. In 1853 a new day school for 500 was built on the site of the old one. By 1857 reading, writing, arithmetic, grammar, geography, history, bookkeeping, and needlework were being taught, to 221 children.[43] The school received annual government grants from 1869, but by 1871 the girls school had declined under an unqualified teacher and from that year it seems to have been supervised by the master.[44] By 1890 the school was attended by some 400 children but its supporters could not afford to improve the building and by 1893 it had been taken over by the school board.[45]

A trust founded in 1790, apparently for teaching boys at the Greencoat school, was applied to the British school. In 1900 the British school building in Priory Street was sold and the proceeds invested in £1,020 stock. Under a Scheme of that year the income was to provide grammar school scholarships for boys of the borough who were educated beyond the usual school leaving standard. Under a Scheme of 1922 the income was to provide exhibitions to technical or secondary schools and to universities.[46] The sale of the Ragged school building in 1899 produced £600 which was invested in the same fund. In 1965 the accumulating capital was £19,040.[47]

BAPTISTS. In 1817 a Sunday school, supported by subscription, opened at Eld Lane chapel. Attendance reached 120 by 1833, but fell to 60 by 1851. A new schoolroom was built in 1868 and the school continued after 1870.[48]

INDEPENDENTS. A Sunday school at Lion Walk church may have been founded as early as 1782; it was included among the group of charity Sunday schools formed in 1786,[49] and in 1812 it was united with the Greencoat school as the central British school.[50]

The Lion Walk congregation opened a number of day and Sunday schools in association with their preaching stations between 1836 and 1848. *Old Heath school*, opened in 1836 in a room at the Bell public house, moved in 1837 to Saville Cottage and was probably the infant school in St. Giles's parish recorded in 1841. A Sunday school was added in 1843.[51] Both schools survived

33 Catholic Poor Schs. Cttee. *Ann. Rep. 1848*, 50; *Essex Recusant*, viii. 99; Foster, *Ch. of St. James*, 19.

34 *E.C.S.* 8 Apr. 1864; *Kelly's Dir. Essex* (1866, 1890); Catholic Poor Schs. Cttee. *Ann. Rep. 1868*, 60; Foster, *Ch. of St. James*, 21–2.

35 Foster, *Ch. of St. James the Less*, 22; P.R.O., ED 21/5494.

36 *Returns Elem. Educ. 1893* [C. 7529], p. 164, H.C. (1894), lxv; P.R.O., ED 21/5494; *Kelly's Dir. Essex* (1902); Foster, *Ch. of St. James*, 25.

37 *Colch. Boro. Council Mins.* 1906–7, pp. 576–7.

38 E.R.O., C/ME 45, p. 338; C/ME 46, p. 130; C/ME 47, p. 673.

39 Ibid. C/ME 57, p. 537; inf. from E.C.C. Educ. (Bldgs. and Maintenance) Dept.; inf. from school.

40 *Essex Educ.* xxi (3), 64; E.R.O., C/ME 63, p. A16.

41 *White's Dir. Essex* (1848), 89; T. Cromwell, *Hist. Colch.* i. 323; *Returns Educ. Poor*, H.C. 224, p. 267 (1819), ix (1).

42 Brit. and Foreign Sch. Soc. *Ann. Reps.* (1815–44); ibid. *Quarterly Extracts from Correspondence*, xvii, 31 Mar. 1831, p. 34; *Educ. Enq. Abstract*, p. 271.

43 J. A. Tabor, *Brief Hist. Independent Chapel, Lion Walk*, 70; E. A. Blaxill, *Hist. Lion Walk Cong. Ch. Colch., 1842–1937*, 41–2; *E.C.S.* 11 May 1855.

44 *Rep. Educ. Cttee. of Council, 1869–70* [C. 165], p. 568, H.C. (1870), xxii; *1879–80* [C. 2562–I], p. 590, H.C. (1880), xxii; *1880–1* [C. 2948–I], p. 576, H.C. (1881), xxxii; Brit. and Foreign Sch. Soc. Correspondence file 373; *Kelly's Dir. Essex* (1878 and later edns.).

45 *E.C.S.* 4 Feb. 1893; *Rep. Educ. Cttee. of Council*, 1893–4 [C. 7437–I], p. 815, H.C. (1894), xxix; Blaxill, *Hist. Lion Walk Cong. Ch.* 36.

46 P.R.O., ED 49/2044.

47 P.R.O., ED 49/2045; inf. from Essex Educ. Dept.

48 E. A. Blaxill, *Nonconf. Chs. Colch.* 15; *Educ. Enq. Abstract*, p. 271; P.R.O., HO 129/8/204.

49 Blaxill, *Hist. Lion Walk Cong. Ch.* 36; N. Forster, *Discourse on the Utility of Sunday Schs.* (1786), 31–3; *D.N.B.* s.v. Fox.

50 Above, this section, British sch.

51 Blaxill, *Hist. Lion Walk Cong. Ch.* 32–3; E.R.O., D/CT 91; D/ACM 12; *White's Dir. Essex* (1848), 89, 99.

in 1851, but the day school seems to have closed by 1863.[52] *Shrub End day and Sunday schools* opened *c.* 1839, and in 1842 a small school chapel was built. Attendance at the day school fell from 30 in 1861[53] to 22 in 1870, but the school survived until *c.* 1878.[54] *East Street Sunday school* opened in 1840 and, although a new school chapel was built in *Harwich Road* in 1844, the East Street room seems to have remained in use as an infant day school until *c.* 1848.[55] The day school in Harwich Road, which survived in 1851, seems to have closed by 1863; the Sunday school alone survived in 1876.[56] *The Hythe Sunday school* was opened by the mission there in 1846 and by 1851 a day school had been added, which survived in 1876 with *c.* 75 children.[57] The *Stockwell Street* congregation had a Sunday school by 1841 or earlier and in 1848 new schoolrooms were built.[58] *Chapel Street (Headgate) Sunday school* opened *c.* 1843 and a day school of 100 infants was added soon afterwards. A schoolroom was built south of the chapel in 1845.[59] The infant school flourished in 1848, but nothing more is known of it. The Sunday school was attended by some 65 children in 1851 and was enlarged in 1875 and 1903.[60]

METHODISTS. In 1837 Wesleyan Methodists built a Sunday school next to their chapel in Culver Street, and by 1841 it was attended by *c.* 185 children.[61] In 1843 a day school was added, which taught elementary and more advanced subjects by the Glasgow system to children who paid from 3*s.* to 9*s.* a quarter.[62] The day school survived in 1850, but had closed by 1863.[63] In 1869 the building was enlarged for 340 and reopened in 1871 as a new higher grade Wesleyan school for 340. It flourished under Henry E. Shaw, master 1871–1916, and in 1882 was said to be among the four best schools in Essex.[64] It received annual government grants from 1872. Attendance rose from 143 in 1874 to 343 in 1886,[65] and by 1887 the school was full. In that year the building was enlarged for 527 and a room for 120 infants was added.[66] By 1909 the building was inadequate, but the site precluded enlargement or alteration, and in 1910 the infant school was closed to make more room for the senior school. The school's fee-paying status and the education it provided, between elementary and grammar school standards, appealed to middle-class parents, and Colchester education committee paid grants to children attending the school. In 1909 the Board of Education, which disapproved of the 'classy' nature of the school, urged the council to replace it with a council school.[67] The First World War delayed the opening of Hamilton Road council school and, although overcrowding remained a problem, the Wesleyan school survived until 1920.[68]

The Hythe Wesleyan school. There was a small Wesleyan Sunday school at the Hythe in 1839, which seems to have survived until *c.* 1848.[69] In 1871 the Culver Street Methodists opened a branch school for 100 children in Back Lane, later Spurgeon Street. It was soon overcrowded and in the 1880s it was often unruly.[70] It was apparently enlarged *c.* 1884, after the closure of a Wesleyan branch school at Elmstead,[71] and by 1891 had 265 children, crowded into two rooms, as its cramped site made enlargement impossible.[72] In 1894 the school board took over the Wesleyan school and in 1896 replaced it by Barrack Street school.[73]

Magdalen Street infant school was opened *c.* 1843, probably by Wesleyan Methodists, who had a chapel there, to serve a poor and thickly populated area where funds were hard to raise. It survived in 1848 but nothing more is known of it.[74]

PRIMITIVE METHODISTS had a Sunday school of *c.* 80 children at their Barrack Ground chapel in 1851. In 1858 the schoolroom was enlarged; the school probably survived after 1870.[75]

PRESBYTERIANS. Henry Dobby gave £50 to a Presbyterian school, which was attended by 18 boys in 1789. It was probably merged in the central British school in 1812. The income from Dobby's charity was £4 11*s.* in 1916.[76]

SOCIETY OF FRIENDS. Schools kept by Quakers are recorded from 1691. From 1722 to 1758 or later there were usually two or three such schools and poor children attending them were maintained by the two-week meeting.[77] John Kendall (d. 1815) left £1,000 in trust to teach reading,

52 P.R.O., HO 129/8/204; *White's Dir. Essex* (1863), 95, 109.

53 Blaxill, *Hist. Lion Walk Cong. Ch.* 34; P.R.O., HO 129/8/204.

54 *E.C.S.* 23 Dec. 1870; *Goody's Colch. Almanac* (1878), 17.

55 Blaxill, *Nonconf. Ch. Colch.* 23; E.R.O., T/M 399 (map 1848); *White's Dir. Essex* (1848), 89.

56 P.R.O., HO 129/8/204; *White's Dir. Essex* (1863), 95; *Goody's Colch. Almanac* (1876), 17.

57 Blaxill, *Hist Lion Walk Cong. Ch.* 34; P.R.O., HO 129/8/204; *Goody's Colch. Almanac* (1876), 17; E.R.O., T/M 399 (map 1848).

58 E.R.O., D/ACM 12; Blaxill, *Nonconf. Ch. Colch.* 14.

59 J. W. Newby, *Story of Headgate 1843–1943*, 25; Blaxill, *Nonconf. Chs. Colch.* 22.

60 E.R.O., T/M 399 (map 1848); P.R.O., HO 129/8/204; Blaxill, *Nonconf. Ch. Colch.* 22.

61 J. A. Baker, *Short Hist. Methodism in Colch.* 11; E.R.O., D/ACM 12; D/P 30/28/12.

62 E.R.O., D/NM 2/4/1; *Essex Countryside*, Nov. 1969, 36–9.

63 *White's Dir. Essex* (1848), 99; (1863), 109; *E.C.S.* 27 Dec. 1850.

64 E.R.O., D/NM 2/4/1; *Essex Countryside*, Nov. 1969, 38; *Rep. Educ. Cttee. of Council 1881–2* [C. 3312–I], p. 404, (1882) xxiii.

65 *Rep. Educ. Cttee. of Council 1872–3* [C. 812], p. 407, H.C. (1873), xxiv; *1874–5* [C. 1265–I], p. 317, H.C. (1875), xxiv; *1886–7* [C. 5123–I], p. 518, H.C. (1887), xxviii.

66 E.R.O., D/NM 2/4/1.

67 Ibid. D/NM 2/4/9; D/NM 2/4/11; P.R.O., ED 21/5494; *Colch. Boro. Council Mins.* 1908–9, p. 872; ibid. 1909–10, p. 901; ibid. 1910–11, p. 879.

68 Below, this section, Board Schs.; E.R.O., D/NM 2/4/11; *Colch. Boro. Council Mins.* 1912–13, p. 997.

69 E.R.O., D/P 30/28/18; ibid. T/M 399 (map 1848).

70 Quinlivan, *Hist. Wilson Marriage Sec. Sch.* 4; C. Reynolds, *Illus. Hist. Wilson Marriage Sch.* 14.

71 E.R.O., D/NM 2/4/2.

72 *E.C.S.* 19 Dec. 1891.

73 E.R.O., D/NM 2/4/3; below, this section Board Schs.

74 *E.C.S.* 19 Jan. 1844; *White's Dir. Essex* (1848), 88; E.R.O., T/M 399 (map 1848).

75 P.R.O., HO 129/8/204; *E.C.S.* 14 May 1858; *White's Dir. Essex* (1863), 91.

76 Anon. *Hist. and Antiq. Colch.* (1789), 221; P.R.O., ED 49/2051.

77 Based on *Jnl. Friends Hist. Soc.* xiii. 87; xxxv. 59–64; S. H. G. Fitch, *Colch. Quakers*, 72–5; 'Jn. Kendall Sch. Trust Foundation' (TS. in E.C.L. Colch.).

writing, and arithmetic to six poor boys from Colchester and the neighbourhood at a boarding school kept by a Quaker master. He also left his library, which was sold in 1865 for the benefit of the school. Kendall's money was added to a gift of £500 received under the will of Francis Freshfield (d.1808).[78] In the period 1817–38 the charity money was paid to three successive private school masters who resigned, complaining of lack of Quaker encouragement for their schools. Edmund Watts, who kept a school in Lexden,[79] taught the Kendall charity boys from 1838 until 1858, when the charity temporarily lapsed. From 1863 until 1867 it was given to Joshua Davy's small school, first in Priory Street and later in Crouch Street.[80] In 1869 the trustees approved Frederick Richardson's new school in Lexden. That school prospered, but by 1903, when Richardson died, the number of Quaker boys attending had dwindled from 24 to 7. The school survived until 1907 when the charity was transferred to Frederick Gröne's boys school.[81] In 1917 Gröne sold the school to a non-Quaker and the trustees withdrew payment of the charity money. Under a Scheme of 1922, which divided the income between the Kendall and Freshfield educational trust and the Kendall book charity, the income from £3,280 stock was to be used to help boys, preferably from Colchester, to attend schools associated with the Society of Friends. In 1951 a supplementary fund was raised by the Essex quarterly meeting. In 1987 the annual income from £4,680 stock, which included the supplementary fund, was £212, from which occasional payments were made for the further education of boys and girls.[82]

OTHER 19TH-CENTURY VOLUNTARY SCHOOLS. *The Ragged school*, Stanwell Street,[83] opened in 1854 at the instigation of A. W. H. Frost, master of a private school. It was held on four evenings a week in a schoolroom in Osborne Street freely provided by John Bawtree the younger. In 1855, when Frost was appointed its salaried master, the school was attended by more than 100 children. Many prominent local people of differing religious and political opinions served on the school's management committee. They supported the school financially, and some of them taught there. At first classes were often unruly, but the school's influence was praised by the police and the clergy. In 1865 a new school for 300 was built in Stanwell Street at Bawtree's expense and leased to the management committee. In 1866 *c.* 138 boys and 85 girls attended,[84] and in 1872 the committee bought the schoolroom. Numbers had fallen to 62 boys and 101 girls by 1871, and the provision of day schools and compulsory attendance under the Education Acts of 1870 and 1876 reduced the number of illiterate children needing evening tuition. The schools closed in 1880.

The Industrial School for Training Girls for Domestic Service was founded in 1867 by Margaret Round in Magdalen Street and supported by subscription. In 1871 it moved, with an associated orphanage, to East Hill, where it survived in 1894 with 12 girls. It seems to have closed by 1902.[85]

An evening school for girls, founded by Margaret Round probably *c.* 1859, was being held at East Hill House in 1869, when it was attended by some 34 girls. It survived until 1878 but seems to have closed soon afterwards.[86]

BOARD SCHOOLS. *St. John's Green school.* In 1892 the school board took over the National schools in Osborne and Stanwell Streets, and the British school in Priory Street,[87] which in 1893 had altogether 676 children. In 1898 those schools were replaced by a new school for 840 at St. John's Green, where attendance rose from 604 in 1899 to 718 in 1905.[88] The school was reorganized in 1938 for 398 juniors and 250 infants and in 1961 those departments were united as a primary school. Although it was threatened with closure in 1973, it survived in 1987 with 115 children, occupying the upstairs rooms only.[89]

East Stockwell Street infant school. The board took over St. Martin's Church infant school[90] in 1892 and in 1898 moved it to a new building for 240 in the same street.[91] Attendance rose from 63 in 1893 to 137 in 1899, and to 178 in 1905.[92] It closed in 1953.[93]

Barrack Street school originated in 1894 when the school board took over St. Leonard's National and Hythe Wesleyan schools.[94] In 1896 the old buildings of those schools were replaced by a new school in Barrack Street for 1,240 mixed and infant children. The building, modelled on

78 S. H. G. Fitch, *Colch. Quakers*, 73.
79 P.R.O., HO 107/344; HO 107/1781; *White's Dir. Essex* (1848), 99.
80 E.R.O., Acc. C210, J. B. Harvey Colln. vi, p. 106; *E.C.S.* 27 Jan. 1865; Brit. and Foreign Sch. Soc. Correspondence file 334.
81 Blaxill, *Nonconf. Ch. Colch.* 10; below, this section, Private Schs.
82 P.R.O., ED 49/2043; inf. from Secretary of Colch. and Coggeshall Monthly Meeting, and from Treasurer of Soc. of Friends.
83 Based on F. Lord, 'Colch. Ragged Schs. 1854–1880' (Essex Univ. B. A. project); Colch. Ragged Schs. *13th Rep. 1873*; *E.C.S.* 22 Sept., 16 Mar., 6 Apr., 9, 11 May 1855; 5 Feb. 1858; 12 May, 1 Dec. 1865; 28 July 1871; 19 Apr. 1879; 5 Nov. 1881; above, this section, Nonconformist Schs. (British Sch.) for charity.
84 P. Sherry, *Portrait Victorian Colch.* 38.
85 *E.C.S.* 2 Nov. 1866; 9 June 1871; 14 Aug. 1874; *Goody's Colch. Almanac* (1876), 13; *Kelly's Dir. Essex* (1894, 1902).
86 E.R.O., D/P 138/28/9; *Essex Tel.* 20 July 1869; 20 July 1878.
87 Above, this section, Other Church of England Schs., Nonconformist Schs.; *E.C.S.* 1 July 1893.
88 *Returns Elem. Educ. 1893* [C. 7529], p. 178, H.C. (1894), lxv; *1899* [Cd. 315], p. 340, H.C. (1900), lxv (2); *Kelly's Dir. Essex* (1902); Sadler, *Rep. Sec. and Higher Educ. in Essex*, 247.
89 P.R.O., ED 21/5495; *Colch. Boro. Council Mins.* 1937–8, p. 546; E.R.O., C/ME 55, p. 198; C/ME 67, p. A67; inf. from sch.
90 Above, this section, Parochial Schs.; *E.C.S.* 20 Aug. 1892.
91 *Kelly's Dir. Essex* (1902).
92 *Returns Elem. Educ. 1893*, p. 178; *1899*, p. 340; Sadler, *Rep. Sec. and Higher Educ. in Essex*, 247.
93 E.R.O., C/ME 47, p. 342; C/ME 65, pp. E150–1.
94 Above, this section, Parochial Schs., Nonconformist Schs.

Medway Street school, Leicester, incorporated many recent developments in school building, including a kitchen for teaching domestic science.[95] Attendance rose from 997 in 1899 to 1,128 in 1905.[96] The school, the largest in the borough, was difficult to run, and in 1933 it was reorganized as separate senior and infant schools, both named after Wilson Marriage.[97] The infant school closed in 1962 and the children moved to St. George's school.[98]

North Street school, John Harper Street, the first school built by the board, was opened in 1894 for 872 mixed and infant children, including those from the workhouse. Attendance rose from 717 in 1899 to 848 in 1905.[99] In 1938 the school was reorganized and the infant school was rebuilt with a nursery department for juniors and infants. The junior and infant departments were amalgamated in 1965.[1]

Old Heath mixed and infant school originated in 1894 when the school board took over St. Giles's parochial school[2] and moved it to new buildings for 160 on an adjoining site. Attendance rose from 95 in 1895 to 139 in 1905.[3] The school was enlarged in 1911 for an additional 80 children. In 1934 it was reorganized for 230 juniors and infants, and in 1936 it was enlarged again for 328.[4]

COUNCIL ELEMENTARY SCHOOLS. *Canterbury Road school* opened in 1903 in a building erected by the school board for 846 mixed and infant children.[5] By 1910 it was attended by 789 children. It was reorganized in 1933 for 738 juniors and infants, and in 1953 was renamed *St. George's*. In 1974 the infants moved to a new building for *c.* 200 in Barrington Road.[6]

St. Anne's temporary school for 100 boys opened in 1906 in St. Anne's mission, Harwich Road, to replace the boys department of St. James's Church school. It closed in 1908 when the boys moved to East Ward school.[7]

Myland school opened in 1907 as an all-standard school for 350 children in a new building to replace Mile End Church school. It was reorganized in 1932 for juniors and infants. It was enlarged in 1975.[8]

East Ward school, Greenstead Road, opened in 1908 as an all-standard school for 550 mixed and infant children from the Greenstead neighbourhood of East Street.[9] In 1932 it was reorganized for seniors, juniors, and infants.[10] It was enlarged to become a senior school in 1934.[11]

Hamilton Road school opened in 1920 for 200 junior mixed children as a department of the central senior school. It closed in 1935.[12]

Lexden school opened in 1925 as an all-standard school in the premises of the former Church school in Spring Lane.[13] In 1928 overcrowding was relieved by the opening of a temporary infant school in Straight Road, and in 1930 the Spring Lane school was replaced by new buildings for 360 in Trafalgar Road, to serve the growing 'garden village'. The new school was soon overcrowded. By 1937 it had 465 children and in 1938 it was reorganized for juniors and infants. In the 1950s and 1960s overcrowding was relieved by use of a church hall and temporary classrooms, and by the opening of Prettygate and Home Farm schools. In 1970 the buildings of the former Shrub End school were annexed to Lexden school.[14]

Harwich Road school, Barnardiston Road, was opened in 1934 for 200 infants. In 1938 a junior school for 400 and a nursery block for 40 were added.[15] The schools were renamed *St. Anne's* in 1957.

PRIMARY SCHOOLS.[16] The following schools are, unless otherwise described, county schools for 320 juniors and 240 infants. Some were completed in two stages. *Montgomery schools*, Baronswood Way, were opened in 1948 as *Berechurch Road school* in the building of the former army school.[17] New buildings on St. Michael's garrison estate were completed in 1966 and 1967. *Hamilton school* opened in 1955 in the premises of the former Hamilton Road secondary modern school. At Shrub End, *King's Ford schools*, Gloucester Avenue, opened in 1953, *Monkwick schools*, School Road, in 1956 and 1958, *Gosbeck's schools*, Owen Ward Close, in 1957, and *Prettygate schools*, Plume Avenue, in 1959 and 1962. *St. Michael's school*, Camulodunum Way, opened in 1971 to serve Montgomery

95 *E.C.S.* 11 Jan. 1896; E.R.O., Colch. Sch. Bd. Mins. i. 70; C. Reynolds, *Illus. Hist. Wilson Marriage Sch.*

96 *Returns Elem. Educ. 1899*, p. 340; Sadler, *Rep. Sec. and Higher Educ. in Essex*, 247.

97 *Colch. Boro. Council Mins* 1921–2, p. 426; below, this section 20th Century Secondary Schs. (Wilson Marriage).

98 E.R.O., C/ME 56, p. 210; Quinlivan, *Hist. Wilson Marriage Sec. Sch.* 29.

99 E.R.O., E/ML 86/1; *Returns Elem. Educ. 1899*. p. 340; Sadler, *Rep. Sec. and Higher Educ. in Essex*, 247.

1 *Colch. Boro. Council Mins* 1937–8, p. 645; 1938–9, p. 15; E.R.O., C/ME 59, p. 438.

2 Above, this section Parochial Schs.

3 E.R.O., Colch. Sch. Bd. Mins. i. 92, 96, 117; *E.C.S.* 22 Feb. 1896; Sadler, *Rep. Sec. and Higher Educ. in Essex*, 247.

4 *Colch. Boro. Council Mins.* 1911–12, p. 1008; 1933–4, p. 689; 1936–7, p. 730; date on rainwater heads.

5 Plaque on bldg.; Colch. Educ. Cttee. *Year Bks.* (1904–8), 46.

6 Plaque on bldg.; *Kelly's Dir. Essex* (1906, 1910); *Colch. Boro. Council Mins.* 1934–5, 760; E.R.O., C/ME 47, p. 10; *St. George's Junior Sch., Canterbury Road, 1903–1983*, ed. D. Jones; inf. from sch.

7 *Colch. Boro. Council Mins.* 1905–6, p. 911; above, this section, Parochial Schs. (St. James's); Colch. Educ. Cttee. *Year Bks.* (1904–8), 66, 68; *E.C.S.* 25 Apr. 1908.

8 *Colch. Boro. Council Mins.* 1905–6, p. 911; 1906–7, p. 982; 1944–5, Final Rep. Educ. Cttee. p. 6; E.R.O., C/ME 65, p. F40; inf. from sch.

9 *E.C.S.* 25 Apr. 1908; *Colch. Boro. Council Mins.* 1944–5, Final Rep. Educ. Cttee. p. 6.

10 *Colch. Boro. Council Mins.* 1932–3, p. 613.

11 Below, this section, 20th-Century Secondary Schs.

12 *Colch. Boro. Council Mins.* 1944–5, Final Rep. Educ. Cttee. p. 6; *Kelly's Dir. Essex* (1922); below, this section 20th-Century Secondary Schs.

13 P.R.O., ED 49/2148.

14 P. C. Spendlove, 'Lexden Sch. 1930–1980' (TS. in E.R.O.); *Colch. Boro. Council Mins.* 1932–3, p. 614; 1944–5, Final Rep. Educ. Cttee. p. 6.

15 *Colch. Boro. Council Mins.* 1933–4, p. 690; 1937–8, p. 786.

16 Section based on Essex Educ. Dept., Lists of schs.; *Educ. in Essex 1952–6*, 21–2; *1956–60*, 21–2; *1960–64*, 19–20; *Essex Educ.* xx (3), 61; xxi (3), 64; xxii (3), 175; inf. from schs.

17 E.R.O., C/ME 41, p. 474; C/ME 42, p. 156; A. F. F. H. Robertson, 'The army in Colch. and its influence on the social, economic and political development of the town 1854–1914' (Essex Univ. Ph.D. thesis, 1991), pp. 84–5.

garrison estate. *Hazelmere schools*, Hawthorn Avenue, Greenstead, opened in 1964. *Friar's Grove school*, Uplands Drive, opened for 320 and *Home Farm school*, Shelley Road, for 220 in 1966, and *St. Andrew's schools*, Hickory Avenue, Greenstead, in 1969 and 1972. *Roach Vale school*, Parson's Heath, opened in 1977 for 280, and its buildings received an award of the Royal Institute of British Architects.[18] *Cherry Tree school*, Holt Drive, Mersea Road, opened in 1979.[19]

20TH-CENTURY SECONDARY SCHOOLS. *Colchester Pupil Teacher centre* opened in 1897 at the Albert school of science and art as a branch of the university extension college. Attendance rose from 85 in 1897 to 172 in 1905, but an official survey of that year found the headmaster struggling against unsuitable accommodation, poor students, and inadequate staff. In 1907 the centre was reorganized as a secondary school for boys and girls. In 1909 the masters and boys moved to the technical institute on North Hill as a junior technical school.[20]

The girls department became *Colchester County secondary*, later *High school*.[21] It remained at the Albert school until 1912, when it moved with *c.* 61 girls to premises for 150 in the technical institute. By 1913 attendance had risen to 144 and in 1914 a preparatory department opened in St. Peter's parish room. Attendance increased rapidly after the First World War to reach 400 in 1920. The school took over more classrooms at the technical institute, but it was still cramped and in 1920 the juniors moved to Greyfriars, East Hill. The school's enrolment and reputation grew rapidly and by 1936 there were 453 girls at the secondary school and 68 in the preparatory school.[22] The county council's plans for a new building were frustrated by the Second World War, and the school continued on two sites until 1958, when it moved to new buildings for 540 in Norman Way.[23] It flourished in 1987 as a selective grammar school for girls.

Colchester junior technical school for boys originated in 1909, when the masters and boys from the pupil teacher centre moved to the new technical institute on North Hill. In 1920 the school took over more classrooms at the institute and in the early 1930s new workshops were added.[24] Under the 1944 Education Act the school became *North-East Essex mixed county technical school*. In 1950 the institute's buildings were extended for the school's use, and in 1958 the school took over all the premises. The buildings were enlarged again in 1961.[25] In 1980 the school, renamed *Gilberd*, became comprehensive and the lower school moved to new buildings for 450 in Brinkley Lane, which were enlarged for 1,200 in 1984.[26] The school continued on two sites until the move to Brinkley Lane was completed in 1987.[27]

Hamilton Road central school was built in 1914, to replace the Wesleyan school, but it was used as a military hospital in the First World War and opened in 1920 as a school for 320 seniors, selected by examination, with a junior department.[28] In 1935 it became a non-selective senior school. Under the 1944 Education Act it became a mixed secondary modern school and in 1955 moved to new premises in Walnut Tree Way, Shrub End, as *Alderman Blaxill school*.[29] In 1976 it became comprehensive.[30]

Wilson Marriage school, Barrack Street, opened as a non-selective senior school for boys and girls in 1933 in the former Barrack Street elementary school building. Under the 1944 Education Act it became a mixed secondary modern school. In 1958 some classes moved to Greyfriars, East Hill, and became the nucleus of Monkwick school.[31] In 1962 Wilson Marriage school took over the buildings of the adjacent infant school and in 1977 it became comprehensive. The school closed in 1987.[32]

East Ward secondary school, Greenstead Road, opened in 1934 in the former elementary school, as a senior school in two departments for boys and girls.[33] It became a mixed secondary modern school under the 1944 Education Act and in 1968 was amalgamated with Sir Charles Lucas school.[34]

St. Helena school, Sheepen Road, was opened in 1938 as a senior school in two departments for 720 boys and girls.[35] It became a mixed secondary modern school under the 1944 Education Act, and in 1976 became comprehensive. It was enlarged for 1,010 in 1977.[36]

SECONDARY SCHOOLS FOUNDED AFTER 1945. All are mixed schools and the first three opened as secondary modern schools. *Monkwick school*, opened in 1958, when classes from Wilson Marriage school moved to Greyfriars, East Hill. It moved in 1960 to new buildings for 450 in Monkwick Avenue, which were enlarged in 1974 for 810 and in 1979 for

[18] E.R.O., N/CME 2, p. D39; N/CME 5, p. D45; Essex C.C. Architect's Dept. *Welshwood Park Sch.* (Plans in E.R.O.).

[19] Essex C.C. Architect's Dept. *Mersea Road Sch.* (Plans in E.R.O.); *E.C.S.* 22 Sept. 1978; inf. from sch.

[20] A. M. Brown, *Colch. County High School: the First Fifty Years*, 6, 9; Sadler, *Rep. on Sec. and Higher Educ. in Essex*, 244–5; E.R.O., E/ML 89; below, this section Colch. junior technical sch.

[21] Based on A. M. Brown, *Colch. High Sch.: the First Fifty Years*; *Colch. County High Sch. Mag.* (1934–71).

[22] E.R.O., C/ME 32, p. 396.

[23] *Educ. in Essex 1956–60*, 24.

[24] E.R.O., C/ME 28, p. 237.

[25] Inf. from sch.; E.R.O., C/ME 52, p. 384; *Educ. in Essex 1960–64*, 22.

[26] E.R.O., N/CME 7, pp. C57, C86; ibid. C/DA 1/1.

[27] Inf. from Essex Educ. Dept.

[28] *Colch. Boro. Council Mins.* 1914–15, p. 923; 1915–16, p. 741; 1944–5, Final Rep. Educ. Cttee. p. 6; above, this section, Nonconformist Schs. (Methodists).

[29] W. Dent, 'Hist. Alderman Blaxill Sch.' (TS. in possession of sch.); *Educ. in Essex 1952–6*, p. 31; E.R.O., C/ME 49, p. 29.

[30] Essex Educ. Dept., List of Schs. (1976).

[31] Quinlivan, *Hist. Wilson Marriage Sec. Sch.* 23, 26, 28; *Colch. Boro. Council Mins.*, 1932–3, 614; above, this section, Board Schs. (Barrack Street).

[32] E.R.O., C/ME 56, p. 210; Essex Educ. Dept., List of Schs. (1977); *E.C.S.* 13 Oct. 1989.

[33] Above, this section, Council Elementary Schs.

[34] Essex Educ. Dept., List of Schs. (1957); E.R.O., C/ME 40, p. 471; *Essex Educ.* xx (3), 54; inf. from Essex Educ. Dept.

[35] Colch. Educ. Cttee. *Official Opening of St. Helena Sch.* (1938).

[36] E.R.O., C/ME 40, p. 632; Essex Educ. Dept., List of Schs. (1976); Essex C.C. Architect's Dept. *St. Helena Sch.* (Plans in E.R.O.); inf. from school.

900.[37] In 1975 it became comprehensive and was renamed *Thomas, Lord Audley, school*.[38] *Philip Morant school* was established in 1963 at Greyfriars, East Hill. It moved in 1965 to new buildings for 450 in Norman Way,[39] which were enlarged for 750 in 1971, when the school became comprehensive. It was enlarged again, for 1,170, in 1973.[40] *Sir Charles Lucas school* originated in 1965 when the county council took over Endsleigh private school at Lexden Park as the nucleus of a comprehensive school. In 1968 it was amalgamated with East Ward school and moved to new buildings for 900 in Hawthorn Avenue where Hazelton's farm had been; the school was enlarged for 1,710 in 1973.[41]

A sixth-form college was established in 1986–7 in the former premises of Gilberd school, North Hill.[42]

FURTHER EDUCATION. A *mechanics institution*, founded in 1833, provided lectures and maintained a library and reading room in High Street, but it operated more as a Liberal club than as an educational institution. In 1849 a rival literary institute was founded by Conservatives and Anglicans and in 1860 the mechanics institution closed.[43]

The *Co-operative Society education centre* was established soon after 1861 at the society's assembly room in Culver Street. From 1875 it provided classes under the auspices of the Science and Arts Department, South Kensington, and in 1894 commercial classes were started for members' sons.[44]

The *Society of Friends' adult schools* were started in 1867 by Wilson Marriage at the East Stockwell Street meeting house on Sunday mornings and Wednesday evenings to provide elementary education for men. A Sunday school, where women and girls were taught writing, was opened *c.* 1871. The schools moved to the new meeting house in Sir Isaac's Walk in 1872, and by 1874 were attended by 100 men, 20 women, and 10 children. Branches were established in outlying parishes. The schools flourished; enrolment reached 498 by 1885 and in 1889 a schoolroom was added to the meeting house. Quakers alone could not supply all the teachers needed and other Nonconformists were recruited. By 1900 the Colchester school had declined for lack of support and although it survived in 1918, by then the outlying schools were failing.[45]

The *Albert school of science and art* was founded in 1885 at the instigation of James Paxman. Day and evening classes for adults were held in the old corn exchange, and in 1887 Paxman, then mayor, organized a subscription and loans to buy the building. The town council made annual grants from 'whiskey money' received under the Local Taxation (Customs and Excise) Act, 1890. In 1894 the management committee ceded the school to the council, which received annual grants from the county council. In 1896 the corn exchange was converted to provide lecture rooms and laboratories for both the Albert school and the university extension centre.[46] In 1912 the Albert school, renamed *Colchester technical institute*, moved to a new building on North Hill and in 1914 an engineering workshop was added. After the Second World War the institute became *North-East Essex technical college and school of art*, and departments of applied science and commerce were added. In 1954 the college moved to new buildings in Sheepen Road, which were completed in 1958 and 1959 and enlarged in 1972.[47] In 1976 the technical college and art school were combined with St. Osyth College, Clacton, as *Colchester institute of higher education*.[48]

A *Cambridge university extension centre*, was established in 1889. It was supported by grants from the town and county councils and by subscription from individuals and local organizations. It was held at the Albert school from 1896 and in 1897 the pupil teacher centre was attached to it.[49]

SPECIAL AND NURSERY SCHOOLS. A special school at Stockwell Street infant school originated in 1906 as a class for *c.* 20 mentally handicapped children. By 1934 it had 28 children of all ages. It survived as a separate school when the infant school was closed in 1953. In 1958 it moved, renamed *Kingswode Hoe*, to Sussex Road.[50] A class for *c.* 22 partially sighted children opened in Barrack Street infant school in 1924. By 1938 only 12 children attended, and the class closed in 1940.[51] *Ramparts school* opened in 1971 for 90 educationally subnormal children. In 1981 the school was amalgamated, as *Lexden Springs school*, with the Royal Eastern Counties Institution's Golden Grove hospital school, which had been held in wooden buildings at Turner village since *c.* 1972. In 1981 the new school took over the buildings of Ramparts

37 Quinlivan, *Hist. Wilson Marriage Sec. Sch.* 28; inf. from Essex Educ. Dept.; Essex C.C. Architect's Dept. *Thomas, Lord Audley Sch.* (Plans in E.R.O.).

38 E.R.O., N/CME 2, pp. C23, D45; *Educ. in Essex 1956–60*, 26.

39 E.R.O., C/ME 57, pp. 21, 796; *Essex Educ.* xix (4), 71.

40 Inf. from Essex Educ. Dept.; *E.C.S.* 7 June 1985.

41 *Essex Educ.* xix (4), 71; *Colch. Boro. Council Mins.* 1964–5, p. 456 ; E.R.O., C/ME 59, pp. 673, 718; C/ME 64, p. G8; inf. from Essex Educ. Dept.; *E.C.S.* 22 Jan. 1988; below, this section, Private Schs. (Endsleigh).

42 Inf. from Essex Educ. Dept.

43 *Rules and Regulations of Colch. Mechanics' Institution* (1838); *White's Dir. Essex* (1848), 86; (1863), 92; Brown, *Colch. 1815– 1914*, 69; E.R.O., T/M 399 (map 1848).

44 Brown, *Colch. 1815–1914*, 71; H. W. Lewington, *Brief Hist. Acct. Colch. Co-op Soc.* section 2, pp. 1–2.

45 S. H. G. Fitch, *Colch. Quakers*, 34–6 ;*Goody's Colch. Almanac* (1876), 13; Sadler, *Rep. Sec. and Higher Educ. in Essex*, 252; Brown, *Colch. 1815–1914*, 71–2.

46 Brown, *Colch. 1815–1914*, 67–8; Colch. Boro. *Technical and University Extension College Inauguration* (1896); Sadler, *Rep. on Sec. and Higher Educ. in Essex*, 252, 255–6; Colch. Technical and University Extension College, *Prospectus 1897–8* (copy in E.C.L. Colch.); P.R.O., ED 29/43.

47 E.R.O., C/ME 8, p. 526; C/ME 10, p. 877; *Official Opening of N.E. Essex Technical Coll. and Sch. of Art 1954* (Pamph. in E.R.O.).

48 E.R.O., N/CME 4, pp. A3–4.

49 Brown, *Colch. 1815–1914*, 70.

50 P.R.O., ED 32/1078; E.R.O., C/ME 48, p. 448; C/ME 52, p. 189.

51 P.R.O., ED 32/300.

52 E.R.O., C/ME 65, p. D9; ibid. N/CME 5, pp. B14, B21; N/CME 8, pp. C19–20; N/CME 9, p. D42; ibid., C/DA 1/13.

school, which were remodelled and enlarged for 100 children.[52] A unit for children with partial hearing, opened in 1912 at Lexden primary school, survived in 1986.[53]

Nursery classes were opened in 1937 at Harwich Road school, in 1938 at Wilson Marriage and St. Anne's schools, and in 1939 at North Street school. Soon after Wilson Marriage infant school closed in 1969, the nursery school was annexed to St. George's school, Barrington Road.[54]

PRIVATE SCHOOLS.[55] In the 1770s there were *c.* 12 private schools in the town.[56] In the period 1780–1804, when the grammar school master neglected his duties, Thomas White, with two or more assistants, kept a school for boys, aged 11–15, including 25 boarders.[57] In the 19th century there were usually *c.* 20 private schools in Colchester, many of them on North Hill, East Hill, Stockwell Street, Crouch Street, and Lexden Road. At least seven schools for boys and one for girls were kept by nonconformists, but from 1870 the master of the grammar school moderated its Anglican bias so that by 1900 about half of its boys were nonconformists,[58] and only one nonconformist private secondary school for boys survived. In the later 19th century private schools probably shared the prosperity which the barracks brought to the town, and a few advertised their suitability for officers' children and 'Indians'.[59] In 1906 there were five private secondary schools for girls, but competition from the county school, established in 1909, led to the closure of three of them by 1920. In 1922 the Board of Education recognized six private schools as efficient.[60] Of those, two had closed by 1926, four survived in 1963, and three were still active in 1987 with another, which opened in 1959.

Of 185 private schools identified in the period 1818–1987 most (149) survived fewer than 20 years and were probably small, but Joseph Cooper's day school with 50 boys, recorded 1825–38 in Botolph Street and later in Priory Street, was the largest of its kind in Colchester.[61] The schools described below flourished for more than 30 years, usually kept by a succession of proprietors.

William Walker's school, established in 1818 in Sir Isaac's Walk, seems to have survived under his successors until 1848,[62] and a boys school in St. John's Street started by John Halls Bare by 1827, survived in the 1850s under a new master.[63] Stockwell, later Arnold, House existed as a boys boarding school at various addresses from 1835 or earlier until *c.* 1878. Its pupils included the Baptist preacher C. H. Spurgeon.[64] The Partridge family's boarding school for girls on East Hill, probably established in 1829, continued until *c.* 1866.[65] St. Mary's classical, mathematical, and commercial school for boys, kept by Methodists, was established in Lion Walk by 1841. It had moved to Crouch Street by 1851, when it had 3 assistant masters and 17 resident boys. It was still open in 1866 but had closed by 1870, when the opening of the Methodist higher grade school was imminent.[66] A girls school on North Hill, opened by Mary Ann Allen before 1853, was kept by Mrs. Donnington 1878–86.[67] A girls school on North Hill kept by Sarah Frost in 1853 moved to Crouch Street in 1894; it may have continued as Durlston House girls school, North Hill, which was kept by E. H. and G. Frost from *c.* 1898 to *c.* 1926.[68] Abraham W. H. Frost, instigator and master of the Ragged school, had a boys boarding school on North Hill from 1861 or earlier until *c.* 1896.[69] Thomas B. Hazell kept a boys day and boarding school in West Stockwell Street from *c.* 1861 until the early 1890s. Frederick Richardson established a boys boarding school in Lexden Road, under Kendall's foundation[70] in 1869. It survived his death in 1903, and in 1907 was apparently taken over by Ferdinand Gröne, a German Quaker,[71] who moved the school to part of the site of his girls school in Wellesley Road. On Gröne's retirement in 1917 the Kendall foundation was withdrawn, but the school was taken over and revived by G. H. Watkin as Colchester high school. It continued under Watkins's successors and numbers increased from 240 in 1947 to 350 in 1982. The school was enlarged in 1975 and 1980, and no. 11 Wellesley Road was acquired for the junior school in 1982.[72] Minden House girls school, Wellesley Road, was opened by Gröne by 1882, and *c.* 1902 it moved to a new building on an adjacent site as Colchester high school for girls. By 1906 it was attended by 71 girls, under a qualified headmistress, and was commended in an official report as the possible nucleus of a county high school.[73] The school remained private and continued under the same management as the boys school until 1922, but had closed by 1926. A girls school on North Hill, kept by Louisa and Emma

53 P. C. Spendlove, 'Lexden Sch. 1930–1980' (TS. in E.R.O.).

54 *Educ. in Essex 1945–52*, 17–18; *1952–6*, 26; *Colch. Boro. Council Mins.* 1937–8, p. 786; inf. from Min. of Educ. and schs.; E.R.O., C/ME 56, p. 210.

55 Based on *Pigot's Lond. and Provincial Dir.* (1823, 1839); *Robson's Dir. Essex c.* 1838; *White's Dir. Essex* (1848), 99; (1863), 109–10; *Kelly's Dir. Essex* (1845 and later edns.); P.R.O., HO 107/344; HO 107/1781; HO 129/8/204; ibid. RG 9/1098–9; RG 10/1685.

56 *Ipswich Jnl.* 8 Dec. 1770.

57 *Chelm. Chron.* 26 Dec. 1794; 10 June 1796; plaque an S. wall of St. Mary's ch. tower.

58 Brown, *Colch. 1815–1914*, 65–6; *E.C.S.* 7 Jan. 1853, 1 Jan. 1858; E.R.O., Acc. C210, J. B. Harvey Colln. v, p. 468 .

59 *E.C.S.* 7 Jan. 1888; 5 Mar. 1892; 4 Feb., 1 July 1893; 2 Jan. 1897; P.R.O., ED 35/758.

60 P.R.O., ED 35/752; ED 15/12.

61 *Educ. Enq. Abstract*, H.C. 62, p. 271 (1835), xli.

62 E.R.O., T/M 268 (map 1818); ibid. D/DCm E9; P.R.O., HO 107/344.

63 *E.C.S.* 18 July 1851; 7 Jan. 1853.

64 *E.R.* i. 75; *E.C.S.* 10 Jan. 1845; 19 Jan. 1849.

65 *Educ. Enq. Abstract*, p. 271.

66 Above, this section, Nonconformist Schs.

67 *E.C.S.* 14 Jan. 1853.

68 Ibid. 15 July 1853; 11 Jan. 1856; P.R.O., RG 10/1685.

69 P.R.O., RG 9/1099; above, this section, Other 19th-Century Schs.

70 Above, this section, Nonconformist Schs. (Soc. of Friends).

71 E.R.O., D/DU 633/8; *Jnl. Friends Hist. Soc.* xxxv. 63; P.R.O., RG 10/1686.

72 Sadler, *Rep. on Sec. and Higher Educ. in Essex*, 239–43; *Royal Blue* (school mag.), N.S. ix (1982), 1–27; inf. from sch.

73 P.R.O., ED 35/753; Sadler, *Rep. Sec. and Higher Educ. in Essex*, 243.

Handscomb in 1872,[74] moved to Wellesley Road and then to Crouch Street, where it survived until *c.* 1913. A girls school, named successively St. Mary's House, St. Martin's, Bracewell House, and Home school, was founded by Elizabeth and Mary Simson and flourished at various addresses from *c.* 1878 until 1919 or later.[75] Endsleigh House school was founded in 1893 by E. A. and L. M. Dobson as a girls day and boarding school in Wellesley Road. In 1906 it was commended as the possible nucleus of a county high school, but it remained a private school. Numbers increased from 106 girls in 1903 to 143 in 1911, and by 1921, when it had 155 girls, two more boarding houses were added.[76] The school moved to Lexden Grange *c.* 1935. A few day boys had been accepted from 1903 or earlier, and after the Second World War the school was extended and opened to boys and girls of all ages. By 1950 Kingswood Hoe, Sussex Road, had been acquired for the preparatory department. The school had moved to Lexden Park by 1958, but attendance declined as more council schools were built and in 1965 the county council took over Endsleigh House school as the nucleus of Sir Charles Lucas county school.[77] St. Mary's girls school, Lexden Road, was founded in 1908 by A. M. Billson. By 1919 it had 45 girls and 16 boys, many of them children of army officers stationed in Colchester. The school continued to expand and in 1987 it had 600 girls in Lexden Road and at Comrie House, Stanway.[78] St. Mary's convent day school, Priory Street, opened in 1919 for girls aged 4 to 18. In 1963 it was reorganized for junior girls, and by 1987 it was attended by 187.[79] Oxford House nursery and preparatory school, opened in 1959 in Wellesley Road. It moved later to Oxford Road and in 1976 to a new building in Lexden Road.[80]

UNIVERSITY OF ESSEX

THE formal application by a county promotion committee for a university in Essex was approved by the University Grants Committee in 1961, and an academic planning board was constituted. In 1962 R. A. Butler (later Lord Butler of Saffron Walden) was appointed chancellor and A. E. (later Sir Albert) Sloman vice-chancellor. The University Grants Committee guaranteed funding to provide for a student population rising to 3,000 in 10 years, but imposed no plan. Essex County Council gave a site of 200 a. at Wivenhoe Park, three miles east of Colchester town centre, and together with three Essex county boroughs promised £120,000 a year. Sponsors raised money through public appeal towards the initial capital cost.[81] A royal charter was granted in 1965.[82] The first students, *c.* 120, were accepted in 1964 and accommodated in Wivenhoe House and its outbuildings and temporary huts. Teaching and research buildings and six residential tower blocks were built in the 1960s designed by Kenneth Capon. Essex students gained a reputation for militancy following their activity in the widespread national student unrest of 1968, although only a minority were extremists.[83]

In the 1970s and 1980s a health centre, a two-storeyed student residence, a 40-bedroom extension to Wivenhoe House, a new building for the biology department, and a building for a printing centre, bookshop, and exhibition gallery were added; Wivenhoe House was converted into Wivenhoe Park Conference Centre. The university concentrated its teaching into large departments. In the late 1970s it faced financial problems which threatened closure, but in the 1980s gained respect nationally and internationally, co-operating with local companies, securing important research contracts, and attracting about a third of its students from overseas.[84]

Four residential blocks of two and three storeys were built in 1991–2 providing 176 study bedrooms.[85] The five-storeyed Rab Butler building was opened in 1991 as a headquarters for the British Household Panel Survey.[86] In 1993 there were 17 departments, more than 5,500 students, 5 industrial units, and the Economic and Social Research Council's data archive; the university employed 1,300 people. A building expansion scheme costing £5.5 million was under way to provide 234 homes for 1,200 students in a new student village, and a 96-place day nursery between Boundary Road and the north towers.[87]

74 *E.C.S.* 12 July 1872.

75 Ibid. 1 Jan. 1881; 4 Feb. 1893; 2 Jan. 1897; 3 Aug. 1907; P.R.O., ED 15/12; Sherry, *Victorian Colch.* 39.

76 P.R.O., ED 35/752; Sadler, *Rep. on Sec. and Higher Educ. in Essex*, 240; *E.C.S.* 3 Aug. 1907.

77 Inf. from Mr. I. T. McMeekan and Mr. P. W. Garrad who attended the sch.; E.R.O., C/TE 1275; C/TE 1912; above, this section, 20th-Century Secondary Schs.

78 P.R.O., ED 35/758; inf. from sch.

79 P.R.O., ED 15/12; *Catholic Dir.* (1943), 160; Sadler, *Rep. Sec. and Higher Educ. in Essex*, 240–1; inf. from convent.

80 *Independent Schs. Assoc. Dir.* (1981), 55, 119; inf. from sch.; *E.C.S.* 18 June 1976; plaque on bldg.

81 A. E. Sloman, *A University in the Making*, 13–17.

82 Inf. from Mr. B. Russell, Publicity Officer.

83 Colch. Charter 800 Assn. *Colch. 800*, 82–3; M. Beloff, *The Plateglass Universities*, 112–21; E.R.O., SA 0653.

84 Colch. Charter 800 Assn. *Colch. 800*, 83–4; E.R.O., SA 0121, 0311.

85 *E.C.S.* 17 Aug. 1990.

86 Ibid. 15 Nov. 1991.

87 Inf. from Mr. Russell; *E.C.S.* 23 Apr. 1993.

CHARITIES FOR THE POOR

CHARITIES FOR THE BOROUGH. ALMSHOUSES.[88] *St. Mary Magdalen Hospital*[89] was re-established by charter in 1610 for a master, who was also to be rector of St. Mary Magdalen's church, and five poor single or widowed people of Colchester. The master, appointed by the Lord Chancellor, was to choose the inhabitants of the hospital and to pay each of them a yearly stipend of 52*s*. A test suit in Chancery 1831–3 and a decree of the court in 1836 established that the almspeople were entitled only to the weekly stipend and that the remaining income of the charity, then amounting to £382 a year, belonged to the master, who was, however, to be resident. In 1837 the almspeople, all women, received a yearly supply of fuel in addition to the stipend.[90] By 1952 the fuel allowance was paid in cash, each almsperson receiving £1 4*s*. every six months,[91] but in 1985 neither stipend nor fuel allowance was paid.[92]

The endowment of the charity consisted in 1837 of over 50 a. of land in St. Mary Magdalen's and adjoining parishes, 3 a. in Ardleigh, 7 a. in Layer-de-la-Haye, and *c*. 49 a. in Stanway. In 1818 the Board of Ordnance paid £5,000 for the use of *c*. 17 a. which were returned to the charity before 1833.[93] Between 1899 and 1932 all the land and houses owned by the charity, except the master's house and the almshouses, were sold and the proceeds invested. Problems arose in the 1940s over the division of income between the hospital and the rectory of St. Mary Magdalen, both still served by the same man, and in 1951, when the mastership and living fell vacant, the Charity Commissioners held an inquiry[94] which, in 1953, resulted in an Act of parliament abolishing the mastership, establishing new trustees, and apportioning the assets of the charity between the hospital and the benefice.[95] In 1985 the charity had an income of £642.[96]

The 17th-century hospital building, adjoining St. Mary Magdalen's churchyard, was demolished in 1832 and rebuilt as six dwellings under one roof, one of which, with an upper storey, was probably for the master.[97] The houses were empty in 1987, awaiting repair or rebuilding.[98] A separate master's house, built about 1880, was compulsorily purchased by the Great Eastern Railway in 1900. Its replacement was sold in 1924, when no. 24 New Town Road was bought and conveyed to the hospital.[99] The house was assigned to the church in 1953.[1]

Arthur Winsley, by will proved 1727, gave Brickhouse Farm in St. Botolph's parish to be converted into almshouses for 12 Colchester men over 60 years old 'that had lived well and fallen into decay'. For the maintenance of the almsmen and of his monument in St. James's church he gave the land of Brickhouse farm, Bocking Hall farm in West Mersea, and the rents of his house on East Hill. After a Chancery suit against the founder's brother Richard, brought in 1730 by the other trustees, the almshouses were established in the main block of the house in 1734.[2] By the later 18th century wives but not widows of almsmen were allowed to live in the almshouses.[3]

Winsley's benefaction had included a weekly stipend of 2*s*. 6*d*. for each almsman, 36 bu. of coal a year, and, on New Year's Day, a sermon in the almshouse chapel followed by a dinner.[4] The stipend rose to 10*s*. in 1879, but was reduced when income was insufficient to meet expenditure, and was finally discontinued in 1956. The gift of coal ceased in 1958. The sermon continued in 1987, but the New Year dinners were replaced in 1873 by gifts of 3*s*. to each almsman, changed to 25p. in 1972.[5] In 1986 the residents paid weekly contributions towards maintenance, hot water, and central heating.[6]

The sale of 23 a. of land to the Barrackmaster General in 1805 raised £2,793 which was invested, and the surplus income, by Chancery decree, was used to build three new almshouses in 1808 and three more in 1811.[7] In spite of reduced income caused by the agricultural depression, the trustees built four more houses in 1845, and later legacies paid for two houses in 1861, and a further 34 between 1900 and 1940, including 14 provided for almsmen's widows by George Rose in 1936 and 1940. The almshouses were remodelled between 1952 and 1962, increasing the accommodation. Ten bungalows were built in 1968, and 11 in 1975,[8] and in 1985 the charity owned 85 almshouses.[9]

In 1811 the charity bought Barn Hall farm, adjacent to Brickhouse farm;[10] parts of it were sold in 1899[11] and 1931, and the remainder in 1945. The land of Brickhouse farm was sold for building between 1893 and 1914; the southern part of the faremhouse, which had been separated from the almshouses and used to house the tenant farmers, was demolished in 1966. Bocking Hall farm was sold in 1916, and Winsley's

88 This section was completed in 1987. A draft hist. of the almshouses, including transcripts of many of the trustees' minutes, was kindly supplied by Mrs. D. Woodward.
89 Above, Religious Houses; *V.C.H. Essex*, ii. 184–5.
90 *32nd Rep. Com. Char.* pp. 546–8.
91 E.R.O., D/P 381/3/10.
92 Inf. from the rector of New Town parish.
93 *32nd Rep. Com. Char.* 546–8.
94 E.R.O., Boro. Mun., Parks and Bathing Places Cttee. Mins. 1896–1907, p. 28; ibid. D/P 381/3/8, 9.
95 1 & 2 Eliz. II, c. 17 (Local).
96 Char. Com. file.
97 *32nd Rep. Com. Char.* 548.
98 Inf. from the rector of New Town parish.
99 E.R.O., D/P 381/3/3.
1 Char. Com. file.
2 *32nd Rep. Com. Char.* 540–1.
3 Ibid. 543.
4 Ibid. 540.
5 E.R.O., Acc. C168, Winsley's Almshos. trustees' mins.
6 Inf. from the clerk to the trustees.
7 *32nd Rep. Com. Char.* 541.
8 E.R.O., Acc. C168, Winsley's Almshos. trustees' mins.
9 Inf. from the clerk to the trustees.
10 E.R.O., D/Q 30/2/66.
11 Ibid. D/Q 30/1/9.

house on East Hill in 1951.[12] In 1985 the charity still owned 15 a. in Elmstead, bought by the trustees in 1735.[13]

John Winnock,[14] by indenture of 1679, conveyed the six houses which he had built in St. Giles's parish in trust for aged poor people of Colchester. The charity was endowed with a yearly rent charge of £41 from Winnock's land and houses in St. Peter's parish, an estate which the trustees had aquired by 1697. Gifts and legacies augmented the charity in the later 18th century, including those of Mrs. Simpson (£200 in 1760) and Hannah Nuthall (£500 in 1779). Further sums totalling £300 were received from Henry Dobby in 1786, Mary Poyner (d. 1810), and Francis Freshfield (d. 1808).

In 1815 the charity housed eight women and its gross income was £135. By 1825 twelve women were living in the original buildings, each occupying a single room, and in 1826 a new building to house four more was built, partly with money given by Mary Barfield. In 1840 another two new dwellings were built. In 1909 four rooms were added at the rear of the existing buildings in Military Road, and in 1914 two houses were built on land bought by the charity on the opposite side of the road. Gifts and bequests enabled two more houses to be built in 1922, and another two in 1931. Between 1933 and 1934 George Rose built and endowed nine almshouses, six in New Square; the last two to be built were endowed with six cottages owned by Rose in Magdalen Street. In the 1950s, with the aid of ministry and local authority grants, an extensive programme of conversion, renovation, and rebuilding was carried out, resulting in the number of almshouses being reduced to 33 in 1954 and to 28 in 1961.

The original terms of the charity allowed each almswoman a stipend of 2*s*. a week and an annual gift of coal. The stipend rose steadily to 4*s*. a week in 1921, but in 1954 it was reduced to 2*s*. for the occupants of the 18 older houses, and discontinued for those of the 15 newer ones. Stipends ceased altogether in 1958, when contributions of not more than 5*s*. a week were requested from the almspeople. The gift of coal ceased in 1955.

John Kendall and his wife Anne, by indenture of 1791, bought and conveyed to trustees a piece of land and a house for eight poor women aged 60 or over, priority to be given to widows of Winsley's almsmen, who were not allowed to remain in Winsley's almshouses.[15] In 1809 John Kendall requested that three of the seven trustees should be Quakers.

A public appeal for an endowment raised £1,045, and in 1793 stipends of 1*s*. a week and an annual coal allowance were paid to the almswomen. The coal allowance ceased in 1962; the stipend ceased for new tenants in 1958 and altogether in 1965. From 1958 new tenants, and from 1965 all tenants, paid 2*s*. a week towards the maintenance of the almshouses, and a Charity Commission Scheme of 1974 enabled charges to be made towards maintenance and heating costs.

Land adjoining the almshouse was bought in 1798, and in 1806 accommodation was built for another eight women. Between 1799 and 1830 the charity received legacies of over £1,400 from Kendall (d. 1815) and fellow Quakers, and by 1837 the investment income was £140 10*s*. a year. George Rose built four bungalows in 1933 and a further ten in 1935, endowing them with £5,000 and farms in East Mersea and Lexden. None of them was to be occupied by a widow from Winsley's almshouses. Between 1935 and 1949 the charity received legacies totalling £4,200, including £100 towards a common room which was opened in 1951.

Under a Scheme of 1976 Winnock's and Kendall's charities were administered and managed as the *Winnock's and Kendall's Combined Almshouse Charity*.[16] In 1984 there were 27 people in Winnock's almshouses and 29 in Kendall's, and the charity had an investment income of £10,889.[17]

In 1896 Charlotte Eleanor Cooper, in memory of three sisters, Elizabeth Cooper, Margaret Round, and Charlotte Borthwick,[18] built *Berryfield Cottages* for 12 poor people aged 60 or more, resident in Colchester and preferably in St. James's parish. She maintained the cottages until her death in 1899. By her will, proved 1900, she established the charity and endowed it with £6,000 to provide, among other things, a weekly stipend of 3*s*. and an annual coal allowance for each almsperson. A meeting room and kitchen for the almshouses were built on adjacent land by Amelia Green, and conveyed to the trustees in 1901. By 1968 the residents contributed towards the maintenance, and by 1982 to the heating. In 1982 the charity had assets of £14,014.[19]

OTHER CHARITIES. *Sir Thomas White* founded a charity in 1566 for the benefit of Bristol and 24 other towns and cities.[20] Colchester, at 24 year intervals, received £104 from which loans of £25 were made to young freemen. Loans were made until 1735, and again in 1766.[21] The charity then apparently lay dormant until 1846 when 15 trustees were appointed under a revised Scheme; in 1849 ten loans, totalling £525, were granted. £710 was available for loan in 1870, but very few freemen were entitled to benefit. In 1924 the terms of the charity were extended to include non-freemen, nevertheless, of 23 applications received in 1938 only one fulfilled all the qualifications. Efforts were again made to revive the charity in 1971 when there were assets of over £1,500 and a mortgage invested in Colchester corporation. Five new trustees were appointed

12 Ibid. Acc. C168, Winsley's Almshos. trustees' mins.; R.C.H.M. *Essex*, iii. 71.

13 E.R.O., T/B 193/1–2; inf. from the clerk to the trustees.

14 Account based on *32nd Rep. Com. Char.* 536–40; Char. Com. file; E.R.O., Winnock's almsho. char., trustees' mins. (uncat.).

15 Account based on *32nd Rep. Com. Char.* 543–6, and E.R.O., Acc. C160, Kendall's almsho. char., trustees' mins.

16 Char. Com. files.

17 Inf. from the clerk to the trustees of Winnock and Kendall's Combined Almsho. Charity.

18 Plaque on wall of cottages.

19 Char. Com. file.

20 *8th Rep. Com. Char.* H.C. 13, pp. 585–7 (1823), viii.

21 E.R.O., D/B 5 Gb1, 30 Sept. 1598; *32nd. Rep. Com. Char.* 552.

in 1973. In 1987 the borough council agreed to take over the management of the charity and was negotiating new terms with the Charity Commission.[22]

John Hunwick,[23] by will dated 1593, gave £300 to the poor of Colchester with the proviso that every fifth year the income should be given to the poor of Ipswich, Sudbury, and Maldon. From 1595 the capital was lent to Colchester tradesmen at 10 per cent interest.[24] The corporation had great difficulty in recovering the money owed, and from 1643 borough revenues were used regularly to make up the arrears.[25] Distributions of the charity continued in 1741 and perhaps later,[26] but had probably ceased by 1782 when Ipswich demanded arrears of £110. In 1837 the charity was deemed to be lost.[27] Mary, widow of Sir Thomas Judd, lord mayor of London, known as *Lady Judd*, by indenture of 1591, gave to the bailiffs and commonalty £100 to buy flax and other materials to set the poor to work. The profits were to be used to help the aged poor and those unable to work. Money was distributed regularly until 1619.[28] The corporation was taking steps to recover lost capital in 1667,[29] but no further reference to distribution of the charity has been found. *Thomas Ingram*, by indenture of 1602, gave to the bailiffs and commonalty £100 to be lent at 5 per cent interest to provide wool for setting to work the poor of St. Peter's parish; the interest was to be distributed among those unable to work. The money was being so used in 1605[30] and possibly until 1660 by which time part at least of the capital had been lost.[31] In 1674 a committee was set up by the corporation to inquire into the charity, and in 1697 and 1698 St. Peter's was being paid £20 a year out of the borough revenues.[32] The state of those three charities was the subject of several corporation inquiries until *c.* 1846, but no record of further payments has been found.[33]

By will proved in 1631, *William Turner*[34] gave to the aged poor of Colchester the rent of a house and land at the Hythe, which he held on a lease from the bailiffs and commonalty. Between 1633 and 1653 distributions of £7 were made reasonably regularly twice a year, but only six payments were made between 1659 and 1693, and the last was recorded in 1699. Later attempts to revive the charity, culminating in a Chancery suit in 1835, were unsuccessful.

William Whorlow Bunting,[35] by will proved 1922, left to trustees, all deacons of Lion Walk Congregational Church, the land and buildings of the Bunting Institute in Culver Street for the benefit of the young men of Colchester. In 1984 the investment income of £264 was supplemented by rent received for the premises. The original hall, built in 1906 as a gymnasium, was sold to developers in 1984, and a new hall built in Lion Walk.

By deed of 1939, *George Rose*[36] gave £6,000 to provide coal for the elderly poor, preferably widows. The charity was to be administered by the trustees of Winnock's charity, but separately from it. In 1985 eleven applicants each received 300 kg. of coal, and the cash balance of the charity was £900.

A *Lying-in charity*, supported by subscriptions, was founded in 1796 and endowed with £50 stock in 1835.[37] It lent to poor married women bedlinen and baby clothes, and gave them a small sum of money for food. Further donations and legacies had increased the investment income to £39 by 1887. With the advent of the National Health Service in 1948, there were very few applications for help from the charity and a Scheme of 1953 allowed larger grants of money to be made. In 1963, after only four grants had been made in five years, a new Scheme altered the terms of the charity to include unmarried mothers. No suitable applications for grants were received between 1973 and 1980, but ten grants of £30 and five of £40 were made in 1985–6.

PAROCHIAL CHARITIES. ALL SAINTS'. *Matthew Stephens*, by will proved in 1599, left to the poor of the parish £10 a year charged on his house in East Hill. In 1639 the occupant, *George Gilbert*, conveyed the house to 18 trustees who were to distribute 16*s.* a year to the poor of All Saints' and give 12*d.* and a penny loaf to 12 aged poor. The buildings were destroyed during the siege of 1648, and the site was let in 1654 to a saymaker for 99 years, 1*s.* a year to be paid to the parish. There is no further record of the charity.[38]

Charles Gray, by indenture enrolled in Chancery in 1772, gave £10 10*s.* yearly to the rector of All Saints' for the use of the poor on condition that he serve the parish himself for at least two months a year, otherwise on the same conditions to be divided between the rectors of St. James's and St. Runwald's parishes. In 1837 the payment was charged on the Castle estate in Colchester.[39] The charity was being distributed regularly in 1886,[40] but no later record of it has been found.

William Goodwin, by will dated 1828, left to the minister and churchwardens £100 for the upkeep of his family vault and three other graves, the residue to be used for the poor. About £3 a year was usually distributed in bread, coals, and money. *John Green Glandfield*,

22 Trustees' Minute Bk. and correspondence in possession of Colch. Boro. Council; inf. from Mr. P. Evans.
23 Account based on Morant, *Colch.* 164–5, and *32nd Rep. Com. Char.* 552.
24 E.R.O., D/B 5 Gb1, 10 Nov. 1595.
25 Ibid. D/B 5 Ab 1/15; D/B 5 Gb5, *passim*; Gb6, p. 342.
26 Morant, *Colch.* 164.
27 E.R.O., D/B 5 Gb8, f. 127.
28 Ibid. D/B 5 Gb2, f. 183v.
29 Ibid. D/B 5 Gb5, f. 15v.
30 Ibid. D/B 5 Gb2, f. 55.
31 Ibid. D/B 5 Gb4, f. 222.
32 Ibid. D/B 5 Gb5, f. 98.
33 *Official Enq. into Colch. Chars. 1886.*
34 Account based on *32nd Rep. Com. Char.* 533–6; Morant, *Colch.* 164; *Official Enq. into Colch. Chars. 1886.*
35 Account based on inf. from trustees of Bunting char. and Char. Com. files.
36 Account based on inf. from trustees of George Rose char. and Char. Com. files.
37 Account based on mins. of trustees of the Lying-in char. in possession of the Town Clerk, Town Hall, Colch.; Char. Com. files and correspondence; inf. from trustees.
38 *32nd Rep. Com. Char.* 553.
39 Ibid. 553.
40 *Official Enq. into Colch. Chars. 1886.*

by will proved in 1845, left to the rector £100 to be invested for the upkeep of his family vault, surplus income to be used for the relief of the poor of the parish. *James Watts*, by will dated 1875, made a similar gift also of £100, the residue to be distributed to the poor in bread on 25 October each year.[41] In 1886 the combined yearly income of the three charities was £8, distributed in bread and coals; in 1986 it was £46, used for general help to the needy.[42]

HOLY TRINITY. Mary (d. 1644), wife of Thomas Darcy, earl Rivers,[43] known as *Lady Darcy*, built for the poor of the parish eight brick almshouses in Eld Lane; at least four of them were built by 1635.[44] Before 1748, when the buildings were used as a workhouse, the parish had added two more houses. They seem to have been used as pauper housing in the early 19th century but had reverted to almshouses by 1886, apart from one house which was used for a school. All the houses were maintained by the vestry, and the rector and churchwardens were trustees of the charity.[45] Six of the houses were rebuilt between 1897 and 1905; the four remaining 17th-century houses were demolished in 1964 and their site was sold in 1971.[46] In 1987 ten new homes, built on East Hill, were given to the charity and the old almshouses in Eld Lane were redeveloped as part of the town centre modernisation.[47]

In the earlier 18th century the almshouses were said to be unendowed, but by 1782 the vestry was leasing 'land belonging to the poor houses', and by the early 19th century two rents of £3 from plots of land adjoining the almshouses had been assigned to the charity.[48] Cottages were built on one plot, fronting Lion Walk, *c.* 1836, and a hall, Darcy Hall, was built on the other *c.* 1910. The cottages were sold in 1955 and 1956 and the hall in 1970.[49]

Rachel, wife of Sir Ralph Creffield, known as *Lady Creffield*, by will proved in 1735, left £3 a year, charged on her house in Culver Street, to the poor of the parish at Christmas. The charity was so distributed in the 19th century, but by 1955 it was being added to the income of Lady Darcy's almshouses, and the arrangement was made permanent in 1958. The rent charge was redeemed in 1972 for £43.50.[50]

The charities are governed by a Scheme of 1959 which requires the almspeople to be resident in the borough of Colchester, preferably in Holy Trinity parish. The six surviving houses were still occupied as almshouses in 1984, and the charity's investment income that year was *c.* £2,660.[51]

ST. BOTOLPH'S. *Jeremiah Daniell*, by will dated 1695, left £10 a year, charged on land in St. Botolph's and St. Giles's parishes, for coal for the poor of four Colchester parishes: St. Botolph's, St. Giles's, St. Mary's-at-the-Walls, and St. Peter's.[52] The rent charge was paid by the War Office from *c.* 1888 until 1912 when it was redeemed.[53] St. Botolph's parish received £2 a year which was distributed regularly as coal until 1940.[54] In 1985 the parish held £60 stock, the income from which, *c.* £3, was used in the vicar's discretionary fund.[55]

By 1734 the parishes of St. Botolph and St. Giles were each receiving £2 12*s.* a year known as the *Poor Widows' Gift* out of a house and 42 a. in Little Totham, Great Totham, and Goldhanger. The payments were confirmed by a Chancery decree in 1740.[56] In 1851 the charity bought bread for 12 widows in each parish.[57] Money was received as late as 1958,[58] but no further reference to the charity has been found.

By will dated 1857, *Mrs. Mary Thorley* left £100 to buy blankets or coal for the poor. The money appears to have been invested and the interest allowed to accumulate until 1885 when a percentage of the accumulated dividend was used as intended.[59] In 1985 the income of £2.50 was used in the vicar's discretionary fund.[60]

ST. GILES'S. The parish shared in *Jeremiah Daniell's* charity, receiving £3 a year which appears to have been combined with the *Poor Widows' Gift* from 1855 or earlier, when the income was distributed in bread and coals.[61] Distribution continued in the 1920s but no later record has been found.[62]

ST. JAMES'S. *Elizabeth Jacobs*, by will dated 1801, left £125 stock and *Susannah Hammant*, by will proved in 1826, left £130, both sums to provide bread yearly at Christmas for the poor of the parish. In 1837 dividends of £10 and £4 10*s.* respectively were distributed in bread.[63] A Scheme in 1900 combined the charities for the general benefit of the poor, and in 1985 the incomes were £46 and £12 respectively.[64] By will proved 1887, *Margaret Round* left £1,500 from the income of which £10 was to be used annually to buy clothes for the poor.[65] In 1985 the combined income of the three charities was used to help the needy.[66]

ST. LEONARD'S. Before 1766 an unknown donor founded a *Bread Charity*, giving the rent from 1 a. of land in the parish to buy bread for poor unmarried people of the parish;[67] in 1864 the

41 E.R.O., D/P 200/8/3.
42 *Official Enq. into Colch. Chars. 1886*; inf. from Char. Com.; inf. from the rector.
43 Morant, *Colch.* 171; *32nd Rep. Com. Char.* 563–4; *Complete Peerage*, iv. 79.
44 Camb. Univ. Libr. Hengrave MS. 91: agreement of 1635.
45 Guildhall MS. 9558, f. 103; *Official Enq. into Colch. Chars. 1886*; E.R.O., D/P 323/8/1, *passim*.
46 E.R.O., D/P 323/8/2, s.a. 1897, 1905; corresp. of trustees of Lady Darcy's char. in possession of Mr. N. Abbott.
47 *E.C.S.* 5 Feb. 1987.
48 Morant, *Colch.* 171; E.R.O., D/P 323/8/1, s.a. 1782; *32nd Rep. Com. Char.* 563–4.
49 Trustees' corresp. and mins.
50 *32nd Rep. Com. Char.* 562; trustees' corresp.; Char. Com. file.
51 Char. Com. file; inf. from trustees.
52 *32nd Rep. Com. Char.* 554–5.
53 E.R.O., T/A 645; ibid. D/P 203/25/3.
54 Inf. from church treasurer.
55 Inf. from churchwarden.
56 Morant, *Colch.* 167.
57 E.R.O., D/P 324/8/1.
58 Church accounts, in possession of church treasurer.
59 *Official Enq. into Colch. Chars. 1886*.
60 Inf. from churchwarden.
61 E.R.O., D/P 324/8/1.
62 Ibid. D/P 324/8/2.
63 *32nd Rep. Com. Char.* 555.
64 Char. Com. file.
65 Ibid.
66 Inf. from the rector of St. James's.
67 Guildhall MS. 9557, f. 70; *32nd Rep. Com. Char.* 555.

land was sold and the proceeds were invested, providing an annual income of £5 6*s*. 8*d*.[68] In 1985 income was £5.32. *Charles Parker-Jarvis*, by will proved in 1840, left £100 to provide coals for poor sailors of the parish. *Emily Nicholls*, by will proved 1918, left £500 to buy blankets and coal at Christmas for the poor of the parish. By will proved 1936, *Elizabeth Everitt* left £100 in memory of her son, John Paxman Everitt, for the poor of the parish.[69] In 1986 the income from all four charities, *c*. £60, was combined and used by the rector of New Town parish, which included the former St. Leonard's parish, to help those in need.[70]

ST. MARTIN'S. None known.

ST. MARY'S-AT-THE-WALLS. By will proved 1689, *Joseph Cox* left £100 to buy land, the rents and profits to be distributed at Christmas to the poor of the parish. In 1711 his executors bought 8 a. of arable land in St. Mary's parish producing £5 10*s*. a year. In 1825 the land, then valuable building land, was exchanged for 28 a. in Mile End.[71] Some land was sold in 1878 and the rest before 1931.[72] In 1855 and again in 1931 the charity was distributed only to poor widows who had lived in the parish for at least a year, but in 1909 recipients included the sick and poor of both sexes.[73] In 1986 the income of £47 was distributed to widows at Christmas.[74]

The parish also shares in the charity of *Jeremiah Daniell,* and holds £80 stock, the income from which was not distributed in 1986.[75]

ST. NICHOLAS'S. *Ralph Finch*,[76] by will proved 1552, devised in trust the four almshouses which he had built in the parish for the use of four poor men or women of the parish, priority being given to Finch's kinsfolk. Each almsperson was to receive 6*d*. a week, to be paid out of a rent of £6 6*s*. 8*d*. a year charged on a brewhouse and land on Balkerne Hill and land in King's meadow and Fordham. After payment of 6*s*. 8*d*. to the trustees, any surplus was to provide firewood for the almspeople. Each almsperson was to leave a 'reasonable' part of his goods towards the maintenance of the almshouse.

By 1809, the full £6 6*s*. 8*d*. was charged on the land on Balkerne Hill, which was bought by the trustees in 1827. A strip of the land was taken by the corporation in 1936 to widen Sheepen Road, and in 1963 the remainder was sold to the Borough Council for £11,000.

Legacies enabled stipends to be raised to 7*d*. in 1791 and to 1*s*. 6*d*. in 1827 when an annuity of £262 10*s*., part of a bequest from William Goodwin, was received. The remainder of Goodwin's bequest, £900 stock to be used to endow four more almshouses, was received in 1835. The trustees demolished the four old, dilapidated houses, and built eight new ones on the same site in Culver Street the following year. By then all eight almsfolk were women, mostly tradesmen's widows; each paid 12*s*. on admission instead of leaving goods at her death. Stipends of 2*s*. were paid to those who had occupied the four original houses, the four new inhabitants had only 1*s*. 6*d*. each, and all received a yearly allowance of coal. In 1857 stipends, which had risen to 2*s*. 6*d*. for all, were cut to 2*s*. They were discontinued in 1948 but by 1970 occupants received £5 a year at Christmas, a gift which continued in 1987.[77] Legacies of £100 from James Watts in 1875 and of £50 from Sophia Ruffles in 1916 were invested.

In 1970 the redevelopment of the town centre led to the demolition of the almshouses in Culver Street and their reconstruction by the developers, Frincon Holdings Ltd., as single-storeyed centrally-heated dwellings on the Riverside estate in St. James's parish. In 1983 the charity, administered under a Scheme of 1926, had a total income of *c*. £3,000.[78]

Robert Franckham, by will dated 1577, gave to the poor of the parish 13*s*. 4*d*. a year charged on a house and lands in West Bergholt. A Chancery decree in 1603 vested the rent in 10 trustees.[79] The money was apparently paid in 1766 and possibly as late as *c*. 1800,[80] but had been lost by 1837.

George Wegg, by will dated 1745, left 40*s*. a year charged on 5 a. in St. James's parish to buy bread monthly from October to March for the poor of St. Nicholas's parish. The wording of the will was apparently insufficient in law, and so by an indenture of 1748, George Wegg, son of the testator, granted the rent charge to the rector of St. Nicholas's.[81] In 1898 the full £2 was spent on bread for poor widows.[82] Under a Scheme of 1945 the charity was administered separately by the trustees of Finch's almshouses.[83] In 1986 the income of £2 was used by the rector of the combined parishes of St. James, All Saints, St. Nicholas, and St. Runwald to assist the poor and needy as occasion arose.[84]

John Lyon, by will proved 1800, gave £5 a year to Finch's almshouse charity, and instituted a weekly bread charity which provided 3*d*. loaves to each of 12 poor widows and widowers, including the almsfolk who attended St. Nicholas's church, and to 12 who attended the Methodist meeting house in the Castle bailey.[85] The bread charity was commuted in 1943 to £15 a year in cash, half of which was paid to the almsfolk, half to the trustees of the Methodist church. From 1945 the almsfolk's share was used for the general expenses of the almshouses.[86] After the closure of the charity Sunday schools in 1812,[87] the *c*. 18*s*. a year which John Lyon had left to

68 E.R.O., D/P 245/8/5; D/P 245/3/7.
69 Char. Com. files.
70 Inf. from rector of the New Town parish.
71 *32nd Rep. Com. Char.* 556–7.
72 E.R.O., D/DMb T49; *Chelm. Dioc. Chron.* Feb. 1932, p. 30.
73 E.R.O., D/P 246/25.
74 Inf. from churchwarden.
75 Ibid.
76 Account based on *32nd Rep. Com. Char.* 557–60; E.R.O., Finch's char. order bk. 1685–1835; transcripts by Mrs. D. Woodward of extracts from later order bks.: in her possession.
77 Inf. from chairman of trustees.
78 Char. Com. file.
79 Morant, *Colch.* 166.
80 Guildhall MSS. 9557, f. 71; 9558, f. 100.
81 Morant, *Colch.* 166; *32nd Rep. Com. Char.* 561.
82 E.R.O., T/A 645.
83 Char. Com. file.
84 Inf. from the rector.
85 *32nd Rep. Com. Char.* 558.
86 Transcript by Mrs. D. Woodward of Finch's charity order bk.
87 Above, Educ.

them was applied to the almshouses. In 1983 Finch's almshouses received dividends of £45 from John Lyon's bequest.[88]

ST. PETER'S. *Agnes Dister* or Leach (d. 1553), daughter of John Woodthorpe, gave an unknown sum of money to be distributed yearly to the poor of the parish. Payment was made in 1786 but was lost by 1837.[89]

In 1570 *George Sayer* built four almshouses in Lower Balkerne Lane. They had no endowment and had been partly demolished by 1748 and completely so by 1768.[90]

The parish share in *Jeremiah Daniell's* charity, £3 a year, was allowed to accumulate in the 19th century; in 1985 the parish held £120 stock. *John Moore*, by will proved 1810, left £200 to buy coal, bread, and meat every New Year's Day for 20 poor people and to provide snuff and tobacco for the old in the workhouse. Only £54 was received, which yielded £2 9*s.* 6*d.* a year. *John Mills*, by will dated 1822, left £166 13*s.* 4*d.* from the income of which £2 10*s.* a year was to provide bread and money yearly at Christmas and Easter for 12 poor widows, and £1 5*s.* a year was to be used for the general relief of the poor of the parish. In 1863 the proceeds of the three charities provided bread and alms for 26 widows and 100 poor people. In 1985 the interest on all three, *c.* £8, was used for the general relief of the sick and poor.[91]

A Charity Commission Scheme of 1905 directed that part of the *c.* £9 income of the *Sears Family Fund*, established by David Sears of Boston, U.S.A., in 1853, be used to help maintain buildings or institutions used in parochial work with the poor,[92] but there is no evidence that the poor have ever benefited from the charity.

ST. RUNWALD'S. None known.

STREET NAMES

THE following section covers the streets in the area of the medieval town as they were before the construction of the inner relief road in 1973. Except where otherwise stated it is based on: E. Blaxill, *Street Names* (1936); J. B. Harvey's *Report* of 1889; *P.N. Essex*; Speed, *Map* (1610); Morant, *Colch.* 3–4, and map (1748); Chapman and André, *Map of Essex* (1777); Benham, *Colch. Map* (1848); MS. notes on Colch. street names by Philip Laver, in E.S.A.H. Libr., Hollytrees, Colch.

Abbeygate Street, 1836:[93] Lodders or Ladders Lane, mid 13th cent.;[94] Clothiers Lane, 1748.

Arthur Street, 1845, named after Arthur Thomas Osborne.[95]

Balkerne Lane, 1429,[96] from Crouch Street to Middleborough: it was Balkerne Hill north of Popes Lane by 1848.

Ball Alley, 1748, because it led to a bowling alley.

Butt Road formerly *Lane*, 1676,[97] because it led to the shooting butts: earlier Holmer, Holmere, Holmer's Lane, 1407;[98] also Lyard Lane, leading to Layer-de-la-Haye, 1748; Holmers Lane, later 18th cent.; Butt Lane, 1818;[99] also Mill Street, 1839, because it led to Butt mill;[1] Butt Road, 1856.[2]

Castle Road, 1861.[3]

Chapel Street, 1845.[4]

Childwell Alley formerly *Lane*, 1748: Cheldervelle Lane, 1340; by 1936 the northern end was Ernulph Walk.

Church Lane, 1399[5] and *St. Mary's Lane*, 1386[6] refer to the lanes leading to the church of St. Mary-at-the-Walls, later called Church Street or Church Walk.

Church Street formerly *Lane*, 1777, 1848: St. Mary's Lane, 1748; Church Street North, 1861;[7] Church Street, 1933.[8]

Church Walk formerly *Lane*, 1748: Church Street South, 1861;[9] perhaps Noah's Ark Lane later 18th cent. from an inn at the junction with Head Street; Church Walk, 1933.[10]

Crouch Street, 1748: Croucher Street, 1385:[11] part may have been known as Maldon Lane, 1389, 1427;[12] cf. Maldon Road.

Culver Street, or *Lane*, 1334–7: probably also Master John's Lane, 1332;[13] Culver Lane or Back Lane, 1748.

East Hill, 1748, from High Street to East Bridge. Earlier not distinguished from East Street which extended to Harwich Road.

Eld Lane, 1482:[14] (le) Oldelond, 1341;[15] Oldelane, 1405; perhaps Thelstreet, 1406; part was Almshouse Lane, 1748; Beast Lane or Stone Street before 1748; also Poor Row (from Trinity Street to Lion Walk), 1848.

George Street formerly *Lane*, 1823:[16] George Yard, 1748.

Head Street, 1173 (Have[d]strata):[17] possibly also Headgate Street, 1458.[18]

High Street, 1399:[19] the western end was called Cornhill, 1337;[20] Hevedstreet, 1412;[21] in front of

88 Char. Com. file.
89 Morant, *Colch.* 165–6; *32nd Rep. Com. Char.* 562.
90 Morant, *Colch.* 171.
91 E.R.O., D/P 178/25/1–2; *32nd Rep. Com. Char.* 561–2; inf. from church treasurer.
92 Scheme in possession of the clerk to the trustees.
93 E.R.O., Boro. Mun., Improvement Com. Mins. ii, p. 59.
94 B.L. Arundel MS. 145, f. 32.
95 *E.C.S.* 18 Sept. 1845.
96 E.R.O., D/B 5 R1, f. 84.
97 P.R.O., ASSI 35/117/3 (Essex) /10.
98 E.R.O., D/B 5 Cr36, rot. 11d.
99 Ibid. Acc. C210, J. B. Harvey Colln. vi, p. 116.
1 Ibid. D/P 246/11/1.
2 Ibid. Acc. C210, J. B. Harvey Colln. v, pp. 153–4.
3 P.R.O., RG 9/1100.
4 E.R.O., T/M 255.
5 Ibid. D/B 5 Cr31, rot. 1d.
6 Ibid. D/B 5 Cr25, rot. 33d.
7 P.R.O., RG 9/1098.
8 *Kelly's Dir. Essex* (1933).
9 P.R.O., RG 9/1098.
10 *Kelly's Dir. Essex* (1933).
11 E.R.O., D/B 5 Cr25, rot. 5d.
12 Ibid. D/B 5 Cr48, rot. 23.
13 Ibid. D/B 5 Cr9, rot. 4.
14 Ibid. D/B 5 Cr79, rot. 17d.
15 Ibid. D/B 5 Cr6, rot. 5d.
16 *Pigot's Lond. and Provincial Dir.* (1823), 291.
17 *Pipe R.* 1174 (P.R.S. xxi), 75.
18 E.R.O., D/B 5 Cr68, rot. 27d.
19 Ibid. D/B 5 Cr31, rot. 1d.
20 Ibid. D/B 5 Cr5, rot. 8d.
21 Ibid. D/B 5 Cr38, rot. 21d.

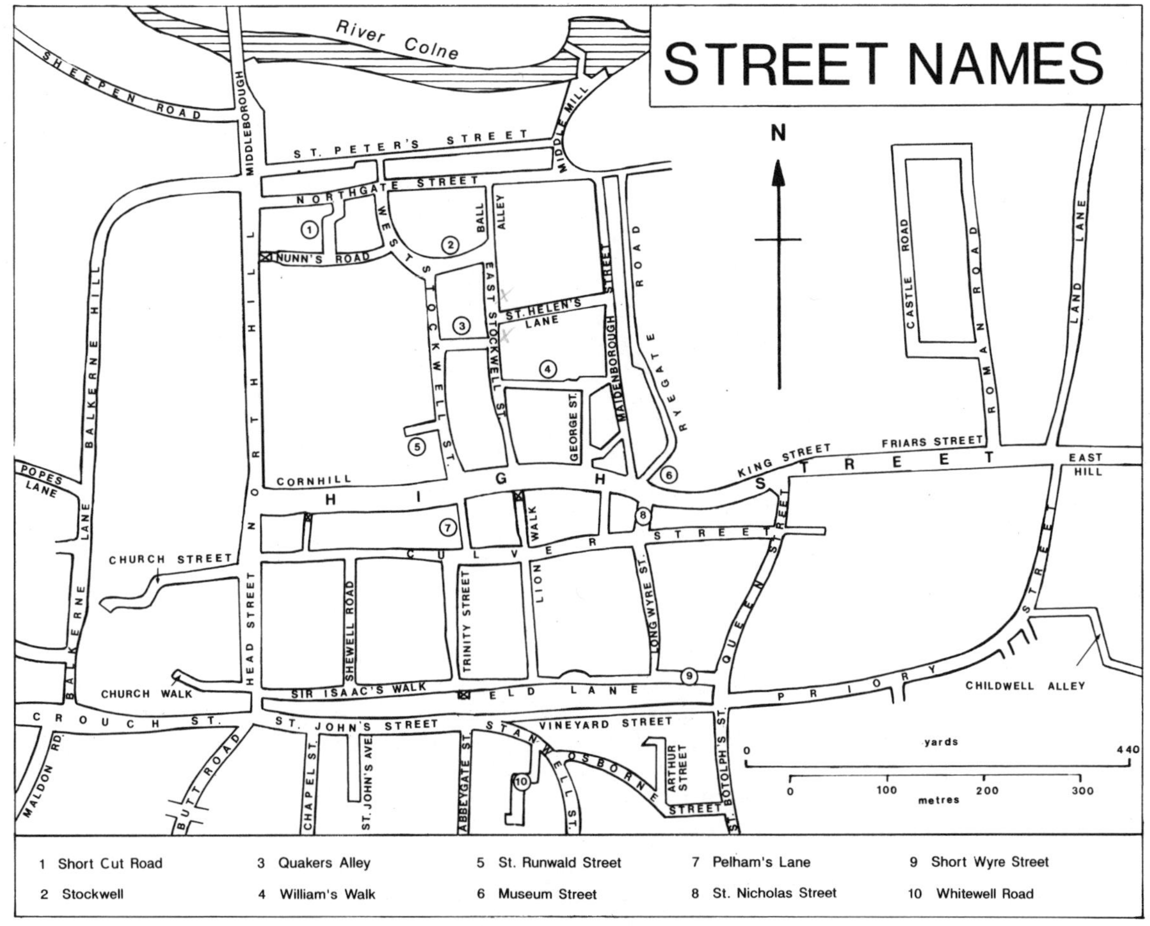

FIG. 32

All Saints' Church was King Street, 1748; in front of Greyfriars was Friars Street, 1388.[22]

Land Lane, 1841:[23] Porthawe, 1477;[24] Lincoln Way, 1976, when the estate was developed.[25]

Lion Walk, 1748: formerly Cat Lane, 1357.

Maidenburgh Street, Maidenborough, 1312:[26] cf. Rob. de Maydenburg, 1248;[27] also St. Helen's Lane, 1387;[28] or St. Helen's Street, 1438;[29] Tennants Lane, a corruption of St. Helen's, 1610; St. Helen's Lane or Maidenburgh Street, 1758.[30]

Maldon Road, formerly *Lane*, 1408:[31] the northern end was sometimes Schrebbe Street; probably also Crowcherche Lane, 1389, 1427.[32]

Middleborough, 1352.

Museum Street, 1851:[33] earlier the entrance to the castle bailey.

North Hill, 1511: North Street, 1196.[34]

Northgate Street, 1854:[35] Duck Lane, 1729;[36] Duck Lane and Little Hill, 1748.

Nunns Road formerly *Cut*, 1860,[37] named after Roger Nunn, mayor 1842: perhaps Grafton Street, 1880.

Osborne Street, 1851:[38] named after Arthur Thomas Osborne whose brewery was nearby.

Pelham's Lane, 1748, named after William Pelham, common councillor 1623–43, who had a shop there: Whitefoot's Lane, 1306.[39]

Popes Lane, 1787:[40] it apparently led to land called Popes Head, 1521; unnamed, 1748; Workhouse Lane or Union Lane, 1876;[41] Popes Lane, 1921.[42]

Priory Street, 1818:[43] More Street, 1275; More Elm Lane, 1610; Moor Lane, 1690.[44]

Quakers Alley, 1748: St. Martin's Lane, 1876.[45]

Queen, or *Queen's Street*, 1748: South Street or Southgate Street, 1333, 1438, because it led to the south gate (St. Botolph's gate); not distinguished from St. Botolph's Street, 1610; perhaps also Silver Street, 1629–30.[46]

22 Ibid. D/B 5 R1, f. 165.
23 P.R.O., HO 107/344.
24 E.R.O., D/B 5 Cr77, rot. 27d.
25 Inf. from Colch. Boro. Council Planning Dept.
26 Ibid. D/B 5 Cr2, rot. 6.
27 P.R.O., JUST 1/231, rot. 34.
28 E.R.O., D/B 5 R1, f. 166v.
29 Ibid. D/B 5 Cr63, rot. 22d.
30 Ibid. D/DHt T72/106.
31 Ibid. D/B 5 Cr36, rot. 11d.
32 Ibid. D/B 5 Cr48, rot. 23.
33 P.R.O., HO 107/1781.
34 *Feet of Fines*, 1182–1196 (P.R.S. xvii), 181.
35 A. F. J. Brown, *Essex People, 1750–1900*, 183.
36 E.R.O., D/B 5 Sr157, rot. 6.
37 Ibid. Boro. Mun., Improvement Com. Mins. iv, p. 317.
38 P.R.O., HO 107/1781.
39 B.L. Campb. Ch. ii. 5.
40 E.R.O., D/DU 728/5.
41 O.S. Map 1/500, Essex XXVII. 12. 5 (1876 edn.).
42 O.S. Map 6", Essex XXXVII. NE. (1924 edn.).
43 E.R.O., Boro. Mun., Improvement Com. Mins. i, p. 112.
44 Ibid. D/B 5 Sr52, *passim*.
45 O.S. Map 1/500, Essex XXVII. 12. 3 (1876 edn.).
46 *E.R.* lviii. 30.

Roman Road, 1861:[47] built in the 1850s.

Ryegate Road, 1891:[48] earlier an unnamed common way.

St. Botolph's Street, 1401:[49] South Street, 1339;[50] St. Botolphs Street, 1610; Southgate Street, Brook Street, or Botolph's Street, 1628;[51] St. Botolph's Street, sometimes called South Street, 1748.

St. Helen's Lane, 1841:[52] Bekelerysbery Lane, 1423;[53] Bucklersbury Lane, Peacock Alley, or Meeting House Alley, 1748.

St. John's Avenue, 1897.[54]

St. John's Street, 1818:[55] Southsherde Street or Southsherdegate Street, 1384;[56] Gutter Street, 1748, from the gutter which ran down the middle of the street.

St. Nicholas Street, 1841:[57] earlier not distinguished from Wyre Street.

St. Peter's Street, 1844:[58] possibly Fowles Lane, 1330;[59] Dead Lane, 1702, or Deadman's Lane, 1748;[60] Dead Lane, 1840;[61] Factory Lane, 1851, after Brown and Moy's silk factory there.[62]

St. Runwald Street, 1936: possibly Hospital Yard, 1748.

Sheepen Road, formerly *Lane*, 1550, because it led to Sheepen farm: Reyners Lane, 1411;[63] Water Lane, 1748; also Water Lane North, 1848; Sheepen Road, 1936.

Shewell Road, 1936, named after a member of the Society of Friends, Joseph Shewell (d. 1875): formerly a private cul-de-sac.

Short Cut Road, 1871:[64] unnamed in 1848.

Sir Isaac's Walk, 1811:[65] Sir Isaac Rebow's Walk, 1748, paved by Sir Isaac Rebow *c.* 1690; earlier part of Eld Lane.

Stanwell Street, 1341:[66] the southern end was Brewery Road in 1876.[67]

Stockwell, Stockwell Street, 1329.[68]

Stockwell Street East, 1311:[69] also called Calayse Street *c.* 1380;[70] Beirs Lane, 1692;[71] Bear Lane, from an inn on the corner with High Street, also St. Martin's Lane, 1748; East Stockwell Street, 1841.[72]

Stockwell Street West, 1327:[73] Angel Lane, 1687;[74] West Stockwell Street, 1841.[75]

Trinity Street, formerly *Lane*, 1610: Trinity Lane or Schere Street, 1748; Trinity Lane or Shiregate Street, 1777.

Vineyard Street, 1861:[76] Beres Lane, 1312;[77] Bere Lane, 1504;[78] Black Boy Lane, 1678;[79] Blackboy or Bear Lane, 1767,[80] 1777; also Brickyard Street, 1861;[81] in 1963 the middle section was closed to make a car park and the western end was incorporated into Osborne Street.

Whitewell Road, 20th cent: Stanwell Road, 1876;[82] perhaps Whitewell Street, 1767.

Williams Walk, 1848.

Wyre Street, 1311:[83] Wyre or Weir Street 1748; Long and Short Wyre Street, 1841.[84]

BAILIFFS AND MAYORS OF COLCHESTER

THE names of the bailiffs for each year were recorded in the borough court rolls (E.R.O., D/B 5 Cr1 onwards) which survive, with some gaps, from 1310 to 1740. The names for the years 1327–1563 were also entered in the Oath Book (E.R.O., D/B 5 R1), which calendars the court rolls, and those for the years 1576 to 1835 were recorded in the assembly books (E.R.O., D/B 5 Gb1–10). Later elections were recorded in the council minutes (E.R.O., Boro. Mun., uncat.) and reported in local newspapers. An incomplete list of bailiffs from the mid 12th century to 1327 can be compiled from various sources. The bailiffs and later mayors took office at Michaelmas until 1835 when the date was changed to November; in 1949 the date was changed to May.

Lists have been published by H. Harrod, *Report on the Records of the Borough of Colchester* (from 1255 to 1865), and by George Rickword, *Bailiffs and Mayors of Colchester* (from before 1086 to 1902). Harrod's list is substantially correct; Rickword's contains a number of errors. The following list is based on Harrod's list, corrected from the Oath Book, for the period 1327–1865, and on council minutes, newspapers, and a list at the town hall for the period 1865–1974; sources are given for any other additions or corrections to Harrod's list, and for all bailiffs for the period before 1327. From 1836 the political parties of the mayors, as known from newspaper reports and from information from the mayor's secretary, are given.

47 P.R.O., RG 9/1100.
48 O.S. Map 1/2,500, Essex XXVII. 12 (1892 edn.).
49 E.R.O., D/B 5 Cr33, rot. 4d.
50 B.L. Arundel MS. 145, f. 25v.
51 E.R.O., D/B 5 Cb1/8, f. 348.
52 P.R.O., HO 107/344.
53 E.R.O., D/B 5 Cr43, rot. 19d.
54 O.S. Map 1/2,500, Essex XXVII. 8 (1897 edn.).
55 E.R.O., Acc. C210, J. B. Harvey Colln. vi, p. 116.
56 Ibid. D/B 5 Cr24, rot. 11d.
57 P.R.O., HO 107/344.
58 Brown, *Essex People, 1750–1900*, 175.
59 E.R.O., D/B 5 Cr3, rot. 2d.
60 Ibid. D/B 5 Sr67, rot. 7.
61 *Pigot's Dir. Essex* (1840).
62 P.R.O., RG 9/1099.
63 E.R.O., D/B 5 Cr38, rot. 2.
64 P.R.O., RG 10/1688.
65 E.R.O., Acc. C210, J. B. Harvey Colln. vi, pp. 115–17.
66 Ibid. D/B 5 Cr6, rot. 9d.
67 O.S. Map 1/500, Essex XXVII. 12. 14 (1876 edn.).
68 E.R.O., D/B 5 Cr3, rot. 1d.
69 Ibid. D/B 5 Cr1, rot. 5d.
70 Ibid. D/B 5 R2, f. 481.
71 Ibid. D/DB T1481.
72 P.R.O., HO 107/344.
73 E.R.O., D/B 5 R1, f. 29v.
74 Ibid. D/B 5 Sr51, rot 6.
75 P.R.O., HO 107/344.
76 Ibid. RG 9/1097.
77 E.R.O., D/B 5 Cr2, rot. 13.
78 Ibid. D/B 5 Cr82, rot. 27.
79 Ibid. D/DC 27/7.
80 Sparrow, *Colch. Map* (1767).
81 E.R.O., Acc. C210, J. B. Harvey Colln. vi, p. 89.
82 O.S. Map 1/500 Essex XXVII. 12. 5 (1876 edn.).
83 E.R.O., D/B 5 Cr1, rot. 12d.
84 P.R.O., HO 107/344.

Bailiffs to 1327

c. 1149 Walter Haning and Benet[85]
1178 Geoffrey son of Benet[86]
1179 Geoffrey son of Benet[87]
1180 Gilbert son of Bruno[88]
1181 Boidin and Geoffrey Spenser[89]
1182 Boidin and Geoffrey Spenser[90]
1183 Gilbert son of Bruno and Richard Ursus[91]
1184 Richard Ursus and [name lost][92]
1186 Boidin and John[93]
1187 Boidin and John[94]
1188 Thomas and [name lost][95]
1191 John and Osbert[96]
1192 Richard son of Gilbert and Nicholas son of Walter[97]
1193 Richard son of Gilbert and Nicholas son of Walter[98]
1194 Walter of Crepping[99]
1195 Walter of Crepping and Simon son of Marcian[1]
1196 Walter of Crepping[2]
1197 Walter of Crepping[3]
1239[4] Nicholas son of Thomas and Ralph son of Peter[5]
1241 Guy Basset and Ralph son of Peter[6]
1242 Guy Basset and Ralph son of Peter[7]
c. 1249 Ralph son of Peter and Walter of East Street[8]
1250 Ralph son of the priest, John son of Ellis, Walter le Mott, and Saer Halferthing (June 1251)[9]
1252 Oliver son of Ellis and Saer Bacun[10]
1254 Ralph son of the priest or chaplain and Simon Eskermissur or Clerk[11]
1267 Walter Goldsmith[12]
1271 Walter Goldsmith and Nicholas Medicus[13]
1272 Robert le Gros and Walter Galingale (son of Roger)[14]
1274? Walter Goldsmith and John Clerk (1275)[15]
1275? Roger Clerk and Thomas Listwine (1275)[16]
1276? Stephen son of Ralph and Henry Goodyear[17]
1276? Geoffrey Goodyear and Richard of Bergholt[18]
1277? Richard Pruet and Saer son of Ralph[19]
1282 John the Clerk and Roger the Clerk[20]
1284 Simon le Gros and Hervey Lightwine[21]
1285 Richard Golafre and Richard Pruet[22]
1289 Ralph Savary and Alexander Tovy or Tony[23]
1292 Saer son of Henry and John of Stanway[24]
1296 John Peacock and Richard Tubbe[25]
1303 Ellis son of John and Alexander the taverner[26]
1304 Ellis son of John and John Ford[27]
1305 Saer le Parmenter and Ralph Savary[28]
1306 Saer of Donyland and Ralph Ode[29]
1307 William Tute, clerk, and Richard Noreys[30]
1309 Warin son of William and Saer of Donyland[31]
1310 Warin son of William and Saer of Donyland[32]
1311 Joseph Eleanor, or Clerk, and William de Sartria[33]
1312 Ellis son of John and Matthew le Verrer[34]
1313 Warin son of William and John le Teynturer[35]
1314 Warin son of William and John Ford[36]
1315 Ellis son of John and Hubert Bosse, or of Colchester[37]
1316 Warin son of William and Adam of the castle[38]
1317 Warin son of William and Joseph Eleanor[39]
1318 Arnold de Mounteny and John of Tendring[40]
1320 William Clerk and Richard of Colne[41]
1321 William le Tote, clerk, and Peter of Aston or le Salter[42]
1324 Warin son of William and Peter of Aston[43]
1325 John Jordan and John Caperun[44]

85 *Colch. Cart.* i. 155.
86 *Pipe R.* 1179 (P.R.S. xxviii), 129.
87 Ibid. 1180 (P.R.S. xxix), 7.
88 Ibid. 1181 (P.R.S. xxx), 106.
89 Ibid. 1182 (P.R.S. xxxi), 102.
90 Ibid. 1183 (P.R.S. xxxii), 26.
91 Ibid. 1184 (P.R.S. xxxiii), 142.
92 Ibid. 1185 (P.R.S. xxxiv), 20.
93 Ibid. 1187 (P.R.S. xxxvii), 129.
94 Ibid. 1188 (P.R.S. xxxviii), 39.
95 Ibid. 1189 (Rec. Com.), 38.
96 Ibid. 1191 & 92 (P.R.S. N.S. ii), 174.
97 Ibid. 1193 (P.R.S. N.S. iii), 8.
98 Ibid. 1194 (P.R.S. N.S. v), 225.
99 Ibid. 1195 (P.R.S. N.S. vi), 14.
1 *Chanc. R.* 1196 (P.R.S. N.S. vii), 120.
2 *Pipe R.* 1197 (P.R.S. N.S. viii), 72.
3 Ibid. 1198 (P.R.S. N.S. ix), 133.
4 *Oath Bk.* ed. W. G. Benham, 223, gives William of Coggeshall as bailiff 1230–1 and Thomas of Coggeshall 1232–3, but they were sheriffs of Essex: E.R.O., D/B 5 R1, f. 176.
5 *Colch. Cart.* ii. 325–6.
6 Ibid. 324.
7 Ibid. 327.
8 P.R.O., JUST 1/233, rot. 58.
9 Ibid. rot. 36; Walter and Saer were presumably underbailiffs.
10 *Abbrev. Plac.* (Rec. Com.), 131; P.R.O., JUST 1/233, rot. 58.
11 *Colch. Cart.* ii. 505; B.L. Arundel MS. 145, f. 19.
12 P.R.O., E 32/12.
13 E.R.O., D/B 5 R2, f. 47.
14 P.R.O., JUST 1/238, rot. 45d.; JUST 1/242, rot. 110.
15 *Cal. Exch. Jews*, ii. 236.
16 Ibid. 276.
17 *Cart. St. John of Jerusalem*, p. 150.
18 E.R.O., D/B 5 R2, f. 1v.
19 Ibid. D/B 5 R1, f. 3.
20 Ibid. D/B 5 R2, f. 107v.
21 P.R.O., JUST 1/242, rot. 36.
22 Ibid.
23 E.R.O., D/B 5 R2, f. 50v.
24 B.L. Arundel MS. 145, f. 25v.
25 Ibid. ff. 20v., 29v.
26 *Cart. St. John of Jerusalem*, p. 159.
27 B.L. Arundel MS. 145, f. 22v.
28 Ibid. Campb. Ch. ii. 5.
29 Ibid. Arundel MS. 145, f. 17.
30 Ibid. ff. 15, 20.
31 Ibid. f. 21; *Colch. Cart.* ii. 639.
32 E.R.O., D/B 5 Cr1, rot. 1.
33 Ibid. D/B 5 Cr2, rot. 1.
34 B.L. Arundel MS. 145, f. 16v.
35 Ibid. f. 18; *Colch. Cart.* ii. 670.
36 E.R.O., St. John's abbey ledger bk. f. 180.
37 Ibid. ff. 179v., 181.
38 Ibid. f. 124v.
39 Ibid. f. 125.
40 Ibid. D/B 5 R2, f. 2; ibid. Acc. A8173.
41 Ibid. St. John's abbey ledger bk. f. 189.
42 B.L. Arundel MS. 145, f. 17v.; E.R.O., St. John's abbey ledger bk. f. 104.
43 E.R.O., St. John's abbey ledger bk. 106v.
44 B.L. Arundel MS. 145, f. 12v.

The following are known to have been bailiffs, but cannot be assigned to a specific year:
Nicholas Spenser, Michael Merchant, and Nicholas son of Thomas, between 1223 and 1245[45]
Nicholas Spenser, Baldwin, and Ralph Bateman, before 1238[46]
Peter Makerel and Nicholas Constable, between 1238 and 1242[47]
Robert of Lexden and Nicholas Constable, before 1254[48]
Saer Bacun and Saer Haning, 1250s or 1260s[49]
Oliver son of Ellis and Saer Bacun, 1250s or 1260s[50]
Henry Goodyear and Ralph Skinner, between 1272 and 1275[51]
Thomas Listwine and John of Horstede, *c.* 1275[52]
Thomas Listwine and Henry Goodyear, before 1276[53]
Ellis son of John and Warin son of William, January 1328 or possibly January 1308[54]

In addition, the following served as coroners, an office normally served by the bailiffs or former bailiffs:
Nicholas of East Street, 1254[55]
Henry Goodyear, Henry the Parmenter, Nicholas Medicus, Richard le Bau, Thomas Listwine, Robert le Gros, and Walter son of Roger, before 1271[56]

Bailiffs 1327–1635
1327 Ralph Knight and Edward Chaloner
1328 Joseph Eleanor and Alan Nayland
1329 Warin son of William and Joseph Eleanor
1330 Warin son of William and Joseph Eleanor
1331 Warin son of William and Joseph Eleanor
1332 Warin son of William and Matthew son of Robert
1333 Warin son of William and Ralph Ode
1334 Warin son of William and Ralph Ode
1335 John Jordan and Robert Belch
1336 John Finch and John Caperun
1337 Matthew son of Robert and John Finch
1338 Ralph Ode and Joseph Eleanor
1339 Warin Atwell and Robert Clerk
1340 Robert Clerk and William Hadleigh
1341 John Fordham and William Buck
1342 Joseph Eleanor and John Fordham
1343 Robert Clerk and Roger Belch
1344 John Warin the elder and William Hadleigh
1345 William Hadleigh and Thomas Dedham
1346 Thomas Dedham and William Hadleigh
1347 Thomas Dedham and William Hadleigh
1348 William Hadleigh and Roger Belch
1349 Matthew son of Robert and Robert Francis
1350 John Ford and Adam Colne
1351 Matthew son of Robert and William Fermery
1352 Adam Colne and Robert Ford
1353 John Dyer and Richard Broadway
1354 John Boyn and Clement Dyer
1355 Adam Atwell and Richard Dyer
1356 John Ford and John Allen
1357 John Ford and Richard Dyer
1358 Adam Warin and Richard Dyer
1359 John Ford and John Dyer
1360 Richard Dyer and William Reyne
1361 Robert Ford and William Reyne
1362 Robert Ford and George Fordham
1363 Alexander Cogger and William Reyne
1364 John Ford and William Reyne
1365 Robert Ford and William Bosse
1366 John Ford and Alexander Cogger
1367 John Ford and Alexander Cogger
1368 Richard Drury and John Keek
1369 Robert Ford and William Mate
1370 Robert Ford and John Lucas
1371 Robert Ford and John Lucas
1372 Alexander Cogger and William Christmas
1373 William Reyne and John Clerk
1374 John Ford and John Pebmarsh
1375 William Reyne and Alexander Pod
1376 Alexander Cogger and Stephen Baron
1377 William Reyne and John Keek
1378 Alexander Cogger and Geoffrey Daw
1379 Robert Ford and Stephen Baron
1380 Alexander Cogger and Ralph Algar
1381 Thomas Francis and Thomas Clerk
1382 Simon Fordham and John Christian
1383 Thomas Francis and Ralph Algar
1384 Alexander Cogger and John Christian
1385 Ralph Algar and William Penne
1386 Simon Fordham and John Christian
1387 Thomas Francis and John Seburgh
1388 Ralph Algar and Stephen Baron
1389 Thomas Francis and Alexander Cogger
1390 Simon Fordham and John Christian
1391 William Reyne and John Seburgh
1392 Thomas Francis and John Christian
1393 Simon Fordham and Ralph Algar
1394 John Seburgh and Thomas Clerk
1395 Simon Fordham and John Dyer
1396 John Christian and John Seburgh
1397 John Dyer and William Mate
1398 Thomas Godstone and Thomas Francis
1399 John Seburgh and John Ford
1400 Thomas Francis and Stephen Flisp
1401 Thomas Godstone and John Seburgh
1402 John Ford and Philip Neggemere
1403 Thomas Francis and John Pod
1404 Thomas Godstone and John Seburgh
1405 John Ford and John Dyer
1406 Thomas Godstone and Henry Bosse
1407 Thomas Francis and John Pod
1408 John Dyer and William Mate
1409 Thomas Francis and John Pod
1410 John Ford and William Mate
1411 Thomas Godstone and John Dyer
1412 Thomas Francis and John Ford
1413 Thomas Godstone and William Mate
1414 Thomas Francis and John Ford
1415 Thomas Godstone and John Kimberley

45 *Colch. Cart.* ii. 544.
46 Ibid. 318.
47 Ibid. 323–4.
48 B.L. Arundel MS. 145, f. 31v.
49 Ibid. ff. 20, 31v.
50 Ibid. f. 31.
51 *Cart. St. John of Jerusalem*, pp. 159–60.
52 Ibid. p. 154.
53 Ibid. pp. 153–4.
54 B.L. Arundel MS. 145, ff. 15v.–16.
55 P.R.O., JUST 1/235, rot. 19.
56 Ibid. JUST 1/238, rot. 58d.

1416 John Ford and William Mate
1417 Thomas Godstone and William Nottingham
1418 John Ford and Austin Bonefaunt
1419 Thomas Godstone and William Nottingham
1420 John Kimberley and William Mate
1421 Thomas Godstone and Henry Bosse
1422 William Nottingham and John Sumpter
1423 Thomas Godstone and Robert Prior
1424 John Sumpter and Henry Bosse
1425 Thomas Godstone and John Kimberley
1426 Henry Bosse and William Nottingham
1427 Simon Mate and Thomas Hoskin
1428 John Beche and Robert Selby
1429 Thomas Godstone and John Beche
1430 Henry Bosse and John Trew
1431 John Beche and Robert Prior
1432 Henry Bosse and John Stevens
1433 John Beche and Robert Prior
1434 Simon Mate and Thomas Hoskin
1435 Robert Selby and Walter Bonefey
1436 John Trew and John Rouge
1437 John Beche and Walter Bonefey
1438 Thomas Hoskin and Robert Selby
1439 Walter Bonefey and John Ode
1440 John Beche and Robert Prior
1441 John Trew and John Rouge
1442 John Beche and Nicholas Peek
1443 John Rouge and Thomas Cent
1444 John Beche and Nicholas Peek
1445 Thomas Hoskin and Thomas Atwood
1446 Robert Selby and Roger Wyke
1447 John Beche and John Rouge
1448 Robert Selby and Roger Wyke
1449 Nicholas Peek and Thomas Atwood
1450 William Leche and William Saxe
1451 John Ford and John Baker
1452 Thomas Atwood and William Saxe
1453 John Ford and William Petworth
1454 William Ford and John Sayer
1455 William Saxe and Seman Youn
1456 John Ford and John Beche (died in office, succeeded by William Saxe)[57]
1457 William Saxe and John Sayer
1458 John Ford and Matthew Drury
1459 William Petworth and William Ford
1460 Matthew Drury and John Baron
1461 William Ford and John Seman
1462 John Ford and John Water
1463 William Smith and John Bishop
1464 John Wright and William Rede
1465 William Ford and William Smith
1466 John Wright and John Ford
1467 Richard Welde and Richard Parker
1468 William Ford and John Bishop
1469 Thomas Smith and John Butler
1470 William Ford and John Wright
1471 John Butler and Richard Marks
1472 Thomas Smith and William Colchester
1473 William Ford and John Butler
1474 William Colchester and Thomas Christmas
1475 John Bishop and John Butler
1476 Thomas Smith and Thomas Christmas
1477 William Smith and William Colchester
1478 William Ford and John Bishop
1479 Richard Marks and Thomas Smith
1480 William Smith and Thomas Stamp (died in office, succeeded by John Gamday)
1481 John Gamday and Thomas Jobson
1482 John Bishop and Thomas Christmas
1483 William Ford and William Smith
1484 Thomas Christmas and Richard Plomer
1485 Thomas Jobson and John Upcher
1486 Richard Marks and Thomas Christmas
1487 Thomas Jobson and Richard Hervey (died in office, succeeded by Richard Plomer)
1488 Richard Haynes and Richard Halke (died in office, succeeded by Thomas Christmas)
1489 John Upcher and Richard Barker
1490 Thomas Jobson and John Bardfield
1491 Thomas Christmas the elder and Nicholas Clere
1492 John Upcher and John Bardfield
1493 Richard Marks and Thomas Christmas the elder
1494 Richard Haynes and Richard Barker
1495 Thomas Christmas the elder and John Thirsk
1496 Richard Haynes and Richard Barker
1497 Thomas Christmas the elder and Thomas Christmas the younger
1498 John Sweyn and John Breton
1499 Thomas Christmas the elder and Richard Barker (died in office, succeeded by Thomas Jobson)
1500 Thomas Christmas the younger and John Sweyn
1501 Robert Cowbridge and John John
1502 John Sweyn and Robert Best
1503 Thomas Christmas and John Mayking
1504 John Sweyn and Richard Pack
1505 John Bardfield (replaced by Thomas Christmas) and William Bennett
1506 Thomas Christmas and John Sweyn
1507 Robert Cowbridge and William Bennett
1508 [unknown]
1509 Thomas Christmas and John Sweyn
1510 John Mayking and Richard Pack
1511 John Sweyn and John Reynold
1512 John Smallpiece and John Bryan
1513 John Sweyn and John Clere
1514 John Smallpiece and John Colle
1515 Thomas Christmas and John Reynold
1516 John Mayking and John Christmas
1517 Thomas Christmas and John Coggeshall
1518 John Clere and John Colle
1519 Thomas Christmas (died in office, succeeded by John Christmas)[58] and William Debenham
1520 John Clere and John Colle
1521 Ambrose Lowth and William Jobson
1522 John Bradman and John Flingaunt
1523 John Mayking and John Colle
1524 John Clere and John Coggeshall
1525 John Christmas and Christopher Hammond
1526 Ambrose Lowth and John Neve
1527 Thomas Flingaunt and John Smallpiece
1528 John Mayking and John Coggeshall
1529 John Colle and William Becket
1530 Ambrose Lowth and John Neve
1531 John Christmas and John Mayking
1532 John Clere and Thomas Cook

57 E.R.O., D/B 5 Cr67, rot. 23d.

58 Ibid. D/B 5 Cr91, rot. 11d.

1533 Thomas Flingaunt and John Smallpiece
1534 John Colle and William Becket
1535 John Christmas and John Neve
1536 John Clere and Thomas Flingaunt
1537 Robert Brown and William Thurston
1538 John Christmas and Thomas Cook
1539 John Neve and Robert Leche
1540 Austin Beriff (resigned, replaced by Thomas Flingaunt who died in office and was succeeded by John Christmas) and George Sayer
1541 Benjamin Clere and Robert Brown the younger
1542 Thomas Cook and William Buxton
1543 Robert Brown the elder and Robert Flingaunt
1544 Benjamin Clere and Austin Beriff
1545 Robert Leche and Thomas Reve
1546 George Sayer and Robert Brown the younger
1547 John Christmas and John Best
1548 Benjamin Clere and Robert Flingaunt
1549 Robert Leche and Thomas Dibney
1550 John Beriff and John Stone (died in office, succeeded by Robert Brown)
1551 John Best and William Mott
1552 George Sayer and Robert Maynard
1553 Benjamin Clere and John Maynard
1554 John Beriff and John Dibney
1555 George Sayer and William Strachey
1556 Robert Brown and Robert Maynard
1557 John Best and John Maynard
1558 Benjamin Clere and William Mott
1559 George Sayer and John Best
1560 Robert Brown and Robert Northen
1561 John Maynard and Robert Middleton
1562 Benjamin Clere and Robert Lambert
1563 George Sayer and John Best
1564 Robert Middleton and Richard Northey
1565 Benjamin Clere and Nicholas Clere
1566 John Maynard and Robert Northen
1567 George Sayer and John Best
1568 Robert Middleton and Robert Lambert
1569 Robert Northen and Richard Northey
1570 Benjamin Clere and John Fowle
1571 John Best and Thomas Turner
1572 Robert Lambert and Thomas Laurence
1573 John Pye and William Simpson (resigned, replaced by Robert Middleton)[59]
1574 Thomas Turner and Richard Thurston
1575 Benjamin Clere and Robert Mott
1576 Robert Lambert and Thomas Laurence
1577 John Pye and John Hunwick
1578 Richard Thurston and Nicholas Clere (died in office, succeeded by William Turner)[60]
1579 Robert Mott and Thomas Cook
1580 Thomas Laurence and Richard Lambert
1581 Robert Lambert and John Pye
1582 John Hunwick and John Bird
1583 William Turner and Robert Bird
1584 Robert Mott and Thomas Cook
1585 Thomas Laurence and Richard Lambert
1586 John Pye and William Earnesby
1587 John Bird and Thomas Barlow
1588 Robert Bird (died in office, succeeded by Thomas Laurence)[61] and Martin Bessell
1589 Robert Mott and Thomas Cook
1590 John Pye and Thomas Reynold
1591 Thomas Laurence and Ralph Northey
1592 Thomas Hazlewood and William Dibney
1593 John Hunwick (died in office, succeeded by Thomas Hazlewood)[62] and John Bird
1594 Robert Mott and Martin Bessell
1595 Thomas Hazlewood and Henry Osborne
1596 Ralph Northey and Thomas Ingram
1597 Thomas Reynold and William Turner
1598 Richard Simnell and Robert Wade
1599 Robert Mott and Thomas Heckford
1600 Martin Bessell and Henry Osborne
1601 John Bird and Ralph Northey
1602 William Turner and Robert Wade
1603 Thomas Hazlewood and Richard Simnell
1604 Martin Bessell and Thomas Heckford
1605 Henry Osborne and Nicholas Clere
1606 John Bird and Ralph Northey
1607 Thomas Hazlewood and William Mott
1608 Thomas Hazlewood and Thomas Thurston
1609 Robert Wade and John Eldred
1610 Martin Bessell and Nicholas Clere
1611 Thomas Heckford and William Turner
1612 Henry Osborne and Robert Talcott
1613 Thomas Thurston and John Cox
1614 William Turner and William Mott
1615 Thomas Hazlewood and John Marshall
1616 Thomas Thurston and William Hall
1617 John Cox and Henry Barrington
1618 William Turner and Robert Talcott
1619 Martin Bessell and John Marshall
1620 Thomas Heckford and John Norton
1621 William Mott and Thomas Thurston
1622 Robert Talcott and John Cox
1623 John Eldred and Geoffrey Langley
1624 John Marshall and John Norton
1625 Sigismund Sewell and Daniel Cole
1626 Robert Talcott and John Badcock
1627 William Mott and Francis Burrows
1628 Daniel Cole and William Johnson
1629 John Marshall and Henry Barrington
1630 John Norton and Thomas Wade
1631 Robert Talcott and Sigismund Sewell
1632 John Badcock and Robert Buxton
1633 Thomas Wade and John Langley
1634 Daniel Cole and Ralph Harrison

Mayors 1635–1973

1635 Daniel Cole
1636 Robert Buxton
1637 Henry Barrington
1638 John Furley
1639 John Langley
1640 Robert Talcott (died in office, succeeded by Henry Barrington)
1641 Thomas Wade
1642 Ralph Harrison
1643 Thomas Laurence
1644 John Cox
1645 Robert Buxton
1646 John Langley
1647 William Cooke
1648 Henry Barrington
1649 Thomas Wade

59 Ibid. D/B 5 Cr137, rot. 14d.
60 Ibid. D/B 5 Cr141, rot. 13.
61 Ibid. D/B 5 Cr150, rot. 15.
62 Ibid. D/B 5 Cr155, rot. 8.

1650 John Furley
1651 Richard Green
1652 John Radhams
1653 Thomas Peek
1654 Thomas Reynolds
1655 John Radhams elected, but apparently did not serve. Thomas Reynolds continued in office until replaced by Thomas Laurence in December.[63]
1656 John Vickers
1657 Nicholas Beacon
1658 Henry Barrington (replaced by John Radhams)[64]
1659 Thomas Peek
1660 John Gale
1661 John Milbank (replaced by Henry Lamb)[65]
1662 Thomas Reynolds
1663 William Moore
1664 Thomas Wade
1665 Thomas Talcott
1666 William Flanner
1667 Andrew Fromanteel
1668 Ralph Creffield
1669 Henry Lamb
1670 William Moore
1671 John Rayner
1672 Nathaniel Laurence
1673 Ralph Creffield
1674 Henry Lamb
1675 Alexander Hindmarsh
1676 Thomas Green
1677 Ralph Creffield
1678 John Rayner
1679 Nathaniel Laurence
1680 Ralph Creffield
1681 William Moore
1682 Thomas Green
1683 Nathaniel Laurence
1684 John Stilman
1685 William Flanner
1686 Samuel Mott
1687 Alexander Hindmarsh (replaced by John Milbank)[66]
1688 John Milbank
1689 John Potter
1690 Benjamin Cock
1691 John Seabrook
1692 John Stilman
1693 Samuel Mott
1694 Wiliam Moore
1695 John Bacon (died in office, succeeded by John Seabrook)[67]
1696 Nathaniel Laurence the younger
1697 Ralph Creffield the younger
1698 William Boys
1699 William Francis
1700 John Potter
1701 Samuel Featherstone
1702 Ralph Creffield the younger
1703 Samuel Angier
1704 Nathaniel Laurence the younger
1705 John Rainham
1706 James Laurence
1707 George Clark
1708 John Pepper (died in office, succeeded by Nathaniel Laurence the elder)
1709 Samuel Angier
1710 Nathaniel Laurence the younger
1711 James Laurence
1712 Peter Johnson
1713 James Laurence
1714 George Clark
1715 Peter Johnson
1716 Sir Isaac Rebow
1717 Thomas Grigson
1718 Robert Clark
1719 Thomas Grigson (died in office, succeeded by Nathaniel Laurence)
1720 Jeremiah Daniell
1721 Arthur Winsley
1722 Edmund Baynham
1723 Samuel Jarrold
1724 Peter Johnson
1725 Jeremiah Daniell
1726 Matthew Martin
1727 Sir Ralph Creffield
1728 John Blatch
1729 James Boys
1730 Joseph Duffield
1731 John Blatch
1732 Thomas Carew
1733 James Boys
1734 Joseph Duffield
1735 John Blatch
1736 Thomas Carew
1737 James Boys
1738 Joseph Duffield
1739 John Blatch
1740 Jeremiah Daniell
1741–63 [Charter in abeyance, no elections held]
1763 Thomas Clamtree
1764 Henry Lodge
1765 Thomas Wilshire
1766 Thomas Bayles
1767 Samuel Ennew
1768 James Robjent
1769 Jordan Harris Lisle
1770 John King
1771 Solomon Smith (died in office, succeeded by Thomas Clamtree)[68]
1772 Thomas Bayles
1773 Thomas Clamtree
1774 John Baker
1775 John King (died in office, succeeded by Thomas Clamtree)
1776 Thomas Boggis
1777 Thomas Clamtree
1778 John King
1779 Thomas Clamtree
1780 Thomas Boggis
1781 John King
1782 Stephen Betts
1783 William Seaber
1784 Samuel Ennew
1785 Edmund Lilley
1786 William Argent
1787 Edward Capstack
1788 Bezaliel Angier

63 Ibid. D/B 5 Cb1/15, ff. 222, 225, 239, 247, 264; Bodl. MS. Rawl. A 34, p. 125.
64 E.R.O., D/B 5 Gb4, f. 194v.
65 Ibid. D/Y 2/10, pp. 71–2.
66 E.R.O., D/B 5 Gb5, f. 296v.
67 Ibid. D/B 5 Gb6, p. 97; ibid. Boro. Mun., 'Colch. MSS.' f. 7.
68 Ibid. D/B 5 Gb8, f. 57.

1789 Edmund Lilley
1790 William Swinborne
1791 John Gibson
1792 Nathaniel Barlow
1793 Newton Tills
1794 William Phillips
1795 William Bunnell
1796 William Mason
1797 Thomas Hedge
1798 William Phillips
1799 Robert Hewes
1800 William Smith
1801 Thomas Hedge
1802 William Phillips
1803 William Bunnell
1804 Thomas Hedge
1805 William Sparling
1806 William Smith
1807 Thomas Hedge the younger
1808 Thomas Hedge
1809 William Smith
1810 Francis Tillett Abell
1811 Francis Smythies
1812 John Bridge (replaced by William Smith)[69]
1813 William Sparling
1814 John King
1815 Edward Clay
1816 William Argent
1817 Edward Clay
1818 William Argent
1819 Francis Tillett Abell
1820 John Clay
1821 James Boggis
1822 William Smith
1823 John Clay
1824 Samuel Clay
1825 John Clay
1826 Edward Clay, of St. Leonard's parish
1827 John Clay
1828 William Sparling
1829 Edward Clay, of Greenstead
1830 William Smith
1831 William Sparling
1832 Edward Clay, of Greenstead
1833 William Smith
1834 Roger Nunn
1835 Roger Nunn (served until Dec. 1835)[70]
1836 George Savill, Lib. (served Jan.–Nov. 1836)[71]
1836 John Chaplin, Lib.
1837 S. G. Cooke, Con.
1838 George Bawtree, Con.
1839 S. G. Cooke, Con.
1840 T. J. Turner, Con.
1841 Henry Vint, Con.
1842 Roger Nunn, Con.
1843 Henry Vint, Con.
1844 Henry Wolton, Con.
1845 Henry Wolton, Con.
1846 W. B. Smith, Con.
1847 Henry Wolton, Con.
1848 C. H. Hawkins, Con.
1849 Edward Williams, Con.
1850 Joseph Cooke, Con.
1851 A. L. Laing, Con.
1852 Francis Smythies, Con.
1853 Henry Wolton, Con.
1854 Edward Williams, Con.
1855 Joseph Cooke, Con.
1856 Henry Wolton, Con.
1857 P. M. Duncan, Con.
1858 A. L. Laing, Con.
1859 Edward Williams, Con.
1860 Francis Smythies, Con.
1861 Henry Wolton, Con.
1862 Edward Williams, Con.
1863 J. F. Bishop, Con.
1864 J. F. Bishop, Con.
1865 C. H. Hawkins, Con.
1866 P. O. Papillon, Con.
1867 J. F. Bishop, Con.
1868 Francis Smythies, Con.
1869 J. F. Bishop, Con.
1870 C. H. Hawkins, Con.
1871 C. H. Hawkins, Con.
1872 J. F. Bishop, Con.
1873 E. A. Round, Con.
1874 J. F. Bishop, Con.
1875 P. O. Papillon, Con.
1876 J. F. Bishop, Con.
1877 Thomas Moy, Con.
1878 Thomas Moy, Con.
1879 John Kent, Lib.
1880 Samuel Chaplin, Lib.
1881 J. B. Harvey, Lib.
1882 J. B. Harvey, Lib.
1883 Alfred Francis, Lib. (died in office, succeeded by J. B. Harvey, Lib.)[72]
1884 H. J. Gurdon-Rebow, Lib.
1885 Henry Laver, Con.
1886 H. G. Egerton-Green, Con.
1887 J. N. Paxman, Lib.
1888 E. J. Sanders, Con.
1889 Asher Prior, Lib.
1890 L. J. Watts, Con.
1891 Wilson Marriage, Lib.
1892 W. G. Benham, Con.
1893 Henry Goody, Lib.
1894 C. E. Egerton-Green, Con.
1895 James Wicks, Lib.
1896 H. G. Egerton-Green, Con.
1897 J. N. Paxman, Lib.
1898 E. J. Sanders, Con.
1899 E. T. Smith, Lib.
1900 C. E. Egerton-Green, Con.
1901 Wilson Marriage, Lib.
1902 H. H. Elwes, Con.
1903 E. H. Barritt, Lib.
1904 E. J. Sanders, Con.
1905 Henry Goody, Lib.
1906 W. B. Sparling, Con.
1907 Wilson Marriage, Lib.
1908 W. G. Benham, Con.
1909 E. A. Blaxill, Lib.
1910 Frank Cant, Con.
1911 R. B. Beard, Lib.
1912 W. C. Hutton, Con.
1913 Wilson Marriage, Lib.
1914 W. C. Hutton, Con.
1915 A. G. Aldridge, Lib.
1916 J. T. Bailey, Con.

69 Ibid. D/B 5 Gb9, pp. 219, 229–30.
70 E.R.O., Boro. Mun., Council Mins. 28 Dec. 1835; 1 Jan. 1836.
71 Ibid. 1 Jan., 9 Nov. 1836.
72 *E.C.S.* 20 Sept. 1884; *Colch. Gaz.* 12 Nov. 1884.

1917 A. M. Jarmin, Lib.
1918 G. F. Wright, Con.
1919 A. O. Ward, Lib.
1920 A. J. Lucking, Con.
1921 Wasey Chopping, Lib.
1922 P. A. Sanders, Con.
1923 Catherine B. Alderton, Lib.
1924 Dame Catherine Hunt, Con.
1925 A. W. Piper, Lib.
1926 C. C. Smallwood, Lab.
1927 E. H. Turner, Con.
1928 John Russell, Lib.
1929 C. J. Jolly, Lab.
1930 W. C. Harper, Con.
1931 G. W. B. Hazell, Con.
1932 Maurice Pye, Lab.
1933 W. G. Benham, Con.
1934 A. H. Cross, Lib.
1935 F. E. Macdonald Docker, Lab.
1936 G. C. Benham, Con.
1937 E. A. Blaxill, Con.
1938 H. H. Fisher, Lab.
1939 P. A. Sanders, Con.
1940 P. A. Sanders, Con.
1941 P. A. Sanders, Con.
1942 P. A. Sanders, Con.
1943 Maurice Pye, Lab.
1944 A. W. Piper, Lib.
1945 H. G. Thompson, Con.
1946 L. M. Worsnop, Lab.
1947–May 1949 L. E. Dansie, Con.[73]
1949 Revd. P. H. Warwick Bailey, Lib.
1950 J. Andrews, Lab.
1951 H. H. Reid, Con.
1952 W. C. Lee, Lab.
1953 Kathleen E. Sanders, Con.
1954 T. H. Morris, Lab.
1955 A. Craig, Con.
1956 C. E. Child, Lab.
1957 C. E. Wheeler, Con.
1958 May Cook, Lab.
1959 A. W. J. Kay, Con.
1960 I. T. Brown, Lab.
1961 D. F. Panton, Con.
1962 W. J. Porter, Lab.
1963 R. A. Harrison, Con.
1964 W. H. Williams, Lab.
1965 S. H. Wooster, Con.
1966 C. W. Pell, Lab.
1967 E. P. Duffield, Con.
1968 C. A. Howe, Lab.
1969 R. W. Hilham, Con.
1970 J. R. Wheeler, Con.
1971 Mrs. A. M. Smith, Con.
1972 W. E. Buckingham, Lab.
1973 A. C. Parsonson, Con.

73 *E.C.S.* 8 Oct. 1948.

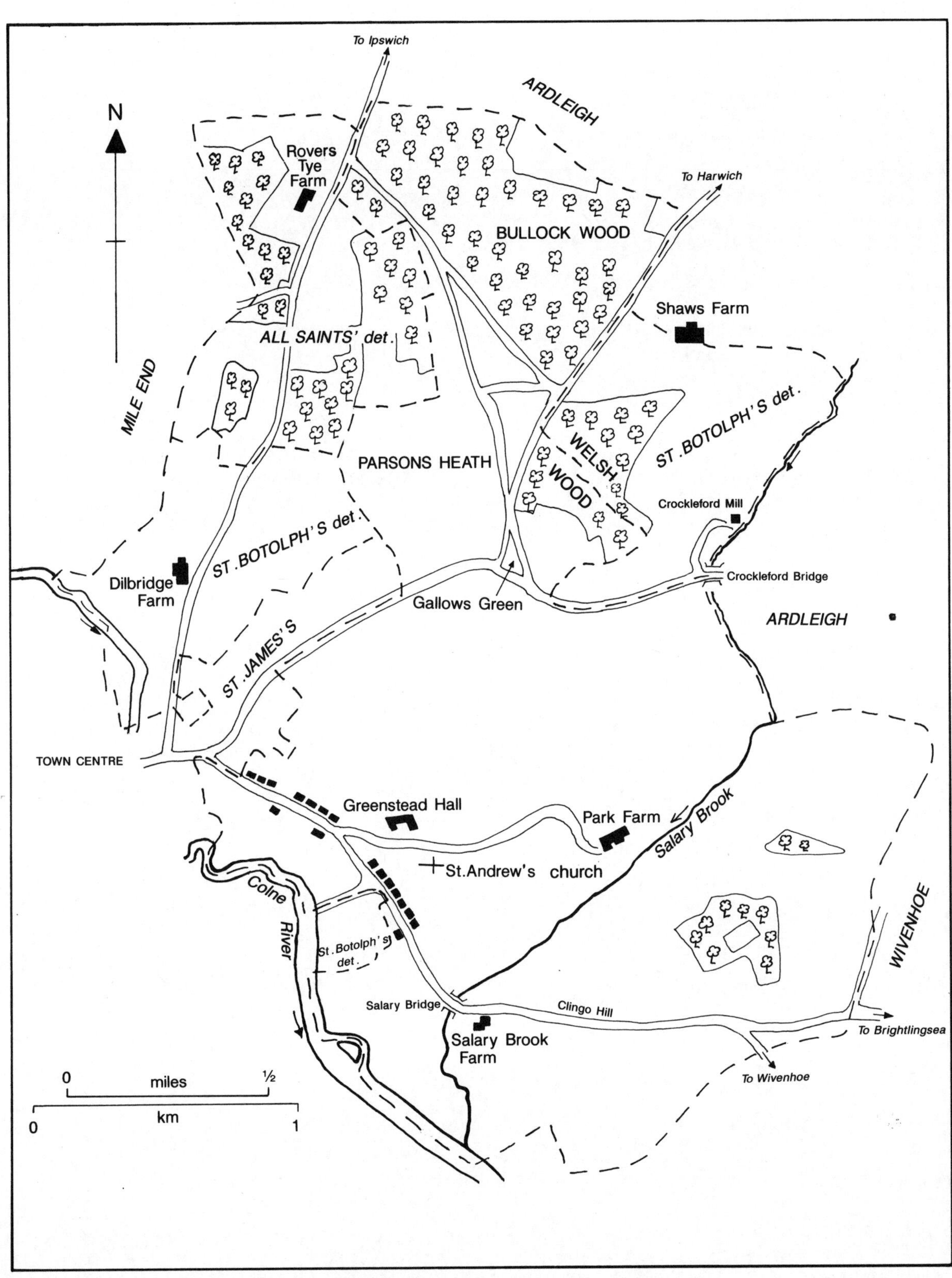

FIG. 33. GREENSTEAD *c.* 1838

OUTLYING PARTS OF THE LIBERTY

THE liberty covered *c.* 10,000 a. around the built-up area of the town, and comprised the outlying parishes of Lexden, Greenstead, Mile End, Berechurch, and St. Giles's, besides the substantial extramural parts of St. Botolph's, All Saints', St. Mary's-at-the-Walls, and St. James's, and smaller, detached, parts of other intramural parishes. All were merged into Colchester civil parish in 1897.[1]

South-east and south-west of the town, until the 19th century, was the arable which was probably once the common fields of the borough. Most of it was cultivated by burgesses throughout the Middle Ages, and most of it lay in the parishes of the intramural churches.[2] In the early Middle Ages much of the pasture in parts of the liberty further from the town was organized into dairy farms or wicks. Canonswick (later Canwick or Cannock) in West Donyland, which belonged to St. Botolph's priory, was recorded in 1160, and an unnamed wick in 1196.[3] Bury St. Edmunds abbey had St. Edmund's wick in Mile End by 1180, and Braiswick in Mile End and Lexden was recorded in 1257–8.[4] The wealthy burgess Adam Warin at his death in 1382 held Braiswick and two other wicks, Oldwick and Cuntingswick, both probably in Lexden, the latter near the road to Botolph's bridge. Tubswick in Mile End was named for Richard Tubbe, its holder in 1296.[5] The occupants of five wicks were assessed for subsidy in 1301: Battleswick in the south-east of the liberty, St. Botolph's wick (Canonswick), St. John's wick (Monkwick or possibly Middlewick), another unidentified wick in Donyland, and Arnoldswick in Lexden. By that date all were mixed farms.[6]

In the early Middle Ages much of the area north of the town was woodland, perhaps divided in the Anglo-Saxon period into Cestrewald, the borough's wood, to the north-west and Kingswood to the north.[7] Kingswood remained woodland and wood pasture throughout the Middle Ages, and regular grants of timber were made from it in the 13th century.[8] As late as 1698 the area, then called Severalls, was 'a sort of deep moor ground and woody'.[9] Cestrewald was cleared in the 13th century, as was some woodland in Greenstead and part of Shrub wood on the border with Stanway in the south-west of the liberty. Further woodland in Mile End and Greenstead was cut down in the 14th century, but much survived into the 18th century.[10]

As late as 1774 Colchester was surrounded by heaths which provided rough grazing.[11] They included Kingswood heath (the former Kingswood), Parson's heath and Rovers Tye heath in Mile End, the small heath at Old Heath, Black heath in West Donyland, and Lexden heath. The Mile End heaths were commonable by all burgesses, but Lexden heath and the heath and marsh at Old Heath were commonable only by the tenants of Lexden and West Donyland and Battleswick manors respectively. All were inclosed in the early 19th century.[12]

The parish boundaries within the liberty were complex and generally did not coincide with the manorial or estate boundaries. In the accounts which follow, detached portions of St. Botolph's and All Saints' parishes have been treated with the neighbouring parish of Greenstead. The area south and south-east of the town, comprising Berechurch and St. Giles's parishes with parts of St. Botolph's, presents particular difficulties; it is treated below under the heading of West Donyland, the name used for it until the 19th century. In the course of the 19th and 20th centuries most of the land in the ancient liberty has been absorbed into the built-up area of Colchester; that process is described above with the history of the borough.[13]

GREENSTEAD

THE ancient parish of Greenstead comprised 1,501 a. (607 ha.) on the east of the built-up area of Colchester.[14] Greenstead was originally a compact estate, but a quarter of it passed to St. Botolph's priory, Colchester, and thus became detached parts of St. Botolph's parish. Earlier the parish was probably bounded on the south-west by the Colne, on the west by Mile End, on the north by woodland, and on the east for a short stretch by Salary brook, while the south-east

1 F. A. Youngs, *Guide to Local Admin. Units of Eng.* i. 135.

2 Above, Common Lands.

3 *Colch. Cart.* ii. 306; *Feet of F. Essex*, i. 10.

4 B.L. Lansdowne MS. 416, ff. 48v., 49v.; *Feud. Docs. of Bury St. Edmunds*, ed. D. C. Douglas, pp. 143–4; *Feet of F. Essex*, i. 227.

5 E.R.O., D/B 5 Cr21, rot. 51d.; ibid. St. John's abbey ledger bk. 212v.; Morant, *Colch.* 46–7.

6 *Rot. Parl.* i. 253, 256–7, 259.

7 *E.A.T.* 3rd ser. xi. 111–12; below Lexden; Mile End (Manors).

8 e.g. *Close R.* 1231–4, 38, 54, 98, 468; 1254–6, 140, 320; 1268–72, 31, 49, 197, 345, 445, 459, 473, 529; *Cal. Close* 1296–1302, 350.

9 *Journeys of Celia Fiennes*, ed. C. Morris, 143.

10 P.R.O., E 32/13, rot. 27d.; E 32/16, rott. 29, 41d.; E 32/299, no. 7; *Essex Map* (1777), sheet IX.

11 *Essex Map* (1777), sheet IX; *Essex Heritage*, ed. K. Neale, 253–4.

12 Below, Mile End (Econ.), Lexden (Econ.), West Donyland (Econ.).

13 Above, Modern Colch. (Town Devt.).

14 *V.C.H. Essex*, ii. 353.

boundary lay across Whitmore heath and Wivenhoe heath. Later the boundary excluded a detached part of St. Botolph's parish in the north-east, and another on the west. Much of the parish lies at over 30 metres, reaching 40 metres on Clingo hill, but the land falls gradually to *c.* 5 metres by the river Colne and more sharply to Salary brook which bisects the main part of the parish.[15] The soil is mostly glacial gravel with some alluvium along the river valleys; a band of London clay runs from south-west to north-east and there is some glacial loam in the east.[16] Much of the parish is good arable land, but the lower ground in the south-east is marshy, and was considered unhealthy in 1723.[17] The abbot of St. John's, Colchester, had fishponds in Greenstead in the 13th century, and before 1286 had created a park, presumably in the area of the later Park farm.[18] Wivenhoe park, landscaped in the late 18th century, extended into the south-west part of the parish.[19]

The Colchester–Harwich road, turnpiked *c.* 1725, crosses the north of the parish. A road, described as a lane in 1608, branches east towards Bromley.[20] The Colchester–Ipswich road runs along the parish boundary for a short distance in the north-west. In the south Greenstead Road, called Greenstead Street in 1372, is part of the Colchester–Wivenhoe road; a branch led eastwards to Greenstead Hall and church and to Park farm.[21] A road called Soleyntye was mentioned in 1498.[22] In the 17th century a road from Greenstead to the Hythe was built.[23]

Sunterforde bridge recorded in 1386, Caterford bridge in 1478, and Cunterfet bridge in 1646 appear to be different names for Salary bridge which carries the Wivenhoe road over Salary brook.[24] Crockleford bridge, which takes the Bromley road over Salary brook, was a ford in 1206; by 1586 there was a bridge, perhaps a footbridge, there.[25] Dilbridge farm seems to have taken its name from a bridge over the Colne, perhaps near the end of Land Lane where signs of an old ford were apparently still visible in the early 20th century.[26]

The railway to Ipswich across the north of the parish was opened in 1846 and the Tendring Hundred railway across the south in the 1860s.[27] There was a sub-post office by 1866, and by 1908 there were two, one in Greenstead Road and one at Parson's Heath.[28]

In the Roman period there may have been one or two villas in the area.[29] An estate which became Greenstead manor existed in the mid 10th century. By 1066 the settlement was well established, with at least four households in addition to the two *servi* who worked the manorial demesne, and had its own church.[30] Thirteen householders were assessed for subsidy in 1296, compared with 7 in Mile End, and 16 in Lexden; William of Greenstead was the most highly taxed inhabitant.[31] Members of the Northen family were substantial tenants of Greenstead manor in the 15th and 16th centuries. Thomas Northen was the wealthiest man in the parish in 1523 when 24 were assessed, more than in West Donyland and Mile End, but fewer than in Lexden.[32] There were 73 households in 1671, of which 44 were exempt from hearth tax.[33] In 1692 there were 107 adults rated to the poll tax. There were significantly more burials than baptisms in the period 1701–31, and by 1768 there were only 26 houses in the parish, many on the road to the Hythe having been demolished. The number of houses increased to 35 in 1790, and in the following decade there were only two thirds as many burials as baptisms.[34]

The population increased rapidly from 309 in 1801 to 598 in 1831, then more slowly to 789 in 1861. There was a slight decline to 752 in 1881 before the population rose again to 1,162 by 1901.[35] The number of inhabited houses increased from 118 in 1821 to 161 in 1851 and 242 in 1901.[36]

Greenstead was for long a sparsely populated, agricultural parish, with the houses concentrated in the south-east nearest Colchester town.[37] From *c.* 1795 another focus developed around Parson's heath in the north, as parts of the former manorial waste on Gallow green were sold in small plots.[38] By 1900 new houses were beginning to fill the gaps along the Greenstead road near the Hythe, and the south-east corner of the parish was increasingly drawn within the compass of the town. Most of Greenstead, however, remained a predominantly agricultural parish, rural rather than suburban, until the mid 20th century.[39]

A charity house, apparently near Clingo hill, was recorded in 1435. It may have been an unendowed almshouse or hospital, or it may simply have been owned by St. Mary Magdalen's hospital.[40] The few buildings from before

15 O.S. Map 6", Essex XXVIII (1881 edn.); O.S. Maps 6", TM 02 NW., SW. (1958 edn.); above, Boundaries.

16 *V.C.H. Essex*, i, map facing p. 1; Essex C.C. *County Development Plan* (1952), Pt. II, Colch. diagram 4: geology.

17 Essex C.C. *Essex Development Plan* (1952), Pt. II, Town map areas, 65; Guildhall MS. 25750/1.

18 *Feet of F. Essex*, i. 92; *Colch. Cart.* ii. 542; E.R.O., D/B 5 R2, loose folio (formerly numbered f. 55v.).

19 E.R.O., T/M 271.

20 Above, Communications (Roads); E.R.O., Q/SR 184, 217.

21 E.R.O., D/B 5 Cr16, rot. 1d.; ibid. Q/SR 440/89; *Essex Map* (1777).

22 E.R.O., D/DHt M148.

23 Ibid. Acc. C210, J. B. Harvey Colln. vi, pp. 136–7.

24 Ibid. D/DHt M145–6; ibid. Q/SR 330/36, 344/36; Essex C.C. Highways Cttee. *Rep.* 1921, p. 1193.

25 *Feet of F. Essex*, i. 37; E.R.O., D/B 5 Sb2/4, f. 61.

26 E.S.A.H. Libr., Laver's Colch. place names; below, this par., Manors (Dilbridge).

27 Above, Communications (Railways).

28 *Kelly's Dir. Essex* (1866, 1908).

29 Essex C.C. sites and monuments record (TM02-019, 092, 094, 121); cropmarks are (TM02-040, 041, 052, 097, 098).

30 *V.C.H. Essex*, i. 574; below, this par., Manor, Church.

31 *E.A.T.* N.S. ix. 132–3.

32 E.R.O., D/B 5 Cr81, rot. 28d.; *E.R.* xxvii. 179; F. G. Emmison, *Essex Wills*, i. 255; P.R.O., E 179/108/162.

33 E.R.O., Q/RTh 5, f. 28v.

34 Morant, *Colch.* 136; E.R.O., D/P 399/1/1; Lambeth Palace Libr., Fulham Papers, Porteus 27.

35 *V.C.H. Essex*, ii. 353.

36 E.R.O., D/P 177/5/1; *Census* 1851, 1901.

37 *Essex Map* (1777).

38 E.R.O., D/DMb T13; D/CT 152A.

39 Ibid. D/DEl T321; above, Modern Colch. (Town Devt.).

40 E.R.O., D/B 5 Cr52, rot. 2.

1800 which survived in 1990 were in Greenstead Road except for Salary Brook Farm, a timber-framed house of the late 16th or early 17th century.[41]

MANORS AND OTHER ESTATES. Ealdorman Aelfgar held an estate at Greenstead which he and his daughters devised to a religious house at Stoke, probably Stoke by Nayland (Suff.).[42] *GREENSTEAD* manor, presumably the same estate, was held in 1066 by Godric, a free man. On his death it was divided between his four sons, and by 1086 half of it was in the king's hands while Eustace of Boulogne and John son of Waleram each held a quarter.[43] Eustace's quarter seems to have passed to St. Botolph's priory, of which he was a benefactor, and to have been merged with the priory's neighbouring manors of Dilbridge and Shaws.[44] The remaining three quarters of Greenstead passed to Eudes the sewer (*dapifer*), the king's moiety presumably with the rest of the royal demesne in Colchester, John son of Waleram's quarter with his other Colchester land which Eudes had acquired by 1119.[45] Eudes apparently gave Greenstead to St. John's abbey, Colchester, but on his death in 1120 it was seized by William of St. Clare. William, with the consent of his brother Hamon of St. Clare and Hamon's son and heir Hubert, restored Greenstead to the abbey between 1141 and 1151.[46] The abbey's estate in Greenstead was enlarged by several grants in the 12th, 13th, and 14th centuries, notably by Hubert of St. Clare between 1148 and 1154, and by William Brome, who gave a total of *c.* 75 a. in 1336.[47]

St. John's retained Greenstead until the Dissolution, when it was granted to Thomas Cromwell, Lord Cromwell.[48] On his attainder in 1540 the estate escheated to the Crown, and was granted in 1548 to Princess, later Queen, Mary.[49] In 1557 Mary granted it to Bernard Hampton, a clerk of the Privy Council, who conveyed it in 1561 to Lawrence Cockson, a London haberdasher, who conveyed it in 1563 to Sir Thomas Lucas.[50] The Lucas family had already acquired Mile End manor in 1544 and Bullock and Soane woods in 1546.[51] From Sir Thomas (d. 1611) the manor passed to his son Sir Thomas (d. 1625) and grandson John Lucas, Baron Lucas of Shenfield. Lord Lucas was succeeded by his daughter Mary, Baroness Lucas of Crudwell (d. 1702), who married Anthony Grey, earl of Kent.[52] The manor then descended with the barony of Lucas of Crudwell until 1917 when it was sold.[53] From 1918 to 1931 the manor was held by C. E. Gooch of Wivenhoe Park, but thereafter manorial rights seem to have lapsed.[54]

Greenstead Hall, where courts were held, was a manor house.[55] The building, demolished *c.* 1967, appears to have been a farmhouse of the 18th and 19th centuries.[56]

The farmstead of *SHAWS*, called a manor from 1542, derived from the holding of John at Shaw in Greenstead, recorded in 1296.[57] It was held of St. Botolph's priory in 1311, and passed into the priory's possession between 1318 and 1351, perhaps on the death of John at Shaw who was last recorded in 1337.[58] By 1542 Shaws, on the boundary between Colchester and Ardleigh, was the centre of an extensive estate comprising land and rents in St. Botolph's, All Saints', St. Giles's, St. Runwald's, St. James's, St. Peter's, St. Nicholas's, St. Leonard's, St. Mary Magdalen's, and Greenstead parishes in Colchester, and in Ardleigh, Bromley, Tendring, Little Bentley, Elmstead, and Wivenhoe, presumably acquired by St. Botolph's at different times. At the Dissolution it was granted to Sir Thomas Audley, later Lord Audley,[59] and escheated to the Crown on his death in 1545.

The Crown retained the manorial rights, but not the demesne land, until 1596,[60] and probably until *c.* 1626 when they were sold to George Whitmore, alderman and later lord mayor of London (d. 1654).[61] He was succeeded by his son William (d. 1678) and grandson, also William Whitmore, who died without issue in 1684. Shaws was sold with the Whitmore's other Essex manor, Wrabness, to Sir Thomas Davall, who held it in 1698.[62] On his death in 1712 it passed to his son, another Sir Thomas Davall (d. 1714), who was succeeded by his infant son Thomas (d. 1718).[63]

On the death of the last Thomas Davall Shaws passed with Wrabness to Daniel Burr, cousin and devisee under the will of the second Sir Thomas Davall. Burr sold the manor in or before 1749 to Nathaniel Garland (d. 1756), who was succeeded by his son Lewis Peak Garland (d. 1780) and by Lewis Peak's son Nathaniel (d. 1845). Nathaniel's son Edgar Wallace Garland died without issue in 1902 and was succeeded by his nephew Arthur Nathaniel Garland who was lord of the manor in 1928, by which time most of the manorial rights had been sold.[64]

41 Dept. of Env. '13th List of Buildings of Archit. or Hist. Interest', f. 50, MS. additions on f. 49v. in copy at Colch. Mus.
42 *A.-S. Wills*, ed. D. Whitelock, 8, 36, 38, 104, 105, 107, 138, 141.
43 *V.C.H. Essex*, i. 415–16, 574.
44 *Cal. Pat.* 1399–1401, 375–6; 1422–9, 414–19; *Reg. Regum Anglo-Norm.* iii, no. 208.
45 *Colch. Cart.* i. 1–3; above, Med. Colch. (Boro. Govt.).
46 *Colch. Cart.* i. 44, 153–60.
47 *Feet of F. Essex*, i. 92; *Colch. Cart.* i. 271; ii. 317, 443; *Cal. Pat.* 1334–8, 315.
48 *L. & P. Hen. VIII*, xv, p. 284.
49 Ibid. xvi, p. 174; *Cal. Pat.* 1548–9, 21–2.
50 *Cal. Pat.* 1557–8, 172–3; 1560–3, 208; 1563–6, 48.
51 Below, Mile End (Manor); *L. & P. Hen. VIII*, xxi (1), p. 767.
52 Morant, *Colch.* 124, 135–6.
53 *Complete Peerage*, viii. 241–4; E.R.O., Sale Cat. B3581.
54 E.R.O., Acc. C47, GR14.
55 *Colch. Cart.* ii. 598.
56 *E.C.S.* 27 Jan. 1967; Dept. of Env. '13th List of Buildings of Archit. or Hist. Interest', f. 49v., MS. addition to copy in Colch. Mus.
57 P.R.O., E 318/2/57; *Rot. Parl.* i. 236.
58 E.R.O., D/B 5 Cr1, rot. 9d.; Cr5, rot. 5; P.R.O., C 260/136, no. 32.
59 P.R.O., E 318/2/57.
60 Ibid. C 142/244, no. 96; E.R.O., D/DU 680/17.
61 E.R.O., D/DLy M103; P.R.O., E 134/9 Chas. I East./18; *D.N.B.*
62 E.R.O., D/DLy M103; P.R.O., PROB 11/357, ff. 273–5; PROB 11/377, f. 70v.; Morant, *Essex*, i. 492.
63 Morant, *Essex*, i. 492; E.R.O., D/DLy M84.
64 Morant, *Colch.* 121; E.R.O., D/DLy M84, 84A; D/DMb T9; *Burke's Landed Gentry* (1937).

The Crown granted the manorial demesne, later Shaws farm, in 1545 to William Beriff, a Colchester clothmaker, and John Multon.[65] Beriff died in 1595 in sole possession of Shaws which he left to his son, another William Beriff (d. 1628), who was succeeded by his son, also William Beriff.[66] By 1640 the farm had passed to Edmund Church. When he died in 1649, his lands were under sequestration for recusancy and Shaws does not seem to have been among those recovered by his daughters Anne and Mary.[67] By 1706 the farm belonged to William Hall;[68] he sold Shaws before 1748 to Thomas Kilham of London (d. 1753)[69] who devised it to his son Leonard. Leonard, of St. James's, Westminster, died in 1799 leaving the farm to his cousin John Roberts (d. 1820). In 1837 Roberts's widow Sarah sold Shaws to Sir Thomas Mash, the principal mortgagee.[70]

By 1425 St. Botolph's priory held a farm at *DILBRIDGE* north-east of the town.[71] It presumably comprised the detached portion of St. Botolph's parish there and was probably the quarter of Greenstead manor held in 1086 by Eustace of Boulogne which he, or more probably his successor another Eustace of Boulogne, gave to the priory before the second Eustace's retirement in 1125.[72] At the Dissolution the farm was granted to Sir Thomas Audley, later Lord Audley, who immediately conveyed it to John Christmas.[73] John and his son George sold it in 1552 to John Lucas, owner of Mile End manor, with which Dilbridge descended thereafter.[74] Baroness Lucas sold the farm to W. Marriage in 1917.[75]

Throwerystye, later *ROVERS TYE*, was recorded in 1353.[76] An estate there was bequeathed by Sir Laurence Rainsford to his son Henry in 1489.[77] In 1544 Edward Smith of Hadleigh (Suff.) and Ursula his wife sold it, with its lands and rents in All Saints', St. Botolph's, Greenstead, and Ardleigh, to John Lucas, and it became part of the Lucas estate in Mile End and Colchester.[78] In 1917 Baroness Lucas sold the farm to its occupier.[79]

The former Rovers Tye farmhouse is an early 17th-century timber-framed house with 18th-century additions along the west side. In 1983, when it was converted into a public house,[80] major timber-framed extensions were made on the west, and a small barn which had stood to the west of the house was rebuilt at the south end.

ECONOMIC HISTORY. In 1066 there were 4 ploughteams. In 1086 only 2 teams with 2 *servi* were recorded, both on the king's demesne. There were 24 a. of meadow and marsh on the king's 2 hides, and presumably an equivalent area on the remaining 2 hides. The king's hides were valued at 30*s*. each, compared with 20*s*. for the remaining 2 hides, suggesting that, although no teams were recorded in 1086, they had not gone out of cultivation and were being cultivated from other Colchester estates.[81]

There was considerable early clearance of woodland. The farm name Shaws, meaning wood or grove, suggests that it was an assart.[82] Other land was also inclosed and used for arable cultivation.[83] Rye and oats were recorded in the 14th century.[84] Some of the cleared land was used for pasture.[85] At Shaws and at Rovers Tye in 1435 pasture was overloaded with 260 sheep.[86] In the 14th century 13 of St. John's abbey's tenants holding a total of 270 a. of arable, 72 a. of wood, and 22 a. of meadow had rights of common for 348 sheep, 50 cows, and 8 pigs beside Crockleford brook and on Parson's heath and Cross heath.[87]

St. John's abbey inclosed some ancient common in the north before 1323 and planted Sowen wood, *c.* 220 a., later known as Soane or Bullock wood, one of the earliest examples of planted woodland in the country. In 1546 trees were still being planted in rotation on 200 a. there. Sixty acres remained in 1986.[88]

An account of the common fields in 1599 recorded 137 a. of arable and pasture and 19 a. of meadow held in severalty, and 10 a. of common meadow.[89] In the 17th century cows' milk was used for cheesemaking.[90] Shaws farm was deteriorating in 1654, but by 1706 was in cultivation. Underwood from the woods there was sold in 1712.[91]

The Lucas family owned Rovers Tye, Dilbridge, and Greenstead farms, as well as Mile End farm, from the mid 16th century.[92] In 1683 Rovers Tye, in Greenstead and other parishes, comprised 2 pasture crofts, and 8 other closes (one called Saffron field) in the detached part of All Saints' parish, probably totalling *c.* 80 a. as they did in 1802; there was also a meadow in Greenstead. By 1730 as much as 12 a. of waste

65 P.R.O., E 318/4/132; *L. & P. Hen. VIII*, xx (1), p. 661.

66 P.R.O., C 142/244, no. 96; C 142/737, no. 171.

67 *Cal. Cttee. for Compounding*, 1643–60, pp. 2402–3, 2405; *Correspondence of Thos. Blount*, ed. T. Bongaerts, 3.

68 P.R.O., E 134/11 Anne Mic./21.

69 Bodl. MS. Eng. Misc. c 660, no. 8; Morant, *Colch.* 121.

70 Bodl. MS. Eng. Misc. c 660, nos. 1–3; E.R.O., D/DMb T7.

71 E.R.O., D/B 5 Cr49, rot. 19d.

72 *V.C.H. Essex*, i. 574; *Reg. Regum Anglo-Norm.* iii, no. 205; Dugdale, *Mon.* vi. 106; R.H.C. Davis, *King Stephen*, 10.

73 *L. & P. Hen. VIII*, x, p. 419; xi, p. 208.

74 *Cal. Pat.* 1550–3, 329–30; Morant, *Colch.* 121, 124, 135; E.R.O., D/DB T516; *White's Dir. Essex* (1848), 82; (1863), 88.

75 Beds. R.O., L 23/660, 669.

76 E.R.O., D/B 5 Cr10, rot. 1.

77 P.R.O., PROB 11/8, f. 208.

78 E.R.O., D/B 5 Cr114, rot. 20d.

79 Ibid. D/DU 906/7.

80 *E.C.S.* 8 Apr. 1983.

81 *V.C.H. Essex*, i. 415–16, 574.

82 Above, this par., Manors (Shaws).

83 e.g. E.R.O., St. John's abbey ledger bk. ff. 97 and v., 101v.–102v.; *E.A.T.* 3rd ser. xix. 159–65.

84 Britnell, *Growth and Decline*, 42–3; E.R.O., St. John's abbey ledger bk. ff. 181v.–183.

85 E.R.O., St. John's abbey ledger bk. ff. 97v.–98v.

86 Ibid. D/B 5 Cr54, rot. 2d.

87 Ibid. St. John's abbey ledger bk. f. 197v.

88 P.R.O., E 32/16, rot. 21d.; E 318/9/352; E.R.O., St. John's ledger bk. f. 40; O. Rackham, *Hist. Countryside*, 153–4.

89 B.L. Stowe MS. 832, f. 31.

90 P.R.O., E 126/15, ff. 167, 260v.

91 Ibid. E 134/11 Anne Mic./21.

92 Above, this par., Manors; below, Mile End (Manors).

along the Ipswich road had been inclosed as part of the farm.[93] In 1699 Dilbridge farm (mainly in St. Botolph's parish) comprised 11 a. of pasture, 9 or 10 arable fields among the burgesses' half year lands, at least 11 other arable fields, and an unspecified amount of meadow and pasture in St. Botolph's, Mile End, St. James's, and St. Nicholas's parishes; in 1711 it was by far the most valuable of the Lucases' Colchester estates.[94]

Greenstead paid £132 land tax in 1778, eleventh of the 16 Colchester parishes; the non-resident lady of the manor, whose Greenstead land was leased in five main farms, paid over half the tax.[95] In 1794 Mary Rebow was the chief of the 39 freeholders and 69 copyholders of the manor.[96] Various members of the Clay family farmed almost three quarters of the manorial estate in 1800 besides a little of their own land.[97]

In 1801 the main crops in the parish were wheat, oats, and barley; some peas, turnips, beans, and potatoes were also grown.[98] At Rovers Tye farm in 1802 fallowing had been entirely eliminated on the 50 a.–60 a. of arable by using beans, peas, turnips, clover, or grass.[99] In 1821 Shaws farm, mainly in St. Botolph's parish but extending into Ardleigh, comprised 181 a.: 178 a. arable (including *c.* 7 a. former meadow presumably along Crockleford brook), 1½ a. of woodland, and the site of the farmhouse and buildings.[1] In 1824 the tenants on the largely arable manorial farms followed a rotation of turnips, barley, clover, wheat, and, if manured, oats, but poor drainage in places diminished yields.[2]

By 1839 about three quarters, 726 a., of tithe-able land was arable. Much of the 239 a. of tithe-free land was woodland. Just over half of the parish was owned by the absentee lord of the manor, who let most of it in three main holdings, of *c.* 245 a., 150 a., and 83 a., and the rest mainly as small parcels of grass or arable or as cottages with gardens.[3] The only other significant land-owner in the parish was the Rebow family, which in the 18th and 19th centuries was gradually consolidating its holdings in the east of the parish and in neighbouring Wivenhoe and Ardleigh.[4] In 1839 Lieut. Gen. Francis Slater Rebow of Wivenhoe Park Lodge owned almost a quarter of Greenstead parish.[5]

Agriculture remained the most important source of employment, particularly for those living in the north part of the parish. However, the farms employed a smaller proportion of the inhabitants in the later 19th century because of agricultural depression and increasing alternative employment in the town.[6]

There was very little industry in the parish before the 19th century. A tilemaker was mentioned in 1370, there was a kiln house for the manufacture of tiles at Dilbridge in 1398–9, and there was brick- and tile-making on a small scale *c.* 1800.[7] The 'thrower' for whom Rovers Tye was named before 1353 may have been a potter, for there is evidence of pottery-making in Mile End.[8] A grazier in 1547 was described as being also a clothier and a salter.[9] In 1810 a mill-wright's and engineer's business was started. Whiting was manufactured in 1842 but no longer by 1900.[10] By 1881 there were nursery gardens along Greenstead Road and an iron and brass foundry near the Hythe.[11]

LOCAL GOVERNMENT. The abbot of St. John's held a manor court in Greenstead in the early 13th century.[12] In 1274 and 1285 he claimed gallows, tumbrel, the assize of bread and of ale, and free warren by charter of Henry III.[13] The gallows presumably stood on or near Gallow green, the triangle of land on the edge of Parson's heath.[14] Manor courts with view of frankpledge were held about three or four times a year from the 14th to the 16th century, usually including one at Whitsun and one near Christmas. An ale-taster, two constables, and one or two rent collectors were elected each year at Whitsun.[15] Between 1572 and 1602 the manor court with view of frankpledge met annually and appointed two constables and two wardens of the commons; thereafter until 1669 it met less regularly. Courts baron were held until 1931.[16]

John at Shaw unsuccessfully claimed heriot from a tenant of Shaw's manor in 1311.[17] St. Botolph's priory and its successors as lords held courts for the manor of Shaws until 1841; from 1558 they apparently held view of frankpledge, but no leet business was recorded, the courts being concerned solely with the transfer of copy-hold land; pleas leading to recoveries were occasionally heard. In 1764 an Ardleigh man was presented for digging brickearth between Harwich Road and Soane wood, and from 1769 encroachments on the waste were presented and licences to inclose small pieces of waste were granted.[18]

Parish stocks were recorded in 1581.[19] Vestry records do not survive, but churchwardens and overseers were mentioned in 1685.[20] A parish

93 Beds. R.O., L 17/193–9; E.R.O., D/DC 23/7.
94 Beds. R.O., L 17/185; E.R.O., T/A 97/2.
95 E.R.O., Q/RPl 1107–8; notes by J. Bensusan-Butt on Beds. R.O., L 17/172–9, 183, 193, 220–1, 233.
96 E.R.O., D/DEt M7.
97 Ibid. Q/RPl 1127.
98 *List & Index Soc.* vol. 189, pp. 139, 154.
99 E.R.O., D/DC 23/7.
1 Ibid. Sale Cat. B1330.
2 Beds. R.O., L 26/981.
3 E.R.O., D/CT 152A.
4 Ibid. D/DB T1496–1502; ibid. Q/RPl 1108, 1127, 1157.
5 Ibid. D/CT 152A.
6 P.R.O., HO 107/344/6; ibid. RG 11/1793; above, Modern Colch. (Econ.).
7 *Cal. Pat.* 1367–70, 357; E.R.O., D/B 5 Cr30, rot. 4; B.L., O.S.D. Sheet 140.
8 Cf. E.R.O., D/B 5 Cr12, rot. 9; Cr14, rot. 11; *P.N. Elements*, ii. 177; *O.E.D.*; below, Mile End (Econ.).
9 P.R.O., REQ 2/16/49; E.R.O., D/B 5 Cr140, rot. 7d.
10 *V.C.H. Essex*, ii. 451, 498.
11 O.S. Map 6", Essex XXVIII (1881 edn.).
12 *Colch. Cart.* ii. 596.
13 E.R.O., D/DCm Z18/1; *Rot. Hund.* (Rec. Com.), i. 163.
14 E.R.O., D/CT 152A.
15 Ibid. D/DHt M145–8.
16 Ibid. D/DHt M149; ibid. Acc. C47, GR 1–18.
17 Ibid. D/B 5 Cr1, rot. 9d.
18 P.R.O., E 318/2/57; E.R.O., D/B 5 Cr39, rot. 19; ibid. D/DU 680/17; D/DLy M84, 84A.
19 Ibid. D/DHt M149.
20 Ibid. D/B 5 Sb3/1.

workhouse was sold in 1815.[21] Annual expenditure on poor relief amounted to £152 in 1776 and *c.* £145 in 1783–5.[22] By 1812 it reached £322, equivalent to *c.* 15*s.* a head, and by 1820 to £487, but fell to £384 in 1821, still *c.* 15*s.* a head, just below the average for Colchester. In 1835 Greenstead became part of the Colchester poor-law union.[23]

CHURCH. The church existed by 1066, and at the Conquest passed with the manor to Eudes the sewer who *c.* 1119 gave to St. John's abbey tithes of Greenstead, presumably of his demesne.[24] After Eudes's death in 1120 William of St. Clare acquired the church and between 1141 and 1151 gave it to the abbey, which kept the advowson until the Dissolution.[25] In 1540 Henry VIII granted the patronage to Thomas Cromwell, but it reverted to the Crown on his attainder and was granted in 1548 to Princess, later Queen, Mary.[26] It has remained with the Crown, from 1863 being exercised by the Lord Chancellor.[27]

The rectory was valued at 13*s.* 4*d.* in 1254 besides a pension to the abbey of 6*s.* (which had increased from 5*s.* in the late 12th century) and 4 lb. of wax a year.[28] The value of the rectory was £1 10*s.* *c.* 1291 and £5 in 1535.[29] In 1443 the living was vacant because of its poverty.[30] The abbot of St. John's retained the tithes of the manorial demesne, presumably as a result of Eudes's grant. In 1620 Thomas Lucas, lord of Greenstead manor, successfully resisted the rector, William Denman's, claim to tithe from Greenstead park, but Denman recovered tithe from two other parcels of land.[31] The house and 11 rods of glebe were worth £6 and the tithes £50 in 1650.[32] The tithes of *c.* 980 a. were commuted for a yearly rent of £293 in 1839, helping to raise the value of the living from £280 in 1835 to £308 10*s.* in 1887.[33]

The parsonage house, almost falling down in 1607, had been either repaired or replaced by the early 18th century, and was in good repair in 1790.[34] A new house was built in Greenstead Road in 1805, and enlarged *c.* 1898.[35] About 1962 a new house was built next to the church.[36]

Before the mid 18th century more than half of the incumbents of the poor living were pluralists.[37] Thomas Juscard, rector 1325–51, was accused in 1324 of assault, and several times between 1330 and 1351 of roaming the town at night with armed men.[38] Richard 'Father' Alvey, rector 1546–8, was one of the most influential of the early protestant preachers. Deprived of his preferments during Mary's reign, he fled abroad and was closely associated with important Marian exiles such as John Pulleyne. He was later Master of the Temple from 1560 until his death in 1584.[39] In 1575 Richard Spencer, curate from the early 1570s until 1580, had to do penance for drunkenness.[40] Robert Holmes, rector 1586–9 and rector of St. James's, Colchester, 1585–92, considered the wearing of the surplice a papal superstition. Three brief incumbencies followed until the institution of William Denman, rector 1599–1624. In 1607 the churchwardens provided a surplice for communion services only.[41] John Jarvis, rector from 1638 and rector of North Fambridge from 1631, was accused in 1644 of speaking against parliament, neglecting his cure on Sundays, swearing, frequenting alehouses, and reading his sermons from a book. He was deprived of both livings in 1646 and, at the request of the parishioners, Greenstead was served by John White, rector of St. James's.[42]

Paul Duckett, appointed in the 1650s, apparently conformed at the Restoration, but was succeeded in 1662 by John Ruting (Johannes Ruytinck), minister of the Dutch church in Colchester 1645–63 and master of Colchester grammar school 1659–62, who held the church in plurality with St. Leonard's, Colchester.[43] In 1683 the rector, Thomas Shaw, was urged to read prayers on Sunday mornings, but a later rector was still neglecting to do so in 1705.[44] Theodore Garland, rector 1706–28, was elderly and infirm by 1723 when a neighbouring clergyman served the cure. By then Garland had moved to the town because his family suffered ague and fevers at Greenstead. Benjamin Owen, resident rector 1730–54 and vicar of Abberton, performed one service on Sundays and administered communion three times a year in each parish.[45] Samuel Forster, rector 1783–97, whose brother Nathaniel was rector of All Saints', Colchester, lived in Oxford where he was registrar of the university, and employed a curate to serve Greenstead.[46]

Charles Hewitt, rector from 1797 until he died aged 96 in 1849, was rector of St. James's 1783–99 and headmaster of Colchester grammar school 1779–1806. He was serving Greenstead himself in 1815, but employed a curate in 1848.[47] Under his successor, the Evangelical Meshach Seaman, rector 1849–82, Greenstead was among

21 Ibid. D/DB T/1500.
22 Ibid. Q/CR 1/1.
23 Ibid. Q/CR 1/10, 12.
24 *V.C.H. Essex*, i. 574; *Colch. Cart.* i. 1–3.
25 Above, this par., Manors; *V.C.H. Essex*, ii. 94.
26 *L. & P. Hen. VIII*, xv, p. 284; *Cal. Pat.* 1548–9, 21–2.
27 *White's Dir. Essex* (1848), 82; (1863), 88; *Chelm. Dioc. Year Bk.* (1986–7), 167.
28 *E.A.T.* N.S. xviii. 123; *Colch. Cart.* i. 86–7.
29 *Tax. Eccl.* (Rec. Com.), 23; *Valor Eccl.* (Rec. Com.), i. 443.
30 Guildhall MS. 9531/6.
31 E.R.O., D/DRe Z9.
32 Smith, *Eccl. Hist. Essex*, 319; Guildhall MS. 9628/2.
33 E.R.O., D/CT 152A; *Rep. Com. Eccl. Revenues*, H.C. 54, pp. 646–7 (1835), xxii; E.R.O., T/A 645.
34 *E.R.* xv. 45; Guildhall MS. 25750/1; Lambeth Palace Libr., Fulham Papers, Porteus 27.
35 *White's Dir. Essex* (1863), 88; E.R.O., T/A 645; ibid. Acc. C296, auction papers for old rectory.
36 E.R.O., D/CP 7/13.
37 Newcourt, *Repertorium*, ii. 286–7; Guildhall MSS. 25750/1; 25753/2.
38 *E.R.* l. 239.
39 *D.N.B.*; *E.R.* lii. 190–4; above, Tudor and Stuart Colch. (Relig. Life).
40 E.R.O., D/AZ 1/8, f. 120v.
41 *E.R.* xv. 45; lii. 94–5; B. Usher, 'Colch. and Diocesan Administration' (TS. in E.R.O.), 25–6, 39–40.
42 *Walker Revised*, ed. A. G. Matthews, 156; T. W. Davids, *Annals of Nonconf. in Essex*, 304.
43 Davids, *Annals of Nonconf. in Essex*, 305 n.; L. Roker, 'Flemish and Dutch Community in Colch.' (Lond. Univ. M.A. thesis, 1963), pp. 157–8: copy in E.R.O.; Morant, *Colch.* 177–8.
44 *E.A.T.* N.S. xxiii. 160; *V.C.H. Essex*, ii. 74.
45 Guildhall MSS. 25750/1; 25753/2; 25754/2.
46 Lambeth Palace Libr., Fulham Papers, Porteus 27; *Alum. Oxon. 1715–1886.*
47 Above, Churches (St. James's); M. I. in Greenstead church; *V.C.H. Essex*, ii. 507; Lambeth Palace Libr., Fulham Papers, Howley 48, no. 191; *White's Dir. Essex* (1848), 82.

the parishes which petitioned Queen Victoria *c.* 1850 against the restoration of the Roman Catholic hierarchy. Seaman was responsible for restoring the church in 1856–7.[48] On Census Sunday 1851 attendances of 77 in the morning and 134 in the afternoon were reported out of a population of 751.[49] In 1869 there were still only eight communion services a year.[50]

In 1920 average church attendance was 50–60 in the morning and 30–40 in the evening, mainly 'well-to-do working men'.[51] St. Edmund's church hall was built in 1966 on Greenstead housing estate to serve both as a church and as a parish hall, but in 1985 it was used mainly as a church hall.[52] In 1981 a parish room at Harwich Road was converted into St. Matthew's church and an assistant curate was appointed to serve the increasing population of Greenstead.[53] St. Andrew's maintained its Evangelical tradition in 1987.

The ecclesiastical parish was reduced in 1863 when the chapelry of St. John the Evangelist was created. In 1911 a small portion of St. Botolph's parish was added to Greenstead.[54] Under the reorganization of Colchester parishes in 1953 one small portion of Greenstead parish became part of the new parish of St. Anne, and another became part of the new parish of St. James with All Saints, St. Nicholas and St. Runwald. In 1961 a small portion of St. John's parish was annexed to Greenstead.[55]

The church of *ST. ANDREW*, Forest Road, Greenstead, comprises a chancel and nave, structurally undivided, a south aisle running the length of the nave and chancel, a west tower, and a north porch.[56] The walls are of mixed rubble, the old work mostly being rendered, the tower is of red brick, and the roofs are of tiles and slates. The simple plan may be of 12th-century origin and the exposed north-west angle incorporates some re-used Roman brick. Until the mid 19th-century restoration two 12th-century windows survived in the chancel, which had other medieval features including a 13th-century lancet and a mid 14th-century east window with reticulated tracery.[57] Two recesses in the east wall are probably early 14th-century and a plain tomb recess in the north wall retains some medieval painting in formal imitation of stonework. The late 16th-century tower is decorated with a simple pattern in dark headers in the red brickwork.

FIG. 34. GREENSTEAD CHURCH *c.* 1824

In 1633 the church was in a poor condition, the buttress on the south side of the chancel having fallen down, and it was presumably damaged during the siege in 1648 when a parliamentary gun battery was erected in the churchyard.[58] About 1705 a buttress, presum-

48 M. Seaman, *Good news for the parishioners of Greenstead* (1852): copy in E.C.L. Colch.; E.R.O., D/P 399/1/1; D. A. Adams, *Story of St. Andrew's*, 8, 15.

49 P.R.O., HO 129/8/204; *V.C.H. Essex*, ii. 353.

50 E.R.O., D/P 399/1/1.

51 Ibid. D/CV 3/2.

52 *Colch. Expr.* 5 May 1966; *Colch. Gaz.* 20 Sept. 1966.

53 *E.C.S.* 25 Oct. 1981.

54 E.R.O., D/CC 14/1; D/CPc 132.

55 Ibid. D/CPc 314, 392.

56 R.C.H.M. *Essex*, iii. 46–7.

57 E.R.O., T/A 641/5, f. 88; etching by J. Greig, *c.* 1824, reproduced above as Fig. 34.

58 *E.A.T.* N.S. xi. 45; Morant, *Colch.* 63.

ably the clasping buttress at the south-east angle in existence in 1824, was built to support the south wall of the chancel. The chancel and east part of the nave were refaced in the late 18th century. By 1824 the south side of the chancel had been heavily buttressed and two dormer windows had been inserted in the nave.[59]

The church was thoroughly restored in 1856–7, largely at the expense of Thomas Philip de Grey, Earl de Grey, and J. G. Rebow, M.P. A south aisle, designed in 13th-century style by G. Sargent, was added and the interior was repewed.[60] After the earthquake of 1884 the nave ceiling was replaced and the tower repaired and stripped of its rendering.[61] Extensive repairs in 1971 included reroofing the tower and rebuilding its parapet.[62]

Victorian oak wall tablets on either side of the chancel east window contain the Lord's prayer, commandments, and creed. The Hanoverian royal arms hang above the north door. There is one bell, of 1723 by Thomas Gardiner; an earlier bell was recorded in 1607. The church plate includes a 17th-century silver cup made by R. Hutchinson of Colchester.[63]

In 1896 Francis Thomas de Grey, Lord Cowper, gave *c.* ½ a. to extend the churchyard,[64] which was still used for burials in 1985.

The dual purpose church hall of *ST. EDMUND*, designed in 1966 by J. Thompson, in brick lined with wood, has a glass south wall surmounted by a cross.[65] The red brick church of *ST. MATTHEW* was converted from a parish room which had previously been a school.[66]

NONCONFORMITY. A small number of Independents was recorded in 1790 and 1810.[67] Later Congregational and Baptist chapels were founded in the parish from churches in the town.[68]

EDUCATION. Three small day schools, presumably dame schools, at which 30 children were educated at their parents' expense, were reported in 1833, but had apparently disappeared by 1841.[69] A National school, which later became Greenstead Church of England primary school, was built in Greenstead Road in 1851 at the instigation of the rector, Meshach Seaman, in a building erected by Thomas Philip de Grey, Earl de Grey, lord of the manor.[70] The site and building remained the property of de Grey's successors until they were given in trust to the rector and churchwardens in 1921.[71] At first the school was maintained solely by Seaman.[72] By 1863 it was attended by *c.* 100 children, and from 1866 it received annual government grants.[73] In 1874 attendance fell as new schools opened in neighbouring parishes, and in 1875, at Seaman's request, the committee of the central National school took over the management of the school.[74] In 1893, when 91 children attended, the school was enlarged by subscription to accommodate 174, and by 1899 attendance had risen to 130.[75] In 1932 the school was reorganized for juniors and infants. It was granted Controlled status in 1951 and closed in 1976.[76]

St. John's Church of England primary school originated in 1863 as a small school for 30 children, associated with St. John's district church and held in a cottage. In 1872 a new school for 90 children was built by subscription and grants on land in Ipswich Road given by Katrine de Grey, Countess Cowper.[77] It received government grants from its opening in 1873.[78] Average attendance was *c.* 60 in 1890, but later that year several children left to go to Kendall Road board school. In 1895 a government inspector found the school inefficient, but it survived falling numbers and frequent staff changes. Attendance rose from 52 in 1898 to 87 in 1910,[79] when the building was enlarged. In 1934 the school was reorganized for juniors and infants. It was granted Controlled status in 1952, and in 1972 moved to new buildings in Clay Lane Grove.[80]

Parson's Heath Church of England primary school originated as a National day and Sunday school for 72 children, hastily built in Greenstead Road in 1890 to forestall a British school. It received annual government grants from its foundation.[81] By 1893 it had 87 children, and in 1894 was enlarged for 121.[82] It was reorganized in 1932 for juniors and infants.[83] In 1951 the school was granted Controlled status and in 1966 it moved to a new building in Templewood Road.[84]

East Ward school, Hazelmere schools, St. Andrew's schools, and Sir Charles Lucas school are described above.[85]

CHARITIES FOR THE POOR. None known.

59 E.R.O., D/ACV 9A, p. 65v.; Greig's etching reproduced above, Fig. 34.
60 *White's Dir. Essex* (1863), 88; E.R.O., D/P 399/1/5.
61 *Essex Notebk.* Jan. 1885, p. 42.
62 Adams, *St. Andrew's*, 9.
63 *Ch. Bells Essex*, 264–5; *E.R.* xv. 45; *Ch. Plate Essex*, 191.
64 E.R.O., D/CC 42/4.
65 *Colch. Expr.* 22 Sept. 1966.
66 Below, this par., Educ.; *E.C.S.* 25 Oct. 1981.
67 Lambeth Palace Libr., Fulham Papers, Porteus 27; ibid. Randolph 9.
68 Above, Protestant Nonconf.
69 *Educ. Enq. Abstract*, H.C. 62, p. 271 (1835), xli; E.R.O., D/ACM 12.
70 *White's Dir. Essex* (1863), 88; *E.C.S.* 15 Apr. 1882.
71 *Chelm. Dioc. Chron.* vii. 120.
72 *Mins. of Educ. Cttee. of Council, 1855–6* [2058], p. 305, H.C. (1856), xlvii.
73 *White's Dir. Essex* (1863), 88; *Rep. of Educ. Cttee. of Council, 1866–7* [3882], p. 570, H.C. (1867), xxii.
74 *E.C.S.* 9 Apr. 1875.
75 *Returns relating to Elem. Educ.* 1893 [C. 7529], p. 164, H.C. (1894), lxv; 1899 [Cd. 315], p. 322, H.C. (1900), lxv (2); E.R.O., D/P 399/1/1.
76 *Colch. Boro. Council Mins.* 1932–3, p. 613; E.R.O., C/ME 45, p. 170; ibid. N/CME 2, pp. C28–9.
77 Nat. Soc. file; E.R.O., E/P 34; E/ML 143; *E.C.S.* 6 Dec. 1872; *Complete Peerage*, iii. 487.
78 *Rep. Educ. Cttee. of Council, 1873–4* [C. 1019-I], p. 323, H.C. (1874), xviii.
79 *Kelly's Dir. Essex* (1890 and later edns.); above, Educ., (Other Ch. of Eng. Schools); E.R.O., E/ML 143.
80 *Colch. Boro. Council Mins.* 1909–10, p. 900; 1933–4, p. 690; E.R.O., C/ME 47, p. 10; inf. from Essex C.C. educ. dept.
81 Nat. Soc. file; *Rep. Educ. Cttee. of Council, 1891–2* [C. 6746–I], p. 626, H.C. (1892), xxviii.
82 *Returns relating to Elem. Educ.* 1893 [C. 7529], p. 164, H.C. (1894), lxv; 1899 [Cd. 315], p. 322, H.C. (1900), lxv (2).
83 *Colch. Boro. Council Mins.* 1932–3, p. 613.
84 E.R.O., C/ME 45, p. 401; C/ME 60, p. 266.
85 Above, Educ.

LEXDEN

THE ancient parish comprised an irregular area of 2,334 a. (945 ha.) west of the town.[86] The Lexden hundred court presumably originally met within the parish, perhaps in the north-west quarter on land owned by the Mott or Mote family from the 14th century, but it had moved to Empford, later Stanway, bridge by 1581.[87] In 1086 Lexden was an outlying estate of Stanway, but the burgesses claimed it had belonged to Greenstead and been rateable with the borough in 1066. It was within the borough and liberty of Colchester by 1296.[88]

Lexden's western boundary with Stanway followed an earthwork and a lane northwards before turning north-west at Chitts Hill to take in a triangular area, which contained a detached part of West Bergholt. The area, which was outside the bounds of Colchester liberty, was perhaps the land in Stanway acquired by John de Burgh before 1243.[89] The name Chitts Hill, recorded as Shitte, Shyt, and Shet Street in the Middle Ages, may derive from *sciete*, a nook or corner.[90] The northern boundary wound along the river Colne and St. Botolph's brook, turning northwards at Botolph's bridge, said in 1304 to be in Mile End, and skirting a small area of inclosed woodland in West Bergholt parish, before turning south-east along field boundaries to join and follow Braiswick Road to a point north of North bridge on the edge of the town. The tongue of Lexden intruding northwards between West Bergholt and Mile End was within Lexden by 1360 and may derive from the clearance of Cestrewald in the 13th century.[91] An exchange of tithes between Lexden and St. Mary's-at-the-Walls *c.* 1699 altered the southern boundary, which thereafter ran from the western earthwork north-east, and then south-east along field boundaries to Maldon Road which it followed for a short way before turning north along field boundaries around intermixed, detached parts of the parishes of Holy Trinity, St. Mary-at-the-Walls, St. James, and St. Peter. In 1817 those parts were consolidated and their boundaries adjusted.[92] A detached area of Lexden comprising 10 a. lay in St. Mary's-at-the-Walls parish.[93]

The land rises from 10 metres by the river Colne to 35 metres near the northern and western extremities. A ridge runs eastwards from Chitts hill for *c.* 1½ mile, roughly following the line of the river. The soil is silty clay with sand and gravel, some London clay and, along the Colne near the eastern boundary, an area of soft alluvial soil.[94] Lexden springs, a group of strong springs rising where sand and gravel beds meet London clay, form a stream which feeds the Colne. In the 19th century the springs were exploited to supplement the town's water supply.[95] Much of the parish is good arable land, with meadow along the Colne. Along its western boundary, however, lay Lexden heath (290 a.) which with the adjoining Stanway heath formed a large area of rough grazing. Before 1237 the lords of Lexden manor created a park between the Colne and Bergholt Road; the Lexden Park which survived in 1990 south of Lexden Street was made in the later 18th century.[96]

The road from Colchester to London, turnpiked in 1696 and 1707,[97] crossed the parish from east to west as Lexden Hill and Lexden Street. A branch from it ran north-west towards Aldham, crossing Chitts Hill, which led from the London road to New bridge. Roads from Colchester to Maldon, West Bergholt, and Mile End form parts of the former southern, northern, and eastern boundaries. Lanes led from those roads to the heath, the mill, and outlying farms. One of them, New Lane, constructed across Lexden heath before 1564, was closed *c.* 1821. After inclosure of the heath in 1821 a lane running south across it from the London road was extended to the Maldon road and named Straight Road.[98] There were four bridges over the Colne. New bridge, recorded from 1204,[99] carries the road from Lexden to West Bergholt near Chitts Hill. Its repair was the joint responsibility of the lords of the manors of West Bergholt, Lexden, and Abbotts in Stanway.[1] The wooden bridge recorded in 1866 was made in three sections to simplify repair by the three parties.[2] The lord of Lexden manor had responsibility for the repair of Lexden bridge between the two mills in Mill Lane, Sheepen bridge carrying a lane to Sheepen Farm, and the lost Cheane bridge, which probably led to the medieval park.[3] Godholves, the name later corrupted to Botolph's, bridge, recorded from the 13th century, carries the Colchester to West Bergholt road over St. Botolph's brook.[4]

There were three medieval crosses in the parish. Lamb's cross, standing where Chitts Hill meets the branch from Lexden Street towards Aldham, was said to have been erected by William de Lanvalei. Stone cross stood almost opposite the junction of the London road with Horsey Lane, where its brick and stone pedestal

86 *V.C.H. Essex*, ii. 353; O.S. Map 6", Essex XXVII (1881 edn.).

87 Bodl. MS. Rawl. D 1480, f. 237; *P.N. Essex*, 359, 376; below, this par., Manors.

88 *V.C.H. Essex*, i. 432, 574; *Rot. Parl.* i. 238.

89 *Cat. Anct. D.* i, A 519.

90 E.R.O., D/B 5 Cr71, rot. 10d.; D/DPa 57/1, f. 9; D/DPa 57/3. f. 8v.; D/DPa 57/4, f. 7; cf. *P.N. Elements*, ii. 108–9.

91 E.R.O., St. John's abbey ledger bk. f. 210; W. R. Fisher, *Forest of Essex*, 236.

92 E.R.O., D/P 273/3/4A; D/P 273/8/1.

93 O.S. Map 6", Essex XXVII (1881 edn.); E.R.O., D/CT 220.

94 O.S. Map 1/25,000, TL 92/TM 02 (1988 edn.); Geol. Surv. Map 6", drift, sheet 224 (1988 edn.).

95 *E. Nat.* xvii. 30; above, Pub. Svces (Water Supply).

96 Below, this par., Manors, Econ.

97 Above, Communications (Roads).

98 *Essex Map* (1777); E.R.O., Q/RDc 19A; ibid. D/DPa 57/3, p. 10.

99 Fisher, *Forest of Essex*, 19.

1 E.R.O., D/DPa 57/3, p. 1; ibid. Q/SBa 1/19; Q/ABp 46; Q/SR 437/29; Morant, *Essex*, ii. 194.

2 E.R.O., Q/ABp 46.

3 Ibid. D/B 5 Cr143, rot. 3; D/B 5 Sb2/5, f. 153v.; D/DEl, f. 2; Morant, *Colch.* 157; cf. Chain meadow: E.R.O., D/CT 220.

4 B.L. Arundel MS. 145, f. 21v.; *P.N. Essex*, 377.

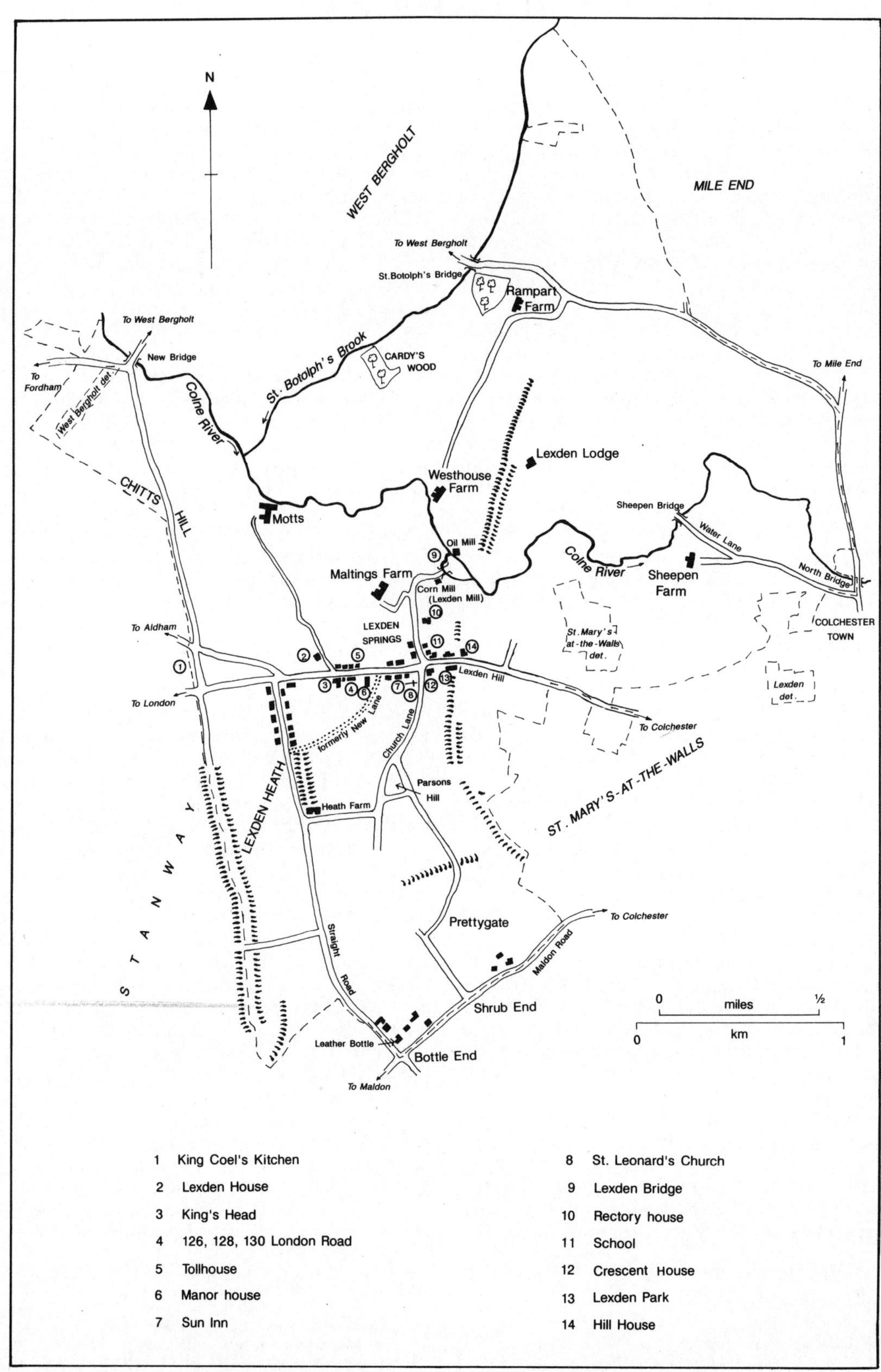

FIG. 35. LEXDEN *c.* 1838

was said in 1748 to have survived within living memory. Peddars cross was at the south end of Lexden heath by a lane to Gosbecks in Stanway.[5]

The Eastern Counties railway from London was built across the north half of the parish in 1843, with a viaduct over the Colne near Motts Farm, and a station, Colchester North, just within the parish.[6] A postal receiving house had been established by 1848.[7]

Three major linear earthworks, part of the Iron-Age dyke system of Camulodunum, cross the parish from north to south. One lies on the western boundary, another east of Straight Road, and the third runs south from Lexden Hill through Lexden park to a hollow way leading to Maldon Road. Numerous tumuli or mounts have been recorded.[8] The earliest known evidence of settlement is a Bronze-Age cemetery near Chitts Hill.[9] The Iron-Age Camulodunum extended over most of the later parish. In the Roman period temples and an industrial site were built on Sheepen farm.[10]

By 1066 a settlement had been established at which 16 or more unfree tenants were recorded, besides 4 *servi* who worked the manorial demesne.[11] Lexden was the wealthiest and perhaps the most populous of the four outlying parishes, with 16 men asessed for subsidy in 1296, 23 in 1524, and 31 in 1604.[12] In the 16th century 25 houses were charged with repairing the churchyard fence.[13] There were 80 households in 1673, and 240 adults were rated to the poll tax in 1692.[14] By 1766 the number of houses had risen to *c.* 94 and remained at that level in 1801, when they were inhabited by 697 people.[15] Therafter, as Colchester expanded westwards, the population of Lexden rose rapidly to 1,603 by 1851 and 4,089 by 1901, the greatest increase occurring in the decades 1821–31 (27 per cent), 1861–71 (25 per cent), and 1881–91 (51 per cent).[16] From 1861 the totals were inflated by the inclusion of Essex Hall asylum, established in 1859.[17]

Lexden village grew up around the church and the springs. The position of a cluster of surviving medieval houses between the lost New Lane and Lexden Road (nos. 126, 128, and 130 Lexden Road)[18] suggests that they encroached on the heath. Among other surviving houses with medieval origins in Lexden Street are Church House, Manor House,[19] and Weavers. Church House (no. 197), opposite the church, is a 15th-century hall house with cross wings. An upper floor was put into the hall in the 17th century and a stair with square newels and turned balusters was inserted behind the hall. A brick service wing was built at the back of the east end in the 19th century. A merchant's mark found in the house[20] was probably that of John Baldwin, tanner, who lived there in the mid 17th century.[21] Weavers (no. 187), perhaps formerly the Angel inn, has a late medieval cross wing. The rest of the house was rebuilt in the early 17th century with a continuous jetty along the street. The jetty was underbuilt, probably in the early 19th century when the interior was refitted, and opened up again in the 20th century. West of Church House a 17th-century timber-framed house survives as two houses (nos. 205 and 207), encased in brick and remodelled internally in 1838.[22] Next to it on the west nos. 209 and 211 are timber-framed houses, originally built as one. East of Weavers a timber-framed house (Jacqueline Court), probably of the 17th century, was fronted in brick in the early 19th century and completely remodelled and enlarged to provide flats in the late 20th century.

There were two small settlements along Shrub End Road on the southern boundary of the parish, Shrub End and Bottle End, both recorded from 1777.[23] They may have been the successors of the medieval settlement of Shrub Street, recorded from *c.* 1200. It was treated as a separate vill by the forest justices in 1276, and at least 11 holdings of arable and one house in Shrub owed rent, called shrebgavel, to the borough in the late 14th century.[24]

Houses on outlying farms recorded in 1655[25] included Coopers (later Prettygate), Sheepen, and West House (Westfields). The first two were pulled down in the late 20th century, but West House survives with a 17th-century main range and cross wing. The house was remodelled and a service wing was added in the 19th century. At Maltings farm the surviving house is possibly a medieval hall with an inserted floor and 18th-century additions. A hedged and moated inclosure in a field called Summerhouse piece in 1838 may have been the site of Summer Hall recorded in 1583 and 1601.[26]

In the 18th century, following the turnpiking of Lexden Street, new houses were built there, including the Sun public house and two adjoining houses (nos. 108 and 110) on the south side, and, on the north side, two houses standing on an embankment and later divided (odd nos. 221–233). West of them a cottage was apparently adapted as a tollhouse and a second tollhouse, stood on the corner of Church Lane and Lexden Street. Lexden House, on the north side of the London road, was enlarged and remodelled,

5 Morant, *Colch.* 132; E.R.O., D/DEl M163, f. 31.
6 E. F. Carter, *Hist. Geography of Railways Br. Isles*, 63; D. I. Gordon, *Regional Hist. Rly.* v. 37; O.S. Map 6", Essex XXVII (1886 edn.); above, Communications (Railways.)
7 *White's Dir. Essex* (1848), 95.
8 O.S. Map 1/2,500, Essex XXVII. 11 (1876 edn.); *V.C.H. Essex*, iii. 91–2; C. F. C. Hawkes and M. R. Hull, *Camulodunum*, 13; J. Foster, *Lexden Tumulus*; *E.A.T.* N.S. xii. 188.
9 *E.A.T.* 3rd ser. ix. 1.
10 Above, Iron-Age and Roman Colch.
11 *V.C.H. Essex*, i. 432.
12 *E.A.T.* N.S. ix. 133; P.R.O., E 179/108/161, rot. 8; E.R.O., Wire 4/1.
13 E.R.O., D/P 273/1/1.
14 Ibid. Q/RTh 8/7; Morant, *Colch.* 133.
15 Lambeth Palace Libr., Fulham Papers, Terrick 14, ff. 745–8; *Census*, 1801.
16 *V.C.H. Essex*, ii. 353.
17 Above, Hospitals (Royal Eastern Counties' Institution); P.R.O., HO 107/344/9; ibid. RG 9/1099; RG 10/1686; RG 11/1790.
18 E.R.O., D/DPa 57, f. 10.
19 Below, this par., Manors.
20 Inf. from Mr. G. Pearson, owner in 1990.
21 E.R.O., D/DPa 57/5, f. 5v.; ibid. D/P 273/1/1.
22 Date on west wall of house.
23 *Essex Map* (1777); E.R.O., Q/RDc 19c.
24 B.L. Arundel MS. 145, f. 31; P.R.O., E 32/12, rot. 4; E.R.O., D/B 5 R1, f. 169v.
25 E.R.O., D/P 273/1/1.
26 Ibid. D/CT 220; D/DPa 57 (Extracts from ct. bk.); D/DRe Z8.

probably by Isaac Green, in the later 18th century.[27] By 1800 four alehouses or inns had been converted to private houses or demolished. The rectory house was rebuilt in 1814 and the church in 1820. Gentlemen's houses with parks or gardens were established at Lexden Park and Hill House. Corner House on the east side of Church Lane near its junction with Lexden Street, recorded in 1528,[28] had become a gentleman's house renamed Crescent House by 1813 and the tollhouse in its garden had been pulled down. Crescent House survived in 1875 but was demolished soon after.[29] Lexden Park was rebuilt in *c.* 1825.[30] In Water Lane on the eastern boundary of the parish terraces of workers' cottages had been built by 1838.[31]

Ten inns were recorded in the 17th century and some of them may have been long established. Five are known to have been in Lexden Street, reflecting its importance as part of the road to London. The Angel was recorded as an inn in 1683 but was a private house by the mid 18th century.[32] Also in Lexden Street in the 17th century were the Ship, the Star, the Sun, and the King's Arms. The first two were apparently closed in the early 18th century, but the King's Arms survived in 1789 and the Sun until the 1790s, when it became a private house.[33] It had reopened as a public house by 1837.[34] The King's Head, near the north-east corner of Lexden heath, was recorded in 1656; in 1721 it was out of repair but seems to have survived as an inn into the late 19th century, when it became a temperance refreshment house.[35] In Bergholt Road were the Fox and Pheasant, recorded 1674–1772,[36] and the Chequers, 1728–1837. The Chequers seems to have been renamed the Railway tavern when the railway was built in 1843 but had closed by 1862.[37] At the south end of Lexden heath the Leather Bottle survives from 1670 or earlier, and the Berechurch Arms, established by 1837 and still trading in the 1980s, may have been the successor of the Fighting Cocks, recorded 1702–40.[38] The Crown at the west end of Lexden Street and the Star in Straight Road opened as beerhouses *c.* 1851.[39] The Queen's Head, mentioned in 1688 and 1701, may have been in St. Mary's-at-the-Walls parish as was the Three Crowns, recorded in field names 1678–1705.[40]

A bowling green in Lexden Street had become a garden by 1726.[41] In 1797 Colchester races were run on Lexden heath, where military camps were occasionally held in the 18th and early 19th century.[42] A village hall was built by a local benefactor in 1884.[43]

A friendly society, the Aldham and United Parishes Insurance Society, founded in 1826, was open to Lexden men aged between 14 and 50. The Lexden members, whose numbers rose from 38 in 1834 to 122 in 1848, included farmers, agricultural labourers, artisans, and servants. The society survived until 1863 or later.[44]

MANORS. Aelfflaed, widow of the ealdorman Brihtnoth, by will of *c.* 1000 bequeathed to the king land in Lexden which was probably the outlying estate of 4 hides belonging to the king's manor of Stanway in 1086, and which became *LEXDEN* manor.[45] The 5 hides at Lexden claimed by the burgesses of Colchester in 1086 as having belonged to Godric's land of Greenstead[46] presumably included those 4 hides, perhaps with other land later in Mile End. The implication that Lexden was transferred from Greenstead to Stanway between *c.* 1066 and 1086 seems to be supported by the statement that Stanway's value increased by half during that period.[47]

Eudes the sewer (*dapifer*), to whom William II granted Colchester and its castle, probably acquired Stanway and Lexden by the same grant, for he certainly held lands in those places.[48] After his death in 1120 both manors descended in chief as part of the honor of Walkern in the families of St. Clare, Lanvalei, and Burgh.[49] John de Burgh (d. 1274), who married Hawise de Lanvalei, was holding Lexden in her right in 1227.[50] Their son John de Burgh (d. 1280) sold Stanway[51] but retained Lexden, which on his death fell to the share of his daughter Dervorguille, first wife of Robert FitzWalter, Lord FitzWalter (d. 1326).[52] After Dervorguille's death in 1284, FitzWalter held by the curtesy of England. In 1313 he bought the reversion of half the manor from their daughter Christine, to whom it had been assigned as her purparty.[53] In 1315 he appears to have bought the reversion of the other half from John Marshal, Lord Marshal, who was probably Christine's nephew.[54] Lexden, therefore, passed on FitzWalter's death to his descendants by his second wife,[55] descending, like Roydon, with the barony of FitzWalter. John Radcliffe, Lord FitzWalter, was attainted

27 Ibid. C/T 523; ibid. D/DEl M166, p. 228; ibid. sale cat. A232. Evidence of an older house survived there in 1993: inf. from Geometric Results, occupiers.

28 E.R.O., D/DPa 57/3. f. 6v.

29 Ibid. D/DPa 63; D/DEl T382; O.S. Map 1/2,500, Essex XXVII. 11 (1876 edn.).

30 Below, this par., Manors.

31 E.R.O., D/CT 220; P.R.O., HO 107/344/9.

32 E.R.O., D/DEl M163, pp. 5–6; D/DEl T395.

33 Ibid. Acc. C47, CPL 1058; ibid. D/DEl 395; D/DEl B24, M163, M180, M182, T356.

34 Ibid. D/CT 220.

35 Ibid. D/DPa 57/3, p. 62; D/DEl M175, M180, M182; D/CT 220; *Kelly's Dir. Essex* (1882 and later edns.).

36 E.R.O., D/P 273/3/1, 2; D/P 273/28/5; D/DEl F1.

37 O.S. Map 6", Essex XXVII (1886 edn.); E.R.O., D/DEl M183; ibid. Lexden Ct. Bk. 1862.

38 E.R.O., D/DEl M156, M163, M175, M179–80, M182, T359; D/CT 220; O.S. Map 1/2,500, Essex XXVII. 15 (1876 edn.); Colch. Boro. Licensing Reg. 1985.

39 P.R.O., HO 107/1781.

40 E.R.O., D/P 273/3/1, 3, 4A; D/P 246/11/2; P.R.O., RG 9/1099.

41 E.R.O., D/DEl M175, f. 2v.; D/P 273/3/3, 4.

42 *Garrison – Ten British Military Towns*, ed. P. Dietz, 9–22; *E.R.* xliv. 125; *V.C.H. Essex*, ii. 241; newspaper cutting in scrapbk. in E.C.L. Colch.

43 *Kelly's Dir. Essex* (1886), 93.

44 E.R.O., D/DHw O12–16; *White's Dir. Essex* (1863), 148.

45 *A.-S. Wills*, ed. D. Whitelock, 39; *V.C.H. Essex*, i. 432.

46 *V.C.H. Essex*, i. 574.

47 *Antiquary*, vi. 7.

48 *Colch. Cart.* i. 96.

49 Sanders, *Eng. Baronies*, 92; cf. *Colch. Cart.* i. 53, 160, 199; ii. 200, 403–4; Morant, *Essex*, ii. 190; W. Farrer, *Honors and Knights' Fees*, iii. 166 sqq.

50 *Bk. of Fees*, ii. 1351.

51 Morant, *Essex*, i. 190.

52 *Cal. Inq. p.m.* ii, p. 198; *Cal. Fine R.* 1272–1307, 126; *Complete Peerage*, v. 474.

53 *Cal. Close*, 1307–13, 523; *Cal. Inq. p.m.* v, p. 238; *Cal. Pat.* 1313–17, 18.

54 *Cal. Pat.* 1313–17, 211; *V.C.H. Essex*, viii. 116–17.

55 *Cal. Inq. p.m.* vi, p. 445; *Cal. Pat.* 1324–7, 214; *Complete Peerage*, v. 474–5.

and executed in 1496 and Lexden was forfeited to the Crown, but in 1505 it was restored to Radcliffe's son Robert, Lord FitzWalter, later earl of Sussex (d. 1542).[56] Lexden remained with the Radcliffes, earls of Sussex, until 1612 when Robert Radcliffe, earl of Sussex, sold it to Sir Thomas Lucas (d. 1625), who settled it on his bastard son Sir Thomas Lucas (d. 1650).[57] The last named Sir Thomas, sequestered as a Royalist during the Civil War, was succeeded at Lexden by his son Charles, Lord Lucas of Shenfield (d. 1688).[58] Lord Lucas settled the manor on his wife Penelope for life, with remainder to their daughters, Anne, wife of Edward Cary, and Penelope, later wife of Isaac Selfe. In 1700 Isaac Selfe bought Anne Cary's reversion of one half and the interest of Robert Lucas; in 1701 Selfe and his wife and her mother sold the manor to Samuel Rawstorn of London (d. 1720).[59]

Thomas Rawstorn, son and heir of Samuel, by his will proved 1768, devised the manor to his widow Sophia, with remainder to his daughter Ann (d. 1816). Ann devised Lexden to the Revd. John Rawstorn Papillon (d. 1837), a distant cousin, who left the manor for life to his sister Elizabeth Papillon (d. 1854), with remainder to his great-nephew Philip O. Papillon.[60] Philip O. Papillon, who was M.P. for Colchester 1859–65 and twice mayor, died in 1899, and was succeeded by his son Pelham R. Papillon (d. 1940).[61] In 1931 the Lexden manor estate was sold and broken up.[62]

The site of the medieval manor house was probably within the moated inclosure where a house known as Lexden Lodge survives. In 1313 the main house, kitchen, granary and chapel stood within the inner courtyard, two barns, a byre, dairy and small garden within the outer courtyard. The existing house, apparently of the 16th century, was probably an addition to an earlier and more substantial building, of which nothing remains. The eastern side of the moat was apparently widened in the early 19th century.[63] In the early 17th century Sir Thomas Lucas acquired the tenter house in Lexden Street, a former copyhold tenement which was in ruins in 1561.[64] He apparently built a new house on that site, where part of an early 17th-century range survives at the south-east corner of the existing house. Its north end appears to have been built late in the same century. Additions were made on the west side in the 18th century and, perhaps at the same time, gardens were laid out around and opposite the house, and Lexden springs were landscaped to give a prospect of ornamental water with plantations. The house was enlarged and remodelled in 1837.[65]

A chapel in or for the park recorded in 1201 was presumably that located in the inner court of Lexden manor house, although a Chapel field survived south of the moated site in 1838.[66]

MOTTS, sometimes styled a manor from 1483, was apparently a free tenement of Lexden manor,[67] which may have taken its name from the family of Arnold de la Mott or Mote (d. by 1310). He gave to the abbey of Waltham Holy Cross land in Lexden,[68] where his son Thomas also held land in the early 14th century.[69] William Mott, who paid tithes in the parish in 1360, may have been Thomas's heir.[70] Clement Spice (fl. 1363) acquired Motts and was succeeded by his sons Richard and Roger, and they in 1459 by Roger's son Clement (d. 1483). Clement's son and heir Humphrey Spice (d. 1485)[71] was succeeded by his daughter Philippa (fl. 1542), whose son, Henry Fortescue, in 1547 conveyed the manor of Motts to George Sayer[72] whose family retained it until 1634, when John Sayer conveyed it to James Lemyng. Lemyng's daughter Mary married Sir Isaac Rebow (d. 1726) from whom Motts passed to his grandson Charles Chamberlain Rebow and Charles's daughter, who married a Capt. Adams. Known as Newbridge farm, it belonged to Thomas Wood in 1821.[73] It was bought soon afterwards by J. F. Mills and became part of the Lexden Park estate.[74] In 1990 it was known as Viaduct farm or Seven Arches farm from its proximity to the railway crossing over the Colne.

LEXDEN PARK ESTATE, named from a park laid out before 1768, lay mainly on the south side of London Road near the junction with Church Lane. It originated in lands acquired by William Mott before 1598.[75] His family extended the estate, retaining it until 1714 when another William Mott sold it to Charles Richardson (d. 1721). Charles devised it to his nephew John Richardson who seems to have laid out the park. By will proved 1768, John left the estate to trustees who sold it to Isaac Bevan. The estate passed to Isaac's son Henry Ennew Bevan (d. 1777) and to Henry's sister Sally, who married William Turner. It was acquired *c.* 1821 by J. F. Mills (d. 1840). He enlarged the estate and devised it to his wife for life and to his son-in-law G. H. Errington (d. 1883), who sold some of the land. In 1889 the house and 90 a. were sold to Sir Mountstuart Elphinstone Grant Duff (d. 1906). In 1908 more land was sold for building and the house and park to E. J. Sanders.[76] They passed to his son Sir Percy Sanders and in 1955

56 *V.C.H. Essex*, iv. 112; viii. 232; *Feet of F. Essex*, iv. 112.
57 Morant, *Colch.* 131; *Complete Peerage*, viii. 245; xii, 527; *Cal. S.P. Dom.* 1627–8, 497; E.R.O., D/DPa 13.
58 *Complete Peerage*, viii. 245–6; Morant, *Colch.* 131–2; E.R.O., D/DPa 13.
59 Morant, *Colch.* 131–2; E.R.O., D/DPa 13.
60 E.R.O., D/DEl E21; D/DEl M163–79; D/DU 906/2.
61 Ibid. D/DU 906/2; *E.R.* iii. 244; xlix. 119.
62 E.R.O., sale cat. B24; *Country Life*, 18 July, 26 Sept. 1931.
63 P.R.O., C134/31, no. 3; E.R.O., D/DPa P9; D/CT 220; O.S. Map 1", sheet 48 (1838 edn.).
64 E.R.O., D/DPa 57; D/DPa 57/3, p. 24.
65 Ibid. D/DPa P7 (Map 1819); D/DEl E12.
66 *E.A.T.* N.S. xvi. 113; *Colch. Cart.* i. 95; E.R.O., D/DPa O1; D/CT 220.
67 P.R.O., C 141/567, no. 28; E.R.O., D/DPa 57, f. 15v.; *Feet of F. Essex*, iii. 186.
68 B.L. Harl. MS. 4809, f. 95.
69 *Feet of F. Essex*, ii. 130, 157; *Medieval Essex Community: Lay Subsidy 1327*, ed. J. C. Ward, 16.
70 E.R.O., St. John's abbey ledger bk. f. 212.
71 P.R.O., C 141/567, no. 28; *Feet of F. Essex*, iii. 137.
72 E.R.O., D/DU 93; *Feet of F. Essex*, v. 2.
73 E.R.O., D/P 273/3/4A; D/DPa O1.
74 Ibid. D/DEl P84; D/CT 220.
75 Ibid. D/B 5 Cr153, rot. 11; Cr160, rot. 9.
76 Ibid. D/DPa 63; Abstract of Title 1908 (copy in possession of Mr. J. Bensusan-Butt.).

were bought by Endsleigh private school, which was taken over by the county council in 1965.[77] The premises were used as the Endsleigh annexe of Colchester Institute[78] until 1990, when the park of *c.* 25 a. was bought by the borough council for public recreation.

The house for which the park was laid out may have been Corner, later Crescent, House[79] but *c.* 1825 a villa was built on the north side of the park to designs by D. Laing.[80] Some fittings, including fireplaces, and some of the walls were re-used in the mid-19th century villa which occupies the site. That house was enlarged and remodelled on more than one occasion in the 19th century and the early 20th. Substantial additions were made to the west end to provide classrooms. In the valley south of the house a small park survives surrounded by a boundary belt of trees and there is a lake close to the house.

ECONOMIC HISTORY. In 1066 on the estate of 4 hides which became Lexden manor there were 2 ploughs on the demesne and 4 on land cultivated by the 6 *villani* and 10 bordars, 18 a. of meadow, and woodland for 100 swine. In 1086 the 5 *villani* and 12 bordars had only 3 ploughs.[81] In 1280 there were on the demesne of Lexden manor 270½ a. of arable land, 22 a. of meadow, and *c.* 150 a. of park pasture and the total value of customary rents and services was 77*s.* 10½*d.*[82] By 1313 the tenants owed winter and autumn week-work, additional ploughing and harrowing services in winter and spring, and renders of chickens and eggs at Christmas and Easter respectively.[83] Their holdings at that time ranged from 8 a. to 50 a. and by the late 14th century appear to have been held in severalty.[84] In 1310 on Thomas Mott's estate, which lay west of Lexden manor, there were 160 a. of arable, 10 a. of meadow, 10 a. of pasture, and 16 a. of alder.[85] Waltham abbey's Stanway manor included arable and meadow land in Lexden, west of Motts.[86]

Rye and oats were grown on the Lexden demesne in 1287 and wheat, oats, barley, and peas in 1351. Income from livestock, hay, and pasture exceeded that from arable crops in both 1287 and 1351. Among livestock cattle apparently predominated; in 1287 the lactage of 40 cows was farmed at 4*s.* each and 25 calves were sold for 1*s.* each. By 1351 the value of the lactage had fallen to 2*s.* 6*d.* for each cow.[87] The name Sheepen, given to lands by the river in the south-east corner of the parish, is derived from 'scipen', cattle pens,[88] suggesting that it was an ancient place for assembling cattle.

The park inclosed by the lord of Lexden manor before 1237 occupied much of the north-east corner of the parish between the river on the south and Bergholt Road on the north. It extended eastwards towards the town at North Street and westwards towards the manor house on the site of Lexden Lodge.[89] In 1287 the rents of its pasture alone amounted to £6 17*s.* ½*d.*[90] Walter FitzWalter, Lord FitzWalter, in 1375 granted to his parker 3*d.* a day, a livery robe every year, pasture for 6 cows, 12 swine, 12 sheep, and 4 mares with their foals, and pasture and hay for his horse. The parker was also keeper of the lord's warren,[91] which may have been in the south-east corner of the parish, along the boundary with St. Mary's-at-the-Walls, where the field names Upper and Lower Warren survived in 1838.[92] The lord of Lexden had a fishery between New bridge and Lexden mill by 1245, and stews on his demesne in 1342.[93]

In the Middle Ages Lexden contained numerous enclosed groves probably providing pasture and underwood.[94] About 1276 the lord of Lexden laid waste part of the ancient wood of Cestrewald in the north-east quarter of the parish, probably the Chesterwelde field recorded in 1360.[95] By 1280 Popeshead (later Cardy's)[96] and Ten Acre woods in the north lay adjacent to two demesne arable fields, West field and the Hide.[97] In the south-east woodland between Lexden and Stanway heaths had been cleared by 1416.[98] The heath was common, and so was Gallow grove, which apparently lay to the north of it and survived in the 1520s.[99] The burgesses of Colchester had half year grazing rights on lands in the south-east quarter of the parish, next to the Borough field in St. Mary's-at-the-Walls.[1] The intermixed, detached parts of West Bergholt on the north-west boundary of Lexden may derive from intercommoning with that parish on the riverside meadows.[2] In the early 19th century only the heath remained common.[3]

The growth of sheep-rearing to serve the local cloth trade increased pressure upon grazing resources. In the 16th century the pasture rights of commoners were limited to 100 sheep, overseers of estovers were appointed, and a pound was set up in Lexden Street.[4] Some arable land, including 50 a. or more in West field, had been converted to grass by 1599 when, of 538 a. of land surveyed, there were 290 a. of pasture, 172

77 Above, Educ. (Private Schs.).
78 E.R.O., C/TE 1912.
79 Above, this par. (Intro.).
80 E.R.O., D/P 273/8/1; T. Wright, *Hist. Essex*, i. 355; Pevsner, *Essex*, 267.
81 *V.C.H. Essex*, i. 432.
82 P.R.O., C 133/24, no. 14.
83 Ibid. C 134/31, no. 3.
84 Ibid.; E.R.O., St. John's abbey ledger bk. f. 212 and v.
85 *Feet of F. Essex*, ii. 130.
86 B.L. Harl. MS. 4809, ff. 89 and v., 95.
87 P.R.O., SC 6/845/13; SC 6/845/15.
88 *P.N. Essex*, 379.
89 *Colch. Cart.* i. 96; Morant, *Essex*, i. 440, ii. 190 (for Lanvalei fam.); Morant, *Colch.* 132, 157; E.R.O., D/B 5 Sb2/5, f. 152v.
90 P.R.O., SC 6/845/13.
91 *Cal. Inq. p.m.* xvi. 138.
92 E.R.O., D/CT 220.
93 *Cat. Anct. D.* i. A519; *Cal. Pat.* 1343–5, 98–9.
94 E.R.O., D/B 5 Cr19, rot. 10d; D/DPa 57/3; B.L. Harl. MS. 4809, f. 90v.; cf. below, Mile End (Econ.).
95 Fisher, *Forest*, 236; E.R.O., St. John's abbey ledger bk. f. 210.
96 E.R.O., D/DPa E1; D/DEl M163, f. 27; D/DEl F2.
97 P.R.O., C 134/31, no. 3.
98 *Cal. Close*, 1413–19, 351.
99 E.R.O., D/DPa 57/3, p. 4; cf. High and Low Gallows fields: ibid. D/CT 220.
1 Ibid. D/DEl T383; above, Common Lands.
2 O.S. Map 6", Essex XXVII (1885–6 edn.).
3 60 Geo. III & 1 Geo. IV, c. 1 (Private, not printed); E.R.O., Q/RDc 19.
4 E.R.O., D/DPa 57/4, f. 7; D/DPa 57/3, pp. 9, 32, 39.

a. of rye ground, and 76 a. of meadow.[5] In 1645 the tithes of Lexden church glebe were payable on 44 a. of rye, 26 a. of oats, 6 a. of barley, 5 a. of flax, 4 a. of wheat, 3 a. of peas, 30 a. of meadow, 22 cows, and 140 sheep.[6] Flax cultivation gave rise to a field name of 1776, and there was a flaxman in 1649.[7] Turnips were being grown as a field crop by 1676, and by 1699 their use as fodder had begun to devalue the meadows.[8] In 1711 a flock of 200 sheep and their lambs was recorded on the Lexden manor pastures.[9]

Much woodland was cleared in the 17th and 18th centuries. Braiswick wood, said to be 140 a. in 1437,[10] survived in 1621,[11] and Shrub wood may have extended into Lexden in 1649,[12] but by 1729 only *c.* 70 a. of woodland remained in the parish.[13] In 1767 another 25 a. was stubbed to make way for corn[14] and by 1821 only 20 a. remained.[15]

In 1729 there were five farms of 100–200 a.; three of them were among the 751 a. owned by Mrs. Rawstorn, lady of Lexden manor, one was owned by Charles Chamberlain Rebow, and the other by Nicholas Corsellis. In the early 18th century farmers were using chalk and town muck to improve the land;[16] leases of the Rawstorns' farms imposed a four-course system of husbandry, with two corn crops followed by summer fallow and clover, the use of farm manure or its equivalent in town muck, penalties for ploughing pasture without consent, and, occasionally, residence in the farmhouse.[17] Rye, which had been a major crop in the Middle Ages, had given way to wheat by the 18th century and in 1801 returns included 294 a. of wheat, 226 a. of barley, 171 a. of oats and 10 a. of rye.[18] In the early 19th century *c.* 14 a. of hops were recorded.[19]

Lexden heath, comprising 290 a., was inclosed by Act of Parliament in 1821.[20] At that time J. R. Papillon of Lexden manor and J. F. Mills of Lexden Park were enlarging their estates; under the award Papillon acquired 151 a. by allotment and bought common rights on 18 a.; Mills acquired *c.* 40 a. by allotment and bought common rights on 41 a. of heath[21] and the burgesses' lammas rights on 39 a. of farmland adjoining his park.[22] By 1838 the Papillon family owned 1,216 a. and J. F. Mills 296 a. out of 2,312 a. in the parish. The titheable acreage then comprised 1,746 a. of arable, 430 a. of pasture, and 37 a. of woodland. There were three farms of over 200 a., three of 100–200 a., three of 50–100 a., and several smaller holdings.[23] Some 40 a. of farmland were lost to the railway in the early 1840s. In 1876 there were 1,637 a. of arable, 423 a. of pasture, and 57 a. of wood.[24]

A common market on the waste beside Lexden Street was mentioned in 1615, but nothing more is known of it.[25]

Henry and John Stow, tenants of Lexden mill in the mid 18th century, were well known locally for their auriculas and tulips.[26] Among nurserymen who flourished in the parish in the 19th century was Isaac Bunting, whose flower nursery in Lexden Road was founded in 1819. By the late 19th century his family had established a second nursery in North Station Road, and in 1935 the Lexden Road nursery was sold.[27] Frank Cant established his rose nursery at Braiswick *c.* 1877.[28]

In 1086 there were two mills in Lexden,[29] probably on the Colne on the sites of the later Lexden mill and North mill. The mill in Lexden which Hubert of St. Clare granted to St. John's abbey before 1154[30] was probably North mill, which by the early 14th century was considered to be in Colchester.[31] The other mill in Lexden remained in the hands of the lords of the manor, being held of John de Burgh in 1233.[32] It was probably the mill on the Colne below New bridge and apparently in Lexden mentioned in the 1240s,[33] and the Lexden mill whose millers were regularly presented at borough lawhundred courts from 1334.[34] It was farmed for 40*s.* in 1352.[35] Thomas Godstone, the farmer in 1403, rebuilt Middle mill in Colchester and may have built the second mill which existed in Lexden by 1431.[36] By 1455 the mills stood on either side of a bridge, presumably the later Lexden bridge where the stream from Lexden springs feeds the Colne.[37] A lease of 1496 reserved the springs to the use of the mills and allowed the lessee to build a dam for the corn mill.[38] From the late 15th century until the early 18th century the mills were farmed together and distinguished as the great or undershot corn mill, north of Lexden bridge, and the little or overshot fulling mill, at the head of a pond south of the bridge.[39]

From 1719 the mills seem to have been farmed separately. The great or undershot mill remained a corn mill until *c.* 1830 when it became an oil mill which was occupied by the Chaplin

5 B.L. Stowe MS. 832, f. 34.
6 Ibid. Stowe MS. 842, ff. 4v.–5.
7 E.R.O., D/DEl F1 (memo. attached to p. 102); D/CT 220; D/ACW 15/92.
8 Ibid. D/P 273/3/1; D/P 273/3/4A (tithe bk.).
9 Ibid. D/P 273/3/2–3.
10 Morant, *Colch.* 143.
11 E.R.O., D/P 273/3/5.
12 Ibid. D/B 5 Sb2/9, f. 28; below, West Donyland.
13 E.R.O., D/P 273/3/4A.
14 A. F. J. Brown, *Essex at Work*, 42.
15 E.R.O., D/DPa O1.
16 Ibid. D/P 273/3/4A.
17 e.g. E.R.O., Acc. C47, CPL 849, 858, 867.
18 *List and Index Soc.* vol. 189, pp. 141, 157.
19 E.R.O., D/DPa O1; D/CT 220.
20 60 Geo. III & 1 Geo. IV, c. 1 (Private, not printed); E.R.O., Q/RDc 19.
21 E.R.O., Q/RDc 19.
22 Ibid. D/DEl T383.
23 Ibid. D/CT 220.
24 *O.S. Area Bk.* (1876).
25 E.R.O., D/DPa 57/4, f. 6v.
26 Morant, *Colch.* 92; *Ipswich Jnl.* 4 May 1754; 5 May 1770; 23 Feb., 11 Apr. 1772; *E.C.S.* 15 Apr. 1966.
27 *Industries of the Eastern Counties Business Review: Essex* (1889–90), 178; sale cat. in E.C.L. Colch.
28 *E.R.* xiii. 168; O.S. Map. 1/2,500, Essex XXVII. 7 (1897 edn.).
29 *V.C.H. Essex*, i. 432.
30 *Colch. Cart.* ii. 599.
31 Above, Mills.
32 *Bracton's Notebk.* ed. Maitland, ii, pp. 596–8.
33 *Cat. Anct. D.* i. A 519.
34 e.g. E.R.O., D/B 5 Cr4, rot. 5d; Cr5, rott. 1d., 7d.; Cr6, rot. 5.
35 P.R.O., SC 6/845/15.
36 E.R.O., D/B 5 Cr33, rot. 14d.; P.R.O., C139/56, no. 46; above, Mills.
37 E.R.O., D/B 5 Cr66, rot. 12; *Essex Map* (1777).
38 *Cal. Pat.* 1494–1509, 60.
39 Guildhall MS. 9628/2; E.R.O., D/P 273/3/1; D/P 273/3/4; D/ABW 50/2.

family until it burnt down in 1878.[40] A corn mill, built adjacent to the undershot mill by 1837 and later driven by an oil engine, remained in use until *c.* 1931 and was converted to a house in 1975.[41] The fulling mill was converted *c.* 1720 for crushing seed for oil. From about the 1740s until 1772 it was occupied by John and Henry Stow. By 1775 it was a bay mill and was leased that year to the Colchester baymakers Tabor and Boggis. Their successor Peter Devall was the lessee in 1821.[42] The bay mill was still working in 1822, but was in ruins by *c.* 1830 and soon afterwards was converted into a corn mill, which was in use until 1898. The building survived in 1931.[43]

A mound south-east of New Lane, described in the 17th century as a former mill mound, may have been the site of the mill belonging to the tenter house.[44]

A medieval tenter house in Lexden Street, used for stretching newly-woven cloth, had fallen into disuse by 1561 and was falling down in 1652.[45] A few weavers were recorded in the parish in the 17th and early 18th century,[46] and there was a tenterfield of unknown date recorded in 1838 on the west side of Water Lane.[47] A tailor lived in the parish *c.* 1568, three in 1588, and about the same number in the 17th century.[48]

A tannery with a bark mill at Church House, Lexden Street, was in use in the 16th and 17th centuries and survived in 1790.[49] There is evidence of malting in the 17th century,[50] and a malthouse established on Maltings farm by 1729 was apparently in use until *c.* 1863.[51]

Gravel was sold from Parsons Hill, south-west of Lexden Park, in the late 17th and early 18th century;[52] throughout the 19th century various gravel and sand pits were exploited, including one on the western boundary known as King Coel's kitchen.[53] The location of the tile kiln recorded in the late 14th and early 15th century is unknown.[54] There were brick kilns on various sites on or near Lodge farm throughout the 19th century; the last of them was worked in 1881 and closed by 1897.[55]

By 1841, although agriculture provided most of the employment within the parish, agricultural labourers and farmers were outnumbered by tradesmen and craftsmen, many of whom may have worked in the town although living in Lexden.[56] In the later 19th century there was much high-standard residential development and Lexden was increasingly seen as a wealthy suburb providing homes for many members of the town's elite.[57]

LOCAL GOVERNMENT. The lord of Lexden manor was holding view of frankpledge by 1280.[58] In 1318 the borough court questioned his right to do so in the absence of its bailiffs,[59] and the tenants were amerced frequently in the 14th and 15th centuries for failing to pay suit to the borough court.[60] Lexden gallows, mentioned in 1379,[61] may have been raised by the lord of the manor. The dispute over borough jurisdiction continued in the 16th century; the manor court, which elected constables and aletasters and maintained stocks, claimed in the early 16th century that Colchester serjeants had no right of arrest in Lexden. In 1571 that exemption was claimed only on Lexden park, and it presumably ceased when the park was disparked in the earlier 17th century.[62]

Extracts from court rolls 1511–1672, recording some leet business,[63] survive with rolls and books of courts baron 1702–1924.[64] In the 18th century courts were held at Lexden Lodge Farm.[65]

A poorhouse mentioned in 1592 was probably an unendowed almshouse, possibly St. Catherine's hospital which was in Lexden manor although in St. Mary's-at-the-Walls parish.[66] A parish workhouse in Spring Lane, recorded in 1751, was sold in 1835 when Lexden became part of Colchester union.[67] A house on Parsons Hill was let to poor people from 1672 until 1693 or later.[68] In 1823 the parish helped Samuel Durrant to build a cottage on its land at Bottle End, granting him life tenancy at a token rent.[69]

Parish records include vestry minutes 1813–57 and overseers' papers 1746–1851.[70] The Easter meeting determined the church rate and elected two churchwardens and two overseers. In the early 19th century the vestry rarely held more than 4 additional meetings, determining the overseer's rate twice a year, but in the period 1820–40 there were 6–8 and occasionally 10

40 H. Benham, *Essex Water Mills*, 91–2; E.R.O., D/CT 220.

41 E.R.O., D/CT 220; ibid. Sale Cat. B24; Benham, *Essex Water Mills*, 93; Colch. Mus., Lexden file.

42 E.R.O., D/P 273/3/4A; D/DEl F1; D/DPa O1; ibid. Acc. C47, CPL 850, 925.

43 E.R.O., D/DPa E1; ibid. Acc. 235 (Laver papers, box 1); ibid. *Sale Cat.* B24; Benham, *Essex Water Mills*, 91.

44 E.R.O., D/DPa 57/4, f. 17; D/DPa 57/3, p. 62.

45 Above, this par. (Manors).

46 E.R.O., D/ABR 8/281; D/ABR 18/67; D/ABW 52/176; D/ACW 15/278; ibid. Q/SR 432/81; ibid. T/A 156; ibid. D/P 273/14 (apprenticeship indentures).

47 Ibid. D/CT 220.

48 Ibid. D/ABW 2/237; D/ABW 28/273; D/ABW 46/77; D/ABR 9/259; D/Y 2/2, p. 193.

49 Emmison, *Essex Wills*, iii, p. 294; E.R.O., D/ABW 218/10; D/ABR 11/308; D/DPa 57/5, f. 5v.; D/DEl M163; D/DEl M166, pp. 77–8; D/B 5 Cr159, rot. 2d.; *Ipswich Jnl.* 18 Mar. 1758.

50 E.R.O., D/B 5 Cb2/6, f. 227v.

51 Ibid. D/P 273/3/2, 3, 4A; ibid. Acc. C47, CPL 859, 891; *White's Dir. Essex* (1848), 109; (1863), 120.

52 E.R.O., D/P 273/3/2.

53 Ibid. D/CT 220; O.S. Map 1/2,500, Essex XXVII. 7, 11, 15 (1876 and 1897 edns.).

54 E.R.O., D/B 5 Cr25, rot. 48d.; Cr48, rot. 10.

55 Ibid. D/DPa E1; D/CT 220; O.S. Map 6", Essex XXVII. NE. (1881); ibid. 1/2,500, Essex XXVII. 4 (1897 edn.).

56 P.R.O., HO 107/344/9.

57 Above, Modern Colch. (Town devt.).

58 P.R.O., C 133/24, no. 14.

59 E.R.O., D/B 5 R2, f. 64v.

60 e.g. ibid. D/B 5 Cr41, rot. 13.

61 Ibid. D/B 5 Cr19, rot. 9d.

62 Ibid. D/DPa 57/3, pp. 2, 12, 16; D/DPa 13, no. 12.

63 Ibid D/DPa 57/3.

64 Ibid. D/DEl M156–179.

65 Ibid. Acc. C47, CPL 879, 908.

66 *Cal. S.P. Dom.* 1591–4, 212; above, Sites and Remains of Religious Ho.

67 E.R.O., D/DEl F2, p. 283; D/DEl M166, p. 84; ibid. D/P 278/8/1; ibid. G/CoM 2.

68 Ibid. D/P 273/3/1.

69 Ibid. D/P 273/8/1.

70 Ibid. D/P 273/8/1, on which the following account is based.

meetings a year, besides the Easter vestry. Their main business was to approve the poor rate quarterly, to nominate a surveyor, and to approve his rate and accounts. Local farmers, and occasionally gentry, served as churchwardens, overseers, and surveyors. George Preston, rector 1804–41, and his successor John Papillon, 1841–90, took the chair at almost every meeting. One or two inhabitants usually attended, workhouse matters and rating assessments attracting a few more. In 1830, although the Easter vestry was attended by only 7 men including the rector and parish officers, 19 parishioners partook of the Easter dinner afterwards and in 1834 many more attended a meeting to elect a new parish surgeon.

In 1673 poor relief was received by 48 of the 80 households assessed for hearth tax.[71] The annual cost of relief averaged £360 a year in 1783–5, above average for the town and liberty. It rose nearly 3-fold to £1,036 in 1813, the second highest payment in Colchester, then fell to £876 in 1814 and to £646 in 1816, a steeper drop than in any other parish in the town or liberty except Mile End. In Lexden as in the other outlying parishes costs rose thereafter, to £849 in 1818. In 1821 the overseers took a 21-year lease on 16 a. of newly inclosed land on Lexden heath for spade husbandry; in that year the amount spent on the poor fell from £827 to £759, which then represented *c.* 16*s.* per head of population, just below the average payment for the town and liberty.[72] By 1833 the overseers employed an apothecary and subscribed to the hospital. In 1836 they continued, with the sanction of Colchester union, to provide spade husbandry on Lexden heath for the term of the lease.[73] In 1867 the vestry set up a fund to pay the expenses of poor parishioners willing to emigrate.[74]

Following local agricultural disturbances in 1830 the vestry raised a subscription, to be supplemented by the poor rate, to select 10 special constables to provide nightly patrols of 5 men paid 2*s.* 6*d.* a night. The system seems to have been abandoned by 1833. The parish was still appointing parish constables in 1837, but by 1841 the borough provided two full-time policemen to patrol Lexden, Mile End, and Greenstead.[75]

CHURCH. St. Leonard's church was established by the early 12th century when Eudes the sewer (d. 1120) gave a share of its tithes to St. John's abbey.[76] The advowson of Lexden was held in 1254 by John de Burgh (d. 1274) in the right of his wife[77] and descended with the manors of Stanway and Lexden in the FitzWalter, Lucas, Rawstorn, and Papillon families.[78] Robert FitzWalter (d. 1326) may have granted turns to others, for in 1328 his widow was to have the presentation on the third vacancy.[79] The king presented in 1386 when Walter FitzWalter (d. 1406) was a minor; Thomas Percy and others did so in 1398 when Walter was in Ireland. Henry Beaufort, bishop of Winchester, presented in 1422 as the heir's guardian and the bishop of London by lapse in 1442. In 1459 and 1461 Sir Thomas Cobham exercised the right of his wife, Elizabeth, widow of Walter FitzWalter (d. 1431). The king presented in 1499 when the manor was forfeit for rebellion.[80] The advowson passed from the Papillon family to the bishop of Chelmsford in 1978.[81]

The rectory was the richest living within the borough and liberty; it was valued at 40*s.* in 1254, £5 6*s.* 8*d.* in 1291, and £12 in 1535.[82] Eudes the sewer endowed St. John's abbey with two thirds of the tithes from the demesne of Lexden manor. Two thirds of the great tithes from all new assarts and of the tithes of Calwood near Chitts Hill also belonged to the abbey by 1254.[83] The rector received the third share and, by agreement with the abbot of St. John's in 1360, all tithes from certain small estates and from the demesne lands in Lexden of Waltham abbey's manor of Abbotts in Stanway.[84] After the Dissolution the Crown leased the abbey's share of tithes to Edward Cole for 21 years,[85] and in 1560 granted them to Sir Francis Jobson.[86] They were acquired by the rector before 1810, perhaps between 1767 and 1776.[87]

In 1621 the rector successfully claimed tithes in kind from Braiswick wood (150 a.) which had belonged to St. John's abbey.[88] In 1650 his income included £8 from glebe, returned apparently in error as *c.* 20 a.,[89] and £80 from tithes.[90] By 1676 most of the rector's tithes had been commuted for money payments, and in 1692 some of the remainder were farmed.[91] By 1810 the glebe comprised *c.* 30 a.[92] and the rector owned all great and small tithes in the parish, except those from Jesus meadow (5 a.), formerly chantry land. A crown rent of £1 13*s.* 4*d.* charged on tithes was redeemed in 1827.[93] The rector's annual income from tithes and glebe rose from £144 in 1705,[94] to £566 in 1835.[95] In 1838 the rector's tithes were commuted for a yearly rent of £660.[96] In 1880 the rector granted an annual rent charge of £60 to the new church of St. Paul's[97] and boundary changes of 1898 resulted in tithe rent charges of £48 being

71 Ibid. Q/RTh 8/7.
72 Ibid. Q/CR 1/1, 1/10, 1/12.
73 Ibid. D/P 273/8/1; ibid. G/CoM 2.
74 Ibid. Acc. C95, vestry mins.
75 Ibid. Acc. C95, vestry mins.; ibid. Boro. Mun. Watch Cttee. Mins. 1840–57, 7 Oct. 1841.
76 *Cal. Chart. R.* 1227–57, 423–6.
77 *E.A.T.* N.S. xviii. 123.
78 Above, this par., Manors; Newcourt, *Repertorium*, ii. 388–9; Morant, *Colch.* 133; Guildhall MSS. 9550, 9556–8.
79 *Cal. Close*, 1327–30, 340.
80 *Cal. Pat.* 1385–9, 241; 1416–22, 78; Newcourt, *Repertorium*, ii. 389; *Complete Peerage*, v. 480, 483.
81 *Chelm. Dioc. Yr. Bk.* (1978).
82 *E.A.T.* N.S. xviii. 123; *Tax. Eccl.* (Rec. Com.), 23; *Valor Eccl.* (Rec. Com.), i. 443.
83 *Colch. Cart.* i. 3; *E.A.T.* N.S. xviii. 123.
84 E.R.O., St. John's abbey ledger bk. f. 212.; ibid. D/DRe Z10 (ii); D/DRe Z9 (xii).
85 *L. & P. Hen. VIII*, xvii, p. 643.
86 *Cal. Pat.* 1558–60, 469.
87 P.R.O., CP 25(2) 1307/7 Geo. III/Hil. no. 5; ibid. 1308/16 Geo. III/Trin. no. 25.
88 E.R.O., D/P 273/3/5.
89 Guildhall MS. 9628/2.
90 Smith, *Eccl. Hist. Essex*, 320.
91 E.R.O., D/P 273/3/1.
92 Ibid. D/DPa O1.
93 Guildhall MS. 9628/2; E.R.O., D/P 273/3/9.
94 E.R.O., Acc. C95 Tithe bk.; ibid. T/R 13.
95 *Rep. Com. Eccl. Revenues*, H.C. 54, pp. 654–5 (1835), xxii.
96 E.R.O., D/CT 220.
97 Ibid. D/CP 3/40.

transferred to St. Mary's-at-the-Walls.[98] Most of the glebe was sold in 1918 and in 1922 only 4 a. remained.[99]

The rectory house mentioned in 1538 adjoined the glebe, which lay off Spring Lane.[1] The house was 'little' in 1610, but in 1662 the rector was taxed on six hearths.[2] The timber and plaster rectory house that stood on the east side of Spring Lane in 1810[3] was replaced in 1814 by a large new house built in Gothic style by George Preston, rector 1804–41.[4] That house was sold in 1910 and replaced by another in Lexden Road, which was replaced in 1975 by a house in Glen Avenue.[5]

The names of rectors are known from 1291. Before the Reformation incumbencies were usually short.[6] Four successive rectors were recorded between 1382 and 1386 when the rectory was held at farm by a chaplain.[7] In 1491 the rector was licensed to hold another benefice in plurality,[8] and a curate was recorded in 1529.[9] Richard Gostelowe, rector 1537–67, resided on another living from *c.* 1548.[10] His successor, John Price, rector 1567–76, was a former fellow of St. Catherine's, Cambridge. By 1574 he failed to serve the benefice and procure regular sermons and may have resigned under pressure. Robert Searle, rector 1576–1610, was one of the four Colchester ministers threatened with deprivation for non conformist practices after 1586, but survived to be designated 'diligent and sufficient' by his puritan brethren in 1604 and died in possession of the benefice.[11]

In contrast, his successor Stephen Nettles, who signed the petition for conformity in 1629, offended puritans by his *Answer* (1625) to John Selden's *History of Tythes*.[12] His contempt for the Covenant of 1643 and his adherence to the Prayer Book led to the sequestration of his livings of Lexden and Steeple in 1644,[13] but he continued to officiate[14] refusing to surrender Lexden rectory to his successor, Gabriel Wyresdale, until he was forced to do so in 1647.[15] Wyresdale, harassed by parishioners who favoured a local clergyman for the living, had left the parish by 1650.[16] John Nettles, rector 1657–69, whose relationship to Stephen is uncertain,[17] may have been assisted in 1657 by George Downs, who in 1669 was associated with the presbyterian Owen Stockton.[18] In 1711 the mayor chose Richard Skingle, rector 1706–29, to preach at the oath-giving ceremony but the town clergy denied him a pulpit; in 1715 Skingle preached at the ceremony in Lexden church and in 1716 the corporation gave thanks there for the suppression of the Jacobite rebellion.[19] In 1717 Skingle successfully challenged the borough's right to poor rates on the rectory.[20]

From the early 18th century the rectors lived in the parish, serving the cure themselves for many years, usually providing two Sunday services and communion 4–6 times a year, catechizing in Lent, and sometimes lecturing in winter evenings.[21] Samuel Sandys, 1769–1804,[22] and his nephew George Preston, 1804–41, sometimes employed assistant curates but both lived in the parish and established schools for the poor.[23] Preston also rebuilt the church and rectory house.[24] His successor John Papillon, a kinsman of the patron, served the church until 1890.[25] Although in 1845 part of Lexden was assigned to a new parish of All Saints, Shrub End,[26] on Census Sunday in 1851 Lexden church, with seats for 577, had a good congregation of different classes in the morning, and was full in the afternoon.[27] In 1869 a chapel of ease, dedicated to St. Paul and served by a curate from Lexden, was built for the growing population near North Street railway station.[28] Part of Lexden parish was assigned to it in 1879, when it became a parish church.[29] Lexden parish was consolidated by exchange of small detached parts with St. Mary's-at-the-Walls in 1898, the transfer of *c.* 41 a. to St. Paul's, and gains from Holy Trinity, St. James's, and St. Mary's in 1911.[30] In the 1930s young people's organizations and a branch of the Mothers' Union were started.[31] In 1990 the church, with 270 on the electoral roll and seven clubs and societies, attracted regular Sunday and weekday congregations.[32]

The medieval church of *ST. LEONARD*, which was demolished in 1820, stood on the south side of Lexden Street. It comprised a chancel, a nave with north chapel or transept, a timbered north porch, a vestry, and a boarded west bellcot with shingled spire.[33] The church and bellcot were in ruins in 1600 and, although

98 Ibid. D/CPc 95.
99 Ibid. Sale Cat. A87; *Kelly's Dir. Essex* (1922).
1 E.R.O., Morant/Holman MS. no. 113 (53), pp. 27–8.
2 Guildhall MS. 9628/2; E.R.O., Q/RTh 1, f. 22v.
3 Guildhall MS. 9628/2.
4 Lambeth Palace Libr., Fulham papers, Howley 48, no. 191.
5 E.R.O., T/A 645; ibid. D/CP 11/29; *Chelm. Dioc. Year Bk.* (1971–2 and later edns.).
6 Newcourt, *Repertorium*, ii. 389; Morant, *Colch.* 132; P. H. Reaney, *Early Essex Clergy*, 111; Smith, *Essex Parochial Clergy*, 123–4; *Reg. Baldock*, 276; *Reg. Simon*, i. 256, 278; *Cal. Close*, 1349–54, 350; *Cal. Pat.* 1385–9, 241; 1422–9, 381; E.R.O., T/A 237; T/A 547/1.
7 E.R.O., D/B 5 Cr24, rot. 36.
8 *Cal. Papal Reg.* x, p. 380.
9 E.R.O. D/B 5 Cr99, rot. 5d.
10 Corpus Christi Coll. Camb., MS. 122, f. 45.
11 B. Usher, 'Colch. and Diocesan Administration' (TS. in E.R.O.), 24, 39; *Seconde Part of a Register*, ed. A. Peel, ii. 164, 261.
12 *D.N.B.*
13 B.L. Add. MS. 15669, ff. 95, 133.
14 E.R.O., D/P 273/1/1.
15 B.L. Stowe MS. 842, f. lv.; T. W. Davids, *Annals of Nonconf. in Essex*, 225–6; Smith, *Eccl. Hist. Essex*, 123–4; E.R.O., D/P 273/1/1.
16 E.R.O., D/B 5 Sb2/9, ff. 7v.–8; B.L. Add. MS. 15669, f. 80; Smith, *Eccl. Hist. Essex*, 320.
17 *Alum. Cantab. to 1751.*
18 Davids, *Annals of Nonconf. in Essex*, 377.
19 E.R.O., Acc. C210, J. B. Harvey Colln. vi, pp. 24, 28; ibid. D/B 5 Gb6, p. 433.
20 Ibid. D/P 273/3/6.
21 Guildhall MS. 25750/1; Lambeth Palace Libr., Fulham papers, Terrick 14, ff. 745–8.
22 *Gent. Mag.* lxxiv (2), 1078.
23 Lambeth Palace Libr., Fulham papers, Randolph 9; E.R.O., D/P 273/1/4; below, this par. (Educ.).
24 Lambeth Palace Libr., Fulham Papers, Randolph 9; ibid. Howley 48, no. 191.
25 E.R.O., T/A 547/1; *Kelly's Dir. Essex* (1908).
26 *Lond. Gaz.* 15 May 1845, p. 2460; above, Churches (Modern Chs.).
27 P.R.O., HO 129/8/204.
28 *Kelly's Dir. Essex* (1870), p. 61; (1878), p. 76.
29 Above, Churches (Modern Chs.).
30 E.R.O., D/CPc 95; D/CPc 132.
31 Ibid. Acc. C115.
32 *Ch. Mag.* May 1990.
33 Morant, *Colch.* 133; Colch. Mus., illus. in Lexden file; Saffron Walden Libr., Scrapbook, iii, p. 356; E.R.O., D/AZ 1/4, f. 143.

some work was done, the church was still decayed in 1607 and the chancel, north porch, and vestry in 1609.[34] A wooden clock tower had been mounted on the north chapel by 1748.[35] A new church was completed in 1822 to the designs of M. G. Thompson in the Early English style, several yards south of the old building, and in 1892 a larger chancel was added in Perpendicular style.[36] The church comprises a chancel with north chapel and south vestry with organ loft above, a nave with north and south porches, and a west tower. The chancel walls are of flint with Box stone bands and dressings; those of the nave and tower are cement rendered. The roofs of the nave and chancel are tiled; the spire is covered with copper.[37] In the period 1946–55 four memorial windows to the Papillon family were inserted on the north side, including one depicting Lexden manor house. The church had one bell in 1683,[38] which may survive as the clock bell. A bell dated 1751, apparently one of a ring, was probably acquired for the new church in 1820. It was cracked by 1859 and in 1899 was recast; in 1901 a chime of 11 small bells was added.[39] The plate includes an inscribed silver cup and paten given before 1683 by Charles Lucas, Lord Lucas, and a silver flagon given in 1763.[40] A marble monument to Richard Hewett (d. 1771) stands against the south wall. The churchyard, enlarged in 1877 and 1926, was closed in 1946.[41] A columbarium for 300 urns was erected in the churchyard in 1950.[42]

NONCONFORMITY. A Primitive Methodist chapel was built in Straight Road in 1859. It had 18 members then and flourished in the later 19th century.[43] In 1972 it had a membership of 18,[44] and it was still open in 1990.

Lexden village mission hall was built in 1885 by Mrs. James Hurnard of Hill House. It was at first used mainly for temperance work, but was registered for services for protestant dissenters in 1890; a full-time missioner was appointed in 1927. In 1971 it became the Lexden Evangelical church.[45] It was still open in 1990.

EDUCATION. A Church Sunday school had been established by 1793, when a house in Mill Lane was provided for the master and mistress.[46] By 1817 two daily dame schools, also maintained by the rector, had been added, and in that year a National day and Sunday school for 100 children was built in Spring Lane, mainly with a legacy of Ann Rawstorn (d. 1816).[47] By 1819 the school, attended by *c.* 70 children and supported by subscriptions, taught all poor children aged 6–12 in the parish.[48] Four small dame schools, supported partly by subscriptions, were teaching *c.* 60 infants by 1833 and the National school had 84 children with 6 more on Sundays, but subscriptions were insufficient to employ a master as well as a mistress and only the daily attendance of George Preston, the rector, and his wife enabled the National school to survive.[49] John Rawstorn Papillon, by will proved 1837, gave £20 a year to the school[50] and by 1839, when it had 70 children, more than half of them received charity clothes. There were then *c.* 40 infants in the dame schools and several older children went to Colchester.[51] A new school and teacher's house were built in Spring Lane in 1842.[52] The school was enlarged in 1861 for 140[53] and in 1893 for 200 children.[54] It received annual government grants from 1866. Attendance rose slowly from 72 in 1866 to 120 in 1886, and more rapidly to 182 in 1904.[55] The school was replaced in 1925 by Lexden council school.[56]

CHARITIES FOR THE POOR. Mary Swinnerton and her son Sir John Swinnerton in 1610 charged their Stanway Hall estate with £5 4*s.* a year to provide bread for 14 old, impotent poor of Lexden. In 1837 the charge, on Chitts Hill farm, provided 20 loaves distributed at church on Sundays to the poor, preferably widows.[57] In 1853 the trustees allocated three loaves to the new All Saints' church, Shrub End, for the poor of Lexden living within that chapelry.[58]

Thomas Love, by will dated 1565, gave to Thomas Rich £120 to buy land to provide a yearly rent of £6 for the poor of Lexden and 11 other parishes, and Rich, by will dated 1570, endowed the charity with land in Lexden. The income was £6 in 1626, £12 in 1676, £24 in 1786, and £30 in 1828.[59] Lexden's share was usually distributed in bread with Swinnerton's charity.[60] In 1964 Lexden received £11 4*s.* 8*d.* from the two charities which was distributed in gifts,[61] and a similar sum in 1990.[62]

34 E.R.O., D/AZ 1/4, ff. 143–4, 154; D/AZ 1/10, f. 55; D/AZ 1/11, f. 8.
35 Morant, *Colch.* (1748 edn.), Bk. II, p. 25.
36 E.R.O., D/CF 31/8; D/P 273/9/3.
37 Ibid. D/P 273/8/1.
38 *E.A.T.* N.S.. xxiii. 147.
39 *Ch. Bells Essex*, 322; E.R.O., Acc. C115.
40 *Ch. Plate Essex*, 192; *E.A.T.* N.S. xxiii. 147.
41 E.R.O., D/CC 28/4; D/CC 77/6; D/P 273/9/3.
42 Pevsner, *Essex*, 267; E.R.O., D/P 273/9/3.
43 E.R.O., D/NM 2/2/1; G.R.O. Worship Reg. no. 13096.
44 *Meth. Statistical Returns*, (1972), i. 12; *Colch. Circuit Plan*, Apr.–June 1972.
45 *Essex Tel.* 27 Sept. 1884; G.R.O. Worship Reg. no. 31963; inf. (1959) from Mrs. M. F. Hurnard.
46 E.R.O., D/P 273/1/5.
47 Ibid. D/P 273/8/1.
48 *Returns Educ. Poor*, H.C. 224, p. 261 (1819), ix (1).
49 *Educ. Enq. Abstract*, H.C. 62, p. 271 (1835), xli.
50 P.R.O., ED 49/2148.
51 E.R.O., D/P 30/28/19.
52 *White's Dir. Essex* (1863), p. 90; O.S. Map 1/2,500, Essex XXVII. 11 (1897 edn.).
53 *E.C.S.* 2 Sept. 1861.
54 *Kelly's Dir. Essex* (1894).
55 *Rep. of Educ. Cttee. of Council, 1866–7* [C. 3882], p. 571, H.C. (1867), xxii; *Colch. Educ. Cttee. Year Bk.* (1904–8), 47.
56 Above, Educ. (Council Elementary Schs.).
57 *32nd Rep. Com. Char.* pp. 565–6 .
58 E.R.O., D/P 273/8/1.
59 *32nd Rep. Com. Char.* pp. 624–6.
60 E.R.O., D/P 273/8/1.
61 Char. Com. files.
62 Inf. from ch. treasurer.

MILE END

THE ancient parish of Mile End, a compact area of 2,352 a. (951.8 ha.),[63] probably took its name from its original settlement a mile north of Colchester town, but by the late 13th century it was sometimes called Myland.[64] It did not become a separate parish until the 13th century.[65]

In the 19th century Mile End's boundary followed natural features on the south along the river Colne and on the north along Black brook and Salary brook except for a small deviation round an intrusive part of Great Horkesley; on the east and west it mainly followed roads and lanes. At the south-west corner the boundary curved inwards round the built-up area of St. Peter's parish as it existed in the 13th century. On the east side the border turned inwards to skirt detached parts of All Saints' and St. Botolph's parishes.[66] From 1841 to 1871 an extra-parochial place of a few acres called 'No Man's Land', on Cock Common in the north-east corner of Mile End next to Ardleigh, was included in Mile End.[67] The land rises from below 15 metres on the Colne in the south to more than 50 metres over much of the north part of the parish, falling away to the east and west.

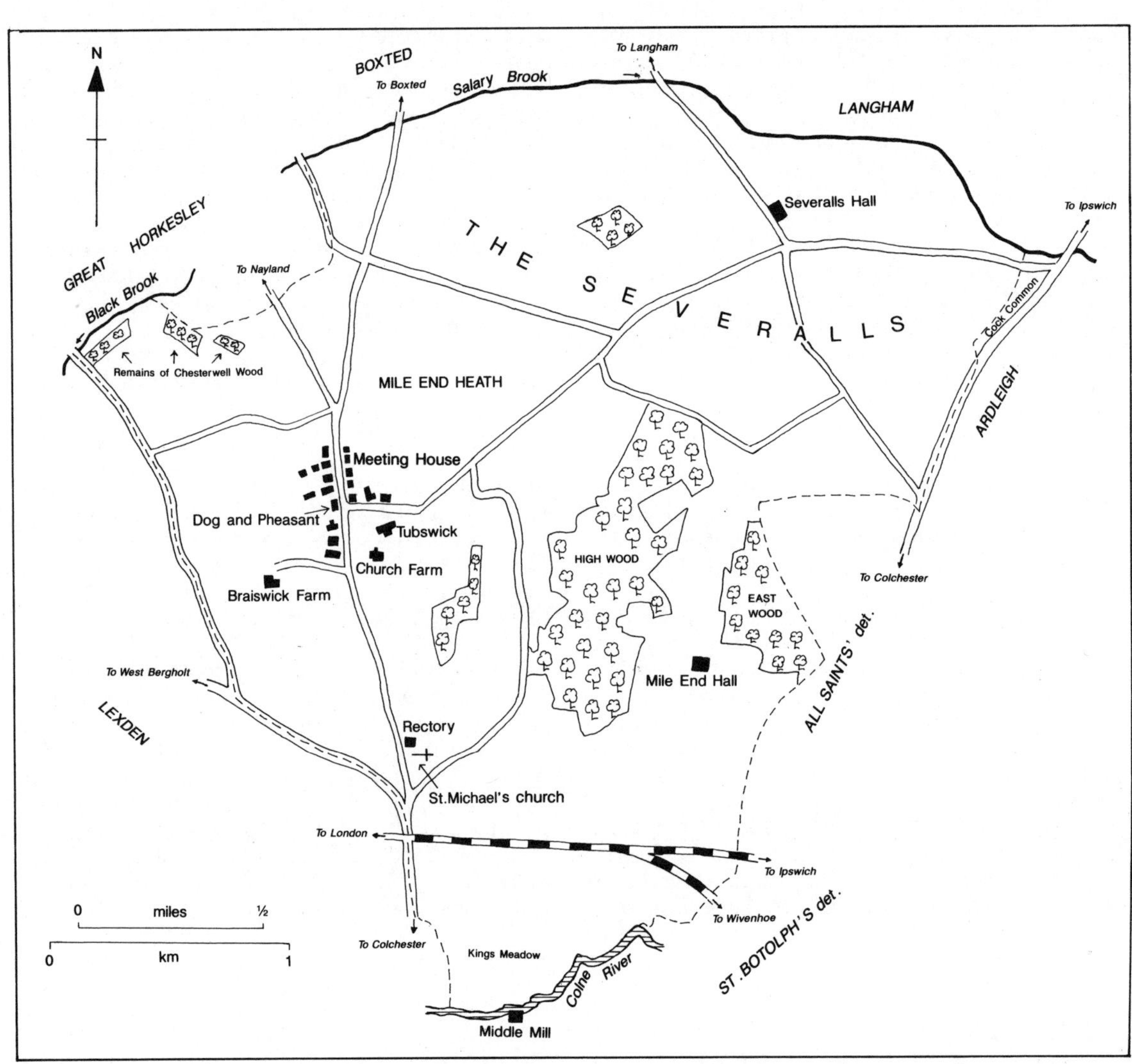

FIG. 36. MILE END *c.* 1846

[63] *V.C.H. Essex*, ii. 353; O.S. Maps 6", Essex. XVIII, XIX, XXVII, XXVIII (1881 edn.); O.S. Maps 6", TL 92 NE., TM 02 NW. (1958 edn.).

[64] *P.N. Essex*, 376.

[65] Below, this par., Church.

[66] E.R.O., Perambulation of Colch., 1801; ibid. D/CT 242A; G. Gilbert, *Colch. Map* [1846].

[67] *V.C.H. Essex*, ii. 351 n.; E.R.O., D/CT 242.

The soil is mainly silty and sandy clay, with some gravel and sand in the north-west corner and some London clay in the south and east.[68]

The main road running northwards through the parish from Colchester to Nayland and Sudbury (Suff.), sometimes called Mile End causeway, was mentioned in 1298.[69] A branch led west to West Bergholt. Severalls Lane, turnpiked in 1696, ran from the main Colchester–Ipswich road, part of which forms the north-east parish boundary, north-west across Mile End towards Langham. Minor roads linked those roads and connected Mile End with neighbouring parishes.[70] Colchester's first railway station, opened in 1843, lay on the road from Colchester to Mile End, just south west of the parish boundary. The railway line from Ipswich to Colchester, opened in 1846, ran across the south part of the parish.[71]

There was presumably a settlement at Mile End by 1254 when the church was recorded.[72] In the Middle Ages settlement seems to have been scattered over the unwooded areas of the parish, including Tubswick recorded from 1295, named from the Tubbe family, and Braiswick.[73] In 1296 only 7 inhabitants were assessed for subsidy, compared with 13 in Greenstead and 16 in Lexden; Simon of Nayland, master of St. Mary Magdalen's hospital in 1301, was the most highly taxed inhabitant.[74] Nineteen men were assessed to the lay subsidy in 1523, fewer than in Lexden and Greenstead, but more than in West Donyland. Of those taxed Robert Northen was worth more than the other 18 together.[75] He was probably Robert Northen of Mile End Hall, cousin of Robert Northen of Colchester, a wealthy clothier.[76] In 1588 twenty three able-bodied men aged between 16 and 60, almost all labourers, were liable for military service.[77] There were 50 households in 1671, of which 29 were exempt from hearth tax.[78] In 1692 the poll tax was assessed on 94 adults.[79] More burials than baptisms were recorded between 1700 and 1720 but baptisms outnumbered burials in most years thereafter until 1800.[80]

By 1801 the population had reached 299 and there were 44 houses. The population doubled between 1801 and 1841, the most rapid growth being between 1811 and 1821, and in the 1830s before the opening of the railway. Between 1841 and 1901 the population increased from 596 to 1,373. The number of inhabited houses increased to 124 in 1841 and 300 in 1901.[81]

In the Middle Ages much of Mile End was woodland and heath, but much of the woodland had been cleared by the end of the 16th century. All of the parish was subject to royal forest jurisdiction. Kingswood included all of the parish except probably the part west of the Nayland road. The north part of Kingswood became the estate called Kingswood and Kingswood heath, later known as the Severalls and Mile End heath.[82] Part of the south became the land of Mile End manor. West of the Nayland road lay part of the ancient wood of Cestrewald or Chesterwell in the north; in the south was part of the Braiswick estate, the rest of which was in Lexden.[83]

There was a race course on Mile End heath in the 1750s, but it had gone by 1821 when the corporation was inclosing *c.* 100 a. of the heath to add to its farmlands.[84] By 1841 much of the parish was arable land, but High wood and part of East wood remained west and east of Mile End manor house.[85] A village focus developed in the 19th century round the new parish church which was built in 1854–5 half a mile north of the old one. An isolation hospital was built in the north of the parish in 1884 and other hospitals in the 20th century.[86]

The medieval manor house, Mile End Hall, is discussed below. The timber-framed back range of Severalls Hall, a farmhouse on the Kingswood estate, was built in the early 17th century. Its western parlour end was refitted in the late 18th century when a bay window was added to the end elevation. Early in the 19th century a brick range containing an entrance hall and new principal rooms was added to the front of the older house. Church Farmhouse is of the early 17th century and has a main frame of oak with subsidiary timbers of elm and pine, and is jettied along the south side. The plan is symmetrical with one room on each side of the chimney stack and a central lobby entrance.[87] It was extended and modernized as a home for 18 mentally handicapped people when Essex Hall hospital closed in 1985.[88]

There was a tenement called the Half Moon, which may have been an inn, on the Severalls estate in the 17th century.[89] The Spread Eagle, sometimes known as the Castle, an inn in 1704, was probably on the site, between the Nayland and Boxted roads, of Eagle Lodge built in the early 19th century.[90] The Dog and Pheasant has a long brick range, of *c.* 1820, with late additions at the back.[91]

MANORS AND OTHER ESTATES. In 1066 St. Peter's church, Colchester, held of the king 2 hides which were probably in what later became Mile End. The church had lost the land to Eudes the sewer and Robert son of Ralf of Hastings by 1086, and the later descent has not

68 Geol. Surv. Map 1/50,000, drift, sheet 224 (1988 edn.).
69 Morant, *Colch.* App. p. 13.
70 *Essex Map* (1777); J. Booker, *Essex and the Industrial Revolution,* 101; above, Communications (Roads).
71 *White's Dir. Essex* (1848), 68; above, Communications (Railways).
72 *E.A.T.* N.S. xviii. 141–2; E.C.C. Sites and Monuments Record (TL92–75).
73 *P.N. Essex*, 378; *E.A.T.* 3rd ser. xix. 162; below, this par., Manors (Braiswick).
74 *E.A.T.* N.S. ix. 132–3.
75 P.R.O., E 179/108/162; Morant, *Colch.* 126.
76 E.R.O., D/ACR 2, ff. 190–1.
77 Ibid. D/Y 2/2, pp. 196–7.
78 Ibid. Q/RTh 5, f. 28v.
79 Morant, *Colch.* 134.
80 E.R.O., D/P 410/1/1–4.
81 *V.C.H. Essex*, ii. 353; *Census* 1801, 1841, 1901.
82 Morant, *Colch.* 12, 134; W. R. Fisher, *Forest of Essex*, 17; Morant, *Colch.* 12; E.R.O., D/DCm Z18/1.
83 Below, this par., Manors and other estates; *E.A.T.* 3rd ser. xi. 111–12.
84 E.C.L. Colch. [Rebow] Scrapbk. of Colch. and Chelmsford, f. 20; Beds. R.O., L 26/1010–11.
85 E.R.O., D/CT 242.
86 Above, Hospitals; *E.C.S.* 4 June 1910.
87 R.C.H.M. *Essex*, iii. 71.
88 *Colch. Gaz.* 24 Apr. 1985; above, Hospitals.
89 E.R.O., D/B 5 Gb4, f. 309v.; Gb5, f. 152v.
90 Ibid. D/B 5 Sr73, rot. 25; ibid. D/DJ 20/4; ibid. sale cat. D678.
91 Beds. R.O., L 26/1010.

been traced.[92] In 1268 the abbot of St. Osyth's was granted free warren in Mile End, presumably the later manor of *MILE END* and *ABBOTS HALL*; the estate was described as a manor in 1359.[93] The abbey kept the manor until the Dissolution when it was granted to Thomas Cromwell, Lord Cromwell.[94] On his attainder in 1540 it reverted to the Crown and was granted in 1544 to John de Vere, earl of Oxford, and Dorothy his wife, who conveyed it the same year to John Lucas.[95] John's son, Sir Thomas Lucas, in 1563 acquired the neighbouring Greenstead manor, with which Mile End descended thereafter.[96] In 1937 the lordship was held by trustees of the late Lord Lucas and Dingwall, by which time manorial rights had lapsed.[97]

Mile End, or Myland, Hall, the manor house, has at its centre a 14th-century two-bayed hall which has a heavily smoke-blackened roof, and there is evidence of a cross-passage at its north end. A southern cross wing is contemporary or slightly later but the northern cross wing has been substantially rebuilt. A central chimney and a first floor were put into the hall in the 16th century. A new range was added alongside the east front of the hall in the 18th century and the north end of the house was enlarged then and in the 19th century. Substantial additions have been made to the north and west since 1980.

BRAISWICK seems to have originated as a medieval freehold and may have been associated with Thomas de Bray who in 1258 acquired 2 messuages, 61 a. of land, 5 a. of meadow, 8 a. of wood, and 12*d.* rent in Mile End and Lexden. Before 1431 Thomas Godstone devised certain lands, rents, and services in Braiswick to his brother John Godstone who appears to have sold the land in 1437.[98] In 1438 John Stopingdon, archdeacon of Colchester, gave St. John's abbey a messuage, 200 a. of land, 3 a. of meadow, and 140 a. of wood in Mile End and Lexden called Braiswick which he held partly of the abbey and partly of Lexden manor.[99] The abbey kept the land until the Dissolution when it was granted to Thomas Cromwell. On his attainder in 1540 it reverted to the Crown and was granted in 1544 to Francis Jobson, his wife Elizabeth, Robert Heneage, and Richard Duke, who conveyed it to George Sayer in 1546 when it was referred to as a manor.[1] The male line of the Sayer family failed in the mid 17th century.[2] Braiswick farm contained 113 a. in Mile End and Lexden in 1803.[3] In 1930 the earl of Winchilsea, a descendant of the Heneage family, claimed to be the lord of Braiswick manor.[4]

Braiswick Farm, Mile End, has at its centre the hall and eastern parlour range of a late medieval house. An upper floor and a chimney were inserted into the hall, which retains its smoke-blackened roof, in the 17th century, and in the 18th century a brick range with a symmetrical eastern elevation was built alongside the parlour wing, which was remodelled internally at the same time. The original service end or wing was rebuilt to a smaller scale, probably in the 18th century, and in the 19th minor additions were made on the north side. The house formed the north side of a courtyard of farm buildings, now destroyed, which included timber-framed and thatched barns.[5]

TUBSWICK took its name from Richard Tubbe, bailiff of Colchester 1296–7, who had crops and stock worth £6 16*s.* 8*d.* there in 1296. It was given for the endowment of Eleanor's chantry in 1349, and on the chantry's dissolution in 1548 it passed to the corporation.[6] The early 18th-century Tubswick farmhouse, part of the Kingswood estate, has a main range of brick and a symmetrical south front of three open and two blind bays. There are 19th- and 20th-century additions along the north side.

Its name, recorded in 1168, implies that *KINGSWOOD* had belonged to the king, but it was in the hands of the burgesses of Colchester from 1130 or earlier until 1168 when Henry II reclaimed it allowing the townsmen to retain their common rights.[7] In 1535 Henry VIII restored Kingswood to the burgesses with the power of inclosure.[8] In 1576, at Queen Elizabeth's request, the Colchester corporation leased to Sir Thomas Heneage for 60 years 800 a. of inclosed land which became known as the Severalls, retaining 300 a. of uninclosed land. When the lease expired the land was let to several persons, notably to Thomas Lucas in 1656.[9] In 1722 the corporation leased to Daniel Defoe for 99 years the estate of Kingswood heath or the Severalls, together with Brinkley farm, and Tubswick.[10] Brinkley farm may have been the messuage called Swaynes and lands opposite Kingswood heath occupied by John Brinkley in 1599, associated with John Sweyn in the 14th century.[11] The corporation sold parts of the Severalls in the mid 19th century, established an isolation hospital in the 1880s on other parts, and sold 300 a. in 1904 for the development of a mental hospital.[12]

ECONOMIC HISTORY. In the Middle Ages the Colchester burgesses had half year lands next to the town in the south of the parish and whole year common rights across the north.[13] There was a certain amount of piecemeal clearance of woodland at Mile End hall manor in the area surrounding Highwoods. In the 13th and 14th centuries the abbot of St. Osyth's and others

92 *V.C.H. Essex*, i. 578.
93 *Cal. Chart. R.* 1257–1300, 100; E.R.O., D/B 5 Cr12, rot. 1.
94 *L. & P. Hen. VIII*, xiv (1), p. 376; xv, p. 284.
95 Ibid. xvi (2), p. 139; xix (1), pp. 286, 383.
96 Above, Greenstead (Manor).
97 *Kelly's Dir. Essex* (1937), 162.
98 P.R.O., C 1/75, no. 38; *Feet of F. Essex*, iii. 245; iv. 26.
99 *Feet of F. Essex*, i. 227; *Cal. Pat.* 1436–41, 223.
1 *L. & P. Hen. VIII*, xv, p. 284; xix (1), p. 625; xxi (2), p. 244.
2 Morant, *Essex*, ii. 199–200.
3 E.R.O., D/DJ 20/26–7.
4 Hist. MSS. Com., Reg. Manorial Docs.
5 Inf. from Mr. P. Borges.
6 B.L. Arundel MS. 145, ff. 19v., 20v., 29v; Morant, *Colch.* 46–7, 155–6.
7 Morant, *Colch.* 134; *Pipe R.* 1130 (Rec. Com.), 138; 1168 (P.R.S. xii), 48.
8 *L. & P. Hen. VIII*, viii, p. 100.
9 Morant, *Colch.* 134.
10 E.R.O., D/DC 5/18.
11 Ibid. D/B 5 Cr25, rot. 42d.; ibid. D/DO T347, T829.
12 Above, Modern Colch. (Political Hist.); Hospitals.
13 Above, Common Lands.

inclosed groves which were apparently used for producing timber and as wood pasture.[14] In the 13th century timber from Kingswood was used at Dover castle and for repairs to Colchester castle.[15] Livestock included sheep: 33 sheep were sold at Mile End hall in 1386.[16] The names Tubswick and Braiswick suggest that they originated as pastoral farms; by 1296 Tubswick was a mixed farm which in 1348 contained 18 a. of arable land and 2 a. of wood; in 1438 Braiswick included 200 a. of land, presumably arable.[17] Smallholdings described as crofts that were hedged and ditched may have contained arable.[18] A field called Little Ryeland was mentioned in 1418 indicating that rye was grown there at some time.[19]

Barley-growing was recorded in 1566 and 1583.[20] A survey of 1599 covering 609 a. of fields in the parish described 22 per cent as arable and 10 per cent as meadow, about three-quarters of each subject to commoning rights, and 68 per cent as coarse pasture and hay ground held in severalty; 100 a. at Mile End hall was included, in similar proportions; and 153 a. of the Severalls, recently inclosed parts of the Kingswood estate, was listed.[21] In the later 17th century grain, including wheat, and peas and beans were grown in Castle grove, former woodland in the south.[22] Arable farming increased as the inclosure of woodland and waste progressed.[23] By 1708 25 a. of the 40 a. of Chesterwell wood had been converted into 5 closes.[24]

In 1767 the Severalls estate, containing 816 a. of 'rich pasture and arable', with common rights on a further 230 a., was said to be let to 'responsible tenants'.[25] In 1778 land tax of £202, the corporation paying over a third of it, was paid by Mile End, seventh of the 16 Colchester parishes. The only other significant landowner was the non-resident lady of the manor.[26] Throughout the 18th century parishioners were still mainly tenant farmers and poor agricultural labourers living in scattered farms and cottages.[27] By 1801 just over half the land in the parish was cultivated: wheat, oats, turnips or rape, and barley were the main crops, but peas, beans, potatoes, and a little rye were also grown.[28] In 1821, when the lease of the Severalls was surrendered, the borough relet the land in smaller units.[29] Mile End hall, mainly an arable farm which was mostly heavy clay and hilly, was 'well managed' by the Lucas family's tenant in 1824, using a rotation of barley, clover or peas, wheat, and beans on the heavier land and turnips on the lighter land.[30] Local farmers in the early 19th century regarded Mile End farm labourers as sober, steady, and hardworking, but low wages and fear of unemployment caused by the new threshing machines led the labourers to participate in 1816 and 1830 in the machine-breaking and incendiarism more widespread in other north Essex parishes.[31]

By 1841 more than three quarters of the parish was arable land, with 16 farmers and 111 agricultural labourers out of a total population of 596. The corporation owned almost half the parish in 1842, nearly a third of it leased to William Wyncoll and the rest in small portions; Thomas Philip, Earl de Grey, lord of the manor, owned almost a quarter of the parish.[32] Although Mile End remained in appearance predominantly agricultural until the end of the 19th century and the number of people employed on the land fluctuated only slightly, farming occupied a declining proportion of the employed population, over half working on the land in 1841, but less than a third in 1881.[33] Employment was increasingly available on the railway and in shops and other service industries in Colchester; few people worked in factories, though much outwork was done for Colchester clothing firms.[34]

There was no large-scale industry in the parish. Potters were living in the north-west part in the late 12th and the 13th century, attracted by the clay, water, and scrub, and by a ready market in Colchester.[35] By the 15th century bricks and tiles were made from clay dug on Kingswood heath, and gravel was extracted in the parish.[36] By the 1840s brickworks east of the railway station employed 10 or more men, and bricks were still being made there at the end of the century.[37] There is evidence of domestic weaving in 1576, perhaps connected with the presence of Dutch people at about that time.[38] Nursery gardening, particularly rose-growing, became important from *c.* 1870 when Messrs. D. Prior and Sons set up their general nurseries. Frank Cant established a rose farm at Braiswick in 1875, and his uncle, Benjamin Cant, developed rose grounds near the station in 1879.[39]

LOCAL GOVERNMENT AND POOR RELIEF.

A manor court was held in the 16th century and presumably earlier.[40] No vestry records before

14 e.g. P.R.O., E 32/13, rot. 35; E 32/16, rot. 29; E32/299, no. 7; E.R.O., D/B 5 Cr4, rot. 4d.; *Arch. in Essex to AD 1500*, ed. D. Buckley, 104–5.

15 *E.A.T.* N.S. xix. 171.

16 E.R.O., D/B 5 Cr25, rot. 42d.

17 Morant, *Colch.* 46–7; *E.A.T.* 3rd ser. xix. 162.

18 e.g. B.L. Arundel MS. 145, f. 21 and v.; *E.A.T.* 3rd ser. xix. 161.

19 E.R.O., D/B 5 Cr41, rot. 31d.

20 Ibid. D/B 5 Sb2/1, ff. 67v., 68v.; Sr5.

21 B.L. Stowe MS. 832, f. 40.

22 P.R.O., E 134/32–3 Chas. II Hil./5.

23 Morant, *Colch.* 12, 134; e.g. E.R.O., D/B 5 Gb2, f. 124v.; Gb4, f. 243v.; Gb9, p. 54.

24 E.R.O., D/DJ 20/4.

25 E.C.L. Colch. [Rebow] Scrapbk. of Colch. and Chelmsford, f. 24.

26 E.R.O., Q/RPl 1107.

27 Guildhall MSS. 25750/1, 25755/1; Lambeth Palace Libr., Fulham Papers, Lowth 4, ff. 317–20.

28 *List & Index Soc.* vol. 189, pp. 137, 150.

29 E.R.O., D/B 5 Gb 9, pp. 464–5, 477–8; Gb10, p. 165.

30 Beds. R.O., L 26/981.

31 A. F. J. Brown, *Chartism in Essex and Suff.*, 23–5; S. W. Amos, 'Social Discontent and Agrarian Disturbances in Essex, 1795–1850' (Durham Univ. M.A. thesis, 1971), 23, 102, 119: copy in E.R.O.; *Ipswich Jnl.* 11 Dec. 1830.

32 E.R.O., D/CT 242A; P.R.O., HO 107/344/13; *V.C.H. Essex*, ii. 353.

33 P.R.O., HO 107/344/13; ibid. RG 11/1790.

34 Ibid. RG 11/1790; above, Modern Colch. (Econ.).

35 *E.A.T.* 3rd ser. vii. 33–60.

36 e.g. E.R.O., D/B 5 Cr47, rot. 23; Cr54, rot. 12; D/B 5 Sb2/6, f. 87; Sr10, rot. 1; D/B 5 Gb4, f. 117.

37 Ibid. D/P 410/28/1; P.R.O., HO 107/344/13; O.S. Map 1/2,500, Essex XXVII. 8 (1897 edn.).

38 F. G. Emmison, *Essex Wills*, iii, p. 334; B.L. Stowe MS. 830, f. 21.

39 *Inds. of E. Counties, Business Rev.: Essex* (1888–90), 190; *V.C.H. Essex*, ii. 481.

40 Beds. R.O., L 26/908–9.

1810 survive,[41] but there were two churchwardens in 1448 and constables *c.* 1655.[42] In the early 19th century two churchwardens, two overseers, and surveyors, constables, and assessors were usually appointed each year, presumably continuing an existing pattern. Vestry meetings were held at Easter and occasionally at other times, usually at the church, but also sometimes at the Dog and Pheasant in the parish, and once at the Waggon and Horses in Colchester. The average attendance was eight and usually included the rector. A committee of five was appointed in 1836 to revise and equalize the rating assessment.

Applications for poor relief were dealt with in 1822–3 at weekly meetings of a select vestry, consisting mainly or entirely of parish officers together with the rector, and between 1824 and 1833 at monthly vestry meetings. Usually from two to seven people attended, but after 1823 the rector was not often present. In 1832–3 one person each week from a rota of wealthier parishioners served with an overseer at the church.

Poor relief was given in cash and kind. In the winter of 1822–3 regular weekly cash payments ranging from 1*s.* to 6*s.* were paid to 29 parishioners. A list of poor families in 1826 included 145 persons, about a third of the population, of whom 60 per cent were children. Financial help was granted for medical, funeral, and lodging expenses. Unemployment was high in the 1820s and 1830s. The parish sometimes employed men, for example at the local gravel pit, but there does not appear to have been any consistent policy. A poor widow was paid to clean the church in 1826–7. Children were sometimes boarded out within the parish; one child was apprenticed to a printer in London in 1829. A workhouse mentioned in 1829 was probably outside the parish.

The annual cost of poor relief was £140 in 1776 and averaged £170 in 1783–5. Expenditure reached £747 in 1812, equivalent to over £2 a head, but fell to £395 in 1814, and then fluctuated between £440 and £695 during the period 1816–25. After rising to £722 in 1831, or £1 10*s.* 3*d.* a head, it had fallen to £493 by 1835 when Mile End parish became part of the Colchester poor law union.[43] Mile End was always a poor parish and before 1835 its expenditure on poor relief per head appears to have been significantly higher than any of the other 16 Colchester parishes. In 1845 low agricultural wages were still often insufficient to support a family, and the vestry agreed to a voluntary levy on ratepayers to supply temporary relief to able-bodied labourers with large families to prevent the break-up of families by the workhouse test.[44]

CHURCH. Mile End was part of St. Peter's parish in the early 13th century, but had become a separate parish by 1254 when St. Botolph's priory held the advowson of the rectory.[45] The patronage remained with the priory until the Dissolution when it was granted to Sir Thomas Audley (d. 1544).[46] He devised it to his brother Thomas, who sold it before 1551 to John Lucas, in whose family it descended, with the manor of Mile End or Abbotts, until 1919 when Nan Ino, Lady Lucas, granted the advowson to Balliol College, Oxford.[47]

The rectory was valued in 1254 at £3 6*s.* 8*d.*, from which 6*s.* 8*d.* a year was paid to the prior of St. Botolph's.[48] The living was vacant in 1443 because of its poverty.[49] In 1535 the value was £7 10*s.*[50] In 1650 the tithes were worth £50 and the house and glebe £30, but in 1681 the tithes of Castle grove and parts of the parish which had belonged to St. John's abbey were in dispute.[51] In 1835 the income was £521.[52] Tithes on 2,164 a. were commuted in 1842 for a yearly rent charge of £567, but in 1851 the living was said to be worth only £572, including £70 from the glebe.[53] In 1898 the tithe rent charge of £567 provided almost all the rector's income.[54]

In 1637 there were *c.* 27 a. of glebe.[55] More land was evidently acquired later. In 1840 and 1844–8 *c.* 30 a. were sold to the Eastern Counties Railway Company, but *c.* 11 a. adjoining the parsonage house were bought for the living in 1847.[56] About 24 a. of glebe were sold in 1919, and most of the remainder in 1927, partly for building plots.[57]

A rectory house was recorded in 1374, and the same or a subsequent house was in ruins in 1584.[58] The house recorded in 1650 may have been the one being repaired in 1723, which in 1727 was still unfit for the rector's family. By 1810 a subsequent rector was living there.[59] The house was demolished in 1842 and a larger one built, apparently on the same site beside the church, to plans by the local builder Samuel Grimes. The house was modernized *c.* 1922, but was itself demolished and replaced in 1972 by a new house, built on part of its garden.[60]

From 1353 a regular succession of rectors was recorded, although many in the Middle Ages served only briefly. A third of the rectors recorded between 1310 and 1542 were pluralists, four of them holding other Colchester livings.[61] A rector named John, presumably John Arrowsmith

41 Account based on E.R.O., D/P 410/8/1 (vestry mins.); D/P 410/11 (overseers' accts.).

42 E.R.O., D/B 5 Cr62, rot 13; D/B 5 Sr44, rot. 18; Sr52; Sr149, rot. 31.

43 E.R.O., Q/CR 1/1, 10, 12; ibid. Acc. C68, overseers' accts. 1819–26, 1831–5.

44 Ibid. D/P 410/8/1; above, Par. Govt. and Poor Relief (Poor Relief after 1834).

45 *Colch. Cart.* ii. 442; *E.A.T.* N.S. xviii. 123.

46 *L. & P. Hen. VIII*, x, p. 419.

47 Above, Manors; Morant, *Colch.* 135; Beds. R.O., L 27/103.

48 *E.A.T.* N.S. xviii. 123.

49 Ibid. N.S. xxiv. 115; Guildhall MS. 9531/6.

50 *Valor Eccl.* (Rec. Com.), i. 443.

51 Smith, *Eccl. Hist. Essex*, 320; P.R.O., E 134/32–3 Chas. II Hil./9.

52 *Rep. Com. Eccl. Revenues*, H.C. 54, pp. 664–5, (1835), xxii.

53 E.R.O., D/CT 242A; P.R.O., HO 129/8/204.

54 E.R.O., T/A 645.

55 Newcourt, *Repertorium*, ii. 419.

56 E.R.O., D/P 410/3/6–8, 11.

57 Ibid. sale cat. A75; Balliol Coll. Mun., Patronage Papers.

58 E.R.O., D/B 5 Cr17, rot. 5; D/AZ 1/7, f. 136v.

59 Smith, *Eccl. Hist. Essex*, 320; Guildhall MSS. 25750/1; 25751; Lambeth Palace Libr., Fulham Papers, Randolph 9, pp. 1010–17.

60 E.R.O., D/P 410/3/2, 3; M. I. Richardson, *St. Michael's Church, Myland* (1980), 14, 20.

61 Newcourt, *Repertorium*, ii. 419–20; *Reg. Sudbury* (Cant. & York Soc.), i. 275; E.R.O., D/B Cr10, rot. 1; ibid. T/A 237.

instituted in 1371, lost a wrestling match in 1372 for two qr. of corn and then refused to hand it over; in 1374 he was accused of violently assaulting another man's female servant and detaining her for five weeks in the rectory.[62]

Churchwardens conformed to the protestant changes of the mid 16th century: by 1548 they had sold church goods, including a rail and hanging for a statue, and a painted cloth from the sepulchre.[63] William Fiske, instituted in 1551, was one of the married clergy deprived by the bishop.[64] William Lyon, rector in 1560, performed his duties uncontroversially but Thomas Knevett, presented by Sir Thomas Lucas in 1585, was suspended the following year for preaching without a licence. He was accused in 1587 of failing to use the ring in marriage, or make the sign of the cross, or wear a surplice, and in 1593 of omitting part of the service when he preached and of failing to hold a service on Easter day. He survived to be listed by his fellow puritans as 'diligent and sufficient' in 1604. He died in possession of Mile End in 1626.[65] The conformist Thomas Talcott, rector of St. Mary's-at-the-Walls 1604–41, was rector from 1625 until his death in 1641.[66] Nevertheless the church was ill equipped in 1633.[67] Thomas Eyres, rector from 1644, was deprived of his other living at Great Horkesley in 1646 but kept Mile End until 1673.[68]

William Smythies, rector 1687–1719, an outspoken critic of popish and High Church tendencies, was a close friend of the writer Daniel Defoe, who held the Severalls estate in the parish.[69] His son Palmer, rector 1720–76, was also master of Colchester grammar school and rector and master of St. Mary Magdalen's church and hospital.[70] He lived in Colchester, for many years at the school, and served both parishes himself, with the help of assistant curates, among them, in 1770, George Pattrick, later a popular preacher in London.[71] Thomas Bland, rector 1777–89, served the cure when his health permitted during the half of each year which he lived in Colchester.[72] In 1723 Palmer Smythies held only one Sunday service and celebrated communion four times a year, an arrangement that continued throughout the 18th century.[73] There were *c.* 40 communicants in 1778.[74]

For most of the 19th century the church was served by two rectors: Philip Strong (1818–49), and Edmund Hall (1855–1903). By 1810 Sunday services had been increased to two, except in winter.[75] In 1841 of the 107 families in the parish 85 were said to belong to the church. In 1851 average attendances of 200 in the morning and 250 in the afternoon (including 60 Sunday school children at each service) were reported out of a population of 870, and the rector claimed that many people were turned away for lack of seats.[76] He started a subscription fund for the new church which was consecrated in 1855. From 1906 the school, built in 1871 with materials from the old church, was used as a church hall.[77]

In 1920 the average church attendance was 150–175. The parish was described in 1922 as 'distinctly Evangelical', but not extreme.[78] Social work was important, and the hymnologist W. J. L. Sheppard, rector 1926–32, found the rapidly growing, poor parish a demanding one.[79] Church life and worship in 1985 centred on the weekly parish communion, and St. Michael's church had close links with Mile End Methodist church, sharing a church magazine.[80]

The medieval church of *ST. MICHAEL*, which was apparently left to fall down in the late 19th century, stood on the east side of Mile End Road a mile north of Colchester, and comprised chancel, aisleless nave, and south porch.[81] Fragments of 14th- or 15th-century stonework survived on the site in 1987. From 1582 the church was frequently reported to be in need of repair, and *c.* 1700 the eastern part of the ruined chancel was demolished and a new east wall built. A western gallery and perhaps the wooden bell turret at the west end of the nave were built at the same time.[82] By the mid 19th century the building was dilapidated and too small for the parish. A new church, designed by E. Hakewill in the Early English style, was built in 1854–5 half a mile north of the old one on a site given by Thomas Philip Weddell, Earl de Grey, the patron. It comprises chancel, nave with north aisle, west tower, and south porch.[83] An organ chamber, choir vestries, and clergy vestry were added on the north side of the chancel in 1933–4.[84]

There was no bell in 1683, and the archdeacon suggested buying one from an abandoned church.[85] If a bell was bought, it was not moved to the

62 E.R.O., D/B 5 Cr16, rot. 4d.; Cr17, rot. 5; *Reg. Sudbury*, i. 275.

63 *E.A.T.* N.S. xiii. 167.

64 *V.C.H. Essex*, ii. 33 n.

65 Corpus Christi Coll. Camb., MS. 122, f. 45; *Seconde Part of a Register*, ed. A. Peel, ii. 164, 261; E.R.O., D/AZ 1/1, ff. 36v., 57v.; D/AZ 1/7, ff. 158v., 195; *A Viewe of the State of the Clargie* (1604), 6.

66 Above, Churches (St. Mary's-at-the-Walls).

67 *E.A.T.* N.S. xi. 42.

68 Guildhall MS. 9531/15; *Walker Revised*, ed. A. G. Matthews, 151.

69 W. Smythies, *Sermon preached at election of Mayor of Colch. 1706*: copy in E.C.L. Colch.; *E.R.* ii. 54.

70 E.C.L. Colch., Crisp MS. 'Colch. Monumental Inscriptions', xiii; *V.C.H. Essex*, ii. 507; Guildhall MSS. 25750/1; 25755/1.

71 E.R.O., D/P 410/1/5–7; *Alum. Cantab. 1752–1900*.

72 Lambeth Palace Libr., Fulham Papers, Lowth 4, ff. 317–20.

73 Guildhall MS. 25750/1.

74 Lambeth Palace Libr., Fulham Papers, Lowth 4, ff. 317–20.

75 Richardson, *St. Michael's*, 23; Lambeth Palace Libr., Fulham Papers, Randolph 9, pp. 1010–17.

76 E.R.O., D/ACM 12; P.R.O., HO 129/8/204; *V.C.H. Essex*, ii. 353.

77 Richardson, *St. Michael's*, 7–8; E.R.O., D/CC 6/5; below, this par., Educ.

78 E.R.O., D/CV 3/2; Balliol Coll. Mun., Patronage Papers.

79 E.R.O., D/CV 4/3; *E.R.* xli. 214; Richardson, *St. Michael's*, 14–15.

80 *Focus* (church mag.), Mar. 1985.

81 Description based on engraving reproduced in Richardson, *St. Michael's*, facing p. 6; mid 19th-century model of church at Hollytrees Mus., Colch; R.C.H.M. *Essex*, iii. 47; *Colch. Arch. Group Bull.* xix. 21.

82 E.R.O., D/AZ 1/2, f. 11; D/AZ 1/4, f. 152v., 157v.; D/AZ 1/8, f. 139v.; D/AZ 1/10, f. 25; D/ACV 9A, p. 66v.; Guildhall MS. 9532/1.

83 E.R.O., D/CC 6/5; Richardson, *St. Michael's*, 7–12.

84 *Chelm. Dioc. Chron.* Nov. 1933, p. 165; Apr. 1934, p. 64.

85 *E.A.T.* N.S. xxiii. 161.

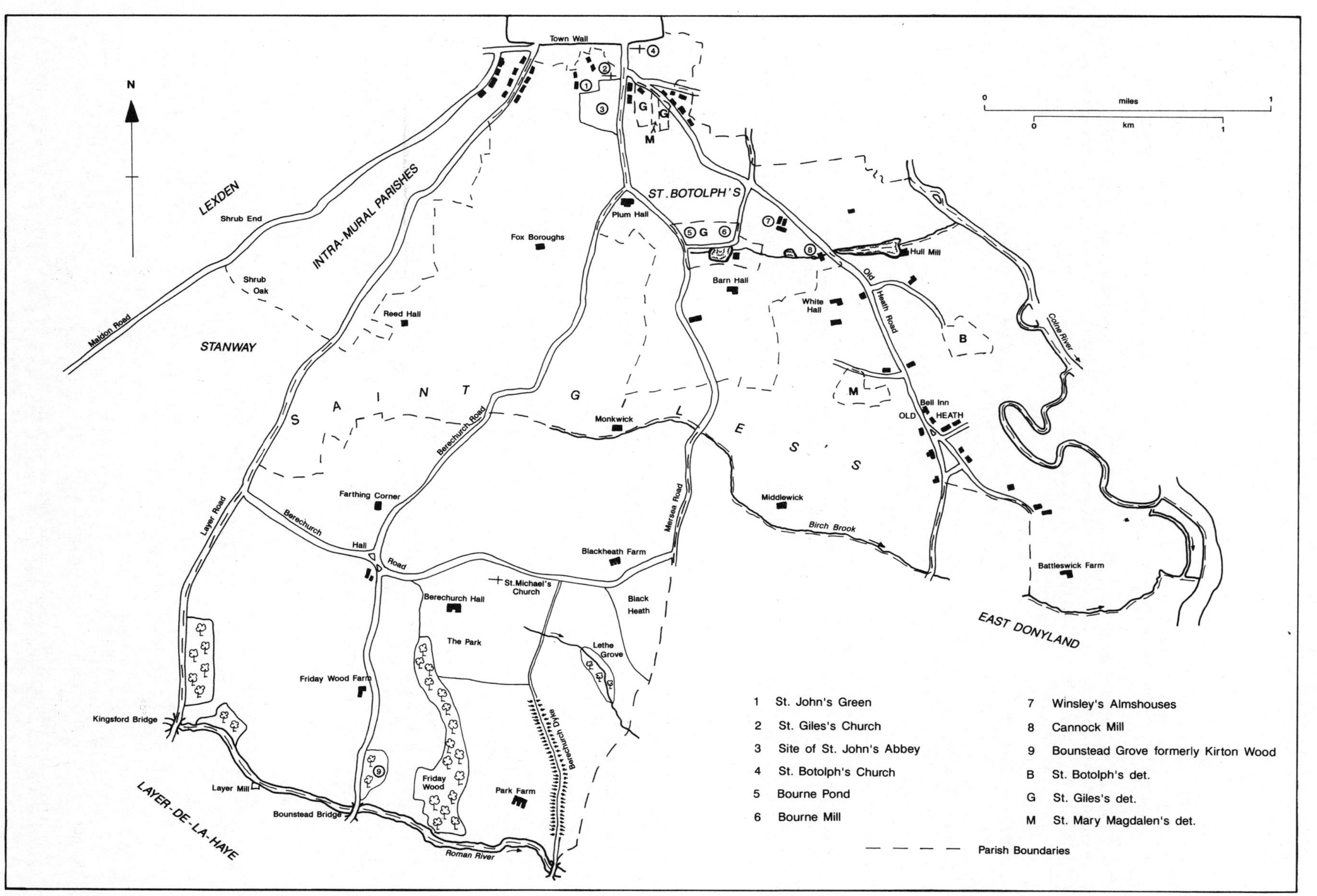

Fig. 37. West Donyland *c.* 1846

19th-century church which has a clock bell of 1887 and two bells of 1897, hung for chiming.[86] The plate includes an inscribed silver chalice and paten of 1660, and a 17th-century almsdish.[87] An early 19th-century octagonal brick font, discovered during excavations on the site of the medieval church *c.* 1972, was placed in the Colchester museum.[88]

NONCONFORMITY. Twelve nonconformists were recorded in 1676, but no more were reported until 1778 when the rector noted one Independent family.[89] There was a licensed Methodist preacher *c.* 1796 and a licensed meeting house with frequent visiting preachers and a considerable following. By 1810 all but three families were alleged by the rector to have returned to the church, but Wesleyan Methodists were meeting in the parish in 1829.[90]

A Primitive Methodist chapel, in the Hadleigh (Suff.) circuit, was built in the high road in 1840 when there were 21 members. It reported congregations of 22 in the afternoon and 38 in the evening on Census Sunday 1851.[91] Mile End had been transferred to the Colchester (Artillery Street) circuit by 1860. By then numbers had fallen to 7 but the chapel was rebuilt in 1866. There was only one member in 1887 and the chapel was closed and let to the Quakers for an adult school.[92]

Mile End (former Wesleyan) Methodist church, Nayland Road, originated in 1884 with mission work by Wesleyans from Culver Street church, Colchester.[93] A small chapel was built in 1895 and a school hall added in 1930.[94] In 1972 the minister also served Boxted, West Bergholt, and Marks Tey.[95]

Mile End chapel, on Mile End heath, registered in 1860 by its minister Henry Wyncoll, a local farmer, for evangelical protestant dissenters, was probably the one in Mill Road known as Providence Independent chapel. It had presumably closed by 1878 when the building was offered to the Wesleyan Methodists.[96]

EDUCATION. In 1833 there was a Church day school with 24 children and a Sunday school with 50, both partly maintained by the rector Philip Strong.[97] The school had failed by 1844 when, because the population was increasing rapidly, Strong invited subscriptions for a new school which was soon established in premises opposite the rectory. By 1846 it had 35 children, 15 more attended on Sundays, and both schools were supported by subscriptions and pence.[98] By 1861 the day school had *c.* 100 children.[99] In 1871 a school for 137 with a teacher's house was built in Mile End Road of materials from the old church.[1] The school received a government building grant and annual grants from 1872.[2] It was enlarged in 1884 for 170 children but by 1891 more than 200 attended.[3] Overcrowding was relieved by the opening of North Street board school in 1894.[4] In 1907 Mile End school was replaced by a new council school for 350 in Mill Road, and the old school was demolished in 1927.[5]

The Gilberd school, North Hill, is discussed above.[6]

CHARITIES FOR THE POOR. None known.

WEST DONYLAND

An estate at Donyland, probably extending from the town wall on the north to Roman river on the south, and from the Colne on the east to Maldon Road on the west, was divided into four in the late 10th century. The two northern quarters were later mainly in the Colchester parishes of St. Giles and St. Botolph; the south-east and south-west quarters became respectively East Donyland parish, in Lexden hundred outside Colchester liberty,[7] and Berechurch parish, within the liberty. The whole of Donyland in Colchester became known as West Donyland, even though parts of it lay in the north-east quarter of the original estate. In the Middle Ages and the 16th century manorial lords occasionally claimed, unsuccessfully, that parts of West Donyland were outside the liberty, and in 1580 four small estates there paid wardsilver to Lexden hundred.[8]

Berechurch, 1,377 a. (551 ha.), was bounded on the south by Roman river, on the north by field boundaries and Birch brook, on the west by Layer Road, and on the east by Mersea Road and a bank running south-west across Black heath.[9] The two northern quarters of Donyland, later in the Colchester parishes of St. Giles and St. Botolph, had been further subdivided by 1086. Several of the smaller estates passed to St.

86 E.R.O., T/A 645; *Ch. Bells Essex*, 344.
87 *Ch. Plate Essex*, 192; inf. from the Revd. J. F. Blore.
88 Richardson, *St. Michael's*, 20; *Colch. Arch. Group Bull.* xix. 21.
89 *Compton Census*, ed. Whiteman, 50; Lambeth Palace Libr., Fulham Papers, Lowth 4, ff. 317–20.
90 Lambeth Palace Libr., Fulham Papers, Randolph 9, pp. 1010–17; E.R.O., Q/CR 3/1/81.
91 E.R.O., D/NM 2/2/1; P.R.O., HO 129/8/204.
92 E.R.O., D/NM 2/2/1, 18, 23–5.
93 Above, Prot. Nonconf. (Wesleyan Methodists).
94 G.R.O. Worship Reg. no. 34957; J. A. A. Baker, *Hist. Methodism in Colch.* 19; E.R.O., D/NM 2/5/18.
95 *Colch. Expr.* 23 Nov. 1972.
96 G.R.O. Worship Reg. no. 9564; O.S. Map 1/2,500, Essex XXVII. 4 (1876 edn.).
97 *Educ. Enq. Abstract*, H.C. 62, p. 272 (1835), xli.
98 Brown, *Colch. 1815–1914*, 57; Richardson, *St. Michael's*, 5–6, pl. III facing p. 18; Nat. Soc. *Inquiry, 1846–7*, Essex, 6–7.
99 *E.C.S.* 16 Aug. 1861.
1 *Kelly's Dir. Essex* (1886); *Return of Schs. 1875–6* [C. 1882], p. 72, H.C. (1877), lxvii.
2 *Rep. of Educ. Cttee. of Council, 1872–3* [C. 812], p. 409, H.C. (1873), xxiv.
3 *Kelly's Dir. Essex* (1886); *E.C.S.* 19 Dec. 1891.
4 Above, Educ. (Board Schs.).
5 *Colch. Educ. Cttee. Year Bks.* 1904–8, pp. 67–8; Colch. Mus., photo. of demolition of school 1927.
6 Above, Educ. (20th-Cent. Secondary Schs.).
7 East Donyland is reserved for treatment in a later volume.
8 Bodl. MS. Rawl. D 1480, ff. 239v., 242; below, this section, Par. Govt.
9 E.R.O., D/B 5 R1, f. 217v.; O.S. Map 6", Essex XXVI, XXVII (1881 edn.).

John's abbey in the 12th and 13th centuries so that the abbey's lands came to extend from St. John's green in the north perhaps as far as Berechurch Hall Road in the south, and from the Layer road in the west to Old Heath Road in the east.[10] Another estate, along the river Colne, became the manor of Battleswick, which, although described as early as 1323 as partly in East Donyland,[11] was entirely within the liberty of Colchester, being bounded on the east by the Colne, on the south by Birch brook, on the north by the stream flowing from Bourne pond, and on the west by field boundaries and the road to East Donyland.

The land rises steeply from the flat marsh on the alluvium along the Colne in the east to 15–20 metres along Old Heath and Rowhedge Roads, and then more gently to 30 metres, on glacial sand and gravel, in much of Berechurch parish in the west. It falls southward to 8 metres along Roman river and eastward to 23 metres at the borough boundary. To the north it falls to 15 metres in the valley of the stream which flows from Bourne pond, before rising again to 25–30 metres near the town wall. The steepness of the slope near the Colne, exposing the underlying London clay, probably gave rise to the surname 'at cliff', recorded in the 15th century.[12] The steep south-eastern slopes are cut by three streams feeding Roman river; a fourth, Birch brook, rises at Monkwick near the Berechurch parish boundary and flows eastwards to the Colne.[13] All four cut through the sand and gravel to the London clay, which is also exposed near Roman river.[14]

The whole area was agricultural land until the 20th century, when the built-up area of Colchester expanded into its northern part. Much of the Berechurch Hall estate in the south was acquired by the War Department between 1926 and 1933 for military training and housing.[15]

The western half of Donyland was within the Iron-Age Camulodunum, whose eastern boundary was formed by Berechurch dyke.[16] Evidence of contemporary occupation has been found inside the dyke, notably on Park farm. Iron-Age was succeeded by Roman occupation at the farm, and there was another Roman settlement to the south-east. Field boundaries and cropmarks north of Maypole green may be those of Roman smallholdings.[17] There were three settlements in West Donyland in the Middle Ages. That at St. John's green was geographically and economically part of the town. The others were at Old Heath, within the manors of West Donyland and Battleswick,[18] and at Berechurch, where Saxon pottery has been found on land adjoining the church.[19]

No major roads ran through Donyland, but the Colchester–Maldon road formed its western boundary; two minor ones, the Colchester to Layer-de-la-Haye road and the Colchester–Mersea road, cross the area from north to south. Berechurch Road and Old Heath Road linked Berechurch and Old Heath to the town. Old Heath Road continued to East Donyland in the Middle Ages, but its eastern branch to Rowhedge was made between 1846 and 1876.[20] Layer Road and Mersea Road are connected by Berechurch Hall Road, which was diverted north of Berechurch church in the 18th century.[21] A medieval road leading directly to the church from a westerly bend in Berechurch Road survives as a footpath. Two lanes, one following Berechurch dyke and the other running from Mersea Road at Black heath, converge at a ford and footbridge over Roman river. Brounsford, where Bounstead Road crosses Roman river to Layer de la Haye and its mill, was recorded from 1384.[22] Brounsford bridge was recorded in 1563; Bounstead bridge, there in 1846, had fallen by 1876 and thereafter the river was forded until a footbridge was built in the late 19th century.[23] An unrepaired footbridge on 'the common church way and market way' in 1501 was probably over one of the streams on Old Heath Road.[24] Kingsford bridge, recorded from 1392, carries Layer Road over Roman river to Layer heath. The county council built a brick bridge there in 1891.[25] Berechurch had a postal service by 1866.[26]

The name Old Heath is a corruption of Old Hythe but no physical evidence of the early harbour or of any settlement associated with it has survived later drainage schemes. Surnames suggest that many of the 25 people assessed for subsidy in West Donyland in 1296 lived at Old Heath.[27] In the mid 14th century there were 14 messuages and 3 cottages on Battleswick manor, most of them probably in Old Heath; by the late 15th century there were at least 2 cottages in West Donyland manor on the west side of Old Heath Road. Fifteen people were assessed for subsidy in Old Heath in 1489–90, and in the early 16th century there were 10 tenements and 11 cottages on Battleswick manor, and at least 2 houses on West Donyland manor.[28] Only 11 people were assessed for subsidy in the whole of West Donyland hamlet in 1523, fewer than in Lexden, Greenstead, or Mile End.[29] There were at least 15 houses in Battleswick manor *c.* 1677, and at least 9 houses on West Donyland manor

[10] P.R.O., SC6/Hen. VIII/976.

[11] Keele Univ. Libr., Raymond Richards Colln. BW 15.

[12] E.R.O., T/B 122.

[13] O.S. Maps 1/10,000, TL 92 SE., TM 02 SW. (1977 edn.).

[14] Geol. Surv. Map 6", sheet 224 (1988 edn.).

[15] Above, Barracks.

[16] C. F. C. Hawkes and M. R. Hull, *Camulodunum*, 9, 14–15; *E.A.T.* 3rd ser. xiv. 137.

[17] Hawkes and Hull, *Camulodunum*, 14–15; Hull, *Roman Colch.* 249; *E.A.T.* 3rd ser. xviii. 93; Colch. Arch. Group, *Bull.* iii (i), 9; iv. 1, 17.

[18] *Colch. Cart.* ii. 307.

[19] Colch. Civic Soc. *Quarterly Bull.* iii. 33.

[20] Gilbert, *Colch. Map* (1846); O.S. Map 6", Essex XXXVII (1876 edn.).

[21] Below, this section, Manors.

[22] E.R.O. D/B 5 Cr23, rot. 37d.; D/B 5 Gb3, ff. 173v.–174; D/B 5 R1, f. 217v.; *Essex Map* (1777).

[23] E.R.O., D/B 5 R1, f. 217v.; Gilbert, *Colch. Map*; O.S. Maps, 1/2,500, Essex XXXVI. 8 (1876 edn.); 6", Essex XXXVI (1881 edn.); 1/2,500, Essex XXXVII. 14 (1923 edn.).

[24] E.R.O., D/DHt M148, rot. 9.

[25] Plaque on bridge; O.S. Maps 6", Essex XXXVI (1881 edn.); E.R.O., D/B 5 Cr27, rot. 28d.

[26] *Kelly's Dir. Essex* (1866).

[27] B.L. Harl. Ch. 54. B. 41; *Rot. Parl.* i. 237–8.

[28] E.R.O., T/B 122; P.R.O., SC 6/Hen. VIII/976, rot. 1d.

[29] P.R.O., E 179/108/162.

in 1737 were probably at Old Heath.[30] By 1846 there was a small group of houses or cottages round the Bell public house; the remaining farmhouses and cottages were scattered over the higher ground; Battleswick Farm, the site of the manorial grange, lay further south, near Birch brook.[31] There were at least two inns, one called the Axe, on West Donyland manor, probably in Old Heath, in 1505.[32] The Bell public house, on Old Heath Road, was recorded by that name from 1652, although not certainly an inn until 1818.[33] Another inn, the Blue Boar, was rebuilt for Ralph Creffield in 1706.[34]

St. James's guild in Old Heath, recorded in 1505, may have acted as a focus for the community before the Reformation; it was probably associated with the light in St. Giles's church which the inhabitants of Old Heath were bound to maintain, and towards which John Argentine, by will dated 1505, gave 40*s*.[35]

The name Berechurch was apparently used solely for the church of St. Michael[36] until *c.* 1536 when Sir Thomas Audley, later Lord Audley, adopted it for his estate. The name, first recorded in the 12th century as Beordescherche and Bierdechurche, appears to be topographical. Its first element may derive from *breord* or from *byrde*; in either case it would describe the location of the church near a rim or edge, either of the Roman river valley or of the land marked out by Berechurch dyke.[37]

Only one of the 25 people assessed for subsidy in West Donyland in 1296, William Frank vicar, certainly lived in Berechurch.[38] Later subsidies also do not distinguish Berechurch from the rest of West Donyland, and there is no evidence for the size of the settlement until 12 households were assessed for hearth tax in 1662 and 1671.[39] Thirty-five adults were rated to the poll tax in 1692, and the population may have declined in the earlier 18th century, there being only *c.* 10 houses in 1766.[40] It had increased to 126 by 1801, then rose slowly to 146 in 1841, declined to 104 by 1871, but reached 167 in 1891, the last year for which separate figures are available.[41] There were 24 houses in 1841 and 27 in 1881.[42] After the rebuilding of Berechurch Hall in 1882 a few estate houses were built.[43] Of the other houses in the parish, the Maypole inn, formerly a farmhouse, and Park Farm may date from the 18th century. An octagonal lodge on Berechurch Hall Road survives from the early 19th century.

The St. Botolph's priory grange of Canonswick, recorded in 1301, was presumably near Canwick mill, so named from 1404.[44] The house cannot certainly be traced after the Dissolution, but it may have been on the site of Brick House, owned by Henry Barrington in the mid 17th century, which became Winsley's almshouses in 1734.[45] The farmhouse on the site of the St. John's abbey grange of Middlewick survived the Dissolution, and continued in use until its farm was sold to the War Office as a rifle range in 1856.[46] Other houses were built at White Hall, Barn Hall, Reed Hall, and Fox Boroughs before 1846.[47]

MANORS. In the late 10th century Aethelflaed, widow of King Edmund and daughter of Ealdorman Aelfgar of Essex, directed that after her death her estate at Donyland should be divided into four: 2 hides to her servant Brihtwold, 2 hides to her priest Aelfwold, 2 hides to her priest Aethelmaer, and 2 hides to her kinsman Aelfgeat.[48] It is tempting to identify the two estates given to priests with the two which became separate parishes, Berechurch and East Donyland. Of the 6 hides of Donyland later in Colchester, little more than 2 can be identified in Domesday book: the 1½ hides and 8 a. held by 4 freemen in 1066 and by Ilbod in 1086, the ½ hide and 12 a. held by Modwin in 1066 and Hagheborn in 1086, and the 1 virgate held by Lagheman in 1066 and Modwin in 1086. None of the estates was said to be in Colchester, and Modwin's was in Lexden hundred.[49] Their relationship to the later medieval manors has not been traced.

WEST DONYLAND manor was probably among the earliest endowments of St. John's abbey, Colchester, and may have been the 2 ploughlands granted by Eudes the sewer (*dapifer*) *c.* 1104.[50] The grant of free warren in Donyland to the abbey *c.* 1127 seems to apply to lands in West Donyland, for only *c.* 1147 did the abbey acquire East Donyland where free warren was granted in 1253.[51] The manor seems to have comprised the northern part of St. Giles's parish, including the land on which the abbey was built, and perhaps 2 tenements in St. Nicholas's, and 3 in St. James's parish.[52] During the 12th and 13th centuries the abbey obtained other tenements in West Donyland, some of which later formed the abbey's granges of Monkwick and Middlewick. About 1150 Hugh son of Stephen, with the consent of Hamon of St. Clare, lord of the fee, granted land formerly Anschetil's to the abbey; a grant later confirmed by his daughters.[53] The land of Pesecroft beside Wick, granted by Ralph son of William de Haye

30 Keele Univ. Libr., Raymond Richards Colln. BW 171, 173; E.R.O., D/DEl M130.

31 Keele Univ. Libr., Raymond Richards Colln. BW 240.

32 E.R.O., D/DHt M148, rot. 21.

33 Keele Univ. Libr., Raymond Richards Colln. BW 11, 240.

34 E.R.O., D/DRc T3/4.

35 Ibid. D/ACR 2, f. 101v.

36 Below, this section, Church.

37 Suggested by the late J. McN. Dodgson.

38 *Rot. Parl.* i. 237.

39 E.R.O., Q/RTh 1, m. 21v.; Q/RTh 5, m. 28v.

40 Morant, *Colch.* 137; Guildhall MS. 9558, f. 89.

41 *V.C.H. Essex*, ii. 353.

42 P.R.O., HO 107/344; HO 107/1781; ibid. RG 9/1098; RG 10/1683; RG 11/1787.

43 E.R.O., Sale Cats. B661, B5164, B5182, B5585.

44 *Rot. Parl.* i. 253; E.R.O., D/B 5 Cr33, rot. 13.

45 E.R.O., D/Q 30/1/4; above, Charities (Almshouses).

46 *Return of Military Stations*, H.C. 305, pp. 32–3 (1862), xxxii.

47 Gilbert, *Colch. Map* (1846).

48 *A.-S. Wills*, ed. D. Whitelock, 37.

49 *V.C.H. Essex*, i. 560–1.

50 *Colch. Cart.* i. 1–3; confirmed by Hen. I in 1104: *Reg. Regum Anglo-Norm.* ii, no. 677.

51 *Reg. Regum. Anglo-Norm.* ii, no. 1513; iii, no. 221; *Colch. Cart.* i. 55.

52 P.R.O., SC6/Hen. VIII/976; E.R.O., D/DHt M145–8; cf. Morant, *Colch.* 117, 119, 123, 137, 143 n. For St. Nic's. see also E.R.O., D/DRe B13; *Colch. Cart.* i. 1–3; *Reg. Regum Anglo-Norm.* ii, no. 1513; iii, no. 221.

53 *Colch. Cart.* i. 162; cf. ibid. 218–20, 222; ii. 514.

probably *c.* 1250, included land with furze lying 'west of the road from the cross to Colchester',[54] a description which suggests that Pesecroft was near Monkwick in Berechurch Road. Before 1248 John de Blondec granted to the abbey his estate in Donyland, later known as Middlewick, a grant confirmed by his tenant Walter Haneng.[55]

St. John's abbey retained West Donyland, including Monkwick and Middlewick, until the Dissolution. In 1547 it, with the site of the abbey, was granted to John Dudley, earl of Warwick, later duke of Northumberland, who in the same year conveyed it to his adherent (Sir) Francis Jobson.[56] Jobson settled at Monkwick, which from 1536 was occasionally described as a separate manor.[57] He died in 1573, having devised West Donyland to one of his younger sons, Edward. The eldest son, John, contested the will, but Edward bought out his claim and retained the manor until his death in 1590.[58]

Edward Jobson left as heirs his infant daughters Mary and Elizabeth. In 1591 his trustees sold West Donyland to Robert Barker of Higham (Suff.);[59] Robert was succeeded *c.* 1618 by his son Bestney Barker (d. 1649) and he by his son Robert Barker. Robert's heir in 1679 was his son Henry Barker (d. *c.* 1717).[60] Henry's successor and perhaps his bastard son, Thomas Perry, sold West Donyland in 1736 to Knox Ward, whose son Ralph succeeded him in 1746.[61] Ralph Ward (d. 1818) left the estate in trust for his daughters Maria (d. 1850) and Elizabeth (d. 1844), wife of Capt. (later Vice-Adm.) Nicholas Tomlinson.[62] In 1850 the manor passed to Elizabeth's sons, John Philip (d. 1892) and William R. Tomlinson (d. 1899), and later descended in the Tomlinson family.[63] In 1941 it was held by the Ward-Tomlinson trust.[64]

The manor house at Monkwick originated as a farmhouse, possibly moated, built by St. John's abbey before 1523.[65] Sir Francis Jobson apparently rebuilt the house and enclosed a park there.[66] The interior of the house was refitted in the mid 17th century; panelling and an overmantel of that date survived in 1989 in Colchester museum. By 1662 the house had 11 hearths.[67] By 1735 it was dilapidated, and the eastern part was demolished to provide material to repair the rest.[68] The two-storeyed, timber-framed and plastered house, with a projecting upper storey and two gables on the south side was occupied as a farmhouse from that time until its demolition in 1963.[69] Medieval fishponds south of the house, fed by Birch brook, survived until the brook was piped in the 20th century. A dovecot recorded in 1814 may have been on the site of that built *c.* 1543.[70]

A freehold estate in the south-west corner of West Donyland, later called *BERECHURCH*, was held in 1385 by Roger Bulbeck. It passed to his daughter Alice who married John Algood of Colchester before 1419, and then descended in the Algood family until 1464 or later.[71] Sir Thomas Audley had acquired it by 1519 when he conveyed it to Elizabeth Barnardiston, mother of his wife Christine, perhaps as part of a marriage settlement.[72] In 1530 it was called Algoods manor.[73] By 1536 Audley had acquired lands adjoining Algoods, including Friday wood and Cannons field which had belonged to St. Botolph's priory, lands held by John Wentworth of the manor of East Mersea, land in West Donyland and Fingringhoe bought from John Christmas, and the glebe of Berechurch church.[74] Kirton wood was probably acquired somewhat later.[75]

Audley gave his estate to his brother Thomas (d. 1558) for life with remainder to Thomas's son Thomas, who died in 1572 leaving as heir his son Robert (d. 1624).[76] The manor passed in the Audley family to Robert's son Sir Henry (d. *c.* 1672), and Henry's sons Thomas (d. 1697) and Henry, who died in debt in 1714, leaving Berechurch mortgaged to James Smyth of Upton in West Ham (d. 1741).[77] The estate, which comprised 774 a. in 1769, passed in successsion to Smyth's nephew Sir Trafford Smyth, Bt. (d. 1765), Sir Trafford's son Sir Robert (d. 1802) and Sir Robert's son Sir George Henry (d. 1852).[78] It was settled upon Sir George's illegitimate daughter Charlotte (d. 1845)[79] and her husband Thomas White (d. 1864) and passed to their son Thomas G. G. White (d. 1877). In 1878, after a suit in Chancery, the estate, then comprising *c.* 3,300 a., was sold to Octavius E. Coope, M.P. (d. 1887). In 1892 Coope's executors sold it to Frederick Gordon of Bentley Priory, Stanmore (Mdx.). Gordon sold the estate in 1898 to Mrs. Frances A. Hetherington, who in 1921 put the estate, then 2,420 a., up for sale; during the next 12 years it was broken up.[80]

Audley entertained Henry VIII at Berechurch

54 Ibid. ii. 332–3. For Ralph de Haye cf. *Feet of F. Essex*, i. 139, 184–5, 195.
55 *Colch. Cart.* i. 251, 444.
56 *Cal. Pat.* 1547–8, 204, 253; *E.R.* iv. 117.
57 e.g. *L. & P. Hen. VIII*, xi, p. 208; *Feet of F. Essex*, v. 185.
58 P.R.O., C 142/176, no. 44; C 142/229, no. 111; E.R.O., D/DCm F1/189; D/DRe T7; D/DR T96.
59 E.R.O., D/DU 507.
60 Ibid. D/DEl M120–6.
61 Ibid. D/DEl M127–31; Morant, *Colch.* 137.
62 E.R.O., D/DEl M132–3; *D.N.B.* s.v. Tomlinson, Nic.; memorial in St. Mic's. ch. yd.
63 E.R.O., D/DU 507/6, 7, 10; *Alum. Cantab. 1752–1900*, iv. 205.
64 E.R.O., D/DEl M133B; Gant, 'Hist. Berechurch', f. 142.
65 P.R.O., SC 6/Hen. VIII/976; Colch. Arch. Group, *Bull.* vi (3), 27.
66 E.R.O., D/B 5 Sb2/2, f. 114; D/DCm F1/189; F. G. Emmison, *Elizabethan Life: Wills of Essex Gentry and Merchants*, 21; Gant, 'Hist. Berechurch', f. 138.
67 E.R.O., Q/RTh 1, m. 21v.
68 Ibid. D/DSr L3; Gant, 'Hist. Berechurch', f. 138.
69 R.C.H.M. *Essex*, iii. 73; inf. from Dept. of Environment; Gant, 'Hist. Berechurch', f. 133v.; Colch. Arch. Group, *Bull.* vi (3), 27; *E.C.S.* 9 Aug. 1963.
70 E.R.O., D/DSr T2; P.R.O., E 318/17/828.
71 E.R.O., D/B 5 Cr38, rot. 9d.; Cr41, rot. 7; Cr73, rot. 30d.
72 *Feet of F. Essex*, iv. 141; *Complete Peerage*, i. 348–9.
73 E.R.O., D/B 5 Cr99, rot. 17; P.R.O., C 54/406, no. 9.
74 *L. & P. Hen. VIII*, xi, p. 209; P.R.O., C 54/406, no. 9.
75 P.R.O., C 142/163, no. 57; C 142/418, no. 92; Colch. Mus., Map of Berechurch (1717).
76 *L. &. P. Hen. VIII*, xix (1), p. 620; P.R.O., C 142/163, no. 57; C 142/418, no. 92.
77 Morant, *Colch.* 139.
78 E.R.O., D/DU 457/27.
79 *Complete Baronetage*, iv. 10.
80 E.R.O., D/DEl T5, T294–6; D/DEl Z11; ibid. Sale Cat. B5164, B5585.

in the 1530s and inclosed a park there *c.* 1540.[81] The manor house was damaged during the Civil War when it was the home of the royalist Sir Henry Audley, but had presumably been repaired by 1662 when it had 20 hearths.[82] That was probably the house depicted standing in a courtyard south-west of the church in 1717.[83] James Smyth rebuilt the house and Sir Robert Smyth (d. 1802) employed Samuel Wyatt to improve it.[84] Most of the Georgian house, which had a parapeted front of 11 bays with central pediment and porch,[85] was demolished in 1882. A new house of *c.* 80 rooms was built on the same foundations in red brick with stone dressings in 'domestic French Gothic' style to the designs of E. C. Lee. The dining room and saloon of the Georgian house were retained. The house, having its own generator in 1882, was one of the earliest to be lit by electricity.[86] A stable block for 30 horses was built west of the house, and new staff houses were built on the estate.[87] After 1921 the house was unoccupied until the War Department requisitioned it during the Second World War. It was demolished in 1952.[88] The park was extended northward in the late 18th century, inclosing the church and diverting Berechurch Hall Road farther from the house.[89] Sir G. H. Smyth (d. 1852) planted Charlotte's wood and Lethe grove, where he made a bathing pool and grotto for his daughter Charlotte.[90]

Ernald or Arnulf de Curton gave to St. Botolph's priory before 1189 land in West Donyland which formed the nucleus of the priory's estate of *CANONSWICK*.[91] Before 1281 the priory had also acquired part of an estate there which had been held in the 12th century by Henry Blondec. His son John gave it before 1202 to St. Ouen abbey, Rouen, of whom the prior of St. Botolph's held in 1281.[92] The overlordship was not recorded thereafter. On the dissolution of St. Botolph's in 1536 the farm, described as a manor, was granted to Sir Thomas Audley, and by him to St. John's abbey.[93] It was presumably merged with West Donyland manor.

BATTLESWICK manor seems to have derived from an estate in Donyland held, with Tendring manor, of the honor of Boulogne in 1205 and *c.* 1217 by Oger or Roger de Curton and *c.* 1222 by his brother William, sons of Arnulf or Ernald de Curton who had given Canonswick to St. Botolph's.[94] The overlordship passed to Richard de Munfitchet, probably the man of that name who died in 1267, and to his heir Giles de Plaiz, Lord Plaiz (d. 1302). It descended with the barony of Plaiz to Sir John Howard, by whose marriage to Joan Walton it was united with the demesne lordship.[95]

The demesne lordship, with that of Tendring, was held by Andrew Blunt (fl. 1259), and passed to his daughter Catherine wife of Richard Battle of Wivenhoe, who gave his name to the Colchester manor.[96] Under an agreement of 1298 Battleswick passed with Wivenhoe to Catherine's daughter and coheir Margery wife of William Sutton,[97] and the manor descended with Wivenhoe until 1624 or 1625.[98] By 1315 the lord was John Sutton and he was followed by two or possibly three other men of the same name.[99] The last John (d. 1393) was succeeded by his brother Richard (d. 1396) and by Richard's son Thomas,[1] but by 1399 the lord was John Walton, husband or son of Thomas Sutton's heir Margery. John was succeeded in 1407 by Richard Walton whose heir was his sister Joan (d. 1424) wife of John Howard, Lord Plaiz. Her daughter and heir Elizabeth married John de Vere, earl of Oxford.[2] In 1473 Elizabeth surrendered her lands, including Wivenhoe and Battleswick, to Richard duke of Gloucester who in 1480 sold them to John Howard, Lord Howard, later duke of Norfolk (d. 1485).[3]

After 1485 the de Veres recovered the manors, which descended with the earldom of Oxford until 1584 when Edward de Vere, earl of Oxford, sold them to Roger Townshend.[4] Townshend died in 1591 and Battleswick was held by his executors during the lifetime of his son John (d. 1603) but passed to his grandson Sir Roger Townshend who sold it in 1624 or 1625 to Robert Buxton.[5] Buxton held in 1653, but by 1658 John Godschall, a London merchant, was lord.[6] He was succeeded in 1693 by his son, another John Godschall,[7] who was followed in 1725 by his son Nicholas. Nicholas was succeeded in 1748 by his daughter Sarah whose husband William Mann assumed the surname Godschall. Sarah died in 1792 and William Mann Godschall in 1803, to be succeeded by his son Samuel Mann Godschall; he sold the manor in 1804 to Joseph Ward who sold it in 1808 to Henry Thorn of Colchester. Thorn was declared bankrupt in 1815, and in 1820 he and his trustee Samuel Blomfield sold the manor to Samuel

81 P.R.O., C 54/406, no. 9; *L. & P. Hen. VIII*, xi, p. 209; xiii, p. 99; xvi, pp. 323, 329.
82 *E.A.T.* N.S. xxii. 93; E.R.O., Q/RTh 1, m. 21v.
83 Colch. Mus., Map of Berechurch (1717).
84 Morant, *Colch.* 138; H. Colvin, *Biog. Dict. Brit. Architects, 1600–1840*, 956.
85 E.R.O., Sale Cat. B101; above, pl. facing p. 328.
86 J. Booker, *Essex and the Industrial Revolution*, 214.
87 *Kelly's Dir. Essex* (1886); E.R.O., Sale Cat. B5164; J. A. Rush, *Seats in Essex*, 37–9; *Building News*, June 16, 1882; M. Girouard, *Victorian Country Ho.* 397.
88 *Kelly's Dir. Essex* (1926 and later edns.); Gant, 'Hist. Berechurch', f. 178.
89 *Essex Map* (1777); O.S. map 1", sheet 48 (1838 edn.).
90 Gant, 'Hist. Berechurch', f. 45.
91 *Rot. Parl.* i. 253; Dugdale, *Mon.* vi. 106.
92 *Cal. Doc. in France*, p. 29; *Cal. Inq. Misc.* i, p. 362.
93 *L. & P. Hen. VIII*, x, p. 419; xi, p. 208.
94 *Bk. of Fees*, i. 234, 238; *Feet of F. Essex*, i. 9, 49, 63; *Pipe R.* 1205 (P.R.S. N.S. xix), 196.
95 *Colch. Cart.* i. 178; *V.C.H. Essex*, iv. 227; vi. 9; *Complete Peerage*, x. 539–42; *Cal. Inq. p.m.* iv, p. 81; vii, p. 26; viii, p. 356; x, p. 466.
96 Morant, *Essex*, i. 470; ii. 187; *Rot. Parl.* i. 238.
97 Morant, *Essex*, ii. 187; *Cal. Inq. p.m.* iv, p. 81; *Feet of F. Essex*, ii. 206.
98 The following paras. are based on Morant, *Essex*, ii. 187; E.R.O., T/B 122; Keele Univ. Libr., Raymond Richards Colln. BW 1–18.
99 E. C. Furber, *Essex Sessions of the Peace*, 17–18.
1 *Cal. Inq. p.m.* xvii, pp. 175, 261–2.
2 P.R.O., C 139/88, no. 56; *Complete Peerage*, x. 238, 542.
3 *Cal. Close*, 1468–76, 334; 1476–85, 216.
4 P.R.O., CP 25/2/132/1693, no. 51.
5 Keele Univ. Libr., Raymond Richards Colln. BW 8–11; P.R.O., PROB 11/77, ff. 127v.–128v.; *Hist. Parl., Commons 1558–1603*, iii. 520.
6 Keele Univ. Libr., Raymond Richards Colln. BW 11.
7 P.R.O., PROB 11/416, ff. 180–2.

John Edgell Martin. Martin sold it in 1825 to John Cutts who sold it in 1848 to James Cuddon of Witham.[8] Thereafter it was held by a succession of absentee lords, Cuddon selling in 1853 to James Manning, deputy steward of the manor, for his daughters Clarissa Peach, Rose Frances, Elizabeth Adelaide, and Louisa Manning. They sold it in 1880 to Richard Henry Wood,[9] who was succeeded *c.* 1908 by Stanley Rose Wood. S. R. Wood was succeeded in 1931 by James Hatton Wood, but by that date the manorial rights had lapsed.[10]

ECONOMIC HISTORY. West Donyland was an area of mixed farming, with some good arable land in Berechurch, poorer pasture and heath at Old Heath, marsh along the Colne, and narrow meadows along Roman river. In 1296 oats seems to have been the main crop, the inhabitants of West Donyland being assessed for subsidy on 37 ½ qr., followed by rye (17½ qr.); small amounts of barley, wheat, and peas were also recorded. Cattle were apparently more important than sheep, 31 cows and 14 calves being recorded compared to 20 sheep, but sheep may have escaped assessment more readily than cattle.[11]

Both Battleswick and Canonswick were mixed farms in 1296 and 1301, although Canonswick may have specialized in sheep: the prior of St. Botolph's was assessed on 20 sheep and 5 lambs there in 1301; in 1464 he had at least 222 sheep there.[12] Oats were grown on the Battleswick demesne in 1325–6, and rye between 1341 and 1344.[13] In 1330–1 there were 20 cows and 40 sheep at the manorial grange, and there were still 20 cows in 1425–6. In 1341–2 as many as 11 customary tenants performed boon works, recorded in 1368 as reaping, binding, and stooking the lord's corn at harvest, receiving from the lord in return food that included bean and fish pottage, bread, eggs, and herrings. By 1425 Battleswick, presumably the demesne, was being farmed for £5 6*s.* 8*d.* a year; the rent fell to £4 in 1426 and did not recover fully until 1492; it then remained at £5 6*s.* 8*d.* until 1518 or later.[14]

On the West Donyland manor belonging to St. John's abbey oats and rye were the main crops in the late 15th century; sheep, cattle, and pigs were kept, some tenants having flocks of 50 or 60 sheep, another as many as 16 cattle. In 1483 one man put 40 more pigs and piglets onto the lord's pasture than he ought to have done; other pigs were grazed in the woods, including Shrub wood, at time of pannage. As late as 1394 a tenant was amerced for failing to work in the lord's hay when summoned to do so.[15] An unidentified Newland in West Donyland, recorded from 1384,[16] was presumably cleared from woodland in the earlier Middle Ages, as perhaps was the area adjoining Lord's wood near the north-west boundary of Berechurch where field names in Breach survived in 1806.[17] There is no evidence for medieval crops in Berechurch, but the rents in kind payable at the Dissolution by the farmer of Monkwick and Middlewick, whose lands may have extended into Berechurch, suggest that rye and barley, of which 30 qr. each were to be paid each year, were the chief crops, although wheat (20 qr. a year payable as rent) was also grown.[18]

Much of Berechurch was probably wooded in the early Middle Ages; Farthing Corner on Berechurch Road, Maypole green at its junction with Layer Road, and Friday wood green are remnants of a chain of greens probably cleared from woodland. Kirton wood, recorded in 1495–6, and the adjoining Friday wood, recorded in 1291–2,[19] were probably associated with the familes of Curton and Friday.[20] Part of Friday wood was taken into Berechurch Hall park *c.* 1540. In 1717 Friday and Kirton woods comprised *c.* 246 a. and the adjoining park of *c.* 390 a. included West Donyland heath.[21] Most of the woodland was cleared in the 18th century, and by 1776 only 21 a. of woodland remained.[22] The park boundary bank north of Park farm survived in 1989. At Monkwick a park laid out in the mid 16th century extended west as far as Black heath.[23]

Most of the recorded medieval tenants of Battleswick manor were agricultural workers. The Colchester merchant John Cleve who acquired 2 messuages, a tenement, 21 a. of land and 4 a. of marsh in 1427 seems to have been a member of an Old Heath family.[24] By *c.* 1500 as many as 11 of the holdings were in the hands of one man, John Fuller of Halstead.[25] From the mid 16th century there was further consolidation of copyholds, notably by George Christmas (d. 1566) who had a freehold house just north of Battleswick. Alderman Thomas Laurence bought 40 a. freehold from George Dibney of Colchester in 1567.[26] By *c.* 1677 John Standly had built up Place farm (60 a.) in the centre of Old Heath. In 1745 there were no owner-occupiers of copyholds in Old Heath.[27] At Berechurch, the Audleys at Berechurch Hall and the Barkers at Monkwick were the largest landowners in the 16th and 17th centuries, but there was a number of smaller holdings. In the 18th and 19th centuries the Smyth family enlarged the Berechurch Hall estate, cultivated parkland and woodland, and established Park, Friday Wood, Maypole, and Blackheath farms.[28]

8 Keele Univ. Libr., Raymond Richards Colln. BW 230, 233.
9 Ibid. BW 223, 235, 238.
10 E.R.O., D/DEl M154.
11 *Rot. Parl.* i. 237–8.
12 Ibid. 238, 253; E.R.O., D/B 5 Cr72, rot. 13d.
13 E.R.O., T/B 122.
14 Ibid.
15 Ibid. D/DHt M145, *passim*; D/DHt M147, rot. 2.
16 Ibid. D/DHt M145, rott. 9, 16.
17 E.R.O., D/DCm P26; *P.N. Essex*, 575.
18 P.R.O., SC 6/Hen. VIII/976.
19 Ibid. E 32/13, rot. 35; Morant, *Essex*, ii. 193.
20 *Bk. of Fees*, i. 238; Morant, *Colch.* 142–3; E.R.O., D/B 5 Cr74, rot. 14.
21 Colch. Mus., Map of Berechurch (1717).
22 E.R.O., D/DEl T5.
23 Ibid. D/B 5 Sb2/2, f. 114; D/DCm P27.
24 Keele Univ. Libr., Raymond Richards Colln. BW 3; E.R.O., T/B 122.
25 E.R.O., T/B 122.
26 Keele Univ. Libr., Raymond Richards Colln. BW 88, 229.
27 Ibid. BW 161/3, 171, 173, 180.
28 E.R.O., D/DE T170; *Essex Map* (1777); O.S. Map 1", sheet 48 (1838 edn.).

In 1599 there were 195 a. of arable land in Berechurch, and rye was apparently the main cereal crop.[29] Eighteenth- and 19th-century leases of Monkwick farm required the tenant to leave the land fallow after two corn crops, but not if beans, peas, or clover were grown, and to return all farm manure to the land. In 1817 frequent planting of peas following wheat was blamed for depletion of the land.[30] Turnips grew well on the light soil if well manured. In the early 19th century Robert Tabor, tenant of Friday Wood farm (350 a.), used a four-course system of turnips, barley, clover, and wheat. Barley, used mainly for malting, was then the most productive crop, each acre yielding 26 bu. a year compared with 20 bu. of wheat and 16 bu. of oats. Having hardly any grass, Tabor fed his turnips and clover to wether sheep, bought as inferior Norfolk lambs at Ipswich fair, and Scottish bullocks, bought at Michaelmas and fattened for the London market. He sometimes fed a little straw but never hay.[31] By 1845 Sir Henry Smyth owned all the land in Berechurch parish, except the Monkwick estate of 110 a.[32] In 1876 the parish contained 1,040 a. of arable, 136 a. of pasture, and 74 a. of wood.[33]

In 1894, of *c.* 104 a. of land in Battleswick farm, *c.* 44 a. were mainly under oats with some barley and rye, *c.* 17 a. were under wheat, and *c.* 40 a. were grass or pasture. When the manor was offered for sale in 1880 the surviving copyholds were valuable chiefly as potential building land.[34]

Old Heath heath or common, along Old Heath Road, and at least part of the marsh along the Colne were common to the tenants of West Donyland and Battleswick from the 14th century or earlier; in the 15th century the tenants of Battleswick pastured or overburdened the common with cows, bullocks, and pigs, the tenants of West Donyland with sheep and horses.[35] There is no evidence for stinting until the mid 17th century when the total stint was said to be 950 sheep. The tenants of the 37 holdings in Battleswick and West Donyland which were responsible for repairing the marsh ditch between Battleswick and Wivenhoe could graze 732 sheep, the stint ranging from 40 to 10.[36] Hull mill, on the northern boundary of Battleswick manor, had commons for 40 sheep in Old Heath marsh in 1690.[37] In 1784 Alexander Carter, the tenant of Berechurch manor, apparently claimed the right to graze 12 head of cattle on Old Heath common.[38] In 1818, under an Act of 1811, a total of *c.* 75 a. of marsh and heath was inclosed, and divided between Henry Thorn, lord of Battleswick manor, and 10 copyholders and freeholders of the manors of West Donyland and Battleswick. About 47 a. of marsh lay along the Colne in the north-east part of the manor, *c.* 20 a. of heath or waste ground lay in two parcels, one north and one south of the Bell inn.[39]

Black heath and Kingsford heath were common to the tenants of West Donyland manor who overburdened them in 1497, 1503, 1504, and 1506,[40] and presumably also to the inhabitants of Berechurch. West Donyland heath was apparently several by 1599.[41]

In the 19th century most of the inhabitants of Berechurch were employed in agriculture or in domestic service; 8 or 9 women in the parish in the period 1861–1881 were laundresses,[42] probably employed at Berechurch Hall, where a separate laundry building survived in 1921.[43] There was a small brickyard north-west of Kingsford bridge in the 1890s.[44] In 1989 Park farm was the only surviving farm, surrounded by military training grounds.

Bourne mill, Cannock mill, and Hull mill, all on the stream leading from Bourne pond, were within West Donyland, as were several windmills, including one at Old Heath built before 1341. All served the town as well as the tenants of the Donyland manors, and their histories are given above.[45] Some inhabitants of Berechurch may have used Layer mill which stood on the boundary between Berechuch and Layer-de-la-Haye and was within the same lordship.[46]

LOCAL GOVERNMENT. Their conflicting rights of jurisdiction in West Donyland led to frequent disputes between the borough on one part and St. John's abbey and later the Audleys on the other.[47] In 1285 the abbot claimed view of frankpledge, the assize of bread and of ale, and right of gallows on his manor of West Donyland under a charter of *c.* 1127. The abbey also claimed unsuccessfully that its manor, like East Donyland, was in Lexden hundred and outside the borough's jurisdiction.[48] Despite protests by the borough court, notably in 1413,[49] it and its successors continued to hold courts with view until 1662, and courts baron until 1916.[50] Brewers, bakers, butchers, and regrators were regularly presented in the late 15th and the early 16th centuries for breaching the assize or taking excessive gain; pleas of debt were heard, and copyholds transferred. In 1392 and 1393 five unfree tenants were presented for living away

29 B.L. Stowe MSS. 832, f. 28; 842, f. 1; Morant, *Colch.* 57.

30 E.R.O., D/DSr T2.

31 A. Young, *Gen. View Agric. Essex*, i. 237, 345, 372; ii. 325–6.

32 P.R.O., IR 18/2222.

33 O.S. *Area Bk.* (1876).

34 Keele Univ. Libr., Raymond Richards Colln. BW 228, 238.

35 Ibid. BW 1–8; E.R.O., D/DHt M145–8; ibid. T/B 122.

36 Keele Univ. Libr., Raymond Richards Colln. BW 248/2.

37 P.R.O., CP 25/2/827/2 Wm. & Mary East. no. 24.

38 E.R.O., D/DSr F6/2.

39 Keele Univ. Libr., Raymond Richards Colln. BW 252; E.R.O. Q/RDc 17A.

40 E.R.O., D/DHt M147, rot. 25 and d.; D/DHt M148, rott. 16 and d., 23d.

41 E.R.O., D/DEl T5; D/B 5 Sb2/9, f. 68; B.L. Stowe MS. 832, f. 28.

42 P.R.O., HO 107/344; HO 107/1781; ibid. RG 9/1098; RG 10/1683; RG 11/1787.

43 E.R.O., Sale Cat. B5164.

44 Ibid. Sale Cat. B661; ibid. D/DEl T296; O.S. Map 1/2,500, Essex XXXVI. 4 (1897 edn.).

45 Above, Mills.

46 E.R.O., D/DBe T21; Morant, *Essex*, i. 412–13.

47 Above, Med. Colch. (Boro. Gov't.); Tudor and Stuart Colch. (Boro. Gov't.).

48 Above, this section, Manors; P.R.O., JUST 1/242, rott. 110, 112d.; E.R.O., D/DCm Z18/1.

49 E.R.O., D/B 5 Cr39, rot. 5.

50 Ibid. D/DHt M145–8; D/DEl M120–33, 133A, 133B.

from the manor without licence, and another paid a fine for his daughter's marriage.[51] In 1484 the court ordered tenants not to put dung and other filth on St. John's green.[52] An aletaster and one or two rent collectors or reeves (*prepositi*) were elected in most years. By the late 16th century court business was largely confined to the transfer of copyholds, but a few tenants were amerced for failing to scour ditches or obstructing footpaths, and in 1612 tenants were ordered not to put swine on St. John's green. Aletasters were elected until 1604, and one under constable until 1607; thereafter two constables were usually elected, one for St. John's green and one for Old Heath, and one or two drivers of the greens, until 1662.[53]

St. Botolph's priory probably held courts for Canonswick, where land was held by copy in 1526.[54] The serjeant of Canwick had custody of a stray horse in 1367.[55]

In the 14th century Battleswick tenants owed suit to the Wivenhoe manor court. In 1412 a jury from Old Heath appeared at that court, and from 1418 separate courts, with view of frankpledge, were held for Battleswick. Tenants of the manor were regularly presented for overloading the common or marsh and for failing to scour ditches. In 1447 several men, including one from Colchester, were presented for taking hares without licence, and in 1594 a Colchester linendraper was presented for digging clay on the heath. In 1562 the court issued orders forbidding the grazing of pigs and restricting the number of sheep on the commons. Constables were appointed from the mid 15th century and drivers of the commons from the mid 16th century to the mid 18th. Until 1668 courts exercised view of frankpledge, but thereafter they were described as courts baron. The transfer of copyholds became their only business from the mid 18th century.[56] The custom of the manor was that copyhold land descended to the youngest son. The last recorded court was held in 1851.[57]

Donyland, except East Donyland parish, also fell within the jurisdiction of the borough court. In 1488 the jury at West Donyland manor court complained that the borough sergeant had entered the manor to distrain on John Argentine of Old Heath, contrary to its liberty.[58] Battleswick tenants were presented in the borough court in the 15th century, several times for unscoured ditches and once for 'a great affray',[59] but there seem to have been no disputes between the borough and the lords of Battleswick manor except in 1577 when the earl of Oxford's tenants were forbidden to yield to the borough, and some claimed that Battleswick was outside the liberty.[60]

In the 17th century the inhabitants of Berechurch were responsible for the repair of the highway from Kingsford bridge to the town gate.[61] The overseers of the roads in Old Heath ordered by the Battleswick manor court in 1644 to repair a bridge,[62] were presumably the surveyors of the highways of St. Giles's parish.

At times in the later 17th century Berechurch parish apparently contributed £8 a year towards poor relief in St. Mary Magdalen's parish.[63] In 1776 the overseers of Berechurch spent £57 15*s* 2*d* on poor relief, the lowest sum in the borough, except for the impoverished St. Mary Magdalen's. By the period 1783–5 the sum had nearly doubled, to £110, a higher proportional increase than in any other parish in the borough. In 1813 the overseers spent £325, the threefold increase since the 1780s being one of the greatest in the borough, and in the period 1814–21 the amount ranged between £255 and £372. The payment per head in 1821, *c.* 16*s*., was the 5th highest in the borough, but considerably less than the £1 9*s*. paid in Mile End.[64]

CHURCH. Berechurch was the only part of West Donyland to become a separate ecclesiastical parish. The ecclesiastical parish was enlarged in 1955 by the addition of those parts of the parishes of St. Botolph and St. Stephen, Colchester, and Fingringhoe which comprised the Monkwick housing estate.[65] Its church, St. Michael's, which was closed in 1975, was recorded in 1170 as Beordescherche and Bierdechurche,[66] a form that suggests it existed by the 11th century. It may have been built by one of the two priests, Aelfwold and Aethelmaer, to whom Aethelflaed gave quarters of her Donyland estate.[67]

By the late 12th century the church, with Holy Trinity, Colchester, belonged to Bury St. Edmunds abbey,[68] which in a complicated transaction between 1200 and 1211 seems to have conveyed the advowsons of both churches to Thomas dean of Colchester.[69] Between 1254 and his death in 1258 or 1259 Richard Champneys of Colchester granted the advowsons to St. John's abbey, Berechurch being then described as a chapel of Holy Trinity.[70] St. Michael's was treated as a chapel in the early 14th century, and the rector of West Donyland to whom money was left for masses in 1401 was presumably the rector of Holy Trinity.[71] William Frank, vicar, who was assessed for subsidy in West Donyland in 1296, presumably served Berechurch,[72] but there is no record of an ordained vicarage.

51 Ibid. D/DHt M145, rott. 29, 30.
52 Ibid. D/DHt M147, rot. 4.
53 Ibid. D/DEl M120–3.
54 Ibid. D/B 5 Cr39, rot. 19; D/ACR 2, ff. 197–8.
55 Ibid. D/B 5 Cr15, rot. 6d.
56 Ibid. T/B 122; Keele Univ. Libr., Raymond Richards Colln. BW 1–18.
57 E.R.O., D/DEl M154.
58 Ibid. D/DHt M147.
59 Ibid. D/B 5 Cr38, rot. 2; Cr39, rot. 2; Cr45, rot. 25; Cr53, rot. 2.
60 Ibid. D/Y 2/6, p. 1.
61 Ibid. Q/SR 411/58.
62 Keele Univ. Libr., Raymond Richards Colln. BW 11.
63 E.R.O., D/B 5 Sb3/1, p. 1; D/B 5 Sr57, rot. 28.
64 Ibid. Q/CR 1/1, 1/10, 1/12.
65 Ibid. D/CPc 331.
66 B.L. Lansdowne MS. 416, f. 47v.
67 *A.-S. Wills*, ed. Whitelock, 37.
68 *Chron. Jocelin of Brakelond*, ed. H. E. Butler, 64.
69 *Kal. Abbot Samson* (Camd. 3rd. ser. lxxxiv), 161–2; B.L. Lansdowne MS. 416, f. 47v.
70 *Colch. Cart.* ii. 439; *Feet of F. Essex*, i. 229.
71 *Reg. Baldock*, pp. 275, 291, 307; E.R.O., D/B 5 Cr32, rot. 19d.
72 *Rot. Parl.* i. 237, 255.

Although the church was generally treated as a chapel, two churchwardens were recorded in 1399, and a parishioner asked to be buried in the graveyard of the parish church of West Donyland in 1500.[73]

In 1536 Sir Thomas Audley was licensed to compensate the rector of Holy Trinity and establish a separate rectory for West Donyland or Berechurch, served by a perpetual chaplain.[74] From that time until *c.* 1913 the chaplains, generally called curates, were appointed by Audley's successors as owners of Berechurch Hall, except in 1650 when the estate of the royalist Sir Henry Audley was sequestered, and in 1835 when Elizabeth Boggis presented by consent of Sir Robert Smyth.[75] From *c.* 1870 the living was a titular vicarage.[76] From 1913 to 1961 the bishop presented by lapse, the identity of the patron being unknown in 1961; from 1964 the bishop was presumed to be the patron.[77] There were no parish officers in 1738, because the church was considered to have been a chapel of Holy Trinity, but churchwardens were recorded in 1852.[78] St. Michael's was closed in 1975,[79] and the former chapel of ease, St. Margaret's on the Monkwick estate, became the parish church.

The living was not separately valued in the Middle Ages. The glebe and tithe of Berechurch passed in the 13th century to the rector of Holy Trinity who held land belonging to 'West Donyland chapel' adjoining John Algood's land in 1427.[80] The 'rectory' of West Donyland occupied by a tenant in 1393,[81] may have been a rectory house, or perhaps the glebe. The tithes of West Donyland which were given to St. John's abbey and passed to Sir Francis Jobson were those of the manor of West Donyland in St. Giles's parish.[82] In 1536 Sir Thomas Audley acquired the glebe, and perhaps the tithes, of Berechurch, from the rector of Holy Trinity, to whom he paid 50*s.* compensation.[83] There is no later reference to glebe, but in 1845 Sir Henry Smyth was said to own the tithes.[84] No living was endowed, but Audley and his successors appear to have paid successive curates a rent of £10 a year charged on land in the parish.[85] The curate's stipend was £20 a year in 1645;[86] it probably fell back to £10, still its value in 1742 and 1748,[87] at the Restoration. The living was augmented in 1749 by £200 from Queen Anne's Bounty, raising its value to £14 a year in 1768.[88] In 1770 the Bounty matched three benefactions of £200, and the money, which seems to have been invested in land, raised the value of the living to £60 2*s.* in 1808.[89] The living was said to be worth £100 in 1835, £110 in 1863, and £144 7*s.* 6*d.* in 1878.[90]

In the Middle Ages the church or chapel was presumably served by the rectors of Holy Trinity or by priests appointed by them. Those appointed by Audley and his successors were usually styled curates, although in 1683 Thomas Parker was called rector.[91] The curate *c.* 1586 was a reputed drunkard and did not preach, and his successor Thomas Holland was imprisoned in 1587 for disturbing the peace.[92] From 1662 until 1912 the cure was served with that of Layer de la Haye.[93] In 1683 and 1707 the communion table at Berechurch was unfurnished.[94] In 1738 the curate complained that he was unable to celebrate communion because the 'impropriator', presumably James Smyth (d. 1741), would not buy communion plate, and Berechurch parishioners received the sacrament at Layer-de-la-Haye. The curate did, however, hold a service every Sunday at Berechurch. By 1742 his successor held communion three times a year and fortnightly prayers, a pattern of services which continued in the later 18th century. Between 1755 and 1767 the cure was often served by assistant curates for the non-resident incumbent.[95] In 1810 a quarter of the population of 93 were nonconformists,[96] and on Census Sunday 1851 out of a population of 120 a morning congregation of 30 was reported.[97] In 1866 and 1870 William Wright, reforming master of Colchester grammar school 1852–76, served the cure for non-resident incumbents.[98] Thomas O. Price, vicar 1870–1913, held one Sunday service and a monthly communion; he was instrumental in effecting the restoration of the church in 1872.[99] The informal union with Layer-de-la-Haye ended on his death and until 1936 Berechurch was held by successive rectors of St. Mary's-at-the-Walls and served by assistant curates.[1] It was held jointly with All Saints', Shrub End, from 1936 to 1953 when the increasing population of the parish made the appointment of a separate vicar of Berechurch necessary.[2] A vicarage house was acquired in

73 E.R.O., D/B 5 Cr31, rot. 1d.; ibid. D/ACR 1/2.

74 *L. & P. Hen. VIII*, xi, pp. 154–5, 208; Newcourt, *Repertorium*, ii. 52–3; E.R.O. D/ACV 9B, p. 3; D/ACV 9A, p. 79.

75 Newcourt, *Repertorium*, ii. 52–3; E.R.O. T/A 547/1; T/A 237; Guildhall MSS. 9550, 9557–8, 9560; *Kelly's Dir. Essex* (1866 and later edns.).

76 *Kelly's Dir. Essex* (1866 and later edns.).

77 *Crockford* (1918–19); *Chelm. Dioc. Yrbk.* (1915–1976).

78 Guildhall MS. 25753/1; E.R.O., D/ACV 28.

79 *Lond. Gaz.* 1 July 1975, p. 8392.

80 E.R.O., D/B 5 Cr47, rot. 24d.

81 Ibid. D/B 5 Cr28, rot. 38.

82 *Colch. Cart.* i. 94–5; *Cal. Pat.* 1558–60, 469.

83 P.R.O., C 54/406, no. 9.

84 Ibid. IR 18/2222.

85 E.R.O., Sale Cat. B5585.

86 Morant, *Colch.* 139.

87 Morant, *Colch.* (1748 edn.), Bk. II, p. 31; Guildhall MS. 25754/1.

88 C. Hodgson, *Queen Anne's Bounty*, 383; Morant, *Colch.* 139.

89 *Livings Augmented by Queen Anne's Bounty, 1703–1815*, H.C. 115, p. 85 (1814–15), xii; E.R.O., Sale Cat. B101.

90 *Rep. Com. Eccl. Revenues*, H.C. 54, pp. 636–7 (1835), xxii; *White's Dir. Essex* (1863), p. 89; E.R.O., T/A 645.

91 E.R.O., D/ACB 9B, p. 3.

92 T. W. Davids, *Annals of Nonconf. in Essex*, 98; E.R.O., D/B 5 Cr148, rot. 38d.; ibid. T/A 547/1.

93 Newcourt, *Repertorium*, ii. 53, 376; *E.C.S.* 27 Dec. 1872; Gant, 'Hist. Berechurch', f. 119.

94 E.R.O., D/ACV 9A, p. 79; D/ACV 9B, p. 3.

95 Guildhall MSS. 9550, 9556–8, 9560; Gant, 'Berechurch', f. 124.

96 Guildhall MS. 9557; E.R.O., D/ACM 12.

97 P.R.O., HO 107/1781; HO 129/8/204.

98 *V.C.H. Essex*, ii. 507; *Kelly's Dir. Essex* (1866, 1870); E.R.O., Libr. Folder, Colch., TS. poem, 'Recollections of an Old Colch. Inhabitant'.

99 E.R.O., D/CV 1/2; *E.C.S.* 27 Dec. 1872.

1 *Kelly's Dir. Essex* (1917 and later edns.); *Chelm. Dioc. Chron.* Nov. 1928, 176; June 1929, 94; July 1933, 107.

2 *Crockford* (1951–2).

1955, and in 1956 a dual purpose church hall, St. Margaret's, was built on the new Monkwick estate off Mersea Road.[3]

The church of *ST. MICHAEL*, so called by 1254,[4] is of brick with stone dressings and comprises nave and chancel in one, north chapel, south porch, and a west tower of three stages with a stair turret and a battlemented parapet.[5] An earlier church, probably on the same site was restored in the 14th century. Stonework of that period was re-used when the church was rebuilt in the late 15th century and survives in the west doorway, the windows of the tower, and the chancel south doorway. Windows which survived in the south wall until 1872 may have belonged to the 14th century. The north chapel, with a richly carved hammerbeam roof bearing the emblems of Henry VIII and Catherine of Aragon, was added in the early 16th century. In the 17th century, when it became the memorial chapel of the Audley family, wooden cartouches, carved and painted with the Audley arms, were fixed to the ends of the hammerbeams and wall posts.

In the 17th century the chancel window was replaced. In the course of restoration in 1872 the walls of the nave and chapel were partly rebuilt, the roofs were raised, the south porch demolished, and new windows inserted in the south wall, where a 14th-century doorway was reset. A new porch was built later.[6]

The building was vandalized after its closure in 1975.[7] In 1981 the Audley chapel was vested in the Redundant Churches Fund and the rest of the building was sold for light industrial use; in 1993 it was occupied as offices by a security firm.[8]

A medieval bell by Richard de Wimbish (fl. 1291) was recast in 1876.[9] The church plate was modern.[10] In the Audley chapel, a tablet commemorating Robert Audley (d. 1624) may be by Gerard Christmas; a life-size white marble effigy of Sir Henry Audley (d. *c.* 1672), reclining on a black and white marble altar tomb with figures of his five children, erected by him in 1648 and surmounted by an inscribed tablet with side pilasters, a pediment, and cartouche of arms, may be by Thomas Stanton (d. 1674). Memorial tablets in the church[11] included one to Charlotte White (d. 1845) by Joseph Edwards.[12]

The church of *ST. MARGARET*, Stansted Road, was built between 1968 and 1972, largely by the vicar and parishioners. The building, of dark, reddish-blue brick, is basically square, but one corner is splayed to lead into the semi-circular sanctuary. The copper-covered, pyramidal roof rises to a height of 40 ft. above the sanctuary.[13] The earlier red brick church hall stands beside the new building.

The church of St. Barnabas, Old Heath, built in 1875 as a chapel of St. Giles's, is discussed above.[14]

NONCONFORMITY. The Audley family made Berechurch a centre of Roman Catholicism in the later 16th century and the 17th.[15]

The 23 Independents or Congregationalists reported in Berechurch in 1810[16] presumably worshipped in Colchester, as there was no Nonconformist church in the parish.

The Congregational church at Old Heath originated in a mission from Lion Walk Church, Colchester, *c.* 1845. Wesleyan Methodists from Colchester had a preaching station at Old Heath in the mid 19th century.[17]

EDUCATION. A day school in Berechurch was opened in 1832 in which *c.* 20 children were taught at their parents' expense.[18] By 1841 it had been succeeded by a National school with 12 children on weekdays and 29 on Sundays, supported by parents and other subscribers, but that had failed by 1846.[19] Another National school survived for a few years in the 1860s, and an attempt to maintain a Church school was made *c.* 1874.[20]

The St. Giles's parish school was founded in Old Heath in 1832, and continued as an infant school until it was replaced by Old Heath mixed and infant school in 1894.[21]

CHARITIES FOR THE POOR. None known.

3 Gant, 'Hist. Berechurch', ff. 120, 132v.; *Essex Churchman*, Nov. 1955; *E.C.S.* 9 Dec. 1983.

4 *Colch. Cart.* ii. 439.

5 Description in E.R.O., T/P 196/4.

6 *E.C.S.* 27 Dec. 1878.

7 *Essex Arch. News*, Autumn 1980, 18.

8 Inf. from the Fund; *E.C.S.* 22 May, 1897; *Essex Chron.* 16 Dec. 1985; sale cat.

9 *Ch. Bells Essex*, 178.

10 *Ch. Plate Essex*, 190.

11 E.C.L. Colch., Crisp MSS. 'Colch. Mon. Inscriptions', xiv; E.R.O., D/DSr F6/1; Colch. Mus., Parish file.

12 R. Gunnis, *Dict. Brit. Sculptors 1660–1851*, 140.

13 *Architect's Jnl.* 2 Jan. 1974; *Colch. Gaz.* 23 Oct. 1970; *E.C.S.* 9 Dec. 1983.

14 Above, Churches (St. Giles's).

15 Above, Roman Catholicism.

16 Guildhall MS. 9668, f. 89.

17 Above, Prot. Nonconf. (Congregationalists, Methodists.).

18 *Educ. Enq. Abstract*, H.C. 62, p. 271 (1835), xli.

19 E.R.O., D/ACM 12; Nat. Soc. *Inquiry, 1846–7*, Essex, 2–3.

20 *Kelly's Dir. Essex* (1866), 60; *E.C.S.* 27 Dec. 1872; Gant, 'Hist. Berechurch', ff. 102–3.

21 Above, Educ. (Parochial Schs.).

INDEX

A page number in italic indicates an illustration on or facing that page. Page numbers in bold type indicate a chapter devoted to the subject or place.

INDEX